FOURTEENTH EDITION

Strategic
Management
and Business
Policy

GLOBALIZATION, INNOVATION, AND SUSTAINABILITY

FOURTEENTH EDITION
GLOBAL EDITION

Strategic Management and Business Policy

GLOBALIZATION, INNOVATION, AND SUSTAINABILITY

Thomas L. Wheelen
Formerly with University of Virginia,
Trinity College, Dublin, Ireland

J. David Hunger
Iowa State University,
St. John's University

Alan N. Hoffman
Bentley University

Charles E. Bamford
University of Notre Dame

PEARSON

Boston Columbus Indianapolis New York San Francisco Upper Saddle River
Amsterdam Cape Town Dubai London Madrid Milan Munich Paris Montreal Toronto
Delhi Mexico City São Paulo Sydney Hong Kong Seoul Singapore Taipei Tokyo

Editor in Chief: Stephanie Wall
Acquisitions Editor: Daniel Tylman
Acquisitions Editor, Global Editions: Debapriya Mukherjee
Project Editor, Global Editions: Suchismita Ukil
Program Management Lead: Ashley Santora
Program Manager: Sarah Holle
Editorial Assistant: Bernard Ollila
Director of Marketing: Maggie Moylan
Marketing Manager: Erin Gardner
Marketing Assistant: Gianni Sandri
Project Management Lead: Judy Leale
Project Manager: Karalyn Holland
Head of Learning Asset Acquisition, Global Editions: Laura Dent
Media Producer, Global Editions: M. Vikram Kumar

Senior Manufacturing Controller, Production, Global Editions: Trudy Kimber
Procurement Specialist: Michelle Klein
Creative Director: Blair Brown
Central Design Manager: Jayne Conte
Cover Design: PreMedia Global
Cover Image: © majeczka/Shutterstock
VP, Director of Digital Strategy & Assessment: Paul Gentile
Digital Editor: Brian Surette
Digital Development Manager: Robin Lazrus
MyLab Project Manager: Joan Waxman
Digital Project Manager: Alana Coles
Media Project Manager: Lisa Rinaldi
Full-Service Project Management: S4Carlisle Publishing Services

Credits and acknowledgments borrowed from other sources and reproduced, with permission, in this textbook appear on the appropriate page within text. Additional photo/image credits: Sustainability issue, LehaKok/Shutterstock; Innovation issue, ssuaphotos/Shutterstock; Global issue, Rob Wilson/Shutterstock; Strategy highlight, Triff/Shutterstock; Chapter opener globe, Nelson Marques/Shutterstock.

Pearson Education Limited
Edinburgh Gate
Harlow
Essex CM20 2JE
England

and Associated Companies throughout the world

Visit us on the World Wide Web at:
www.pearsonglobaleditions.com

© Pearson Education Limited 2015

The rights of Thomas L. Wheelen, J. David Hunger, Alan N. Hoffman, and Charles E. Bamford to be identified as the authors of this work have been asserted by them in accordance with the Copyright, Designs and Patents Act 1988.

Authorized adaptation from the United States edition, entitled Strategic Management and Business Policy, 14th edition, ISBN 978-0-13-312614-3, by Thomas L. Wheelen, J. David Hunger, Alan N. Hoffman, and Charles E. Bamford, published by Pearson Education © 2015.

ISBN 10: 1-292-06081-6
ISBN 13: 978-1-292-06081-1

British Library Cataloguing-in-Publication Data
A catalogue record for this book is available from the British Library

10 9 8 7 6 5 4 3 2 1
14

Typeset in 10/12 Times LT Std by S4Carlisle Publishing Services

Printed and bound by Courier Kendallville in The United States of America

Brief Contents

Contents

Dedicated to

SPECIAL DEDICATION TO TOM WHEELEN

Tom originated this book in the late 1970s and with his friend David Hunger brought the first edition to fruition in 1982. What a ride it has been! After battling bone cancer, Tom died in Saint Petersburg, Florida, on December 24, 2011. It was Tom's idea from the very beginning to include the latest research and useful material written in such a way that the typical student could read and understand the book without outside assistance. That has been a key reason for the success of the book through its many editions. Tom's last months were spent working with the two new co-authors to map out the direction for the 14th edition. We thank you, Tom, and bid you a fond farewell! This 14th edition is for you.

J. David Hunger
Alan N. Hoffman
Charles E. Bamford

This is a special dedication to Thomas L. Wheelen, co-author, father, and best friend, May 30, 1935 – December 24, 2011. This is the 14th edition of SMBP the creation you and Mr. Hunger started due to your friendship at the McIntire School of Commerce at UVA with that adjoining door! It is not very often that two co-authors become the best of friends, but you both did. That was a very special gift that Tom treasured until the end. We are so glad you were able to meet as the dynamic foursome to discuss the 14th edition of SMBP! The new addition of co-authors Alan Hoffman and Chuck Bamford gave you and Mr. Hunger the ability to relax and smell the roses. We have come full circle with you being back at UVA! You were an amazing friend, visionary, teacher, and leader! Thank you for pushing us to be who we are today! You were very blessed to have two children as your best friends! You will never know how much you are missed!

Dad – chailleann againn go mbainfidh tú agus grá agat. Tá do Spiorad na hÉireann le linn i gcónaí!

GNPD KEW and RDW

Betty, Kari and Jeff, Maddie and Megan, Suzi and Nick, Summer and Kacey, Lori, Merry, Dylan, and newborn Edan. Also to Wolfie (arf!).

David Hunger

To Will Hoffman, the greatest son in the world. . . . and to our saint Wendy Appel. In memory of my good friend, Tom Wheelen, via con dios. Thank you, Tom and David.

Alan Hoffman

To Yvonne, for your support, advice, encouragement, love, and confidence. To David and Tom, for your confidence, council, and mental energy in the revision of this remarkable text.

Chuck Bamford

Preface

Welcome to the 14th edition of *Strategic Management and Business Policy*! All of the chapters have been updated, and most of the cases are new and different. We have added several brand-new cases (**Early Warning: Concussion Risk** and the **Case of the Impact Sensing Chinstrap, A123, Amazon, Blue Nile, Groupon, Netflix, Zynga, Under Armour, General Electric, AB Electrolux, Tesla Motors, Delta Airlines,** and **The U.S. Digital Signage Industry Note**) for a **total of 13 new cases**! Many of the cases are exclusive to this edition! Although we still make a distinction between full-length and mini cases, we have interwoven them throughout the book to better identify them with their industries.

This edition revamps the theme that runs throughout all 12 chapters. We utilize a three-legged approach consisting of *globalization, innovation, and sustainability*. These three strategic issues comprise the cornerstone that all organizations must build upon to push their businesses forward. Each chapter incorporates specific vignettes about these three themes. We continue to be the most comprehensive and practical strategy book on the market, with chapters ranging from corporate governance and social responsibility to competitive strategy, functional strategy, and strategic alliances.

FEATURES NEW TO THIS 14TH EDITION

For the first time in 30 years, the 14th edition has added two new authors to the text. Alan Hoffman, a major contributor to the 13th edition, is a former textbook author and world-renowned author of strategy business cases, and Chuck Bamford, who was a student of Tom Wheelen and David Hunger back in 1980 at the University of Virginia (McIntire School of Commerce), has authored four other textbooks. They join J. David Hunger and bring a fresh perspective to this extraordinarily well-researched and practically crafted text. In that vein, this edition of the text has:

- Vignettes on Sustainability (which is widely defined as Business Sustainability), Globalization (which we view as an expectation of business), and Innovation (which is the single most important element in achieving competitive advantage) appear in every chapter of the text.
- Every example, chapter opening, and story has been updated. This includes chapter opening vignettes examining companies such as: Five Guys, RIM (BlackBerry), HP's Board of Directors, Tata Motors, Costco, and Pfizer among many others.
- Resource-based analysis (Chapter 5) has been added to the toolbox of students' understanding of competitive advantage.
- Extensive additions have been made to the text on strategy research.
- Current consulting practices have been added to the topics of strategy formulation and strategy implementation.
- Thirteen new full-length cases have been added:

Twelve new comprehensive cases and one new Industry Note have been added to support the 13 popular full-length cases and 8 mini-cases carried forward from past editions. Thirteen of the cases in the 14th edition are brand new and one case is an updated favorite from past editions. Of the 34 cases appearing in this book, 20 are exclusive and do not appear in other books.

- One of the new cases deals with corporate social responsibility issues (**Early Warning: Concussion Risk and the Case of the Impact Sensing Chinstrap**).
- Two of the new cases deal with international issues (**A123, AB Electrolux**).
- Two of the new cases involve Internet companies (**Amazon, Blue Nile**).
- Three of the new cases deal with Entertainment and Leisure (**Groupon, Netflix, and Zynga**).
- One new case deals with sports and apparel clothing (**Under Armour**).
- One new Industry Note concerns digital signage. (**Daktronics**).
- One new case concerns the financial crisis of 2008 (**GE Capital**).
- Two new cases deal with transportation (**Delta Airlines, Tesla Motors**)

HOW THIS BOOK IS DIFFERENT FROM OTHER STRATEGY TEXTBOOKS

This book contains a **Strategic Management Model** that runs through the first 11 chapters and is made operational through the **Strategic Audit**, a complete case analysis methodology. The Strategic Audit provides a professional framework for case analysis in terms of external and internal factors and takes the student through the generation of strategic alternatives and implementation programs.

To help the student synthesize the many factors in a complex strategy case, we developed three useful techniques:

- **The External Factor Analysis (EFAS) Table in Chapter 4**
  This reduces the external opportunities and threats to the 8 to 10 most important external factors facing management.

- **The Internal Factor Analysis (IFAS) Table in Chapter 5**
  This reduces the internal strengths and weaknesses to the 8 to 10 most important internal factors facing management.

- **The Strategic Factor Analysis Summary (SFAS) Matrix in Chapter 6**
  This condenses the 16 to 20 factors generated in the EFAS and IFAS tables into the 8 to 10 most important (strategic) factors facing the company. These strategic factors become the basis for generating alternatives and act as a recommendation for the company's future direction.

Suggestions for case analysis are provided in **Appendix 12.B (end of Chapter 12)** and contain step-by-step procedures on how to use a strategic audit in analyzing a case. This appendix includes an example of a student-written strategic audit. Thousands of students around the world have applied this methodology to case analysis with great success. *The Case Instructor's Manual* contains examples of student-written strategic audits for each of the full-length comprehensive strategy cases.

FEATURES

This edition contains many of the same features and content that helped make previous editions successful. Some of the features include the following:

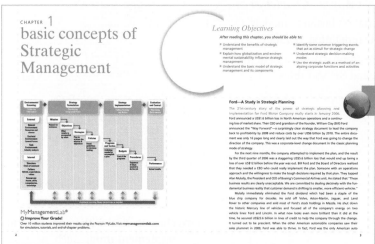

- A **strategic management model** runs throughout the first 11 chapters as a unifying concept. (Explained in *Chapter 1*)

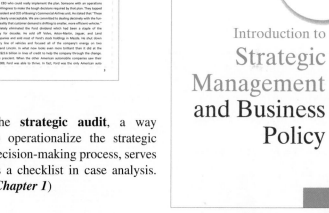

PART 1

Introduction to
Strategic
Management
and Business
Policy

- The **strategic audit**, a way to operationalize the strategic decision-making process, serves as a checklist in case analysis. (*Chapter 1*)

- **Corporate governance** is examined in terms of the roles, responsibilities, and interactions of top management and the board of directors and includes the impact of the Sarbanes–Oxley Act. (*Chapter 2*)

- **Social responsibility and managerial ethics** are examined in detail in terms of how they affect strategic decision making. They include the process of stakeholder analysis and the concept of social capital. (*Chapter 3*)

- Equal emphasis is placed on **environmental scanning** of the societal environment as well as on the task environment. Topics include forecasting and Miles and Snow's typology in addition to competitive intelligence techniques and Porter's industry analysis. (***Chapter 4***)

- **Core and distinctive competencies** are examined within the framework of the resource-based view of the firm. (***Chapter 5***)

- **Organizational analysis** includes material on business models, supply chain management, and corporate reputation. (***Chapter 5***)

- Internal and external strategic factors are emphasized through the use of specially designed **EFAS**, **IFAS**, and **SFAS tables**. (***Chapters 4, 5, and 6***)

- **Functional strategies** are examined in light of **outsourcing**. (***Chapter 8***)

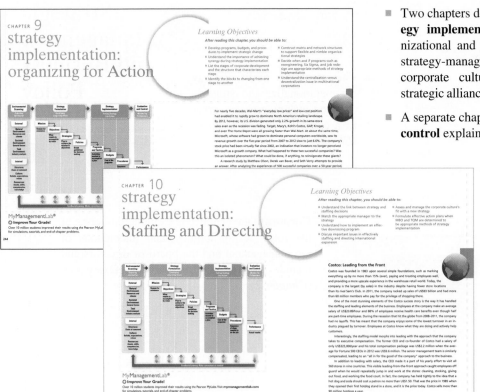

- Two chapters deal with issues in **strategy implementation**, such as organizational and job design, as well as strategy-manager fit, action planning, corporate culture, and international strategic alliances. (***Chapters 9 and 10***)

- A separate chapter on **evaluation and control** explains the importance of measurement and incentives to organizational performance. (***Chapter 11***)

- **Suggestions for in-depth case analysis** provide a complete listing of financial ratios, recommendations for oral and written analysis, and ideas for further research. (***Chapter 12***)

■ The **strategic audit worksheet** is based on the time-tested strategic audit and is designed to help students organize and structure daily case preparation in a brief period of time. The worksheet works exceedingly well for checking the level of daily student case preparation—especially for open class discussions of cases. (*Chapter 12*)

Strategic Audit Heading	Analysis		
	(+) Factors	(−) Factors	Comments
I. Current Situation			
A. Past Corporate Performance Indexes			
B. Strategic Posture: Current Mission Current Objectives Current Strategies Current Policies			
SWOT Analysis Begins:			
II. Corporate Governance			
A. Board of Directors			
B. Top Management			
III. External Environment (EFAS): Opportunities and Threats (SWOT)			
A. Natural Environment			
B. Societal Environment			
C. Task Environment (Industry Analysis)			
IV. Internal Environment (IFAS): Strengths and Weaknesses (SWOT)			
A. Corporate Structure			
B. Corporate Culture			
C. Corporate Resources			
1. Marketing			
2. Finance			
3. Research and Development			
4. Operations and Logistics			
5. Human Resources			
6. Information Technology			
V. Analysis of Strategic Factors (SFAS)			
A. Key Internal and External Strategic Factors (SWOT)			
B. Review of Mission and Objectives			
SWOT Analysis Ends. Recommendation Begins:			
VI. Alternatives and Recommendations			
A. Strategic Alternatives—pros and cons			
B. Recommended Strategy			
VII. Implementation			
VIII. Evaluation and Control			

NOTE: See the complete Strategic Audit on pages 34–41. It lists the pages in the book that discuss each of the eight headings.
SOURCE: T. L. Wheelen and J. D. Hunger, "Strategic Audit Worksheet." Copyright © 1985, 1986, 1987, 1988, 1989, 2005, and 2009 by T. L. Wheelen. Copyright © 1989, 2005, and 2009 by Wheelen and Hunger Associates. Revised 1991, 1994, and 1997. Reprinted by permission. Additional copies available for classroom use in Part D of the Case Instructor's Manual and on the Prentice Hall Web site (www.prenhall.com/wheelen).

End of Chapter SUMMARY

Every day, about 17 truckloads of used diesel engines and other parts are dumped at a receiving facility at Caterpillar's remanufacturing plant in Corinth, Mississippi. The filthy iron engines are then broken down by two workers, who manually hammer and drill for half a day until they have taken every bolt off the engine and put each component into its own bin. The engines are then cleaned and remade at half of the cost of a new engine and sold for a tidy profit. This system works at Caterpillar because, as a general rule, 70% of the cost to build something new is in the materials and 30% is in the labor. Remanufacturing simply starts the manufacturing process over again with materials that are essentially free and which already contain most of the energy costs needed to make them. The would-be discards become fodder for the next product, eliminating waste, and cutting costs. Caterpillar's management was so impressed by the remanufacturing operation that they made the business a separate division in 2005. The unit earned more than US$1 billion in sales in 2005 and in 2012 employed more than 8500 workers in 16 countries.

Caterpillar's remanufacturing unit was successful not only because of its capability of wringing productivity out of materials and labor, but also because it designed its products for reuse. Before they are built new, remanufactured products must be designed for disassembly. In order to achieve this, Caterpillar asks its designers to check a "Reman" box on Caterpillar's product development checklist. The company also needs to know where its products are being used in order to take them back—known as the art of *reverse logistics*. This is achieved by Caterpillar's excellent relationship with its dealers throughout the world, as well as through financial incentives. For example, when a customer orders a crankshaft, that customer is offered a remanufactured one for half the cost of a new one—assuming the customer turns in the old

■ An **experiential exercise** focusing on the material covered in each chapter helps the reader apply strategic concepts to an actual situation.

■ A list of **key terms** and the pages in which they are discussed let the reader keep track of important concepts as they are introduced in each chapter.

End of Chapter SUMMARY

Strategy implementation is where "the rubber hits the road." Environmental scanning and strategy formulation are crucial to strategic management but are only the beginning of the process. The failure to carry a strategic plan into the day-to-day operations of the workplace is a major reason why strategic planning often fails to achieve its objectives. It is discouraging to note that in one study nearly 70% of the strategic plans were never successfully implemented.[84]

For a strategy to be successfully implemented, it must be made action-oriented. This is done through a series of programs that are funded through specific budgets and contain new detailed procedures. This is what Sergio Marchionne did when he implemented a turnaround strategy as the new Fiat Group CEO in 2004. He attacked the lethargic, bureaucratic system by flattening Fiat's structure and giving younger managers a larger amount of authority and responsibility. He and other managers worked to reduce the number of auto platforms from 19 to six by 2012. The time from the completion of the design process to new car production was cut from 26 to 18 months. By 2008, the Fiat auto unit was again profitable. Marchionne reintroduced Fiat to the United States market in 2012 after a 27-year absence.[85]

This chapter explains how jobs and organizational units can be designed to support a change in strategy. We will continue with staffing and directing issues in strategy implementation in the next chapter.

MyManagementLab®

Go to **mymanagementlab.com** to complete the problems marked with this icon. ⬡

KEY TERMS

budget (p. 251)
cellular/modular organization (p. 263)
geographic-area structure (p. 269)
job design (p. 265)
matrix of change (p. xx)
matrix structure (p. 260)
multinational corporation (MNC) (p. 266)

network structure (p. 262)
organizational life cycle (p. 258)
procedure (p. 252)
product-group structure (p. 269)
program (p. 248)
reengineering (p. 263)
Six Sigma (p. 264)

stages of corporate development (p. 255)
stages of international development (p. 267)
strategy implementation (p. 246)
structure follows strategy (p. 253)
synergy (p. 252)
virtual organization (p. 262)

- **Learning objectives** begin each chapter.
- **Timely, well-researched, and class-tested cases** deal with interesting companies and industries. Many of the cases are about well-known, publicly held corporations—ideal subjects for further research by students wishing to "update" the cases.

Both the text and the cases have been class-tested in strategy courses and revised based on feedback from students and instructors. The first 11 chapters are organized around a strategic management model that begins each chapter and provides a structure for both content and case analysis. We emphasize those concepts that have proven to be most useful in understanding strategic decision making and in conducting case analysis. Our goal was to make the text as comprehensive as possible without getting bogged down in any one area. Extensive endnote references are provided for those who wish to learn more about any particular topic. All cases are about actual organizations. The firms range in size from large, established multinationals to small, entrepreneurial ventures, and cover a broad variety of issues. As an aid to case analysis, we propose the strategic audit as an analytical technique.

SUPPLEMENTS

Instructor Resource Center

At **www.pearsonglobaleditions.com/Wheelen**, instructors can access teaching resources available with this text in a downloadable, digital format. Registration is simple and gives you immediate access to new titles and editions. Please contact your Pearson sales representative for your access code. As a registered faculty member, you can download resource files and receive immediate access and instructions for installing course management content on your campus server. In case you ever need assistance, our dedicated technical support team is ready to assist instructors with questions about the media supplements that accompany this text. Visit **http://247.pearsoned.com** for answers to frequently asked questions and toll-free user support phone numbers. The Instructor Resource Center provides the following electronic resources.

Instructor's Manuals

Two comprehensive Instructor's Manuals have been carefully constructed to accompany this book. The first one accompanies the concepts chapters; the second one accompanies the cases.

Concepts Instructor's Manual
To aid in discussing the 12 strategy chapters, the *Concepts Instructor's Manual* includes:

- **Suggestions for Teaching Strategic Management:** These include various teaching methods and suggested course syllabi.
- **Chapter Notes:** These include summaries of each chapter, suggested answers to discussion questions, and suggestions for using end-of-chapter cases/exercises and part-ending cases, plus additional discussion questions (with answers) and lecture modules.

Case Instructor's Manual
To aid in case method teaching, the *Case Instructor's Manual* includes detailed suggestions for its use, teaching objectives, and examples of student analyses for each of the full-length comprehensive cases. This is the most comprehensive instructor's manual available in strategic management. A standardized format is provided for each case:

1. Case Abstract
2. Case Issues and Subjects
3. Steps Covered in the Strategic Decision-Making Process

4. Case Objectives

5. Suggested Classroom Approaches

6. Discussion Questions

7. Case Author's Teaching Note (if available)

8. Student-Written Strategic Audit (if appropriate)

9. EFAS, IFAS, and SFAS Exhibits

10. Financial Analysis—ratios and common-size income statements (if appropriate)

PowerPoint Slides

PowerPoint slides, provided in a comprehensive package of text outlines and figures corresponding to the text, are designed to aid the educator and supplement in-class lectures.

Test Item File

The Test Item File contains over 1200 questions, including multiple-choice, true/false, and essay questions. Each question is followed by the correct answer, AACSB category, and difficulty rating.

TestGen

TestGen software is preloaded with all of the *Test Item File* questions. It allows instructors to manually or randomly view test questions, and to add, delete, or modify test-bank questions as needed to create multiple tests.

VIDEO LIBRARY

Videos illustrating the most important subject topics are available at:

- MyLab – available for instructors and students, provides round the clock instant access to videos and corresponding assessment and simulations for Pearson textbooks.

  Contact your local Pearson representative to request access.

CourseSmart* eTextbooks Online

CourseSmart eTextbooks were developed for students looking to save the cost on required or recommended textbooks. Students simply select their eText by title or author and purchase immediate access to the content for the duration of the course using any major credit card. With a CourseSmart eText, students can search for specific keywords or page numbers, take notes online, print out reading assignments that incorporate lecture notes, and bookmark important passages for later review. For more information or to purchase a CourseSmart eTextbook, visit **www.coursesmart.co.uk**.

Acknowledgments

We would like to thank the many people at Pearson who helped make this edition possible. We are especially grateful to our senior project manager, Karalyn Holland, who managed to keep everything on an even keel. We also would like to thank Stephanie Wall, Sarah Holle, Norine Strang, Judy Leale, Estelle Simpson, Michael Joyce, Michael McGee, Bernard Ollila, Erin Gardner, and Brooks Hill-Whilton and everyone at Pearson who guided the book through the production and marketing processes. Special thanks to Dave Ostrow at Pearson for his hard work in the trenches.

---

*This product may not be available in all markets. For more details, please visit www.coursesmart.co.uk or contact your local Pearson representative.

We are very thankful to Paul D. Maxwell, *St. Thomas University, Miami, FL*; Terry J. Schindler, *University of Indianapolis*; Anne Walsh, *La Salle University*; Angelo Camillo, *Woodbury University*; Jeannine L Scherenberg, *Rockford College*; William Reisel, *St. John's University*; Ronaldo Parente, *Florida International University*; Roxana Wright, *Plymouth State University*; J. Barry Dickinson, *Holy Family University*; Theodore E Davis, *Jr., PhD, SUNY College at Buffalo*; Manzoor Chowdhury, *Lincoln University*; David Olson, *California State University at Bakersfield*; and Janis Dietz, *University of La Verne* for their constructive criticism of the 14th edition.

We are especially thankful to the many students who tried out the cases we chose to include in this book. Their comments helped us find any flaws in the cases before the book went to the printer.

We also offer a big thanks to the many case authors who have provided us with excellent cases for the 14th edition of this book. We consider many of these case authors to be our friends. A special thanks to you!! The adage is true: The path to greatness is through others.

Alan Hoffman would like to thank the following colleagues for their valuable insight, support, and feedback during the writing process: Janet Forte, Kathy Connolly, Robert Frisch, Barbara Gottfried, Bonnie Kornman, Gail Goldman, Janyce Lee, Raj Sisodia, Ken Kornman, Donna Gallo, Jeff Shuman, Linda Edelman, Anna Forte, Emily Murphy, Tatiana Manolova, Michael Montalbano, Goli Eshghi, Marie Rock, Deb Kennedy, Linda Bee, Alex Zampieron, Alyssa Goldman, Jill Brown, Natalia Gold, Jayne Pollack, Aileen Cordette, Andrea Harding, Martha Bailey, Lew Sudarsky, Ed Ottensmeyer, Tim Stearns, Gloria Larson, Christopher Forte, Sam Vitali, Michael Page, Chip Wiggins, Vicki Lafarge, Dorothy Feldmann, Duncan Spelman, Josh Senn, Gary Cordette, Bob Cronin, Joe Goldman, Ed Harding, Anne Nelson, Tao Yue, Dianne Bevelander, Rick Vitali, Catherine Usoff, Beverley Earle, and William Wiggins. Special thanks to Joyce Vincelette, Kathryn Wheelen, Patricia Ryan, Jim Schwartz and Pamela Goldberg.

Lastly, to the many strategy instructors and students who have relayed to us their thoughts about teaching the strategy course: We have tried to respond to your problems and concerns as best we could by providing a comprehensive yet usable text coupled with recent and complex cases. To you, the people who work hard in the strategy trenches, we acknowledge our debt. This book is yours.

T. L. W.
Saint Petersburg, Florida

J. D. H.
St. Joseph, Minnesota

A. N. H.
Waltham, Massachusetts

C. E. B.
Charlotte, North Carolina

Pearson would like to thank and acknowledge the following people for their work on the Global Edition:

Contributors
Caroline Akhras
Notre Dame University, Lebanon

Jon and Diane Sutherland
Freelance Writers, UK

Krish Saha
Coventry University, UK

Reviewers
Hadijah Iberahim
Universiti Teknologi MARA, Malaysia

Goh Yuan Sheng Victor
Singapore Management University, Singapore

Khalil Ghazzawi
Rafik Hariri University, Lebanon

About the Authors

THOMAS L. WHEELEN, *May 30, 1935 – December 24, 2011.* DBA, MBA, BS Cum Laude (George Washington University, Babson College, and Boston College, respectively), College, MBA (1961); Boston College, BS cum laude (1957). Teaching Experience: Visiting Professor— *Trinity College—University of Dublin* (Fall 1999); *University of South Florida*—Professor of Strategic Management (1983–2008); University of Virginia - *McIntire School of Commerce*; Ralph A. Beeton Professor of Free Enterprise (1981–1985); Professor (1974–1981); Associate Professor (1971–1974); and Assistant Professor (1968–1971); Visiting Professor—*University of Arizona* (1979–1980 and *Northeastern University* (Summer 1975, 1977, and 1979). **Academic, Industry and Military Experience:** *University of Virginia College of Continuing Education:* (1) Coordinator for Business Education (1978–1983, 1971–1976)—approved all undergraduate courses offered at seven Regional Centers and approved faculty; (2) Liaison Faculty and Consultant to the National Academy of the FBI Academy (1972–1983) and; (3) developed, sold, and conducted over 200 seminars for local, state, and national governments, and companies for the McIntire School of Commerce and Continuing Education. *General Electric Company* - various management positions (1961–1965); *U.S. Navy Supply Corps* (SC)—Lt. (SC) USNR—assistant supply officer aboard nuclear support tender (1957–1960). **Publications:** (1) *Monograph, An Assessment of Undergraduate Business Education in the United States* (with J. D. Hunger), 1980; (2) *Books: **60 books published**; **14 books translated into eight languages** (Arabic, Bahasa-Indonesian, Chinese, Chinese Simplified, Greek, Italian, Japanese, Portuguese, and Thai);* (3) *Books*—co-author with J. D. Hunger—five active books: *Strategic Management and Business Policy*, 10th edition (2006); *Cases in Strategic Management and Business Policy*, 10th edition (2006); *Concepts in Strategic Management and Business Policy*, 10th edition (2006); *Strategic Management and Business Policy*, 10th edition; *International Edition* (2006); and *Essentials of Strategic Management*, 3rd edition (2003); (4) *Co-editor*: *Developments in Information Systems* (1974) and *Collective Bargaining in the Public Sector* (1977); and (5) *Co-developer of software*—STrategic Financial ANalyzer (ST. FAN) (1993, 1990, 1989—different versions); (6) *Articles*—authored over 40 articles that have appeared in such journals as the *Journal of Management, Business Quarterly, Personnel Journal, SAM Advanced Management Journal, Journal of Retailing, International Journal of Management,* and the *Handbook of Business Strategy*; (6) *Cases*—have about 280 cases appearing in over 83 text and case books, as well as the *Business Case Journal, Journal of Management Case Studies, International Journal of Case Studies and Research*, and the *Case Research Journal.* **Awards:** (1) *Fellow* elected by the *Society for Advancement of Management* in 2002; (2) *Fellow* elected by the *North American Case Research Association* in 2000; (3) *Fellow* elected by the *Text and Academic Authors Association* in 2000; (4) the 1999 Phil Carroll Advancement of Management Award in Strategic Management from the Society for Advancement of Management; (5) 1999 McGuffey Award for *Excellence and Longevity for Strategic Management and Business Policy*, 6th edition, from the Text and Academic Authors Association; (6) 1996/97 Teaching Incentive Program Award for teaching undergraduate strategic management; (7) Fulbright, 1996–1997, to Ireland but had to turn it down; (8) Endowed Chair, Ralph A. Beeton Professor, at University of Virginia (1981–1985); (9) a Sesquicentennial Associateship research grant from the Center for Advanced Studies at the University of Virginia, 1979–1980; (10) Small Business Administration (Small Business Institute), supervised undergraduate team that won District, Regional III, and Honorable Mention Awards; and (11) awards for two articles. **Associations:** Dr. Wheelen served on the Board of Directors of the Adhia Mutual Fund, the Society for Advancement of Management, and on the Editorial Board and as Associate Editor of *SAM Advanced Management Journal*. He served on the Board of Directors of Lazer Surgical Software Inc. and the Southern Management Association, and on the Editorial Boards of the *Journal of Management* and *Journal of Management Case Studies,* the *Journal of Retail Banking,* the *Case Research Journal,* and *the Business Case Journal.* He was Vice President of *Strategic Management* for the *Society for the Advancement of Management,* and President of the *North American Case Research Association.* Dr. Wheelen was a member of the *Academy of Management, Beta Gamma Sigma,* the *Southern Management Association,* the *North American Case Research Association,* the *Society for Advancement of Management,* the *Society for Case Research,* the *Strategic Management Association,* and the *World Association for Case Method Research and Application.* He has been listed in *Who's Who in Finance and Industry, Who's Who in the South and Southwest,* and *Who's Who in American Education.*

J. DAVID HUNGER, Ph.D. (Ohio State University), is currently Strategic Management Scholar in Residence at Saint John's University in Minnesota. He is also Professor Emeritus at Iowa State University where he taught for 23 years. He previously taught at George Mason University, the University of Virginia, and Baldwin-Wallace College. He worked in brand management at Procter & Gamble Company, as a selling supervisor at Lazarus Department Store, and served as a Captain in U.S. Army Military Intelligence. He has been active as a consultant and trainer to business corporations, as well as to state and federal government agencies. He has written numerous articles and cases that have appeared in the *Academy of Management Journal, International Journal of Management, Human Resource Management, Journal of Business Strategies, Case Research Journal, Business Case Journal, Handbook of Business Strategy, Journal of Management Case Studies, Annual Advances in Business Cases, Journal of Retail Banking, SAM Advanced Management Journal,* and *Journal of Management,* among others. Dr. Hunger is a member of the Academy of Management, the North American Case Research Association, the Society for Case Research, the North American Management Society, the Textbook and Academic Authors Association, and the Strategic Management Society. He is past-President of the North American Case Research Association, the Society for Case Research, and the Iowa State University Press Board of Directors. He also served as a Vice President of the U.S. Association for Small Business and Entrepreneurship. He was Academic Director of the Pappajohn Center for Entrepreneurship at Iowa State University. He has served on the editorial review boards of *SAM Advanced Management Journal, the Journal of Business Strategies,* and *Journal of Business Research*. He has served on the board of directors of the North American Case Research Association, the Society for Case Research, the Iowa State University Press, and the North American Management Society. He is co-author with Thomas L. Wheelen of *Strategic Management and Business Policy* and *Essentials of Strategic Management* plus *Concepts in Strategic Management and Business Policy and Cases in Strategic Management and Business Policy*, as well as *Strategic Management Cases* (PIC: Preferred Individualized Cases), and a monograph assessing undergraduate business education in the United States. The 8th edition of *Strategic Management and Business Policy* received the McGuffey Award for Excellence and Longevity in 1999 from the Text and Academic Authors Association. Dr. Hunger received the Best Case Award given by the McGraw-Hill Publishing Company and the Society for Case Research in 1991 for outstanding case development. He is listed in various versions of *Who's Who*, including *Who's Who in the United States* and *Who's Who in the World*. He was also recognized in 1999 by the Iowa State University College of Business with its Innovation in Teaching Award and was elected a Fellow of the Teaching and Academic Authors Association and of the North American Case Research Association.

ALAN N. HOFFMAN, MBA, DBA (Indiana University), is Professor of Strategic Management at Bentley University in Waltham, Massachusetts. He is the former Director of the MBA Program at Bentley University. He served as the course coordinator and Visiting Professor of Strategic Management for the Global Strategy course in the OneMBA Program at the Rotterdam School of Management at Erasmus University, Rotterdam, The Netherlands. He is also the owner of Dr. Alan N. Hoffman Investment Management, founded in 1995. His major areas of interest include strategic management, global competition, investment strategy, design thinking, and technology. Professor Hoffman is coauthor of *The Strategic Management Casebook and Skill Builder* textbook (with Hugh O'Neill). His academic publications have appeared in the *Academy of Management Journal*, *Human Relations*, the *Journal of Business Ethics*, the *Journal of Business Research*, and *Business Horizons*. He has authored more than 30 strategic management cases, including The Boston YWCA, Ryka Inc., Liz Claiborne, Ben & Jerry's, Cisco Systems, Sun Microsystems, Palm Inc., Handspring, eBay, AOL/Time Warner, McAfee, Apple Computer, TiVo Inc., Wynn Resorts, TomTom, Blue Nile, GE, Amazon, Netflix, Delta Airlines, A123, Tesla Motors, and Whole Foods Market. He is the recipient of the 2004 Bentley University Teaching Innovation Award for his course: "The Organizational Life Cycle—The Boston Beer Company Brewers of Samuel Adams Lager Beer." He teaches strategic management in many executive programs and also teaches business to artists at The Massachusetts College of Art and Design.

CHARLES E. BAMFORD, Ph.D. (University of Tennessee), MBA (Virginia Tech), and BS (University of Virginia). He is an adjunct professor at the University of Notre Dame, where he has been awarded the EMBA Professor of the Year Award three times. Chuck worked in industry for 12 years prior to pursuing his Ph.D. His last position was as the Manager of Business Analysis (Mergers & Acquisitions, Dispositions, and Business Consulting) for Dominion Bankshares Corporation (now Wells Fargo). For the past 20 years, Chuck has been an active consultant as the Founder of Bamford Associates, LLC. He has worked with thousands of managers in the development of implementable strategic plans and an entrepreneurial orientation to growth.

His research has been published in the *Strategic Management Journal, Journal of Business Venturing, Entrepreneurship Theory & Practice, Journal of Business Research, Journal of Business Strategies, Journal of Technology Transfer*, and *Journal of Small Business Management,* among others. Chuck has co-authored four textbooks and is the author of the fiction novel *Some Things Are Never Forgiven* (Penguin Press).

He has taught courses in strategy and entrepreneurship at the undergraduate, graduate, and executive levels. His teaching experience includes courses taught at universities in Scotland, Hungary, and the Czech Republic. He was a Professor and held the Dennis Thompson Chair of Entrepreneurship at Queens University of Charlotte and previously held positions as an Associate Professor at Texas Christian University and at the University of Richmond. He has taught Executive MBA courses at The University of Notre Dame, Texas Christian University, Tulane University, and at Queens University of Charlotte.

Chuck has won 18 individual teaching excellence awards during his career, including 9 Executive MBA Professor of the Year Awards. He is also a Noble Foundation Fellow in Teaching Excellence.

Introduction to Strategic Management and Business Policy

basic concepts of Strategic Management

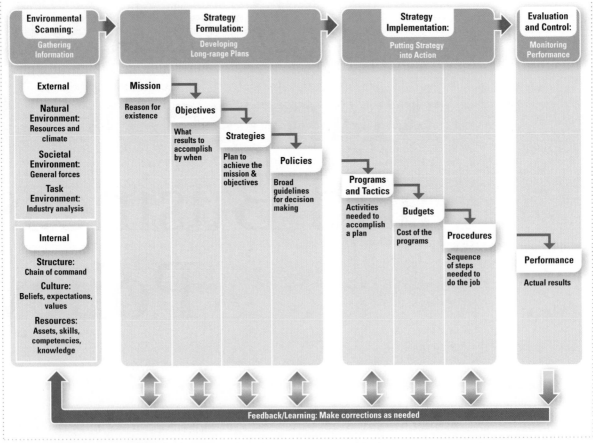

| Environmental Scanning: Gathering Information | Strategy Formulation: Developing Long-range Plans | Strategy Implementation: Putting Strategy into Action | Evaluation and Control: Monitoring Performance |

External

Natural Environment: Resources and climate

Societal Environment: General forces

Task Environment: Industry analysis

Internal

Structure: Chain of command

Culture: Beliefs, expectations, values

Resources: Assets, skills, competencies, knowledge

Mission — Reason for existence

Objectives — What results to accomplish by when

Strategies — Plan to achieve the mission & objectives

Policies — Broad guidelines for decision making

Programs and Tactics — Activities needed to accomplish a plan

Budgets — Cost of the programs

Procedures — Sequence of steps needed to do the job

Performance — Actual results

Feedback/Learning: Make corrections as needed

MyManagementLab®

⭐ Improve Your Grade!

Over 10 million students improved their results using the Pearson MyLabs. Visit **mymanagementlab.com** for simulations, tutorials, and end-of-chapter problems.

Learning Objectives

After reading this chapter, you should be able to:

- Understand the benefits of strategic management
- Explain how globalization and environmental sustainability influence strategic management
- Understand the basic model of strategic management and its components
- Identify some common triggering events that act as stimuli for strategic change
- Understand strategic decision-making modes
- Use the strategic audit as a method of analyzing corporate functions and activities

Ford—A Study in Strategic Planning

The 21st-century story of the power of strategic planning and implementation for Ford Motor Company really starts in January 2006. Ford announced a US$1.6 billion loss in North American operations and a continuing loss of market share. Then CEO and grandson of the founder, William Clay (Bill) Ford announced the "Way Forward"—a surprisingly clear strategy document to lead the company back to profitability by 2008 and reduce costs by over US$6 billion by 2010. The entire document was only 16 pages long and clearly laid out the way that Ford was going to change the direction of the company. This was a corporate-level change document in the classic planning mode of strategy.

For the next nine months, the company attempted to implement the plan, and the result by the third quarter of 2006 was a staggering US$5.6 billion loss that would end up being a loss of over US$12 billion before the year was out. Bill Ford and the Board of Directors realized that they needed a CEO who could really implement the plan. Someone with an operations approach and the willingness to make the tough decisions required by that plan. They tapped Alan Mulally, the President and CEO of Boeing's Commercial Airlines unit. He stated that "These business results are clearly unacceptable. We are committed to dealing decisively with the fundamental business reality that customer demand is shifting to smaller, more efficient vehicles."

Mulally immediately eliminated the Ford dividend which had been a staple of the blue chip company for decades. He sold off Volvo, Aston-Martin, Jaguar, and Land Rover to other companies and sold most of Ford's stock holdings in Mazda. He shut down the historic Mercury line of vehicles and focused all of the company's energy on two vehicle lines: Ford and Lincoln. In what now looks even more brilliant than it did at the time, he secured US$23.6 billion in lines of credit to help the company through the change. It turned out to be prescient. When the other American automobile companies saw their sales plummet in 2009, Ford was able to thrive. In fact, Ford was the only American auto company that didn't require a government bailout. If not for the bailout moneys from the U.S. government, Ford may well have become the only American automaker that remained.

The results speak for themselves. In early 2012, Ford announced that for the calendar year of 2011 it earned US$20.2 billion in net income and US$8.8 billion in pre-tax profit, which was the third year in a row it reported an increase in annual profits. Ford has moved into the solid #2 spot for worldwide sales of vehicles and has reduced its total debt position to less than US$13 billion. Mulally credits the results to a companywide focus on a strategy that matters to customers.

SOURCES: R. Jones, "'Way Forward' for Ford Looking Long and Hard," MSNBC (2011), http://www .msnbc.msn.com/id/10988134/ns/business-autos/t/way-forward-ford-looking-long-hard/; "Ford Hits Another Big Pothole," BusinessWeek (October 23, 2006), http://www.businessweek.com/ stories/2006-10-23/ford-hits-another-big-potholebusinessweek-business-news-stock-market-and- financial-advice; http://media.ford.com/article_display.cfm?article_id=24203/; N. Vardy, "Ford: An All American Success Story," MSN Money (December 14, 2011), http://money.msn.com/top- stocks/post.aspx?post=f7a06d6b-9b5f-48fd-ac35-0a1d0747a582; http://topics.nytimes.com/top/news/ business/companies/ford_motor_company/index.html; http://media.ford.com/article_display.cfm?article_ id=35878.

The Study of Strategic Management

Strategic management is a set of managerial decisions and actions that help determine the long-term performance of an organization. It includes environmental scanning (both external and internal), strategy formulation (strategic or long-range planning), strategy implementation, and evaluation and control. Originally called *business policy*, strategic management has advanced substantially with the concentrated efforts of researchers and practitioners. Today we recognize both a science and an art to the application of strategic management techniques.

PHASES OF STRATEGIC MANAGEMENT

Many of the concepts and techniques that deal with strategic management have been developed and used successfully by business corporations as large as General Electric and as small as the newest startup. Over time, business practitioners and academic researchers have expanded and refined these concepts. Initially, strategic management was of most use to large corporations operating in multiple industries. Increasing risks of error, costly mistakes, and even economic ruin are causing today's professional managers in all organizations to take strategic management seriously in order to keep their companies competitive in an increasingly volatile environment.

As managers attempt to better deal with their changing world, a firm generally evolves through the following four **phases of strategic management:**[1]

Phase 1—Basic financial planning: Managers initiate serious planning when they are requested to propose the following year's budget. Projects are proposed on the basis of very little analysis, with most information coming from within the firm. The sales force usually provides the small amount of environmental information. Such simplistic operational planning only pretends to be strategic management, yet it is quite time consuming. Normal company activities are often suspended for weeks while managers try to cram ideas into the proposed budget. The time horizon is usually one year.

Phase 2—Forecast-based planning: As annual budgets become less useful at stimulating long-term planning, managers attempt to propose five-year plans. At this point, they consider projects that may take more than one year. In addition to internal information, managers gather any available environmental data—usually on an ad hoc basis—and extrapolate current trends five years into the future. This phase is also time consuming, often involving a full month or more of managerial activity to make sure all the proposed budgets fit together. The process gets very political as managers compete for larger shares of limited funds. Seemingly endless meetings take place to evaluate proposals and justify assumptions. The time horizon is usually three to five years.

Phase 3—Externally oriented (strategic) planning: Frustrated with highly political yet ineffectual five-year plans, top management takes control of the planning process by initiating strategic planning. The company seeks to increase its responsiveness to changing markets and competition by thinking strategically. Planning is taken out of the hands of lower-level managers and concentrated in a planning staff whose task is to develop strategic plans for the corporation. Consultants often provide the sophisticated and innovative techniques that the planning staff uses to gather information and forecast future trends. Organizations start competitive intelligence units. Upper-level managers meet once a year at a resort "retreat" led by key members of the planning staff to evaluate and update the current strategic plan. Such top-down planning emphasizes formal strategy formulation and leaves the implementation issues to lower-management levels. Top management typically develops five-year plans with help from consultants but minimal input from lower levels.

Phase 4—Strategic management: Realizing that even the best strategic plans are worthless without the input and commitment of lower-level managers, top management forms planning groups of managers and key employees at many levels, from various departments and workgroups. They develop and integrate a series of strategic plans aimed at achieving the company's primary objectives. Strategic plans at this point detail the implementation, evaluation, and control issues. Rather than attempting to perfectly forecast the future, the plans emphasize probable scenarios and contingency strategies. The sophisticated annual five-year strategic plan is replaced with strategic thinking at all levels of the organization throughout the year. Strategic information, previously available only centrally to top management, is available virtually to people throughout the organization. Instead of a large centralized planning staff, internal and external planning consultants are available to help guide group strategy discussions. Although top management may still initiate the strategic planning process, the resulting strategies may come from anywhere in the organization. Planning is typically interactive across levels and is no longer strictly top down. People at all levels are now involved.

General Electric, one of the pioneers of strategic planning, led the transition from strategic planning to strategic management during the 1980s.[2] By the 1990s, most other corporations around the world had also begun the conversion to strategic management.

BENEFITS OF STRATEGIC MANAGEMENT

Strategic management emphasizes long-term performance. Many companies can manage short-term bursts of high performance, but only a few can sustain it over a longer period of time. For example, of the original *Fortune 500* companies listed in 1955, only 6 of the Top 25 in that original list are still in the Top 25 as of 2012 and 10 of the original companies are no longer in business. To be successful in the long-run, companies must not only be able to *execute* current activities to satisfy an existing market, but they must also *adapt* those activities to satisfy new and changing markets.[3]

Research reveals that organizations that engage in strategic management generally outperform those that do not.[4] The attainment of an appropriate match, or "fit," between an organization's environment and its strategy, structure, and processes has positive effects on the organization's performance.[5] Strategic planning becomes increasingly important as the environment becomes more unstable.[6] For example, studies of the impact of deregulation on the U.S. railroad and trucking industries found that companies that changed their strategies and structures as their environment changed outperformed companies that did not change.[7]

A survey of nearly 50 corporations in a variety of countries and industries found the three most highly rated benefits of strategic management to be:

- A clearer sense of strategic vision for the firm.
- A sharper focus on what is strategically important.
- An improved understanding of a rapidly changing environment.[8]

A survey by McKinsey & Company of 800 executives found that formal strategic planning processes improved overall satisfaction with strategy development.[9] To be effective, however, strategic management need not always be a formal process. It can begin with a few simple questions:

1. Where is the organization now? (Not where do we hope it is!)

2. If no changes are made, where will the organization be in one year? Two years? Five years? Ten years? Are the answers acceptable?

3. If the answers are not acceptable, what specific actions should management undertake? What are the risks and payoffs involved?

Although Bain & Company's *2011 Management Tools and Trends* survey of 1,230 global executives revealed that benchmarking had replaced strategic planning as the perennial number one tool used by businesses, this was most likely a reaction to the global slowdown of the past few years. Strategic planning was listed as second and was said to be particularly effective at identifying new opportunities for growth and in ensuring that all managers have the same goals.[10] Other highly ranked strategic management tools were mission and vision statements, core competencies, change management programs and balanced scorecards.[11] A study by Joyce, Nohria, and Roberson of 200 firms in 50 subindustries found that devising and maintaining an engaged, focused strategy was the first of four essential management practices that best differentiated between successful and unsuccessful companies.[12] Based on these and other studies, it can be concluded that strategic management is crucial for long-term organizational success.

Research into the planning practices of companies in the oil industry concludes that the real value of modern strategic planning is more in the *strategic thinking* and *organizational learning* that is part of a future-oriented planning process than in any resulting written strategic plan.[13] Small companies, in particular, may plan informally and irregularly. Nevertheless, studies of small- and medium-sized businesses reveal that the greater the level of planning intensity, as measured by the presence of a formal strategic plan, the greater the level of financial performance, especially when measured in terms of sales increases.[14]

Planning the strategy of large, multidivisional corporations can be complex and time consuming. It often takes slightly more than a year for a large company to move from situation assessment to a final decision agreement. For example, strategic plans in the global oil industry tend to cover 4 to 5 years. The planning horizon for oil exploration is even longer—up to 15 years.[15] Because of the relatively large number of people affected by a strategic decision in a large firm, a formalized, more sophisticated system is needed to ensure that strategic planning leads to successful performance. Otherwise, top management becomes isolated from developments in the business units, and lower-level managers lose sight of the corporate mission and objectives.

Globalization, Innovation, and Sustainability: Challenges to Strategic Management

Not too long ago, a business corporation could be successful by focusing only on making and selling goods and services within its national boundaries. International considerations were minimal. Profits earned from exporting products to foreign lands were considered frosting on the cake, but not really essential to corporate success. During the 1960s, for example, most U.S. companies organized themselves around a number of product divisions that made and sold goods only in the United States. All manufacturing and sales outside the United States were typically managed through one international division. An international assignment was usually considered a message that the person was no longer promotable and should be looking for another job.

For a very long time, many established companies viewed innovation as the domain of the new entrant. The efficiencies that came with size were considered to be the competitive advantage of the large organization. That view has been soundly defeated during the past 30 years. The ability to create unique value and grow an organization organically requires innovation skills. A strategic management approach suggests that if an organization stands still, it will be run over by the competition. What was extraordinary last year is the standard expectation of customers this year. We have watched many large corporations succumb to the lack of innovation in their organization. Sears was the dominant retailer in the United States for more 70 years. Today, it is struggling to find an approach that will give it a competitive advantage. IBM was a company that dominated mainframe computing and was fortunate enough to find a visionary CEO when the mainframe market was crushed by the advent of the PC. That CEO (Louis V. Gerstner, Jr.) transformed the organization with innovation that was cultural, structural, and painful for the company employees. Innovation is rarely easy and it is almost never painless. Nonetheless, it is a core element of successful strategic management.

Similarly, until the later part of the 20th century, a business firm could be very successful without considering sustainable business practices. Companies dumped their waste products in nearby streams or lakes and freely polluted the air with smoke containing noxious gases. Responding to complaints, governments eventually passed laws restricting the freedom to pollute the environment. Lawsuits forced companies to stop old practices. Nevertheless, until the dawn of the 21st century, most executives considered pollution abatement measures to be a cost of business that should be either minimized or avoided. Rather than clean up a polluting manufacturing site, they often closed the plant and moved manufacturing offshore to a developing nation with fewer environmental restrictions. Similarly, the issues of recycling and refurbishing, as well as a company's responsibility to both the local inhabitants and the environment where it operated, were not considered appropriate business approaches, because it was felt these concerns did not help maximize shareholder value. In those days, the word *sustainability* was used to describe competitive advantage, not the environment.

Today, the term used to describe a business's sustainability is the **triple bottom line.** This phrase was first used by John Elkington in 1994 to suggest that companies prepare three different bottom lines in their annual report.[16]

1. Traditional Profit/Loss
2. People Account – The social responsibility of the organization
3. Planet Account – The environmental responsibility of the organization

This triple bottom line has become increasingly important to business today. Companies seek LEED certification for their buildings and mold a reputation for being a business that is friendly to the world. LEED (Leadership in Energy and Environmental Design) certification is available for all structures and includes a number of levels depending upon the efforts made to have a building be self-sustaining or to have as little impact (the smallest footprint) on the environment as possible.[17]

IMPACT OF GLOBALIZATION

Today, everything has changed. **Globalization,** the integrated internationalization of markets and corporations, has changed the way modern corporations do business. As Thomas Friedman points out in *The World Is Flat*, jobs, knowledge, and capital are now able to move across borders with far greater speed and far less friction than was possible only a few years ago.[18]

For example, the interconnected nature of the global financial community meant that the mortgage lending problems of U.S. banks led to a global financial crisis that started in 2008 and impacted economies for years. The worldwide availability of the Internet and supply-chain logistical improvements, such as containerized shipping, mean that companies can now locate anywhere and work with multiple partners to serve any market. For companies seeking a low-cost approach, the internationalization of business has been a new avenue for competitive advantage. Nike and Reebok manufacture their athletic shoes in various countries throughout Asia for sale on every continent. Many other companies in North America and Western Europe are outsourcing their manufacturing, software development, or customer service to companies in China, Eastern Europe, or India. English language proficiency, lower wages in India, and large pools of talented software programmers now enable IBM to employ an estimated 100,000 people in its global delivery centers in Bangalore, Delhi, or Kolkata to serve the needs of clients in Atlanta, Munich, or Melbourne.[19] Instead of using one international division to manage everything outside the home country, large corporations are now using matrix structures in which product units are interwoven with country or regional units. Today, international assignments are considered key for anyone interested in reaching top management.

As more industries become global, strategic management is becoming an increasingly important way to keep track of international developments and position a company for long-term competitive advantage. For example, General Electric moved a major research and development lab for its medical systems division from Japan to China in order to learn more about developing new products for developing economies. Microsoft's largest research center outside Redmond, Washington, is in Beijing.

The formation of regional trade associations and agreements, such as the European Union, NAFTA, Mercosur, Andean Community, CAFTA, and ASEAN, is changing how international business is being conducted. See the **Global Issue** feature to learn how regional trade associations are forcing corporations to establish a manufacturing presence wherever they wish to market goods or else face significant tariffs. These associations have led to the increasing harmonization of standards so that products can more easily be sold and moved across national boundaries. International considerations have led to the strategic alliance between British Airways and American Airlines and to the acquisition of the Anheuser-Busch Companies by the Belgium company InBev, creating AB InBev, among others.

IMPACT OF INNOVATION

Innovation, as the term is used in business, is meant to describe new products, services, methods and organizational approaches that allow the business to achieve extraordinary returns. Innovation has become such an important part of business that *Bloomberg Businessweek* has a weekly section of articles on the topic. A 2012 survey of more than 160 CEOs in the United States administered by consulting group PWC found that CEOs expected the following areas of change in their innovation portfolios:[20]

- New Business Models—56%
- New Products/Services—72%
- Significant Changes to Existing Products/Services—57%
- Cost Reductions for Existing Processes—6%

Innovation is the machine that generates business opportunities in the market; however, it is the implementation of potential innovations that truly drives businesses to be remarkable. While there is a value in being a first mover, there is also a tremendous value in being a second

GLOBAL issue

REGIONAL TRADE ASSOCIATIONS REPLACE NATIONAL TRADE BARRIERS

Formed as the European Economic Community in 1957, the **European Union (EU)** is the most significant trade association in the world. The goal of the EU is the complete economic integration of its 27 member countries so that goods made in one part of Europe can move freely without ever stopping for a customs inspection. The EU includes Austria, Belgium, Bulgaria, Cyprus, the Czech Republic, Denmark, Estonia, Finland, France, Germany, Greece, Hungary, Ireland, Italy, Latvia, Lithuania, Luxembourg, Malta, the Netherlands, Poland, Portugal, Romania, Slovakia, Slovenia, Spain, Sweden, and the United Kingdom. Croatia is an acceding country and Macedonia, Iceland, Montenegro, Serbia, and Turkey are candidate countries in the process of applying. The EU is less than half the size of the United States of America, but has 50% more people. One currency, the euro, is being used throughout the region (with the exception of the United Kingdom) as members integrate their monetary systems. The steady elimination of barriers to free trade is providing the impetus for a series of mergers, acquisitions, and joint ventures among business corporations. The requirement of at least 60% local content to avoid tariffs has forced many U.S. and Asian companies to abandon exporting in favor of having a strong local presence in Europe.

Canada, the United States, and Mexico are affiliated economically under the **North American Free Trade Agreement (NAFTA).** The goal of NAFTA is improved trade among the three member countries rather than complete economic integration. Launched in 1994, the agreement required all three members to remove all tariffs among themselves over 15 years, but they were allowed to have their own tariff arrangements with nonmember countries. Cars and trucks must have 62.5% North American content to qualify for duty-free status. Transportation restrictions and other regulations have been being significantly reduced. A number of Asian and European corporations, such as Sweden's Electrolux, have built manufacturing facilities in Mexico to take advantage of the country's lower wages and easy access to the entire North American region.

or third mover with the right implementation. PC tablets had been developed and even sold almost two decades before the iPad stormed the market. Many people forget that Apple released the Newton tablet back in 1992.[21] Not only was the timing not right, but the product was not promoted in a way that consumers felt a compelling need to buy one. Many elements have to come together for an innovation to bring long-term success to a company.

IMPACT OF SUSTAINABILITY

Sustainability refers to the use of business practices to manage the triple bottom line as was discussed earlier. That triple bottom line involves (1) the management of traditional profit/loss; (2) the management of the company's social responsibility; and (3) the management of its environmental responsibility.

The company has a relatively obvious long-term responsibility to the shareholders of the organization. That means that the company has to be able to thrive despite changes in the industry, society, and the physical environment. This is the focus of much of this textbook and the focus of strategy in business.

The company that pursues a sustainable approach to business has a responsibility to its employees, its customers, and the community in which it operates. Companies that have embraced sustainable practices have seen dramatic increases in risk mitigation and innovation, and an overall feeling of corporate social responsibility. A 2010 research study out of the University of Notre Dame found that employees at companies who focused on business sustainability report higher levels of engagement, high-quality connections, and more creative involvement.[22] In fact, a Gallop research study found that these engaged organizations had 3.9 times the earnings per share (EPS) growth rates when compared to organizations with lower engagement in the same industry.[23]

The company also has a responsibility to treat the environment well. This is usually defined as trying to achieve (or approach) zero impact on the environment. Recycling, increased use of renewable resources, reduction of waste, and refitting buildings to reduce their impact on the environment, among many other techniques, are included in this element of the triple bottom line. The most recognized worldwide standard for environmental efficiency is the ISO 14001 designation. It is not a set of standards, but a framework of activities aimed at effective environmental management.[24]

South American countries are also working to harmonize their trading relationships with each other and to form trade associations. The establishment of the **Mercosur** (**Mercosul** in Portuguese) free-trade area among Argentina, Brazil, Uruguay, and Venezuela means that a manufacturing presence within these countries is becoming essential to avoid tariffs for non-member countries. Paraguay was an original member but is currently suspended following the hasty impeachment of its President Fernando Lugo. The **Andean Community** (Comunidad Andina de Naciones) is a free-trade alliance composed of Columbia, Ecuador, Peru, and Bolivia. On May 23, 2008, the **Union of South American Nations** was formed to unite the two existing free-trade areas with a secretariat in Ecuador and a parliament in Bolivia. It consists of 12 South American countries.

In 2004, the five Central American countries of El Salvador, Guatemala, Honduras, Nicaragua, and Costa Rica, plus the United States, signed the **Central American Free Trade Agreement (CAFTA).** The Dominican Republic joined soon thereafter. Previously, Central American textile manufacturers had to pay import duties of 18%–28% to sell their clothes in the United States unless they bought their raw material from U.S. companies. Under CAFTA, members can buy raw material from anywhere, and their exports are duty free. In addition, CAFTA eliminated import duties on 80% of U.S. goods exported to the region, with theremaining tariffs being phased out over 10 years.

The **Association of Southeast Asian Nations (ASEAN)**—composed of Brunei Darussalam, Cambodia, Indonesia, Laos, Malaysia, Myanmar, Philippines, Singapore, Thailand, and Vietnam—is in the process of linking its members into a borderless economic zone by 2020. Tariffs had been significantly reduced among member countries by 2008 and a new agreement is expected by early 2013. Increasingly referred to as ASEAN+3, ASEAN now includes China, Japan, and South Korea in its annual summit meetings. The ASEAN nations negotiated linkage of the ASEAN Free Trade Area (AFTA) with the existing free-trade area of Australia and New Zealand. With the EU extending eastward and NAFTA extending southward to someday connect with CAFTA and the Union of South American Nations, pressure is building on the independent Asian nations to join ASEAN.

Porter and Reinhardt warn that "in addition to understanding its emissions costs, every firm needs to evaluate its vulnerability to climate-related effects such as regional shifts in the availability of energy and water, the reliability of infrastructures and supply chains, and the prevalence of infectious diseases."[25] Swiss Re, the world's second-largest reinsurer, estimated that the overall economic costs of climate catastrophes related to climate change threatens to double to US$150 billion per year by 2014. The insurance industry's share of this loss would be US$30–$40 billion annually.[26]

Although global warming remains a controversial topic, the best argument in favor of working toward environmental sustainability is a variation of Pascal's Wager on the existence of God:

> The same goes for global warming. If you accept it as reality, adapting your strategy and practices, your plants will use less energy and emit fewer effluents. Your packaging will be more biodegradable, and your new products will be able to capture any markets created by severe weather effects. Yes, global warming might not be as damaging as some predict, and you might have invested more than you needed, but it's just as Pascal said: Given all the possible outcomes, the upside of being ready and prepared for a "fearsome event" surely beats the alternative.[27]

Theories of Organizational Adaptation

Globalization, innovation, and sustainability present real challenges to the strategic management of businesses. How can any one company keep track of all the changing technological, economic, political–legal, and sociocultural trends around the world in order to make the necessary adjustments? This is not an easy task. Various theories have been proposed to account for how organizations obtain fit with their environment and how these approaches have been used to varying degrees by researchers trying to understand firm performance. The theory of **population ecology** suggests that once an organization is successfully established in a particular environmental niche, it is unable to adapt to changing conditions. Inertia prevents the organization from changing in any significant manner. The company is thus replaced (is bought out or goes bankrupt) by other organizations more suited to the new environment. Although it is a popular theory in sociology, research fails to support the arguments of population ecology.[28] **Institution theory,** in contrast, proposes that organizations can and do adapt to changing conditions by imitating other successful organizations. To its credit, many examples can be found of companies that have adapted to changing circumstances by imitating an admired firm's strategies and management techniques.[29] The theory does not, however, explain how or by whom successful new strategies are developed in the first place. The **strategic choice perspective** goes one step further by proposing that not only do organizations adapt to a changing environment, but they also have the opportunity and power to reshape their environment. This perspective is supported by research indicating that the decisions of a firm's management have at least as great an impact on firm performance as overall industry factors.[30] Because of its emphasis on managers making rational strategic decisions, the strategic choice perspective is the dominant one taken in strategic management. Its argument that adaptation is a dynamic process fits with the view of **organizational learning theory,** which says that an organization adjusts defensively to a changing environment and uses knowledge offensively to improve the fit between itself and its environment. This perspective expands the strategic choice perspective to include people at all levels becoming involved in providing input into strategic decisions.[31]

In agreement with the concepts of organizational learning theory, an increasing number of companies are realizing that they must shift from a vertically organized, top-down type of organization to a more horizontally managed, interactive organization. They are attempting to adapt more quickly to changing conditions by becoming "learning organizations."

Creating a Learning Organization

Strategic management has now evolved to the point that its primary value is in helping an organization operate successfully in a dynamic, complex environment. To be competitive in dynamic environments, corporations are becoming less bureaucratic and more flexible. In stable environments such as those that existed in years past, a competitive strategy simply involved defining a competitive position and then defending it. As it takes less and less time for one product or technology to replace another, companies are finding that there is no such thing as a permanent competitive advantage. Many agree with Richard D'Aveni, who says in his book *Hypercompetition* that any sustainable competitive advantage lies not in doggedly following a centrally managed five-year plan but in stringing together a series of strategic short-term thrusts (as Apple does by cutting into the sales of its own offerings with periodic introductions of new products).[32] This means that corporations must develop *strategic flexibility*—the ability to shift from one dominant strategy to another.[33]

Strategic flexibility demands a long-term commitment to the development and nurturing of critical resources. It also demands that the company become a **learning organization**—an organization skilled at creating, acquiring, and transferring knowledge and at modifying its behavior to reflect new knowledge and insights. Organizational learning is a critical component of competitiveness in a dynamic environment. It is particularly important to innovation and new product development.[34] Siemens, a major electronics company, created a global knowledge-sharing network, called ShareNet, in order to quickly spread information technology throughout the firm. Based on its experience with ShareNet, Siemens established PeopleShareNet, a system that serves as a virtual expert marketplace for facilitating the creation of cross-cultural teams composed of members with specific knowledge and competencies.[35]

Learning organizations are skilled at four main activities:

- Solving problems systematically
- Experimenting with new approaches
- Learning from their own experiences and past history as well as from the experiences of others
- Transferring knowledge quickly and efficiently throughout the organization[36]

Business historian Alfred Chandler proposes that high-technology industries are defined by "paths of learning" in which organizational strengths derive from learned capabilities.[37] According to Chandler, companies spring from an individual entrepreneur's knowledge, which then evolves into organizational knowledge. This organizational knowledge is composed of three basic strengths: technical skills, mainly in research; functional knowledge, such as production and marketing; and managerial expertise. This knowledge leads to new businesses where the company can succeed and creates an entry barrier to new competitors. Chandler points out that once a corporation has built its learning base to the point where it has become a core company in its industry, entrepreneurial startups are rarely able to successfully enter. Thus, organizational knowledge becomes a competitive advantage that is difficult to understand and imitate.

Strategic management is essential for learning organizations to avoid stagnation through continuous self-examination and experimentation. People at all levels, not just top management, participate in strategic management—helping to scan the environment for critical information, suggesting changes to strategies and programs to take advantage of environmental shifts, and working with others to continuously improve work methods, procedures, and evaluation techniques. The Toyota production system is famous for empowering employees to improve. If an employee spots a problem on the line, he/she pulls the andon cord, which immediately starts a speedy diagnosis. The line continues if the problem can be solved within one minute. If not, the production line is shut down until the problem is solved. At Toyota, they learn from their mistakes as much as they learn from their successes. Improvements are sent to all factories worldwide.[38]

Organizations that are willing to experiment and are able to learn from their experiences are more successful than those that are not.[39] This was seen in a study of U.S. manufacturers of diagnostic imaging equipment, the most successful firms were those that improved products sold in the United States by incorporating some of what they had learned from their manufacturing and sales experiences in other nations. The less successful firms used the foreign operations primarily as sales outlets, not as important sources of technical knowledge.[40] Research also reveals that multidivisional corporations that establish ways to transfer knowledge across divisions are more innovative than other diversified corporations that do not.[41]

Basic Model of Strategic Management

Strategic management consists of four basic elements:

- Environmental scanning
- Strategy formulation
- Strategy implementation
- Evaluation and control

Figure 1–1 illustrates how these four elements interact; **Figure 1–2** expands each of these elements and serves as the model for this book. This model is both rational and prescriptive. It is a planning model that presents what a corporation *should* do in terms of the strategic management process, not what any particular firm may actually do. The rational planning model predicts that as environmental uncertainty increases, corporations that work more diligently to analyze and predict more accurately the changing situation in which they operate will outperform those that do not. Empirical research studies support this model.[42] The terms used in Figure 1–2 are explained in the following pages.

FIGURE 1–1
**Basic Elements
of the Strategic
Management
Process**

FIGURE 1–2   Strategic Management Model

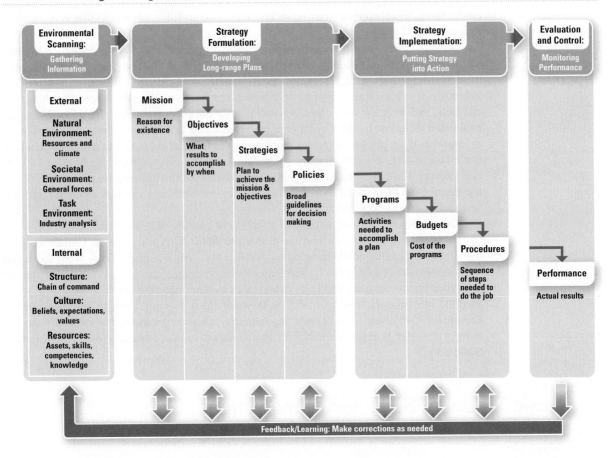

SOURCE: T. L. Wheelen, "Strategic Management Model," adapted from "Concepts of Management," presented to Society for Advancement of Management (SAM), International Meeting, Richmond, VA, 1981. Kathryn E. Wheelen solely owns all of (Dr.) Thomas L. Wheelen's copyright materials. Kathryn E. Wheelen requires written reprint permission for each book that this material is to be printed in. Copyright © 1981 by T. L. Wheelen and SAM. Copyright © 1982, 1985, 1988, and 2005 by T. L. Wheelen and J. D. Hunger. Revised 1989, 1995, 1998, 2000, 2005, 2009, and 2013. Reprinted by permission of the copyright holders.

ENVIRONMENTAL SCANNING

Environmental scanning is the monitoring, evaluating, and disseminating of information from the external and internal environments to key people within the corporation. Its purpose is to identify **strategic factors**—those external and internal elements that will assist in the analysis in deciding the strategic decisions of the corporation. The simplest way to conduct environmental scanning is through **SWOT analysis.** SWOT is an acronym

FIGURE 1–3   Environmental Variables

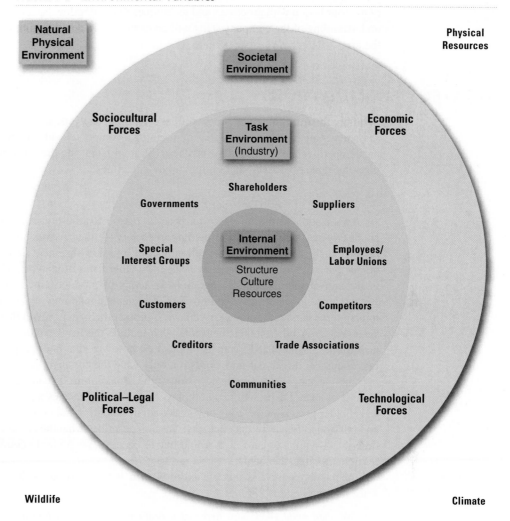

used to describe the particular **S**trengths, **W**eaknesses, **O**pportunities, and **T**hreats that are strategic factors for a specific company. The **external environment** consists of variables (**O**pportunities and **T**hreats) that are outside the organization and not typically within the short-run control of top management. These variables form the context within which the corporation exists. **Figure 1–3** depicts key environmental variables. They may be general forces and trends within the natural or societal environments or specific factors that operate within an organization's specific task environment—often called its *industry*. The analysis techniques available for the examination of these environmental variables are the focus of **Chapter 4.**

The **internal environment** of a corporation consists of variables (**S**trengths and **W**eaknesses) that are within the organization itself and are not usually within the short-run control of top management. These variables form the context in which work is done. They include the corporation's structure, culture, and resources. Key strengths form a set of core competencies that the corporation can use to gain competitive advantage. While strategic management is fundamentally concerned with strengths, weaknesses, opportunities, and threats, the methods to analyze each has developed substantially in the past two decades. No longer do we simply list the SWOT variables and have employees try to populate the quadrants. Each of the four is rich with processes and techniques that will allow for a robust and sophisticated understanding of the company. This will be examined in detail beginning with **Chapter 5** of the text.

STRATEGY FORMULATION

Strategy formulation is the process of investigation, analysis, and decision making that provides the company with the criteria for attaining a competitive advantage. It includes defining the competitive advantages of the business (Strategy), crafting the corporate mission, specifying achievable objectives, and setting policy guidelines.

Mission: Stating Purpose

An organization's **mission** is the purpose or reason for the organization's existence. It announces what the company is providing to society—either a service such as consulting or a product such as automobiles. A well-conceived mission statement defines the fundamental, unique purpose that sets a company apart from other firms of its type and identifies the scope or domain of the company's operations in terms of products (including services) offered. Research reveals that firms with mission statements containing explicit descriptions of customers served and technologies used have significantly higher growth than firms without such statements.[43] A mission statement may also include the firm's values and philosophy about how it does business and treats its employees; however, that is usually better kept as a separate document. It can put into words not only what the company is now but what it wants to become—management's strategic vision of the firm's future. The mission statement promotes a sense of shared expectations in employees and communicates a public image to important stakeholder groups in the company's task environment. Some people like to consider vision and mission as two different concepts: Mission describes what the organization is now; **vision** describes what the organization would like to become. We prefer to combine these ideas into a single mission statement.[44]

A classic example is that etched in bronze at Newport News Shipbuilding, unchanged since its founding in 1886:

> We shall build good ships here—at a profit if we can—at a loss if we must—but always good ships.[45]

A mission may be defined narrowly or broadly in scope. An example of a *broad* mission statement is that used by many corporations: "Serve the best interests of shareowners, customers, and employees." A broadly defined mission statement such as this keeps the company from restricting itself to one field or product line, but it fails to clearly identify either what it makes or which products/markets it plans to emphasize. Because this broad statement is so general, a *narrow* mission statement, such as the preceding example by Newport News Shipbuilding, is significantly more useful. A narrow mission very clearly states the organization's primary business and will limit the scope of the firm's activities in terms of the product or service offered, the technology used, and probably the market served.

Objectives: Listing Expected Results

Objectives are the end results of planned activity. They should be stated as *action verbs* and tell what is to be accomplished by when and quantified if possible. The achievement of corporate objectives should result in the fulfillment of a corporation's mission. In effect, this is what society gives back to the corporation when the corporation does a good job of fulfilling its mission. Coca-Cola has set the standard of a focused, international company. In their new Vision 2020 plan, they have laid out specific objectives including reducing the overall carbon footprint of their business operations by 15% by 2020, as compared to the 2007 baseline, and reducing the impact of their packaging by maximizing their use of renewable, reusable, and recyclable resources to recover the equivalent of 100% of their packaging. This type of focus has made Coca-Cola a perennial member of the Fortune 500, one of the Fortune 50 Most Admired Companies, one of Barron's Most Respected Companies in the World and a Diversity, Inc. Top 50 company. Over the past 10 years they have raised their dividend an average of 9.8% per year and the company's earnings per share have jumped 11.3% per year over the past 5 years.[46]

The term *goal* is often used interchangeably with the term objective. In this book, we prefer to differentiate the two terms. In contrast to an objective, we consider a *goal* as an open-ended statement of what one wants to accomplish, with no quantification of what is to be achieved and no time criteria for completion. For example, a simple statement of "increased profitability" is thus a goal, not an objective, because it does not state how much profit the firm wants to make the next year. A good objective should be action-oriented and begin with the word *to*. An example of an objective is "to increase the firm's profitability in 2014 by 10% over 2013."

Some of the areas in which a corporation might establish its goals and objectives are:

- Profitability (net profits)
- Efficiency (low costs, etc.)
- Growth (increase in total assets, sales, etc.)
- Shareholder wealth (dividends plus stock price appreciation)
- Utilization of resources (ROE or ROI)
- Reputation (being considered a "top" firm)
- Contributions to employees (employment security, wages, diversity)
- Contributions to society (taxes paid, participation in charities, providing a needed product or service)
- Market leadership (market share)
- Technological leadership (innovations, creativity)
- Survival (avoiding bankruptcy)
- Personal needs of top management (using the firm for personal purposes, such as providing jobs for relatives)

Strategy: Defining the Competitive Advantages

An organization must examine the external environment in order to determine who constitutes the perfect customer for the business as it exists today, who the most direct competitors are for that customer, what the company does that is necessary to compete and what the company does that truly sets it apart from its competitors. These elements can be rephrased into the strengths of the business, the understanding of its weaknesses relative to its competitors, what opportunities would be most prudent, and what threats might affect the business's primary competitive advantages.

A **strategy** of a corporation forms a comprehensive master approach that states how the corporation will achieve its mission and objectives. It maximizes competitive advantage and minimizes competitive disadvantage. Pfizer, the giant drug company has embraced the need for this type of approach. Faced with the rapid fall-off of its biggest blockbuster drugs (patents expiring), Pfizer was faced with the question of how to generate the R&D to create new drugs. Historically, the company had relied upon its cadre of scientists, but this changed in the past few years. Pfizer plans to have 50 drug development projects running with university research centers by 2015. They opened their first one in 2010. This is the crucial new ground from which they hope to replace such blockbusters as Lipitor, which expects to see sales drop by more than 80% (from US$12 billion in 2012) when the patent expired.[47]

The typical business firm usually considers three types of strategy: corporate, business, and functional.

1. **Corporate strategy** describes a company's overall direction in terms of its general attitude toward growth and the management of its various businesses and product lines. Corporate strategies typically fit within the three main categories of stability, growth, and retrenchment.

2. **Business strategy** usually occurs at the business unit or product level, and it emphasizes improvement of the competitive position of a corporation's products or services in the specific industry or market segment served by that business unit. Business strategies may fit within the two overall categories: *competitive* and *cooperative* strategies. For example, Staples, the U.S. office supply store chain, has used a competitive strategy to differentiate its retail stores from its competitors by adding services to its stores, such as copying, UPS shipping, and hiring mobile technicians who can fix computers and install networks. British Airways has followed a cooperative strategy by forming an alliance with American Airlines in order to provide global service. Cooperative strategy may thus be used to provide a competitive advantage. Intel, a manufacturer of computer microprocessors, uses its alliance (cooperative strategy) with Microsoft to differentiate itself (competitive strategy) from AMD, its primary competitor.

3. **Functional strategy** is the approach taken by a functional area to achieve corporate and business unit objectives and strategies by maximizing resource productivity. It is concerned with developing and nurturing a distinctive competence to provide a company or business unit with a competitive advantage. Examples of research and development (R&D) functional strategies are technological followership (imitation of the products of other companies) and technological leadership (pioneering an innovation). For years, Magic Chef had been a successful appliance maker by spending little on R&D but by quickly imitating the innovations of other competitors. This helped the company keep its costs lower than those of its competitors and consequently to compete with lower prices. In terms of marketing functional strategies, Procter & Gamble (P&G) is a master of marketing "pull"—the process of spending huge amounts on advertising in order to create customer demand. This supports P&G's competitive strategy of differentiating its products from those of its competitors.

Business firms use all three types of strategy simultaneously. A **hierarchy of strategy** is a grouping of strategy types by level in the organization. Hierarchy of strategy is a nesting of one strategy within another so that they complement and support one another. (See **Figure 1–4.**) Functional strategies support business strategies, which, in turn, support the corporate strategy(ies).

Policies: Setting Guidelines

A **policy** is a broad guideline for decision making that links the formulation of a strategy with its implementation. Companies use policies to make sure that employees throughout the firm make decisions and take actions that support the corporation's mission, objectives, and

FIGURE 1–4
Hierarchy of
Strategy

Corporate Strategy:
Overall Direction of
Company and Management
of Its Businesses

**Business
Strategy:**
Competitive and
Cooperative Strategies

**Functional
Strategy:**
Maximize Resource
Productivity

strategies. For example, when Cisco decided on a strategy of growth through acquisitions, it established a policy to consider only companies with no more than 75 employees, 75% of whom were engineers.[48] Consider the following company policies:

- **3M:** 3M says researchers should spend 15% of their time working on something other than their primary project. (This supports 3M's strong product development strategy.)

- **Google:** Google's health care plan includes their onsite medical staff. Any employee who feels ill at work can make an appointment with the doctor at the Googleplex. This supports the Google HRM functional strategy to support its employees.

- **General Electric:** GE must be number one or two wherever it competes. (This supports GE's objective to be number one in market capitalization.)

- **Starbucks:** All Starbucks employees are offered a Total Pay Package that includes a 401(k) savings plan, stock options, and an employee stock purchase plan. This goes a long way toward their goal of having every employee feel like a partner in the business.

- **Ryanair:** Ryanair charges for everything a passenger might want or need on a flight. The only thing you get with your ticket is the right to a seat on the plane (and that seat depends upon how fast you can run to the plane).

Policies such as these provide clear guidance to managers throughout the organization. (Strategy formulation is discussed in greater detail in **Chapters 6, 7**, and **8.**)

STRATEGY IMPLEMENTATION

Strategy implementation is a process by which strategies and policies are put into action through the development of programs, budgets, and procedures. This process might involve changes within the overall culture, structure, and/or management system of the entire organization. Except when such drastic corporatewide changes are needed, however, the implementation of strategy is typically conducted by middle- and lower-level managers, with review by top management. Sometimes referred to as *operational planning*, strategy implementation often involves day-to-day decisions in resource allocation.

Programs and Tactics: Defining Actions

A **program** or a **tactic** is a statement of the activities or steps needed to support a strategy. The terms are interchangeable. In practice, a program is a collection of tactics where a tactic is the individual action taken by the organization as an element of the effort to accomplish a plan. A program or tactic makes a strategy action-oriented. It may involve restructuring the corporation, changing the company's internal culture, or beginning a new research effort. For example, Boeing's strategy to regain industry leadership with its new 787 Dreamliner meant that the company had to increase its manufacturing efficiency in order to keep the price low. To significantly cut costs, management decided to implement a series of tactics:

- Outsource approximately 70% of manufacturing.
- Reduce final assembly time to three days (compared to 20 for its 737 plane) by having suppliers build completed plane sections.
- Use new, lightweight composite materials in place of aluminum to reduce inspection time.
- Resolve poor relations with labor unions caused by downsizing and outsourcing.

Another example is a set of programs or tactics used by automaker BMW to achieve its objective of increasing production efficiency by 5% each year: (a) shorten new model development time from 60 to 30 months, (b) reduce preproduction time from a year to no more than 5 months, and (c) build at least two vehicles in each plant so that production can shift among models depending upon demand.

Budgets: Costing Programs

A **budget** is a statement of a corporation's programs in terms of dollars. Used in planning and control, a budget lists the detailed cost of each program. Many corporations demand a certain percentage return on investment, often called a "hurdle rate," before management will approve a new program. This is done so that the new program has the potential to significantly add to the corporation's profit performance and thus build shareholder value. The budget thus not only serves as a detailed plan of the new strategy in action, it also specifies through pro forma financial statements the expected impact on the firm's financial future.

A company that has really invested in the future is Atlantic Gulf & Pacific Company (AG&P) based in the Philippines. The company makes modular units for large construction projects (e.g., power plants) and sees modular building to be the wave of the future as skilled labor costs go up. In the past year, it has expanded its facility from 450,000 square meters to over 1.5 million square meters in anticipation of future work flow. The CEO expects to invest another US$250 million into the business by the end of 2013.[49]

Procedures: Detailing Activities

Procedures, sometimes termed Standard Operating Procedures (SOP), are a system of sequential steps or techniques that describe in detail how a particular task or job is to be done. They typically detail the various activities that must be carried out in order to complete the corporation's program. For example, when the home improvement retailer Home Depot noted that sales were lagging because its stores were full of clogged aisles, long checkout times, and too few salespeople, management changed its procedures for restocking shelves and pricing the products. Instead of requiring its employees to do these activities at the same time they were working with customers, management moved these activities to when the stores were closed at night. Employees were then able to focus on increasing customer sales during the day. Both UPS and FedEx put such an emphasis on consistent, quality service that both companies have strict rules for employee behavior, ranging from how a driver dresses to how keys are held when approaching a customer's door. (Strategy implementation is discussed in more detail in **Chapters 9** and **10.**)

EVALUATION AND CONTROL

Evaluation and control is a process in which corporate activities and performance results are monitored so that actual performance can be compared with desired performance. Managers at all levels use the resulting information to take corrective action and resolve problems. Although evaluation and control is the final major element of strategic management, it can also pinpoint weaknesses in previously implemented strategic plans and thus stimulates the entire process to begin again.

Performance is the end result of activities.[50] It includes the actual outcomes of the strategic management process. The practice of strategic management is justified in terms of its ability to improve an organization's performance, typically measured in terms of profits and return on investment. For evaluation and control to be effective, managers must obtain clear, prompt, and unbiased information from the people below them in the corporation's hierarchy. Using this information, managers compare what is actually happening with what was originally planned in the formulation stage.

Starbucks had created a mystique around the enjoyment of coffee. Carefully designed stores and an experience that encouraged people to stay and chat had built Starbucks into a powerhouse. In 2000, Howard Schultz (Founder and CEO) stepped down from active management of the business. In 2005, Jim Donald took over as CEO and drove the company toward efficiency and diversification. The company went from an American success story to one with a 97% drop in net income and same store sales in the negative territory. Despite a well-known e-mail from Schultz to Donald in 2007 encouraging him to return to core elements of the business, things did not improve, and in January 2008 Schultz replaced Donald as CEO. In February 2008, all 7,100+ Starbucks in North America shut their doors for a three-hour video conference with Schultz so they could reset the Starbucks experience. The turnaround at Starbucks has been a remarkable story of regaining the cache they almost lost.[51]

The evaluation and control of performance completes the strategic management model. Based on performance results, management may need to make adjustments in its strategy formulation, in implementation, or in both. (Evaluation and control is discussed in more detail in **Chapter 11.**)

FEEDBACK/LEARNING PROCESS

Note that the strategic management model depicted in **Figure 1–2** includes a feedback/learning process. Arrows are drawn coming out of each part of the model and taking information to each of the previous parts of the model. As a firm or business unit develops strategies, programs, and the like, it often must go back to revise or correct decisions made earlier in the process.

For example, poor performance (as measured in evaluation and control) usually indicates that something has gone wrong with either strategy formulation or implementation. It could also mean that a key variable, such as a new competitor, was ignored during environmental scanning and assessment. In the case of Starbucks, the recession had hit and the mantra in the country had become, "save money, don't buy Starbucks." The business was built on an image as the comfortable place away from home, but had trended toward a fast-food operation. Schultz eliminated hot sandwiches which were filing the place with the smell of burnt cheese instead of coffee. Starbucks needed to reassess the environment and find a better way to profitably apply its core competencies.

Initiation of Strategy: Triggering Events

After much research, Henry Mintzberg discovered that strategy formulation is typically not a regular, continuous process: "It is most often an irregular, discontinuous process, proceeding in fits and starts. There are periods of stability in strategy development, but also there are periods of flux, of groping, of piecemeal change, and of global change."[52] This view of strategy formulation as an irregular process can be explained by the very human tendency to continue on a particular course of action until something goes wrong or a person is forced to question his or her actions. This period of strategic drift may result from inertia on the part of the organization, or it may reflect management's belief that the current strategy is still appropriate and needs only some fine-tuning.

Most large organizations tend to follow a particular strategic orientation for a period of years (often 15–20 years) before making a significant change in direction.[53] This phenomenon, called *punctuated equilibrium*, describes corporations as evolving through relatively long periods of stability (equilibrium periods) punctuated by relatively short bursts of fundamental change (revolutionary periods).[54] After this rather long period of fine-tuning an existing strategy, some sort of shock to the system is needed to motivate management to seriously reassess the corporation's situation.

A **triggering event** is something that acts as a stimulus for a change in strategy. Some possible triggering events are:[55]

- **New CEO:** By asking a series of embarrassing questions, a new CEO cuts through the veil of complacency and forces people to question the very reason for the corporation's existence.

- **External intervention:** A firm's bank suddenly refuses to approve a new loan or suddenly demands payment in full on an old one. A key customer complains about a serious product defect.

- **Threat of a change in ownership:** Another firm may initiate a takeover by buying a company's common stock.

- **Performance gap:** A *performance gap* exists when performance does not meet expectations. Sales and profits either are no longer increasing or may even be falling.

- **Strategic inflection point:** Coined by Andy Grove, past-CEO of Intel Corporation, a *strategic inflection point* is what happens to a business when a major change takes place due to the introduction of new technologies, a different regulatory environment, a change in customers' values, or a change in what customers prefer.[56]

Strategic Decision Making

The distinguishing characteristic of strategic management is its emphasis on strategic decision making. As organizations grow larger and more complex, with more uncertain environments, decisions become increasingly complicated and difficult to make. In agreement with the strategic choice perspective mentioned earlier, this book proposes a strategic decision-making framework that can help people make these decisions regardless of their level and function in the corporation.

WHAT MAKES A DECISION STRATEGIC

Unlike many other decisions, **strategic decisions** deal with the long-term future of an entire organization and have three characteristics:

1. **Rare:** Strategic decisions are unusual and typically have no precedent to follow.
2. **Consequential:** Strategic decisions commit substantial resources and demand a great deal of commitment from people at all levels.
3. **Directive:** Strategic decisions set precedents for lesser decisions and future actions throughout an organization.[57]

One example of a strategic decision with all of these characteristics was that made by Genentech, a biotechnology company that had been founded in 1976 to produce protein-based drugs from cloned genes. After building sales to US$9 billion and profits to US$2 billion in 2006, the company's sales growth slowed and its stock price dropped in 2007. The company's products were reaching maturity with few new ones in the pipeline. To regain revenue growth, management decided to target autoimmune diseases, such as multiple sclerosis, rheumatoid arthritis, lupus, and 80 other ailments for which there was no known lasting treatment. This was an enormous opportunity, but also a very large risk for the company. Existing drugs in this area either weren't effective for many patients or caused side effects that were worse than the disease. Competition from companies like Amgen and Novartis were already vying for leadership in this area. A number of Genentech's first attempts in the area had failed to do well against the competition.

The strategic decision to commit resources to this new area was based on a report from a British physician that Genentech's cancer drug Rituxan eased the agony of rheumatoid arthritis in five of his patients. CEO Arthur Levinson was so impressed with this report that he immediately informed Genentech's board of directors. He urged them to support a full research program for Rituxan in autoimmune disease. With the board's blessing, Levinson launched a program to study the drug as a treatment for rheumatoid arthritis, MS, and lupus. The company deployed a third of its 1,000 researchers to pursue new drugs to fight autoimmune diseases. In 2006, Rituxan was approved to treat rheumatoid arthritis and captured 10% of the market. By 2012, Rituxan had sales of more than US$3 billion. The research mandate was to consider ideas others might overlook. This has led to a series of FDA-approved drugs for breast cancer and vision loss. "There's this tremendous herd instinct out there," said Levinson. "That's a great opportunity, because often the crowd is wrong."[58]

MINTZBERG'S MODES OF STRATEGIC DECISION MAKING

Some strategic decisions are made in a flash by one person (often an entrepreneur or a powerful chief executive officer) who has a brilliant insight and is quickly able to convince others to adopt his or her idea. Other strategic decisions seem to develop out of a series of small incremental choices that over time push an organization more in one direction than another. According to Henry Mintzberg, the three most typical approaches, or modes, of strategic decision making are entrepreneurial, adaptive, and planning (a fourth mode, logical incrementalism, was added later by Quinn):[59]

- **Entrepreneurial mode:** Strategy is made by one powerful individual. The focus is on opportunities; problems are secondary. Strategy is guided by the founder's own vision of direction and is exemplified by large, bold decisions. The dominant goal is growth of the corporation. Amazon.com, founded by Jeff Bezos, is an example of this mode of strategic decision making. The company reflected Bezos' vision of using the Internet to market books and more. Although Amazon's clear growth strategy was certainly an advantage of the entrepreneurial mode, Bezos' eccentric management style made it difficult to retain senior executives.[60]

- **Adaptive mode:** Sometimes referred to as "muddling through," this decision-making mode is characterized by reactive solutions to existing problems, rather than a proactive search for new opportunities. Much bargaining goes on concerning priorities of objectives. Strategy is fragmented and is developed to move a corporation forward incrementally. This mode is typical of most universities, many large hospitals, a large number of governmental agencies, and a surprising number of large corporations. Encyclopædia Britannica Inc. operated successfully for many years in this mode, but it continued to rely on the door-to-door selling of its prestigious books long after dual-career couples made that marketing approach obsolete. Only after it was acquired in 1996 did the company change its door-to-door sales to television advertising and Internet marketing. The company now charges libraries and individual subscribers for complete access via its Web site and has apps for the iPad and iPhone that cost users US$70. In May 2012, the company stopped producing the bound set of encyclopedias that had been in print for over 244 years.[61]

- **Planning mode:** This decision-making mode involves the systematic gathering of appropriate information for situation analysis, the generation of feasible alternative strategies, and the rational selection of the most appropriate strategy. It includes both the proactive search for new opportunities and the reactive solution of existing problems. IBM under CEO Louis Gerstner is an example of the planning mode. When Gerstner accepted the position of CEO in 1993, he realized that IBM was in serious difficulty. Mainframe computers, the company's primary product line, were suffering a rapid decline both in sales and market share. One of Gerstner's first actions was to convene a two-day meeting on corporate strategy with senior executives. An in-depth analysis of IBM's product lines revealed that the only part of the company that was growing was services, but it was a relatively small segment and not very profitable. Rather than focusing on making and selling its own computer hardware, IBM made the strategic decision to invest in services that integrated information technology. IBM thus decided to provide a complete set of services from building systems to defining architecture to actually running and managing the computers for the customer—regardless of who made the products. Because it was no longer important that the company be completely vertically integrated, it sold off its DRAM, disk-drive, and laptop computer businesses and exited software application development. Since making this strategic decision in 1993, 80% of IBM's revenue growth has come from services. Most of this is chronicled in an outstanding business practices book written by Gerstner himself entitled "Who Says Elephants Can't Dance." It should be one of the top reads for anyone really interested in this topic.[62]

■ **Logical incrementalism:** A fourth decision-making mode can be viewed as a synthesis of the planning, adaptive, and, to a lesser extent, the entrepreneurial modes. In this mode, top management has a reasonably clear idea of the corporation's mission and objectives, but, in its development of strategies, it chooses to use "an interactive process in which the organization probes the future, experiments, and learns from a series of partial (incremental) commitments rather than through global formulations of total strategies."[63] Thus, although the mission and objectives are set, the strategy is allowed to emerge out of debate, discussion, and experimentation. This approach appears to be useful when the environment is changing rapidly and when it is important to build consensus and develop needed resources before committing an entire corporation to a specific strategy. In his analysis of the petroleum industry, Grant described strategic planning in this industry as "planned emergence." Corporate headquarters established the mission and objectives but allowed the business units to propose strategies to achieve them.[64]

STRATEGIC DECISION-MAKING PROCESS: AID TO BETTER DECISIONS

Good arguments can be made for using either the entrepreneurial or adaptive modes (or logical incrementalism) in certain situations.[65] This book proposes, however, that in most situations the planning mode, which includes the basic elements of the strategic management process, is a more rational and thus better way of making strategic decisions. Research indicates that the planning mode is not only more analytical and less political than are the other modes, but it is also more appropriate for dealing with complex, changing environments.[66] We therefore propose the following eight-step **strategic decision-making process** to improve the making of strategic decisions (see **Figure 1–5**):

1. **Evaluate current performance results** in terms of (a) return on investment, profitability, and so forth, and (b) the current mission, objectives, strategies, and policies.

2. **Review corporate governance**—that is, the performance of the firm's board of directors and top management.

3. **Scan and assess the external environment** to determine the strategic factors that pose **O**pportunities and **T**hreats.

4. **Scan and assess the internal corporate environment** to determine the strategic factors that are **S**trengths (especially core competencies) and **W**eaknesses.

5. **Analyze strategic factors** to (a) pinpoint problem areas and (b) review and revise the corporate mission and objectives, as necessary.

6. **Generate, evaluate, and select the best alternative strategy** in light of the analysis conducted in step 5.

7. **Implement selected strategies** via programs, budgets, and procedures.

8. **Evaluate implemented strategies** via feedback systems, and the control of activities to ensure their minimum deviation from plans.

This rational approach to strategic decision making has been used successfully by corporations such as Warner-Lambert, Target, General Electric, IBM, Avon Products, Bechtel Group Inc., and Taisei Corporation.

FIGURE 1–5
Strategic Decision-
Making Process

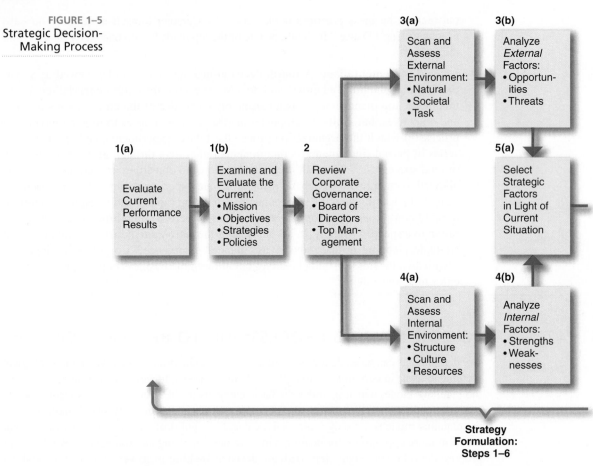

SOURCE: T. L. Wheelen and J. D. Hunger, "Strategic Decision-Making Process." Copyright © 1994 and 1977 by Wheelen and Hunger Associates. Reprinted by permission.

The Strategic Audit: Aid to Strategic Decision Making

One effective means of putting the strategic decision-making process into action is through a technique known as the strategic audit. A **strategic audit** provides a checklist of questions, by area or issue, that enables a systematic analysis to be made of various corporate functions and activities. (See **Appendix 1.A** at the end of this chapter.) Note that the numbered primary headings in the audit are the same as the numbered blocks in the strategic decision-making process in **Figure 1–5**. Beginning with an evaluation of current performance, the audit continues with environmental scanning, strategy formulation, and strategy implementation, and it concludes with evaluation and control. A strategic audit is a type of management audit and is extremely useful as a diagnostic tool to pinpoint corporatewide problem areas and to highlight organizational strengths and weaknesses.[67] A strategic audit can help determine why a certain area is creating problems for a corporation and help generate solutions to the problem.

A strategic audit is not an all-inclusive list, but it presents many of the critical questions needed for a detailed strategic analysis of any business corporation. Some questions or even

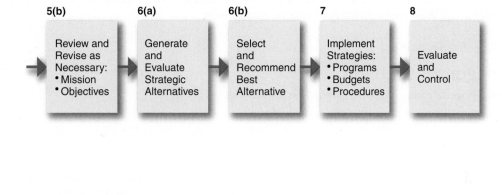

some areas might be inappropriate for a particular company; in other cases, the questions may be insufficient for a complete analysis. However, each question in a particular area of a strategic audit can be broken down into an additional series of subquestions. An analyst can develop these subquestions when they are needed for a complete strategic analysis of a company.

End of Chapter SUMMARY

Strategy scholars Donald Hambrick and James Fredrickson propose that a good strategy has five elements, providing answers to five questions:

1. **Arenas:** Where will we be active?
2. **Vehicles:** How will we get there?
3. **Differentiators:** How will we win in the marketplace?
4. **Staging:** What will be our speed and sequence of moves?
5. **Economic logic:** How will we obtain our returns?[68]

This chapter introduces you to a well-accepted model of strategic management (**Figure 1–2**) in which environmental scanning leads to strategy formulation, strategy implementation, and evaluation and control. It further shows how that model can be put into action through the strategic decision-making process (**Figure 1–5**) and a strategic audit (**Appendix 1.A**). As pointed out by Hambrick and Fredrickson, "strategy consists of an integrated set of choices."[69] The questions "Where will we be active?" and "How will we get there?" are dealt with by a company's mission, objectives, and corporate strategy. The question "How will we win in the marketplace?" is the concern of business strategy. The question "What will be our speed and sequence of moves?" is answered not only by business strategy and tactics but also by functional strategy and by implemented programs, budgets, and procedures. The question "How will we obtain our returns?" is the primary emphasis of the evaluation and control element of the strategic management model. Each of these questions and topics will be dealt with in greater detail in the chapters to come. Welcome to the study of strategic management!

MyManagementLab®

Go to **mymanagementlab.com** to complete the problems marked with this icon .

KEY TERMS

budget (p. 54)
business strategy (p. 52)
corporate strategy (p. 52)
environmental scanning (p. 48)
evaluation and control (p. 55)
external environment (p. 49)
functional strategy (p. 52)
globalization (p. 42)
hierarchy of strategy (p. 52)
innovation (p. 43)
institution theory (p. 45)
internal environment (p. 49)
learning organization (p. 46)

mission (p. 50)
objective (p. 50)
organizational learning theory (p. 46)
performance (p. 55)
phases of strategic management (p. 38)
policy (p. 52)
population ecology (p. 45)
procedure (p. 54)
program (p. 54)
strategic audit (p. 60)
strategic choice perspective (p. 45)
strategic decision (p. 57)

strategic decision-making process (p. 59)
strategic factor (p. 48)
strategic management (p. 38)
strategy (p. 51)
strategy formulation (p. 50)
strategy implementation (p. 53)
sustainability (p. 44)
SWOT analysis (p. 48)
tactic (p. 54)
triggering event (p. 56)
triple bottom line (p. 42)
vision (p. 50)

MyManagementLab®

Go to **mymanagmentlab.com** for the following Assisted-graded writing questions:

1-1. How do the three elements of Globalization, Innovation and Sustainability impact your understanding of Strategy?

1-2. Organizational strategy can be divided roughly into two categories: a) formulation and b) implementation. While there is legitimate crossover between the two, how would you characterize the issues involved in each effort?

DISCUSSION QUESTIONS

1-3. Why has strategic management become so important to today's corporations?

1-4. What is the impact of sustainability on business practice?

1-5. What is a learning organization? Is this approach to strategic management better than the more traditional top-down approach in which strategic planning is primarily done by top management?

1-6. What is a triggering event? List a few triggering events that stimulate strategic changes.

1-7. When is the planning mode of strategic decision making superior to the entrepreneurial and adaptive modes?

STRATEGIC PRACTICE EXERCISES

Advanced economies are emerging from the worst financial recessions in modern times. Many developed nations have implemented austerity measures to adjust the deficit caused by massive spending during the years of cheap and available credit facilities. New industrial policies are also implemented at national and regional levels to police banks and financial institutions as measures of avoiding further economic problems in the future. The austerity measures and policy changes have forced industries and business practices to change. How do you think these act as strategic change stimuli?

1. What changes do you think this might cause in the immediate task environment for a business operating within the financial service industry? Look at the *Financial Times* online for information.

2. How do these changes impact on corporate, business, and functional level strategies of financial service businesses? Are these changes going to affect you as customers?

3. How do you think a learning organization would act in this dynamic environment? What survival chances do the stagnant organizations have?

NOTES

1. F. W. Gluck, S. P. Kaufman, and A. S. Walleck, "The Four Phases of Strategic Management," *Journal of Business Strategy* (Winter 1982), pp. 9–21.
2. M. R. Vaghefi and A. B Huellmantel, "Strategic Leadership at General Electric," *Long Range Planning* (April 1998), pp. 280–294. For a detailed description of the evolution of strategic management at GE, see W. Ocasio and J. Joseph, "Rise and Fall—or Transformation?" *Long Range Planning* (June 2008), pp. 248–272.
3. E. D. Beinhocker, "The Adaptable Corporation," *McKinsey Quarterly* (2006, Number 2), pp. 77–87.
4. B. W. Wirtz, A. Mathieu, and O. Schilke, "Strategy in High-Velocity Environments," *Long Range Planning* (June 2007), pp. 295–313; L. F. Teagarden, Y. Sarason, J. S. Childers, and D. E. Hatfield, "The Engagement of Employees in the Strategy Process and Firm Performance: The Role of Strategic Goals and Environment," *Journal of Business Strategies* (Spring 2005), pp. 75–99; T. J. Andersen, "Strategic Planning, Autonomous Actions and Corporate Performance," *Long Range Planning* (April 2000), pp. 184–200; C. C. Miller and L. B. Cardinal, "Strategic Planning and Firm Performance: A Synthesis of More than Two Decades of Research," *Academy of Management Journal* (December 1994), pp. 1649–1665; P. Pekar Jr., and S. Abraham, "Is Strategic Management Living Up to Its Promise?" *Long Range Planning* (October 1995), pp. 32–44; W. E. Hopkins and S. A. Hopkins, "Strategic Planning— Financial Performance Relationship in Banks: A Causal Examination," *Strategic Management Journal* (September 1997), pp. 635–652.
5. E. J. Zajac, M. S. Kraatz, and R. F. Bresser, "Modeling the Dynamics of Strategic Fit: A Normative Approach to Strategic Change," *Strategic Management Journal* (April 2000), pp. 429–453; M. Peteraf and R. Reed, "Managerial Discretion and Internal Alignment Under Regulatory Constraints and Change," *Strategic Management Journal* (November 2007), pp. 1089–1112; C. S. Katsikeas, S. Samiee, and M. Theodosiou, "Strategy Fit and Performance Consequences of International Marketing Standardization," *Strategic Management Journal* (September 2006), pp. 867–890.
6. P. Brews and D. Purohit, "Strategic Planning in Unstable Environments," *Long Range Planning* (February 2007), pp. 64–83.
7. K. G. Smith and C. M. Grimm, "Environmental Variation, Strategic Change and Firm Performance: A Study of Railroad Deregulation," *Strategic Management Journal* (July–August 1987), pp. 363–376; J. A. Nickerson and B. S. Silverman, "Why Firms Want to Organize Efficiently and What Keeps Them from Doing So: Inappropriate Governance, Performance, and Adaptation in a Deregulated Industry," *Administrative Science Quarterly* (September 2003), pp. 433–465.
8. I. Wilson, "Strategic Planning Isn't Dead—It Changed," *Long Range Planning* (August 1994), p. 20.
9. R. Dye and O. Sibony, "How to Improve Strategic Planning," *McKinsey Quarterly* (2007, Number 3), pp. 40–48.
10. W. M. Becker and V. M. Freeman, "Going from Global Trends to Corporate Strategy," *McKinsey Quarterly* (2006, Number 2), pp. 17–27
11. D. Rigby and B. Bilodeau, *Management Tools and Trends 2007* (Bain & Company, 2007); D. Rigby and B. Bilodeau, *Management Tools and Trends 2011* (Bain & Company, 2011).
12. W. Joyce, "What Really Works: Building the 4+2 Organization," *Organizational Dynamics* (Vol. 34, Issue 2, 2005), pp. 118–129. See also W. Joyce, N. Nohria, and B. Roberson, *What Really Works: The 4+2 Formula for Sustained Business Success* (HarperBusiness, 2003).
13. R. M. Grant, "Strategic Planning in a Turbulent Environment: Evidence from the Oil Majors," *Strategic Management Journal* (June 2003), pp. 491–517.
14. M. J. Peel and J. Bridge, "How Planning and Capital Budgeting Improve SME Performance," *Long Range Planning* (December 1998), pp. 848–856; L. W. Rue and N. A. Ibrahim, "The Relationship Between Planning Sophistication and Performance in Small Businesses," *Journal of Small Business Management* (October 1998), pp. 24–32; J. C. Carland and J. W. Carland, "A Model of Entrepreneurial Planning and Its Effect on Performance," paper presented to Association for Small Business and Entrepreneurship (Houston, TX, 2003).
15. R. M. Grant, "Strategic Planning in a Turbulent Environment: Evidence from the Oil Majors," *Strategic Management Journal* (June 2003), pp. 491–517.
16. "Triple Bottom Line," *The Economist* (November 17, 2009), (www.economist.com/node/14301663).
17. www.usgbc.org/.
18. T. L. Friedman, *The World Is Flat* (NY: Farrar, Strauss & Giroux, 2005).
19. R. Cohen, "America Abroad," *The New York Times*, January 9, 2012, (www.nytimes.com/2012/01/10/opinion/america-abroad.html); A. K. Gupta, V. Govindarajan, and H. Wang, *The*

Quest for Global Dominance, 2nd ed. (San Francisco: Jossey-Bass, 2008).

20. "The CEO Agenda for Innovation," 2012, (www.pwc.com/us/en/issues/ceo-agenda-for-innovation-and-technology/index.jhtml).

21. http://www.ign.com/articles/2010/01/26/apples-first-tablet.

22. A. Glavas and S. Piderit. "How Does Doing Good Matter," *Journal of Corporate Citizenship*, Winter, 36 (2009), pp. 51–70.

23. R. Sylvan and K. Rainey, "2012 Workplace Trends Report: Workplaces that Promote Sustainabilty," (www.sodexousa.com/usen/roles/facilmgmt/workplaces_that_promote_sustainability.asp).

24. www.iso.org/iso/iso14000.

25. M. E. Porter and F. L. Reinhardt, "A Strategic Approach to Climate," *Harvard Business Review* (October 2007), p. 22.

26. "The Rising Costs of Global Warming," *Futurist* (November–December 2005), p. 13.

27. J. Welch and S. Welch, "The Global Warming Wager," *BusinessWeek* (February 26, 2007), p. 130.

28. J. A. C. Baum, "Organizational Ecology," in *Handbook of Organization Studies*, edited by S. R. Clegg, C. Handy, and W. Nord (London: Sage, 1996), pp. 77–114.

29. B. M. Staw and L. D. Epstein, "What Bandwagons Bring: Effects of Popular Management Techniques on Corporate Performance, Reputation, and CEO Pay," *Administrative Science Quarterly* (September 2000), pp. 523–556; M. B. Lieberman and S. Asaba, "Why Do Firms Imitate Each Other?" *Academy of Management Review* (April 2006), pp. 366–385.

30. T. W. Ruefli and R. R. Wiggins, "Industry, Corporate, and Segment Effects and Business Performance: A Non-Parametric Approach," *Strategic Management Journal* (September 2003), pp. 861–879; Y. E. Spanos, G. Zaralis, and S. Lioukas, "Strategy and Industry Effects on Profitability: Evidence from Greece," *Strategic Management Journal* (February 2004), pp. 139–165; E. H. Bowman and C. E. Helfat, "Does Corporate Strategy Matter?" *Strategic Management Journal* (January 2001), pp. 1–23; T. H. Brush, P. Bromiley, and M. Hendrickx, "The Relative Influence of Industry and Corporation on Business Segment Performance: An Alternative Estimate," *Strategic Management Journal* (June 1999), pp. 519–547; K. M. Gilley, B. A. Walters, and B. J. Olson, "Top Management Team Risk Taking Propensities and Firm Performance: Direct and Moderating Effects," *Journal of Business Strategies* (Fall 2002), pp. 95–114.

31. For more information on these theories, see A. Y. Lewin and H. W. Voloberda, "Prolegomena on Coevolution: A Framework for Research on Strategy and New Organizational Forms," *Organization Science* (October 1999), pp. 519–534, and H. Aldrich, *Organizations Evolving* (London: Sage, 1999), pp. 43–74.

32. R. A. D'Aveni, *Hypercompetition* (New York: The Free Press, 1994). Hypercompetition is discussed in more detail in Chapter 4.

33. R. S. M. Lau, "Strategic Flexibility: A New Reality for World-Class Manufacturing," *SAM Advanced Management Journal* (Spring 1996), pp. 11–15.

34. M. A. Hitt, B. W. Keats, and S. M. DeMarie, "Navigating in the New Competitive Landscape: Building Strategic Flexibility and Competitive Advantage in the 21st Century," *Academy of Management Executive* (November 1998), pp. 22–42.

35. S. C. Voelpel, M. Dous, and T. H. Davenport, "Five Steps to Creating a Global Knowledge-Sharing System: Siemens' ShareNet," *Academy of Management Executive* (May 2005), pp. 9–23.

36. D. A. Garvin, "Building a Learning Organization," *Harvard Business Review* (July/August 1993), p. 80. See also P. M. Senge, *The Fifth Discipline: The Art and Practice of the Learning Organization* (New York: Doubleday, 1990).

37. A. D. Chandler, *Inventing the Electronic Century* (New York: The Free Press, 2001).

38. N. Collier, F. Fishwick, and S. W. Floyd, "Managerial Involvement and Perceptions of Strategy Process," *Long Range Planning* (February 2004), pp. 67–83; J. A. Parnell, S. Carraher, and K. Holt, "Participative Management's Influence on Effective Strategic Planning," *Journal of Business Strategies* (Fall 2002), pp. 161–179; M. Ketokivi and X. Castaner, "Strategic Planning as an Integrative Device," *Administrative Science Quarterly* (September 2004), pp. 337–365; Edmondson, A. 2011. "Strategies for Learning from Failure," *Harvard Business Review* (April 2011).

39. E. W. K. Tsang, "Internationalization as a Learning Process: Singapore MNCs in China," *Academy of Management Executive* (February 1999), pp. 91–101; J. M. Shaver, W. Mitchell, and B. Yeung, "The Effect of Own-Firm and Other Firm Experience on Foreign Direct Investment Survival in the U.S., 1987–92," *Strategic Management Journal* (November 1997), pp. 811–824; P. Kale and H. Singh, "Building Firm Capabilities through Learning: The Role of the Alliance Learning Process in Alliance Capability and Firm-Level Alliance Success," *Strategic Management Journal* (October 2007), pp. 981–1000; H. Barkema and M. Schijven, "How Do Firms Learn to Make Acquisitions? A Review of Past Research and an Agenda for the Future," *Journal of Management* (June 2008), pp. 594–634; D. D. Bergh and E. N-K Lim, "Learning How to Restructure: Absorptive Capacity and Improvisational Views of Restructuring Actions and Performance," *Strategic Management Journal* (June 2008), pp. 593–616.

40. W. Mitchell, J. M. Shaver, and B. Yeung, "Getting There in a Global Industry: Impacts on Performance of Changing International Presence," *Strategic Management Journal* (September 1992), pp. 419–432.

41. D. J. Miller, M. J. Fern, and L. B. Cardinal, "The Use of Knowledge for Technological Innovation Within Diversified Firms," *Academy of Management Journal* (April 2007), pp. 308–326.

42. R. Wiltbank, N. Dew, S. Read, and S. D. Sarasvathy, "What to Do Next? The Case for Non-Predictive Strategy," *Strategic Management Journal* (October 2006), pp. 981–998; J. A. Smith, "Strategies for Start-Ups," *Long Range Planning* (December 1998), pp. 857–872.

43. J. S. Sidhu, "Business-Domain Definition and Performance: An Empirical Study," *SAM Advanced Management Journal* (Autumn 2004), pp. 40–45.

44. See A. Campbell and S. Yeung, "Brief Case: Mission, Vision, and Strategic Intent," *Long Range Planning* (August 1991), pp. 145–147; S. Cummings and J. Davies, "Mission, Vision, Fusion," *Long Range Planning* (December 1994), pp. 147–150.

45. J. Cosco, "Down to the Sea in Ships," *Journal of Business Strategy* (November/December 1995), p. 48.

46. "Is PepsiCo a Better Dividend Stock than Coca-Cola?" *Seeking Alpha* (August 7, 2012), (www.seekingalpha.com/article/786211-is-pepsi-a-better-dividend-stock-than-coca-cola); www.thecoca-coalacompany.com.

47. D. Armstrong, "Pfizer Sees Harvard Collaboration as Spark for New Drugs," *Bloomberg Businessweek* (June 15, 2012), (www.bloomberg.com/news/2012-06-15/pfizer-sees-harvard-collaboration-as-spark-for-new-drugs.html).

48. K. M. Eisenhardt and D. N. Sull, "Strategy as Simple Rules," *Harvard Business Review* (January 2001), p. 110.

49. M. Wood, "Facebook Buys Instagram . . . But for What?" CBS News, April 10, 2012, (http://www.cbsnews.com/8301-205_162-57411761/facebook-buys-instagram-...but-for-what/); D. Dumlao. "American Entrepreneur Bets Big on PH," *Philippine Daily Inquirer* (August 11, 2012), (http://business.inquirer.net/76323/american-entrepreneur-bets-big-on-ph).

50. H. A. Simon, *Administrative Behavior*, 2nd edition (New York: The Free Press, 1957), p. 231.

51. "Starbucks to Close All U.S. Stores for Training," MSNBC (February 26, 2008), (www.msnbc.com/id/23351151/ns/business-us_business/t/starbucks-close-all-us-stores-trainign/#.uco_I2t5mk0); "Howard Schultz on How Starbucks Got Its Groove Back," careerbuilder.com (June 3, 2011), (http://thehiringsite.careerbuilder.com/2011/06/03/howard-schultz-on-how-starbucks-got-its-groove-back/); B. Stone. "Starbucks Profits Down Sharply on Restructuring Costs," *The New York Times* (November 10, 2008), (http://www.nytimes.com/2008/11/11/business/11sbux.html).

52. H. Mintzberg, "Planning on the Left Side and Managing on the Right," *Harvard Business Review* (July–August 1976), p. 56.

53. R. A. Burgelman and A. S. Grove, "Let Chaos Reign, Then Reign in Chaos—Repeatedly: Managing Strategic Dynamics for Corporate Longevity," *Strategic Management Journal* (October 2007), pp. 965–979.

54. E. Romanelli and M. L. Tushman, "Organizational Transformation as Punctuated Equilibrium: An Empirical Test," *Academy of Management Journal* (October 1994), pp. 1141–1166.

55. S. S. Gordon, W. H. Stewart, Jr., R. Sweo, and W. A. Luker, "Convergence versus Strategic Reorientation: The Antecedents of Fast-Paced Organizational Change," *Journal of Management* (Vol. 26, No. 5, 2000), pp. 911–945.

56. Speech to the 1998 Academy of Management, reported by S. M. Puffer, "Global Executive: Intel's Andrew Grove on Competitiveness," *Academy of Management Executive* (February 1999), pp. 15–24.

57. D. J. Hickson, R. J. Butler, D. Cray, G. R. Mallory, and D. C. Wilson, *Top Decisions: Strategic Decision Making in Organizations* (San Francisco: Jossey-Bass, 1986), pp. 26–42.

58. A. Weintraub, "Genentech's Gamble," *BusinessWeek* (December 17, 2007), pp. 44–48; http://www.fiercepharma.com/special-reports/top-10-best-selling-cancer-drugs/rituxan-3-billion; http://diabetes.webmd.com/news/20120814/new-drug-for-diabetes-related-vision-loss.

59. H. Mintzberg, "Strategy-Making in Three Modes," *California Management Review* (Winter 1973), pp. 44–53.

60. F. Vogelstein, "Mighty Amazon," *Fortune* (May 26, 2003), pp. 60–74.

61. Stern, J. 2012, "Encyclopedia Britannica Kills Its Print Edition," *ABC News* (March 13, 2012), (http://abcnews.go.com/blogs/technology/2012/03/encyclopaedia-britannica-kills-its-print-edition/).

62. L. V. Gerstner, *Who Says Elephants Can't Dance?* (New York: HarperCollins, 2002).

63. J. B. Quinn, *Strategies for Change: Logical Incrementalism* (Homewood, IL.: Irwin, 1980), p. 58.

64. R. M. Grant, "Strategic Planning in a Turbulent Environment: Evidence from the Oil Majors," *Strategic Management Journal* (June 2003), pp. 491–517.

65. G. Gavetti and J. W. Rivkin, "Seek Strategy the Right Way at the Right Time," *Harvard Business Review* (January 2008), pp. 22–23.

66. P. J. Brews and M. R. Hunt, "Learning to Plan and Planning to Learn: Resolving the Planning School/Learning School Debate," *Strategic Management Journal* (October 1999), pp. 889–913; I. Gold and A. M. A. Rasheed, "Rational Decision-Making and Firm Performance: The Moderating Role of the Environment," *Strategic Management Journal* (August 1997), pp. 583–591; R. L. Priem, A. M. A. Rasheed, and A. G. Kotulic, "Rationality in Strategic Decision Processes, Environmental Dynamism and Firm Performance," *Journal of Management*, Vol. 21, No. 5 (1995), pp. 913–929; J. W. Dean, Jr., and M. P. Sharfman, "Does Decision Process Matter? A Study of Strategic Decision-Making Effectiveness," *Academy of Management Journal* (April 1996), pp. 368–396.

67. T. L. Wheelen and J. D. Hunger, "Using the Strategic Audit," *SAM Advanced Management Journal* (Winter 1987), pp. 4–12; G. Donaldson, "A New Tool for Boards: The Strategic Audit," *Harvard Business Review* (July–August 1995), pp. 99–107.

68. D. C. Hambrick and J. W. Fredrickson, "Are You Sure You Have a Strategy?" *Academy of Management Executive* (November, 2001), pp. 48–59.

69. Hambrick and Fredrickson, p. 49.

1.A
Strategic Audit of a Corporation

I. Current Situation

A. Current Performance

How did the corporation perform in the past year overall in terms of return on investment, market share, and profitability?

B. Strategic Posture

What are the corporation's current mission, objectives, strategies, and policies?

1. Are they clearly stated, or are they merely implied from performance?
2. **Mission:** What business(es) is the corporation in? Why?
3. **Objectives:** What are the corporate, business, and functional objectives? Are they consistent with each other, with the mission, and with the internal and external environments?
4. **Strategies:** What strategy or mix of strategies is the corporation following? Are they consistent with each other, with the mission and objectives, and with the internal and external environments?
5. **Policies:** What are the corporation's policies? Are they consistent with each other, with the mission, objectives, and strategies, and with the internal and external environments?
6. Do the current mission, objectives, strategies, and policies reflect the corporation's international operations, whether global or multidomestic?

II. Corporate Governance

A. Board of Directors

1. Who is on the board? Are they internal (employees) or external members?
2. Do they own significant shares of stock?
3. Is the stock privately held or publicly traded? Are there different classes of stock with different voting rights?
4. What do the board members contribute to the corporation in terms of knowledge, skills, background, and connections? If the corporation has international operations, do board members have international experience? Are board members concerned with environmental sustainability?

SOURCE: T. L. Wheelen and J. D. Hunger, *Strategic Audit of a Corporation*, Copyright © 1982 and 2005 by Wheelen and Hunger Associates. Thomas L. Wheelen, "A Strategic Audit," paper presented to Society for Advancement of Management (SAM). Presented by J. D. Hunger and T. L. Wheelen in "The Strategic Audit: An Integrative Approach to Teaching Business Policy," *Academy of Management* (August 1983). Published in "Using the Strategic Audit," by T. L. Wheelen and J. D. Hunger in *SAM Advanced Management Journal* (Winter 1987), pp. 4–12. Reprinted by permission of the copyright holders. Revised 1988, 1994, 1997, 2000, 2002, 2004, 2005, 2009, and 2013.

5. How long have the board members served on the board?

6. What is their level of involvement in strategic management? Do they merely rubber-stamp top management's proposals or do they actively participate and suggest future directions? Do they evaluate management's proposals in terms of environmental sustainability?

B. Top Management

1. What person or group constitutes top management?

2. What are top management's chief characteristics in terms of knowledge, skills, background, and style? If the corporation has international operations, does top management have international experience? Are executives from acquired companies considered part of the top management team?

3. Has top management been responsible for the corporation's performance over the past few years? How many managers have been in their current position for less than three years? Were they promoted internally or externally hired?

4. Has top management established a systematic approach to strategic management?

5. What is top management's level of involvement in the strategic management process?

6. How well does top management interact with lower-level managers and with the board of directors?

7. Are strategic decisions made ethically in a socially responsible manner?

8. Are strategic decisions made in an environmentally sustainable manner?

9. Do top executives own significant amounts of stock in the corporation?

10. Is top management sufficiently skilled to cope with likely future challenges?

III. External Environment: Opportunities and Threats (SW**OT**)

A. Natural Physical Environment: Sustainability Issues

1. What forces from the natural physical environmental are currently affecting the corporation and the industries in which it competes? Which present current or future threats? Opportunities?
   a. Climate, including global temperature, sea level, and fresh water availability
   b. Weather-related events, such as severe storms, floods, and droughts
   c. Solar phenomena, such as sunspots and solar wind

2. Do these forces have different effects in other regions of the world?

B. Societal Environment

1. What general environmental forces are currently affecting both the corporation and the industries in which it competes? Which present current or future threats? Opportunities?
   a. Economic
   b. Technological
   c. Political–legal
   d. Sociocultural

2. Are these forces different in other regions of the world?

C. Task Environment

1. What forces drive industry competition? Are these forces the same globally or do they vary from country to country? Rate each force as **high**, **medium**, or **low**.
   a. Threat of new entrants

   b. Bargaining power of buyers
   c. Threat of substitute products or services
   d. Bargaining power of suppliers
   e. Rivalry among competing firms
   f. Relative power of unions, governments, special interest groups, etc.

2. What key factors in the immediate environment (that is, customers, competitors, suppliers, creditors, labor unions, governments, trade associations, interest groups, local communities, and shareholders) are currently affecting the corporation? Which are current or future threats? Opportunities?

D. Summary of External Factors (List in the EFAS Table 4–5, p. 155)

Which of these forces and factors are the most important to the corporation and to the industries in which it competes at the present time? Which will be important in the future?

IV. Internal Environment: Strengths and Weaknesses (**SW**OT)

A. Corporate Structure

1. How is the corporation structured at present?
   a. Is the decision-making authority centralized around one group or decentralized to many units?
   b. Is the corporation organized on the basis of functions, projects, geography, or some combination of these?
2. Is the structure clearly understood by everyone in the corporation?
3. Is the present structure consistent with current corporate objectives, strategies, policies, and programs, as well as with the firm's international operations?
4. In what ways does this structure compare with those of similar corporations?

B. Corporate Culture

1. Is there a well-defined or emerging culture composed of shared beliefs, expectations, and values?
2. Is the culture consistent with the current objectives, strategies, policies, and programs?
3. What is the culture's position on environmental sustainability?
4. What is the culture's position on other important issues facing the corporation (that is, on productivity, quality of performance, adaptability to changing conditions, and internationalization)?
5. Is the culture compatible with the employees' diversity of backgrounds?
6. Does the company take into consideration the values of the culture of each nation in which the firm operates?

C. Corporate Resources

1. **Marketing**
   a. What are the corporation's current marketing objectives, strategies, policies, and programs?
      i. Are they clearly stated or merely implied from performance and/or budgets?
      ii. Are they consistent with the corporation's mission, objectives, strategies, and policies and with internal and external environments?

b. How well is the corporation performing in terms of analysis of market position and marketing mix (that is, product, price, place, and promotion) in both domestic and international markets? How dependent is the corporation on a few customers? How big is its market? Where is it gaining or losing market share? What percentage of sales comes from developed versus developing regions? Where are current products in the product life cycle?
  i. What trends emerge from this analysis?
  ii. What impact have these trends had on past performance and how might these trends affect future performance?
  iii. Does this analysis support the corporation's past and pending strategic decisions?
  iv. Does marketing provide the company with a competitive advantage?
c. How well does the corporation's marketing performance compare with that of similar corporations?
d. Are marketing managers using accepted marketing concepts and techniques to evaluate and improve product performance? (Consider product life cycle, market segmentation, market research, and product portfolios.)
e. Does marketing adjust to the conditions in each country in which it operates?
f. Does marketing consider environmental sustainability when making decisions?
g. What is the role of the marketing manager in the strategic management process?

2. **Finance**
a. What are the corporation's current financial objectives, strategies, and policies and programs?
  i. Are they clearly stated or merely implied from performance and/or budgets?
  ii. Are they consistent with the corporation's mission, objectives, strategies, and policies and with internal and external environments?
b. How well is the corporation performing in terms of financial analysis? (Consider ratio analysis, common size statements, and capitalization structure.) How balanced, in terms of cash flow, is the company's portfolio of products and businesses? What are investor expectations in terms of share price?
  i. What trends emerge from this analysis?
  ii. Are there any significant differences when statements are calculated in constant versus reported dollars?
  iii. What impact have these trends had on past performance and how might these trends affect future performance?
  iv. Does this analysis support the corporation's past and pending strategic decisions?
  v. Does finance provide the company with a competitive advantage?
c. How well does the corporation's financial performance compare with that of similar corporations?
d. Are financial managers using accepted financial concepts and techniques to evaluate and improve current corporate and divisional performance? (Consider financial leverage, capital budgeting, ratio analysis, and managing foreign currencies.)
e. Does finance adjust to the conditions in each country in which the company operates?
f. Does finance cope with global financial issues?
g. What is the role of the financial manager in the strategic management process?

3. **Research and Development (R&D)**
a. What are the corporation's current R&D objectives, strategies, policies, and programs?
  i. Are they clearly stated or merely implied from performance or budgets?
  ii. Are they consistent with the corporation's mission, objectives, strategies and policies, and with internal and external environments?
  iii. What is the role of technology in corporate performance?

      iv. Is the mix of basic, applied, and engineering research appropriate given the corporate mission and strategies?

      v. Does R&D provide the company with a competitive advantage?

b. What return is the corporation receiving from its investment in R&D?

c. Is the corporation competent in technology transfer? Does it use concurrent engineering and cross-functional work teams in product and process design?

d. What role does technological discontinuity play in the company's products?

e. How well does the corporation's investment in R&D compare with the investments of similar corporations? How much R&D is being outsourced? Is the corporation using value-chain alliances appropriately for innovation and competitive advantage?

f. Does R&D adjust to the conditions in each country in which the company operates?

g. Does R&D consider environmental sustainability in product development and packaging?

h. What is the role of the R&D manager in the strategic management process?

4. **Operations and Logistics**

a. What are the corporation's current manufacturing/service objectives, strategies, policies, and programs?

      i. Are they clearly stated or merely implied from performance or budgets?

      ii. Are they consistent with the corporation's mission, objectives, strategies, and policies and with internal and external environments?

b. What are the type and extent of operations capabilities of the corporation? How much is done domestically versus internationally? Is the amount of outsourcing appropriate to be competitive? Is purchasing being handled appropriately? Are suppliers and distributors operating in an environmentally sustainable manner? Which products have the highest and lowest profit margins?

      i. If the corporation is product-oriented, consider plant facilities, type of manufacturing system (continuous mass production, intermittent job shop, or flexible manufacturing), age and type of equipment, degree and role of automation and/or robots, plant capacities and utilization, productivity ratings, and availability and type of transportation.

      ii. If the corporation is service-oriented, consider service facilities (hospital, theater, or school buildings), type of operations systems (continuous service over time to the same clientele or intermittent service over time to varied clientele), age and type of supporting equipment, degree and role of automation and use of mass communication devices (diagnostic machinery, video machines), facility capacities and utilization rates, efficiency ratings of professional and service personnel, and availability and type of transportation to bring service staff and clientele together.

c. Are manufacturing or service facilities vulnerable to natural disasters, local or national strikes, reduction or limitation of resources from suppliers, substantial cost increases of materials, or nationalization by governments?

d. Is there an appropriate mix of people and machines (in manufacturing firms) or of support staff to professionals (in service firms)?

e. How well does the corporation perform relative to the competition? Is it balancing inventory costs (warehousing) with logistical costs (just-in-time)? Consider costs per unit of labor, material, and overhead; downtime; inventory control management and scheduling of service staff; production ratings; facility utilization percentages; and number of clients successfully treated by category (if service firm) or percentage of orders shipped on time (if product firm).

      i. What trends emerge from this analysis?

      ii. What impact have these trends had on past performance and how might these trends affect future performance?

      iii. Does this analysis support the corporation's past and pending strategic decisions?

      iv. Does operations provide the company with a competitive advantage?

    f. Are operations managers using appropriate concepts and techniques to evaluate and improve current performance? Consider cost systems, quality control and reliability systems, inventory control management, personnel scheduling, TQM, learning curves, safety programs, and engineering programs that can improve efficiency of manufacturing or of service.

    g. Do operations adjust to the conditions in each country in which it has facilities?

    h. Do operations consider environmental sustainability when making decisions?

    i. What is the role of the operations manager in the strategic management process?

5. **Human Resources Management (HRM)**

    a. What are the corporation's current HRM objectives, strategies, policies, and programs?

       i. Are they clearly stated or merely implied from performance and/or budgets?

       ii. Are they consistent with the corporation's mission, objectives, strategies, and policies and with internal and external environments?

    b. How well is the corporation's HRM performing in terms of improving the fit between the individual employee and the job? Consider turnover, grievances, strikes, layoffs, employee training, and quality of work life.

       i. What trends emerge from this analysis?

       ii. What impact have these trends had on past performance and how might these trends affect future performance?

       iii. Does this analysis support the corporation's past and pending strategic decisions?

       iv. Does HRM provide the company with a competitive advantage?

    c. How does this corporation's HRM performance compare with that of similar corporations?

    d. Are HRM managers using appropriate concepts and techniques to evaluate and improve corporate performance? Consider the job analysis program, performance appraisal system, up-to-date job descriptions, training and development programs, attitude surveys, job design programs, quality of relationships with unions, and use of autonomous work teams.

    e. How well is the company managing the diversity of its workforce? What is the company's record on human rights? Does the company monitor the human rights record of key suppliers and distributors?

    f. Does HRM adjust to the conditions in each country in which the company operates? Does the company have a code of conduct for HRM for itself and key suppliers in developing nations? Are employees receiving international assignments to prepare them for managerial positions?

    g. What is the role of outsourcing in HRM planning?

    h. What is the role of the HRM manager in the strategic management process?

6. **Information Technology (IT)**

    a. What are the corporation's current IT objectives, strategies, policies, and programs?

       i. Are they clearly stated or merely implied from performance and/or budgets?

       ii. Are they consistent with the corporation's mission, objectives, strategies, and policies and with internal and external environments?

    b. How well is the corporation's IT performing in terms of providing a useful database, automating routine clerical operations, assisting managers in making routine decisions, and providing information necessary for strategic decisions?

       i. What trends emerge from this analysis?

       ii. What impact have these trends had on past performance and how might these trends affect future performance?

       iii. Does this analysis support the corporation's past and pending strategic decisions?

       iv. Does IT provide the company with a competitive advantage?

    c. How does this corporation's IT performance and stage of development compare with that of similar corporations? Is it appropriately using the Internet, intranet, and extranets?

    d. Are IT managers using appropriate concepts and techniques to evaluate and improve corporate performance? Do they know how to build and manage a complex database, establish Web sites with firewalls and virus protection, conduct system analyses, and implement interactive decision-support systems?

    e. Does the company have a global IT and Internet presence? Does it have difficulty with getting data across national boundaries?

    f. What is the role of the IT manager in the strategic management process?

D. Summary of Internal Factors
(List in the IFAS Table 5–2, p. 188)

Which of these factors are core competencies? Which, if any, are distinctive competencies? Which of these factors are the most important to the corporation and to the industries in which it competes at the present time? Which might be important in the future? Which functions or activities are candidates for outsourcing?

V. Analysis of Strategic Factors (SWOT)

A. Situational Analysis
(List in SFAS Matrix, Figure 6–1, pp. 200–201)

Of the external (EFAS) and internal (IFAS) factors listed in III.D and IV.D, which are the strategic (most important) factors that strongly affect the corporation's present and future performance?

B. Review of Mission and Objectives

1. Are the current mission and objectives appropriate in light of the key strategic factors and problems?

2. Should the mission and objectives be changed? If so, how?

3. If they are changed, what will be the effects on the firm?

VI. Strategic Alternatives and Recommended Strategy

A. Strategic Alternatives

1. Can the current or revised objectives be met through more careful implementation of those strategies presently in use (for example, fine-tuning the strategies)?

2. What are the major feasible alternative strategies available to the corporation? What are the pros and cons of each? Can corporate scenarios be developed and agreed on? (Alternatives must fit the natural physical environment, societal environment, industry, and corporation for the next three to five years.)

    a. Consider *stability*, *growth*, and *retrenchment* as corporate strategies.

    b. Consider *cost leadership* and *differentiation* as business strategies.

    c. Consider any functional strategic alternatives that might be needed for reinforcement of an important corporate or business strategic alternative.

B. Recommended Strategy

1. Specify which of the strategic alternatives you are recommending for the corporate, business, and functional levels of the corporation. Do you recommend different business or functional strategies for different units of the corporation?

2. Justify your recommendation in terms of its ability to resolve both long- and short-term problems and effectively deal with the strategic factors.

3. What policies should be developed or revised to guide effective implementation?

4. What is the impact of your recommended strategy on the company's core and distinctive competencies?

VII. Implementation

A. What Kinds of Programs or Tactics (for Example, Restructuring the Corporation or Instituting TQM) Should Be Developed to Implement the Recommended Strategy?

1. Who should develop these programs/tactics?

2. Who should be in charge of these programs/tactics?

B. Are the Programs/Tactics Financially Feasible? Can Pro Forma Budgets Be Developed and Agreed On? Are Priorities and Timetables Appropriate to Individual Programs/Tactics?

C. Will New Standard Operating Procedures Need to Be Developed?

VIII. Evaluation and Control

A. Is the Current Information System Capable of Providing Sufficient Feedback on Implementation Activities and Performance? Can It Measure Strategic Factors?

1. Can performance results be pinpointed by area, unit, project, or function?

2. Is the information timely?

3. Is the corporation using benchmarking to evaluate its functions and activities?

B. Are Adequate Control Measures in Place to Ensure Conformance with the Recommended Strategic Plan?

1. Are appropriate standards and measures being used?

2. Are reward systems capable of recognizing and rewarding good performance?

corporate Governance

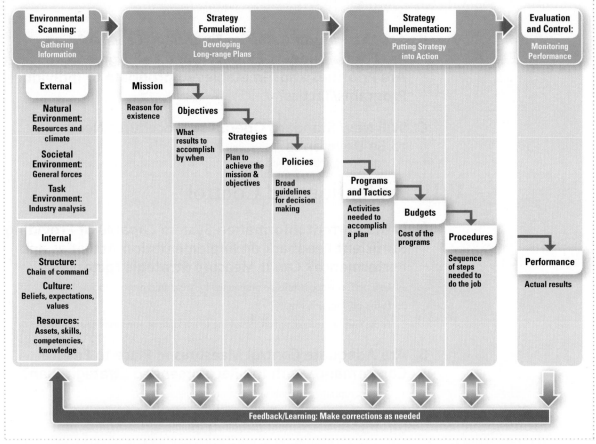

External

Natural Environment: Resources and climate

Societal Environment: General forces

Task Environment: Industry analysis

Internal

Structure: Chain of command

Culture: Beliefs, expectations, values

Resources: Assets, skills, competencies, knowledge

Mission Reason for existence

Objectives What results to accomplish by when

Strategies Plan to achieve the mission & objectives

Policies Broad guidelines for decision making

Programs and Tactics Activities needed to accomplish a plan

Budgets Cost of the programs

Procedures Sequence of steps needed to do the job

Performance Actual results

Feedback/Learning: Make corrections as needed

MyManagementLab®

⭐ Improve Your Grade!

Over 10 million students improved their results using the Pearson MyLabs. Visit **mymanagementlab.com** for simulations, tutorials, and end-of-chapter problems.

Learning Objectives

After reading this chapter, you should be able to:

- Describe the role and responsibilities of the board of directors in corporate governance
- Understand how the composition of a board can affect its operation
- Describe the impact of the Sarbanes–Oxley Act on corporate governance in the United States
- Discuss trends in corporate governance
- Explain how executive leadership is an important part of strategic management

Disarray with the HP Board of Directors

Sometimes an activist or even catalyst board does more harm than good. This has certainly been the case at Hewlett-Packard Company, the Palo Alto pioneer in technology.

Lewis Platt was only the fourth CEO in the history of the company, and like his predecessor (John A. Young), he was a long-time engineering employee of the company. Under his leadership, the company prospered as it had through most of its 50-year history up to that point. With the support of the board, he spun off the Medical Instruments division and made tentative moves toward the new information age, but was slow to recognize the importance of the Internet.

In 1999, along with the board of directors, he decided to look outside the company for the first time and try to hire a visible, passionate leader for the staid engineering-oriented firm. On July 19, 1999, HP announced that Carly Fiorina would be the new CEO, making her the first woman to head a DOW 30 company. Fiorina made her name at Lucent Technologies where she was President of a company that made a remarkable turnaround in the face of the huge changes in technology of the day.

Some of the same board members that hired her then turned against her in one of the most public proxy battles of our times when she announced a US$25 billion merger with Compaq Computer Company in September 2001. Walter Hewlett and Lewis Platt openly opposed the merger. The plan to move HP into an innovation machine in the Internet age was now moving to put most of its resources in a low-margin, shrinking PC manufacturing business. Wall Street hated the idea. HP stock lost 18% of its value on the day the merger was announced and many analysts in the industry thought this was a bad move. Fiorina forced the merger forward with the support of the majority of the board of directors.

On February 22, 2002, the HP Board of Directors sent a very public and stinging letter of criticism against Hewlett to all of its shareholders. Hewlett responded by taking out ads in major newspapers opposing the acquisition. In the end, the merger was approved, but by only a scant 3% majority.

The history of acquisitions is not a good one. Very few bring real value to the companies that are the acquirer. The bigger the acquisition, the more likely this is the case. Such was the fate of HP. By the end of 2004, the board was fed up with Carly Fiorina's inability to move the new, huge HP forward. The board began meeting in private without their high-profile CEO. On February 6, 2005, the board met with Fiorina at Chicago's O'Hare Hyatt Hotel and expressed their frustration with her leadership and her unwillingness to work with the board of directors on the future of the company. The next day they asked her to resign.

Believing that it was a failure of execution, the board moved to hire someone with strict operating credentials. The result was Mark Hurd, the 25-year veteran CEO at NCR Corporation. Hurd roared into the company, eliminating 15,000+ jobs, cutting R&D, and attempting to automate consulting services. A leak of information discussed at a board of directors strategy meeting in late 2005 led then–Board Chairman Patricia Dunn and CEO Mark Hurd to initiate an investigation of fellow board members. Using detectives who posed as reporters, they obtained phone records of those people on the board that they suspected, and the spying scandal exploded into the open.

Dunn was fired from her board seat in 2006 and *Newsweek* magazine put her on the cover with the title "The Boss Who Spied on Her Board." Mark Hurd escaped any serious repercussions from the scandal and announced a new, very strict code of conduct for the corporation.

By all accounts, Mark Hurd was successful at turning the company around and was listed as one of the best CEOs in 2009. However, another scandal broke, with Hurd being accused of sexual harassment with an HP marketing consultant. While the board found that he did not actually violate the company's sexual-harassment policies, they did find that he submitted inaccurate expense reports intended to conceal the relationship. He was forced to resign in August 2010 by a powerful but small group of directors.

In the wake of the Hurd resignation, there was a major board shakeup. Four directors involved in forcing the Hurd resignation resigned their board seats and five new board members were named. In November, 2010, the board named Leo Apotheker as the new CEO. He was the former head of Global Field Operations at SAP, and would remain the company's CEO for little more than 10 months.

Apotheker's move to push forward the HP TouchPad tablet was a commercial failure at the same time that HP phones were taking a beating in the market. In a stunning announcement in September 2011, he stated that HP would exit the PC business entirely. HP was the leader in PC sales both within the United States and globally. The outrage was immediate and overwhelming. The company reversed position two weeks later, but the board was appalled at his lack of leadership. After firing Apotheker, the board named one of its own members, former eBay CEO Meg Whitman to run the company.

One of the most important responsibilities that a board of directors has is to effectively recruit and work with management that will lead the business. The CEO revolving door at HP has cost the company more than US$83 million in severance pay for CEOs that the board no longer wants to run the company. *CNN Money* reported in 2012 that "Before Apotheker ever came to HP, the company was known for its fractious board. Individual directors would cycle in and out, yet somehow the group seemed constantly divided by personal rivalries, bickering, and leaks to the press."

SOURCES: Bandler, J. and Burke, D. "How Hewlett-Packard Lost Its Way," Accessed 5/30/13, www.tech
.fortune.cnn.com/2012/05/08/500-hp-apotheker/; Lohr, S. "Lewis E. Platt, 64, Chief of Hewlett-Packard
in 1990's Dies," nytimes.com, Accessed 5/30/13, www.nytimes.com/2005/09/10/technology/10platt
.html; Stanford Graduate School of Business Case SM-130. "HP and Compaq Combined: In Search
of Scale and Scope," Accessed 5/30/13, www.cendix.com/downloads/education/HP%20Compaq
.pdf; Elgin, B. "The Inside Story of Carly's Ouster," Accessed 5/30/13, www.businessweek.com/
stories/2005-02-20/the-inside-story-of-carlys-ouster; Oracle.com, "Mark Hurd – President," Accessed,
5/30/13, www.oracle.com/us/corporate/press/executives/mark-hurd-170533.html; Gregory, S. "Corporate Scandals: Why HP had to Oust Mark Hurd," Accessed 5/30/13, www.time.com/time/business/
article/0,8599,2009617,00.html; Arnold, L. and Turner, N. "Patricia Dunn, HP Chairman Fired in Spying
Scandal, Dies at 58," Accessed 5/30/13, www.businessweek.com/news/2011-12-05/patricia-dunn-
hp-chairman-fired-in-spying-scandal-dies-at-58.html.

Role of the Board of Directors

A *corporation* is a mechanism established to allow different parties to contribute capital, expertise, and labor for their mutual benefit. The investor/shareholder participates in the profits (in the form of dividends and stock price increases) of the enterprise without taking responsibility for the operations. Management runs the company without being responsible for personally providing the funds. To make this possible, laws have been passed that give shareholders limited liability and, correspondingly, limited involvement in a corporation's activities. That involvement does include, however, the right to elect directors who have a legal duty to represent the shareholders and protect their interests. As representatives of the shareholders, directors have both the authority and the responsibility to establish basic corporate policies and to ensure that they are followed.[1]

The board of directors, therefore, has an obligation to approve all decisions that might affect the long-term performance of the corporation. This means that the corporation is fundamentally governed by the *board of directors* overseeing *top management*, with the concurrence of the *shareholder*. The term **corporate governance** refers to the relationship among these three groups in determining the direction and performance of the corporation.[2]

Over the past decade and a half, shareholders and various interest groups have seriously questioned the role of the board of directors in corporations. They are concerned that inside board members may use their position to feather their own nests and that outside board members often lack sufficient knowledge, involvement, and enthusiasm to do an adequate job of monitoring and providing guidance to top management. Instances of widespread corruption and questionable accounting practices at Enron, Global Crossing, WorldCom, Tyco, and Qwest, among others, seem to justify their concerns. The board at HP appeared to be incapable of deciding upon the direction of the business, moving CEOs in and out as its ideas changed.

The general public has not only become more aware and more critical of many boards' apparent lack of responsibility for corporate activities, it has begun to push government to demand accountability. As a result, the board as a rubber stamp of the CEO or as a bastion of the "old-boy" selection system is slowly being replaced by more active, more professional boards.

RESPONSIBILITIES OF THE BOARD

Laws and standards defining the responsibilities of boards of directors vary from country to country. For example, board members in Ontario, Canada, face more than 100 provincial and federal laws governing director liability. The United States, however, has no clear national standards or federal laws. Specific requirements of directors vary, depending on the state in which the corporate charter is issued. There is, nevertheless, a developing worldwide consensus concerning the major responsibilities of a board. An article by Spencer Stuart written by an international team of contributors suggested the following five **board of director responsibilities**:

1. Effective Board Leadership including the processes, makeup and output of the board
2. Strategy of the Organization
3. Risk vs. initiative and the overall risk profile of the organization
4. Succession planning for the board and top management team
5. Sustainability[3]

These results are in agreement with a survey by the National Association of Corporate Directors, in which U.S. CEOs reported that the four most important issues boards should address are corporate performance, CEO succession, strategic planning, and corporate governance.[4] Directors in the United States must make certain, in addition to the duties just listed, that the corporation is managed in accordance with the laws of the state in which it is incorporated. Because more than half of all publicly traded companies in the United States are incorporated in the state of Delaware, this state's laws and rulings have more impact than do those of any other state.[5] Directors must also ensure management's adherence to laws and regulations, such as those dealing with the issuance of securities, insider trading, and other conflict-of-interest situations. They must also be aware of the needs and demands of constituent groups so that they can achieve a judicious balance among the interests of these diverse groups while ensuring the continued functioning of the corporation.

In a legal sense, the board is required to direct the affairs of the corporation but not to manage them. It is charged by law to act with **due care**. If a director or the board as a whole fails to act with due care and, as a result, the corporation is in some way harmed, the careless director or directors can be held personally liable for the harm done. This is no small concern given that one survey of outside directors revealed that more than 40% had been named as part of lawsuits against corporations.[6] For example, board members of Equitable Life in Britain were sued for up to US$5.4 billion for their failure to question the CEO's reckless policies.[7] For this reason, corporations have found that they need directors' and officers' liability insurance in order to attract people to become members of boards of directors.

A 2011 global survey of directors by McKinsey & Company revealed the average amount of time boards spend on a given issue during their meetings. The top 5 are:[8]

- Strategy (development and analysis of strategies)—23%
- Execution (prioritizing programs and approving mergers and acquisitions)—22%
- Performance management (development of incentives and measuring performance)—18%
- Governance and compliance (nominations, compensation, audits)—14%
- Talent management—10%

Role of the Board in Strategic Management

How does a board of directors fulfill these many responsibilities? The *role of the board of directors in strategic management* is to carry out three basic tasks:

- **Monitor:** By acting through its committees, a board can keep abreast of developments inside and outside the corporation, bringing to management's attention developments it might have overlooked. A board should at the minimum carry out this task.

- **Evaluate and influence:** A board can examine management's proposals, decisions, and actions; agree or disagree with them; give advice and offer suggestions; and outline alternatives. More active boards perform this task in addition to monitoring.

- **Initiate and determine:** A board can delineate a corporation's mission and specify strategic options to its management. Only the most active boards take on this task in addition to the two previous ones.

Board of Directors' Continuum

A board of directors is involved in strategic management to the extent that it carries out the three tasks of monitoring, evaluating and influencing, and initiating and determining. The **board of directors' continuum** shown in **Figure 2–1** shows the possible degree of involvement (from low to high) in the strategic management process. Boards can range from phantom boards with no real involvement to catalyst boards with a very high degree of involvement.[9] Research suggests that active board involvement in strategic management is positively related to a corporation's financial performance and its credit rating.[10]

Highly involved boards tend to be very active. They take their tasks of monitoring, evaluating and influencing, and initiating and determining very seriously; they provide advice when necessary and keep management alert. As depicted in **Figure 2–1**, their heavy involvement in the strategic management process places them in the active participation or even catalyst positions. Although 74% of public corporations have periodic board meetings devoted primarily to the review of overall company strategy, the boards may not have had much influence in generating the plan itself.[11] The same 2011 global survey of directors by McKinsey & Company found that 44% of respondents reviewed and approved management's proposed strategy, 41% developed strategy with management, and 11% developed strategy, which management was then assigned to execute. Those boards reporting high influence typically shared a common

FIGURE 2–1   Board of Directors' Continuum

		DEGREE OF INVOLVEMENT IN STRATEGIC MANAGEMENT			
Low (Passive)					**High** (Active)
Phantom	**Rubber Stamp**	**Minimal Review**	**Nominal Participation**	**Active Participation**	**Catalyst**
Never knows what to do, if anything; no degree of involvement.	Permits officers to make all decisions. It votes as the officers recommend on action issues.	Formally reviews selected issues that officers bring to its attention.	Involved to a limited degree in the performance or review of selected key decisions, indicators, or programs of managment.	Approves, questions, and makes final decisions on mission, strategy, policies, and objectives. Has active board committees. Performs fiscal and management audits.	Takes the leading role in establishing and modifying the mission, objectives, strategy, and policies. It has a very active strategy committee.

SOURCE: T. L. Wheelen and J. D. Hunger, "Board of Directors' Continuum," Copyright © 1994 by Wheelen and Hunger Associates. Reprinted by permission.

plan for creating value and had healthy debate about what actions the company should take to create value. Together with top management, these high-influence boards considered global trends and future scenarios and developed plans. In contrast, those boards with low influence tended not to do any of these things.[12] Nevertheless, studies indicate that boards are becoming increasingly active.

These and other studies suggest that most large publicly owned corporations have boards that operate at some point between nominal and active participation. Some corporations with actively participating boards are Target, Medtronic, Best Western, Service Corporation International, Bank of Montreal, Mead Corporation, Rolm and Haas, Whirlpool, 3M, Apria Healthcare, General Electric, Pfizer, and Texas Instruments.[13] Target, a corporate governance leader, has a board that each year sets three top priorities, such as strategic direction, capital allocation, and succession planning. Each of these priority topics is placed at the top of the agenda for at least one meeting. Target's board also devotes one meeting a year to setting the strategic direction for each major operating division.[14]

As a board becomes less involved in the affairs of the corporation, it moves farther to the left on the continuum (see **Figure 2–1**). On the far left are passive phantom or rubber-stamp boards that typically never initiate or determine strategy unless a crisis occurs. In these situations, the CEO also serves as Chairman of the Board, personally nominates all directors, and works to keep board members under his or her control by giving them the "mushroom treatment"—throw manure on them and keep them in the dark!

Generally, the smaller the corporation, the less active is its board of directors in strategic management.[15] In an entrepreneurial venture, for example, the privately held corporation may be 100% owned by the founders—who also manage the company. In this case, there is no need for an active board to protect the interests of the owner-manager shareholders—the interests of the owners and the managers are identical. In this instance, a board is really unnecessary and only meets to satisfy legal requirements. If stock is sold to outsiders to finance growth, however, the board becomes more active. Key investors want seats on the board so they can oversee their investment. To the extent that they still control most of the stock, however, the founders dominate the board. Friends, family members, and key shareholders usually become members, but the board acts primarily as a rubber stamp for any proposals put forward by the owner-managers. In this type of company, the founder tends to be both CEO and Chairman of the Board and the board includes few people who are not affiliated with the firm or family.[16] This cozy relationship between the board and management should change, however, when the corporation goes public and stock is more widely dispersed. The founders, who are still acting as management, may sometimes make decisions that conflict with the needs of the other shareholders (especially if the founders own less than 50% of the common stock). In this instance, problems could occur if the board fails to become more active in terms of its roles and responsibilities. This situation can occur in large organizations as well. Even after the high profile IPO, Facebook was still more than 50% controlled by founder Mark Zuckerberg and he used his position to make significant strategic decisions without input from the board of directors. In 2012, just ahead of the IPO of Facebook, he bought Instagram for roughly US$1 billion and only then informed the board of his move. [17]

MEMBERS OF A BOARD OF DIRECTORS

The boards of most publicly owned corporations are composed of both inside and outside directors. **Inside directors** (sometimes called management directors) are typically officers or executives employed by the corporation. **Outside directors** (sometimes called non-management directors) may be executives of other firms but are not employees of the board's corporation. Although there is yet no clear evidence indicating that a high proportion of outsiders on a board results in improved financial performance,[18] there is a trend in

INNOVATION issue

JCPENNEY AND INNOVATION

Ron Johnson joined erstwhile retailer JCPenney in November 2011 with a mandate from the board of directors to shake up the organization. The board members were not interested in another decade of classic retailer wisdom, they wanted someone who would create a new JCPenney. They got exactly what they were looking for. The question is whether that bold move will allow the company to thrive or force it out of business.

Johnson was the architect behind the "cheap chic" approach at Target before he moved to Apple with the mandate to create "THE" store experience. He designed an Apple retail approach that is the envy of the retailer world and in the process created the world's most profitable stores. Johnson was personally recruited to take over JCPenney by Bill Ackman. His company (Pershing Square Capital Management) owns 18% of JCPenney.

Johnson's vision was to create a company that was not dependent upon sales coupons or continuous promotions for its survival. He joined a 110-year-old company that was running 590 different promotions a year that cost the company (in promotion costs alone) more than US$1 billion. Ninety-nine percent of those promotions were ignored by

their primary customer group. The real sales price for virtually every product in the store was substantially less than the list price on the shelf.

The fundamental strategic approach was sound. He was separating the company from its competitors and doing so with an approach that was rare in the retailing world, durable as long as the competitors didn't believe that approach would work, and might have been valuable for the company both from a cost containment approach as well as its potential to draw in new customers. The story was over almost before it began. Sales plummeted, profits evaporated and after 18 months on the job, Johnson was fired only to be replaced by the former CEO of the company. Perhaps Johnson's biggest failure was rollout. Rather than experimenting with the new concept to refine the effort, he demanded that it be put in place systemwide. He had the support of the board until his unwillingness to compromise or re-evaluate his strategy drove the board to act.

....

SOURCES: Berfield, S. and Maheshwari, S. 2012. "J.C. Penney vs. The Bargain Hunters," *Bloomberg Businessweek*, May 28 – June 3, 2012, pg. 21–22. Rooney, J. "JCPenney's New Strategy a Tough Sell on the Sales Floor," Forbes.com, Accessed 5/30/13, www.forbes.com/sites/jenniferrooney/2012/03/14/jc-penneys-new-strategy-a-tough-sell-on-the-sales-floor/

---

the United States to increase the number of outsiders on boards and to reduce the total size of the board.[19] The board of directors of a typical large U.S. corporation has an average of 10 directors, 2 of whom are insiders.[20]

Outsiders thus account for 80% of the board members in large U.S. corporations (approximately the same as in Canada). Boards in the UK typically have 5 inside and 5 outside directors, whereas in France boards usually consist of 3 insiders and 8 outsiders. Japanese boards, in contrast, contain 2 outsiders and 12 insiders.[21] The board of directors in a typical small U.S. corporation has 4 to 5 members, of whom only 1 or 2 are outsiders.[22] Research from large and small corporations reveals a negative relationship between board size and firm profitability.[23]

People who favor a high proportion of outsiders state that outside directors are less biased and more likely to evaluate management's performance objectively than are inside directors. This is the main reason why the U.S. Securities and Exchange Commission (SEC) in 2003 required that a majority of directors on the board be independent outsiders. The SEC also required that all listed companies staff their audit, compensation, and nominating/corporate governance committees entirely with independent, outside members. This view is in agreement with **agency theory**, which states that problems arise in corporations because the agents (top management) are not willing to bear responsibility for their decisions unless they own a substantial amount of stock in the corporation. The theory suggests that a majority of a board needs to be from outside the firm so that top management is prevented from acting selfishly to the detriment of the shareholders. For example, proponents of agency theory argue that managers in management-controlled firms (contrasted with owner-controlled firms in which the founder or family still own a significant amount of stock) select less risky strategies with quick payoffs in order to keep their jobs.[24] This view is supported by research revealing that manager controlled firms (with weak boards) are more likely to go into debt to diversify into unrelated markets (thus quickly boosting sales and assets to justify higher salaries for themselves). These actions result in poorer long-term performance than owner-controlled firms.[25] Boards with a larger proportion of outside directors tend to favor growth through international expansion and innovative venturing activities than do boards with a smaller proportion of outsiders.[26] Outsiders tend to be more objective and critical of corporate activities. For example, research reveals that the likelihood of a firm engaging in illegal behavior or being sued declines with the addition of outsiders on the board.[27] Research on family businesses has found that boards with a larger number of outsiders on the board tended to have better corporate governance and better performance than did boards with fewer outsiders.[28]

In contrast, those who prefer inside over outside directors contend that outside directors are less effective than are insiders because the outsiders are less likely to have the necessary interest, availability, or competency. **Stewardship theory** proposes that, because of their long tenure with the corporation, insiders (senior executives) tend to identify with the corporation and its success. Rather than use the firm for their own ends, these executives are thus most interested in guaranteeing the continued life and success of the corporation. (See the Strategy Highlight feature for a discussion of Agency Theory contrasted with Stewardship Theory.) Excluding all insiders but the CEO reduces the opportunity for outside directors to see potential successors in action or to obtain alternate points of view of management decisions. Outside directors may sometimes serve on so many boards that they spread their time and interest too thin to actively fulfill their responsibilities. The average board member of a U.S. Fortune 500 firm serves on three boards. Research indicates that firm performance decreases as the number of directorships held by the average board member increases.[29] Although only 40% of surveyed U.S. boards currently limit the number of directorships a board member may hold in other corporations, 60% limit the number of boards on which their CEO may be a member.[30]

Those who question the value of having more outside board members point out that the term *outsider* is too simplistic because some outsiders are not truly objective and should be considered more as insiders than as outsiders. For example, there can be:

1. **Affiliated directors**, who, though not really employed by the corporation, handle the legal or insurance work for the company or are important suppliers (and thus dependent on the current management for a key part of their business). These outsiders face a conflict of interest and are not likely to be objective. As a result of recent actions by the U.S. Congress, the Securities and Exchange Commission, the New York Stock Exchange, and NASDAQ, affiliated directors are being banned from U.S. corporate boardrooms. U.S. boards can no longer include representatives of major suppliers or customers or even professional organizations that might do business with the firm, even though these people could provide valuable knowledge and expertise.[31] The New York Stock Exchange decided in 2004 that anyone paid by the company during the previous three years could not be classified as an independent outside director.[32]

2. **Retired executive directors**, who used to work for the company, such as the past CEO who is partly responsible for much of the corporation's current strategy and who probably groomed the current CEO as his or her replacement. In the recent past, many boards of large firms kept the firm's recently retired CEO on the board for a year or two after retirement as a courtesy, especially if he or she had performed well as the CEO. It is almost certain, however, that this person will not be able to objectively evaluate the corporation's

STRATEGY highlight

AGENCY THEORY VERSUS STEWARDSHIP THEORY IN CORPORATE GOVERNANCE

Managers of large, modern publicly held corporations are typically not the owners. In fact, most of today's top managers own only nominal amounts of stock in the corporation they manage. The real owners (shareholders) elect boards of directors who hire managers as their agents to run the firm's day-to-day activities. Once hired, how trustworthy are these executives? Do they put themselves or the firm first? There are two significant schools of thought on this.

Agency Theory. As suggested in the classic study by Berle and Means, top managers are, in effect, "hired hands" who are very likely more interested in their personal welfare than that of the shareholders. For example, management might emphasize strategies, such as acquisitions, that increase the size of the firm (to become more powerful and to demand increased pay and benefits) or that diversify the firm into unrelated businesses (to reduce short-term risk and to allow them to put less effort into a core product line that may be facing difficulty) but that result in a reduction of dividends and/or stock price.

Agency theory is concerned with analyzing and resolving two problems that occur in relationships between principals (owners/shareholders) and their agents (top management):

1. *Conflict of interest* arises when the desires or objectives of the owners and the agents conflict. For example, attitudes toward risk may be quite different. Agents may shy away from riskier strategies in order to protect their jobs.

2. *Moral hazard* refers to the situation where it is difficult or expensive for the owners to verify what the agents are actually doing.

According to agency theory, the likelihood that these problems will occur increases when stock is widely held (that is, when no one shareholder owns more than a small percentage of the total common stock), when the board of directors is composed of people who know little of the company or who are personal friends of top management, and when a high percentage of board members are inside (management) directors.

To better align the interests of the agents with those of the owners and to increase the corporation's overall performance, agency theory suggests that top management have a significant degree of ownership in the firm and/or have a strong financial stake in its long-term performance. In support of this argument, research indicates a positive relationship between corporate performance and the amount of stock owned by directors.

Stewardship Theory. In contrast, stewardship theory suggests that executives tend to be more motivated to act in the best interests of the corporation than in their own self-interests. Whereas agency theory focuses on extrinsic rewards that serve lower-level needs, such as pay and security, stewardship theory focuses on the higher-order needs, such as achievement and self-actualization. Stewardship theory argues that senior executives over time tend to view the corporation as an extension of themselves. Rather than use the firm for their own ends, these executives are most interested in guaranteeing the continued life and success of the corporation. The relationship between the board and top management is thus one of principal and steward, not principal and agent ("hired hand"). Stewardship theory notes that in a widely held corporation, the shareholder is free to sell his or her stock at any time. In fact, the average share of stock is held less than 10 months. A diversified investor or speculator may care little about risk at the company level—preferring management to assume extraordinary risk so long as the return is adequate. Because executives in a firm cannot easily leave their jobs when in difficulty, they are more interested in a merely satisfactory return and put heavy emphasis on the firm's continued survival. Thus, stewardship theory argues that in many instances top management may care more about a company's long-term success than do more short-term–oriented shareholders.

. . . .

SOURCES: For more information about agency and stewardship theory, see A. A. Berle and G. C. Means, *The Modern Corporation and Private Property* (NY: Macmillan, 1936). Also see J. H. Davis, F. D. Schoorman, and L. Donaldson, "Toward a Stewardship Theory of Management," *Academy of Management Review* (January 1997), pp. 20–47; P. J. Lane, A. A. Cannella, Jr., and M. H. Lubatkin, "Agency Problems as Antecedents to Unrelated Mergers and Diversification: Amihud and Lev Reconsidered," *Strategic Management Journal* (June 1998), pp. 555–578; M. L. Hayward and D. C. Hambrick, "Explaining the Premiums Paid for Large Acquisitions: Evidence of CEO Hubris," *Administrative Science Quarterly* (March 1997), pp. 103–127; and C. M. Christensen and S. D. Anthony, "Put Investors in Their Place," *BusinessWeek* (May 28, 2007), p. 108.

performance. Because of the likelihood of a conflict of interest, only 30% of boards in the Americas and 28% in Europe now include the former CEO on their boards.[33]

3. **Family directors,** who are descendants of the founder and own significant blocks of stock (with personal agendas based on a family relationship with the current CEO). The Schlitz Brewing Company, for example, was unable to complete its turnaround strategy with a non-family CEO because family members serving on the board wanted their money out of the company, forcing it to be sold.[34]

The majority of outside directors are active or retired CEOs and COOs of other corporations. Others are major investors/shareholders, academicians, attorneys, consultants, former government officials, and bankers. Given that 66% of the outstanding stock in the largest U.S. and UK corporations is now owned by institutional investors, such as mutual funds and pension plans, these investors are taking an increasingly active role in board membership and activities.[35] For example, TIAA-CREF's Corporate Governance team monitors governance practices of the 4000 companies in which it invests its pension funds through its Corporate Assessment Program. If its analysis of a company reveals problems, TIAA-CREF first sends letters stating its concerns, followed up by visits, and it finally sponsors a shareholder resolution in opposition to management's actions.[36] Institutional investors are also powerful in many other countries. In Germany, bankers are represented on almost every board—primarily because they own large blocks of stock in German corporations. In Denmark, Sweden, Belgium, and Italy, however, investment companies assume this role. For example, the investment company Investor casts 42.5% of the Electrolux shareholder votes, thus guaranteeing itself positions on the Electrolux board.

Boards of directors have been working to increase the number of women and minorities serving on boards and well they should. A 2012 study of 2360 companies found that shares of companies with female board members outperformed comparable businesses with all-male boards by 26% worldwide over a six-year time period.[37] Korn/Ferry International reported that amongst the 100 largest companies listed in 2011 that 96% of boards of directors had at least one female director, while at the same time women made up only 16% of all directors.

This number was quite different when we look at the situation in some other countries. A 2011 study by Korn/Ferry examined the 100 largest companies in seven countries across the Pacific Rim (Australia, China, Hong Kong, India, Malaysia, Singapore, and New Zealand). They found female board representation to be:

- Australia—(11.2%)
- China—(8.1%)
- Hong Kong—(8.6%)
- India—(4.7%)
- Malaysia—(7.8%)
- Singapore—(6.4%)
- New Zealand—(7.5%)[38]

Korn/Ferry's survey also revealed that 78% of the U.S. boards had at least one ethnic minority in 2007 (African-American, 47%; Latino, 19%; Asian, 11%) as director compared to only 47% in 1995, comprising around 14% of total directors.[39] Among the top 200 S&P companies in the U.S., however, 84% have at least one African-American director.[40] The globalization of business is having an impact on board membership. According to the Spencer Stuart executive recruiting firm, 33% of U.S. boards had an international director.[41] Europe was the most "globalized" region of the world, with most companies reporting one or more non-national directors.[42] Although Asian and Latin American boards are still predominantly staffed by nationals, they are working to add more international directors.[43]

A 2011 study of the top 100 public firms in the U.S. found that 3.7% of the companies paid their directors more than US$150K as a cash retainer (not counting money paid for meeting attendance or other obligations). The same study found that the median cash retainer was between US$75K and US$100K (26.7%).[44] Directors serving on the boards of small companies usually received much less compensation (around US$10,000). One study found directors of a sample of large U.S. firms to hold, on average, 3% of their corporations' outstanding stock.[45]

The vast majority of inside directors are the chief executive officer and either the chief operating officer (if not also the CEO) or the chief financial officer. Presidents or vice presidents of key operating divisions or functional units sometimes serve on the board. Few, if any, inside directors receive any extra compensation for assuming this extra duty. Very rarely does a U.S. board include any lower-level operating employees.

Codetermination: Should Employees Serve on Boards?

Codetermination, the inclusion of a corporation's workers on its board, began only recently in the United States. Corporations such as Chrysler, Northwest Airlines, United Airlines (UAL), and Wheeling-Pittsburgh Steel added representatives from employee associations to their boards as part of union agreements or Employee Stock Ownership Plans (ESOPs). For example, United Airlines workers traded 15% in pay cuts for 55% of the company (through an ESOP) and 3 of the firm's 12 board seats. In this instance, workers represent themselves on the board not so much as employees but primarily as owners. At Chrysler, however, the United Auto Workers union obtained a temporary seat on the board as part of a union contract agreement in exchange for changes in work rules and reductions in benefits. This was at a time when Chrysler was facing bankruptcy in the late 1970s. In situations like this when a director represents an internal stakeholder, critics raise the issue of conflict of interest. Can a member of the board, who is privy to confidential managerial information, function, for example, as a union leader whose primary duty is to fight for the best benefits for his or her members? Although the movement to place employees on the boards of directors of U.S. companies shows little likelihood of increasing (except through employee stock ownership), the European experience reveals an increasing acceptance of worker participation (without ownership) on corporate boards.

Germany pioneered codetermination during the 1950s with a two-tiered system: (1) a supervisory board elected by shareholders and employees to approve or decide corporate strategy and policy and (2) a management board (composed primarily of top management) appointed by the supervisory board to manage the company's activities. Most other Western European countries have either passed similar codetermination legislation (as in Sweden, Denmark, Norway, and Austria) or use worker councils to work closely with management (as in Belgium, Luxembourg, France, Italy, Ireland, and the Netherlands).

Interlocking Directorates

CEOs often nominate chief executives (as well as board members) from other firms to membership on their own boards in order to create an interlocking directorate. A *direct* **interlocking directorate** occurs when two firms share a director or when an executive of one firm sits on the board of a second firm. An *indirect* interlock occurs when two corporations have directors who also serve on the board of a third firm, such as a bank.

Although the Clayton Act and the Banking Act of 1933 prohibit interlocking directorates by U.S. companies competing in the same industry, interlocking continues to occur in almost all corporations, especially large ones. Interlocking occurs because large firms have a large impact on other corporations and these other corporations, in turn, have some control over the firm's inputs and marketplace. For example, most large corporations in the United States, Japan, and Germany are interlocked either directly or indirectly with financial institutions.[46]

Eleven of the 15 largest U.S. corporations have at least two board members who sit together on another board. Twenty percent of the 1000 largest U.S. firms share at least one board member.[47]

Interlocking directorates are useful for gaining both inside information about an uncertain environment and objective expertise about potential strategies and tactics.[48] For example, Kleiner Perkins, a high-tech venture capital firm, not only has seats on the boards of the companies in which it invests, but it also has executives (which Kleiner Perkins hired) from one entrepreneurial venture who serve as directors on others. Kleiner Perkins refers to its network of interlocked firms as its *keiretsu*, a Japanese term for a set of companies with interlocking business relationships and share-holdings.[49] Family-owned corporations, however, are less likely to have interlocking directorates than are corporations with highly dispersed stock ownership, probably because family-owned corporations do not like to dilute their corporate control by adding outsiders to boardroom discussions.

There is some concern, however, when the chairs of separate corporations serve on each other's boards. Twenty-two such pairs of corporate chairs (who typically also served as their firm's CEO) existed in 2003. In one instance, the three chairmen of Anheuser-Busch, SBC Communications, and Emerson Electric served on all three of the boards. Typically, a CEO sits on only one board in addition to his or her own—down from two additional boards in previous years. Although such interlocks may provide valuable information, they are increasingly frowned upon because of the possibility of collusion.[50] Nevertheless, evidence indicates that well-interlocked corporations are better able to survive in a highly competitive environment.[51]

NOMINATION AND ELECTION OF BOARD MEMBERS

Traditionally, the CEO of a corporation decided whom to invite to board membership and merely asked the shareholders for approval in the annual proxy statement. All nominees were usually elected. There are some dangers, however, in allowing the CEO free rein in nominating directors. The CEO might select only board members who, in the CEO's opinion, will not disturb the company's policies and functioning. Given that the average length of service of a U.S. board member is three 3-year terms (but can range up to 20 years for some boards), CEO-friendly, passive boards are likely to result. This is especially likely given that only 7% of surveyed directors indicated that their company had term limits for board members. Nevertheless, 60% of U.S. boards and 58% of European boards have a mandatory retirement age—typically around 70.[52] Research reveals that boards rated as least effective by the Corporate Library, a corporate governance research firm, tend to have members serving longer (an average of 9.7 years) than boards rated as most effective (7.5 years).[53] Directors selected by the CEO often feel that they should go along with any proposal the CEO makes. Thus board members find themselves accountable to the very management they are charged to oversee. Because this is likely to happen, more boards are using a nominating committee to nominate new outside board members for the shareholders to elect. Ninety-seven percent of large U.S. corporations now use nominating committees to identify potential directors. This practice is less common in Europe where 60% of boards use nominating committees.[54]

Many corporations whose directors serve terms of more than one year divide the board into classes and stagger elections so that only a portion of the board stands for election each year. This is called a *staggered board*. Sixty-three percent of U.S. boards currently have staggered boards.[55] Arguments in favor of this practice are that it provides continuity by reducing the chance of an abrupt turnover in its membership and that it reduces the likelihood of electing people unfriendly to management (who might be interested in a hostile takeover) through cumulative voting. An argument against staggered boards is that they make it more difficult for concerned shareholders to curb a CEO's power—especially when that CEO is also Chairman of the board. An increasing number of shareholder resolutions to replace staggered boards with annual elections of all board members are currently being passed at annual meetings.

When nominating people for election to a board of directors, it is important that nominees have previous experience dealing with corporate issues. For example, research reveals that a firm makes better acquisition decisions when the firm's outside directors have had experience with such decisions.[56]

A survey of directors of U.S. corporations revealed the following criteria in a good director:

- Willing to challenge management when necessary—95%
- Special expertise important to the company—67%
- Available outside meetings to advise management—57%
- Expertise on global business issues—41%
- Understands the firm's key technologies and processes—39%
- Brings external contacts that are potentially valuable to the firm—33%
- Has detailed knowledge of the firm's industry—31%
- Has high visibility in his or her field—31%
- Is accomplished at representing the firm to stakeholders—18%[57]

ORGANIZATION OF THE BOARD

The size of a board in the United States is determined by the corporation's charter and its bylaws, in compliance with state laws. Although some states require a minimum number of board members, most corporations have quite a bit of discretion in determining board size. The average large, publicly held U.S. firm has 10 directors on its board. The average small, privately held company has 4 to 5 members. The average size of boards elsewhere is Japan, 14; Non-Japan Asia, 9; Germany, 16; UK, 10; and France, 11.[58]

Approximately 68% of the 100 largest U.S. company's top executives hold the dual designation of Chairman and CEO.[59] The combined Chair/CEO position is being increasingly criticized because of the potential for conflict of interest. The CEO is supposed to concentrate on strategy, planning, external relations, and responsibility to the board. The Chairman's responsibility is to ensure that the board and its committees perform their functions as stated in the board's charter. Further, the Chairman schedules board meetings and presides over the annual shareholders' meeting. Critics of having one person in the two offices ask how the board can properly oversee top management if the Chairman is also a part of top management. For this reason, the Chairman and CEO roles are separated by law in Germany, the Netherlands, South Africa, and Finland. A similar law has been considered in the United Kingdom and Australia. Although research is mixed regarding the impact of the combined Chair/CEO position on overall corporate financial performance, firm stock price and credit ratings both respond negatively to announcements of CEOs also assuming the Chairman position.[60] Research also shows that corporations with a combined Chair/CEO have a greater likelihood of fraudulent financial reporting when CEO stock options are not present.[61]

Many of those who prefer that the Chairman and CEO positions be combined agree that the outside directors should elect a **lead director**. This person is consulted by the Chair/CEO regarding board affairs and coordinates the annual evaluation of the CEO.[62] The lead director position is very popular in the United Kingdom, where it originated. Of those U.S. companies combining the Chairman and CEO positions, 96% had a lead director.[63] Korn/Ferry found that in 2003 72% of respondents thought a lead director was the right thing to do, while 85%

thought so in 2007. A lead director creates a balance in power when the CEO is also the Chair of the Board. The same survey showed that board members are spending 16 hours a month on board business and that 86% were either very satisfied or extremely satisfied with their role in the business. The lead director becomes increasingly important because 94% of U.S. boards in 2007 (compared to only 41% in 2002) held regular executive sessions without the CEO being present.[64] Nevertheless, there are many ways in which an unscrupulous Chair/CEO can guarantee a director's loyalty. Research indicates that an increase in board independence often results in higher levels of CEO ingratiation behavior aimed at persuading directors to support CEO proposals. Long-tenured directors who support the CEO may use social pressure to persuade a new board member to conform to the group. Directors are more likely to be recommended for membership on other boards if they "don't rock the boat" and engage in low levels of monitoring and control behavior.[65] Even in those situations when the board has a nominating committee composed only of outsiders, the committee often obtains the CEO's approval for each new board candidate.[66]

The most effective boards accomplish much of their work through committees. Although they do not usually have legal duties, most committees are granted full power to act with the authority of the board between board meetings. Typical standing committees (in order of prevalence) are the audit (100%), compensation (99%), nominating (97%), corporate governance (94%), stock options (84%), director compensation (52%), and executive (43%) committees.[67] The executive committee is usually composed of two inside and two outside directors located nearby who can meet between board meetings to attend to matters that must be settled quickly. This committee acts as an extension of the board and, consequently, may have almost unrestricted authority in certain areas.[68] Except for the executive, finance, and investment committees, board committees are now typically staffed only by outside directors. Although each board committee typically meets four to five times annually, the average audit committee met nine times during 2007.[69]

IMPACT OF THE SARBANES–OXLEY ACT ON U.S. CORPORATE GOVERNANCE

In response to the many corporate scandals uncovered since 2000, the U.S. Congress passed the **Sarbanes–Oxley Act** in June 2002. This act was designed to protect shareholders from the excesses and failed oversight that characterized criminal activities at Enron, Tyco, WorldCom, Adelphia Communications, Qwest, and Global Crossing, among other prominent firms. Several key elements of Sarbanes–Oxley were designed to formalize greater board independence and oversight. For example, the act requires that all directors serving on the audit committee be independent of the firm and receive no fees other than for services of the director. In addition, boards may no longer grant loans to corporate officers. The act has also established formal procedures for individuals (known as "whistleblowers") to report incidents of questionable accounting or auditing. Firms are prohibited from retaliating against anyone reporting wrongdoing. Both the CEO and CFO must certify the corporation's financial information. The act bans auditors from providing both external and internal audit services to the same company. It also requires that a firm identify whether it has a "financial expert" serving on the audit committee who is independent from management.

Although the cost to a large corporation of implementing the provisions of the law was US$8.5 million in 2004, the first year of compliance, the costs to a large firm fell to US$1–$5 million annually during the following years as accounting and information processes were refined and made more efficient.[70] Pitney Bowes, for example, saved more than US$500,000 in 2005 simply by consolidating four accounts receivable offices into one. Similar savings were realized at Cisco and Genentech.[71] An additional benefit of the increased disclosure requirements is more reliable corporate financial statements. Companies are now reporting numbers with fewer adjustments for unusual charges and write-offs, which in the past have been used to boost reported earnings.[72] The new rules have also made it more difficult for firms to post-date executive stock options. "This is an unintended consequence of disclosure," remarked Gregory Taxin, CEO of Glass, Lewis & Company, a stock research firm.[73] See the **Global Issue** feature to learn how board activism affects the managing of a global company.

Improving Governance

In implementing the Sarbanes–Oxley Act, the U.S. Securities and Exchange Commission (SEC) required in 2003 that a company disclose whether it has adopted a code of ethics that applies to the CEO and to the company's principal financial officer. Among other things, the SEC requires that the audit, nominating, and compensation committees be staffed entirely by outside directors. The New York Stock Exchange reinforced the mandates of Sarbanes–Oxley by requiring that companies have a nominating/governance committee composed entirely of independent outside directors. Similarly, NASDAQ rules require that nominations for new directors be made by either a nominating committee of independent outsiders or by a majority of independent outside directors.[74]

Partially in response to Sarbanes–Oxley, a survey of directors of Fortune 1000 U.S. companies by Mercer Delta Consulting and the University of Southern California revealed that 60% of directors were spending more time on board matters than before Sarbanes–Oxley, with 85% spending more time on their company's accounts, 83% more on governance practices, and 52% on monitoring financial performance.[75] Newly elected outside directors with financial management experience increased to 10% of all outside directors in 2003 from only 1% of outsiders in 1998.[76] Seventy-eight percent of Fortune 1000 U.S. boards in 2006 required that directors own stock in the corporation, compared to just 36% in Europe, and 26% in Asia.[77]

Evaluating Governance

To help investors evaluate a firm's corporate governance, a number of independent rating services, such as Standard & Poor's (S&P), Moody's, Morningstar, The Corporate Library, Institutional Shareholder Services (ISS), and Governance Metrics International (GMI), have established criteria for good governance. *Bloomberg Businessweek* annually publishes a list of the best and worst boards of U.S. corporations. Whereas rating service firms like S&P, Moody's, and The Corporate Library use a wide mix of research data and criteria to evaluate companies, ISS and GMI have been criticized because they primarily use public records to score firms, using simple checklists.[78] In contrast, the S&P Corporate Governance Scoring System researches four major issues:

- Ownership Structure and Influence
- Financial Stakeholder Rights and Relations
- Financial Transparency and Information Disclosure
- Board Structure and Processes

Although the S&P scoring system is proprietary and confidential, independent research using generally accepted measures of S&P's four issues revealed that moving from the poorest to the best-governed categories nearly doubled a firm's likelihood of receiving an investment-grade credit rating.[79]

Avoiding Governance Improvements

A number of corporations are concerned that various requirements to improve corporate governance will constrain top management's ability to effectively manage the company. For

GLOBAL issue

GLOBAL BUSINESS BOARD ACTIVISM AT YAHOO!

In the digital age in general and with Internet-based companies in particular, the impact of board activism now cuts across geographic boundaries like nothing has in the past. Yahoo grew to become the largest Internet search engine company in the world used by individuals in their own language.

Yahoo! was founded in a Stanford University campus trailer in early 1994 by Ph.D. candidates David Filo and Jerry Yang as a means for people to keep track of their favorite interests on the Internet. Yahoo! is an acronym for "Yet Another Hierarchical Officious Oracle." Young companies often see dramatic moves by the board of directors who are unaccustomed to the growth phases in a business. An activist board will hold management responsible for their actions and may take on the role of a catalyst board in some circumstances.

Yahoo! grew quickly before the Internet bubble nearly bankrupted the company. Terry Semel, a legendary Hollywood dealmaker who didn't even use e-mail, was hired to turn the company into a media giant. In the summer of 2002, Semel tried to buy Google for roughly US$3 billion (this was two years before Google went public). At the time, Google's revenue stood at a paltry US$240 million, while Yahoo!'s was in excess of US$800 million. Despite failures to purchase Google, Facebook, and YouTube, Yahoo! became an Internet search giant serving more than 345 million individuals a month. By 2005, Yahoo! was the number one global Internet brand. Forbes listed Semel's total compensation as US$230.6 million. His reign saw both the rise and fall of the company. The board grew increasingly dissatisfied. By 2007, the company was losing market share and repeated acquisitions had failed to produce any real bump in the stock price. The board moved to act in June 2007. Semel assumed the role of non-executive chairman and Jerry Yang became the CEO once again.

Things did not improve. There were regular calls for Yang's resignation as the company continued to flounder. At a time when tech companies were growing dramatically, Yahoo! continued its long, slow slide. Frustrated by his inability to strike deals with rivals Microsoft and Google, Yang and the board agreed that it was best for him to resign as CEO. His tenure lasted a scant 18 months.

Carol Bartz was hired in January 2009 to turn the company around and help it regain its stature. She was the former CEO of Autodesk and was viewed as a no-nonsense industry veteran. She instituted layoffs, reshuffled management, and turned over search operations to Microsoft in a deal that brought US$900 million to Yahoo!. However, shares remained effectively flat during her tenure and market share continued to drop. The board became increasingly dissatisfied with her performance and acted suddenly in September 2011. Without a replacement in hand, she was notified via a phone call from the Chairman of the Board that she was fired.

After a lengthy search, Scott Thompson was hired as the CEO in January 2012. He had previously been the CEO of eBay's PayPal unit and had done what most experts believed was a very good job. Unfortunately, he listed a computer science degree from Stonehill College that he had not earned. He did graduate, but with an accounting degree. Activist shareholder group Third Point (who has a chair on the board and owns 5.8% of the company) released details about his resumé padding. The information was part of a proxy fight that led to a board shakeup in February of 2012. That shakeup saw most of the previous board members removed and a new group of members (approved of by Third Point) elected.

Thompson resigned and Ross Levinsohm, the former head of global media for the company, was named the interim CEO while the company did yet another search. That search ended in July 2012 when the company named Marissa Mayer as the new CEO. Mayer was a longtime Google executive who ran their search group.

The continuous changes at Yahoo! have served to damage the company's ability to perform. It is difficult to gain any momentum in an industry when the top management changes so often and with such dramatic flair. The board of directors has a responsibility to the shareholders. The question is: At what point have they failed to do their job?

. . . .

SOURCES: B. Stone. "Marissa Mayer Is Yahoo's New CEO," *Bloomberg Businessweek* (July 16, 2012), (www.businessweek.com/articles/2012-07-16/marissa-mayer-is the-new-yahoo-ceo); Yahoo! Website - http://pressroom.yahoo.net/pr/ycorp/overview.aspx; Damouni, N. "Yahoo CEO Search down to Leninsohn, Hulu CEO's Jason Kilar," Accessed 5/30/13, www.huffingtonpost.com/2012/07/05/yahoo-ceo-search-down-to-levinsohn-kilar_n_1652674.html; Temin, D. "Little Lies; Big Lies - Yahoo! CEO Scott Thompson's Revisionist History", Accessed 5/30/13; www.forbes.com/sites/daviatemin/2012/05/07/little-lies-big-lies-yahoo-ceo-scott-thomponson-revisionist-history.html; Pepitone, J. "Yahoo confirms CEO is out after resume scandal," Accessed 5/30/13. www.money.cnn.com/2012/05/13/technology/yahoo-ceo-out/index.html; Kopytoff, V. and Miller, C. "Yahoo Board Fires Chief Executive," Accessed 5/30/13 www.nytimes.com/2011/09/07/technology/carol-bartz-yahoos-chief-executive-is-fired.html; Carmody, T. "Co-Founder, Ex-CEO Jerry Yang Resigns From Yahoo's Board," Accessed 5/30/13, www.wired.com/business/2012/01/jerry-yang-resigns-yahoo/; Compensation - Terry S Semel, Accessed 5/30/13, www.forbes.com/static/pvp2005/LIRXC25.html; Vogelstein, F. "How Yahoo! Blew It," Accessed 5/30/13, www.wired.com/wired/archive/15.02/yahoo.html.

example, more U.S. public corporations have gone private in the years since the passage of Sarbanes–Oxley than before its passage. Other companies use multiple classes of stock to keep outsiders from having sufficient voting power to change the company. Insiders, usually the company's founders, get stock with extra votes, while others get second-class stock with fewer votes. For example, in 2012 Mark Zuckerberg, the CEO of Facebook, owned approximately 28% of the outstanding shares, but because of a two-class stock system, he controlled 57% of the voting shares.[80] A comprehensive analysis of firms completed in 2006 reported that approximately 6% of the companies had multiple classes of stock.[81]

Another approach to sidestepping new governance requirements is being used by corporations such as Google, Infrasource Services, Orbitz, and W&T Offshore. If a corporation in which an individual group or another company controls more than 50% of the voting shares decides to become a "controlled company," the firm is then exempt from requirements by the New York Stock Exchange and NASDAQ that a majority of the board and all members of key board committees be independent outsiders. It is easy to see that the minority shareholders have virtually no power in these situations.

TRENDS IN CORPORATE GOVERNANCE

The role of the board of directors in the strategic management of a corporation is likely to be more active in the future. Although neither the composition of boards nor the board leadership structure has been consistently linked to firm financial performance, better governance does lead to higher credit ratings and stock prices. A McKinsey survey reveals that investors are willing to pay 16% more for a corporation's stock if it is known to have good corporate governance. The investors explained that they would pay more because, in their opinion (1) good governance leads to better performance over time, (2) good governance reduces the risk of the company getting into trouble, and (3) governance is a major strategic issue.[82]

Some of today's trends in governance (particularly prevalent in the United States and the United Kingdom) that are likely to continue include the following:

- Boards are getting more involved not only in reviewing and evaluating company strategy but also in shaping it.

- Institutional investors, such as pension funds, mutual funds, and insurance companies, are becoming active on boards and are putting increasing pressure on top management to improve corporate performance. This trend is supported by a U.S. SEC requirement that a mutual fund must publicly disclose the proxy votes cast at company board meetings in its portfolio. This reduces the tendency for mutual funds to rubber-stamp management proposals.[83]

- Shareholders are demanding that directors and top managers own more than token amounts of stock in the corporation. Research indicates that boards with equity ownership use quantifiable, verifiable criteria (instead of vague, qualitative criteria) to evaluate the CEO.[84] When compensation committee members are significant shareholders, they tend to offer the CEO less salary but with a higher incentive component than do compensation committee members who own little to no stock.[85]

- Non-affiliated outside (non-management) directors are increasing their numbers and power in publicly held corporations as CEOs loosen their grip on boards. Outside members are taking charge of annual CEO evaluations.

- Women and minorities are being increasingly represented on boards.

- Boards are establishing mandatory retirement ages for board members—typically around age 70.

- Boards are evaluating not only their own overall performance, but also that of individual directors.

- Boards are getting smaller—partially because of the reduction in the number of insiders but also because boards desire new directors to have specialized knowledge and expertise instead of general experience.

- Boards continue to take more control of board functions by either splitting the combined Chair/CEO into two separate positions or establishing a lead outside director position.

- Boards are eliminating 1970s anti-takeover defenses that served to entrench current management. In just one year, for example, 66 boards repealed their staggered boards and 25 eliminated poison pills.[86]

- As corporations become more global, they are increasingly looking for board members with international experience.

- Instead of merely being able to vote for or against directors nominated by the board's nominating committee, shareholders may eventually be allowed to nominate board members. This was originally proposed by the U.S. Securities and Exchange Commission in 2004, but was not implemented. Supported by the AFL-CIO, a more open nominating process would enable shareholders to vote out directors who ignore shareholder interests.[87]

- Society, in the form of special interest groups, increasingly expects boards of directors to balance the economic goal of profitability with the social needs of society. Issues dealing with workforce diversity and environmental sustainability are now reaching the board level.

The Role of Top Management

The top management function is usually conducted by the CEO of the corporation in coordination with the COO (Chief Operating Officer) or president, executive vice president, and vice presidents of divisions and functional areas.[88] Even though strategic management involves everyone in the organization, the board of directors holds top management primarily responsible for the strategy and implementation of that strategy at the firm.[89]

RESPONSIBILITIES OF TOP MANAGEMENT

Top management responsibilities, especially those of the CEO, involve getting things accomplished through and with others in order to meet the corporate objectives. Top management's job is thus multidimensional and is oriented toward the welfare of the total organization. Specific top management tasks vary from firm to firm and are developed from an analysis of the mission, objectives, strategies, and key activities of the corporation. Tasks are typically divided among the members of the top management team. A diversity of skills can thus be very important. Research indicates that top management teams with a diversity of functional backgrounds, experiences, and length of time with the company tend to be significantly related to improvements in corporate market share and profitability.[90] In addition, highly diverse teams with some international experience tend to emphasize international growth strategies and strategic innovation, especially in uncertain environments, as a means to boost financial performance.[91] The CEO, with the support of the rest of the top management team, has two primary responsibilities when it comes to strategic management. The first is to provide

SUSTAINABILITY issue

CEO PAY AND CORPORATE PERFORMANCE

What leads a CEO to perform in the best interests of the shareholders? This has been a question for some time (see Strategy Highlight). Egregious pay for CEOs who don't perform has been a contention for many years. Leo Apotheker was paid over US$30 million dollars during his 11-month tenure at HP despite making strategic choices that cost the company hundreds of millions in sales and a share price that dropped almost in half. Financial research firm Obermatt did a study on CEO pay and company performance between 2008 and 2010. They calculated a "deserved pay" based upon earnings growth and shareholder return. They found that there is no correlation in the S&P 100 between CEO pay and company performance.

The 2011 median pay for the nation's 200 top-paid CEOs was US$14.5 million, according to a study conducted for *The New York Times*.

In 2010, the Dodd–Frank financial reform law was enacted, which requires companies to submit executive compensation packages for a nonbinding shareholder vote at least once every six years. The changes in the boardroom to the means and methods of executive compensation have been affected because of the potential for public embarrassment. While less than 2% of "say-on-pay" proposals were rejected in 2012, those rejections have led to more alignment in compensation packages throughout public corporations. In 2011, shareholders rejected CEO Vikram Pandit's (Citigroup) US$14.8 million pay package after the stock dropped over 40%, and in 2012 shareholders rejected Chiquita Brands CEO pay package by a 4-to-1 margin.

BusinessWeek reported that companies who suffered shareholder rejections of executive pay packages, as well as those that received yes votes, changed their compensation systems to align them with the interest of shareholders. By 2012, a *Wall Street Journal* analysis of the top 300 U.S. companies found that pay now generally tracked performance. Balancing the interests of the owners of a corporation with those who run the corporation is one of the most important issues in sustainable business practices.

....

SOURCES: *"Executive Pay and Performance,"* Accessed 5/30/13, www.economist.com/blogs/graphicdetail/2012/02/focus-O; Brady, D. "Say on Pay: Boards Listen When Shareholders Speak," Accessed 5/30/13, www.businessweek.com/articles/2012-06-07/say-on-pay-boards-listen-when-shareholders-speak.html; Popper, N. "C.E.O. Pay Is Rising Despite the Din," Accessed 5/30/13, www.nytimes.com/2012/06/17/business/executive-pay-still-climbing-despite-a-shareholder-din.html.

executive leadership and a vision for the firm. The second is to manage a strategic planning process. (See the **Sustainability Issue** feature for an example of how CEO pay is affecting the economic viability of corporations.)

Executive Leadership and Strategic Vision

Executive leadership is the directing of activities toward the accomplishment of corporate objectives. Executive leadership is important because it sets the tone for the entire corporation. A **strategic vision** is a description of what the company is capable of becoming. It is often communicated in the company's vision statement (as described in Chapter 1). People in an organization want to have a sense of direction, but only top management is in the position to specify and communicate their unique strategic vision to the general workforce. Top management's enthusiasm (or lack of it) about the corporation tends to be contagious. The importance of executive leadership is wonderfully illustrated by the quote in the United States Infantry Journal from 1948: "No man is a leader until his appointment is ratified in the minds and hearts of his men."[92]

Successful CEOs are noted for having a clear strategic vision, a strong passion for their company, and an ability to communicate with others. They are often perceived to be dynamic and charismatic leaders—which is especially important for high firm performance and investor confidence in uncertain environments.[93] They have many of the characteristics of **transformational leaders**—that is, leaders who provide change and movement in an organization by providing a vision for that change.[94] For instance, the positive attitude characterizing many well-known current and former leaders—such as Bill Gates at Microsoft, Anita Roddick at the Body Shop, Richard Branson at Virgin, Steve Jobs at Apple Computer, Meg Whitman at eBay and now HP, Howard Schultz at Starbucks, and Herb Kelleher at Southwest Airlines—energized their respective corporations at important times. These transformational leaders have been able to command respect and execute effective strategy formulation and implementation because they have exhibited three key characteristics:[95]

1. **The CEO articulates a strategic vision for the corporation:** The CEO envisions the company not as it currently is but as it can become. The new perspective that the CEO's vision brings gives renewed meaning to everyone's work and enables employees to see beyond the details of their own jobs to the functioning of the total corporation.[96] Louis Gerstner proposed a new vision for IBM when he proposed that the company change its business model from computer hardware to services: "If customers were going to look to an integrator to help them envision, design, and build end-to-end solutions, then the companies playing that role would exert tremendous influence over the full range of technology decisions—from architecture and applications to hardware and software choices."[97] In a survey of 1,500 senior executives from 20 different countries, when asked the most important behavioral trait a CEO must have, 98% responded that the CEO must convey "a strong sense of vision."[98]

2. **The CEO presents a role for others to identify with and to follow:** The leader empathizes with followers and sets an example in terms of behavior, dress, and actions. The CEO's attitudes and values concerning the corporation's purpose and activities are clear-cut and constantly communicated in words and deeds. For example, when design engineers at General Motors had problems with monitor resolution using the Windows operating system, Steve Ballmer, CEO of Microsoft, personally crawled under conference room tables to plug in PC monitors and diagnose the problem.[99] People need to know what to expect and have trust in their CEO. Research indicates that businesses in which the general manager has the trust of the employees have higher sales and profits with lower turnover than do businesses in which there is a lesser amount of trust.[100]

3. **The CEO communicates high performance standards and also shows confidence in the followers' abilities to meet these standards:** The leader empowers followers by raising their beliefs in their own capabilities. No leader ever improved performance by setting easily attainable goals that provided no challenge. Communicating high expectations to others can often lead to high performance.[101] The CEO must be willing to follow through by coaching people. As a result, employees view their work as very important and thus motivating.[102] Ivan Seidenberg, chief executive of Verizon Communications, was closely involved in deciding Verizon's strategic direction, and he showed his faith in his people by letting his key managers handle important projects and represent the company in public forums. "All of these people could be CEOs in their own right. They are warriors and they are on a mission," explained Seidenberg. Grateful for his faith in them, his managers were fiercely loyal both to him and the company.[103]

The negative side of confident executive leaders is that their very confidence may lead to *hubris*, in which their confidence blinds them to information that is contrary to a decided course of action. For example, overconfident CEOs tend to charge ahead with mergers and acquisitions even though they are aware that most acquisitions destroy shareholder value. Research by Tate and Malmendier found that "overconfident CEOs are more likely to conduct mergers than rational CEOs at any point in time. Overconfident CEOs view their company as undervalued by outside investors who are less optimistic about the prospects of the firm." Overconfident CEOs were most likely to make acquisitions when they could avoid selling new stock to finance them, and they were more likely to do deals that diversified their firm's lines of businesses.[104] Carly Fiorina used the power of her office and her considerable influence with a relatively weak board of directors to push through the Compaq Computer acquisition.

Managing the Strategic Planning Process

As business corporations adopt more of the characteristics of the learning organization, strategic planning initiatives can come from any part of an organization. A survey of 156 large corporations throughout the world revealed that, in two-thirds of the firms, strategies were first proposed in the business units and sent to headquarters for approval.[105] However, unless top management encourages and supports the planning process, it is unlikely to result in a strategy. In most corporations, top management must initiate and manage the strategic planning process. It may do so by first asking business units and functional areas to propose strategic plans for themselves, or it may begin by drafting an overall corporate plan within which the units can then build their own plans. Research suggests that bottom-up strategic planning may be most appropriate in multidivisional corporations operating in relatively stable environments but that top-down strategic planning may be most appropriate for firms operating in turbulent environments.[106] Other organizations engage in concurrent strategic planning in which all the organization's units draft plans for themselves after they have been provided with the organization's overall mission and objectives.

Regardless of the approach taken, the typical board of directors expects top management to manage the overall strategic planning process so that the plans of all the units and functional areas fit together into an overall corporate plan. Top management's job therefore includes the tasks of evaluating unit plans and providing feedback. To do this, it may require each unit to justify its proposed objectives, strategies, and programs in terms of how well they satisfy the organization's overall objectives in light of available resources. If a company is not organized into business units, top managers may work together as a team to do strategic planning. CEO Jeff Bezos tells how this is done at Amazon.com:

> We have a group called the S Team—S meaning "senior" [management]—that stays abreast of what the company is working on and delves into strategy issues. It meets for about four hours every Tuesday. Once or twice a year the S Team also gets together in a two-day meeting where different ideas are explored. Homework is assigned ahead of time. . . . Eventually we have to choose just a couple of things, if they're big, and make bets.[107]

In contrast to the seemingly continuous strategic planning being done at Amazon.com, most large corporations conduct the strategic planning process just once a year—often at offsite strategy workshops attended by senior executives.[108]

Many large organizations have a *strategic planning staff* charged with supporting both top management and the business units in the strategic planning process. This staff may prepare the background materials used in senior management's offsite strategy workshop. This planning staff typically consists of fewer than 10 people, headed by a senior executive with the title of Director of Corporate Development or Chief Strategy Officer. The staff's major responsibilities are to:

1. Identify and analyze companywide strategic issues, and suggest corporate strategic alternatives to top management.
2. Work as facilitators with business units to guide them through the strategic planning process.[109]

End of Chapter SUMMARY

Who determines a corporation's performance? According to the popular press, it is the Chief Executive Officer who seems to be personally responsible for a company's success or failure. When a company is in trouble, one of the first alternatives usually presented is to fire the CEO. That was certainly the case at the Walt Disney Company under Michael Eisner, as well as Hewlett-Packard under Carly Fiorina. Both CEOs were first viewed as transformational leaders who made needed strategic changes to their companies. Later both were perceived to be the primary reason for their company's poor performance and were fired by their boards. The truth is rarely this simple.

According to research by Margarethe Wiersema, firing the CEO rarely solves a corporation's problems. In a study of CEO turnover caused by dismissals and retirements in the 500 largest public U.S. companies, 71% of the departures were involuntary. In those firms in which the CEO was fired or asked to resign and replaced by another, Wiersema found *no* significant improvement in the company's operating earnings or stock price. She couldn't find a single measure suggesting that CEO dismissal had a positive effect on corporate performance! Wiersema placed the blame for the poor results squarely on the shoulders of the boards of directors. Boards typically lack an in-depth understanding of the business and consequently rely too heavily on executive search firms that know even less about the business. According to Wiersema, boards that successfully managed the executive succession process had three things in common:

- The board set the criteria for candidate selection based on the strategic needs of the company.
- The board set realistic performance expectations rather than demanding a quick fix to please the investment community.
- The board developed a deep understanding of the business and provided strong strategic oversight of top management, including thoughtful annual reviews of CEO performance.[110]

As noted at the beginning of this chapter, corporate governance involves not just the CEO or the board of directors. It involves the combined active participation of the board, top management, and shareholders. One positive result of the many corporate scandals occurring over the past decade is the increased interest in governance. Institutional investors are no longer content to be passive shareholders. Thanks to new regulations, boards of directors are taking their responsibilities more seriously and including more independent outsiders on key oversight committees. Top managers are beginning to understand the value of working with boards as partners, not just as adversaries or as people to be manipulated. Although there will always be passive shareholders, rubber-stamp boards, and dominating CEOs, the simple truth is that good corporate governance means better strategic management.

MyManagementLab®

Go to **mymanagementlab.com** to complete the problems marked with this icon 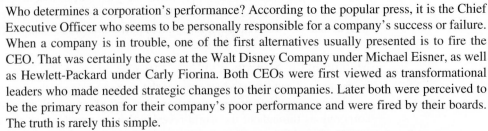.

KEY TERMS

affiliated director (p. 82)

agency theory (p. 81)

board of directors' continuum (p. 79)

board of director responsibilities (p. 78)

codetermination (p. 85)

corporate governance (p. 77)

due care (p. 78)

executive leadership (p. 93)

inside director (p. 80)

interlocking directorate (p. 85)   retired director (p. 82)   strategic vision (p. 93)
lead director (p. 87)   Sarbanes–Oxley Act (p. 88)   top management responsibilities (p. 92)
outside director (p. 80)   stewardship theory (p. 82)   transformational leader (p. 93)

MyManagementLab®

Go to **mymanagementlab.com** for the following Assisted-graded writing questions:

2-1. What are the roles and responsibilities of an effective and active Board of Directors?

2-2. What are the issues that suggest the need for oversight of a particular company's management team?

DISCUSSION QUESTIONS

2-3. Explain the role of executive leadership in building the strategic vision in corporations.

✪ **2-4.** Who should and should not serve on a board of directors? What about environmentalists or union leaders?

✪ **2-5.** Should a CEO be allowed to serve on another company's board of directors? Why or why not?

2-6. What is the role of codetermination? In your opinion, is the incorporation of lower-level employees on the board appropriate?

✪ **2-7.** Should all CEOs be transformational leaders? Would you like to work for a transformational leader?

STRATEGIC PRACTICE EXERCISE

Innovation Issue: Blackberry's Lost Empire

RIM, renamed Blackberry, was once the market leader in smartphones. By 2014, it was on the verge of collapse. They had reported a staggering U.S. $965 million loss. This was largely due to its Z10 smartphone being a massive failure. The company was now poised to trim 4,500 jobs, equating to around 40 percent of its workforce.

To the beleaguered shareholders of Blackberry this was just another failure to build on the failures of the past. Since 2008, they had seen over U.S. $75 billion wiped off the value of the company. This was a business that had been at the forefront of smartphone technology, design, and innovation, now reduced to a company desperately fighting a losing battle against Apple and its other competitors.

Time after time, Blackberry had the chance to continue to dominate the smartphone market. Time after time, the board of directors had either terminated innovative projects or had disagreed with one another to such an extent that nothing happened. Back in 2007, just after the launch of the first iPhone,

Blackberry had been approached to create a touch screen smartphone. Their research and development had failed them. Verizon turned to Google and the Android was born.

In 2012, the board had clashed over Jim Balsillie's (then co-CEO) plans to focus on instant messaging software. The scheme was violently opposed by Blackberry's founder, Mike Lazaridis. The plan was terminated by the new CEO Thorsten Heins. In turn, Heins disagreed with Lazaridis about the continued focus on the keyboard rather than the smart screen. Heins opted for touch screen technology for the Z10.

Blackberry had earned its reputation and fortune by creating a smartphone for corporate clients. What the board failed to notice was that the real growth and innovation was in the consumer market. It was here that Apple was scoring with each successive development of the iPhone. It was also the consumer that was buying Android devices in steadily increasing numbers.

A potentially lucrative venture in the Chinese market was also shelved in 2013 because the Blackberry board had taken too long to make decisions. They had also left its Asian partners out of the loop.

SOURCES: Jesse Hicks, "Research, no motion: How the BlackBerry CEOs lost an empire," *The Verge* (February 21, 2012), www.theverge. com/2012/2/21/2789676/rim-blackberry-mike-lazaridis-jim-balsillie-lost-empire; Sean Silcoff, Jacquie Mcnish, and Steve Ladurantaye, "Inside the fall of BlackBerry: How the smartphone inventor failed to adapt," *The Globe and Mail* (September 27, 2013), www.theglobeandmail.com/report-on-business/the-inside-story-of-why-blackberry-is-failing/article14563602/?page=all; Sam Gustin, "The Fatal Mistake That Doomed BlackBerry," *Time* (September 24, 2013), business.time.com/2013/09/24/the-fatal-mistake-that-doomed-blackberry/.

NOTES

1. A. G. Monks and N. Minow, *Corporate Governance* (Cambridge, MA: Blackwell Business, 1995), pp. 8–32.

2. Ibid., p. 1.

3. C. Corsi, G. Dale, J. H. Daum, J. W. Mumm, and W. Schoppen, "5 Things Boards of Directors Should Be Thinking About," *Point of View*: A special issue focusing on today's board and CEO agenda (2010), Spencer Stuart. © 2010 Spencer Stuart. All rights reserved. For information about copying, distributing, and displaying this work, contact permissions@spencerstuart.com.

4. Reported by E. L. Biggs in "CEO Succession Planning: An Emerging Challenge for Boards of Directors," *Academy of Management Executive* (February 2004), pp. 105–107.

5. A. Borrus, "Less Laissez-Faire in Delaware?" *BusinessWeek* (March 22, 2004), pp. 80–82.

6. L. Light, "Why Outside Directors Have Nightmares," *Business-Week* (October 23, 1996), p. 6.

7. "Where's All the Fun Gone?" *The Economist* (March 20, 2004), p. 76.

8. A. Chen, J. Osofsky, and E. Stephenson, "Making the Board More Strategic: A McKinsey Global Survey," *McKinsey Quarterly* (March 2008), pp. 1–10.

9. Nadler proposes a similar five-step continuum for board involvement ranging from the least involved "passive board" to the most involved "operating board," plus a form for measuring board involvement in D. A. Nadler, "Building Better Boards," *Harvard Business Review* (May 2004), pp. 102–111.

10. H. Ashbaugh, D. W. Collins, and R. LaFond, "The Effects of Corporate Governance on Firms' Credit Ratings," unpublished paper (March, 2004); W. Q. Judge Jr., and C. P. Zeithaml, "Institutional and Strategic Choice Perspectives on Board Involvement in the Strategic Choice Process," *Academy of Management Journal* (October 1992), pp. 766–794; J. A. Pearce II, and S. A. Zahra, "Effective Power-Sharing Between the Board of Directors and the CEO," *Handbook of Business Strategy*, 1992/93 Yearbook (Boston: Warren, Gorham, and Lamont, 1992), pp. 1.1–1.16.

11. *Current Board Practices*, American Society of Corporate Secretaries, 2002 as reported by B. Atkins in "Directors Don't Deserve such a Punitive Policy," *Directors & Boards* (Summer 2002), p. 23.

12. A. Chen, J. Osofsky, and E. Stephenson, "Making the Board More Strategic: A McKinsey Global Survey," *McKinsey Quarterly* (March 2008), pp. 1–10.

13. D. A. Nadler, "Building Better Boards," *Harvard Business Review* (May 2004), pp. 102–111; L. Lavelle, "The Best and Worst Boards," *BusinessWeek* (October 7, 2002), pp. 104–114.

14. Nadler, p. 109.

15. M. K. Fiegener, "Determinants of Board Participation in the Strategic Decisions of Small Corporations," *Entrepreneurship Theory and Practice* (September 2005), pp. 627–650.

16. A. L. Ranft and H. M. O'Neill, "Board Composition and High-Flying Founders: Hints of Trouble to Come?" *Academy of Management Executive* (February 2001), pp. 126–138.

17. B. Stone, D. MacMilan, A. Vance, A. Satariano, and D. Bass, "How Zuck Hacked the Valley," *BusinessWeek* (May 21, 2012).

18. D. R. Dalton, M. A. Hitt, S. Trevis Certo, and C. M. Dalton, "The Fundamental Agency Problem and Its Mitigation," Chapter One in *Academy of Management Annals*, edited by J. F. Westfall and A. F. Brief (London: Rutledge, 2007); Y. Deutsch, "The Impact of Board Composition on Firms' Critical Decisions: A Meta-Analytic Review," *Journal of Management* (June 2005), pp. 424–444; D. F. Larcher, S. A. Richardson, and I. Tuna, "Does Corporate Governance Really Matter?" *Knowledge @ Wharton* (September 8–21, 2004); J. Merritt and L. Lavelle, "A Different Kind of Governance Guru," *BusinessWeek* (August 9, 2004), pp. 46–47; A. Dehaene, V. DeVuyst, and H. Ooghe, "Corporate Performance and Board Structure in Belgian Companies," *Long Range Planning* (June 2001), pp. 383–398; M. W. Peng, "Outside Directors and Firm Performance During Institutional Transitions," *Strategic Management Journal* (May 2004), pp. 453–471.

19. D. R. Dalton, M. A. Hitt, S. Trevis Certo, and C. M. Dalton, "The Fundamental Agency Problem and Its Mitigation," Chapter One in *Academy of Management Annals*, edited by J. F. Westfall and A. F. Brief (London: Rutledge, 2007).

20. *33rd Annual Board of Directors Study* (New York: Korn/Ferry International, 2007), p. 11.

21. *30th Annual Board of Directors Study* (New York: Korn/Ferry International, 2003).

22. M. K. Fiegerer, "Determinants of Board Participation in the Strategic Decisions of Small Corporations," *Entrepreneurship Theory and Practice* (September 2005), pp. 627–650; S. K. Lee and G. Filbeck, "Board Size and Firm Performance: Case of Small Firms," *Proceedings of the Academy of Accounting and Financial Studies* (2006), pp. 43–46; W. S. Schulze, M. H. Lubatkin, R. N. Dino, and A. K. Buchholtz, "Agency Relationships in Family Firms: Theory and Evidence," *Organization Science* (March–April, 2001), pp. 99–116.

23. S. K. Lee and G. Filbeck, "Board Size and Firm Performance: The Case of Small Firms," *Proceedings of the Academy of Accounting and Financial Studies* (2006), pp. 43–46.

24. J. J. Reur and R. Ragozzino, "Agency Hazards and Alliance Portfolios," *Strategic Management Journal* (January 2006), pp. 27–43.

25. M. Goranova, T. M. Alessandri, P. Brades, and R. Dharwadkar, "Managerial Ownership and Corporate Diversification: A Longitudinal View," *Strategic Management Journal* (March 2007), pp. 211–225; B. K. Boyd, S. Gove, and M. A. Hitt, "Consequences of Measurement Problems in Strategic Management Research: The Case of Amihud and Lev," *Strategic Management Journal* (April 2005), pp. 367–375; J. P. Katz and B. P. Niehoff, "How Owners Influence Strategy—A Comparison of Owner-Controlled and Manager-Controlled Firms," *Long Range Planning* (October 1998), pp. 755–761; M. Kroll, P. Wright, L. Toombs, and H. Leavell, "Form of Control: A Critical Determinant of Acquisition Performance and CEO Rewards," *Strategic Management Journal* (February 1997), pp. 85–96.

26. L. Tihanyi, R. A. Johnson, R. E. Hoskisson, and M. A. Hitt, "Institutional Ownership Differences and International Diversification: The Effects of Boards of Directors and Technological Opportunity," *Academy of Management Journal* (April 2003), pp. 195–211; A. E. Ellstrand, L. Tihanyi, and J. L. Johnson, "Board Structure and International Political Risk," *Academy of Management Journal* (August 2002), pp. 769–777; S. A. Zahra, D. O. Neubaum, and M. Huse, "Entrepreneurship in Medium-Size Companies: Exploring the Effects of Ownership and Governance Systems," *Journal of Management* (Vol. 26, No. 5, 2000), pp. 947–976.

27. G. Kassinis and N. Vafeas, "Corporate Boards and Outside Stake-holders as Determinants of Environmental Litigation," *Strategic Management Journal* (May 2002), pp. 399–415; P. Dunn, "The Impact of Insider Power on Fraudulent Financial Reporting," *Journal of Management* (Vol. 30, No. 3, 2004), pp. 397–412.

28. R. C. Anderson and D. M. Reeb, "Board Composition: Balancing Family Influence in S&P 500 Firms," *Administrative Science Quarterly* (June 2004), pp. 209–237; W. S. Schulze, M. H. Lubatkin, R. N. Dino, and A. K. Buchholtz, "Agency Relationships in Family Firms: Theory and Evidence," *Organization Science* (March–April, 2001), pp. 99–116.

29. M. N. Young, A. K. Buchholtz, and D. Ahlstrom, "How Can Board Members Be Empowered If They Are Spread Too Thin?" *SAM Advanced Management Journal* (Autumn 2003), pp. 4–11.

30. *33rd Annual Board of Directors Study* (New York: Korn/Ferry International, 2007), p. 21.

31. C. M. Daily and D. R. Dalton, "The Endangered Director," *Journal of Business Strategy*, (Vol. 25, No. 3, 2004), pp. 8–9.

32. I. Sager, "The Boardroom: New Rules, New Loopholes," *BusinessWeek* (November 29, 2004), p. 13.

33. *34th Annual Board of Directors Study* (New York: Korn/Ferry International, 2008), pp. 25–32.

34. See S. Finkelstein, and D. C. Hambrick, *Strategic Leadership: Top Executives and Their Impact on Organizations* (St. Paul, MN: West, 1996), p. 213.

35. D. R. Dalton, M. A. Hitt, S. Trevis Certo, and C. M. Dalton, "The Fundamental Agency Problem and Its Mitigation," Chapter One in *Academy of Management Annals*, edited by J. F. Westfall and A. F. Brief (London: Rutledge, 2007).

36. "TIAA-CREF's Role in Corporate Governance," *Investment Forum* (June 2003), p. 13.

37. Credit Suisse Research Institutes (July 31, 2012), (www.credit-suisse.com/news/en/media_release.jsp).

38. M. Teen, "The Diversity Scorecard," (Korn/Ferry Institute, 2011).

39. *33rd Annual Board of Directors Study* (New York: Korn/Ferry International, 2007), p. 11; T. Neff and J. H. Daum, "The Empty Boardroom," *Strategy + Business* (Summer 2007), pp. 57–61.

40. R. O. Crockett, "The Rising Stock of Black Directors," *BusinessWeek* (February 27, 2006), p. 34.

41. J. Daum, "Portrait of Boards on the Cusp of Historic Change," *Directors & Boards* (Winter 2003), p. 56; J. Daum, "SSBI: Audit Committees Are Leading the Change," *Directors & Boards* (Winter 2004), p. 59.

42. *30th Annual Board of Directors Study* (New York: Korn/Ferry International, 2003) p. 38

43. *Globalizing the Board of Directors: Trends and Strategies* (New York: The Conference Board, 1999).

44. "The Korn/Ferry Market Cap 100 – 2011," p. 20.

45. R. W. Pouder and R. S. Cantrell, "Corporate Governance Reform: Influence on Shareholder Wealth," *Journal of Business Strategies* (Spring 1999), pp. 48–66.

46. M. L. Gerlach, "The Japanese Corporate Network: A Block-Model Analysis," *Administrative Science Quarterly* (March 1992), pp. 105–139.

47. W. E. Stead and J. G. Stead, *Sustainable Strategic Management* (Armonk, NY: M. E. Sharp, 2004), p. 47.

48. J. D. Westphal, M. L. Seidel, and K. J. Stewart, "Second-Order Imitation: Uncovering Latent Effects of Board Network Ties," *Administrative Science Quarterly* (December 2001),

pp. 717–747; M. A. Geletkanycz, B. K. Boyd, and S. Finkelstein, "The Strategic Value of CEO External Directorate Networks: Implications for CEO Compensation," *Strategic Management Journal* (September 2001), pp. 889–898; M. A. Carpenter and J. D. Westphal, "The Strategic Context of External Network Ties: Examining the Impact of Director Appointments on Board Involvement in Strategic Decision Making," *Academy of Management Journal* (August 2001), pp. 639–660.

49. M. Warner, "Inside the Silicon Valley Money Machine," *Fortune* (October 26, 1998), pp. 128–140.

50. D. Jones and B. Hansen, "Chairmen Still Doing Do-Si-Do," *USA Today* (November 5, 2003), p. 3B; J. H. Daum and T. J. Neff, "SSBI: Audit Committees Are Leading the Charge," *Directors & Boards* (Winter 2003), p. 59.

51. J. A. C. Baum and C. Oliver, "Institutional Linkages and Organizational Mortality," *Administrative Science Quarterly* (June 1991) pp. 187–218; J. P. Sheppard, "Strategy and Bankruptcy: An Exploration into Organizational Death," *Journal of Management* (Winter 1994), pp. 795–833.

52. *33rd Annual Board of Directors Study* (New York: Korn/Ferry International, 2007), p. 44, and *Directors' Compensation and Board Practices in 2003*, Research Report R-1339-03-RR (New York: Conference Board, 2003) Table 49, p. 38.

53. J. Canavan, B. Jones, and M. J. Potter, "Board Tenure: How Long Is Too Long?" *Boards & Directors* (Winter 2004), pp. 39–42.

54. *34th Annual Board of Directors Study* (New York: Korn/Ferry International, 2008), p. 18, and *30th Annual Board of Directors Study Supplement: Governance Trends of the Fortune 1000* (New York: Korn/Ferry International, 2004), p. 5.

55. D. F. Larcker and S. A. Richardson, "Does Governance Really Matter?" *Knowledge @ Wharton* (September 8–21, 2004).

56. M. L. McDonald, J. D. Westphal, and M. E. Graebner, "What Do they Know? The Effects of Outside Director Acquisition Experience on Firm Acquisition Experience," *Strategic Management Journal* (November 2008), pp. 1155–1177.

57. *26th Annual Board of Directors Study* (New York: Korn/Ferry International, 1999), p. 30.

58. *30th Annual Board of Directors Study* (New York: Korn/Ferry International, 2003), pp. 8, 31, 44.

59. D. R. Dalton, M. A. Hitt, S. Trevis Certo, and C. M. Dalton, "The Fundamental Agency Problem and Its Mitigation," Chapter One in *Academy of Management Annals*, edited by J. F. Westfall and A. F. Brief (London: Rutledge, 2007); P. Coombes and S. C-Y Wong, "Chairman and CEO—One Job or Two?" *McKinsey Quarterly* (2004, No. 2), pp. 43–47; "The Korn/Ferry Market Cap 100 – 2011."

60. A. Desai, M. Kroll, and P. Wright, "CEO Duality, Board Monitoring, and Acquisition Performance," *Journal of Business Strategies* (Fall 2003), pp. 147–156; D. Harris and C. E. Helfat, "CEO Duality, Succession, Capabilities and Agency Theory: Commentary and Research Agenda," *Strategic Management Journal* (September 1998), pp. 901–904; C. M. Daily and D. R. Dalton, "CEO and Board Chair Roles Held Jointly or Separately: Much Ado About Nothing," *Academy of Management Executive* (August 1997), pp. 11–20; D. L. Worrell, C. Nemec, and W. N. Davidson III, "One Hat Too Many: Key Executive Plurality and Shareholder Wealth," *Strategic Management Journal* (June 1997), pp. 499–507; J. W. Coles and W. S. Hesterly, "Independence of the Chairman and Board Composition: Firm Choices and Shareholder Value,"

Journal of Management, Vol. 26, No. 2 (2000), pp. 195–214; H. Ashbaugh, D. W. Collins, and R. LaFond, "The Effects of Corporate Governance on Firms' Credit Ratings," unpublished paper, March 2004.

61. J. P. O'Connor, R. I. Priem, J. E. Coombs, and K. M. Gilley, "Do CEO Stock Options Prevent or Promote Fraudulent Financial Reporting?" *Academy of Management Journal* (June 2006), pp. 483–500.

62. N. R. Augustine, "How Leading a Role for the Lead Director?" *Directors & Boards* (Winter 2004), pp. 20–23.

63. D. R. Dalton, M. A. Hitt, S. Trevis Certo, and C. M. Dalton, "The Fundamental Agency Problem and Its Mitigation," Chapter One in *Academy of Management Annals*, edited by J. F. Westfall and A. F. Brief (London: Rutledge, 2007).

64. *34th Annual Board of Directors Study* (New York: Korn/Ferry International, 2008), p. 19.

65. J. D. Westphal and I. Stern, "Flattery Will Get You Everywhere (Especially If You Are a Male Caucasian): How Ingratiation, Boardroom Behavior, and Demographic Minority Status Affect Additional Board Appointments at U.S. Companies," *Academy of Management Journal* (April 2007), pp. 267–288; J. D. Westphal, "Board Games: How CEOs Adapt to Increases in Structural Board Independence from Management," *Administrative Science Quarterly* (September 1998), pp. 511–537; J. D. Westphal and P. Khanna, "Keeping Directors in Line: Social Distancing as a Control Mechanism in the Corporate Elite," *Administrative Science Quarterly* (September 2003), pp. 361–398.

66. H. L. Tosi, W. Shen, and R. J. Gentry, "Why Outsiders on Boards Can't Solve the Corporate Governance Problem," *Organizational Dynamics* (Vol. 32, No. 2, 2003), pp. 180–192.

67. *33rd Annual Board of Directors Study* (New York: Korn/Ferry International, 2007), p. 12. Other committees are succession planning (39%), finance (30%), corporate responsibility (17%), and investment (15%).

68. Perhaps because of their potential to usurp the power of the board, executive committees are being used less often.

69. *34th Annual Board of Directors Study* (New York: Korn/Ferry International, 2008), p. 19.

70. "The Trial of Sarbanes–Oxley," *The Economist* (April 22, 2006), pp. 59–60; *33rd Annual Board of Directors Study* (New York: Korn/Ferry International, 2007), p. 14; S. Wagner and L. Dittmar, "The Unexpected Benefits of Sarbanes–Oxley," *Harvard Business Review* (April 2006), pp. 133–140.

71. A. Borrus, "Learning to Love Sarbanes–Oxley," *BusinessWeek* (November 21, 2005), pp. 126–128.

72. D. Henry, "Not Everyone Hates SarbOx," *BusinessWeek* (January 29, 2007), p. 37.

73. D. Henry, "A SarbOx Surprise," *BusinessWeek* (January 12, 2006), p. 38.

74. *30th Annual Board of Directors Study Supplement: Governance Trends of the Fortune 1000* (New York: Korn/Ferry International, 2004), p. 5.

75. "Where's All the Fun Gone?" *The Economist* (March 20, 2004), pp. 75–77.

76. Daum and Neff (2004), p. 58.

77. *33rd Annual Board of Directors Study* (New York: Korn/Ferry International, 2007), p. 7.

78. J. Sonnenfeld, "Good Governance and the Misleading Myths of Bad Metrics." *Academy of Management Executive* (February 2004), pp. 108–113.

79. H. Ashbaugh, D. W. Collins, and R. LaFond, "The Effects of Corporate Governance on Firms' Credit Ratings," unpublished paper (March 2002).

80. M. Hiltzik, "Facebook Shareholders Are Wedded to the Whims of Mark Zuckerberg," *The Los Angeles Times* (May 20, 2012), (www.articles.latimes.com/2012/may/20/business/la-fi-hiltzik-20120517).

81. P. A. Gompers, J. Ishii, and A. Metrick, *Extreme Governance: An Analysis of Dual-Class Firms in the United States*," (2006), (www.hbs.edu/units/am/pdf/dual.pdf), pp. 1–48.

82. D. R. Dalton, C. M. Daily, A. E. Ellstrand, and J. L. Johnson, "Meta-Analytic Reviews of Board Composition, Leadership Structure, and Financial Performance," *Strategic Management Journal* (March 1998), pp. 269–290; G. Beaver, "Competitive Advantage and Corporate Governance—Shop Soiled and Needing Attention!" *Strategic Change* (September–October 1999), p. 330.

83. A. Borrus and L. Young, "Nothing Like a Little Exposure," *BusinessWeek* (September 13, 2004), p. 92.

84. P. Silva, "Do Motivation and Equity Ownership Matter in Board of Directors' Evaluation of CEO Performance?" *Journal of Management Issues* (Fall 2005), pp. 346–362.

85. L. He and M. J. Conyon, "The Role of Compensation Committees in CEO and Committee Compensation Decisions," paper presented to *Academy of Management* (Seattle, WA, 2003).

86. P. Coy, E. Thornton, M. Arndt, B. Grow, and A. Park, "Shake, Rattle, and Merge," *BusinessWeek* (January 10, 2005), pp. 32–35.

87. L. Lavelle, "A Fighting Chance for Boardroom Democracy," *BusinessWeek* (June 9, 2003), p. 50; L. Lavelle, "So That's Why Boards Are Waking Up," *BusinessWeek* (January 19, 2004), pp. 72–73.

88. For a detailed description of the COO's role, see N. Bennett and S. A. Miles, "Second in Command," *Harvard Business Review* (May 2006), pp. 71–78.

89. S. Finkelstein and D. C. Hambrick, *Strategic Leadership: Top Executives and Their Impact on Organizations* (St. Louis: West, 1996).

90. H. G. Barkema and O. Shvyrkov, "Does Top Management Team Diversity Promote or Hamper Foreign Expansion?" *Strategic Management Journal* (July 2007), pp. 663–680; D. C. Hambrick, T. S. Cho, and M-J Chen, "The Influence of Top Management Team Heterogeneity on Firms' Competitive Moves," *Administrative Science Quarterly* (December 1996), pp. 659–684.

91. P. Pitcher and A. D. Smith, "Top Management Heterogeneity: Personality, Power, and Proxies," *Organization Science* (January–February 2001), pp. 1–18; M. A. Carpenter and J. W. Fredrickson, "Top Management Teams, Global Strategic Posture, and the Moderating Role of Uncertainty," *Academy of Management Journal* (June 2001), pp. 533–545; M. A. Carpenter, "The Implications of Strategy and Social Context for the Relationship Between Top Management Team Heterogeneity and Firm Performance," *Strategic Management Journal* (March 2002), pp. 275–284; L. Tihanyi, A. E. Ellstrand, C. M. Daily, and D. R. Dalton, "Composition of the Top Management Team and Firm International Expansion," *Journal of Management* (Vol. 26, No. 6, 2000), pp. 1157–1177.

92. "One on One with Steve Reinemund," *BusinessWeek* (December 17, 2001), special advertising insert on leadership by Heidrick & Struggles, executive search firm.

93. D. A. Waldman, G. G. Ramirez, R. J. House, and P. Puranam, "Does Leadership Matter? CEO Leadership Attributes and Profitability Under Conditions of Perceived Environmental Uncertainty,"

Academy of Management Journal (February 2001), pp. 134–143; F. J. Flynn and B. M. Staw, "Lend Me Your Wallets: The Effect of Charismatic Leadership on External Support for an Organization," *Strategic Management Journal* (April 2004), pp. 309–330.

94. J. Burns, *Leadership* (New York: HarperCollins, 1978); B. Bass, "From Transactional to Transformational Leadership: Learning to Share the Vision," *Organizational Dynamics* (Vol. 18, 1990), pp. 19–31; W. Bennis and B. Nanus, *Leaders: Strategies for Taking Charge* (New York: HarperCollins, 1997).

95. Based on R. J. House, "A 1976 Theory of Charismatic Leadership," in J. G. Hunt and L. L. Larson (Eds.), *Leadership: The Cutting Edge* (Carbondale, IL: Southern Illinois University Press, 1976), pp. 189–207. Also see J. Choi, "A Motivational Theory of Charismatic Leadership: Envisioning, Empathy, and Empowerment," *Journal of Leadership and Organizational Studies* (Vol. 13, No. 1, 2006), pp. 24–43.

96. I. D. Colville and A. J. Murphy, "Leadership as the Enabler of Strategizing and Organizing," *Long Range Planning* (December 2006), pp. 663–677.

97. L. V. Gerstner Jr., *Who Says Elephants Can't Dance?* (New York: HarperCollins, 2002), p. 124.

98. M. Lipton, "Demystifying the Development of an Organizational Vision," *Sloan Management Review* (Summer 1996), p. 84.

99. S. Hahn, "Why High Tech Has to Stay Humble," *BusinessWeek* (January 19, 2004), pp. 76–77.

100. J. H. David, F. D. Schoorman, R. Mayer, and H. H. Tan, "The Trusted General Manager and Business Unit Performance: Empirical Evidence of a Competitive Advantage," *Strategic Management Journal* (May 2000), pp. 563–576.

101. D. B. McNatt and T. A. Judge, "Boundary Conditions of the Galatea Effect: A Field Experiment and Constructive Replication," *Academy of Management Journal* (August 2004), pp. 550–565.

102. R. F. Piccolo and J. A. Colquitt, "Transformational Leadership and Job Behaviors: The Mediating Role of Core Job Characteristics," *Academy of Management Journal* (April 2006), pp. 327–340; J. E. Bono and T. A. Judge, "Self-Concordance at Work: Toward Understanding the Motivational Effects of Transformational Leaders," *Academy of Management Journal* (October 2003), pp. 554–571.

103. T. Lowry, R. O. Crockett, and I. M. Kunii, "Verizon's Gutsy Bet," *BusinessWeek* (August 4, 2003), pp. 52–62.

104. G. Tate and U. Malmendier, "Who Makes Acquisitions? CEO Overconfidence and the Market's Reaction," summarized by *Knowledge @ Wharton* (February 25, 2004).

105. M. C. Mankins and R. Steele, "Stop Making Plans, Start Making Decisions," *Harvard Business Review* (January 2006), pp. 76–84.

106. T. R. Eisenmann and J. L. Bower, "The Entrepreneurial M Form: Strategic Integration in Global Media Firms," *Organization Science* (May–June 2000), pp. 348–355.

107. J. Kirby and T. A. Stewart, "The Institutional Yes," *Harvard Business Review* (October 2007), p. 76.

108. M. C. Mankins and R. Steele, "Stop Making Plans, Start Making Decisions," *Harvard Business Review* (January 2006), pp. 76–84; G. P. Hodgkinson, R. Whittington, G. Johnson, and M. Schwarz, "The Role of Strategy Workshops in Strategy Development Processes: Formality, Communication, Co-ordination and Inclusion," *Long Range Planning* (October 2006), pp. 479–496; B. Frisch and L. Chandler, "Off-Sites that Work," *Harvard Business Review* (June 2006), pp. 117–126.

109. For a description of the Chief Strategy Officer, see R. T. S. Breene, P. F. Nunes, and W. E. Shill, "The Chief Strategy Officer," *Harvard Business Review* (October 2007), pp. 84–93; R. Dye, "How Chief Strategy Officers Think about Their Role: A Roundtable," *McKinsey Quarterly* (May 2008), pp. 1–8.

110. M. Wiersema, "Holes at the Top: Why CEO Firings Backfire," *Harvard Business Review* (December 2002), pp. 70–77.

social responsibility and Ethics in Strategic Management

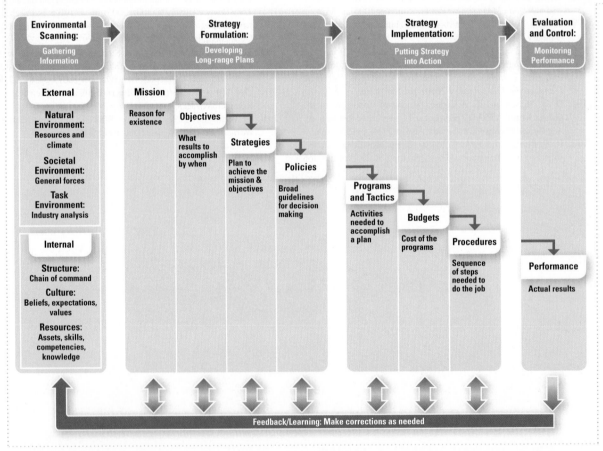

MyManagementLab®

⭐ Improve Your Grade!

Over 10 million students improved their results using the Pearson MyLabs. Visit **mymanagementlab.com** for simulations, tutorials, and end-of-chapter problems.

Learning Objectives

After reading this chapter, you should be able to:

- Compare and contrast Friedman's traditional view with Carroll's contemporary view of social responsibility
- Understand the relationship between social responsibility and corporate performance
- Explain the concept of sustainability

- Conduct a stakeholder analysis
- Explain why people may act unethically
- Describe different views of ethics according to the utilitarian, individual rights, and justice approaches

Coca-Cola and Environmental Stewardship

Each year, Fortune magazine publishes its list of the most admired companies. Companies are rated in innovation, people management, use of corporate assets, social responsibility, quality of management, financial soundness, long-term investment, quality of products/services, and global competitiveness. When the 2012 list was announced, it was no surprise to see Coca-Cola in the top five. Coca-Cola has been a consistent member of this elite group for some time. They were cited for their environmental efforts, including water conservation and their PlantBottle Packaging Platform.

The PlantBottle is the only bottle in the market that is made partially with plants (30%), is commercially recyclable, and meets all the high-performance standards set by Coke. However, Coca-Cola's biggest impact has been in the use and reuse of water. Water is obviously critical to the operations of the company, but they have gone far beyond the classic business approach in creating their supply. By 2020, the company plans to return both to nature and the communities where it operates an amount of water equivalent to what is used in all of its beverages and their production. The company has written in a Water Stewardship code that applies to all 900 bottling plants worldwide. It is committed to watershed stewardship, and since 2005 has been involved with more than 300 community water partnership projects.

One such effort is with the United Nations Development Program in China. Coca-Cola has donated more than US$5 million to support the quality and quantity of high-quality drinking water in underserved rural areas. This work is outside the classic bounds of business and is being done far from the operating plants in China.

Coca-Cola has not always been on the front end of this issue, and some would argue that it should not be there now. In its 2002 annual filing, Coca-Cola did not even list water under its raw materials, but today it is listed as the main ingredient in its processes. It takes approximately 2.5 liters of water to produce 1 liter of its products. By 2002, the company was under worldwide pressure to improve its business practices. That year, the residents of Plachimada, a village in India, accused the company of sucking the wells dry and polluting the ground water. In 2004, the local government forced Coca-Cola to shut down their plant. The public relations impact around the world was substantial. The company announced that "if people are perceiving that we're using water at their expense, that's not a sustainable operation. . . and for us, having the goodwill in the community is an important thing." In response, the company spent US$10 million establishing a foundation to improve water in India, installed 320 rainwater harvesting systems, and was providing clean drinking water to more than 1000 schools in the country.

Did Coca-Cola over compensate for their business use of water? What is the proper role for a company? Are sustainable business practices part of a business's responsibilities?

SOURCES: Coca-Cola Stories, Accessed 5/30/13, www.thecoca-colacompany.com/citizenship/water_main.html; "World's Most Admired Companies," CNNmoney.com, Accessed 5/30/13, http://money.cnn.com/magazines/fortune/most-admired/2012/full_list; "Coca-Cola Helps Advance Water Sustainability Projects in the Pacific Region," May 12, 2011, Environmental Protection, (www.epoline.com/articles/2011/05/12/coca-cola-advances-water-sustainability-projects-in-pacific-region.aspx); Liu, L.W. 2008, "Water Pressure," Time, June 12, 2008 (www.time.com/time/magazine/article/0,9171,1814261,00.html);.

Social Responsibilities of Strategic Decision Makers

Should strategic decision makers be responsible only to shareholders, or do they have broader responsibilities? The concept of **social responsibility** proposes that a private corporation has responsibilities to society that extend beyond making a profit. Strategic decisions often affect more than just the corporation. A decision to retrench by closing some plants and discontinuing product lines, for example, affects not only the firm's workforce but also the communities where the plants are located and the customers with no other source for the discontinued product. Such situations raise questions about the appropriateness of certain missions, objectives, and strategies of business corporations. Managers must be able to deal with these conflicting interests in an ethical manner to formulate a viable strategic plan.

RESPONSIBILITIES OF A BUSINESS FIRM

What are the responsibilities of a business firm and how many of them must be fulfilled? Milton Friedman and Archie Carroll offer two contrasting views of the responsibilities of business firms to society.

Friedman's Traditional View of Business Responsibility

Urging a return to a laissez-faire worldwide economy with minimal government regulation, Milton Friedman argues against the concept of social responsibility as a function of business. A business person who acts "responsibly" by cutting the price of the firm's product to aid the poor, or by making expenditures to reduce pollution, or by hiring the hard-core unemployed, according to Friedman, is spending the shareholder's money for a general social interest. Even if the businessperson has shareholder permission or encouragement to do so, he or she is still acting from motives other than economic and may, in the long run, harm the very society the firm is trying to help. By taking on the burden of these social costs, the business becomes less efficient—either prices go up to pay for the increased costs or investment in new activities and research is postponed. These results negatively affect—perhaps fatally—the long-term efficiency of a business. Friedman thus referred to the social responsibility of business as a "fundamentally subversive doctrine" and stated that:

> *There is one and only one social responsibility of business—to use its resources and engage in activities designed to increase its profits so long as it stays within the rules of the game, which is to say, engages in open and free competition without deception or fraud.*[1]

Following Friedman's reasoning, the management of Coca-Cola was clearly guilty of misusing corporate assets and negatively affecting shareholder wealth. The millions spent in social services could have been invested in new product development or given back as dividends to the shareholders. Instead of Coca-Cola's management acting on its own, shareholders could have decided which charities to support.

Carroll's Four Responsibilities of Business

Friedman's contention that the primary goal of business is profit maximization is only one side of an ongoing debate regarding corporate social responsibility (CSR). According to William J. Byron, Distinguished Professor of Ethics at Georgetown University and past President of Catholic University of America, profits are merely a means to an end, not an end in itself. Just as a person needs food to survive and grow, so does a business corporation need profits to survive and grow. "Maximizing profits is like maximizing food." Thus, contends Byron, maximization of profits cannot be the primary obligation of business.[2]

As shown in **Figure 3–1**, Archie Carroll proposed that the managers of business organizations have four responsibilities: economic, legal, ethical, and discretionary.[3]

1. **Economic** responsibilities of a business organization's management are to produce goods and services of value to society so that the firm may repay its creditors and increase the wealth of its shareholders.

2. **Legal** responsibilities are defined by governments in laws that management is expected to obey. For example, U.S. business firms are required to hire and promote people based on their credentials rather than to discriminate on non-job-related characteristics such as race, gender, or religion.

3. **Ethical** responsibilities of an organization's management are to follow the generally held beliefs about behavior in a society. For example, society generally expects firms to work with the employees and the community in planning for layoffs, even though no law may require this. The affected people can get very upset if an organization's management fails to act according to generally prevailing ethical values.

4. **Discretionary** responsibilities are the purely voluntary obligations a corporation assumes. Examples are philanthropic contributions, training the hard-core unemployed, and providing day-care centers. The difference between ethical and discretionary responsibilities is that few people expect an organization to fulfill discretionary responsibilities, whereas many expect an organization to fulfill ethical ones.[4]

FIGURE 3–1
Responsibilities of Business

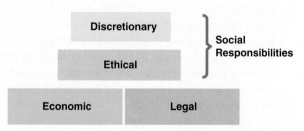

SOURCE: Suggested by Archie Carroll in A. B. Carroll, "A Three Dimensional Conceptual Model of Corporate Performance," *Academy of Management Review* (October 1979), pp. 497–505; A. B. Carroll, "Managing Ethically with Global Stakeholders: A Present and Future Challenge," *Academy of Management Executive* (May 2004), pp. 114–120; and A. B. Carroll, "The Pyramid of Corporate Social Responsibility: Toward the Moral Management of Organizational Stakeholders," *Business Horizons* (July–August 1991), pp. 39–48.

Carroll lists these four responsibilities *in order of priority*. A business firm must first make a profit to satisfy its economic responsibilities. To continue in existence, the firm must follow the laws, thus fulfilling its legal responsibilities. There is evidence that companies found guilty of violating laws have lower profits and sales growth after conviction.[5] On this point, Carroll and Friedman are in agreement. Carroll, however, goes further by arguing that business managers have responsibilities beyond economic and legal ones.

Having satisfied the two basic responsibilities, according to Carroll, a firm should look to fulfilling its social responsibilities. Social responsibility, therefore, includes both ethical and discretionary, but not economic and legal, responsibilities. A firm can fulfill its ethical responsibilities by taking actions that society tends to value but has not yet put into law. When ethical responsibilities are satisfied, a firm can focus on discretionary responsibilities— purely voluntary actions that society has not yet decided to expect from every company. For example, when Cisco Systems decided to dismiss 6000 full-time employees, it provided a novel severance package. Those employees who agreed to work for a local nonprofit organization for a year would receive one-third of their salaries plus benefits and stock options and be the first to be rehired. Nonprofits were delighted to hire such highly qualified people and Cisco was able to maintain its talent pool for when it could hire once again.[6]

As societal values evolve, the discretionary responsibilities of today may become the ethical responsibilities of tomorrow. For example, in 1990, 86% of people in the United States believed that obesity was caused by the individuals themselves, with only 14% blaming either corporate marketing or government guidelines. By 2003, however, only 54% blamed obesity on individuals and 46% put responsibility on corporate marketing and government guidelines. Thus, the offering of healthy, low-calorie food by food processors and restaurants is moving rapidly from being a discretionary to an ethical responsibility.[7] In recent years, school cafeterias across the United States have added fresh vegetables, removed soda machines, and in 2012, many school systems also moved to eliminate the much maligned *pink slime* from their beef product lines.

Carroll suggests that to the extent that business corporations fail to acknowledge discretionary or ethical responsibilities, society, through government, will act, making them legal responsibilities. Government may do this, moreover, without regard to an organization's economic responsibilities. As a result, the organization may have greater difficulty in earning a profit than it would have if it had voluntarily assumed some ethical and discretionary responsibilities.

Both Friedman and Carroll argue their positions based on the impact of socially responsible actions on a firm's profits. Friedman says that socially responsible actions hurt a firm's efficiency. Carroll proposes that a lack of social responsibility results in increased government regulations, which reduce a firm's efficiency because it must not only comply with the law, but must prove its compliance with regulators.

Friedman's position on social responsibility appears to be losing traction with business executives. For example, a 2006 survey of business executives across the world by McKinsey & Company revealed that only 16% felt that business should focus solely on providing the highest possible returns to investors while obeying all laws and regulations, contrasted with 84% who stated that business should generate high returns to investors but balance it with contributions to the broader public good.[8] The United National Global Compact was started in 2001 as an initiative for a company to voluntarily commit to aligning their operations with 10 principles covering human rights, the environment, labor and corruption among others. By 2012, over 6,800 companies in 140 countries had signed the compact. Those CEOs have agreed to report on their activities annually.[9]

Empirical research now indicates that socially responsible actions may have a positive effect on a firm's financial performance. Although a number of studies in the past have found no significant relationship,[10] an increasing number are finding a small, but positive relationship.[11]

A recent in-depth analysis by Margolis and Walsh of 127 studies found that "there is a positive association and very little evidence of a negative association between a company's social performance and its financial performance."[12] Another meta-analysis of 52 studies on social responsibility and performance reached this same conclusion.[13]

According to Porter and Kramer, "social and economic goals are not inherently conflicting, but integrally connected."[14] Being known as a socially responsible firm may provide a company with *social capital*, the goodwill of key stakeholders, that can be used for competitive advantage.[15] Target, for example, tries to attract socially concerned younger consumers by offering brands from companies that can boast ethical track records and community involvement.[16] A 2008 study conducted by Grant Thornton found that privately held businesses were forgoing the big publicity campaigns run by multinational companies and focusing their attention on CSR as a means for recruitment and retention of the best employees. In the same report, they found that 58% of these private companies had formally adopted transparent CSR policies as a means of influencing larger companies that may use their services/products.[17]

Being socially responsible does provide a firm with a more positive overall reputation.[18] A survey of more than 700 global companies by The Conference Board reported that 60% of the managers state that citizenship activities had led to (1) goodwill that opened doors in local communities and (2) an enhanced reputation with consumers.[19] Another survey of 140 U.S. firms revealed that being more socially responsible regarding environmental sustainability resulted not only in competitive advantages but also in cost savings.[20] For example, companies that take the lead in being environmentally friendly, such as by using recycled materials, preempt attacks from environmental groups and enhance their corporate image. Programs to reduce pollution, for example, can actually reduce waste and maximize resource productivity. One study that examined 70 ecological initiatives taken by 43 companies found the average payback period to be 18 months.[21] Other examples of benefits received from being socially responsible are:[22]

- Their environmental concerns may enable them to charge premium prices and gain brand loyalty (for example, Stoneyfield Yogurt, Whole Foods, and Ben & Jerry's Ice Cream).
- Their trustworthiness may help them generate enduring relationships with suppliers and distributors without requiring them to spend a lot of time and money policing contracts.
- They can attract outstanding employees who prefer working for a responsible firm (for example, Procter & Gamble and Starbucks).
- They are more likely to be welcomed into a foreign country (for example, Levi Strauss).
- They can utilize the goodwill of public officials for support in difficult times.
- They are more likely to attract capital infusions from investors who view reputable companies as desirable long-term investments. For example, mutual funds investing only in socially responsible companies more than doubled in size from 1995 to 2007 and outperformed the S&P 500 list of stocks.[23]

SUSTAINABILITY

As we pointed out in Chapter 1, sustainability includes much more than just ecological concerns and the natural environment. Crane and Matten point out that the concept of sustainability should be broadened to include economic and social as well as environmental concerns. They argue that it is sometimes impossible to address the sustainability of the natural environment without considering the social and economic aspects of relevant communities and their activities. For example, even though environmentalists may oppose road-building programs because of their effect on wildlife and conservation efforts, others point to the benefits to local communities of less traffic congestion and more jobs.[24] Dow Jones & Company, a leading provider of global business news and information, developed a sustainability index that considers not only environmental, but also economic and social factors. See the **Sustainability Issue** feature to learn how a global company is using environmental sustainability efforts to improve its bottom line.

The broader concept of sustainability has much in common with Carroll's list of business responsibilities presented earlier. In order for a business corporation to be sustainable—that is, to be successful over a long period of time—it must satisfy all of its economic, legal, ethical, and discretionary responsibilities. Sustainability thus involves many issues, concerns, and tradeoffs—leading us to an examination of corporate stakeholders.

CORPORATE STAKEHOLDERS

The concept that business must be socially responsible sounds appealing until we ask, "Responsible to whom?" A corporation's task environment includes a large number of groups with interest in a business organization's activities. These groups are referred to as **stakeholders** because they affect or are affected by the achievement of the firm's objectives.[25] Should a corporation be responsible only to some of these groups, or does business have an equal responsibility to all of them?

A survey of the U.S. general public by Penn Schoen Berland of Corporate Social Responsibility found that companies utilize a number of activities to appease their stakeholders and provide something back to a wide range of stakeholders. This included 33% who practiced recycling and energy savings approaches and 24% who donated to charities.[26] As scandal after scandal breaks in the press, support for corporate leaders plunges. A 2012 survey of

SUSTAINABILITY issue

MARKS & SPENCER LEADS THE WAY

There have been many moves over the past few years to increase the sustainability of business practices. The idea that waste is not a given in the operation of businesses has led to new ways of doing business that not only make a business a good citizen, but save a company a substantial amount of money. None has been more focused than Marks and Spencer Group (M&S), the enormous retailer of goods from clothing to food that is based in the UK. M&S announced in June 2012 that it had achieved its goal of going "carbon neutral."

A huge financial incentive exists in the UK to do so. There is a landfill tax of 64 pounds (roughly US$100) per ton, and that number is slated to increase by 8 pounds a year indefinitely because the country is rapidly running out of landfill space. M&S now recycles 89% of its food waste from its 511 UK stores. That waste goes to biogas facilities, and in the past 12 months has saved the company more than 105 million pounds.

The effort was started in 2007 with what the company called Plan A. Plan A was designed to transform the company into the carbon neutral firm it is today. The company's efforts in this area extend to everything in their operation. Over the past five years, they have worked with suppliers and cut food packaging by 20%, made hanger recycling the norm, and reduced food carrier bag use by 80%.

Management takes the whole business very seriously. Progress on Plan A is reviewed by a "how we do business" committee and reported annually. Furthermore, progress on Plan A constitutes 20% of the bonuses for the CEO and the directors of the company.

M&S is not done, however. In 2010, they started a new five-year plan aimed at making M&S the most sustainable major retailer in the world. Their efforts have been good for their business and good for society at large.

....

SOURCES: www.marksandspencer.com; "Finally, a Use for Sandwich Crusts," *BusinessWeek* (June 18, 2012); L. Thorpe, "Marks & Spencer – An Ambitious Commitment to Tackling Waste," *The Guardian* (2011), (http://www.guardian.co.uk/sustainable-business/marks-spencer-waste-recycling).

169 Chief Financial Officers at publicly traded companies in the U.S. found that 20% intentionally misrepresented their economic performance primarily to influence stock price.[27]

In any one strategic decision, the interests of one stakeholder group can conflict with those of another. For example, a business firm's decision to use only recycled materials in its manufacturing process may have a positive effect on environmental groups, but a negative effect on shareholder dividends. In another example, arguably the worst environmental disaster in the past decade occurred in the Gulf of Mexico when the Deepwater Horizon platform exploded, killing 11 workers and unleashing the worst oil spill in the nation's history. Much of the investigation since that explosion centered on a series of cost-saving approaches used by Trans Ocean (under contract to BP). On the one hand, shareholders were being rewarded with lower costs and higher profits. Had the rig not exploded, the focus would have remained on extracting the oil at the least possible cost. On the other hand, officials and the population along the gulf coast were decimated by the economic and environmental impact of a spill that was entirely preventable.[28] Which group's interests should have priority?

In order to answer this question, the corporation may need to craft an *enterprise strategy*—an overarching strategy that explicitly articulates the firm's ethical relationship with its stakeholders. This requires not only that management clearly state the firm's key ethical values, but also that it understands the firm's societal context, and undertakes stakeholder analysis to identify the concerns and abilities of each stakeholder.[29]

Stakeholder Analysis

Stakeholder analysis is the identification and evaluation of corporate stakeholders. This can be done in a three-step process.

The *first step* in stakeholder analysis is to identify primary stakeholders, those who have a *direct connection* with the corporation and who have sufficient bargaining power to *directly* affect corporate activities. Primary stakeholders include customers, employees, suppliers, shareholders, and creditors.

Unfortunately, determining exactly who constitutes the firm's customers and exactly what they want is difficult. This is particularly difficult when companies sell items for other companies (many retail organizations are simply flow-through operations for the products on their shelf, e.g., Wal-Mart, Target, etc.) or they sell items for which they have only limited influence. Coca-Cola Bottling Company Consolidated (CCBCC) is the largest independent bottler for Coca-Cola. While they are in direct contact with the retailers who display their products, most of those products are controlled by Coca-Cola in Atlanta, Georgia. Furthermore, these retailers while customers of CCBCC, are really just conduits for the consumer of the beverage. Marketing outwardly focuses on the end consumer of the beverage, while that same consumer probably has no idea that CCBCC has done all the work to ensure that the shelves are stocked. Coca-Cola in Atlanta may create a new flavor or drink brand (think Coconut Water) and pressure CCBCC to find a way to get those products accepted by the retailer who really only wants the product if it will outsell what was on the shelf before it arrived.

While difficult to determine at times, it is nonetheless important for businesses to determine who their stakeholders are and what they want. The corporation systematically monitors these stakeholders because they are important to a firm meeting its economic and legal responsibilities. Employees want a fair pay and fringe benefits. Customers want safe products and a value for price they pay. Shareholders want dividends and stock price appreciation. Suppliers want predictable orders and bills paid. Creditors want commitments to be met on time. In the normal course of affairs, the relationship between a firm and many of its primary stakeholders is regulated by written or verbal agreements and laws. Once a problem is identified, negotiation takes place based on costs and benefits to each party. (Government is not usually considered a primary stakeholder because laws apply to everyone in a particular category and usually cannot be negotiated.)

The *second step* in stakeholder analysis is to identify the *secondary stakeholders*—those who have only an *indirect* stake in the corporation but who are also affected by corporate activities. These usually include nongovernmental organizations (NGOs, such as Greenpeace), activists, local communities, trade associations, competitors, and governments. Because the corporation's relationship with each of these stakeholders is usually not covered by any written or verbal agreement, there is room for misunderstanding. As in the case of NGOs and activists, there actually may be no relationship until a problem develops—usually brought up by the stakeholder. In the normal course of events, these stakeholders do not affect the corporation's ability to meet its economic or legal responsibilities. Aside from competitors, these secondary stakeholders are not usually monitored by the corporation in any systematic fashion. As a result, relationships are usually based on a set of questionable assumptions about each other's needs and wants. Although these stakeholders may not directly affect a firm's short-term profitability, their actions could impact a corporation's reputation and thus its long-term performance.

The *third step* in stakeholder analysis is to estimate the effect on each stakeholder group from any particular strategic decision. Since the primary decision criteria used by management is generally economic, this is the point where secondary stakeholders may be ignored or discounted as unimportant. For a firm to fulfill its ethical or discretionary responsibilities, it must seriously consider the needs and wants of its secondary stakeholders in any strategic decision. For example, how much will specific stakeholder groups lose or gain? What other alternatives do they have to replace what may be lost?

Stakeholder Input

Once stakeholder impacts have been identified, managers should decide whether stakeholder input should be invited into the discussion of the strategic alternatives. A group is more likely to accept or even help implement a decision if it has some input into which alternative is chosen and how it is to be implemented. In the case of the huge BP oil spill, the company committed more than US$20 billion to the restoration of the gulf coast and the reimbursement of lost earnings to businesses affected by the spill. While there are still outstanding lawsuits and many claim to not have been made whole, the main effort by BP has been made without any legal requirement.

Given the wide range of interests and concerns present in any organization's task environment, one or more groups, at any one time, probably will be dissatisfied with an organization's activities—even if management is trying to be socially responsible. A company may have some stakeholders of which it is only marginally aware and in some cases does not seem interested in appeasing. For example, when Chick-fil-A announced their support for a ban on gay marriage, a firestorm of protests erupted. The mayors of Chicago and Boston opposed moves by Chick-fil-A to add stores in their area, The Jim Henson Company pulled their Muppet toys from the kids meals and gay-rights groups called for a boycott. On the other hand, the company found a quick and vocal group of supporters. Radio talk show host and former Presidential candidate, Mike Huckabee called for a "Chick-fil-A Appreciation Day."[30]

Therefore, before making a strategic decision, strategic managers should consider how each alternative will affect various stakeholder groups. What seems at first to be the best decision because it appears to be the most profitable may actually result in the worst set of consequences to the corporation. One example of a company that does its best to consider its responsibilities to its primary and secondary stakeholders when making strategic decisions is Johnson & Johnson. See the **Strategy Highlight** feature for the J & J Credo.

STRATEGY highlight

JOHNSON & JOHNSON CREDO

We believe our first responsibility is to the doctors, nurses, and patients, to mothers and fathers and all others who use our products and services. In meeting their needs everything we do must be of high quality. We must constantly strive to reduce our costs in order to maintain reasonable prices. Customers' orders must be serviced promptly and accurately. Our suppliers and distributors must have an opportunity to make a fair profit.

We are responsible to our employees, the men and women who work with us throughout the world. Everyone must be considered as an individual. We must respect their dignity and recognize their merit. They must have a sense of security in their jobs. Compensation must be fair and adequate, and working conditions clean, orderly, and safe. We must be mindful of ways to help our employees fulfill their family responsibilities. Employees must feel free to make suggestions and complaints. There must be equal opportunity for employment, development, and advancement for those qualified. We must provide competent management, and their actions must be just and ethical.

We are responsible to the communities where we live and work and to the world community as well. We must be good citizens—support good works and charities and bear our fair share of taxes. We must encourage civic improvements and better health and education. We must maintain in good order the property we are privileged to use, protecting the environment and natural resources.

Our final responsibility is to our stockholders. Business must make a sound profit. We must experiment with new ideas. Research must be carried on, innovative programs developed, and mistakes paid for. New equipment must be purchased, new facilities provided, and new products launched. Reserves must be created for adverse times. When we operate according to these principles, the stockholders should realize a fair return.

. . . .

Ethical Decision Making

Some people joke that there is no such thing as "business ethics." They call it an oxymoron—a concept that combines opposite or contradictory ideas. Unfortunately, there is some truth to this sarcastic comment. The 2011 (released in 2012) survey by the Ethics Resource Center of more than 4600 employees found that 45% of employees surveyed said that they had witnessed misconduct at work, but only 65% reported it.[31] The most commonly reported types of misconduct were misuse of company time (33%), abusive behavior (21%), lying to employees (20%), and violating company Internet use policies (16%). However, there were other more egregious observed behaviors including stealing (12%), falsifying time reports or hours worked (12%), and environmental violation (7%).[32] In a survey from 1996 to 2005 of top managers at 2270 firms, researchers found that 29.2% of the firms analyzed had backdated or otherwise manipulated stock option grants to take advantage of favorable share-price movements.[33]

The Financial Crimes Enforcement Network found that mortgage fraud cases jumped by over 88% from 2010 to 2011 to just over 29,500. The most common type of mortgage fraud are debt-elimination scams, falsifying information on loan applications and identity theft.[34] In one instance, Allison Bice, office manager at Leonard Fazio's RE/MAX A-1 Best Realtors in Urbandale, Iowa, admitted that she submitted fake invoices and copies of checks drawn on a closed account as part of a scheme to obtain more money from Homecoming Financial, a mortgage company that had hired Fazio's agency to resell foreclosed homes.

A study of more than 5000 graduate students at 32 colleges and universities in the United States and Canada revealed that 56% of business students and 47% of non-business students admitted to cheating at least once during the past year. Cheating was more likely when a student's peers also cheated.[35] In another example, 6000 people paid US$30 to enter a VIP section on ScoreTop.com's Web site to obtain access to actual test questions posted by those who had recently taken the Graduate Management Admission Test (GMAT). In response, the Graduate Management Admission Council promised to cancel the scores of anyone who posted "live" questions to the site or knowingly read them.[36] Given this lack of ethical behavior among students, it is easy to understand why some could run into trouble if they obtained a job at a corporation having an unethical culture, such as Enron, World-Com, or Tyco.

SOME REASONS FOR UNETHICAL BEHAVIOR

Why are many business people perceived to be acting unethically? It may be that the involved people are not even aware that they are doing something questionable. There is no worldwide standard of conduct for business people. This is especially important given the global nature of business activities. Cultural norms and values vary between countries and even between different geographic regions and ethnic groups within a country. For example, what is considered in one country to be a bribe to expedite service is sometimes considered in another country to be normal business practice. Some of these differences may derive from whether a country's governance system is *rule-based* or *relationship-based*. Relationship-based countries tend to be less transparent and have a higher degree of corruption than do rule-based countries.[37] See the **Global Issue** feature for an explanation of country governance systems and how they may affect business practices

Another possible reason for what is often perceived to be unethical behavior lies in differences in values between business people and key stakeholders. Some businesspeople may believe profit maximization is the key goal of their firm, whereas concerned interest groups may have other priorities, such as the hiring of minorities and women or the safety of their neighborhoods. Of the six values measured by the Allport-Vernon-Lindzey Study of Values test (aesthetic, economic, political, religious, social, and theoretical), both U.S. and UK executives consistently score highest on economic and political values and lowest on social and religious ones. This is similar to the value profile of managers from Japan, Korea, India, and Australia, as well as those of U.S. business school students. U.S. Protestant ministers, in contrast, score highest on religious and social values and very low on economic values.[38]

This difference in values can make it difficult for one group of people to understand another's actions. For example, Michael Bloomberg, mayor of New York City has pushed through regulations that changed the type of oil that fast-food companies could use in their fryers, mandated calorie listings for all eating establishments, and in 2012 pushed through a plan that prohibited food-service establishments from selling sodas and similarly sweet drinks in sizes larger than 16 oz. "*Let the buyer beware*" is a traditional saying by free-market proponents who argue that customers in a free market democracy have the right to choose how they spend their money and live their lives. Social progressives contend that business people working in tobacco, alcoholic beverages, gambling, and maybe now the soft drink industries are acting unethically by making and advertising products with potentially dangerous and expensive side effects, such as cancer, alcoholism, obesity, and addiction. People working in these industries could respond by asking whether it is ethical for people who don't smoke, drink, or gamble to reject another person's right to do so.

GLOBAL issue

HOW RULE-BASED AND RELATIONSHIP-BASED GOVERNANCE SYSTEMS AFFECT ETHICAL BEHAVIOR

The developed nations of the world operate under governance systems quite different from those used by developing nations. Developed nations and the business firms within them follow well-recognized rules in their dealings and financial reporting. To the extent that a country's rules force business corporations to publicly disclose in-depth information about the company to potential shareholders and others, that country's financial and legal system is said to be *transparent*. Transparency helps simplify transactions and reduces the temptation to behave illegally or unethically. Finland, the United Kingdom, Hong Kong, the United States, and Australia have very transparent business climates. The Kurtzman Group, a consulting firm, developed an *opacity index* that measures the risks associated with unclear legal systems, regulations, economic policies, corporate governance standards, and corruption in 48 countries. The countries with the most opaque/least transparent ratings are Indonesia, Venezuela, China, Nigeria, India, Egypt, and Russia.

Developing nations tend to have *relationship-based governance*. Transactions are based on personal and implicit agreements, not on formal contracts enforceable by a court. Information about a business is largely local and private—thus, it cannot be easily verified by a third party. In contrast, *rule-based governance* relies on publicly verifiable information—the type of information that is typically not available in a developing country. The rule-based system has an infrastructure, based on accounting, auditing, ratings systems, legal cases, and codes, to provide and monitor this information. If present in a developing nation, the infrastructure is not very sophisticated. This is why investing in a developing country is very risky. The relationship-based system in a developing

nation is inherently nontransparent due to the local and non-verifiable nature of its information. A business person needs to develop and nurture a wide network of personal relationships. *What* you know is less important than *who* you know.

The investment in time and money needed to build the necessary relationships to conduct business in a developing nation creates a high entry barrier for any newcomers to an industry. Thus, key industries in developing nations tend to be controlled by a small number of companies, usually privately owned, family-controlled conglomerates. Because public information is unreliable and insufficient for decisions, strategic decisions may depend more on a CEO playing golf with the prime minister than with questionable market share data. In a relationship-based system, the culture of the country (and the founder's family) strongly affects corporate culture and business ethics. What is "fair" depends on whether one is a family member, a close friend, a neighbor, or a stranger. Because behavior tends to be less controlled by laws and agreed-upon standards than by tradition, businesspeople from a rule-based developed nation perceive the relationship-based system in a developing nation to be less ethical and more corrupt. According to Larry Smeltzer, ethics professor at Arizona State University: "The lack of openness and predictable business standards drives companies away. Why would you want to do business in, say Libya, where you don't know the rules?"

....

SOURCES: S. Li, S. H. Park, and S. Li, "The Great Leap Forward: The Transition from Relation-Based Governance to Rule-Based Governance," *Organizational Dynamics* (Vol. 33, No. 1, 2003), pp. 63–78; M. Davids, "Global Standards, Local Problems," *Journal of Business Strategy* (January/February 1999), pp. 38–43; "The Opacity Index," *The Economist* (September 18, 2004), p. 106.

Seventy percent of executives representing 111 diverse national and multinational corporations reported that they bend the rules to attain their objectives.[39] The three most common reasons given were:

- Organizational performance required it—74%

- Rules were ambiguous or out of date—70%

- Pressure from others and everyone does it—47%

The financial community's emphasis on short-term earnings performance is a significant pressure for executives to "manage" quarterly earnings. For example, a company achieving its forecasted quarterly earnings figure signals the investment community that its strategy and operations are proceeding as planned. Failing to meet its targeted objective signals that the company is in trouble—thus causing the stock price to fall and shareholders to become worried. Research by Degeorge and Patel involving more than 100,000 quarterly earnings reports revealed that a preponderance (82%) of reported earnings *exactly* matched analysts' expectations or exceeded them by 1%. The disparity between the number of earnings reports that missed estimates by a penny and the number that exceeded them by a penny suggests that executives who risked falling short of forecasts "borrowed" earnings from future quarters.[40]

In explaining why executives and accountants at Enron engaged in unethical and illegal actions, former Enron Vice-President Sherron Watkins used the *"frogs in boiling water"* analogy. If, for example, one were to toss a frog into a pan of boiling water, according to the folk tale, the frog would quickly jump out. It might be burned, but the frog would survive. However, if one put a frog in a pan of cold water and turned up the heat very slowly, the frog would not sense the increasing heat until it was too lethargic to jump out and would be boiled.

Moral Relativism

Some people justify their seemingly unethical positions by arguing that there is no one absolute code of ethics and that morality is relative. Simply put, **moral relativism** claims that morality is relative to some personal, social, or cultural standard and that there is no method for deciding whether one decision is better than another.

At one time or another, most managers have probably used one of the four types of moral relativism—naïve, role, social group, or cultural—to justify questionable behavior.[41]

Naïve relativism: Based on the belief that all moral decisions are deeply personal and that individuals have the right to run their own lives, adherents of moral relativism argue that each person should be allowed to interpret situations and act on his or her own moral values. This is not so much a belief as it is an excuse for not having a belief or is a common excuse for not taking action when observing others lying or cheating.

Role relativism: Based on the belief that social roles carry with them certain obligations to that role, adherents of role relativism argue that a manager in charge of a work unit must put aside his or her personal beliefs and do instead what the role requires—that is, act in the best interests of the unit. Blindly following orders was a common excuse provided by Nazi war criminals after World War II.

Social group relativism: Based on a belief that morality is simply a matter of following the norms of an individual's peer group, social group relativism argues that a decision is considered legitimate if it is common practice, regardless of other considerations ("everyone's doing it"). A real danger in embracing this view is that the person may incorrectly believe that a certain action is commonly accepted practice in an industry when it is not.

Cultural relativism: Based on the belief that morality is relative to a particular culture, society, or community, adherents of cultural relativism argue that people should understand the practices of other societies, but not judge them. This view not only suggests that one should not criticize another culture's norms and customs, but also that it is acceptable to personally follow these norms and customs ("When in Rome, do as the Romans do.").

Although each of these arguments have some element that may be understandable, moral relativism could enable a person to justify almost any sort of decision or action, so long as it is not declared illegal.

Kohlberg's Levels of Moral Development

Another reason why some business people might be seen as unethical is that they may have no well-developed personal sense of ethics. A person's ethical behavior is affected by his or her level of moral development, certain personality variables, and such situational factors as the job itself, the supervisor, and the organizational culture.[42] Kohlberg proposes that a person progresses through three **levels of moral development**.[43] Similar in some ways to Maslow's hierarchy of needs, in Kohlberg's system, the individual moves from total self-centeredness to a concern for universal values. Kohlberg's three levels are as follows:

1. **The preconventional level:** This level is characterized by a concern for self. Small children and others who have not progressed beyond this stage evaluate behaviors on the basis of personal interest—avoiding punishment or quid pro quo.

2. **The conventional level:** This level is characterized by considerations of society's laws and norms. Actions are justified by an external code of conduct.

3. **The principled level:** This level is characterized by a person's adherence to an internal moral code. An individual at this level looks beyond norms or laws to find universal values or principles. See the Innovation Issue to see how someone turned a pressing world need into a viable business.

Kohlberg places most people in the conventional level, with fewer than 20% of U.S. adults in the principled level of development.[44] Research appears to support Kohlberg's concept. For example, one study found that individuals higher in cognitive moral development, lower in Machiavellianism, with a more internal locus of control, a less-relativistic moral philosophy, and higher job satisfaction are less likely to plan and enact unethical choices.[45]

INNOVATION issue

TURNING A NEED INTO A BUSINESS TO SOLVE THE NEED

Tying an innovative idea to a social problem and turning it into a viable business is no small feat. Putting those three concepts together was exactly what David Auerbach accomplished. After returning from a two-year fellowship in China's Hunan province, he and several of his MIT classmates put their heads together to solve a horrifying problem that he encountered. He found that vast rural stretches of the Chinese provinces had no adequate sanitation. Pit latrines that spread disease and made life miserable were more the norm than he realized.

Today, 2.6 billion people on the earth have no access to adequate sanitation. The resulting disease and pollution cause more than 1.7 million deaths and the loss of some US$84 billion in worker time each year. A particularly poor area of the world is Kenya, where some 8 million people lack any access to adequate sanitation.

The key was to turn this issue into something more than a charity. Charities come and go with the interest level of donors. If Auerbach and his team could figure out how to make it into a business, then the potential for vastly improving the lives of millions might be possible. With that, he and his classmates put together a business plan and won the 2009 business plan competition at MIT. Armed with their prize money and US$20,000 from the Eleos Foundation (a nonprofit that makes venture capital investments in social businesses), they set off to start a company in Kenya.

Today that company is Sanergy (http://saner.gy). They build prefab concrete toilets and sell them to local entrepreneurs for US$500. Those entrepreneurs charge "customers" roughly 5 cents per use. The units are well stocked with toilet paper, soap, and water. The waste is collected by the company at the end of each day and is processed and sold as fertilizer. By July 2012, they had 30 franchises and 50 toilets serving more than 2000 residents. The team is now looking at pitching the toilets to landlords as a means for them to charge a bit more in rent but provide better sanitation to their tenants.

There are no easy answers in addressing some of these almost intractable problems, but a consistent theme of success is turning a "good" into a business that thrives for local residents.

....

SOURCES: "Getting to Sanitation for All: Always Be Closing," (July 9, 2012), (http://saner.gy/2012/07/09/getting-to-sanitation-for-all-always-be-closing); P. Clark, "Innovator Cleaning Up," *BusinessWeek* (October 17, 2011).

ENCOURAGING ETHICAL BEHAVIOR

Following Carroll's work, if business people do not act ethically, government will be forced to pass laws regulating their actions—and usually increasing their costs. For self-interest, if for no other reason, managers should be more ethical in their decision making. One way to do that is by developing codes of ethics. Another is by providing guidelines for ethical behavior.

Codes of Ethics

A **code of ethics** specifies how an organization expects its employees to behave while on the job. Developing a code of ethics can be a useful way to promote ethical behavior, especially for people who are operating at Kohlberg's conventional level of moral development. Such codes are currently being used by more than half of U.S. business corporations. A code of ethics (1) clarifies company expectations of employee conduct in various situations and (2) makes clear that the company expects its people to recognize the ethical dimensions in decisions and actions.[46]

Various studies indicate that an increasing number of companies are developing codes of ethics and implementing ethics training workshops and seminars. However, research also indicates that when faced with a question of ethics, managers tend to ignore codes of ethics and try to solve dilemmas on their own.[47] To combat this tendency, the management of a company that wants to improve its employees' ethical behavior should not only develop a comprehensive code of ethics but also communicate the code in its training programs, in its performance appraisal system, policies and procedures, and through its own actions.[48] It may even include key values in its values and mission statements. According to a 2011 survey conducted by the National Business Ethics Survey (NBES), the strength of ethics cultures declined dramatically in 2011 with 42% of respondents finding that their corporate ethics culture was either weak or weak leaning. This was an increase from the 2009 survey that found only 35% in the same situation. Specific findings of interest were:

- 90% of employees who observed corporate misconduct rated their cultures as Weak.
- 34% of employees felt that their supervisor did not display ethical behavior.
- 34% said their management watches them more closely.[49]

In addition, U.S. corporations have attempted to support **whistle-blowers**, those employees who report illegal or unethical behavior on the part of others. The U.S. False Claims Act gives whistle-blowers 15% to 30% of any damages recovered in cases where the government is defrauded. Even though the Sarbanes–Oxley Act forbids firms from retaliating against anyone reporting wrongdoing, 22% of employees who reported misconduct in one study said they experienced retaliation, which was up from 15% in 2009 and 12% in 2007.[50]

Corporations appear to benefit from well-conceived and implemented ethics programs. For example, companies with strong ethical cultures and enforced codes of conduct have fewer unethical choices available to employees—thus fewer temptations.[51] A study by the Open Compliance and Ethics Group found that no company with an ethics program in place for 10 years or more experienced "reputational damage" in the last five years.[52] Some of the companies identified in surveys as having strong moral cultures are Canon, Hewlett-Packard, Johnson & Johnson, Levi Strauss, Medtronic, Motorola, Newman's Own, Patagonia, S. C. Johnson, Shorebank, Smucker, and Sony.[53]

A corporation's management should consider establishing and enforcing a code of ethical behavior not only for itself, but also for those companies with which it does business—especially if it outsources its manufacturing to a company in another country. Apple is one of the most profitable and powerful companies in the world. Much of their product manufacturing is outsourced to Chinese factories that have a reputation for harsh working conditions.

Apple has a supplier code of conduct and a relatively vigorous auditing effort. Despite those efforts, *The New York Times* reported in 2012 that some of the suppliers audited by Apple had violated at least one aspect of the code every year since 2007. Critics have pointed out that for a variety of reasons Apple is relatively lax in its enforcement of the code. *The New York Times* reported that Apple conducted 312 audits over a three-year time period finding more than half the companies in violation and 70 core violations. Yet, despite all the evidence, Apple has terminated only 15 contracts over the past 5 years.[54]

Recent surveys of over one hundred companies in the Global 2000 uncovered that 64% have some code of conduct that regulates supplier conduct, but only 40% require suppliers to actually take any action with respect to the code, such as disseminating it to employees, offering training, certifying compliance, or even reading or acknowledging receipt of the code.[55]

It is important to note that having a code of ethics for suppliers does not prevent harm to a corporation's reputation if one of its offshore suppliers is able to conceal abuses. Numerous Chinese factories, for example, keep double sets of books to fool auditors and distribute scripts for employees to recite if they are questioned. Consultants have found new business helping Chinese companies evade audits.[56]

Guidelines for Ethical Behavior

Ethics is defined as the consensually accepted standards of behavior for an occupation, a trade, or a profession. **Morality**, in contrast, constitutes one's rules of personal behavior based on religious or philosophical grounds. **Law** refers to formal codes that permit or forbid certain behaviors and may or may not enforce ethics or morality.[57] Given these definitions, how do we arrive at a comprehensive statement of ethics to use in making decisions in a specific occupation, trade, or profession? A starting point for such a code of ethics is to consider the three basic approaches to ethical behavior:[58]

1. **Utilitarian approach:** The **utilitarian approach** proposes that actions and plans should be judged by their consequences. People should therefore behave in a way that will produce the greatest benefit to society and produce the least harm or the lowest cost. A problem with this approach is the difficulty in recognizing all the benefits and costs of any particular decision. Research reveals that only the stakeholders who have the most *power* (ability to affect the company), *legitimacy* (legal or moral claim on company resources), and *urgency* (demand for immediate attention) are given priority by CEOs.[59] It is therefore likely that only the most obvious stakeholders will be considered, while others are ignored.

2. **Individual rights approach:** The **individual rights approach** proposes that human beings have certain fundamental rights that should be respected in all decisions. A particular decision or behavior should be avoided if it interferes with the rights of others. A problem with this approach is in defining "fundamental rights." The U.S. Constitution includes a Bill of Rights that may or may not be accepted throughout the world. The approach can also encourage selfish behavior when a person defines a personal need or want as a "right."

3. **Justice approach:** The **justice approach** proposes that decision makers be equitable, fair, and impartial in the distribution of costs and benefits to individuals and groups. It follows the principles of *distributive justice* (people who are similar on relevant dimensions such as job seniority should be treated in the same way) and *fairness* (liberty should be equal for all persons). The justice approach can also include the concepts of *retributive justice* (punishment should be proportional to the offense) and *compensatory justice* (wrongs should be compensated in proportion to the offense). Affirmative action issues such as reverse discrimination are examples of conflicts between distributive and compensatory justice.

Cavanagh proposes that we solve ethical problems by asking the following three questions regarding an act or a decision:

1. **Utility:** Does it optimize the satisfactions of all stakeholders?
2. **Rights:** Does it respect the rights of the individuals involved?
3. **Justice:** Is it consistent with the canons of justice?[60]

For example, what if a company allows one vice-president to fly first class to Europe, but not others? Using the utility criterion, this action increases the company's costs and thus does not optimize benefits for shareholders or customers. Using the rights approach, the VP allowed to fly first class might argue that he or she is owed this type of reward for the extra strain that an international trip puts on personal relationships or work performance. Using the justice criterion, unless everyone at the VP level is allowed to fly first class, the privilege is not justifiable.

Another approach to resolving ethical dilemmas is by applying the logic of the philosopher Immanuel Kant. Kant presents two principles (called **categorical imperatives**) to guide our actions:

1. A person's action is ethical only if that person is willing for that same action to be taken by everyone who is in a similar situation. This is the same as the Golden Rule: Treat others as you would like them to treat you. For example, staying at upscale hotels while on the trip to Europe is only ethical if the same opportunity is available to others in the company at the same level.
2. A person should never treat another human being simply as a means but always as an end. This means that an action is morally wrong for a person if that person uses others merely as a means for advancing his or her own interests. To be moral, the act should not restrict other people's actions so they are disadvantaged in some way.[61]

End of Chapter SUMMARY

In his book *Defining Moments*, Joseph Badaracco states that most ethics problems deal with "right versus right" problems in which neither choice is wrong. These are what he calls "dirty hands problems" in which a person has to deal with very specific situations that are covered only vaguely in corporate credos or mission statements. For example, many mission statements endorse fairness but fail to define the term. At the personal level, *fairness* could mean playing by the rules of the game, following basic morality, treating everyone alike and not playing favorites, treating others as you would want to be treated, being sensitive to individual needs, providing equal opportunity for everyone, or creating a level playing field for the disadvantaged. According to Badaracco, codes of ethics are not always helpful because they tend to emphasize problems of misconduct and wrongdoing, not a choice between two acceptable alternatives, such as keeping an inefficient plant operating for the good of the community or closing the plant and relocating to a more efficient location to lower costs.[62]

This chapter provides a framework for evaluating the social responsibilities of a business. Following Carroll, it proposes that a manager should consider not only the economic and legal responsibilities of the business but also its ethical and discretionary responsibilities. It also provides a method for making ethical choices, whether they are right versus right or some combination of right and wrong. It is important to consider Cavanaugh's questions about using the utilitarian, individual rights, and justice approaches, plus Kant's categorical imperatives, when making a strategic decision. In general, a corporation should try to move from Kohlberg's conventional development to a principled level of ethical development. If nothing else, the frameworks should contribute to well-reasoned strategic decisions that a person can defend when interviewed by hostile media or questioned in a court room.

MyManagementLab®

Go to **mymanagementlab.com** to complete the problems marked with this icon .

KEY TERMS

categorical imperatives (p. 118)
code of ethics (p. 116)
ethics (p. 117)
individual rights approach (p. 117)
justice approach (p. 117)

law (p. 117)
levels of moral development (p. 115)
morality (p. 117)
moral relativism (p. 114)
social responsibility (p. 104)

stakeholder analysis (p. 109)
stakeholders (p. 108)
utilitarian approach (p. 117)
whistle-blowers (p. 116)

MyManagementLab®

Go to **mymanagmentlab.com** for the following Assisted-graded writing questions:

3-1. How has moral relativism led to criminal activities by some employees in companies?

3-2. How does a company ensure that its code of ethics is integrated into the daily decision-making process of the company and is not just a symbolic trophy or plaque hanging on the wall?

DISCUSSION QUESTIONS

3-3. What is hypercompetition? Is the outcome positive for corporations in the IT industry?

3-4. What is your opinion of Apple having a code of conduct for its suppliers? What would Milton Friedman say? Contrast his view with Archie Carroll's view.

3-5. Does a company have to act selflessly to be considered socially responsible? For example, when building a new plant, a corporation voluntarily invested in additional equipment that enabled it to reduce its pollution emissions beyond any current laws. Knowing that it would be very expensive for its competitors to do the same, the firm lobbied the government to make pollution regulations more restrictive on the entire industry. Is this company socially responsible? Were its managers acting ethically?

3-6. What is stakeholder analysis? Explain the steps taken to achieve the identification and evaluation.

3-7. Given that people rarely use a company's code of ethics to guide their decision making, what good are the codes?

STRATEGIC PRACTICE EXERCISE

It was certainly not the first time it had happened to the new social gaming company, but it was more of a worry this time. It was taking a lot longer to release the first version of the game being designed than had ever been anticipated. The firm had raised money four times already, but this round was more of an issue. The company probably needed an additional US$25 million, and more and more it was looking like the sales projections were far too optimistic.

The original idea for the game had morphed quite a bit and now was slated to use Facebook as its platform. The problem had occurred during the almost three years it had taken to bring the product to market. Two other games had been released that had taken the wind out of the new offering.

Knowing this, the company had quietly begun work on a new gaming platform. The problem was that it would take another 18 months before it has any marketability, and investors were unlikely to provide the type of valuations the company needed to keep afloat. The key to raising the funds needed was to keep talking about the existing game and getting it released into the market.

Private company valuations and market potential is difficult under the best circumstances. They are not required to provide audited financials, the risk of failure is quite high, and sales projections are at best a guess. They do not exist in the marketplace, so there is no history from which to judge their performance. In addition, competitor reactions to their entry is unknown.

All of this is hard enough for investors, let alone the issue of management trying to hide known issues. The management of the business is convinced that they can be a big player in the market with their newer product, however to get there they need the finances that may only be available if they act as if the product closer to release will be THE ONE. What should the manager do? Why do you believe so? What are the ethical implications of your decision?

NOTES

1. M. Friedman, "The Social Responsibility of Business Is to Increase Its Profits," *The New York Times Magazine* (September 13, 1970), pp. 30, 126–127; M. Friedman, *Capitalism and Freedom* (Chicago: University of Chicago Press, 1963), p. 133.

2. W. J. Byron, *Old Ethical Principles for the New Corporate Culture*, presentation to the College of Business, Iowa State University, Ames, Iowa (March 31, 2003).

3. A. B. Carroll, "A Three-Dimensional Conceptual Model of Corporate Performance," *Academy of Management Review* (October 1979), pp. 497–505. This model of business responsibilities was reaffirmed in A. B. Carroll, "Managing Ethically with Global Stakeholders: A Present and Future Challenge," *Academy of Management Executive* (May 2004), pp. 114–120.

4. Carroll refers to discretionary responsibilities as philanthropic responsibilities in A. B. Carroll, "The Pyramid of Corporate Social Responsibility: Toward the Moral Management of Organizational Stakeholders," *Business Horizons* (July–August 1991), pp. 39–48.

5. M. S. Baucus and D. A. Baucus, "Paying the Piper: An Empirical Examination of Longer-Term Financial Consequences of Illegal Corporate Behavior," *Academy of Management Journal* (February 1997), pp. 129–151.

6. J. Oleck, "Pink Slips with a Silver Lining," *BusinessWeek* (June 4, 2001), p. 14.

7. S. M. J. Bonini, L. T. Mendonca, and J. M. Oppenheim, "When Social Issues Become Strategic," *McKinsey Quarterly* (2006, Number 2), pp. 20–31.

8. "The McKinsey Global Survey of Business Executives: Business and Society," *McKinsey Quarterly*, Web edition (March 31, 2006).

9. "Corporate Social Responsibility Now a Staple at Davos," *CNBC* (January 22, 2012), (www.cnbc.com/id/45856248/corporate_social_responsibility_now_a_staple_at_Davos).

10. A. McWilliams and D. Siegel, "Corporate Social Responsibility and Financial Performance: Correlation or Misspecification?" *Strategic Management Journal* (May 2000), pp. 603–609; P. Rechner and K. Roth, "Social Responsibility and Financial Performance: A Structural Equation Methodology," *International Journal of Management* (December 1990), pp. 382–391; K. E. Aupperle, A. B. Carroll, and J. D. Hatfield, "An Empirical Examination of the Relationship Between Corporate Social Responsibility and Profitability," *Academy of Management Journal* (June 1985), p. 459.

11. M. M. Arthur, "Share Price Reactions to Work-Family Initiatives: An Institutional Perspective," *Academy of Management Journal* (April 2003), pp. 497–505; S. A. Waddock and S. B. Graves, "The Corporate Social Performance—Financial Performance Link," *Strategic Management Journal* (April 1997), pp. 303–319; M. V. Russo and P. A. Fouts, "Resource Based Perspective on Corporate Environmental Performance and Profitability" *Academy of Management Journal* (July 1997), pp. 534–559; H. Meyer, "The Greening of Corporate America," *Journal of Business Strategy* (January/February 2000), pp. 38–43.

12. J. D. Margolis and J. P. Walsh, "Misery Loves Companies: Re-thinking Social Initiatives by Business," *Administrative Science Quarterly* (June 2003), pp. 268–305.

13. M. F. L. Orlitzky, F. L. Schmidt, and S. L. Rynes, "Corporate Social and Financial Performance: A Meta Analysis," *Organization Studies* (Vol. 24, 2003), pp. 403–441.

14. M. Porter and M. R. Kramer, "The Competitive Advantage of Corporate Philanthropy," *Harvard Business Review* (December 2002), p. 59.

15. P. S. Adler and S. W. Kwon, "Social Capital: Prospects for a New Concept," *Academy of Management Journal* (January 2002), pp. 17–40. Also called "moral capital" in P. C. Godfrey, "The Relationship Between Corporate Philanthropy and Shareholder Wealth: A Risk Management Perspective," *Academy of Management Review* (October 2005), pp. 777–799.

16. L. Gard, "We're Good Guys, Buy from Us," *BusinessWeek* (November 22, 2004), pp. 72–74.

17. G. Thornton, "Corporate Social Responsibility – A Necessity Not a Choice for Privately Held Businesses," (2008), (www.internationalbusinessreport.com/2008/corporate-social-responsibility.asp).

18. C. J. Fombrun, "Corporate Reputation as an Economic Asset," in M. A. Hitt, E. R. Freeman, and J. S. Harrison (Eds.), *The Blackwell Handbook of Strategic Management* (Oxford: Blackwell Publishers, 2001), pp. 289–310.

19. S. A. Muirhead, C. J. Bennett, R. E. Berenbeim, A. Kao, and D. J. Vidal, *Corporate Citizenship in the New Century* (New York: The Conference Board, 2002), p. 6.

20. *2002 Sustainability Survey Report*, PriceWaterhouseCoopers, reported in "Corporate America's Social Conscience," Special Advertising Section, *Fortune* (May 26, 2003), pp. 149–157.

21. C. L. Harman and E. R. Stafford, "Green Alliances: Building New Business with Environmental Groups" *Long Range Planning* (April 1997), pp. 184–196.

22. D. B. Turner and D. W. Greening, "Corporate Social Performance and Organizational Attractiveness to Prospective Employees," *Academy of Management Journal* (July 1997), pp. 658–672; S. Preece, C. Fleisher, and J. Toccacelli, "Building a Reputation Along the Value Chain at Levi Strauss," *Long Range Planning* (December 1995), pp. 88–98; J. B. Barney and M. H. Hansen, "Trustworthiness as a Source of Competitive Advantage," *Strategic Management Journal* (Special Winter Issue, 1994), pp. 175–190: R. V. Aguilera, D. E. Rupp, C. A. Williams, and J. Ganapathi, "Putting the S Back in Corporate Social Responsibility: A Multilevel Theory of Social Change in Organizations," *Academy of Management Review* (July 2007), pp. 836–863; S. Bonini and S. Chenevert, "The State of Corporate Philanthropy: A McKinsey Global Survey," *McKinsey Quarterly*, Web edition (March 1, 2008); P. Kotler and N. Lee (Eds.), *Corporate Social Responsibility: Doing the Most Good for Your Company and Your Cause* (Hoboken, NJ: Wiley, 2005).

23. "Numbers: Do-Good Investments Are Holding Up Better," *BusinessWeek* (July 14 and 21, 2008), p. 15.

24. A. Crane and D. Matten, *Business Ethics: A European Perspective* (Oxford: Oxford University Press, 2004), p. 22.

25. R. E. Freeman and D. R. Gilbert, *Corporate Strategy and the Search for Ethics* (Upper Saddle River, NJ: Prentice Hall, 1988), p. 6.

26. "CSR Branding Survey 2010," (www.slideshare.net/bmglobalnews/csr-branding-survey-2010-final).

27. M. Boesler, "Study: 20% of Companies Lie on Earnings Reports, Top Reason Is to Boost Stock Price," *Business Insider* (July 25, 2012), (www.businessinsider.com/study-20-of-companies-lie-earnings-stock-prices-2012-7).

28. "BP expert defends controversial cost saving decision before blast," ProjectNola.com (July 22, 2010), (http://projectnola .com/the-news/news/42-fox-8/98578-bp-expert-defends-controversial-cost-saving-decision-before-blast).

29. W. E. Stead and J. G. Stead, *Sustainable Strategic Management* (Armonk, NY: M. E. Sharpe, 2004), p. 41.

30. B. Barrow, "Chick-fil-A Sandwiches at Center of Latest Political Storm," *The Charlotte Observer* (July 27, 2012), pg. A1.

31. M. Oxley and P. Harned, "2011 National Business Ethics Survey," (2012), pp. 1–62.

32. Ibid.

33. "Dates from Hell," *The Economist* (July 22, 2006), pp. 59–60.

34. B. O'Connell, "Mortgage Fraud Cases Climbing," NuWire Investor (2011), www.nuwireinvestor.com/articles/mortgage-fraud-cases-climbing-57871.aspx.

35. D. L. McCabe, K. D. Butterfield, and L. K. Trevino, "Academic Dishonesty in Graduate Business Programs: Prevalence, Causes, and Proposed Action," *Academy of Management Learning & Education* (September 2006), pp. 294–305.

36. L. Lavelle, "The GMAT Cheat Sheet," *BusinessWeek* (July 14 and 21, 2008), p. 34.

37. S. Li, S. H. Park, and S. Li, "The Great Leap Forward: The Transition from Relation-Based Governance to Rule-Based Governance," *Organizational Dynamics* (Vol. 33, No. 1, 2004), pp. 63–78; M. Davids, "Global Standards, Local Problems," *Journal of Business Strategy* (January/February 1999), pp. 38–43; "The Opacity Index," *The Economist* (September 18, 2004), p. 106.

38. K. Kumar, "Ethical Orientation of Future American Executives: What the Value Profiles of Business School Students Portend," *SAM Advanced Management Journal* (Autumn 1995), pp. 32–36, 47; M. Gable and P. Arlow, "A Comparative Examination of the Value Orientations of British and American Executives," *International Journal of Management* (September 1986), pp. 97–106; W. D. Guth and R. Tagiuri, "Personal Values and Corporate Strategy," *Harvard Business Review* (September–October 1965), pp. 126–127; G. W. England, "Managers and Their Value Systems: A Five Country Comparative Study," *Columbia Journal of World Business* (Summer 1978), p. 35.

39. J. F. Veiga, T. D. Golden, and K. Dechant, "Why Managers Bend Company Rules," *Academy of Management Executive* (May 2004), pp. 84–91.

40. H. Collingwood, "The Earnings Game," *Harvard Business Review* (June 2001), pp. 65–74; J. Fox, "Can We Trust Them Now?" *Fortune* (March 3, 2003), pp. 97–99.

41. R. E. Freeman and D. R. Gilbert, Jr., *Corporate Strategy and the Search for Ethics* (Englewood Cliffs, NJ: Prentice Hall, 1988), pp. 24–41.

42. L. K. Trevino, "Ethical Decision Making in Organizations: A Person-Situation Interactionist Model," *Academy of Management Review* (July 1986), pp. 601–617.

43. L. Kohlberg, "Moral Stage and Moralization: The Cognitive-Development Approach," in T. Lickona (Ed.), *Moral Development and Behavior* (New York: Holt, Rinehart & Winston, 1976).

44. L. K. Trevino, "Ethical Decision Making in Organizations: A Person-Situation Interactionist Model," *Academy of Management Review* (July 1986), p. 606; L. K. Trevino, G. R. Weaver, and S. J. Reynolds, "Behavioral Ethics in Organizations: A Review," *Journal of Management* (December 2006), pp. 951–990.

45. J. K. Gephart, D. A. Harrison, and L. K. Trevino, "The Who, When, and Where of Unethical Choices: Meta-Analytic Answers to Fundamental Ethics Questions." Paper presented to the *Academy of Management* annual meeting, Philadelphia, PA (2007).

46. J. Keogh (Ed.), *Corporate Ethics: A Prime Business Asset* (New York: The Business Roundtable, 1988), p. 5.

47. G. F. Kohut, and S. E. Corriher, "The Relationship of Age, Gender, Experience and Awareness of Written Ethics Policies to Business Decision Making," *SAM Advanced Management Journal* (Winter 1994), pp. 32–39; J. C. Lere and B. R. Gaumitz, "The Impact of Codes of Ethics on Decision Making: Some Insights from Information Economics," *Journal of Business Ethics* (Vol. 48, 2003), pp. 365–379.

48. W. I. Sauser, "Business Ethics: Back to Basics," *Management in Practice* (2005, No. 2), pp. 2–3; J. M. Stevens, H. K. Steensma, D. A. Harrison, and P. L. Cochran, "Symbolic or Substantive Document? The Influence of Ethics Codes on Financial Executives' Decisions," *Strategic Management Journal* (February 2005), pp. 181–195.

49. M. Oxley and P. Harned, "2011 National Business Ethics Survey," (2012), pp. 1–62.

50. Ibid.

51. J. K. Gephart, D. A. Harrison, and L. K. Trevino, "The Who, When, and Where of Unethical Choices: Meta-Analytic Answers to Fundamental Ethics Questions." Paper presented to the *Academy of Management* annual meeting, Philadelphia, PA (2007).

52. "A 'How Am I Doing?' Guide for Ethics Czars," *Business Ethics* (Fall 2005), p. 11.

53. S. P. Feldman, "Moral Business Cultures: The Keys to Creating and Maintaining Them," *Organizational Dynamics* (Vol. 36, No. 2, 2007), pp. 156–170. Also see the "World's Most Ethical Companies," published annually by Ethisphere at http://ethisphere.com.

54. "In China, Human Costs Are Built into an iPad," *The New York Times* (January 25, 2012), (www.nytimes.com/2012/01/26/business/ieconomy-apples-ipad-and-the-human-costs-for-workers-in-china.html).

55. M. Levin, "Building an Ethical Supply Chain," *Sarbanes-Oxley Compliance Journal* (April 3, 2008).

56. A. Bernstein, S. Holmes, and X. Ji, "Secrets, Lies, and Sweatshops," *BusinessWeek* (November 27, 2006), pp. 50–58.

57. T. J. Von der Embse, and R. A. Wagley, "Managerial Ethics: Hard Decisions on Soft Criteria," *SAM Advanced Management Journal* (Winter 1988), p. 6.

58. G. F. Cavanagh, *American Business Values*, 3rd ed. (Upper Saddle River, NJ: Prentice Hall, 1990), pp. 186–199.

59. B. R. Agle, R. K. Mitchell, and J. A. Sonnenfeld, "Who Matters Most to CEOs? An Investigation of Stakeholder Attributes and Salience, Corporate Performance, and CEO Values," *Academy of Management Journal* (October 1999), pp. 507–525.

60. G. F. Cavanagh, *American Business Values*, 3rd ed. (Upper Saddle River, NJ: Prentice Hall, 1990), pp. 195–196.

61. I. Kant, "The Foundations of the Metaphysic of Morals," in *Ethical Theory: Classical and Contemporary Readings*, 2nd ed., by L. P. Pojman (Belmont, CA: Wadsworth Publishing, 1995), pp. 255–279.

62. J. L. Badaracco Jr., *Defining Moments* (Boston: Harvard Business School Press, 1997).

PART 2

Scanning the
Environment

CHAPTER 4

environmental scanning and Industry Analysis

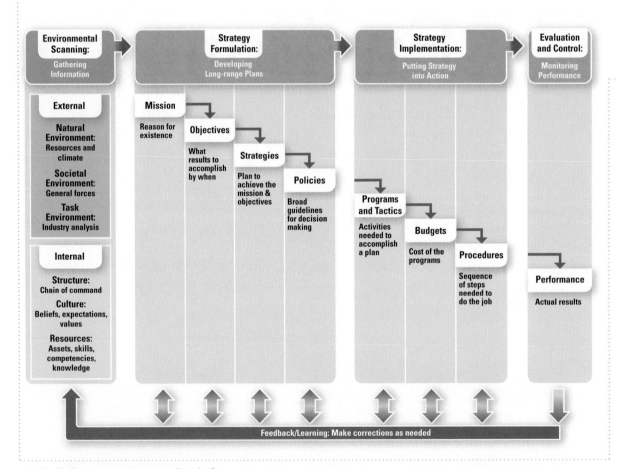

Environmental Scanning:	Strategy Formulation:	Strategy Implementation:	Evaluation and Control:
Gathering Information	Developing Long-range Plans	Putting Strategy into Action	Monitoring Performance

External

Natural Environment: Resources and climate

Societal Environment: General forces

Task Environment: Industry analysis

Internal

Structure: Chain of command

Culture: Beliefs, expectations, values

Resources: Assets, skills, competencies, knowledge

Mission
Reason for existence

Objectives
What results to accomplish by when

Strategies
Plan to achieve the mission & objectives

Policies
Broad guidelines for decision making

Programs and Tactics
Activities needed to accomplish a plan

Budgets
Cost of the programs

Procedures
Sequence of steps needed to do the job

Performance
Actual results

Feedback/Learning: Make corrections as needed

MyManagementLab®
⭐ Improve Your Grade!

Learning Objectives

After reading this chapter, you should be able to:

- Recognize aspects of an organization's environment that can influence its long-term decisions
- Identify the aspects of an organization's environment that are most strategically important
- Conduct an industry analysis to understand the competitive forces that influence the intensity of rivalry within an industry
- Understand how industry maturity affects industry competitive forces
- Categorize international industries based on their pressures for coordination and local responsiveness

- Construct strategic group maps to assess the competitive positions of firms in an industry
- Identify key success factors and develop an industry matrix
- Use publicly available information to conduct competitive intelligence
- Know how to develop an industry scenario
- Be able to construct an EFAS Table that summarizes external environmental factors

No More Oil

Depending upon whom you listen to, the world will either run out of oil within 50 years or there will be oil for much longer because of new oil extraction techniques and undiscovered reserves. Both approaches suggest significant price increases to keep using oil as we do; however, the view you take for your business is likely to cause significantly different decisions.

According to a study by HSBC (the second largest bank in the world), at our current worldwide consumption rate (that does not include growth), the world is likely to have little or no oil left in 50 years. Enormous oil price increases will no doubt cause a significant drop in consumption and the associated extension of oil's availability. However, a change away from oil as a primary input to business will impact every economic enterprise on the earth. These changes are generally being ignored by the vast majority of businesses, and yet it's one area where proper planning can make a difference.

On the other side of this debate is an argument that there are many means with which to attain energy in a useable form. This includes oil sands, deep-water drilling, new oil extraction techniques like horizontal drilling, fracking, synthetic oils, and coal liquefaction to name a few. This supply/demand approach suggests that as price and demand rises, so will the means by which businesses satisfy those needs.

What might this mean for the economies of the world and the speed with which this event will arrive? What companies are working on alternative approaches to the use of oil? It is incumbent upon business leaders to think about the future and prepare their organizations for changes in the environment—be it the natural environment, competitive environment, political environment, technological environment, or social environment.

SOURCES: J. C. Rudolf, "Less than 50 Years of Oil Left, HSBC Warns," *The New York Times* (March 30, 2011), (http://green.blogs.nytimes.com/2011/01/20/less-than-50-years-of-oil-left-hsbc-warns/); C. Krauss, "There Will Be Fuel," *The New York Times* (November 16, 2010), (http://www.nytimes.com/2010/11/17/business/energy-environment/17fuel.html).

A changing environment can help as well as hurt a company. Many pioneering companies have gone out of business because of their failure to adapt to environmental change or, even worse, because of their failure to create change. For example, Baldwin Locomotive, the major manufacturer of steam locomotives, was very slow in making the switch to diesel locomotives. General Electric and General Motors soon dominated the diesel locomotive business and Baldwin went out of business. The dominant manufacturers of vacuum tubes failed to make the change to transistors and consequently lost this market. Eastman Kodak, the pioneer and market leader of chemical-based film photography, has been in a long decline as it struggles to find its place in the post-film world. Failure to adapt is, however, only one side of the coin. The aforementioned oil example shows how a changing environment usually creates new opportunities at the same time it destroys old ones. The lesson is simple: To be successful over time, an organization needs to be in tune with its external environment. There must be a strategic fit between what the environment wants and what the corporation has to offer, as well as between what the corporation needs and what the environment can provide.

Current predictions are that the environment for all organizations will become even more uncertain with every passing year. What is **environmental uncertainty**? It is the *degree of complexity* plus the *degree of change* that exists in an organization's external environment. As more and more markets become global, the number of factors a company must consider in any decision increases in size and difficulty. With new technologies being discovered every year, markets change and products must change with them.

On the one hand, environmental uncertainty is a threat to strategic managers because it hampers their ability to develop long-range plans and to make strategic decisions to keep the corporation in equilibrium with its external environment. On the other hand, environmental uncertainty is an opportunity because it creates a new playing field in which creativity and innovation can play a major part in strategic decisions.

Environmental Scanning

Before managers can begin strategy formulation, they must understand the context of the environment in which it competes. It is virtually impossible for a company to design a strategy without a deep understanding of the external environment. Once management has framed the aspects of the environment that impact the business, they are in a position to determine the firm's competitive advantages. **Environmental scanning** is an overarching term encompassing the monitoring, evaluation, and dissemination of information relevant to the organizational development of strategy. A corporation uses this tool to avoid strategic surprise and to ensure its long-term health. Research has found a positive relationship between environmental scanning and profits.[1] A 2011 study by McKinsey & Company found that executives ranked Macrolevel trends as the most important input to be considered when developing corporate strategy.[2]

IDENTIFYING EXTERNAL ENVIRONMENTAL VARIABLES

In undertaking environmental scanning, strategic managers must first be aware of the many variables within a corporation's natural, societal, and task environments (see **Figure 1–3**). The **natural environment** includes physical resources, wildlife, and climate that are an inherent part of existence on Earth. These factors form an ecological system of interrelated life. The **societal environment** is mankind's social system that includes general forces that do not directly touch on the short-run activities of the organization, but that can influence its long-term decisions. These factors affect multiple industries and are as follows:

- **Economic forces** that regulate the exchange of materials, money, energy, and information.
- **Technological forces** that generate problem-solving inventions.
- **Political–legal forces** that allocate power and provide constraining and protecting laws and regulations.
- **Sociocultural forces** that regulate the values, mores, and customs of society.

The **task environment** includes those elements or groups that directly affect a corporation and, in turn, are affected by it. These are governments, local communities, suppliers, competitors, customers, creditors, employees/labor unions, special-interest groups, and trade associations. A corporation's task environment is typically focused on the industry within which the firm operates. **Industry analysis** (popularized by Michael Porter) refers to an in-depth examination of key factors within a corporation's task environment. The natural, societal, and task environments must be monitored to examine the strategic factors that have a strong impact on corporate success or failure. Significant changes in the natural environment tend to impact the societal environment of the business (resource availability and costs), and finally the task environment because it impacts the growth or decline of whole industries.

Scanning the Natural Environment

The natural environment includes physical resources, wildlife, and climate that are an inherent part of existence on Earth. Until the 20th century, the natural environment was generally perceived by business people to be a given—something to exploit, not conserve. It was viewed as a free resource, something to be taken or fought over, like arable land, diamond mines, deep water harbors, or fresh water. Once they were controlled by a person or entity, these resources were considered assets and thus valued as part of the general economic system—a resource to be bought, sold, or sometimes shared. Side effects, such as pollution, were considered to be *externalities*, costs not included in a business firm's accounting system, but felt by others. Eventually these externalities were identified by governments, which passed regulations to force business corporations to deal with the side effects of their activities.

The concept of sustainability argues that a firm's ability to continuously renew itself for long-term success and survival is dependent not only upon the greater economic and social system of which it is a part, but also upon the natural ecosystem in which the firm is embedded.[3] For more information on innovative approaches to this issue, see the **Sustainability Issue** feature.

A business must scan the natural environment for factors that might previously have been taken for granted, such as the availability of fresh water and clean air. Global warming means that aspects of the natural environment, such as sea level, weather, and climate, are becoming increasingly uncertain and difficult to predict. Management must therefore scan not only the natural environment for possible strategic factors, but also include in its strategic decision-making processes the impact of its activities upon the natural environment. In a world concerned with climate change, a company could measure and reduce its *carbon footprint*—the amount of greenhouse gases it is emitting into the air. Research reveals that scanning the market for environmental issues is positively related to firm performance because it helps management identify opportunities to fulfill future market demand based upon environmentally friendly products or processes.[4] See the Sustainability Issue feature to learn how the high-end car companies saw an opportunity in green cars.

SUSTAINABILITY issue

GREEN SUPERCARS

The move to greener cars has finally reached ultra-high-end car companies, including Porsche, Ferrari, and Bentley. The push to get car manufacturing companies to increase gas mileage and reduce emissions has come from a combination of regulations, purchasing patterns, and pressure from environmental groups. Although some form of hybrid vehicle technology has been around since the beginning of the automobile, the Toyota Prius, introduced to the Japanese market in 1997, quickly became the standard of economy in the industry.

Higher-end car makers have been making hybrid vehicles for some time, even though the price of these vehicles has kept their sales relatively modest. BMW offers the 750i, four-door sedan for US$101,000, while the equivalent Mercedes sedan (S400) goes for roughly US$92,000. Despite this, ultra-luxury car makers waited until the 2013 model year to release their hybrid models.

Ferrari announced the F70, which has two electric motors along with a 12-cylinder gasoline engine that cuts fuel consumption by more than 40%. The price tag is something to see, however. The vehicle will most likely be priced above US$850,000. Porsche already has hybrid versions of its Cayenne SUV and Panamera four-door cars, clocking in at US$70,000 and US$96,000, respectively. However, they are also gearing up for a new 918 Spyder sports coupe to be released for the 2014 model year, which will cost more than US$950,000. Even venerable Bentley is planning a plug-in hybrid version of its SUV that will come with a price tag of around US$250,000.

All of these vehicles require battery packs that weigh in excess of 1000 pounds and must be disposed of when the vehicle is no longer useful. The increase in sustainability from an environmental approach on one end triggers an environmental issue at the other end of the product's useful life. So what is the right answer for these companies? And what about the environment?

....
SOURCES: http://www.hybridcars.com/history/history-of-hybrid-vehicles.html; T. Ebhardt, "Supercar Makers Seek a Different Shade of Green," *BusinessWeek* (May 28, 2012), (www.businessweek.com).

Scanning the Societal Environment: STEEP Analysis

The number of possible strategic factors in the societal environment is very high. The number becomes enormous when we realize that, generally speaking, each country in the world can be represented by its own unique set of societal forces—some of which are very similar to those of neighboring countries and some of which are very different.

For example, even though Korea and China share Asia's Pacific Rim area with Thailand, Taiwan, and Hong Kong (sharing many similar cultural values), they have very different views about the role of business in society. It is generally believed in Korea and China (and to a lesser extent in Japan) that the role of business is primarily to contribute to national development. However, in Hong Kong, Taiwan, and Thailand (and to a lesser extent in the Philippines, Indonesia, Singapore, and Malaysia), the role of business is primarily to make profits for the shareholders.[5] Such differences may translate into different trade regulations and varying difficulty in the *repatriation of profits* (the transfer of profits from a foreign subsidiary to a corporation's headquarters) from one group of Pacific Rim countries to another.

STEEP Analysis: Monitoring Trends in the Societal and Natural Environments.   As shown in **Table 4–1,** large corporations categorize the natural and societal environments in any one geographic region into five areas and focus their scanning in each area on trends that have corporatewide relevance. For ease of remembering the approach, this scanning can be called **STEEP Analysis**, the scanning of Sociocultural, Technological, Economic, Ecological, and Political–legal environmental forces.[6] (It may also be called *PESTEL Analysis* for Political, Economic, Sociocultural, Technological, Ecological, and Legal forces.) Obviously, trends in any one area may be very important to firms in one industry but of lesser importance to firms in other industries.

Demographic trends are part of the *sociocultural* aspect of the societal environment. Even though the world's population has grown from 3.71 billion people in 1970 to 7.03 billion in

TABLE 4–1	Some Important Variables in the Societal Environment			
Sociocultural	**Technological**	**Economic**	**Ecological**	**Political–Legal**
Lifestyle changes	Total government spending for R&D	GDP trends	Environmental protection laws	Antitrust regulations
Career expectations	Total industry spending for R&D	Interest rates	Global warming impacts	Environmental protection laws
Consumer activism	Focus of technological efforts	Money supply	Non-governmental organizations	Global warming legislation
Rate of family formation	Patent protection	Inflation rates	Pollution impacts	Immigration laws
Growth rate of population	New products	Unemployment levels	Reuse	Tax laws
Age distribution of population	New developments in technology transfer from lab to marketplace	Wage/price controls	Triple bottom line	Special incentives
Regional shifts in population		Devaluation/ revaluation	Recycling	Foreign trade regulations
Life expectancies	Productivity improvements through automation	Energy alternatives		Attitudes toward foreign companies
Birthrates	Internet availability	Energy availability and cost		Laws on hiring and promotion
Pension plans	Telecommunication infrastructure	Disposable and discretionary income		Stability of government
Health care	Computer hacking activity	Currency markets		Outsourcing regulation
Level of education		Global financial system		Foreign "sweatshops"
Living wage				
Unionization				

2012 and is expected to increase to 8.72 billion by 2040, not all regions will grow equally. Most of the growth will be in the developing nations. It is predicted that the population of the developed nations will fall from 14% of the total world population in 2000 to only 10% in 2050.[7] Around 75% of the world will live in a city by 2050, compared to little more than half in 2008.[8] Developing nations will continue to have more young than old people, but it will be the reverse in the industrialized nations. For example, the demographic bulge in the U.S. population caused by the baby boom after WWII continues to affect market demand in many industries. This group of 77 million people now in their 50s and 60s is the largest age group in all developed countries, especially in Europe. (See **Table 4–2.**) Although the median age in the United States will rise from 35 in 2000 to 40 by 2050, it will increase from 40 to 47 during the same time period in Germany, and it will increase to up to 50 in Italy as soon as 2025.[9] By 2050, one in three Italians will be over 65, nearly double the number in 2005.[10] With its low birthrate, Japan's population is expected to fall from 127.6 million in 2004 to around 100 million by 2050.[11] China's stringent birth control policy is predicted to cause the ratio of workers to retirees to fall from 20 to 1 during the early 1980s to 2.5 to one by 2020.[12] Companies with an eye on the future can find many opportunities to offer products and services to the growing number of "woofies" (well-off old folks)—defined as people over 50 with money to spend.[13] These people are very likely to purchase recreational vehicles (RVs), take ocean cruises, and enjoy leisure sports, in addition to needing financial services and health care. Anticipating the needs of seniors for prescription drugs is one reason Walgreens opened 261 new stores in 2011![14]

To attract older customers, retailers will need to place seats in their larger stores so aging shoppers can rest. Washrooms will need to be more handicap-accessible. Signs will need to be larger. Restaurants will need to raise the level of lighting so people can read their menus. Home appliances will require simpler and larger controls. Automobiles will need larger door openings and more comfortable seats. Zimmer Holdings, an innovative manufacturer

TABLE 4–2		Generation	Born	Age in 2010	% of Total Adult Population
Current U.S. Generations	Current U.S. Generations	WWII / Silent Generation	1936–1945	65–74	16%
		Baby Boomers	1946–1964	46–64	34%
		Generation X	1965–1976	43–45	19%
		Millennials	1977–1992	18–33	30%

SOURCES: Developed from K. Zickuhr, "Generations 2010," Pew Research Center (December 16, 2010), (www.pewinternet.org/reports/2010/generations-2010.aspx).

of artificial joints, is looking forward to its market growing rapidly over the next 20 years. According to J. Raymond Elliot, Chair and CEO of Zimmer, "It's simple math. Our best years are still in front of us."[15]

Eight current sociocultural trends are transforming North America and the rest of the world:

1. **Increasing environmental awareness:** Recycling and conservation are becoming more than slogans. Busch Gardens, for example, has eliminated the use of disposable Styrofoam trays in favor of washing and reusing plastic trays.

2. **Growing health consciousness:** Concerns about personal health fuel the trend toward physical fitness and healthier living. There has been a general move across the planet to attack obesity. The U.S. Centers for Disease Control and Prevention cites that more than two-thirds of American adults and one-third of American youth are now obese or overweight. A number of states have enacted provisions to encourage grocery stores to open in so-called "food deserts" where the population has virtually no access to fresh foods.[16] In 2012, Chile decided to ban toys that are included in various fast-food meals aimed at children in order to increase the fight against childhood obesity.[17]

3. **Expanding seniors market:** As their numbers increase, people over age 55 will become an even more important market. Already some companies are segmenting the senior population into Young Matures, Older Matures, and the Elderly—each having a different set of attitudes and interests. Both mature segments, for example, are good markets for the health care and tourism industries; whereas, the elderly are the key market for long-term care facilities. The desire for companionship by people whose children are grown is causing the pet care industry to grow by more than 5% annually in the United States. In 2012, for example, 72.9 million households in the United States spent US$52 billion on their pets. That was up from just above US$41 billion just five years ago.[18]

4. **Impact of Millennials:** Born between 1977 and 1992 to the baby boomers and Generation Xers, this cohort is almost as large as the baby boom generation. In 1957, the peak year of the postwar boom, 4.3 million babies were born. In 1990, there were 4.2 million births in Millennials peak year. By 2000, they were overcrowding elementary and high schools and entering college in numbers not seen since the baby boomers. Now in its 20s and 30s, this cohort is expected to have a strong impact on future products and services.

5. **Declining mass market:** Niche markets are defining the marketers' environment. People want products and services that are adapted more to their personal needs. For example, Estée Lauder's "All Skin" and Maybelline's "Shades of You" lines of cosmetic products are specifically made for African-American women. "Mass customization"—the making and marketing of products tailored to a person's requirements is replacing the mass production and marketing of the same product in some markets. The past 10 years have seen a real fracturing of the chocolate market with the advent of craft chocolate making

and flavored chocolates. These products command significantly higher margins and have become a force in the retailing environment. By 2010, 43% of chocolate sales occurred in nontraditional channels.[19]

6. **Changing pace and location of life:** Instant communication via e-mail, cell phones, and overnight mail enhances efficiency, but it also puts more pressure on people. Merging the personal or tablet computer with the communication and entertainment industries through telephone lines, satellite dishes, and Internet connections increases consumers' choices and allows workers to telecommute from anywhere.

7. **Changing household composition:** Single-person households, especially those of single women with children, could soon become the most common household type in the United States. According to the U.S. Census, married-couple households slipped from nearly 80% in the 1950s to 48% of all households by 2010.[20] By 2007, for the first time in U.S. history, more than half the adult female population were single.[21] Those women are also having more children. As of 2012, 41% of all births in the United States were to unmarried women.[22] A typical family household is no longer the same as it was once portrayed in *Happy Days* in the 1970s or *The Cosby Show* in the 1980s.

8. **Increasing diversity of workforce and markets:** Between now and 2050, minorities will account for nearly 90% of population growth in the United States. Over time, group percentages of the total U.S. population are expected to change as follows: Non- Hispanic Whites—from 90% in 1950 to 74% in 1995 to 53% by 2050; Hispanic Whites—from 9% in 1995 to 22% in 2050; Blacks—from 13% in 1995 to 15% in 2050; Asians—from 4% in 1995 to 9% in 2050; American Indians—1%, with slight increase.[23]

Heavy immigration from developing to developed nations is increasing the number of minorities in all developed countries and forcing an acceptance of the value of diversity in races, religions, and lifestyles. For example, 24% of the Swiss population was born elsewhere.[24] Traditional minority groups are increasing their numbers in the workforce and are being identified as desirable target markets. Coca-Cola, Nestlé, and Pepsi have targeted African-American and Latino communities for the sale of bottled water after a study by the department of pediatrics at the Medical College of Wisconsin in 2011 found that African-American and Latino families were three times more likely to give their children bottled water as compared to white families.[25]

Changes in the *technological* part of the societal environment can also have a great impact on multiple industries. Improvements in computer microprocessors have not only led to the widespread use of personal computers but also to better automobile engine performance in terms of power and fuel economy through the use of microprocessors to monitor fuel injection. Digital technology allows movies and music to be available instantly over the Internet or through cable service, but it has also meant falling fortunes for movie rental shops such as Blockbuster and CD stores like Tower Records. Advances in nanotechnology are enabling companies to manufacture extremely small devices that are very energy efficient. Developing biotechnology, including gene manipulation techniques, is already providing new approaches to dealing with disease and agriculture. Researchers at George Washington University have identified a number of technological breakthroughs that are already having a significant impact on many industries:

- **Portable information devices and electronic networking:** Combining the computing power of the personal computer, the networking of the Internet, the images of television, and the convenience of the telephone, tablets and Smartphones will soon be used by a majority of the population of industrialized nations to make phone calls, stay connected in business and personal relationships, and transmit documents and other data. Homes, autos, and offices are rapidly being connected (via wires and wirelessly) into intelligent networks that interact with one another. This trend is being accelerated by the development of *cloud computing*, in which a person can access their data anywhere through a Web connection.[26] This is being dramatically improved by companies like Microsoft who are releasing *cloud* versions of their Office package available for rent.[27] The traditional stand-alone desktop computer will someday join the manual typewriter as a historical curiosity.

■ **Alternative energy sources:** The use of wind, geothermal, hydroelectric, solar, biomass, and other alternative energy sources should increase considerably. Over the past two decades, the cost of manufacturing and installing a photovoltaic solar-power system has decreased by 20% with every doubling of installed capacity.[28]

■ **Precision farming:** The computerized management of crops to suit variations in land characteristics will make farming more efficient and sustainable. Farm equipment dealers such as Case and John Deere now add this equipment to tractors for an additional US$6,000 or so. It enables farmers to reduce costs, increase yields, and decrease environmental impact. The old system of small, low-tech farming is becoming less viable as large corporate farms increase crop yields on limited farmland for a growing population.

■ **Virtual personal assistants:** Very smart computer programs that monitor e-mail, faxes, and phone calls will be able to take over routine tasks, such as writing a letter, retrieving a file, making a phone call, or screening requests. Acting like a secretary, a person's virtual assistant could substitute for a person at meetings or in dealing with routine actions.

■ **Genetically altered organisms:** A convergence of biotechnology and agriculture is creating a new field of life sciences. Plant seeds can be genetically modified to produce more needed vitamins or to be less attractive to pests and more able to survive. Animals (including people) could be similarly modified for desirable characteristics and to eliminate genetic disabilities and diseases.

■ **Smart, mobile robots:** Robot development has been limited by a lack of sensory devices and sophisticated artificial intelligence systems. Improvements in these areas mean that robots will be created to perform more sophisticated factory work, run errands, do household chores, and assist the disabled.[29]

Trends in the *economic* part of the societal environment can have an obvious impact on business activity. For example, an increase in interest rates means fewer sales of major home appliances. Why? A rising interest rate tends to be reflected in higher mortgage rates. Because higher mortgage rates increase the cost of buying a house, the demand for new and used houses tends to fall. Because most major home appliances are sold when people change houses, a reduction in house sales soon translates into a decline in sales of refrigerators, stoves, and dishwashers and reduced profits for everyone in the appliance industry. Changes in the price of oil have a similar impact upon multiple industries, from packaging and automobiles to hospitality and shipping.

The rapid economic development of Brazil, Russia, India, and China (often called the *BRIC* countries) is having a major impact on the rest of the world. By 2007, China had become the world's second-largest economy according to the World Bank. With India graduating more English-speaking scientists, engineers, and technicians than all other nations combined, it has become the primary location for the outsourcing of services, computer software, and telecommunications.[30] Eastern Europe has become a major manufacturing supplier to the European Union countries. According to the International Monetary Fund, emerging markets make up less than one-third of total world gross domestic product (GDP), but account for more than half of GDP growth.[31]

Trends in the *ecological* part of the environment have been accelerating at a pace that is difficult to stay up with. This element is focused upon the natural environment and its consideration/impacts upon the operation of a business. The effects of climate change on companies can be grouped into six categories of risks: regulatory, supply chain, product and technology, litigation, reputational, and physical.[32]

1. **Regulatory Risk:** Companies in much of the world are already subject to the *Kyoto Protocol,* which requires the developed countries (and thus the companies operating within them) to reduce carbon dioxide and other greenhouse gases by an average of 6% from 1990 levels by 2012. The European Union has an emissions trading program that allows companies that emit greenhouse gases beyond a certain point to buy additional allowances from other companies whose emissions are lower than that allowed. Companies can also earn credits toward their emissions by investing in emissions abatement projects outside their own firms. Although the United States withdrew from the Kyoto Protocol, various regional, state, and local government policies affect company activities in the United States. For example, seven Northeastern states, six Western states, and four Canadian provinces have adopted proposals to cap carbon emissions and establish carbon-trading programs.

2. **Supply Chain Risk:** Suppliers will be increasingly vulnerable to government regulations—leading to higher component and energy costs as they pass along increasing carbon-related costs to their customers. Global supply chains will be at risk from an increasing intensity of major storms and flooding. Higher sea levels resulting from the melting of polar ice will create problems for seaports. China, where much of the world's manufacturing is currently being outsourced, is becoming concerned with environmental degradation. Twelve Chinese ministries produced a report on global warming foreseeing a 5%–10% reduction in agricultural output by 2030; more droughts, floods, typhoons, and sandstorms; and a 40% increase in population threatened by plague.[33]

   The increasing scarcity of fossil-based fuel is already boosting transportation costs significantly. For example, Tesla Motors, the maker of an electric-powered sports car, transferred assembly of battery packs from Thailand to California because Thailand's low wages were more than offset by the costs of shipping thousand-pound battery packs across the Pacific Ocean.[34]

3. **Product and Technology Risk:** Environmental sustainability can be a prerequisite to profitable growth. Sixty percent of U.S. respondents to an Environics study stated that knowing a company is mindful of its impact on the environment and society makes them more likely to buy their products and services.[35] Carbon-friendly products using new technologies are becoming increasingly popular with consumers. Those automobile companies, for example, that were quick to introduce hybrid or alternative energy cars gained a competitive advantage.

4. **Litigation Risk:** Companies that generate significant carbon emissions face the threat of lawsuits similar to those in the tobacco, pharmaceutical, and building supplies (e.g., asbestos) industries. For example, oil and gas companies were sued for greenhouse gas emissions in the federal district court of Mississippi, based on the assertion that these companies contributed to the severity of Hurricane Katrina.

5. **Reputational Risk:** A company's impact on the environment can affect its overall reputation. The Carbon Trust, a consulting group, found that in some sectors the value of a company's brand could be at risk because of negative perceptions related to climate change. In contrast, a company with a good record of environmental sustainability may create a competitive advantage in terms of attracting and keeping loyal consumers, employees, and investors. For example, Wal-Mart's pursuit of environmental sustainability as a core business strategy has helped soften its negative reputation as a low-wage, low-benefit employer. By setting objectives for its retail stores of reducing greenhouse

gases by 20%, reducing solid waste by 25%, increasing truck fleet efficiency by 25%, and using 100% renewable energy, it is also forcing its suppliers to become more environmentally sustainable.[36] Tools have recently been developed to measure sustainability on a variety of factors. For example, the SAM (Sustainable Asset Management) Group of Zurich, Switzerland, has been assessing and documenting the sustainability performance of over 1000 corporations annually since 1999. SAM lists the top 15% of firms in its *Sustainability Yearbook* and classifies them into gold, silver, and bronze categories.[37]

BusinessWeek published its first list of the world's 100 most sustainable corporations January 29, 2007. The *Dow Jones Sustainability Indexes* and the *KLD Broad Market Social Index*, which evaluate companies on a range of environmental, social, and governance criteria are used for investment decisions.[38] Financial services firms, such as Goldman Sachs, Bank of America, JPMorgan Chase, and Citigroup have adopted guidelines for lending and asset management aimed at promoting clean-energy alternatives.[39]

6. **Physical Risk:** The direct risk posed by climate change includes the physical effects of droughts, floods, storms, and rising sea levels. Average Arctic temperatures have risen four to five degrees Fahrenheit (two to three degrees Celsius) in the past 50 years, leading to melting glaciers and sea levels rising one inch per decade.[40] Industries most likely to be affected are insurance, agriculture, fishing, forestry, real estate, and tourism. Physical risk can also affect other industries, such as oil and gas, through higher insurance premiums paid on facilities in vulnerable areas. Coca-Cola, for example, studies the linkages between climate change and water availability in terms of how this will affect the location of its new bottling plants. The warming of the Tibetan plateau has led to a thawing of the permafrost—thereby threatening the newly-completed railway line between China and Tibet.[41]

Trends in the *political–legal* part of the societal environment have a significant impact not only on the level of competition within an industry but also on which strategies might be successful.[42] For example, periods of strict enforcement of U.S. antitrust laws directly affect corporate growth strategy. As large companies find it more difficult to acquire another firm in the same or a related industry, they are typically driven to diversify into unrelated industries.[43] High levels of taxation and constraining labor laws in Western European countries stimulate companies to alter their competitive strategies or find better locations elsewhere. It is because Germany has some of the highest labor and tax costs in Europe that German companies have been forced to compete at the top end of the market with high-quality products or else move their manufacturing to lower-cost countries.[44] Government bureaucracy can create regulations that make it almost impossible for a business firm to operate profitably in some countries. The World Bank's 2012 report on red tape around the world found amazing examples of government bureaucracy, including: 1) A company in the Congo with a profit margin of 20% or more faces a tax bill of 340% of profits; 2) obtaining a construction permit in Russia requires 51 steps; 3) enforcing a contract through the courts takes 150 days in Singapore and 1,420 in India; 4) while winding up an insolvent firm, creditors in Japan can recover 92.7 cents on the dollar, those in Chad get nothing.[45]

The US$66 trillion global economy operates through a set of rules established by the World Trade Organization (WTO). Composed of 155 member nations and 29 observer nations, the WTO is a forum for governments to negotiate trade agreements and settle trade disputes. Originally founded in 1947 as the General Agreement on Tariffs and Trade (GATT), the WTO was created in 1995 to extend the ground rules for international commerce. The system's purpose is to encourage free trade among nations with the least undesirable side effects. Among its principles is trade without discrimination. This is exemplified by its *most-favored nation* clause, which states that a country cannot grant a trading partner lower customs duties without granting them to all other WTO member nations. Another principle is that of lowering trade barriers gradually though negotiation. It implements this principle through a series of rounds of trade negotiations. As a result of these negotiations, industrial countries' tariff rates on industrial goods had fallen steadily to less than 4% by the mid-1990s. The WTO is currently negotiating its latest round of negotiations, called the Doha Round. The WTO is also in favor of fair competition, predictability of member markets, and the encouragement of economic development and reform. As a result of many negotiations, developed nations have started to allow duty-free and quota-free imports from almost all products from the least-developed countries.[46]

International Societal Considerations.   Each country or group of countries in which a company operates presents a unique societal environment with a different set of sociocultural, technological, economic, ecological, and political-legal variables for the company to face. International societal environments vary so widely that a corporation's internal environment and strategic management process must be very flexible. Cultural trends in Germany, for example, have resulted in the inclusion of worker representatives in corporate strategic planning. Because Islamic law (*sharia*) forbids interest (*riba*), loans of capital in Islamic countries must be arranged on the basis of profit-sharing instead of interest rates.[47]

Differences in societal environments strongly affect the ways in which a **multinational corporation (MNC)**, a company with significant assets and activities in multiple countries, conducts its marketing, financial, manufacturing, and other functional activities. For example, Europe's lower labor productivity, due to a shorter work week and restrictions on the ability to lay off unproductive workers, forces European-based MNCs to expand operations in countries where labor is cheaper and productivity is higher.[48] Moving manufacturing to a lower-cost location, such as China, was a successful strategy during the 1990s, but a country's labor costs rise as it develops economically. For example, China required all firms in January 2008 to consult employees on material work-related issues, enabling the country to achieve its stated objective of having trade unions in all of China's non-state-owned enterprises. By September 2008, the All-China Federation of Trade Unions had signed with 80% of the largest foreign companies.[49] See the **Global Issues** feature to see how demand for SUVs has exploded in China.

To account for the many differences among societal environments from one country to another, consider **Table 4–3.** It includes a list of economic, technological, political–legal, and sociocultural variables for any particular country or region. For example, an important economic variable for any firm investing in a foreign country is currency convertibility. Without convertibility, a company cannot convert its money. Almost all nations allow for some method of currency conversion. As of 2012, only the Cuban national peso and the North Korean won are nonconvertible. In terms of sociocultural variables, many Asian cultures (especially China) are less concerned with a Western version of human rights than are European and North American cultures. Some Asians actually contend that U.S. companies are trying to impose Western human rights requirements on them in an attempt to make Asian products less competitive by raising their costs.[50]

Before planning its strategy for a particular international location, a company must scan that country's environment(s) for its similarities and differences with the company's home country. Focusing only on developed nations may cause a corporation to miss important market opportunities. Although those nations may not have developed to the point that they have significant demand for a broad spectrum of products, they may very likely be on the threshold of rapid growth in the demand for specific products. Using the concept of entering where the competition is not, this may be an opportunity for a company to enter this market—before competition is established. The key is to be able to identify the *trigger point* when demand for a particular product or service is ready to boom.

Creating a Scanning System.   Although the Internet has opened up a tremendous volume of information, scanning and making sense of that data is one of the important skills in an effective manager.

TABLE 4-3	Some Important Variables in *International* Societal Environments			
Sociocultural	**Technological**	**Economic**	**Ecological**	**Political–Legal**
Customs, norms, values	Regulations on technology transfer	Economic development	Non-governmental groups	Form of government
Language	Energy availability/cost	Per capita income	Passion for environmental causes	Political ideology
Demographics	Natural resource availability	Climate	Infrastructure to handle recycling	Tax laws
Life expectancies		GDP trends		Stability of government
Social institutions	Transportation network	Monetary and fiscal policies		Government attitude toward foreign companies
Status symbols	Skill level of workforce	Unemployment levels		
Lifestyle		Currency convertibility		Regulations on foreign ownership of assets
Religious beliefs	Patent-trademark protection	Wage levels		Strength of opposition groups
Attitudes toward foreigners		Nature of competition		Trade regulations
Literacy level	Internet availability	Membership in regional economic associations—e.g., EU, NAFTA, ASEAN		Protectionist sentiment
Human rights	Telecommunication infrastructure			Foreign policies
Environmentalism	Computer hacking technology			Terrorist activity
"Sweatshops"	New energy sources	Membership in World Trade Organization (WTO)		Legal system
Pension plans				Global warming laws
Health care		Outsourcing capability		Immigration laws
Slavery		Global financial system		

GLOBAL issue

SUVs POWER ON IN CHINA

U.S. and European automakers are looking to China for most of their growth potential in the next two decades. The Chinese middle class is expected to grow to between 600 million and 800 million consumers in the next 10 to 15 years. That is a market that is equivalent to the ENTIRE population of the Unites States AND every country in the European Union combined.

This growing middle class in China (it stood at less than 300 million in 2012) has spurred a huge demand for sport utility vehicles (SUVs). Ford, BMW, Mercedes-Benz, and Porsche are all selling SUVs at a significant clip. The total SUV market in China is predicted to grow by more than 100% in the next three years. BMW reported that they sold more than 20,000 SUVs in the first quarter of 2012. That was a 92% increase over the same quarter a year earlier.

Growing prosperity is leading to this push by consumers. *BusinessWeek* reported seeing the same trend in China that has been seen in the United States, with women in particular being drawn to the flexibility of the SUV. A Ford spokesperson said that "For Tiger Moms—and other moms—SUVs offer great appeal as the whole family can be transported safely and in style." The sharp increase in demand has drawn in the ultra-high-end car companies as well. Maserati and Lamborghini have both announced new SUVs for the Chinese market starting in 2013 and 2014, respectively.

BMW has approached the market with products that they sell around the world, including the BMW X5. This is an example of a global organization. On the other hand, Mercedes-Benz is producing a Chinese-built GLK SUV that is tailored to the market. This is an example of a multidomestic organization. Figuring out how to address global markets is a key strategic area for any management team.

....
SOURCES: "China's Soccer Moms Want SUVs, Too," *Bloomberg BusinessWeek* (May 7, 2012), (www.businessweek.com/articles/2012-05-03/chinas-soccer-moms-want-suvs-too); Eurostat news release, "EU27 population 502.5 million at 1 January 2011". Accessed 5/30/13, http://epp.eurostat.ec.europa.eu/cache/ITY_PUBLIC/3-28072011-AP/EN/3-28072011-AP-EN.PDF).

FIGURE 4–1
Scanning External
Environment

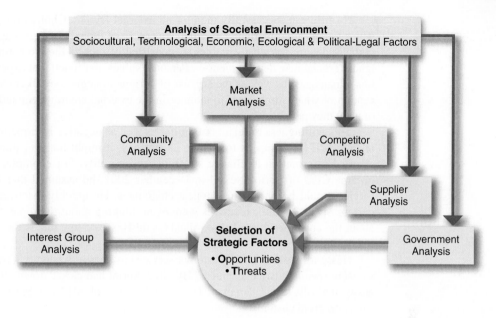

As shown in **Figure 4–1** caption:
Analysis of Societal Environment — Sociocultural, Technological, Economic, Ecological & Political-Legal Factors; Market Analysis; Community Analysis; Competitor Analysis; Supplier Analysis; Interest Group Analysis; Selection of Strategic Factors — Opportunities, Threats; Government Analysis

It is a daunting task for even a large corporation with many resources. To deal with this problem, in 2002 IBM created a tool called *WebFountain* to help the company analyze the vast amounts of environmental data available on the internet. WebFountain is an advanced information discovery system designed to help extract trends, detect patterns, and find relationships within vast amounts of raw data. For example, IBM sought to learn whether there was a trend toward more positive discussions about e-business. Within a week, the company had data that experts within the company used to replace their hunches with valid conclusions.

Scanning the Task Environment

As shown in **Figure 4–1**, a corporation's scanning of the environment includes analyses of all the relevant elements in the task environment. These analyses take the form of individual reports written by various people in different parts of the firm. At Procter & Gamble (P&G), for example, people from each of the brand management teams work with key people from the sales and market research departments to research and write a "competitive activity report" each quarter on each of the product categories in which P&G competes. People in purchasing also write similar reports concerning new developments in the industries that supply P&G. These and other reports are then summarized and transmitted up the corporate hierarchy for top management to use in strategic decision making. If a new development is reported regarding a particular product category, top management may then send memos asking people throughout the organization to watch for and report on developments in related product areas. The many reports resulting from these scanning efforts, when boiled down to their essentials, act as a detailed list of external strategic factors.

IDENTIFYING EXTERNAL STRATEGIC FACTORS

The origin of competitive advantage lies in the ability to identify and respond to environmental change well in advance of competition.[51] Although this seems obvious, why are some companies better able to adapt than others? One reason is because of differences in the ability of managers to recognize and understand external strategic issues and factors. Booz & Company found that companies that are most successful at avoiding surprises had a well-defined system that integrated planning, budgeting, and business reviews.[52]

No firm can successfully monitor all external factors. Choices must be made regarding which factors are important and which are not. Even though managers agree that strategic importance determines what variables are consistently tracked, they sometimes miss or choose to ignore crucial new developments.[53] Personal values and functional experiences of a corporation's managers, as well as the success of current strategies, are likely to bias both their perception of what is important to monitor in the external environment and their interpretations of what they perceive.[54]

This willingness to reject unfamiliar as well as negative information is called *strategic myopia*.[55] If a firm needs to change its strategy, it might not be gathering the appropriate external information to change strategies successfully. For example, when Daniel Hesse became CEO of Sprint Nextel in December 2007, he assumed that improving customer service would be one of his biggest challenges. He quickly discovered that none of the current Sprint Nextel executives were even thinking about the topic. "We weren't talking about the customer when I first joined," said Hesse. "Now this is the No. 1 priority of the company."[56]

Hesse insists that "great customer service costs less—when we were last in the industry, we were spending twice as much." By 2012, Sprint had closed down 29 call centers and was answering calls faster than ever. The second quarter of 2012 saw Sprint receiving the fewest calls ever from customers.[57]

Industry Analysis: Analyzing the Task Environment

An **industry** is a group of firms that produces a similar product or service, such as soft drinks or financial services. An examination of the important stakeholder groups, like suppliers and customers, in a particular corporation's task environment is a part of industry analysis.

PORTER'S APPROACH TO INDUSTRY ANALYSIS

Michael Porter, an authority on competitive strategy, contends that a corporation is most concerned with the intensity of competition within its industry. The level of this intensity is determined by basic competitive forces, as depicted in **Figure 4–2**. "The collective strength of these forces," he contends, "determines the ultimate profit potential in the industry, where profit potential is measured in terms of long-run return on invested capital."[58] In carefully scanning its industry, a corporation must assess the importance to its success of each of six forces: threat of new entrants, rivalry among existing firms, threat of substitute products or services, bargaining power of buyers, bargaining power of suppliers, and relative power of other stakeholders.[59] The stronger each of these forces are, the more limited companies are in their ability to raise prices and earn greater profits. Although Porter mentions only five forces, a sixth—other stakeholders—is added here to reflect the power that governments, local communities, and other groups from the task environment wield over industry activities.

Using the model in **Figure 4–2**, a high force can be regarded as a threat because it is likely to reduce profits. A low force, in contrast, can be viewed as an opportunity because it may allow the company to earn greater profits. In the short run, these forces act as constraints on a company's activities. In the long run, however, it may be possible for a company, through its choice of strategy, to change the strength of one or more of the forces to the company's advantage. For example, Dell's early use of the Internet to market its computers was an effective way to negate the bargaining power of distributors in the PC industry.

FIGURE 4–2
Forces Driving
Industry
Competition

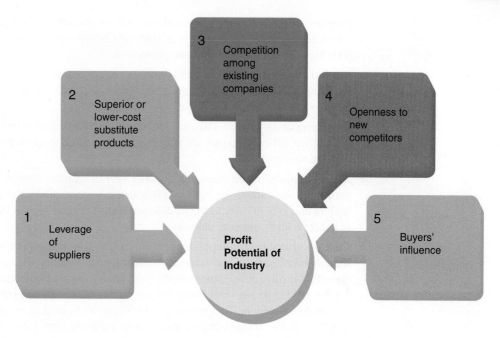

A strategist can analyze any industry by rating each competitive force as high, medium, or low in strength. For example, the global athletic shoe industry could be rated as follows: rivalry is high (Nike, Reebok, New Balance, Converse, and Adidas are strong competitors worldwide), threat of potential entrants is high (the industry has seen clothing firms such as UnderArmour and Fila as well as specialty shoe brands like the wildly popular Vibram Five Fingers shoes), threat of substitutes is low (other shoes don't provide support for sports activities), bargaining power of suppliers is medium but rising (suppliers in Asian countries are increasing in size and ability), bargaining power of buyers is medium but increasing (prices are falling as the low-priced shoe market has grown to be half of the U.S.-branded athletic shoe market), and threat of other stakeholders is medium to high (government regulations and human rights concerns are growing). Based on current trends in each of these competitive forces, the industry's level of competitive intensity will continue to be high—meaning that sales increases and profit margins should continue to be modest for the industry as a whole.[60]

Threat of New Entrants

New entrants to an industry typically bring to it new capacity, a desire to gain market share, and potentially substantial resources. They are, therefore, threats to an established corporation. The threat of entry depends on the presence of entry barriers and the reaction that can be expected from existing competitors. An **entry barrier** is an obstruction that makes it difficult for a company to enter an industry. For example, no new, full-line domestic automobile companies have been successfully established in the United States since the 1930s because of the high capital requirements to build production facilities and to develop a dealer distribution network. Some of the possible barriers to entry are:

- **Economies of scale:** Scale economies in the production and sale of microprocessors, for example, gave Intel a significant cost advantage over any new rival.

- **Product differentiation:** Corporations such as Procter & Gamble and General Mills, which manufacture products such as Tide and Cheerios, create high entry barriers through their high levels of advertising and promotion.

- **Capital requirements:** The need to invest huge financial resources in manufacturing facilities in order to produce large commercial airplanes creates a significant barrier to entry to any competitor for Boeing and Airbus.

- **Switching costs:** Once a software program such as Excel or Word becomes established in an office, office managers are very reluctant to switch to a new program because of the high training costs.

- **Access to distribution channels:** Smaller new firms often have difficulty obtaining supermarket shelf space for their goods because large retailers charge for space on their shelves and give priority to the established firms who can pay for the advertising needed to generate high customer demand.

- **Cost disadvantages independent of size:** Once a new product earns sufficient market share to be accepted as the *standard* for that type of product, the maker has a key advantage. Microsoft's development of the first widely adopted operating system (MS-DOS) for the IBM-type personal computer gave it a significant competitive advantage over potential competitors. Its introduction of Windows helped to cement that advantage so that the Microsoft operating system is now on more than 90% of personal computers worldwide.

- **Government policy:** Governments can limit entry into an industry through licensing requirements by restricting access to raw materials, such as oil-drilling sites in protected areas.

Rivalry among Existing Firms

In most industries, corporations are mutually dependent. A competitive move by one firm can be expected to have a noticeable effect on its competitors and thus may cause retaliation. For example, the successful entry by companies such as Samsung, Amazon and unsuccessful entries by HP and RIM into a Tablet industry previously dominated by Apple changed the level of competitive activity to such an extent that each new product change was quickly followed by similar moves from other tablet makers. The same is true of prices in the United States airline industry. According to Porter, intense rivalry is related to the presence of several factors, including:

- **Number of competitors:** When competitors are few and roughly equal in size, such as in the auto and major home appliance industries, they watch each other carefully to make sure they match any move by another firm with an equal countermove.

- **Rate of industry growth:** Any slowing in passenger traffic tends to set off price wars in the airline industry because the only path to growth is to take sales away from a competitor.

- **Product or service characteristics:** A product can be very unique, with many qualities differentiating it from others of its kind, or it may be a *commodity*, a product whose characteristics are the same, regardless of who sells it. For example, most people choose a gas station based on location and pricing because they view gasoline as a commodity.

- **Amount of fixed costs:** Because airlines must fly their planes on a schedule, regardless of the number of paying passengers for any one flight, some offer cheap standby fares whenever a plane has empty seats.

- **Capacity:** If the only way a manufacturer can increase capacity is in a large increment by building a new plant (as in the paper industry), it will run that new plant at full capacity to keep its unit costs as low as possible—thus producing so much that the selling price falls throughout the industry.

- **Height of exit barriers: Exit barriers** keep a company from leaving an industry. The brewing industry, for example, has a low percentage of companies that voluntarily leave the industry because breweries are specialized assets with few uses except for making beer.

- **Diversity of rivals:** Rivals that have very different ideas of how to compete are likely to cross paths often and unknowingly challenge each other's position. This happens frequently in the retail clothing industry when a number of retailers open outlets in the same location—thus taking sales away from each other. This is also likely to happen in some countries or regions when multinational corporations compete in an increasingly global economy.

Threat of Substitute Products or Services

A **substitute product** is a product that appears to be different but can satisfy the same need as another product. For example, texting is a substitute for e-mail, Nutrasweet is a substitute for sugar, the Internet is a substitute for video stores, and bottled water is a substitute for a cola. According to Porter, "Substitutes limit the potential returns of an industry by placing a ceiling on the prices firms in the industry can profitably charge."[61] To the extent that switching costs are low, substitutes may have a strong effect on an industry. Tea can be considered a substitute for coffee. If the price of coffee goes up high enough, coffee drinkers will slowly begin switching to tea. The price of tea thus puts a price ceiling on the price of coffee. Sometimes a difficult task, the identification of possible substitute products or services means searching for products or services that can perform the same function, even though they have a different appearance and may not appear to be easily substitutable.

The Bargaining Power of Buyers

Buyers affect an industry through their ability to force down prices, bargain for higher quality or more services, and play competitors against each other. A buyer or a group of buyers is powerful if some of the following factors hold true:

- A buyer purchases a large proportion of the seller's product or service (for example, oil filters purchased by a major automaker).

- A buyer has the potential to integrate backward by producing the product itself (for example, a newspaper chain could make its own paper).

- Alternative suppliers are plentiful because the product is standard or undifferentiated (for example, motorists can choose among many gas stations).

- Changing suppliers costs very little (for example, office supplies are easy to find).

- The purchased product represents a high percentage of a buyer's costs, thus providing an incentive to shop around for a lower price (for example, gasoline purchased for resale by convenience stores makes up half their total costs).

- A buyer earns low profits and is thus very sensitive to costs and service differences (for example, grocery stores have very small margins).

- The purchased product is unimportant to the final quality or price of a buyer's products or services and thus can be easily substituted without affecting the final product adversely (for example, electric wire bought for use in lamps).

The Bargaining Power of Suppliers

Suppliers can affect an industry through their ability to raise prices or reduce the quality of purchased goods and services. A supplier or supplier group is powerful if some of the following factors apply:

- The supplier industry is dominated by a few companies, but it sells to many (for example, the petroleum industry).

■ Its product or service is unique and/or it has built up switching costs (for example, word processing software).

■ Substitutes are not readily available (for example, electricity).

■ Suppliers are able to integrate forward and compete directly with their present customers for example, a microprocessor producer such as Intel can make PCs).

■ A purchasing industry buys only a small portion of the supplier group's goods and services and is thus unimportant to the supplier (for example, sales of lawn mower tires are less important to the tire industry than are sales of auto tires).

The Relative Power of Other Stakeholders

A sixth force should be added to Porter's list to include a variety of stakeholder groups from the task environment. Some of these groups are governments (if not explicitly included elsewhere), local communities, creditors (if not included with suppliers), trade associations, special-interest groups, unions (if not included with suppliers), shareholders, and complementors. According to Andy Grove, Chairman and past CEO of Intel, a **complementor** is a company (e.g., Microsoft) or an industry whose product works well with a firm's (e.g., Intel's) product and without which the product would lose much of its value.[62] An example of complementary industries is the tire and automobile industries. Key international stakeholders who determine many of the international trade regulations and standards are the World Trade Organization, the European Union, NAFTA, ASEAN, and Mercosur.

The importance of these stakeholders varies by industry. For example, environmental groups in Maine, Michigan, Oregon, and Iowa successfully fought to pass bills outlawing disposable bottles and cans, and thus deposits for most drink containers are now required. This effectively raised costs across the board, with the most impact on the marginal producers who could not internally absorb all these costs. The traditionally strong power of national unions in the United States' auto and railroad industries has effectively raised costs throughout these industries but is of little importance in computer software.

INDUSTRY EVOLUTION

Over time, most industries evolve through a series of stages from growth through maturity to eventual decline. The strength of each of the six forces mentioned earlier varies according to the stage of industry evolution. The industry life cycle is useful for explaining and predicting trends among the six forces that drive industry competition. For example, when an industry is new, people often buy the product, regardless of price, because it uniquely fulfills an existing need. This usually occurs in a **fragmented industry**—where no firm has large market share, and each firm serves only a small piece of the total market in competition with others (for example, cleaning services).[63] As new competitors enter the industry, prices drop as a result of competition. Companies use the experience curve (discussed in Chapter 5) and economies of scale to reduce costs faster than the competition. Companies integrate to reduce costs even further by acquiring their suppliers and distributors. Competitors try to differentiate their products from one another's in order to avoid the fierce price competition common to a maturing industry.

By the time an industry enters maturity, products tend to become more like commodities. This is now a **consolidated industry**—dominated by a few large firms, each of which struggles to differentiate its products from those of the competition. As buyers become more sophisticated over time, purchasing decisions are based on better information. Price becomes a dominant concern, given a minimum level of quality and features, and profit margins decline. The automobile, petroleum, and major home appliance industries are examples of mature,

INNOVATION issue

TAKING STOCK OF AN OBSESSION

It is worth periodically taking stock of innovations to understand their profound impact upon consumers, competitors, and perhaps in this case, every business operation in the world. The Apple iPhone was released to great fanfare on June 29, 2007 and by mid-2012 more than 217 million had been sold. Cisco Systems estimates that by 2016 there will be more mobile devices than people in the world. In his book *iDisorder: Understanding Our Obsession with Technology and Overcoming Its Hold on Us*, psychologist Larry Rosen observes that "the iPhone has changed everything about how we relate to technology, for both good and bad."

The iPhone led the way to using a touchscreen for every aspect of the phone's use. The Apple focus on simplicity in design and functionality changed the way that phones would look and be used. The laptop computer was the state-of-the-art mobile business platform when the iPhone was released. More and more people not only realized that they could use their phone to keep up with e-mails, make calls, and check Web pages, but more importantly, they were exposed to the App for the first time.

The app (a staple of the iPhone's capability) provides people with a means to achieve a result with a minimum of additional effort. Besides playing games, the business application apps have become a time-saver and confidence builder for people throughout the world. By 2012, there were more than half a million apps in the iTunes App Store. Apps run the gamut from games that probably waste productive time, to translators that quickly help international travelers, to digital books that allow one to take any book with them wherever they go, to programs that allow one to access all their files wherever they may be.

Mobile access is accelerating with the introduction of the iPad tablet, along with the many look-alike tablets and Smartphones. Where will this all go? What will business communication look like in 10 years? No one predicted that a phone would become our computer.

....

SOURCES: P. Burrows, "The First Five Years of Mass Obsession," *Bloomberg BusinessWeek* (June 25, 2012), www.apple.com/iphone/built-in-apps/app-store.html.

consolidated industries, each controlled by a few large competitors. In the case of the United States' major home appliance industry, the industry changed from being a fragmented industry (pure competition) composed of hundreds of appliance manufacturers in the industry's early years to a consolidated industry (mature oligopoly) composed of three companies controlling over 90% of U.S. appliance sales. A similar consolidation is occurring now in European major home appliances.

As an industry moves through maturity toward possible decline, its products' growth rate of sales slows and may even begin to decrease. To the extent that exit barriers are low, firms begin converting their facilities to alternate uses or sell them to other firms. The industry tends to consolidate around fewer but larger competitors. The tobacco industry is an example of an industry currently in decline.

CATEGORIZING INTERNATIONAL INDUSTRIES

According to Porter, worldwide industries vary on a continuum from multidomestic to global (see **Figure 4–3**).[64] **Multidomestic industries** are specific to each country or group of countries. This type of international industry is a collection of essentially domestic industries, such as retailing and insurance. The activities in a subsidiary of a multinational corporation (MNC) in this type of industry are essentially independent of the activities of the MNC's subsidiaries in other countries. Within each country, it has a manufacturing facility to produce goods for sale within that country. The MNC is thus able to tailor its products or services to the very specific needs of consumers in a particular country or group of countries having similar societal environments.

FIGURE 4–3
Continuum of
International
Industries

Multidomestic ⟵————————————————————⟶ **Global**

Industry in which companies tailor
their products to the specific needs
of consumers in a particular country.
• Retailing
• Insurance
• Banking

Industry in which companies manufacture
and sell the same products, with only minor
adjustments made for individual countries
around the world.
• Automobiles
• Tires
• Television sets

Global industries, in contrast, operate worldwide, with MNCs making only small adjustments for country-specific circumstances. In a global industry an MNC's activities in one country are not significantly affected by its activities in other countries. MNCs in global industries produce products or services in various locations throughout the world and sell them, making only minor adjustments for specific country requirements. Examples of global industries are commercial aircraft, television sets, semiconductors, copiers, automobiles, watches, and tires. The largest industrial corporations in the world in terms of sales revenue are, for the most part, MNCs operating in global industries.

The factors that tend to determine whether an industry will be primarily multidomestic or primarily global are:

1. *Pressure for coordination* within the MNCs operating in that industry
2. *Pressure for local responsiveness* on the part of individual country markets

To the extent that the pressure for coordination is strong and the pressure for local responsiveness is weak for MNCs within a particular industry, that industry will tend to become global. In contrast, when the pressure for local responsiveness is strong and the pressure for coordination is weak for multinational corporations in an industry, that industry will tend to be multidomestic. Between these two extremes lie a number of industries with varying characteristics of both multidomestic and global industries. These are **regional industries**, in which MNCs primarily coordinate their activities within regions, such as the Americas or Asia.[65] The major home appliance industry is a current example of a regional industry becoming a global industry. Japanese appliance makers, for example, are major competitors in Asia, but only minor players in Europe or America. The dynamic tension between the pressure for coordination and the pressure for local responsiveness is contained in the phrase, "*Think globally but act locally.*"

INTERNATIONAL RISK ASSESSMENT

Some firms develop elaborate information networks and computerized systems to evaluate and rank investment risks. Small companies may hire outside consultants, such as Boston's Arthur D. Little Inc., to provide political-risk assessments. Among the many systems that exist to assess political and economic risks are the Business Environment Risk Index, the Economist Intelligence Unit, and Frost and Sullivan's World Political Risk Forecasts. The Economist Intelligence Unit, for example, provides a constant flow of analysis and forecasts on more than 200 countries and eight key industries. Regardless of the source of data, a firm must develop its own method of assessing risk. It must decide on its most important risk factors and then assign weights to each.

STRATEGIC GROUPS

A **strategic group** is a set of business units or firms that "pursue similar strategies with similar resources."[66] Categorizing firms in any one industry into a set of strategic groups is very useful as a way of better understanding the competitive environment.[67] Research shows that some strategic groups in the same industry are more profitable than others.[68] Because a corporation's structure and culture tend to reflect the kinds of strategies it follows, companies or business units belonging to a particular strategic group within the same industry tend to be strong rivals and tend to be more similar to each other than to competitors in other strategic groups within the same industry.[69]

For example, although McDonald's and Olive Garden are a part of the same industry, the restaurant industry, they have different missions, objectives, and strategies, and thus they belong to different strategic groups. They generally have very little in common and pay little attention to each other when planning competitive actions. Burger King and Wendy's, however, have a great deal in common with McDonald's in terms of their similar strategy of producing a high volume of low-priced meals targeted for sale to the average family. Consequently, they are strong rivals and are organized to operate similarly.

Strategic groups in a particular industry can be mapped by plotting the market positions of industry competitors on a two-dimensional graph, using two strategic variables as the vertical and horizontal axes (**Figure 4–4**):

1. Select two broad characteristics, such as price and menu, that differentiate the companies in an industry from one another.

2. Plot the firms, using these two characteristics as the dimensions.

3. Draw a circle around those companies that are closest to one another as one strategic group, varying the size of the circle in proportion to the group's share of total industry sales. (You could also name each strategic group in the restaurant industry with an identifying title, such as quick fast food or buffet-style service.)

FIGURE 4–4
Mapping Strategic Groups in the U.S. Restaurant Chain Industry

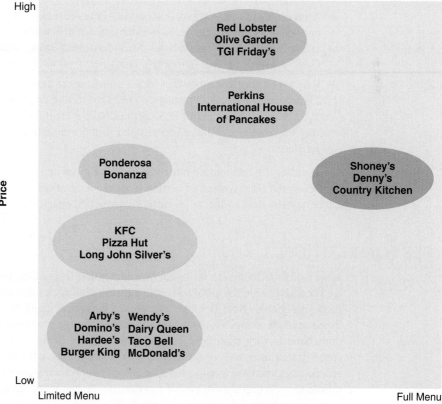

Other dimensions, such as quality, service, location, or degree of vertical integration, could also be used in additional graphs of the restaurant industry to gain a better understanding of how the various firms in the industry compete. Keep in mind, however, that the two dimensions should not be highly correlated; otherwise, the circles on the map will simply lie along the diagonal, providing very little new information other than the obvious.

STRATEGIC TYPES

In analyzing the level of competitive intensity within a particular industry or strategic group, it is useful to characterize the various competitors for predictive purposes. A **strategic type** is a category of firms based on a common strategic orientation and a combination of structure, culture, and processes consistent with that strategy. According to Miles and Snow, competing firms within a single industry can be categorized into one of four basic types on the basis of their general strategic orientation.[70] This distinction helps explain why companies facing similar situations behave differently and why they continue to do so over long periods of time.[71] These general types have the following characteristics:

- **Defenders** are companies with a limited product line that *focus on improving the efficiency of their existing operations*. This cost orientation makes them unlikely to innovate in new areas. With its emphasis on efficiency, Lincoln Electric is an example of a defender.

- **Prospectors** are companies with fairly broad product lines that *focus on product innovation and market opportunities*. This sales orientation makes them somewhat inefficient. They tend to emphasize creativity over efficiency. Frito Lay's emphasis on new product development makes it an example of a prospector.

- **Analyzers** are corporations that *operate in at least two different product-market areas*, one stable and one variable. In the stable areas, efficiency is emphasized. In the variable areas, innovation is emphasized. Multidivisional firms, such as BASF and Procter & Gamble, which operate in multiple industries, tend to be analyzers.

- **Reactors** are corporations that *lack a consistent strategy-structure-culture relationship*. Their (often ineffective) responses to environmental pressures tend to be piecemeal strategic changes. Most major U.S. airlines have recently tended to be reactors—given the way they have been forced to respond to more nimble airlines such as Southwest and JetBlue.

Dividing the competition into these four categories enables the strategic manager not only to monitor the effectiveness of certain strategic orientations, but also to develop scenarios of future industry developments (discussed later in this chapter).

HYPERCOMPETITION

Most industries today are facing an ever-increasing level of environmental uncertainty. They are becoming more complex and more dynamic. Industries that used to be multidomestic are becoming global. New flexible, aggressive, innovative competitors are moving into established markets to rapidly erode the advantages of large previously dominant firms. Distribution channels vary from country to country and are being altered daily through the use of sophisticated information systems. Closer relationships with suppliers are being forged to reduce costs, increase quality, and gain access to new technology. Companies learn to quickly imitate the successful strategies of market leaders, and it becomes harder to sustain any competitive advantage for very long. Consequently, the level of competitive intensity is increasing in most industries.

Richard D'Aveni contends that as this type of environmental turbulence reaches more industries, competition becomes **hypercompetition**. According to D'Aveni:

In hypercompetition the frequency, boldness, and aggressiveness of dynamic movement by the players accelerates to create a condition of constant disequilibrium and change. Market stability is threatened by short product life cycles, short product design cycles, new technologies, frequent entry by unexpected outsiders, repositioning by incumbents, and tactical redefinitions of market boundaries as diverse industries merge. In other words, environments escalate toward higher and higher levels of uncertainty, dynamism, heterogeneity of the players and hostility.[72]

In hypercompetitive industries such as information technology, competitive advantage comes from an up-to-date knowledge of environmental trends and competitive activity, coupled with a willingness to risk a current advantage for a possible new advantage. Companies must be willing to *cannibalize* their own products (that is, replace popular products before competitors do so) in order to sustain their competitive advantage. (Hypercompetition is discussed in more detail in Chapter 6.)

USING KEY SUCCESS FACTORS TO CREATE AN INDUSTRY MATRIX

Within any industry, there are usually certain variables—key success factors—that a company's management must understand in order to be successful. **Key success factors** are variables that can significantly affect the overall competitive positions of companies within any particular industry. They typically vary from industry to industry and are crucial to determining a company's ability to succeed within that industry. They are usually determined by the economic and technological characteristics of the industry and by the competitive weapons on which the firms in the industry have built their strategies.[73] For example, in the major home appliance industry, a firm must achieve low costs, typically by building large manufacturing facilities dedicated to making multiple versions of one type of appliance, such as washing machines. Because 60% of major home appliances in the United States are sold through "power retailers" such as Sears and Best Buy, a firm must have a strong presence in the mass merchandiser distribution channel. It must offer a full line of appliances and provide a just-in-time delivery system to keep store inventory and ordering costs to a minimum. Because the consumer expects reliability and durability in an appliance, a firm must have excellent process R&D. Any appliance manufacturer that is unable to deal successfully with these key success factors will not survive long in the U.S. market.

An **industry matrix** summarizes the key success factors within a particular industry. As shown in **Table 4–4**, the matrix gives a weight for each factor based on how important that factor is for success within the industry. The matrix also specifies how well various competitors in the industry are responding to each factor. To generate an industry matrix

TABLE 4–4   Industry Matrix

Key Success Factors	Weight	Company A Rating	Company A Weighted Score	Company B Rating	Company B Weighted Score
1	2	3	4	5	6
Total	1.00		—		—

SOURCE: T. L. Wheelen and J. D. Hunger, *Industry Matrix*. Copyright © 1997, 2001, and 2005 by Wheelen & Hunger Associates. Reprinted with permission.

using two industry competitors (called A and B), complete the following steps for the industry being analyzed:

1. In **Column 1** (*Key Success Factors*), list the 8 to 10 factors that appear to determine success in the industry.

2. In **Column 2** (*Weight*), assign a weight to each factor, from **1.0** (*Most Important*) to **0.0** (*Not Important*) based on that factor's probable impact on the overall industry's current and future success. (**All weights must sum to 1.0 regardless of the number of strategic factors.**)

3. In **Column 3** (*Company A Rating*), examine a particular company within the industry—for example, Company A. Assign a rating to each factor from **5** (*Outstanding*) to **1** (*Poor*) based on Company A's current response to that particular factor. Each rating is a judgment regarding how well that company is specifically dealing with each key success factor.

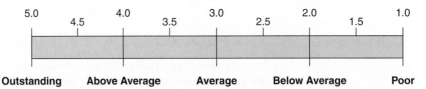

4. In **Column 4** (*Company A Weighted Score*) multiply the weight in **Column 2** for each factor by its rating in **Column 3** to obtain that factor's weighted score for Company A.

5. In **Column 5** (*Company B Rating*) examine a second company within the industry—in this case, Company B. Assign a rating to each key success factor from **5.0** (Outstanding) to **1.0** (Poor), based on Company B's current response to each particular factor.

6. In **Column 6** (*Company B Weighted Score*) multiply the weight in **Column 2** for each factor times its rating in **Column 5** to obtain that factor's weighted score for Company B.

7. Finally, add the weighted scores for all the factors in **Columns 4** and **6** to determine the total weighted scores for companies A and B. **The total weighted score indicates how well each company is responding to current and expected key success factors in the industry's environment.** Check to ensure that the total weighted score truly reflects the company's current performance in terms of profitability and market share. (An average company should have a total weighted score of 3.)

The industry matrix can be expanded to include all the major competitors within an industry through the addition of two additional columns for each additional competitor.

Competitive Intelligence

Most external environmental scanning is done on an informal and individual basis. Information is obtained from a variety of sources—suppliers, customers, industry publications, employees, industry experts, industry conferences, and the Internet.[74] For example, scientists and engineers working in a firm's R&D lab can learn about new products and competitors' ideas at professional meetings; someone from the purchasing department, speaking with supplier- representatives' personnel, may also uncover valuable bits of information about a competitor. A study of product innovation found that 77% of all product innovations in scientific instruments and 67% in semiconductors and printed circuit boards were initiated by the customer in the form of inquiries and complaints.[75] In these industries, the sales force and service departments must be especially vigilant.

A recent survey of global executives by McKinsey & Company found that the single factor contributing most to the increasing competitive intensity in their industries was the improved capabilities of competitors.[76] Yet, without competitive intelligence, companies run the risk of flying blind in the marketplace. According to work by Ryall, firms can have competitive advantages simply because their rivals have erroneous beliefs about them.[77] This is why competitive intelligence has become an important part of environmental scanning in most companies.

Competitive intelligence is a formal program of gathering information on a company's competitors. Often called *business intelligence*, it is one of the fastest growing fields within strategic management. Research indicates that there is a strong association between corporate performance and competitive intelligence activities.[78] According to a 2011 survey of competitive intelligence by the Global Intelligence Alliance, nearly 70% of North American companies plan to increase their budgets for competitive intelligence. 94% felt that they had benefited from their competitive intelligence efforts, while 42% of those companies without a competitive intelligence program intend to start one within the year.[79]

In about a third of the firms, the competitive/business intelligence function is housed in its own unit, with the remainder being housed within marketing, strategic planning, information services, business development (merger and acquisitions), product development, or other units.[80] Competitive Intelligence software maker GoodData estimated the size of the total spent on competitive intelligence activities was more than US$25 Billion in 2012.[81] At General Mills, for example, all employees have been trained to recognize and tap sources of competitive information. Janitors no longer simply place orders with suppliers of cleaning materials; they also ask about relevant practices at competing firms!

SOURCES OF COMPETITIVE INTELLIGENCE

Most corporations use outside organizations to provide them with environmental data. Firms such as A. C. Nielsen Co. provide subscribers with bimonthly data on brand share, retail prices, percentages of stores stocking an item, and percentages of stock-out stores. Strategists can use this data to spot regional and national trends as well as to assess market share. Information on market conditions, government regulations, industry competitors, and new products can be bought from "information brokers" such as Market Research.com (Findex), Lexis-Nexis (company and country analyses), and Finsbury Data Services. Company and industry profiles are generally available from the Hoover's Web site at www.hoovers.com. Many business corporations have established their own in-house libraries and computerized information systems to deal with the growing mass of available information.

The Internet has changed the way strategists engage in environmental scanning. It provides the quickest means to obtain data on almost any subject. Although the scope and quality of Internet information is increasing geometrically, it is also littered with "noise," misinformation, and utter nonsense. Unlike the library, the Internet lacks the tight bibliographic control standards that exist in the print world. There is no ISBN or Dewey Decimal System to identify, search, and retrieve a document. Many Web documents lack the name of the author and the date of publication. A Web page providing useful information may be accessible on the Web one day and gone the next. Unhappy ex-employees, far-out environmentalists, and prank-prone hackers create "blog" Web sites to attack and discredit an otherwise reputable corporation. Rumors with no basis in fact are spread via chat rooms and personal Web sites. This creates a serious problem for researchers. How can one evaluate the information found on the Internet? For a way to evaluate intelligence information, see the Strategy Highlight on the next page.

Some companies choose to use industrial espionage or other intelligence-gathering techniques to get their information straight from their competitors. According to a survey by the American Society for Industrial Security, PricewaterhouseCoopers, and the United States

Chamber of Commerce, Fortune 1000 companies lost an estimated US$59 billion in one year alone due to the theft of trade secrets.[82] By using current or former competitors' employees and private contractors, some firms attempt to steal trade secrets, technology, business plans, and pricing strategies. For example, Avon Products hired private investigators to retrieve from a public dumpster documents (some of them shredded) that Mary Kay Corporation had thrown away. Oracle Corporation also hired detectives to obtain the trash of a think tank that had defended the pricing practices of its rival Microsoft. Studies reveal that 32% of the trash typically found next to copy machines contains confidential company data, in addition to personal data (29%) and gossip (39%).[83] Even P&G, which defends itself like a fortress from information leaks, is vulnerable. A competitor was able to learn the precise launch date of a concentrated laundry detergent in Europe when one of its people visited the factory where machinery was being made. Simply asking a few questions about what a certain machine did, whom it was for, and when it would be delivered was all that was necessary.

Some of the firms providing investigatory services are Altegrity Inc. with 11,000 employees in 30 countries, Fairfax, Security Outsourcing Solutions, Trident Group, and Diligence Inc.[84]

Trident, for example, specializes in helping American companies enter the Russian market and is a U.S.-based corporate intelligence firm founded and managed by former veterans of Russian intelligence services, like the KGB.[85]

STRATEGY highlight

EVALUATING COMPETITIVE INTELLIGENCE

A basic rule in intelligence gathering is that before a piece of information can be in any report or briefing, it must first be evaluated in two ways. *First*, the source of the information should be judged in terms of its truthfulness and reliability. How trustworthy is the source? How well can a researcher rely upon it for truthful and correct information? One approach is to rank the reliability of the source on a scale from A (extremely reliable), B (reliable), C (unknown reliability), D (probably unreliable), to E (very questionable reliability). The reliability of a source can be judged on the basis of the author's credentials, the organization sponsoring the information, and past performance, among other factors. *Second*, the information or data should be judged in terms of its likelihood of being correct. The correctness of the data may be ranked on a scale from 1 (correct), 2 (probably correct), 3 (unknown), 4 (doubtful), to 5 (extremely doubtful). The correctness of a piece of data or information can be judged on the basis of its agreement with other bits of separately obtained information or with a general trend supported by previous data. For every piece of information found on the Internet, for example, list not only the URL of the Web page, but also the evaluation of the information from A1 (good stuff) to E5 (bad doodoo). Information found through library research in sources such as Moody's Industrials, Standard & Poor's, or Value Line can generally be evaluated as having a reliability of A. The correctness of the data can still range anywhere from 1 to 5, but in most instances is likely to be either 1 or 2, but probably no worse than 3 or 4. Web sites are quite different.

Web sites, such as those sponsored by the U.S. Securities and Exchange Commission (www.sec.gov), *The Economist* (www.economist.com), or Hoovers Online (www.hoovers.com) are extremely reliable. Company-sponsored Web sites are generally reliable, but are not the place to go for trade secrets, strategic plans, or proprietary information. For one thing, many firms think of their Web sites primarily in terms of marketing and provide little data aside from product descriptions and distributors. Other companies provide their latest financial statements and links to other useful Web sites. Nevertheless, some companies in very competitive industries may install software on their Web site to ascertain a visitor's Web address. Visitors from a competitor's domain name are thus screened before they are allowed to access certain Web sites. They may not be allowed beyond the product information page or they may be sent to a bogus Web site containing misinformation. Cisco Systems, for example, uses its Web site to send visitors coming in from other high-tech firm web sites to a special Web page asking if they would like to apply for a job at Cisco!

To combat the increasing theft of company secrets, the U.S. government passed the Economic Espionage Act in 1996. The law makes it illegal (with fines up to US$5 million and 10 years in jail) to steal any material that a business has taken "reasonable efforts" to keep secret and that derives its value from not being known.[86] The Society of Competitive Intelligence Professionals (www.scip.org) urges strategists to stay within the law and to act ethically when searching for information. The society states that illegal activities are foolish because the vast majority of worthwhile competitive intelligence is available publicly via annual reports, Web sites, and libraries. Unfortunately, a number of firms hire "kites," consultants with questionable reputations, who do what is necessary to get information when the selected methods do not meet SPIC ethical standards or are illegal. This allows the company that initiated the action to deny that it did anything wrong.[87]

MONITORING COMPETITORS FOR STRATEGIC PLANNING

The primary activity of a competitive intelligence unit is to monitor **competitors**—organizations that offer same, similar, or substitutable products or services in the business area in which a particular company operates. To understand a competitor, it is important to answer the following 10 questions:

1. Why do your competitors exist? Do they exist to make profits or just to support another unit?

2. Where do they add customer value—higher quality, lower price, excellent credit terms, or better service?

3. Which of your customers are the competitors most interested in? Are they cherry-picking your best customers, picking the ones you don't want, or going after all of them?

4. What is their cost base and liquidity? How much cash do they have? How do they get their supplies?

5. Are they less exposed with their suppliers than your firm? Are their suppliers better than yours?

6. What do they intend to do in the future? Do they have a strategic plan to target your market segments? How committed are they to growth? Are there any succession issues?

7. How will their activity affect your strategies? Should you adjust your plans and operations?

8. How much better than your competitor do you need to be in order to win customers? Do either of you have a competitive advantage in the marketplace?

9. Will new competitors or new ways of doing things appear over the next few years? Who is a potential new entrant?

10. If you were a customer, would you choose your product over those offered by your competitors? What irritates your current customers? What competitors solve these particular customer complaints?[88]

To answer these and other questions, competitive intelligence professionals utilize a number of analytical techniques. In addition to the previously discussed industry forces analysis, and strategic group analysis, some of these techniques are Porter's four-corner exercise, Treacy and Wiersema's value disciplines, Gilad's blind spot analysis, and war gaming.[89] Done right, competitive intelligence is a key input to strategic planning.

Forecasting

Environmental scanning provides reasonably hard data on the present situation and current trends, but intuition and luck are needed to accurately predict whether these trends will continue. The resulting forecasts are, however, usually based on a set of assumptions that may or may not be valid.

DANGER OF ASSUMPTIONS

Faulty underlying assumptions are the most frequent cause of forecasting errors. Nevertheless, many managers who formulate and implement strategic plans rarely consider that their success is based on a series of basic assumptions. Many strategic plans are simply based on projections of the current situation. For example, few people in 2007 expected the price of oil (light, sweet crude, also called West Texas intermediate) to rise above US$80 per barrel and were extremely surprised to see the price approach US$150 by July 2008, especially since the price had been around US$20 per barrel in 2002. U.S. auto companies in particular had continued to design and manufacture large cars, pick-up trucks, and SUVs under the assumption of gasoline being available for around US$2.00 a gallon. Market demand for these types of cars collapsed when the price of gasoline passed US$3.00 to reach US$4.00 a gallon in July 2008. While the price of gas modified some by 2012, at US$112 a barrel and retail gas prices in the mid US$3 range, the car makers are trying to move to vehicles with increasing efficiency. In another example, many banks made a number of questionable mortgages based on the assumption that housing prices would continue to rise as they had in the past. When housing prices began to fall in late 2006, these "sub-prime" mortgages were almost worthless—causing the banking crisis that gripped the nation for the next three plus years. The lesson here: Assumptions can be dangerous to your business's health!

USEFUL FORECASTING TECHNIQUES

Various techniques are used to forecast future situations. They do not tell the future; they merely state what can be, not what will be. As such, they can be used to form a set of reasonable assumptions about the future. Each technique has its proponents and its critics. A study of nearly 500 of the world's largest corporations revealed trend extrapolation to be the most widely practiced form of forecasting—over 70% use this technique either occasionally or frequently.[90] Simply stated, *extrapolation* is the extension of present trends into the future. It rests on the assumption that the world is reasonably consistent and changes slowly in the short run. Time-series methods are approaches of this type. They attempt to carry a series of historical events forward into the future. The basic problem with extrapolation is that a historical trend is based on a series of patterns or relationships among so many different variables that a change in any one can drastically alter the future direction of the trend. As a rule of thumb, the further back into the past you can find relevant data supporting the trend, the more confidence you can have in the prediction.

Brainstorming, expert opinion, and statistical modeling are also very popular forecasting techniques. *Brainstorming* is a non-quantitative approach that simply requires the presence of people with some knowledge of the situation in order to concept out the future. The basic ground rule is to propose ideas without first mentally screening them. No criticism is allowed. "Wild" ideas are encouraged. Ideas should build on previous ideas until a consensus is reached.[91] This is a good technique to use with operating managers who have more faith in "gut feel" than in more quantitative number-crunching techniques. *Expert opinion* is a nonquantitative technique in which experts in a particular area attempt to forecast likely developments. This type of forecast is based on the ability of a knowledgeable person(s) to construct probable future developments based on the interaction of key variables. One application, developed by the RAND Corporation, is the *Delphi Technique*, in which separated experts independently assess the likelihoods of specified events. These assessments are combined and sent back to each expert for fine-tuning until agreement is reached. These assessments are most useful if they are shaped into several possible scenarios that allow decision makers to more fully understand their implication.[92] *Statistical modeling* is a quantitative technique that attempts to discover causal or at least explanatory factors that link two or more time series together. Examples of statistical modeling are regression analysis and other econometric methods. Although very useful in the grasping of historic trends, statistical modeling, such as trend extrapolation, is based on historical data. As the patterns of relationships change, the accuracy of the forecast deteriorates.

Prediction markets is a recent forecasting technique enabled by easy access to the Internet. As emphasized by James Surowiecki in *The Wisdom of Crowds*, the conclusions of large groups can often be better than those of experts because such groups can aggregate a large amount of dispersed wisdom.[93] Prediction markets are small-scale electronic markets, frequently open to any employee, that tie payoffs to measurable future events, such as sales data for a computer workstation, the number of bugs in an application, or product usage patterns. These markets yield prices on prediction contracts—prices that can be interpreted as market- aggregated forecasts.[94] Companies including Microsoft, Google, and Eli Lilly have asked their employees to participate in prediction markets by betting on whether products will sell, when new offices will open, and whether profits will be high in the next quarter. Early predictions have been exceedingly accurate.[95] Intrade.com offers a free Web site in which people can buy or sell various predictions in a manner similar to buying or selling common stock. On August 17, 2012, for example, Intrade.com listed the bidding price for democratic presidential candidate Barack Obama as US$5.62 compared to US$4.26 for Mitt Romney. Thus far, prediction markets have not been documented for long-term forecasting, so its value in strategic planning has not yet been established. Other forecasting techniques, such as *cross-impact analysis (CIA)* and *trend-impact analysis (TIA)*, have not established themselves successfully as regularly employed tools.[96]

Scenario writing is the most widely used forecasting technique after trend extrapolation. Originated by Royal Dutch Shell, *scenarios* are focused descriptions of different likely futures presented in a narrative fashion. A scenario thus may be merely a written description of some future state, in terms of key variables and issues, or it may be generated in combination with other forecasting techniques. Often called scenario planning, this technique has been successfully used by 3M, Levi-Strauss, General Electric, United Distillers, Electrolux, British Airways, and Pacific Gas and Electricity, among others.[97] According to Mike Eskew, Chairman and CEO of United Parcel Service, UPS uses scenario writing to envision what its customers might need 5 to 10 years in the future.[98]

An **industry scenario** is a forecasted description of a particular industry's likely future. Such a scenario is developed by analyzing the probable impact of future societal forces on key groups in a particular industry. The process may operate as follows:[99]

1. Examine possible shifts in the natural environment and in societal variables globally.

2. Identify uncertainties in each of the six forces of the task environment (that is, potential entrants, competitors, likely substitutes, buyers, suppliers, and other key stakeholders).

3. Make a range of plausible assumptions about future trends.

4. Combine assumptions about individual trends into internally consistent scenarios.

5. Analyze the industry situation that would prevail under each scenario.

6. Determine the sources of competitive advantage under each scenario.

7. Predict competitors' behavior under each scenario.

8. Select the scenarios that are either most likely to occur or most likely to have a strong impact on the future of the company. Use these scenarios as assumptions in strategy formulation.

The Strategic Audit: A Checklist for Environmental Scanning

One way of scanning the environment to identify opportunities and threats is by using the Strategic Audit found in **Appendix 1.A** at the end of Chapter 1. The audit provides a checklist of questions by area of concern. For example, Part III of the audit examines the natural, societal, and task environments. It looks at the societal environment in terms of economic, technological, political–legal, and sociocultural forces. It also considers the task environment (industry) in terms of the threat of new entrants, the bargaining power of buyers and suppliers, the threat of substitute products, rivalry among existing firms, and the relative power of other stakeholders.

Synthesis of External Factors—EFAS

After strategic managers have scanned the natural, societal, and task environments and identified a number of likely external factors for their particular corporation, they may want to refine their analysis of these factors by using a form such as that given in **Table 4–5.** Using an **EFAS (External Factors Analysis Summary) Table** is one way to organize the external factors into the generally accepted categories of opportunities and threats, as well as to analyze how well a particular company's management (rating) is responding to these specific factors in light of the perceived importance (weight) of these factors to the company. To generate an EFAS Table for the company being analyzed, complete the following steps:

1. In **Column 1 (*External Factors*)**, list the 8 to 10 most important opportunities and threats facing the company.

2. In **Column 2 (*Weight*)**, assign a weight to each factor from **1.0** (*Most Important*) to **0.0** (*Not Important*) based on that factor's probable impact on a particular company's current strategic position. The higher the weight, the more important is this factor to the current and future success of the company. **(All weights must sum to 1.0 regardless of the number of factors.)**

3. In **Column 3 (*Rating*)**, assign a rating to each factor from **5.0** (*Outstanding*) to **1.0** (*Poor*) based on that particular company's specific response to that particular factor. Each rating is a judgment regarding how well the company is currently dealing with each specific external factor.

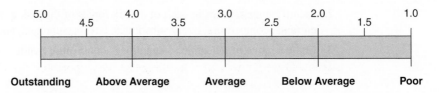

TABLE 4–5	External Factor Analysis Summary (EFAS Table): Maytag as Example				
External Factors	**Weight**	**Rating**	**Weighted Score**	**Comments**
1	2	3	4	5
Opportunities				
▪ Economic integration of European Community	.20	4.1	.82	Acquisition of Hoover
▪ Demographics favor quality appliances	.10	5.0	.50	Maytag quality
▪ Economic development of Asia	.05	1.0	.05	Low Maytag presence
▪ Opening of Eastern Europe	.05	2.0	.10	Will take time
▪ Trend to "Super Stores"	.10	1.8	.18	Maytag weak in this channel
Threats				
▪ Increasing government regulations	.10	4.3	.43	Well positioned
▪ Strong U.S. competition	.10	4.0	.40	Well positioned
▪ Whirlpool and Electrolux strong globally	.15	3.0	.45	Hoover weak globally
▪ New product advances	.05	1.2	.06	Questionable
▪ Japanese appliance companies	.10	1.6	.16	Only Asian presence in Australia
Total Scores	1.00		3.15	

NOTES:

1. List opportunities and threats (8–10) in Column 1.
2. Weight each factor from 1.0 (Most Important) to 0.0 (Not Important) in Column 2 based on that factor's probable impact on the company's strategic position. **The total weights must sum to 1.00.**
3. Rate each factor from 5.0 (Outstanding) to 1.0 (Poor) in Column 3 based on the company's response to that factor.
4. Multiply each factor's weight times its rating to obtain each factor's weighted score in Column 4.
5. Use Column 5 (comments) for the rationale used for each factor.
6. Add the individual weighted scores to obtain the total weighted score for the company in Column 4. This tells how well the company is responding to the factors in its external environment.

SOURCE: Thomas L. Wheelen. Copyright © 1982, 1985, 1987, 1988, 1989, 1990, 1991, 1998, and every year after that. Kathryn E. Wheelen solely owns all of (Dr.) Thomas L. Wheelen's copyright materials. Kathryn E. Wheelen requires written reprint permission for each book that this material is to be printed in. Thomas L. Wheelen and J. David Hunger, copyright © 1991–first year "External Factor Analysis Summary" (EFAS) appeared in this text (4th ed.). Reprinted by permission of the copyright holders.

4. In **Column 4** (*Weighted Score*), multiply the weight in **Column 2** for each factor times its rating in **Column 3** to obtain that factor's weighted score.

5. In **Column 5** (*Comments*), note why a particular factor was selected and how its weight and rating were estimated.

6. Finally, add the weighted scores for all the external factors in **Column 4** to determine the total weighted score for that particular company. The **total weighted** score indicates how well a particular company is responding to current and expected factors in its external environment. The score can be used to compare that firm to other firms in the industry. Check to ensure that the total weighted score truly reflects the company's current performance in terms of profitability and market share. **The total weighted score for an average firm in an industry is always 3.0.**

As an example of this procedure, **Table 4–5** includes a number of external factors for Maytag Corporation with corresponding weights, ratings, and weighted scores provided. This table is appropriate for 1995, long before Maytag was acquired by Whirlpool. Note that Maytag's total weight was 3.15, meaning that the corporation was slightly above average in the major home appliance industry at that time.

End of Chapter SUMMARY

Wayne Gretzky was one of the most famous people ever to play professional ice hockey. He wasn't very fast. His shot was fairly weak. He was usually last in his team in strength training. He tended to operate in the back of his opponent's goal, anticipating where his team members would be long before they got there and fed them passes so unsuspected that he would often surprise his own team members. In an interview with *Time* magazine, Gretzky stated that the key to winning is skating not to where the puck is but to where it is going to be. "People talk about skating, puck handling and shooting, but the whole sport is angles and caroms, forgetting the straight direction the puck is going, calculating where it will be diverted, factoring in all the interruptions," explained Gretzky.[100]

Environmental scanning involves monitoring, collecting, and evaluating information in order to understand the current trends in the natural, societal, and task environments. The information is then used to forecast whether these trends will continue or whether others will take their place. How will developments in the natural environment affect the world? What kind of developments can we expect in the societal environment to affect our industry? What will an industry look like in 10 to 20 years? Who will be the key competitors? Who is likely to fall by the wayside? We use this information to make certain assumptions about the future—assumptions that are then used in strategic planning. In many ways, success in the business world is like ice hockey: The key to winning is not to assume that your industry will continue as it is now but to assume that the industry will change and to make sure your company will be in position to take advantage of those changes.

MyManagementLab®

Go to **mymanagementlab.com** to complete the problems marked with this icon 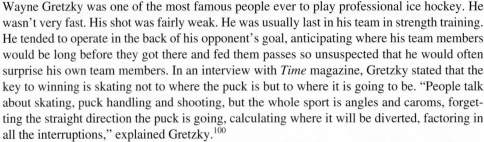.

KEY TERMS

competitive intelligence (p. 149)
competitors (p. 151)
complementor (p. 142)
consolidated industry (p. 142)
EFAS Table (p. 154)
entry barrier (p. 139)
environmental scanning (p. 126)
environmental uncertainty (p. 126)
exit barrier (p. 141)
fragmented industry (p. 142)

global industry (p. 144)
hypercompetition (p. 147)
industry (p. 138)
industry analysis (p. 127)
industry matrix (p. 147)
industry scenario (p. 153)
key success factor (p. 147)
multidomestic industry (p. 143)
multinational corporation (MNC) (p. 135)

natural environment (p. 126)
new entrant (p. 139)
regional industries (p. 144)
societal environment (p. 127)
STEEP analysis (p. 128)
strategic group (p. 144)
strategic type (p. 146)
substitute product (p. 141)
task environment (p. 127)

MyManagementLab®

Go to **mymanagementlab.com** for the following Assisted-graded writing questions:

4-1. How does STEEP analysis aid in the development of the strategy of a company?

4-2. The effects of climate change on companies can be grouped into six categories of risks. Use any two of these to explain the impact upon the resort hotel industry?

DISCUSSION QUESTIONS

⊛ **4-3.** Discuss how a development in a corporation's natural and societal environments can affect the corporation through its task environment.

4-4. How do corporations analyze the societal environment? Is STEEP Analysis an appropriate tool?

4-5. Clarify the difference in fragmented and consolidated industry.

⊛ **4-6.** How can a decision maker identify strategic factors in a corporation's external international environment?

⊛ **4-7.** Compare and contrast trend extrapolation with the writing of scenarios as forecasting techniques.

STRATEGIC PRACTICE EXERCISE

Vying for Shares

Competition is fierce in the Lebanese banking sector as local banks are vying for the shares of local, regional, and/or international banks. London-based Standard Chartered bank is up for bids, and domestic banks are rolling up their sleeves in anticipation. Standard Chartered is headquartered in a key urban area, has three branches, and has licenses to open two more branches – a very lucrative prospect for any investment bank with no branches or trained employees. Its total deposits are only U.S. $80 million, a very small amount compared to deposits of other Lebanese lenders. Even though Standard Chartered's operations in Lebanon are relatively small compared to its activities in other emerging countries, the bank is attractive. Four banks stand out as the main competitors: International Bank of Lebanon, First National Bank, Audi Bank, and Cedrus Invest Bank.

Audi Bank is mainly interested in the retail operations of Standard Chartered and has begun talks in that domain. On the other hand, Cedrus Invest Bank seems to have a larger objective in mind. Cedrus Invest Bank is the largest specialized bank in Lebanon in terms of capitalization, with a paid-up capital of U.S. $52 million and more than U.S. $400 million in assets under management and administration. It can take advantage of Standard Chartered's opportunities. Cedrus is keen to realize the full potential of Standard Chartered in Lebanon, and plans to do so by acquiring the license and assets of the bank and expanding its business to commercial banking.

1. How far should banks go to gather competitive intelligence?

2. Where should the line be drawn?

....
SOURCE: O. Habib, "Four banks vie for shares of Standard Chartered Bank" *The Daily Star* (January 10, 2014), p. 5.

NOTES

1. J. B. Thomas, S. M. Clark, and D. A. Gioia, "Strategic Sensemaking and Organizational Performance: Linkages Among Scanning, Interpretation, Action, Outcomes," *Academy of Management Journal* (April 1993), pp. 239–270; J. A. Smith, "Strategies for Start-Ups," *Long Range Planning* (December 1998), pp. 857–872.
2. M. Birshan, R. Dye, and S. Hall, "Creating More Value with Corporate Strategy: McKinsey Global Survey Results," (2011), (www.mckinseyquarterly.com/surveys/creating_more_value_with_corporate_strategy_McKinsey_Global_Survey_results_2733).
3. W. E. Stead and J. G. Stead, *Sustainable Strategic Management* (Armonk, NY: M. E. Sharpe, 2004), p. 6.
4. F. Montabon, R. Sroufe, and R. Narasimhan, "An Examination of Corporate Reporting, Environmental Management Practices and Firm Performance," *Journal of Operations Management* (August 2007), pp. 998–1014.
5. P. Lasserre and J. Probert, "Competing on the Pacific Rim: High Risks and High Returns," *Long Range Planning* (April 1994), pp. 12–35.
6. J. J. McGonagle, "Mapping and Anticipating the Competitive Landscape," *Competitive Intelligence Magazine* (March–April 2007), p. 49.
7. M. J. Cetron and O. Davies, "Trends Now Shaping the Future," *The Futurist* (March–April 2005), pp. 28–29; M. Cetron and O. Davies, "Trends Shaping Tomorrow's World," *The Futurist* (March–April 2008), pp. 35–52.
8. "Trend: Urbane Urban Portraits," *BusinessWeek* (April 28, 2008), p. 57.
9. "Old Europe," *The Economist* (October 2, 2004), pp. 49–50.
10. M. J. Cetron and O. Davies, "Trends Now Shaping the Future," *The Futurist* (March–April 2005), p. 30.
11. "The Incredible Shrinking Country," *The Economist* (November 13, 2004), pp. 45–46.
12. D. Levin, "Tradition Under Stress," *AARP Bulletin* (July–August 2008), pp. 16–18.
13. J. Wyatt, "Playing the Woofie Card," *Fortune* (February 6, 1995), pp. 130–132.
14. www.news.walgreens.com/article_display.cfm?article_id=831.
15. M. Arndt, "Zimmer: Growing Older Gracefully," *BusinessWeek* (June 9, 2003), pp. 82–84.
16. "Healthy Eating" Public Health Law Center—William Mitchell College of Law (2012), (www.publichealthlawcenter.org/topics/healthy-eating).
17. "Chile Bans Toys in Fast Food to Attack Child Obesity," *Fox News Latino* (August 2, 2012), (www.latino.foxnews.com/latino/lifestyle/2012/08/02/chile-bans-toys-in-fast-food-to-attack-child-obesity)
18. H. Yen, "Empty Nesters Push Growth of Pet Health Care Businesses," *The (Ames, IA) Tribune* (September 27, 2003), p. C8; "Industry Statistics and Trends—2012," American Pet Products Association, (www.americanpetproducts.org/press_industrytrends.asp); "Pampering Your Pet," *St. Cloud (MN) Times* (September 8, 2007), p. 3A.
19. "Chocolate Candy Market in the U.S.: Trends and Opportunities in Premium, Gourmet and Mass Market Products," *Packaged Facts* (www.packagedfacts.com/chocolate-2505082).

20. S. Tavernise, "Married Couples Are No Longer a Majority, Census Finds," *The New York Times*, May 26, 2011, (www.nytimes.com/2011/05/26/us/26marry.html).

21. "The Power of One," *Entrepreneur* (June 2007), p. 28.

22. "Unmarried Childbearing," Centers for Disease Control and Prevention, 2012, (www.cdc.gov/nchs/fastats/unmarry.html).

23. N. Irvin, II, "The Arrival of the Thrivals," *The Futurist* (March–April 2004), pp. 16–23.

24. "The Trouble with Migrants," *The Economist* (November 24, 2007), pp. 56–57.

25. G. Cheeseman, "Bottled Water Marketing Campaigns Target Minorities," (November 29, 2011), (www.triplepundit.com/2011/11/bottled-water-brands-target-minorities/).

26. E. Knorr and G. Gruman, "What Cloud Computing Really Means," *InfoWorld* (2012), (www.infoworld.com/d/cloud-computing/what-cloud-computing-really-means-031).

27. K. Boehret, "Is Hotmail Hotter Now than It's Outlook.com?" *The Wall Street Journal* (August 1, 2012), (http://online.wsj.com/article/SB10000872396390444226904577756113154505 2576.html?KEYWORDS=microsoft+and+cloud)

28. P. Lorenz, D. Pinner, and T. Seitz, "The Economics of Solar Power," *McKinsey Quarterly* (June 2008), p. 2.

29. W. E. Halal, "The Top 10 Emerging Technologies," *Special Report* (World Future Society, 2000).

30. M. J. Cetron, "Economics: Prospects for the 'Dragon' and the 'Tiger,'" *Futurist* (July–August 2004), pp. 10–11; "A Less Fiery Dragon," *The Economist* (December 1, 2007), p. 92.

31. "Investing Without Borders: A Different Approach to Global Investing," *T. Rowe Price Report* (Fall 2007), p. 1.

32. J. Lash and F. Wellington, "Competitive Advantage on a Warming Planet," *Harvard Business Review* (March 2007), pp. 95–102.

33. "Melting Asia," *The Economist* (June 7, 2008), pp. 29–32.

34. P. Engardia, "Can the U.S. Bring Jobs Back from China?" *BusinessWeek* (June 30, 2008), pp. 39–43.

35. D. Rigby, "Growth through Sustainability," Presentation to the 2008 Annual Meeting of the Consumer Industries Governors, World Economic Forum (January 24, 2008).

36. J. Carey and L. Woellert, "Global Warming: Here Comes the Lawyers," *BusinessWeek* (October 30, 2006), pp. 34–36.

37. C. Laszlo, *Sustainable Value: How the World's Leading Companies Are Doing Well by Doing Good* (Stanford: Stanford University Press, 2008), pp. 89–99.

38. R. Ringger and S. A. DiPizza, *Sustainability Yearbook 2008* (PricewaterhouseCoopers, 2008).

39. L. T. Mendonca and J. Oppenheim, "Investing in Sustainability: An Interview with Al Gore and David Blood," *McKinsey Quarterly* (May 2007).

40. A. J. Hoffman, *Getting Ahead of the Curve: Corporate Strategies that Address Climate Change* (Ann Arbor: University of Michigan, 2006), p. 2.

41. J. K. Bourne, Jr., "Signs of Change," *National Geographic* (Special report on Changing Climate, 2008), pp. 7–21.

42. F. Dobbin and T. J. Dowd, "How Policy Shapes Competition: Early Railroad Foundings in Massachusetts," *Administrative Science Quarterly* (September 1997), pp. 501–529.

43. A. Shleifer and R. W. Viskny, "Takeovers in the 1960s and the 1980s: Evidence and Implications," in R. P. Rumelt, D. E. Schendel, and D. J. Teece (Eds.), *Fundamental Issues in Strategy: A Research Agenda* (Boston: Harvard Business School Press, 1994), pp. 403–418.

44. "The Problem with Solid Engineering," *The Economist* (May 20, 2006), pp. 71–73.

45. "Doing Business," *The Economist* (October 22, 2011), (www.economist.com/node/21533395).

46. Web site, *World Trade Organization*, www.wto.org (accessed August 3, 2012).

47. "Islamic Finance: West Meets East," *The Economist* (October 25, 2003), p. 69.

48. "Giants Forced to Dance," *The Economist* (May 26, 2007), pp. 67–68.

49. "Membership Required," *The Economist* (August 2, 2008), p. 66.

50. J. Naisbitt, *Megatrends Asia* (New York: Simon & Schuster, 1996), p. 79.

51. I. M. Cockburn, R. M. Henderson, and S. Stern, "Untangling the Origins of Competitive Advantage," *Strategic Management Journal* (October–November, 2000), Special Issue, pp. 1123–1145.

52. J. Kerins and C. McNeese, "No Surprises: Creating an Effective "Early Warning" System, (October 2008), (www.booz.com/media/uploads/no_surprises.pdf).

53. H. Wissema, "Driving through Red Lights," *Long Range Planning* (October 2002), pp. 521–539; B. K. Boyd and J. Fulk, "Executive Scanning and Perceived Uncertainty: A Multidimensional Model," *Journal of Management* (Vol. 22, No. 1, 1996), pp. 1–21.

54. P. G. Audia, E. A. Locke, and K. G. Smith, "The Paradox of Success: An Archival and a Laboratory Study of Strategic Persistence Following Radical Environmental Change," *Academy of Management Journal* (October 2000), pp. 837–853; M. L. McDonald and J. D. Westphal, "Getting By with the Advice of Their Friends: CEOs Advice Networks and Firms' Strategic Responses to Poor Performance," *Administrative Science Quarterly* (March 2003), pp. 1–32; R. A. Bettis and C. K. Prahalad, "The Dominant Logic: Retrospective and Extension," *Strategic Management Journal* (January 1995), pp. 5–14; J. M. Stofford and C. W. F. Baden-Fuller, "Creating Corporate Entrepreneurship," *Strategic Management Journal* (September 1994), pp. 521–536; J. M. Beyer, P. Chattopadhyay, E. George, W. H. Glick, and D. Pugliese, "The Selective Perception of Managers Revisited," *Academy of Management Journal* (June 1997), pp. 716–737.

55. H. I. Ansoff, "Strategic Management in a Historical Perspective," in *International Review of Strategic Management* (Vol. 2, No. 1, 1991), D. E. Hussey (Ed.), (Chichester, England: Wiley, 1991), p. 61.

56. S. E. Ante, "Sprint's Wake-Up Call," *BusinessWeek* (March 3, 2008), p. 54.

57. I. Fried, "Sprint CEO Hesse: Good Customer Service Costs Less," *All Things D* (August 7, 2012), (www.allthingsd.com/20120807/sprint-ceo-hesse-good-customer-service-costs-less).

58. M. E. Porter, *Competitive Strategy* (New York: The Free Press, 1980), p. 3.

59. This summary of the forces driving competitive strategy is taken from Porter, *Competitive Strategy*, pp. 7–29.

60. M. McCarthy, "Rivals Scramble to Topple Nike's Sneaker Supremacy," *USA Today* (April 3, 2003), pp. B1–B2; S. Holmes, "Changing the Game on Nike," *BusinessWeek* (January 22, 2007), p. 80.

61. Porter, *Competitive Strategy*, p. 23.

62. A. S. Grove, "Surviving a 10x Force," *Strategy & Leadership* (January/February 1997), pp. 35–37.

63. A fragmented industry is defined as one whose market share for the leading four firms is equal to or less than 40% of total industry sales. See M. J. Dollinger, "The Evolution of Collective Strategies in Fragmented Industries," *Academy of Management Review* (April 1990), pp. 266–285.

64. M. E. Porter, "Changing Patterns of International Competition," *California Management Review* (Winter 1986), pp. 9–40.

65. A. M. Rugman, *The Regional Multinationals: MNEs and Global Strategic Management* (Cambridge: Cambridge University Press, 2005).

66. K. J. Hatten and M. L. Hatten, "Strategic Groups, Asymmetrical Mobility Barriers, and Contestability," *Strategic Management Journal* (July–August 1987), p. 329.

67. J. C. Short, D. J. Ketchen Jr., T. B. Palmer, and G. T. M. Hult, "Firm, Strategic Group, and Industry Influences on Performance," *Strategic Management Journal* (February 2007), pp. 147–167; J. D. Osborne, C. I. Stubbart, and A. Ramaprasad, "Strategic Groups and Competitive Enactment: A Study of Dynamic Relationships Between Mental Models and Performance," *Strategic Management Journal* (May 2001), pp. 435–454; A. Fiegenbaum and H. Thomas, "Strategic Groups as Reference Groups: Theory, Modeling and Empirical Examination of Industry and Competitive Strategy," *Strategic Management Journal* (September 1995), pp. 461–476; H. R. Greve, "Managerial Cognition and the Mimities Adoption of Market Positions: What You See Is What You Do," *Strategic Management Journal* (October 1998), pp. 967–988.

68. G. Leask and D. Parker, "Strategic Groups, Competitive Groups and Performance Within the U.K. Pharmaceutical Industry: Improving Our Understanding of the Competitive Process," *Strategic Management Journal* (July 2007), pp. 723–745.

69. C. C. Pegels, Y. I. Song, and B. Yang, "Management Heterogeneity, Competitive Interaction Groups, and Firm Performance," *Strategic Management Journal* (September 2000), pp. 911–923; W. S. Desarbo and R. Grewal, "Hybrid Strategic Groups," *Strategic Management Journal* (March 2008), pp. 293–317.

70. R. E. Miles and C. C. Snow, *Organizational Strategy, Structure, and Process* (New York: McGraw-Hill, 1978). See also D. J. Ketchen Jr., "An Interview with Raymond E. Miles and Charles C. Snow," *Academy of Management Executive* (November 2003), pp. 97–104.

71. B. Kabanoff and S. Brown, "Knowledge Structures of Prospectors, Analyzers, and Defenders: Content, Structure, Stability, and Performance," *Strategic Management Journal* (February 2008), pp. 149–171.

72. R. A. D'Aveni, *Hypercompetition* (New York: The Free Press, 1994), pp. xiii–xiv.

73. C. W. Hofer and D. Schendel, *Strategy Formulation: Analytical Concepts* (St. Paul, MN: West Publishing Co., 1978), p. 77.

74. "Information Overload," *Journal of Business Strategy* (January–February 1998), p. 4.

75. E. Von Hipple, *Sources of Innovation* (New York: Oxford University Press, 1988), p. 4.

76. "An Executive Takes on the Top Business Trends: A McKinsey Global Survey," *McKinsey Quarterly* (April 2006).

77. M. D. Ryall, "Subjective Rationality, Self-Confirming Equilibrium, and Corporate Strategy," *Management Science* (Vol. 49, 2003), pp. 936–949.

78. C. H. Wee and M. L. Leow, "Competitive Business Intelligence in Singapore," *Journal of Strategic Marketing* (Vol. 2, 1994), pp. 112–139.

79. Miller, G. 2011. "Online Retailers will spend more $$$ on competitive intelligence in 2012," Upstream Commerce (November 19, 2011), (www.upstreamcommerce.com/blog/2011/11/19/north-american-companies-spend-bit-on-competitive-intelligence-2012).

80. D. Fehringer, B. Hohhof, and T. Johnson, "State of the Art: Competitive Intelligence," Research Report of the *Competitive Intelligence Foundation* (2006), p. 6.

81. A. Andreescu, "GoodData Delivers Record-Breaking Second Quarter 2012," (August 6, 2012), (www.gooddata.com/blog/gooddata-delivers-record-breaking-second-quarter-2012).

82. E. Iwata, "More U.S. Trade Secrets Walk Out Door with Foreign Spies," *USA Today* (February 13, 2003), pp. B1, B2.

83. "Twenty-nine Percent Spy on Co-Workers," *USA Today* (August 19, 2003), p. B1.

84. M. Orey, "Corporate Snoops," *BusinessWeek* (October 9, 2006), pp. 46–49; E. Javers, "Spies, Lies, & KPMG," *BusinessWeek* (February 26, 2007), pp. 86–88; "Altegrity to Acquire Kroll, the World's Leading Risk Consulting Firm," from Marsh & McLennan, *Business Wire* (www.businesswire.com/news/home/20100607005989/en/altegrity-acquire-kroll-world-leading-risk-consulting)

85. E. Javers, "I Spy—For Capitalism," *BusinessWeek* (August 13, 2007), pp. 54–56.

86. B. Flora, "Ethical Business Intelligence in NOT Mission Impossible," *Strategy & Leadership* (January/February 1998), pp. 40–41.

87. A. L. Penenberg and M. Berry, *Spooked: Espionage in Corporate America* (Cambridge, MA: Perseus Publishing, 2000).

88. T. Kendrick and J. Blackmore, "Ten Things You Really Need to Know About Competitors," *Competitive Intelligence Magazine* (September–October 2001), pp. 12–15.

89. For the percentage of CI professionals using each analytical technique, see A. Badr, E. Madden, and S. Wright, "The Contributions of CI to the Strategic Decision Making Process: Empirical Study of the European Pharmaceutical Industry," *Journal of Competitive Intelligence and Management* (Vol. 3, No. 4, 2006), pp. 15–35; and D. Fehringer, B. Hohhof, and T. Johnson, "State of the Art: Competitive Intelligence," Research Report of the *Competitive Intelligence Foundation* (2006).

90. H. E. Klein and R. E. Linneman, "Environmental Assessment: An International Study of Corporate Practices," *Journal of Business Strategy* (Summer 1984), p. 72.

91. A. F. Osborn, *Applied Imagination* (NY: Scribner, 1957); R. C. Litchfield, "Brainstorming Reconsidered: A Goal-Based View," *Academy of Management Review* (July 2008), pp. 649–668; R. I. Sutton, "The Truth About Brainstorming," *Inside Innovation*, insert to *BusinessWeek* (September 26, 2006), pp. 17–21.

92. R. S. Duboff, "The Wisdom of Expert Crowds," *Harvard Business Review* (September 2007), p. 28.

93. J. Surowiecki, *The Wisdom of Crowds* (NY: Doubleday, 2004).

94. R. Dye, "The Promise of Prediction Markets: A Roundtable," *McKinsey Quarterly* (April 2008), pp. 83–93.

95. C. R. Sunstein, "When Crowds Aren't Wise," *Harvard Business Review* (September 2006), pp. 20–21.

96. See L. E. Schlange and U. Juttner, "Helping Managers to Identify the Key Strategic Issues," *Long Range Planning* (October 1997), pp. 777–786, for an explanation and application of the cross-impact matrix.

97. G. Ringland, *Scenario Planning: Managing for the Future* (Chichester, England: Wiley, 1998); N. C. Georgantzas and W. Acar, *Scenario-Driven Planning: Learning to Manage Strategic Uncertainty* (Westport, CN: Quorum Books, 1995); L. Fahey and R. M. Randall (Eds.), *Learning from the Future: Competitive Foresight Scenarios* (New York: John Wiley & Sons, 1998).

98. M. Eskew, "Stick with Your Vision," *Harvard Business Review* (July–August 2007), pp. 56–57. This process of scenario development is adapted from M. E. Porter, *Competitive Advantage* (New York: The Free Press, 1985), pp. 448–470.

99. This process of scenario development is adapted from M. E. Porter, *Competitive Advantage* (New York: The Free Press, 1985), pp. 448–470.

100. H. C. Sashittal and A. R. Jassawalla, "Learning from Wayne Gretzky," *Organizational Dynamics* (Spring 2002), pp. 341–355.

internal scanning: Organizational Analysis

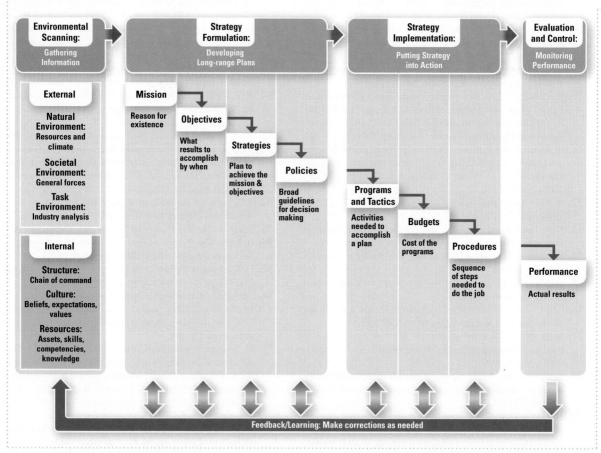

Environmental Scanning: Gathering Information	Strategy Formulation: Developing Long-range Plans	Strategy Implementation: Putting Strategy into Action	Evaluation and Control: Monitoring Performance

External

Natural Environment: Resources and climate

Societal Environment: General forces

Task Environment: Industry analysis

Internal

Structure: Chain of command

Culture: Beliefs, expectations, values

Resources: Assets, skills, competencies, knowledge

Mission — Reason for existence

Objectives — What results to accomplish by when

Strategies — Plan to achieve the mission & objectives

Policies — Broad guidelines for decision making

Programs and Tactics — Activities needed to accomplish a plan

Budgets — Cost of the programs

Procedures — Sequence of steps needed to do the job

Performance — Actual results

Feedback/Learning: Make corrections as needed

MyManagementLab®

⭐ Improve Your Grade!

Over 10 million students improved their results using the Pearson MyLabs. Visit **mymanagementlab.com** for simulations, tutorials, and end-of-chapter problems.

Learning Objectives

After reading this chapter, you should be able to:

- Apply the resource-based view of the firm to determine core and distinctive competencies
- Use the VRIO framework and the value chain to assess an organization's competitive advantage and how it can be sustained
- Understand a company's business model and how it could be imitated

- Assess a company's corporate culture and how it might affect a proposed strategy
- Scan functional resources to determine their fit with a firm's strategy
- Construct an IFAS Table that summarizes internal factors

The Nano Tries to Change the Auto Industry

Tata Motors introduced the world to the Nano at the Indian Auto Show in New Delhi back in 2008. Called the *People's Car*, the new auto was developed to sell for US$2500 in India. Even though many manufacturers were hoping to introduce cheap small cars into India and other developing nations, Tata Motors seemed to have significant advantages that other companies lacked. India's low labor costs meant that Tata could engineer a new model for 20% of the US$350 million it would cost in developed nations. A factory worker in Mumbai earned just US$1.20 per hour, less than autoworkers earned in China. The car was kept very simple. The company would save about US$900 per car by skipping equipment that the United States, Europe, and Japan required for emissions control. The engineers questioned everything about car design, putting the engine in the rear and the gas tank up front, and using fiber and plastic instead of steel. The People's Car did not have features like antilock brakes, air bags, or support beams to protect passengers in case of a crash. The dashboard contained just a speedometer, fuel gauge, and oil light. It lacked a radio, reclining seats, or power steering. It came with a small 650 cc engine that generated only 70 horsepower, but obtained 50 to 60 miles per gallon. The car's suspension system used old technology that was cheap and resulted in a rougher ride than in more expensive cars.

The vehicle was a smash success at its introduction. Tata used a lottery to choose the first 100,000 customers from more than 206,000 initial orders for the car. Then the fires started. Five cars caught fire in a short period in 2009 and sales plummeted. There was a reworking of some parts and the company extended the warranty to cover the first 60,000 miles; however, the standard line from the company was that there were no significant issues with the car other than a minor part that was defective.

The company built a plant capable of producing 20,000 Nano cars a month, but by July 2012 they sold only 5485. That was a 68% increase over a year earlier. The company sells approximately 75,000 Nanos a year. Although Tata Motors had intended to initially sell the people's car in India and then offer it in other developing markets, management has really retrenched and the Nano looks to be based in India for a long time to come.

SOURCES: S. Philip, "Chairman Tata Seeks to Salvage World's Cheapest Nano Car," *Bloomberg* (August 21, 2012), (www.bloomberg.com/news/2012-08-21/chairman-tata-seeks-to-salvage-world-s-cheapest-nan-car-html); A. K. Mishra, "Tata's Nano:Fire!" *Forbes* (May 21, 2010), (www.forbes.com/2010/05/20/forbes-india-wheels-of-fire-tata-motors.html); D. Welch and N. Lakshman, "My Other Car Is a Tata," *Business Week* (January 14, 2008), pp. 33–34.

A Resource-Based Approach to Organizational Analysis

Scanning and analyzing the external environment for opportunities and threats is necessary for the firm to be able to understand its competitive environment and its place in that environment; however, it is not enough to provide an organization with a competitive advantage. Once this external examination has been completed, the attention must turn to look within the corporation itself to identify *internal strategic factors*—critical *strengths and weaknesses* that are likely to determine whether a firm will be able to take advantage of opportunities while avoiding threats. This internal scanning, often referred to as **organizational analysis**, is concerned with identifying, developing, and taking advantage of an organization's resources and competencies.

CORE AND DISTINCTIVE COMPETENCIES

Resources are an organization's assets and are thus the basic building blocks of the organization. They include *tangible assets* (such as its plant, equipment, finances, and location), *human assets* (the number of employees, their skills, and motivation), and *intangible assets* (such as its technology [patents and copyrights], culture, and reputation).[1] **Capabilities** refer to a corporation's ability to exploit its resources. They consist of business processes and routines that manage the interaction among resources to turn inputs into outputs. For example, a company's marketing capability can be based on the interaction among its marketing specialists, distribution channels, and salespeople. A capability is functionally based and is resident in a particular function. Thus, there are marketing capabilities, manufacturing capabilities, and human resource management capabilities. When these capabilities are constantly being changed and reconfigured to make them more adaptive to an uncertain environment, they are called *dynamic capabilities*.[2] A **competency** is a cross-functional integration and coordination of capabilities. For example, a competency in new product development in one division of a corporation may be the consequence of integrating information systems capabilities, marketing capabilities, R&D capabilities, and production capabilities within the division. A **core competency** is a collection of competencies that crosses divisional boundaries, is widespread within the corporation, and is something that the corporation can do exceedingly well. Thus, new product development is a core competency if it goes beyond one division.[3] For example, a core competency of Avon Products is its expertise in door-to-door selling. FedEx has a core competency in its application of information technology to all its operations. A company must continually reinvest in a core competency or risk its becoming a *core rigidity* or *deficiency*—that is, a strength that over time matures and may become a weakness.[4] Although it is typically not an asset in the accounting sense, a core competency is a very valuable resource—it does not "wear out" with use. In general, the more core competencies are used, the more refined they get, and the more valuable they become. When core competencies are superior to those of the competition, they are called **distinctive competencies**. For example, General Electric is well known for its distinctive competency in management development. Its executives are sought out by other companies hiring top managers.[5]

Barney, in his **VRIO framework** of analysis, proposes four questions to evaluate a firm's competencies:

1. **Value:** Does it provide customer value and competitive advantage?
2. **Rareness:** Do no other competitors possess it?
3. **Imitability:** Is it costly for others to imitate?
4. **Organization:** Is the firm organized to exploit the resource?

If the answer to each of these questions is *yes* for a particular competency, it is considered to be a strength and thus a distinctive competence.[6] This should give the company a competitive advantage and lead to higher performance.[7]

It is important to evaluate the importance of a company's resources, capabilities, and competencies to ascertain whether they are internal strategic factors—that is, particular strengths and weaknesses that will help determine the future of the company. This can be done by comparing measures of these factors with measures of (1) the company's past performance, (2) the company's key competitors, and (3) the industry as a whole. To the extent that a resource (such as a firm's cash situation), capability, or competency is significantly different from the firm's own past resource, its key competitors', or the industry average, that resource is likely to be a strategic factor and should be considered in strategic decisions.

Even though a distinctive competency is certainly considered to be a corporation's key strength, a key strength may not always be a distinctive competency. As competitors attempt to imitate another company's competency (especially during hypercompetition), what was once a distinctive competency becomes a minimum requirement to compete in the industry.[8] Even though the competency may still be a core competency and thus a strength, it is no longer unique. Apple is well known for their functional design ability. The iPod, iPad, and mostly the iPhone are examples of their distinctive competency. As other phone manufacturers (in particular) imitated Apple's designs and released ever more stylish phones, we would say that this continued to be a key strength (that is, a core competency) of Apple, but it was less and less a distinctive competency.

USING RESOURCES TO GAIN COMPETITIVE ADVANTAGE

Proposing that a company's sustained competitive advantage is primarily determined by its resource endowments, Grant proposes a five-step, resource-based approach to strategy analysis.

1. Identify and classify the firm's resources in terms of strengths and weaknesses.
2. Combine the firm's strengths into specific capabilities and core competencies.
3. Appraise the profit potential of these capabilities and competencies in terms of their potential for sustainable competitive advantage and the ability to harvest the profits resulting from their use. Are there any distinctive competencies?
4. Select the strategy that best exploits the firm's capabilities and competencies relative to external opportunities.
5. Identify resource gaps and invest in upgrading weaknesses.[9]

Where do these competencies come from? A corporation can gain access to a distinctive competency in four ways:

- It may be an asset endowment, such as a key patent, coming from the founding of the company. Such was the case with Xerox, which grew on the basis of its original copying patent.

- It may be acquired from someone else. Disney bought Pixar in order to reestablish itself in the animated movie market.

- It may be shared with another business unit or alliance partner. LG has taken its electronics and production expertise into appliances with astonishing success in the market.

- It may be carefully built and accumulated over time within the company. For example, Honda carefully extended its expertise in small motor manufacturing from motorcycles to autos, boat engines, generators, and lawnmowers.[10]

There is some evidence that the best corporations prefer organic internal growth over acquisitions. One study of large global companies identified firms that outperformed their peers on both revenue growth and profitability over a decade. These excellent performers generated value from knowledge-intensive intangibles, such as copyrights, trade secrets, or strong brands, not from acquisitions.[11]

The desire to build or upgrade a core competency is one reason entrepreneurial and other fast-growing firms often tend to locate close to their competitors. They form *clusters*—geographic concentrations of interconnected companies and industries. Examples in the United States are computer technology in Silicon Valley in northern California; biotechnology in the Research Triangle area of North Carolina; financial services in New York City; clean energy in Colorado; and electric car batteries in Michigan.[12] According to Michael Porter, clusters provide access to employees, suppliers, specialized information, and complementary products.[13] Being close to one's competitors makes it easier to measure and compare performance against rivals. Capabilities may thus be formed externally through a firm's network resources. An example is the presence of many venture capitalists located in Silicon Valley who provide financial support and assistance to high-tech startup firms in the region. Employees from competitive firms in these clusters often socialize. As a result, companies learn from each other while competing with each other. Interestingly, research reveals that companies with strong core competencies have little to gain from locating in a cluster with other firms and therefore do not do so. In contrast, firms with the weakest technologies, human resources, training programs, suppliers, and distributors are strongly motivated to cluster. They have little to lose and a lot to gain from locating close to their competitors.[14]

DETERMINING THE SUSTAINABILITY OF AN ADVANTAGE

Just because a firm is able to use its resources, capabilities, and competencies to develop a competitive advantage does not mean it will be able to sustain it. Two characteristics determine the sustainability of a firm's distinctive competency(ies): durability and imitability.

Durability is the rate at which a firm's underlying resources, capabilities, or core competencies depreciate in value or become obsolete. New technology can make a company's core competency obsolete or irrelevant. However, more often we simply see that, over time, any core competency that is not continually updated and reinforced is likely to depreciate to the mean expectation in the industry and therefore cease to exist as an advantage. Sears was the dominant player in the department store industry for decades. It was not undone by a new technology, but by complacency. The management at Sears simply assumed that people would continue to shop at Sears even in the face of competitors who were catering to the new demographics in the market. Those seismic changes included the move toward designer clothes at Macy's and Target on the higher end, while on the low end Wal-Mart's explosive growth ate into sales, as well as the wave of discount tire-only retailers, and the move by Best Buy to sell appliances.

Imitability is the rate at which a firm's underlying resources, capabilities, or core competencies can be duplicated by others. To the extent that a firm's distinctive competency gives it competitive advantage in the marketplace, competitors will do what they can to learn and imitate that set of skills and capabilities. Competitors' efforts may range from *reverse engineering* (which involves taking apart a competitor's product in order to find out how it works), to hiring employees from the competitor, to outright patent infringement. A core competency can be easily imitated to the extent that it is transparent, transferable, and replicable.

- **Transparency** is the speed with which other firms can understand the relationship of resources and capabilities supporting a successful firm's strategy. Gillette has always supported its dominance in the marketing of razors with excellent R&D. A competitor could never understand how the Fusion razor was produced simply by taking one apart. Gillette's razor designs are very difficult to copy, partly because the manufacturing equipment needed to produce it is so expensive and complicated.

- **Transferability** is the ability of competitors to gather the resources and capabilities necessary to support a competitive challenge. For example, it may be very difficult for a winemaker to duplicate a French winery's key resources of land and climate, especially if the imitator is located in Iowa.

- **Replicability** is the ability of competitors to use duplicated resources and capabilities to imitate the other firm's success. For example, even though many companies have tried to imitate Procter & Gamble's success with brand management by hiring brand managers away from P&G, they have often failed to duplicate P&G's success. The competitors failed to identify less visible P&G coordination mechanisms or to realize that P&G's brand management style conflicted with the competitor's own corporate culture.

It is relatively easy to learn and imitate another company's core competency or capability if it comes from **explicit knowledge**—that is, knowledge that can be easily articulated and communicated. This is the type of knowledge that competitive intelligence activities can quickly identify and communicate. **Tacit knowledge**, in contrast, is knowledge that is *not* easily communicated because it is deeply rooted in employee experience or in a corporation's culture.[15] Tacit knowledge is more valuable and more likely to lead to a sustainable competitive advantage than is explicit knowledge because it is much harder for competitors to imitate.[16] The knowledge may be complex and combined with other types of knowledge in an unclear fashion in such a way that even management cannot clearly explain the competency.[17] Tacit knowledge is thus subject to a paradox. For a corporation to be successful and grow, its tacit knowledge must be clearly identified and codified if the knowledge is to be spread throughout the firm. Once tacit knowledge is identified and written down, however, it is easily imitable by competitors.[18] This forces companies to establish complex security systems to safeguard their key knowledge.

An organization's resources and capabilities can be placed on a continuum to the extent they are durable and can't be imitated (that is, aren't transparent, transferable, or replicable) by another firm. At one extreme are resources which are sustainable because they are shielded by patents, geography, strong brand names, or tacit knowledge. These resources and capabilities are distinctive competencies because they provide a sustainable competitive advantage. Gillette's razor technology is a good example of a product built around slow-cycle resources. The other extreme includes resources which face the highest imitation pressures because they are based on a concept or technology that can be easily duplicated, such as streaming movies. To the extent that a company has fast-cycle resources, the primary way it can compete successfully is through increased speed from lab to marketplace. Otherwise, it has no real sustainable competitive advantage.

With its low-cost position and innovative marketing strategy, Tata Motors appeared to have a competitive advantage in making and selling its new People's Car at the lowest price in the industry. Is a low-cost approach sustainable? In terms of durability, the car's lack of safety or emissions equipment could be a disadvantage when India and other developing nations begin to require such technology. Given that most developing nations also have low labor costs, Tata's low wages could be easily imitated—probably fairly quickly. In fact, Renault and Nissan had already formed an alliance in 2008 with Indian motorcycle maker Bajaj Auto to launch a US$3000 car in India in 2009.[19] That car never made it off the drawing board. By late 2011, Bajaj announced that it was reassessing the whole project because they felt the low-cost car was "unviable."[20] Overall, the sustainability of Tata Motors' potential competitive advantage seemed fairly low, given the fast-cycle nature of its resources.

Business Models

When analyzing a company, it is helpful to learn what sort of business model it is following. A **business model** is a company's method for making money in the current business environment. It includes the key structural and operational characteristics of a firm—how it earns revenue and makes a profit. A business model is usually composed of five elements:

- Who it serves
- What it provides
- How it makes money
- How it differentiates and sustains competitive advantage
- How it provides its product/service[21]

The simplest business model is to provide a good or service that can be sold such that revenues exceed costs and all expenses. Other models can be much more complicated. Some of the many possible business models are:

- **Customer solutions model:** IBM uses this model to make money not by selling IBM products, but by selling its expertise to improve its customers' operations. This is a consulting model.

- **Profit pyramid model:** General Motors offers a full line of automobiles in order to close out any niches where a competitor might find a position. The key is to get customers to buy in at the low-priced, low-margin entry point (Chevrolet Aveo – MSRP US$10235) and move them up to high-priced, high-margin products (Cadillac and Buick) where the company makes its money.

- **Multicomponent system/installed base model:** Gillette invented this classic model to sell razors at break-even pricing in order to make money on higher-margin razor blades. HP does the same with printers and printer cartridges. The product is thus a system, not just one product, with one component providing most of the profits.

- **Advertising model:** Similar to the multicomponent system/installed base model, this model offers its basic product free in order to make money on advertising. Originating in the newspaper industry, this model is used heavily in commercial radio and television. Internet-based firms, such as Google and Facebook, offer free services to users in order to expose them to the advertising that pays the bills.

- **Switchboard model:** In this model, a firm acts as an intermediary to connect multiple sellers to multiple buyers. Financial planners juggle a wide range of products for sale to multiple customers with different needs. This model has been successfully used by eBay and Amazon.com.

- **Time model:** Product R&D and speed are the keys to success in the time model. Being the first to market with a new innovation allows a pioneer like Google to earn extraordinary returns. By the time the rest of the industry catches up, Google has moved on to a newer, more innovative approach to keep people coming back.

- **Efficiency model:** In this model, a company waits until a product becomes standardized and then enters the market with a low-priced, low-margin product that appeals to the mass market. This model is used by Wal-Mart, KIA Motors, and Vanguard.

- **Blockbuster model:** In some industries, such as pharmaceuticals and motion picture studios, profitability is driven by a few key products. The focus is on high investment in a few products with high potential payoffs—especially if they can be protected by patents.

- **Profit multiplier model:** The idea of this model is to develop a concept that may or may not make money on its own but, through synergy, can spin off many profitable products. Walt Disney invented this concept by using cartoon characters to develop high-margin theme parks, merchandise, and licensing opportunities.

- **Entrepreneurial model:** In this model, a company offers specialized products/services to market niches that are too small to be worthwhile to large competitors but have the potential to grow quickly. Small, local brew pubs have been very successful in a mature industry dominated by AB InBev and MillerCoors. This model has often been used by small high-tech firms that develop innovative prototypes in order to sell off the companies (without ever selling a product) to Microsoft or DuPont.

- **De Facto industry standard model:** In this model, a company offers products free or at a very low price in order to saturate the market and become the industry standard. Once users are locked in, the company offers higher-margin products using this standard. Zynga uses this model with its famous Farmville game, and TurboTax makes its most basic program free.

In order to understand how some of these business models work, it is important to learn where on the value chain the company makes its money. Although a company might offer a large number of products and services, one product line might contribute most of the profits. At Hewlett-Packard, the printer and imaging division represents more than 20% of the company's revenues, with operating margins that exceed 15% compared to the PC division's 6% margins. However, the printer division's revenue is down 12% from 2008 as more people share pictures and documents in the cloud.[22]

Value-Chain Analysis

A **value chain** is a linked set of value-creating activities that begin with basic raw materials coming from suppliers, moving on to a series of value-added activities involved in producing and marketing a product or service, and ending with distributors getting the final goods into the hands of the ultimate consumer. Value-chain analysis works for every type of business regardless of whether they provide a service or manufacture a product. See **Figure 5–1** for an example of a typical value chain for a manufactured product. The focus of value-chain analysis is to examine the corporation in the context of the overall chain of value-creating activities, of which the firm may be only a small part.

FIGURE 5–1
Typical Value
Chain for a Manu-
factured Product

Very few corporations have a product's entire value chain in-house. Ford Motor Company did when it was managed by its founder, Henry Ford. During the 1920s and 1930s, the company owned its own iron mines, ore-carrying ships, and a small rail line to bring ore to its mile-long River Rouge plant in Detroit. Visitors to the plant would walk along an elevated walkway, where they could watch iron ore being dumped from the rail cars into huge furnaces. The resulting steel was poured and rolled out onto a moving belt to be fabricated into auto frames and parts while the visitors watched in awe. As visitors walked along the walkway, they observed an automobile being built piece by piece. Reaching the end of the moving line, the finished automobile was driven out of the plant into a vast adjoining parking lot. Ford trucks would then load the cars for delivery to dealers. Interestingly, Ford dealers had almost no power in the value-chain of the company. Dealerships were awarded by the company and taken away if a dealer was at all disloyal. Dealers received new vehicles not necessarily because they needed those particular models, but because Ford Motor chose those vehicles for sale at that dealership. Ford Motor Company at that time was completely vertically integrated—that is, it controlled (usually by ownership) every stage of the value chain, from the iron mines to the retailers.

INDUSTRY VALUE-CHAIN ANALYSIS

The value chains of most industries can be split into two segments, *upstream* and *downstream*. In the petroleum industry, for example, *upstream* refers to oil exploration, drilling, and moving the crude oil to the refinery, and *downstream* refers to refining the oil plus transporting and marketing gasoline and refined oil to distributors and gas station retailers. Even though most large oil companies are completely integrated, they often vary in the amount of expertise they have at each part of the value chain. Amoco, for example, had strong expertise downstream in marketing and retailing. British Petroleum, in contrast, was more dominant in upstream activities like exploration. That's one reason the two companies merged to form BP Amoco in 1998. The company has since changed its name to simply BP.[23]

An industry can be analyzed in terms of the profit margin available at any point along the value chain. For example, the U.S. auto industry's revenues and profits are divided among many value-chain activities, including manufacturing, new and used car sales, gasoline retailing, insurance, after-sales service and parts, and lease financing. From a revenue standpoint, auto manufacturers dominate the industry, accounting for almost 60% of total industry revenues. Profits, however, are a different matter. The various North American automakers have gone from earning most of their profit from leasing, insurance, and financing operations just a few years ago, to a resurgence of the manufacturing part of the value chain as the driver of profits. After undergoing a painful few years from 2008–2010, the automakers have emerged again as manufacturing-driven organizations. In 2012, the once bankrupt General Motors reported profits of US$7.6 Billion and Ford Motor Company which took no bailout from the government, reported profits of US$8.8 Billion.[24]

In analyzing the complete value chain of a product, note that even if a firm operates up and down the entire industry chain, it usually has an area of expertise where its primary activities lie. A company's *center of gravity* is the part of the chain where the company's greatest expertise and capabilities lie—its core competencies. According to Galbraith, a company's center of gravity is usually the point at which the company started. After a firm successfully establishes itself at this point by obtaining a competitive advantage, one of its first strategic moves is to move forward or backward along the value chain in order to reduce costs, guarantee access to key raw materials, or to guarantee distribution.[25] This process, called *vertical integration*, is discussed in more detail in **Chapter 7**.

In the paper industry, for example, Weyerhauser's center of gravity is in the raw materials and primary manufacturing parts of the value chain shown in **Figure 5–2**. Weyerhauser's expertise is in lumbering and pulp mills, which is where the company started. It integrated forward by using its wood pulp to make paper and boxes, but its greatest capability still lay in getting the greatest return from its lumbering activities. In contrast, P&G is primarily a consumer products company that also owned timberland and operated pulp mills. Its expertise is in the fabrication and distribution parts of the **Figure 5–2** value chain. P&G purchased these assets to guarantee access to the large quantities of wood pulp it needed to expand its disposable diaper, toilet tissue, and napkin products. P&G's strongest capabilities have always been in the downstream activities of product development, marketing, and brand management. It has never been as efficient in upstream paper activities as Weyerhauser. It had no real distinctive competency on that part of the value chain. When paper supplies became more plentiful (and competition got rougher), P&G gladly sold its land and mills to focus more on the part of the value chain where it could provide the greatest value at the lowest cost—creating and marketing innovative consumer products. As was the case with P&G's experience in the paper industry, it may make sense for a company to outsource any weak areas it may control internally on the industry value chain.

CORPORATE VALUE-CHAIN ANALYSIS

Each corporation has its own internal value chain of activities. See **Figure 5–2** for an example of a corporate value chain. Porter proposes that a manufacturing firm's *primary activities* usually begin with inbound logistics (raw materials handling and warehousing), go through an operations process in which a product is manufactured, and continue on to outbound logistics (warehousing and distribution), to marketing and sales, and finally to service (installation, repair, and sale of parts). Several *support activities*, such as procurement (purchasing),

FIGURE 5–2
A Corporation's
Value Chain

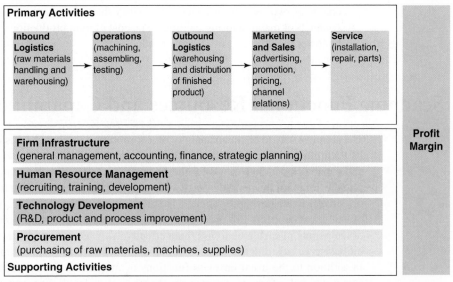

technology development (R&D), human resource management, and firm infrastructure (accounting, finance, strategic planning), ensure that the primary value-chain activities operate effectively and efficiently. Each of a company's product lines has its own distinctive value chain. Because most corporations make several different products or services, an internal analysis of the firm involves analyzing a series of different value chains.

The systematic examination of individual value activities can lead to a better understanding of a corporation's strengths and weaknesses. According to Porter, "Differences among competitor value chains are a key source of competitive advantage."[26] Corporate value-chain analysis involves the following three steps:

1. **Examine each product line's value chain in terms of the various activities involved in producing that product or service:** Which activities can be considered strengths (core competencies) or weaknesses (core deficiencies)? Do any of the strengths provide competitive advantage and can they thus be labeled distinctive competencies?

2. **Examine the "linkages" within each product line's value chain:** *Linkages* are the connections between the way one value activity (for example, marketing) is performed and the cost of performance of another activity (for example, quality control). In seeking ways for a corporation to gain competitive advantage in the marketplace, the same function can be performed in different ways with different results. For example, quality inspection of 100% of output by the workers themselves instead of the usual 10% by quality control inspectors might increase production costs, but that increase could be offset by the savings obtained from reducing the number of repair people needed to fix defective products and increasing the amount of salespeople's time devoted to selling instead of exchanging already-sold but defective products. It could also be used by the overall company as a differentiator when compared to competitors and allow the company to charge more.

3. **Examine the potential synergies among the value chains of different product lines or business units:** Each value element, such as advertising or manufacturing, has an inherent economy of scale in which activities are conducted at their lowest possible cost per unit of output. If a particular product is not being produced at a high enough level to reach economies of scale in distribution, another product could be used to share the same distribution channel. This is an example of **economies of scope**, which result when the value chains of two separate products or services share activities, such as the same marketing channels or manufacturing facilities. The cost of joint production of multiple products can be lower than the cost of separate production.

Scanning Functional Resources and Capabilities

The simplest way to begin an analysis of a corporation's value chain is by carefully examining its traditional functional areas for potential strengths and weaknesses. Functional resources and capabilities include not only the financial, physical, and human assets in each area but also the ability of the people in each area to formulate and implement the necessary functional objectives, strategies, and policies. These resources and capabilities include the knowledge of analytical concepts and procedural techniques common to each area, as well as the ability of the people in each area to use them effectively. If used properly, these resources and capabilities serve as strengths to carry out value-added activities and support strategic decisions. In addition to the usual business functions of marketing, finance, R&D, operations, human resources, and information systems/technology, we also discuss structure and culture as key parts of a business corporation's value chain.

BASIC ORGANIZATIONAL STRUCTURES

Although there is an almost infinite variety of structural forms, certain basic types predominate in modern complex organizations. **Figure 5–3** illustrates three basic **organizational structures**. The conglomerate structure is a variant of divisional structure and is thus not depicted as a fourth structure. Generally speaking, each structure tends to support some corporate strategies better than others:

- **Simple structure** has no functional or product categories and is appropriate for a small, entrepreneur-dominated company with one or two product lines that operates in a reasonably small, easily identifiable market niche. Employees tend to be generalists and jacks-of-all-trades. In terms of stages of development (to be discussed in **Chapter 9**), this is a Stage I company.

- **Functional structure** is appropriate for a medium-sized firm with several product lines in one industry. Employees tend to be specialists in the business functions that are important to that industry, such as manufacturing, marketing, finance, and human resources. In terms of stages of development (discussed in **Chapter 9**), this is a Stage II company.

- **Divisional structure** is appropriate for a large corporation with many product lines in several related industries. Employees tend to be functional specialists organized according to product/market distinctions. The Clorox Company is made up of five big divisions: (1) Cleaning (i.e., Clorox, 409, and Tilex); (2) Household (i.e., Glad, Kingsford and Fresh

FIGURE 5–3 Basic Organizational Structures

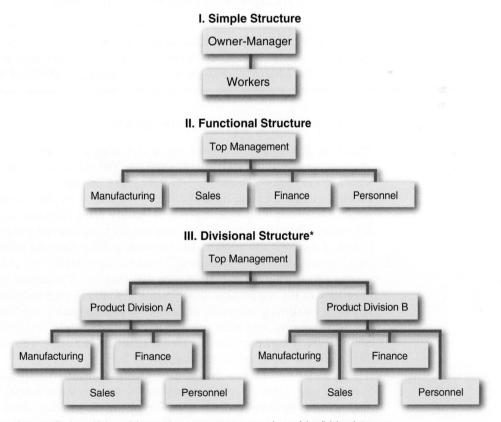

*Strategic Business Units and the conglomerate structure are variants of the divisional structure.

Step); (3) Lifestyle (i.e., Brita and Burt's Bees); (4) Professional (Commercial Solutions); and (5) International (i.e., Chux and Poett).[27] Management attempts to find some synergy among divisional activities through the use of committees and horizontal linkages. In terms of stages of development (to be discussed in **Chapter 9**), this is a Stage III company.

- **Strategic business units (SBUs)** are a modification of the divisional structure. Strategic business units are divisions or groups of divisions composed of independent product-market segments that are given primary responsibility and authority for the management of their own functional areas. *An SBU may be of any size or level, but it must have (1) a unique mission, (2) identifiable competitors, (3) an external market focus, and (4) control of its business functions.*[28] The idea is to decentralize on the basis of strategic elements rather than on the basis of size, product characteristics, or span of control and to create horizontal linkages among units previously kept separate. For example, rather than organize products on the basis of packaging technology like frozen foods, canned foods, and bagged foods, General Foods organized its products into SBUs on the basis of consumer-oriented menu segments: breakfast food, beverage, main meal, dessert, and pet foods. In terms of stages of development (to be discussed in **Chapter 9**), this is also a Stage III company.

- **Conglomerate structure** is appropriate for a large corporation with many product lines in several unrelated industries. A variant of the divisional structure, the conglomerate structure (sometimes called a holding company) is typically an assemblage of legally independent firms (subsidiaries) operating under one corporate umbrella but controlled through the subsidiaries' boards of directors. The unrelated nature of the subsidiaries prevents any attempt at gaining synergy among them. In terms of stages of development (discussed in **Chapter 9**), this is also a Stage III company.

If the current basic structure of a corporation does not easily support a strategy under consideration, top management must decide whether the proposed strategy is feasible or whether the structure should be changed to a more complicated structure such as a matrix or network. (Other structural designs such as the matrix and network are discussed in **Chapter 9.**)

CORPORATE CULTURE: THE COMPANY WAY

There is an oft-told story of a person new to a company asking an experienced co-worker what an employee should do when a customer calls. The old-timer responded: "There are three ways to do any job—the right way, the wrong way, and the company way. Around here, we always do things the company way." In most organizations, the "company way" is derived from the corporation's culture. **Corporate culture** is the collection of beliefs, expectations, and values learned and shared by a corporation's members and transmitted from one generation of employees to another. The corporate culture generally reflects the values of the founder(s) and the mission of the firm.[29] It gives a company a sense of identity: "This is who we are. This is what we do. This is what we stand for." The culture includes the dominant orientation of the company, such as R&D at 3M, shared responsibility at Nucor, customer service at Nordstrom, innovation at Google, or product quality at BMW. It often includes a number of informal work rules (forming the "company way") that employees follow without question. These work practices over time become part of a company's unquestioned tradition. The culture, therefore, reflects the company's values.

Corporate culture has two distinct attributes, intensity and integration.[30] *Cultural intensity* is the degree to which members of a unit accept the norms, values, or other cultural content associated with the unit. This shows the culture's depth. Organizations with strong norms promoting a particular value, such as quality at BMW, have intensive cultures, whereas new firms (or those in transition) have weaker, less intensive cultures. Employees in an intensive culture tend to exhibit consistent behavior—that is, they tend to act similarly over time. *Cultural integration* is the extent to which units throughout an organization share a common culture. This is the culture's breadth. Organizations with a pervasive dominant culture may be hierarchically controlled and power-oriented, such as a military unit, and have highly integrated cultures. All employees tend to hold the same cultural values and norms. In contrast, a company that is structured into diverse units by functions or divisions usually exhibits some strong subcultures (for example, R&D versus manufacturing) and a less integrated corporate culture.

Corporate culture fulfills several important functions in an organization:

1. Conveys a sense of identity for employees.
2. Helps generate employee commitment to something greater than themselves.
3. Adds to the stability of the organization as a social system.
4. Serves as a frame of reference for employees to use to make sense of organizational activities and to use as a guide for appropriate behavior.[31]

Corporate culture shapes the behavior of people in a corporation, thus affecting corporate performance. For example, corporate cultures that emphasize the socialization of new employees have less employee turnover, leading to lower costs.[32] Because corporate cultures have a powerful influence on the behavior of people at all levels, they can strongly affect a corporation's ability to shift its strategic direction. A strong culture should not only promote survival, but it should also create the basis for a superior competitive position by increasing motivation and facilitating coordination and control.[33] For example, a culture emphasizing constant renewal may help a company adapt to a changing, hypercompetitive environment.[34] To the extent that a corporation's distinctive competence is embedded in an organization's culture, it will be a form of tacit knowledge and very difficult for a competitor to imitate. The **Global Issue** feature shows the differences between ABB Asea Brown Boveri AG and Panasonic Corporation in terms of how they manage their corporate cultures in a global industry.

A change in mission, objectives, strategies, or policies is not likely to be successful if it is in opposition to the accepted culture of a firm. Foot-dragging and even sabotage may result, as employees fight to resist a radical change in corporate philosophy. As with structure, if an organization's culture is compatible with a new strategy, it is an internal strength. On the other hand, if the corporate culture is not compatible with the proposed strategy, it is a serious weakness. Circuit City ceased operations in January 2009 after a disastrous set of moves by then CEO Philip Schoonover. The history of Circuit City and its competitive advantage for years had been built around a level of expertise simply not available at other big box stores like Best Buy. However, in a move to save money, Schoonover fired 3400 of Circuit City's most experienced employees and replaced them with low-wage, low-level clerks. Analysts blasted the move for the devastating loss of morale and associated decline in customer service. The misalignment with the organization's culture spelled doom for the organization.[35]

Corporate culture is also important when considering an acquisition. The merging of two dissimilar cultures, if not handled wisely, can create some serious internal conflicts. Procter & Gamble's management knew, for example, that their 2005 acquisition of Gillette might create some cultural problems. Even though both companies were strong consumer goods marketers, they each had a fundamental difference that led to many, subtle differences between the cultures: Gillette sold its razors, toothbrushes, and batteries to men; whereas, P&G sold its health and beauty aids to women. Art Lafley, P&G's CEO, admitted a year after the merger that it would take an additional year to 15 months to align the two companies.[36]

GLOBAL issue

MANAGING CORPORATE CULTURE FOR GLOBAL COMPETITIVE ADVANTAGE: ABB VS. PANASONIC

Zurich-based ABB Asea Brown Boveri AG is a world-builder of power plants and electrical equipment with industrial factories in 140 countries. By establishing one set of multicultural values throughout its global operations, ABB's management believes that the company will gain an advantage over its rivals Siemens AG of Germany, France's Alcatel-Alsthom NV, and the U.S.'s General Electric Company. ABB is a company with no geographic base. Instead, it has many "home" markets where it can draw on expertise from around the globe. ABB created a set of 500 global managers who could adapt to local cultures while executing ABB's global strategies. These people are multilingual and move around each of ABB's 5000 profit centers in 140 countries. Their assignment is to cut costs, improve efficiency, and integrate local businesses with the ABB worldview.

Few multinational corporations are as successful as ABB in getting global strategies to work with local operations. In agreement with the resource-based view of the firm, the past Chairman of ABB, Percy Barnevik stated, "Our strength comes from pulling together. . . . If you can make this work real well, then you get a competitive edge out of the organization which is very, very difficult to copy."

Contrast ABB's globally oriented corporate culture with the more parochial culture of Panasonic Corporation of Japan. Panasonic is the third-largest electrical company in the world. Konosuke Matsushita founded the company in 1918. His management philosophy led to the company's success but became institutionalized in the corporate culture—a culture that was more focused on Japanese values than on cross-cultural globalization. As a result, Panasonic corporate culture does not adapt well to local conditions. Not only is Panasonic's top management *exclusively* Japanese, its subsidiary managers are *overwhelmingly* Japanese. The company's distrust of non-Japanese managers in the United States and some European countries results in a "rice-paper ceiling" that prevents non-Japanese people from being promoted into Panasonic subsidiaries' top management. Foreign employees are often confused by the corporate philosophy that has not been adapted to suit local realities. Panasonic's corporate culture perpetuates a cross-cultural divide that separates the Japanese from the non-Japanese managers, leaving the non-Japanese managers feeling frustrated and undervalued. This divide prevents the flow of knowledge and experience from regional operations to the headquarters and may hinder Panasonic's ability to compete globally.

. . . .

SOURCES: Summarized from J. Guyon, "ABB Fuses Units with One Set of Values," *The Wall Street Journal* (October 2, 1996), p. A15, and N. Holden, "Why Globalizing with a Conservative Corporate Culture Inhibits Localization of Management: The Telling Case of Matsushita Electric," *International Journal of Cross Cultural Management* (Vol. 1, No. 1, 2001), pp. 53–72.

STRATEGIC MARKETING ISSUES

The marketing manager is a company's primary link to the customer and the competition. The manager, therefore, must be especially concerned with the market position and marketing mix of the firm as well as with the overall reputation of the company and its brands.

Market Position and Segmentation

Market position deals with the question, "Who are our customers?" It refers to the selection of specific areas for marketing concentration and can be expressed in terms of market, product, and geographic locations. Through market research, corporations are able to practice *market segmentation* with various products or services so that managers can discover what niches to seek, which new types of products to develop, and how to ensure that a company's many products do not directly compete with one another.

Marketing Mix

Marketing mix refers to the particular combination of key variables under a corporation's control that can be used to affect demand and to gain competitive advantage. These variables

TABLE 5–1	**Product**	**Place**	**Promotion**	**Price**
Marketing Mix Variables	Quality Features Options Style Brand name Packaging Sizes Services Warranties Returns	Channels Coverage Locations Inventory Transport	Advertising Personal selling Sales promotion Publicity	List price Discounts Allowances Payment periods Credit items

SOURCE: Philip Kotler, *Marketing Management*, 11th edition © 2003, p. 16. Reprinted by Pearson Education Inc., Upper Saddle River, NJ.

are product, place, promotion, and price. Within each of these four variables are several sub-variables, listed in **Table 5–1**, that should be analyzed in terms of their effects on divisional and corporate performance.

Product Life Cycle

As depicted in **Figure 5–4**, the **product life cycle** is a graph showing time plotted against the sales of a product as it moves from introduction through growth and maturity to decline. This concept is used by marketing managers to discuss the marketing mix of a particular product or group of products in terms of where it might exist in the life cycle. From a strategic management perspective, this concept is of little value because the real position of any product can only be ascertained in hindsight. Strategy is about making decisions in real-time for the future of the business. The Innovation Issue feature shows how a company can use the conventional wisdom of the product life cycle to its advantage against leading-edge competitors.

FIGURE 5–4
Product Life Cycle

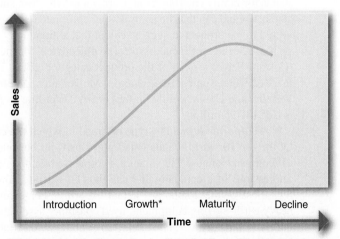

* The right end of the Growth stage is often called Competitive Turbulence because of price and distribution competition that shakes out the weaker competitors. For further information, see C. R. Wasson, *Dynamic Competitive Strategy and Product Life Cycles*. 3rd ed. (Austin, TX: Austin Press, 1978).

INNOVATION issue

DOCOMO MOVES AGAINST THE GRAIN

Years ago, DoCoMo (Japan's largest cell phone service provider in Japan) chose not to be a part of the iPhone phenomenon. The expense of the iPhone to the company was key in this decision. Sometimes innovation is needed because of strategic decisions. In this case, the iPhone has come to symbolize what constitutes "hip," so the company went on a search for opportunities in the market where they had core strengths that were not being addressed.

The fastest-growing demographic in Japan is the elderly. People age 65 and older make up 23% of the population and their needs are substantially different than the younger set. This is especially true in the cell phone market, where the latest iPhone helped push the percentage of adults age 20–29 with a Smartphone in Japan to over 51%. That compares to less than 6% of people age 65 or older who own a Smartphone.

The small screen and apps designed for the latest desires of the younger set simply don't appeal to an audience with weaker eyesight and a focus on more practical applications. DoCoMo seized on this apparent opportunity and went to work to create a must-have Smartphone experience for those over 60.

Today, the company is offering phones with larger keys, apps that are easier to understand and use, a new voice-recognition software that allows its customers to send e-mails, and is holding training sessions around the country to teach older customers how to use a Smartphone. By March of 2012, they had run more than 1100 such sessions. In each of these areas, they are separating themselves from the competition, which is far more interested in being seen as the most cutting-edge in the industry. While other competitors battle it out for the younger set, DoCoMo has captured the imagination of the older set. People over the age of 60 now account for more than 24% of the company's business, and DoCoMo's goal is to stay in the lead with the elderly market by anticipating their desires and providing innovative solutions that in some cases are more retro than cutting-edge.

....

SOURCES: R. Martin, "DoCoMo Shuns iPhone, Pushes Android Options," *The Japan Times* (May 23, 2012), (http://www.japantimes.co.jp/text/nc20120523ga.html); M. Yasu and S. Ozasa, "DoCoMo Savors an Older Vintage," *Bloomberg Businessweek* (July 2, 2012), (http://www.businessweek.com/articles/2012-06-28/docomo-looks-for-growth-among-japans-elderly).

Brand and Corporate Reputation

A **brand** is a name given to a company's product which embodies all of the characteristics of that item in the mind of the consumer. Over time and with effective advertising and execution, a brand connotes various characteristics in the consumers' minds. For example, Disney stands for family entertainment. Carnival has the "fun ships." BMW means high-performance autos. A brand can thus be an important corporate resource. If done well, a brand name is connected to the product to such an extent that a brand may stand for an entire product category, such as Kleenex for facial tissue. The objective is for the customer to ask for the brand name (Coke or Pepsi) instead of the product category (cola). The world's 10 most valuable brands in 2012 were Apple, IBM, Google, McDonald's, Microsoft, Coca-Cola, Marlboro, AT&T, Verizon, and China Mobile, in that order. According to *Forbes*, the value of the Apple brand is US$182.95 billion.[37]

A *corporate brand* is a type of brand in which the company's name serves as the brand. Of the top 10 world brands listed previously, all but one (Marlboro is part of Altria Group) are company names. The value of a corporate brand is that it typically stands for consumers' impressions of a company and can thus be extended onto products not currently offered—regardless of the company's actual expertise. For example, Caterpillar, a manufacturer of heavy earth-moving equipment, used consumer associations with the Caterpillar brand (*rugged, masculine, construction-related*) to market work boots. While this type of move may not be strategically advisable, consumer impressions of a brand can at least suggest new product categories to enter even though a company may have no competencies in making or marketing that type of product or service.[38]

A **corporate reputation** is a widely held perception of a company by the general public. It consists of two attributes: (1) stakeholders' perceptions of a corporation's ability to produce quality goods and (2) a corporation's prominence in the minds of stakeholders.[39] A good corporate reputation can be a strategic resource. It can serve in marketing as both a signal and an entry barrier. It contributes to its goods having a price premium.[40] Reputation is especially important when the quality of a company's product or service is not directly observable and can be learned only through experience. For example, retail stores are willing to stock a new product from P&G or Coca-Cola because they know that both companies market only good-quality products that are highly advertised. Like tacit knowledge, reputation tends to be long-lasting and hard for others to duplicate—thus providing a potential sustainable competitive advantage.[41] It might also have a significant impact on a firm's stock price.[42] Research reveals a positive relationship between corporate reputation and financial performance.[43]

STRATEGIC FINANCIAL ISSUES

A financial manager must ascertain the best sources of funds, uses of funds, and the control of funds. All strategic issues have financial implications. Cash must be raised from internal or external (local and global) sources and allocated for different uses. The flow of funds in the operations of an organization must be monitored. To the extent that a corporation is involved in international activities, currency fluctuations must be dealt with to ensure that profits aren't wiped out by the rise or fall of the dollar versus the yen, euro, or other currencies. Benefits in the form of returns, repayments, or products and services must be given to the sources of outside financing. All these tasks must be handled in a way that complements and supports overall corporate strategy. A firm's capital structure (amounts of debt and equity) can influence its strategic choices. Corporations with increased debt tend to be more risk-averse and less willing to invest in R&D.[44]

Financial Leverage

The mix of externally generated short-term and long-term funds in relation to the amount and timing of internally generated funds should be appropriate to the corporate objectives, strategies, and policies. The concept of **financial leverage** (the ratio of total debt to total assets) is helpful in describing how debt is used to increase the earnings available to common shareholders. When the company finances its activities by sales of bonds or notes instead of through stock, the earnings per share are boosted: the interest paid on the debt reduces taxable income, but fewer shareholders share the profits than if the company had sold more stock to finance its activities. The debt, however, does raise the firm's break-even point above what it would have been if the firm had financed from internally generated funds only. High leverage may therefore be perceived as a corporate strength in times of prosperity and ever-increasing sales, or as a weakness in times of a recession and falling sales. This is because leverage acts to magnify the effect on earnings per share of an increase or decrease in dollar sales. Research indicates that greater leverage has a positive impact on performance for firms in stable environments, but a negative impact for firms in dynamic environments.[45]

Capital Budgeting

Capital budgeting is the analyzing and ranking of possible investments in fixed assets such as land, buildings, and equipment in terms of the additional outlays and additional receipts that will result from each investment. A good finance department will be able to prepare such capital budgets and to rank them on the basis of some accepted criteria or *hurdle rate* (for example, years to pay back investment, rate of return, or time to break-even point) for the purpose of strategic decision making. Most firms have more than one hurdle rate and vary it as a function of the type of project being considered. Projects with high strategic significance, such as entering new markets or defending market share, will often have lower hurdle rates.[46]

STRATEGIC RESEARCH AND DEVELOPMENT (R&D) ISSUES

The R&D manager is responsible for suggesting and implementing a company's technological strategy in light of its corporate objectives and policies. The manager's job, therefore, involves (1) choosing among alternative new technologies to use within the corporation, (2) developing methods of embodying the new technology in new products and processes, and (3) deploying resources so that the new technology can be successfully implemented.

R&D Intensity, Technological Competence, and Technology Transfer

The company must make available the resources necessary for effective research and development. A company's **R&D intensity** (its spending on R&D as a percentage of sales revenue) is a principal means of gaining market share in global competition. The amount spent on R&D often varies by industry. For example, the U.S. computer software industry traditionally spends 13.5% of its sales dollar for R&D, whereas the paper and forest products industry spends only 1.0%.[47] A good rule of thumb for R&D spending is that a corporation should spend at a "normal" rate for that particular industry unless its strategic plan calls for unusual expenditures.

Simply spending money on R&D or new projects does not mean, however, that the money will produce useful results. Apple is one of the most profitable companies in the world and yet they ranked #18 on the 2012 S&P 500 in terms of R&D spending The top 5 on the list of companies that invest in R&D were Microsoft (US$9.4B), Pfizer (US$8.4B), Intel (US$8.4B), Merck (US$8.3B) and J&J (US$7.5B).[48]

A company's R&D unit should be evaluated for **technological competence** in both the development and the use of innovative technology. Not only should the corporation make a consistent research effort (as measured by reasonably constant corporate expenditures that result in usable innovations), it should also be proficient in managing research personnel and integrating their innovations into its day-to-day operations. A company should also be proficient in **technology transfer**, the process of taking a new technology from the laboratory to the marketplace. Aerospace parts maker Rockwell Collins, for example, is a master of developing new technology, such as the "heads-up display" (transparent screens in an airplane cockpit that tell pilots speed, altitude, and direction), for the military and then using it in products built for the civilian market.[49]

R&D Mix

Basic R&D is conducted by scientists in well-equipped laboratories where the focus is on theoretical problem areas. The best indicators of a company's capability in this area are its patents and research publications. *Product R&D* concentrates on marketing and is concerned with product or product-packaging improvements. The best measurements of ability in this area are the number of successful new products introduced and the percentage of total sales and profits coming from products introduced within the past five years. *Engineering (or process) R&D* is concerned with engineering, concentrating on quality control, and the development of design specifications and improved production equipment. A company's capability in this area can be measured by consistent reductions in unit manufacturing costs and by the number of product defects.

Most corporations will have a mix of basic, product, and process R&D, which varies by industry, company, and product line. The balance of these types of research is known as the

R&D mix and should be appropriate to the strategy being considered and to each product's life cycle. For example, it is generally accepted that product R&D normally dominates the early stages of a product's life cycle (when the product's optimal form and features are still being debated), whereas process R&D becomes especially important in the later stages (when the product's design is solidified and the emphasis is on reducing costs and improving quality).

Impact of Technological Discontinuity on Strategy

The R&D manager must determine when to abandon present technology and when to develop or adopt new technology. Richard Foster of McKinsey and Company states that the displacement of one technology by another (**technological discontinuity**) is a frequent and strategically important phenomenon. Such a discontinuity occurs when a new technology cannot simply be used to enhance the current technology, but actually substitutes for that technology to yield better performance. For each technology within a given field or industry, according to Foster, the plotting of product performance against research effort/expenditures on a graph results in an S-shaped curve.

Information technology is still on the steep upward slope of its S-curve in which relatively small increments in R&D effort result in significant improvement in performance. This is an example of *Moore's Law* (which is really a rule of thumb and not a scientific law), which states that the number of transistors that can be fit on a computer chip (microprocessors) will double (in other words, computing power will double) every 18 months.[50] The presence of a technological discontinuity in the world's steel industry during the 1960s explains why the large capital expenditures by U.S. steel companies failed to keep them competitive with the Japanese firms that adopted the new technologies. As Foster points out, "History has shown that as one technology nears the end of its S-curve, competitive leadership in a market generally changes hands."[51]

Christensen explains in *The Innovator's Dilemma* why this transition occurs when a "disruptive technology" enters an industry. In a study of computer disk drive manufacturers, he explains that established market leaders are typically reluctant to move in a timely manner to a new technology. This reluctance to switch technologies (even when the firm is aware of the new technology and may have even invented it!) is because the resource allocation process in most companies gives priority to those projects (typically based on the old technology) with the greatest likelihood of generating a good return on investment—those projects appealing to the firm's current customers (whose products are also based on the characteristics of the old technology). For example, in the 1980s a disk drive manufacturer's customers (PC manufacturers) wanted a better (faster) 5¼″ drive with greater capacity. These PC makers were not interested in the new 3½″ drives based on the new technology because (at that time) the smaller drives were slower and had less capacity. Smaller size was irrelevant since these companies primarily made desktop personal computers, which were designed to hold large drives.

The new technology is generally riskier and of little appeal to the current customers of established firms. Products derived from the new technology are more expensive and do not meet the customers' requirements—requirements based on the old technology. New entrepreneurial firms are typically more interested in the new technology because it is one way to appeal to a developing market niche in a market currently dominated by established companies. Even though the new technology may be more expensive to develop, it offers performance improvements in areas that are attractive to this small niche, but of no consequence to the customers of the established competitors.

This was the case with the entrepreneurial manufacturers of 3½″ disk drives. These smaller drives appealed to the PC makers who were trying to increase their small PC market share by offering laptop computers. Size and weight were more important to these customers than were capacity and speed. By the time the new technology was developed to the point that the 3½″ drive matched and even surpassed the 5¼″ drive in terms of speed and capacity (in addition to size and weight), it was too late for the established 5¼″ disk drive firms to switch to the new technology. Once their customers begin demanding smaller products using the new technology, the established firms were unable to respond quickly and lost their leadership position in the industry. They were able to remain in the industry (with a much reduced market share) only if they were able to utilize the new technology to be competitive in the new product line.[52]

The same phenomenon can be seen in many product categories ranging from flat-panel display screens to railroad locomotives to digital photography to musical recordings. For example, George Heilmeier created the first practical liquid-crystal display (LCD) in 1964 at RCA Labs. RCA unveiled the new display in 1968 with much fanfare about LCDs being the future of TV sets, but then refused to fund further development of the new technology. In contrast, Japanese television and computer manufacturers invested in long-term development of LCDs. Today, Japanese, Korean, and Taiwanese companies dominate the US$34 billion LCD business, and RCA no longer makes televisions. Interestingly, Heilmeier received the Kyoto Prize in 2005 for his LCD invention.[53]

STRATEGIC OPERATIONS ISSUES

The primary task of the operations (manufacturing or service) manager is to develop and operate a system that will produce the required number of products or services, with a certain quality, at a given cost, within an allotted time. Many of the key concepts and techniques popularly used in manufacturing can be applied to service businesses.

In very general terms, manufacturing can be intermittent or continuous. In *intermittent systems* (job shops), the item is normally processed sequentially, but the work and sequence of the process vary. An example is an auto body repair shop. At each location, the tasks determine the details of processing and the time required for them. These job shops can be very labor-intensive. For example, a job shop usually has little automated machinery and thus a small amount of fixed costs. It has a fairly low break-even point, but its variable cost line (composed of wages and the costs of special parts) has a relatively steep slope. Because most of the costs associated with the product are variable (many employees earn piece-rate wages), a job shop's variable costs are higher than those of automated firms. Its advantage over other firms is that it can operate at low levels and still be profitable. After a job shop's sales reach break-even, however, the huge variable costs as a percentage of total costs keep the profit per unit at a relatively low level. In terms of strategy, this firm should look for a niche in the marketplace for which it can produce and sell a reasonably small quantity of custom-made goods.

In contrast, *continuous systems* are those laid out as lines on which products can be continuously assembled or processed. An example is an automobile assembly line. A firm using continuous systems invests heavily in fixed investments such as automated processes and highly sophisticated machinery. Its labor force, relatively small but highly skilled, earns salaries rather than piece-rate wages. Consequently, this firm has a high amount of fixed costs. It also has a relatively high break-even point, but its variable cost line rises slowly. This is an example of **operating leverage**, the impact of a specific change in sales volume on net operating income. The advantage of high operating leverage is that once the firm reaches break-even, its profits rise faster than do those of less automated firms having lower operating leverage. Continuous systems reap benefits from economies of scale. In terms of strategy, this firm needs to find a high-demand niche in the marketplace for which it can produce and sell a large quantity of goods. However, a firm with high operating leverage is likely to suffer huge losses during a recession. During an economic downturn, the firm with less automation and thus less leverage is more likely to survive comfortably because a drop in sales primarily affects variable costs. It is often easier to lay off labor than to sell off specialized plants and machines.

Experience Curve

A conceptual framework that many large corporations have used successfully is the experience curve (originally called the learning curve). The **experience curve** suggests that unit production costs decline by some fixed percentage (commonly 20%–30%) each time the total accumulated volume of production in units doubles. The actual percentage varies by industry and is based on many variables: the amount of time it takes a person to learn a new task, scale economies, product and process improvements, and lower raw materials cost, among others. For example, in an industry with an 85% experience curve, a corporation might expect a 15% reduction in unit costs for every doubling of volume. The total costs per unit can be expected to drop from US$100 when the total production is 10 units, to US$85 (US$100 $\times$ 85%) when production increases to 20 units, and to US$72.25 (US$85 $\times$ 85%) when it reaches 40 units. Achieving these results often means investing in R&D and fixed assets; higher fixed costs and less flexibility thus result. Nevertheless, the manufacturing strategy is one of building capacity ahead of demand in order to achieve the lower unit costs that develop from the experience curve. On the basis of some future point on the experience curve, the corporation should price the product or service very low to preempt competition and increase market demand. The resulting high number of units sold and high market share should result in high profits, based on the low unit costs.

Management commonly uses the experience curve in estimating the production costs of (1) a product never before made with the present techniques and processes or (2) current products produced by newly introduced techniques or processes. The concept was first applied in the airframe industry and can be applied in the service industry as well. For example, a cleaning company can reduce its costs per employee by having its workers use the same equipment and techniques to clean many adjacent offices in one office building rather than just cleaning a few offices in multiple buildings. Although many firms have used experience curves extensively, an unquestioning acceptance of the industry norm (such as 80% for the airframe industry or 70% for integrated circuits) is very risky. The experience curve of the industry as a whole might not hold true for a particular company for a variety of reasons.[54]

Flexible Manufacturing for Mass Customization

The use of large, continuous, mass-production facilities to take advantage of experience-curve economies has recently been criticized. The use of **C**omputer-**A**ssisted **D**esign and **C**omputer-**A**ssisted **M**anufacturing (CAD/CAM) and robot technology means that learning times are shorter and products can be economically manufactured in small, customized batches in a process called *mass customization*—the low-cost production of individually customized goods and services.[55] Economies of scope (in which common parts of the manufacturing activities of various products are combined to gain economies even though small numbers of each product are made) replace **economies of scale** (in which unit costs are reduced by making large numbers of the same product) in flexible manufacturing. *Flexible manufacturing* permits the low-volume output of custom-tailored products at relatively low unit costs through economies of scope. It is thus possible to have the cost advantages of continuous systems with the customer-oriented advantages of intermittent systems. The automaker Hyundai/Kia is designing all of its manufacturing facilities so that any assembly line can build any car in the fleet with minimal change. They are automating plants so that robots are able to handle parts regardless of the model being produced. Previously, robots were capable of only handling parts for only one model line at a time.[56]

STRATEGIC HUMAN RESOURCE (HRM) ISSUES

The primary task of the manager of human resources is to improve the match between individuals and jobs. Research indicates that companies with good HRM practices have higher profits and a better survival rate than do firms without these practices.[57] A good HRM department should know how to use attitude surveys and other feedback devices to assess employees' satisfaction with their jobs and with the corporation as a whole. HRM managers should also use job analysis to obtain job description information about what each job needs to accomplish in terms of quality and quantity. Up-to-date job descriptions are essential not only for proper employee selection, appraisal, training, and development for wage and salary administration, and for labor negotiations, but also for summarizing the corporatewide human resources in terms of employee-skill categories. Just as a company must know the number, type, and quality of its manufacturing facilities, it must also know the kinds of people it employs and the skills they possess. The best strategies are meaningless if employees do not have the skills to carry them out or if jobs cannot be designed to accommodate the available workers. IBM, Procter & Gamble, and Hewlett-Packard, for example, use employee profiles to ensure that they have the best mix of talents to implement their planned strategies. Because project managers at IBM are now able to scan the company's databases to identify employee capabilities and availability, the average time needed to assemble a team has declined 20% for a savings of US$500 million overall.[58]

Increasing Use of Teams

Management is beginning to realize that it must be more flexible in its utilization of employees in order for human resources to be classified as a strength. Human resource managers, therefore, need to be knowledgeable about work options such as part-time work, job sharing, flex-time, extended leaves, and contract work, and especially about the proper use of teams. Over two- thirds of large U.S. companies are successfully using *autonomous (self-managing) work teams* in which a group of people work together without a supervisor to plan, coordinate, and evaluate their own work.[59] Connecticut Spring & Stamping is using self-directed work teams to achieve the dual goals of 100% on-time delivery and 100% quality. Since installing the work teams, the company has gone from what it referred to as a "very low on-time delivery performance" to an on-time delivery rate of 96%.[60]

As a way to move a product more quickly through its development stage, companies like Harley-Davidson, KPMG, Wendy's, LinkedIn, and Pfizer are using *cross-functional work teams*. Instead of developing products/services in a series of steps, companies are tearing down the traditional walls separating the departments so that people from each discipline can get involved in projects early on. In a process called *concurrent engineering*, the once-isolated specialists now work side by side and compare notes constantly in an effort to design cost-effective products with features customers want. Taking this approach enabled Chrysler Corporation to reduce its product development cycle from 60 to 36 months.[61] For such cross-functional work teams to be successful, the groups must receive training and coaching. Otherwise, poorly implemented teams may worsen morale, create divisiveness, and raise the level of cynicism among workers.[62]

Virtual teams are groups of geographically and/or organizationally dispersed co-workers that are assembled using a combination of telecommunications and information technologies to accomplish an organizational task.[63] A study conducted in 2012 found that 46% of organizations polled used virtual teams and that multinational companies were twice as likely (66%) to use virtual teams as compared to those having U.S.-based operations (28%).[64] According to the Gartner Group, more than 60% of professional employees now work in virtual teams.[65] Internet, intranet, and extranet systems are combining with other new technologies, such as desktop videoconferencing and collaborative software, to create a new workplace in which teams of workers are no longer restrained by geography, time, or organizational boundaries. This technology allows about 12% of the U.S. workforce, who have no permanent office at their companies, to do team projects over the Internet and report to a manager thousands of miles away. While the definition of telecommuting varies somewhat, the U.S. government reported that in 2012 approximately 24% of the workforce did at least part of their job from home. They define telecommuting as employees who work regularly, but not exclusively at home.[66]

As more companies outsource some of the activities previously conducted internally, the traditional organizational structure is being replaced by a series of virtual teams, which rarely, if ever, meet face to face. Such teams may be established as temporary groups to accomplish a specific task or may be more permanent to address continuing issues such as strategic planning. Membership on these teams is often fluid, depending upon the task to be accomplished. They may include not only employees from different functions within a company, but also members of various stakeholder groups, such as suppliers, customers, and law or consulting firms. The use of virtual teams to replace traditional face-to-face work groups is being driven by five trends:

1. Flatter organizational structures with increasing cross-functional coordination need
2. Turbulent environments requiring more interorganizational cooperation
3. Increasing employee autonomy and participation in decision making
4. Higher knowledge requirements derived from a greater emphasis on service
5. Increasing globalization of trade and corporate activity[67]

Union Relations and Temporary/Part-Time Workers

If the corporation is unionized, a good human resource manager should be able to work closely with the union. Even though union membership had dropped to only 11.8% of the U.S. work-force by 2011 compared to 20.1% in 1983, it still included 14.8 million people. Nevertheless, only 6.9% of private sector employees belonged to a union (compared to 37% of public sector employees).[68] To save jobs, U.S. unions are increasingly willing to support new strategic initiatives and employee involvement programs. For example, United Steel Workers hired Ron Bloom, an investment banker, to propose a strategic plan to make Goodyear Tire & Rubber globally competitive in a way that would preserve as many jobs as possible. In their landmark 2003 contract, the union gave up US$1.15 billion in wage and benefit concessions over three years in return for a promise by Goodyear's top management to invest in 12 of its 14 U.S. factories, to limit imports from its factories in Brazil and Asia, and to maintain 85% of its 19,000-person workforce. The company also agreed to aggressively restructure the firm's US$5 billion debt. According to Bloom, "We told Goodyear, 'We'll make you profitable, but you're going to adopt this strategy.'. . . We think the company should be a patient, long-term builder of value for the employees and shareholders." In their most recent contract, the U.S. tire maker expects to save some US$500+ million over four years and invest US$600 million in unionized plants.[69]

Outside the United States, the average proportion of unionized workers among major industrialized nations is around 50%. European unions tend to be militant, politically oriented, and much less interested in working with management to increase efficiency. Nationwide strikes can occur quickly. In contrast, Japanese unions are typically tied to individual companies and are usually supportive of management. These differences among countries have significant implications for the management of multinational corporations.

To increase flexibility, avoid layoffs, and reduce labor costs, corporations are using more temporary (also known as contingent) workers. Over 90% of U.S. and European firms use temporary workers in some capacity; 43% use them in professional and technical functions.[70] Approximately 23% of the U.S. workforce are part-time workers. The percentage is even higher in Japan, where 26% of workers are part-time, and in the Netherlands, where 36% of all employees work part-time.[71] Labor unions are concerned that companies use temps to avoid hiring costlier unionized workers.

Quality of Work Life and Human Diversity

Human resource departments have found that to reduce employee dissatisfaction and unionization efforts (or, conversely, to improve employee satisfaction and existing union relations), they must consider the *quality of work life* in the design of jobs. Partially a reaction to the traditionally heavy emphasis on technical and economic factors in job design, quality of work life emphasizes improving the human dimension of work. The knowledgeable human resource manager, therefore, should be able to improve the corporation's quality of work life by (1) introducing participative problem solving, (2) restructuring work, (3) introducing innovative reward systems, and (4) improving the work environment. It is hoped that these improvements will lead to a more participative corporate culture and thus higher productivity and quality products. Ford Motor Company, for example, rebuilt and modernized its famous River Rouge plant using flexible equipment and new processes. Employees work in teams and use Internet-connected PCs on the shop floor to share their concerns instantly with suppliers or product engineers. Workstations were redesigned to make them more ergonomic and reduce repetitive-strain injuries. "If you feel good while you're working, I think quality and productivity will increase, and Ford thinks that too, otherwise they wouldn't do this," observed Jerry Sullivan, president of United Auto Workers Local 600.[72]

Companies are also discovering that by redesigning their plants and offices for improved energy efficiency, they can receive a side effect of improving their employees' quality of work life—that is, raising labor productivity. See the **Sustainability Issue** feature to learn how improved environmental sustainability programs have changed the Olympic Games.

Human diversity refers to the mix in the workplace of people from different races, cultures, and backgrounds. Realizing that the demographics are changing toward an increasing percentage

SUSTAINABILITY issue

THE OLYMPIC GAMES—SOCHI 2014 AND RIO 2016

Prior to the 2012 Olympic Games in London, there had never been a plan in place for any sustainability standards for the event sector. The 2012 London Olympic Committee decided to not only make sustainability a cornerstone of that Olympics, but also to establish standards for future Olympics and other major events.

Rather than dictating a set of specific targets or checklists, the committee established a method for organizers to work with the local community, suppliers, and participants to identify the key impact areas of the event and a means to mitigate the negative impacts, measure progress, make improvements, and report those results. The committee worked with representatives from over 30 countries including the hosts for the 2014 and 2016 games. There were five areas of focus for the group: (1) Climate Change; (2) Waste; (3) Bio-diversity; (4) Inclusion; and (5) Healthy Living.

The results were stunning. Not only did the committee succeed in codifying the new standards (now referred to as ISO 20121), they also used the standards to design and run the games. Here are two of many examples of their success:

1. An industrial dump had existed in East London for over 100 years. The site was famous with the locals as an eyesore and a dangerous place. The committee took this on as one of their sustainability projects by cleaning the entire area up, putting many of the new sports venues on the site and creating what is now one of Europe's largest urban parks. The area has been transformed and eventually will see thousands of new homes in the heart of London.

2. The "Food Vision" program aimed to mitigate the impact of having to serve more than 14 million meals across 40 different venues during the 17 days of the Olympics. It required suppliers to use local sources as much as possible, and certify that food met a number of food-related standards including Fairtrade, Marine Stewardship Council Certified Fish, and Farm Assured Red Tractor. Sponsor companies such as McDonald's, Coca-Cola, and Cadbury voluntarily applied the standards to all of their meals.

While there is no way to have a zero-impact event with something the size of the Olympic games, the work done for the 2012 Olympics will change the way that all organizations plan for large events.

SOURCES: "London 2012 – Helping Set Sustainability Standards," *The Guardian* (August 10, 2012), (http://www.guardian.co.uk/sustainable-business/blog/london-2012-helping-set-sustainability-standards); http://www.london2012.com/about-us/publications/publication=london-2012-sustainability-plan-summary/; http://ukinjapan.fco.gov.uk/en/visiting-the-uk/london-2012-olympics/sustainability/.

of minorities and women in the U.S. workforce, companies are now concerned with hiring and promoting people without regard to ethnic background. Research does indicate that an increase in racial diversity leads to an increase in firm performance.[73] In a survey of 131 leading European companies, 67.2% stated that a diverse workforce can provide competitive advantage.[74] A manager from Nestlé stated: "To deliver products that meet the needs of individual consumers, we need people who respect other cultures, embrace diversity, and never discriminate on any basis."[75] Good human resource managers should be working to ensure that people are treated fairly on the job and not harassed by prejudiced co-workers or managers. Otherwise, they may find themselves subject to lawsuits. Coca-Cola Company, for example, agreed to pay US$192.5 million because of discrimination against African-American salaried employees in pay, promotions, and evaluations from 1995 and 2000. According to then Chairman and CEO Douglas Daft, "Sometimes things happen in an unintentional manner. And I've made it clear that can't happen anymore."[76]

An organization's human resources may be a key to achieving a sustainable competitive advantage. Advances in technology are copied almost immediately by competitors around the world. People, however, are not as willing to move to other companies in other countries. This means that the only long-term resource advantage remaining to corporations operating in the industrialized nations may lie in the area of skilled human resources.[77] Research does reveal that competitive strategies are more successfully executed in those companies with a high level of commitment to their employees than in those firms with less commitment.[78]

STRATEGIC INFORMATION SYSTEMS/TECHNOLOGY ISSUES

The primary task of the manager of information systems/technology is to design and manage the flow of information in an organization in ways that improve productivity and decision making. Information must be collected, stored, and synthesized in such a manner that it will answer important operating and strategic questions. A corporation's information system can be a strength or a weakness in multiple areas of strategic management. It can not only aid in environmental scanning and in controlling a company's many activities, it can also be used as a strategic weapon in gaining competitive advantage.

Impact on Performance

Information systems/technology offers four main contributions to corporate performance. *First*, (beginning in the 1970s with mainframe computers) it is used to automate existing back-office processes, such as payroll, human resource records, accounts payable and receivable, and to establish huge databases. *Second*, (beginning in the 1980s) it is used to automate individual tasks, such as keeping track of clients and expenses, through the use of personal computers with word processing and spreadsheet software. Corporate databases are accessed to provide sufficient data to analyze the data and create what-if scenarios. These first two contributions tend to focus on reducing costs. *Third*, (beginning in the 1990s) it is used to enhance key business functions, such as marketing and operations. This third contribution focuses on productivity improvements. The system provides customer support and help in distribution and logistics. For example, In an early effort on the Internet, FedEx found that by allowing customers to directly access its package-tracking database via the Web instead of their having to ask a human operator, the company saved up to US$2 million annually.[79] Business processes are analyzed to increase efficiency and productivity via reengineering. Enterprise resource planning (ERP) application software, such as SAP, PeopleSoft, Oracle, Baan, and J.D. Edwards (discussed further in **Chapter 10**), is used to integrate worldwide business activities so that employees need to enter information only once and that information is available to all corporate systems (including accounting) around the world. *Fourth*, (beginning in 2000) it is used to develop competitive advantage. For example, American Hospital Supply (AHS), a leading manufacturer and distributor of a broad line of products for doctors, laboratories, and hospitals, developed an order entry distribution system that directly linked the majority of its customers to AHS computers. The system was successful because it simplified ordering processes for customers, reduced costs for both AHS and the customer, and allowed AHS to provide pricing incentives to the customer. As a result, customer loyalty was high and AHS's share of the market became large.

A current trend in corporate information systems/technology is the increasing use of the Internet for marketing, intranets for internal communication, and extranets for logistics and distribution. An *intranet* is an information network within an organization that also has access to the external worldwide Internet. Intranets typically begin as ways to provide employees with company information such as lists of product prices, fringe benefits, and company policies. They are then converted into extranets for supply chain management. An *extranet* is an information network within an organization that is available to key suppliers and customers. The key issue in building an extranet is the creation of "fire walls" to block extranet users from accessing the firm's or other users' confidential data. Once this is accomplished, companies can allow employees, customers, and suppliers to access information and conduct business on the Internet in a completely automated manner. By connecting these groups, companies hope to obtain a competitive advantage by reducing the time needed to design and bring new products to market, slashing inventories, customizing manufacturing, and entering new markets.[80]

A recent development in information systems/technology is Web 2.0. *Web 2.0* refers to the use of wikis, blogs, RSS (Really Simple Syndication), social networks (e.g., LinkedIn and Facebook), podcasts, and mash-ups through company Web sites to forge tighter links with customers and suppliers and to engage employees more successfully. A 2010 survey by McKinsey revealed the percentage of companies using individual Web 2.0 technologies now exceeded 67% with the top uses being social networking (40%), and blogs (38%). The most heavily used tool is Web services, software that makes it easier to exchange information and conduct transactions. Satisfied users of these information technologies report that they are using these tools to interact with their customers, suppliers, and outside experts in product development efforts known as *co-creation*. For example, LEGO invited customers to suggest new models interactively and then financially rewarded the people whose ideas proved marketable.[81]

Supply Chain Management

The expansion of the marketing-oriented Internet into intranets and extranets is making significant contributions to organizational performance through supply chain management. **Supply chain management** is the forming of networks for sourcing raw materials, manufacturing products or creating services, storing and distributing the goods, and delivering them to customers and consumers.[82] Research indicates that supplier network resources have a significant impact on firm performance.[83] A survey of global executives revealed that their interest in supply chains was first to reduce costs, and then to improve customer service and get new products to market faster.[84] More than 85% of senior executives stated that improving their firm's supply-chain performance was a top priority. Companies like Wal-Mart, Dell, and Toyota, who are known to be exemplars in supply-chain management, spend only 4% of their revenues on supply-chain costs compared to 10% by the average firm.[85]

Industry leaders are integrating modern information systems into their corporate value chains to harmonize companywide efforts and to achieve competitive advantage. For example, Heineken beer distributors input actual depletion figures and replenishment orders to the Netherlands brewer through their linked Web pages. This interactive planning system generates time-phased orders based on actual usage rather than on projected demand. Distributors are then able to modify plans based on local conditions or changes in marketing. Heineken uses these modifications to adjust brewing and supply schedules. As a result of this system, lead times have been reduced from the traditional 10–12 weeks to 4–6 weeks. This time savings is especially useful in an industry competing on product freshness. In another example, Procter & Gamble participates in an information network to move the company's line of consumer products through Wal-Mart's many stores. *Radio-frequency identification (RFID)* tags containing product information are used to track goods through inventory and distribution channels. As part of the network with Wal-Mart, P&G knows by cash register and by store what products have passed through the system every hour of each day. The network is linked by satellite communications on a real-time basis. With actual point-of-sale information, products are replenished to meet current demand and minimize stockouts while maintaining exceptionally low inventories.[86]

The Strategic Audit: A Checklist for Organizational Analysis

One way of conducting an organizational analysis to ascertain a company's strengths and weaknesses is by using the Strategic Audit found in **Appendix 1.A** at the end of **Chapter 1**. The audit provides a checklist of questions by area of concern. For example, Part IV of the audit examines corporate structure, culture, and resources. It looks at organizational resources and capabilities in terms of the functional areas of marketing, finance, R&D, operations, human resources, and information systems, among others.

Synthesis of Internal Factors

After strategists have scanned the internal organizational environment and identified factors for their particular corporation, they may want to summarize their analysis of these factors using a form such as that given in **Table 5–2**. This **IFAS (Internal Factor Analysis Summary) Table** is one way to organize the internal factors into the generally accepted categories of strengths and weaknesses as well as to analyze how well a particular company's management is responding to these specific factors in light of the perceived importance of these factors to the company. Use the VRIO framework (**V**alue, **R**areness, **I**mitability, and **O**rganization) to assess the importance of each of the factors that might be considered strengths. Except for its internal orientation, this IFAS Table is built the same way as the EFAS Table described in **Chapter 4** (in **Table 4–5**). To use the IFAS Table, complete the following steps:

1. In **Column 1** (*Internal Factors*), list the 8 to 10 most important strengths and weaknesses facing the company.

2. In **Column 2** (*Weight*), assign a weight to each factor from **1.0** (*Most Important*) to **0.0** (*Not Important*) based on that factor's probable impact on a particular company's current strategic position. The higher the weight, the more important is this factor to the current and future success of the company. **All weights must sum to 1.0 regardless of the number of factors.**

3. In **Column 3** (*Rating*), assign a rating to each factor from **5.0** (*Outstanding*) to **1.0** (*Poor*) based on management's specific response to that particular factor. Each rating is a judgment regarding how well the company's management is currently dealing with each specific internal factor.

TABLE 5–2   Internal Factor Analysis Summary (IFAS Table): Maytag as Example

Internal Factors	Weight	Rating	Weighted Score	Comments
1	2	3	4	5
Strengths				
▪ Quality Maytag culture	.15	5.0	.75	Quality key to success
▪ Experienced top management	.05	4.2	.21	Know appliances
▪ Vertical integration	.10	3.9	.39	Dedicated factories
▪ Employer relations	.05	3.0	.15	Good, but deteriorating
▪ Hoover's international orientation	.15	2.8	.42	Hoover name in cleaners
Weaknesses				
▪ Process-oriented R&D	.05	2.2	.11	Slow on new products
▪ Distribution channels	.05	2.0	.10	Superstores replacing small dealers
▪ Financial position	.15	2.0	.30	High debt load
▪ Global positioning	.20	2.1	.42	Hoover weak outside the United Kingdom and Australia
▪ Manufacturing facilities	.05	4.0	.20	Investing now
Total Scores	1.00		3.05	

NOTES:

1. List strengths and weaknesses (8–10) in Column 1.
2. Weight each factor from **1.0** (Most Important) to **0.0** (Not Important) in Column 2 based on that factor's probable impact on the company's strategic position. **The total weights must sum to 1.00.**
3. Rate each factor from **5.0** (Outstanding) to **1.0** (Poor) in Column 3 based on the company's response to that factor.
4. Multiply each factor's weight times its rating to obtain each factor's weighted score in Column 4.
5. Use Column 5 (comments) for the rationale used for each factor.
6. Add the individual weighted scores to obtain the total weighted score for the company in Column 4. This tells how well the company is responding to the factors in its internal environment.

SOURCE: Thomas L. Wheelen, copyright © 1982, 1985, 1987, 1988, 1989, 1990, 1991, 1995, and every year after that. Kathryn E. Wheelen solely owns all of (Dr.) Thomas L. Wheelen's copyright materials. Kathryn E. Wheelen requires written reprint permission for each book that this material is to be printed in. Thomas L. Wheelen and J. David Hunger, copyright © 1991—first year "Internal Factor Analysis Summary (IFAS) appeared in this text (4th ed.) Reprinted by permission of the copyright holders.

4. In **Column 4** (*Weighted Score*), multiply the weight in **Column 2** for each factor times its rating in **Column 3** to obtain that factor's weighted score.

5. In **Column 5** (*Comments*), note why a particular factor was selected and/or how its weight and rating were estimated.

6. Finally, add the weighted scores for all the internal factors in **Column 4** to determine the total weighted score for that particular company. The **total weighted score** indicates how well a particular company is responding to current and expected factors in its internal environment. The score can be used to compare that firm to other firms in its industry. Check to ensure that the total weighted score truly reflects the company's current performance in terms of profitability and market share. **The total weighted score for an average firm in an industry is always 3.0**.

As an example of this procedure, **Table 5–2** includes a number of internal factors for Maytag Corporation in 1995 (before Maytag was acquired by Whirlpool) with corresponding weights, ratings, and weighted scores provided. Note that Maytag's total weighted score is 3.05, meaning that the corporation is about average compared to the strengths and weaknesses of others in the major home appliance industry.

End of Chapter SUMMARY

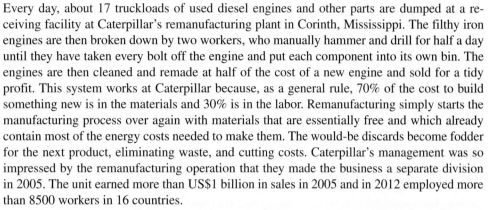

Every day, about 17 truckloads of used diesel engines and other parts are dumped at a receiving facility at Caterpillar's remanufacturing plant in Corinth, Mississippi. The filthy iron engines are then broken down by two workers, who manually hammer and drill for half a day until they have taken every bolt off the engine and put each component into its own bin. The engines are then cleaned and remade at half of the cost of a new engine and sold for a tidy profit. This system works at Caterpillar because, as a general rule, 70% of the cost to build something new is in the materials and 30% is in the labor. Remanufacturing simply starts the manufacturing process over again with materials that are essentially free and which already contain most of the energy costs needed to make them. The would-be discards become fodder for the next product, eliminating waste, and cutting costs. Caterpillar's management was so impressed by the remanufacturing operation that they made the business a separate division in 2005. The unit earned more than US$1 billion in sales in 2005 and in 2012 employed more than 8500 workers in 16 countries.

Caterpillar's remanufacturing unit was successful not only because of its capability of wringing productivity out of materials and labor, but also because it designed its products for reuse. Before they are built new, remanufactured products must be designed for disassembly. In order to achieve this, Caterpillar asks its designers to check a "Reman" box on Caterpillar's product development checklist. The company also needs to know where its products are being used in order to take them back—known as the art of *reverse logistics*. This is achieved by Caterpillar's excellent relationship with its dealers throughout the world, as well as through financial incentives. For example, when a customer orders a crankshaft, that customer is offered a remanufactured one for half the cost of a new one—assuming the customer turns in the old crankshaft to Caterpillar. The products also should be built for performance with little regard for changing fashion. Since diesel engines change little from year to year, a remanufactured engine is very similar to a new engine and might perform even better.

Monitoring the external environment is only one part of environmental scanning. Strategists also need to scan a corporation's internal environment to identify its resources, capabilities, and competencies. What are its strengths and weaknesses? At Caterpillar, management clearly noted that the environment was changing in a way to make its remanufactured product more desirable. It took advantage of its strengths in manufacturing and distribution to offer a recycling service for its current customers and a low-cost alternative product for those who could not afford a new Caterpillar engine. It also happened to be an environmentally friendly, sustainable business model. Caterpillar's management felt that remanufacturing thus provided them with a strategic advantage over competitors who don't remanufacture. This is an example of a company using its capabilities in key functional areas to expand its business by moving into a new profitable position on its value chain.[87]

MyManagementLab®

Go to **mymanagementlab.com** to complete the problems marked with this icon .

KEY TERMS

brand (p. 176)

business model (p. 166)

capabilities (p. 162)

capital budgeting (p. 177)

competency (p. 162)

conglomerate structure (p. 172)

core competencies (p. 162)

corporate culture (p. 172)

corporate reputation (p. 177)

MyManagementLab®

Go to **mymanagmentlab.com** for the following Assisted-graded writing questions:

5-1. How does the Resource-Based View of the Firm provide a superior means of evaluating a company's competitive advantage?

5-2. Explain how using an IFAS table impacts the understanding of a company's internal resources and capabilities?

DISCUSSION QUESTIONS

5-3. How does the resource-based view of firms help in determining the sustainability of a competitive advantage?

5-4. How does VRIO framework analysis help in evaluating a company's competencies?

5-5. In what ways can a corporation's structure and culture be internal strengths or weaknesses?

5-6. What are the pros and cons of management's using the experience curve to determine strategy?

5-7. How might a firm's management decide whether it should continue to invest in current known technology or in new, but untested technology? What factors might encourage or discourage such a shift?

STRATEGIC PRACTICE EXERCISES

Today, the primary means of information collection is through the Internet. Try the following exercise.

1. Form into teams of around three to five people. Select a well-known publicly-owned company to research. Inform the instructor of your choice.

2. Assign each person a separate task. One task might be to find the latest financial statements. Another would be to learn as much as possible about its top management and board of directors. Yet another might be to identify its business model, or its key competitors. Conduct research on the company *using the Internet only*.
   a. Apply the resource-based view of the firm to determine core and distinctive competencies of your selected company.
   b. Use the VRIO framework and the value chain to assess the company's competitive advantage, and how it can be sustained.
   c. Understand the company's business model, and how it could be imitated.
   d. Assess the company's corporate culture, and how it might affect a proposed strategy.
   e. Scan functional resources to determine their fit with the company strategy.
   f. What is your prediction about the future of this firm if it continues on its current path?

3. Would you buy a stock in this company? Assume that your team has U.S. $25,000 to invest. Allocate the money among the four or five primary competitors in this industry. List the companies, the number of shares purchased of each, the cost of each share as of a given date, and the total cost for each purchase assuming a typical commission used by an Internet broker, such as E-Trade or Scottrade.

NOTES

1. R. M. Grant, *Contemporary Strategy Analysis*, 6th edition (Malden, MA: Blackwell Publishing, 2008), pp. 130–131.

2. G. Schreyogg and M. Kliesch-Eberl, "How Dynamic Can Organizational Capabilities Be? Towards a Dual-Process Model of Capability Dynamization," *Strategic Management Journal* (September 2007), pp. 913–933.

3. M. Javidan, "Core Competence: What Does It Mean in Practice?" *Long Range Planning* (February 1998), pp. 60–71.

4. M. A. Hitt, B. W. Keats, and S. M. DeMarie, "Navigating in the New Competitive Landscape: Building Strategic Flexibility and Competitive Advantage in the 21st Century," *Academy of Management Executive* (November 1998), pp. 22–42; C. E. Helfat and M. A. Peteraf, "The Dynamic Resources-Based View: Capability Life Cycles," *Strategic Management Journal* (October 2003), pp. 997–1010.

5. D. Brady and K. Capell, "GE Breaks the Mold to Spur Innovation," *BusinessWeek* (April 26, 2004), pp. 88–89.

6. J. B. Barney, *Gaining and Sustaining Competitive Advantage*, 2nd ed. (Upper Saddle River, NJ: Prentice Hall, 2002), pp. 159–172. Barney's VRIO questions are very similar to those proposed by G. Hamel and S. K. Prahalad in their book, *Competing for the Future* (Boston: Harvard Business School Press, 1994) on pages 202–207 in which they state that to be distinctive, a competency must (a) provide customer value, (b) be competitor unique, and (c) be extendable to develop new products and/or markets.

7. S. L. Newbert, "Value, Rareness, Competitive Advantage, and Performance: A Conceptual-Level Empirical Investigation of the Resource-Based View of the Firm," *Strategic Management Journal* (July 2008), pp. 745–768.

8. Barney, p. 161.

9. R. M. Grant, "The Resource-Based Theory of Competitive Advantage: Implications for Strategy Formulation," *California Management Review* (Spring 1991), pp. 114–135.

10. P. J. Verdin, and P. J. Williamson, "Core Competencies, Competitive Advantage and Market Analysis: Forging the Links," in G. Hamel and A. Heene (Eds.), *Competence-Based Competition* (New York: John Wiley and Sons, 1994), pp. 83–84; S. K. Ethiraj, P. Kale, M. S. Krishnan, and J. V. Singh, "Where Do Capabilities Come From and How Do They Matter? A Study in the Software Services Industry," *Strategic Management Journal* (January 2005), pp. 701–719.

11. J. Devan, M. B. Klusas, and T. W. Ruefli, "The Elusive Goal of Corporate Outperformance," *McKinsey Quarterly Online* (April 2007).

12. Davidson, P. 2011. "To Get Jobs, Areas Develop Industry Hubs in Emerging Fields," *USA Today* (June 7, 2011).

13. M. E. Porter, "Clusters and the New Economics of Competition," *Harvard Business Review* (November–December 1998), pp. 77–90.

14. J. M. Shaver and F. Flyer, "Agglomeration Economies, Firm Heterogeneity, and Foreign Direct Investment in the United States," *Strategic Management Journal* (December 2000), pp. 1175–1193; W. Chung and A. Kalnins, "Agglomeration Effects and Performance: A Test of the Texas Lodging Industry," *Strategic Management Journal* (October 2001), pp. 969–988.

15. M. Polanyi, *The Tacit Dimension* (London: Routledge & Kegan Paul, 1966).

16. S. K. McEvily and B. Chakravarthy, "The Persistence of Knowledge-Based Advantage: An Empirical Test for Product Performance and Technological Knowledge," *Strategic Management Journal* (April 2002), pp. 285–305.

17. P. E. Bierly III, "Development of a Generic Knowledge Strategy Typology," *Journal of Business Strategies* (Spring 1999), p. 3.

18. R. W. Coff, D. C. Coff, and R. Eastvold, "The Knowledge-Leveraging Paradox: How to Achieve Scale Without Making Knowledge Imitable," *Academy of Management Review* (April 2006), pp. 452–465.

19. D. Welch and N. Lakshman "My Other Car Is a Tata," *Business Week* (January 14, 2008), p. 33.

20. P. Doval, "Renault, Nissan Tight-Lipped on Bajaj's Views on Low-Cost Car," *The Times of India* (July 16, 2011), (Articles .timesofindia.indiatimes.com/2011-07-16/delhi/29781096_1_ low-cost-car-bajaj-auto-renault-and-nissan).

21. S. Abraham, "Experiencing Strategic Conversations about the Central Forces of Our Time," *Strategy & Leadership* (Vol. 31, No. 2, 2003), pp. 61–62.

22. K. Kelleher, "HP's Printer Problem," *CNNMoney* (March 29, 2012), (www.tech.fortune.cnn.com/2012/03/29/hps-printer-problem/); P. Burrows, "Ever Wonder Why Ink Costs So Much?" *Business-Week* (November 14, 2005), pp. 42–44.

23. http://www.bp.com/sectiongenericarticle.do?categoryId=9014 445&contentId=7027526.

24. http://corporate.ford.com/our-company/investors/investor-quarterly-results/quarterly-results-detail/pr-ford-posts-2011-pretax-operating-35878?releaseId=1244755137166;http:// articles.latimes.com/2012/feb/16/business/la-fi-mo-general-motors-profits-20120215.

25. J. R. Galbraith, "Strategy and Organization Planning," in H. Mintzberg and J. B. Quinn (Eds.), *The Strategy Process: Concepts, Contexts, and Cases*, 2nd ed. (Englewood Cliffs, N.J.: Prentice Hall, 1991), pp. 315–324.

26. M. Porter, *Competitive Advantage: Creating and Sustaining Superior Performance* (New York: The Free Press, 1985), p. 36.

27. www.thecloroxcompany.com/products/our-brands/.

28. M. Leontiades, "A Diagnostic Framework for Planning," *Strategic Management Journal* (January–March 1983), p. 14.

29. E. H. Schein, *The Corporate Culture Survival Guide* (San Francisco: Jossey-Bass, 1999), p. 12; L. C. Harris and E. Ogbonna, "The Strategic Legacy of Company Founders," *Long Range Planning* (June 1999), pp. 333–343.

30. D. M. Rousseau, "Assessing Organizational Culture: The Case for Multiple Methods," in B. Schneider (Ed.), *Organizational Climate and Culture* (San Francisco: Jossey-Bass, 1990), pp. 153–192.

31. L. Smircich, "Concepts of Culture and Organizational Analysis," *Administrative Science Quarterly* (September 1983), pp. 345–346; D. Ravasi and M. Schultz, "Responding to Organizational Identity Threats: Exploring the Role of Organizational Culture," *Academy of Management Journal* (June 2006), pp. 433–458.

32. D. G. Allen, "Do Organizational Socialization Tactics Influence Newcomer Embeddedness and Turnover?" *Journal of Management* (April 2006), pp. 237–256.

33. J. B. Sorensen, "The Strength of Corporate Culture and the Reliability of Firm Performance," *Administrative Science Quarterly*

(March 2002), pp. 70–91; R. E. Smerek and D. R. Denison, "Social Capital in Organizations: Understanding the Link to Firm Performance," presentation to the *Academy of Management* (Philadelphia, 2007).

34. K. E. Aupperle, "Spontaneous Organizational Reconfiguration: A Historical Example Based on Xenophon's Anabasis," *Organization Science* (July–August 1996), pp. 445–460.

35. P. Gogoi, "Circuit City: Due for a Change?" *Bloomberg Businessweek* (February 29, 2008), (www.businessweek.com/stories/2008-02-29/circuit-city-due-for-a-change-businessweek-business-news-stock-market-and-financial-advice; E. Gruenwedel, "Circuit City Ceases Operations," *HomeMedia Magazine* (January 16, 2009), (http://www.homemediamagazine.com/news/circuit-city-ceases-operations-14346).

36. "Face Value: A Post-Modern Proctoid," *The Economist* (April 15, 2006), p. 68.

37. E. Savitz, "Apple Tops Ranking of World's Most Valuable Brands," *Forbes* (May 22, 2012), (www.forbes.com/sites/ericsavitz/2012/05/22/apple-tops-ranking-of-worlds-most-valuable-brands/ Kiley).

38. R. T. Wilcox, "The Hidden Potential of Powerful Brands," *Batten Briefings* (Summer 2003), pp. 1, 4–5.

39. V. P. Rindova, I. O. Williamson, A. P. Petkova, and J. M. Sever, "Being Good or Being Known: An Empirical Examination of the Dimensions, Antecedents, and Consequences of Organizational Reputation," *Academy of Management Journal* (December 2005), pp. 1033–1049.

40. Ibid.

41. C. Fombrun and C. Van Riel, "The Reputational Landscape," *Corporate Reputation Review* (Vol. 1, Nos. 1&2, 1997), pp. 5–13.

42. P. Engardio and M. Arndt, "What Price Reputation?" *BusinessWeek* (July 9 and 16, 2007), pp. 70–79.

43. P. W. Roberts and G. R. Dowling, "Corporate Reputation and Sustained Financial Performance," *Strategic Management Journal* (December 2002), pp. 1077–1093; J. Shamsie, "The Context of Dominance: An Industry-Driven Framework for Exploiting Reputation," *Strategic Management Journal* (March 2003), pp. 199–215; M. D. Michalisin, D. M. Kline, and R. D. Smith, "Intangible Strategic Assets and Firm Performance: A Multi-Industry Study of the Resource-Based View," *Journal of Business Strategies* (Fall 2000), pp. 91–117; S. S. Standifird, "Reputation and E-Commerce: eBay Auctions and the Asymmetrical Impact of Positive and Negative Ratings," *Journal of Management* (Vol. 27, No. 3, 2001), pp. 279–295.

44. R. L. Simerly and M. Li, "Environmental Dynamism, Capital Structure and Performance: A Theoretical Integration and an Empirical Test," *Strategic Management Journal* (January 2000), pp. 31–49.

45. R. L. Simerly and M. Li, "Environmental Dynamism, Capital Structure and Performance: A Theoretical Integration and an Empirical Test," *Strategic Management Journal* (January 2000), pp. 31–49; A. Heisz and S. LaRochelle-Cote, "Corporate Financial Leverage in Canadian Manufacturing: Consequences for Employment and Inventories," *Canadian Journal of Administrative Science* (June 2004), pp. 111–128.

46. J. M. Poterba and L. H. Summers, "A CEO Survey of U.S. Companies' Time Horizons and Hurdle Rates," *Sloan Management Review* (Fall 1995), pp. 43–53.

47. "R&D Scoreboard," *BusinessWeek* (June 27, 1994), pp. 81–103.

48. M. Krantz, "Microsoft, Intel, Google Outspend Apple on R&D," *USA Today* (March 21, 2012), (www.usatoday.com/money/perfi/columnist/krantz/story/2012-02-20/apple-marketing-research-and-development-spending/53673126/1).

49. C. Palmeri, "Swords to Plowshares—And Back Again," *BusinessWeek* (February 11, 2008), p. 66.

50. G. E. Moore, "Cramming More Components onto Integrated Circuits," *Electronics* (38(8), April 19, 1965); D. J. Yang, "Leaving Moore's Law in the Dust," *U.S. News & World Report* (July 10, 2000), pp. 37–38; R. Fishburne and M. Malone, "Laying Down the Laws: Gordon Moore and Bob Metcalfe in Conversation," *Forbes ASAP* (February 21, 2000), pp. 97–100.

51. P. Pascarella, "Are You Investing in the Wrong Technology?" *Industry Week* (July 25, 1983), p. 38

52. C. M. Christensen, *The Innovator's Dilemma* (Boston: Harvard Business School Press, 1997).

53. O. Port, "Flat-Panel Pioneer," *BusinessWeek* (December 12, 2005), p. 22. This phenomenon has also been discussed in terms of paradigm shifts in which a new development makes the old game obsolete—See Joel A. Barker, *Future Edge* (New York: William Morrow and Company, 1992).

54. For examples of experience curves for various products, see M. Gottfredson, S. Schaubert, and H. Saenz, "The New Leader's Guide to Diagnosing the Business," *Harvard Business Review* (February 2008), pp. 63–73.

55. B. J. Pine, *Mass Customization: The New Frontier in Business Competition* (Boston: Harvard Business School Press, 1993).

56. J. Buckley, "Korea's Flexible Carmakers," *AMS* (May/June 2009), pp. 18–29.

57. S. L Rynes, K. G. Brown, and A. E. Colbert, "Seven Common Misconceptions about Human Resource Practices: Research Findings Versus Practitioner Belief," *Academy of Management Executive* (August 2002), pp. 92–103; R. S. Schuler and S. E. Jackson, "A Quarter-Century Review of Human Resource Management in the U.S.: The Growth in Importance of the International Perspective," in R. S. Schuler and S. E. Jackson (Eds.), *Strategic Human Resource Management*, 2nd ed. (Malden, MA: Blackwell Publishing, 2007), pp. 214–240; M. Guthridge and A. B. Komm, "Why Multinationals Struggle to Manage Talent," *McKinsey Quarterly* (May 2008), pp. 1–5.

58. J. McGregor and S. Hamm, "Managing the Global Workforce," *BusinessWeek* (January 28, 2008), pp. 34–48; D. A. Ready and J. A. Conger, "Make Your Company a Talent Factory," *Harvard Business Review* (June 2007), pp. 68–77.

59. E. E. Lawler, S. A. Mohrman, and G. E. Ledford, Jr., *Creating High Performance Organizations* (San Francisco: Jossey-Bass, 1995), p. 29.

60. "Building Perfection: Self-Directed Work Teams Deliver on Quality," *QualityDigest* (February 1, 2012), (www.qualtydigest.com/inside/quality-insider-article/connecticut-company-uses-self-directed-work-teams-improve-time.html).

61. R. Sanchez, "Strategic Flexibility in Product Competition," *Strategic Management Journal* (Summer 1995), p. 147.

62. A. R. Jassawalla and H. C. Sashittal, "Building Collaborative Cross-Functional New Product Teams," *Academy of Management Executive* (August 1999), pp. 50–63.

63. A. M. Townsend, S. M. DeMarie, and A. R. Hendrickson, "Virtual Teams' Technology and the Workplace of the Future," *Academy of Management Executive* (August 1998), pp. 17–29.

64. S. A. Furst, M. Reeves, B. Rosen, and R. S. Blackburn, "Managing the Life Cycle of Virtual Teams," *Academy of Management Executive* (May 2004), pp. 6–20; L. L. Martins,

L. L. Gilson, and M. T. Maynard, "Virtual Teams: What Do We Know and Where Do We Go From Here?" *Journal of Management* (Vol. 30, No. 6, 2004), pp. 805–835; T. Minton-Eversole, "Virtual Teams Used Most by Global Organizations, Survey Says," *SHRM* (July 19, 2012), (www.shrm.org/hrdisciplines/orgempdev/articles/pages/virtualteamsusedmostbyglobalorganizations,surveysays.aspx).

65. C. B. Gibson and J. L. Gibbs, "Unpacking the Concept of Virtuality: The Effects of Geographic Dispersion, Electronic Dependence, Dynamic Structure, and National Diversity on Team Innovation," *Administrative Science Quarterly* (September 2006), pp. 451–495.

66. M. C. Noonan and J. L. Glass, "The Hard Truth about Telecommuting," *Monthly Labor Review* (June 2012), (www.bls.gov/opbu/mir/2012/06/art3full.pdf).

67. Townsend, DeMarie, and Hendrickson, p. 18.

68. "Economic News Release," *Bureau of Labor Statistics*, U.S. Department of Labor (January 27, 2012).

69. D. Welsh, "What Goodyear Got from Its Union," *BusinessWeek* (October 20, 2003), pp. 148–149; "Update 1 – Goodyear Union Contract Saves $215 Mln over 4-Yrs," *Reuters* (September 29, 2009), (www.reuters.com/articles/2009/09/29/goodyear-idUSN2915419220090929).

70. S. F. Matusik and C. W. L. Hill, "The Utilization of Contingent Work, Knowledge Creation, and Competitive Advantage," *Academy of Management Executive* (October 1998), pp. 680–697; W. Mayrhofer and C. Brewster, "European Human Resource Management: Researching Developments Over Time," in *Strategic Human Resource Management*, 2nd ed. (Malden, MA: Blackwell Publishing, 2007), pp. 241–269.

71. "Part-Time Work," *The Economist* (June 24, 2006), p. 112, (www.statistica.com/statistics/192342/unadjusted-monthly-number-of-part-time-employees-in-the-us/).

72. J. Muller, "A Ford Redesign," *BusinessWeek* (November 13, 2000), Special Report.

73. O. C. Richard, B. P. S. Murthi, and K. Ismail, "The Impact of Racial Diversity on Intermediate and Long-Term Performance: The Moderating Role of Environmental Context," *Strategic Management Journal* (December 2007), pp. 1213–1233; G. Colvin, "The 50 Best Companies for Asians, Blacks, and Hispanics," *Fortune* (July 19, 1999), pp. 53–58.

74. V. Singh and S. Point, "Strategic Responses by European Companies to the Diversity Challenge: An Online Comparison," *Long Range Planning* (August 2004), pp. 295–318.

75. Singh and Point, p. 310.

76. J. Bachman, "Coke to Pay $192.5 Million to Settle Lawsuit," *The* (Ames, IA) *Tribune* (November 20, 2000), p. D4.

77. O. Gottschalg and M. Zollo, "Interest Alignment and Competitive Advantage," *Academy of Management Review* (April 2007), pp. 418–437.

78. J. Lee and D. Miller, "People Matter: Commitment to Employees, Strategy, and Performance in Korean Firms," *Strategic Management Journal* (June 1999), pp. 579–593.

79. A. Cortese, "Here Comes the Intranet," *BusinessWeek* (February 26, 1996), p. 76.

80. D. Bartholomew, "Blue-Collar Computing," *Information Week* (June 19, 1995), pp. 34–43.

81. J. Bughin, J. Manyika, A. Miller, and M. Cjhui, "Building the Web 2.0 Enterprise," *McKinsey Quarterly Online* (December 2010); J. Bughin and M. Chui, "The Rise of the Networked Enterprise: Web 2.0 Finds Its Payday," *McKinsey Quarterly Online* (December 2010), pp. 1–4.

82. C. C. Poirier, *Advanced Supply Chain Management* (San Francisco: Berrett-Koehler Publishers, 1999), p. 2.

83. J. H. Dyer and N. W. Hatch, "Relation-Specific Capabilities and Barriers to Knowledge Transfers: Creating Advantage through Network Relationships," *Strategic Management Journal* (August 2006), pp. 701–719.

84. D. Paulonis and S. Norton, "Managing Global Supply Chains," *McKinsey Quarterly Online* (August 2008).

85. M. Cook and R. Hagey, "Why Companies Flunk Supply-Chain 101: Only 33 Percent Correctly Measure Supply-Chain Performance; Few Use the Right Incentives," *Journal of Business Strategy* (Vol. 24, No. 4, 2003), pp. 35–42.

86. C. C. Poirer, pp. 3–5. For further information on RFID technology, see F. Taghaboni-Dutta and B. Velthouse, "RFID Technology is Revolutionary: Who Should Be Involved in This Game of Tag?" *Academy of Management Perspectives* (November 2006), pp. 65–78.

87. M. Arndt, "Everything Old Is New Again," *BusinessWeek* (September 25, 2006), pp. 64–70, (www.cat.com/).

PART 3

Strategy
Formulation

CHAPTER 6

strategy formulation: situation analysis and Business Strategy

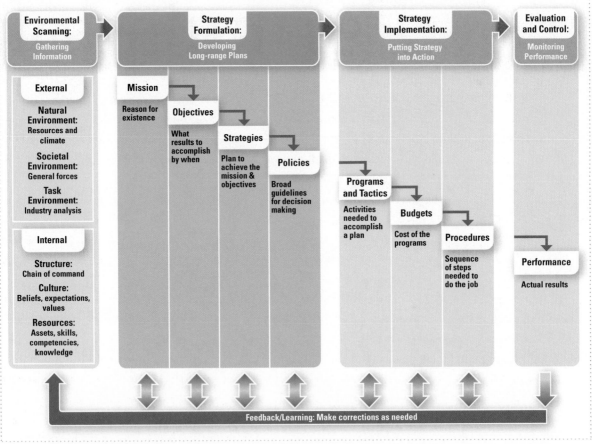

Environmental Scanning:	Strategy Formulation:	Strategy Implementation:	Evaluation and Control:
Gathering Information	Developing Long-range Plans	Putting Strategy into Action	Monitoring Performance

External

Natural Environment: Resources and climate

Societal Environment: General forces

Task Environment: Industry analysis

Internal

Structure: Chain of command

Culture: Beliefs, expectations, values

Resources: Assets, skills, competencies, knowledge

Mission
Reason for existence

Objectives
What results to accomplish by when

Strategies
Plan to achieve the mission & objectives

Policies
Broad guidelines for decision making

Programs and Tactics
Activities needed to accomplish a plan

Budgets
Cost of the programs

Procedures
Sequence of steps needed to do the job

Performance
Actual results

Feedback/Learning: Make corrections as needed

MyManagementLab®

⭐ Improve Your Grade!

Over 10 million students improved their results using the Pearson MyLabs. Visit **mymanagementlab.com** for simulations, tutorials, and end-of-chapter problems.

Learning Objectives

After reading this chapter, you should be able to:

- Organize environmental and organizational information using a SWOT approach and the SFAS matrix
- Understand the competitive and cooperative strategies available to corporations

- List the competitive tactics that would accompany competitive strategies
- Identify the basic types of strategic alliances

Target Makes a Strategic Move

Target started with a store in Roseville, Minnesota, in 1962 and for most of the next 50 years it followed families out to the suburbs with a cheap chic approach. Today, it boasts more than 1700 stores in the United States. The big-box stores carry everything from the latest Michael Graves teapot to groceries. Filling up the family minivan has served the company well. However, by 2012 the company realized that its growth days were ending. Had it not been for its wildly successful credit card that offered 5% off purchases and Target's robust sales in groceries, the company sales would have been virtually flat in 2011.

Monitoring the movement of young professionals back into city centers in Chicago, Seattle, Charlotte, Los Angeles, and San Francisco has spurred Target to try and differentiate itself in a whole new way. The company has created a new store concept called CITY Target. The stores are two-thirds the size of traditional Target stores and aim to cater to the needs of people in the city.

Gone will be 24 packs of toilet paper, replaced by 4 packs. The store eliminates lawn furniture and carries more air mattresses. It features a fresh foods section designed to pull people into the store more often. All of this is counter to the business model that is so successful outside of the city and represents a fairly risky strategic move.

The company plans to open 10 CITY locations by the end of 2013 and then evaluate their success. Other big-box retailers have tried to move into city locations, but their appeal has fallen flat with customers who walk home or take public transportation. Target's first store will be on State Street in the LOOP area of Chicago, just a block from Macy's and across the street from Forever 21.

Combining a low-cost strategy with a differentiation strategy is one of the more difficult approaches in business. This and other means of trying to achieve a sustainable competitive advantage will be discussed in this chapter.

SOURCES: http://sites.target.com/site/en/company/page.jsp?contentId=WCMP04-031761; M. Townsend, "Target's City Ambitions," *Bloomberg Businessweek* (June 4, 2012), (http://www.businessweek.com/articles/2012-05-31/targets-city-ambitions).

Situational Analysis: SWOT Approach

Strategy formulation, often referred to as strategic planning or long-range planning, is concerned with developing a corporation's mission, objectives, strategies, and policies. It begins with situation analysis: the process of finding a strategic fit between external opportunities and internal strengths while working around external threats and internal weaknesses. As shown in the Strategic Decision-Making Process in **Figure 1–5**, step 5(a) is analyzing strategic factors in light of the current situation using a SWOT approach. **SWOT** is an acronym used to describe the particular **S**trengths, **W**eaknesses, **O**pportunities, and **T**hreats that are potential strategic factors for a specific company. A SWOT approach should not only result in the identification of a corporation's distinctive competencies—the particular capabilities and resources that a firm possesses and the superior way in which they are used—but also in the identification of opportunities that the firm is not currently able to take advantage of due to a lack of appropriate resources.

It can be said that the essence of strategy is opportunity divided by capacity.[1] An opportunity by itself has no real value unless a company has the capacity (i.e., resources) to take advantage of that opportunity. By itself, a distinctive competency in a key resource or capability is no guarantee of competitive advantage. Weaknesses in other resource areas can prevent a strategy from being successful. SWOT can thus be used to take a broader view of strategy through the formula $SA = O/(S-W)$—that is, (Strategic Alternative equals Opportunity divided by Strengths minus Weaknesses). This reflects an important issue strategic managers face: Should we invest more in our strengths to make them even stronger (a distinctive competence) or should we invest in our weaknesses to at least make them competitive?

SWOT, by itself, is just a start to a strategic analysis. Some of the primary criticisms of SWOT are:

- It is simply the opinions of those filling out the boxes
- Virtually everything that is a strength is also a weakness
- Virtually everything that is an opportunity is also a threat
- Adding layers of effort does not improve the validity of the list
- It uses a single point in time approach
- There is no tie to the view from the customer
- There is no validated evaluation approach

Originally developed in the 1970s, SWOT was one of the original approaches as the field moved from business policy (looking at examples and inferring long-range plans) to strategy. In the intervening years, many techniques have developed that provide strategists with a keener insight into the elements of SWOT. However, as strategists, we need to understand our strengths, calculate the impact of weaknesses (whether they are real or perceived), take advantage of opportunities that match our strengths and minimize the impact of outside threats to the success of the organization. Thus, SWOT as a means of conceptualizing the organization is quite effective.

GENERATING A STRATEGIC FACTORS ANALYSIS SUMMARY (SFAS) MATRIX

The EFAS and IFAS Tables plus the SFAS Matrix have been developed to deal with the criticisms of SWOT analysis. When used together, they are a powerful analytical set of tools for strategic analysis. The **SFAS (Strategic Factors Analysis Summary) Matrix** summarizes an organization's strategic factors by combining the external factors from the EFAS Table with the internal factors from the IFAS Table. The EFAS and IFAS examples given of Maytag Corporation (as it was in 1995) in **Table 4–5** and **Table 5–2** list a total of 20 internal and external factors. These are too many factors for most people to use in strategy formulation. The SFAS Matrix requires a strategic decision maker to condense these strengths, weaknesses, opportunities, and threats into fewer than 10 strategic factors. This is done by reviewing and revising the weight given each factor. The revised weights reflect the priority of each factor as a determinant of the company's future success. The highest-weighted EFAS and IFAS factors should appear in the SFAS Matrix.

As shown in **Figure 6–1**, you can create an SFAS Matrix by following these steps:

1. In **Column 1** *(Strategic Factors)*, list the most important EFAS and IFAS items. After each factor, indicate whether it is a Strength (**S**), Weakness (**W**), an Opportunity (**O**), or a Threat (**T**).

2. In **Column 2** *(Weight)*, assign weights for all of the internal and external strategic factors. As with the EFAS and IFAS Tables presented earlier, the **weight column must total 1.00**. This means that the weights calculated earlier for EFAS and IFAS will probably have to be adjusted.

3. In **Column 3** *(Rating)* assign a rating of how the company's management is responding to each of the strategic factors. These ratings will probably (but not always) be the same as those listed in the EFAS and IFAS Tables.

4. In **Column 4** *(Weighted Score)* multiply the weight in **Column 2** for each factor by its rating in **Column 3** to obtain the factor's rated score.

5. In **Column 5** *(Duration)*, depicted in **Figure 6–1**, indicate **short-term** (less than one year), **intermediate-term** (one to three years), or **long-term** (three years and beyond).

6. In **Column 6** *(Comments)*, repeat or revise your comments for each strategic factor from the previous EFAS and IFAS Tables. **The total weighted score for the average firm in an industry is always 3.0.**

The resulting SFAS Matrix is a listing of the firm's external and internal strategic factors in one table. The example given in **Figure 6–1** is for Maytag Corporation in 1995, before the firm sold its European and Australian operations and it was acquired by Whirlpool. The SFAS Matrix includes only the most important factors gathered from environmental scanning, and thus provides information that is essential for strategy formulation. The use of EFAS and IFAS Tables together with the SFAS Matrix deals with some of the criticisms of SWOT analysis. For example, the use of the SFAS Matrix reduces the list of factors to a manageable number, puts weights on each factor, and allows one factor to be listed as both a strength and a weakness (or as an opportunity and a threat).

FINDING A PROPITIOUS NICHE

One desired outcome of analyzing strategic factors is identifying a niche where an organization can use its core competencies to take advantage of a particular market opportunity. A niche is a need in the marketplace that is currently unsatisfied. The goal is to find a **propitious niche**—an extremely favorable niche—that is so well suited to the firm's internal and external environment that other corporations are not likely to challenge or dislodge it.[2] A niche is propitious to the extent that it currently is just large enough for one firm to satisfy its demand. After a firm has found and filled that niche, it is not worth a potential competitor's time or money to also go after the same niche.

FIGURE 6–1   Strategic Factor Analysis Summary (SFAS) Matrix

Internal Strategic Factors	Weight	Rating	Weighted Score	Comments
	1	2	3	4 5
Strengths				
S1 Quality Maytag culture	.15	5.0	.75	Quality key to success
S2 Experienced top management	.05	4.2	.21	Know appliances
S3 Vertical integration	.10	3.9	.39	Dedicated factories
S4 Employee relations	.05	3.0	.15	Good, but deteriorating
S5 Hoover's international orientation	.15	2.8	.42	Hoover name in cleaners
Weaknesses				
W1 Process-oriented R&D	.05	2.2	.11	Slow on new products
W2 Distribution channels	.05	2.0	.10	Superstores replacing small dealers
W3 Financial position	.15	2.0	.30	High debt load
W4 Global positioning	.20	2.1	.42	Hoover weak outside the United Kingdom and Australia
W5 Manufacturing facilities	.05	4.0	.20	Investing now
Total Scores	1.00		3.05	

External Strategic Factors	Weight	Rating	Weighted Score	Comments
	1	2	3	4 5
Opportunities				
O1 Economic integration of European Community	.20	4.1	.82	Acquisition of Hoover
O2 Demographics favor quality appliances	.10	5.0	.50	Maytag quality
O3 Economic development of Asia	.05	1.0	.05	Low Maytag presence
O4 Opening of Eastern Europe	.05	2.0	.10	Will take time
O5 Trend to "Super Stores"	.10	1.8	.18	Maytag weak in this channel
Threats				
T1 Increasing government regulations	.10	4.3	.43	Well positioned
T2 Strong U.S. competition	.10	4.0	.40	Well positioned
T3 Whirlpool and Electrolux strong globally	.15	3.0	.45	Hoover weak globally
T4 New product advances	.05	1.2	.06	Questionable
T5 Japanese appliance companies	.10	1.6	.16	Only Asian presence is Australia
Total Scores	1.00		3.15	

*The most important external and internal factors are identified in the EFAS and IFAS Tables as shown here by shading these factors.

Strategic Factors (Select the most important opportunities/threats from EFAS, Table 4–5 and the most important strengths and weaknesses from IFAS, Table 5–2)	1 Weight	2 Rating	3 Weighted Score	4 SHORT	Duration INTERMEDIATE	5 LONG	6 Comments
S1 Quality Maytag culture (S)	.10	5.0	.50			X	Quality key to success
S5 Hoover's international orientation (S)	.10	2.8	.28	X	X		Name recognition
W3 Financial position (W)	.10	2.0	.20	X	X		High debt
W4 Global positioning (W)	.15	2.2	.33		X	X	Only in N.A., U.K., and Australia
O1 Economic integration of European Community (O)	.10	4.1	.41			X	Acquisition of Hoover
O2 Demographics favor quality (O)	.10	5.0	.50		X		Maytag quality
O5 Trend to super stores (O + T)	.10	1.8	.18	X			Weak in this channel
T3 Whirlpool and Electrolux (T)	.15	3.0	.45	X			Dominate industry
T5 Japanese appliance companies (T)	.10	1.6	.16			X	Asian presence
Total Scores	1.00		3.01				

NOTES:
1. List each of the most important factors developed in your IFAS and EFAS Tables in Column 1.
2. Weight each factor from **1.0** (Most Important) to **0.0** (Not Important) in Column 2 based on that factor's probable impact on the company's strategic position. **The total weights must sum to 1.00.**
3. Rate each factor from **5.0** (Outstanding) to **1.0** (Poor) in Column 3 based on the company's response to that factor.
4. Multiply each factor's weight times its rating to obtain each factor's weighted score in Column 4.
5. For the duration in Column 5, check the appropriate column (short term—less than 1 year; intermediate—1 to 3 years; long term—over 3 years).
6. Use Column 6 (comments) for rationale used for each factor.

Finding such a niche or sweet spot is not easy. A firm's management must continually look for a *strategic window*—that is, a unique market opportunity that is available only for a particular time. The first firm through a strategic window can occupy a propitious niche and discourage competition (if the firm has the required internal strengths). One company that successfully found a propitious niche was Frank J. Zamboni & Company, the manufacturer of the machines that smooth the ice at ice skating rinks. Frank Zamboni invented the unique tractor-like machine in 1949 and no one has found a substitute for what it does. Before the machine was invented, people had to clean and scrape the ice by hand to prepare the surface for skating. Now hockey fans look forward to intermissions just to watch "the Zamboni" slowly drive up and down the ice rink, turning rough, scraped ice into a smooth mirror surface—almost like magic. So long as Zamboni's company was able to produce the machines in the quantity and quality desired, at a reasonable price, it was not worth another company's while to go after Frank Zamboni & Company's propitious niche.

As a niche grows, so can a company within that niche—by increasing its operations' capacity or through alliances with larger firms. The key is to identify a market opportunity in which the first firm to reach that market segment can obtain and keep dominant market share. For example, Church & Dwight was the first company in the United States to successfully market sodium bicarbonate for use in cooking. Its Arm & Hammer brand baking soda is still found in 95% of all U.S. households. The propitious niche concept is crucial to the software industry. Small initial demand in emerging markets allows new entrepreneurial ventures to go after niches too small to be noticed by established companies. When Microsoft developed its first disk operating system (DOS) in 1980 for IBM's personal computers, for example, the demand for such open systems software was very small—a small niche for a then very small Microsoft. The company was able to fill that niche and to successfully grow with it.

Niches can also change—sometimes faster than a firm can adapt to that change. A company's management may discover in their situation analysis that they need to invest heavily in the firm's capabilities to keep them competitively strong in a changing niche. South African Breweries (SAB), for example, took this approach when management realized that the only way to keep competitors out of its market was to continuously invest in increased productivity and infrastructure in order to keep its prices very low.

Review of Mission and Objectives

A reexamination of an organization's current mission and objectives must be made before alternative strategies can be generated and evaluated. Even when formulating strategy, decision makers tend to concentrate on the alternatives—the action possibilities—rather than on a mission to be fulfilled and objectives to be achieved. This tendency is so attractive because it is much easier to deal with alternative courses of action that exist right here and now than to really think about what you want to accomplish in the future. The end result is that we often choose strategies that set our objectives for us rather than having our choices incorporate clear objectives and a mission statement.

Problems in performance can derive from an inappropriate statement of mission, which may be too narrow or too broad. If the mission does not provide a **common thread** (a unifying theme) for a corporation's businesses, managers may be unclear about where the company is heading. Objectives and strategies might be in conflict with each other. Divisions might be competing against one another rather than against outside competition—to the detriment of the corporation as a whole.

A company's objectives can also be inappropriately stated. They can either focus too much on short-term operational goals or be so general that they provide little real guidance. There may be a gap between planned and achieved objectives. When such a gap occurs, either the strategies have to be changed to improve performance or the objectives need to be adjusted downward to be more realistic. Consequently, objectives should be constantly reviewed to ensure their usefulness. This is what happened at Boeing when management decided to change its primary objective from being the largest in the industry to being the most profitable. This had a significant effect on its strategies and policies. Following its new objective, the company canceled its policy of competing with Airbus on price and abandoned its commitment to maintaining a manufacturing capacity that could produce more than half a peak year's demand for airplanes.[3]

Business Strategies

Business strategy focuses on improving the competitive position of a company's or business unit's products or services within the specific industry or market segment that the company or business unit serves. Business strategy is extremely important because research shows that business unit effects have double the impact on overall company performance than do either corporate or industry effects.[4] Business strategy can be competitive (battling against all competitors for advantage) and/or cooperative (working with one or more companies to gain advantage against other competitors). Just as corporate strategy asks what industry(ies) the company should be in, business strategy asks how the company or its units should compete or cooperate in each industry.

PORTER'S COMPETITIVE STRATEGIES

Competitive strategy raises the following questions:

- Should we compete on the basis of lower cost (and thus price), or should we differentiate our products or services on some basis other than cost, such as quality or service?
- Should we compete head to head with our major competitors for the biggest but most sought-after share of the market, or should we focus on a niche in which we can satisfy a less sought-after but also profitable segment of the market?

Michael Porter proposed three "generic" competitive strategies for outperforming other corporations in a particular industry: overall cost leadership, differentiation, and focus.[5] These strategies are called generic because they can be pursued by any type or size of business firm, even by not-for-profit organizations:

- **Cost leadership** is the ability of a company or a business unit to design, produce, and market a comparable product more efficiently than its competitors.

- **Differentiation** is the ability of a company to provide unique and superior value to the buyer in terms of product quality, special features, or after-sale service.

- **Focus** is the ability of a company to provide unique and superior value to a particular buyer group, segment of the market line, or geographic market.

Porter proposed that a firm's competitive advantage in an industry is determined by its **competitive scope**—that is, the breadth of the company's or business unit's target market. Simply put, a company or business unit can choose a broad target (that is, aim at the middle of the mass market) or a narrow target (that is, aim at a market niche). Combining these two types of target markets with the three competitive strategies results in the four variations of generic strategies. When the lower-cost and differentiation strategies have a broad mass-market target, they are simply called *cost leadership* and *differentiation*. When they are focused on a market niche (narrow target), however, they are called *cost focus* and *differentiation focus*. Research does indicate that established firms pursuing broad-scope strategies outperform firms following narrow-scope strategies in terms of ROA (Return on Assets). Even though research has found that new entrepreneurial firms increase their chance of survival if they follow a narrow-scope strategy, it has unfortunately also found that new firms that take the risk and pursue a broad-scope strategy will significantly outperform those that follow a narrow-scope strategy regardless of the size and breadth of their initial resources.[6]

Cost leadership is a lower-cost competitive strategy that aims at the broad mass market and requires "aggressive construction of efficient-scale facilities, vigorous pursuit of cost reductions from experience, tight cost and overhead control, avoidance of marginal customer accounts, and cost minimization in areas like R&D, service, sales force, advertising, and so on."[7] Because of its lower costs, the cost leader is able to charge a lower price for its products than its competitors and still make a satisfactory profit. Although it may not necessarily have the lowest costs in the industry, it has lower costs than its competitors. Some companies successfully following this strategy are Wal-Mart (discount retailing), Taco Bell (fast-food restaurants), HP (computers), Enterprise (rental cars), Aldi (grocery stores), Southwest Airlines, and Timex (watches). Having a lower-cost position also gives a company or business unit a defense against rivals. Its lower costs allow it to continue to earn profits during times of heavy competition. Its high market share means that it will have high bargaining power relative to its suppliers (because it buys in large quantities). Its low price will also serve as a barrier to entry because few new entrants will be able to match the leader's cost advantage. As a result, cost leaders are likely to earn above-average returns on investment.

Differentiation is aimed at the broad mass market and involves the creation of a product or service that is perceived throughout its industry as unique. The company or business unit may then charge a premium for its product. This specialty can be associated with design or brand image, technology, features, a dealer network, or customer service. Differentiation is a viable strategy for earning above-average returns in a specific business because the resulting brand loyalty lowers customers' sensitivity to price. Increased costs can usually be passed on to the buyers. Buyer loyalty also serves as an entry barrier; new firms must develop their own distinctive competence to differentiate their products in some way in order to compete successfully. Examples of companies that successfully use a **differentiation strategy** are Walt Disney Company (entertainment), BMW (automobiles), Apple (computers, tablets, and cell phones), and Five Guys (fast food). Research does suggest that a differentiation strategy is more likely to generate higher profits than does a **lower-cost strategy** because differentiation creates a better entry barrier. A low-cost strategy is more likely, however, to generate increases in market share.[8] For an example of how two companies approach generic strategies, see the **Global Issue** feature on Nike versus New Balance.

Cost focus is a low-cost competitive strategy that focuses on a particular buyer group or geographic market and attempts to serve only this niche, to the exclusion of others. In using cost focus, the company or business unit seeks a cost advantage in its target segment. A good example of this strategy is Potlach Corporation, a manufacturer of toilet tissue. Rather than compete directly against Procter & Gamble's Charmin, Potlach makes the house brands for Albertson's, Safeway, Jewel, and many other grocery store chains. It matches the quality of the well-known brands, but keeps costs low by eliminating advertising and promotion expenses. As a result, Spokane-based Potlach makes 92% of the private-label bathroom tissue and one-third of all bathroom tissue sold in Western U.S. grocery stores. The phenomenal growth of store brand purchases is a testament to the power of a cost focus as a means to sell at lower prices. A 2012 study by Accenture found that annual sales of store brands had increased 40% over the past decade. A total of 64% of U.S. shoppers said that store brands comprised 50% of their groceries. The same study asked why people purchased store brands. They found that 66% of shoppers bought store brands because they were cheaper, and 87% said they would buy brand-name products but only if they were the same price as the store brand.[9]

Differentiation focus, like cost focus, concentrates on a particular buyer group, product line segment, or geographic market. This is the strategy successfully followed by Midamar Corporation (distributor of halal foods), Morgan Motor Car Company (a manufacturer of classic British sports cars), Nickelodeon (a cable channel for children), OrphageniX (pharmaceuticals), and local ethnic grocery stores. In using differentiation focus, a company or business unit seeks differentiation in a targeted market segment. This strategy is valued by those who

GLOBAL issue

THE NIKE SHOE STRATEGY VS. THE NEW BALANCE SHOE STRATEGY

Nike (based in Beaverton, Oregon) and New Balance (based in Boston, Massachusetts) are direct competitors in the shoe industry. While both companies concentrate on athletic shoes, they also carry a wide variety of shoes, from sandals to boots. Both companies continually push out new models to appeal to the sports enthusiast while maintaining a line of athletic shoes that spans the entire market. New Balance has shoes that range from US$19 to their latest creation, the Minimus, that is priced around $100, all the way up to their New Balance 2040, which runs $275.

However, the battlefield is really played out using unique generic strategies. Nike produces virtually all of its shoes in Indonesia, China, and Vietnam. The focus is on strict cost controls and the ability to bring a shoe into the U.S. market cheaper than their competitors. New Balance produces a majority of its shoes (though not all) in the United States (primarily in Maine). New Balance claims that the approach allows it the ability to react faster to demand from U.S. stores and thus help those stores maintain a lower inventory. The company also believes that their U.S. workers maintain better quality control than workers abroad.

This strategy difference is being put to the test with the latest free-trade effort currently in negotiations. The Trans-Pacific Partnership Free Trade agreement aims to open up markets by reducing or eliminating tariffs. Currently, there is a 20% tariff on imported athletic shoes, and New Balance argues that this tariff is necessary to keep production in the United States. Nike (and for that matter virtually every other athletic shoe maker) argues that this is a restriction of trade and favors one company over the desires of an entire industry. Nike would be able to take full advantage of their cost advantage if the trade tariffs were removed, while New Balance would have to find more compelling competitive advantages if it wanted to keep production in the United States. The tariffs provide an artificial leveling of the cost advantage approach.

SOURCES: K. Miller, "Congress Members, New Balance Workers Fight to Save Shoe Tariffs," *Morning Sentinel* (July 19, 2012). (http://www.onlinesentinel.com/news/mainers-in-congress-workers-fight-to-save-shoe-tariffs_2012-07-18.html); http://www.newbalance.com/men/new-and-popular/17000,default,sc.html; Global Exchange, "Nike FAQ's" Accessed 6/1/13, http://www.globalexchange.org/sweatfree/nike/faq; E. Martin, "New Balance Wants its Tariffs. Nike Doesn't," *Bloomberg Businessweek* (May 7, 2012), (http://www.businessweek.com/articles/2012-05-03/new-balance-wants-its-tariffs-dot-nike-doesnt).

believe that a company or a unit that focuses its efforts is better able to serve the special needs of a narrow strategic target more effectively than can its competition. For example, Orphage-niX is a small biotech pharmaceutical company that avoids head-to-head competition with big companies like AstraZenica and Merck by developing drug therapies for "orphan" diseases. That is, diseases that are rare and often life threatening but do not have effective treatment options—for instance, diseases such as sickle cell anemia and spinal muscular atrophy that big drug makers are overlooking.[10]

Risks in Competitive Strategies

No one competitive strategy is guaranteed to achieve success, and some companies that have successfully implemented one of Porter's competitive strategies have found that they could not sustain the strategy. Each of the generic strategies has risks. For example, a company following a differentiation strategy must ensure that the higher price it charges for its higher quality is not too far above the price of the competition, otherwise customers will not see the extra quality as worth the extra cost. For years, Deere & Company was the leader in farm machinery until low-cost competitors from India and other developing countries began making low-priced products. Deere responded by building high-tech flexible manufacturing plants using mass-customization to cut its manufacturing costs and using innovation to create differentiated products which, although higher-priced, reduced customers' labor and fuel expenses.[11]

Issues in Competitive Strategies

Porter argues that to be successful, a company or business unit must achieve one of the previously mentioned generic competitive strategies. Otherwise, the company or business unit is *stuck in the middle* of the competitive marketplace with no competitive advantage and is doomed to below-average performance. A classic example of a company that found itself stuck in the middle was K-Mart. The company spent a lot of money trying to imitate both Wal-Mart's low-cost strategy and Target's quality differentiation strategy. The result was a bankruptcy filing and its continuation today as a floundering company with poor performance and no clear strategy. Although some studies do support Porter's argument that companies tend to sort themselves into either lower cost or differentiation strategies and that successful companies emphasize only one strategy,[12] other research suggests that some combination of the two competitive strategies may also be successful.[13]

The Toyota and Honda auto companies are often presented as examples of successful firms able to achieve both of these generic competitive strategies. Thanks to advances in technology, a company may be able to design quality into a product or service in such a way that it can achieve both high quality and lower costs thus achieving a higher market share.[14] Although Porter agrees that it is possible for a company or a business unit to achieve low cost and differentiation simultaneously, he continues to argue that this state is often temporary.[15] Porter does admit, however, that many different kinds of potentially profitable competitive strategies exist. Although there is generally room for only one company to successfully pursue the mass- market cost leadership strategy (because it is so often tied to maintaining a dominant market share), there is room for an almost unlimited number of differentiation and focus strategies (depending on the range of possible desirable features and the number of identifiable market niches).

Most entrepreneurial ventures follow focus strategies. The successful ones differentiate their product or service from those of others by focusing on customer wants in a segment of the market, thereby achieving a dominant share of that part of the market. Adopting guerrilla warfare tactics, these companies often go after opportunities in market niches too small to justify retaliation from the market leaders.

Industry Structure and Competitive Strategy

Although each of Porter's generic competitive strategies may be used in any industry, certain strategies are more likely to succeed depending upon the type of industry. In a **fragmented industry**, for example, where many small- and medium-sized local companies compete for relatively small shares of the total market, focus strategies will likely predominate. Fragmented industries are typical for products in the early stages of their life cycles. If few economies are to be gained through size, no large firms will emerge and entry barriers will be low—allowing a stream of new entrants into the industry. Sandwich shops, veterinary care, used-car lots, dry cleaners, and nail salons are examples. Even though P.F. Chang's and the Panda Restaurant Group have firmly established themselves as chains in the United States, local family-owned restaurants still comprise 86% of Asian casual dining restaurants.[16]

If a company is able to overcome the limitations of a fragmented market, however, it can reap the benefits of a broadly targeted cost-leadership or differentiation strategy. Until Pizza Hut was able to use advertising to differentiate itself from local competitors, the pizza fast-food business was a fragmented industry composed primarily of locally owned pizza parlors, each with its own distinctive product and service offering. Subsequently, Domino's used the cost-leadership strategy to achieve the number 2 U.S. national market share.

As an industry matures, fragmentation is overcome, and the industry tends to become a **consolidated industry** dominated by a few large companies. Although many industries start out being fragmented, battles for market share and creative attempts to overcome local or niche market boundaries often increase the market share of a few companies. After product standards become established for minimum quality and features, competition shifts to a greater emphasis on cost and service. Slower growth, overcapacity, and knowledgeable buyers combine to put a premium on a firm's ability to achieve cost leadership or differentiation along the dimensions most desired by the market. R&D shifts from product to process improvements. Overall product quality improves, and costs are reduced significantly.

The *strategic rollup* was developed in the mid-1990s as an efficient way to quickly consolidate a fragmented industry. With the aid of money from venture capitalists and private equity firms, a single company acquires hundreds of owner-operated small businesses. The resulting large firm creates economies of scale by building regional or national brands, applies best practices across all aspects of marketing and operations, and hires more sophisticated managers than the small businesses could previously afford. Rollups differ from conventional mergers and acquisitions in three ways: (1) they involve large numbers of firms, (2) the acquired firms are typically owner operated, and (3) the objective is not to gain incremental advantage, but to reinvent an entire industry.[18] Rollups are currently under way in the anti-freeze (waste glycol) recycling industry led by GlyEco Inc. and legendary rollup artist John Lorenz, and in the shredding and record storage industry led by Business Records Management and Cornerstone Records Management. Cornerstone has completed 24 acquisitions in the past four years as it attempts to consolidate this very local and fragmented industry.[19]

Once consolidated, an industry will become one in which cost leadership and differentiation tend to be combined to various degrees, even though one competitive strategy may be primarily emphasized. A firm can no longer gain and keep high market share simply through low price. The buyers are more sophisticated and demand a certain minimum level of quality for price paid. Colgate Palmolive Company, a leader in soap, toothpaste, and toothbrushes used the U.S. obsession for whiter teeth to create Colgate Optic White toothpaste (at a premium price) helping increase the company's overall market share in toothpaste to almost 37% and helping the company grow organic sales by an astonishing 6.5% in 2012.[20] The same is true for firms emphasizing high quality. Either the quality must be high enough and valued by the customer enough to justify the higher price, or the price must be dropped (through lowering costs) to compete effectively with the lower-priced products. Apple has consistently chosen to increase the capabilities of their products instead of dropping the price. Even though tablets are now available in a wide variety of sizes, capabilities, and price points, Apple has chosen to maintain their premium price and add features. They allow no discounting and no sales of their products. Consolidation is taking place worldwide in the banking, airline, cell phone, and home appliance industries. For an example of a how a company can challenge what is still a fragmented industry and change the way the whole industry operates, see the **Innovation Issue** feature on CHEGG.

Hypercompetition and Competitive Advantage Sustainability

Some firms are able to sustain their competitive advantage for many years,[21] but most find that competitive advantage erodes over time. In his book *Hypercompetition*, D'Aveni proposes that it is becoming increasingly difficult to sustain a competitive advantage for very long. "Market stability is threatened by short product life cycles, short product design cycles, new technologies, frequent entry by unexpected outsiders, repositioning by incumbents, and tactical redefinitions of market boundaries as diverse industries merge."[22] Consequently, a company or business unit must constantly work to improve its competitive advantage. It is not enough to be just the lowest-cost competitor. Through continuous improvement programs, competitors are usually working to lower their costs as well. Firms must find new ways not only to reduce costs further but also to add value to the product or service being provided.

INNOVATION issue

CHEGG AND COLLEGE TEXTBOOKS

Innovation in strategy sometimes means being able to gain advantage in an industry that refuses to acknowledge a change in customer behavior. One market that has remained mired in the past has been that of college textbooks. The business model dates back a long time and most colleges and universities used (or still use) the on-campus bookstore as a cash generator. Textbooks are chosen by professors, not students, to fit the mindset the professor wants for that particular class. Once chosen, the professors post the required material to their syllabus and let the bookstore know what they have chosen.

For many decades, students lined up to buy their books and pay whatever the bookstore charged (usually an amount that was staggering). The advent of the Internet and some very creative companies have changed the entire industry, upending both the bookstores and the publishers' means for generating income. Beyond the obvious avenue of used textbook sales, there were innovative companies taking advantage of the stagnation in the industry.

In 2007, CHEGG launched its online rental site for textbooks. Rather than paying hundreds of dollars for an "Introduction to Biology" textbook, you could rent it from CHEGG for as much as 80% off the cover price. CHEGG quickly became known as the Netflix of textbooks and their bright orange boxes became a staple at campuses throughout the United States. The company had sales of over US$200 million by 2012. However, not all was well at the company. Book rentals started to level off long before CHEGG hit any type of market saturation.

The winds had started changing again with the move to digital books, digital rentals, and a number of companies who were reimagining an industry where the textbook was not the center of the learning environment. CHEGG chose to move as well, but it moved in a different direction. The company saw the college experience as the new center for their business model and moved with it, spending US$50 million and buying up six companies in an effort to become the hub of the college student experience, offering discounts on dorm room decorations, homework help, professor recommendations, digital books, and connecting the whole operation to Facebook. CHEGG's rental book market acts as the core of its business, while CHUBB.com is used as a focused networking site for college students.

....

SOURCES: http://www.chegg.com/; A. Levy, "A College Hub. Togas Not Included," *Bloomberg Businessweek* (June 4, 2012), (http://www.businessweek.com/articles/2012-05-31/chegg-a-college-hub-dot-togas-not-included).

The same is true of a firm or unit that is following a differentiation strategy. Maytag Corporation, for example, was successful for many years by offering the most reliable brand in North American major home appliances. It was able to charge the highest prices for Maytag brand washing machines. When other competitors improved the quality of their products, however, it became increasingly difficult for customers to justify Maytag's significantly higher price. Consequently, Maytag Corporation was forced not only to add new features to its products but also to reduce costs through improved manufacturing processes so that its prices were no longer out of line with those of the competition. D'Aveni's theory of hypercompetition is supported by developing research on the importance of building *dynamic capabilities* to better cope with uncertain environments (discussed previously in Chapter 5 in the resource-based view of the firm).

D'Aveni contends that when industries become hypercompetitive, they tend to go through escalating stages of competition. Firms initially compete on cost and quality, until an abundance of high-quality, low-priced goods result. This occurred in the U.S. major home appliance industry up through 1980. In a second stage of competition, the competitors move into untapped markets. Others usually imitate these moves until their actions become too risky or expensive. This epitomized the major home appliance industry during the 1980s and 1990s, as strong U.S. and European firms like Whirlpool, Electrolux, and Bosch-Siemens established a presence in both Europe and the Americas and then moved into Asia. Strong Asian firms like LG and Haier likewise entered Europe and the Americas in the late 1990s.

According to D'Aveni, firms then raise entry barriers to limit competitors. Economies of scale, distribution agreements, and strategic alliances made it all but impossible for a new firm to enter the major home appliance industry by the end of the 20th century. After the established players have entered and consolidated all new markets, the next stage is for the remaining firms to attack and destroy the strongholds of other firms. Maytag's inability to hold onto its North American stronghold led to its acquisition by Whirlpool in 2006. Eventually, according to D'Aveni, the remaining large global competitors can work their way to a situation of perfect competition in which no one has any advantage and profits are minimal.

Before hypercompetition, strategic initiatives provided competitive advantage for many years, perhaps for decades. Except for a few stable industries, this is no longer the case. According to D'Aveni, as industries become hypercompetitive, there is no such thing as a sustainable competitive advantage. Successful strategic initiatives in this type of industry typically last only months to a few years. According to D'Aveni, the only way a firm in this kind of dynamic industry can sustain any competitive advantage is through a continuous series of multiple short-term initiatives aimed at replacing a firm's current successful products with the next generation of products before the competitors can do so. Consumer product companies like Procter & Gamble, Kraft, and Kimberly Clark are taking this approach in the hypercompetitive household products industry.

Hypercompetition views competition, in effect, as a distinct series of ocean waves on what used to be a fairly calm stretch of water. As industry competition becomes more intense, the waves grow higher and require more dexterity to handle. Although a strategy is still needed to sail from point A to point B, more turbulent water means that a craft must continually adjust course to suit each new large wave. One danger of D'Aveni's concept of hypercompetition, however, is that it may lead to an overemphasis on short-term tactics (discussed in the next section) over long-term strategy. Too much of an orientation on the individual waves of hyper-competition could cause a company to focus too much on short-term temporary advantage and not enough on achieving its long-term objectives through building sustainable competitive advantage. Nevertheless, research supports D'Aveni's argument that sustained competitive advantage is increasingly a matter not of a single advantage maintained over time, but more a matter of sequencing advantages over time.[23]

For an example of a how a company can achieve sustainable competitive advantages in a hypercompetitive market, see the **Sustainability Issue** feature about ESPN.

COOPERATIVE STRATEGIES

A company uses competitive strategies to gain competitive advantage within an industry by battling against other firms. These are not, however, the only business strategy options available to a company or business unit for competing successfully within an industry. A company can also use **cooperative strategies** to gain competitive advantage within an industry by working with other firms. The two general types of cooperative strategies are collusion and strategic alliances.

Collusion

Collusion is the active cooperation of firms within an industry to reduce output and raise prices in order to get around the normal economic law of supply and demand. Collusion may be explicit, in which case firms cooperate through direct communication and negotiation, or tacit, in which case firms cooperate indirectly through an informal system of signals. Explicit collusion is illegal in most countries and in a number of regional trade associations, such as the European Union. For example, Archer Daniels Midland (ADM), the large U.S. agricultural products firm, conspired with its competitors to limit the sales volume and raise the price of the food additive lysine. Executives from three Japanese and South Korean lysine

SUSTAINABILITY issue

STRATEGIC SUSTAINABILITY—ESPN

A sustainable strategy has many components. This is especially true in the hyper-competitive sports entertainment industry. Around the world, there is an almost maniacal love of sports, sports teams, sports superstars, and sports trivia. While this phenomenon is nothing new, technology advances have raised this "want" to an instant gratification level.

This was not always the way it was. Way back in the 1970s, we watched sports when the three networks deemed that we were to watch sports. We watched only the teams that they chose and it was rare to see any sports that were not considered to be mainstream. When you think about the staggering number of sporting events that occur every day around the world, it was amazing how few were shown on television.

All that changed with the founding of ESPN (Entertainment and Sports Programming Network) in 1979 in Bristol, Connecticut. Aired with little content, a show called *Sports Center*, and a lot of Australian Rules Football, the company sought out an approach in a field that had been dominated by the major league sports teams. The new ESPN moved to 24-hour broadcasting on September 1, 1980. ESPN quickly realized that a sustainable competitive advantage required contracts. All the analysis in the world would not make up for the fact that fans were watching other channels. The top management at ESPN also realized that it would not just be about keeping viewers tied to a single television channel as the industry standard was at the time.

The company opened up new television channels, created a radio station broadcast for stations across the country, moved aggressively into the Internet, and is the leader in mobile broadcasting of sports. Today, ESPN is the undisputed king of Sports broadcasting. Its projected 2013 revenues of over US$9 billion put it on a par with traditional media powerhouse CBS. ESPN charges cable companies US$5.13 per month/per subscriber in an industry where the average is US$.20/month/subscriber. The company has bet its sustainability in this market on its contracts with the NFL (through 2021), MLB (2021), NBA (2016), NASCAR (2013), and Wimbledon (2023), as well as a series of exclusive or partially shared contracts with major colleges and conferences. It caters to the sports enthusiast by providing that customer with the access and information they desire in the manner they desire it. The company then takes each successful platform to advertisers and monetizes the platform. ESPN is unconcerned about cannibalizing platforms because they seek to continually reinvent the company. John Skipper (ESPN President) believes that the company's dominance comes from a competitive approach that he calls "build, build, build."

....

SOURCES: K. T. Greenfeld, "ESPN Is Running Up the Score," *Bloomberg Businessweek* (September 3, 2012), pp. 58–64; http://frontrow.espn.go.com/category/espn-history/; http://a.espncdn.com/espninc/pressreleases/chronology.html; Hawkins, S. "Big 12 reaches $2.6B deal with ESPN, Fox Sports," Accessed 6/1/13, http://www.boston.comsports/colleges/2012/09/07/big-reaches-deal-with-espn-fox-sports/MbkpeOW4xEyX78F3FfHPcl/story.html.

manufacturers admitted meeting in hotels in major cities throughout the world to form a "lysine trade association." The three companies were fined more than US$20 million by the U.S. federal government.[24] Professional sports is big business and a fascinating collusion lawsuit was filed in May 2012 (*Reggie White, et al. v. NFL*) against the National Football League. The players contended they lost US$1 billion because of a secret salary cap for the 2010 season. As stipulated by collectively bargained language, such damages, if proved, would be automatically trebled to US$3 billion.[25]

Collusion can also be tacit, in which case there is no direct communication among competing firms. According to Barney, tacit collusion in an industry is most likely to be successful if (1) there are a small number of identifiable competitors, (2) costs are similar among firms, (3) one firm tends to act as the price leader, (4) there is a common industry culture that accepts cooperation, (5) sales are characterized by a high frequency of small orders, (6) large inventories and order backlogs are normal ways of dealing with fluctuations in demand, and (7) there are high entry barriers to keep out new competitors.[26]

Even tacit collusion can, however, be illegal. For example, when General Electric wanted to ease price competition in the steam turbine industry, it widely advertised its prices and publicly committed not to sell below those prices. Customers were even told that if GE reduced turbine prices in the future, it would give customers a refund equal to the price reduction. GE's message was not lost on Westinghouse, the major competitor in steam turbines. Both prices and profit margins remained stable for the next 10 years in this industry. The U.S. Department of Justice then sued both firms for engaging in "conscious parallelism" (following each other's lead to reduce the level of competition) in order to reduce competition.

Strategic Alliances

A **strategic alliance** is a long-term cooperative arrangement between two or more independent firms or business units that engage in business activities for mutual economic gain.[27] Alliances between companies or business units have become a fact of life in modern business. Each of the top 500 global business firms now averages 60 major alliances.[28] Some alliances are very short term, only lasting long enough for one partner to establish a beachhead in a new market. Over time, conflicts over objectives and control often develop among the partners. For these and other reasons, around half of all alliances (including international alliances) perform unsatisfactorily.[29] Others are more long-lasting and may even be preludes to full mergers between companies.

Many alliances do increase profitability of the members and have a positive effect on firm value.[30] A study by Cooper & Lybrand found that firms involved in strategic alliances had 11% higher revenue and a 20% higher growth rate than did companies not involved in alliances.[31]

Forming and managing strategic alliances is a capability that is learned over time. Research reveals that the more experience a firm has with strategic alliances, the more likely that its alliances will be successful.[32] (There is some evidence, however, that too much partnering experience with the same partners generates diminishing returns over time and leads to reduced performance.)[33] Consequently, leading firms are making investments in building and developing their partnering capabilities.[34]

Companies or business units may form a strategic alliance for a number of reasons, including:

1. **To obtain or learn new capabilities:** In May 2012, Hallmark formed an alliance with Shutterfly that put more than 1000 exclusive Hallmark-designed customizable cards on Shutterfly's new personalized greeting card site, Treat.com, as well as the core Shutterfly site.[35] Alliances are especially useful if the desired knowledge or capability is based on tacit knowledge or on new poorly understood technology.[36] A study found that firms with strategic alliances had more modern manufacturing technologies than did firms without alliances.[37]

2. **To obtain access to specific markets:** Rather than buy a foreign company or build breweries of its own in other countries, AB InBev chose to license the right to brew and market Budweiser to other brewers, such as Labatt in Canada, Modelo in Mexico, and Kirin in Japan. As another example, U.S. defense contractors and aircraft manufacturers selling to foreign governments are typically required by these governments to spend a percentage of the contract/purchase value, either by purchasing parts or obtaining sub-contractors, in that country. This is often achieved by forming value-chain alliances with foreign companies either as parts suppliers or as sub-contractors.[38] In a survey by the *Economist Intelligence Unit*, 59% of executives stated that their primary reason for engaging in alliances was the need for fast and low-cost expansion into new markets.[39]

3. **To reduce financial risk:** Alliances take less financial resources than do acquisitions or going it alone and are easier to exit if necessary.[40] For example, because the costs of developing new large jet airplanes were becoming too high for any one manufacturer, Aerospatiale of France, British Aerospace, Construcciones Aeronáuticas of Spain, and Daimler-Benz Aerospace of Germany formed a joint consortium called Airbus Industrie

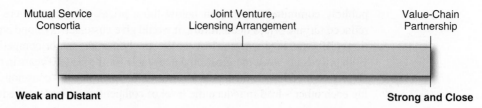

FIGURE 6–2
Continuum of
Strategic Alliances

to design and build such planes. Using alliances with suppliers is a popular means of outsourcing an expensive activity.

4. **To reduce political risk:** Forming alliances with local partners is a good way to overcome deficiencies in resources and capabilities when expanding into international markets.[41] To gain access to China while ensuring a positive relationship with the often restrictive Chinese government, Maytag Corporation formed a joint venture with the Chinese appliance maker, RSD.

Cooperative arrangements between companies and business units fall along a continuum from weak and distant to strong and close. (See **Figure 6–2**.) The types of alliances range from mutual service consortia to joint ventures and licensing arrangements to value-chain partnerships.[42]

Mutual Service Consortia. A **mutual service consortium** is a partnership of similar companies in similar industries that pool their resources to gain a benefit that is too expensive to develop alone, such as access to advanced technology. For example, IBM established a research alliance with Sony Electronics and Toshiba to build its next generation of computer chips. The result was the "cell" chip, a microprocessor running at 256 gigaflops—around 10 times the performance of the fastest chips currently used in desktop computers. Referred to as a "supercomputer on a chip," cell chips were to be used by Sony in its PlayStation 3, by Toshiba in its high-definition televisions, and by IBM in its super computers.[43] The mutual service consortia is a fairly weak and distant alliance—appropriate for partners that wish to work together but not share their core competencies. There is very little interaction or communication among the partners.

Joint Venture. A **joint venture** is a "cooperative business activity, formed by two or more separate organizations for strategic purposes, that creates an independent business entity and allocates ownership, operational responsibilities, and financial risks and rewards to each member, while preserving their separate identity/autonomy."[44] Along with licensing arrangements, joint ventures lie at the midpoint of the continuum and are formed to pursue an opportunity that needs a capability from two or more companies or business units, such as the technology of one and the distribution channels of another.

Joint ventures are the most popular form of strategic alliance. They often occur because the companies involved do not want to or cannot legally merge permanently. Joint ventures provide a way to temporarily combine the different strengths of partners to achieve an outcome of value to all. For example, Proctor & Gamble formed a joint venture with Clorox to produce food-storage wraps. P&G brought its cling-film technology and 20 full-time employees to the venture, while Clorox contributed its bags, containers, and wraps business.[45]

Extremely popular in international undertakings because of financial and political–legal constraints, forming joint ventures is a convenient way for corporations to work together without losing their independence. Between 30% and 55% of international joint ventures include three or more partners.[46] The disadvantages of joint ventures include loss of control, lower profits, probability of conflicts with partners, and the likely transfer of technological advantage to the partner. Joint ventures are often meant to be temporary, especially by some companies that may view them as a way to rectify a competitive weakness until they can achieve long-term dominance in the partnership. Partially for this reason, joint ventures have a high failure rate. Research indicates, however, that joint ventures tend to be more successful when both partners have equal ownership in the venture and are mutually dependent on each other for results.[47]

Licensing Arrangements. A **licensing arrangement** is an agreement in which the licensing firm grants rights to another firm in another country or market to produce and/or sell a product. The licensee pays compensation to the licensing firm in return for technical expertise. Licensing is an especially useful strategy if the trademark or brand name is well known but the MNC does not have sufficient funds to finance its entering the country directly. For example, Yum! Brands successfully used franchising and licensing to establish its KFC, Pizza Hut, Taco Bell, Long John Silver's, and A&W restaurants throughout the world. By 2012, Yum! Brands had used that strategy to open more than 3700 restaurants in China and had plans to open 700 more by year's end.[48] This strategy also becomes important if the country makes entry via investment either difficult or impossible. The danger always exists, however, that the licensee might develop its competence to the point that it becomes a competitor to the licensing firm. Therefore, a company should never license its distinctive competence, even for some short-run advantage.

Value-Chain Partnerships. A **value-chain partnership** is a strong and close alliance in which one company or unit forms a long-term arrangement with a key supplier or distributor for mutual advantage. For example, P&G, the maker of Folgers and Millstone coffee, worked with coffee appliance makers Mr. Coffee, Krups, and Hamilton Beach to use technology licensed from Black & Decker to market a pressurized, single-serve coffee-making system called Home Cafe. This was an attempt to reverse declining at-home coffee consumption at a time when coffeehouse sales were rising.[49]

To improve the quality of parts it purchases, companies in the U.S. auto industry, for example, have decided to work more closely with fewer suppliers and to involve them more in product design decisions. Activities that had previously been done internally by an automaker are being outsourced to suppliers specializing in those activities. The benefits of such relationships do not just accrue to the purchasing firm. Research suggests that suppliers that engage in long-term relationships are more profitable than suppliers with multiple short-term contracts.[50]

All forms of strategic alliances involve uncertainty. Many issues need to be dealt with when an alliance is initially formed, and others, which emerge later. Many problems revolve around the fact that a firm's alliance partners may also be its competitors, either immediately or in the future. According to Professor Peter Lorange, one thorny issue in any strategic alliance is how to cooperate without giving away the company or business unit's core competence: "Particularly when advanced technology is involved, it can be difficult for partners in an alliance to cooperate and openly share strategic know-how, but it is mandatory if the joint venture is to succeed."[51] It is therefore important that a company or business unit that is interested in joining or forming a strategic alliance consider the strategic alliance success factors listed in **Table 6–1**.

TABLE 6–1	<ul><li>Have a clear strategic purpose. Integrate the alliance with each partner's strategy. Ensure that mutual value is created for all partners.</li><li>Find a fitting partner with compatible goals and complementary capabilities.</li><li>Identify likely partnering risks and deal with them when the alliance is formed.</li><li>Allocate tasks and responsibilities so that each partner can specialize in what it does best.</li><li>Create incentives for cooperation to minimize differences in corporate culture or organization fit.</li><li>Minimize conflicts among the partners by clarifying objectives and avoiding direct competition in the marketplace.</li><li>In an international alliance, ensure that those managing it have comprehensive cross-cultural knowledge.</li><li>Exchange human resources to maintain communication and trust. Don't allow individual egos to dominate.</li><li>Operate with long-term time horizons. The expectation of future gains can minimize short-term conflicts.</li><li>Develop multiple joint projects so that any failures are counterbalanced by successes.</li><li>Agree on a monitoring process. Share information to build trust and keep projects on target. Monitor customer responses and service complaints.</li><li>Be flexible in terms of willingness to renegotiate the relationship in terms of environmental changes and new opportunities.</li><li>Agree on an exit strategy for when the partners' objectives are achieved or the alliance is judged a failure.</li></ul>
Strategic Alliance Success Factors	

SOURCES: Compiled from B. Gomes-Casseres, "Do You Really Have an Alliance Strategy?" *Strategy & Leadership* (September/October 1998), pp. 6–11; L. Segil, "Strategic Alliances for the 21st Century," *Strategy & Leadership* (September/October 1998), pp. 12–16; and A. C. Inkpen and K-Q Li, "Joint Venture Formation: Planning and Knowledge Gathering for Success," *Organizational Dynamics* (Spring 1999), pp. 33–47. Inkpen and Li provide a checklist of 17 questions on p. 46.

End of Chapter SUMMARY

Once environmental scanning is completed, situational analysis calls for the integration of this information. Using a SWOT approach is one of the more popular methods for examining external and internal information. We recommend using the SFAS Matrix as one way to identify a corporation's strategic factors.

Business strategy is composed of both competitive and cooperative strategy. As the external environment becomes more uncertain, an increasing number of corporations are choosing to simultaneously compete *and* cooperate with their competitors. These firms may cooperate to obtain efficiency in some areas, while each firm simultaneously tries to differentiate itself for competitive purposes. Raymond Noorda, Novell's founder and former CEO, coined the term *co-opetition* to describe such simultaneous competition and cooperation among firms.[52] One example is the collaboration between competitors DHL and UPS in the express delivery market. DHL's American delivery business was losing money and UPS' costly airfreight network had excess capacity. Under the terms of a 10-year agreement signed back in 2008, UPS carries DHL packages in its American airfreight network for a fee. The agreement covers only air freight, leaving both firms free to compete in the rest of the express parcel business.[53] A careful balancing act, co-opetition involves the careful management of alliance partners so that each partner obtains sufficient benefits to keep the alliance together. A long-term view is crucial. An unintended transfer of knowledge could be enough to provide one partner a significant competitive advantage over the others.[54] Unless that company forebears from using that knowledge against its partners, the alliance will be doomed.

MyManagementLab®

Go to **mymanagementlab.com** to complete the problems marked with this icon ⭐.

KEY TERMS

business strategy (p. 203)
collusion (p. 209)
common thread (p. 202)
competitive scope (p. 203)
competitive strategy (p. 203)
consolidated industry (p. 206)
cooperative strategy (p. 209)
cost focus (p. 204)
cost leadership (p. 203)

differentiation (p. 203)
differentiation focus (p. 204)
differentiation strategy (p. 204)
fragmented industry (p. 206)
joint venture (p. 212)
licensing arrangement (p. 213)
lower cost strategy (p. 204)
mutual service consortium (p. 212)
propitious niche (p. 199)

SFAS (Strategic Factors Analysis
    Summary) Matrix (p. 198)
strategic alliance (p. 211)
strategy formulation (p. 198)
SWOT (p. 198)
tactics (p. 209)
value-chain partnership (p. 213)

MyManagementLab®

Go to **mymanagementlab**.com for the following Assisted-graded writing questions:

6-1. How does a hypercompetitive environment change the strategic approach for a company?

6-2. Explain how our understanding of the three generic strategic approaches available to companies can be used to direct the efforts of all employees at those companies.

DISCUSSION QUESTIONS

6-3. Discuss how industry structure impacts competitive strategy choice.

⭐ **6-4.** What does a business have to consider when trying to follow a cost leadership strategy and a differentiation strategy simultaneously? Can you name a company doing this?

⭐ **6-5.** How can a company achieve a sustainable competitive advantage when its industry becomes hypercompetitive?

⭐ **6-6.** Why are many strategic alliances temporary?

STRATEGIC PRACTICE EXERCISE

Select two publicly-owned companies within a particular industry, and perform a comparative SWOT analysis for the selected companies.

INDUSTRY: _____

Companies:_____

Strengths:_____

Weaknesses:_____

Opportunities:_____

Threats:_____

NOTES

1. T. Brown, "The Essence of Strategy," *Management Review* (April 1997), pp. 8–13.
2. W. H. Newman, "Shaping the Master Strategy of Your Firm," *California Management Review* (Vol. 9, No. 3, 1967), pp. 77–88.
3. D. J. Collis and M. G. Rukstad, "Can You Say What Your Strategy Is?" *Harvard Business Review* (April 2008), pp.86.
4. V. F. Misangyi, H. Elms, T. Greckhamer, and J. A Lepine, "A New Perspective on a Fundamental Debate: A Multilevel Approach to Industry, Corporate, and Business Unit Effects," *Strategic Management Journal* (June 2006), pp. 571–590.
5. M. E. Porter, *Competitive Strategy* (New York: The Free Press, 1980), pp. 34–41 as revised in M. E. Porter, *The Competitive Advantage of Nations* (New York: The Free Press, 1990), pp. 37–40.
6. J. O. DeCastro and J. J. Chrisman, "Narrow-Scope Strategies and Firm Performance: An Empirical Investigation," *Journal of Business Strategies* (Spring 1998), pp. 1–16; T. M. Stearns, N. M. Carter, P. D. Reynolds, and M. L. Williams, "New Firm Survival: Industry, Strategy, and Location," *Journal of Business Venturing* (January 1995), pp. 23–42; C. E. Bamford, T. J. Dean, and P. P. McDougall, "Reconsidering the Niche Prescription for New Ventures: A Study of Initial Strategy and Growth," *Advances in Entrepreneurship: Firm Emergence and Growth* (Vol. 11, 2009). pp. 9–39.
7. Porter, *Competitive Strategy*, p. 35.
8. R. E. Caves, and P. Ghemawat, "Identifying Mobility Barriers," *Strategic Management Journal* (January 1992), pp. 1–12.
9. "Private Label Brands Winning the Retail Sales Game," *Food Product Design* (July 27, 2012), (http://www.foodproductdesign.com/news/2012/07/private-label-brands-winning-the-retail-sales-gam.aspx).
10. "Company Targets 'Orphan Drugs,'" *St. Cloud (MN) Times* (May 9, 2007), p. 2A, http://www.orphagenix.com/Home/research-technology-1.
11. M. Arndt, "Deere's Revolution on Wheels," *BusinessWeek* (July 2, 2007), pp. 78–79.
12. S. Thornhill and R. E. White, "Strategic Purity: A Multi-Industry Evaluation of Pure vs. Hybrid Business Strategies," *Strategic Management Journal* (May 2007), pp. 553–561; M. Delmas, M. V. Russo, and M. J. Montes-Sancho, "Deregulation and Environmental Differentiation in the Electric Utility Industry," *Strategic Management Journal* (February 2007), pp. 189–209.
13. C. Campbell-Hunt, "What Have We Learned About Generic Competitive Strategy? A Meta Analysis," *Strategic Management Journal* (February 2000), pp. 127–154.
14. M. Kroll, P. Wright, and R. A. Heiens, "The Contribution of Product Quality to Competitive Advantage: Impacts on Systematic Variance and Unexplained Variance in Returns," *Strategic Management Journal* (April 1999), pp. 375–384.
15. R. M. Hodgetts, "A Conversation with Michael E. Porter: A 'Significant Extension' Toward Operational Improvement and Positioning," *Organizational Dynamics* (Summer 1999), pp. 24–33.
16. M. Morrison, "Table Set for Fast Casual Asian Invasion," *Advertising Age* (May 16, 2011), (http://adage.com/article/news/table-set-fast-casual-asian-invasion/227577/); D. Banerjee and L. Patton, "P.F. Chang's to Be Bought by Centerbridge for $1Billion," *BloombergBusinessweek* (May1,2012),(http://www.businessweek.com/news/2012-05-01/p-dot-f-dot-chang-s-is-bought-by-centerbridge-for-1-dot-1-billion).
17. Pizza Industry Report 2011, (http://www.franchisedirect.com/foodfranchises/pizzafranchises/pizzaindustryreport2011productdiversitymarketleadersbusinessmodels2/80/294).
18. P. F. Kocourek, S. Y. Chung, and M. G. McKenna, "Strategic Rollups: Overhauling the Multi-Merger Machine," *Strategy + Business* (2nd Quarter 2000), pp. 45–53.
19. J. A. Tannenbaum, "Acquisitive Companies Set Out to 'Roll Up' Fragmented Industries," *The Wall Street Journal* (March 3, 1997), pp. A1, A6; 2007 Form 10-K and Quarterly Report (July 2008); VCA Antech Inc. "A Best Idea", "Legendary Roll-Up Virtuoso John Lorenz Inks Acquisition #7 in just over Four Months," *SmallCap Network* (June 14, 2012), (http://www.smallcapnetwork.com/A-Best-Idea-Legendary-roll-up-virtuoso-John-Lorenz-inks-acquisition-7-in-just-over-four-months/s/via/8996/article/view/p/mid/1/id/43/); "BRM Acquires Paper Exchange," *Shred Nations* (August 31, 2012), (http://www.shrednations.com/news/category/acquisition/).
20. "Colgate Announces First Quarter Results," (April 26, 2012), (http://finance.yahoo.com/news/colgate-announces-1st-quarter-results-110000350.html).
21. J. C. Bou and A. Satorra, "The Persistence of Abnormal Returns at Industry and Firm Levels: Evidence from Spain," *Strategic Management Journal* (July 2007), pp. 707–722.
22. R. A. D'Aveni, *Hypercompetition* (New York: The Free Press, 1994), pp. xiii–xiv.
23. R. R. Wiggins and T. W. Ruefli, "Schumpeter's Ghost: Is Hypercompetition Making the Best of Times Shorter?" *Strategic Management Journal* (October 2005), pp. 887–911.
24. T. M. Burton, "Archer-Daniels Faces a Potential Blow as Three Firms Admit Price-Fixing Plot," *The Wall Street Journal* (August 28, 1996), pp. A3, A6; R. Henkoff, "The ADM Tale Gets Even Stranger," *Fortune* (May 13, 1996), pp. 113–120.
25. M. McCann, "Proving that NFL Teams Agreed to a Secret Salary Cap Will Not Be Easy," *Sports Illustrated* (May 24, 2012), (http://sportsillustrated.cnn.com/2012/writers/michael_mccann/05/23/nfl/index.html).
26. Much of the content on cooperative strategies was summarized from J. B. Barney, *Gaining and Sustaining Competitive Advantage* (Reading, MA: Addison-Wesley, 1997), pp. 255–278.
27. A. C. Inkpen and E. W. K. Tsang, "Learning and Strategic Alliances," *Academy of Management Annals* (Vol. 1, December 2007), J. F. Walsh and A. F. Brief (Eds.), pp. 479–511.
28. R. D. Ireland, M. A. Hitt, and D. Vaidyanath, "Alliance Management as a Source of Competitive Advantage," *Journal of Management* (Vol. 28, No. 3, 2002), pp. 413–446.
29. S. H. Park and G. R. Ungson, "Interfirm Rivalry and Managerial Complexity: A Conceptual Framework of Alliance Failure," *Organization Science* (January–February 2001), pp. 37–53.; D. C. Hambrick, J. Li, K. Xin, and A. S. Tsui, "Compositional Gaps and Downward Spirals in International Joint Venture Management Groups," *Strategic Management Journal* (November 2001), pp. 1033–1053; T. K. Das and B. S. Teng, "Instabilities of Strategic Alliances: An Internal Tensions Perspective," *Organization Science* (January–February 2000),

pp. 77–101; J. F. Hennart, D. J. Kim, and M. Zeng, "The Impact of Joint Venture Status on the Longevity of Japanese Stakes in U.S. Manufacturing Affiliates," *Organization Science* (May–June 1998), pp. 382–395.

30. N. K. Park, J. M. Mezias, and J. Song, "A Resource-Based View of Strategic Alliances and Firm Value in the Electronic Marketplace," *Journal of Management* (Vol. 30, No. 1, 2004), pp. 7–27; T. Khanna and J. W. Rivkin, "Estimating the Performance Effects of Business Groups in Emerging Markets," *Strategic Management Journal* (January 2001), pp. 45–74; G. Garai, "Leveraging the Rewards of Strategic Alliances," *Journal of Business Strategy* (March–April 1999), pp. 40–43.

31. L. Segil, "Strategic Alliances for the 21st Century," *Strategy & Leadership* (September/October 1998), pp. 12–16.

32. R. C. Sampson, "Experience Effects and Collaborative Returns in R&D Alliances," *Strategic Management Journal* (November 2005), pp. 1009–1031; J. Draulans, A-P de Man, and H. W. Volberda, "Building Alliance Capability: Management Techniques for Superior Alliance Performance," *Long Range Planning* (April 2003), pp. 151–166; P. Kale, J. H. Dyer, and H. Singh, "Alliance Capability, Stock Market Response, and Long-Term Alliance Success: The Role of the Alliance Function," *Strategic Management Journal* (August 2002), pp. 747–767.

33. H. Hoang and F. T. Rothaermel, "The Effect of General and Partner-Specific Alliance Experience on Joint R&D Project Performance," *Academy of Management Journal* (April 2005), pp. 332–345; A. Goerzen, "Alliance Networks and Firm Performance: The Impact of Repeated Partnerships," *Strategic Management Journal* (May 2007), pp. 487–509.

34. A. MacCormack and T. Forbath, "Learning the Fine Art of Global Collaboration," *Harvard Business Review* (January 2008), pp. 24–26.

35. "Hallmark Announces Strategic Alliance with Shutterfly," *PR Newswire* (June 20, 2012), (http://www.prnewswire.com/news-releases/hallmark-announces-strategic-alliance-with-shutterfly-159781365.html).

36. H. Bapuji and M. Crossan, "Knowledge Types and Knowledge Management Strategies," in M. Gibbert and T. Durand (Eds.) *Strategic Networks: Learning to Compete* (Malden, MA: Blackwell Publishing, 2007), pp. 8–25; F. T. Rothaermel and W. Boeker, "Old Technology Meets New Technology: Complementarities, Similarities, and Alliance Formation," *Strategic Management Journal* (January 2008), pp. 47–77.

37. M. M. Bear, "How Japanese Partners Help U.S. Manufacturers to Raise Productivity," *Long Range Planning* (December 1998), pp. 919–926.

38. According to M. J. Thome of Rockwell Collins in a June 26, 2008, e-mail, these are called "international offsets."

39. P. Anslinger and J. Jenk, "Creating Successful Alliances," *Journal of Business Strategy* (Vol. 25, No. 2, 2004), p. 18.

40. X. Yin and M. Shanley, "Industry Determinants of the 'Merger Versus Alliance' Decision," *Academy of Management Review* (April 2008), pp. 473–491.

41. J. W. Lu and P. W. Beamish, "The Internationalization and Performance of SMEs," *Strategic Management Journal* (June–July 2001), pp. 565–586.

42. R. M. Kanter, "Collaborative Advantage: The Art of Alliances," *Harvard Business Review* (July–August 1994), pp. 96–108.

43. "The Cell of the New Machine," *The Economist* (February 12, 2005), pp. 77–78.

44. R. P. Lynch, *The Practical Guide to Joint Ventures and Corporate Alliances* (New York: John Wiley and Sons, 1989), p. 7.

45. "Will She, Won't She?" *The Economist* (August 11, 2007), pp. 61–63.

46. Y Gong, O Shenkar, Y. Luo, and M-K Nyaw, "Do Multiple Parents Help or Hinder International Joint Venture Performance? The Mediating Roles of Contract Completeness and Partner Cooperation," *Strategic Management Journal* (October 2007), pp. 1021–1034.

47. L. L. Blodgett, "Factors in the Instability of International Joint Ventures: An Event History Analysis," *Strategic Management Journal* (September 1992), pp. 475–481; J. Bleeke and D. Ernst, "The Way to Win in Cross-Border Alliances," *Harvard Business Review* (November–December 1991), pp. 127–135; J. M. Geringer, "Partner Selection Criteria for Developed Country Joint Ventures," in H. W. Lane and J. J. DiStephano (Eds.), *International Management Behavior*, 2nd ed. (Boston: PWS-Kent, 1992), pp. 206–216.

48. Schreiner, B. 2012, "YUM Brands Posts Rare Profit Setback in China," *USA Today* (July 18, 2012), (http://www.usatoday.com/money/companies/earnings/story/2012-07-18/yum-brands-earnings/56321222/1).

49. B. Horovitz, "New Coffee Maker May Jolt Industry," *USA Today* (February 18, 2004), pp. 1E–2E.

50. K. Z. Andrews, "Manufacturer/Supplier Relationships: The Supplier Payoff," *Harvard Business Review* (September–October 1995), pp. 14–15.

51. P. Lorange, "Black-Box Protection of Your Core Competencies in Strategic Alliances," in P. W. Beamish and J. P. Killing (Eds.), *Cooperative Strategies: European Perspectives* (San Francisco: The New Lexington Press, 1997), pp. 59–99.

52. E. P. Gee, "Co-opetition: The New Market Milieu," *Journal of Healthcare Management* (Vol. 45, 2000), pp. 359–363.

53. "Make Love—and War," *The Economist* (August 9, 2008), pp. 57–58.

54. D. J. Ketchen Jr., C. C. Snow, and V. L. Hoover, "Research on Competitive Dynamics: Recent Accomplishments and Future Challenges," *Journal of Management* (Vol. 30, No. 6, 2004), pp. 779–804.

CHAPTER 7

strategy formulation:
Corporate Strategy

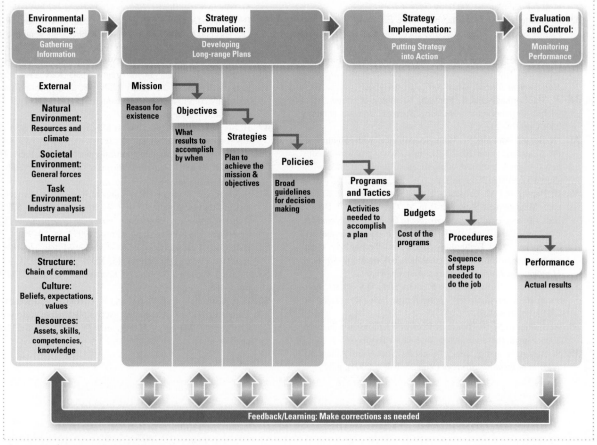

MyManagementLab®

⭐ **Improve Your Grade!**

Over 10 million students improved their results using the Pearson MyLabs. Visit **mymanagementlab.com** for simulations, tutorials, and end-of-chapter problems.

Learning Objectives

After reading this chapter, you should be able to:

- Understand the three aspects of corporate strategy
- Apply the directional strategies of growth, stability, and retrenchment
- Understand the differences between vertical and horizontal growth as well as concentric and conglomerate diversification

- Identify strategic options to enter a foreign country
- Apply portfolio analysis to guide decisions in companies with multiple products and businesses
- Develop a parenting strategy for a multiple-business corporation

How Does a Company Grow if Its Primary Business Is Maturing?

Pfizer Remakes the Company

Pfizer, Inc. was founded in 1849 by Charles Pfizer and Charles Erhart. The company was the breakthrough leader in the development of the means for producing Penicillin on a large scale. In fact, most of the Penicillin carried by troops on D-Day in 1944 was made by Pfizer. The company became a major research lab for the development of drugs. In 1972, Pfizer increased funding of research and development from 5% of sales (an astounding figure in any industry) to 20% of sales. The company viewed its mission as discovering and developing innovative pharmaceuticals. By 2011, the company had sales of US$67.4 billion but had also absorbed several very large acquisitions from 1999–2009, including Wyeth, Warner-Lambert, and Pharmacia. A number of blockbuster drugs had or were coming off patent protection and new ones were becoming increasingly difficult to find. Most of the diseases that still lacked effective treatment, such as Alzheimer's, were more complicated.

By 2012, new drug successes were becoming increasingly difficult to find. The company poured US$2.8 billion into an inhalable insulin (Exubera) and a cholesterol-reducing replacement for Lipitor (Torcetrapib), but both failed to take hold in the market. History has shown that only 16% of drugs under development ever get regulatory approval.

In a bold move, Pfizer's CEO, Ian Read, made the decision in 2012 to consolidate around five areas: cardiovascular diseases, cancer, neuroscience, vaccines, and inflammation/immunology. Redirecting resources in the company, Pfizer closed the famed Sandwich, England, research campus (the birthplace of Viagra) laying off more than 2000 employees because its focus was on areas not included in the new direction of the company. It then divested its animal health and infant nutrition businesses. It also cut more than 3000 research jobs at its flagship New London, Connecticut, campus.

All of the cuts were being plowed back into one of the five areas the company will focus on in the future. This type of corporate repositioning is a hallmark of portfolio management and the techniques described in this chapter.

SOURCES: "Pfizer Embarks on an Overdue Crash Diet," *Bloomberg Businessweek* (March 12, 2012), pp. 24–25; http://www.pfizer.com/about/history/history.jsp; http://www.pfizer.com/about/history/1951_1999.jsp.

Corporate Strategy

The vignette about Pfizer illustrates the importance of corporate strategy to a firm's survival and success. Corporate strategy addresses three key issues facing the corporation as a whole:

1. The firm's overall orientation toward growth, stability, or retrenchment (**directional strategy**)
2. The industries or markets in which the firm competes through its products and business units (**portfolio analysis**)
3. The manner in which management coordinates activities and transfers resources and cultivates capabilities among product lines and business units (**parenting strategy**)

Corporate strategy is primarily about the choice of direction for a firm as a whole and the management of its business or product portfolio.[1] This is true whether the firm is a small company or a large multinational corporation (MNC). In a large multiple-business company, in particular, corporate strategy is concerned with managing various product lines and business units for maximum value. In this instance, corporate headquarters must play the role of the organizational "parent," in that it must deal with various product and business unit "children." Even though each product line or business unit has its own competitive or cooperative strategy that it uses to obtain its own competitive advantage in the marketplace, the corporation must coordinate these different business strategies so that the corporation as a whole succeeds as a "family."[2]

Corporate strategy, therefore, includes decisions regarding the flow of financial and other resources to and from a company's product lines and business units. Through a series of coordinating devices, a company transfers skills and capabilities developed in one unit to other units that need such resources. In this way, it attempts to obtain synergy among numerous product lines and business units so that the corporate whole is greater than the sum of its individual business unit parts.[3] All corporations, from the smallest company offering one product in only one industry to the largest conglomerate operating in many industries with many products, must at one time or another consider one or more of these issues.

To deal with each of the key issues, this chapter is organized into three parts that examine corporate strategy in terms of *directional strategy* (orientation toward growth), *portfolio analysis* (coordination of cash flow among units), and *corporate parenting* (the building of corporate synergies through resource sharing and development).[4]

Directional Strategy

Just as every product or business unit must follow a business strategy to improve its competitive position, every corporation must decide its orientation toward growth by asking the following three questions:

1. Should we expand, cut back, or continue our operations unchanged?

2. Should we concentrate our activities within our current industry, or should we diversify into other industries?

3. If we want to grow and expand nationally and/or globally, should we do so through internal development or through external acquisitions, mergers, or strategic alliances?

A corporation's **directional strategy** is composed of three general orientations (sometimes called *grand strategies*):

- **Growth strategies** expand the company's activities.
- **Stability strategies** make no change to the company's current activities.
- **Retrenchment strategies** reduce the company's level of activities.

Having chosen the general orientation (such as growth), a company's managers can select from several more specific corporate strategies such as concentration within one product line/industry or diversification into other products/industries. (See **Figure 7–1**.) These strategies are useful both to corporations operating in only one industry with one product line and to those operating in many industries with many product lines.

GROWTH STRATEGIES

By far, the most widely pursued corporate directional strategies are those designed to achieve growth in sales, assets, profits, or some combination of these. Companies that do business in expanding industries must grow to survive. Continuing growth means increasing sales and a chance to take advantage of the experience curve to reduce the per-unit cost of products sold, thereby increasing profits. This cost reduction becomes extremely important if a corporation's industry is growing quickly or consolidating and if competitors are engaging in price wars in attempts to increase their shares of the market. Firms that have not reached "critical mass" (that is, gained the necessary economy of large-scale production) face large losses unless they can find and fill a small, but profitable, niche where higher prices can be offset by special product or service features. That is why Oracle has been on the acquisition trail for the past seven years. In that time period, Oracle acquired 85 businesses in a wide variety of areas. Although still growing, the software industry is maturing around a handful of large firms. According to CEO Larry Ellison, Oracle needed to double or even triple in size by buying smaller and weaker rivals if it wants to compete with SAP and Microsoft.[5] Growth is a popular strategy because larger businesses tend to survive longer than smaller companies due to the greater availability of financial resources, organizational routines, and external ties.[6]

A corporation can grow internally by expanding its operations both globally and domestically, or it can grow externally through mergers, acquisitions, and strategic alliances. In practice, the line between mergers and acquisitions has been blurred to the point where it is

FIGURE 7–1 Corporate Directional Strategies

• GROWTH	• STABILITY	• RETRENCHMENT
Concentration Vertical Growth Horizontal Growth **Diversification** Concentric Conglomerate	Pause/Proceed with Caution No Change Profit	Turnaround Captive Company Sell-Out/Divestment Bankruptcy/Liquidation

difficult to tell the difference. In general, we regard a **merger** as a transaction involving two or more corporations in which both companies exchange stock in order to create one new corporation. Mergers that occur between firms of somewhat similar size are referred to as a "merger of equals." Most mergers are "friendly"—that is, both parties believe it is in their best interests to combine their companies. The resulting firm is likely to have a name derived from its composite firms. One example is the merging of Allied Corporation and Signal Companies to form Allied Signal. An **acquisition** is a 100% purchase of another company. In some cases, the company continues to operate as an independent entity and in others it is completely absorbed as an operating subsidiary or division of the acquiring corporation. In July 2012, Duke Energy acquired Progress Energy, making the latter a wholly owned unit of Duke Energy. With the acquisition, Duke Energy became the largest utility in the United States.[7] Acquisitions usually occur between firms of different sizes and can be either friendly or hostile. Hostile acquisitions are often called *takeovers*.

From management's perspective (but perhaps not a stockholder's), growth is very attractive for two key reasons:

- Growth based on increasing market demand may mask flaws in a company—flaws that would be immediately evident in a stable or declining market. A growing flow of revenue into a highly leveraged corporation can create a large amount of *organization slack* (unused resources) that can be used to quickly resolve problems and conflicts between departments and divisions. Growth also provides a big cushion for turnaround in case a strategic error is made. Larger firms also have more bargaining power than do small firms and are more likely to obtain support from key stakeholders in case of difficulty.

- A growing firm offers more opportunities for advancement, promotion, and interesting jobs. Growth itself is exciting and ego-enhancing for everyone. The marketplace and potential investors tend to view a growing corporation as a "winner" or "on the move." Executive compensation tends to get bigger as an organization increases in size. Large firms are also more difficult to acquire than smaller ones—thus, an executive's job in a large firm is more secure.

The two basic growth strategies are **concentration** on the current product line(s) in one industry and **diversification** into other product lines in other industries.

Concentration

If a company's current product lines have real growth potential, the concentration of resources on those product lines makes sense as a strategy for growth. The two basic concentration strategies are vertical growth and horizontal growth. Growing firms in a growing industry tend to choose these strategies before they try diversification.

Vertical Growth. **Vertical growth** can be achieved by taking over a function previously provided by a supplier or distributor. The company, in effect, grows by making its own supplies and/or by distributing its own products. This may be done in order to reduce costs, gain control over a scarce resource, guarantee quality of a key input, or obtain access to potential customers. This growth can be achieved either internally by expanding current operations or externally through acquisitions. Henry Ford, for example, used internal company resources to build his River Rouge plant outside Detroit. The manufacturing process was integrated to the point that iron ore entered one end of the long plant, and finished automobiles rolled out the other end into a huge parking lot. In contrast, Cisco Systems, a maker of Internet hardware, chose the external route to vertical growth by purchasing Scientific-Atlanta Inc., a maker of set-top boxes for television programs and movies-on-demand. This acquisition gave Cisco access to technology for distributing television to living rooms through the Internet.[8]

Vertical growth results in **vertical integration**—the degree to which a firm operates vertically in multiple locations on an industry's value chain from extracting raw materials to manufacturing to retailing. More specifically, assuming a function previously provided by a supplier is called **backward integration** (going backward on an industry's value chain). The purchase of Carroll's Foods for its hog-growing facilities by Smithfield Foods, the world's largest pork processor, is an example of backward integration.[9] Assuming a function previously provided by a distributor is labeled **forward integration** (going forward on an industry's value chain). FedEx, for example, used forward integration when it purchased Kinko's in order to provide store-front package drop-off and delivery services for the small-business market.[10]

Vertical growth is a logical strategy for a corporation or business unit with a strong competitive position in a highly attractive industry—especially when technology is predictable and markets are growing.[11] To keep and even improve its competitive position, a company may use backward integration to minimize resource acquisition costs and inefficient operations, as well as forward integration to gain more control over product distribution. The firm, in effect, builds on its distinctive competence by expanding along the industry's value chain to gain greater competitive advantage.

Although backward integration is often more profitable than forward integration (because of typical low margins in retailing), it can reduce a corporation's strategic flexibility. The resulting encumbrance of expensive assets that might be hard to sell could create an exit barrier, preventing the corporation from leaving that particular industry. Examples of single-use assets are blast furnaces and refineries. When demand drops in either of these industries (steel or oil and gas), these assets have no alternative use, but continue to cost money in terms of debt payments, property taxes, and security expenses.

Transaction cost economics proposes that vertical integration is more efficient than contracting for goods and services in the marketplace when the transaction costs of buying goods on the open market become too great. When highly vertically integrated firms become excessively large and bureaucratic, however, the costs of managing the internal transactions may become greater than simply purchasing the needed goods externally—thus justifying outsourcing over vertical integration. This is why vertical integration and outsourcing are situation specific. Neither approach is best for all companies in all situations.[12] See the Strategy Highlight feature on how transaction cost economics helps explain why firms vertically integrate or outsource important activities. Research thus far provides mixed support for the predictions of transaction cost economics.[13]

Harrigan proposes that a company's degree of vertical integration can range from total ownership of the value chain needed to make and sell a product to no ownership at all.[14] (See **Figure 7–2**.) Under **full integration**, a firm internally makes 100% of its key supplies and completely controls its distributors. Large oil companies, such as British Petroleum and Royal Dutch Shell, are fully integrated. They own the oil rigs that pump the oil out of the ground, the ships and pipelines that transport the oil, the refineries that convert the oil to gasoline, and the trucks that deliver the gasoline to company-owned and franchised gas

FIGURE 7–2 Vertical Integration Continuum

Full Integration	Taper Integration	Quasi-Integration	Long-Term Contract

SOURCE: *Suggested by K. R. Harrigan, Strategies for Vertical Integration* (Lexington, MA: Lexington Books, D.C. Heath, 1983), pp. 16–21.

stations. Sherwin-Williams Company, which not only manufactures paint, but also sells it in its own chain of 3000 retail stores, is another example of a fully integrated firm.[15] If a corporation does not want the disadvantages of full vertical integration, it may choose either taper or quasi-integration strategies.

With **taper integration** (also called concurrent sourcing), a firm internally produces less than half of its own requirements and buys the rest from outside suppliers (backward taper integration).[16] In the case of Smithfield Foods, its purchase of Carroll's allowed it to produce 27% of the hogs it needed to process into pork. In terms of forward taper integration, a firm sells part of its goods through company-owned stores and the rest through general wholesalers. Although Apple had 246 of its own retail stores in 2012, much of the company's sales continued to be through national chains such as Best Buy and through independent local and regional dealers.

With **quasi-integration**, a company does not make any of its key supplies but purchases most of its requirements from outside suppliers that are under its partial control (backward quasi-integration). A company may not want to purchase outright a supplier or distributor, but it still may want to guarantee access to needed supplies, new products, technologies, or distribution channels. For example, the pharmaceutical company Bristol-Myers Squibb purchased 17% of the common stock of ImClone in order to gain access to new drug products being developed through biotechnology. An example of forward quasi-integration would be a paper company acquiring part interest in an office products chain in order to guarantee that its products had access to the distribution channel. Purchasing part interest in another company usually provides a company with a seat on the other firm's board of directors, thus guaranteeing the acquiring firm both information and control. As in the case of Bristol-Myers Squibb and ImClone, a quasi-integrated firm may later decide to buy the rest of a key supplier that it did not already own.[17]

Long-term contracts are agreements between two firms to provide agreed-upon goods and services to each other for a specified period of time. This cannot really be considered to be vertical integration unless it is an *exclusive* contract that specifies that the supplier or distributor cannot have a similar relationship with a competitive firm. In that case, the supplier or distributor is really a *captive company* that, although officially independent, does most of its business with the contracted firm and is formally tied to the other company through a long-term contract.

Recently, there has been a movement away from vertical growth strategies (and thus vertical integration) toward cooperative contractual relationships with suppliers and even with competitors.[18] These relationships range from *outsourcing*, in which resources are purchased from outsiders through long-term contracts instead of being done in-house (Coca-Cola Enterprises eliminated jobs in three U.S. centers by contracting with Capgemini for accounting and financial services), to strategic alliances, in which partnerships, technology licensing agreements, and joint ventures supplement a firm's capabilities (Toshiba has used strategic alliances with GE, Siemens, Motorola, and Ericsson to become one of the world's leading electronic companies).[19]

Horizontal Growth. A firm can achieve **horizontal growth** by expanding its operations into other geographic locations and/or by increasing the range of products and services offered to current markets. Research indicates that firms that grow horizontally by broadening their product lines have high survival rates.[20] Horizontal growth results in **horizontal integration**—the degree to which a firm operates in multiple geographic locations at the same point on an industry's value chain. For example, Procter & Gamble (P&G) continually adds additional sizes and multiple variations to its existing product lines to reduce possible niches that competitors may enter. In addition, it introduces successful products from one part of the world to other regions. P&G has been introducing into China a steady stream of popular

STRATEGY highlight

TRANSACTION COST ECONOMICS ANALYZES VERTICAL GROWTH STRATEGY

Why do corporations use vertical growth to permanently own suppliers or distributors when they could simply purchase individual items when needed on the open market? Transaction cost economics is a branch of institutional economics that attempts to answer this question. Transaction cost economics proposes that owning resources through vertical growth is more efficient than contracting for goods and services in the marketplace when the transaction costs of buying goods on the open market become too great. Transaction costs include the basic costs of drafting, negotiating, and safeguarding a market agreement (a contract) as well as the later managerial costs when the agreement is creating problems (goods aren't being delivered on time or quality is lower than needed), renegotiation costs (e.g., costs of meetings and phone calls), and the costs of settling disputes (e.g., lawyers' fees and court costs).

According to Williamson, three conditions must be met before a corporation will prefer internalizing a vertical transaction through ownership over contracting for the transaction in the marketplace: (1) a high level of uncertainty must surround the transaction, (2) assets involved in the transaction must be highly specialized to the transaction, and (3) the transaction must occur frequently. If there is a high level of uncertainty, it will be impossible to write a contract covering all contingencies, and it is likely that the contractor will act opportunistically to exploit any gaps in the written agreement—thus creating problems and increasing costs. If the assets being contracted for are highly specialized (e.g., goods or services with few alternate uses), there are likely to be few alternative suppliers—thus allowing the contractor to take advantage of the situation and increase costs. The more frequent the transactions, the more opportunity for the contractor to demand special treatment and thus increase costs further.

Vertical integration is not always more efficient than the marketplace, however. When highly vertically integrated firms become excessively large and bureaucratic, the costs of managing the internal transactions may become greater than simply purchasing the needed goods externally—thus justifying outsourcing over ownership. The usually hidden management costs (e.g., excessive layers of management, endless committee meetings needed for interdepartmental coordination, and delayed decision making due to excessively detailed rules and policies) add to the internal transaction costs—thus reducing the effectiveness and efficiency of vertical integration. The decision to own or to outsource is, therefore, based on the particular situation surrounding the transaction and the ability of the corporation to manage the transaction internally both effectively and efficiently.

....

SOURCES: O. E. Williamson and S. G. Winter (Eds.), *The Nature of the Firm: Origins, Evolution, and Development* (New York: Oxford University Press, 1991); E. Mosakowski, "Organizational Boundaries and Economic Performance: An Empirical Study of Entrepreneurial Computer Firms," *Strategic Management Journal* (February 1991), pp. 115–133; P. S. Ring and A. H. Van de Ven, "Structuring Cooperative Relationships Between Organizations," *Strategic Management Journal* (October 1992), pp. 483–498.

American brands, such as Head & Shoulders, Crest, Olay, Tide, Pampers, and Whisper. By 2012, it had sales of more than US$6 billion in China, and 10 manufacturing plants.[21]

Horizontal growth can be achieved through internal development or externally through acquisitions and strategic alliances with other firms in the same industry. For example, Delta Airlines acquired Northwest Airlines in 2008 to obtain access to Northwest's Asian markets and those American markets that Delta was not then serving. In contrast, many small commuter airlines engage in long-term contracts with major airlines in order to offer a complete arrangement for travelers. For example, the regional carrier Mesa Airlines arranged contractual agreements with United Airlines and U.S. Airways to be listed on their computer reservations, respectively, as United Express and U.S. Airways Express.

Horizontal growth is increasingly being achieved in today's world through international expansion. America's Wal-Mart, France's Carrefour, and Britain's Tesco are examples of national supermarket discount chains expanding horizontally throughout the world. This type of growth can be achieved internationally through many different strategies.

INTERNATIONAL ENTRY OPTIONS FOR HORIZONTAL GROWTH

Research indicates that growing internationally is positively associated with firm profitability.[22] A corporation can select from several strategic options the most appropriate method for entering a foreign market or establishing manufacturing facilities in another country. The options vary from simple exporting to acquisitions to management contracts. See the **Global Issue** feature to see how U.S.-based firms do not always succeed when using international entry options in a horizontal growth strategy to expand throughout the world.

Some of the most popular options for international entry are as follows:

- **Exporting:** A good way to minimize risk and experiment with a specific product is **exporting**, shipping goods produced in the company's home country to other countries for marketing. The company could choose to handle all critical functions itself, or it could contract these functions to an export management company. Exporting is becoming increasingly popular for small businesses because of the Internet, fax machines, toll-free numbers, and overnight express services, which reduce the once-formidable costs of going international.

- **Licensing:** Under a **licensing** agreement, the licensing firm grants rights to another firm in the host country to produce and/or sell a product. The licensee pays compensation to the licensing firm in return for technical expertise. This is an especially useful strategy if the trademark or brand name is well known but the company does not have sufficient

GLOBAL issue

GLOBAL EXPANSION IS NOT ALWAYS A PATH TO EXPANSION

The mantra in U.S. business growth for the past few decades has been to look to international markets for growth, and especially to China. Company after company poured into China with their successful U.S. business models and touted their global growth plans. Entering a new market, and especially a new market that is in a new country, often requires an adjustment to the nuances of that market.

McDonald's learned that lesson long ago when it modified its menu for the Indian market by eliminating pork and beef products and offering such unique offerings as the McAloo Tikkiburger with a mashed potato patty and the McPuff, which is a vegetable and cheese pastry. In China-based McDonald's outlets, a favorite drink is "bubble tea," which is tea with tapioca balls in the bottom. Unfortunately, many large U.S. companies are pulling out of China completely or are having to completely rewrite their business models in order to succeed.

Home Depot Inc. closed all seven of its remaining Chinese big-box stores in 2012 (they started with 12 stores through an acquisition in 2006). Unlike the U.S. market, the Chinese consumer is far more interested in finished goods and paying someone to complete a project than they are in doing it themselves. IKEA struggled for years in the Chinese market until they began offering assembly and delivery services. The DIY (do-it-yourself) market does not appear to translate well into some cultures.

Best Buy closed all of its nine stores in 2011 after discovering that Chinese consumers were far more interested in appliances than its predominantly entertainment-based product line. Best Buy is now experimenting with a small-sized appliance store.

This is not to say that some businesses don't translate easily. Yum Brands Inc. has opened nearly 4000 KFC and Pizza Hut outlets in the past few years following its business model (much like McDonald's) but modifying the approach (which is selling fast food) to its market. KFC sells egg tarts and soy milk in China while not offering those menu items outside the Chinese market.

Global success is a function of many different elements. Some businesses that are wildly successful in their home country will not find an easy path to growth in international expansion.

SOURCES: "McDonald's Going Vegetarian," *Bloomberg Businessweek* (September 10, 2012), p. 30; L. Burkitt, "Home Depot: Chinese Prefer Do-It-for-Me,'" *The Wall Street Journal* (September 15, 2012), p. B1.

funds to finance its entering the country directly. AB InBev used this strategy to produce and market Budweiser beer in the United Kingdom, Japan, Israel, Australia, Korea, and the Philippines. This strategy is also important if the country makes entry via investment either difficult or impossible.

- **Franchising:** Under a **franchising** agreement, the franchiser grants rights to another company to open a retail store using the franchiser's name and operating system. In exchange, the franchisee pays the franchiser a percentage of its sales as a royalty. Franchising provides an opportunity for a firm to establish a presence in countries where the population or per capita spending is not sufficient for a major expansion effort.[23] Franchising accounts for 32% of total U.S. retail sales. Close to half of U.S. franchisers, such as Yum! Brands, franchise internationally.[24]

- **Joint ventures:** Forming a **joint venture** between a foreign corporation and a domestic company is the most popular strategy used to enter a new country.[25] Companies often form joint ventures to combine the resources and expertise needed to develop new products or technologies. A joint venture may be an association between a company and a firm in the host country or a government agency in that country. A quick method of obtaining local management, it also reduces the risks of expropriation and harassment by host country officials. A joint venture may also enable a firm to enter a country that restricts foreign ownership. The corporation can enter another country with fewer assets at stake and thus lower risk. Under Indian law, for example, foreign retailers are permitted to own no more than 51% of shops selling single-brand products, or to sell to others on a wholesale basis. These and other restrictions deterred supermarket giants Tesco and Carrefour from entering India. As a result, 97% of Indian retailing is composed of small, family-run stores. Eager to enter India, Wal-Mart's management formed an equal partnership joint venture in 2007 with Bharti Enterprises to start wholesale operations. Under the name Best Price, the new company had opened 17 retail stores by 2012 and had plans to open 5 more stores before the end of 2012.[26]

- **Acquisitions:** A relatively quick way to move into an international area is through acquisitions—purchasing another company already operating in that area. Synergistic benefits can result if the company acquires a firm with strong complementary product lines and a good distribution network. For example, Belgium's InBev purchased Anheuser-Busch in 2008 for US$52 billion to obtain a solid position in the profitable North American beer market. Before the acquisition, InBev had only a small presence in the U.S., but a strong one in Europe and Latin American, where Anheuser-Busch was weak.[27] Research suggests that wholly owned subsidiaries are more successful in international undertakings than are strategic alliances, such as joint ventures.[28] This is one reason why firms more experienced in international markets take a higher ownership position when making a foreign investment.[29] Cross-border acquisitions by U.S. firms amounted to more than US$930 billion in 2011, up almost 11% from 2010.[30] In some countries, however, acquisitions can be difficult to arrange because of a lack of available information about potential candidates. Government restrictions on ownership, such as the U.S. requirement that limits foreign ownership of U.S. airlines to 49% of nonvoting and 25% of voting stock, can also discourage acquisitions.

- **Green-field development:** If a company doesn't want to purchase another company's problems along with its assets, it may choose **green-field development** and build its own manufacturing plant and distribution system. Research indicates that firms possessing high levels of technology, multinational experience, and diverse product lines prefer green-field development to acquisitions.[31] This is usually a far more complicated and expensive operation than acquisition, but it allows a company more freedom in designing the plant, choosing suppliers, and hiring a workforce. For example, Nissan, Honda, and

Toyota built auto factories in rural areas of Great Britain and then hired a young work-force with no experience in the industry. BMW did the same thing when it built its auto plant in Spartanburg, South Carolina, to make its Z3 and Z4 sports cars.

- **Production sharing:** Coined by Peter Drucker, the term **production sharing** means the process of combining the higher labor skills and technology available in developed countries with the lower-cost labor available in developing countries. Often called *outsourcing*, one example is Maytag's moving some of its refrigeration production to a new plant in Reynosa, Mexico, in order to reduce labor costs. Many companies have moved data processing, programming, and customer service activities "offshore" to Ireland, India, Barbados, Jamaica, the Philippines, and Singapore, where wages are lower, English is spoken, and telecommunications are in place. IBM's U.S. workforce dropped by almost 30,000 employees in the past decade and now numbers less than 105,000, while its Indian workforce grew by 9000 to 75,000. Now, less than one-fourth of the people it employs worldwide are in the United States.[32]

- **Turnkey operations: Turnkey operations** are typically contracts for the construction of operating facilities in exchange for a fee. The facilities are transferred to the host country or firm when they are complete. The customer is usually a government agency of, for example, a Middle East country that has decreed that a particular product must be produced locally and under its control. For example, Fiat built an auto plant in Tagliatti, Russia, for the Soviet Union in the late 1960s to produce an older model of Fiat under the brand name of Lada. MNCs that perform turnkey operations are frequently industrial equipment manufacturers that supply some of their own equipment for the project and that commonly sell replacement parts and maintenance services to the host country. They thereby create customers as well as future competitors. Interestingly, Renault purchased a 25% stake in the same Tagliatti factory built by Fiat to help the Russian carmaker modernize, using Renault's low-cost Logan as the base for the plant's new Lada model.[33]

- **BOT concept:** The **BOT (Build, Operate, Transfer) concept** is a variation of the turn-key operation. Instead of turning the facility (usually a power plant or toll road) over to the host country when completed, the company operates the facility for a fixed period of time during which it earns back its investment, plus a profit. It then turns the facility over to the government at little or no cost to the host country.[34]

- **Management contracts:** A large corporation operating throughout the world is likely to have a large amount of management talent at its disposal. **Management contracts** offer a means through which a corporation can use some of its personnel to assist a firm in a host country for a specified fee and period of time. Management contracts are common when a host government expropriates part or all of a foreign-owned company's holdings in its country. The contracts allow the firm to continue to earn some income from its investment and keep the operations going until local management is trained.[35]

Diversification Strategies

According to strategist Richard Rumelt, companies begin thinking about diversification when their growth has plateaued and opportunities for growth in the original business have been depleted.[36] This often occurs when an industry consolidates, becomes mature, and most of the surviving firms have reached the limits of growth using vertical and horizontal growth strategies. Unless the competitors are able to expand internationally into less mature markets, they may have no choice but to diversify into different industries if they want to continue growing. The two basic diversification strategies are concentric and conglomerate and both require very sophisticated management techniques in order to keep the elements of the company moving in relatively the same direction.

Concentric (Related) Diversification. Growth through **concentric diversification** into a related industry may be a very appropriate corporate strategy when a firm has a strong competitive position but industry attractiveness is low.

Research indicates that the probability of succeeding by moving into a related business is a function of a company's position in its core business. For companies in leadership positions, the chances for success are nearly three times higher than those for followers.[37] By focusing on the characteristics that have given the company its distinctive competence, the company uses those very strengths as its means of diversification. The firm attempts to secure strategic fit in a new industry where the firm's product knowledge, its manufacturing capabilities, and/or the marketing skills it used so effectively in the original industry can be put to good use.[38] The corporation's products or processes are related in some way: They possess some common thread.

The search is for **synergy**, the concept that two businesses will generate more profits together than they could separately. The point of commonality may be similar technology, customer usage, distribution, managerial skills, or product similarity. This is the rationale taken by Quebec-based Bombardier, the world's third-largest aircraft manufacturer. In the 1980s, the company expanded beyond snowmobiles into making light rail equipment. Defining itself as a transportation company, it entered the aircraft business in 1986, with its purchase of Canadair, then best known for its fire-fighting airplanes. It later bought Learjet, a well-known maker of business jets. Over a 14-year period, Bombardier launched 14 new aircraft. In July 2008, the company announced its C Series Aircraft Program to manufacture a 110–130-seat "green" single-aisle family of airplanes to directly compete with Airbus and Boeing. By 2012, the company had received orders for 150 C Series aircraft and the company's goal was to start delivering the aircraft by 2013.[39]

A firm may choose to diversify concentrically through either internal or external means. Bombardier, for example, diversified externally through acquisitions. Toro, in contrast, grew internally in North America by using its current manufacturing processes and distributors to make and market snow blowers in addition to lawn mowers.

Conglomerate (Unrelated) Diversification. When management realizes that the current industry is unattractive and that the firm lacks outstanding abilities or skills that it could easily transfer to related products or services in other industries, the most likely strategy is **conglomerate diversification**—diversifying into an industry unrelated to its current one. Rather than maintaining a common thread throughout their organization, strategic managers who adopt this strategy are primarily concerned with financial considerations of cash flow or risk reduction. This is also a good strategy for a firm when its core capability is its own excellent management systems. General Electric and Berkshire Hathaway are examples of companies that have used conglomerate diversification to grow successfully. Managed by Warren Buffet, Berkshire Hathaway has interests in furniture retailing, railroads, razor blades, airlines, paper, broadcasting, soft drinks, and publishing.[40]

The emphasis in conglomerate diversification is on sound investment and value-oriented management rather than on the product-market synergy common to concentric diversification. A cash-rich company with few opportunities for growth in its industry might, for example, move into another industry where opportunities are great but cash is hard to find. Another instance of conglomerate diversification might be when a company with a seasonal and, therefore, uneven cash flow purchases a firm in an unrelated industry with complementing seasonal sales that will level out the cash flow. CSX management considered the purchase of a natural gas transmission business (Texas Gas Resources) by CSX Corporation (a railroad-dominated transportation company) to be a good fit because most of the gas transmission revenue was realized in the winter months—the lean period in the railroad business.

CONTROVERSIES IN DIRECTIONAL GROWTH STRATEGIES

Is vertical growth better than horizontal growth? Is concentration better than diversification? Is concentric diversification better than conglomerate diversification? Research reveals that companies following a related diversification strategy appear to be higher performers and survive longer than do companies with narrower scope following a pure concentration strategy.[41] Although the research is not in complete agreement, growth into areas related to a company's current product lines is generally more successful than is growth into completely unrelated areas.[42] For example, one study of various growth projects examined how many were considered successful—that is, still in existence after 22 years. The results were vertical growth, 80%; horizontal growth, 50%; concentric diversification, 35%; and conglomerate diversification, 28%.[43] This supports the conclusion from a study of 40 successful European companies that companies should first exploit their existing assets and capabilities before exploring for new ones, but that they should also diversify their portfolio of products.[44]

In terms of diversification strategies, research suggests that the relationship between relatedness and performance follows an inverted U-shaped curve. If a new business is very similar to that of the acquiring firm, it adds little new to the corporation and only marginally improves performance. If the new business is completely different from the acquiring company's businesses, there may be very little potential for any synergy. If, however, the new business provides new resources and capabilities in a different but similar business, the likelihood of a significant performance improvement is high.[45]

Is internal growth better than external growth? Corporations can follow the growth strategies of either concentration or diversification through the internal development of new products and services, or through external acquisitions, mergers, and strategic alliances. The value of global acquisitions and mergers has steadily increased from less than US\$1 trillion in 1990 to US\$3.1 trillion in 2011.[46] According to a McKinsey & Company survey, managers are primarily motivated to purchase other companies in order to add capabilities, expand geographically, and buy growth.[47] Research generally concludes, however, that firms growing through acquisitions do not perform financially as well as firms that grow through internal means.[48] For example, on September 3, 2001, the day *before* HP announced that it was purchasing Compaq, HP's stock was selling at US\$23.11. After the announcement, the stock price fell to US\$18.87. Three years later, on September 21, 2004, the shares sold at US\$18.70.[49] One reason for this poor performance may be that acquiring firms tend to spend less on R&D than do other firms.[50] Another reason may be the typically high price of the acquisition itself. Studies reveal that over half to two-thirds of acquisitions are failures primarily because the premiums paid were too high for them to earn their cost of capital.[51] Another reason for the poor stock performance is that 50% of the customers of a merged firm are less satisfied with the combined company's service two years after the merger.[52] It is likely that neither strategy is best by itself and that some combination of internal and external growth strategies is better than using one or the other.[53]

What can improve acquisition performance? For one thing, the acquisition should be linked to strategic objectives and support corporate strategy. Some consultants have suggested that a corporation must be prepared to identify roughly 100 candidates and conduct due diligence investigation on around 40 companies in order to ultimately purchase 10 companies. This kind of effort requires the capacity to sift through many candidates while simultaneously integrating previous acquisitions.[54] A study by Bain & Company of more than 11,000 acquisitions by companies throughout the world concluded that successful acquirers make small, low-risk acquisitions before moving on to larger ones.[55] Previous experience between an acquirer and a target firm in terms of R&D, manufacturing, or marketing alliances improves the likelihood of a successful acquisition.[56]

STABILITY STRATEGIES

A corporation may choose stability over growth by continuing its current activities without any significant change in direction. Although sometimes viewed as a lack of strategy, the stability family of corporate strategies can be appropriate for a successful corporation operating in a reasonably predictable environment.[57] They are very popular with small business owners who have found a niche and are happy with their success and the manageable size of their firms. Stability strategies can be very useful in the short run, but they can be dangerous if followed for too long. Some of the more popular of these strategies are the pause/proceed-with-caution, no-change, and profit strategies.

Pause/Proceed-with-Caution Strategy

A **pause/proceed-with-caution strategy** is, in effect, a timeout—an opportunity to rest before continuing a growth or retrenchment strategy. It is a very deliberate attempt to make only incremental improvements until a particular environmental situation changes. It is typically conceived as a temporary strategy to be used until the environment becomes more hospitable or to enable a company to consolidate its resources after prolonged rapid growth. This was the strategy Dell followed after its growth strategy had resulted in more growth than it could handle. Explained CEO Michael Dell, "We grew 285% in two years, and we're having some growing pains." Selling personal computers by mail enabled Dell to underprice competitors, but it could not keep up with the needs of a US$2 billion, 5600-employee company selling PCs in 95 countries. Dell did not give up on its growth strategy though. It merely put it temporarily in limbo until the company was able to hire new managers, improve the structure, and build new facilities.[58] Dell spent the next few years diversifying its revenue base in the face of weakened consumer demand, giving up low-margin computer sales to consumers and moving into higher-margin, higher-cost areas, such as catering to the technology needs of small and medium businesses.[59]

No-Change Strategy

A **no-change strategy** is a decision to do nothing new—a choice to continue current operations and policies for the foreseeable future. Rarely articulated as a definite strategy, a no-change strategy's success depends on a lack of significant change in a corporation's situation. The relative stability created by the firm's modest competitive position in an industry facing little or no growth encourages the company to continue on its current course, making only small adjustments for inflation in its sales and profit objectives. There are no obvious opportunities or threats, nor is there much in the way of significant strengths or weaknesses. Few aggressive new competitors are likely to enter such an industry. The corporation has probably found a reasonably profitable and stable niche for its products. Unless the industry is undergoing consolidation, the relative comfort a company in this situation experiences is likely to encourage the company to follow a no-change strategy in which the future is expected to continue as an extension of the present. Many small-town businesses followed this strategy before Wal-Mart moved into their areas and forced them to rethink their strategy.

Profit Strategy

A **profit strategy** is a decision to do nothing new in a worsening situation but instead to act as though the company's problems are only temporary. The profit strategy is an attempt to artificially support profits when a company's sales are declining by reducing investment and short-term discretionary expenditures. Rather than announce the company's poor position to shareholders and the investment community at large, top management may be tempted to follow this very seductive strategy. Blaming the company's problems on a hostile environment (such as anti-business government policies, unethical competitors, finicky customers, and/or greedy lenders), management defers investments and/or cuts expenses (such as R&D, maintenance, and advertising) to stabilize profits during this period. It may even sell one of its product lines for the cash-flow benefits.

The profit strategy is useful only to help a company get through a temporary difficulty. It may also be a way to boost the value of a company in preparation for going public via an initial public offering (IPO). Unfortunately, the strategy is seductive and if continued long enough it will lead to a serious deterioration in a corporation's competitive position. The profit strategy is typically top management's passive, short-term, and often self-serving response to a difficult situation. In such situations, it is often better to face the problem directly by choosing a retrenchment strategy.

RETRENCHMENT STRATEGIES

A company may pursue retrenchment strategies when it has a weak competitive position in some or all of its product lines resulting in poor performance—sales are down and profits are becoming losses. These strategies impose a great deal of pressure to improve performance. In an attempt to eliminate the weaknesses that are dragging the company down, management may follow one of several retrenchment strategies, ranging from turnaround or becoming a captive company to selling out, bankruptcy, or liquidation.

Turnaround Strategy

Turnaround strategy emphasizes the improvement of operational efficiency and is probably most appropriate when a corporation's problems are pervasive but not yet critical. Research shows that poorly performing firms in mature industries have been able to improve their performance by cutting costs and expenses and by selling off assets.[60] Analogous to a weight- reduction diet, the two basic phases of a turnaround strategy are contraction and consolidation.[61]

Contraction is the initial effort to quickly "stop the bleeding" with a general, across-the-board cutback in size and costs. For example, when Howard Stringer was selected to be CEO of Sony Corporation in 2005, he immediately implemented the first stage of a turnaround plan by eliminating 10,000 jobs, closing 11 of 65 plants, and divesting many unprofitable electronics businesses.[62] The second phase, *consolidation*, implements a program to stabilize the now- leaner corporation. To streamline the company, plans are developed to reduce unnecessary overhead and to make functional activities cost-justified. This is a crucial time for the organization. If the consolidation phase is not conducted in a positive manner, many of the best people leave the organization. An overemphasis on downsizing and cutting costs coupled with a heavy hand by top management is usually counterproductive and can actually hurt performance.[63] If, however, all employees are encouraged to get involved in productivity improvements, the firm is likely to emerge from this retrenchment period a much stronger and better-organized company. It has improved its competitive position and is able once again to expand the business.[64]

Captive Company Strategy

A **captive company strategy** involves giving up independence in exchange for security. A company with a weak competitive position may not be able to engage in a full-blown turnaround strategy. The industry may not be sufficiently attractive to justify such an effort from either the current management or investors. Nevertheless, a company in this situation faces poor sales and increasing losses unless it takes some action. Management desperately searches for an "angel" by offering to be a captive company to one of its larger customers in order to guarantee the company's continued existence with a long-term contract. In this way, the corporation may be able to reduce the scope of some of its functional activities, such as marketing, thus significantly reducing costs. The weaker company gains certainty of sales and production in return for becoming heavily dependent on another firm for at least 75% of its sales. For example, to become the sole supplier of an auto part to General Motors, Simpson Industries of Birmingham, Michigan, agreed to let a special team from GM inspect its engine parts facilities and books and interview its employees. In return, nearly 80% of the company's production was sold to GM through long-term contracts.[65]

Sell-Out/Divestment Strategy

If a corporation with a weak competitive position in an industry is unable either to pull itself up by its bootstraps or to find a customer to which it can become a captive company, it may have no choice but to sell out. The **sell-out strategy** makes sense if management can still obtain a good price for its shareholders and the employees can keep their jobs by selling the entire company to another firm. The hope is that another company will have the necessary resources and determination to return the company to profitability. Marginal performance in a troubled industry was one reason American Airlines was willing to talk to US Airways in 2012.

If the corporation has multiple business lines and it chooses to sell off a division with low growth potential, this is called **divestment**. This was the strategy Ford used when it sold its struggling Jaguar and Land Rover units to Tata Motors in 2008 for US$2 billion. Ford had paid US$2.8 billion for Land Rover in 2000, and had spent US$10 billion trying to turn around Jaguar after spending US$2.5 billion to buy it in 1990.[66] General Electric's management used the same reasoning when it decided to sell or spin off its slow-growth appliance business in 2008.

Divestment is often used after a corporation acquires a multi-unit corporation in order to shed the units that do not fit with the corporation's new strategy. This is why Whirlpool sold Maytag's Hoover vacuum cleaner unit after Whirlpool purchased Maytag. Divestment was also a key part of Lego's turnaround strategy when management decided to divest its theme parks to concentrate more on its core business of making toys.[67]

Bankruptcy/Liquidation Strategy

When a company finds itself in the worst possible situation with a poor competitive position in an industry with few prospects, management has only a few alternatives—all of them distasteful. Because no one is interested in buying a weak company in an unattractive industry, the firm must pursue a bankruptcy or liquidation strategy. **Bankruptcy** involves giving up management of the firm to the courts in return for some settlement of the corporation's obligations. Top management hopes that once the court decides the claims on the company, the company will be stronger and better able to compete in a more attractive industry. Faced with a recessionary economy and increasing costs of operation, American Airlines (AMR) finally succumbed to bankruptcy in 2012. AMR was the only major airline that did not file for bankruptcy reorganization during the early part of the millennia. Its inefficient cost structure put it at a major disadvantage with the newly reorganized competition. It merged with USAir just before emerging from bankruptcy and the new company took the American Airlines name. A controversial approach was used by Delphi Corporation when it filed for Chapter 11 bankruptcy only for its U.S. operations, which employed 32,000 high-wage union workers, but not for its foreign factories in low-wage countries.[68]

In contrast to bankruptcy, which seeks to perpetuate a corporation, **liquidation** is the termination of the firm. When the industry is unattractive and the company too weak to be sold as a going concern, management may choose to convert as many saleable assets as possible to cash, which is then distributed to the shareholders after all obligations are paid. Liquidation is a prudent strategy for distressed firms with a small number of choices, all of which are problematic.[69] This was Circuit City's situation when it liquidated its retail stores. The benefit of liquidation over bankruptcy is that the board of directors, as representatives of the share-holders, together with top management, make the decisions instead of turning them over to the bankruptcy court, which may choose to ignore shareholders completely.

At times, top management must be willing to select one of these less desirable retrench-ment strategies. Unfortunately, many top managers are unwilling to admit that their com-pany has serious weaknesses for fear that they may be personally blamed. Even worse, top management may not even perceive that crises are developing. When these top managers eventually notice trouble, they are prone to attribute the problems to temporary environ-mental disturbances and tend to follow profit strategies. Even when things are going terribly wrong, top management is greatly tempted to avoid liquidation in the hope of a miracle. Top management then enters a *cycle of decline*, in which it goes through a process of secrecy and denial, followed by blame and scorn, avoidance and turf protection, ending with passivity and helplessness.[70] Thus, a corporation needs a strong board of directors who, to safeguard shareholders' interests, can tell top management when to quit.

Portfolio Analysis

Chapter 6 dealt with how individual product lines and business units can gain competitive advantage in the marketplace by using competitive and cooperative strategies. Companies with multiple product lines or business units must also ask themselves how these various products and business units should be managed to boost overall corporate performance:

- How much of our time and money should we spend on our best products and business units to ensure that they continue to be successful?

- How much of our time and money should we spend developing new costly products, most of which will never be successful?

One of the most popular aids to developing corporate strategy in a multiple-business cor-poration is portfolio analysis. Although its popularity has dropped since the 1970s and 1980s, when more than half of the largest business corporations used portfolio analysis, it is still used by around 27% of Fortune 500 firms in corporate strategy formulation.[71] Portfolio analysis puts corporate headquarters into the role of an internal banker. In **portfolio analysis**, top management views its product lines and business units as a series of investments from which it expects a profitable return. The product lines/business units form a portfolio of investments that top management must constantly juggle to ensure the best return on the corporation's invested money. A McKinsey & Company study of the performance of the 200 largest U.S. corporations found that companies that actively managed their business portfolios through acquisitions and divestitures created substantially more shareholder value than those compa-nies that passively held their businesses.[72] Given the increasing number of strategic alliances in today's corporations, portfolio analysis is also being used to evaluate the contribution of alliances to corporate and business unit objectives.

Two of the most popular portfolio techniques are the BCG Growth-Share Matrix and **GE Business Screen**.

BCG GROWTH-SHARE MATRIX

Using the **BCG (Boston Consulting Group) Growth-Share Matrix** depicted in **Figure 7–3** is the simplest way to portray a corporation's portfolio of investments. Each of the corpora-tion's product lines or business units is plotted on the matrix according to both the growth rate of the industry in which it competes and its relative market share. A unit's relative competitive position is defined as its market share in the industry divided by that of the largest other competitor. By this calculation, a relative market share above 1.0 belongs to the market leader. The business growth rate is the percentage of market growth—that is, the percentage by which sales of a particular business unit classification of products have increased. The matrix assumes that, other things being equal, a growing market is attractive.

The line separating areas of high and low relative competitive position is set at 1.5 times. A product line or business unit must have relative strengths of this magnitude to ensure that it will have the dominant position needed to be a "star" or "cash cow." On the other hand, a product line or unit having a relative competitive position less than 1.0 has "dog" status.[73] Each product or unit is represented in **Figure 7–3** by a circle. The area of the circle represents the relative significance of each business unit or product line to the corporation in terms of assets used or sales generated.

The BCG Growth-Share Matrix has some common attributes with the product life cycle. As a product moves through its life cycle, it is generally categorized into one of four types for the purpose of funding decisions:

- **Question marks** (sometimes called "problem children" or "wildcats") are new products with the potential for success, but they need a lot of cash for development. If such a product is to gain enough market share to become a market leader and thus a star, money must be taken from more mature products and spent on the question mark. This is a "fish or cut bait" decision in which management must decide if the business is worth the investment needed. For example, after years of fruitlessly experimenting with an electric car, General Motors finally decided in 2006 to take a chance on developing the Chevrolet Volt.[74] To learn more of GM's decision to build the electric car, see the **Sustainability Issue** feature.

- **Stars** are market leaders that are typically at or nearing the peak of their product life cycle and are able to generate enough cash to maintain their high share of the market and usually contribute to the company's profits. The iPhone business has been called Apple's "crown jewel" because of its 52% market share and the extensive app network available on iTunes.[75]

- **Cash cows** typically bring in far more money than is needed to maintain their market share. In this declining stage of their life cycle, these products are "milked" for cash that will be invested in new question marks. Expenses such as advertising and R&D are

FIGURE 7–3   BCG Growth- Share Matrix

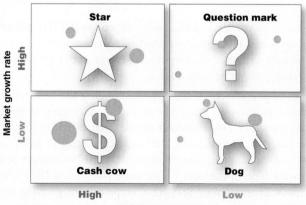

SOURCE: Based on *Long Range Planning,* Vol. 10, No. 2, 1977, Hedley, "Strategy and the Business Portfolio." p. 12. Copyright © 1977

SUSTAINABILITY issue

GENERAL MOTORS AND THE ELECTRIC CAR

In 2003, top management at General Motors (GM) decided to discontinue further work on its EV1 electric automobile. Working versions of the car had been leased to a limited number of people, but never sold. GM required every EV1 to be returned to the company. Environmentalists protested that GM stopped making the car just to send a message to government policy makers that an electric car was bad business. Management responded by stating that the car would never have made a profit.

In an April 2005 meeting of GM's top management team, Vice Chairman Robert Lutz suggested that it might be time to build another electric car. He noted that Toyota's Prius hybrid had made Toyota look environmentally sensitive, whereas GM was viewed as making gas "hogs." The response was negative. Lutz recalled one executive saying, "We lost $1 billion on the last one. Do you want to lose $1 billion on the next one?"

Even though worldwide car ownership was growing 5% annually, rising fuel prices in 2005 reduced sales of GM's profitable SUVs—resulting in a loss of US$11 billion. Board members began signaling that it was time for management to take some riskier bets to get the company out of financial trouble. In February 2006, management reluctantly approved developmental work on another electric car. At the time, no one in GM knew if batteries could be made small enough to power a car, but they knew that choices were limited. According to Larry Burns, Vice President of R&D and Strategic Planning, "This industry is 98% dependent on petroleum. GM has concluded that that's not sustainable."

Chairman and CEO Richard Wagoner Jr. surprised the world at the January 2007 Detroit Auto Show with a vow to start developing an electric car called the Chevrolet Volt. It would plug into a regular electric outlet, leapfrog the competition, and be on sale in 2010.

Management created a new team dedicated to getting hybrid and electric cars to market. The R&D budget was increased from US$6.6 billion in 2006 to US$8.1 billion in 2007. Several new models were canceled to free up resources. The battery lab was under pressure to design batteries that could propel the Volt 40 miles before a small gasoline engine would recharge the battery and extend the range to 600 miles. Douglas Drauch, battery lab manager, said. "Fifty years from now, people will remember the Volt—like they remember a '53 Corvette."

The Volt was released with much fanfare in October, 2010, and by 2012 GM was selling 2500 a month at just over US$40,000 per car. The company was still struggling to match manufacturing with sales and still make a profit. In the meantime, Nissan, Ford, and Toyota were making significant moves in the battery powered car business. Nissan released the Leaf, Ford released the electric Focus, and Toyota offered the Plug-in Prius and the all-electric RAV4, which claimed to get 103 MPG.

....

SOURCES: J. Bennett, "GM Expects Volt Sales to Set Monthly Record," *The Wall Street Journal* (August 30, 2012), (http://blogs.wsj.com/drivers-seat/2012/08/30/gm-expects-volt-sales-to-set-monthly-record/?KEYWORDS=volt); "12 Electric Cars for 2012," *CNN Money*, (http://money.cnn.com/galleries/2012/autos/1201/gallery.electric-hybrid-cars.fortune/9.html); D. Welch, "GM: Live Green or Die," *BusinessWeek* (May 26, 2008), pp. 36–41; "The Drive for Low Emissions," *The Economist's Special Report on Business and Climate Change* (June 2, 2007), pp. 26–28.

....

reduced. Panasonic's videocassette recorders (VCRs) moved to this category when sales declined and DVD player/recorders replaced them. Question marks unable to obtain dominant market share (and thus become stars) by the time the industry growth rate inevitably slows become dogs.

- **Dogs** have low market share and do not have the potential (because they are in an unattractive industry) to bring in much cash. According to the BCG Growth-Share Matrix, dogs should be either sold off or managed carefully for the small amount of cash they can generate. For example, DuPont, the inventor of nylon, sold its textiles unit in 2003 because the company wanted to eliminate its low-margin products and focus more on its growing biotech business.[76] The same was true of IBM when it sold its PC business to China's Lenovo Group in order to emphasize its growing services business.

Underlying the BCG Growth-Share Matrix is the concept of the experience curve (discussed in **Chapter 5**). The key to success with this model is assumed to be market share. Firms with the highest market share tend to have a cost leadership position based on economies of scale, among many other things. If a company is able to use the experience curve to its advantage, it should be able to manufacture and sell new products at a price low enough to garner early market share leadership (assuming no successful imitation by competitors).

Having plotted the current positions of its product lines or business units on a matrix, a company can project its future positions; however, this assumes no change in strategy by either the company with the portfolio or its competitors—a very unrealistic assumption. That said, present and projected matrixes can be used to help identify major strategic issues facing the organization. The goal of any company using a portfolio approach is to maintain a balanced portfolio so it can be self-sufficient in cash and always working to harvest mature products in declining industries to support new ones in growing industries.

The BCG Growth-Share Matrix is a very well-known portfolio concept with some clear advantages. It is quantifiable and easy to use. *Cash cow*, *dog*, *question mark*, and *star* are easy- to-remember terms for referring to a corporation's business units or products. Unfortunately, the BCG Growth-Share Matrix also has some serious limitations:

- The use of highs and lows to form four categories is too simplistic.
- The link between market share and profitability is questionable.[77] Low-share businesses can also be profitable.[78] For example, Olivetti is still profitably selling manual typewriters through mail-order catalogs.
- Growth rate is only one aspect of industry attractiveness.
- Product lines or business units are considered only in relation to one competitor: the market leader. Small competitors with fast-growing market shares are ignored.
- Market share is only one aspect of overall competitive position.

ADVANTAGES AND LIMITATIONS OF PORTFOLIO ANALYSIS

Portfolio analysis is commonly used in strategy formulation because it offers certain *advantages:*

- It encourages top management to evaluate each of the corporation's businesses individually and to set objectives and allocate resources for each.
- It stimulates the use of externally oriented data to supplement management's judgment.
- It raises the issue of cash-flow availability for use in expansion and growth.
- Its graphic depiction facilitates communication.

Portfolio analysis does, however, have some very real *limitations* that have caused some companies to reduce their use of this approach:

- Defining product/market segments is difficult.
- It suggests the use of standard strategies that can miss opportunities or be impractical.
- It provides an illusion of scientific rigor, when in reality positions are based on subjective judgments.
- Its value-laden terms such as cash cow and dog can lead to self-fulfilling prophecies.

- It is not always clear what makes an industry attractive or where a product is in its life cycle.

- Naively following the prescriptions of a portfolio model may actually reduce corporate profits if they are used inappropriately. For example, General Mills' Chief Executive H. Brewster Atwater cited his company's Bisquick brand of baking mix as a product that would have been written off years ago based on portfolio analysis. "This product is 57 years old. By all rights it should have been overtaken by newer products. But with the proper research to improve the product and promotion to keep customers excited, it's doing very well."[79]

MANAGING A STRATEGIC ALLIANCE PORTFOLIO

Just as product lines/business units form a portfolio of investments that top management must constantly juggle to ensure the best return on the corporation's invested money, strategic alliances can also be viewed as a portfolio of investments—investments of money, time, and energy. The way a company manages these intertwined relationships can significantly influence corporate competitiveness. Alliances are thus recognized as an important source of competitive advantage and superior performance.[80]

Managing groups of strategic alliances is primarily the job of the business unit. Its decisions may escalate, however, to the corporate level. Toman Corporation, for example, has 195 international joint ventures containing 422 alliance partners.

A study of 25 leading European corporations found four tasks of multi-alliance management that are necessary for successful alliance portfolio management:

1. **Developing and implementing a portfolio strategy for each business unit and a corporate policy for managing all the alliances of the entire company:** Alliances are primarily determined by business units. The corporate level develops general rules concerning when, how, and with whom to cooperate. The task of alliance policy is to strategically align all of the corporation's alliance activities with corporate strategy and corporate values. Every new alliance is thus checked against corporate policy before it is approved.

2. **Monitoring the alliance portfolio in terms of implementing business unit strategies and corporate strategy and policies:** Each alliance is measured in terms of achievement of objectives (e.g., market share), financial measures (e.g., profits and cash flow), contributed resource quality and quantity, and the overall relationship. The more a firm is diversified, the less the need for monitoring at the corporate level.

3. **Coordinating the portfolio to obtain synergies and avoid conflicts among alliances:** Because the interdependencies among alliances within a business unit are usually greater than among different businesses, the need for coordination is greater at the business level than at the corporate level. The need for coordination increases as the number of alliances in one business unit and the company as a whole increases, the average number of partners per alliance increases, and/or the overlap of the alliances increases.

4. **Establishing an alliance management system to support other tasks of multi-alliance management:** This infrastructure consists of formalized processes, standardized tools and specialized organizational units. All but two of the 25 companies established centers of competence for alliance management. The centers were often part of a department for corporate development or a department of alliance management at the corporate level. In other corporations, specialized positions for alliance management were created at both the corporate and business unit levels or only at the business unit level. Most corporations prefer a system in which the corporate level provides the methods and tools to support alliances centrally, but decentralizes day-to-day alliance management to the business units.[81]

Corporate Parenting

It has been suggested that corporate strategists address two crucial questions:

- What businesses should this company own and why?
- What organizational structure, management processes, and philosophy will foster superior performance from the company's business units?[82]

Portfolio analysis typically attempts to answer these questions by examining the attractiveness of various industries and by managing business units for cash flow—that is, by using cash generated from mature units to build new product lines. Unfortunately, portfolio analysis fails to deal with the question of what industries a corporation should enter or how a corporation can attain synergy among its product lines and business units. As suggested by its name, portfolio analysis tends to primarily view matters financially, regarding business units and product lines as separate and independent investments. Calculating the impact and fit of a new industry or a new business acquisition can be quite difficult as shown in the Innovation Issue feature.

Corporate parenting, or parenting strategy, in contrast, views a corporation in terms of resources and capabilities that can be used to build business unit value as well as generate synergies across business units. According to Campbell, Goold, and Alexander:

> *Multibusiness companies create value by influencing—or parenting—the businesses they own. The best parent companies create more value than any of their rivals would if they owned the same businesses. Those companies have what we call parenting advantage.*[83]

INNOVATION issue

TO RED HAT OR NOT?

Many large, established organizations including IBM, Hewlett-Packard, Oracle, and Intel were looking closely at acquiring a business that had grown to a US$1 billion business in a niche area of the industry. Red Hat was a business founded on supporting what amounts to a free software system called Linux.

The precursor to the Internet was born in 1968, and in 1969 a researcher at Bell Labs created UNIX as an open-source operating system. Being open sourced meant that anyone who wanted to volunteer their time could add to the capability of the software. Fast forward to 1995 and a new company called Red Hat was born as an accessory, books, and magazine company focused on what had then become known as Linux.

Red Hat based in Durham, North Carolina, released a version of Linux in 1995 and promised to support companies who used that version. It was still freeware, but now it had a company of engineers to support it at that particular point in time. This became the core of the business. The company would freeze Linux periodically and then support that "version" for a 10-year period of time. This gave corporate managers the confidence to use Linux as their operating system.

The company experienced phenomenal growth by focusing on Data Centers and supporting each version with more than 150 engineers. Red Hat charged a substantial premium to its customers who pay a subscription fee for Red Hat support.

With the winds of a potential acquisition behind it, the company's share price surged 66% between 2010 and 2012. Red Hat was the only company that had found a business model that made substantial profits on open-sourced software. Whether this fit with the needs of such major companies as IBM or not was the open question.

····················
SOURCES: http://www.redhat.com/about/company/history.html; "Red Hat Sees Lots of Green," *Bloomberg Businessweek* (April 2, 2012), pp. 41–43.

Corporate parenting generates corporate strategy by focusing on the core competencies of the parent corporation and on the value created from the relationship between the parent and its businesses. In the form of corporate headquarters, the parent has a great deal of power in this relationship. If there is a good fit between the parent's skills and resources and the needs and opportunities of the business units, the corporation is likely to create value. If, however, there is not a good fit, the corporation is likely to destroy value.[84] Research indicates that companies that have a good fit between their strategy and their parenting roles are better performers than those companies that do not have a good fit.[85] This approach to corporate strategy is useful not only in deciding what new businesses to acquire but also in choosing how each existing business unit should be best managed. This appears to have been the secret to the success of General Electric under CEO Jack Welch.

The primary job of corporate headquarters is, therefore, to obtain synergy among the business units by providing needed resources to units, transferring skills and capabilities among the units, and coordinating the activities of shared unit functions to attain economies of scope (as in centralized purchasing).[86] This is in agreement with the concept of the learning organization discussed in **Chapter 1** in which the role of a large firm is to facilitate and transfer the knowledge assets and services throughout the corporation.[87] This is especially important given that 75% or more of a modern company's market value stems from its intangible assets—the organization's knowledge and capabilities.[88] At Proctor & Gamble, for example, the various business units are expected to work together to develop innovative products. Crest Whitestrips, which controls 68% of the at-home tooth-whitening market, was based on the P&G laundry division's knowledge of whitening agents.[89]

DEVELOPING A CORPORATE PARENTING STRATEGY

The search for appropriate corporate strategy involves three analytical steps:

1. **Examine each business unit (or target firm in the case of acquisition) in terms of its strategic factors:** People in the business units probably identified the strategic factors when they were generating business strategies for their units. One popular approach is to establish centers of excellence throughout the corporation. A **center of excellence** is "an organizational unit that embodies a set of capabilities that has been explicitly recognized by the firm as an important source of value creation, with the intention that these capabilities be leveraged by and/or disseminated to other parts of the firm."[90]

2. **Examine each business unit (or target firm) in terms of areas in which performance can be improved:** These are considered to be parenting opportunities. For example, two business units might be able to gain economies of scope by combining their sales forces. In another instance, a unit may have good, but not great, manufacturing and logistics skills. A parent company having world-class expertise in these areas could improve that unit's performance. The corporate parent could also transfer some people from one business unit who have the desired skills to another unit that is in need of those skills. People at corporate headquarters may, because of their experience in many industries, spot areas where improvements are possible that even people in the business unit may not have noticed. Unless specific areas are significantly weaker than the competition, people in the business units may not even be aware that these areas could be improved, especially if each business unit monitors only its own particular industry.

3. **Analyze how well the parent corporation fits with the business unit (or target firm):** Corporate headquarters must be aware of its own strengths and weaknesses in terms of resources, skills, and capabilities. To do this, the corporate parent must ask whether it has the characteristics that fit the parenting opportunities in each business unit. It must also ask whether there is a misfit between the parent's characteristics and the critical success factors of each business unit.

HORIZONTAL STRATEGY AND MULTIPOINT COMPETITION

A **horizontal strategy** is a corporate strategy that cuts across business unit boundaries to build synergy between business units and to improve the competitive position of one or more business units.[91] When used to build synergy, it acts like a parenting strategy. When used to improve the competitive position of one or more business units, it can be thought of as a corporate competitive strategy. In **multipoint competition**, large multibusiness corporations compete against other large multibusiness firms in a number of markets. These multipoint competitors are firms that compete with each other not only in one business unit, but also in a number of business units. At one time or another, a cash-rich competitor may choose to build its own market share in a particular market to the disadvantage of another corporation's business unit. Although each business unit has primary responsibility for its own business strategy, it may sometimes need some help from its corporate parent, especially if the competitor business unit is getting heavy financial support from its corporate parent. In this instance, corporate headquarters develops a horizontal strategy to coordinate the various goals and strategies of related business units.

For example, P&G, Kimberly-Clark, Scott Paper, and Johnson & Johnson (J&J) compete with one another in varying combinations of consumer paper products, from disposable diapers to facial tissue. If (purely hypothetically) J&J had just developed a toilet tissue with which it chose to challenge Procter & Gamble's high-share Charmin brand in a particular district, it might charge a low price for its new brand to build sales quickly. P&G might not choose to respond to this attack on its share by cutting prices on Charmin. Because of Charmin's high market share, P&G would lose significantly more sales dollars in a price war than J&J would with its initially low-share brand. To retaliate, P&G might challenge J&J's high-share baby shampoo with P&G's own low-share brand of baby shampoo in a different district. Once J&J had perceived P&G's response, it might choose to stop challenging Charmin so that P&G would stop challenging J&J's baby shampoo.

Multipoint competition and the resulting use of horizontal strategy may actually slow the development of hypercompetition in an industry. The realization that an attack on a market leader's position could result in a response in another market leads to mutual forbearance in which managers behave more conservatively toward multimarket rivals and competitive rivalry is reduced.[92] In one industry, for example, multipoint competition resulted in firms being less likely to exit a market. "Live and let live" replaced strong competitive rivalry.[93]

Multipoint competition is likely to become even more prevalent in the future, as corporations become global competitors and expand into more markets through strategic alliances.[94]

End of Chapter SUMMARY

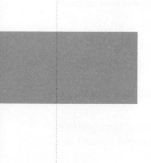

Corporate strategy is primarily about the choice of direction for the firm as a whole. It deals with three key issues that a corporation faces: (1) the firm's overall orientation toward growth, stability, or retrenchment; (2) the industries or markets in which the firm competes through its products and business units; and (3) the manner in which management coordinates activities and transfers resources and cultivates capabilities among product lines and business units. These issues are dealt with through directional strategy, portfolio analysis, and corporate parenting.

Managers must constantly examine their corporation's entire portfolio of products, businesses, and opportunities as if they were planning to reinvest all of its capital.[95] One of the most complex and well-known collections of businesses (a conglomerate) is run by Berkshire Hathaway and headed by icon, Warren Buffett. By 2012, Berkshire owned and managed more than 80 businesses, with profits approaching US$12 billion/year. Over the years, the company has moved resources around to benefit the whole corporation. This meant moving away from insurance and investing in railroads, utilities, and manufacturing companies using the profits from the more successful cash generating businesses to fund investments in promising new business ideas. Some of the more well-known companies are BNSF Railroad, GEICO Insurance, See's Candies, Dairy Queen, and Fruit of the Loom.[96]

MyManagementLab®

Go to **mymanagementlab.com** to complete the problems marked with this icon .

KEY TERMS

acquisition (p. 227)
backward integration (p. 223)
bankruptcy (p. 233)
BCG (Boston Consulting Group) Growth-Share Matrix (p. 234)
BOT (Build, Operate, Transfer) concept (p. 228)
captive company strategy (p. 232)
cash cows (p. 235)
center of excellence (p. 240)
concentration (p. 222)
concentric diversification (p. 229)
conglomerate diversification (p. 229)
corporate parenting (p. 239)
corporate strategy (p. 220)
directional strategy (p. 221)
diversification (p. 222)
divestment (p. 233)
dogs (p. 236)

exporting (p. 226)
forward integration (p. 223)
franchising (p. 227)
full integration (p. 223)
GE business screen (p. 234)
green-field development (p. 227)
growth strategy (p. 221)
horizontal growth (p. 224)
horizontal integration (p. 224)
horizontal strategy (p. 241)
joint venture (p. 227)
licensing (p. 226)
liquidation (p. 233)
long-term contracts (p. 224)
management contracts (p. 228)
merger (p. 222)
multipoint competition (p. 241)
no-change strategy (p. 231)
parenting strategy (pp. 220)

pause/proceed-with-caution strategy (p. 231)
portfolio analysis (p. 220)
production sharing (p. 228)
profit strategy (p. 231)
quasi-integration (p. 224)
question marks (p. 235)
retrenchment strategies (p. 221)
sell-out strategy (p. 233)
stability strategy (p. 221)
stars (p. 235)
synergy (p. 229)
taper integration (p. 224)
transaction cost economics (p. 223)
turnaround strategy (p. 232)
turnkey operations (p. 228)
vertical growth (p. 222)
vertical integration (p. 223)

MyManagementLab®

Go to **mymanagementlab.com** for the following Assisted-graded writing questions:

7-1. List the means available to a company for Horizontal Growth and explain why a company might pursue one over another?

7-2. Evaluate the types of retrenchment strategies that might be used by companies in stagnant industries.

DISCUSSION QUESTIONS

⭐ **7-3.** How does horizontal growth differ from vertical growth as a corporate strategy? From concentric diversification?

⭐ **7-4.** What are the trade-offs between an internal and an external growth strategy? Which approach is best as an international entry strategy?

7-5. Explain the vertical integration continuum.

7-6. Explain Green Field Development, and provide examples to clarify.

⭐ **7-7.** How is corporate parenting different from portfolio analysis? How is it alike? Is it a useful concept in a global industry?

STRATEGIC PRACTICE EXERCISE

Steps Taken

Political measures taken in emerging countries are important when carefully thought-out, especially when small nations have an opportunity to build ongoing relations with powerful multinational companies. It seems that Gebran Bassil, the caretaker Minister of Energy and Water Resources of Lebanon, has been taking a lot of time to think through his steps as he makes his way through an entrenched and vociferous cabinet that refuses to budge even though competitive advantage is lost along the way. He stressed that the cabinet should support and encourage the oil march.

An American firm plans to conduct an airborne survey to research the oil and gas potential of Lebanon, after being given the full support of the caretaker minister. Bassil has encouraged the U.S. and other international firms, that have expressed their interest in conducting onshore oil surveys, in an effort to discover oil and gas both onshore and offshore. He has worked alongside the Vice President and General Manager of NEOS Geosolutions MENA, Frank Jreij who has signed an agreement with the ministry to establish "Cedar Oil," a project that will survey 6,000 square kilometers over the northern part of the country.

Cedar Oil will reduce the time needed to examine the entire area. The survey intends to use six different sensors to survey parts of Lebanon's geological layers. The data collected from the sensors is to quickly analyze and establish if the country has oil and gas onshore. Jreij said that analyzing the data collected from the plane's sensors would be much quicker than conventional methods. Phase One takes up two months, while the data acquisition will be completed within seven months. Jreij estimated that the entire project would be completed within 18 months. The British-based Spectrum company began a 2-D seismic onshore survey of the Batroun region last year, and intends to complete the survey by the end of this year. The caretaker Energy Minister assured the cabinet and the country that the initial onshore survey was promising, though he did not provide any details. With this Bassil hoped to limit too many contradicting opinions, and stop the local politicians from obstructing the drive to tap the country's oil and gas wealth.

1. Form small groups to discuss the problem.
2. Discuss whether the manner taken to address it was appropriate.
3. Arrive at a solution to the problem.
4. Discuss the group's solution with the class.
5. What strategies should the company follow to enter the Lebanese market and gain the governmental contract?

....

SOURCE: "U.S. firm to conduct airborne survey of onshore oil," *The Daily Star* (January 11, 2014), p. 4.

NOTES

1. R. P. Rumelt, D. E. Schendel, and D. J. Teece, "Fundamental Issues in Strategy," in R. P. Rumelt, D. E. Schendel, and D. J. Teece (Eds.), *Fundamental Issues in Strategy: A Research Agenda* (Boston: HBS Press, 1994), p. 42.
2. This analogy of corporate parent and business unit children was initially proposed by A. Campbell, M. Goold, and M. Alexander. See "Corporate Strategy: The Quest for Parenting Advantage," *Harvard Business Review* (March–April, 1995), pp. 120–132.
3. M. E. Porter, "From Competitive Strategy to Corporate Strategy," in D. E. Husey (Ed.), *International Review of Strategic Management, Vol. 1* (Chichester, England: John Wiley & Sons, 1990), p. 29.
4. This is in agreement with Toyohiro Kono when he proposes that corporate headquarters has three main functions: formulate corporate strategy, identify and develop the company's core competencies, and provide central resources. See T. Kono, "A Strong Head Office Makes a Strong Company," *Long Range Planning* (April 1999), pp. 225–236.
5. "Larry Ups the Ante," *The Economist* (February 7, 2004), pp. 59–60, (http://www.oracle.com/us/corporate/acquisitions/index.html).
6. J. Bercovitz and W. Mitchell, "When Is More Better? The Impact of Business Scale and Scope on Long-Term Business Survival, While Controlling for Profitability," *Strategic Management Journal* (January 2007), pp. 61–79.
7. http://finance.yahoo.com/news/duke-energy-acquires-progress-energy-184514127.html.
8. "Cisco Inc. Buys Top Technology Innovator," *St. Cloud (MN) Times* (November 19, 2005), p. 6A.
9. J. Perkins, "It's a Hog Predicament," *Des Moines Register* (April 11, 1999), pp. J1–J2.
10. C. Woodyard, "FedEx Ponies Up $2.4B for Kinko's," *USA Today* (December 31, 2003), p. B1.
11. J. W. Slocum Jr., M. McGill, and D. T. Lei, "The New Learning Strategy: Anytime, Anything, Anywhere," *Organizational Dynamics* (Autumn 1994), p. 36.
12. M. J. Leiblein, J. J. Reuer, and F. Dalsace, "Do Make or Buy Decisions Matter? The Influence of Organizational Governance on Technological Performance," *Strategic Management Journal* (September 2002), pp. 817–833.
13. I. Geyskens, J-B. E. M. Steenkamp, and N. Kumar, "Make, Buy, or Ally: A Transaction Cost Theory Meta-Analysis,"

Academy of Management Journal (June 2006), pp. 519–543; R. Carter and G. M. Hodgson, "The Impact of Empirical Tests of Transaction Cost Economics on the Debate on the Nature of the Firm," *Strategic Management Journal* (May 2006), pp. 461–476; T. A. Shervani, G. Frazier, and G. Challagalla, "The Moderating Influence of Firm Market Power on the Transaction Cost Economics Model: An Empirical Test in a Forward Channel Integration Context," *Strategic Management Journal* (June 2007), pp. 635–652; K. J. Mayer and R. M. Solomon, "Capabilities, Contractual Hazards, and Governance: Integrating Resource-Based and Transaction Cost Perspectives," *Academy of Management Journal* (October 2006), pp. 942–959.

14. K. R. Harrigan, *Strategies for Vertical Integration* (Lexington, MA.: Lexington Books, 1983), pp. 16–21.

15. M. Arndt, "Who's Afraid of a Housing Slump?" *BusinessWeek* (April 30, 2007), p. 76.

16. A. Parmigiani, "Why Do Firms Both Make and Buy? An Investigation of Concurrent Sourcing," *Strategic Management Journal* (March 2007), pp. 285–311; F. T. Rothaermel, M. A. Hitt, and L. A. Jobe, "Balancing Vertical Integration and Strategic Outsourcing: Effects on Product Portfolio, Product Success, and Firm Performance," *Strategic Management Journal* (November 2006), pp. 1033–1056.

17. "Converge or Conflict?" *The Economist* (August 30, 2008), pp. 61–62.

18. M. G. Jacobides, "Industry Change Through Vertical Disintegration: How and Why Markets Emerged in Mortgage Banking," *Academy of Management Journal* (June 2005), pp. 465–498.

19. For a discussion of the pros and cons of contracting versus vertical integration, see J. T. Mahoney, "The Choice of Organizational Form: Vertical Financial Ownership Versus Other Methods of Vertical Integration," *Strategic Management Journal* (November 1992), pp. 559–584; J. Helyar, "Outsourcing: A Passage Out of India," *Bloomberg Businessweek* (March 15, 2012), (www.businessweek.com/articles/2012-03-15/outsourcing-a-passage-out-of-india).

20. G. Dowell, "Product Line Strategies of New Entrants in an Established Industry: Evidence from the U.S. Bicycle Industry," *Strategic Management Journal* (October 2006), pp. 959–979; C. Sorenson, S. McEvily, C. R. Ren, and R. Roy, "Niche Width Revisited: Organizational Scope, Behavior and Performance," *Strategic Management Journal* (October 2006), pp. 915–936.

21. "Procter & Gamble CEO Takes on New role as USCBC Board Chair," *China Business Review* (July–September 2012), (www.chinabusinessreview.com/public/1207/interview.html); D. Roberts, "Scrambling to Bring Crest to the Masses," *BusinessWeek* (June 25, 2007), pp. 72–73.

22. A. Delios and P. W. Beamish, "Geographic Scope, Product Diversification, and the Corporate Performance of Japanese Firms," *Strategic Management Journal* (August 1999), pp. 711–727.

23. E. Elango and V. H. Fried, "Franchising Research: A Literature Review and Synthesis," *Journal of Small Business Management* (July 1997), pp. 68–81.

24. Franchise Business Economic Outlook: 2011 (December 16, 2011), (http://emarket.franchise.org/News_Release/Franchise%20Business%20Outlook%20Report%202011%20final.pdf); T. Thilgen, "Corporate Clout Replaces 'Small Is Beautiful,'" *The Wall Street Journal* (March 27, 1997), p. B14.

25. J. E. McCann III, "The Growth of Acquisitions in Services," *Long Range Planning* (December 1996), pp. 835–841.

26. Mukherjee, A. 2012. "Update 1 – Wal-Mart Plans 3-5 More India Stores This Year," *Reuters* (September 11, 2012), (http://in.reuters.com/article/2012/09/11/walmart-india-idINL3E8KB4O320120911); "Gently Does It," *The Economist* (August 11, 2007), p. 59.

27. A Bid for Bud," *The Economist* (June 21, 2008), p. 77.

28. B. Voss, "Strategic Federations Frequently Falter in Far East," *Journal of Business Strategy* (July/August 1993), p. 6; S. Douma, "Success and Failure in New Ventures," *Long Range Planning* (April 1991), pp. 54–60.

29. A. Delios and P. W. Beamish, "Ownership Strategy of Japanese Firms: Transactional, Institutional, and Experience Approaches," *Strategic Management Journal* (October 1999), pp. 915–933.

30. "Cross Border M&A," (January 3, 2012), (http://www.wlrk.com/webdocs/wlrknew/WLRKMemos/WLRK/WLRK.21572.12.pdf).

31. K. D. Brouthers and L. E. Brouthers, "Acquisition or Greenfield Start-up? Institutional, Cultural, and Transaction Cost Influences," *Strategic Management Journal* (January 2000), pp. 89–97.

32. P. Hill, "The MEAN Economy: IBM Workers Suffer Culture Change as Jobs Go Global," *The Washington Times* (August 26, 2012), (http://www.washingtontimes.com/news/2012/aug/26/innovators-working-their-way-out-of-a-job/?page=all).

33. C. Matlack, "Carlos Ghosn's Russian Gambit," *BusinessWeek* (March 17, 2008), pp. 57–58.

34. J. Naisbitt, *Megatrends Asia* (New York: Simon & Schuster, 1996), p. 143.

35. For additional information on international entry modes, see D. F. Spulber, *Global Competitive Strategy* (Cambridge, UK: Cambridge University Press, 2007) and K. D. Brouthers and J-F Hennart, "Boundaries of the Firm: Insights from International Entry Mode Research," *Journal of Management* (June 2007), pp. 395–425.

36. D. P. Lovallo and L. T. Mendonca, "Strategy's Strategist: An Interview with Richard Rumelt," *McKinsey Quarterly Online* (2007, No. 4).

37. C. Zook, "Increasing the Odds of Successful Growth: The Critical Prelude to Moving 'Beyond the Core.'" *Strategy & Leadership* (Vol. 32, No. 4, 2004), pp. 17–23.

38. A. Y. Ilinich and C. P. Zeithaml, "Operationalizing and Testing Galbraith's Center of Gravity Theory," *Strategic Management Journal* (June 1995), pp. 401–410; H. Tanriverdi and N. Venkatraman, "Knowledge Relatedness and the Performance of Multibusiness Firms," *Strategic Management Journal* (February 2005), pp. 97–119.

39. E. Duffner and B. Kammel, "Bombardier CSeries Boosted on Agreement to Sell 15 Jets," *Bloomberg* (July 9, 2012), (http://www.bloomberg.com/news/2012-07-08/bombardier-wins-1-02-billion-deal-for-15-cseries-jetliners-1-.html); "Flying into Battle," *The Economist* (May 8, 2004), p. 60 and corporate Web site (www.bombardier.com) accessed September 27, 2008.

40. R. F. Bruner, "Corporation Diversification May Be Okay After All," *Batten Briefings* (Spring 2003), pp. 2–3, 12.

41. J. Bercovitz and W. Mitchell, "When Is More Better? The Impact of Business Scale and Scope on Long-Term Business Survival, While Controlling for Profitability," *Strategic Management Journal* (January 2007), pp. 61–79; D. J. Miller, "Technological Diversity, Related Diversification, and Firm Performance," *Strategic Management Journal* (July 2006), pp. 601–619; C. Stadler, "The Four Principles of Enduring

Success," *Harvard Business Review* (July–August 2007), pp. 62–72.

42. K. Carow, R. Heron, and T. Saxton, "Do Early Birds Get the Returns? An Empirical Investigation of Early-Mover Advantages in Acquisitions," *Strategic Management Journal* (June 2004), pp. 563–585; K. Ramaswamy, "The Performance Impact of Strategic Similarity in Horizontal Mergers: Evidence from the U.S. Banking Industry," *Academy of Management Journal* (July 1997), pp. 697–715; D. J. Flanagan, "Announcements of Purely Related and Purely Unrelated Mergers and Shareholder Returns: Reconciling the Relatedness Paradox," *Journal of Management* (Vol. 22, No. 6, 1996), pp. 823–835; D. D. Bergh, "Predicting Diversification of Unrelated Acquisitions: An Integrated Model of Ex Ante Conditions," *Strategic Management Journal* (October 1997), pp. 715–731.

43. J. M. Pennings, H. Barkema, and S. Douma, "Organizational Learning and Diversification," *Academy of Management Journal* (June 1994), pp. 608–640.

44. C. Stadler, "The Four Principles of Enduring Success," *Harvard Business Review* (July–August 2007), pp. 62–72.

45. L. E. Palich, L. B. Cardinal, and C. C. Miller, "Curvilinearity in the Diversification-Performance Linkage: An Examination of over Three Decades of Research," *Strategic Management Journal* (February 2000), pp. 155–174; M. S. Gary, "Implementation Strategy and Performance Outcomes in Related Diversification," *Strategic Management Journal* (July 2005), pp. 643–664; G. Yip and G. Johnson, "Transforming Strategy," *Business Strategy Review* (Spring 2007), pp. 11–15.

46. "The Great Merger Wave Breaks," *The Economist* (January 27, 2001), pp. 59–60; http://www.mondaq.com/unitedstates/x/181456/Corporate+Governance/2012+MA+Report.

47. R. N. Palter and D. Srinivasan, "Habits of Busiest Acquirers," *McKinsey on Finance* (Summer 2006), pp. 8–13.

48. D. R. King, D. R. Dalton, C. M. Daily, and J. G. Covin, "Meta-Analyses of Post-Acquisition Performance: Indications of Unidentified Moderators," *Strategic Management Journal* (February 2004), pp. 187–200; W. B. Carper, "Corporate Acquisitions and Shareholder Wealth: A Review and Exploratory Analysis" *Journal of Management* (December 1990), pp. 807–823; P. G. Simmonds, "Using Diversification as a Tool for Effective Performance," in H. E. Glass and M. A. Hovde (Eds.), *Handbook of Business Strategy, 1992/93 Yearbook* (Boston: Warren, Gorham & Lamont, 1992), pp. 3.1–3.7; B. T. Lamont and C. A. Anderson, "Mode of Corporate Diversification and Economic Performance," *Academy of Management Journal* (December 1985), pp. 926–936.

49. "The HP–Compaq Merger Two Years Out: Still Waiting for the Upside," *Knowledge @ Wharton* (October 6–19, 2004).

50. D. J. Miller, "Firms' Technological Resources and the Performance Effects of Diversification: A Longitudinal Study," *Strategic Management Journal* (November 2004), pp. 1097–1119.

51. A. Hinterhuber, "When Two Companies Become One," in S. Crainer and D. Dearlove (Eds.), *Financial Times Handbook of Management*, 3rd ed. (Harlow, UK: Pearson Education, 2004), pp. 824–833; D. L. Laurie, Y. L. Doz, and C. P. Sheer, "Creating New Growth Platforms," *Harvard Business Review* (May 2006), pp. 80–90; R. Langford and C. Brown III, "Making M&A Pay: Lessons from the World's Most Successful Acquirers," *Strategy & Leadership* (Vol. 32, No. 1, 2004), pp. 5–14; J. G. Lynch and B. Lind, "Escaping Merger and Acquisition

Madness," *Strategy & Leadership* (Vol. 30, No. 2, 2002), pp. 5–12; M. L. Sirower, *The Synergy Trap* (New York: Free Press, 1997); B. Jensen, "Make It Simple! How Simplicity Could Become Your Ultimate Strategy," *Strategy & Leadership* (March/April 1997), p. 35.

52. E. Thornton, "Why Consumers Hate Mergers," *BusinessWeek* (December 6, 2004), pp. 58–64.

53. S. Karim and W. Mitchell, "Innovating through Acquisition and Internal Development: A Quarter-Century of Boundary Evolution at Johnson & Johnson," *Long Range Planning* (December 2004), pp. 525–547; L. Selden and G. Colvin, "M&A Needn't Be a Loser's Game," *Harvard Business Review* (June 2003), pp. 70–79; E. C. Busija, H. M. O'Neill, and C. P. Zeithaml, "Diversification Strategy, Entry Mode, and Performance: Evidence of Choice and Constraints," *Strategic Management Journal* (April 1997), pp. 321–327; A. Sharma, "Mode of Entry and Ex-Post Performance," *Strategic Management Journal* (September 1998), pp. 879–900.

54. R. T. Uhlaner and A. S. West, "Running a Winning M&A Shop," *McKinsey Quarterly* (March 2008), pp. 1–7.

55. S. Rovitt, D. Harding, and C. Lemire, "A Simple M&A Model for All Seasons," *Strategy & Leadership* (Vol. 32, No. 5, 2004), pp. 18–24.

56. P. Porrini, "Can a Previous Alliance Between an Acquirer and a Target Affect Acquisition Performance?" *Journal of Management* (Vol. 30, No. 4, 2004), pp. 545–562; L. Wang and E. J. Zajac, "Alliance or Acquisition? A Dyadic Perspective on Interfirm Resource Combinations," *Strategic Management Journal* (December 2007), pp. 1291–1317.

57. A. Inkpen and N. Choudhury, "The Seeking of Strategy Where It Is Not: Towards a Theory of Strategy Absence," *Strategic Management Journal* (May 1995), pp. 313–323.

58. P. Burrows and S. Anderson, "Dell Computer Goes into the Shop," *BusinessWeek* (July 12, 1993), pp. 138–140.

59. P. Gupta, "Dell's Strategy Questioned after Shares Dive," *Reuters*, May 23, 2012. (http://www.reuters.com/article/2012/05/23/us-dell-research-idUSBRE84M0OR20120523).

60. M. Brauer, "What Have We Acquired and What Should We Acquire in Divestiture Research? A Review and Research Agenda," *Journal of Management* (December 2006), pp. 751–785; J. L. Morrow Jr., R. A. Johnson, and L. W. Busenitz, "The Effects of Cost and Asset Retrenchment on Firm Performance: The Overlooked Role of a Firm's Competitive Environment," *Journal of Management* (Vol. 30, No. 2, 2004), pp. 189–208.

61. J. A. Pearce II and D. K. Robbins, "Retrenchment Remains the Foundation of Business Turnaround," *Strategic Management Journal* (June 1994), pp. 407–417.

62. Y. Kageyama, "Sony Turnaround Plan Draws Yawns," *Des Moines Register* (September 23, 2005), p. 3D.

63. F. Gandolfi, "Reflecting on Downsizing: What Have We Learned?" *SAM Advanced Management Journal* (Spring 2008), pp. 46–55; C. Chadwick, L. W. Hunter, and S. L. Walston, "Effects of Downsizing Practices on the Performance of Hospitals," *Strategic Management Journal* (May 2004), pp. 405–427; J. R. Morris, W. F. Cascio, and C. E. Young, "Downsizing After All These Years," *Organizational Dynamics* (Winter 1999), pp. 78–87; P. H. Mirvis, "Human Resource Management: Leaders, Laggards, and Followers," *Academy of Management Executive* (May 1997), pp. 43–56; J. K. DeDee and D. W. Vorhies, "Retrenchment Activities of Small Firms During

Economic Downturn: An Empirical Investigation," *Journal of Small Business Management* (July 1998), pp. 46–61.

64. C. Chadwick, L. W. Hunter, and S. L. Walston, "Effects of Downsizing Practices on the Performance of Hospitals," *Strategic Management Journal* (May 2004), pp. 405–427.

65. J. B. Treece, "U.S. Parts Makers Just Won't Say 'Uncle,'" *BusinessWeek* (August 10, 1987), pp. 76–77.

66. S. S. Carty, "Ford Plans to Park Jaguar, Land Rover with Tata Motors," *USA Today* (March 26, 2008), p. 1B–2B.

67. For more on divestment, see C. Dexter and T. Mellewight, "Thirty Years After Michael E. Porter: What Do We Know about Business Exit?" *Academy of Management Perspectives* (May 2007), pp. 41–55.

68. D. Welch, "Go Bankrupt, Then Go Overseas," *BusinessWeek* (April 24, 2006), pp. 52–55.

69. D. D. Dawley, J. J. Hoffman, and B. T. Lamont, "Choice Situation, Refocusing, and Post-Bankruptcy Performance," *Journal of Management* (Vol. 28, No. 5, 2002), pp. 695–717.

70. R. M. Kanter, "Leadership and the Psychology of Turnarounds," *Harvard Business Review* (June 2003), pp. 58–67.

71. B. C. Reimann and A. Reichert, "Portfolio Planning Methods for Strategic Capital Allocation: A Survey of Fortune 500 Firms," *International Journal of Management* (March 1996), pp. 84–93; D. K. Sinha, "Strategic Planning in the Fortune 500," in H. E. Glass and M. A. Hovde (Eds.), *Handbook of Business Strategy, 1991/92 Yearbook*, (Boston: Warren, Gorham & Lamont, 1991), p. 96.

72. L. Dranikoff, T. Koller, and A. Schneider, "Divestiture: Strategy's Missing Link," *Harvard Business Review* (May 2002), pp. 74–83.

73. B. Hedley, "Strategy and the Business Portfolio," *Long Range Planning* (February 1977), p. 9.

74. D. Welch, "GM: Live Green or Die," *BusinessWeek* (May 26, 2008), pp. 36–41.

75. "Android vs. iPhone Market Share, 52 against 33 percent," *Phones Review* (September 5, 2012), (http://www.phonesreview.co.uk/2012/09/05/android-vs-iphone-market-share-52-against-33-percent/).

76. A. Fitzgerald, "Going Global," *Des Moines Register* (March 14, 2004), p. 1M, 3M.

77. C. Anterasian, J. L. Graham, and R. B. Money, "Are U.S. Managers Superstitious About Market Share?" *Sloan Management Review* (Summer 1996), pp. 67–77.

78. D. Rosenblum, D. Tomlinson, and L. Scott, "Bottom-Feeding for Blockbuster Businesses," *Harvard Business Review* (March 2003), pp. 52–59.

79. J. J. Curran, "Companies that Rob the Future," *Fortune* (July 4, 1988), p. 84.

80. W. H. Hoffmann, "Strategies for Managing a Portfolio of Alliances," *Strategic Management Journal* (August 2007), pp. 827–856; D. Lavie, "Alliance Portfolios and Firm Performance: A Study of Value Creation and Appropriation in the U.S. Software Industry," *Strategic Management Journal* (December 2007), pp. 1187–1212.

81. W. H. Hoffmann, "How to Manage a Portfolio of Alliances," *Long Range Planning* (April 2005), pp. 121–143.

82. A. Campbell, M. Goold, and M. Alexander, *Corporate-Level Strategy: Creating Value in the Multibusiness Company* (New York: John Wiley & Sons, 1994). See also M. Goold, A. Campbell, and M. Alexander, "Corporate Strategy and Parenting Theory," *Long Range Planning* (April 1998), pp. 308–318, and M. Goold and A. Campbell, "Parenting in Complex Structures," *Long Range Planning* (June 2002), pp. 219–243.

83. A. Campbell, M. Goold, and M. Alexander, "Corporate Strategy: The Quest for Parenting Advantage," *Harvard Business Review* (March–April 1995), p. 121.

84. Ibid., p. 122.

85. A. van Oijen and S. Douma, "Diversification Strategy and the Roles of the Centre," *Long Range Planning* (August 2000), pp. 560–578.

86. D. J. Collis, "Corporate Strategy in Multibusiness Firms," *Long Range Planning* (June 1996), pp. 416–418; D. Lei, M. A. Hitt, and R. Bettis, "Dynamic Core Competencies Through Meta-Learning and Strategic Context," *Journal of Management* (Vol. 22, No. 4, 1996), pp. 549–569.

87. D. J. Teece, "Strategies for Managing Knowledge Assets: The Role of Firm Structure and Industrial Context," *Long Range Planning* (February 2000), pp. 35–54.

88. R. S. Kaplan and D. P. Norton, "The Strategy Map: Guide to Aligning Intangible Assets," *Strategy & Leadership* (Vol. 32, No. 5, 2004), pp. 10–17; L. Edvinsson, "The New Knowledge Economics," *Business Strategy Review* (September 2002), pp. 72–76; C. Havens and E. Knapp, "Easing into Knowledge Management," *Strategy & Leadership* (March/April 1999), pp. 4–9.

89. J. Scanlon, "Cross-Pollinators," *BusinessWeek's Inside Innovation* (September 2007), pp. 8–11.

90. T. S. Frost, J. M. Birkinshaw, and P. C. Ensign, "Centers of Excellence in Multinational Corporations," *Strategic Management Journal* (November 2002), pp. 997–1018.

91. M. E. Porter, *Competitive Advantage* (New York: The Free Press, 1985), pp. 317–382.

92. H. R. Greve, "Multimarket Contact and Sales Growth: Evidence from Insurance," *Strategic Management Journal* (March 2008), pp. 229–249; L. Fuentelsaz and J. Gomez, "Multipoint Competition, Strategic Similarity and Entry Into Geographic Markets," *Strategic Management Journal* (May 2006), pp. 477–499; J. Gimeno, "Reciprocal Threats in Multimarket Rivalry: Staking Out 'Spheres of Influence' in the U.S. Airline Industry," *Strategic Management Journal* (February 1999), pp. 101–128; J. Baum and H. J. Korn, "Dynamics of Dyadic Competitive Interaction," *Strategic Management Journal* (March 1999), pp. 251–278; J. Gimeno and C. Y. Woo, "Hypercompetition in a Multimarket Environment: The Role of Strategic Similarity and Multimarket Contact in Competitive De-escalation," *Organization Science* (May/June 1996), pp. 322–341.

93. W. Boeker, J. Goodstein, J. Stephan, and J. P. Murmann, "Competition in a Multimarket Environment: The Case of Market Exit," *Organization Science* (March/April 1997), pp. 126–142.

94. J. Gimeno and C. Y. Woo, "Multimarket Contact, Economies of Scope, and Firm Performance," *Academy of Management Journal* (June 1999), pp. 239–259.

95. L. Carlesi, B. Verster, and F. Wenger, "The New Dynamics of Managing the Corporate Portfolio," *McKinsey Quarterly Online* (April 2007).

96. http://www.berkshirehathaway.com/subs/sublinks.html; J. Funk, "Warren Buffet's Successors Inherit Complex Conglomerate," *USA Today* (August 31, 2012), (www.usatoday.com/money/industries/manufacturing/story/2012-09-03/Warren-Buffet-evolving-conglomerate/57488280/1).

97. "Learning to E-Read," *The Economist Survey E-Entertainment* (October 7, 2000), p. 22.

98. J. Greenfield, "Lies, Lies and Damned E-Book Lies: Where WSJ Got It Wrong," *Forbes* (July 12, 2012), (www.forbes.com/sites/jeremygreenfield/2012/07/12/lies-lies-and-damed-e-book-lies-where-wsj-got-it-wrong/2/).

99. J. Pepitone, "Amazon Unveils Kindle Fire HD, but Sales Will Remain a Mystery," *CNN Money* (September 6, 2012), (money.cnn.com/2012/09/06/technology/kindle-fire-sales/index.html).

CHAPTER 8

Strategy Formulation: Functional Strategy and Strategic Choice

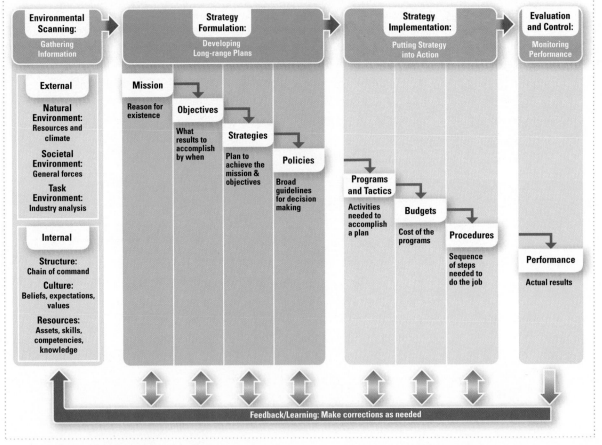

MyManagementLab®

⭐ **Improve Your Grade!**

Over 10 million students improved their results using the Pearson MyLabs. Visit **mymanagementlab.com** for simulations, tutorials, and end-of-chapter problems.

Learning Objectives

After reading this chapter, you should be able to:

- Identify a variety of functional strategies that can be used to achieve organizational goals and objectives
- Understand what activities and functions are appropriate to outsource in order to gain or strengthen competitive advantage
- Recognize strategies to avoid and understand why they are dangerous
- Construct corporate scenarios to evaluate strategic options
- Develop policies to implement corporate, business, and functional strategies

Research in Motion—BlackBerry

Research in Motion was founded in 1984 by Jim Balsillie and Mike Lazaridis as a business focused on providing the backbone for the two-way pager market. In 1999, they released the first BlackBerry device, which quickly set the bar for the connected business person. The term "crack berry" was even coined for those business people who could not put down their BlackBerry. The company focused almost exclusively on the integrity of the network on which their phones operated. They provided security measures that made RIM the choice of data managers.

When developing a strategy, all companies have to bring together all the elements in a manner that provides them with a unique position relative to their competitors. At the time of its release, most competitors provided cell phones that could make calls and little more. BlackBerry sales peaked in 2008 about the same time that Apple released the iPhone. Sales have plummeted since that point, the stock has lost 95% of its value between 2009 and 2013, and it has consistently reporting losses.

Despite that, the company still has 80 million users worldwide, a cash hoard in excess of US$2 billion and a reputation for being a best-in-class device for the business community. The company has made a number of missteps along the way, including a touchscreen BlackBerry that didn't catch on, a tablet that lacked e-mail connectivity, and an approach to the market that made it clear that the company believed the backbone was of more value than the device used.

The two founders stepped down in 2012 and the company continued to fumble with its strategy. New CEO Thorsten Heins asserted in January 2012 that RIM needed to focus on consumers rather than the enterprise. Then, in March 2012, he told analysts that RIM will focus on the enterprise instead of consumers. How can RIM align the elements of its strategy?

SOURCES: S. Jakab, "RIM Seeks to Avoid Its Own Waterloo," *The Wall Street Journal* (September 27, 2012), (http://online.wsj.com/article/SB10000872396390444549204578020473252582296.html?KEYWORDS=RIM+waterloo); D. Meyer, "How RIM Found Itself on the Wrong Side of History," *ZDNet* (July 1, 2012), (http://www.zdnet.com/how-rim-found-itself-on-the-wrong-side-of-history-3040155462/); http://www.rim.com/company/index.shtml; "Research in Motion Co-founders Step Down," (New York)*Daily News* (January 23, 2012), (http://articles.nydailynews.com/2012-01-23/news/30653912_1_balsillie-and-mike-lazaridis-rim-founders).

Functional Strategy

Functional strategy is the approach a functional area takes to achieve corporate and business unit objectives and strategies by maximizing resource productivity. It is concerned with developing and nurturing a distinctive competence to provide a company or business unit with a competitive advantage. Just as a multidivisional corporation has several business units, each with its own business strategy, each business unit has its own set of departments, each with its own functional strategy.

The orientation of a functional strategy is dictated by its parent business unit's strategy.[1] For example, a business unit following a competitive strategy of differentiation through high quality needs a manufacturing functional strategy that emphasizes expensive quality assurance processes over cheaper, high-volume production; a human resource functional strategy that emphasizes the hiring and training of a highly skilled, but costly, workforce; and a marketing functional strategy that emphasizes distribution channel "pull," using advertising to increase consumer demand, over "push," using promotional allowances to retailers. If a business unit were to follow a low-cost competitive strategy, however, a different set of functional strategies would be needed to support the business strategy.

Just as competitive strategies may need to vary from one region of the world to another, functional strategies may need to vary from region to region. When Mr. Donut expanded into Japan, for example, it had to market donuts not as breakfast, but as snack food. Because the Japanese had no breakfast coffee-and-donut custom, they preferred to eat the donuts in the afternoon or evening. Mr. Donut restaurants were thus located near railroad stations and supermarkets. All signs were in English to appeal to the Western interests of the Japanese.

MARKETING STRATEGY

Marketing strategy deals with pricing, selling, and distributing a product. Using a **market development** strategy, a company or business unit can (1) capture a larger share of an existing market for current products through market saturation and market penetration or (2) develop new uses and/or markets for current products. Consumer product giants such as P&G, Colgate-Palmolive, and Unilever are experts at using advertising and promotion to implement a market saturation/penetration strategy to gain the dominant market share in a product category. As seeming masters of the product life cycle, these companies are able to extend product life almost indefinitely through "new and improved" variations of product and packaging that appeal to most market niches. A company, such as Church & Dwight, follows the second market development strategy by finding new uses for its successful current product: Arm & Hammer brand baking soda.

Using the **product development** strategy, a company or unit can (1) develop new products for *existing markets* or (2) develop new products for *new markets*. Church & Dwight has had great success by following the first product development strategy developing new products to sell to its current customers in its existing markets. Acknowledging the widespread appeal of its Arm & Hammer brand baking soda, the company has generated new uses for its sodium bicarbonate by reformulating it as toothpaste, deodorant, and detergent. In another example, Ocean Spray developed Craisins, mock berries, more than 50 variations of juice, sauces, flavored snacks and juice boxes in order to market its cranberries to current customers.[2] Using a successful brand name to market other products is called *brand extension*, and it is a good way to appeal to a company's current customers. Smith & Wesson, famous for its handguns, has taken this approach by using licensing to put its name on men's cologne and other products like the Smith & Wesson 357 Magnum Wood Pellet Smoker (for smoking meats).[3] Church & Dwight has successfully followed the second product development strategy (new products for new markets) by developing new pollution-reduction products (using sodium bicarbonate compounds) for sale to coal-fired electric utility plants—a very different market from grocery stores.

There are numerous other marketing strategies. For advertising and promotion, for example, a company or business unit can choose between "push" and "pull" marketing strategies. Many large food and consumer products companies in the United States and Canada follow a *push strategy* by spending a large amount of money on trade promotion in order to gain or hold shelf space in retail outlets. Trade promotion includes discounts, in-store special offers, and advertising allowances designed to "push" products through the distribution system. The Kellogg Company decided a few years ago to change its emphasis from a push to a *pull strategy*, in which advertising "pulls" the products through the distribution channels. The company now spends more money on consumer advertising designed to build brand awareness so that shoppers will ask for the products. Research has found that a high level of advertising (a key part of a pull strategy) is beneficial to leading brands in a market.[4] Strong brands provide a competitive advantage to a firm because they act as entry barriers and usually generate higher market share.[5]

Other marketing strategies deal with distribution and pricing. Should a company use distributors and dealers to sell its products, should it sell directly to mass merchandisers, or should it use the direct marketing model by selling straight to the consumers via the Internet? Using multiple channels simultaneously can lead to problems. In order to increase the sales of its lawn tractors and mowers, for example, John Deere decided to sell the products not only through its current dealer network but also through mass merchandisers such as Home Depot. Deere's dealers, however, were furious. They considered Home Depot to be a key competitor. The dealers were concerned that Home Depot's ability to underprice them would eventually lead to their becoming little more than repair facilities for their competition and be left with insufficient sales to stay in business. However, the bulk (US$23 billion) of John Deere's US$32 billion in revenue comes from equipment sold to farmers. Home Depot sells the average lawn mower/tractor that was never a big part of the dealer's business.[6]

When pricing a new product, a company or business unit can follow one of two strategies. For new-product pioneers, *skim pricing* offers the opportunity to "skim the cream" from the top of the demand curve with a high price while the product is novel and competitors are few. *Penetration pricing*, in contrast, attempts to hasten market development and offers the pioneer the opportunity to use the experience curve to gain market share with a low price and then dominate the industry. Depending on corporate and business unit objectives and strategies, either of these choices may be desirable to a particular company or unit. Penetration pricing is, however, more likely than skim pricing to raise a unit's operating profit in the long term.[7] The use of the Internet to market goods directly to consumers allows a company to use *dynamic pricing*, a practice in which prices vary frequently based upon demand, market segment, and product availability.[8]

FINANCIAL STRATEGY

Financial strategy examines the financial implications of corporate and business-level strategic options and identifies the best financial course of action. It can also provide competitive advantage through a lower cost of funds and a flexible ability to raise capital to support a business strategy. Financial strategy usually attempts to maximize the financial value of a firm.

The trade-off between achieving the desired debt-to-equity ratio and relying on internal long-term financing via cash flow is a key issue in financial strategy. Many small-and medium-sized family-owned companies such as Urschel Laboratories try to avoid all external sources of funds in order to avoid outside entanglements and to keep control of the company within the family. Few large publicly held firms have no long-term debt and instead keep a large amount of money in cash and short-term investments. One of these is Apple Inc., which had more than a US$100 million cash hoard at the end of 2011. According to Apple's Chief Financial Officer, Peter Oppenheimer, "Our preference is to maintain a strong balance sheet in order to preserve our flexibility."[9] Many financial analysts believe, however, that only by financing through long-term debt can a corporation use financial leverage to boost earnings per share—thus raising stock price and the overall value of the company. Research indicates that higher debt levels not only deter takeover by other firms (by making the company less attractive) but also lead to improved productivity and improved cash flows by forcing management to focus on core businesses.[10] High debt can be a problem, however, when the economy falters and a company's cash flow drops.

Research reveals that a firm's financial strategy is influenced by its corporate diversification strategy. Equity financing, for example, is preferred for related diversification, whereas debt financing is preferred for unrelated diversification.[11] The trend away from unrelated to related acquisitions explains why the number of acquisitions being paid for entirely with stock increased from only 2% in 1988 to 50% in 1998.[12]

A very popular financial strategy that ebbs and flows with the economy is the leveraged buyout (LBO). The LBO market made up only 6% of the M&A deals completed in 2010, far below the peak of 25% seen in 2006.[13] In a **leveraged buyout**, a company is acquired in a transaction financed largely by debt, usually obtained from a third party, such as an insurance company or an investment banker. Ultimately, the debt is paid with money generated from the acquired company's operations or by sales of its assets. The acquired company, in effect, pays for its own acquisition. Management of the LBO is then under tremendous pressure to keep the highly leveraged company profitable. Unfortunately, the huge amount of debt on the acquired company's books may actually cause its eventual decline by focusing management's attention on short-term matters. For example, one year after the buyout, the cash flow of eight of the largest LBOs made during 2006–2007 was barely enough to cover interest payments.[14] One study of LBOs (also called MBOs—Management BuyOuts if they are led by company's current management) revealed that the financial performance of the typical LBO usually falls below the industry average in the fourth year after the buyout. The firm declines because of inflated expectations, utilization of all slack, management burnout, and a lack of strategic management.[15] Often, the only solutions are to sell the company or to again go public by selling stock to finance growth.[16]

The management of dividends and stock price is an important part of a corporation's financial strategy. Corporations in fast-growing industries such as computers and computer software often do not declare dividends. They use the money they might have spent on dividends to finance rapid growth. If the company is successful, its growth in sales and profits is reflected in a higher stock price, eventually resulting in a hefty capital gain when shareholders sell their common stock. Other corporations, such as Whirlpool Corporation, that do not face rapid growth, must support the value of their stock by offering consistent dividends. Instead of raising dividends when profits are high, a popular financial strategy is to use excess cash (or even use debt) to buy back a company's own shares of stock. In just the second quarter of 2012, U.S.-based publicly traded companies declared more than US$112 billion worth of stock repurchase plans. Because stock buybacks increase earnings per share, they typically increase a firm's stock price and make unwanted takeover attempts more difficult. Such buybacks do send a signal to investors that management may not have been able to find any profitable investment opportunities for the company or that it is anticipating reduced future earnings.[17]

A number of firms have been supporting the price of their stock by using *reverse stock splits*. Contrasted with a typical forward 2-for-1 stock split in which an investor receives an additional share for every share owned (with each share being worth only half as much), in a reverse 1-for-2 stock split, an investor's shares are split in half for the same total amount of money (with each share now being worth twice as much). Thus, 100 shares of stock worth US$10 each are exchanged for 50 shares worth US$20 each. A reverse stock split may successfully raise a company's stock price, but it does not solve underlying problems. A study by Credit Suisse First Boston revealed that almost all 800 companies that had reverse stock splits in a five-year period underperformed their peers over the long term.[18]

A rather novel financial strategy is the selling of a company's patents. Companies such as AT&T, Bellsouth, American Express, Kimberly Clark, and 3Com have been selling patents for products that they no longer wish to commercialize or are not a part of their core business. Kodak has been selling off virtually its entire portfolio of patents in a desperate attempt to raise enough money to survive while management tries to figure out what the company should do if it can emerge from bankruptcy. Companies like Apple, Microsoft, and Google have bought patents in order to protect their competitive positions. Patents are also bought by patent accumulators who seek to sell groups of patents to other companies.[19]

RESEARCH AND DEVELOPMENT (R&D) STRATEGY

R&D strategy deals with product and process innovation and improvement. It also deals with the appropriate mix of different types of R&D (basic, product, or process) and with the question of how new technology should be accessed—through internal development, external acquisition, or strategic alliances. RIM has floundered by going back and forth among these approaches rather than choosing an approach and investing their resources.

One of the R&D choices is to be either a **technological leader**, pioneering an innovation, or a **technological follower**, imitating the products of competitors.

One example of an effective use of the *leader* R&D functional strategy to achieve a differentiation competitive advantage is Nike Inc. Nike spends more than most in the industry on R&D to differentiate the performance of its athletic shoes from that of its competitors. As a result, its products have become the favorite of serious athletes. This despite the fact that Nike simultaneously pursues a low-cost manufacturing approach. An example of the use of the *follower* R&D functional strategy to achieve a low-cost competitive advantage is Dean Foods Company.

An increasing number of companies are working with their suppliers to help them keep up with changing technology. They are beginning to realize that a firm cannot be competitive technologically only through internal development. For example, Chrysler Corporation's skillful use of parts suppliers to design everything from car seats to drive shafts has enabled it to spend consistently less money than its competitors to develop new car models. Using strategic technology alliances is one way to combine the R&D capabilities of two companies. Maytag Company worked with one of its suppliers to apply fuzzy logic technology to its IntelliSense dishwasher. The partnership enabled Maytag to complete the project in a shorter amount of time than if it had tried to do it alone.[20] One UK study found that 93% of UK auto assemblers and component manufacturers use their suppliers as technology suppliers.[21]

A newer approach to R&D is *open innovation*, in which a firm uses alliances and connections with corporate, government, academic labs, and consumers to develop new products and processes. For example, Intel opened four small-scale research facilities adjacent to universities to promote the cross-pollination of ideas. Thirteen U.S. university labs engaging in nanotechnology research have formed the National Nanotechnology Infrastructure Network in order to offer their resources to businesses for a fee.[22] Mattel, Wal-Mart, and other toy manufacturers and retailers use idea brokers such as Big Idea Group to scout for new toy ideas. Another big player in this type of business is Everyday Edisons which runs a nationally broadcast, Emmy-award winning PBS television show and also invites inventors to submit ideas to its Web site (www.everydayedisons.com). Everyday Edisons works with companies to put out calls for ideas, then helps sift through those ideas in order to put the best ones in front of companies that are interested.[23] IBM adopted the open operating system Linux for some of its computer products and systems, drawing on a core code base that is continually improved and enhanced by a massive global community of software developers, of whom only a fraction work for IBM.[24] To open its own labs to ideas being generated elsewhere, P&G's CEO Art Lafley decreed that half of the company's ideas must come from outside, up from 10% in 2000. P&G instituted the use of *technology scouts* to search beyond the company for promising innovations. By 2007, the objective was achieved: 50% of the company's innovations originated outside P&G. Unfortunately, the unintended consequence was a sharp reduction in breakthrough products overall. Most of the innovations were relatively minor changes to existing products or products with very limited markets.[25]

A slightly different approach to technology development is for a large firm such as IBM or Microsoft to purchase minority stakes in relatively new high-tech entrepreneurial ventures that need capital to continue operation. Investing corporate venture capital is one way to gain access to promising innovations at a lower cost than by developing them internally.[26]

OPERATIONS STRATEGY

Operations strategy determines how and where a product or service is to be manufactured, the level of vertical integration in the production process, the deployment of physical resources, and relationships with suppliers. It should also deal with the optimum level of technology the firm should use in its operations processes. See the **Global Issue** feature to see how operational differences in national conditions can impact the global efforts of a worldwide brand.

Advanced Manufacturing Technology (AMT) is revolutionizing operations worldwide and should continue to have a major impact as corporations strive to integrate diverse business activities by using computer-assisted design and manufacturing (CAD/CAM) principles. The use of CAD/CAM, flexible manufacturing systems, computer numerically controlled systems, automatically guided vehicles, robotics, manufacturing resource planning (MRP II), optimized production technology, and just-in-time techniques contribute to increased flexibility, quick response time, and higher productivity. Such investments also act to increase the company's fixed costs and could cause significant problems if the company is unable to achieve economies of scale or scope. Baldor Electric Company, the largest maker of industrial electric motors in the United States, built a new factory using new technology to eliminate undesirable jobs with high employee turnover. With one-tenth the employees of its foreign plants, the plant was cost-competitive with motors produced in Mexico or China.[27]

A firm's manufacturing strategy is often affected by a product's life cycle. As the sales of a product increase, there will be an increase in production volume ranging from lot sizes as low as one in a *job shop* (one-of-a-kind production using skilled labor) through *connected line batch flow* (components are standardized; each machine functions such as a job shop but is positioned in the same order as the parts are processed) to lot sizes as high as 100,000 or more per year for *flexible manufacturing systems* (parts are grouped into manufacturing families to produce a wide variety of mass-produced items) and *dedicated transfer lines* (highly automated assembly lines making one mass-produced product using little human labor). According to this concept, the product becomes standardized into a commodity over time in conjunction with increasing demand. Flexibility thus gives way to efficiency.[28]

Increasing competitive intensity in many industries has forced companies to switch from traditional mass production using dedicated transfer lines to a continuous improvement production strategy. A *mass-production* system was an excellent method to produce a large number of low-cost, standard goods and services. Employees worked on narrowly defined, repetitive tasks under close supervision in a bureaucratic and hierarchical structure. Quality, however, often tended to be fairly low. Learning how to do something better was the prerogative of management; workers were expected only to learn what was assigned to them. This system tended to dominate manufacturing until the 1970s. Under the *continuous improvement* system developed W. Edwards Deming and perfected by Japanese firms, companies empowered cross-functional teams to constantly strive to improve production processes. Managers are more like coaches than bosses. The result is a large quantity of low-cost, standard goods and services, but with high quality. The key to continuous improvement is the acknowledgment that workers' experience and knowledge can help managers solve production problems and contribute to tightening variances and reducing errors. Because continuous improvement enables firms to use the same low-cost competitive strategy as do mass-production firms but at a significantly higher level of quality, it is rapidly replacing mass production as an operations strategy.

The automobile industry is currently experimenting with the strategy of *modular manufacturing* in which preassembled subassemblies are delivered as they are needed (i.e., just-in-time) to a company's assembly-line workers, who quickly piece the modules together into a finished product. For example, General Motors built a new automotive complex in Brazil to make its new subcompact, the Celta. Sixteen of the 17 buildings were occupied by suppliers, including Delphi, Lear, and Goodyear. These suppliers delivered preassembled modules (which comprised 85% of the final value of each car) to GM's building for assembly. In a process new to the industry, the suppliers acted as a team to build a single module comprising the motor, transmission, fuel lines, rear axle, brake-fluid lines, and exhaust system, which

GLOBAL issue

WHY DOESN'T STARBUCKS WANT TO EXPAND TO ITALY?

The concept of the Starbucks café (as it exists today) started in Milan, Italy, when Howard Schultz, then the Marketing Director for a coffee roasting business called Starbucks, saw how people talked to the folks making their coffee at the many coffee houses there. He came back to the United States and unable to convince his bosses about the idea, started up his own café in Seattle. Within three years, he had grown his company to such a size that he bought out the original roasting business.

Today, Starbucks has more than 11,000 locations in the United States, as well as 925 outlets in Japan, 730 in the UK, 314 in Mexico, and a significant presence in, among other places, Spain, France, Germany, Switzerland, Austria, Greece, Turkey, Lebanon, and Saudi Arabia. Interestingly, it does not have one outlet in Italy.

Why are there no Starbucks in Italy? Italy is the home of coffee culture and their approach to coffee is quite different. Italians primarily drink espresso and do so in one quick gulp. Cappuccino is strictly a breakfast drink, and while coffee stands are a gathering point, people rarely hang out after they have received their coffee.

That said, McDonald's has had significant success with its McCafé offering of traditional American style coffee, as well as Italian espresso. It encourages customers to linger much like the Starbucks model. McDonald's has opened 411 locations in Italy that serve coffee, including more than 100 that have a traditional Italian coffee bar.

So, should Starbucks make the move into Italy?

SOURCES: S. Faris, "Grounds Zero," *Bloomberg Businessweek* (February 13, 2012), (http://www.businessweek.com/magazine/grounds-zero-a-starbucksfree-italy-02092012.html); http://www.starbucks.com/about-us/our-heritage; "Starbucks Outlines Strategy for Accelerating Profitable Global Growth" (http://news.starbucks.com/article_display.cfm?article_id=342).

was then installed as one piece. GM hoped that this manufacturing strategy would enable it to produce 100 vehicles annually per worker compared to the standard rate of 30 to 50 autos per worker.[29] Ford and Chrysler have also opened similar modular facilities in Brazil.

The concept of a product's life cycle eventually leading to one-size-fits-all mass production is being increasingly challenged by the newer concept of mass customization. Appropriate for an ever-changing environment, *mass customization* requires that people, processes, units, and technology reconfigure themselves to give customers exactly what they want, when they want it. In the case of Dell Computer, customers can still use the Internet to design their own computers. In contrast to continuous improvement, mass customization requires flexibility and quick responsiveness. Managers coordinate independent, capable individuals. An efficient linkage system is crucial. The result is low-cost, high-quality, customized goods and services appropriate for a large number of market niches.

A contentious issue for manufacturing companies throughout the world is the availability of resources needed to operate a modern factory. The increasing cost of oil in the past decade has drastically boosted costs, only some of which could be passed on to the customers in a competitive environment. The likelihood that fresh water will become an equally scarce resource is causing many companies to rethink water-intensive manufacturing processes. To learn how companies are beginning to deal with global warming and increasing fresh water scarcity, see the **Sustainability Issue** feature.

PURCHASING STRATEGY

Purchasing strategy deals with obtaining the raw materials, parts, and supplies needed to perform the operations function. Purchasing strategy is important because materials and components purchased from suppliers comprise 50% of total manufacturing costs of manufacturing companies in the United Kingdom, United States, Australia, Belgium, and Finland.[30] The basic purchasing choices are multiple, sole, and parallel sourcing. Under *multiple sourcing*, the purchasing company orders a particular part from several vendors. Multiple sourcing has traditionally been considered superior to other purchasing approaches because (1) it forces suppliers to compete for the business of an important buyer, thus reducing purchasing costs, and (2) if one supplier cannot deliver, another usually can, thus guaranteeing that parts and supplies are always on hand when needed. Multiple sourcing has been one way for a purchasing firm to control the relationship with its suppliers. So long as suppliers can provide evidence that they can meet the product specifications, they are kept on the purchaser's list of acceptable vendors for specific parts and supplies. Unfortunately, the common practice of accepting the lowest bid often compromises quality.

W. Edwards Deming, a well-known management consultant, strongly recommended *sole sourcing* as the only manageable way to obtain high supplier quality. Sole sourcing relies on only one supplier for a particular part. Given his concern with designing quality into a product in its early stages of development, Deming argued that the buyer should work closely with the supplier at all stages. This reduces both cost and time spent on product design and it also improves quality. It can also simplify the purchasing company's production process by using the *just-in-time* (JIT) concept of having the purchased parts arrive at the plant just when they are needed rather than keeping inventories. The concept of sole sourcing is taken one step further in JIT II, in which vendor sales representatives actually have desks next to the purchasing company's factory floor, attend production status meetings, visit the R&D lab, and analyze the purchasing company's sales forecasts. These in-house suppliers then write sales orders for which the purchasing company is billed. Developed by Lance Dixon at Bose Corporation, JIT II is also being used at IBM, Honeywell, and Ingersoll-Rand. Karen Dale, purchasing manager for Honeywell's office supplies, said she was very concerned about confidentiality when JIT II was first suggested to her. Soon she had five suppliers working with her 20 buyers and reported few problems.[31]

SUSTAINABILITY issue

HOW HOT IS HOT?

July 2012 was the hottest month in the recorded history of the United States and the summer of 2012 ended up the third hottest on record. The United States has recorded 7 of the hottest 10 summers since 2000. The U.S. National Weather Service began recording temperatures in 1895 and only two other summers topped the one in 2012 (2011 and 1936).

The impact on freshwater availability is more than significant not only to individuals, but also the operations of companies. The United Nations reported that by the mid-1990s, some 40 percent of the world's population was suffering water shortages. They predict that in less than 25 years, two-thirds of the world's population will be living in water-stressed countries.

Nestlé, Unilever, Coca-Cola, Anheuser-Busch, and Danone consume almost 575 billion liters of water a year, enough to satisfy the daily water needs of every person on the planet. It takes about 13 cubic meters of freshwater to produce a single 200-mm semiconductor wafer. As a result, chip making is believed to account for 25% of the water consumption in Silicon Valley. According to José Lopez, Nestlé's COO, it takes four liters of water to make one liter of product in Nestlé's factories, but 3000 liters of water are needed to grow the agricultural produce that supplies them. Each year, around 40% of the freshwater withdrawn from lakes and aquifers in America is used to cool power plants. Separating one liter of oil from Canada's tar sands requires up to five liters of water!

"Water is the oil of the 21st century," contends Andrew Liveris, CEO of the chemical company Dow. Like oil, supplies of clean, easily accessible fresh water are under a growing strain because of the growing population and widespread improvements in living standards. Industrialization in developing nations is contaminating rivers and aquifers. Climate change is altering the patterns of fresh water availability so that droughts are more likely in many parts of the world. According to a survey by the Marsh Center for Risk Insights, 40% of Fortune 1000 companies stated that the impact of a water shortage on their business would be "severe" or "catastrophic," but only 17% said that they were prepared for such a crisis. Of Nestlé's 481 factories worldwide, 49 are located in water-scarce regions. Environmental activists have attacked PepsiCo and Coca-Cola for allegedly depleting groundwater in India to make bottled drinks.

There are a number of companies that are taking action to protect their future supply of freshwater. Dow has reduced the amount of water it uses by over a third since 1995. During 1997–2006, when Nestlé almost doubled the volume of food it produced, it reduced the amount of water used by 29%. China's Elion Chemical is working with General Electric to recycle 90% of its wastewater to comply with the government's new "zero-liquid" discharge rules.

....
SOURCES: D. Rice, "Summer 2012 Was the U.S.A.'s Third Hottest on Record," *USA Today* (September 11, 2012), (http://usatoday30.usatoday.com/weather/climate/story/2012-08-30/summer-temperatures/57729858/1); "The Impact of Global Change on Water Resources," UNESCO Report, (http://unesdoc.unesco.org/images/0019/001922/192216e.pdf); K. Kube, "Into the Wild Brown Yonder," *Trains* (November 2008), pp. 68–73; "Running Dry," *The Economist* (August 23, 2008), pp. 53–54.

Sole sourcing reduces transaction costs and builds quality by having the purchaser and supplier work together as partners rather than as adversaries. With sole sourcing, more companies will have longer relationships with fewer suppliers. Research has found that buyer-supplier collaboration and joint problem solving with both parties dependent upon the other results in the development of competitive capabilities, higher quality, lower costs, and better scheduling.[32] Sole sourcing does, however, have limitations. If a supplier is unable to deliver a part, the purchaser has no alternative but to delay production. Multiple suppliers can provide the purchaser with better information about new technology and performance capabilities. The limitations of sole sourcing have led to the development of parallel sourcing. In *parallel sourcing*, two suppliers are the sole suppliers of two different parts, but they are also backup suppliers for each other's parts. If one vendor cannot supply all of its parts on time, the other vendor is asked to make up the difference.[33]

The Internet is being increasingly used both to find new sources of supply and to keep inventories replenished. For example, Hewlett-Packard introduced a Web-based procurement system to enable its 84,000 employees to buy office supplies from a standard set of suppliers. The new system enabled the company to save US$60 to US$100 million annually in purchasing costs.[34] Research indicates that companies using Internet-based technologies are able to lower administrative costs and purchase prices.[35] Sometimes innovations tied to the use of the Internet for one strategy are adopted by other areas. See the Innovation Issue regarding the use and misuse of QR Codes.

LOGISTICS STRATEGY

Logistics strategy deals with the flow of products into and out of the manufacturing process. Three trends related to this strategy are evident: centralization, outsourcing, and the use of the Internet. To gain logistical synergies across business units, corporations began centralizing logistics in the headquarters group. This centralized logistics group usually contains specialists with expertise in different transportation modes such as rail or trucking. They work to aggregate shipping volumes across the entire corporation to gain better contracts with shippers. Companies such as Georgia-Pacific, Marriott, and Union Carbide view the logistics function as an important way to differentiate themselves from the competition, to add value, and to reduce costs.

Many companies have found that outsourcing logistics reduces costs and improves delivery time. For example, HP contracted with Roadway Logistics to manage its inbound raw materials warehousing in Vancouver, Canada. Nearly 140 Roadway employees replaced 250 HP workers, who were transferred to other HP activities.[36]

INNOVATION issue

WHEN AN INNOVATION FAILS TO LIVE UP TO EXPECTATIONS

Sometimes a promising innovation has to find the right application for it to have an impact on strategy formulation. Such has been the fate of QR Codes. QR Codes, or Quick Response Codes, are those dense, square, grids of black and white that seem to be everywhere. Invented in 1994 by Denso Wave (a subsidiary of Toyota Group), the original intent of the little block was to improve the inventory tracking of auto parts. While the QR code is patented, the company published complete specifications online and allowed anyone to use the codes for free.

Over the past few years, the codes have been adopted by advertisers as a means to improve the connection between a company and its customers. In December 2011, more than 8% of magazine ads contained the codes, up from just over 3% at the beginning of the year. Unfortunately, most companies seem to have little idea how to use the codes to engage the consumer. Most direct the consumer's cell phone to the corporate Web site, and therein lies much of the issue with using this as a part of a company's strategy. The QR code requires the consumer to download an app that reads the codes onto their cell phone and then hold the phone very steady as they take a picture of the code that they want to follow.

The codes have found a real value in the movie theater business as more people buy their tickets online. The codes are downloaded to a consumer's Smartphone and scanned as a ticket upon entering the theater. They could also be used to help prevent counterfeit goods, but some companies have put the codes on billboards (virtually impossible to scan), the inside of liquor bottles, and on subway posters (low light prevents the app from working).

Not all innovations that businesses can adopt should be adopted. Finding the value and aligning the innovation with the competitive advantages of the business are crucial. Where do you believe QR codes could be put to their best use?

....

SOURCES: "QR Code Fatigue," *Bloomberg Businessweek* (July 2, 2012), pp. 28–29; https://www.denso-wave.com/en/; http://www.qrcode.com/en/index.html.

Many companies are using the Internet to simplify their logistical system. For example, Ace Hardware created an online system for its retailers and suppliers. An individual hardware store can now see on the Web site that ordering 210 cases of wrenches is cheaper than ordering 200 cases. Because a full pallet is composed of 210 cases of wrenches, an order for a full pallet means that the supplier doesn't have to pull 10 cases off a pallet and repackage them for storage. There is less chance that loose cases will be lost in delivery, and the paperwork doesn't have to be redone. As a result, Ace's transportation costs are down 18%, and warehouse costs have been cut 28%.[37]

HUMAN RESOURCE MANAGEMENT (HRM) STRATEGY

HRM strategy, among other things, addresses the issue of whether a company or business unit should hire a large number of low-skilled employees who receive low pay, perform repetitive jobs, and will most likely quit after a short time (the fast-food restaurant strategy) or hire skilled employees who receive relatively high pay and are cross-trained to participate in *self-managing work teams*. As work increases in complexity, the more suited it is for teams, especially in the case of innovative product development efforts. Multinational corporations are increasingly using self-managing work teams in their foreign affiliates as well as in home-country operations.[38] Research indicates that the use of work teams leads to increased quality and productivity as well as to higher employee satisfaction and commitment.[39]

Companies following a competitive strategy of differentiation through high quality use input from subordinates and peers in performance appraisals to a greater extent than do firms following other business strategies.[40] A complete *360-degree appraisal*, in which performance input is gathered from multiple sources, is now being used by more than 90% of the Fortune 500 (according to Fortune magazine) and has become one of the most popular tools in developing employees and new managers.[41] One Indian company, HCL Technologies, publishes the appraisal ratings for the top 20 managers on the company's intranet for all to see.[42]

Companies are finding that having a *diverse workforce* can be a competitive advantage. Research reveals that firms with a high degree of racial diversity following a growth strategy have higher productivity than do firms with less racial diversity.[43] Avon Company, for example, was able to turn around its unprofitable inner-city markets by putting African-American and Hispanic managers in charge of marketing to these markets.[44] Diversity in terms of age and national origin also offers benefits. DuPont's use of multinational teams has helped the company develop and market products internationally. McDonald's has discovered that older workers perform as well as, if not better than, younger employees. According to Edward Rensi, CEO of McDonald's USA, "We find these people to be particularly well motivated, with a sort of discipline and work habits hard to find in younger employees."[45]

INFORMATION TECHNOLOGY STRATEGY

Corporations are increasingly using **information technology strategy** to provide business units with competitive advantage. When FedEx first provided its customers with PowerShip computer software to store addresses, print shipping labels, and track package location, its sales jumped significantly. UPS soon followed with its own MaxiShips software. Viewing its information system as a distinctive competency, FedEx continued to push for further advantage over UPS by using its Web site to enable customers to track their packages. FedEx uses this competency in its advertisements by showing how customers can track the progress of their shipments. Soon thereafter, UPS provided the same service. Although it can be argued that information technology has now become so pervasive that it no longer offers companies a competitive advantage, corporations worldwide continue to spend over US$3.6 trillion annually on information technology.[46]

Multinational corporations are finding that having a sophisticated intranet allows employees to practice *follow-the-sun management*, in which project team members living in one country can pass their work to team members in another country in which the work day is just beginning. Thus, night shifts are no longer needed.[47] The development of instant translation software is also enabling workers to have online communication with co-workers in other countries who use a different language.[48] For example, Mattel has cut the time it takes to develop new products by 10% by enabling designers and licensees in other countries to collaborate on toy design. IBM uses its intranet to allow its employees to collaborate and improve their skills, thus reducing its training and travel expenses.[49]

Many companies, such as Lockheed Martin, General Electric, and Whirlpool, use information technology to form closer relationships with both their customers and suppliers through sophisticated extranets. For example, General Electric's Trading Process Network allows suppliers to electronically download GE's requests for proposals, view diagrams of parts specifications, and communicate with GE purchasing managers. According to Robert Livingston, GE's head of worldwide sourcing for the Lighting Division, going on the Web reduces processing time by one-third.[50] Thus, the use of information technology through extranets makes it easier for a company to buy from others (outsource) rather than make it themselves (vertically integrate).[51]

The Sourcing Decision: Location of Functions

For a functional strategy to have the best chance of success, it should be built on a distinctive competency residing within that functional area. If a corporation does not have a distinctive competency in a particular functional area, that functional area could be a candidate for outsourcing.

Outsourcing is purchasing from someone else a product or service that had been previously provided internally. Thus, it is the reverse of vertical integration. Outsourcing is becoming an increasingly important part of strategic decision making and an important way to increase efficiency and often quality. In a study of 30 firms, outsourcing resulted on average in a 9% reduction in costs and a 15% increase in capacity and quality.[52] For example, Boeing used outsourcing as a way to reduce the cost of designing and manufacturing its new 787 Dreamliner. Up to 70% of the plane was outsourced. In a break from past practice, suppliers make large parts of the fuselage, including plumbing, electrical, and computer systems, and ship them to Seattle for assembly by Boeing.[53]

According to a 2012 survey by Deloitte Consulting, The most popular outsourced activities are Information Technology (76%), operations (42%), legal (40%), finance (37%), real-estate/facilities (32%), HR (30%), procurement (24%), and sales/marketing support (11%). The survey also reveals that the top factors in a successful outsourcing relationship are a spirit of partnership, a well-designed agreement, joint governance, and consistent communication.[54] Authorities not only expect the number of companies engaging in outsourcing to increase, they also expect companies to outsource an increasing number of functions, especially those in customer service, bookkeeping, financial/clerical, sales/telemarketing, and the mailroom.[55] It is estimated that 50% of U.S. manufacturing will be outsourced to firms in 28 developing countries by 2015.[56]

Offshoring is the outsourcing of an activity or a function to a wholly owned company or an independent provider in another country. Offshoring is a global phenomenon that has been supported by advances in information and communication technologies, the development of stable, secure, and high-speed data transmission systems, and logistical advances like containerized shipping. According to Bain & Company, 51% of large firms in North America, Europe, and Asia outsource offshore.[57] Although India currently has 70% of the offshoring market, countries such as Brazil, China, Russia, the Philippines, Malaysia, Hungary, the Czech Republic, and Israel are growing in importance. These countries have low-cost qualified labor and an educated workforce. These are important considerations because more than 93% of offshoring companies do so to reduce costs.[58] For example, Mexican assembly line workers average US$4.00 an hour plus benefits compared to US$28 an hour plus benefits at a GM or Ford plant in the United States. Less-skilled Mexican workers at auto parts makers earn as little as US$1.50 per hour with fewer benefits.[59]

Software programming and customer service, in particular, are being outsourced to India. For example, General Electric's back-office services unit, GE Capital International Services which was spun off into a new company called Genpact, is one of the oldest and biggest of India's outsourcing companies. From only US$26 million in 1999, its annual revenues grew to over US$1.6 billion by 2011.[60] As part of this trend, IBM acquired Daksh eServices Ltd., one of India's biggest suppliers of remote business services.[61]

Outsourcing, including offshoring, has significant disadvantages. For example, mounting complaints forced Dell Computer to stop routing corporate customers to a technical support call center in Bangalore, India.[62] GE's introduction of a new washing machine was delayed three weeks because of production problems at a supplier's company to which it had contracted out key work. Some companies have found themselves locked into long-term contracts with outside suppliers that were no longer competitive.[63] Some authorities propose that the cumulative effects of continued outsourcing steadily reduces a firm's ability to learn new skills and to develop new core competencies.[64] One survey of 129 outsourcing firms revealed that half the outsourcing projects undertaken in one year failed to deliver anticipated savings. This is in agreement with a survey by Bain & Company in which 51% of large North American, European, and Asian firms stated that outsourcing (including offshoring) did not meet their expectations.[65] Another survey of software projects, by MIT, found that the median Indian project had 10% more software bugs than did comparable U.S. projects.[66] The increasing cost of oil was making offshoring less economical. Since 2003, crude oil increased in price from US$28 to over US$90 a barrel in 2012.[67]

A study of 91 outsourcing efforts conducted by European and North American firms found seven major errors that should be avoided:

1. **Outsourcing activities that should not be outsourced:** Companies failed to keep core activities in-house.

2. **Selecting the wrong vendor:** Vendors were not trustworthy or lacked state-of-the-art processes.

3. **Writing a poor contract:** Companies failed to establish a balance of power in the relationship.

4. **Overlooking personnel issues:** Employees lost commitment to the firm.

5. **Losing control over the outsourced activity:** Qualified managers failed to manage the outsourced activity.[68]

6. **Overlooking the hidden costs of outsourcing:** Transaction costs overwhelmed other savings.

7. **Failing to plan an exit strategy:** Companies failed to build reversibility clauses into the contract.[69]

The key to outsourcing is to purchase from outside only those activities that are not key to the company's distinctive competencies. Otherwise, the company may give up the very capabilities that made it successful in the first place—thus putting itself on the road to eventual decline. This is supported by research reporting that companies that have more experience with a particular manufacturing technology tend to keep manufacturing in-house.[70] J. P. Morgan Chase & Company terminated a seven-year technology outsourcing agreement with IBM because the bank's management realized that information technology (IT) was too important strategically to be outsourced.[71]

In determining functional strategy, the strategist must:

- Identify the company's or business unit's core competencies.
- Ensure that the competencies are continually being strengthened.
- Manage the competencies in such a way that best preserves the competitive advantage they create.

An outsourcing decision depends on the fraction of total value added that the activity under consideration represents and on the amount of potential competitive advantage in that activity for the company or business unit. See the outsourcing matrix in **Figure 8–1**. A firm should consider outsourcing any activity or function that has low potential for competitive advantage. If that activity constitutes only a small part of the total value of the firm's products or services, it should be purchased on the open market (assuming that quality providers of the activity are plentiful). If, however, the activity contributes highly to the company's products or services, the firm should purchase it through long-term contracts with trusted suppliers or distributors. A firm should always produce at least some of the activity or function (i.e., taper vertical integration) if that activity has the potential for providing the company some competitive advantage. However, full vertical integration should be considered only when that activity or function adds significant value to the company's products or services in addition to providing competitive advantage.[72]

FIGURE 8–1
Proposed Outsourcing Matrix

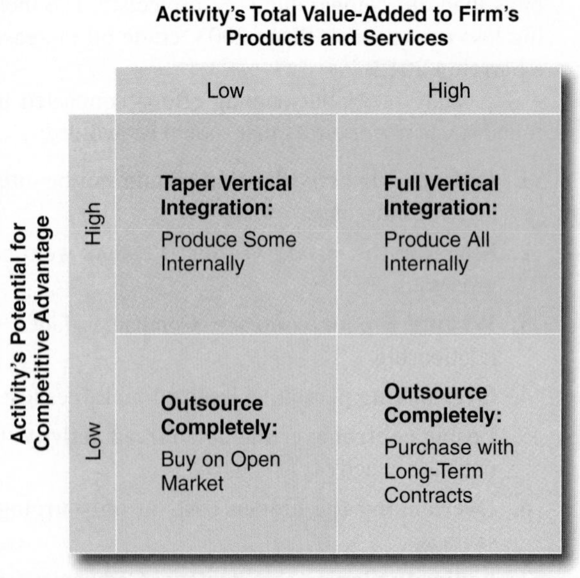

SOURCE: J. D. Hunger and T. L. Wheelen, "Proposed Outsourcing Matrix." Copyright © 1996 and 2005 by Wheelen and Hunger Associates. Reprinted by permission.

Strategies to Avoid

Several strategies that could be considered corporate, business, or functional are very dangerous. Managers who have made poor analyses or lack creativity may be trapped into considering some of the following strategies to avoid:

- **Follow the leader:** Imitating a leading competitor's strategy might seem to be a good idea, but it ignores a firm's particular competitive advantages and the possibility that the leader may be wrong. Fujitsu Ltd., the world's second-largest computer maker, had been driven since the 1960s by the sole ambition of catching up to IBM. Like IBM at the time, Fujitsu competed primarily as a mainframe computer maker. So devoted was it to catching IBM, however, that it failed to notice that the mainframe business had reached maturity by 1990 and was no longer growing.

- **Hit another home run:** If a company is successful because it pioneered an extremely successful product, it tends to search for another super product that will ensure growth and prosperity. As in betting on long shots in horse races, the probability of finding a second winner is slight. Polaroid spent a lot of money developing an "instant" movie camera, but the public ignored it in favor of the camcorder.

- **Arms race:** Entering into a spirited battle with another firm for increased market share might increase sales revenue, but that increase will probably be more than offset by increases in advertising, promotion, R&D, and manufacturing costs. Since the deregulation of airlines, price wars and rate specials have contributed to the low profit margins and bankruptcies of many major airlines, such as Eastern, Pan American, TWA, and virtually every major airline still operating today.

- **Do everything:** When faced with several interesting opportunities, management might tend to leap at all of them. At first, a corporation might have enough resources to develop each idea into a project, but money, time, and energy are soon exhausted as the many projects demand large infusions of resources. The Walt Disney Company's expertise in the entertainment industry led it to acquire the ABC network. As the company churned out new motion pictures and television programs such as *Who Wants to Be a Millionaire?* it spent US$750 million to build new theme parks and buy a cruise line and a hockey team. By 2000, even though corporate sales had continued to increase, net income was falling.[73]

- **Losing hand:** A corporation might have invested so much in a particular strategy that top management is unwilling to accept its failure. Believing that it has too much invested to quit, management may continue to "throw good money after bad." RIM's BlackBerry phone was the undisputed leader in Smartphone technology and acceptance. They were so focused on their approach to how users needed to access information that they missed seeing how the new entrants in the industry had changed the industry. By the time they accepted that a change had really occurred, they were so far behind that catching up was virtually impossible.

Strategic Choice: Selecting the Best Strategy

After the pros and cons of the potential strategic alternatives have been identified and evaluated, one must be selected for implementation. By now, it is likely that many feasible alternatives will have emerged. How is the best strategy determined?

Perhaps the most important criterion is the capability of the proposed strategy to deal with the specific strategic factors developed earlier using the SWOT approach. If the alternative doesn't take advantage of environmental opportunities and corporate strengths/competencies, and lead away from environmental threats and corporate weaknesses, it will probably fail.

Another important consideration in the selection of a strategy is the ability of each alternative to satisfy agreed-upon objectives with the least resources and the fewest negative side effects. It is, therefore, important to develop a tentative implementation plan in order to address the difficulties that management is likely to face. This should be done in light of societal trends, the industry, and the company's situation based on the construction of scenarios.

CONSTRUCTING CORPORATE SCENARIOS

Corporate scenarios are *pro forma* (estimated future) balance sheets and income statements that forecast the effect each alternative strategy and its various programs will likely have on division and corporate return on investment. (Pro forma financial statements are discussed in **Chapter 12**.) In a survey of Fortune 500 firms, 84% reported using computer simulation models in strategic planning. Most of these were simply spreadsheet-based simulation models dealing with what-if questions.[74]

The recommended scenarios are simply extensions of the industry scenarios discussed in **Chapter 4**. If, for example, industry scenarios suggest the probable emergence of a strong market demand in a specific country for certain products, a series of alternative strategy scenarios can be developed. The alternative of acquiring another firm having these products in that country can be compared with the alternative of a green-field development (e.g., building new operations in that country). Using three sets of estimated sales figures (optimistic, pessimistic, and most likely) for the new products over the next five years, the two alternatives can be evaluated in terms of their effect on future company performance as reflected in the company's probable future financial statements. Pro forma balance sheets and income statements can be generated with spreadsheet software, such as Excel, on a personal computer. Pro forma statements are based on financial and economic scenarios.

To construct a corporate scenario, follow these steps:

1. Use industry scenarios (as discussed in **Chapter 4**) to develop a set of assumptions about the task environment (in the specific country under consideration). For example, 3M requires the general manager of each business unit to describe annually what his or her industry will look like in 15 years. List *optimistic,pessimistic*, and *most likely* assumptions for key economic factors such as the GDP (Gross Domestic Product), CPI (consumer price index), and prime interest rate and for other key external strategic factors such as governmental regulation and industry trends. This should be done for every country/region in which the corporation has significant operations that will be affected by each strategic alternative. These same underlying assumptions should be listed for each of the alternative scenarios to be developed.

2. Develop common-size financial statements (as discussed in **Chapter 12**) for the company's or business unit's previous years to serve as the basis for the trend analysis projections of pro forma financial statements. Use the *Scenario Box* form shown in **Table 8–1**:

   a. Use the historical common-size percentages to estimate the level of revenues, expenses, and other categories in estimated pro forma statements for future years.

   b. Develop for each strategic alternative a set of *optimistic(O),pessimistic(P)*, and *most likely(ML)* assumptions about the impact of key variables on the company's future financial statements.

   c. Forecast three sets of sales and cost of goods sold figures for at least five years into the future.

   d. Analyze historical data and make adjustments based on the environmental assumptions listed earlier. Do the same for other figures that can vary significantly.

TABLE 8–1	Scenario Box for Use in Generating Financial Pro Forma Statements												
				Projections[1]									
				200–			200–			200–			
Factor	Last Year	Historical Average	Trend Analysis	O	P	ML	O	P	ML	O	P	ML	Comments
GDP													
CPI													
Other													
Sales units													
Dollars													
COGS													
Advertising and marketing													
Interest expense													
Plant expansion													
Dividends													
Net profits													
EPS													
ROI													
ROE													
Other													

NOTE 1: O = Optimistic; P = Pessimistic; ML = Most Likely.

SOURCE: T. L. Wheelen and J. D. Hunger. Copyright © 1987, 1988, 1989, 1990, 1992, 2005, and 2009 by T. L. Wheelen. Copyright © 1993 and 2005 by Wheelen and Hunger Associates. Reprinted with permission.

    e. Assume for other figures that they will continue in their historical relationship to sales or some other key determining factor. Plug in expected inventory levels, accounts receivable, accounts payable, R&D expenses, advertising and promotion expenses, capital expenditures, and debt payments (assuming that debt is used to finance the strategy), among others.

    f. Consider not only historical trends but also programs that might be needed to implement each alternative strategy (such as building a new manufacturing facility or expanding the sales force).

3. Construct detailed pro forma financial statements for each strategic alternative:

    a. List the actual figures from this year's financial statements in the left column of the spreadsheet.

    b. List to the right of this column the optimistic figures for years 1 through 5.

    c. Go through this same process with the same strategic alternative, but now list the pessimistic figures for the next five years.

    d. Do the same with the most likely figures.

    e. Develop a similar set of optimistic (O), pessimistic (P), and most likely (ML) pro forma statements for the second strategic alternative. This process generates six different pro forma scenarios reflecting three different situations (O, P, and ML) for two strategic alternatives.

    f. Calculate financial ratios and common-size income statements and create balance sheets to accompany the pro forma statements.

    g. Compare the assumptions underlying the scenarios with the financial statements and ratios to determine the feasibility of the scenarios. For example, if cost of goods sold drops from 70% to 50% of total sales revenue in the pro forma income statements, this drop should result from a change in the production process or a shift to cheaper raw materials or labor costs rather than from a failure to keep the cost of goods sold in its usual percentage relationship to sales revenue when the predicted statement was developed.

The result of this detailed scenario construction should be anticipated net profits, cash flow, and net working capital for each of three versions of the two alternatives for five years into the future. A strategist might want to go further into the future if the strategy is expected to have a major impact on the company's financial statements beyond five years. The result of this work should provide sufficient information on which forecasts of the likely feasibility and probable profitability of each of the strategic alternatives could be based.

Obviously, these scenarios can quickly become very complicated, especially if three sets of acquisition prices and development costs are calculated. Nevertheless, this sort of detailed what-if analysis is needed to realistically compare the projected outcome of each reasonable alternative strategy and its attendant programs, budgets, and procedures. Regardless of the quantifiable pros and cons of each alternative, the actual decision will probably be influenced by several subjective factors such as those described in the following sections.

Management's Attitude Toward Risk

The attractiveness of a particular strategic alternative is partially a function of the amount of risk it entails. **Risk** is composed not only of the *probability* that the strategy will be effective but also of the *amount of assets* the corporation must allocate to that strategy and the *length of time* the assets will be unavailable for other uses. Because of variation among countries in terms of customs, regulations, and resources, companies operating in global industries must deal with a greater amount of risk than firms operating only in one country.[75] The greater the assets involved and the longer they are committed, the more likely top management is to demand a high probability of success. Managers with no ownership position in a company are unlikely to have much interest in putting their jobs in danger with risky decisions. Research indicates that managers who own a significant amount of stock in their firms are more likely to engage in risk-taking actions than are managers with no stock.[76]

A high level of risk was why Intel's board of directors found it difficult to vote for a proposal in the early 1990s to commit US$5 billion to making the Pentium microprocessor chip—five times the amount of money needed for its previous chip. In looking back on that board meeting, then-CEO Andy Grove remarked, "I remember people's eyes looking at that chart and getting big. I wasn't even sure I believed those numbers at the time." The proposal committed the company to building new factories—something Intel had been reluctant to do. A wrong decision would mean that the company would end up with a killing amount of overcapacity. Based on Grove's presentation, the board decided to take the gamble. Intel's resulting manufacturing expansion eventually cost US$10 billion but resulted in Intel's obtaining 75% of the microprocessor business and huge cash profits.[77]

Risk might be one reason that significant innovations occur more often in small firms than in large, established corporations. A small firm managed by an entrepreneur is often willing to accept greater risk than is a large firm of diversified ownership run by professional managers.[78] It is one thing to take a chance if you are the primary shareholder and are not concerned with periodic changes in the value of the company's common stock. It is something else if the corporation's stock is widely held and acquisition-hungry competitors or takeover artists surround the company like sharks every time the company's stock price falls below some external assessment of the firm's value.

A new approach to evaluating alternatives under conditions of high environmental uncertainty is to use the real-options theory. According to the **real-options** approach, when the future is highly uncertain, it pays to have a broad range of options open. This is in contrast to using *net present value (NPV)* to calculate the value of a project by predicting its payouts, adjusting them for risk, and subtracting the amount invested. By boiling everything down to one scenario, NPV doesn't provide any flexibility in case circumstances change. NPV is also difficult to apply to projects in which the potential payoffs are currently unknown. The real-options approach, however, deals with these issues by breaking the investment into stages.

Management allocates a small amount of funding to initiate multiple projects, monitors their development, and then cancels the projects that aren't successful and funds those that are doing well.[79] This approach is very similar to the way venture capitalists fund an entrepreneurial venture in stages of funding based on the venture's performance.

A survey of 4000 CFOs found that 27% of them always or almost always used some sort of options approach to evaluating and deciding upon growth opportunities.[80] Research indicates that the use of the real-options approach does improve organizational performance.[81] Some of the corporations using the real-options approach are Chevron for bidding on petroleum reserves, Airbus for calculating the costs of airlines changing their orders at the last minute, and the Tennessee Valley Authority for outsourcing electricity generation instead of building its own plant. Because of its complexity, the real-options approach is not worthwhile for minor decisions or for projects requiring a full commitment at the beginning.[82]

Pressures from Stakeholders

The attractiveness of a strategic alternative is affected by its perceived compatibility with the key stakeholders in a corporation's task environment. Creditors want to be paid on time. Unions exert pressure for comparable wage and employment security. Governments and interest groups demand social responsibility. Shareholders want dividends. All these pressures must be given some consideration in the selection of the best alternative.

Stakeholders can be categorized in terms of their (1) interest in the corporation's activities and (2) relative power to influence the corporation's activities. As shown in **Figure 8–2**, each stakeholder group can be shown graphically based on its *level of interest* (from low to high) in a corporation's activities and on its *relative power* (from low to high) to influence a corporation's activities.

Strategic managers should ask four questions to assess the importance of stakeholder concerns in a particular decision:

1. How will this decision affect each stakeholder, especially those given high and medium priority?

2. How much of what each stakeholder wants is he or she likely to get under this alternative?

FIGURE 8–2
Stakeholder
Priority Matrix

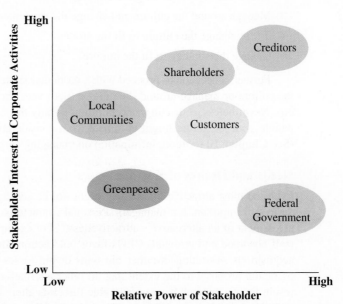

SOURCE: Suggested by C. Anderson in "Values-Based Management," *Academy of Management Executive* (November 1997), pp. 25–46.

3. What are the stakeholders likely to do if they don't get what they want?

4. What is the probability that they will do it?

Strategy makers should choose strategic alternatives that minimize external pressures and maximize the probability of gaining stakeholder support. Managers may, however, ignore or take some stakeholders for granted—leading to serious problems later. The Tata Group, for example, failed to consider the unwillingness of farmers in Singur, India, to accept the West Bengal government's compensation for expropriating their land so that Tata could build its Nano auto plant. Farmers formed rallies against the plant, blocked roads, and even assaulted an employee of a Tata supplier.[83]

Top management can also propose a political strategy to influence its key stakeholders. A **political strategy** is a plan to bring stakeholders into agreement with a corporation's actions. Some of the most commonly used political strategies are constituency building, political action committee contributions, advocacy advertising, lobbying, and coalition building. Research reveals that large firms, those operating in concentrated industries, and firms that are highly dependent upon government regulation are more politically active.[84] Political support can be critical in entering a new international market, especially in transition economies where free market competition did not previously exist.[85]

Pressures from the Corporate Culture

If a strategy is incompatible with a company's corporate culture, the likelihood of its success is very low. Foot-dragging and even sabotage will result as employees fight to resist a radical change in corporate philosophy. Precedents from the past tend to restrict the kinds of objectives and strategies that are seriously considered.[86] The "aura" of the founders of a corporation can linger long past their lifetimes because their values are imprinted on a corporation's members.

In evaluating a strategic alternative, strategy makers must consider pressures from the corporate culture and assess a strategy's compatibility with that culture. If there is little fit, management must decide if it should:

- Take a chance on ignoring the culture.
- Manage around the culture and change the implementation plan.
- Try to change the culture to fit the strategy.
- Change the strategy to fit the culture.

Further, a decision to proceed with a particular strategy without a commitment to change the culture or manage around the culture (both very tricky and time consuming) is dangerous. Nevertheless, restricting a corporation to only those strategies that are completely compatible with its culture might eliminate from consideration the most profitable alternatives. (See **Chapter 10** for more information on managing corporate culture.)

Needs and Desires of Key Managers

Even the most attractive alternative might not be selected if it is contrary to the needs and desires of important top managers. Personal characteristics and experience affect a person's assessment of an alternative's attractiveness.[87] For example, one study found that narcissistic (self-absorbed and arrogant) CEOs favor bold actions that attract attention, like many large acquisitions—resulting in either big wins or big losses.[88] A person's ego may be tied to a particular proposal to the extent that all other alternatives are strongly lobbied against. As a result, the person may have unfavorable forecasts altered so that they are more in agreement with the desired alternative.[89] In a study by McKinsey & Company of 2507 executives from around the world, 36% responded that managers hide, restrict, or misrepresent information at least "somewhat" frequently when submitting capital-investment proposals. In addition, an executive might influence other people in top management to favor a particular alternative so that objections to it are overruled. In the same McKinsey study of global executives, more than 60% of the managers reported that business unit and divisional heads form alliances with peers or lobby someone more senior in the organization at least "somewhat" frequently when resource allocation decisions are being made.[90]

Industry and cultural backgrounds affect strategic choice. For example, executives with strong ties within an industry tend to choose strategies commonly used in that industry. Other executives who have come to the firm from another industry and have strong ties outside the industry tend to choose different strategies from what is being currently used in their industry.[91] Country of origin often affects preferences. For example, Japanese managers prefer a cost-leadership strategy more than do United States managers.[92] Research reveals that executives from Korea, the United States, Japan, and Germany tend to make different strategic choices in similar situations because they use different decision criteria and weights. For example, Korean executives emphasize industry attractiveness, sales, and market share in their decisions, whereas U.S. executives emphasize projected demand, discounted cash flow, and ROI.[93]

There is a tendency to maintain the status quo, which means that decision makers continue with existing goals and plans beyond the point when an objective observer would recommend a change in course.[94] Some executives show a self-serving tendency to attribute the firm's problems not to their own poor decisions but to environmental events out of their control, such as government policies or a poor economic climate.[95] For example, a CEO is more likely to divest a poorly performing unit when its poor performance does not incriminate that same CEO who had acquired it.[96] Negative information about a particular course of action to which a person is committed may be ignored because of a desire to appear competent or because of strongly held values regarding consistency. It may take a crisis or an unlikely event to cause strategic decision makers to seriously consider an alternative they had previously ignored or discounted.[97] For example, it wasn't until the CEO of ConAgra, a multinational food products company, had a heart attack that ConAgra started producing the Healthy Choice line of low-fat, low-cholesterol, low-sodium frozen-food entrees.

THE PROCESS OF STRATEGIC CHOICE

Strategic choice is the evaluation of alternative strategies and selection of the best alternative. According to Paul Nutt, an authority in decision making, half of the decisions made by managers are failures.[98] After analyzing 400 decisions, Nutt found that failure almost always stems from the actions of the decision maker, not from bad luck or situational limitations. In these instances, managers commit one or more key blunders: (1) their desire for speedy actions leads to a rush to judgment, (2) they apply failure-prone decision-making practices such as adopting the claim of an influential stakeholder, and (3) they make poor use of resources by investigating only one or two options. These three blunders cause executives to limit their search for feasible alternatives and look for a quick consensus. Only 4% of the 400 managers set an objective and considered several alternatives. The search for innovative options was attempted in only 24% of the decisions studied.[99] Another study of 68 divestiture decisions found a strong tendency for managers to rely heavily on past experience when developing strategic alternatives.[100]

There is mounting evidence that when an organization is facing a dynamic environment, the best strategic decisions are not arrived at through **consensus** when everyone agrees on one alternative. They actually involve a certain amount of heated disagreement, and even conflict.[101] Many diverse opinions are presented, participants trust in one another's abilities and competencies, and conflict is task-oriented, not personal.[102] This is certainly the case for firms operating in global industries. Because unmanaged conflict often carries a high emotional cost, authorities in decision making propose that strategic managers use "programmed conflict" to raise different opinions, regardless of the personal feelings of the people involved.[103] Two techniques help strategic managers avoid the consensus trap that Alfred Sloan found:

1. **Devil's advocate:** The idea of the **devil's advocate** originated in the medieval Roman Catholic Church as a way of ensuring that impostors were not canonized as saints. One trusted person was selected to find and present all the reasons why a person should not be canonized. When this process is applied to strategic decision making, a devil's advocate (who may be an individual or a group) is assigned to identify potential pitfalls and problems with a proposed alternative strategy in a formal presentation.

2. **Dialectical inquiry:** The dialectical philosophy, which can be traced back to Plato and Aristotle and more recently to Hegel, involves combining two conflicting views—the thesis and the antithesis—into a synthesis. When applied to strategic decision making, **dialectical inquiry** requires that two proposals using different assumptions be generated for each alternative strategy under consideration. After advocates of each position present and debate the merits of their arguments before key decision makers, either one of the alternatives or a new compromise alternative is selected as the strategy to be implemented.

Research generally supports the conclusion that the devil's advocate and dialectical inquiry methods are equally superior to consensus in decision making, especially when the firm's environment is dynamic. The debate itself, rather than its particular format, appears to improve the quality of decisions by formalizing and legitimizing constructive conflict and by encouraging critical evaluation. Both lead to better assumptions and recommendations and to a higher level of critical thinking among the people involved.[104]

Regardless of the process used to generate strategic alternatives, each resulting alternative must be rigorously evaluated in terms of its ability to meet four criteria:

1. **Mutual exclusivity:** Doing any one alternative would preclude doing any other.
2. **Success:** It must be feasible and have a good probability of success.
3. **Completeness:** It must take into account all the key strategic issues.
4. **Internal consistency:** It must make sense on its own as a strategic decision for the entire firm and not contradict key goals, policies, and strategies currently being pursued by the firm or its units.[105]

Developing Policies

The selection of the best strategic alternative is not the end of strategy formulation. The organization must then engage in developing policies. Policies define the broad guidelines for implementation. Flowing from the selected strategy, policies provide guidance for decision making and actions throughout the organization. They are the principles under which the corporation operates on a day-to-day basis. At General Electric, for example, Chairman Jack Welch initiated the policy that any GE business unit must be number one or number two in whatever market it competes. This policy gave clear guidance to managers throughout the organization.

When crafted correctly, an effective policy accomplishes three things:

- It forces trade-offs between competing resource demands.

- It tests the strategic soundness of a particular action.
- It sets clear boundaries within which employees must operate, while granting them the freedom to experiment within those constraints.[106]

Policies tend to be rather long lived and can even outlast the particular strategy that created them. These general policies—such as "The customer is always right" (Nordstrom) or "Always Low Prices" (Wal-Mart)—can become, in time, part of a corporation's culture. Such policies can make the implementation of specific strategies easier. They can also restrict top management's strategic options in the future. Thus a change in strategy should be followed quickly by a change in policies. Managing policy is one way to manage the corporate culture.

End of Chapter SUMMARY

This chapter completes the part of this book on strategy formulation and sets the stage for strategy implementation. Functional strategies must be formulated to support business and corporate strategies; otherwise, the company will move in multiple directions and eventually pull itself apart. For a functional strategy to have the best chance of success, it should be built on a distinctive competency residing within that functional area. If a corporation does not have a distinctive competency in a particular functional area, that functional area could be a candidate for outsourcing.

When evaluating a strategic alternative, the most important criterion is the ability of the proposed strategy to deal with the specific strategic factors developed earlier, in the SWOT approach. If the alternative doesn't take advantage of environmental opportunities and corporate strengths/competencies, and lead away from environmental threats and corporate weaknesses, it will probably fail. Developing corporate scenarios and pro forma projections for each alternative are rational aids for strategic decision making. This logical approach fits Mintzberg's planning mode of strategic decision making, as discussed earlier in **Chapter 1**. Nevertheless, some strategic decisions are inherently risky and are often resolved on the basis of one person's "gut feel." This is an aspect of the entrepreneurial mode and is seen in large established corporations as well as in new venture startups. Various management studies have found that executives routinely rely on their intuition to solve complex problems. The effective use of intuition has been found to differentiate successful top executives and board members from lower-level managers and dysfunctional boards.[107] According to Ralph Larsen, former Chair and CEO of Johnson & Johnson, "Often there is absolutely no way that you could have the time to thoroughly analyze every one of the options or alternatives available to you. So you have to rely on your business judgment."[108] For managerial intuition to be effective, however, it requires years of experience in problem solving and is founded upon a complete understanding of the details of the business.[109]

For example, when Bob Lutz, then President of Chrysler Corporation, was enjoying a fast drive in his Cobra roadster one weekend in 1988, he wondered why Chrysler's cars were so dull. "I felt guilty: there I was, the president of Chrysler, driving this great car that had such a strong Ford association," said Lutz, referring to the original Cobra's Ford V-8 engine. That Monday, Lutz enlisted allies at Chrysler to develop a muscular, outrageous sports car that would turn heads and stop traffic. Others in management argued that the US$80 million investment would be better spent elsewhere. The sales force warned that no U.S. auto maker had ever succeeded in selling a US$50,000 car. With only his gut instincts to support him, he pushed the project forward with unwavering commitment. The result was the Dodge Viper—a car that single-handedly changed the public's perception of Chrysler. Years later, Lutz had trouble describing exactly how he had made this critical decision. "It was this subconscious, visceral feeling. And it just felt right," explained Lutz.[110]

MyManagementLab®

Go to **mymanagementlab.com** to complete the problems marked with this icon ⭐.

KEY TERMS

consensus (p. 269)

corporate scenarios (p. 264)

devil's advocate (p. 270)

dialectical inquiry (p. 270)

financial strategy (p. 251)

functional strategy (p. 250)

HRM strategy (p. 259)

information technology strategy
  (p. 259)

leveraged buyout (p. 252)

logistics strategy (p. 258)

market development (p. 250)

marketing strategy (p. 250)

offshoring (p. 260)

operations strategy (p. 254)

outsourcing (p. 260)

political strategy (p. 268)

product development (p. 250)

purchasing strategy (p. 256)

R&D strategy (p. 253)

real options (p. 266)

risk (p. 266)

strategic choice (p. 269)

technological follower (p. 253)

technological leader (p. 253)

MyManagementLab®

Go to **mymanagmentlab.com** for the following Assisted-graded writing questions:

8-1. How can an Operations Strategy be used to understand and exploit a particular product offering?

8-2. How are corporate scenarios used in the development of an effective strategy?

DISCUSSION QUESTIONS

⭐**8-3.** Are functional strategies interdependent, or can they be formulated independently of other functions?

⭐**8-4.** Do you believe that penetration pricing or skim pricing will be better at raising a company's or a business unit's operating profit in the long run?

8-5. Explain the new real-options approach used in conditions of high environmental uncertainty.

⭐**8-6.** When should a corporation or business unit consider outsourcing a function or an activity?

8-7. How does a business evaluate its strategic choices?

STRATEGIC PRACTICE EXERCISE

Solidere

The political situation in Lebanon always seems to be changing. At times, like the saying goes, political calm only precedes chaos. At others, this political calm truly stabilizes the economy and growth follows. Encouraging news about the potential formation of a new government, at one point, pushed

the Beirut Stock Exchange (BSE) higher with Solidere A and B shares having gained 7.87 percent and 6.18 percent, respectively. Investors, whether local or foreign, seemed optimistic. The beneficial impact of this rise led to more sales: the trade of Solidere A was 86,111 while Solidere B was 24,060. The total number of shares traded that day was

307,667 with a trading value of $4.47 million, meaning that the stock capitalization of the listed companies increased by 1.30 percent to reach $10.848 billion rather than the $10.707 billion for the previous session. Despite the increase in trades on the BSE following the news, the volume remained relatively low compared to historic levels. Trade was local; it was not foreign. Foreign investors who normally do not buy less than 50,000 shares are rarely found on the Beirut Stock Exchange. It is their capital that is acutely needed in Lebanon today!

1. What is the problem Solidere faces?

2. Should Solidere adopt a marketing strategy? Why? Why not?

3. If you were part of the decision-making team in Solidere, which functional level strategy would you adopt to improve the position of Solidere?

....

SOURCE: Dana Halawi, "Hope for cabinet lift Solidere Shares," *The Daily Star* (January 15, 2014), p. 5.

NOTES

1. S. F. Slater and E. M. Olson, "Market's Contribution to the Implementation of Business Strategy: An Empirical Analysis," *Strategic Management Journal* (November 2001), pp. 1055–1067; B. C. Skaggs and T. R. Huffman, "A Customer Interaction Approach to Strategy and Production Complexity Alignment in Service Firms," *Academy of Management Journal* (December 2003), pp. 775–786.

2. A. Pressman, "Ocean Spray's Creative Juices," *BusinessWeek* (May 15, 2006), pp. 88–89; http://www.oceanspray.com/Products.aspx.

3. A. Pressman, "Smith & Wesson: A Gunmaker Loaded with Offshoots," *BusinessWeek* (June 4, 2007), p. 66. A *line extension,* in contrast to brand extension, is the introduction of additional items in the same category under the same brand name, such as new flavors, added ingredients, or package sizes.

4. S. M. Oster, *Modern Competitive Analysis*, 2nd ed. (New York: Oxford University Press, 1994), p. 93.

5. J. M. de Figueiredo and M. K. Kyle, "Surviving the Gales of Creative Destruction: The Determinants of Product Turnover," *Strategic Management Journal* (March 2006), pp. 241–264.

6. J. Gruley and S. D. Singh, "Deere's Big Green Profit Machine," *Bloomberg Businessweek* (July 5, 2012), (http://www.businessweek.com/articles/2012-07-05/deeres-big-green-profit-machine); M. Springer, "Plowed Under," *Forbes* (February 21, 2000), p. 56.

7. W. Redmond, "The Strategic Pricing of Innovative Products," *Handbook of Business Strategy, 1992/1993 Yearbook*, edited by H. E. Glass and M. A. Hovde (Boston: Warren, Gorham & Lamont, 1992), pp. 16.1–16.13; A. Hinterhuber, "Towards Value-Based Pricing—An Integrative Framework for Decision Making," *Industrial Marketing Management* (Vol. 33, 2004), pp. 765–778.

8. A. Kambil, H. J. Wilson III, and V. Agrawal, "Are You Leaving Money on the Table?" *Journal of Business Strategy* (January/February 2002), pp. 40–43.

9. N. Wingfield, "Flush with Cash, Apple Plans Buyback and Dividend," *The New York Times* (March 19, 2012), (http://www.nytimes.com/2012/03/20/technology/apple-to-use-cash-for-stock-dividend-and-buyback.html?pagewanted=all&_r=0); P. Burrows, "Apple's Cash Conundrum,"

10. A. Safieddine and S. Titman in April 1999 *Journal of Finance,* as summarized by D. Champion, "The Joy of Leverage," *Harvard Business Review* (July–August 1999), pp. 19–22.

11. R. Kochhar and M. A. Hitt, "Linking Corporate Strategy to Capital Structure: Diversification Strategy, Type and Source of Financing," *Strategic Management Journal* (June 1998), pp. 601–610.

12. A. Rappaport and M. L. Sirower, "Stock or Cash?" *Harvard Business Review* (November–December 1999), pp. 147–158.

13. M. Davies, "Dealtalk – Plain Vanilla LBOs Few and Far Between," *Reuters* (April 28, 2011), (http://www.reuters.com/article/2011/04/28/dealtalk-lbos-idUSN2828850720110428).

14. "Private Investigations," *The Economist* (July 5, 2008), pp. 84–85.

15. D. Angwin and I. Contardo, "Unleashing Cerberus: Don't Let Your MBOs Turn on Themselves," *Long Range Planning* (October 1999), pp. 494–504.

16. For information on different types of LBOs, see M. Wright, R. E. Hoskisson, and L. W. Busenitz, "Firm Rebirth: Buyouts as Facilitators of Strategic Growth and Entrepreneurship," *Academy of Management Executive* (February 2001), pp. 111–125.

17. J. Brown, "The Buyback Epidemic," (October 12, 2012), (http://www.thereformedbroker.com/2012/10/12/the-buyback-epidemic/); D. N. Hurtt, J. G. Kreuze, and S. A. Langsam, "Stock Buybacks and Their Association with Stock Options Exercised in the IT Industry," *American Journal of Business* (Spring 2008), pp. 13–21.

18. B. Deener, "Back Up and Look at Reasons for Reverse Stock Split," *The (St. Petersburg, FL) Times* (December 29, 2002), p. 3H.

19. T. Francis, "Can You Get a Patent on Being a Patent Troll?" NPR, August 2, 2012. (http://www.npr.org/blogs/money/2012/08/01/157743897/can-you-get-a-patent-on-being-a-patent-troll); M. Orey, "A Sotheby's for Investors," *BusinessWeek* (February 13, 2006), p. 39.

20. S. Stevens, "Speeding the Signals of Change," *Appliance* (February 1995), p. 7.

21. L-E. Gadde and H. Hakansson, "Teaching in Supplier Networks," in M. Gibbert and T. Durand (Eds.), *Strategic Networks: Learning to Compete* (Malden, MA: Blackwell Publishing, 2007), pp. 40–57.

22. "Schools Rent Out Labs to Businesses," *St. Cloud (MN) Times* (December 11, 2007), p. 3A.

23. H. W. Chesbrough, "A Better Way to Innovate," *Harvard Business Review* (July 2003), pp. 12–13; Everydayedisons.com.

24. J. Bughin, M. Chui, and B. Johnson, "The Next Step in Open Innovation," *McKinsey Quarterly* (June 2008), pp. 1–8.

25. L. Coleman-Lochner and C. Hymowitz, "At P&G, the Innovation Well Runs Dry," *Bloomberg Businessweek* (September 10, 2012), pp. 24–26; J. Greene, J. Carey, M. Arndt, and O. Port,

"Reinventing Corporate R&D," *BusinessWeek* (September 22, 2003), pp. 74–76; J. Birkinshaw, S. Crainer, and M. Mol, "From R&D to Connect + Develop at P&G," *Business Strategy Review* (Spring 2007), pp. 66–69; L. Huston and N. Sakkab, "Connect and Develop: Inside Proctor & Gamble's New Model for Innovation," *Harvard Business Review* (March 2006), pp. 58–66.

26. G. Dushnitsky and M. J. Lenox, "When Do Firms Undertake R&D by Investing in New Ventures?" Paper presented to the annual meeting of the *Academy of Management*, Seattle, WA (August 2003).

27. A. Aston and M. Arndt, "The Flexible Factory," *BusinessWeek* (May 5, 2003), pp. 90–91.

28. J. R. Williams and R. S. Novak, "Aligning CIM Strategies to Different Markets," *Long Range Planning* (February 1990), pp. 126–135.

29. J. Wheatley, "Super Factory—or Super Headache," *Business-Week* (July 31, 2000), p. 66.

30. M. Tayles and C. Drury, "Moving from Make/Buy to Strategic Sourcing: The Outsource Decision Process," *Long Range Planning* (October 2001), pp. 605–622.

31. F. R. Bleakley, "Some Companies Let Supplies Work on Site and Even Place Orders," *The Wall Street Journal* (January 13, 1995), pp. A1, A6.

32. M. Hoegl and S. M. Wagner, "Buyer-Supplier Collaboration in Product Development Projects," *Journal of Management* (August 2005), pp. 530–548; B. McEvily and A. Marcus, "Embedded Ties and the Acquisition of Competitive Capabilities," *Strategic Management Journal* (November 2005), pp. 1033–1055; R. Gulati and M. Sytch, "Dependence Asymmetry and Joint Dependence in Interorganizational Relationships: Effects of Embeddedness on a Manufacturer's Performance in Procurement Relationships," *Administrative Science Quarterly* (March 2007), pp. 32–69.

33. J. Richardson, "Parallel Sourcing and Supplier Performance in the Japanese Automobile Industry," *Strategic Management Journal* (July 1993), pp. 339–350.

34. S. Roberts-Witt, "Procurement: The HP Way," *PC Magazine* (November 21, 2000), pp. 21–22.

35. D. H. Pearcy, D. B. Parker, and L. C. Giunipero, "Using Electronic Procurement to Facilitate Supply Chain Integration: An Exploratory Study of U.S.-Based Firms," *American Journal of Business* (Spring 2008), pp. 23–35.

36. J. Bigness, "In Today's Economy, There Is Big Money to Be Made in Logistics," *The Wall Street Journal* (September 6, 1995), pp. A1, A9.

37. F. Keenan, "Logistics Gets a Little Respect," *BusinessWeek* (November 20, 2000), pp. 112–116.

38. B. L. Kirkman and Debra L. Shapiro, "The Impact of Cultural Values on Employee Resistance to Teams: Toward a Model of Globalized Self-Managing Work Team Effectiveness," *Academy of Management Review* (July 1997), pp. 730–757.

39. R. D. Banker, J. M. Field, R. G. Schroeder, and K. K. Sinha, "Impact of Work Teams on Manufacturing Performance: A Longitudinal Field Study," *Academy of Management Journal* (August 1996), pp. 867–890; B. L. Kirkman and B. Rosen, "Beyond Self-Management: Antecedents and Consequences of Team Empowerment," *Academy of Management Journal* (February 1999), pp. 58–74.

40. V. Y. Haines III, S. St. Onge, and A. Marcoux, "Performance Management Design and Effectiveness in Quality-Driven Organizations," *Canadian Journal of Administrative Sciences* (June 2004), pp. 146–160.

41. A. S. DeNisi and A. N. Kluger, "Feedback Effectiveness: Can 360-Degree Appraisals Be Improved?" *Academy of Management Executive* (February 2000), pp. 129–139; S. Thornton, "The History of 360 Degree Feedback," (2012), (http://www.ehow.com/about_5163489_history-degree-feedback.html); G. Toegel and J. A. Conger, "360-Degree Assessment: Time for Reinvention," *Academy of Management Learning and Education* (September 2003), pp. 297–311; F. Shipper, R. C. Hoffman, and D. M. Rotondo, "Does the 360 Feedback Process Create Actionable Knowledge Equally Across Cultures?" *Academy of Management Learning & Education* (March 2007), pp. 33–50.

42. J. McGregor, "The Employee Is Always Right," *BusinessWeek* (November 19, 2007), pp. 80–82.

43. O. C. Richard, "Racial Diversity, Business Strategy, and Firm Performance: A Resource-Based View," *Academy of Management Journal* (April 2000), pp. 164–177.

44. G. Robinson and K. Dechant, "Building a Business Case for Diversity," *Academy of Management Executive* (August 1997), pp. 21–31.

45. K. Labich, "Making Diversity Pay," *Fortune* (September 9, 1996), pp. 177–180.

46. "Gartner Says Worldwide IT Spend on Pace to Surpass $3.6 Trillion in 2012," (July 9, 2012), (http://www.gartner.com/it/page.jsp?id=2074815); N. G. Carr, "IT Doesn't Matter," *Harvard Business Review* (May 2003), pp. 41–50.

47. J. Greco, "Good Day Sunshine," *Journal of Business Strategy* (July/August 1998), pp. 4–5.

48. W. Howard, "Translate Now," *PC Magazine* (September 19, 2000), p. 81.

49. H. Green, "The Web Smart 50," *BusinessWeek* (November 24, 2003), p. 84.

50. T. Smart, "Jack Welch's Cyber-Czar," *BusinessWeek* (August 5, 1996), p. 83.

51. S. M. Kim and J. T. Mahoney, "Mutual Commitment to Support Exchange: Relation-Specific IT System as a Substitute for Managerial Hierarchy," *Strategic Management Journal* (May 2006), pp. 401–423.

52. B. Kelley, "Outsourcing Marches On," *Journal of Business Strategy* (July/August 1995), p. 40.

53. S. Holmes and M. Arndt, "A Plane that Could Change the Game," *BusinessWeek* (August 9, 2004), p. 33.

54. "2012 Global Outsourcing and Insourcing Survey," (February 2012), (http://www.deloitte.com/assets/Dcom-UnitedStates/Local%20Assets/Documents/IMOs/Shared%20Services/us_sdt_2012GlobalOutsourcingandInsourcingSurveyExecutiveSummary_050112.pdf).

55. J. Greco, "Outsourcing: The New Partnership," *Journal of Business Strategy* (July/August 1997), pp. 48–54.

56. W. M. Fitzpatrick and S. A. DiLullo, "Outsourcing and the Personnel Paradox," *SAM Advanced Management Journal* (Summer 2007), pp. 4–12.

57. Outsourcing: Time to Bring It Back Home?" *The Economist* (March 5, 2005), p. 63.

58. A. Y. Lewin and C. Peeters, "Offshoring Work: Business Hype or the Onset of Fundamental Transformation?" *Long Range Planning* (June 2006), pp. 221–239; A. Y. Lewing and C. Peeters, "The Top-Line Allure of Offshoring," *Harvard Business Review* (March 2006), pp. 22–24.

59. N. Miroff, "In Mexico, Auto Industry fuels the Middle Class," *The Washington Post* (April 3, 2012), (http://www.washingtonpost.com/world/the_americas/in-mexico-auto-industry-fuels-middle-class/2012/04/03/gIQApKdntS_story.html); G. Smith, "Factories Go South; So Does Pay," *BusinessWeek* (April 9, 2007), p. 76.

60. http://www.genpact.com/docs/pr/q4-and-ye-2011-earnings-release-final02062012.

61. "IBM's Plan to Buy India Firm Points to Demand for Outsourcing," *Des Moines Register* (April 11, 2004), p. 2D.

62. A. Castro, "Complaints Push Dell to Use U.S. Call Centers," *Des Moines Register* (November 25, 2003), p. 1D.

63. J. A. Byrne, "Has Outsourcing Gone Too Far?" *BusinessWeek* (April 1, 1996), pp. 26–28.

64. R. C. Insinga and M. J. Werle, "Linking Outsourcing to Business Strategy," *Academy of Management Executive* (November 2000), pp. 58–70; D. Lei and M. A. Hitt, "Strategic Restructuring and Outsourcing: The Effect of Mergers and Acquisitions and LBOs on Building Firm Skills and Capabilities," *Journal of Management* (Vol. 21, No. 5, 1995), pp. 835–859.

65. "Outsourcing: Time to Bring It Back Home*?" The Economist* (May 5, 2005), p. 63.

66. S. E. Ante, "Shifting Work Offshore? Outsourcer Beware," *BusinessWeek* (January 12, 2004), pp. 36–37.

67. http://www.oil-price.net/.

68. A. Takeishi, "Bridging Inter- and Intra-Firm Boundaries: Management of Supplier Involvement in Automobile Product Development," *Strategic Management Journal* May 2001), pp. 40-433.

69. J. Barthelemy, "The Seven Deadly Sins of Outsourcing," *Academy of Management Executive* (May 2003), pp. 87–98.

70. M. J. Leiblein and D. J. Miller, "An Empirical Examination of Transaction and Firm-Level Influences on the Vertical Boundaries of the Firm," *Strategic Management Journal* (September 2003), pp. 839–859.

71. S. Hamm, "Is Outsourcing on the Outs?" *BusinessWeek* (October 4, 2004), p. 42.

72. For further information on effective offshoring, see R. Aron and J. V. Singh, "Getting Offshoring Right," *Harvard Business Review* (December 2005), pp. 135–143.

73. R. Grover and D. Polek, "Millionaire Buys Disney Time," *BusinessWeek* (June 26, 2000), pp. 141–144.

74. D. K. Sinha, "Strategic Planning in the Fortune 500," in H. E. Glass and M. A. Hovde (Eds.), *Handbook of Business Strategy, 1991/1992 Yearbook* (Boston: Warren, Gorham & Lamont, 1991), pp. 9.6–9.8.

75. N. Checa, J. Maguire, and J. Berry, "The New World Disorder," *Harvard Business Review* (August 2003), pp. 70–79.

76. T. B. Palmer and R. M. Wiseman, "Decoupling Risk Taking from Income Stream Uncertainty: A Holistic Model of Risk," *Strategic Management Journal* (November 1999), pp. 1037–1062; W. G. Sanders and D. C. Hambrick, "Swinging for the Fences: The Effects of CEO Stock Options on Company Risk Taking and Performance," *Academy of Management Journal* (October 2007), pp. 1055–1078.

77. D. Clark, "All the Chips: A Big Bet Made Intel What It Is Today; Now It Wagers Again," *The Wall Street Journal* (June 6, 1995), pp. A1, A5.

78. L. W. Busenitz and J. B. Barney, "Differences Between Entrepreneurs and Managers in Large Organizations: Biases and Heuristics in Strategic Decision-Making," *Journal of Business Venturing* (January 1997), pp. 9–30.

79. J. J. Janney and G. G. Dess, "Can Real-Options Analysis Improve Decision-Making? Promises and Pitfalls," *Academy of Management Executive* (November 2004), pp. 60–75; S. Maklan, S. Knox, and L. Ryals, "Using Real Options to Help Build the Business Case for CRM Investment," *Long Range Planning* (August 2005), pp. 393–410.

80. T. Copeland and P. Tufano, "A Real-World Way to Manage Real Options," *Harvard Business Review* (March 2004), pp. 90–99.

81. J. Rosenberger and K. Eisenhardt, "What Are Real Options: A Review of Empirical Research," Paper presented to annual meeting of the *Academy of Management*, Seattle, WA (August 2003).

82. P. Coy, "Exploiting Uncertainty," *BusinessWeek* (June 7, 1999), pp. 118–124. For further information on real options, see M. Amram and N. Kulatilaka, *Real Options* (Boston, Harvard University Press, 1999). For a simpler summary, see R. M. Grant, *Contemporary Strategy Analysis*, 5th ed. (Malden, MA: Blackwell Publishing, 2005), pp. 48–50.

83. "Nano Wars," *The Economist* (August 30, 2008), p. 63.

84. J-P. Bonardi, A. J. Hillman, and G. D. Keim, "The Attractiveness of Political Markets: Implications for Firm Strategy," *Academy of Management Review* (April 2005), pp. 397–413.

85. J. G. Frynas, K. Mellahi, and G. A. Pigman, "First Mover Advantages in International Business and Firm-Specific Political Resources," *Strategic Management Journal* (April 2006), pp. 321–345. For additional information about political strategies, see C. Oliver and I. Holzinger, "The Effectiveness of Strategic Political Management: A Dynamic Capabilities Framework," *Academy of Management Review* (April 2008), pp. 496–520.

86. H. M. O'Neill, R. W. Pouder, and A. K. Buchholtz, "Patterns in the Diffusion of Strategies Across Organizations: Insights from the Innovation Diffusion Literature," *Academy of Management Executive* (January 1998), pp. 98–114; C. G. Gilbert, "Unbundling the Structure of Inertia: Resource Versus Routine Rigidity," *Academy of Management Journal* (October 2005), pp. 741–763.

87. B. B. Tyler and H. K. Steensma. "Evaluating Technological Collaborative Opportunities: A Cognitive Modeling Perspective," *Strategic Management Journal* (Summer 1995), pp. 43–70; D. Duchan, D. P. Ashman, and M. Nathan, "Mavericks, Visionaries, Protestors, and Sages: Toward a Typology of Cognitive Structures for Decision Making in Organizations," *Journal of Business Strategies* (Fall 1997), pp. 106–125; P. Chattopadhyay, W. H. Glick, C. C. Miller, and G. P. Huber, "Determinants of Executive Beliefs: Comparing Functional Conditioning and Social Influence," *Strategic Management Journal* (August 1999), pp. 763–789; B. Katey and G. G. Meredith, "Relationship Among Owner/Manager Personal Values, Business Strategies, and Enterprise Performance," *Journal of Small Business Management* (April 1997), pp. 37–64.

88. A. Chatterjee and D. C. Hambrick, "It's All About Me: Narcissistic Executive Officers and Their Effects on Company Strategy and Performance," *Administrative Science Quarterly* (September 2007), pp. 351–386.

89. C. S. Galbraith and G. B. Merrill, "The Politics of Forecasting: Managing the Truth*," California Management Review* (Winter 1996), pp. 29–43.

90. M. Garbuio, D. Lovallo, and P. Viguerie, "How Companies Spend Their Money: A McKinsey Global Survey," *McKinsey Quarterly Online* (June 2007).

91. M. A. Geletkanycz and D. C. Hambrick, "The External Ties of Top Executives: Implications for Strategic Choice and Performance," *Administrative Science Quarterly* (December 1997), pp. 654–681.

92. M. Song, R. J. Calantone, and C. A. Di Benedetto, "Competitive Forces and Strategic Choice Decisions: An Experimental Investigation in the United States and Japan," *Strategic Management Journal* (October 2002), pp. 969–978.

93. M. A. Hitt, M. T. Dacin, B. B. Tyler, and D. Park, "Understanding the Differences in Korean and U.S. Executives' Strategic Orientation," *Strategic Management Journal* (February 1997), pp. 159–167; L. G. Thomas III and G. Waring, "Competing Capitalisms: Capital Investment in American, German, and Japanese Firms,"*Strategic Management Journal* (August 1999), pp. 729–748.

94. M. H. Bazerman and D. Chugh, "Decisions Without Blinders," *Harvard Business Review* (January 2006), pp. 88–97.

95. J. A. Wagner III and R. Z. Gooding, "Equivocal Information and Attribution: An Investigation of Patterns of Managerial Sensemaking," *Strategic Management Journal* (April 1997), pp. 275–286; K. Shimizu and M. A. Hitt, "Strategic Flexibility: Organizational Preparedness to Reverse Ineffective Strategic Decisions," *Academy of Management Executive* (November 2004), pp. 44–59.

96. M. L. A. Hayward and K. Shimizu, "De-Commitment to Losing Strategic Action: Evidence from the Divestiture of Poorly Performing Acquisitions," *Strategic Management Journal* (June 2006), pp. 541–557.

97. J. Ross and B. M. Staw, "Organizational Escalation and Exit: Lessons from the Shoreham Nuclear Power Plant," *Academy of Management Journal* (August 1993), pp. 701–732; P. W. Mulvey, J. F. Veiga, and P. M. Elsass, "When Teammates Raise a White Flag," *Academy of Management Executive* (February 1996), pp. 40–49.

98. P. C. Nutt, *Why Decisions Fail* (San Francisco: Berrett-Koehler, 2002).

99. P. C. Nutt, "Expanding the Search for Alternatives During Strategic Decision-Making," *Academy of Management Executive* (November 2004), pp. 13–28.

100. K. Shimizu, "Prospect Theory, Behavioral Theory, and the Threat-Rigidity Thesis: Combinative Effects on Organizational Decisions to Divest Formerly Acquired Units," *Academy of Management Journal* (December 2007), pp. 1495–1514.

101. G. P. West III and G. D. Meyer, "To Agree or Not to Agree? Consensus and Performance in New Ventures," *Journal of Business Venturing* (September 1998), pp. 395–422; L. Markoczy, "Consensus Formation During Strategic Change," *Strategic Management Journal* (November 2001), pp. 1013–1031.

102. B. J. Olson, S. Parayitam, and Y. Bao, "Strategic Decision Making: The Effects of Cognitive Diversity, Conflict, and Trust on Decision Outcomes," *Journal of Management* (April 2007), pp. 196–222.

103. A. C. Amason, "Distinguishing the Effects of Functional and Dysfunctional Conflict on Strategic Decision Making: Resolving a Paradox for Top Management Teams," *Academy of Management Journal* (February 1996), pp. 123–148; A. C. Amason and H. J. Sapienza, "The Effects of Top Management Team Size and Interaction Norms on Cognitive and Affective Conflict," *Journal of Management* (Vol. 23, No. 4, 1997), pp. 495–516.

104. D. M. Schweiger, W. R. Sandberg, and P. L. Rechner, "Experiential Effects of Dialectical Inquiry, Devil's Advocacy, and Consensus Approaches to Strategic Decision Making," *Academy of Management Journal* (December 1989), pp. 745–772; G. Whyte, "Decision Failures: Why They Occur and How to Prevent Them," *Academy of Management Executive* (August 1991), pp. 23–31; R. L. Priem, D. A. Harrison, and N. K. Muir, "Structured Conflict and Consensus Outcomes in Group Decision Making," *Journal of Management* (Vol. 21, No. 4, 1995), pp. 691–710.

105. S. C. Abraham, "Using Bundles to Find the Best Strategy," *Strategy & Leadership* (July/August/September 1999), pp. 53–55.

106. O. Gadiesh and J. L Gilbert, "Transforming Corner-Office Strategy into Frontline Action," *Harvard Business Review* (May 2001), pp. 73–79.

107. E. Dane and M. G. Pratt, "Exploring Intuition and Its Role in Managerial Decision Making," *Academy of Management Review* (January 2007), pp. 33–54.

108. A. M. Hayashi, "When to Trust Your Gut," *Harvard Business Review* (February 2001), pp. 59–65.

109. E. Dane and M. G. Pratt, "Exploring Intuition and Its Role in Managerial Decision Making," *Academy of Management Review* (January 2007), pp. 33–54.

110. A. M. Hayashi, pp. 59–60.

111. C. Holahan, "Going, Going . . . Everywhere," *BusinessWeek* (June 18, 2007), pp. 62–64.

112. "The Skype Hyper," *The Economist* (October 6, 2007), p. 80.

113. D. Kucera, "eBay Poised to Gain 30% Chasing Amazon Without PayPal: Real M&A," *Bloomberg Businessweek* (January 9, 2012), (www.bloomberg.com/news/2012-01-08/ebay-poised-to-gain-30-chasing-amazon-without-paypal-real-m-a.html); C. Holahan, "eBay's New Tough Love CEO," *BusinessWeek* (February 4, 2008), pp. 58–59; PayPal Really Does Want to Be Your Pal," *Bloomberg Businessweek* (October 1, 2012), pg. 47.

PART 4

Strategy
Implementation
and Control

strategy implementation: organizing for Action

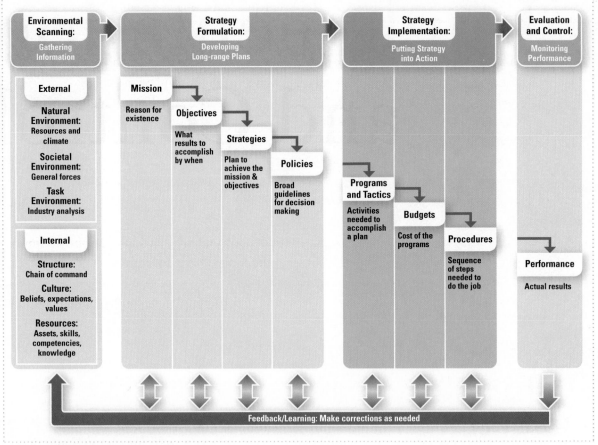

MyManagementLab®

★ Improve Your Grade!

Over 10 million students improved their results using the Pearson MyLabs. Visit **mymanagement.com** for simulations, tutorials, and end-of-chapter problems.

Learning Objectives

After reading this chapter, you should be able to:

- Develop programs, budgets, and procedures to implement strategic change
- Understand the importance of achieving synergy during strategy implementation
- List the stages of corporate development and the structure that characterizes each stage
- Identify the blocks to changing from one stage to another
- Construct matrix and network structures to support flexible and nimble organizational strategies
- Decide when and if programs such as reengineering, Six Sigma, and job redesign are appropriate methods of strategy implementation
- Understand the centralization versus decentralization issue in multinational corporations

The Rhythms of Business

For nearly five decades, Wal-Mart's "everyday low prices" and low-cost position had enabled it to rapidly grow to dominate North America's retailing landscape. By 2012, however, its U.S. division generated only 2.2% growth in its same-store sales even as the recession was fading. Target, Macy's, Kohl's Costco, GAP, Kroger, and even The Home Depot were all growing faster than Wal-Mart. At about the same time, Microsoft, whose software had grown to dominate personal computers worldwide, saw its revenue growth over the five-year period from 2007 to 2012 slow to just 6.6%. The company's stock price had been virtually flat since 2002, an indication that investors no longer perceived Microsoft as a growth company. What had happened to these two successful companies? Was this an isolated phenomenon? What could be done, if anything, to reinvigorate these giants?

A research study by Matthew Olson, Derek van Bever, and Seth Verry attempts to provide an answer. After analyzing the experiences of 500 successful companies over a 50-year period, they found that 87% of the firms had suffered one or more serious declines in sales and profits. This included a diverse set of corporations, such as Levi Strauss, 3M, Apple, Bank One, Caterpillar, Daimler-Benz, Toys"R"Us, and Volvo. After years of prolonged growth in sales and profits, revenue growth at each of these firms suddenly stopped and even turned negative! Olson, van Bever, and Verry called these long-term reversals in company growth *stall points*. On average, corporations lost 74% of their market capitalization in the decade surrounding a growth stall. Even though the CEO and other members of top management were typically replaced, only 46% of the firms were able to return to moderate or high growth within the decade. When slow growth was allowed to persist for more than 10 years, the delay was usually fatal. Only 7% of this group was able to return to moderate or high growth.

At Levi Strauss & Company, for example, sales topped US$7 billion in 1996—extending growth that had more than doubled over the previous decade. From that high-water mark, sales plummeted to US$4.6 billion in 2000—a 35% decline. Market share in its U.S. jeans market dropped from 31% in 1990 to 14% by 2000. After replacing management, the company underwent a companywide transformation, however, and by 2012, sales had dropped to US$4.3 billion.

According to Olson, van Bever, and Verry, these stall points occurred primarily because of a poor choice in strategy or organizational design. The root causes fell into four categories:

1. **Premium position backfires:** This happens to a firm that has developed a premium position in the market but is unable to respond effectively to new, low-cost competitors or a shift in customer valuation of product features. Management teams go through a process of disdain, denial, and rationalization that precedes the fall.

2. **Innovation management breaks down:** Management processes for updating existing products and creating new ones falter and become systemic inefficiencies.

3. **Core business abandoned:** Management fails to exploit growth opportunities in existing core businesses and instead engages in growth initiatives in areas remote from existing customers, products, and distribution channels.

4. **Talent and capabilities run short:** Strategies are not executed properly because of a lack of managers and staff with the skills and capabilities needed for strategy implementation. Often supported by promote-from-within policies, top management has a narrow experience base, which too often replicates the skill set of past top managers.

SOURCES: S. Clifford, "Sales at Wal-Mart, Though Still Rising, Suggest Wary Shoppers," *The New York Times* (August 16, 2012), http://www.nytimes.com/2012/08/17/business/wal-marts-earnings-suggest-strained-shoppers.html?_r=0); "U.S. Retail Sales Rise in October Before Sandy," *Fox Business* (November 1, 2012), http://www.foxbusiness.com/news/2012/11/01/us-retail-sales-rise-in-october-before-sandy/#ixzz2B0GC4zhd; A. Wiedmerman, "Walmart Rolls into Battle against the 'Big Three' Grocery Chains," *Daily Finance* (August 2, 2012), http://www.dailyfinance.com/2012/08/02/walmart-battles-big-three-grocery-chains/; A. Bianco, M. Der Hovanesian, L. Young, and P. Gogoi, "Wal-Mart's Midlife Crisis," *BusinessWeek* (April 30, 2007), pp. 46–56; "The Bulldozer of Bentonville Slows," *The Economist* (February 17, 2007), p. 64; D. Kirkpatrick, "Microsoft's New Brain," *Fortune* (May 1, 2006), pp. 56–68; "Spot the Dinosaur," *The Economist* (April 1, 2006), pp. 53–54; J. Greene, "Microsoft's Midlife Crisis," *BusinessWeek* (April 19, 2004), pp. 88–98. M. S. Olson, D. van Bever, and S. Verry, "When Growth Stalls," *Harvard Business Review* (March 2008), pp. 50–61. This phenomenon was called the "burnout syndrome" by G. Probst and S. Raisch in "Organizational Crisis: The Logic of Failure," *Academy of Management Executive* (February 2005), pp. 90–105. Ibid.

Strategy Implementation

Strategy implementation is the sum total of the activities and choices required for the execution of a strategic plan. It is the process by which objectives, strategies, and policies are put into action through the development of programs and tactics, budgets, and procedures. Although implementation is often considered only after strategy has been formulated, implementation is a key part of strategic management. Strategy formulation and strategy implementation should thus be considered as two sides of the same coin.

Poor implementation has been blamed for a number of strategic failures. For example, studies show that half of all acquisitions fail to achieve what was expected of them, and one out of four international ventures does not succeed.[1] The most mentioned problems reported in post-merger integration were poor communication, unrealistic synergy expectations, structural problems, missing master plans, lost momentum, lack of top management commitment, and unclear strategic fit. A study by A. T. Kearney found that a company has just two years in which to make an acquisition perform. After the second year, the window of opportunity for forging synergies has mostly closed. Kearney's study was supported by further independent research by Bert, MacDonald, and Herd. Among the most successful acquirers studied, 70% to 85% of all merger synergies were realized within the first 12 months, with the remainder being realized in year two.[2]

To begin the implementation process, strategy makers must consider these questions:

- *Who* are the people who will carry out the strategic plan?
- *What* must be done to align the company's operations in the new intended direction?
- *How* is everyone going to work together to do what is needed?

These questions and similar ones should have been addressed initially when the pros and cons of strategic alternatives were analyzed. They must also be addressed again before appropriate implementation plans can be made. Unless top management can answer these basic questions satisfactorily, even the best planned strategy is unlikely to provide the desired outcome.

A survey of 93 Fortune 500 firms revealed that more than half of the corporations experienced the following 10 problems when they attempted to implement a strategic change. These problems are listed in order of frequency:

1. Implementation took more time than originally planned.
2. Unanticipated major problems arose.
3. Activities were ineffectively coordinated.
4. Competing activities and crises took attention away from implementation.
5. The involved employees had insufficient capabilities to perform their jobs.
6. Lower-level employees were inadequately trained.
7. Uncontrollable external environmental factors created problems.
8. Departmental managers provided inadequate leadership and direction.
9. Key implementation tasks and activities were poorly defined.
10. The information system inadequately monitored activities.[3]

Who Implements Strategy?

Depending on how a corporation is organized, those who implement strategy will probably be a much more diverse set of people than those who formulate it. In most large, multi-industry corporations, the implementers are everyone in the organization. Vice presidents of functional areas and directors of divisions or strategic business units (SBUs) work with their subordinates to put together large-scale implementation plans. Plant managers, project managers, and unit heads put together plans for their specific plants, departments, and units. Therefore, every operational manager down to the first-line supervisor and every employee is involved in some way in the implementation of corporate, business, and functional strategies.

Many of the people in the organization who are crucial to successful strategy implementation probably had little to do with the development of the corporate and even business strategy. Therefore, they might be entirely ignorant of the vast amount of data and work that went into the formulation process. Unless changes in mission, objectives, strategies, and policies and their importance to the company are communicated clearly to all operational managers, there can be a lot of resistance and foot-dragging. Managers might hope to influence top management into abandoning its new plans and returning to its old ways. This is one reason why involving people from all organizational levels in the formulation and implementation of strategy tends to result in better organizational performance.[4]

What Must Be Done?

The managers of divisions and functional areas work with their fellow managers to develop programs, budgets, and procedures for the implementation of strategy. They also work to achieve synergy among the divisions and functional areas in order to establish and maintain a company's distinctive competence.

DEVELOPING PROGRAMS, BUDGETS, AND PROCEDURES

Strategy implementation involves establishing programs and tactics to create a series of new organizational activities, budgets to allocate funds to the new activities, and procedures to handle the day-to-day details.

Programs and Tactics

The purpose of a **program** or a tactic is to make a strategy action-oriented. As we discussed in **Chapter 1**, the terms are somewhat interchangeable. In practice, a program is a collection of tactics where a tactic is the individual action taken by the organization as an element of the effort to accomplish a plan. For example, when Xerox Corporation undertook a turnaround strategy, it needed to significantly reduce its costs and expenses. Management introduced a program called *Lean Six Sigma*. This program was developed to identify and improve a poorly performing process. Xerox first trained its top executives in the program and then launched around 250 individual Six Sigma projects throughout the corporation. The result was US$6 million in savings in one year, with even more expected the next.[5] (Six Sigma is explained later in this chapter.)

Most corporate headquarters have around 10 to 30 programs in effect at any one time.[6] One of the programs initiated by Ford Motor Company was to find an organic substitute for petroleum-based foam being used in vehicle seats. Apple used a recycled and yet elegant pulp tray to hold the original iPhone that became the inspiration for a business out to change the way bottles are produced. For more information on this innovative approach to bottle design, see the **Sustainability Issue** feature.

Competitive Tactics

Studies of decision making report that half the decisions made in organizations fail because of poor tactics.[7] A tactic is a specific operating plan that details how a strategy is to be implemented in terms of when and where it is to be put into action. By their nature, tactics are narrower in scope and shorter in time horizon than are strategies. Tactics, therefore, may be viewed (like policies) as a link between the formulation and implementation of strategy. Some of the tactics available to implement competitive strategies are timing tactics and market location tactics.

Timing Tactics: When to Compete

A **timing tactic** deals with *when* a company implements a strategy. The first company to manufacture and sell a new product or service is called the **first mover** (or pioneer). Some

SUSTAINABILITY issue

A BETTER BOTTLE—ECOLOGIC BRANDS

Some of the ideas that transform business practice are born in the simplest of places. Julie Corbett's started when she bought her first iPhone in 2007. She was fascinated by the paper pulp tray that it arrived in. The tray was elegant, sturdy, and biodegradable. She immediately thought of how it could be used to reduce the vast amounts of plastic needed for plastic bottles holding liquids. Combining the sturdiness of the paper pulp with an interior bladder to hold the liquid, she created Ecologic Brands.

Winner of the 2012 Gold Award from the Industrial Designers Society of America, the "bottle" is instantly recognizable as eco-friendly and yet extremely comfortable to touch and use. The bottles use 70% less plastic than regular ones and are the first of their type to hit store shelves. In addition, the bottle shells are made from 100% recycled cardboard and newspaper. The company didn't need to use any exotic materials or techniques to create the bottles. However, they have patents on the processes for connecting the components and have new products on the way. Ecologic is creating a demand for pulp paper in an industry that has been battered for many years.

Seventh Generation Laundry Detergent was one of the first brands to use the bottles and saw a 19% increase in sales after switching. In 2012, Ecologic shipped 2 million eco bottles, and with a new plant coming on line in 2013, it expects to ship 9 million bottles a year for the biggest brands in the United States.

....

SOURCES: "Bottles Inspired by the iPhone," *Bloomberg Businessweek,* October 29, 2012, p. 45; http://www.ecologicbrands.com/about_eco.html; http://www.fastcodesign.com/1664838/tk-years-in-the-making-a-cardboard-jug-for-laundry-detergent.

of the advantages of being a first mover are that the company is able to establish a reputation as an industry leader, move down the learning curve to assume the cost-leader position, and earn temporarily high profits from buyers who value the product or service very highly. A successful first mover can also set the standard for all subsequent products in the industry. A company that sets the standard "locks in" customers and is then able to offer further products based on that standard.[8] Microsoft was able to do this in software with its Windows operating system, and Netscape garnered over an 80% share of the Internet browser market by being the first to commercialize the product successfully. Research does indicate that moving first or second into a new industry or foreign country results in greater market share and shareholder wealth than does moving later.[9] Being first provides a company profit advantages for about 10 years in consumer goods and about 12 years in industrial goods.[10] This is true, however, only if the first mover has sufficient resources to both exploit the new market and to defend its position against later arrivals with greater resources.[11] Gillette, for example, has been able to keep its leadership of the razor category (70% market share) by continuously introducing new products.[12]

Being a first mover does, however, have its disadvantages. These disadvantages can be, conversely, advantages enjoyed by late-mover firms. **Late movers** may be able to imitate the technological advances of others (and thus keep R&D costs low), keep risks down by waiting until a new technological standard or market is established, and take advantage of the first mover's natural inclination to ignore market segments.[13] Research indicates that successful late movers tend to be large firms with considerable resources and related experience.[14] Microsoft is one example. Once Netscape had established itself as the standard for Internet browsers in the 1990s, Microsoft used its huge resources to directly attack Netscape's position with its Internet Explorer. It did not want Netscape to also set the standard in the developing and highly lucrative intranet market inside corporations. By 2004, Microsoft's Internet Explorer dominated Web browsers, and Netscape was only a minor presence. Nevertheless, research suggests that the advantages and disadvantages of first and late movers may not always generalize across industries because of differences in entry barriers and the resources of the specific competitors.[15]

Market Location Tactics: Where to Compete

A **market location tactic** deals with *where* a company implements a strategy. A company or business unit can implement a competitive strategy either offensively or defensively. An *offensive tactic* usually takes place in an established competitor's market location. A *defensive tactic* usually takes place in the firm's own current market position as a defense against possible attack by a rival.[16]

Offensive Tactics. Some of the methods used to attack a competitor's position are:

- **Frontal assault:** The attacking firm goes head to head with its competitor. It matches the competitor in every category from price to promotion to distribution channel. To be successful, the attacker must have not only superior resources, but also the willingness to persevere. This is generally a very expensive tactic and may serve to awaken a sleeping giant, depressing profits for the whole industry. This is what Kimberly-Clark did when it introduced Huggies disposable diapers against P&G's market-leading Pampers. The resulting competitive battle between the two firms depressed Kimberly-Clark's profits.[17]

- **Flanking maneuver:** Rather than going straight for a competitor's position of strength with a frontal assault, a firm may attack a part of the market where the competitor is weak. Texas Instruments, for example, avoided competing directly with Intel by developing microprocessors for consumer electronics, cell phones, and medical devices instead of computers. Taken together, these other applications are worth more in terms of dollars and influence than are computers, where Intel dominates.[18]

- **Bypass attack:** Rather than directly attacking the established competitor frontally or on its flanks, a company or business unit may choose to change the rules of the game. This tactic attempts to cut the market out from under the established defender by offering a new type of product that makes the competitor's product unnecessary. For example, instead of competing directly against Microsoft's Pocket PC and Palm Pilot for the handheld computer market, Apple introduced the iPod as a personal digital music player. It was the most radical change to the way people listen to music since the Sony Walkman. By redefining the market, Apple successfully sidestepped both Intel and Microsoft, leaving them to play "catch-up."[19]

- **Encirclement:** Usually evolving out of a frontal assault or flanking maneuver, encirclement occurs as an attacking company or unit encircles the competitor's position in terms of products or markets or both. The encircler has greater product variety (e.g., a complete product line, ranging from low to high price) and/or serves more markets (e.g., it dominates every secondary market). For example, Steinway was a major manufacturer of pianos in the United States until Yamaha entered the market with a broader range of pianos, keyboards, and other musical instruments. Although Steinway still dominates concert halls, it has only a 2% share of the U.S. market.[20] Oracle is using this strategy in its battle against market leader SAP for enterprise resource planning (ERP) software by "surrounding" SAP with acquisitions.[21]

- **Guerrilla warfare:** Instead of a continual and extensive resource-expensive attack on a competitor, a firm or business unit may choose to "hit and run." Guerrilla warfare is characterized by the use of small, intermittent assaults on different market segments held by the competitor. In this way, a new entrant or small firm can make some gains without seriously threatening a large, established competitor and evoking some form of retaliation.

To be successful, the firm or unit conducting guerrilla warfare must be patient enough to accept small gains and avoid pushing the established competitor to the point that it must respond or else lose face. Microbreweries, which make beer for sale to local customers, use this tactic against major brewers such as Anheuser-Busch.

Defensive tactics. According to Porter, defensive tactics aim to lower the probability of attack, divert attacks to less threatening avenues, or lessen the intensity of an attack. Instead of increasing competitive advantage per se, they make a company's or business unit's competitive advantage more sustainable by causing a challenger to conclude that an attack is unattractive. These tactics deliberately reduce short-term profitability to ensure long-term profitability.[22]

- **Raise structural barriers.** Entry barriers act to block a challenger's logical avenues of attack. Some of the most important, according to Porter, are to:
  1. Offer a full line of products in every profitable market segment to close off any entry points (for example, Coca-Cola offers unprofitable noncarbonated beverages to keep competitors off store shelves).
  2. Block channel access by signing exclusive agreements with distributors.
  3. Raise buyer switching costs by offering low-cost training to users.
  4. Raise the cost of gaining trial users by keeping prices low on items new users are most likely to purchase.
  5. Increase scale economies to reduce unit costs.
  6. Foreclose alternative technologies through patenting or licensing.
  7. Limit outside access to facilities and personnel.
  8. Tie up suppliers by obtaining exclusive contracts or purchasing key locations.
  9. Avoid suppliers that also serve competitors.
  10. Encourage the government to raise barriers, such as safety and pollution standards or favorable trade policies.

- **Increase expected retaliation:** This tactic is any action that increases the perceived threat of retaliation for an attack. For example, management may strongly defend any erosion of market share by drastically cutting prices or matching a challenger's promotion through a policy of accepting any price-reduction coupons for a competitor's product. This counterattack is especially important in markets that are very important to the defending company or business unit. For example, when Clorox Company challenged P&G in the detergent market with Clorox Super Detergent, P&G retaliated by test marketing its liquid bleach, Lemon Fresh Comet, in an attempt to scare Clorox into retreating from the detergent market. Research suggests that retaliating quickly is not as successful in slowing market share loss as a slower, but more concentrated and aggressive response.[23]

- **Lower the inducement for attack:** A third type of defensive tactic is to reduce a challenger's expectations of future profits in the industry. Like Southwest Airlines, a company can deliberately keep prices low and constantly invest in cost-reducing measures. With prices kept very low, there is little profit incentive for a new entrant.[24]

Budgets

After programs and tactical plans have been developed, the **budget** process begins. Planning a budget is the last real check a corporation has on the feasibility of its selected strategy. An ideal strategy might be found to be completely impractical only after specific implementation programs and tactics are costed in detail. For example, once Cadbury Schweppes' management realized how dependent the company was on cocoa from Ghana to continue the company's growth strategy, it developed a program to show cocoa farmers how to increase yields using fertilizers and by working with each other. Ghana produced 70% of Cadbury's worldwide supply of the high-quality cocoa necessary to provide the distinctive taste of Dairy Milk, Crème Egg, and other treats. Management introduced the "Cadbury Cocoa Partnership" on January 28, 2008, and budgeted US$87 million for this program over a 10-year period.[25]

Procedures

After the divisional and corporate budgets are approved, **procedures** must be developed. Often called *Standard Operating Procedures (SOPs)*, they typically detail the various activities that must be carried out to complete a corporation's programs and tactical plans. Also known as *organizational routines*, procedures are the primary means by which organizations accomplish much of what they do.[26] Once in place, procedures must be updated to reflect any changes in technology as well as in strategy. For example, a company following a differentiation competitive strategy manages its sales force more closely than does a firm following a low-cost strategy. Differentiation requires long-term customer relationships created out of close interaction with the sales force. An in-depth understanding of the customer's needs provides the foundation for product development and improvement.[27]

In a retail store, procedures ensure that the day-to-day store operations will be consistent over time (that is, next week's work activities will be the same as this week's) and consistent among stores (that is, each store will operate in the same manner as the others). Properly planned procedures can help eliminate poor service by making sure that employees do not use excuses to justify poor behavior toward customers. Even though McDonald's, the fast-food restaurant, has developed very detailed procedures to ensure that customers have high-quality service, not every business is so well managed.

Before a new strategy can be successfully implemented, current procedures may need to be changed. For example, in order to implement The Home Depot's strategic move into services, such as kitchen and bathroom installation, the company had to first improve its productivity. Store managers were drowning in paperwork designed for a smaller and simpler company. "We'd get a fax, an e-mail, a call, and a memo, all on the same project," reported store manager Michael Jones. One executive used just three weeks of memos to wallpaper an entire conference room, floor to ceiling, windows included. Then CEO Robert Nardelli told his top managers to eliminate duplicate communications and streamline work projects. Directives not related to work orders had to be sent separately and only once a month. The company also spent US$2 million on workload-management software.[28]

ACHIEVING SYNERGY

One of the goals to be achieved in strategy implementation is synergy between and among functions and business units. This is the reason corporations commonly reorganize after an acquisition. **Synergy** is said to exist for a divisional corporation if the return on investment (ROI) of each division is greater than what the return would be if each division were an independent business. According to Goold and Campbell, synergy can take place in one of six forms:

- **Shared know-how:** Combined units often benefit from sharing knowledge or skills. This is a leveraging of core competencies. One reason that Procter & Gamble purchased Gillette was to combine P&G's knowledge of the female consumer with Gillette's knowledge of the male consumer.
- **Coordinated strategies:** Aligning the business strategies of two or more business units may give a corporation significant advantage by reducing inter-unit competition and developing a coordinated response to common competitors (horizontal strategy). The merger between Comcast and NBC Universal in 2011 gave the combined company significant bargaining strength and flexibility with advertisers in the increasingly competitive television media industry.

- **Shared tangible resources:** Combined units can sometimes save money by sharing resources, such as a common manufacturing facility or R&D lab. The big pharmaceutical companies were all looking for savings with the big mergers in the industry, such as Pfizer-Wyeth, Novartis-Alcon, and Roche-Genentech.

- **Economies of scale or scope:** Coordinating the flow of products or services of one unit with that of another unit can reduce inventory, increase capacity utilization, and improve market access. This was a reason United Airlines bought Continental Airlines.

- **Pooled negotiating power:** Units can combine their volume of purchasing to gain bargaining power over common suppliers to reduce costs and improve quality. The same can be done with common distributors. The acquisitions of Macy's and the May Company enabled Federated Department Stores (which changed its name to Macy's in 2007) to gain purchasing economies for all of its stores.

- **New business creation:** Exchanging knowledge and skills can facilitate new products or services by extracting discrete activities from various units and combining them in a new unit or by establishing joint ventures among internal business units. Google acquired, on average, one company a week from 2010 to 2012—more than 100 companies—as it tried to organize the world's information and make it universally accessible and useful.[29]

How Is Strategy to Be Implemented? Organizing for Action

Before plans can lead to actual performance, a corporation should be appropriately organized, programs should be adequately staffed, and activities should be directed toward achieving desired objectives. (Organizing activities are reviewed briefly in this chapter; staffing, directing, and control activities are discussed in **Chapters 10** and **11**.)

Any change in corporate strategy is very likely to require some sort of change in the way an organization is structured and in the kind of skills needed in particular positions. Managers must therefore closely examine the way their company is structured in order to decide what, if any, changes should be made in the way work is accomplished. Should activities be grouped differently? Should the authority to make key decisions be centralized at headquarters or decentralized to managers in distant locations? Should the company be managed like a "tight ship" with many rules and controls, or "loosely" with few rules and controls? Should the corporation be organized into a "tall" structure with many layers of managers, each having a narrow span of control (that is, few employees per supervisor) to better control his or her subordinates; or should it be organized into a "flat" structure with fewer layers of managers, each having a wide span of control (that is, more employees per supervisor) to give more freedom to his or her subordinates?

STRUCTURE FOLLOWS STRATEGY

In a classic study of large U.S. corporations such as DuPont, General Motors, Sears, and Standard Oil, Alfred Chandler concluded that **structure follows strategy**—that is, changes in corporate strategy lead to changes in organizational structure.[30] He also concluded that organizations follow a pattern of development from one kind of structural arrangement to another as they expand. According to Chandler, these structural changes occur because the old structure, having been pushed too far, has caused inefficiencies that have become too obviously detrimental to bear. Chandler, therefore, proposed the following as the sequence of what occurs:

1. New strategy is created.
2. New administrative problems emerge.

3. Economic performance declines.

4. New appropriate structure is created.

5. Economic performance rises.

Chandler found that in their early years, corporations such as DuPont tend to have a centralized functional organizational structure that is well suited to producing and selling a limited range of products. As they add new product lines, purchase their own sources of supply, and create their own distribution networks, they become too complex for highly centralized structures. To remain successful, this type of organization needs to shift to a decentralized structure with several semiautonomous divisions (referred to in **Chapter 5** as *divisional structure*).

Alfred P. Sloan, past CEO of General Motors, detailed how GM conducted such structural changes in the 1920s.[31] He saw decentralization of structure as "centralized policy determination coupled with decentralized operating management." After top management had developed a strategy for the total corporation, the individual divisions (Chevrolet, Buick, and so on) were free to choose how to implement that strategy. Patterned after DuPont, GM found the decentralized multidivisional structure to be extremely effective in allowing the maximum amount of freedom for product development. Return on investment was used as a financial control. (ROI is discussed in more detail in **Chapter 11**.)

Research generally supports Chandler's proposition that structure follows strategy (as well as the reverse proposition that structure influences strategy).[32] As mentioned earlier, changes in the environment tend to be reflected in changes in a corporation's strategy, thus leading to changes in a corporation's structure. In 2008, Arctic Cat, the recreational vehicles firm, reorganized its ATV (all terrain vehicles), snowmobile and parts, and garments and accessories product lines into three separate business units, each led by a general manager focused on expanding the business. True to Chandler's findings, the restructuring of Arctic Cat came after seven consecutive years of record growth followed by its first loss in 25 years. By 2012, sales were increasing by double digits and the company had sales in excess of half a billion dollars.[33]

Strategy, structure, and the environment need to be closely aligned; otherwise, organizational performance will likely suffer.[34] For example, a business unit following a differentiation strategy needs more freedom from headquarters to be successful than does another unit following a low-cost strategy.[35]

Although it is agreed that organizational structure must vary with different environmental conditions, which, in turn, affect an organization's strategy, there is no agreement about an optimal organizational design. What was appropriate for DuPont and General Motors in the 1920s might not be appropriate today. Firms in the same industry do, however, tend to organize themselves similarly to one another. For example, automobile manufacturers tend to emulate General Motors' divisional concept, whereas consumer-goods producers tend to emulate the brand-management concept (a type of matrix structure) pioneered by Procter & Gamble Company. See the Innovation Issues feature to see how P&G's structural decisions ended up derailing their innovation efforts. The general conclusion seems to be that firms following similar strategies in similar industries tend to adopt similar structures.

STAGES OF CORPORATE DEVELOPMENT

Successful, large conglomerate organizations have tended to follow a pattern of structural development as they grow and expand. Beginning with the simple structure of the entrepreneurial firm (in which everybody does everything), these organizations tend to get larger and organize along functional lines, with marketing, production, and finance departments. With continuing success, the company adds new product lines in different industries and organizes

INNOVATION issues

THE P&G INNOVATION MACHINE STUMBLES

As we have discussed throughout this text, innovation is a key element to organically grow a company. Developing an ever-widening portfolio of businesses has been a strategic approach used by many companies. None has been more successful with this approach than Procter & Gamble (P&G). Their 175-year history is filled with consumer-oriented product innovations including Ivory Soap (1879), Crisco (1911), Dreft which became Tide (1933), Crest (1955), Pampers (1961), Pringles (1968), Fabreze (1993), Swiffer (1998), and Crest Whitestrips (2002).

Known for their heavy investment in research and development, the company invested more than US$2 billion in R&D in 2012. For most of its history, the company used a highly centralized R&D group to generate new ideas. This all came to an end in 2000 when then-CEO A.G. Lafley decentralized the operations to the operating units and opened product innovation to outside partners. Taking his cue for the dramatic growth in social media and crowdsourcing, Lafley sought to have 50% of innovative new products generated from people not employed by the company. The operating units were expected to be more closely tied to the consumers and thus be in a better position to know the potential for each new product idea.

Between 2003 and 2008, the sales of new launches shrank by half. The company's pipeline became focused on reformulating old products, adding scents to successful product lines, and adjusting the sizes that were sold.

In 2009, new CEO Bob McDonald started recentralizing R&D operations in an attempt to reverse the deterioration of innovation at the company. By 2012, between 20 and 30 percent of R&D had been centralized. The loss of focus cost the company a decade of innovations while competitors rolled out new products in virtually every product category in which P&G competes. There is no single means for generating innovative ideas or for turning those ideas into a blockbuster new product. Companies seek to organize their businesses so they can own the next big "thing."

SOURCES: L. Coleman-Lochner and C. Hymowitz, "At P&G, the Innovation Well Runs Dry," *Bloomberg Businessweek* (September 10, 2012), pp. 24–26; http://www.pg.com/en_US/brands/index.shtml.

---

itself into interconnected divisions. The differences among these three structural **stages of corporate development** in terms of typical problems, objectives, strategies, reward systems, and other characteristics are specified in detail in **Table 9–1**.

Stage I: Simple Structure

Stage I is typified by the entrepreneur or a small team, who founds a company to promote an idea (a product or a service). The entrepreneur or team tend to make all the important decisions and is involved in every detail and phase of the organization. The Stage I company has little formal structure, which allows the entrepreneur or team to directly supervise the activities of every employee (see **Figure 5–4** for an illustration of the simple, functional, and divisional structures). Planning is usually short range or reactive. The typical managerial functions of planning, organizing, directing, staffing, and controlling are usually performed to a very limited degree, if at all. The greatest strengths of a Stage I corporation are its flexibility and dynamism. The drive of the entrepreneur energizes the organization in its struggle for growth. Its greatest weakness is its extreme reliance on the entrepreneur to decide general strategies as well as detailed procedures. If the entrepreneur falters, the company usually flounders. This is labeled by Greiner as a *crisis of leadership*.[36]

Stage I describes the early life of Oracle Corporation, the computer software firm, under the management of its co-founder and CEO Lawrence Ellison. The company adopted a pioneering approach to retrieving data, called Structured Query Language (SQL). When IBM made SQL its standard, Oracle's success was assured. Unfortunately, Ellison's technical wizardry was not sufficient to manage the company. Often working at home, he lost sight of details outside his technical interests. Although the company's sales were rapidly increasing,

TABLE 9–1	Factors Differentiating Stage I, II, and III Companies		
Function	Stage I	Stage II	Stage III
1. Sizing up: Major problems	Survival and growth dealing with short-term operating problems.	Growth, rationalization, and expansion of resources, providing for adequate attention to product problems.	Trusteeship in management and investment and control of large, increasing, and diversified resources. Also, important to diagnose and take action on problems at division level.
2. Objectives	Personal and subjective.	Profits and meeting functionally oriented budgets and performance targets.	ROI, profits, earnings per share.
3. Strategy	Implicit and personal; exploitation of immediate opportunities seen by owner-manager.	Functionally oriented moves restricted to "one product" scope; exploitation of one basic product or service field.	Growth and product diversification; exploitation of general business opportunities.
4. Organization: Major characteristic of structure	One unit, "one-man show."	One unit, functionally specialized group.	Multiunit general staff office and decentralized operating divisions.
5. (a) Measurement and control	Personal, subjective control based on simple accounting system and daily communication and observation.	Control grows beyond one person; assessment of functional operations necessary; structured control systems evolve.	Complex formal system geared to comparative assessment of performance measures, indicating problems and opportunities and assessing management ability of division managers.
5. (b) Key performance indicators	Personal criteria, relationships with owner, operating efficiency, ability to solve operating problems.	Functional and internal criteria such as sales, performance compared to budget, size of empire, status in group, personal, relationships, etc.	More impersonal application of comparisons such as profits, ROI, P/E ratio, sales, market share, productivity, product leadership, personnel development, employee attitudes, public responsibility.
6. Reward–punishment system	Informal, personal, subjective; used to maintain control and divide small pool of resources for key performers to provide personal incentives.	More structured; usually based to a greater extent on agreed policies as opposed to personal opinion and relationships.	Allotment by "due process" of a wide variety of different rewards and punishments on a formal and systematic basis. Companywide policies usually apply to many different classes of managers and workers with few major exceptions for individual cases.

SOURCE: Donald H. Thain, "Stages of Corporate Development," *Ivey Business Journal* (formerly *Ivey Business Quarterly*), Winter 1969, p. 37. Copyright © 1969, Ivey Management Services. One-time permission to reproduce granted by Ivey Management Services.

its financial controls were so weak that management had to restate an entire year's results to rectify irregularities. After the company recorded its first loss, Ellison hired a set of functional managers to run the company while he retreated to focus on new product development.

Stage II: Functional Structure

Stage II is the point when the entrepreneur is replaced by a team of managers who have functional specializations. The transition to this stage requires a substantial managerial style change for the chief officer of the company, especially if he or she was the Stage I entrepreneur. He or she must learn to delegate; otherwise, having additional staff members yields no benefits to the organization. The previous example of Ellison's retreat from top management at Oracle Corporation to new product development manager is one way that technically brilliant founders are able to get out of the way of the newly empowered functional managers. In Stage II, the corporate strategy favors protectionism through dominance of the industry, often through vertical and horizontal growth. The great strength of a Stage II corporation lies in its concentration and specialization in one industry. Its great weakness is that all its eggs are in one basket.

By concentrating on one industry while that industry remains attractive, a Stage II company, such as Oracle Corporation in computer software, can be very successful. Once a functionally structured firm diversifies into other products in different industries, however, the advantages of the functional structure break down. A *crisis of autonomy* can now develop, in which people managing diversified product lines need more decision-making freedom than top management is willing to delegate to them. The company needs to move to a different structure.

Stage III: Divisional Structure

Stage III is typified by the corporation's managing diverse product lines in numerous industries; it decentralizes the decision-making authority. Stage III organizations grow by diversifying their product lines and expanding to cover wider geographical areas. They move to a divisional structure with a central headquarters and decentralized operating divisions—with each division or business unit a functionally organized Stage II company. They may also use a conglomerate structure if top management chooses to keep its collection of Stage II subsidiaries operating autonomously. A *crisis of control* can now develop, in which the various units act to optimize their own sales and profits without regard to the overall corporation, whose headquarters seems far away and almost irrelevant.

Over time, divisions have been evolving into SBUs to better reflect product–market considerations. Headquarters attempts to coordinate the activities of its operating divisions or SBUs through performance, results-oriented control, and reporting systems, and by stressing corporate planning techniques. The units are not tightly controlled but are held responsible for their own performance results. Therefore, to be effective, the company has to have a decentralized decision process. The greatest strength of a Stage III corporation is its almost unlimited resources. Its most significant weakness is that it is usually so large and complex that it tends to become relatively inflexible. General Electric, DuPont, and General Motors are examples of Stage III corporations.

Stage IV: Beyond SBUs

Even with the evolution into SBUs during the 1970s and 1980s, the divisional structure is not the last word in organization structure. The use of SBUs may result in a *red tape crisis* in which the corporation has grown too large and complex to be managed through formal programs and rigid systems, and procedures take precedence over problem solving.[37] For example, Pfizer's acquisitions of Warner-Lambert and Pharmacia resulted in 14 layers of management between scientists and top executives and thus forced researchers to spend most of their time in meetings.[38] Under conditions of (1) increasing environmental uncertainty, (2) greater use of sophisticated technological production methods and information systems, (3) the increasing size and scope of worldwide business corporations, (4) a greater emphasis on multi-industry competitive strategy, and (5) a more educated cadre of managers and employees, new advanced forms of organizational structure are emerging. These structures emphasize collaboration over competition in the managing of an organization's multiple overlapping projects and developing businesses.

The matrix and the network are two possible candidates for a fourth stage in corporate development—a stage that not only emphasizes horizontal over vertical connections between people and groups but also organizes work around temporary projects in which sophisticated information systems support collaborative activities. According to Greiner, it is likely that this stage of development will have its own crisis as well—a sort of *pressure-cooker crisis*. He predicts that employees in these collaborative organizations will eventually grow emotionally and physically exhausted from the intensity of teamwork and the heavy pressure for innovative solutions.[39]

Blocks to Changing Stages

Corporations often find themselves in difficulty because they are blocked from moving into the next logical stage of development. Blocks to development may be internal (such as lack of resources, lack of ability, or refusal of top management to delegate decision making to others) or external (such as economic conditions, labor shortages, and lack of market growth). For example, Chandler noted in his study that the successful founder/CEO in one stage was rarely the person who created the new structure to fit the new strategy, and as a result, the transition from one stage to another was often painful. This was true of General Motors Corporation under the management of William Durant, Ford Motor Company under Henry Ford I, Polaroid Corporation under Edwin Land, eBay under Pierre Omidyar, and Yahoo under Jerry Yang and David Filo.

Entrepreneurs who start businesses generally have four tendencies that work very well for small new ventures but become Achilles' heels for these same individuals when they try to manage a larger firm with diverse needs, departments, priorities, and constituencies:

- **Loyalty to comrades:** This is good at the beginning but soon becomes a liability as "favoritism."
- **Task oriented:** Focusing on the job is critical at first but then becomes excessive attention to detail.
- **Single-mindedness:** A grand vision is needed to introduce a new product but can become tunnel vision as the company grows into more markets and products.
- **Working in isolation:** This is good for a brilliant scientist but disastrous for a CEO with multiple constituencies.[40]

This difficulty in moving to a new stage is compounded by the founder's tendency to maneuver around the need to delegate by carefully hiring, training, and grooming his or her own team of managers. The team tends to maintain the founder's influence throughout the organization long after the founder is gone. This is what happened at Walt Disney Productions when the family continued to emphasize Walt's policies and plans long after he was dead. The refrain that was often heard was "What would Walt have done?" Although in some cases this may be an organization's strength, it can also be a weakness—to the extent that the culture supports the status quo and blocks needed change.

ORGANIZATIONAL LIFE CYCLE

Instead of considering stages of development in terms of structure, the organizational life cycle approach places the primary emphasis on the dominant issue facing the corporation. Organizational structure becomes a secondary concern. The **organizational life cycle** describes how organizations grow, develop, and eventually decline. It is the organizational equivalent of the product life cycle in marketing. These stages are Birth (Stage I), Growth (Stage II), Maturity (Stage III), Decline (Stage IV), and Death (Stage V). The impact of these stages on corporate strategy and structure is summarized in **Table 9–2**. Note that the first three stages

TABLE 9–2	Organizational Life Cycle				
	Stage I	**Stage II**	**Stage III***	**Stage IV**	**Stage V**
Dominant Issue	Birth	Growth	Maturity	Decline	Death
Popular Strategies	Concentration in a niche	Horizontal and vertical growth	Concentric and conglomerate diversification	Profit strategy followed by retrenchment	Liquidation or bankruptcy
Likely Structure	Entrepreneur dominated	Functional management emphasized	Decentralization into profit or investment centers	Structural surgery	Dismemberment of structure

NOTE: *An organization may enter a Revival phase either during the Maturity or Decline stages and thus extend the organization's life.

of the organizational life cycle are similar to the three commonly accepted stages of corporate development mentioned previously. The only significant difference is the addition of the Decline and Death stages to complete the cycle. Even though a company's strategy may still be sound, its aging structure, culture, and processes may be such that they prevent the strategy from being executed properly. Its core competencies become *core rigidities* that are no longer able to adapt to changing conditions—thus the company moves into Decline.[41]

Movement from Growth to Maturity to Decline and finally to Death is not, however, inevitable. A Revival phase may occur sometime during the Maturity or Decline stages. The corporation's life cycle can be extended by managerial and product innovations.[42] Developing new combinations of existing resources to introduce new products or acquiring new resources through acquisitions can enable firms with declining performance to regain growth—so long as the action is valuable and difficult to imitate.[43] We have seen this play out with Apple. It was clearly in decline in the mid-1980s and many believe well on its way to dying. The company was rejuvenated with the return of Steve Jobs and a seemingly continuous stream of new products that took the company into numerous new markets. This can occur during the implementation of a turnaround strategy.[44] Nevertheless, the fact that firms in decline are less likely to search for new technologies suggests that it is difficult to revive a company in decline.[45]

Eastman Kodak is an example of a firm in decline, and quite nearly dead, that has been attempting to develop new combinations of its existing resources to introduce new products, and thus, revive the corporation. When Antonio Perez left Hewlett-Packard to become Kodak's President in 2003, Kodak was in the midst of its struggle to make the transition from chemical film technology to digital technology and digital cameras. Instead of focusing the company's efforts on acquisitions to find growth, Perez looked at technologies that Kodak already owned, but was not utilizing. He noticed that Kodak scientists had developed new ink to yield photo prints with vivid colors that would last a lifetime. He suddenly realized that Kodak's distinctive competence was not in digital photography, where other competitors led the market, but in color printing. Perez initiated project *Goza* to go head to head with HP in the consumer inkjet printer business. In 2007, Kodak unveiled its new line of multipurpose machines that not only handled photographs and documents, but also made copies and sent faxes. The printers were designed to print high-quality photos with ink that would stay vibrant for 100 rather than the usual 15 years. Most importantly, replacement ink cartridges would cost half the price of competitors' cartridges. According to Perez, "We think it will give us the opportunity to disrupt the industry's business model and address consumers' key dissatisfaction: the high cost of ink." Perez then predicted that Kodak's inkjet printers would become a multibillion-dollar product line.[46]

Kodak's printer business had grown to 6% of the U.S. market by 2012 but had not made a dent in the 60% market share owned by HP. Kodak continued to sell off its patent portfolio in order to pay for the move into a printer market that is expected to be flat or declining in the future.[47]

Unless a company is able to resolve the critical issues facing it in the Decline stage, it is likely to move into Stage V, Death—also known as bankruptcy. This is what happened to Montgomery Ward, Pan American Airlines, Mervyn's, Borders, Eastern Airlines, Circuit City, Orion Pictures, and Levitz Furniture, as well as many other firms. As in the cases of Johns-Manville, Bennigan's, Macy's, and Kmart—all of which went bankrupt—a corporation can rise like a phoenix from its own ashes and live again under the same or a different name. The company may be reorganized or liquidated, depending on individual circumstances. For example, Kmart emerged from Chapter 11 bankruptcy in 2003 with a new CEO and a plan to sell a number of its stores to The Home Depot and Sears. These sales earned the company close to US$1 billion. Although store sales continued to erode, Kmart had sufficient cash reserves to continue with its turnaround.[48] It used that money to acquire Sears in 2005. Unfortunately, however, fewer than 20% of firms entering Chapter 11 bankruptcy in the United States emerge as going concerns; the rest are forced into liquidation (also known as Chapter 7).[49]

Few corporations will move through these five stages in order. Some corporations, for example, might never move past Stage II. Others, such as General Motors, might go directly from Stage I to Stage III. A large number of entrepreneurial ventures jump from Stage I or II directly into Stage IV or V. Hayes Microcomputer Products, for example, went from the Growth to Decline stage under its founder Dennis Hayes. The key is to be able to identify indications that a firm is in the process of changing stages and to make the appropriate strategic and structural adjustments to ensure that corporate performance is maintained or even improved.

ADVANCED TYPES OF ORGANIZATIONAL STRUCTURES

The basic structures (simple, functional, divisional, and conglomerate) are discussed in **Chapter 5** and summarized under the first three stages of corporate development in this chapter. A new strategy may require more flexible characteristics than the traditional functional or divisional structure can offer. Today's business organizations are becoming less centralized with a greater use of cross-functional work teams. Although many variations and hybrid structures exist, two forms stand out: the matrix structure and the network structure.

The Matrix Structure

Most organizations find that organizing around either functions (in the functional structure) or products and geography (in the divisional structure) provides an appropriate organizational structure. The matrix structure, in contrast, may be very appropriate when organizations conclude that neither functional nor divisional forms, even when combined with horizontal linking mechanisms such as SBUs, are right for their situations. In **matrix structures**, functional and product forms are combined simultaneously at the same level of the organization. (See **Figure 9–1**.) Employees have two superiors, a product or project manager, and a functional manager. The "home" department—that is, engineering, manufacturing, or sales—is usually functional and is reasonably permanent. People from these functional units are often assigned temporarily to one or more product units or projects. The product units or projects are usually temporary and act like divisions in that they are differentiated on a product-market basis.

Pioneered in the aerospace industry, the matrix structure was developed to combine the stability of the functional structure with the flexibility of the product form. The matrix structure is very useful when the external environment (especially its technological and market aspects) is very complex and changeable. It does, however, produce conflicts revolving around duties, authority, and resource allocation. To the extent that the goals to be achieved are vague and the technology used is poorly understood, a continuous battle for power between product and

FIGURE 9–1
Matrix
and Network
Structures

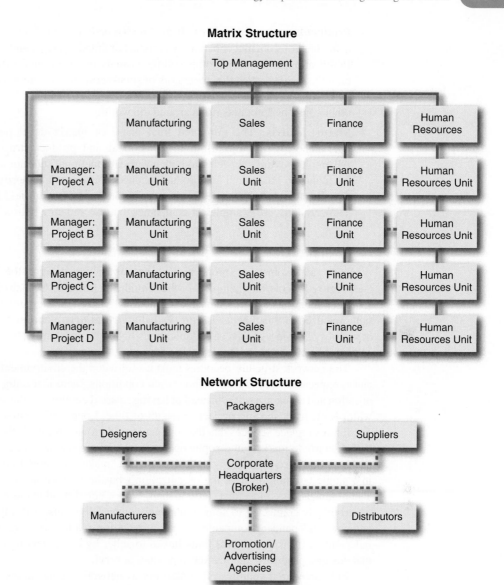

functional managers is likely. The matrix structure is often found in an organization or SBU when the following three conditions exist:

- Ideas need to be cross-fertilized across projects or products.
- Resources are scarce.
- Abilities to process information and to make decisions need to be improved.[50]

Davis and Lawrence, authorities on the matrix form of organization, propose that *three distinct phases* exist in the development of the matrix structure:[51]

- **Temporary cross-functional task forces:** These are initially used when a new product line is being introduced. A project manager is in charge as the key horizontal link. J&J's experience with cross-functional teams in its drug group led it to emphasize teams crossing multiple units.

■ **Product/brand management:** If the cross-functional task forces become more permanent, the project manager becomes a product or brand manager and a second phase begins. In this arrangement, function is still the primary organizational structure, but product or brand managers act as the integrators of semi-permanent products or brands. Considered by many a key to the success of P&G, brand management has been widely imitated by other consumer products firms around the world.

■ **Mature matrix:** The third and final phase of matrix development involves a true dual-authority structure. Both the functional and product structures are permanent. All employees are connected to both a vertical functional superior and a horizontal product manager. Functional and product managers have equal authority and must work well together to resolve disagreements over resources and priorities. Boeing, Philips, and TRW Systems are examples of companies that use a mature matrix.

Network Structure—The Virtual Organization

A newer and somewhat more radical organizational design, the **network structure** (see **Figure 9–1**) is an example of what could be termed a "non-structure" because of its virtual elimination of in-house business functions. Many activities are outsourced. A corporation organized in this manner is often called a **virtual organization** because it is composed of a series of project groups or collaborations linked by constantly changing nonhierarchical, cobweb-like electronic networks.[52]

The network structure becomes most useful when the environment of a firm is unstable and is expected to remain so.[53] Under such conditions, there is usually a strong need for innovation and quick response. Instead of having salaried employees, the company may contract with people for a specific project or length of time. Long-term contracts with suppliers and distributors replace services that the company could provide for itself through vertical integration. Electronic markets and sophisticated information systems reduce the transaction costs of the marketplace, thus justifying a "buy" over a "make" decision. Rather than being located in a single building or area, the organization's business functions are scattered worldwide. The organization is, in effect, only a shell, with a small headquarters acting as a "broker," electronically connected to some completely owned divisions, partially owned subsidiaries, and other independent companies. In its ultimate form, a network organization is a series of independent firms or business units linked together by computers in an information system that designs, produces, and markets a product or service.[54]

Entrepreneurial ventures often start out as network organizations. For example, Randy and Nicole Wilburn of Dorchester, Massachusetts, run real estate, consulting, design, and baby food companies out of their home. Nicole, a stay-at-home mom and graphic designer, farms out design work to freelancers and cooks her own line of organic baby food. For US$300, an Indian artist designed the logo for Nicole's "Baby Fresh Organic Baby Foods." A London freelancer wrote promotional materials. Instead of hiring a secretary, Randy hired "virtual assistants" in Jerusalem to transcribe voicemail, update his Web site, and design PowerPoint graphics. Retired brokers in Virginia and Michigan deal with his real estate paperwork.[55]

Large companies such as Nike, Reebok, and Benetton use the network structure in their operations function by subcontracting (outsourcing) manufacturing to other companies in low-cost locations around the world. For control purposes, the Italian-based Benetton maintains what it calls an "umbilical cord" by assuring production planning for all its subcontractors, planning materials requirements for them, and providing them with bills of labor and standard prices and costs, as well as technical assistance to make sure their quality is up to Benetton's standards.

The network organizational structure provides an organization with increased flexibility and adaptability to cope with rapid technological change and shifting patterns of international trade and competition. It allows a company to concentrate on its distinctive competencies, while gathering efficiencies from other firms that are concentrating their efforts in their areas of expertise. The network does, however, have disadvantages. Some believe that the network is really only a transitional structure because it is inherently unstable and subject to tensions.[56] The availability of numerous potential partners can be a source of trouble. Contracting out individual activities to separate suppliers/distributors may keep the firm from discovering any internal synergies by combining these activities. If a particular firm overspecializes on only a few functions, it runs the risk of choosing the wrong functions and thus becoming noncompetitive.

Cellular/Modular Organization: A New Type of Structure?

Some authorities in the field propose that the evolution of organizational forms is leading from the matrix and the network to the cellular (also called modular) organizational form. According to Miles and Snow et al., "a **cellular organization** is composed of cells (self-managing teams, autonomous business units, etc.) which can operate alone but which can interact with other cells to produce a more potent and competent business mechanism." This combination of independence and interdependence allows the cellular/modular organizational form to generate and share the knowledge and expertise needed to produce continuous innovation. The cellular/modular form includes the dispersed entrepreneurship of the divisional structure, customer responsiveness of the matrix, and self-organizing knowledge and asset sharing of the network.[57] Bombardier, for example, broke up the design of its Continental business jet into 12 parts provided by internal divisions and external contractors. The cockpit, center, and forward fuselage were produced in-house, but other major parts were supplied by manufacturers spread around the globe. The cellular/modular structure is used when it is possible to break up a company's products into self-contained modules or cells and where interfaces can be specified such that the cells/modules work when they are joined together.[58] The cellular/modular structure is similar to a current trend in industry of using internal joint ventures to temporarily combine specialized expertise and skills within a corporation to accomplish a task which individual units alone could not accomplish.[59]

The impetus for such a new structure is the pressure for a continuous process of innovation in all industries. Each cell/module has an entrepreneurial responsibility to the larger organization. Beyond knowledge creation and sharing, the cellular/modular form adds value by keeping the firm's total knowledge assets more fully in use than any other type of structure.[60] It is beginning to appear in firms that are focused on rapid product and service innovation—providing unique or state-of-the-art offerings in industries such as automobile manufacture, bicycle production, consumer electronics, household appliances, power tools, computing products, and software.[61]

REENGINEERING AND STRATEGY IMPLEMENTATION

Reengineering is the radical redesign of business processes to achieve major gains in cost, service, or time. It is not in itself a type of structure, but it is an effective program to implement a turnaround strategy.

Business process reengineering strives to break away from the old rules and procedures that develop and become ingrained in every organization over the years. They may be a combination of policies, rules, and procedures that have never been seriously questioned because they were established years earlier. These may range from "Credit decisions are made by the credit department" to "Local inventory is needed for good customer service." These rules of organization and work design may have been based on assumptions about technology, people, and organizational goals that may no longer be relevant. Rather than attempting to fix existing problems through minor adjustments and the fine-tuning of existing processes, the key to reengineering is asking "If this were a new company, how would we run this place?"

Michael Hammer, who popularized the concept of reengineering, suggests the following principles for reengineering:

- **Organize around outcomes, not tasks:** Design a person's or a department's job around an objective or outcome instead of a single task or series of tasks.

- **Have those who use the output of the process perform the process:** With computer-based information systems, processes can now be reengineered so that the people who need the result of the process can do it themselves.

- **Subsume information-processing work into the real work that produces the information:** People or departments that produce information can also process it for use instead of just sending raw data to others in the organization to interpret.

- **Treat geographically dispersed resources as though they were centralized:** With modern information systems, companies can provide flexible service locally while keeping the actual resources in a centralized location for coordination purposes.

- **Link parallel activities instead of integrating their results:** Instead of having separate units perform different activities that must eventually come together, have them communicate while they work so they can do the integrating.

- **Put the decision point where the work is performed and build control into the process:** The people who do the work should make the decisions and be self-controlling.

- **Capture information once and at the source:** Instead of having each unit develop its own database and information processing activities, the information can be put on a network so all can access it.[62]

Studies of the performance of reengineering programs show mixed results. Several companies have had success with business process reengineering. For example, the Mossville Engine Center, a business unit of Caterpillar Inc., used reengineering to decrease process cycle times by 50%, reduce the number of process steps by 45%, reduce human effort by 8%, and improve cross-divisional interactions and overall employee decision making.[63]

One study of North American financial firms found that "the average reengineering project took 15 months, consumed 66 person-months of effort, and delivered cost savings of 24%."[64] In a survey of 782 corporations using reengineering, 75% of the executives said their companies had succeeded in reducing operating expenses and increasing productivity.[65] A study of 134 large and small Canadian companies found that reengineering programs resulted in (1) an increase in productivity and product quality, (2) cost reductions, and (3) an increase in overall organization quality, for both large and small firms.[66] Other studies report, however, that anywhere from 50% to 70% of reengineering programs fail to achieve their objectives.[67] Reengineering thus appears to be more useful for redesigning specific processes like order entry, than for changing an entire organization.[68]

SIX SIGMA

Originally conceived by Motorola as a quality improvement program in the mid-1980s, Six Sigma has become a cost-saving program for all types of manufacturers. Briefly, **Six Sigma** is an analytical method for achieving near-perfect results on a production line. Although the emphasis is on reducing product variance in order to boost quality and efficiency, it is increasingly being applied to accounts receivable, sales, and R&D. In statistics, the Greek letter *sigma* denotes variation in the standard bell-shaped curve. One sigma equals 690,000 defects per 1 million. Most companies are able to achieve only three sigma, or 66,000 defects per million. Six Sigma reduces the defects to only 3.4 defects per million—thus saving money by preventing waste. The process of Six Sigma encompasses five steps.

1. *Define* a process where results are poorer than average.
2. *Measure* the process to determine exact current performance.
3. *Analyze* the information to pinpoint where things are going wrong.
4. *Improve* the process and eliminate the error.
5. *Establish* controls to prevent future defects from occurring.[69]

Savings attributed to Six Sigma programs have ranged from 1.2% to 4.5% of annual revenue for a number of Fortune 500 firms. Firms that have successfully employed Six Sigma include General Electric, Allied Signal, ABB, and Ford Motor Company.[70] Fifty-three percent of the Fortune 500 companies now have a Six Sigma program in place and more than 83% of the Fortune 100 have it in place despite its manufacturing origins.[71] At Dow Chemical, each Six Sigma project has resulted in cost savings of US$500,000 in the first year. According to Jack Welch, GE's past CEO, Six Sigma is an appropriate change program for the entire organization.[72] Six Sigma experts at 3M have been able to speed up R&D and analyze why its top salespeople sold more than others. A disadvantage of the program is that training costs in the beginning may outweigh any savings. The expense of compiling and analyzing data, especially in areas where a process cannot be easily standardized, may exceed what is saved.[73] Another disadvantage is that Six Sigma can lead to less-risky incremental innovation based on previous work than on riskier "blue-sky" projects.[74]

A new program called *Lean Six Sigma* is becoming increasingly popular in companies. This program incorporates the statistical approach of Six Sigma with the lean manufacturing program originally developed by Toyota. Like reengineering, it includes the removal of unnecessary steps in any process and fixing those that remain. This is the "lean" addition to Six Sigma. Xerox used Lean Six Sigma to resolve a problem with a US$500,000 printing press it had just introduced. Teams from supply, manufacturing, and R&D used Lean Six Sigma to find the cause of the problem and to resolve it by working with a supplier to change the chemistry of the oil on a roller.[75]

DESIGNING JOBS TO IMPLEMENT STRATEGY

Organizing a company's activities and people to implement strategy involves more than simply redesigning a corporation's overall structure; it also involves redesigning the way jobs are done. With the increasing emphasis on reengineering, many companies are beginning to rethink their work processes with an eye toward phasing unnecessary people and activities out of the process. Process steps that have traditionally been performed sequentially can be improved by performing them concurrently using cross-functional work teams. Harley-Davidson, for example, has managed to reduce total plant employment by 25% while reducing by 50% the time needed to build a motorcycle. Restructuring through needing fewer people requires broadening the scope of jobs and encouraging teamwork. The design of jobs and subsequent job performance are, therefore, increasingly being considered as sources of competitive advantage.

Job design refers to the study of individual tasks in an attempt to make them more relevant to the company and to the employee(s). To minimize some of the adverse consequences of task specialization, corporations have turned to new job design techniques: *job enlargement* (combining tasks to give a worker more of the same type of duties to perform), *job rotation* (moving workers through several jobs to increase variety), *job characteristics* (using task characteristics to improve employee motivation), and *job enrichment* (altering the jobs by giving the worker more autonomy and control over activities). Although each of these methods has its adherents, no one method seems to work in all situations.

A good example of modern job design is the introduction of team-based production by the glass manufacturer Corning Inc., in its Blacksburg, Virginia, plant. With union approval, Corning reduced job classifications from 47 to 4 to enable production workers to rotate jobs after learning new skills. The workers were divided into 14-member teams that, in effect, managed themselves. The plant had only two levels of management: Plant Manager Robert Hoover and two line leaders who only advised the teams. Employees worked very demanding 12½;-hour shifts, alternating three-day and four-day weeks. The teams made managerial decisions, imposed discipline on fellow workers, and were required to learn three "skill modules" within two years or else lose their jobs. As a result of this new job design, a Blacksburg team, made up of workers with interchangeable skills, can retool a line to produce a different type of filter in only 10 minutes—six times faster than workers in a traditionally designed filter plant. The Blacksburg plant earned a US$2 million profit in its first eight months of production instead of losing the US$2.3 million projected for the startup period. The plant performed so well that Corning's top management acted to convert the company's 27 other factories to team-based production.[76]

International Issues in Strategy Implementation

An international company is one that engages in any combination of activities, from exporting/importing to full-scale manufacturing, in foreign countries. A **multinational corporation (MNC)**, in contrast, is a highly developed international company with a deep involvement throughout the world, plus a worldwide perspective in its management and decision making. For an MNC to be considered global, it must manage its worldwide operations as if they were totally interconnected. This approach works best when the industry has moved from being *multidomestic* (each country's industry is essentially separate from the same industry in other countries) to *global* (each country is a part of one worldwide industry).

The global MNC faces the dual challenge of achieving scale economies through standardization while at the same time responding to local customer differences.

The design of an organization's structure is strongly affected by the company's stage of development in international activities and the types of industries in which the company is involved. Strategic alliances may complement or even substitute for an internal functional activity. The issue of centralization versus decentralization becomes especially important for an MNC operating in both multidomestic and global industries.

INTERNATIONAL STRATEGIC ALLIANCES

Strategic alliances, such as joint ventures and licensing agreements, between an MNC and a local partner in a host country are becoming increasingly popular as a means by which a corporation can gain entry into other countries, especially less developed countries. The key to the successful implementation of these strategies is the selection of the local partner. Each party needs to assess not only the strategic fit of each company's project strategy but also the fit of each company's respective resources. A successful joint venture may require as much as two years of prior contacts between the parties. A prior relationship helps to develop a level of trust, which facilitates openness in sharing knowledge and a reduced fear of opportunistic behavior by the alliance partners. This is especially important when the environmental uncertainty is high.[77] Research reveals that firms favor past partners when forming new alliances.[78]

Key drivers for strategic fit between alliance partners are the following:

- Partners must agree on fundamental values and have a shared vision about the potential for joint value creation.
- Alliance strategy must be derived from business, corporate, and functional strategy.
- The alliance must be important to both partners, especially to top management.
- Partners must be mutually dependent for achieving clear and realistic objectives.
- Joint activities must have added value for customers and the partners.
- The alliance must be accepted by key stakeholders.
- Partners contribute key strengths but protect core competencies.[79]

STAGES OF INTERNATIONAL DEVELOPMENT

Corporations operating internationally tend to evolve through five common stages, both in their relationships with widely dispersed geographic markets and in the manner in which they structure their operations and programs. These **stages of international development** are:

- **Stage 1 (Domestic company):** The primarily domestic company exports some of its products through local dealers and distributors in the foreign countries. The impact on the organization's structure is minimal because an export department at corporate headquarters handles everything.

- **Stage 2 (Domestic company with export division):** Success in Stage 1 leads the company to establish its own sales company with offices in other countries to eliminate the middlemen and to better control marketing. Because exports have now become more important, the company establishes an export division to oversee foreign sales offices.

- **Stage 3 (Primarily domestic company with international division):** Success in earlier stages leads the company to establish manufacturing facilities in addition to sales and service offices in key countries. The company now adds an international division with responsibilities for most of the business functions conducted in other countries.

- **Stage 4 (Multinational corporation with multidomestic emphasis):** Now a full-fledged MNC, the company increases its investments in other countries. The company establishes a local operating division or company in the host country, such as Ford of Britain, to better serve the market. The product line is expanded, and local manufacturing capacity is established. Managerial functions (product development, finance, marketing, and so on) are organized locally. Over time, the parent company acquires other related businesses, broadening the base of the local operating division. As the subsidiary in the host country successfully develops a strong regional presence, it achieves greater autonomy and self-sufficiency. The operations in each country are, nevertheless, managed separately as if each is a domestic company.

- **Stage 5 (MNC with global emphasis):** The most successful MNCs move into a fifth stage in which they have worldwide human resources, R&D, and financing strategies. Typically operating in a global industry, the MNC denationalizes its operations and plans product design, manufacturing, and marketing around worldwide considerations. Global considerations now dominate organizational design. The global MNC structures itself in a matrix form around some combination of geographic areas, product lines, and functions. All managers are responsible for dealing with international as well as domestic issues.

GLOBAL issue

OUTSOURCING COMES FULL CIRCLE

What happens when international companies who have developed their business model on cheaper labor in remote countries have to hire employees back in the originating country because the work demands local labor? That is exactly what is happening to many Indian firms who established their businesses as U.S. companies were seeking highly skilled, well-educated employees who worked for one-tenth the wage of U.S. workers. This was the classic cost-cutting model of the past two decades and no area on earth benefited as much as India. In 2011, U.S. companies spent just shy of US$28 billion on outsourcing.

The mood of the U.S. swung during the recession of 2009–2011 and the U.S. instituted tough new regulations limiting the number of foreign nationals who could work in the United States. This effort coincided with a wave of companies trying to pitch speed, local knowledge, and U.S. employment growth as competitive factors in their business.

In 2012, Bangalore-based Infosys acquired Marsh Consumer BPO and its 87 employees based in Des Moines, Iowa, and the gigantic Cognizant Technology Solutions, which, while based in New Jersey, has most of its 145,000 employees in India, and acquired centers in Iowa and North Dakota employing almost 1000 employees. Tata Consultancy Services employees 93% of their staff in India and less than 1% in the United States.

Bloomberg Businessweek pointed out that "with jobs and outsourcing such hot political issues in the U.S., it pays for Indian companies to hire some Americans, even though they're more expensive." The complexity of managing the workforces and catering to clients that simultaneously want cost controls, efficient work, and local expertise can be daunting.

....

SOURCES: "Indian Companies Seek a Passage to America," *Bloomberg Businessweek* (October 29, 2012), pp. 26–27; D. Thoppil, "Indian Outsourcing Firms Hire in the U.S.," *The Wall Street Journal* (August 7, 2012); http://online.wsj.com/article/SB1 0000872396390443517104577572930208453186.html.

Research provides some support for stages of international development, but it does not necessarily support the preceding sequence of stages. For example, a company may initiate production and sales in multiple countries without having gone through the steps of exporting or having local sales subsidiaries. In addition, any one corporation can be at different stages simultaneously, with different products in different markets at different levels. Firms may also leapfrog across stages to a global emphasis. In addition, most firms that are considered to be stage 5 global MNCs are actually regional. Around 88% of the world's biggest MNCs derive at least half of their sales from their home regions. Just 2% (a total of nine firms) derive 20% or more of their sales from each of the North American, European, and Asian regions.[80]

Developments in information technology are changing the way business is being done internationally. See the **Global Issue** feature to learn about the latest issue related to international outsourcing of IT.

The stages concept provides a useful way to illustrate some of the structural changes corporations undergo when they increase their involvement in international activities.

CENTRALIZATION VERSUS DECENTRALIZATION

A basic dilemma an MNC faces is how to organize authority centrally so it operates as a vast interlocking system that achieves synergy and at the same time decentralize authority so that local managers can make the decisions necessary to meet the demands of the local market or host government.[81] To deal with this problem, MNCs tend to structure themselves either along product groups or geographic areas. They may even combine both in a matrix structure—the design chosen by 3M Corporation, Philips, and Asea Brown Boveri (ABB), among others.[82]

One side of 3M's matrix represents the company's product divisions; the other side includes the company's international country and regional subsidiaries.

Two examples of the usual international structure are Nestlé and American Cyanamid. Nestlé's structure is one in which significant power and authority have been decentralized to geographic entities. This structure is similar to that depicted in **Figure 9–2**, in which each geographic set of operating companies has a different group of products. In contrast, American Cyanamid has a series of centralized product groups with worldwide responsibilities. To depict Cyanamid's structure, the geographical entities in **Figure 9–2** would have to be replaced by product groups or SBUs.
The **product-group structure** of American Cyanamid enables the company to introduce and manage a similar line of products around the world. This enables the corporation to centralize decision making along product lines and to reduce costs. The **geographic-area structure** of Nestlé, in contrast, allows the company to tailor products to regional differences and to achieve regional coordination. For instance, Nestlé markets 200 different varieties of its instant coffee, Nescafé. The geographic-area structure decentralizes decision making to the local subsidiaries.

As industries move from being multidomestic to more globally integrated, MNCs are increasingly switching from the geographic-area to the product-group structure. Nestlé, for example, found that its decentralized area structure had become increasingly inefficient. As a result, operating margins at Nestlé have trailed those at rivals Unilever, Group Danone, and Kraft Foods by as much as 50%. Then CEO Peter Brabeck-Letmathe acted to eliminate country-by-country responsibilities for many functions. In one instance, he established five centers worldwide to handle most coffee and cocoa purchasing.[83]

Simultaneous pressures for decentralization to be locally responsive and centralization to be maximally efficient are causing interesting structural adjustments in most large corporations. This is what is meant by the phrase "think globally, act locally." Companies are attempting to decentralize those operations that are culturally oriented and closest to the customers—manufacturing, marketing, and human resources. At the same time, the companies are consolidating less visible internal functions, such as research and development, finance, and information systems, where there can be significant economies of scale.

FIGURE 9–2
Geographic Area Structure for an MNC

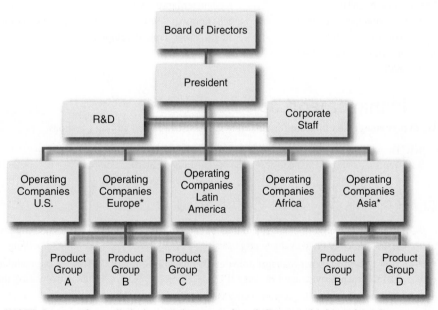

*NOTE: Because of space limitations, product groups for only Europe and Asia are shown here.

End of Chapter SUMMARY

Strategy implementation is where "the rubber hits the road." Environmental scanning and strategy formulation are crucial to strategic management but are only the beginning of the process. The failure to carry a strategic plan into the day-to-day operations of the workplace is a major reason why strategic planning often fails to achieve its objectives. It is discouraging to note that in one study nearly 70% of the strategic plans were never successfully implemented.[84]

For a strategy to be successfully implemented, it must be made action-oriented. This is done through a series of programs that are funded through specific budgets and contain new detailed procedures. This is what Sergio Marchionne did when he implemented a turnaround strategy as the new Fiat Group CEO in 2004. He attacked the lethargic, bureaucratic system by flattening Fiat's structure and giving younger managers a larger amount of authority and responsibility. He and other managers worked to reduce the number of auto platforms from 19 to six by 2012. The time from the completion of the design process to new car production was cut from 26 to 18 months. By 2008, the Fiat auto unit was again profitable. Marchionne reintroduced Fiat to the United States market in 2012 after a 27-year absence.[85]

This chapter explains how jobs and organizational units can be designed to support a change in strategy. We will continue with staffing and directing issues in strategy implementation in the next chapter.

MyManagementLab®

Go to **mymanagementlab.com** to complete the problems marked with this icon .

KEY TERMS

budget (p. 285)
cellular/modular organization (p. 297)
first mover (p. 282)
geographic-area structure (p. 303)
job design (p. 299)
late movers (p. 283)
market location tactic (p. 284)
matrix structure (p. 294)
multinational corporation (MNC)
   (p. 300)

network structure (p. 296)
organizational life cycle (p. 292)
procedure (p. 286)
product-group structure (p. 303)
program (p. 282)
reengineering (p. 297)
Six Sigma (p. 298)
stages of corporate development
   (p. 289)

stages of international development
   (p. 301)
strategy implementation (p. 280)
structure follows strategy (p. 287)
synergy (p. 286)
timing tactic (p. 282)
virtual organization (p. 296)

MyManagementLab®

Go to **mymanagementlab.com** for the following Assisted-graded writing questions:

9-1. How do timing tactics impact the strategy implementation efforts of a company?
9-2. What issues would you consider to be the most important for a company that is considering the use of a functional structure?

DISCUSSION QUESTIONS

9-3. What is the matrix of change, and how often do managers implement it to evaluate proposals?

9-4. How should an owner-manager prepare a company for its movement from Stage I to Stage II?

9-5. Show how reengineering as promoted by Michael Hammer is an appropriate method of strategy implementation.

9-6. Is reengineering just another management fad, or does it offer something of lasting value?

9-7. How is the cellular/modular structure different from the network structure?

STRATEGIC PRACTICE EXERCISE

Offense and Defense

Set Up

The instructor/moderator needs to prepare a series of cards. One set of cards (five of them) are marked with "Offense" on one side and "frontal assault," "flanking maneuver," "by-pass attack," "encirclement," or "guerrilla warfare" on the other. The second set of cards (three of them) are marked with "Defense" on one side and "structural barrier," "increase expected retaliation," or "lower inducement for attack" on the other side. The third set of cards should comprise of pairs of cards with the names of competitors in either the local or regional market. The instructor will need to make as many of the third set of pairs as there are groups in the class.

The instructor/moderator should also set up a relevant number of chairs either side of a table at the front of the class for the head-to-head encounters.

Procedure

The instructor/moderator should divide the class into teams of three to five people. The names of the competitor pairs of businesses are revealed to the class. Each group should then be allocated one of the businesses. There needs to be an even number of groups. The groups will now know who they will be paired against in the head-to-head part of the exercise.

The groups should be told to consider potential offensive and defensive tactics that the businesses could take. The instructor/moderator should allow the groups 15 minutes to come up with a series of potential tactics.

Once this time is up, the first pair of groups is called to the head-to-head table. The instructor/moderator can decide which of the two groups is going to present offensive and defensive strategies.

The "Offense" pack is shuffled and the team picks the card from the top. This will determine the offensive tactic it need to present to the other team. The "Defense" pack is also shuffled and the Defense team takes the card from the top of the pack. This will determine the defensive tactic that it must use to combat the offensive move from its competitor. If the team chooses the "structural barriers" card, then it can choose any of the tactics outlined by Porter (p. 253).

The Offense team is given five minutes to present its offensive move to take market share away from the Defense team's business. Likewise, the Defense team is then given five minutes to outline its defensive tactic to combat the attack.

The instructor/moderator must then call time. The other groups are then asked to vote on which team they think has presented the most compelling argument, and whether its tactics would work in the situation presented.

The head-to-head encounters continue until all of the groups have had a chance to either make an offensive or defensive presentation. If time permits, then the roles should be reversed with all the Offense teams becoming Defense teams in the next round of head-to-heads.

Notes

Ideally, pairs of competing businesses should be drawn from the broadest possible range of markets and industries. Care should be taken to choose businesses that most of the class will have some knowledge and understanding of, as well as be aware of their strengths and weaknesses. This exercise could be preceded by the issuing of brief notes on the backgrounds and strategic directions of the businesses, or the class could be instructed to research specific businesses in advance with this exercise in mind.

NOTES

1. J. W. Gadella, "Avoiding Expensive Mistakes in Capital Investment," *Long Range Planning* (April 1994), pp. 103–110; B. Voss, "World Market Is Not for Everyone," *Journal of Business Strategy* (July/August 1993), p. 4.
2. A. Bert, T. MacDonald, and T. Herd, "Two Merger Integration Imperatives: Urgency and Execution," *Strategy & Leadership*, Vol. 31, No. 3 (2003), pp. 42–49.
3. L. D. Alexander, "Strategy Implementation: Nature of the Problem," *International Review of Strategic Management*, Vol. 2, No. 1, edited by D. E. Hussey (New York: John Wiley & Sons, 1991), pp. 73–113. See also L. G. Hrebiniak, "Obstacles to Effective Strategy Implementation," *Organizational Dynamics* (Vol. 35, Issue 1, 2006), pp. 12–31 for six obstacles to implementation.
4. L. G. Hrebiniak (2006).
5. F. Arner and A. Aston, "How Xerox Got Up to Speed," *Bloomberg Businessweek* (May 3, 2004), pp. 103–104.
6. J. Darragh and A. Campbell, "Why Corporate Initiatives Get Stuck?" *Long Range Planning* (February 2001), pp. 33–52.
7. P. C. Nutt, "Surprising But True: Half the Decisions in Organizations Fail," *Academy of Management Executive* (November 1999), pp. 75–90.
8. Some refer to this as the economic concept of "increasing returns." Instead of the curve leveling off when the company reaches a point of diminishing returns when a product saturates a market, the curve continues to go up as the company takes advantage of setting the standard to spin off new products that use the new standard to achieve higher performance than competitors. See J. Alley, "The Theory That Made Microsoft," *Fortune* (April 29, 1996), pp. 65–66.
9. H. Lee, K. G. Smith, C. M. Grimm and A. Schomburg, "Timing, Order and Durability of New Product Advantages with Imitation," *Strategic Management Journal* (January 2000), pp. 23–30; Y. Pan and P. C. K. Chi, "Financial Performance and Survival of Multinational Corporations in China," *Strategic Management Journal* (April 1999), pp. 359–374; R. Makadok, "Can First-Mover and Early-Mover Advantages Be Sustained

in an Industry with Low Barriers to Entry/Imitation?" *Strategic Management Journal* (July 1998), pp. 683–696; B. Mascarenhas, "The Order and Size of Entry into International Markets," *Journal of Business Venturing* (July 1997), pp. 287–299.

10. At these respective points, cost disadvantages vis-à-vis later entrants fully eroded the earlier returns to first movers. See W. Boulding and M. Christen, "Idea—First Mover Disadvantage," *Harvard Business Review* (Vol. 79, No. 9, 2001), pp. 20–21 as reported by D. J. Ketchen Jr., C. C. Snow, and V. L. Hoover, "Research on Competitive Dynamics: Recent Accomplishments and Future Challenges," *Journal of Management* (Vol. 30, No. 6, 2004), pp. 779–804.

11. M. B. Lieberman and D. B. Montgomery, "First-Mover (Dis) Advantages: Retrospective and Link with the Resource-Based View," *Strategic Management Journal* (December, 1998), pp. 1111–1125; G. J. Tellis and P. N. Golder, "First to Market, First to Fail? Real Causes of Enduring Market Leadership," *Sloan Management Review* (Winter 1996), pp. 65–75.

12. J. Pope, "Schick Entry May Work Industry into a Lather," *Des Moines Register* (May 15, 2003), p. 6D.

13. S. K. Ethiraj and D. H. Zhu, "Performance Effects of Imitative Entry," *Strategic Management Journal* (August 2008), pp. 797–817; G. Dowell and A. Swaminathan, "Entry Timing, Exploration, and Firm Survival in the Early U.S. Bicycle Industry," *Strategic Management Journal* (December 2006), pp. 1159–1182. For an in-depth discussion of first- and late-mover advantages and disadvantages, see D. S. Cho, D. J. Kim, and D. K. Rhee, "Latecomer Strategies: Evidence from the Semiconductor Industry in Japan and Korea," *Organization Science* (July–August 1998), pp. 489–505.

14. J. Shamsie, C. Phelps, and J. Kuperman, "Better Late than Never: A Study of Late Entrants in Household Electrical Equipment," *Strategic Management Journal* (January 2004), pp. 69–84.

15. T. S. Schoenecker and A. C. Cooper, "The Role of Firm Resources and Organizational Attributes in Determining Entry Timing: A Cross-Industry Study," *Strategic Management Journal* (December 1998), pp. 1127–1143.

16. Summarized from various articles by L. Fahey in *The Strategic Management Reader*, edited by L. Fahey (Englewood Cliffs, NJ: Prentice Hall, 1989), pp. 178–205.

17. M. Boyle, "Dueling Diapers," *Fortune* (February 17, 2003), pp. 115–116.

18. C. Edwards, "To See Where Tech Is Headed, Watch TI," *Bloomberg Businessweek* (November 6, 2006), p. 74.

19. P. Burrows, "Show Time," *Bloomberg Businessweek* (February 2, 2004), pp. 56–64.

20. A. Serwer, "Happy Birthday, Steinway," *Fortune* (March 17, 2003), pp. 94–97.

21. "Programmed for a Fight," *The Economist* (October 20, 2007), p. 85.

22. This information on defensive tactics is summarized from M. E. Porter, *Competitive Advantage* (New York: The Free Press, 1985), pp. 482–512.

23. H. D. Hopkins, "The Response Strategies of Dominant U.S. Firms to Japanese Challengers," *Journal of Management* (Vol. 29, No. 1, 2003), pp. 5–25.

24. For additional information on defensive competitive tactics, see G. Stalk, "Curveball Strategies to Fool the Competition," *Harvard Business Review* (September 2006), pp. 115–122.

25. "Cocoa Farming: Fair Enough?" *The Economist* (February 2, 2008), p. 74.

26. M. S. Feldman and B. T. Pentland, "Reconceptualizing Organizational Routines as a Source of Flexibility and Change," *Administrative Science Quarterly* (March 2003), pp. 94–118.

27. S. F. Slater and E. M. Olson, "Strategy Type and Performance: The Influence of Sales Force Management," *Strategic Management Journal* (August 2000), pp. 813–829.

28. B. Grow, "Thinking Outside the Box," *Bloomberg Businessweek* (October 25, 2004), pp. 70–72.

29. http://www.google.com/about/company/.

30. A. D. Chandler, *Strategy and Structure* (Cambridge, MA: MIT Press, 1962).

31. A. P. Sloan Jr., *My Years with General Motors* (Garden City, NY: Doubleday, 1964).

32. T. L. Amburgey and T. Dacin, "As the Left Foot Follows the Right? The Dynamics of Strategic and Structural Change," *Academy of Management Journal* (December 1994), pp. 1427–1452; M. Ollinger, "The Limits of Growth of the Multidivisional Firm: A Case Study of the U.S. Oil Industry from 1930–90," *Strategic Management Journal* (September 1994), pp. 503–520.

33. "Arctic Cat 2012 First Quarter Net Sales Up 18 Percent," *Sled Racer.com* (2012), http://www.sledracer.com/2011/07/arctic-cat-2012-first-quarter-net-sales-up-18-percent/.

34. D. F. Jennings and S. L. Seaman, "High and Low Levels of Organizational Adaptation: An Empirical Analysis of Strategy, Structure, and Performance," *Strategic Management Journal* (July 1994), pp. 459–475; L. Donaldson, "The Normal Science of Structured Contingency Theory," in *Handbook of Organization Studies*, edited by S. R. Clegg, C. Hardy, and W. R. Nord (London: Sage Publications, 1996), pp. 57–76.

35. A. K. Gupta, "SBU Strategies, Corporate-SBU Relations, and SBU Effectiveness in Strategy Implementation," *Academy of Management Journal* (September 1987), pp. 477–500.

36. L. E. Greiner, "Evolution and Revolution as Organizations Grow," *Harvard Business Review* (May–June 1998), pp. 55–67. This is an updated version of Greiner's classic 1972 article.

37. K. Shimizu and M. A. Hitt, "What Constrains or Facilitates Divestitures of Formerly Acquired Firms? The Effects of Organizational Inertia," *Journal of Management* (February 2005), pp. 50–72.

38. A. Weintraub, "Can Pfizer Prime the Pipeline?" *Bloomberg Businessweek* (December 31, 2007), pp. 90–91.

39. Ibid, p. 64. Although Greiner simply labeled this as the *"?" crisis*, the term *pressure-cooker* seems apt.

40. J. Hamm, "Why Entrepreneurs Don't Scale," *Harvard Business Review* (December 2002), pp. 110–115. See also C. B. Gibson and R. M. Rottner, "The Social Foundations for Building a Company Around an Inventor," *Organizational Dynamics* (Vol. 37, Issue 1, January–March 2008), pp. 21–34.

41. W. P. Barnett, "The Dynamics of Competitive Intensity," *Administrative Science Quarterly* (March 1997), pp. 128–160; D. Miller, *The Icarus Paradox: How Exceptional Companies Bring About Their Own Downfall* (New York: Harper Business, 1990).

42. D. Miller and P. H. Friesen, "A Longitudinal Study of the Corporate Life Cycle," *Management Science* (October 1984), pp. 1161–1183.

43. J. L. Morrow Jr., D. G. Sirmon, M. A. Hitt, and T. R. Holcomb, "Creating Value in the Face of Declining Performance: Firm Strategies and Organizational Recovery," *Strategic Management Journal* (March 2007), pp. 271–283; C. Zook, "Finding

Your Next Core Business," *Harvard Business Review* (April 2007), pp. 66–75.

44. J. P. Sheppard and S. D. Chowdhury, "Riding the Wrong Wave: Organizational Failure as a Failed Turnaround," *Long Range Planning* (June 2005), pp. 239–260.

45. W-R. Chen and K. D. Miller, "Situational and Institutional Determinants of Firms' R&D Search Intensity," *Strategic Management Journal* (April 2007), pp. 369–381.

46. S. Hamm, "Kodak's Moment of Truth," *Bloomberg Businessweek* (February 19, 2007), pp. 42–49.

47. A. Martin, "Negative Exposure for Kodak," *The New York Times* (October 20, 2011), http://www.nytimes.com/2011/10/21/business/kodaks-bet-on-its-printers-fails-to-quell-the-doubters.html?pagewanted=all&_r=0.

48. R. Berner, "Turning Kmart into a Cash Cow," *Bloomberg Businessweek* (July 12, 2004), p. 81.

49. H. Tavakolian, "Bankruptcy: An Emerging Corporate Strategy," *SAM Advanced Management Journal* (Spring 1995), p. 19.

50. L. G. Hrebiniak and W. F. Joyce, *Implementing Strategy* (New York: Macmillan, 1984), pp. 85–86.

51. S. M. Davis and P. R. Lawrence, *Matrix* (Reading, MA: Addison-Wesley, 1977), pp. 11–24.

52. J. G. March, "The Future Disposable Organizations and the Rigidities of Imagination," *Organization* (August/November 1995), p. 434.

53. M. A. Schilling and H. K. Steensma, "The Use of Modular Organizational Forms: An Industry-Level Analysis," *Academy of Management Journal* (December 2001), pp. 1149–1168.

54. M. P. Koza and A. Y. Lewin, "The Coevolution of Network Alliances: A Longitudinal Analysis of an International Professional Service Network," *Organization Science* (September/October 1999), pp. 638–653.

55. P. Engardio, "Mom-and-Pop Multinationals," *Bloomberg Businessweek* (July 14 and 21, 2008), pp. 77–78.

56. For more information on managing a network organization, see G. Lorenzoni and C Baden-Fuller, "Creating a Strategic Center to Manage a Web of Partners," *California Management Review* (Spring 1995), pp. 146–163.

57. R. E. Miles, C. C. Snow, J. A. Mathews, G. Miles, and H. J. Coleman Jr., "Organizing in the Knowledge Age: Anticipating the Cellular Form," *Academy of Management Executive* (November 1997), pp. 7–24.

58. N. Anand and R. L. Daft, "What Is the Right Organization Design?" *Organizational Dynamics* (Vol. 36, No. 4, 2007), pp. 329–344.

59. J. Naylor and M. Lewis, "Internal Alliances: Using Joint Ventures in a Diversified Company," *Long Range Planning* (October 1997), pp. 678–688.

60. G. Hoetker, "Do Modular Products Lead to Modular Organizations?" *Strategic Management Journal* (June 2006), pp. 501–518.

61. Anand and Daft, pp. 336–338.

62. Summarized from M. Hammer, "Reengineering Work: Don't Automate, Obliterate," *Harvard Business Review* (July–August 1990), pp. 104–112.

63. D. Paper, "BPR: Creating the Conditions for Success," *Long Range Planning* (June 1998), pp. 426–435.

64. S. Drew, "BPR in Financial Services: Factors for Success," *Long Range Planning* (October 1994), pp. 25–41.

65. "Do As I Say, Not As I Do," *Journal of Business Strategy* (May/June 1997), pp. 3–4.

66. L. Raymond and S. Rivard, "Determinants of Business Process Reengineering Success in Small and Large Enterprises: An Empirical Study in the Canadian Context," *Journal of Small Business Management* (January 1998), pp. 72–85.

67. K. Grint, "Reengineering History: Social Resonances and Business Process Reengineering," *Organization* (July 1994), pp. 179–201; A. Kleiner, "Revisiting Reengineering," *Strategy + Business* (3rd Quarter 2000), pp. 27–31.

68. E. A. Hall, J. Rosenthal, and J. Wade, "How to Make Reengineering *Really* Work," McKinsey Quarterly (1994, No. 2), pp. 107–128.

69. M. Arndt, "Quality Isn't Just for Widgets," *Bloomberg Businessweek* (July 22, 2002), pp. 72–73.

70. T. M. Box, "Six Sigma Quality: Experiential Learning," *SAM Advanced Management Journal* (Winter 2006), pp. 20–23.

71. L. Bodell, "5 Ways Process Is Killing Your Productivity," *Fast Company* (May 15, 2012), http://www.fastcompany.com/1837301/5-ways-process-killing-your-productivity.

72. J. Welch and S. Welch, "The Six Sigma Shotgun," *Bloomberg Businessweek* (May 21, 2007), p. 110.

73. Arndt, p. 73.

74. B. Hindo, "At 3M, a Struggle Between Efficiency and Creativity," *Bloomberg Businessweek IN* (June 11, 2007), pp. 8–16.

75. F. Arner and A. Aston, "How Xerox Got Up to Speed," *Bloomberg Businessweek* (May 3, 2004), pp. 103–104.

76. J. Hoerr, "Sharpening Minds for a Competitive Edge," *Bloomberg Businessweek* (December 17, 1990), pp. 72–78.

77. R. Krishnan, X. Martin, and N. G. Noorderhaven, "When Does Trust Matter to Alliance Performance," *Academy of Management Journal* (October 2006), pp. 894–917.

78. S. X. Li and T. J. Rowley, "Inertia and Evaluation Mechanisms in Interorganizational Partner Selection: Syndicate Formation Among U.S. Investment Banks," *Academy of Management Journal* (December 2002), pp. 1104–1119.

79. M. U. Douma, J. Bilderbeek, P. J. Idenburg, and J. K. Loise, "Strategic Alliances: Managing the Dynamics of Fit," *Long Range Planning* (August 2000), pp. 579–598; W. Hoffmann and R. Schlosser, "Success Factors of Strategic Alliances in Small and Medium-Sized Enterprises—An Empirical Survey," *Long Range Planning* (June 2001), pp. 357–381; Y. Luo, "How Important Are Shared Perceptions of Procedural Justice in Cooperative Alliances?" *Academy of Management Journal* (August 2005), pp. 695–709.

80. Alan M. Rugman, *The Regional Multinationals* (Cambridge, UK: Cambridge University Press, 2005); P. Ghemawat, "Regional Strategies for Global Leadership," *Harvard Business Review* (December 2005), pp. 98–108.

81. J. H. Taggart, "Strategy Shifts in MNC Subsidiaries," *Strategic Management Journal* (July 1998), pp. 663–681.

82. C. A. Bartlett and S. Ghoshal, "Beyond the M-Form: Toward a Managerial Theory of the Firm," *Strategic Management Journal* (Winter 1993), pp. 23–46.

83. C. Matlack, "Nestle Is Starting to Slim Down at Last," *Bloomberg Businessweek* (October 27, 2003), pp. 56–57; "Daring, Defying to Grow," *The Economist* (August 7, 2004), pp. 55–58.

84. J. Sterling, "Translating Strategy into Effective Implementation: Dispelling the Myths and Highlighting What Works," *Strategy & Leadership* (Vol. 31, No. 3, 2003), pp. 27–34.

85. "Rebirth of a Carmaker," *The Economist* (April 26, 2008), pp. 87–89; D. Kiley, "Fiat Headed Back to U.S. after 27 Years," *AOL Autos* (February 14, 2011), http://autos.aol.com/article/fiat-500-coming-to-america/.

strategy implementation: Staffing and Directing

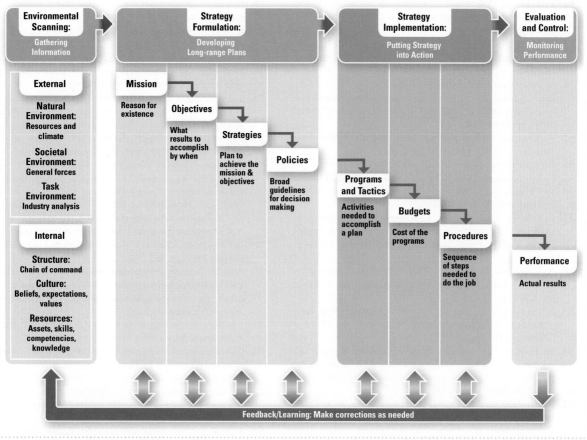

Environmental Scanning:	Strategy Formulation:	Strategy Implementation:	Evaluation and Control:
Gathering Information	Developing Long-range Plans	Putting Strategy into Action	Monitoring Performance

External

Natural Environment: Resources and climate

Societal Environment: General forces

Task Environment: Industry analysis

Internal

Structure: Chain of command

Culture: Beliefs, expectations, values

Resources: Assets, skills, competencies, knowledge

Mission — Reason for existence

Objectives — What results to accomplish by when

Strategies — Plan to achieve the mission & objectives

Policies — Broad guidelines for decision making

Programs and Tactics — Activities needed to accomplish a plan

Budgets — Cost of the programs

Procedures — Sequence of steps needed to do the job

Performance — Actual results

Feedback/Learning: Make corrections as needed

MyManagementLab®

⭐ Improve Your Grade!

Over 10 million students improved their results using the Pearson MyLabs. Visit **mymanagementlab.com** for simulations, tutorials, and end-of-chapter problems.

Learning Objectives

After reading this chapter, you should be able to:

- Understand the link between strategy and staffing decisions
- Match the appropriate manager to the strategy
- Understand how to implement an effective downsizing program
- Discuss important issues in effectively staffing and directing international expansion

- Assess and manage the corporate culture's fit with a new strategy
- Formulate effective action plans when MBO and TQM are determined to be appropriate methods of strategy implementation

Costco: Leading from the Front

Costco was founded in 1983 upon several simple foundations, such as marking everything up by no more than 15% (ever), paying and treating employees well, and providing a more upscale experience in the warehouse retail world. Today, the company is the largest (by sales) in the industry despite having fewer store locations than its rival Sam's Club. In 2011, the company racked up sales of US$93 billion and had more than 60 million members who pay for the privilege of shopping there.

One of the most stunning elements of the Costco success story is the way it has handled the staffing and leading elements of the business. Employees at the company make an average salary of US$20.89/hour and 88% of employees receive health care benefits even though half are part-time employees. During the recession that hit the globe from 2008–2011, the company had no layoffs. This has meant that the company enjoys some of the lowest turnover in an industry plagued by turnover. Employees at Costco know what they are doing and actively help customers.

Interestingly, the staffing model morphs into leading with the approach that the company takes to executive compensation. The former CEO and co-founder of Costco had a salary of only US$325,000/year and his total compensation package was US$2.2 million when the average for Fortune 500 CEOs in 2012 was US$9.6 million. The senior management team is similarly compensated, leading to an "all in for the good of the company" approach to the business.

In addition to leading with salary, the CEO made it a part of his yearly effort to visit all 560 stores in nine countries. This visible leading-from-the-front approach caught employees off guard when he would repeatedly jump in and work at the stores: cleaning, stocking, giving out food, and working the food court. In fact, the company has held tightly to the idea that a hot dog and soda should cost a patron no more than US$1.50. That was the price in 1985 when they opened their first hotdog stand in a store, and it is the price today. Costco sells more than 90 million hotdogs a year.

This chapter discusses strategy implementation in terms of staffing and leading. **Staffing** focuses on the selection and use of employees. **Leading** emphasizes the use of programs to better align employee interests and attitudes with a new strategy.

SOURCES: Stone, B. "How Cheap is Craig Jelinek," *Bloomberg BusinessWeek,* (June 10–16, 2013), pg. 54–60. C. Rexrode and B. Condon, "Average CEO Pay 2011 Nearly $10 Million at Public Companies: AP Study," *The Huffington Post* (May 25, 2012), http://www.huffingtonpost.com/2012/05/25/average-ceo-pay-2011_n_1545225.html; "The Costco Craze: Inside the Warehouse Giant," CNBC (2012), http://www.cnbc.com/id/46603589; "Fortune 50 CEO Pay vs. Our Salaries," Fortune (2012), http://money.cnn.com/magazines/fortune/fortune500/2012/ceo-pay-ratios/; A. Ruggeri, "Jim Sinegal: Costco CEO Focuses on Employees," *U.S. News & World Report* (October 22, 2009), http://www.usnews.com/news/best-leaders/articles/2009/10/22/jim-sinegal-costco-ceo-focuses-on-employees; T. Ferguson, "Sinegal Ends an Era at Costco," *Forbes* (September 1, 2011), http://www.forbes.com/sites/timferguson/2011/09/01/sinegal-ends-an-era-at-costco/.

Staffing

The implementation of new strategies and policies often calls for new human resource management priorities and a different use of personnel. Such staffing issues can involve hiring new people with new skills, firing people with inappropriate or substandard skills, and/or training existing employees to learn new skills. Research demonstrates that companies with enlightened talent-management policies and programs have higher returns on sales, investments, assets, and equity.[1] This is especially important given that the total U.S. market for talent acquisition is currently about US$124 billion and the average cost per hire is US$5700.[2]

If growth strategies are to be implemented, new people may need to be hired and trained. Experienced people with the necessary skills need to be found for promotion to newly created managerial positions. When a corporation follows a growth through acquisition strategy, it may find that it needs to replace several managers in the acquired company. The percentage of an acquired company's top management team that either quit or is asked to leave is around 25% after the first year, 35% after the second year, 48% after the third year, 55% after the fourth year, and 61% after five years.[3] In addition, executives who join an acquired company after the acquisition quit at significantly higher-than-normal rates beginning in their second year. Executives continue to depart at higher-than-normal rates for nine years after the acquisition.[4] Turnover rates of executives in firms acquired by foreign firms are significantly higher than for firms acquired by domestic firms, primarily in the fourth and fifth years after the acquisition.[5]

It is one thing to lose excess employees after a merger, but it is something else to lose highly skilled people who are difficult to replace. In a study of 40 mergers, 90% of the acquiring companies in the 15 successful mergers identified key employees and targeted them for retention within 30 days after the announcement. In contrast, this task was carried out only in one-third of the unsuccessful acquisitions.[6] To deal with integration issues such as these, some companies are appointing special **integration managers** to shepherd companies through the implementation process. The job of the integrator is to prepare a competitive profile of the combined company in terms of its strengths and weaknesses, draft an ideal profile of what the combined company should look like, develop action plans to close the gap between the actuality and the ideal, and establish training programs to unite the combined company and make it more competitive.[7] To be a successful integration manager, a person should have (1) a deep knowledge of the acquiring company, (2) a flexible management style, (3) an ability to work in cross-functional project teams, (4) a willingness to work independently, and (5) sufficient emotional and cultural intelligence to work well with people from all backgrounds.[8]

If a corporation adopts a retrenchment strategy, however, a large number of people may need to be laid off or fired (in many instances, being laid off is the same as being fired)—and top management, as well as the divisional managers, needs to specify the criteria to be used in making these personnel decisions. Should employees be fired on the basis of low seniority or on the basis of poor performance? Sometimes corporations find it easier to close or sell off an entire division than to choose which individuals to fire.

STAFFING FOLLOWS STRATEGY

As in the case of structure, staffing requirements should follow a change in strategy. For example, promotions should be based not only on current job performance but also on whether a person has the skills and abilities to do what is needed to implement the new strategy.

Changing Hiring and Training Requirements

Having formulated a new strategy, a corporation may find that it needs to either hire different people or retrain current employees to implement the new strategy. Consider the introduction of team-based production at Corning's filter plant mentioned in **Chapter 9**. Employee selection and training were crucial to the success of the new manufacturing strategy. Plant Manager Robert Hoover sorted through 8000 job applications before hiring 150 people with the best problem-solving abilities and a willingness to work in a team setting. Those selected received extensive training in technical and interpersonal skills. During the first year of production, 25% of all hours worked were devoted to training, at a cost of US$750,000.[9]

One way to implement a company's business strategy, such as overall low cost, is through training and development. According to the American Society of Training and Development, the average annual expenditure per employee on corporate training and development is US$1182 per employee.[10] A study of 155 U.S. manufacturing firms revealed that those with training programs had 19% higher productivity than those without such programs. Another study found that a doubling of formal training per employee resulted in a 7% reduction in scrap.[11] Training is especially important for a differentiation strategy emphasizing quality or customer service. At innovative online retailer Zappos, the whole company strategy is built around extraordinary customer service. Employees are screened and then screened again. At the end of each new employee training session, Zappos offers new employees US$4000 to quit. CEO Tony Hsieh said that about two to three percent of trainees accept that offer each year. They are not interested in employees that are simply there to get a paycheck. Training lasts seven weeks and there are tests along the way. A trainee has to graduate to be an employee.[12] Training is also important when implementing a retrenchment strategy. As suggested earlier, successful downsizing means that a company has to invest in its remaining employees. General Electric's Aircraft Engine Group used training to maintain its share of the market even though it had cut its workforce from 42,000 to 33,000 in the 1990s.[13]

Matching the Manager to the Strategy

Executive characteristics influence strategic outcomes for a corporation.[14] It is possible that a current CEO may not be appropriate to implement a new strategy. Research indicates that there may be a career life cycle for top executives. During the early years of executives' tenure, for example, they tend to experiment intensively with product lines to learn about their business. This is their learning stage. Later, their accumulated knowledge allows them to reduce experimentation and increase performance. This is their harvest stage. They enter a decline stage in their later years, when they reduce experimentation still further, and performance declines. Thus, there is an inverted U-shaped relationship between top executive tenure and the firm's financial performance. Some executives retire before any decline occurs. Others stave off decline longer than their counterparts. Because the length of time spent in each stage varies among CEOs, it is up to the board to decide when a top executive should be replaced.[15]

The most appropriate type of general manager needed to effectively implement a new corporate or business strategy depends on the desired strategic direction of that firm or business unit. Executives with a particular mix of skills and experiences may be classified as an **executive type** and paired with a specific corporate strategy. For example, a corporation following a concentration strategy emphasizing vertical or horizontal growth would probably want an aggressive new chief executive with a great deal of experience in that particular industry—a *dynamic industry expert*. A diversification strategy, in contrast, might call for someone with an analytical mind who is highly knowledgeable in other industries and can manage diverse product lines—an *analytical portfolio manager*. A corporation choosing to follow a stability strategy would probably want as its CEO a *cautious profit planner*, a person with a conservative style, a production or engineering background, and experience with controlling budgets, capital expenditures, inventories, and standardization procedures.

Weak companies in a relatively attractive industry tend to turn to a type of challenge-oriented executive known as a *turnaround specialist* to save the company. Julia Stewart started her career as an IHOP (International House of Pancakes) waitress. Years later she left the Applebee's restaurant chain to become CEO of IHOP, she worked to rebuild the company with better food, better ads, and a better atmosphere. Six years later, a much improved IHOP acquired the struggling Applebee's restaurant chain. CEO Stewart vowed to turnaround Applebee's within a year by improving service and food quality and by focusing the menu on what the restaurant does best: riblets, burgers, and salads. She wanted Applebee's to again be the friendly, neighborhood bar and grill that it once was.[16]

If a company cannot be saved, a *professional liquidator* might be called on by a bankruptcy court to close the firm and liquidate its assets. This is what happened to Montgomery Ward Inc., the nation's first catalog retailer, which closed its stores for good in 2001, after declaring bankruptcy for the second time.[17] Research supports the conclusion that as a firm's environment changes, it tends to change the type of top executive needed to implement a new strategy.[18]

For example, during the 1990s when the emphasis was on growth in a company's core products/services, the most desired background for a U.S. CEO was either in marketing or international experience. With the current decade's emphasis on mergers, acquisitions, and divestitures, the most desired background is finance. Currently, one out of five American and UK CEOs are former Chief Financial Officers, twice the percentage during the previous decade.[19]

This approach is in agreement with Chandler, who proposes (see **Chapter 9**) that the most appropriate CEO of a company changes as a firm moves from one stage of development to another. Because priorities certainly change over an organization's life, successful corporations need to select managers who have skills and characteristics appropriate to the organization's particular stage of development and position in its life cycle. For example, founders of firms tend to have functional backgrounds in technological specialties, whereas successors tend to have backgrounds in marketing and administration.[20] A change in the environment leading to a change in a company's strategy also leads to a change in the top management team. For example, a change in the U.S. utility industry's environment in 1992 supporting internally focused, efficiency-oriented strategies, led to top management teams being dominated by older managers with longer company and industry tenure, and with efficiency-oriented backgrounds in operations, engineering, and accounting.[21] Research reveals that executives having a specific personality characteristic (external locus of control) are more effective in regulated industries than are executives with a different characteristic (internal locus of control).[22]

Other studies have found a link between the type of CEO and a firm's overall strategic type. (Strategic types were presented in **Chapter 4**). For example, successful prospector firms tended to be headed by CEOs from research/engineering and general management backgrounds. High-performance defenders tended to have CEOs with accounting/finance, manufacturing/production, and general management experience. Analyzers tended to have CEOs with a marketing/sales background.[23]

A study of 173 firms over a 25-year period revealed that CEOs in these companies tended to have the same functional specialization as the former CEO, especially when the past CEO's strategy continued to be successful. This may be a pattern for successful corporations.[24] In particular, it explains why so many prosperous companies tend to recruit their top executives from one particular area. At Procter & Gamble (P&G)—a good example of an analyzer firm—the route to the CEO's position has traditionally been through brand management, with a strong emphasis on marketing—and more recently international experience. In other firms, the route may be through manufacturing, marketing, accounting, or finance—depending on what the corporation has always considered its core capability (and its overall strategic orientation).

SELECTION AND MANAGEMENT DEVELOPMENT

Selection and development are important not only to ensure that people with the right mix of skills and experiences are initially hired but also to help them grow on the job so they might be prepared for future promotions. For an interesting view of executive selection, take a look at the Innovation Issue on keeping Apple "cool."

INNOVATION issue

HOW TO KEEP APPLE "COOL"

Arguably, one of the most iconic "cool" companies in the past few decades has to be Apple. The designs, the feel of the products, and the ease with which the products work has made the company a standout with consumers. The innovative demands of a company that has the "cool" cache requires a balance of creative new products while maintaining a feel for what it means to be an Apple product. Much of this innovative ability was attributed to cofounder Steve Jobs. With his death in 2011, the company turned to Steve Schiller (then–Vice President of Product Marketing) to maintain the cache of the brand. Inside Apple, Steve Schiller was known as "mini-me"—a reference from the Austin Powers films that equated Steve Schiller with Steve Jobs.

Apple determined long ago that it took a consistent and persistent voice to develop and maintain the look and feel of something that would be called an Apple. Eschewing the approach of much of corporate America, Apple places that authority in one person. This exposes the innovation engine of an organization to both a staffing issue as well as a leading issue.

Schiller has been referred to as overly controlling and virtually dictatorial. Insiders called him "Dr. NO" for the

way he dealt with most new ideas. While potentially a positive when controlling content, this approach may be seen as a reticence within the corporation to be creative. If anything happens to Schiller, the company would face a big issue if it tried to either pass the baton to another executive or revert to standard corporate practice and create guidelines for designers to follow. This is a very similar path to that taken by Sony as it transitioned in the 1990s. Unfortunately, SONY became mired in its own procedures and lost its cache as the "cool" product company.

In 2012, Apple released both the iPhone 5 and the iPad Mini. These products were viewed by most analysts as catch-up products because Apple had fallen behind. They looked like Apple products, but were virtually void of anything innovative.

Does Apple still have that "cool" feel to it? Are the products innovative?

SOURCES: P. Burrows and A. Satariano, "Can This Guy Keep Apple Cool?" *Bloomberg Businessweek* (June 11, 2012), pp. 47–48; http://www.apple.com/pr/bios/philip-w-schiller.html; E. Kolawole, "Apple Reveals iPhone 5: But Is It Innovative?" *The Washington Post* (September 12, 2012), http://www.washingtonpost.com/blogs/innovations/post/apple-reveals-iphone-5-but-is-it-innovative/2012/09/12/ffb257a4-fcda-11e1-8adc-499661afe377_blog.html.

Executive Succession: Insiders vs. Outsiders

Executive succession is the process of replacing a key top manager. The average tenure of a chief executive of a large U.S. company declined from nearly 10 years in 2000 to 8.4 years in 2011.[25] Given that two-thirds of all major corporations worldwide replace their CEO at least once in a five-year period, it is important that the firm plan for this eventuality.[26] It is especially important for a company that usually promotes from within to prepare its current managers for promotion. For example, companies using so-called "relay" executive succession, in which a particular candidate is groomed to take over the CEO position, have significantly higher performance than those that hire someone from the outside or hold a competition between internal candidates.[27] These "heirs apparent" are provided special assignments including membership on other firms' boards of directors.[28] Nevertheless, only half of large U.S. companies have CEO succession plans in place.[29]

Companies known for being excellent training grounds for executive talent are Allied-Signal, Bain & Company, Bankers Trust, Boeing, Bristol Myers Squibb, Cititcorp, General Electric, Hewlett-Packard, McDonald's, McKinsey & Company, Microsoft, Nike, Pfizer, and P&G. For example, one study showed that hiring 19 GE executives into CEO positions added US$24.5 billion to the share prices of the companies that hired them. One year after people from GE started their new jobs, 11 of the 19 companies they joined were outperforming their competitors and the overall market.[30]

Some of the best practices for top management succession are encouraging boards to help the CEO create a succession plan, identifying succession candidates below the top layer, measuring internal candidates against outside candidates to ensure the development of a comprehensive set of skills, and providing appropriate financial incentives.[31] Succession planning has become the most important topic discussed by boards of directors.[32]

Prosperous firms tend to look outside for CEO candidates only if they have no obvious internal candidates.[33] For example, 78% of the CEOs selected to run S&P 500 companies in 2011 were insiders, according to executive search firm Spencer Stuart.[34] Hiring an outsider to be a CEO is a risky gamble. CEOs from the outside tend to introduce significant change and high turnover among the current top management.[35] For example, in one study, the percentage of senior executives that left a firm after a new CEO took office was 20% when the new CEO was an insider, but increased to 34% when the new CEO was an outsider.[36] CEOs hired from outside the firm tend to have a low survival rate. According to RHR International, 40% to 60% of high-level executives brought in from outside a company failed within two years.[37] A study of 392 large U.S. firms revealed that only 16.6% of them had hired outsiders to be their CEOs. The outsiders tended to perform slightly worse than insiders but had a very high variance in performance. Compared to that of insiders, the performance of outsiders tended to be either very good or very poor. Although outsiders performed much better (in terms of shareholder returns) than insiders in the first half of their tenures, they did much worse in their second half. As a result, the average tenure of an outsider was significantly less than for insiders.[38]

Firms in trouble, however, overwhelmingly choose outsiders to lead them.[39] For example, one study of 22 firms undertaking turnaround strategies over a 13-year period found that the CEO was replaced in all but two companies. Of 27 changes of CEO (several firms had more than one CEO during this period), only seven were insiders—20 were outsiders.[40] The probability of an outsider being chosen to lead a firm in difficulty increases if there is no internal heir apparent, if the last CEO was fired, and if the board of directors is composed of a large percentage of outsiders.[41] Boards realize that the best way to force a change in strategy is to hire a new CEO who has no connections to the current strategy.[42] For example, outsiders have been found to be very effective in leading strategic change for firms in Chapter 11 bankruptcy.[43]

Identifying Abilities and Potential

A company can identify and prepare its people for important positions in several ways. One approach is to establish a sound *performance appraisal system* to identify good performers with promotion potential. A survey of 34 corporate planners and human resource executives from 24 large U.S. corporations revealed that approximately 80% made some attempt to identify managers' talents and behavioral tendencies so they could place a manager with a likely fit to a given competitive strategy.[44] Companies select those people with promotion potential to be in their executive development training program. GE's spends more than US$1 billion per year for employee training at the company's famous Leadership Development Center in Crotonville, New York.[45] Doug Pelino, chief talent officer at Xerox, keeps a list of about 100 managers in middle management and at the vice presidential levels who have been selected to receive special training, leadership experience, and mentorship to become the next generation of top management.[46]

A company should examine its human resource system to ensure not only that people are being hired without regard to their racial, ethnic, or religious background, but also that they are being identified for training and promotion in the same manner. Management diversity can be a competitive advantage in a multi-ethnic world. With more women in the workplace, an increasing number are moving into top management, but are demanding more flexible career ladders to allow for family responsibilities.

Many large organizations are using *assessment centers* to evaluate a person's suitability for an advanced position. Corporations such as AT&T, Standard Oil, IBM, Sears, and GE have successfully used assessment centers. Because each is specifically tailored to its corporation, these assessment centers are unique. They use special interviews, management games, in-basket exercises, leaderless group discussions, case analyses, decision-making exercises, and oral presentations to assess the potential of employees for specific positions. Promotions into these positions are based on performance levels in the assessment center. Assessment centers have generally been able to accurately predict subsequent job performance and career success.[47]

Job rotation—moving people from one job to another—is also used in many large corporations to ensure that employees are gaining the appropriate mix of experiences to prepare them for future responsibilities. Rotating people among divisions is one way that a corporation can improve the level of organizational learning. General Electric, for example, routinely rotates its executives from one sector to a completely different one to learn the skills of managing in different industries. Jeffrey Immelt, who took over as CEO from Jack Welch, had managed businesses in plastics, appliances, and medical systems.[48] Companies that pursue related diversification strategies through internal development make greater use of interdivisional transfers of people than do companies that grow through unrelated acquisitions. Apparently, the companies that grow internally attempt to transfer important knowledge and skills throughout the corporation in order to achieve some sort of synergy.[49]

PROBLEMS IN RETRENCHMENT

In May 2012, Hewlett-Packard announced that it would lay off 27,000 employees (almost 8% of its workforce) in an effort to return the company to health. Meanwhile, major U.S. retail chains like Sears, Blockbuster, The Gap, and Abercrombie & Fitch announced triple-digit store closing plans for 2012.[50] **Downsizing** (sometimes called "rightsizing" or "resizing") refers to the planned elimination of positions or jobs. This program is often used to implement retrenchment strategies. Because the financial community is likely to react favorably to announcements of downsizing from a company in difficulty, such a program may provide some short-term benefits such as raising the company's stock price. If not done properly, however, downsizing may result in less, rather than more, productivity. One study found that a 10% reduction in people resulted in only a 1.5% reduction in costs, profits increased in only half the firms downsizing, and the stock prices of downsized firms increased over three years, but not as much as did those of firms that did not downsize.[51] Why were the results so marginal?

A study of downsizing at automobile-related U.S. industrial companies revealed that at 20 out of 30 companies, either the wrong jobs were eliminated or blanket offers of early retirement prompted managers, even those considered invaluable, to leave. After the layoffs, the remaining employees had to do not only their work but also the work of the people who had gone. Because the survivors often didn't know how to do the work of those who had left the company, morale and productivity plummeted.[52] Downsizing can seriously damage the learning capacity of organizations.[53] Creativity drops significantly (affecting new product development), and it becomes very difficult to keep high performers from leaving the company.[54] In addition, cost-conscious executives tend to defer maintenance, skimp on training, delay new product introductions, and avoid risky new businesses—all of which leads to lower sales and eventually to lower profits.[55] These are some of the reasons why layoffs worry customers and have a negative effect on a firm's reputation.[56]

A good retrenchment strategy can thus be implemented well in terms of organizing but poorly in terms of staffing. A situation can develop in which retrenchment feeds on itself and acts to further weaken instead of strengthen the company. Research indicates that companies undertaking cost-cutting programs are four times more likely than others to cut costs again, typically by reducing staff.[57] This has been the story at such well-known operations like Sears, Gannet, RIM, HSBC, and Borders, which eventually went into bankruptcy.[58] In contrast, successful downsizing firms undertake a strategic reorientation, not just a bloodletting of employees. Research shows that when companies use downsizing as part of a larger restructuring program to narrow company focus, they enjoy better performance.[59] This was the situation at Starbucks in 2008 as it closed stores and laid off more than 7000 people in its effort to refocus the business on the coffee experience. In the ensuing years, the company roared back to life without having to revert to layoffs again.

Consider the following guidelines that have been proposed for successful downsizing:

- **Eliminate unnecessary work instead of making across-the-board cuts:** Spend the time to research where money is going and eliminate the task, not the workers, if it doesn't add value to what the firm is producing. Reduce the number of administrative levels rather than the number of individual positions. Look for interdependent relationships before eliminating activities. Identify and protect core competencies.

- **Contract out work that others can do cheaper:** For example, Bankers Trust of New York contracted out its mailroom and printing services and some of its payroll and accounts payable activities to a division of Xerox. Outsourcing may be cheaper than vertical integration.

- **Plan for long-run efficiencies:** Don't simply eliminate all postponable expenses, such as maintenance, R&D, and advertising, in the unjustifiable hope that the environment will become more supportive. Continue to hire, grow, and develop—particularly in critical areas.

- **Communicate the reasons for actions:** Tell employees not only why the company is downsizing but also what the company is trying to achieve. Promote educational programs.

- **Invest in the remaining employees:** Because most "survivors" in a corporate downsizing will probably be doing different tasks from what they were doing before the change, firms need to draft new job specifications, performance standards, appraisal techniques, and compensation packages. Additional training is needed to ensure that everyone has the proper skills to deal with expanded jobs and responsibilities. Empower key individuals/groups and emphasize team building. Identify, protect, and mentor people who have leadership talent.

- **Develop value-added jobs to balance out job elimination:** When no other jobs are currently available within the organization to transfer employees to, management must consider other staffing alternatives. For example, Harley-Davidson worked with the company's unions to find other work for surplus employees by moving into Harley plants work that had previously been done by suppliers.[60]

INTERNATIONAL ISSUES IN STAFFING

Implementing a strategy of international expansion takes a lot of planning and can be very expensive. Nearly 80% of midsize and larger companies send some of their employees abroad, and 45% plan to increase the number they have on foreign assignment. A complete package for one executive working in another country costs from US$300,000 to US$1 million annually. Nevertheless, between 10% and 20% of all U.S. managers sent abroad returned early because of job dissatisfaction or difficulties in adjusting to a foreign country. Of those who stayed for the duration of their assignment, nearly one-third did not perform as well as expected. One-fourth of those completing an assignment left their company within one year of returning home—often leaving to join a competitor.[61] One common mistake is failing to educate the person about the customs and values in other countries.

Primarily due to cultural differences, managerial style and human resource practices must be tailored to fit the particular situations in other countries. Only 11% of human resource managers have ever worked abroad, most have little understanding of a global assignment's unique personal and professional challenges and thus fail to develop the training necessary for such an assignment.[62] This is complicated by the fact that 90% of companies select employees for an international assignment based on their technical expertise while ignoring other areas.[63] A lack of knowledge of national and ethnic differences can make managing an international operation extremely difficult. One such example that shows the issues that have to be dealt with exists in Malaysia. Three ethnic groups live in Malaysia (Malay, Chinese, and Indian), each with their own language and religion, attending different schools, and a preference to not work in the same factories with each other. Because of the importance of cultural distinctions such as these, multinational corporations (MNCs) are now putting more emphasis on intercultural training for managers being sent on an assignment to a foreign country. This type of training is one of the commonly cited reasons for the lower expatriate failure rates—6% or less—for European and Japanese MNCs, which have emphasized cross-cultural experiences, compared with a 35% failure rate for U.S.-based MNCs.[64]

To improve organizational learning, many MNCs are providing their managers with international assignments lasting as long as five years. Upon their return to headquarters, these expatriates have an in-depth understanding of the company's operations in another part of the world. This has value to the extent that these employees communicate this understanding to others in decision-making positions. Research indicates that an MNC performs at a higher level when its CEO has international experience.[65] Global MNCs, in particular, emphasize international experience, have a greater number of senior managers who have been expatriates, and have a strong focus on leadership development through the expatriate experience.[66] Unfortunately, not all corporations appropriately manage international assignments. While out of the country, a person may be overlooked for an important promotion (out of sight, out of mind). Upon his or her return to the home country, co-workers may discount the out-of-country experience as a waste of time. The perceived lack of organizational support for international assignments increases the likelihood that an expatriate will return home early.[67]

One study of 750 U.S., Japanese, and European companies, found that the companies that do a good job of managing foreign assignments follow three general practices:

- When making international assignments, they focus on transferring knowledge and developing global leadership.

- They make foreign assignments to people whose technical skills are matched or exceeded by their cross-cultural abilities.

- They end foreign assignments with a deliberate repatriation process, with career guidance and jobs where the employees can apply what they learned in their assignments.[68]

Once a corporation has established itself in another country, it hires and promotes people from the host country into higher-level positions. For example, most large MNCs attempt to fill managerial positions in their subsidiaries with well-qualified citizens of the host countries. Unilever and IBM have traditionally taken this approach to international staffing. This policy serves to placate nationalistic governments and to better attune management practices to the host country's culture. The danger in using primarily foreign nationals to staff managerial positions in subsidiaries is the increased likelihood of suboptimization (the local subsidiary ignores the needs of the larger parent corporation). This makes it difficult for an MNC to meet its long-term, worldwide objectives. To a local national in an MNC subsidiary, the corporation as a whole can be an abstraction. Communication and coordination across subsidiaries become more difficult. As it becomes harder to coordinate the activities of several international subsidiaries, an MNC will have serious problems operating in a global industry.

Another approach to staffing the managerial positions of MNCs is to use people with an "international" orientation, regardless of their country of origin or host country assignment. This is a widespread practice among European firms. For example, Electrolux, a Swedish firm, had a French director in its Singapore factory. Using third-country "nationals" can allow for more opportunities for promotion than does Unilever's policy of hiring local people, but it can also result in more misunderstandings and conflicts with the local employees and with the host country's government.

Some corporations take advantage of immigrants and their children to staff key positions when negotiating entry into another country and when selecting an executive to manage the company's new foreign operations. For example, when General Motors wanted to learn more about business opportunities in China, it turned to Shirley Young, a Vice President of Marketing at GM. Born in Shanghai and fluent in Chinese language and customs, Young was instrumental in helping GM negotiate a US$1 billion joint venture with Shanghai Automotive to build a Buick plant in China. With other Chinese-Americans, Young formed a committee to advise GM on relations with China. Although just a part of a larger team of GM employees working on the joint venture, Young coached GM employees on Chinese customs and traditions.[69]

MNCs with a high level of international interdependence among activities need to provide their managers with significant international assignments and experiences as part of their training and development. Such assignments provide future corporate leaders with a series of valuable international contacts in addition to a better personal understanding of international issues and global linkages among corporate activities.[70] Research reveals that corporations using cross-national teams, whose members have international experience and communicate frequently with overseas managers, have greater product development capabilities than others.[71] Executive recruiters report that more major corporations are now requiring candidates to have international experience.[72] To increase its own top management's global expertise, Cisco Systems introduced a staffing program in 2007 with the objective of locating 20% of its senior managers at its new Bangalore, India, Globalization Center by 2010.[73]

Since an increasing number of multinational corporations are primarily organized around business units and product lines instead of geographic areas, product and SBU managers who are based at corporate headquarters are often traveling around the world to work personally with country managers. These managers and other mobile workers are being called *stealth expatriates* because they are either cross-border commuters (especially in the EU) or the accidental expatriate who goes on many business trips or temporary assignments due to offshoring and/or international joint ventures.[74]

Leading

Implementation also involves leading through coaching people to use their abilities and skills most effectively and efficiently to achieve organizational objectives. Without direction, people tend to do their work according to their personal view of what tasks should be done, how, and in what order. They may approach their work as they have in the past or emphasize those tasks that they most enjoy—regardless of the corporation's priorities. This can create real problems, particularly if the company is operating internationally and must adjust to customs and traditions in other countries. This direction may take the form of management leadership, communicated norms of behavior from the corporate culture, or agreements among workers in autonomous work groups. For an example of how a company can lead by radically changing the business model and the way it is staffed, see the **Sustainability Issue** feature. It may be accomplished more formally through action planning or through programs, such as Management By Objectives and Total Quality Management. Procedures can be changed to provide incentives to motivate employees to align their behavior with corporate objectives.

SUSTAINABILITY issue

PANERA AND THE "PANERA CARES COMMUNITY CAFÉ"

Sometimes the staffing model for a business can be adapted to provide long-term value to the community and help that company lead an industry. Panera Bread Company, with more than 1600 restaurants, had sales of more than US$1.8 billion and profits of US$136 million in 2011. The company had grown into an institution in the United States, catering to those who could afford to eat there (in other words, those who are employed). They steadfastly refused to lower prices during the latest recession and posted sales gains through that time period.

In an effort to lead in the business community as well as provide work for individuals in training programs supported by the company, Panera came up with a creative business approach when it opened its pilot "Panera Cares Community Café" in Clayton, Missouri, in 2010. Known by most as the "pay what you want" restaurant, the restaurant offered suggested donation levels instead of prices.

To make the business model work, the company created a foundation in order to separate it from the for-profit business. Consumers who are most able to pay are asked to donate extra, while those who are short on cash can pay less, and those who can't pay anything can volunteer for an hour to pay for their meal.

It is interesting to note that all three of the first locations in Clayton, Missouri, Dearborn, Michigan, and Portland, Oregon, turn a profit. The profit is used by the foundation to provide money to social service organizations that provide job training for at-risk youth. Panera then hires those who have received the training. This full-circle approach to staffing led Panera to convert two more stores—one in Chicago and one in Boston. The Chicago store was well known as the place where the founder wrote the company mission statement and he thought the location was perfect because it was a place where there are "million-dollar townhomes and people on the street."

·················

SOURCES: D. Goodison, "Pay-What-You-Can Panera Donation Café Will Grace Hub," (November 5, 2012), E. York, "Panera to Open First Local Pay-What-You-Can Café in Lakeview," *Chicago Tribune* (June 20, 2012), http://articles.chicagotribune.com/2012-06-20/business/chi-panera-adds-paywhatyoucan-cafe-in-chicago-20120620_1_ron-shaich-lakeview-open-first;http://www.panerabread.com/about/company/?ref=/about/community/index.php.

MANAGING CORPORATE CULTURE

Because an organization's culture can exert a powerful influence on the behavior of all employees, it can strongly affect a company's ability to shift its strategic direction. A problem for a strong culture is that a change in mission, objectives, strategies, or policies and tactics is not likely to be successful if it is in opposition to the accepted culture of the company. Corporate culture has a strong tendency to resist change because its very reason for existence often rests on preserving stable relationships and patterns of behavior. For example, when Robert Nardelli became CEO at The Home Depot in 2000, he changed the corporate strategy to growing the company's small professional supply business (sales to building contractors) through acquisitions and making the mature retail business cost-effective. He attempted to replace the old informal entrepreneurial collaborative culture with one of military efficiency. Before Nardelli's arrival, most store managers had based their decisions upon their personal knowledge of their customers' preferences. Under Nardelli, they were given weekly sales and profit targets. Underperforming managers were asked to leave the company. The once-heavy ranks of full-time employees were replaced with cheaper part-timers who had far less experience to help the DIY customer. In this "culture of fear," morale fell and The Home Depot's customer satisfaction score dropped to last place among major U.S. retailers. Nardelli was asked to leave the company in 2007 and the company's resurgence over the next four years as it moved back to its roots is a testament to the strength of corporate culture.

There is no one best corporate culture. An optimal culture is one that best supports the mission and strategy of the company of which it is a part. This means that *corporate culture should support the strategy.* Unless strategy is in complete agreement with the culture, any significant change in strategy should be followed by a modification of the organization's culture. Although corporate culture can be changed, it often takes a long time, and it requires a lot of effort. At The Home Depot, for example, CEO Nardelli attempted to change the corporate culture by hiring GE veterans like himself into top management positions, hiring ex-military officers as store managers, and instituting a top-down command structure.

A key job of management involves managing corporate culture. In doing so, management must evaluate what a particular change in strategy means to the corporate culture, assess whether a change in culture is needed, and decide whether an attempt to change the culture is worth the likely costs.

Assessing Strategy-Culture Compatibility

When implementing a new strategy, a company should take the time to assess *strategy-culture compatibility.* (See **Figure 10–1**.) Consider the following questions regarding a corporation's culture:

1. **Is the proposed strategy compatible with the company's current culture?** *If yes*, full steam ahead. Tie organizational changes into the company's culture by identifying how the new strategy will achieve the mission better than the current strategy does. *If not . . .*

2. **Can the culture be easily modified to make it more compatible with the new strategy?** *If yes*, move forward carefully by introducing a set of culture-changing activities such as minor structural modifications, training and development activities, and/or hiring new managers who are more compatible with the new strategy. When Proctor & Gamble's top management decided to implement a strategy aimed at reducing costs, for example, it made some changes in how things were done, but it did not eliminate its brand-management system. The culture adapted to these modifications over a couple of years and productivity increased. *If not . . .*

FIGURE 10–1 Assessing Strategy–Culture Compatibility

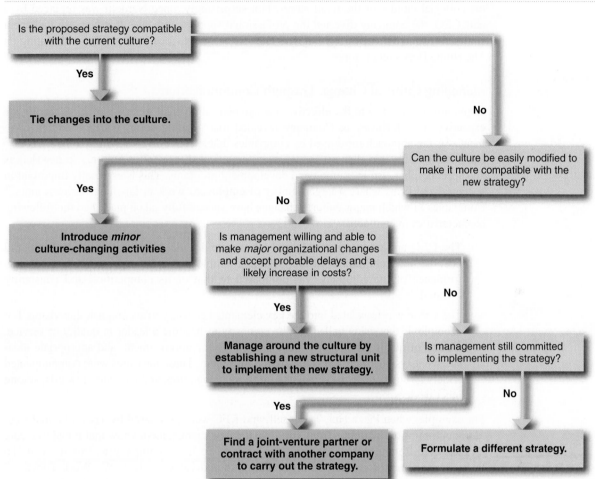

3. **Is management willing and able to make major organizational changes and accept probable delays and a likely increase in costs?** *If yes*, manage around the culture by establishing a new structural unit to implement the new strategy. In 2012, Saab Automobile Parts AB established a subsidiary to provide original parts in the United States after running into a decade of issues resulting from a lack of focus on U.S. Saab owners. By creating a separate subsidiary whose sole responsibility was providing U.S. customers with spare parts for their cars, the company was able to bypass the established focus of the company, which was clearly not on U.S. Saab owners. *If not . . .*

4. **Is management still committed to implementing the strategy?** *If yes*, find a joint-venture partner or contract with another company to carry out the strategy. *If not*, formulate a different strategy.

Based on Robert Nardelli's decisions when he initially started as The Home Depot's CEO, he probably answered "no" to the first question and "yes" to the second question—thus justifying his many changes in staffing and leading. Unfortunately, these changes didn't work very well. Instead, he should have replied "no" to the first and second questions and stopped at the third question. As suggested by this question, he should have considered a different corporate strategy, such as growing the professional side of the business without changing the collegial culture of the retail stores. Not surprisingly, once Nardelli was replaced by a new CEO, the company divested the professional supply companies that Nardelli had spent so much time and money acquiring and returned to its previous strategy of concentrating on The Home Depot retail stores.

Managing Cultural Change Through Communication

Communication is key to the effective management of change. A survey of 3199 worldwide executives by McKinsey & Company revealed that ongoing communication and involvement was the approach most used by companies that successfully transformed themselves.[75] Rationale for strategic changes should be communicated to workers not only in newsletters and speeches, but also in training and development programs. This is especially important in decentralized firms where a large number of employees work in far-flung business units.[76] Companies in which major cultural changes have successfully taken place had the following characteristics in common:

- The CEO and other top managers had a strategic vision of what the company could become and communicated that vision to employees at all levels. The current performance of the company was compared to that of its competition and constantly updated.

- The vision was translated into the key elements necessary to accomplish that vision. For example, if the vision called for the company to become a leader in quality or service, aspects of quality and service were pinpointed for improvement, and appropriate measurement systems were developed to monitor them. These measures were communicated widely through contests, formal and informal recognition, and monetary rewards, among other devices.[77]

For example, when Pizza Hut, Taco Bell, and KFC were purchased by Tricon Global Restaurants (now Yum! Brands) from PepsiCo, the new management knew that it had to create a radically different culture than the one at PepsiCo if the company was to succeed. To begin, management formulated a statement of shared values—"How We Work Together" principles. They declared their differences with the "mother country" (PepsiCo) and wrote a "Declaration of Independence" stating what the new company would stand for. Restaurant managers participated in team-building activities at the corporate headquarters and finished by signing the company's "Declaration of Independence" as "founders" of the company. Since then, "Founders Day" has become an annual event celebrating the culture of the company. Headquarters was renamed the "Restaurant Support Center," signifying the cultural value the restaurants held as the central focus of the company. People measures were added to financial measures and customer measures, reinforcing the "putting people first" value. In an unprecedented move in the industry, restaurant managers were given stock options and stock was added to the list of performance incentives. The company created values-focused 360-degree performance reviews, which were eventually pushed to the restaurant manager level.[78]

Managing Diverse Cultures Following an Acquisition

When merging with or acquiring another company, top management must give some consideration to a potential clash of corporate cultures. According to a Hewitt Associates survey of 218 major U.S. corporations, integrating culture was a top challenge for 69% of the reporting companies.[79] Cultural differences are even more problematic when a company acquires a firm in another country. Daimler-Benz has dealt with this on a number of occasions, including its merger with Chrysler in 1998 and its purchase of a controlling interest in Mitsubishi Motors in 2001. Resistance to change led Daimler-Benz to eject both organizations from the parent company.[80] It's dangerous to assume that the firms can simply be integrated into the same reporting structure. The greater the gap between the cultures of the acquired firm and the acquiring firm, the faster executives in the acquired firm quit their jobs and valuable talent is lost. Conversely, when corporate cultures are similar, performance problems are minimized.[81]

There are four general methods of managing two different cultures. (See **Figure 10–2**.) The choice of which method to use should be based on *(1) how much members of the acquired firm value preserving their own culture* and *(2) how attractive they perceive the culture of the acquirer to be.*[82]

1. *Integration* involves a relatively balanced give-and-take of cultural and managerial practices between the merger partners, and no strong imposition of cultural change on either company. It merges the two cultures in such a way that the separate cultures of both firms are preserved in the resulting culture. This is what occurred when France's Renault purchased a controlling interest in Japan's Nissan Motor Company and installed Carlos Ghosn as Nissan's new CEO to turn the company around. Ghosn was very sensitive to Nissan's culture and allowed the company room to develop a new corporate culture based on the best elements of Japan's national culture. His goal was to form one successful auto group from two very distinct companies.[83]

2. *Assimilation* involves the domination of one organization over the other. The domination is not forced, but it is welcomed by members of the acquired firm, who may feel for many reasons that their culture and managerial practices have not produced success. The acquired firm surrenders its culture and adopts the culture of the acquiring company. This was the case when Maytag Company (now part of Whirlpool) acquired Admiral. Because Admiral's previous owners had not kept the manufacturing facilities up to date, quality had drastically fallen over the years. Admiral's employees were willing to accept the dominance of Maytag's strong quality-oriented culture because they respected it and knew that without significant changes at Admiral, they would soon be out of work. In turn, they expected to be treated with some respect for their skills in refrigeration technology.

FIGURE 10–2
Methods of Managing the Culture of an Acquired Firm

Integration

Equal merger of both cultures into a new corporate culture

Assimilation

Acquiring firm's culture kept intact, but subservient to that of acquiring firm's corporate culture

Separation

Conflicting cultures kept intact, but kept separate in different units

Deculturation

Forced replacement of conflicting acquired firm's culture with that of the acquiring firm's culture

SOURCES: Suggested by A. R. Malezadeh and A. Nahavandi in "Making Mergers Work in Managing Cultures," *Journal of Business Strategy* (May/June 1990), pp. 53–57 and "Acculturation in Mergers and Acquisitions," *Academy of Management Review* (January 1988), pp. 79–90.

3. *Separation* is characterized by a separation of the two companies' cultures. They are structurally separated, without cultural exchange. When Boeing acquired McDonnell-Douglas, known for its expertise in military aircraft and missiles, Boeing created a separate unit to house both McDonnell's operations and Boeing's own military business. McDonnell executives were given top posts in the new unit and other measures were taken to protect the strong McDonnell culture. On the commercial side, where Boeing had the most expertise, McDonnell's commercial operations were combined with Boeing's in a separate unit managed by Boeing executives.[84]

4. *Deculturation* involves the disintegration of one company's culture resulting from unwanted and extreme pressure from the other to impose its culture and practices. This is the most common and most destructive method of dealing with two different cultures. It is often accompanied by much confusion, conflict, resentment, and stress. This is a primary reason why so many executives tend to leave after their firm is acquired. Such a merger typically results in poor performance by the acquired company and its eventual divestment. This is what happened when AT&T acquired NCR Corporation in 1990 for its computer business. It replaced NCR managers with an AT&T management team, reorganized sales, forced employees to adhere to the AT&T code of values (called the "Common Bond"), and even dropped the proud NCR name (successor to National Cash Register) in favor of a sterile GIS (Global Information Solutions) nonidentity. By 1995, AT&T was forced to take a US$1.2 billion loss and lay off 10,000 people.[85] The NCR unit was consequently sold.

ACTION PLANNING

Activities can be directed toward accomplishing strategic goals through action planning. At a minimum, an **action plan** states what actions are going to be taken, by whom, during what time frame, and with what expected results. After a program has been selected to implement a particular strategy, an action plan should be developed to put the program in place. **Table 10–1** shows an example of an action plan for a new advertising and promotion program.

Take the example of a company choosing forward vertical integration through the acquisition of a retailing chain as its growth strategy. Once it owns its own retail outlets, it must integrate the stores into the company. One of the many programs it would have to develop is a new advertising program for the stores. The resulting action plan to develop a new advertising program should include much of the following information:

1. **Specific actions to be taken to make the program operational:** One action might be to contact three reputable advertising agencies and ask them to prepare a proposal for a new radio and newspaper ad campaign based on the theme "Jones Surplus is now a part of Ajax Continental. Prices are lower. Selection is better."

2. **Dates to begin and end each action:** Time would have to be allotted not only to select and contact three agencies, but to allow them sufficient time to prepare a detailed proposal. For example, allow one week to select and contact the agencies, plus three months for them to prepare detailed proposals to present to the company's marketing director. Also allow some time to decide which proposal to accept.

3. **Person (identified by name and title) responsible for carrying out each action:** List someone—such as Jan Lewis, advertising manager—who can be put in charge of the program.

4. **Person responsible for monitoring the timeliness and effectiveness of each action:** Indicate that Jan Lewis is responsible for ensuring that the proposals are of good quality and are priced within the planned program budget. She will be the primary company

TABLE 10–1 Example of an Action Plan

Action Plan for Jan Lewis, Advertising Manager, and Rick Carter, Advertising Assistant, Ajax Continental

Program Objective: To Run a New Advertising and Promotion Campaign for the Combined Jones Surplus/Ajax Continental Retail Stores for the Coming Christmas Season within a Budget of $XX.

Program Activities:

1. Identify Three Best Ad Agencies for New Campaign.
2. Ask Three Ad Agencies to Submit a Proposal for a New Advertising and Promotion Campaign for Combined Stores.
3. Agencies Present Proposals to Marketing Manager.
4. Select Best Proposal and Inform Agencies of Decision.
5. Agency Presents Winning Proposal to Top Management.
6. Ads Air on TV and Promotions Appear in Stores.
7. Measure Results of Campaign in Terms of Viewer Recall and Increase in Store Sales.

Action Steps	Responsibility	Start–End
1. A. Review previous programs	Lewis & Carter	1/1–2/1
B. Discuss with boss	Lewis & Smith	2/1–2/3
C. Decide on three agencies	Lewis	2/4
2. A. Write specifications for ad	Lewis	1/15–1/20
B. Assistant writes ad request	Carter	1/20–1/30
C. Contact ad agencies	Lewis	2/5–2/8
D. Send request to three agencies	Carter	2/10
E. Meet with agency acct. execs	Lewis & Carter	2/16–2/20
3. A. Agencies work on proposals	Acct. Execs	2/23–5/1
B. Agencies present proposals	Carter	5/1–5/15
4. A. Select best proposal	Lewis	5/15–5/20
B. Meet with winning agency	Lewis	5/22–5/30
C. Inform losers	Carter	6/1
5. A. Fine-tune proposal	Acct. Exec	6/1–7/1
B. Presentation to management	Lewis	7/1–7/3
6. A. Ads air on TV	Lewis	9/1–12/24
B. Floor displays in stores	Carter	8/20–8/30
7. A. Gather recall measures of ads	Carter	9/1–12/24
B. Evaluate sales data	Carter	1/1–1/10
C. Prepare analysis of campaign	Carter	1/10–2/15

contact for the ad agencies and will report on the progress of the program once a week to the company's marketing director.

5. **Expected financial and physical consequences of each action:** Estimate when a completed ad campaign will be ready to show top management and how long it will take after approval to begin to air the ads. Estimate the expected increase in store sales over the six-month period after the ads are first aired. Indicate whether "recall" measures will be used to help assess the ad campaign's effectiveness, plus how, when, and by whom the recall data will be collected and analyzed.

6. **Contingency plans:** Indicate how long it will take to get an acceptable ad campaign to show top management if none of the initial proposals is acceptable.

Action plans are important for several reasons. First, action plans serve as a link between strategy formulation and evaluation and control. Second, the action plan specifies what needs to be done differently from the way operations are currently carried out. Third, during the evaluation and control process that comes later, an action plan helps in both the appraisal of performance and in the identification of any remedial actions, as needed. In addition, the explicit assignment of responsibilities for implementing and monitoring the programs may contribute to better motivation.

MANAGEMENT BY OBJECTIVES

Management By Objectives (MBO) is a technique that encourages participative decision making through shared goal setting at all organizational levels and performance assessment based on the achievement of stated objectives.[86] MBO links organizational objectives and the behavior of individuals. Because it is a system that links plans with performance, it is a powerful implementation technique.

The MBO process involves:

1. Establishing and communicating organizational objectives.
2. Setting individual objectives (through superior-subordinate interaction) that help implement organizational ones.
3. Developing an action plan of activities needed to achieve the objectives.
4. Periodically (at least quarterly) reviewing performance as it relates to the objectives and including the results in the annual performance appraisal.[87]

MBO provides an opportunity for the corporation to connect the objectives of people at each level to those at the next higher level. MBO, therefore, acts to tie together corporate, business, and functional objectives, as well as the strategies developed to achieve them. Although MBO originated in the 1950s, 90% of surveyed practicing managers feel that MBO is applicable today.[88] The principles of MBO are a part of self-managing work teams and quality circles.[89]

One of the real benefits of MBO is that it can reduce the amount of internal politics operating within a large corporation. Political actions within a firm can cause conflict and create divisions between the very people and groups who should be working together to implement strategy. People are less likely to jockey for position if the company's mission and objectives are clear and they know that the reward system is based not on game playing, but on achieving clearly communicated, measurable objectives.

TOTAL QUALITY MANAGEMENT

Total Quality Management (TQM) is an operational philosophy committed to *customer satisfaction* and *continuous improvement*. TQM is committed to quality/excellence and to being the best in all functions. Because TQM aims to reduce costs and improve quality, it can be used as a program to implement an overall low-cost or a differentiation business strategy. About 92% of manufacturing companies and 69% of service firms have implemented some form of quality management practices.[90] Not all TQM programs have been successes. Nevertheless, a recent survey of 325 manufacturing firms in Canada, Hungary, Italy, Lebanon, Taiwan, and the United States revealed that total quality management and just-in-time were the two highest-ranked improvement programs to improve company performance. An analysis of the successes and failures of TQM concluded that the key ingredient is top management. Successful TQM programs occur in those companies in which "top managers move beyond defensive and tactical orientations to embrace a developmental orientation."[91]

According to TQM, faulty processes, not poorly motivated employees, are the cause of defects in quality. The program involves a significant change in corporate culture, requiring strong leadership from top management, employee training, empowerment of lower-level employees (giving people more control over their work), and teamwork in order to succeed in a company. TQM emphasizes prevention, not correction. Inspection for quality still takes place, but the emphasis is on improving the process to prevent errors and deficiencies. Thus, quality circles or quality improvement teams are formed to identify problems and to suggest how to improve the processes that may be causing the problems.

TQM's essential ingredients are:

- **An intense focus on customer satisfaction:** Everyone (not just people in the sales and marketing departments) understands that their jobs exist only because of customer needs. Thus all jobs must be approached in terms of how they will affect customer satisfaction.

- **Internal as well as external customers:** An employee in the shipping department may be the internal customer of another employee who completes the assembly of a product, just as a person who buys the product is a customer of the entire company. An employee must be just as concerned with pleasing the internal customer as in satisfying the external customer.

- **Accurate measurement of every critical variable in a company's operations:** This means that employees have to be trained in what to measure, how to measure, and how to interpret the data. A rule of TQM is that *you only improve what you measure.*

- **Continuous improvement of products and services:** Everyone realizes that operations need to be continuously monitored to find ways to improve products and services.

- **New work relationships based on trust and teamwork:** Important is the idea of empowerment—giving employees wide latitude in how they go about achieving the company's goals. Research indicates that the keys to TQM success lie in executive commitment, an open organizational culture, and employee empowerment.[92]

INTERNATIONAL CONSIDERATIONS IN LEADING

In a study of 53 different national cultures, Hofstede found that each nation's unique culture could be identified using five dimensions. He found that national culture is so influential that it tends to overwhelm even a strong corporate culture. (See the numerous sociocultural societal variables that compose another country's culture listed in **Table 4–3**.) In measuring the differences among these **dimensions of national culture** from country to country, he was able to explain why a certain management practice might be successful in one nation but fail in another:[93]

1. **Power distance (PD)** is the extent to which a society accepts an unequal distribution of power in organizations. Malaysia and Mexico scored highest, whereas Germany and Austria scored lowest. People in those countries scoring high on this dimension tend to prefer autocratic to more participative managers.

2. **Uncertainty avoidance (UA)** is the extent to which a society feels threatened by uncertain and ambiguous situations. Greece and Japan scored highest on disliking ambiguity, whereas the United States and Singapore scored lowest. People in those nations scoring high on this dimension tend to want career stability, formal rules, and clear-cut measures of performance.

3. **Individualism-collectivism (I-C)** is the extent to which a society values individual freedom and independence of action compared with a tight social framework and loyalty to the group. The United States and Canada scored highest on individualism, whereas

Mexico and Guatemala scored lowest. People in nations scoring high on individualism tend to value individual success through competition, whereas people scoring low on individualism (thus high on collectivism) tend to value group success through collective cooperation.

4. **Masculinity-femininity (M-F)** is the extent to which society is oriented toward money and things (which Hofstede labels masculine) or toward people (which Hofstede labels feminine). Japan and Mexico scored highest on masculinity, whereas France and Sweden scored lowest (thus highest on femininity). People in nations scoring high on masculinity tend to value clearly defined sex roles where men dominate, and to emphasize performance and independence, whereas people scoring low on masculinity (and thus high on femininity) tend to value equality of the sexes where power is shared, and to emphasize the quality of life and interdependence.

5. **Long-term orientation (LT)** is the extent to which society is oriented toward the long- versus the short-term. Hong Kong and Japan scored highest on long-term orientation, whereas Pakistan scored the lowest. A long-term time orientation emphasizes the importance of hard work, education, and persistence as well as the importance of thrift. Nations with a long-term time orientation tend to value strategic planning and other management techniques with a long-term payback.

Hofstede's work was extended by Project GLOBE, a team of 150 researchers who collected data on cultural values, practices, and leadership attributes from 18,000 managers in 62 countries. The project studied the nine cultural dimensions of assertiveness, future orientation, gender differentiation, and uncertainty avoidance, and power distance, institutional emphasis on collectivism versus individualism, in-group collectivism, performance orientation, and humane orientation.[94]

The dimensions of national culture help explain why some management practices work well in some countries but not in others. For example, MBO, which originated in the United States, succeeded in Germany, according to Hofstede, because the idea of replacing the arbitrary authority of the boss with the impersonal authority of mutually agreed-upon objectives fits the low power distance that is a dimension of the German culture. It failed in France, however, because the French are used to high power distances; they are used to accepting orders from a highly personalized authority. In countries with high levels of uncertainty avoidance, such as Switzerland and Austria, communication should be clear and explicit, based on facts. Meetings should be planned in advance and have clear agendas. In contrast, in low-uncertainty-avoidance countries such as Greece or Russia, people are not used to structured communication and prefer more open-ended meetings. Because Thailand has a high level of power distance, Thai managers feel that communication should go from the top to the bottom of a corporation. As a result, 360-degree performance appraisals are seen as dysfunctional.[95] Some of the difficulties experienced by U.S. companies in using Japanese-style quality circles in TQM may stem from the extremely high value U.S. culture places on individualism. The differences between the United States and Mexico in terms of the power distance (Mexico 104 vs. U.S. 46) and individualism-collectivism (U.S. 91 vs. Mexico 30) dimensions may help explain why some companies operating in both countries have difficulty adapting to the differences in customs.[96] In addition, research has found that technology alliance formation is strongest in countries that value cooperation and avoid uncertainty.[97]

When one successful company in one country merges with another successful company in another country, the clash of corporate cultures is compounded by the clash of national cultures. For example, when two companies, one from a high-uncertainty-avoidance society and one from a low-uncertainty-avoidance country, are considering a merger, they should investigate each other's management practices to determine potential areas of conflict. Given the growing number of cross-border mergers and acquisitions, the management of cultures is becoming a key issue in strategy implementation. See the **Global Issue** feature to learn how differences in national and corporate cultures created conflict when Upjohn Company of the United States and Pharmacia AB of Sweden merged.

MNCs must pay attention to the many differences in cultural dimensions around the world and adjust their management practices accordingly. Cultural differences can easily go unrecognized by a headquarters staff that may interpret these differences as personality defects, whether the people in the subsidiaries are locals or expatriates. When conducting strategic planning in an MNC, top management must be aware that the process will vary based upon the national culture where a subsidiary is located. The values embedded in national culture have a profound and enduring effect on an executive's orientation, regardless of the impact of industry experience or corporate culture.[98]

GLOBAL issue

CULTURAL DIFFERENCES CREATE IMPLEMENTATION PROBLEMS IN MERGER

When Upjohn Pharmaceuticals of Kalamazoo, Michigan, and Pharmacia AB of Stockholm, Sweden, merged in 1995, employees of both sides were optimistic for the newly formed Pharmacia & Upjohn, Inc. Both companies were second-tier competitors fighting for survival in a global industry. Together, the firms would create a global company that could compete scientifically with its bigger rivals.

Because Pharmacia had acquired an Italian firm in 1993, it also had a large operation in Milan. U.S. executives scheduled meetings throughout the summer of 1996—only to cancel them when their European counterparts could not attend. Although it was common knowledge in Europe that most Swedes take the entire month of July for vacation and that Italians take off all of August, this was not common knowledge in Michigan. Differences in management styles became a special irritant. Swedes were used to an open system, with autonomous work teams. Executives sought the whole group's approval before making an important decision. Upjohn executives followed the more traditional American top-down approach. Upon taking command of the newly merged firm, Dr. Zabriskie (who had been Upjohn's CEO), divided the company into departments reporting to the new London headquarters. He required frequent reports, budgets, and staffing updates. The Swedes reacted negatively to this top-down management hierarchical style. "It was degrading," said Stener Kvinnsland, head of Pharmacia's cancer research in Italy before he quit the new company.

The Italian operations baffled the Americans, even though the Italians felt comfortable with a hierarchical management style. Italy's laws and unions made layoffs difficult. Italian data and accounting were often inaccurate. Because the Americans didn't trust the data, they were constantly asking for verification. In turn, the Italians were concerned that the Americans were trying to take over Italian operations. At Upjohn, all workers were subject to testing for drug and alcohol abuse. Upjohn also banned smoking. At Pharmacia's Italian business center, however, waiters poured wine freely every afternoon in the company dining room. Pharmacia's boardrooms were stocked with humidors for executives who smoked cigars during long meetings. After a brief attempt to enforce Upjohn's policies, the company dropped both the no-drinking and no-smoking policies for European workers.

In order to assert more control over the whole operation, the company moved its HQ back to the United States in 1998. In 2000, the company acquired Monsanto and Searle, both large pharmaceutical companies. The new company, called Pharmacia, didn't last long. The company was bought out by Pfizer in 2003.

....

SOURCES: Summarized from R. Frank and T. M. Burton, "Cross-Border Merger Results in Headaches for a Drug Company," *The Wall Street Journal* (February 4, 1997), pp. A1, A12; http://www.pfizer.com/about/history/pfizer_pharmacia.jsp.

End of Chapter SUMMARY

Strategy is implemented by modifying structure (organizing), selecting the appropriate people to carry out the strategy (staffing), and communicating clearly how the strategy can be put into action (leading). A number of programs, such as organizational and job design, reengineering, Six Sigma, MBO, TQM, and action planning, can be used to implement a new strategy. Executives must manage the corporate culture and find the right mix of qualified people to put a strategy in place.

Research on executive succession reveals that it is very risky to hire new top managers from outside the corporation. Although this is often done when a company is in trouble, it can be dangerous for a successful firm. This is also true when hiring people for non-executive positions. An in-depth study of 1052 stock analysts at 78 investment banks revealed that hiring a star (an outstanding performer) from another company did not improve the hiring company's performance. When a company hires a star, the star's performance plunges, there is a sharp decline in the functioning of the team the person works with, and the company's market value declines. Their performance dropped about 20% and did not return to the level before the job change—even after five years. Interestingly, around 36% of the stars left the investment banks that hired them within 36 months. Another 29% quit in the next 24 months.

This phenomenon occurs not because a star doesn't suddenly become less intelligent when switching firms, but because the star cannot take to the new firm the firm-specific resources that contributed to her or his achievements at the previous company. As a result, the star is unable to repeat the high performance in another company until he or she learns the new system. This may take years, but only if the new company has a good support system in place. Otherwise, the performance may never improve. For these reasons, companies cannot obtain competitive advantage by hiring stars from the outside. Instead, they should emphasize growing their own talent and developing the infrastructure necessary for high performance.[99]

It is important to not ignore the majority of the workforce who, while not being stars, are the solid performers that keep a company going over the years. An undue emphasis on attracting stars often wastes money and destroys morale. The CEO of McKesson, a pharmaceutical wholesaler, calls these B players "performers in place. . . . They are happy living in Dubuque. I have more time and admiration for them than the A player who is at my desk every six months asking for the next promotion." With few exceptions, coaches who try to forge a sports team composed of stars courts disaster.

MyManagementLab®

Go to **mymanagementlab.com** to complete the problems marked with this icon .

KEY TERMS

action plan (p. 324)
dimensions of national culture (p. 327)
downsizing (p. 315)
executive succession (p. 314)
executive type (p. 312)
individualism-collectivism (I-C) (p. 327)

integration manager (p. 310)
leading (p. 310)
long-term orientation (LT) (p. 328)
Management By Objectives (MBO) (p. 326)
masculinity-femininity (M-F) (p. 328)
power distance (PD) (p. 327)

staffing (p. 310)
Total Quality Management (TQM) (p. 326)
uncertainty avoidance (UA) (p. 327)

MyManagementLab®

Go to **mymanagementlab.com** for the following Assisted-graded writing questions:

10-1. What are the critical issues that a company must consider when trying to match its staffing to its strategy?

10-2. What are the unique impacts on a company that must staff in international settings?

DISCUSSION QUESTIONS

⭐**10-3.** What skills should a person have for managing a business unit following a differentiation strategy? Why? What should a company do if no one is available internally and the company has a policy of promotion from within?

10-4. Does staffing really follow strategy? Are the job applicants' knowledge, skills, and abilities the key, or is it the corporate strategy?

⭐**10-5.** What are some ways to implement a retrenchment strategy without creating a lot of resentment and conflict with labor unions?

⭐**10-6.** How can corporate culture be changed?

10-7. Provide local examples to show how relevant Hofstede's dimensions are in effective staffing and directing.

STRATEGIC PRACTICE EXERCISE

HRM in the United Arab Emirates

The role of human resources has grown increasingly more complex and challenging in today's fast-paced, ever-evolving business world. The truth is, in recent years, there has been a slew of unparalleled transformations in companies in the Emirates that have punctuated the region's workforce. Tenured staff has to handle technological breakthroughs, fluctuating market environments, and the global crises. The additional challenge, of course, is the Millennial Generation! These fresh-driven, young graduates born between 1982 and 2002 come from shifting demographics and changing organizational structures. They are diversified: the new, powered globalization's workforce! The youth has changed the very fabric of the Middle East's ultra-competitive employment landscape, reaffirming the need for world-class human resource practices that place employment engagement at the core of every corporation's business ethos. The third millennium needs a corporate environment that is conducive to productivity, creativity, and innovation, one which is the key to optimizing peak performance, maintaining low employee turnover, and achieving long-term business goals.

An example of such a company, at present operating in the Arab Gulf, is Proctor & Gamble (P&G). At P&G, the human resource managers, who have generated an approach that has helped guide the company, are its building blocks of success. The business world is riddled with instability, cynicism, and doubt. Fresh graduates are not readily employed nor do they easily build a career within that organization up until retirement. The rules of the game have radically changed. Every industry suffers from increased job mobility, mounting recruitment costs, and low retention rates. P&G understood the importance of cultivating a high-performing, collaborative, and loyal workforce. The company's vision led to a nomination in Aon Hewitt's Top 5 Best Employers list for 2013.

Corporations today need to foster a corporate culture where workers identify with and are motivated by their employer. What this means is nurturing a heightened connection between an employee and his/her job, organization, manager, and co-workers. In fact, recent studies show that employees who are committed and dedicated to their work on an emotional level tend to outperform those who are not. This, of course, begs the question: how can organizations effectively deliver human resource services that can meet the needs of today's layered, multigenerational workforce as it simultaneously guarantees organizational success?

Layer and Divide the Work

Companies need to include everyone in the HRM plan. The ecosystem structures organizational outcomes, and safeguards employee engagement. Leadership skills drive excellence, and create meaningful challenging work that employees "own" and are held accountable for. Pivotal engagement drivers not only motivate employees but also help build strong teams. The new ecosystem shapes a flexible learning and development path: providing employees with deserving rewards, recognition, and enhanced compensation; offering a career trajectory forecast and related guidance; embedding the company's core values; celebrating the organization's overall success and individual accomplishments; creating a transparent, direct line of communication with employees; developing a culture of interdependent teamwork; and lastly, involving employees in corporate social responsibilities initiatives. The new ecosystem is a corporate climate that centers on value, accomplishment, and commitment in the UAE, and across the global market.

- Based on what you read, what are P&G's concepts on handling its staff?

- List P&G's guidelines.

- Do you believe that P&G's guidelines are universal, or should they be tailored to fit different cultures?

SOURCE: Fahad Al Abdulkarim, "Middle East's changing jobs market calls for sustainable HR practices," *National* (November 4, 2013).

NOTES

1. S. Caudron, "How HR Drives Profits," *Workforce Management* (December 2001), pp. 26–31 as reported by L. L. Bryan, C. I. Joyce, and L. M. Weiss in "Making a Market in Talent," *McKinsey Quarterly* (2006, No. 2), pp. 1–7.

2. "Talent Acquisition Up 6% in 2011 and Average Cost Per Hire About $3,500 per New Bersin & Assoc. Factbook," *Shaker* (November 28, 2011), http://shakerrecruitment.ning.com/profiles/blogs/talent-acquisition-up-6-in-2011-and-average-cost-per-hire-about-3.

3. The numbers are approximate averages from three separate studies of top management turnover after mergers. See M. Lubatkin, D. Schweiger, and Y. Weber, "Top Management Turnover in Related M&Ss: An Additional Test of the Theory of Relative Standing," *Journal of Management* (Vol. 25, No. 1, 1999), pp. 55–73.

4. J. A. Krug, "Executive Turnover in Acquired Firms: A Longitudinal Analysis of Long-Term Interaction Effects," paper presented to the annual meeting of *Academy of Management*, Seattle, WA (2003).

5. J. A. Krug and W. H. Hegarty, "Post-Acquisition Turnover Among U.S. Top Management Teams: An Analysis of the Effects of Foreign vs. Domestic Acquisitions of U.S. Targets," *Strategic Management Journal* (September 1997), pp. 667–675; J. A. Frug and W. H. Hegarty, "Predicting Who Stays and Leaves After an Acquisition: A Study of Top Managers in Multinational Firms," *Strategic Management Journal* (February 2001), pp. 185–196.

6. D. Harding and T. Rouse, "Human Due Diligence," *Harvard Business Review* (April 2007), pp. 124–131.

7. A. Hinterhuber, "Making M&A Work," *Business Strategy Review* (September 2002), pp. 7–9.

8. R. N. Ashkenas and S. C. Francis, "Integration Managers: Special Leaders for Special Times," *Harvard Business Review* (November–December 2000), pp. 108–116.

9. J. Hoerr, "Sharpening Minds for a Competitive Edge," *Business Week* (December 17, 1990), pp. 72–78.

10. "ASTD 2012 State of the Industry Report: Organizations Continue to Invest in Workplace Learning," *ASTD* (November 8, 2012), http://www.astd.org/Publications/Magazines/TD/TD-Archive/2012/11/ASTD-2012-State-of-the-Industry-Report.

11. *High Performance Work Practices and Firm Performance* (Washington, DC: U.S. Department of Labor, Office of the American Workplace, 1993), pp. i, 4.

12. "The Happy Wackiness of Zappos.com," *ABC News* (October 26, 2011), http://abcnews.go.com/blogs/business/2011/10/the-happy-wackiness-of-zappos-com/; J. Edwards, "Check Out the Insane Lengths Zappos Customer Service Reps Will Go To," *Business Insider* (January 29, 2012), http://articles.businessinsider.com/2012-01-09/news/30606433_1_customer-service-zappos-center-services.

13. R. Henkoff, "Companies that Train Best," *Fortune* (March 22, 1993), pp. 62–75.

14. D. C. Hambrick, "Upper Echelons Theory: An Update," *Academy of Management Review* (April 2007), pp. 334–343.

15. D. Miller and J. Shamsie, "Learning Across the Life Cycle: Experimentation and Performance Among the Hollywood Studio Heads," *Strategic Management Journal* (August 2001), pp. 725–745. An exception to these findings may be the computer software industry in which CEOs are at their best when they start their jobs and steadily decline during their tenures. See A. D. Henderson, D. Miller, and D. C. Hambrick, "How Quickly Do CEOs Become Obsolete? Industry Dynamism, CEO Tenure, and Company Performance," *Strategic Management Journal* (May 2006), pp. 447–460.

16. B. Hrowvitz, "New CEO Puts Comeback on the Menu at Applebee's," *USA Today* (April 28, 2008), pp. 1B, 2B.

17. A study of former General Electric executives who became CEOs categorized them as cost controllers, growers, or cycle managers on the basis of their line experience at GE. See B. Groysberg, A. N. McLean, and N. Nohria, "Are Leaders Portable?" *Harvard Business Review* (May 2006), pp. 92–100.

18. D. K. Datta and N. Rajagopalan, "Industry Structure and CEO Characteristics: An Empirical Study of Succession Events," *Strategic Management Journal* (September 1998), pp. 833–852; A. S. Thomas and K. Ramaswamy, "Environmental Change and Management Staffing: A Comment," *Journal of Management* (Winter 1993), pp. 877–887; J. P. Guthrie, C. M. Grimm, and K. G. Smith, "Environmental Change and Management Staffing: An Empirical Study," *Journal of Management* (December 1991), pp. 735–748.

19. J. Greco, "The Search Goes On," *Journal of Business Strategy* (September/October 1997), pp. 22–25; W. Ocasio and H. Kim, "The Circulation of Corporate Control: Selection of Functional Backgrounds on New CEOs in Large U.S. Manufacturing Firms, 1981–1992," *Administrative Science Quarterly* (September 1999), pp. 532–562; R. Dobbs, D. Harris, and A. Rasmussen, "When Should CFOs Take the Helm?" *McKinsey Quarterly Online* (November 2006); "How to Get to the Top," *The Economist* (May 31, 2008), p. 70.

20. R. Drazin and R. K. Kazanjian, "Applying the Del Technique to the Analysis of Cross-Classification Data: A Test of CEO Succession and Top Management Team Development," *Academy of Management Journal* (December 1993), pp. 1374–1399; W. E. Rothschild, "A Portfolio of Strategic Leaders," *Planning Review* (January/February 1996), pp. 16–19.

21. R. Subramanian and C. M. Sanchez, "Environmental Change and Management Staffing: An Empirical Examination of the Electric Utilities Industry," *Journal of Business Strategies* (Spring 1998), pp. 17–34.

22. M. A. Carpenter and B. R. Golden, "Perceived Managerial Discretion: A Study of Cause and Effect," *Strategic Management Journal* (March 1997), pp. 187–206.

23. J. A. Parnell, "Functional Background and Business Strategy: The Impact of Executive-Strategy Fit on Performance," *Journal of Business Strategies* (Spring 1994), pp. 49–62.

24. M. Smith and M. C. White, "Strategy, CEO Specialization, and Succession," *Administrative Science Quarterly* (June 1987), pp. 263–280.

25. "Average Tenure of CEOs Declined to 8.4 Years, the Conference Board Reports," The Conference Board (April 12, 2012), http://www.conference-board.org/press/pressdetail.cfm?pressid=4453; "Making Companies Work," *The Economist* (October 25, 2003), p. 14; C. H. Mooney, C. M. Dalton, D. R. Dalton, and S. T. Cero, "CEO Succession as a Funnel: The Critical, and Changing Role of Inside Directors," *Organizational*

Dynamics (Vol. 36, No. 4, 2007), pp. 418–428. Note, however, that the tenures of CEOs of family firms typically exceed 15 years. See I. Le Breton-Miller and D. Miller, "Why Do Some Family Businesses Out-Compete? Governance, Long-Term Orientations, and Sustainable Capability," *Entrepreneurship Theory and Practice* (November 2006), pp. 731–746.

26. A. Bianco, L. Lavelle, J. Merrit, and A. Barrett, "The CEO Trap," *BusinessWeek* (December 11, 2000), pp. 86–92.

27. Y. Zhang and N. Rajagopalan, "When the Known Devil Is Better than an Unknown God: An Empirical Study of the Antecedents and Consequences of Relay CEO Succession," *Academy of Management Journal* (August 2004), pp. 483–500; W. Sheen and A. A. Cannella Jr., "Will Succession Planning Increase Shareholder Wealth? Evidence from Investor Reactions to Relay CEO Successions," *Strategic Management Journal* (February 2003), pp. 191–198.

28. G. A. Bigley and M. F. Wiersema, "New CEOs and Corporate Strategic Refocusing: How Experience as Heir Apparent Influences the Use of Power," *Administrative Science Quarterly* (December 2002), pp. 707–727.

29. J. L. Bower, "Solve the Succession Crisis by Growing Inside-Outside Leaders," *Harvard Business Review* (November 2007), pp. 91–96; Y. Zhang and N. Rajagopalan, "Grooming for the Top Post and Ending the CEO Succession Crisis," *Organizational Dynamics* (Vol. 35, Issue 1, 2006), pp. 96–105.

30. "Coming and Going," Survey of Corporate Leadership," *The Economist* (October 25, 2003), pp. 12–14.

31. D. C. Carey and D. Ogden, *CEO Succession: A Window on How Boards Do It Right When Choosing a New Chief Executive* (New York: Oxford University Press, 2000).

32. "The King Lear Syndrome," *The Economist* (December 13, 2003), p. 65.

33. Y. Zang and N. Rajagopalan, "Grooming for the Top Post and Ending the CEO Succession Crisis," *Organizational Dynamics* (Vol. 35, Issue 1, 2006), pp. 96–105.

34. "2011 CEO Transitions," *Spencer Stuart* (March 2012), http://www.spencerstuart.com/research/ceo/1580/.

35. M. S. Kraatz and J. H. Moore, "Executive Migration and Institutional Change," *Academy of Management Journal* (February 2002), pp. 120–143; Y. Zhang and N. Rajagopalan, "When the Known Devil Is Better than an Unknown God: An Empirical Study of the Antecedents and Consequences of Relay CEO Succession" *Academy of Management Journal* (August 2004), pp. 483–500; W. Shen and A. A. Cannella Jr., "Revisiting the Performance Consequences of CEO Succession: The Impacts of Successor Type, Post-Succession Senior Executive Turnover, and Departing CEO Tenure," *Academy of Management Journal* (August 2002), pp. 717–733.

36. K. P. Coyne and E. J. Coyne Sr., "Surviving Your New CEO," *Harvard Business Review* (May 2007), pp. 62–69.

37. N. Byrnes and D. Kiley, "Hello, You Must Be Going," *Business Week* (February 12, 2007), pp. 30–32.

38. C. Lucier and J. Dyer, "Hiring an Outside CEO: A Board's Best Moves," *Directors & Boards* (Winter 2004), pp. 36–38. These findings are supported by a later study by Booz Allen Hamilton in which 1595 worldwide companies during 1995 to 2005 showed the same results. See J. Webber, "The Accidental CEO," *BusinessWeek* (April 23, 2007), pp. 64–72.

39. Q. Yue, "Antecedents of Top Management Successor Origin in China," paper presented to the annual meeting of the *Academy of Management*, Seattle, WA (2003); A. A. Buchko and D. DiVerde, "Antecedents, Moderators, and Consequences of CEO Turnover: A Review and Reconceptualization," paper presented to *Midwest Academy of Management* (Lincoln, NE: 1997), p. 10; W. Ocasio, "Institutionalized Action and Corporate Governance: The Reliance on Rules of CEO Succession," *Administrative Science Quarterly* (June 1999), pp. 384–416.

40. C. Gopinath, "Turnaround: Recognizing Decline and Initiating Intervention," *Long Range Planning* (December 1991), pp. 96–101.

41. K. B. Schwartz and K. Menon, "Executive Succession in Failing Firms," *Academy of Management Journal* (September 1985), pp. 680–686; A. A. Cannella Jr., and M. Lubatkin, "Succession as a Sociopolitical Process: Internal Impediments to Outsider Selection," *Academy of Management Journal* (August 1993), pp. 763–793; W. Boeker and J. Goodstein, "Performance and Succession Choice: The Moderating Effects of Governance and Ownership," *Academy of Management Journal* (February 1993), pp. 172–186.

42. W. Boeker, "Executive Migration and Strategic Change: The Effect of Top Manager Movement on Product-Market Entry," *Administrative Science Quarterly* (June 1997), pp. 213–236.

43. E. Brockmann, J. J. Hoffman, and D. Dawley, "A Contingency Theory of CEO Successor Choice and Post-Bankruptcy Strategic Change," paper presented to annual meeting of *Academy of Management*, Seattle, WA (2003).

44. P. Lorange, and D. Murphy, "Bringing Human Resources into Strategic Planning: System Design Characteristics," in C. J. Fombrun, N. M. Tichy, and M. A. Devanna (Eds.), *Strategic Human Resource Management* (New York: John Wiley & Sons, 1984), pp. 281–283.

45. http://www.ge.com/company/culture/leadership_learning.html.

46. S. Armour, "Playing the Succession Game," *USA Today* (November 24, 2003), p. 3B.

47. D. A. Waldman and T. Korbar, "Student Assessment Center Performance in the Prediction of Early Career Success," *Academy of Management Learning and Education* (June 2004), pp. 151–167.

48. "Coming and Going, Survey of Corporate Leadership," *The Economist* (October 25, 2003), pp. 12–14.

49. R. A. Pitts, "Strategies and Structures for Diversification," *Academy of Management Journal* (June 1997), pp. 197–208.

50. D. Poeter, "HP Announces 27,000 Layoffs in Major Restructuring," *PC Magazine* (May 23, 2012), http://www.pcmag.com/article2/0,2817,2404820,00.asp; http://retailindustry.about.com/od/storeclosingsandopenings/a/2012-Store-Closings-US-Retail-Industry-Liquidations-Roundup-Chains-Going-Out-Business.htm.

51. K. E. Mishra, G. M. Spreitzer, and A. K. Mishra, "Preserving Employee Morale During Downsizing," *Sloan Management Review* (Winter 1998), pp. 83–95.

52. B. O'Reilly, "Is Your Company Asking Too Much?" *Fortune* (March 12, 1990), p. 41. For more information on the emotional reactions of survivors of downsizing, see C. R. Stoner and R. I. Hartman, "Organizational Therapy: Building Survivor Health & Competitiveness," *SAM Advanced Management Journal* (Summer 1997), pp. 15–31, 41.

53. S. R. Fisher and M. A. White, "Downsizing in a Learning Organization: Are There Hidden Costs?" *Academy of Management Review* (January 2000), pp. 244–251.

54. T. M. Amabile and R. Conti, "Changes in the Work Environment for Creativity During Downsizing," *Academy of Management Journal* (December 1999), pp. 630–640; A. G. Bedeian and A. A. Armenakis, "The Cesspool Syndrome: How Dreck Floats to the Top of Declining Organizations," *Academy of Management Executive* (February 1998), pp. 58–67.

55. For a more complete listing of the psychological and behavioral reactions to downsizing, see M. L. Marks and K. P. De Meuse, "Resizing the Organization: Maximizing the Gain While Minimizing the Pain of Layoffs, Divestitures, and Closings," *Organizational Dynamics* (Vol. 34, No. 1, 2005), pp. 19–35.

56. D. J. Flanagan and K. C. O'Shaughnessy, "The Effect of Layoffs on Firm Reputation," *Journal of Management* (June 2005), pp. 445–463.

57. *The Wall Street Journal* (December 22, 1992), p. B1.

58. V. Giang, "14 of the Biggest Mass Layoffs of 2011," *Business Insider* (August 28, 2011), http://www.businessinsider.com/companies-with-the-biggest-layoffs-in-2011-2011-8?op=1.

59. R. D. Nixon, M. A. Hitt, H. Lee, and E. Jeong, "Market Reactions to Announcements of Corporate Downsizing Actions and Implementation Strategies," *Strategic Management Journal* (November 2004), pp. 1121–1129; G. D. Bruton, J. K. Keels, and C. L. Shook, "Downsizing the Firm: Answering the Strategic Questions," *Academy of Management Executive* (May 1996), pp. 38–45; E. G. Love and N. Nohria, "Reducing Slack: The Performance Consequences of Downsizing by Large Industrial Firms, 1977–93," *Strategic Management Journal* (December 2005), pp. 1087–1108; C. D. Zatzick and R. D. Iverson, "High-Involvement Management and Workforce Reduction: Competitive Advantage or Disadvantage?" *Academy of Management Journal* (October 2006), pp. 999–1015.

60. M. A. Hitt, B. W. Keats, H. F. Harback, and R. D. Nixon, "Rightsizing: Building and Maintaining Strategic Leadership and Long-Term Competitiveness," *Organizational Dynamics* (Autumn 1994), pp. 18–32. For additional suggestions, see W. F. Cascio, "Strategies for Responsible Restructuring," *Academy of Management Executive* (August 2002), pp. 80–91, and T. Mroczkowski and M. Hanaoka, "Effective Rightsizing Strategies in Japan and America: Is There a Convergence of Employment Practices?" *Academy of Management Executive* (May 1997), pp. 57–67. For an excellent list of cost-reduction programs for use in short, medium, and long-term time horizons, see F. Gandolfi, "Cost Reductions, Downsizing-Related Layoffs, and HR Practices," *SAM Advanced Management Journal* (Spring 2008), pp. 52–58.

61. J. S. Black and H. B. Gregersen, "The Right Way to Manage Expats," *Harvard Business Review* (March–April 1999), pp. 52–61.

62. Ibid, p. 54.

63. J. I. Sanchez, P. E. Spector, and C. L. Cooper, "Adapting to a Boundaryless World: A Developmental Expatriate Model," *Academy of Management Executive* (May 2000), pp. 96–106.

64. R. L. Tung, *The New Expatriates* (Cambridge, MA: Ballinger, 1988); J. S. Black, M. Mendenhall, and G. Oddou, "Toward a Comprehensive Model of International Adjustment: An Integration of Multiple Theoretical Perspectives," *Academy of Management Review* (April 1991), pp. 291–317.

65. M. A. Carpenter, W. G. Sanders, and H. B. Gregersen, "Bundling Human Capital with Organizational Context: The Impact of International Assignment Experience on Multinational Firm Performance and CEO Pay," *Academy of Management Journal* (June 2001), pp. 493–511.

66. P. M. Caligiuri and S. Colakoglu, "A Strategic Contingency Approach to Expatriate Assignment Management," *Human Resource Management Journal* (Vol. 17, No. 4, 2007), pp. 393–410.

67. M. A. Shaffer, D. A. Harrison, K. M. Gilley, and D. M. Luk, "Struggling for Balance Amid Turbulence on International Assignments: Work-Family Conflict, Support, and Commitment," *Journal of Management* (Vol. 27, No. 1, 2001), pp. 99–121.

68. J. S. Black and H. B. Gregersen, "The Right Way to Manage Ex-pats," *Harvard Business Review* (March–April 1999), p. 54.

69. G. Stern, "GM Executive's Ties to Native Country Help Auto Maker Clinch Deal in China," *The Wall Street Journal* (November 2, 1995), p. B7.

70. K. Roth, "Managing International Interdependence: CEO Characteristics in a Resource-Based Framework," *Academy of Management Journal* (February 1995), pp. 200–231.

71. M. Subramaniam and N. Venkatraman, "Determinants of Transnational New Product Development Capability: Testing the Influence of Transferring and Deploying Tacit Overseas Knowledge," *Strategic Management Journal* (April 2001), pp. 359–378.

72. J. S. Lublin, "An Overseas Stint Can Be a Ticket to the Top," *The Wall Street Journal* (January 29, 1996), pp. B1, B2.

73. "Cisco Shifts Senior Executives to India," *St. Cloud* (MN) *Times* (January 13, 2007), p. 6A.

74. "Expatriate Employees: In Search of Stealth," *The Economist* (April 23, 2005), pp. 62–64.

75. M. Meaney, C. Pung, and S. Kamath, "Creating Organizational Transformations," *McKinsey Quarterly Online* (September 10, 2008).

76. L. G. Love, R. L. Priem, and G. T. Lumpkin, "Explicitly Articulated Strategy and Firm Performance Under Alternative Levels of Centralization," *Journal of Management* (Vol. 28, No. 5, 2002), pp. 611–627.

77. G. G. Gordon, "The Relationship of Corporate Culture to Industry Sector and Corporate Performance," in R. H. Kilmann, M. J. Saxton, R. Serpa, and Associates (Eds.), *Gaining Control of the Corporate Culture* (San Francisco: Jossey-Bass, 1985), p. 123; T. Kono, "Corporate Culture and Long-Range Planning," *Long Range Planning* (August 1990), pp. 9–19.

78. B. Mike and J. W. Slocum Jr., "Changing Culture at Pizza Hut and Yum! Brands," *Organizational Dynamics* (Vol. 32, No. 4, 2003), pp. 319–330.

79. T. J. Tetenbaum, "Seven Key Practices that Improve the Chance for Expected Integration and Synergies," *Organizational Dynamics* (Autumn 1999), pp. 22–35.

80. B. Bremner and G. Edmondson, "Japan: A Tale of Two Mergers," *BusinessWeek* (May 10, 2004), p. 42; http://www.worldcarfans.com/10805221239/mercedes-benz-admits-to-chrysler-merger-mistake.

81. P. Very, M. Lubatkin, R. Calori, and J. Veiga, "Relative Standing and the Performance of Recently Acquired European Firms," *Strategic Management Journal* (September 1997), pp. 593–614.

82. A. R. Malekzadeh and A. Nahavandi, "Making Mergers Work by Managing Cultures," *Journal of Business Strategy* (May/June 1990), pp. 53–57; A. Nahavandi, and A. R. Malekzadeh, "Acculturation in Mergers and Acquisitions," *Academy of Management Review* (January 1988), pp. 79–90.

83. C. Ghosn, "Saving the Business Without Losing the Company," *Harvard Business Review* (January 2002), pp. 37–45;

B. Bremner, G. Edmondson, C. Dawson, D. Welch, and K. Kerwin, "Nissan's Boss," *BusinessWeek* (October 4, 2004), pp. 50–60.

84. D. Harding and T. Rouse, "Human Due Diligence," *Harvard Business Review* (April 2007), pp. 124–131.

85. J. J. Keller, "Why AT&T Takeover of NCR Hasn't Been a Real Bell Ringer," *The Wall Street Journal* (September 19, 1995), pp. A1, A5.

86. J. W. Gibson and D. V. Tesone, "Management Fads: Emergence, Evolution, and Implications for Managers," *Academy of Management Executive* (November 2001), pp. 122–133.

87. For additional information, see S. J. Carroll, Jr., and M. L. Tosi Jr., *Management by Objectives: Applications and Research* (New York: Macmillan, 1973), and A. P. Aria, *Managing by Objectives* (Glenview, IL: Scott, Foreman, and Company, 1974).

88. J. W. Gibson, D. V. Tesone, and C. W. Blackwell, "Management Fads: Here Yesterday, Gone Today?" *SAM Advanced Management Journal* (Autumn 2003), pp. 12–17.

89. J. W. Gibson and D. V. Tesone, "Management Fads: Emergence, Evolution, and Implications for Managers," *Academy of Management Executive* (November 2001), p. 125.

90. S. S. Masterson, and M. S. Taylor, "Total Quality Management and Performance Appraisal: An Integrative Perspective," *Journal of Quality Management* (Vol. 1, No. 1, 1996), pp. 67–89.

91. T. Y. Choi and O. C. Behling, "Top Managers and TQM Success: One More Look After All These Years," *Academy of Management Executive* (February 1997), pp. 37–47.

92. T. C. Powell, "Total Quality Management as Competitive Advantage: A Review and Empirical Study," *Strategic Management Journal* (January 1995), pp. 15–37.

93. G. Hofstede, "Culture's Recent Consequences: Using Dimensional Scores in Theory and Research," *International Journal of Cross Cultural Management* (Vol. 1, No. 1, 2001), pp. 11–17; G. Hofstede, *Cultures and Organizations: Software of the Mind* (London: McGraw-Hill, 1991); G. Hofstede and M. H. Bond, "The Confucius Connection: From Cultural Roots to Economic Growth," *Organizational Dynamics* (Spring 1988), pp. 5–21; R. Hodgetts, "A Conversation with Geert Hofstede," *Organizational Dynamics* (Spring 1993), pp. 53–61.

94. M. Javidan and R. J. House, "Cultural Acumen for the Global Manager: Lessons from Project GLOBE," *Organizational Dynamics* (Vol. 29, No. 4, 2001), pp. 289–305; R. J. House, P. J. Hanges, M. Javidan, P. W. Dorfman, and V. Gupta (Eds.), *Culture, Leadership and Organizations: The GLOBE Study of 62 Societies* (Thousand Oaks, CA: Sage, 2004).

95. M. Javidan and R. J. House, "Cultural Acumen for the Global Manager: Lessons from Project GLOBE," *Organizational Dynamics* (Vol. 29, No. 4, 2001), p. 303.

96. See G. Hofstede and M. H. Bond, "The Confucius Connection, From Cultural Roots to Economic Growth," *Organizational Dynamics* (Spring 1988), pp. 12–13.

97. H. K. Steensma, L. Marino, K. M. Weaver, and P. H. Dickson, "The Influence of National Culture on the Formation of Technology Alliances by Entrepreneurial Firms," *Academy of Management Journal* (October 2000), pp. 951–973.

98. M. A. Geletkancz, "The Salience of 'Culture's Consequences': The Effects of Cultural Values on Top Executive Commitment to the Status Quo," *Strategic Management Journal* (September 1997), pp. 615–634.

99. B. Groysberg, A. Nanda, and N. Nohria, "The Risky Business of Hiring Stars," *Harvard Business Review* (May 2004), pp. 92–100.

100. D. Keirsey, *Please Understand Me II* (Del Mar, CA: Prometheus Nemesis Book Co., 1998).

CHAPTER 11

Evaluation and Control

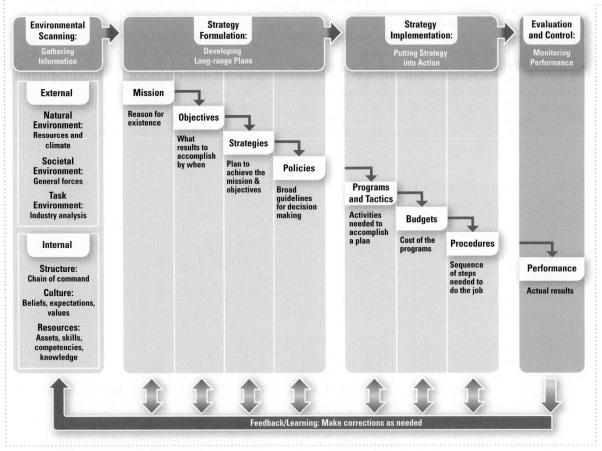

Environmental Scanning:	Strategy Formulation:	Strategy Implementation:	Evaluation and Control:
Gathering Information	Developing Long-range Plans	Putting Strategy into Action	Monitoring Performance

External

Natural Environment: Resources and climate

Societal Environment: General forces

Task Environment: Industry analysis

Internal

Structure: Chain of command

Culture: Beliefs, expectations, values

Resources: Assets, skills, competencies, knowledge

Mission

Reason for existence

Objectives

What results to accomplish by when

Strategies

Plan to achieve the mission & objectives

Policies

Broad guidelines for decision making

Programs and Tactics

Activities needed to accomplish a plan

Budgets

Cost of the programs

Procedures

Sequence of steps needed to do the job

Performance

Actual results

Feedback/Learning: Make corrections as needed

MyManagementLab®

⭐ Improve Your Grade!

Over 10 million students improved their results using the Pearson MyLabs. Visit **mymanagementlab.com** for simulations, tutorials, and end-of-chapter problems.

Learning Objectives

After reading this chapter, you should be able to:

- Understand the basic control process
- Choose among traditional measures, such as ROI, and shareholder value measures, such as economic value added, to properly assess performance
- Use the balanced scorecard approach to develop key performance measures
- Apply the benchmarking process to a function or an activity
- Develop appropriate control systems to support specific strategies including performance measurement

Five Guys and Execution

If you want to be in a business with thousands of competitors, then you must execute exceptionally well. That is the hallmark of Five Guys Burgers and Fries. Five Guys started in 1986 with a single location that had no seating. They decided to put in controls for the business that might not make sense right out of the box.

In fact, they were unable to raise any capital or get any loans for their business idea. They wanted to create a burger place that used the finest ingredients in the business, paying top dollar for their meat, getting a renowned local bakery to produce their rolls, buying the most expensive bacon, and cooking only in peanut oil, which cost five times as much as the oil other burger restaurants were using. These standards would become the key to their success. They don't start cooking until you order, peanuts are provided for free while you wait, and they so overload each customer with French fries that they gained the reputation that one order of their small fries will feed four people.

They have more than 1000 locations in the United States and Canada, with the founding family (the parents and five sons) owning 200 and the rest franchised. In 2011, they had revenues of $976 million, up from $720 million in 2010.

The whole business is built on consistency and controls. They don't comparison shop for ingredients and are rigorous in their evaluation of standards. The company employs their own employees as secret shoppers to make sure each store lives up to the Five Guys' standard of service. There are weekly, monthly, and quarterly programs that award crew members based on the shoppers' reports.

SOURCES: http://www.fiveguys.com/; L. Joyner, "Five Guys Found Simple Recipe for Success: Do It Right," *USA Today* (August 2, 2012), http://usatoday30.usatoday.com/money/economy/story/2012-07-29/five-guys-ceo-jerry-murrell/56541886/1; K. Weise, "Behind Five Guys' Beloved Burgers," *Bloomberg Businessweek* (August 11, 2011), http://www.businessweek.com/magazine/behind-five-guys-beloved-burgers-08112011.html.

FIGURE 11–1
Evaluation and
Control Process

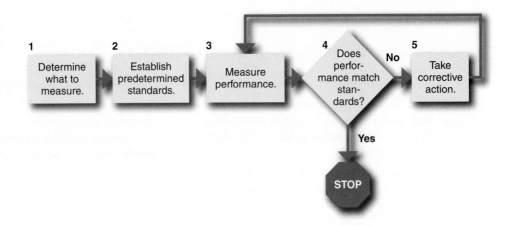

Evaluation and Control in Strategic Management

Evaluation and control information consists of performance data and activity reports (gathered in Step 3 in **Figure 11–1**). If undesired performance results because the strategic management processes were inappropriately used, operational managers must know about it so they can correct the employee activity. Top management need not be involved. If, however, undesired performance results from the processes themselves, top managers, as well as operational managers, must know about it so they can develop new implementation programs or procedures. Evaluation and control information must be relevant to what is being monitored. One of the obstacles to effective control is the difficulty in developing appropriate measures of important activities and outputs.

Measuring Performance

Performance is the end result of activity. Select measures to assess performance based on the organizational unit to be appraised and the objectives to be achieved. The objectives that were established earlier in the strategy formulation part of the strategic management process (dealing with profitability, market share, and cost reduction, among others) should certainly be used to measure corporate performance once the strategies have been implemented.

APPROPRIATE MEASURES

Some measures, such as return on investment (ROI) and earnings per share (EPS), are appropriate for evaluating a corporation's or a division's ability to achieve a profitability objective. This type of measure, however, is inadequate for evaluating additional corporate objectives such as social responsibility or employee development. Even though profitability is a corporation's major objective, ROI and EPS can be computed only after profits are totaled for a period. It tells what happened after the fact—not what is happening or what will happen. A firm, therefore, needs to develop measures that predict likely profitability. These are referred to as **steering controls** because they measure variables that influence future profitability. Every industry has its own set of key metrics that tend to predict profits. Airlines, for example, closely monitor cost per available seat mile (ASM). In 2002, Southwest's cost per passenger mile was 7.5¢, the lowest in the industry, contrasted with United's 11.5¢, the highest in the industry. Its low costs gave Southwest a significant competitive advantage. By 2011, Southwest's costs had risen substantially to 12.5¢, while United had moved to 16.6¢. In the meantime, Southwest had been replaced as the most low-cost airline by Spirit Airlines, whose cost per ASM in 2011 was 10.1¢.[1]

An example of a steering control used by retail stores is the *inventory turnover ratio*, in which a retailer's cost of goods sold is divided by the average value of its inventories. This measure shows how hard an investment in inventory is working; the higher the ratio, the better. Not only does quicker moving inventory tie up less cash in inventories, it also reduces the risk that the goods will grow obsolete before they're sold—a crucial measure for computers and other technology items. For example, Office Depot increased its inventory turnover ratio from 6.9 in one year to 7.5 the next year, leading to improved annual profits.[2]

Another steering control is customer satisfaction. Research reveals that companies that score high on the *American Customer Satisfaction Index (ACSI)*, a measure developed by the University of Michigan's National Research Center, have higher stock returns and better cash flows than those companies that score low on the ACSI. A change in a firm's customer satisfaction typically works its way through a firm's value chain and is eventually reflected in quarterly profits.[3] Other approaches to measuring customer satisfaction include Oracle's use of the ratio of quarterly sales divided by customer service requests and the total number of hours that technicians spend on the phone solving customer problems. To help executives keep track of important steering controls, Netsuite developed *dashboard* software that displays critical information in easy-to-read computer graphics assembled from data pulled from other corporate software programs.[4]

TYPES OF CONTROLS

Controls can be established to focus on actual performance results (output), the activities that generate the performance (behavior), or on resources that are used in performance (input). **Output controls** specify what is to be accomplished by focusing on the end result of the behaviors through the use of objectives and performance targets or milestones. **Behavior controls** specify how something is to be done through policies, rules, standard operating procedures, and orders from a superior. **Input controls** emphasize resources, such as knowledge, skills, abilities, values, and motives of employees.[5]

Output, behavior, and input controls are not interchangeable. Output controls (such as sales quotas, specific cost-reduction or profit objectives, and surveys of customer satisfaction) are most appropriate when specific output measures have been agreed on but the cause–effect connection between activities and results is not clear. Behavior controls (such as following company procedures, making sales calls to potential customers, and getting to work on time) are most appropriate when performance results are hard to measure, but the cause–effect connection between activities and results is relatively clear. Input controls (such as number of years of education and experience) are most appropriate when output is difficult to measure and there is no clear cause–effect relationship between behavior and performance (such as in college teaching). Corporations following the strategy of conglomerate diversification tend to emphasize output controls with their divisions and subsidiaries (presumably because they are managed independently of each other), whereas, corporations following concentric diversification use all three types of controls (presumably because synergy is desired).[6] Even if all three types of control are used, one or two of them may be emphasized more than another depending on the circumstances. For example, Muralidharan and Hamilton propose that as a multinational corporation moves through its stages of development, its emphasis on control should shift from being primarily output at first, to behavioral, and finally to input control.[7]

Examples of increasingly popular behavior controls are the ISO 9000 and 14000 Standards Series on quality and environmental assurance, developed by the International Standards Association of Geneva, Switzerland. Using the **ISO 9000 Standards Series** (now a family of standards with eight management principles) is a way of objectively documenting a company's high level of quality operations. The **ISO 14000 Standards Series** establishes how to document the company's impact on the environment. A company wanting ISO 9000 certification would document its process for product introductions, among other things. ISO 9001 would require this firm to separately document design input, design process, design output, and design verification—a large amount of work. ISO 14001 would specify how companies should establish, maintain and continually improve an environmental management system. The benefits from ISO certification are partially in cost savings, but primarily they are a signal to suppliers and buyers about the focus of the company.[8] For an example of how one company that is steeped in controls is using an innovative idea to improve their systems, see the Innovation Issue feature.

Many corporations view ISO 9000 certification as assurance that a supplier sells quality products. Firms such as DuPont, Hewlett-Packard, and 3M have facilities registered to ISO standards. Companies in more than 60 countries, such as Canada, Mexico, Japan, the United States (including the entire U.S. auto industry), and the European Union, require ISO 9000 certification of their suppliers.[9] The same is happening for ISO 14000. Both Ford and General Motors require their suppliers to follow ISO 14001. In a survey of manufacturing executives, 51% of the executives found that ISO 9000 certification increased their international competitiveness. Other executives noted that it signaled their commitment to quality and gave them a strategic advantage over noncertified competitors.[10]

Since its ISO 14000 certification, SWD Inc. has become a showplace for environmental awareness. According to SWD's Delawder, ISO 14000 certification improves environmental

INNOVATION issue

REUSE OF ELECTRIC VEHICLE BATTERIES

No industry is more concerned about established procedures and minimizing fluctuations in their business model than the electric utility industry. Beyond storms that bring down the power grid, the biggest issue is dealing with fluctuations in power demand. Backup generators, purchasing power from other utilities, and keeping excess power available has been used for decades. However, the wide-scale introduction of solar arrays has added a whole new wrinkle to the issue in the industry. While solar arrays work quite well when the sun is shining, even modest cloud cover can cause large fluctuations in output.

Duke Energy in partnership with General Motors and ABB (the huge power technology company) is now exploring the reuse of electric vehicle batteries to smooth out fluctuations in the power grid. Not only would the system be good for the environment, but it would provide an innovative solution to a known problem in the industry.

A typical electric vehicle battery weighs more than 700 pounds and has 70% or more of its useful life left when it is no longer usable in an electric vehicle. General Motors estimates that it will have 500,000 vehicles with battery packs on the road by 2017, meaning that there is a huge recycling/reuse/waste issue that will have to be dealt with shortly.

Duke sees battery systems (EV battery packs that are linked together in a series) as a means for smoothing out sudden swings in output from solar arrays, thus helping the whole grid work more smoothly. The solar arrays could be used to provide power (when the sun is shining) to the grid, as well as to the recharging of battery systems. The system was demonstrated in San Francisco in 2012 and will be tested in undisclosed locations before being utilized on any scale.

SOURCES: M. Ramsey, "Ford Reveals How Much Electric Car Batteries Cost," *The Wall Street Journal* (April 17, 2012), http://blogs.wsj.com/drivers-seat/2012/04/17/ford-reveals-how-much-electric-car-batteries-cost/; B. Henderson, "Duke to Test Uses for EV Batteries," *The Charlotte Observer* (November 16, 2012), pg. 2B.

awareness among employees, reduces risks of violating regulations, and improves the firm's image among customers and the local community.[11]

Another example of a behavior control is a company's monitoring of employee phone calls and PCs to ensure that employees are behaving according to company guidelines. In a study by the American Management Association, nearly two-thirds of U.S. companies actively monitored their workers' Web site visits in order to prevent inappropriate surfing while 65% use software to block connections to Web sites deemed off limits for employees. 43% of companies monitor e-mail, and 28% of employers have fired workers for e-mail misuse. (For example, Xerox fired 40 employees for visiting pornographic Web sites.[12])

ACTIVITY-BASED COSTING

Activity-based costing (ABC) is a recently developed accounting method for allocating indirect and fixed costs to individual products or product lines based on the value-added activities going into that product.[13] This accounting method is thus very useful in doing a value-chain analysis of a firm's activities for making outsourcing decisions. Traditional cost accounting, in contrast, focuses on valuing a company's inventory for financial reporting purposes. To obtain a unit's cost, cost accountants typically add direct labor to the cost of materials. Then they compute overhead from rent to R&D expenses, based on the number of direct labor hours it takes to make a product. To obtain unit cost, they divide the total by the number of items made during the period under consideration.

Traditional cost accounting is useful when direct labor accounts for most of total costs and a company produces just a few products requiring the same processes. This may have been true of companies during the early part of the twentieth century, but it is no longer relevant today, when overhead may account for as much as 70% of manufacturing costs. According to Bob Van Der Linde, CEO of a contract manufacturing services firm in San Diego, California: "Overhead is 80% to 90% in our industry, so allocation errors lead to pricing errors, which could easily bankrupt the company."[14] The appropriate allocation of indirect costs and overhead has thus become crucial for decision making. The traditional volume-based cost-driven system systematically understates the cost per unit of products with low sales volumes and products with a high degree of complexity. Similarly, it overstates the cost per unit of products with high sales volumes and a low degree of complexity.[15] When Chrysler used ABC, it discovered that the true cost of some of the parts used in making cars was 30 times what the company had previously estimated.[16]

ABC accounting allows accountants to charge costs more accurately than the traditional method because it allocates overhead far more precisely. For example, imagine a production line in a pen factory where black pens are made in high volume and blue pens in low volume. Assume that it takes eight hours to retool (reprogram the machinery) to shift production from one kind of pen to the other. The total costs include supplies (the same for both pens), the direct labor of the line workers, and factory overhead. In this instance, a very significant part of the overhead cost is the cost of reprogramming the machinery to switch from one pen to another. If the company produces 10 times as many black pens as blue pens, 10 times the cost of the reprogramming expenses will be allocated to the black pens as to the blue pens under traditional cost accounting methods. This approach underestimates, however, the true cost of making the blue pens.

ABC accounting, in contrast, first breaks down pen manufacturing into its activities. It is then very easy to see that it is the activity of changing pens that triggers the cost of retooling. The ABC accountant calculates an average cost of setting up the machinery and charges it against each batch of pens that requires retooling, regardless of the size of the run. Thus a product carries only those costs for the overhead it actually consumes. Management is now able to discover that its blue pens cost almost twice as much as do the black pens. Unless the company is able to charge a higher price for its blue pens, it cannot make a profit on these pens. Unless there is a strategic reason why it must offer blue pens (such as a key customer who must have a small number of blue pens with every large order of black pens or a marketing trend away from black to blue pens), the company will earn significantly greater profits if it completely stops making blue pens.[17]

ENTERPRISE RISK MANAGEMENT

Enterprise Risk Management (ERM) is a corporatewide, integrated process for managing the uncertainties that could negatively or positively influence the achievement of the corporation's objectives. In the past, managing risk was done in a fragmented manner within functions or business units. Individuals would manage process risk, safety risk, and insurance, financial, and other assorted risks. As a result of this fragmented approach, companies would take huge risks in some areas of the business while over-managing substantially smaller risks in other areas. ERM is being adopted because of the increasing amount of environmental uncertainty that can affect an entire corporation. As a result, the position Chief Risk Officer is one of the fastest growing executive positions in U.S. corporations.[18] Microsoft uses scenario analysis to identify key business risks. According to Microsoft's treasurer, Brent Callinicos, "The scenarios are really what we're trying to protect against."[19] The scenarios were the possibility of an earthquake in the Seattle region and a major downturn in the stock market.

The process of rating risks involves three steps:

1. Identify the risks using scenario analysis or brainstorming or by performing risk self-assessments.

2. Rank the risks, using some scale of impact and likelihood.

3. Measure the risks, using some agreed-upon standard.

Some companies are using value at risk, or VAR (effect of unlikely events in normal markets), and stress testing (effect of plausible events in abnormal markets) methodologies to measure the potential impact of the financial risks they face. DuPont uses earnings at risk (EAR) measuring tools to measure the effect of risk on reported earnings. It can then manage risk to a specified earnings level based on the company's "risk appetite." With this integrated view, DuPont can view how risks affect the likelihood of achieving certain earnings targets.[20] Research has shown that companies with integrative risk management capabilities achieve superior economic performance.[21]

PRIMARY MEASURES OF CORPORATE PERFORMANCE

The days when simple financial measures such as ROI or EPS were used alone to assess overall corporate performance are coming to an end. Analysts now recommend a broad range of methods to evaluate the success or failure of a strategy. Some of these methods are stakeholder measures, shareholder value, and the balanced scorecard approach. Even though each of these methods has supporters as well as detractors, the current trend is clearly toward more complicated financial measures and an increasing use of non-financial measures of corporate performance. For example, research indicates that companies pursuing strategies founded on innovation and new product development now tend to favor non-financial over financial measures.[22]

Traditional Financial Measures

The most commonly used measure of corporate performance (in terms of profits) is **return on investment (ROI)**. It is simply the result of dividing net income before taxes by the total amount invested in the company (typically measured by total assets). Although using ROI has several advantages, it also has several distinct limitationsROI gives the impression of objectivity and precision, it can be easily manipulated.

Earnings per share (EPS), which involves dividing net earnings by the amount of common stock, also has several deficiencies as an evaluation of past and future performance. First, because alternative accounting principles are available, EPS can have several different but equally acceptable values, depending on the principle selected for its computation. Second, because EPS is based on accrual income, the conversion of income to cash can be near term or delayed. Therefore, EPS does not consider the time value of money. **Return on equity (ROE)**, which involves dividing net income by total equity, also has limitations because it is also derived from accounting-based data. In addition, EPS and ROE are often unrelated to a company's stock price.

Operating cash flow, the amount of money generated by a company before the cost of financing and taxes, is a broad measure of a company's funds. This is the company's net income plus depreciation, depletion, amortization, interest expense, and income tax expense.[23] Some takeover specialists look at a much narrower **free cash flow**: the amount of money a new owner can take out of the firm without harming the business. This is net income plus depreciation, depletion, and amortization less capital expenditures and dividends. The free cash flow ratio is very useful in evaluating the stability of an entrepreneurial venture.[24] Although cash flow may be harder to manipulate than earnings, the number can be increased by selling accounts receivable, classifying outstanding checks as accounts payable, trading securities, and capitalizing certain expenses, such as direct-response advertising.[25]

Because of these and other limitations, ROI, EPS, ROE, and operating cash flow are not by themselves adequate measures of corporate performance. At the same time, these traditional financial measures are very appropriate when used with complementary financial and non-financial measures. For example, some non–financial performance measures used by Internet business ventures are *stickiness* (length of Web site visit), *eyeballs* (number of people who visit a Web site), and *mindshare* (brand awareness). Mergers and acquisitions may be priced on multiples of *MUUs* (monthly unique users) or even on registered users.

Shareholder Value

Because of the belief that accounting-based numbers such as ROI, ROE, and EPS are not reliable indicators of a corporation's economic value, many corporations are using shareholder value as a better measure of corporate performance and strategic management effectiveness.

Shareholder value can be defined as the present value of the anticipated future stream of cash flows from the business plus the value of the company if liquidated. Arguing that the purpose of a company is to increase shareholder wealth, shareholder value analysis concentrates on cash flow as the key measure of performance. The value of a corporation is thus the value of its cash flows discounted back to their present value, using the business's cost of capital as the discount rate. As long as the returns from a business exceed its cost of capital, the business will create value and be worth more than the capital invested in it. For example, Deere and Company charges each business unit a cost of capital of 1% of assets a month. Each business unit is required to earn a shareholder value-added profit margin of 20%, on average, over the business cycle. Financial rewards are linked to this measure.[26]

The New York consulting firm Stern Stewart & Company devised and popularized two shareholder value measures: economic value added (EVA) and market value added (MVA). A basic tenet of EVA and MVA is that businesses should not invest in projects unless they can generate a profit above the cost of capital. Stern Stewart argues that a deficiency of traditional accounting-based measures is that they assume the cost of capital to be zero.[27] Well-known companies, such as Coca-Cola, General Electric, AT&T, Whirlpool, Quaker Oats, Eli Lilly, Georgia-Pacific, Polaroid, Sprint, Toyota, and Tenneco have adopted MVA and/or EVA as the best yardstick for corporate performance.

Economic value added (EVA) has become an extremely popular shareholder value method of measuring corporate and divisional performance and may be on its way to replacing ROI as the standard performance measure. EVA measures the difference between the pre- strategy and post-strategy values for the business. Simply put, EVA is after-tax operating income minus the total annual cost of capital. The formula to measure EVA is:

$$EVA = \text{after-tax operating income} - (\text{investment in assets} \times \text{weighted average cost of capital})^{28}$$

The cost of capital combines the cost of debt and equity. The annual cost of borrowed capital is the interest charged by the firm's banks and bondholders. To calculate the cost of equity, assume that shareholders generally earn about 6% more on stocks than on government bonds. If long-term treasury bills are selling at 2.5%, the firm's cost of equity should be 8.5%—more if the firm is in a risky industry. A corporation's overall cost of capital is the weighted-average cost of the firm's debt and equity capital. The investment in assets is the total amount of capital invested in the business, including buildings, machines, computers, and investments in R&D and training (allocating costs annually over their useful life). Because the typical balance sheet understates the investment made in a company, Stern Stewart has identified more than 160 possible adjustments, before EVA is calculated.[29] Multiply the firm's total investment in assets by the weighted-average cost of capital. Subtract that figure from after-tax operating income. If the difference is positive, the strategy (and the management employing it) is generating value for the shareholders. If it is negative, the strategy is destroying shareholder value.[30]

Roberto Goizueta, past-CEO of Coca-Cola, explained, "We raise capital to make concentrate, and sell it at an operating profit. Then we pay the cost of that capital. Shareholders pocket the difference."[31] Managers can improve their company's or business unit's EVA by: (1) earning more profit without using more capital, (2) using less capital, and (3) investing capital in high-return projects. Studies have found that companies using EVA outperform their median competitor by an average of 8.43% of total return annually.[32] EVA does, however, have some limitations. For one thing, it does not control for size differences across plants or divisions. As with ROI, managers can manipulate the numbers. As with ROI, EVA is an after-the-fact measure and cannot be used like a steering control.[33] Although proponents of EVA argue that EVA (unlike return on investment, equity, or sales) has a strong relationship to stock price, other studies do not support this contention.[34]

Market value added (MVA) is the difference between the market value of a corporation and the capital contributed by shareholders and lenders. Like net present value, it measures the stock market's estimate of the net present value of a firm's past and expected capital investment projects. As such, MVA is the present value of future EVA.[35] To calculate MVA:

1. Add all the capital that has been put into a company—from shareholders, bondholders, and retained earnings.

2. Reclassify certain accounting expenses, such as R&D, to reflect that they are actually investments in future earnings. This provides the firm's total capital. So far, this is the same approach taken in calculating EVA.

3. Using the current stock price, total the value of all outstanding stock, adding it to the company's debt. This is the company's market value. If the company's market value is greater than all the capital invested in it, the firm has a positive MVA—meaning that management (and the strategy it is following) has created wealth. In some cases, however, the market value of the company is actually less than the capital put into it, which means shareholder wealth is being destroyed.

Microsoft, General Electric, Intel, and Coca-Cola have tended to have high MVAs in the United States, whereas General Motors and RJR Nabisco have had low ones.[36]Studies have shown that EVA is a predictor of MVA. Consecutive years of positive EVA generally lead to a soaring MVA.[37] Research also reveals that CEO turnover is significantly correlated with MVA and EVA, whereas ROA and ROE are not. This suggests that EVA and MVA may be more appropriate measures of the market's evaluation of a firm's strategy and its management than are the traditional measures of corporate performance.[38] Nevertheless, these measures consider only the financial interests of the shareholder and ignore other stakeholders, such as environmentalists and employees.

Climate change is likely to lead to new regulations, technological remedies, and shifts in consumer behavior. It will thus have a significant impact on the financial performance of many corporations. To see how companies are using new techniques that are simultaneously good for the environment as well as being good for the company, see the **Sustainability Issue** feature.

BALANCED SCORECARD APPROACH: USING KEY PERFORMANCE MEASURES

Rather than evaluate a corporation using a few financial measures, Kaplan and Norton argue for a "balanced scorecard" that includes non-financial as well as financial measures.[39] This approach is especially useful given that research indicates that non-financial assets explain 50% to 80% of a firm's value.[40] The **balanced scorecard** combines financial measures that tell the results of actions already taken with operational measures on customer satisfaction, internal processes, and the corporation's innovation and improvement activities—the drivers of future financial performance. Thus steering controls are combined with output controls. In the balanced scorecard, management develops goals or objectives in each of four areas:

- **Financial:** How do we appear to shareholders?
- **Customer:** How do customers view us?

SUSTAINABILITY issue

E-RECEIPTS

More than nine million trees are cut down each year to make cash register receipts in the United States and most of those receipts are simply thrown away. A number of companies were moving toward e-receipts in the late 1990s, but the dot-com bust brought all that to a temporary end. In 2005, Apple introduced e-receipts at its stylish Apple stores and the wave began.

E-receipts not only save on necessary printing and landfill waste, they also provide the customer with an electronic record of purchases (for taxes, expense reports, or gift returns). A number of national retailers now offer e-receipts, including Best Buy, Whole Foods, Nordstrom, Gap Inc. (which owns Old Navy and Banana Republic), Anthropologie, Patagonia, Sears, and Kmart. The advantage beyond cost savings for the retailer is having the customer's e-mail address for use with promotions.

Some companies are using this new opportunity to provide value to the consumer. At Nordstrom's, they are looking at making e-receipts more appealing by adding a picture of the item to the receipt so a shopper can post it to a Facebook wall or remember exactly what they bought last time.

According to a 2012 survey of 3900 retailers, more than 35% now offer e-receipts as an option. At Wells Fargo, 12% of their customers are choosing e-receipts for their ATM transactions. The audit trail is improved for both customer and company by providing a new level of improved control.

....
SOURCES: W. Koch, "Retailers Find Profits with Paperless Receipts," *USA Today* (November 3, 2012), http://www.usatoday.com/story/news/nation/2012/11/03/retailers-e-mail-digital-paperless-receipts/1675069/#; S. Clifford, "Shopper Receipts Join Paperless Age," *The New York Times* (August 7, 2011), http://www.nytimes.com/2011/08/08/technology/digital-receipts-at-stores-gain-in-popularity.html?_r=0.

- **Internal business perspective:** What must we excel at?
- **Innovation and learning:** Can we continue to improve and create value?[41]

Each goal in each area (for example, avoiding bankruptcy in the financial area) is then assigned one or more measures, as well as a target and an initiative. These measures can be thought of as **key performance measures**—measures that are essential for achieving a desired strategic option.[42] For example, a company could include cash flow, quarterly sales growth, and ROE as measures for success in the financial area. It could include market share (competitive position goal), customer satisfaction, and percentage of new sales coming from new products (customer acceptance goal) as measures under the customer perspective. It could include cycle time and unit cost (manufacturing excellence goal) as measures under the internal business perspective. It could include time to develop next-generation products (technology leadership objective) under the innovation and learning perspective.

A 2011 global survey by Bain & Company reported that 63% of Fortune 1000 companies in North America use a version of the balanced scorecard.[43] A study of the Fortune 500 firms in the United States and the Post 300 firms in Canada revealed the most popular non-financial measures to be customer satisfaction, customer service, product quality, market share, productivity, service quality, and core competencies. New product development, corporate culture, and market growth were not far behind.[44] DuPont's Engineering Polymers Division uses the balanced scorecard to align employees, business units, and shared services around a common strategy involving productivity improvements and revenue growth.[45] Corporate experience with the balanced scorecard reveals that a firm should tailor the system to suit its situation, not just adopt it as a cookbook approach. When the balanced scorecard complements corporate strategy, it improves performance. Using the method in a mechanistic fashion without any link to strategy hinders performance and may even decrease it.[46]

Evaluating Top Management and the Board of Directors

Through its strategy, audit, and compensation committees, a board of directors closely evaluates the job performance of the CEO and the top management team. The vast majority of American (91%), European (75%), and Asian (75%) boards review the CEO's performance using a formalized process.[47] Objective evaluations of the CEO by the board are very important given that CEOs tend to evaluate senior management's performance significantly more positively than do other executives.[48] The board is concerned primarily with overall corporate profitability as measured quantitatively by ROI, ROE, EPS, and shareholder value. The absence of short-run profitability certainly contributes to the firing of any CEO. The board, however, is also concerned with other factors.

Members of the compensation committees of today's boards of directors generally agree that a CEO's ability to establish strategic direction, build a management team, and provide leadership are more critical in the long run than are a few quantitative measures. The board should evaluate top management not only on the typical output-oriented quantitative measures, but also on behavioral measures—factors relating to its strategic management practices. According to a survey by Korn/Ferry International, the criteria used by American boards are financial (81%), ethical behavior (63%), thought leadership (58%), corporate reputation (32%), stock price performance (22%), and meeting participation (10%).[49] The specific items that a board uses to evaluate its top management should be derived from the objectives that both the board and top management agreed on earlier. If better relations with the local community and improved safety practices in work areas were selected as objectives for the year (or for five years), these items should be included in the evaluation. In addition, other factors that tend to lead to profitability might be included, such as market share, product quality, or investment intensity.

Performance evaluations of the overall board's performance are standard practice for 87% of directors in the Americas, 72% in Europe, and 62% in Asia.[50] Evaluations of individual directors are less common. According to a PricewaterhouseCoopers survey of 1100 directors, 77% of the directors agreed that individual directors should be appraised regularly on their performance, but only 37% responded that they actually do so.[51] Corporations that have successfully used board performance appraisal systems are Goldman Sachs, Boeing, Ingersoll Rand, McDonald's, Google, and Ford Motor.

Chairman-CEO Feedback Instrument. An increasing number of companies are evaluating their CEO by using a 17-item questionnaire developed by Ram Charon, an authority on corporate governance. The questionnaire focuses on four key areas: (1) company performance, (2) leadership of the organization, (3) team-building and management succession, and (4) leadership of external constituencies.[52] After taking an hour to complete the questionnaire, the board of KeraVision Inc. used it as a basis for a lengthy discussion with the CEO, Thomas Loarie. The board criticized Loarie for "not tempering enthusiasm with reality" and urged Loarie to develop a clear management succession plan. The evaluation caused Loarie to more closely involve the board in setting the company's primary objectives and discussing "where we are, where we want to go, and the operating environment."[53]

Management Audit. Management audits are very useful to boards of directors in evaluating management's handling of various corporate activities. Management audits have been developed to evaluate activities such as corporate social responsibility, functional areas like the marketing department, and divisions such as the international division. These can be helpful if the board has selected particular functional areas or activities for improvement.

Strategic Audit. The strategic audit, presented in the **Chapter 1 Appendix 1.A**, is a type of management audit. The strategic audit provides a checklist of questions, by area or issue, that enables a systematic analysis of various corporate functions and activities to be made. It is a type of management audit and is extremely useful as a diagnostic tool to pinpoint corporatewide problem areas and to highlight organizational strengths and weaknesses.[54] A strategic audit can help determine why a certain area is creating problems for a corporation and help generate solutions to the problem. As such, it can be very useful in evaluating the performance of top management.

PRIMARY MEASURES OF DIVISIONAL AND FUNCTIONAL PERFORMANCE

Companies use a variety of techniques to evaluate and control performance in divisions, strategic business units (SBUs), and functional areas. If a corporation is composed of SBUs or divisions, it will use many of the same performance measures (ROI or EVA, for instance) that it uses to assess overall corporate performance. To the extent that it can isolate specific functional units such as R&D, the corporation may develop responsibility centers. It will also use typical functional measures, such as market share and sales per employee (marketing), unit costs and percentage of defects (operations), percentage of sales from new products and number of patents (R&D), and turnover and job satisfaction (HRM). For example, FedEx uses Enhanced Tracker software with its COSMOS database to track the progress of its 2.5 to 3.5 million shipments daily. As a courier is completing her or his day's activities, the Enhanced Tracker asks whether the person's package count equals the Enhanced Tracker's count. If the count is off, the software helps reconcile the differences.[55]

During strategy formulation and implementation, top management approves a series of programs and supporting *operating budgets* from its business units. During evaluation and control, actual expenses are contrasted with planned expenditures, and the degree of variance is assessed. This is typically done on a monthly basis. In addition, top management will probably require *periodic statistical reports* summarizing data on such key factors as the number of new customer contracts, the volume of received orders, and productivity figures.

RESPONSIBILITY CENTERS

Control systems can be established to monitor specific functions, projects, or divisions. Budgets are one type of control system that is typically used to control the financial indicators of performance. **Responsibility centers** are used to isolate a unit so it can be evaluated separately from the rest of the corporation. Each responsibility center, therefore, has its own budget and is evaluated on its use of budgeted resources. It is headed by the manager responsible for the center's performance. The center uses resources (measured in terms of costs or expenses) to produce a service or a product (measured in terms of volume or revenues). There are five major types of responsibility centers. The type is determined by the way the corporation's control system measures these resources and services or products.

- **Standard cost centers: Standard cost centers** are primarily used in manufacturing facilities. Standard (or expected) costs are computed for each operation on the basis of historical data. In evaluating the center's performance, its total standard costs are multiplied by the units produced. The result is the *expected* cost of production, which is then compared to the *actual* cost of production.

- **Revenue centers:** With **revenue centers**, production, usually in terms of unit or dollar sales, is measured without consideration of resource costs (for example, salaries). The center is thus judged in terms of effectiveness rather than efficiency. The effectiveness of a sales region, for example, is determined by comparing its actual sales to its projected or previous year's sales. Profits are not considered because sales departments have very limited influence over the cost of the products they sell.

- **Expense centers:** Resources are measured in dollars, without consideration for service or product costs. Thus budgets will have been prepared for engineered expenses (costs that can be calculated) and for discretionary expenses (costs that can be only estimated). Typical **expense centers** are administrative, service, and research departments. They cost a company money, but they only indirectly contribute to revenues.

- **Profit centers:** Performance is measured in terms of the difference between revenues (which measure production) and expenditures (which measure resources). A **profit center** is typically established whenever an organizational unit has control over both its resources and its products or services. By having such centers, a company can be organized into divisions of separate product lines. The manager of each division is given autonomy to the extent that he or she is able to keep profits at a satisfactory (or better) level.

Some organizational units that are not usually considered potentially autonomous can, for the purpose of profit center evaluations, be made so. A manufacturing department, for example, can be converted from a standard cost center (or expense center) into a profit center; it is allowed to charge a transfer price for each product it "sells" to the sales department. The difference between the manufacturing cost per unit and the agreed-upon transfer price is the unit's "profit."

Transfer pricing is commonly used in vertically integrated corporations and can work well when a price can be easily determined for a designated amount of product. Even though most experts agree that market-based transfer prices are the best choice, A 2010 global survey completed by E&Y found that only 27% of companies use market price to set the transfer price.[56] When a price cannot be set easily, however, the relative bargaining power of the centers, rather than strategic considerations, tends to influence the agreed-upon price. Top management has an obligation to make sure that these political considerations do not overwhelm the strategic ones. Otherwise, profit figures for each center will be biased and provide poor information for strategic decisions at both the corporate and divisional levels.

- **Investment centers:** Because many divisions in large manufacturing corporations use significant assets to make their products, their asset base should be factored into their performance evaluation. Thus it is insufficient to focus only on profits, as in the case of profit centers. An **investment center's** performance is measured in terms of the difference between its resources and its services or products. For example, two divisions in a corporation made identical profits, but one division owns a $3 million plant, whereas the other owns a $1 million plant. Both make the same profits, but one is obviously more efficient; the smaller plant provides the shareholders with a better return on their investment. The most widely used measure of investment center performance is ROI.

Most single-business corporations, such as Buffalo Wild Wings, tend to use a combination of cost, expense, and revenue centers. In these corporations, most managers are functional specialists and manage against a budget. Total profitability is integrated at the corporate level. Multidivisional corporations with one dominating product line (such as ABInBev) that have diversified into a few businesses but that still depend on a single product line (such as beer) for most of their revenue and income, generally use a combination of cost, expense, revenue, and profit centers. Multidivisional corporations, such as General Electric, tend to emphasize investment centers—although in various units throughout the corporation other types of responsibility centers are also used. One problem with using responsibility centers, however, is that the separation needed to measure and evaluate a division's performance can diminish the level of cooperation among divisions that is needed to attain synergy for the corporation as a whole. (This problem is discussed later in this chapter, under "Suboptimization.")

USING BENCHMARKING TO EVALUATE PERFORMANCE

According to Xerox Corporation, the company that pioneered this concept in the United States, **benchmarking** is "the continual process of measuring products, services, and practices against the toughest competitors or those companies recognized as industry leaders."[57] Benchmarking, an increasingly popular program, is based on the concept that it makes no sense to reinvent something that someone else is already using. It involves openly learning how others do something better than one's own company so that the company not only can imitate, but perhaps even improve upon its techniques. The benchmarking process usually involves the following steps:

1. Identify the area or process to be examined. It should be an activity that has the potential to determine a business unit's competitive advantage.

2. Find behavioral and output measures of the area or process and obtain measurements.

3. Select an accessible set of competitors and best-in-class companies against which to benchmark. These may very often be companies that are in completely different industries, but perform similar activities. For example, when Xerox wanted to improve its order fulfillment, it went to L.L.Bean, the successful mail order firm, to learn how it achieved excellence in this area.

4. Calculate the differences among the company's performance measurements and those of the best-in-class and determine why the differences exist.

5. Develop tactical programs for closing performance gaps.

6. Implement the programs and then compare the resulting new measurements with those of the best-in-class companies.

Benchmarking has been found to produce best results in companies that are already well managed. Apparently poorer performing firms tend to be overwhelmed by the discrepancy between their performance and the benchmark—and tend to view the benchmark as too difficult to reach.[58] Nevertheless, a survey by Bain & Company of companies of various sizes across all U.S. industries indicated that about 65% were using benchmarking.[59] Cost reductions range from 15% to 45%.[60] Benchmarking can also increase sales, improve goal setting, and boost employee motivation.[61] The average cost of a benchmarking study is around $100,000 and involves 30 weeks of effort.[62] Manco Inc., a small Cleveland-area producer of duct tape, regularly benchmarks itself against Wal-Mart, Rubbermaid, and PepsiCo to enable it to better compete with giant 3M. APQC (American Productivity & Quality Center), a Houston research group, established the Open Standards Benchmarking Collaborative database, composed of more than 1200 commonly used measures and individual benchmarks, to track the performance of core operational functions. Firms can submit their performance data to this online database to learn how they compare to top performers and industry peers (see www.apqc.org).

INTERNATIONAL MEASUREMENT ISSUES

The three most widely used techniques for international performance evaluation are ROI, budget analysis, and historical comparisons. In one study, 95% of the corporate officers interviewed stated that they use the same evaluation techniques for foreign and domestic operations. Rate of return was mentioned as the single most important measure.[63] However, ROI can cause problems when it is applied to international operations: Because of foreign currencies, different accounting systems, different rates of inflation, different tax laws, and the use of transfer pricing, both the net income figure and the investment base may be seriously distorted.[64] To deal with different accounting systems throughout the world, the London-based International Accounting Standards Board developed International Financial Reporting Standards (IFRS) to harmonize accounting practices. The Financial Accounting Standards Board (FASB) oversees the Generally Accepted Accounting Principles (GAAP) that is used in the United States. Over the past decade, these two groups have worked to merge their systems and there was hope that there would be a single set of standards by 2015. Nevertheless, enforcement and cultural interpretations of the international rules can still vary by country and may undercut what is hoped to be a uniform accounting system.[65]

A study of 79 MNCs revealed that *international transfer pricing* from one country unit to another is primarily used not to evaluate performance but to minimize taxes.[66] Taxes are an important issue for MNCs, given that corporate tax rates vary from 40% in the United States to 38% in Japan, 32% in India, 30% in Mexico, 24% in the U.K. and South Korea, 26% in Canada, 25% in China, 17% in Singapore, 10% in Albania, and 0% in Bahrain and the Cayman Islands.[67] For example, the U.S. Internal Revenue Service contended in the early 1990s that many Japanese firms doing business in the United States artificially inflated the value of U.S. deliveries in order to reduce the profits and thus the taxes of their American subsidiaries.[68]

Parts made in a subsidiary of a Japanese MNC in a low-tax country such as Singapore could be shipped to its subsidiary in a high-tax country like the United States at such a high price that the U.S. subsidiary reports very little profit (and thus pays few taxes), while the Singapore subsidiary reports a very high profit (but also pays few taxes because of the lower tax rate). A Japanese MNC could, therefore, earn more profit worldwide by reporting less profit in high-tax countries and more profit in low-tax countries. Transfer pricing can thus be one way the parent company can reduce taxes and "capture profits" from a subsidiary. Other common ways of transferring profits to the parent company (often referred to as the *repatriation of profits*) are through dividends, royalties, and management fees.[69]

Among the most important barriers to international trade are the different standards for products and services. There are at least three categories of standards: safety/environmental, energy efficiency, and testing procedures. Existing standards have been drafted by such bodies as the British Standards Institute (BSI-UK) in the United Kingdom, the Japanese Industrial Standards Committee (JISC), AFNOR in France, DIN in Germany, CSA in Canada, and the American Standards Institute in the United States. These standards traditionally created entry barriers that served to fragment various industries, such as major home appliances, by country. The International Electrotechnical Commission (IEC) standards were created to harmonize standards in the European Union and eventually to serve as worldwide standards, with some national deviations to satisfy specific needs. Because the European Union (EU) was the first to harmonize the many different standards of its member countries, the EU is shaping standards for the rest of the world. In addition, the International Organization for Standardization (ISO) is preparing and publishing international standards. These standards provide a foundation for regional associations to build upon. CANENA, the Council for Harmonization of Electrotechnical Standards of the Nations of the Americas, was created in 1992 to further coordinate the harmonization of standards in North and South America. Efforts are also under way in Asia to harmonize standards.[70]

An important issue in international trade is counterfeiting/piracy. Firms in developing nations around the world make money by making counterfeit/pirated copies of well-known name-brand products and selling them globally as well as locally. See the **Global Issue** feature to learn how this is being done.

Authorities in international business recommend that the control and reward systems used by a global MNC be different from those used by a multidomestic MNC.[71]

A *MNC* should use loose controls on its foreign units. The management of each geographic unit should be given considerable operational latitude, but it should be expected to meet some performance targets. Because profit and ROI measures are often unreliable in international operations, it is recommended that the MNC's top management, in this instance, emphasize budgets and non-financial measures of performance such as market share, productivity, public image, employee morale, and relations with the host country government.[72] Multiple measures should be used to differentiate between the worth of the subsidiary and the performance of its management.

A *global MNC*, however, needs tight controls over its many units. To reduce costs and gain competitive advantage, it is trying to spread the manufacturing and marketing operations of a few fairly uniform products around the world. Therefore, its key operational decisions must be centralized. Its environmental scanning must include research not only into each of the national markets in which the MNC competes but also into the "global arena" of the interaction between markets. Foreign units are thus evaluated more as cost centers, revenue centers, or expense centers than as investment or profit centers because MNCs operating in a global industry do not often make the entire product in the country in which it is sold.

GLOBAL issue

COUNTERFEIT GOODS AND PIRATED SOFTWARE: A GLOBAL PROBLEM

"We know that 15% to 20% of all goods in China are counterfeit," states Dan Chow, a law professor at Ohio State University. This includes products from Tide detergent and Budweiser beer to Marlboro cigarettes. There is a saying in Shanghai, China: "We can copy everything except your mother." Yamaha estimates that five out of every six bikes bearing its brand name are fake. Fake Cisco network routers (known as "Chiscos") and counterfeit Nokia mobile phones can be easily found throughout China. Procter & Gamble estimates that 15% of the soaps and detergents under its Head & Shoulders, Vidal Sassoon, Safeguard, and Tide brands in China are counterfeit, costing the company $150 million in lost sales.

In Yiwu, a few hours from Shanghai, one person admitted to a *60 Minutes* reporter that she could make 1000 pairs of counterfeit Nike shoes in 10 days for $4.00 a pair. According to the market research firm Automotive Resources, the profit margins on counterfeit shock absorbers can reach 80% versus only 15% for the real ones. The World Custom Organization estimates that 7% of the world's merchandise is bogus.

Tens of thousands of counterfeiters are active in China. They range from factories mixing shampoo and soap in back rooms to large state-owned enterprises making copies of soft drinks and beer. Other factories make everything from car batteries to automobiles. Mobile CD factories with optical disc-mastering machines counterfeit music and software. *60 Minutes* found a small factory in Donguan making fake Callaway golf clubs and bags at a rate of 500 bags per week. Factories in the southern Guangdong and Fujian provinces truck their products to a central distribution center, such as the one in Yiwu. They may also be shipped across the border into Russia, Pakistan, Vietnam, or Burma. Chinese counterfeiters have developed a global reach through their connections with organized crime.

As much as 35% of software on personal computers worldwide is pirated, according to the Business Software Alliance and ISDC, a market research firm. The worldwide cost of software piracy was around $63 billion in 2011. For example, 21% of the software sold in the United States is pirated. That figure increases to 26%–30% in the European Union, 83% in Russia, Algeria, and Bolivia, to 86% in China, 87% in Indonesia, and 90% in Vietnam.

....

SOURCES: "Head in the Clouds," *The Economist* (July 25, 2012), http://www.economist.com/blogs/graphicdetail/2012/07/online-software-piracy; "The Sincerest Form of Flattery," *The Economist* (April 7, 2007), pp. 64–65; F. Balfour, "Fakes!" *BusinessWeek* (February 7, 2005), pp. 54–64; "PC Software Piracy," *The Economist* (June 10, 2006), p. 102; "The World's Greatest Fakes," *60 Minutes*, CBS News (August 8, 2004); "Business Software Piracy," *Pocket World in Figures 2004* (London: Economist & Profile Book, 2003), p. 60; D. Roberts, F. Balfour, P. Magnusson, P. Engardio, and J. Lee, "China's Piracy Plague," *BusinessWeek* (June 5, 2000), pp. 44–48.

Strategic Information Systems

Before performance measures can have any impact on strategic management, they must first be communicated to the people responsible for formulating and implementing strategic plans. Strategic information systems can perform this function. They can be computer-based or manual, formal or informal. One of the key reasons given for the bankruptcy of International Harvester was the inability of the corporation's top management to precisely determine income by major class of similar products. Because of this inability, management kept trying to fix ailing businesses and was unable to respond flexibly to major changes and unexpected events. In contrast, one of the key reasons for the success of Wal-Mart has been management's use of the company's sophisticated information system to control purchasing decisions. Cash registers in Wal-Mart retail stores transmit information hourly to computers at the company headquarters. Consequently, managers know every morning exactly how many of each item were sold the day before, how many have been sold so far in the year, and how this year's sales compare to last year's. The information system allows all reordering to be done automatically by computers, without any managerial input. It also allows the company to experiment with new products without committing to big orders in advance. In effect, the system allows the customers to decide through their purchases what gets reordered.

ENTERPRISE RESOURCE PLANNING (ERP)

Many corporations around the world have adopted **enterprise resource planning (ERP)** software. ERP unites all of a company's major business activities, from order processing to production, within a single family of software modules. The system provides instant access to critical information to everyone in the organization, from the CEO to the factory floor worker. Because of the ability of ERP software to use a common information system throughout a company's many operations around the world, it is becoming the business information systems' global standard. The major providers of this software are SAP AG, Oracle (including PeopleSoft), J. D. Edwards, Baan, and SSA Global Technologies.

The German company SAP AG originated the concept with its R/3 software system. Microsoft, for example, used R/3 to replace a tangle of 33 financial tracking systems in 26 subsidiaries. Even though it cost the company $25 million and took 10 months to install, R/3 annually saves Microsoft $18 million. Coca-Cola uses the R/3 system to enable a manager in Atlanta to use her personal computer to check the latest sales of 20-ounce bottles of Coke Classic in India. Owens-Corning envisioned that its R/3 system allowed salespeople to learn what was available at any plant or warehouse and to quickly assemble orders for customers.

ERP may not fit every company, however. The system is extremely complicated and demands a high level of standardization throughout a corporation. Its demanding nature often forces companies to change the way they do business. There are three reasons ERP could fail: (1) insufficient tailoring of the software to fit the company, (2) inadequate training, and (3) insufficient implementation support.[73] Over the two-year period of installing R/3, Owens-Corning had to completely overhaul its operations. Because R/3 was incompatible with Apple's very organic corporate culture, the company was able to apply it only to its order management and financial operations, but not to manufacturing. Other companies that had difficulty installing and using ERP are Whirlpool, Hershey Foods, Volkswagen, and Stanley Works. At Whirlpool, SAP's software led to missed and delayed shipments, causing The Home Depot to cancel its agreement for selling Whirlpool products.[74] One survey found that 65% of executives believed that ERP had a moderate chance of hurting their business because of implementation problems. Nevertheless, the payoff from ERP software can be worth the effort. In an industry where one company implements ERP ahead of its competitors, it can be used to gain some competitive advantage, streamline operations, and help manage a lean manufacturing system.[75]

RADIO FREQUENCY IDENTIFICATION (RFID)

Radio frequency identification (RFID) is an electronic tagging technology used in a number of companies to improve supply-chain efficiency. By tagging containers and items with tiny chips, companies use the tags as wireless barcodes to track inventory more efficiently. Both Wal-Mart and the U.S. Department of Defense began requiring their largest suppliers to incorporate RFID tags in their goods in 2003. After trying to implement RFID for the past decade, the UK-based supermarket chain Tesco postponed their full implementation of RFID technology in late 2012. Tesco had planned to deploy RFID tags and readers in 1400 stores and in its distribution centers by the middle of 2012. However, it had installed RFID tags in only 40 stores and one depot before it brought the program to a halt.[76] Nevertheless, some suppliers and retailers of expensive consumer products view the cost of the tag as worthwhile because it reduces losses from counterfeiting and theft. RFID technology is currently in wide use as wireless commuter passes for toll roads, tunnels, and bridges. Even though RFID standards may vary among companies, individual firms like Audi, Sony, and Dole Food use the tags to track goods within their own factories and warehouses.[77] According to Dan Mullen of AIM Global, "RFID will go through a process similar to what happened in barcode technology 20 years ago. . . . As companies implement the technology deeper within their operations, the return on investment will grow and applications will expand."[78]

DIVISIONAL AND FUNCTIONAL IS SUPPORT

At the divisional or SBU level of a corporation, the information system should be used to support, reinforce, or enlarge its business-level strategy through its decision support system. An SBU pursuing a strategy of overall cost leadership could use its information system to reduce costs either by improving labor productivity or improving the use of other resources such as inventory or machinery. Kaiser Health has 37 hospitals, 15,857 physicians, and 9 million plus members all tied together in a single system that has made for better health services and an increased ability to reduce problems in the system. An internal study of heart attacks among 46,000 patients in Northern California who were 30 years and older showed a decline of 24 percent. Kaiser has also reduced mortality rates by 40% since 2008 for its hospital patients who contract sepsis, a dangerous infectious disease.[79] Another SBU, in contrast, might want to pursue a differentiation strategy. It could use its information system to add uniqueness to the product or service and contribute to quality, service, or image through the functional areas. FedEx wanted to use superior service to gain a competitive advantage. It invested significantly in several types of information systems to measure and track the performance of its delivery service. Together, these information systems gave FedEx the fastest error-response time in the overnight delivery business.

Problems in Measuring Performance

The measurement of performance is a crucial part of evaluation and control. The lack of quantifiable objectives or performance standards and the inability of the information system to provide timely and valid information are two obvious control problems. According to Meg Whitman, former CEO of eBay, "If you can't measure it, you can't control it." That's why eBay has a multitude of measures, from total revenues and profits to *take rate*, the ratio of revenues to the value of goods traded on the site.[80] Without objective and timely measurements, it would be extremely difficult to make operational, let alone strategic, decisions. Nevertheless, the use of timely, quantifiable standards does not guarantee good performance. The very act of monitoring and measuring performance can cause side effects that interfere with overall corporate performance. Among the most frequent negative side effects are a short-term orientation and goal displacement.

SHORT-TERM ORIENTATION

Top executives report that in many situations, they analyze neither the long-term implications of present operations on the strategy they have adopted nor the operational impact of a strategy on the corporate mission. Long-term evaluations may not be conducted because executives

(1) don't realize their importance, (2) believe that short-term considerations are more important than long-term considerations, (3) aren't personally evaluated on a long-term basis, or (4) don't have the time to make a long-term analysis.[81] There is no real justification for the first and last reasons. If executives realize the importance of long-term evaluations, they make the time needed to conduct them. Even though many chief executives point to immediate pressures from the investment community and to short-term incentive and promotion plans to support the second and third reasons, evidence does not always support their claims.[82]

At one international heavy-equipment manufacturer, managers were so strongly motivated to achieve their quarterly revenue target that they shipped unfinished products from their plant in England to a warehouse in the Netherlands for final assembly. By shipping the incomplete products, they were able to realize the sales before the end of the quarter—thus fulfilling their budgeted objective and making their bonuses. Unfortunately, the high cost of assembling the goods at a distant location (requiring not only renting the warehouse but also paying additional labor) ended up reducing the company's overall profit.[83]

Many accounting-based measures, such as EPS and ROI, encourage a **short-term orientation** in which managers consider only current tactical or operational issues and ignore long-term strategic ones. Because growth in EPS (earnings per share) is an important driver of near-term stock price, top managers are biased against investments that might reduce short-term EPS.[84] This is compounded by pressure from financial analysts and investors for quarterly *earnings guidance*—that is, estimates of future corporate earnings.[85] Hewlett-Packard (HP) acquired British firm Autonomy for $11.1 billion in 2011 and had to write down $8.8 billion of that amount in 2012 as the company found significant accounting errors. Multiple lawsuits were filed against HP, its officers, directors, and the accounting firms involved with Autonomy before the acquisition.[86]

One of the limitations of ROI as a performance measure is its short-term nature. In theory, ROI is not limited to the short run, but in practice it is often difficult to use this measure to realize long-term benefits for a company. Because managers can often manipulate both the numerator (earnings) and the denominator (investment), the resulting ROI figure can be meaningless. Advertising, maintenance, and research efforts can be reduced. Estimates of pension-fund profits, unpaid receivables, and old inventory, are easy to adjust. Optimistic estimates of returned products, bad debts, and obsolete inventory inflate the present year's sales and earnings.[87] Expensive retooling and plant modernization can be delayed as long as a manager can manipulate figures on production defects and absenteeism. In a recent survey of financial executives, 80% of the managers stated that they would decrease spending on research and development, advertising, maintenance, and hiring in order to meet earnings targets. More than half said they would delay a new project even if it meant sacrificing value.[88]

Mergers can be undertaken that will do more for the present year's earnings (and the next year's paycheck) than for the division's or corporation's future profits. For example, research on 55 firms that engaged in major acquisitions revealed that even though the firms performed poorly after the acquisition, the acquiring firms' top management still received significant increases in compensation.[89] Determining CEO compensation on the basis of firm size rather than performance is typical and is particularly likely for firms that are not monitored closely by independent analysts.[90]

Research supports the conclusion that many CEOs and their friends on the board of directors' compensation committee manipulate information to provide themselves a pay raise.[91] For example, CEOs tend to announce bad news—thus reducing the company's stock price—just before the issuance of stock options. Once the options are issued, the CEOs tend to announce good news—thus raising the stock price and making their options more valuable.[92] Board compensation committees tend to expand the peer group comparison outside their industry to include lower-performing firms to justify a high raise to the CEO. They tend to do this when the company performs poorly, the industry performs well, the CEO is already highly paid, and shareholders are powerful and active.[93]

GOAL DISPLACEMENT

If not carefully done, monitoring and measuring of performance can actually result in a decline in overall corporate performance. **Goal displacement** is the confusion of means with ends and occurs when activities originally intended to help managers attain corporate objectives become ends in themselves—or are adapted to meet ends other than those for which they were intended. Two types of goal displacement are behavior substitution and suboptimization.

Behavior Substitution

Behavior substitution refers to the phenomenon of when people substitute activities that do not lead to goal accomplishment for activities that do lead to goal accomplishment because the wrong activities are being rewarded. Managers, like most other people, tend to focus more of their attention on behaviors that are clearly measurable than on those that are not. Employees often receive little or no reward for engaging in hard-to-measure activities such as cooperation and initiative. However, easy-to-measure activities might have little or no relationship to the desired good performance. Rational people, nevertheless, tend to work for the rewards that the system has to offer. Therefore, people tend to substitute behaviors that are recognized and rewarded for behaviors that are ignored, without regard to their contribution to goal accomplishment. A research study of 157 corporations revealed that most of the companies made little attempt to identify areas of non-financial performance that might advance their chosen strategy. Only 23% consistently built and verified cause-and-effect relationships between intermediate controls (such as number of patents filed or product flaws) and company performance.[94]

A U.S. Navy quip sums up this situation: "What you inspect (or reward) is what you get." If the reward system emphasizes quantity while merely asking for quality and cooperation, the system is likely to produce a large number of low-quality products and unsatisfied customers.[95] A proposed law governing the effect of measurement on behavior is that *quantifiable measures drive out non-quantifiable measures.*

A classic example of behavior substitution happened a few years ago at Sears. Sears' management thought it could improve employee productivity by tying performance to rewards. It, therefore, paid commissions to its auto shop employees as a percentage of each repair bill. Behavior substitution resulted as employees altered their behavior to fit the reward system. The results were over-billed customers, charges for work never done, and a scandal that tarnished Sears' reputation for many years.[96]

Suboptimization

Suboptimization refers to the phenomenon of a unit optimizing its goal accomplishment to the detriment of the organization as a whole. The emphasis in large corporations on developing separate responsibility centers can create some problems for the corporation as a whole. To the extent that a division or functional unit views itself as a separate entity, it might refuse to cooperate with other units or divisions in the same corporation if cooperation could in some way negatively affect its performance evaluation. The competition between divisions to achieve a high ROI can result in one division's refusal to share its new technology or work process improvements. One division's attempt to optimize the accomplishment of its goals can cause other divisions to fall behind and thus negatively affect overall corporate performance. One common example of suboptimization occurs when a marketing department approves an early shipment overtime production for that one order. Production costs are raised, which reduces the manufacturing department's overall efficiency. The end result might be that, although marketing achieves its sales goal, the corporation as a whole fails to achieve its expected profitability.[97]

Guidelines for Proper Control

In designing a control system, top management should remember that controls should follow strategy. Unless controls ensure the use of the proper strategy to achieve objectives, there is a strong likelihood that dysfunctional side effects will completely undermine the implementation of the objectives. The following guidelines are recommended:

1. **Control should involve only the minimum amount of information needed to give a reliable picture of events:** Too many controls create confusion. Focus on the strategic factors by following the **80/20 rule**: *Monitor those 20% of the factors that determine 80% of the results.*

2. **Controls should monitor only meaningful activities and results, regardless of measurement difficulty:** If cooperation between divisions is important to corporate performance, some form of qualitative or quantitative measure should be established to monitor cooperation.

3. **Controls should be timely so that corrective action can be taken before it is too late:** Steering controls, controls that monitor or measure the factors influencing performance, should be stressed so that advance notice of problems is given.

4. **Long-term *and* short-term controls should be used:** If only short-term measures are emphasized, a short-term managerial orientation is likely.

5. **Controls should aim at pinpointing exceptions:** Only activities or results that fall outside a predetermined tolerance range should call for action.

6. **Emphasize the reward of meeting or exceeding standards rather than punishment for failing to meet standards:** Heavy punishment of failure typically results in goal displacement. Managers will "fudge" reports and lobby for lower standards.

If corporate culture complements and reinforces the strategic orientation of a firm, there is less need for an extensive formal control system. In their book *In Search of Excellence*, Peters and Waterman state that "the stronger the culture and the more it was directed toward the marketplace, the less need was there for policy manuals, organization charts, or detailed procedures and rules. In these companies, people way down the line know what they are supposed to do in most situations because the handful of guiding values is crystal clear."[98] For example, at Eaton Corporation, the employees are expected to enforce the rules themselves. If someone misses too much work or picks fights with co-workers, other members of the production team point out the problem. According to Randy Savage, a long-time Eaton employee, "They say there are no bosses here, but if you screw up, you find one pretty fast."[99]

Strategic Incentive Management

To ensure congruence between the needs of a corporation as a whole and the needs of the employees as individuals, management and the board of directors should develop an incentive program that rewards desired performance. This reduces the likelihood of the agency problems (when employees act to feather their own nests instead of building shareholder value) mentioned earlier in **Chapter 2**. Incentive plans should be linked in some way to corporate and divisional strategy. Research reveals that firm performance is affected by its compensation policies.[100] Companies using different strategies tend to adopt different pay policies. For example, a survey of 600 business units indicates that the pay mix associated with a growth strategy emphasizes bonuses and other incentives over salary and benefits, whereas the pay mix associated with a stability strategy has the reverse emphasis.[101] Research indicates that SBU managers having long-term performance elements in their compensation program favor a long-term perspective and thus greater investments in R&D, capital equipment, and employee training.[102] Although the typical CEO pay package is composed of 21% salary, 27% short-term annual incentives, 16% long-term incentives, and 36% stock options,[103] there is some evidence that stock options are being replaced by greater emphasis on performance-related pay.[104]

The following three approaches are tailored to help match measurements and rewards with explicit strategic objectives and time frames:[105]

- **Weighted-factor method:** The weighted-factor method is particularly appropriate for measuring and rewarding the performance of top SBU managers and group-level executives when performance factors and their importance vary from one SBU to another. Using portfolio analysis, one corporation's measurements might contain the following variations: the performance of high-performing (star) SBUs is measured equally in terms of ROI, cash flow, market share, and progress on several future-oriented strategic projects; the performance of low-growth, but strong (cash cow) SBUs, in contrast, is measured in terms of ROI, market share, and cash generation; and the performance of developing question mark SBUs is measured in terms of development and market share growth with no weight on ROI or cash flow. (Refer to **Figure 11–2**.)

- **Long-term evaluation method:** The **long-term evaluation method** compensates managers for achieving objectives set over a multiyear period. An executive is promised some compensation based on long-term performance. A board of directors, for example, might set a particular objective in terms of growth in earnings per share during a five-year period. The giving of awards would be contingent on the corporation's meeting that objective within the designated time. Any executive who leaves the corporation before the objective is met receives nothing. The typical emphasis on stock prices makes this approach more applicable to top management than to business unit managers. Because rising stock markets tend to raise the stock price of mediocre companies, there is a developing trend to index stock options to competitors or to the Standard & Poor's 500.[106]

FIGURE 11–2
Business Strength/ Competitive Position

Business Strength/Competitive Position

Industry Attractiveness		High	Low
High		**Star**	**Question Mark**
		ROI (25%)	ROI (0%)
		Cash Flow (25%)	Cash Flow (0%)
		Strategic Funds (25%)	Strategic Funds (50%)
		Market Share (25%)	Market Share Growth (50%)
Low		**Cash Cow**	**DOG**
		ROI (20%)	ROI (50%)
		Cash Flow (60%)	Cash Flow (50%)
		Strategic Funds (0%)	Strategic Funds (0%)
		Market Share (20%)	Market Share (0%)

SOURCE: Suggested by Paul J. Stomach in "The Performance Measurement and Reward System: Critical to Strategic Management," *Organizational Dynamics,* (Winter 1984), pp. 45–57.

General Electric, for example, offered its CEO 250,000 performance share units (PSUs) tied to performance targets achieved over five years. Half of the PSUs convert into GE stock only if GE achieves a 10% average annual growth in operations. The other half converts to stock only if total shareholder return meets or beats the S&P 500.[107]

- **Strategic-funds method:** The **strategic-funds method** encourages executives to look at developmental expenses as being different from expenses required for current operations. The accounting statement for a corporate unit enters strategic funds as a separate entry below the current ROI. It is, therefore, possible to distinguish between expense dollars consumed in the generation of current revenues and those invested in the future of a business. Therefore, a manager can be evaluated on both a short- and a long-term basis and has an incentive to invest strategic funds in the future. For example, begin with the total sales of a unit ($12,300,000). Subtract cost of goods sold ($6,900,000) leaving a gross margin of $5,400,000. Subtract general and administrative expenses ($3,700,000) leaving an operating profit/ROI of $1,700,000. So far, this is standard accounting procedure. The strategic-funds approach goes one step further by subtracting an additional $1,000,000 for "strategic funds/development expenses." This results in a pretax profit of $700,000. This strategic-funds approach is a good way to ensure that the manager of a high-performing unit (e.g., star) not only generates $700,000 in ROI, but also invests $1 million in the unit for its continued growth. It also ensures that a manager of a developing unit is appropriately evaluated on the basis of market share growth and product development and not on ROI or cash flow.

An effective way to achieve the desired strategic results through a reward system is to combine the three approaches:

1. Segregate strategic funds from short-term funds, as is done in the strategic-funds method.
2. Develop a weighted-factor chart for each SBU.
3. Measure performance on three bases: The pretax profit indicated by the strategic-funds approach, the weighted factors, and the long-term evaluation of the SBUs' and the corporation's performance.

Walt Disney Company, Dow Chemical, IBM, and General Motors are just some firms in which top management compensation is contingent upon the company's achieving strategic objectives.

The board of directors and top management must be careful to develop a compensation plan that achieves the appropriate objectives. One reason why top executives are often criticized for being overpaid (the ratio of CEO to average worker pay is currently 400 to 1)[108] is that in a large number of corporations the incentives for sales growth exceed those for shareholder wealth, resulting in too many executives pursuing growth to the detriment of shareholder value.[109]

End of Chapter SUMMARY

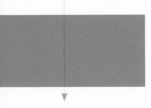

Having strategic management without evaluation and control is like playing football without any scoring or referees. Unless strategic management improves performance, it is only an exercise. In business, the bottom-line measure of performance is making a profit that exceeds that of our competitors. If people aren't willing to pay more than what it costs to make a product or provide a service, that business will not continue to exist. **Chapter 1** explains that organizations engaging in strategic management outperform those that do not. The sticky issue is: How should we measure performance? Is measuring profits sufficient? Does an income statement tell us what we need to know? The accrual method of accounting enables us to count a sale even when the cash has not yet been received. Therefore, a firm might be profitable, but still go bankrupt because it can't pay its bills. Is profit the amount of cash on hand at the end of the year after paying costs and expenses? What if you made a big sale in December and must wait until January to get paid? Many retail stores use a fiscal year ending January 31 (to include returned Christmas items that were bought in December) instead of a calendar year ending December 31. Should two managers receive the same bonus when their divisions earn the same profit, even though one division is much smaller than the other? What of the manager who is managing a new product introduction that won't make a profit for another two years?

Evaluation and control is one of the most difficult parts of strategic management. No one measure can tell us what we need to know. That's why we need to use not only the traditional measures of financial performance, such as net earnings, ROI, and EPS, but we need to consider using EVA or MVA and a balanced scorecard, among other possibilities. On top of that, science informs us that just attempting to measure something changes what is being measured. The measurement of performance can and does result in short-term–oriented actions and goal displacement. That's why experts suggest we use multiple measures of only those things that provide a meaningful and reliable picture of events: Measure those 20% of the factors that determine 80% of the results. Once the appropriate performance measurements are taken, it is possible to get closer to determining whether the strategy was successful. As shown in the model of strategic management depicted at the beginning this chapter, the measured results of corporate performance allow us to decide whether we need to reformulate the strategy, improve its implementation, or gather more information about our competition.

MyManagementLab®

Go to **mymanagementlab.com** to complete the problems marked with this icon .

KEY TERMS

80/20 rule (p. 357)
activity-based costing (ABC) (p. 341)
balanced scorecard (p. 345)
behavior control (p. 339)
behavior substitution (p. 356)
benchmarking (p. 349)
earnings per share (EPS) (p. 343)
economic value added (EVA) (p. 344)
enterprise resource planning (ERP) (p. 353)
enterprise risk management (ERM) (p. 342)
expense center (p. 348)

free cash flow (p. 343)
goal displacement (p. 356)
input controls (p. 339)
investment center (p. 349)
ISO 9000 Standards Service (p. 340)
ISO 14000 Standards Service (p. 340)
key performance measures (p. 346)
long-term evaluation method (p. 358)
management audit (p. 347)
market value added (p. 344)
operating cash flow (p. 343)
output controls (p. 339)
performance (p. 338)

profit center (p. 348)
responsibility center (p. 348)
return on equity (ROE) (p. 343)
return on investment (ROI) (p. 342)
revenue center (p. 348)
shareholder value (p. 343)
short-term orientation (p. 355)
standard cost center (p. 348)
steering control (p. 338)
strategic-funds method (p. 359)
suboptimization (p. 356)
transfer pricing (p. 348)
weighted-factor method (p. 358)

MyManagementLab®

Go to **mymanagementlab.com** for the following Assisted-graded writing questions:

11-1. Explain why ROI might not be the best measure of firm performance.

11-2. What are the best methods for evaluating the performance of the top management team?

DISCUSSION QUESTIONS

11-3. Define steering control? Explain its role in influencing the corporations' profitability.

⭐**11-4.** What are some examples of behavior controls? Output controls? Input controls?

⭐**11-5.** How does EVA improve our knowledge of performance over ROI, ROE, or EPS?

11-6. What role does strategic incentive management play in corporations today given the need to ensure congruence between the in-house needs of stakeholders?

⭐**11-7.** Is the evaluation and control process appropriate for a corporation that emphasizes creativity? Are control and creativity compatible?

STRATEGIC PRACTICE EXERCISE

Dubai Handles Its Debt

A noteworthy investment company, Dubai Group, based in the United Arab Emirates, is the subsidiary of Dubai Holdings. Originally founded in 2000 as The Investment Office, the company was renamed Dubai Group in 2005. Through its companies, the group focuses on banking, investments, and insurance both in the United Arab Emirates and globally. Dubai Group has been able to maintain its success through appropriate control despite difficult times.

Based on a clear objective, Dubai Group restructured its debt of U.S. $10 billion. Borrowing from banks between 2006 and 2008 to fund its acquisitions across the boom years led to a credit-market that was dried-up to its core. As a result of the global financial and the real-estate crises, local government was forced to reassess itself. It found itself unable to manage its obligations, and was forced to renegotiate tens of billions of dollars of debt. Consequently, Dubai Holdings, that includes France's Natixis and Dubai's Emirates NBD, agreed to loan the money. "It's not perfect, but it's a major milestone for both the Emirate and the banks that were exposed to the Dubai government-related entities," noted a creditor bank. The final deal involves creditors extending maturities up to 12 years, with the length of time dependent on the level of security against specific debts. This means that Dubai Group's assets can recover in value before being sold to meet obligations. While the company has signed the document, formal completion means that lenders have to sign an amended inter-creditor agreement that removes references to the loan secured against Dubai Group's holding in Malaysia's Bank Islam. The stake was sold at the end of last year to BIMB Holdings, when the money from the divestment had been delivered to those banks that held security against the asset. Some of these lenders had held off signing the restructuring deal until the cash was placed with them. This, in effect, meant that the formal deal-closing time was missed—the end of 2013. Creditors have two parts to the restructuring document: Part One – specific claim against the company which has been formally completed, and Part Two – inter-creditor agreement that manages the overall restructuring. Out of its U.S. $10 billion total debt, U.S. $6 billion is owed to banks, and the remaining U.S. $4 billion is classed as intercompany loans.

- How well has Dubai Group monitored its performance?
- Which steps should be taken to properly monitor its ongoing performance as a leading investment bank?

....

SOURCE: D. French, "Dubai signs $10 B debt restructuring," *The Daily Star* (January 17, 2014), p. 6.

NOTES

1. http://www.airlinefinancials.com/airline_data_comparisons.html; http://www.bts.gov/press_releases/2012/bts011_12/html/bts011_12.html.

2. R. Barker, "A Surprise in Office Depot's In-Box," *BusinessWeek* (October 25, 2004), p. 122.

3. C. W. Hart, "Customer Service: Beating the Market with Customer Satisfaction," *Harvard Business Review* (March 2007), pp. 30–32.

4. S. E. Ante, "Giving the Boss the Big Picture," *BusinessWeek* (February 13, 2006), pp. 48–51.

5. R. Muralidharan and R. D. Hamilton III, "Aligning Multinational Control Systems," *Long Range Planning* (June 1999), pp. 352–361. These types are based on W. G. Ouchy, "The Relationship Between Organizational Structure and Organizational Control," *Administrative Science Quarterly* (Vol. 20, 1977), pp. 95–113 and W. G. Ouchi, "A Conceptual Framework for the Design of Organizational Control Mechanisms," *Management Science* (Vol. 25, 1979), pp. 833–848. Muralidhara and Hamilton refer to Ouchi's clan control as input control.

6. W. G. Rowe and P. M. Wright, "Related and Unrelated Diversification and Their Effect on Human Resource Management Controls," *Strategic Management Journal* (April 1997), pp. 329–338.

7. R. Muralidharan and R. D. Hamilton III, "Aligning Multinational Control Systems," *Long Range Planning* (June 1999) pp. 356–359.

8. B. Manders and H. de Vries, "Does ISO 9001 Pay? Analysis of 42 Studies," *ISO* (October 2012), http://www.iso.org/iso/home/news_index/news_archive/news.htm?refid=Ref1665.

9. M. V. Uzumeri, "ISO 9000 and Other Metastandards: Principles for Management Practice?" *Academy of Management Executive* (February 1997), pp. 21–36.

10. A. M. Hormozi, "Understanding and Implementing ISO 9000: A Manager's Guide," *SAM Advanced Management Journal* (Autumn 1995), pp. 4–11.

11. M. Henricks, "A New Standard," *Entrepreneur* (October 2002) p. 84.

12. L. Armstrong, "Someone to Watch Over You," *BusinessWeek* (July 10, 2000), pp. 189 -190; https://www.privacyrights.org/fs/fs7-work.htm.

13. J. K. Shank and V. Govindarajan, *Strategic Cost Management* (New York: The Free Press, 1993).

14. S. S. Rao, "ABCs of Cost Control," *Inc. Technology* (No. 2, 1997), pp. 79–81.

15. R. Gruber, "Why You Should Consider Activity-Based Costing," *Small Business Forum* (Spring 1994), pp. 20–36.

16. "Easier Than ABC," *The Economist* (October 25, 2003), p. 56.

17. T. P. Pare, "A New Tool for Managing Costs," *Fortune* (June 14, 1993), pp. 124–129. For further information on the use of ABC with EVA, see T. L. Pohlen and B. J. Coleman, "Evaluating Internal Operations and Supply Chain Performance Using EVA and ABC," *SAM Advanced Management Journal* (Spring 2005), pp. 45–58.

18. K. Hopkins, "The Risk Agenda," *BusinessWeek*, Special Advertising Section (November 22, 2004), pp. 166–170.

19. T. L. Barton, W. G. Shenkir, and P. L. Walker, "Managing Risk: An Enterprise-wide Approach," *Financial Executive* (March/April 2001), p. 51.

20. T. L. Barton, W. G. Shenkir, and P. L. Walker, "Managing Risk: An Enterprise-Wide Approach," pp. 48–51; P. L. Walker, W. G. Shenkir, and T. L. Barton, "Enterprise Risk Management: Putting It All Together," *Internal Auditor* (August 2003), pp. 50–55.

21. T. J. Andersen, "The Performance Relationship of Effective Risk Management: Exploring the Firm-Specific Investment Rationale," *Long Range Planning* (April 2008), pp. 155–176.

22. C. K. Brancato, *New Corporate Performance* Measures(New York: Conference Board, 1995); C. D. Ittner, D. F. Larcker, and M. V. Rajan, "The Choice of Performance Measures in Annual Bonus Contracts," working paper reported by K. Z. Andrews in "Executive Bonuses," *Harvard Business Review* (January–February 1996), pp. 8–9; J. Low and T. Siesfeld, "Measures That Matter: Wall Street Considers Non-Financial Performance More Than You Think," *Strategy & Leadership* (March/April 1998), pp. 24–30.

23. A similar measure, EBITDA (Earnings Before Interest, Taxes, Depreciation, and Amortization), is sometimes used, but is *not* determined in accordance with generally accepted accounting principles and is thus subject to varying calculations.

24. J. M. Laderman, "Earnings, Schmernings: Look at the Cash," *BusinessWeek* (July 24, 1989), pp. 56–57.

25. H. Greenberg, "Don't Count on Cash Flow," *Fortune* (May 13, 2002), p. 176; A. Tergesen, "Cash-Flow Hocus-Pocus," *BusinessWeek* (July 15, 2002), pp. 130–132.

26. "Green Revolutionary," *The Economist* (April 7, 2007), p. 66.

27. E. H. Hall, Jr., and J. Lee, "Diversification Strategies: Creating Value of Generating Profits?" paper presented to the annual meeting of the *Decision Sciences Institute*, Orlando, FL (November 18–21, 2000).

28. P. C. Brewer, G. Chandra, and C. A. Hock, "Economic Value Added (EVA): Its Uses and Limitations," SAM *Advanced Management Journal* (Spring 1999), pp. 4–11.

29. D. J. Skyrme and D. M. Amidon, "New Measures of Success," *Journal of Business Strategy* (January/February 1998), p. 23; http://www.investopedia.com/articles/fundamental/03/031203.asp#axzz2Cgj4StE0.

30. G. B. Stewart III, "EVA Works—But Not if You Make These Common Mistakes," *Fortune* (May 1, 1995), pp. 117–118.

31. S. Tully, "The Real Key to Creating Wealth," *Fortune* (September 20, 1993), p. 38.

32. A. Ehrbar, "Using EVA to Measure Performance and Assess Strategy," *Strategy & Leadership* (May/June 1999), pp. 20–24.

33. P. C. Brewer, G. Chandra, and C. A. Hock, "Economic Value Added (EVA): Its Uses and Limitations," *SAM Advanced Management Journal* (Spring 1999), pp. 7–9.

34. R. Sarbapriya, "Efficacy of Economic Value Added Concept in Business Performance Measurement," *Advances in Information Technology and Management* (Vol. 2, No. 2), pp. 260–267; Pro: K. Lehn and A. K. Makhija, "EVA and MVA as Performance Measures and Signals for Strategic Change," *Strategy & Leadership* (May/June 1996), pp. 34–38; Con: D. I. Goldberg, "Shareholder Value Debunked," *Strategy & Leadership* (January/ February 2000), pp. 30–36.

35. A. Ehrbar, "Using EVA to Measure Performance and Assess Strategy," *Strategy & Leadership* (May/June 1999), p. 21.

36. S. Tully, "America's Wealth Creators," *Fortune* (November 22, 1999), pp. 275–284; A. B. Fisher, "Creating Stockholder Wealth: Market Value Added," *Fortune* (December 11, 1995), pp. 105–116.

37. A. B. Fisher, "Creating Stockholder Wealth: Market Value Added," *Fortune* (December 11, 1995), pp. 105–116.

38. K. Lehn and A. K. Makhija, "EVA and MVA as Performance Measures and Signals for Strategic Change," p. 37.

39. R. S. Kaplan and D. P. Norton, "Using the Balanced Scorecard as a Strategic Management System," *Harvard Business Review* (January–February 1996), pp. 75–85; R. S. Kaplan and D. P. Norton, "The Balanced Scorecard—Measures That Drive Performance," *Harvard Business Review* (January–February, 1992), pp. 71–79.

40. D. I. Goldenberg, "Shareholder Value Debunked," p. 34.

41. In later work, Kaplan and Norton used the term "perspectives" and replaced "internal business perspective" with "process perspective" and "innovation and learning" with "learning and growth perspective." See R. S. Norton and D. P. Norton, "How to Implement a New Strategy Without Disrupting Your Organization," *Harvard Business Review* (March 2006), pp. 100–109.

42. C. K. Brancato, *New Performance Measures* (New York: Conference Board, 1995).

43. D. Rigby and B. Bilodeau, "Management Tools and Trends 2011," *Bain and Company*, http://www.bain.com/Images/BAIN_BRIEF_Management_Tools.pdf.

44. B. P. Stivers and T. Joyce, "Building a Balanced Performance Management System," *SAM Advanced Management Journal* (Spring 2000), pp. 22–29.

45. Kaplan and Norton (March, 2006), p. 107.

46. G. J. M. Braam and E. Nijssen, "Performance Effects of Using the Balanced Scorecard: A Note on the Dutch Experience," *Long Range Planning* (August 2004), pp. 335–349; H. Ahn, "Applying the Balanced Scorecard Concept: An Experience Report," *Long Range Planning* (August 2001), pp. 441–461.

47. S. P. Mader, D. Vuchot, and S. Fukushima of Korn/Ferry International, *33rd Annual Board of Directors Study* (2006), p. 9.

48. R. M. Rosen and F. Adair, "CEOs Misperceive Top Teams' Performance," *Harvard Business Review* (September 2007), p. 30.

49. S. P. Mader, D. Vuchot, and S. Fukushima of Korn/Ferry International, *33rd Annual Board of Directors Study* (2006), p. 33.

50. Ibid., p. 9.

51. J. L. Kerr and W. B. Werther Jr., "The Next Frontier in Corporate Governance: Engaging the Board in Strategy," *Organizational Dynamics* (Vol. 37, No. 2, 2008), pp. 112–124. This agrees with figures (73% and 38%, respectively) reported by Korn/Ferry International in its *33rd Annual Board of Directors Study* from data gathered in 2006, p. 8.

52. R. Charan, *Boards at Work* (San Francisco: Jossey-Bass, 1998), pp. 176–177.

53. T. D. Schellhardt, "Directors Get Tough: Inside a CEO Performance Review," *The Wall Street Journal Interactive Edition* (April 27, 1998).

54. T. L. Wheelen and J. D. Hunger, "Using the Strategic Audit," *SAM Advanced Management Journal* (Winter 1987), pp. 4–12; G. Donaldson, "A New Tool for Boards: The Strategic Audit," *Harvard Business Review* (July–August 1995), pp. 99–107.

55. H. Threat, "Measurement Is Free," *Strategy & Leadership* (May/June 1999), pp. 16–19; http://www.fedex.com/ma/about/overview/innovation.html.

56. 2010 Global Transfer Pricing Survey, Ernst & Young; http://www.ey.com/Publication/vwLUAssets/Global_transfer_pricing_survey_-_2010/$FILE/2010-Globaltransferpricingsurvey_17Jan.pdf.

57. H. Rothman, "You Need Not Be Big to Benchmark," *Nation's Business* (December 1992), p. 64.

58. C. W. Von Bergen and B. Soper, "A Problem with Benchmarking: Using Shaping as a Solution," *SAM Advanced Management Journal* (Autumn 1995), pp. 16–19.

59. http://www.bain.com/publications/articles/management-tools-2011-benchmarking.aspx.

60. R. J. Kennedy, "Benchmarking and Its Myths," *Competitive Intelligence Magazine* (April–June 2000), pp. 28–33.

61. "Just the Facts: Numbers Runners," *Journal of Business Strategy* (July/August 2002), p. 3; L. Mann, D. Samson, and D. Dow, "A Field Experiment on the Effects of Benchmarking and Goal Setting on Company Sales Performance," *Journal of Management* (Vol. 24, No. 1, 1998), pp. 73–96.

62. S. A. W. Drew, "From Knowledge to Action: The Impact of Benchmarking on Organizational Performance," *Long Range Planning* (June 1997), pp. 427–441.

63. S. M. Robbins and R. B. Stobaugh, "The Bent Measuring Stick for Foreign Subsidiaries," *Harvard Business Review* (September–October 1973), p. 82.

64. J. D. Daniels and L. H. Radebaugh, *International Business*, 5th ed. (Reading, MA: Addison-Wesley, 1989), pp. 673–674.

65. D. Henry, "A Better Way to Keep the Books," *BusinessWeek* (September 15, 2008), p. 35; "International Accounting: Speaking in Tongues," *The Economist* (May 19, 2007), pp. 77–78; C. Hackett, "Convergence of U.S. GAAP and IFRS: Where Do Things Stand?" (http://www.cshco.com/News/Articles/Convergence_of_U.S._GAAP_and_IFRS%3A_Where_do_things_stand%3F/).

66. W. A. Johnson and R. J. Kirsch, "International Transfer Pricing and Decision Making in United States Multinationals," *International Journal of Management* (June 1991), pp. 554–561.

67. *KPMG's Corporate Tax Rate Table 2012*, (http://www.kpmg.com/global/en/services/tax/tax-tools-and-resources/pages/corporate-tax-rates-table.aspx).

68. "Fixing the Bottom Line," *Time* (November 23, 1992), p. 20.

69. J. M. L. Poon, R. Ainuddin, and H. Affrim, "Management Policies and Practices of American, British, European, and Japanese Subsidiaries in Malaysia: A Comparative Study," *International Journal of Management* (December 1990), pp. 467–474.

70. M. Egan, "Setting Standards: Strategic Advantages in International Trade," *Business Strategy Review* (Vol. 13, No. 1, 2002), pp. 51–64; L. Swatkowski, "Building Towards International Standards," *Appliance* (December 1999), p. 30.

71. C. W. L. Hill, P. Hwang, and W. C. Kim, "An Eclectic Theory of the Choice of International Entry Mode," *Strategic Management Journal* (February 1990), pp. 117–128; D. Lei, J. W. Slocum, Jr., and R. W. Slater, "Global Strategy and Reward Systems: The Key Roles of Management Development and Corporate Culture," *Organizational Dynamics* (Autumn 1990), pp. 27–41; W. R. Fannin and A. F. Rodrigues, "National or Global?—Control vs. Flexibility," *Long Range Planning* (October 1986), pp. 84–188.

72. A. V. Phatak, *International Dimensions of Management*, 2nd ed. (Boston: Kent, 1989), pp. 155–157.

73. S. McAlary, "Three Pitfalls in ERP Implementation," *Strategy & Leadership* (October/November/December 1999), pp. 49–50.

74. J. B. White, D. Clark, and S. Ascarelli, "This German Software Is Complex, Expensive—And Wildly Popular," *The Wall Street Journal* (March 14, 1997), pp. A1, A8; D. Ward, "Whirlpool Takes a Dive with Software Snarl," *Des Moines Register* (April 29, 2000), p. 8D.

75. J. Verville, R. Palanisamy, C. Bernadas, and A. Halingten, "ERP Acquisition Planning: A Critical Dimension for Making the Right Choice," *Long Range Planning* (February 2007), pp. 45–63.

76. http://www.rfidblog.org/entry/tesco-postpones-rfid-implementation-at-its-stores/.

77. "Radio Silence," *The Economist* (June 9, 2007), pp. 20–21.

78. C. Krivda, "RFID After Compliance: Integration and Payback," Special Advertising Section, *BusinessWeek* (December 20, 2004), pp. 91–98.

79. D. Leonard and J. Tozzi, "Why Don't More Hospitals Use Electronic Health Records?" *Bloomberg Businessweek* (June 21, 2012), http://www.businessweek.com/articles/2012-06-21/why-dont-more-hospitals-use-electronic-health-records.

80. A. Lashinsky, "Meg and the Machine," *Fortune* (September 1, 2003), pp. 68–78.

81. R. M. Hodgetts and M. S. Wortman, *Administrative Policy*, 2nd ed. (New York: John Wiley & Sons, 1980), p. 128.

82. J. R. Wooldridge and C. C. Snow, "Stock Market Reaction to Strategic Investment Decisions," *Strategic Management Journal* (September 1990), pp. 353–363.

83. M. C. Jensen, "Corporate Budgeting Is Broken—Let's Fix It," *Harvard Business Review* (November 2001), pp. 94–101.

84. C. M. Christensen, S. P. Kaufman, and W. C. Smith, "Innovation Killers: How Financial Tools Destroy Your Capacity to Do New Things," *Harvard Business Review* (January 2008), pp. 98–105.

85. P. Hsieh, T. Keller, and S. R. Rajan, "The Misguided Practice of Earnings Guidance," *McKinsey Quarterly* (Spring 2006), pp. 1–5.

86. "Audit Firms Sued in HP's Autonomy Acquisition," *Reuters* (November 28, 2012), (http://www.reuters.com/article/2012/11/29/hp-autonomy-auditors-idUSL1E8MS8ZX20121129).

87. D. Henry "Fuzzy Numbers," *BusinessWeek* (October 4, 2004), pp. 79–88.

88. A. Rappaport, "10 Ways to Create Shareholder Value," *Harvard Business Review* (September 2006), pp. 66–77.

89. D. R. Schmidt and K. L. Fowler, "Post-Acquisition Financial Performance and Executive Compensation," *Strategic Management Journal* (November–December 1990), pp. 559–569.

90. H. L. Tosi, S. Werner, J. P. Katz, and L. R. Gomez-Mejia, "How Much Does Performance Matter? A Meta-Analysis of CEO Pay Studies," *Journal of Management* (Vol. 26, No. 2, 2000), pp. 301–339; P. Wright, M. Kroll, and D. Elenkov, "Acquisition Returns, Increase in Firm Size, and Chief Executive Officer Compensation: The Moderating Role of Monitoring," *Academy of Management Journal* (June 2002), pp. 599–608; S. Werner, H. L. Tosi, and L. Gomez-Mejia, "Organizational Governance and Employee Pay: How Ownership Structure Affects the Firm's Compensation Strategy," *Strategic Management Journal* (April 2005), pp. 377–384.

91. X. Zhang, K. M. Bartol, K. G. Smith, M. D. Pfarrer, and D. M. Khanin, "CEOs on the Edge: Earnings Manipulation and Stock-based Incentive Misalignment," *Academy of Management Journal* (April 2008), pp. 241–258; L. Bebchuk and J. Fried, *Pay Without Performance: The Unfulfilled Promise of Executive Compensation* (Boston: Harvard University Press, 2004); L. A. Benchuk and J. M. Fried, "Pay Without Performance: Overview of the Issues," *Academy of Management Perspectives* (February 2006), pp. 5–24.

92. D. Jones, "Bad News Can Enrich Executives," *Des Moines Register* (November 26, 1999), p. 8S.

93. J. F. Porac, J. B. Wade, and T. G. Pollock, "Industry Categories and the Politics of the Comparable Firm in CEO Compensation," *Administrative Science Quarterly* (March 1999), pp. 112–144. For summaries of current research on executive compensation and performance, see C. E. Devers, A. A. Cannella Jr., G. P. Reilly, and M. E. Yoder, "Executive Compensation: A Multidisciplinary Review of Recent Developments," *Journal of Management* (December 2007), pp. 1016–1072; M. Chan, "Executive Compensation," *Business and Society Review* (March 2008), pp. 129–161; and S. N. Kaplan, "Are CEOs Overpaid?" *Academy of Management Perspective* (May 2008), pp. 5–20.

94. C. D. Ittner and D. F. Larcker, "Coming Up Short," *Harvard Business Review* (November 2003), pp. 88–95.

95. See the classic article by S. Kerr, "On the Folly of Rewarding A, While Hoping for B," *Academy of Management Journal* (Vol. 18, December 1975), pp. 769–783.

96. W. Zellner, E. Schine, and G. Smith, "Trickle-Down Is Trickling Down at Work," *BusinessWeek* (March 18, 1996), p. 34.

97. For more information on how goals can have dysfunctional side effects, see D. C. Kayes, "The Destructive Pursuit of Idealized Goals," *Organizational Dynamics* (Vol. 34, Issue 4, 2005), pp. 391–401.

98. T. J. Peters and R. H. Waterman, *In Search of Excellence* (New York: Harper Collins, 1982), pp. 75–76.

99. T. Aeppel, "Not All Workers Find Idea of Empowerment as Neat as It Sounds," *The Wall Street Journal* (September 8, 1997), pp. A1, A13.

100. R. S. Allen and M. M. Helms, "Employee Perceptions of the Relationship Between Strategy, Rewards, and Organizational Performance," *Journal of Business Strategies* (Fall 2002), pp. 115–140; M. A. Carpenter, "The Price of Change: The Role of CEO Compensation in Strategic Variation and Deviation from Industry Strategy Norms," *Journal of Management* (Vol. 26, No. 6, 2000), pp. 1179–1198; M. A. Carpenter and W. G. Sanders, "The Effects of Top Management Team Pay and Firm Internationalization on MNC Performance," *Journal of Management* (Vol. 30, No. 4, 2004), pp. 509–528; J. D. Shaw, N. Gupta, and J. E. Delery, "Congruence Between Technology and Compensation Systems: Implications for Strategy Implementation," *Strategic Management Journal* (April 2001), pp. 379–386; E. F. Montemazon, "Congruence Between Pay Policy and Competitive Strategy in High-Performing Organizations," *Journal of Management* (Vol. 22, No. 6, 1996), pp. 889–908.

101. D. B. Balkin and L. R. Gomez-Mejia, "Matching Compensation and Organizational Strategies," *Strategic Management Journal* (February 1990), pp. 153–169.

102. C. S. Galbraith, "The Effect of Compensation Programs and Structure on SBU Competitive Strategy: A Study of Technology-Intensive Firms," *Strategic Management Journal* (July 1991), pp. 353–370.

103. T. A. Stewart, "CEO Pay: Mom Wouldn't Approve," *Fortune* (March 31, 1997), pp. 119–120.

104. "The Politics of Pay," *The Economist* (March 24, 2007), pp. 71–72.

105. P. J. Stonich, "The Performance Measurement and Reward System: Critical to Strategic Management," *Organizational Dynamics* (Winter 1984), pp. 45–57.

106. A. Rappaport, "New Thinking on How to Link Executive Pay with Performance," *Harvard Business Review* (March–April 1999), pp. 91–101.

107. Motley Fool, "Fool's School: Hooray for GE," *The* (Ames, IA) *Tribune* (October 27, 2003), p. 1D.

108. M. Chan, "Executive Compensation," *Business and Society Review* (March 2008), pp. 129–161.

109. S. E. O'Byrne and S. D. Young, "Why Executive Pay Is Failing," *Harvard Business Review* (June 2006), p. 28.

110. *Fortune* magazine Web site accessed on December 4, 2012, at http://money.cnn.com/magazines/fortune/most-admired/2012/full_list/.

111. A. Harrington, "America's Most Admired Companies," *Fortune* (March 8, 2004), pp. 80–81.

PART 5

Introduction to
Case Analysis

CHAPTER 12
Suggestions for Case Analysis

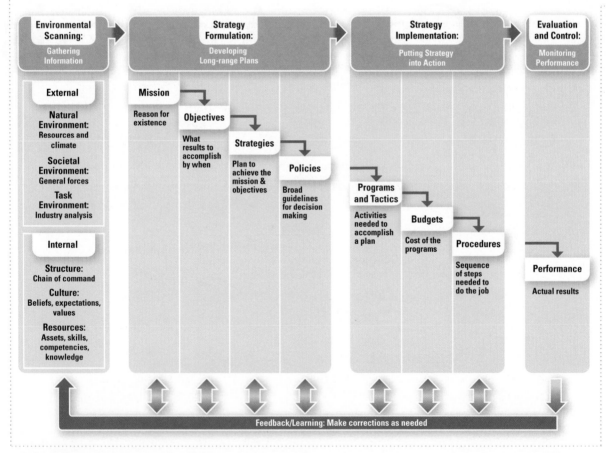

MyManagementLab®
⭐ Improve Your Grade!

Over 10 million students improved their results using the Pearson MyLabs. Visit **mymanagementlab.com** for simulations, tutorials, and end-of-chapter problems.

Learning Objectives

After reading this chapter, you should be able to:

- Research the case situation as needed
- Analyze financial statements by using ratios and common-size statements
- Use the strategic audit as a method of organizing and analyzing case information

Identifying Red Flags

Howard Schilit, founder of the Center for Financial Research & Analysis (CFRA), works with a staff of 15 analysts to screen financial databases and analyze public financial filings of 3600 companies, looking for inconsistencies and aggressive accounting methods. Schilit calls this search for hidden weaknesses in a company's performance *forensic accounting*. He advises anyone interested in analyzing a company to look deeply into its financial statements. For example, when the CFRA noticed that Kraft Foods made $122 million in acquisitions in 2002, but claimed $539 million as "goodwill" assets related to the purchases, it concluded that Kraft was padding its earnings with one-time gains. According to Schilit, unusually high goodwill gains related to recent acquisitions is a *red flag* that suggests an underlying problem.

Schilit proposes a short checklist of items to examine for red flags:

- **Cash flow from operations should exceed net income:** If cash flow from operations drops below net income, it could mean that the company is propping up its earnings by selling assets, borrowing cash, or shuffling numbers. Says Schilit, "You could have spotted the problems at Enron by just doing this."

- **Accounts receivable should not grow faster than sales:** A firm facing slowing sales can make itself look better by inflating accounts receivable with expected future sales and by making sales to customers who are not creditworthy. "It's like mailing a contract to a dead person and then counting it as a sale," says Schilit.

- **Gross margins should not fluctuate over time:** A change of more than 2% in either direction from year to year is worth a closer look. It could mean that the company is using other revenue, such as sales of assets or write-offs to boost profits. Sunbeam reported an increase of 10% in gross margins just before it was investigated by the SEC.

- **Examine carefully information about top management and the board:** When Schilit learned that the chairman of Checkers Restaurants had put his two young sons on the board, he warned investors of nepotism. Two years later, Checkers' huge debt caused its stock to fall 85% and all three family members were forced out of the company.
- **Footnotes are important:** When companies change their accounting assumptions to make the statements more attractive, they often bury their rationale in the footnotes.

Schilit makes his living analyzing companies and selling his reports to investors. Annual reports and financial statements provide a lot of information about a company's health, but it's hard to find problem areas when management is massaging the numbers to make the company appear more attractive than it is. That's why Michelle Leder created her Web site, www.footnoted.org. She likes to highlight "the things that companies bury in their routine SEC filings." This type of in-depth, investigative analysis is a key part of analyzing strategy cases. This chapter provides various analytical techniques and suggestions for conducting this kind of case analysis.

SOURCES: M. Heimer, "Wall Street Sherlock," *Smart Money* (July 2003), pp. 103–107. D. Stead, "The Secrets in SEC Filings," *BusinessWeek* (September 1, 2008), p. 12.

The Case Method

The analysis and discussion of case problems has been the most popular method of teaching strategy and policy for many years. The case method offers the opportunity to move from a narrow, specialized view that emphasizes functional techniques to a broader, less precise analysis of the overall corporation. Cases present actual business situations and enable you to examine both successful and unsuccessful corporations. In case analysis, you might be asked to critically analyze a situation in which a manager had to make a decision of long-term corporate importance. This approach gives you a feel for what it is like to face making and implementing strategic decisions.

Researching the Case Situation

You should not restrict yourself only to the information written in the case unless your instructor states otherwise. You should, if possible, undertake outside research about the environmental setting. Check the decision date of each case (typically the latest date mentioned in the case) to find out when the situation occurred and then screen the business periodicals for that time period. An understanding of the economy during that period will help you avoid making a serious error in your analysis—for example, suggesting a sale of stock when the stock market is at an all-time low or taking on more debt when the prime interest rate is over 15%. Information about the industry will provide insights into its competitive activities. *Important Note: Don't go beyond the decision date of the case in your research unless directed to do so by your instructor.*

Use computerized company and industry information services such as Compustat, Compact Disclosure, and a wide variety of information sources available on the Internet including

Hoover's online corporate directory (www.hoovers.com) and the U.S. Securities and Exchange Commission's EDGAR database (www.sec.gov) provide access to corporate annual reports and 10-K forms. This background will give you an appreciation for the situation as it was experienced by the participants in the case. Use a search engine such as Google or Bing to find additional information about the industry and the company.

A company's **annual report** and **SEC 10-K form** from the year of the case can be very helpful. According to the Yankelovich Partners survey firm, 8 out of 10 portfolio managers and 75% of security analysts use annual reports when making decisions.[1] They contain not only the usual income statements and balance sheets, but also cash flow statements and notes to the financial statements indicating why certain actions were taken. 10-K forms include detailed information not usually available in an annual report. **SEC 10-Q forms** include quarterly financial reports. **SEC 14-A forms** include detailed information on members of a company's board of directors and proxy statements for annual meetings. Some resources available for research into the economy and a corporation's industry are suggested in **Appendix 12.A**.

A caveat: Before obtaining additional information about the company profiled in a particular case, ask your instructor if doing so is appropriate for your class assignment. Your strategy instructor may want you to stay within the confines of the case information provided in the book. In this case, it is usually acceptable to at least learn more about the societal environment at the time of the case.

Financial Analysis: A Place to Begin

Once you have read a case, a good place to begin your analysis is with the financial statements. **Ratio analysis** is the calculation of ratios from data in these statements. It is done to identify possible financial strengths or weaknesses. Thus it is a valuable part of the SWOT approach. A review of key financial ratios can help you assess a company's overall situation and pinpoint some problem areas. Ratios are useful regardless of firm size and enable you to compare a company's ratios with industry averages. **Table 12–1** lists some of the most important financial ratios, which are (1) **liquidity ratios**, (2) **profitability ratios**, (3) **activity ratios**, and (4) **leverage ratios**.

ANALYZING FINANCIAL STATEMENTS

In your analysis, do not simply make an exhibit that includes all the ratios (unless your instructor requires you to do so), but select and discuss only those ratios that have an impact on the company's problems. For instance, accounts receivable and inventory may provide a source of funds. If receivables and inventories are double the industry average, reducing them may provide needed cash. In this situation, the case report should include not only sources of funds but also the number of dollars freed for use. Compare these ratios with industry averages to discover whether the company is out of line with others in the industry. Annual and quarterly industry ratios can be found in the library or on the Internet. (See the resources for case research in **Appendix 12.A**.) In the years to come, expect to see financial entries for the trading of CERs (Certified Emissions Reductions). This is the amount of money a company earns from reducing carbon emissions and selling them on the open market.

TABLE 12–1   Financial Ratio Analysis

	Formula	How Expressed	Meaning
1. Liquidity Ratios			
Current ratio	$\dfrac{\text{Current assets}}{\text{Current liabilities}}$	Decimal	A short-term indicator of the company's ability to pay its short-term liabilities from short-term assets; how much of current assets are available to cover each dollar of current liabilities.
Quick (acid test) ratio	$\dfrac{\text{Current assets} - \text{Inventory}}{\text{Current liabilities}}$	Decimal	Measures the company's ability to pay off its short-term obligations from current assets, excluding inventories.
Inventory to net working capital	$\dfrac{\text{Inventory}}{\text{Current assets} - \text{Current liabilities}}$	Decimal	A measure of inventory balance; measures the extent to which the cushion of excess current assets over current liabilities may be threatened by unfavorable changes in inventory.
Cash ratio	$\dfrac{\text{Cash} + \text{Cash equivalents}}{\text{Current liabilities}}$	Decimal	Measures the extent to which the company's capital is in cash or cash equivalents; shows how much of the current obligations can be paid from cash or near-cash assets.
2. Profitability Ratios			
Net profit margin	$\dfrac{\text{Net profit after taxes}}{\text{Net sales}}$	Percentage	Shows how much after-tax profits are generated by each dollar of sales.
Gross profit margin	$\dfrac{\text{Sales} - \text{Cost of goods sold}}{\text{Net sales}}$	Percentage	Indicates the total margin available to cover other expenses beyond cost of goods sold and still yield a profit.
Return on investment (ROI)	$\dfrac{\text{Net profit after taxes}}{\text{Total assets}}$	Percentage	Measures the rate of return on the total assets utilized in the company; a measure of management's efficiency, it shows the return on all the assets under its control, regardless of source of financing.
Return on equity (ROE)	$\dfrac{\text{Net profit after taxes}}{\text{Shareholders' equity}}$	Percentage	Measures the rate of return on the book value of shareholders' total investment in the company.
Earnings per share (EPS)	$\dfrac{\text{Net profit after taxes} - \text{Preferred stock dividends}}{\text{Average number of common shares}}$	Dollars per share	Shows the after-tax earnings generated for each share of common stock.
3. Activity Ratios			
Inventory turnover	$\dfrac{\text{Net sales}}{\text{Inventory}}$	Decimal	Measures the number of times that average inventory of finished goods was turned over or sold during a period of time, usually a year.
Days of inventory	$\dfrac{\text{Inventory}}{\text{Cost of goods sold} + 365}$	Days	Measures the number of one day's worth of inventory that a company has on hand at any given time.

TABLE 12–1   Financial Ratio Analysis, (continued)

	Formula	How Expressed	Meaning
Net working capital turnover	$\dfrac{\text{Net sales}}{\text{Net working capital}}$	Decimal	Measures how effectively the net working capital is used to generate sales.
Asset turnover	$\dfrac{\text{Sales}}{\text{Total assets}}$	Decimal	Measures the utilization of all the company's assets; measures how many sales are generated by each dollar of assets.
Fixed asset turnover	$\dfrac{\text{Sales}}{\text{Fixed assets}}$	Decimal	Measures the utilization of the company's fixed assets (i.e., plant and equipment); measures how many sales are generated by each dollar of fixed assets.
Average collection period	$\dfrac{\text{Accounts receivable}}{\text{Sales for year} + 365}$	Days	Indicates the average length of time in days that a company must wait to collect a sale after making it; may be compared to the credit terms offered by the company to its customers.
Accounts receivable turnover	$\dfrac{\text{Annual credit sales}}{\text{Accounts receivable}}$	Decimal	Indicates the number of times that accounts receivable are cycled during the period (usually a year).
Accounts payable period	$\dfrac{\text{Accounts payable}}{\text{Purchase for year} \div 365}$	Days	Indicates the average length of time in days that the company takes to pay its credit purchases.
Days of cash	$\dfrac{\text{Cash}}{\text{Net sales for year} \div 365}$	Days	Indicates the number of days of cash on hand, at present sales levels.
4. Leverage Ratios Debt-to-asset ratio	$\dfrac{\text{Total debt}}{\text{Total assets}}$	Percentage	Measures the extent to which borrowed funds have been used to finance the company's assets.
Debt-to-equity ratio	$\dfrac{\text{Total debt}}{\text{Shareholders' equity}}$	Percentage	Measures the funds provided by creditors versus the funds provided by owners.
Long-term debt to capital structure	$\dfrac{\text{Long-term debt}}{\text{Shareholders' equity}}$	Percentage	Measures the long-term component of capital structure.
Times interest earned	$\dfrac{\text{Profit before taxes} + \text{Interest charges}}{\text{Interest charges}}$	Decimal	Indicates the ability of the company to meet its annual interest costs.
Coverage of fixed charges	$\dfrac{\text{Profit before taxes} + \text{Interest charges} + \text{Lease charges}}{\text{Interest charges} + \text{Lease obligations}}$	Decimal	A measure of the company's ability to meet all of its fixed-charge obligations.
Current liabilities to equity	$\dfrac{\text{Current liabilities}}{\text{Shareholders' equity}}$	Percentage	Measures the short-term financing portion versus that provided by owners.

continued

TABLE 12–1 Financial Ratio Analysis, (continued)

	Formula	How Expressed	Meaning
5. Other Ratios Price/earnings ratio	$\dfrac{\text{Market price per share}}{\text{Earnings per share}}$	Decimal	Shows the current market's evaluation of a stock, based on its earnings; shows how much the investor is willing to pay for each dollar of earnings.
Divided payout ratio	$\dfrac{\text{Annual dividends per share}}{\text{Annual earnings per share}}$	Percentage	Indicates the percentage of profit that is paid out as dividends.
Dividend yield on common stock	$\dfrac{\text{Annual dividends per share}}{\text{Current market price per share}}$	Percentage	Indicates the dividend rate of return to common shareholders at the current market price.

NOTE: In using ratios for analysis, calculate ratios for the corporation and compare them to the average and quartile ratios for the particular industry. Refer to Standard & Poor's and Robert Morris Associates for average industry data. Special thanks to Dr. Moustafa H. Abdelsamad, Dean, Business School, Texas A&M University—Corpus Christi, Corpus Christi, Texas, for his definitions of these ratios.

A typical financial analysis of a firm would include a study of the operating statements for five or so years, including a trend analysis of sales, profits, earnings per share, debt-to-equity ratio, return on investment, and so on, plus a ratio study comparing the firm under study with industry standards. As a minimum, undertake the following five steps in basic financial analysis.

1. **Scrutinize historical income statements and balance sheets:** These two basic statements provide most of the data needed for analysis. Statements of cash flow may also be useful.

2. **Compare historical statements over time** if a series of statements is available.

3. **Calculate changes that occur in individual categories from year to year,** as well as the cumulative total change.

4. **Determine the change as a percentage** as well as an absolute amount.

5. **Adjust for inflation** if that was a significant factor.

Examination of this information may reveal developing trends. Compare trends in one category with trends in related categories. For example, an increase in sales of 15% over three years may appear to be satisfactory until you note an increase of 20% in the cost of goods sold during the same period. The outcome of this comparison might suggest that further investigation into the manufacturing process is necessary. If a company is reporting strong net income growth but negative cash flow, this would suggest that the company is relying on something other than operations for earnings growth. Is it selling off assets or cutting R&D? If accounts receivable are growing faster than sales revenues, the company is not getting paid for the products or services it is counting as sold. Is the company dumping product on its distributors at the end of the year to boost its reported annual sales? If so, expect the distributors to return the unordered product the next month, thus drastically cutting the next year's reported sales.

Other "tricks of the trade" need to be examined. Until June 2000, firms growing through acquisition were allowed to account for the cost of the purchased company, through the pooling of both companies' stock. This approach was used in 40% of the value of mergers between 1997 and 1999. The pooling method enabled the acquiring company to disregard the premium it paid for the other firm (the amount above the fair market value of the purchased company often called "good will"). Thus, when PepsiCo agreed to purchase Quaker Oats for $13.4 billion in PepsiCo stock, the $13.4 billion was not found on PepsiCo's balance sheet. As of June 2000, merging firms must use the "purchase" accounting rules in which the true purchase price is reflected in the financial statements.[2]

The analysis of a multinational corporation's financial statements can get very complicated, especially if its headquarters is in another country that uses different accounting standards.

COMMON-SIZE STATEMENTS

Common-size statements are income statements and balance sheets in which the dollar figures have been converted into percentages. These statements are used to identify trends in each of the categories, such as cost of goods sold as a percentage of sales (sales is the denominator). For the income statement, net sales represent 100%: calculate the percentage for each category so that the categories sum to the net sales percentage (100%). For the balance sheet, give the total assets a value of 100% and calculate other asset and liability categories as percentages of the total assets with total assets as the denominator. (Individual asset and liability items, such as accounts receivable and accounts payable, can also be calculated as a percentage of net sales.)

When you convert statements to this form, it is relatively easy to note the percentage that each category represents of the total. Look for trends in specific items, such as cost of goods sold, when compared to the company's historical figures. To get a proper picture, however, you need to make comparisons with industry data, if available, to see whether fluctuations are merely reflecting industrywide trends. If a firm's trends are generally in line with those of the rest of the industry, problems are less likely than if the firm's trends are worse than industry averages. If ratios are not available for the industry, calculate the ratios for the industry's best and worst firms and compare them to the firm you are analyzing. Common-size statements are especially helpful in developing scenarios and pro forma statements because they provide a series of historical relationships (for example, cost of goods sold to sales, interest to sales, and inventories as a percentage of assets) from which you can estimate the future with your scenario assumptions for each year.

Z-VALUE AND THE INDEX OF SUSTAINABLE GROWTH

If the corporation being studied appears to be in poor financial condition, use **Altman's Z-Value Bankruptcy Formula** to calculate its likelihood of going bankrupt. The *Z-value* formula combines five ratios by weighting them according to their importance to a corporation's financial strength. The formula is:

$$Z = 1.2x_1 + 1.4x_2 + 3.3x_3 + 0.6x_4 + 1.0x_5$$

where:

x_1 = Working capital/Total assets (%)
x_2 = Retained earnings/Total assets (%)
x_3 = Earnings before interest and taxes/Total assets (%)
x_4 = Market value of equity/Total liabilities (%)
x_5 = Sales/Total assets (number of times)

A score below 1.81 indicates significant credit problems, whereas a score above 3.0 indicates a healthy firm. Scores between 1.81 and 3.0 indicate question marks.[3] The Altman Z model has achieved a remarkable 94% accuracy in predicting corporate bankruptcies. Its accuracy is excellent in the two years before financial distress, but diminishes as the lead time increases.[4]

The **index of sustainable growth** is useful to learn whether a company embarking on a growth strategy will need to take on debt to fund this growth. The index indicates how much of the growth rate of sales can be sustained by internally generated funds. The formula is:

$$g^* = \frac{[P(1-D)(1+L)]}{[T - P(1-D)(1+L)]}$$

where:

P = (Net profit before tax/Net sales) $\times$ 100
D = Target dividends/Profit after tax
L = Total liabilities/Net worth
T = (Total assets/Net sales) $\times$ 100

If the planned growth rate calls for a growth rate higher than its g^*, external capital will be needed to fund the growth unless management is able to find efficiencies, decrease dividends, increase the debt-equity ratio, or reduce assets through renting or leasing arrangements.[5]

USEFUL ECONOMIC MEASURES

If you are analyzing a company over many years, you may want to adjust sales and net income for inflation to arrive at a "true" financial performance in constant dollars. **Constant dollars** are dollars adjusted for inflation to make them comparable over various years. One way to adjust for inflation in the United States is to use the consumer price index (CPI), as given in **Table 12–2**. Dividing sales and net income by the CPI factor for that year will change the figures to 1982–1984 U.S. constant dollars (when the CPI was 1.0). Adjusting for inflation is especially important for companies operating in emerging economies like China and Russia. China's inflation rate was 8.7% in 2008, which was the highest it had been in 10 years. The Russian inflation rate in 2011 was expected to top 6%.[6]

Another helpful analytical aid provided in **Table 12–2** is the **prime interest rate**, the rate of interest banks charge on their lowest-risk loans. For better assessments of strategic decisions, it can be useful to note the level of the prime interest rate at the time of the case. A decision to borrow money to build a new plant would have been a good one in 2003 at 4.1%, but less practical in 2007 when the average rate was 8.05%.

In preparing a scenario for your pro forma financial statements, you may want to use the **gross domestic product (GDP)** from **Table 12–2**. GDP is used worldwide and measures the total output of goods and services within a country's borders. The amount of change from one year to the next indicates how much that country's economy is growing. Remember that scenarios have to be adjusted for a country's specific conditions. For other economic information, see the resources for case research in **Appendix 12.A**.

TABLE 12–2 U.S. Economic Indicators	Year	GDP (in $ billions) Gross Domestic Product	CPI (for all items) Consumer Price Index	PIR (in %) Prime Interest Rate
	1980	2788.1	.824	15.26
	1985	4217.5	1.076	9.93
	1990	5800.4	1.307	10.01
	1995	7414.7	1.524	8.83
	2000	9951.5	1.722	9.23
	2001	10,286.2	1.771	6.91
	2002	10,642.3	1.799	4.67
	2003	11,142.2	1.840	4.12
	2004	11,853.3	1.889	4.34
	2005	12,623.0	1.953	6.19
	2006	13.377.2	2.016	7.96
	2007	14,028.7	2.073	8.05
	2008	14,291.5	2.153	5.09
	2009	13,973.7	2.145	3.25
	2010	1,498.9	2.180	3.25
	2011	15,075.7	2.249	3.25

NOTES: Gross domestic product (GDP) in billions of dollars; Consumer price index for all items (CPI) (1982–84 = 1.0); Prime interest rate (PIR) in percentages.

SOURCES: Gross domestic product (GDP) from U.S. Bureau of Economic Analysis, National Economic Accounts (www.bea.gov). Consumer price index (CPI) from U.S. Bureau of Labor Statistics (www.bls.gov). Prime interest rate (PIR) (www.federalreserve.gov).

Format for Case Analysis: The Strategic Audit

There is no one best way to analyze or present a case report. Each instructor has personal preferences for format and approach. Nevertheless, in **Appendix 12.B** we suggest an approach for both written and oral reports that provides a systematic method for successfully attacking a case. This approach is based on the strategic audit, which is presented at the end of **Chapter 1** in **Appendix 1.A**. We find that this approach provides structure and is very helpful for the typical student who may be a relative novice in case analysis. Regardless of the format chosen, be careful to include a complete analysis of key environmental variables—especially of trends in the industry and of the competition. Look at international developments as well.

If you choose to use the strategic audit as a guide to the analysis of complex strategy cases, you may want to use the **strategic audit worksheet** in **Figure 12–1**. Print a copy of the worksheet to use to take notes as you analyze a case. See **Appendix 12.C** for an example of a completed student-written analysis of a 1993 Maytag Corporation case done in an outline form using the strategic audit format. This is one example of what a case analysis in outline form may look like.

Case discussion focuses on critical analysis and logical development of thought. A solution is satisfactory if it resolves important problems and is likely to be implemented successfully. How the corporation actually dealt with the case problems has no real bearing on the analysis because management might have analyzed its problems incorrectly or implemented a series of flawed solutions.

FIGURE 12–1
Strategic Audit
Worksheet

Strategic Audit Heading	Analysis		Comments
	(+) Factors	(–) Factors	
I. Current Situation			
A. Past Corporate Performance Indexes			

B. Strategic Posture:
  Current Mission
  Current Objectives
  Current Strategies
  Current Policies			

SWOT Analysis Begins:			
II. Corporate Governance			
A. Board of Directors			
B. Top Management			
III. External Environment (EFAS): **Opportunities and Threats (SW<u>OT</u>)**			
A. Natural Environment			
B. Societal Environment			
C. Task Environment (Industry Analysis)			
IV. Internal Environment (IFAS): **Strengths and Weaknesses (<u>SW</u>OT)**			
A. Corporate Structure			
B. Corporate Culture			
C. Corporate Resources			
1. Marketing			
2. Finance			
3. Research and Development			
4. Operations and Logistics			
5. Human Resources			
6. Information Technology			
V. Analysis of Strategic Factors (SFAS)			
A. Key Internal and External Strategic Factors (SWOT)			
B. Review of Mission and Objectives			
SWOT Analysis Ends. Recommendation Begins:			
VI. Alternatives and Recommendations			
A. Strategic Alternatives—pros and cons			
B. Recommended Strategy			
VII. Implementation			
VIII. Evaluation and Control			

NOTE: See the complete Strategic Audit on pages 66–73. It lists the pages in the book that discuss each of the eight headings.

End of Chapter SUMMARY

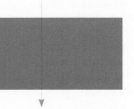

Using case analysis is one of the best ways to understand and remember the strategic management process. By applying to cases the concepts and techniques you have learned, you will be able to remember them long past the time when you have forgotten other memorized bits of information. The use of cases to examine actual situations brings alive the field of strategic management and helps build your analytic and decision-making skills. These are just some of the reasons why the use of cases in disciplines from agribusiness to health care is increasing throughout the world.

MyManagementLab®

Go to **mymanagementlab.com** to complete the problems marked with this icon .

KEY TERMS

activity ratio (p. 369)

Altman's Z-Value Bankruptcy Formula (p. 373)

annual report (p. 369)

common-size statement (p. 373)

constant dollars (p. 374)

gross domestic product (GDP) (p. 374)

index of sustainable growth (p. 374)

leverage ratio (p. 369)

liquidity ratio (p. 369)

prime interest rate (p. 374)

profitability ratio (p. 369)

ratio analysis (p. 369)

SEC 10-K form (p. 369)

SEC 10-Q form (p. 369)

SEC 14-A form (p. 369)

strategic audit worksheet (p. 375)

MyManagementLab®

Go to **mymanagementlab.com** for the following Assisted-graded writing questions:

12-1. What ratios would you use to begin your analysis of a case?

12-2. What are the five crucial steps to follow in basic financial analysis?

DISCUSSION QUESTIONS

12-3. Why should you begin a case analysis with a financial analysis? When are other approaches appropriate?

12-4. Why has the discussion of case analysis become so popular today in teaching strategy and policy?

12-5. When should you gather information outside a case? What should you look for?

12-6. When is inflation an important issue in conducting case analysis? Why bother?

12-7. Why is strategic audit commonly used as the format for case analysis?

STRATEGIC PRACTICE EXERCISE

Read the short article drawn from *The Economist*. What is the impact of currency on corporate industry, especially in the emerging marketplace?

Currency and Strategy

It is clear that emerging markets have been affected by the "tapering" carried out in the United States. Ben Bernanke, the outgoing Fed. Chairman, stated that America had tapered bond-buying. Argentina witnessed this, as have other markets: since January 22nd, the Argentine peso has fallen by 14 percent. Turkey, South Africa, and India among others are trying, each in their own way, to handle this crisis as their currency is weakened against the American dollar.

A sizable loss in the value of a nation's currency of 10 percent to 20 percent is difficult to manage, especially as each emerging country has its own political and economic headache. Argentina is using up its international reserves to prop up its peso. South Africa and Turkey have gaping current account deficits whereas Ukraine and Thailand have internal political discontent. Furthermore, Brazil is susceptible to China's economic slowdown. When markets start falling, there tends to be a domino effect.

....

SOURCE: "The plunging currency club," *The Economist* (January 24, 2014).

NOTES

1. M. Vanac, "What's a Novice Investor to Do?" *Des Moines Register* (November 30, 1997), p. 3G.
2. A. R. Sorking, "New Path on Mergers Could Contain Loopholes," *The* (Ames, IA) *Daily Tribune* (January 9, 2001), p. B7; "Firms Resist Effort to Unveil True Costs of Doing Business," *USA Today* (July 3, 2000), p. 10A.
3. M. S. Fridson, *Financial Statement Analysis* (New York: John Wiley & Sons, 1991), pp. 192–194.
4. E. I. Altman, "Predicting Financial Distress of Companies: Revisiting the Z-Score and Zeta Models," working paper at pages.stern.nyu.edu/~ealtman/Zscores.pdf (July 2000).
5. D. H. Bangs, *Managing by the Numbers* (Dover, NH: Upstart Publications, 1992), pp. 106–107.
6. http://ycharts.com/indicators/china_inflation_rate; http://www.bloomberg.com/news/2012-10-03/russia-september-inflation-rate-probably-surged-to-10-month-high.html.

Resources
for Case Research

Company Information

1. Annual reports

2. Moody's *Manuals on Investment* (a listing of companies within certain industries that contains a brief history and a five-year financial statement of each company)

3. Securities and Exchange Commission Annual Report Form 10-K (annually) and 10-Q (quarterly)

4. Standard & Poor's *Register of Corporations, Directors, and Executives*

5. Value Line's *Investment Survey*

6. Findex's *Directory of Market Research Reports, Studies, and Surveys* (a listing by Find/SVP of more than 11,000 studies conducted by leading research firms)

7. Compustat, Compact Disclosure, CD/International, and Hoover's online corporate directory (computerized operating and financial information on thousands of publicly held corporations)

8. Shareholders meeting notices in SEC Form 14-A (proxy notices)

Economic Information

1. Regional statistics and local forecasts from large banks

2. *Business Cycle Development* (Department of Commerce)

3. Chase Econometric Associates' publications

4. U.S. Census Bureau publications on population, transportation, and housing

5. *Current Business Reports* (U.S. Department of Commerce)

6. *Economic Indicators* (U.S. Joint Economic Committee)

7. *Economic Report of the President to Congress*

8. *Long-Term Economic Growth* (U.S. Department of Commerce)

9. *Monthly Labor Review* (U.S. Department of Labor)

10. *Monthly Bulletin of Statistics* (United Nations)

11. *Statistical Abstract of the United States* (U.S. Department of Commerce)

12. *Statistical Yearbook* (United Nations)

13. *Survey of Current Business* (U.S. Department of Commerce)

14. *U.S. Industrial Outlook* (U.S. Department of Defense)

15. *World Trade Annual* (United Nations)

16. *Overseas Business Reports* (by country, published by the U.S. Department of Commerce)

Industry Information

1. Analyses of companies and industries by investment brokerage firms

2. *Bloomberg Businessweek* (provides weekly economic and business information, as well as quarterly profit and sales rankings of corporations)

3. *Fortune* (each April publishes listings of financial information on corporations within certain industries)

4. *Industry Survey* (published quarterly by Standard & Poor's)

5. *Industry Week* (late March / early April issue provides information on 14 industry groups)

6. *Forbes* (mid-January issue provides performance data on firms in various industries)

7. *Inc.* (May and December issues give information on fast-growing entrepreneurial companies)

Directory and Index Information on Companies and Industries

1. *Business Periodical Index* (on computers in many libraries)

2. *Directory of National Trade Associations*

3. *Encyclopedia of Associations*

4. Funk and Scott's *Index of Corporations and Industries*

5. Thomas's *Register of American Manufacturers*

6. *The Wall Street Journal Index*

Ratio Analysis Information

1. *Almanac of Business and Industrial Financial Ratios* (Prentice Hall)

2. *Annual Statement Studies* (Risk Management Associates; also Robert Morris Associates)

3. *Dun's Review* (Dun & Bradstreet; published annually in September–December issues)

4. *Industry Norms and Key Business Ratios* (Dun & Bradstreet)

Online Information

1. *Hoover's Online*—financial statements and profiles of public companies (www.hoovers.com)

2. U.S. Securities and Exchange Commission—official filings of public companies in the EDGAR database (www.sec.gov)

3. Fortune 500—statistics for largest U.S. corporations (www.fortune.com)

4. Dun & Bradstreet's Online—short reports on 10 million public and private U.S. companies (smallbusiness.dnb.com)

5. Competitive Intelligence Guide—information on company resources (www.fuld.com)

6. Society of Competitive Intelligence Professionals (www.scip.org)

7. *The Economist*—provides international information and surveys (www.economist.com)

8. *CIA World Fact Book*—international information by country (http://www.cia.gov)

9. Bloomberg—information on interest rates, stock prices, currency conversion rates, and other general financial information (www.bloomberg.com)

10. CEOExpress—links to many valuable sources of business information (www.ceoexpress.com)

11. *The Wall Street Journal*—business news (www.wsj.com)

12. Forbes—America's largest private companies (http://www.forbes.com/lists/)

13. CorporateInformation.com—subscription service for company profiles (www.corporateinformation.com)

14. Kompass International—industry information (www.kompass.com)

15. CorpTech—database of technology companies (www.corptech.com)

16. ADNet—information technology industry (www.companyfinders.com)

17. CNN company research—provides company information (http://money.cnn.com/news/)

18. Paywatch—database of executive compensation (http://www.aflcio.org/corporatewatch/paywatch/)

19. Global Edge Global Resources—international resources (http://globaledge.msu.edu/resourceDesk/)

20. Google Finance—data on North American stocks (http://www.google.com/finance)

21. World Federation of Exchanges—international stock exchanges (www.world-exchanges.org/)

22. SEC International Registry—data on international corporations (http://www.sec.gov/divisions/corpfin/internatl/companies.shtml)

23. Yahoo Finance—data on North American companies (http://finance.yahoo.com)

Suggested Case Analysis Methodology Using the Strategic Audit

First Reading of the Case

- Develop a general overview of the company and its external environment.
- Begin a list of the possible strategic factors facing the company at this time.
- List the research information you may need on the economy, industry, and competitors.

Over the past six years, increases in yearly revenues have consistently reached 12%. Byte Products Inc., headquartered in the U.S. Midwest, is regarded as one of the largest-volume suppliers of specialized components and is easily the industry leader.

Second Reading of the Case

- Read the case a second time, using the strategic audit as a framework for in-depth analysis. (See **Appendix 1.A** on pages 66–73.) You may want to make a copy of the strategic audit worksheet (**Figure 12–1**) to use to keep track of your comments as you read the case.
- The questions in the strategic audit parallel the strategic decision-making process shown in **Figure 1–5** (pages 60–61).
- The audit provides you with a conceptual framework to examine the company's mission, objectives, strategies, and policies, as well as problems, symptoms, facts, opinions, and issues.
- Perform a financial analysis of the company, using ratio analysis (see **Table 12–1**), and do the calculations necessary to convert key parts of the financial statements to a common-size basis.

Library and Online Computer Services

- Each case has a decision date indicating when the case actually took place. Your research should be based on the time period for the case.
- See **Appendix 12.A** for resources for case research. Your research should include information about the environment at the time of the case. Find average industry ratios. You may also want to obtain further information regarding competitors and the company itself (10-K forms and annual reports). This information should help you conduct an industry analysis. *Check with your instructor to see what kind of outside research is appropriate for your assignment.*
- Don't try to learn what actually happened to the company discussed in the case. What management actually decided may not be the best solution. It will certainly bias your analysis and will probably cause your recommendation to lack proper justification.
- Analyze the natural and societal environments to see what general trends are likely to affect the industry(s) in which the company is operating.

- Conduct an industry analysis using Porter's competitive forces from **Chapter 4**. Develop an Industry Matrix (**Table 4–4** on page 147).
- Generate 8 to 10 external factors. These should be the *most important* opportunities and threats facing the company at the time of the case.
- Develop an EFAS Table, as shown in **Table 4–5** (page 155), for your list of external strategic factors.
- **Suggestion:** Rank the 8 to 10 factors from most to least important. Start by grouping the three top factors and then the three bottom factors.

Internal Organizational Analysis: IFAS

- Generate 8 to 10 internal factors. These should be the *most important* strengths and weaknesses of the company at the time of the case.
- Develop an IFAS Table, as shown in **Table 5–2** (page 188), for your list of internal strategic factors.
- **Suggestion:** Rank the 8 to 10 factors from most to least important. Start by grouping the three top factors and then the three bottom factors.
- Review the student-written audit of an old Maytag case in **Appendix 12.C** for an example.
- Write Parts I to IV of the strategic audit. Remember to include the factors from your EFAS and IFAS Tables in your audit.

Strategic Factor Analysis Summary: SFAS

- Condense the list of factors from the 16 to 20 identified in your EFAS and IFAS Tables to only the 8 to 10 most important factors.
- Select the most important EFAS and IFAS factors. Recalculate the weights of each. The weights still need to add to 1.0.
- This is a good time to reexamine what you wrote earlier in Parts I to IV. You may want to add to or delete some of what you wrote. Ensure that each one of the strategic factors you have included in your SFAS Matrix is discussed in the appropriate place in Parts I to IV. Part V of the audit is *not* the place to mention a strategic factor for the first time.
- Write Part V of your strategic audit. This completes your SWOT analysis.
- This is the place to suggest a revised mission statement and a better set of objectives for the company. The SWOT analysis coupled with revised mission and objectives for the company set the stage for the generation of strategic alternatives.

A. Alternatives

- Develop around three mutually exclusive strategic alternatives. If appropriate to the case you are analyzing, you might propose one alternative for growth, one for stability, and one for retrenchment. Within each corporate strategy, you should probably propose an appropriate business/competitive.
- Construct a corporate scenario for each alternative. Use the data from your outside research to project general societal trends (GDP, inflation, and etc.) and industry trends. Use these as the basis of your assumptions to write pro forma financial statements (particularly income statements) for each strategic alternative for the next five years.
- List pros and cons for each alternative based on your scenarios.

B. Recommendation

- Specify which one of your alternative strategies you recommend. Justify your choice in terms of dealing with the strategic factors you listed in Part V of the strategic audit.
- Develop policies to help implement your strategies.

Implementation

- Develop programs to implement your recommended strategy.
- Specify who is to be responsible for implementing each program and how long each program will take to complete.

■ Refer to the pro forma financial statements you developed earlier for your recommended strategy. Use common-size historical income statements as the basis for the pro forma statement. Do the numbers still make sense? If not, this may be a good time to rethink the budget numbers to reflect your recommended programs.

Evaluation and Control

■ Specify the type of evaluation and controls you need to ensure that your recommendation is carried out successfully. Specify who is responsible for monitoring these controls.

■ Indicate whether sufficient information is available to monitor how the strategy is being implemented. If not, suggest a change to the information system.

Final Draft of Your Strategic Audit

■ Check to ensure that your audit is within the page limits set out by your professor. You may need to cut some parts and expand others.

■ Make sure your recommendation clearly deals with the strategic factors.

■ **Attach your EFAS and IFAS Tables, and SFAS Matrix,** plus your ratio analysis and pro forma statements. Label them as numbered exhibits and refer to each of them within the body of the audit.

■ Proof your work for errors. If on a computer, use a spell checker.

SPECIAL NOTE: Depending on your assignment, it is relatively easy to use the strategic audit you have just developed to write a written case analysis in essay form or to make an oral presentation. The strategic audit is just a detailed case analysis in an outline form and can be used as the basic framework for any sort of case analysis and presentation.

Example of Student-Written Strategic Audit

(For the 1993 Maytag Corporation Case)

I. Current Situation

A. Current Performance

Poor financials, high debt load, first losses since 1920s, price/earnings ratio negative.

- First loss since 1920s.
- Laid off 4500 employees at Magic Chef.
- Hoover Europe still showing losses.

B. Strategic Posture

1. **Mission**
   - Developed in 1989 for the Maytag Company: "To provide our customers with products of unsurpassed performance that last longer, need fewer repairs, and are produced at the lowest possible cost."
   - Updated in 1991: "Our collective mission is world class quality." Expands Maytag's belief in product quality to all aspects of operations.

2. **Objectives**
   - "To be the profitability leader in the industry for every product line Maytag manufactures." Selected profitability rather than market share.
   - "To be number one in total customer satisfaction." Doesn't say how to measure satisfaction.
   - "To grow the North American appliance business and become the third largest appliance manufacturer (in unit sales) in North America."
   - To increase profitable market share growth in the North American appliance and floor care business, 6.5% return on sales, 10% return on assets, 20% return on equity, beat competition in satisfying customers, dealer, builder, and endorser, and move into third place in total units shipped per year. Nicely quantified objectives.

3. **Strategies**
   - Global growth through acquisition, and alliance with Bosch-Siemens.
   - Differentiate brand names for competitive advantage.
   - Create synergy between companies, product improvement, investment in plant and equipment.

4. **Policies**
   - Cost reduction is secondary to high quality.
   - Promotion from within.
   - Slow but sure R&D: Maytag slow to respond to changes in market.

II. Strategic Managers

A. Board of Directors

1. Fourteen members—eleven are outsiders.
2. Well-respected Americans, most on board since 1986 or earlier.
3. No international or marketing backgrounds.
4. Time for a change?

B. Top Management

1. Top management promoted from within Maytag Company. Too inbred?
2. Very experienced in the industry.
3. Responsible for current situation.
4. May be too parochial for global industry. May need new blood.

III. External Environment (EFAS Table; see Exhibit 1)

A. Natural Environment

1. Growing water scarcity
2. Energy availability a growing problem

B. Societal Environment

1. **Economic**
   a. Unstable economy but recession ending, consumer confidence growing—could increase spending for big ticket items like houses, cars, and appliances. **(O)**
   b. Individual economies becoming interconnected into a world economy. **(O)**
2. **Technological**
   a. Fuzzy logic technology being applied to sense and measure activities. **(O)**
   b. Computers and information technology increasingly important. **(O)**
3. **Political–Legal**
   a. NAFTA, European Union, other regional trade pacts opening doors to markets in Europe, Asia, and Latin America that offer enormous potential. **(O)**
   b. Breakdown of communism means less chance of world war. **(O)**
   c. Environmentalism being reflected in laws on pollution and energy usage. **(T)**
4. **Sociocultural**
   a. Developing nations desire goods seen on TV. **(O)**
   b. Middle-aged baby boomers want attractive, high-quality products, like BMWs and Maytag. **(O)**
   c. Dual-career couples increases need for labor-saving appliances, second cars, and day care. **(O)**
   d. Divorce and career mobility means need for more houses and goods to fill them. **(O)**

C. Task Environment

1. North American market mature and extremely competitive—vigilant consumers demand high quality with low price in safe, environmentally sound products. **(T)**

2. Industry going global as North American and European firms expand internationally. **(T)**

3. European design popular and consumer desire for technologically advanced appliances. **(O)**

4. **Rivalry High**. Whirlpool, Electrolux, GE have enormous resources and developing global presence. **(T)**

5. **Buyers' Power Low**. Technology and materials can be sourced worldwide. **(O)**

6. **Power of Other Stakeholders Medium**. Quality, safety, environmental regulations increasing. **(T)**

7. **Distributors' Power High**. Super retailers more important: mom and pop dealers less. **(T)**

8. **Threat of Substitutes Low**. **(O)**

9. **Entry Barriers High**. New entrants unlikely except for large international firms. **(T)**

IV. Internal Environment (IFAS Table; see Exhibit 2)

A. Corporate Structure

1. Divisional structure: appliance manufacturing and vending machines. Floor care managed separately. **(S)**

2. Centralized major decisions by Newton corporate staff, with a time line of about three years. **(S)**

B. Corporate Culture

1. Quality key ingredient—commitment to quality shared by executives and workers. **(S)**

2. Much of corporate culture is based on founder F. L. Maytag's personal philosophy, including concern for quality, employees, local community, innovation, and performance. **(S)**

3. Acquired companies, except for European, seem to accept dominance of Maytag culture. **(S)**

C. Corporate Resources

1. **Marketing**
   a. Maytag brand lonely repairman advertising successful but dated. **(W)**
   b. Efforts focus on distribution—combining three sales forces into two, concentrating on major retailers. (Cost $95 million for this restructuring.) **(S)**
   c. Hoover's well-publicized marketing fiasco involving airline tickets. **(W)**

2. **Finance** (see **Exhibits 4 and 5**)
   a. Revenues are up slightly, operating income is down significantly. **(W)**
   b. Some key ratios are troubling, such as a 57% debt/asset ratio, 132% long-term debt/equity ratio. No room for more debt to grow company. **(W)**
   c. Net income is 400% less than 1988, based on common-size income statements. **(W)**

3. **R&D**
   a. Process-oriented with focus on manufacturing process and durability. **(S)**
   b. Maytag becoming a technology follower, taking too long to get product innovations to market (competitors put out more in last six months than prior two years combined), lagging in fuzzy logic and other technological areas. **(W)**

4. **Operations**
   a. Maytag's core competence. Continual improvement process kept it dominant in the U.S. market for many years. **(S)**
   b. Plants aging and may be losing competitiveness as rivals upgrade facilities. Quality no longer distinctive competence? **(W)**

5. **Human Resources**
   a. Traditionally very good relations with unions and employees. **(S)**
   b. Labor relations increasingly strained, with two salary raise delays, and layoffs of 4500 employees at Magic Chef. **(W)**
   c. Unions express concern at new, more distant tone from Maytag Corporation. **(W)**

6. **Information Systems**
   a. Not mentioned in case. Hoover fiasco in Europe suggests information systems need significant upgrading. **(W)**
   b. Critical area where Maytag may be unwilling or unable to commit resources needed to stay competitive. **(W)**

V. Analysis of Strategic Factors

A. Situational Analysis (SWOT) (SFAS Matrix; see Exhibit 3)

1. **Strengths**
   a. Quality Maytag culture.
   b. Maytag well-known and respected brand.
   c. Hoover's international orientation.
   d. Core competencies in process R&D and manufacturing.

2. **Weaknesses**
   a. Lacks financial resources of competitors.
   b. Poor global positioning. Hoover weak on European continent.
   c. Product R&D and customer service innovation are areas of serious weakness.
   d. Dependent on small dealers.
   e. Marketing needs improvement.

3. **Opportunities**
   a. Economic integration of European community.
   b. Demographics favor quality.
   c. Trend to superstores.

4. **Threats**
   a. Trend to superstores.
   b. Aggressive rivals—Whirlpool and Electrolux.
   c. Japanese appliance companies—new entrants?

B. Review of Current Mission and Objectives

1. Current mission appears appropriate.
2. Some of the objectives are really goals and need to be quantified and given time horizons.

VI. Strategic Alternatives and Recommended Strategy

A. Strategic Alternatives

1. *Growth through Concentric Diversification*: Acquire a company in a related industry such as commercial appliances.
   a. *[Pros]:* Product/market synergy created by acquisition of related company.
   b. *[Cons]:* Maytag does not have the financial resources to play this game.

2. *Pause Strategy*: Consolidate various acquisitions to find economies and to encourage innovation among the business units.

   a. *[Pros]:* Maytag needs to get its financial house in order and get administrative control over its recent acquisitions.

   b. *[Cons]:* Unless it can grow through a stronger alliance with Bosch-Siemens or some other backer, Maytag is a prime candidate for takeover because of its poor financial performance in recent years, and it is suffering from the initial reduction in efficiency inherent in acquisition strategy.

3. *Retrenchment*: Sell Hoover's foreign major home appliance businesses (Australia and UK) to emphasize increasing market share in North America.

   a. *[Pros]:* Divesting Hoover improves bottom line and enables Maytag Corp. to focus on North America while Whirlpool, Electrolux, and GE are battling elsewhere.

   b. *[Cons]:* Maytag may be giving up its only opportunity to become a player in the coming global appliance industry.

B. Recommended Strategy

1. Recommend pause strategy, at least for a year, so Maytag can get a grip on its European operation and consolidate its companies in a more synergistic way.

2. Maytag quality must be maintained, and continued shortage of operating capital will take its toll, so investment must be made in R&D.

3. Maytag may be able to make the Hoover UK investment work better since the recession is ending and the EU countries are closer to integrating than ever before.

4. Because it is only an average competitor, Maytag needs the Hoover link to Europe to provide a jumping off place for negotiations with Bosch-Siemens that could strengthen their alliance.

VII. Implementation

A. The only way to increase profitability in North America is to further involve Maytag with the superstore retailers; sure to anger the independent dealers, but necessary for Maytag to compete.

B. Board members with more global business experience should be recruited, with an eye toward the future, especially with expertise in Asia and Latin America.

C. R&D needs to be improved, as does marketing, to get new products online quickly.

VIII. Evaluation and Control

A. MIS needs to be developed for speedier evaluation and control. While the question of control vs. autonomy is "under review," another Hoover fiasco may be brewing.

B. The acquired companies do not all share the Midwestern work ethic or the Maytag Corporation culture, and Maytag's managers must inculcate these values into the employees of all acquired companies.

C. Systems should be developed to decide if the size and location of Maytag manufacturing plants is still correct and to plan for the future. Industry analysis indicates that smaller automated plants may be more efficient now than in the past.

EXHIBIT 1 EFAS Table for Maytag Corporation 1993

External Factors	Weight	Rating	Weighted Score	Comments
1	2	3	4	5
Opportunities				
▪ Economic integration of European Community	.20	4.1	.82	Acquisition of Hoover
▪ Demographics favor quality appliances	.10	5.0	.50	Maytag quality
▪ Economic development of Asia	.05	1.0	.05	Low Maytag presence
▪ Opening of Eastern Europe	.05	2.0	.10	Will take time
▪ Trend to "Super Stores"	.10	1.8	.18	Maytag weak in this channel
Threats				
▪ Increasing government regulations	.10	4.3	.43	Well positioned
▪ Strong U.S. competition	.10	4.0	.40	Well positioned
▪ Whirlpool and Electrolux strong globally	.15	3.0	.45	Hoover weak globally
▪ New product advances	.05	1.2	.06	Questionable
▪ Japanese appliance companies	.10	1.6	.16	Only Asian presence in Australia
Total Scores	1.00		3.15	

EXHIBIT 2 IFAS Table for Maytag Corporation 1993

Internal Factors	Weight	Rating	Weighted Score	Comments
1	2	3	4	5
Strengths				
▪ Quality Maytag culture	.15	5.0	.75	Quality key to success
▪ Experienced top management	.05	4.2	.21	Know appliances
▪ Vertical integration	.10	3.9	.39	Dedicated factories
▪ Employer relations	.05	3.0	.15	Good, but deteriorating
▪ Hoover's international orientation	.15	2.8	.42	Hoover name in cleaners
Weaknesses				
▪ Process-oriented R&D	.05	2.2	.11	Slow on new products
▪ Distribution channels	.05	2.0	.10	Superstores replacing small dealers
▪ Financial position	.15	2.0	.30	High debt load
▪ Global positioning	.20	2.1	.42	Hoover weak outside the United Kingdom and Australia
▪ Manufacturing facilities	.05	4.0	.20	Investing now
Total scores	1.00		3.05	

| EXHIBIT 3 | SFAS Matrix for Maytag Corporation 1993 |

Strategic Factors (Select the most important opportunities/threats from EFAS, Table 4–5 and the most important strengths and weaknesses from IFAS, Table 5–2)	Weight	Rating	Weighted Score	SHORT	INTERMEDIATE	LONG	Comments
▶S1 Quality Maytag culture (S)	.10	5.0	.50			X	Quality key to success
▶S5 Hoover's international orientation (S)	.10	2.8	.28	X	X		Name recognition
▶W3 Financial position (W)	.10	2.0	.20	X	X		High debt
▶W4 Global positioning (W)	.15	2.2	.33		X	X	Only in N.A., U.K., and Australia
▶O1 Economic integration of European Community (O)	.10	4.1	.41			X	Acquisition of Hoover
▶O2 Demographics favor quality (O)	.10	5.0	.50		X		Maytag quality
▶O5 Trend to super stores (O + T)	.10	1.8	.18	X			Weak in this channel
▶T3 Whirlpool and Electrolux (T)	.15	3.0	.45	X			Dominate industry
▶T5 Japanese appliance companies (T)	.10	1.6	.16			X	Asian presence
Total Scores	1.00		3.01				

EXHIBIT 4		1990	1991	1992	1993
Ratio Analysis for Maytag Corporation 1993	**1. LIQUIDITY RATIOS**				
	Current	2.1	1.9	1.8	1.6
	Quick	1.1	1.0	1.1	1.0
	2. LEVERAGE RATIOS				
	Debt to Total Assets	61%	60%	76%	57%
	Debt to Equity	155%	151%	317%	254%
	3. ACTIVITY RATIOS				
	Inventory turnover—sales	5.7	6.1	7.6	6.9
	Inventory Turnover—cost of sales	4.3	4.6	5.8	6.5
	Avg. Collection Period—days	57	55	56	0
	Fixed Asset Turnover	3.9	3.6	3.6	3.6
	Total Assets Turnover	1.2	1.2	1.2	1.1
	4. PROFITABILITY RATIOS				
	Gross Profit Margin	24%	24%	23%	5%
	Net Operating Margin	8%	6%	3%	5%
	Profit Margin on Sales	3%	3%	−0%	2%
	Return on Total Assets	4%	3%	−0%	2%
	Return on Equity	10%	8%	−1%	8%

EXHIBIT 5		1992	1991	1990
Common Size Income Statements for Maytag Corporation 1993	Net sales	100.0%	100.0%	100.0%
	Cost of sales	76.92	75.88	75.50
	Gross profit	23.08	24.12	24.46
	Selling, general/admin. Expenses	17.37	17.67	16.90
	Reorganization expenses	.031	——	——
	Operating income	.026	.064	.075
	Interest expense	(.025)	(.025)	(0.26)
	Other—net	.001	.002	.009
	Income before accounting changes	.002	.042	.052
	Income taxes	.005	.015	.020
	Income before accounting changes	(.002)	.026	.032
	Effect of accounting changes for postretirement benefits other than pensions and income taxes	(.101)	——	——
	Total operating costs and expenses	<u>74.9</u>	<u>76.0</u>	<u>76.3</u>
	Net income	**(.104)**	**.026**	**.032**

EXHIBIT 6   Implementation, Evaluation, and Control Plan for Maytag Corporation 1993

Strategic Factor	Action Plan	Priority System (1–5)	Who Will Implement	Who Will Review	How Often Review	Criteria Used
Quality Maytag culture	Build quality in acquired units	1	Heads of acquired units	Manufacturing VP	Quarterly	Number defects & customer satisfaction
Hoover's international orientation	Identify ways to expand sales	2	Head of Hoover	Marketing VP	Quarterly	Feasible alternatives generated
Financial position	Pay down debt	1	CFO	CEO	Monthly	Leverage ratios
Global positioning	Find strategic alliance partners	2	VP of Business Development	COO	Quarterly	Feasible alternatives generated
EU economic integration	Grow sales throughout EU	3	Hoover UK Head	Marketing VP	Annually	Sales growth
Demographics favor quality	Simplify controls	3	Manufacturing VP	COO	Annually	Market research user satisfaction
Trend to super stores	Market through Sears	1	Marketing VP	CEO	Monthly	Sales growth
Whirlpool & Electrolux	Monitor competitor performance	1	Competition committee	COO	Quarterly	Competitor sales & new products
Japanese appliance companies	Monitor expansion	4	Head of Hoover Australia	Competition committee	Semi-annually	Sales growth outside Japan

Cases in

Strategic Management

cases in
strategic management

CONTENTS

alphabetical listing of cases

CASE **1**

The Recalcitrant Director at Byte Products, Inc.

CORPORATE LEGALITY VERSUS CORPORATE RESPONSIBILITY

Dan R. Dalton, Richard A. Cosier, and Cathy A. Enz

BYTE PRODUCTS, INC., IS PRIMARILY INVOLVED IN THE PRODUCTION OF ELECTRONIC components that are used in personal computers. Although such components might be found in a few computers in home use, Byte products are found most frequently in computers used for sophisticated business and engineering applications. Annual sales of these products have been steadily increasing over the past several years; Byte Products, Inc., currently has total sales of approximately $265 million.

Over the past six years, increases in yearly revenues have consistently reached 12%. Byte Products, Inc., headquartered in the midwestern United States, is regarded as one of the largest-volume suppliers of specialized components and is easily the industry leader, with some 32% market share. Unfortunately for Byte, many new firms—domestic and foreign—have entered the industry. A dramatic surge in demand, high profitability, and the relative ease of a new firm's entry into the industry explain in part the increased number of competing firms.

Although Byte management—and presumably shareholders as well—is very pleased about the growth of its markets, it faces a major problem: Byte simply cannot meet the demand for these components. The company currently operates three manufacturing facilities in various locations throughout the United States. Each of these plants operates three production shifts (24 hours per day), seven days a week. This activity constitutes virtually all of the company's production capacity. Without an additional manufacturing plant, Byte simply cannot increase its output of components.

....

James M. Elliott, Chief Executive Officer and Chairman of the Board, recognizes the gravity of the problem. If Byte Products cannot continue to manufacture components in sufficient numbers to meet the demand, buyers will go elsewhere. Worse yet is the possibility that any continued lack of supply will encourage others to enter the market. As a long-term solution to this problem, the board of directors unanimously authorized the construction of a new, state-of-the-art manufacturing facility in the southwestern United States. When the planned capacity of this plant is added to that of the three current plants, Byte should be able to meet demand for many years to come. Unfortunately, an estimated three years will be required to complete the plant and bring it online.

Jim Elliott believes very strongly that this three-year period is far too long and has insisted that there also be a shorter-range, stopgap solution while the plant is under construction. The instability of the market and the pressure to maintain leader status are two factors contributing to Elliott's insistence on a more immediate solution. Without such a move, Byte management believes it will lose market share and, again, attract competitors into the market.

Several Solutions

A number of suggestions for such a temporary measure were offered by various staff specialists but rejected by Elliott. For example, licensing Byte's product and process technology to other manufacturers in the short run to meet immediate demand was possible. This licensing authorization would be short term, or just until the new plant could come online. Top management, as well as the board, was uncomfortable with this solution for several reasons. They thought it unlikely that any manufacturer would shoulder the fixed costs of producing appropriate components for such a short term. Any manufacturer that would do so would charge a premium to recover its costs. This suggestion, obviously, would make Byte's own products available to its customers at an unacceptable price. Nor did passing any price increase to its customers seem sensible, for this too would almost certainly reduce Byte's market share as well as encourage further competition.

Overseas facilities and licensing also were considered but rejected. Before it became a publicly traded company, Byte's founders had decided that its manufacturing facilities would be domestic. Top management strongly felt that this strategy had served Byte well; moreover, Byte's majority stockholders (initial owners of the then privately held Byte) were not likely to endorse such a move. Beyond that, however, top management was reluctant to foreign license their goods—or make available by any means the technologies for others to produce Byte products—as they could not then properly control patents. Top management feared that foreign licensing would essentially give away costly proprietary information regarding the company's highly efficient means of product development. There also was the potential for initial low product quality—whether produced domestically or otherwise—especially for such a short-run operation. Any reduction in quality, however brief, would threaten Byte's share of this sensitive market.

The Solution!

One recommendation that has come to the attention of the Chief Executive Officer could help solve Byte's problem in the short run. Certain members of his staff have notified him that an abandoned plant currently is available in Plainville, a small town in the northeastern United States. Before its closing eight years earlier, this plant was used primarily for the manufacture of electronic components. As is, it could not possibly be used to produce Byte products, but it could be inexpensively refitted to do so in as few as three months. Moreover, this plant is available at a very attractive price. In fact, discreet inquiries by Elliott's staff indicate that this plant could probably be leased immediately from its present owners because the building has been vacant for some eight years.

All the news about this temporary plant proposal, however, is not nearly so positive. Elliott's staff concedes that this plant will never be efficient and its profitability will be low. In addition, the Plainville location is a poor one in terms of high labor costs (the area is highly unionized), warehousing expenses, and inadequate transportation links to Byte's major markets and suppliers. Plainville is simply not a candidate for a long-term solution. Still, in the short run, a temporary plant could help meet the demand and might forestall additional competition.

The staff is persuasive and notes that this option has several advantages: (1) there is no need for any licensing, foreign or domestic, (2) quality control remains firmly in the company's hands, and (3) an increase in the product price will be unnecessary. The temporary plant, then, would be used for three years or so until the new plant could be built. Then the temporary plant would be immediately closed.

CEO Elliott is convinced.

Taking the Plan to the Board

The quarterly meeting of the board of directors is set to commence at 2:00 P.M. Jim Elliott has been reviewing his notes and agenda for the meeting most of the morning. The issue of the temporary plant is clearly the most important agenda item. Reviewing his detailed presentation of this matter, including the associated financial analyses, has occupied much of his time for several days. All the available information underscores his contention that the temporary plant in Plainville is the only responsible solution to the demand problems. No other option offers the same low level of risk and ensures Byte's status as industry leader.

At the meeting, after the board has dispensed with a number of routine matters, Jim Elliott turns his attention to the temporary plant. In short order, he advises the 11-member board (himself, 3 additional inside members, and 7 outside members) of his proposal to obtain and refit the existing plant to ameliorate demand problems in the short run, authorizes the construction of the new plant (the completion of which is estimated to take some three years), and plans to switch capacity from the temporary plant to the new one when it is operational. He also briefly reviews additional details concerning the costs involved, advantages of this proposal versus domestic or foreign licensing, and so on.

All the board members except one are in favor of the proposal. In fact, they are most enthusiastic; the overwhelming majority agree that the temporary plant is an excellent—even inspired—stopgap measure. Ten of the eleven board members seem relieved because the board was most reluctant to endorse any of the other alternatives that had been mentioned.

The single dissenter—T. Kevin Williams, an outside director—is, however, steadfast in his objections. He will not, under any circumstances, endorse the notion of the temporary plant and states rather strongly that "I will not be party to this nonsense, not now, not ever."

T. Kevin Williams, the senior executive of a major nonprofit organization, is normally a reserved and really quite agreeable person. This sudden, uncharacteristic burst of emotion clearly startles the remaining board members into silence. The following excerpt captures the ensuing, essentially one-on-one conversation between Williams and Elliott:

Williams: How many workers do your people estimate will be employed in the temporary plant?

Elliott: Roughly 1200, possibly a few more.

Williams: I presume it would be fair, then, to say that, including spouses and children, something on the order of 4000 people will be attracted to the community.

Elliott: I certainly would not be surprised.

Williams: If I understand the situation correctly, this plant closed just over eight years ago, and that closing had a catastrophic effect on Plainville. Isn't it true that a large portion of the community was employed by this plant?

Elliott: Yes, it was far and away the majority employer.

Williams: And most of these people have left the community, presumably to find employment elsewhere?

Elliott: Definitely. There was a drastic decrease in the area's population.

Williams: Are you concerned, then, that our company must attract the 1200 employees to Plainville from other parts of New England?

Elliott: Not in the least. We are absolutely confident that we will attract 1200—even more, for that matter, virtually any number we need. That, in fact, is one of the chief advantages of this proposal. I would think that the community would be very pleased to have us there.

Williams: On the contrary, I would suspect that the community will rue the day we arrived. Beyond that, though, this plan is totally unworkable if we are candid. On the other hand, if we are less than candid, the proposal will work for us, but only at great cost to Plainville. In fact, quite frankly, the implications are appalling. Once again, I must enter my serious objections.

Elliott: I don't follow you.

Williams: The temporary plant would employ some 1200 people. Again, this means the infusion of over 4000 to the community and surrounding areas. Byte Products, however, intends to close this plant in three years or less. If Byte informs the community or the employees that the jobs are temporary, the proposal simply won't work. When the new people arrive in the community, there will be a need for more schools, instructors, utilities, housing, restaurants, and so forth. Obviously, if the banks and local government know that the plant is temporary, no funding will be made available for these projects and certainly no credit for the new employees to buy homes, appliances, automobiles, and so forth.

   If, on the other hand, Byte Products does not tell the community of its "temporary" plans, the project can go on. But, in several years when the plant closes (and we here have agreed today that it will close), we will have created a ghost town. The tax base of the community will have been destroyed; property values will decrease precipitously; practically the whole town will be unemployed. This proposal will place Byte Products in an untenable position and in extreme jeopardy.

Elliott: Are you suggesting that this proposal jeopardizes us legally? If so, it should be noted that the legal department has reviewed this proposal in its entirety and has indicated no problem.

Williams: No! I don't think we are dealing with an issue of legality here. In fact, I don't doubt for a minute that this proposal is altogether legal. I do, however, resolutely believe that this proposal constitutes gross irresponsibility.

   I think this decision has captured most of my major concerns. These, along with a host of collateral problems associated with this project, lead me to strongly suggest that you and the balance of the board reconsider and not endorse this proposal. Byte Products must find another way.

The Dilemma

After a short recess, the board meeting reconvened. Presumably because of some discussion during the recess, several other board members indicated that they were no longer inclined to support the proposal. After a short period of rather heated discussion, the following exchange took place:

Elliott: It appears to me that any vote on this matter is likely to be very close. Given the gravity of our demand capacity problem, I must insist that the stockholders' equity be protected. We cannot wait three years; that is clearly out of the question. I still feel that licensing—domestic or foreign—is not in our long-term interests for any number of reasons, some of which have been discussed here. On the other hand, I do not want to take this project forward on the strength of a mixed vote. A vote of 6–5 or 7–4, for example, does not indicate that the board is remotely close to being of one mind. Mr. Williams, is there a compromise to be reached?

Williams: Respectfully, I have to say no. If we tell the truth—namely, the temporary nature of our operations—the proposal is simply not viable. If we are less than candid in this respect, we do grave damage to the community as well as to our image. It seems to me that we can only go one way or the other. I don't see a middle ground.

CASE **2**

The Wallace Group

Laurence J. Stybel

FRANCES RAMPAR, PRESIDENT OF RAMPAR ASSOCIATES, DRUMMED HER FINGERS ON THE desk. Scattered before her were her notes. She had to put the pieces together in order to make an effective sales presentation to Harold Wallace.

Hal Wallace was the President of The Wallace Group. He had asked Rampar to conduct a series of interviews with some key Wallace Group employees, in preparation for a possible consulting assignment for Rampar Associates.

During the past three days, Rampar had been talking with some of these key people and had received background material about the company. The problem was not in finding the problem. The problem was that there were too many problems!

Background on The Wallace Group

The Wallace Group, Inc., is a diversified company dealing in the manufacture and development of technical products and systems (see **Exhibit 1**). The company currently consists of three operational groups and a corporate staff. The three groups include Electronics, Plastics, and Chemicals, each operating under the direction of a Group Vice President (see **Exhibits 2**, **3**, and **4**). The company generates $70 million in sales as a manufacturer of plastics, chemical products, and electronic components and systems. Principal sales are to large contractors in governmental and automotive markets. With respect to sales volume, Plastics and Chemicals are approximately equal in size, and both of them together equal the size of the Electronics Group.

Electronics offers competence in the areas of microelectronics, electromagnetic sensors, antennas, microwaves, and minicomputers. Presently, these skills are devoted primarily to the engineering and manufacture of countermeasure equipment for aircraft. This includes radar detection systems that allow an aircraft crew to know that they are being tracked by radar units on the ground, on ships, or on other aircraft. Further, the company manufactures displays that provide the crew with a visual "fix" on where they are relative to the radar units that are tracking them.

This case was prepared by Dr. Laurence J. Stybel. It was prepared for class discussion rather than to illustrate either effective or ineffective handling of an administrative situation. Unauthorized duplication of copyright materials is a violation of federal law. This case was edited for the *SMBP*–9th, 10th, 11th, 12th, 13th and 14th Editions. The copyright holders are solely responsible for case content. Reprint permission is solely granted to the publisher, Prentice Hall, for the book, *Strategic Management and Business Policy* – 14th Edition by copyright holder, Dr. Laurence J. Stybel. Any other publication of this case (translation, any form of electronic or other media), or sale (any form of partnership) to another publisher will be in violation of copyright laws, unless the copyright holder has granted an additional written reprint permission.

EXHIBIT 1
An Excerpt from the
Annual Report

To the Shareholders:

This past year was one of definite accomplishment for The Wallace Group, although with some admitted soft spots. This is a period of consolidation, of strengthening our internal capacity for future growth and development. Presently, we are in the process of creating a strong management team to meet the challenges we will set for the future.

Despite our failure to achieve some objectives, we turned a profit of $3,521,000 before taxes, which was a growth over the previous year's earnings. And we have declared a dividend for the fifth consecutive year, albeit one that is less than the year before. However, the retention of earnings is imperative if we are to lay a firm foundation for future accomplishment.

Currently, The Wallace Group has achieved a level of stability. We have a firm foothold in our current markets, and we could elect to simply enact strong internal controls and maximize our profits. However, this would not be a growth strategy. Instead, we have chosen to adopt a more aggressive posture for the future, to reach out into new markets wherever possible and to institute the controls necessary to move forward in a planned and orderly fashion.

The Electronics Group performed well this past year and is engaged in two major programs under Defense Department contracts. These are developmental programs that provide us with the opportunity for ongoing sales upon testing of the final product. Both involve the creation of tactical display systems for aircraft being built by Lombard Aircraft for the Navy and the Air Force. Future potential sales from these efforts could amount to approximately $56 million over the next five years. Additionally, we are developing technical refinements to older, already installed systems under Army Department contracts.

In the future, we will continue to offer our technological competence in such tactical display systems and anticipate additional breakthroughs and success in meeting the demands of this market. However, we also believe that we have unique contributions to make to other markets, and to that end we are making the investments necessary to expand our opportunities.

Plastics also turned in a solid performance this past year and has continued to be a major supplier to Chrysler, Martin Tool, Foster Electric, and, of course, to our Electronics Group. The market for this group continues to expand, and we believe that additional investments in this group will allow us to seize a larger share of the future.

Chemicals' performance, admittedly, has not been as satisfactory as anticipated during the past year. However, we have been able to realize a small amount of profit from this operation and to halt what was a potentially dangerous decline in profits. We believe that this situation is only temporary and that infusions of capital for developing new technology, plus the streamlining of operations, has stabilized the situation. The next step will be to begin more aggressive marketing to capitalize on the group's basic strengths.

Overall, the outlook seems to be one of modest but profitable growth. The near term will be one of creating the technology and controls necessary for developing our market offerings and growing in a planned and purposeful manner. Our improvement efforts in the various company groups can be expected to take hold over the years with a positive effect on results.

We wish to express our appreciation to all those who participated in our efforts this past year.

Harold Wallace
Chairman and President

In addition to manufacturing tested and proven systems developed in the past, The Wallace Group is currently involved in two major and two minor programs, all involving display systems. The Navy-A Program calls for the development of a display system for a tactical fighter plane; Air Force-B is another such system for an observation plane. Ongoing production orders are anticipated following flight testing. The other two minor programs, Army-LG and OBT-37, involve the incorporation of new technology into existing aircraft systems.

EXHIBIT 2
Organizational Chart: The Wallace Group (Electronics)

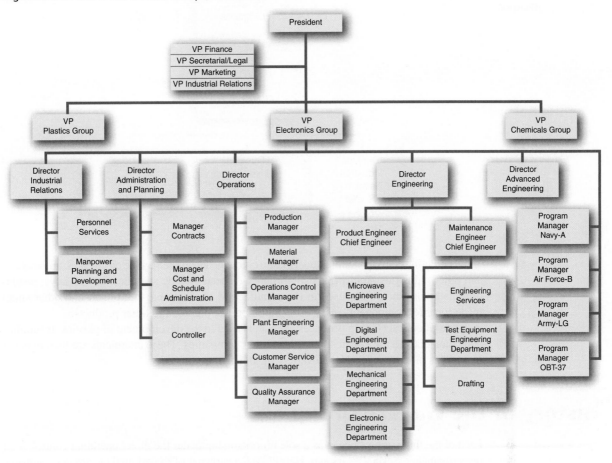

EXHIBIT 3
The Wallace Group
(Chemicals)

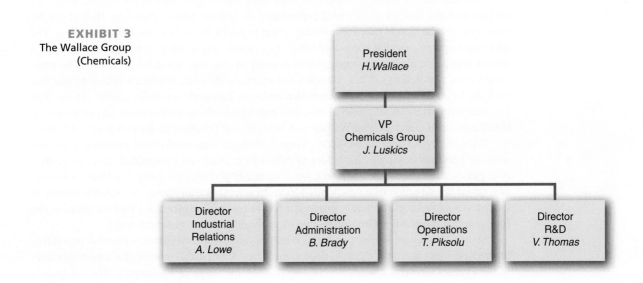

EXHIBIT 4
The Wallace Group
(Plastics)

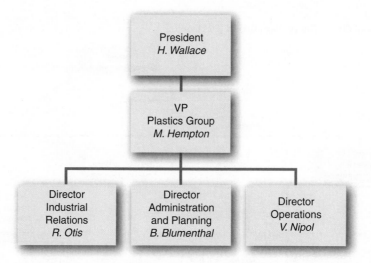

The Plastics Group manufactures plastic components utilized by the electronics, automotive, and other industries requiring plastic products. These include switches, knobs, keys, insulation materials, and so on, used in the manufacture of electronic equipment and other small made-to-order components installed in automobiles, planes, and other products.

The Chemicals Group produces chemicals used in the development of plastics. It supplies bulk chemicals to the Plastics Group and other companies. These chemicals are then injected into molds or extruded to form a variety of finished products.

History of the Wallace Group

Each of the three groups began as a sole proprietorship under the direct operating control of an owner/manager. Several years ago, Harold Wallace, owner of the original electronics company, determined to undertake a program of diversification. Initially, he attempted to expand his market through product development and line extensions entirely within the electronics industry. However, because of initial problems, he drew back and sought other opportunities. Wallace's primary concern was his almost total dependence on defense-related contracts. He had felt for some time that he should take some strong action to gain a foothold in the private markets. The first major opportunity that seemed to satisfy his various requirements was the acquisition of a former supplier, a plastics company whose primary market was not defense-related. The company's owner desired to sell his operation and retire. At the time, Wallace's debt structure was such that he could not manage the acquisition and so he had to attract equity capital. He was able to gather a relatively small group of investors and form a closed corporation. The group established a board of directors with Wallace as Chairman and President of the new corporate entity.

With respect to operations, little changed. Wallace continued direct operational control over the Electronics Group. As holder of 60% of the stock, he maintained effective control over policy and operations. However, because of his personal interests, the Plastics Group, now under the direction of a newly hired Vice President, Martin Hempton, was left mainly to its own devices except for yearly progress reviews by the President. All Wallace asked at the time was that the Plastics Group continue its profitable operation, which it did.

Several years ago, Wallace and the board decided to diversify further because two-thirds of their business was still defense-dependent. They learned that one of the major suppliers of the Plastics Group, a chemical company, was on the verge of bankruptcy. The company's owner, Jerome Luskics, agreed to sell. However, this acquisition required a public stock offering, with most of the funds going to pay off debts incurred by the three groups, especially the Chemicals Group. The net result was that Wallace now holds 45% of The Wallace Group and Jerome Luskics 5%, with the remainder distributed among the public.

Organization and Personnel

Presently, Harold Wallace serves as Chairman and President of The Wallace Group. The Electronics Group had been run by LeRoy Tuscher, who just resigned as Vice President. Hempton continued as Vice President of Plastics, and Luskics served as Vice President of the Chemicals Group.

Reflecting the requirements of a corporate perspective and approach, a corporate staff has grown up, consisting of Vice Presidents for Finance, Secretarial/Legal, Marketing, and Industrial Relations. This staff has assumed many functions formerly associated with the group offices.

Because these positions are recent additions, many of the job accountabilities are still being defined. Problems have arisen over the responsibilities and relationships between corporate and group positions. President Wallace has settled most of the disputes himself because of the inability of the various parties to resolve differences amongst themselves.

Current Trends

Presently, there is a mood of lethargy and drift within The Wallace Group. Most managers feel that each of the three groups functions as an independent company. And, with respect to group performance, not much change or progress has been made in recent years. Electronics and Plastics are still stable and profitable, but both lack growth in markets and profits. The infusion of capital breathed new life and hope into the Chemicals operation but did not solve most of the old problems and failings that had caused its initial decline. For all these reasons, Wallace decided that strong action was necessary. His greatest disappointment was with the Electronics Group, in which he had placed high hopes for future development. Thus he acted by requesting and getting the Electronics Group Vice President's resignation. Hired from a computer company to replace LeRoy Tuscher, Jason Matthews joined The Wallace Group a week ago.

As of last week, Wallace's annual net sales were $70 million. By group, they were:

Electronics	$35,000,000
Plastics	$20,000,000
Chemicals	$15,000,000

On a consolidated basis, the financial highlights of the past two years are as follows:

	Last Year	Two Years Ago
Net sales	$70,434,000	$69,950,000
Income (pre-tax)	3,521,000	3,497,500
Income (after-tax)	2,760,500	1,748,750
Working capital	16,200,000	16,088,500
Shareholders' equity	39,000,000	38,647,000
Total assets	59,869,000	59,457,000
Long-term debt	4,350,000	3,500,000
Per Share of Common Stock		
Net income	$.37	$.36
Cash dividends paid	.15	.25

Of the net income, approximately 70% came from Electronics, 25% from Plastics, and 5% from Chemicals.

The Problem Confronting Frances Rampar

As Rampar finished reviewing her notes (see **Exhibits 5–11**), she kept reflecting on what Hal Wallace had told her:

> Don't give me a laundry list of problems, Fran. Anyone can do that. I want a set of priorities I should focus on during the next year. I want a clear action plan from you. And I want to know how much this plan is going to cost me!

Fran Rampar again drummed her fingers on the desk.

EXHIBIT 5
Selected Portions of a Transcribed Interview with H. Wallace

Rampar: What is your greatest problem right now?

Wallace: That's why I called you in! Engineers are a high-strung, temperamental lot. Always complaining. It's hard to take them seriously.

Last month we had an annual stockholders' meeting. We have an Employee Stock Option Plan, and many of our long-term employees attended the meeting. One of my managers—and I won't mention any names—introduced a resolution calling for the resignation of the President—me!

The vote was defeated. But, of course, I own 45% of the stock!

Now I realize that there could be no serious attempt to get rid of me. Those who voted for the resolution were making a dramatic effort to show me how upset they are with the way things are going.

I could fire those employees who voted against me. I was surprised by how many did. Some of my key people were in that group. Perhaps I ought to stop and listen to what they are saying.

Businesswise, I think we're okay. Not great, but okay. Last year we turned in a profit of $3.5 million before taxes, which was a growth over previous years' earnings. We declared a dividend for the fifth consecutive year.

We're currently working on the creation of a tactical display system for aircraft being built by Lombard Aircraft for the Navy and the Air Force. If Lombard gets the contract to produce the prototype, future sales could amount to $56 million over the next five years.

Why are they complaining?

Rampar: You must have thoughts on the matter.

Wallace: I think the issue revolves around how we manage people. It's a personnel problem. You were highly recommended as someone with expertise in high-technology human resource management.

I have some ideas on what is the problem. But I'd like you to do an independent investigation and give me your findings. Give me a plan of action.

Don't give me a laundry list of problems, Fran. Anyone can do that. I want a set of priorities I should focus on during the next year. I want a clear action plan from you. And I want to know how much this plan is going to cost me!

Other than that, I'll leave you alone and let you talk to anyone in the company you want.

EXHIBIT 6
Selected Portions of
a Transcribed
Interview with
Frank Campbell,
Vice President of
Industrial Relations

Rampar: What is your greatest problem right now?

Campbell: Trying to contain my enthusiasm over the fact that Wallace brought you in!
Morale is really poor here. Hal runs this place like a one-man operation, when it's grown too big for that. It took a palace revolt to finally get him to see the depths of the resentment. Whether he'll do anything about it, that's another matter.

Rampar: What would you like to see changed?

Campbell: Other than a new President?

Rampar: Uh-huh.

Campbell: We badly need a management development program for our group. Because of our growth, we have been forced to promote technical people to management positions who have had no prior managerial experience. Mr. Tuscher agreed on the need for a program, but Hal Wallace vetoed the idea because developing such a program would be too expensive. I think it is too expensive *not* to move ahead on this.

Rampar: Anything else?

Campbell: The IEWU negotiations have been extremely tough this time around, due to the excessive demands they have been making. Union pay scales are already pushing up against our foreman salary levels, and foremen are being paid high in their salary ranges. This problem, coupled with union insistence on a no-layoff clause, is causing us fits. How can we keep all our workers when we have production equipment on order that will eliminate 20% of our assembly positions?

Rampar: Wow.

Campbell: We have been sued by a rejected candidate for a position on the basis of discrimination. She claimed our entrance qualifications are excessive because we require shorthand. There is some basis for this statement since most reports are given to secretaries in handwritten form or on audio cassettes. In fact, we have always required it and our executives want their secretaries to have skill in taking dictation. Not only is this case taking time, but I need to reconsider if any of our position entrance requirements, in fact, are excessive. I am sure we do not want another case like this one.

Rampar: That puts The Wallace Group in a vulnerable position, considering the amount of government work you do.

Campbell: We have a tremendous recruiting backlog, especially for engineering positions. Either our pay scales are too low, our job specs are too high, or we are using the wrong recruiting channels. Kane and Smith [Director of Engineering and Director of Advanced Systems] keep rejecting everyone we send down there as being unqualified.

Rampar: Gee.

Campbell: Being head of human resources around here is a tough job. We don't act. We react.

EXHIBIT 7

Selected Portions of a Transcribed Interview with Matthew Smith, Director of Advanced Systems

Rampar: What is your greatest problem right now?

Smith: Corporate brass keeps making demands on me and others that don't relate to the job we are trying to get done. They say that the information they need is to satisfy corporate planning and operations review requirements, but they don't seem to recognize how much time and effort is required to provide this information. Sometimes it seems like they are generating analyses, reports, and requests for data just to keep themselves busy. Someone should be evaluating how critical these corporate staff activities really are. To me and the Electronics Group, these activities are unnecessary.

An example is the Vice President, Marketing (L. Holt), who keeps asking us for supporting data so he can prepare a corporate marketing strategy. As you know, we prepare our own group marketing strategic plans annually, but using data and formats that are oriented to our needs, rather than Corporate's. This planning activity, which occurs at the same time as Corporate's, coupled with heavy workloads on current projects, makes us appear to Holt as though we are being unresponsive.

Somehow we need to integrate our marketing planning efforts between our group and Corporate. This is especially true if our group is to successfully grow in nondefense-oriented markets and products. We do need corporate help, but not arbitrary demands for information that divert us from putting together effective marketing strategies for our group.

I am getting too old to keep fighting these battles.

Rampar: This is a long-standing problem?

Smith: You bet! Our problems are fairly classic in the high-tech field. I've been at other companies and they're not much better. We spend so much time firefighting, we never really get organized. Everything is done on an ad hoc basis.

I'm still waiting for tomorrow.

EXHIBIT 8

Selected Portions of a Transcribed Interview with Ralph Kane, Director of Engineering

Rampar: What is your greatest problem right now?

Kane: Knowing you were coming, I wrote them down. They fall into four areas:

1. Our salary schedules are too low to attract good, experienced EEs. We have been told by our Vice President (Frank Campbell) that corporate policy is to hire new people below the salary grade midpoint. All qualified candidates are making more than that now and in some cases are making more than our grade maximums. I think our Project Engineer job is rated too low.

2. Chemicals Group asked for—and the former Electronics Vice President (Tuscher) agreed to—"lend" six of our best EEs to help solve problems it is having developing a new battery. That is great for the Chemicals Group, but meanwhile how do we solve the engineering problems that have cropped up in our Navy-A and OBT-37 programs?

3. As you know, Matt Smith (Director of Advanced Systems) is retiring in six months. I depend heavily on his group for technical expertise, and in some areas he depends heavily on some of my key engineers. I have lost some people to the Chemicals Group, and Matt has been trying to lend me some of his people to fill in. But he and his staff have been heavily involved in marketing planning and trying to identify or recruit a qualified successor long enough before his retirement to be able to train him or her. The result is that his people are up to their eyeballs in doing their own stuff and cannot continue to help me meet my needs.

4. IR has been preoccupied with union negotiations in the plant and has not had time to help me deal with this issue of management planning. Campbell is working on some kind of system that will help deal with this kind of problem and prevent them in the future. That's great, but I need help now—not when his "system" is ready.

EXHIBIT 9
Selected Portions of a Transcribed Interview with Brad Lowell, Program Manager, Navy-A

Rampar: What is your . . .?

Lowell: . . . great problem? I'll tell you what it is. I still cannot get the support I need from Kane in Engineering. He commits and then doesn't deliver, and it has me quite concerned. The excuse now is that in "his judgment," Sid Wright needs the help for the Air Force program more than I do. Wright's program is one week ahead of schedule, so I disagree with "his judgment." Kane keeps complaining about not having enough people.

Rampar: Why do you think Kane says he doesn't have enough people?

Lowell: Because Hal Wallace is a tight-fisted S.O.B. who won't let us hire the people we need!

EXHIBIT 10
Selected Portions of a Transcribed Interview with Phil Jones, Director of Administration and Planning

Rampar: What is your greatest problem right now?

Jones: Wheel spinning—that's our problem! We talk about expansion, but we don't do anything about it. Are we serious or not?

For example, a bid request came in from a prime contractor seeking help in developing a countermeasure system for a medium-range aircraft. They needed an immediate response and concept proposal in one week. Tuscher just sat on my urgent memo to him asking for a go/no go decision on bidding. I could not give the contractor an answer (because no decision came from Tuscher), so they gave up on us.

I am frustrated because (1) we lost an opportunity we were "naturals" to win, and (2) my personal reputation was damaged because I was unable to answer the bid request. Okay, Tuscher's gone now, but we need to develop some mechanism so an answer to such a request can be made quickly.

Another thing, our MIS is being developed by the Corporate Finance Group. More wheel spinning! They are telling us what information we need rather than asking us what we want! E. Kay (our Group Controller) is going crazy trying to sort out the input requirements they need for the system and understanding the complicated reports that came out. Maybe this new system is great as a technical achievement, but what good is it to us if we can't use it?

EXHIBIT 11
Selected Portions of
a Transcribed
Interview with
Burt Williams,
Director of
Operations

Rampar: What is your biggest problem right now?

Williams: One of the biggest problems we face right now stems from corporate policy regarding transfer pricing. I realize we are "encouraged" to purchase our plastics and chemicals from our sister Wallace groups, but we are also committed to making a profit! Because manufacturing problems in those groups have forced them to raise their prices, should *we* suffer the consequences? We can get some materials cheaper from other suppliers. How can we meet our volume and profit targets when we are saddled with noncompetitive material costs?

Rampar: And if that issue was settled to your satisfaction, then would things be okay?

Williams: Although out of my direct function, it occurs to me that we are not planning effectively our efforts to expand into nondefense areas. With minimal alteration to existing production methods, we can develop both end-use products (e.g., small motors, traffic control devices, and microwave transceivers for highway emergency communications) and components (e.g., LED and LCD displays, police radar tracking devices, and word processing system memory and control devices) with large potential markets.

The problems in this regard are:

1. Matt Smith (Director, Advanced Systems) is retiring and has had only defense-related experience. Therefore, he is not leading any product development efforts along these lines.
2. We have no marketing function at the group level to develop a strategy, define markets, and research and develop product opportunities.
3. Even if we had a marketing plan and products for industrial/commercial application, we would still have no sales force or rep network to sell the stuff.

Maybe I am way off base, but it seems to me we need a Groups/Marketing/Sales function to lead us in this business expansion effort. It should be headed by an experienced technical marketing manager with a proven track record in developing such products and markets.

Rampar: Have you discussed your concerns with others?

Williams: I have brought these ideas up with Mr. Matthews and others at the Group Management Committee. No one else seems interested in pursuing this concept, but they won't say this outright and don't say why it should not be addressed. I guess that in raising the idea with you I am trying to relieve some of my frustrations.

CASE **3**

Everyone Does It

Steven M. Cox and Shawana P. Johnson

JIM WILLIS WAS THE VICE PRESIDENT OF MARKETING AND SALES FOR INTERNATIONAL Satellite Images (ISI). ISI had been building a satellite to image the world at a resolution of one meter. At that resolution, a trained photo interpreter could identify virtually any military and civilian vehicle, as well as numerous other military and non-military objects. The ISI team had been preparing a proposal for a Japanese government contractor. The contract called for a commitment of a minimum imagery purchase of $10 million per year for five years. In a recent executive staff meeting, it became clear that the ISI satellite camera subcontractor was having trouble with the development of a thermal stabilizer for the instrument. It appeared that the development delay would be at least one year and possibly 18 months.

When Jim approached Fred Ballard, the President of ISI, for advice on what launch date to put into the proposal, Fred told Jim to use the published date because that was still the official launch date. When Jim protested that the use of an incorrect date was clearly unethical, Fred said, "Look Jim, no satellite has ever been launched on time. Everyone, including our competitors, publishes very aggressive launch dates. Customers understand the tentative nature of launch schedules. In fact, it is so common that customers factor into their plans the likelihood that spacecraft will not be launched on time. If we provided realistic dates, our launch dates would be so much later than those published by our competitors that we would never be able to sell any advanced contracts. So do not worry about it, just use the published date and we will revise it in a few months." Fred's words were not very comforting to Jim. It was true that satellite launch dates were seldom met, but putting a launch date into a proposal that ISI knew was no longer possible seemed underhanded. He wondered about the ethics of such a practice and the effect on his own reputation.

The Industry

Companies from four nations—the United States, France, Russia, and Israel—controlled the satellite imaging industry. The U.S. companies had a clear advantage in technology and imagery clarity. In the United States, three companies dominated: Lockart, Global Sciences, and ISI. Each of these companies had received a license from the U.S. government to build and launch a satellite able to identify objects as small as one square meter. However, none had yet been able to successfully launch a commercial satellite with such a fine resolution. Currently, all of the companies had announced a launch date within six months of the ISI published launch date. Further, each company had to revise its launch date at least once, and in the case of Global Sciences, twice. Each time a company had revised its launch date, ongoing international contract negotiations with that company had been either stalled or terminated.

Financing a Satellite Program

The construction and ongoing operations of each of the programs was financed by venture capitalists. The venture capitalists relied heavily on advance contract acquisition to ensure the success of their investment. As a result, if any company was unable to acquire sufficient advance contracts, or if one company appeared to be gaining a lead on the others, there was a real possibility that the financiers would pull the plug on the other projects and the losing companies would be forced to stop production and possibly declare bankruptcy. The typical advance contract target was 150% of the cost of building and launching a satellite. Since the cost to build and launch was $200 million, each company was striving to acquire $300 million in advance contracts.

Advance contracts were typically written like franchise licensing agreements. Each franchisee guaranteed to purchase a minimum amount of imagery per year for five years, the engineered life of the satellite. In addition, each franchisee agreed to acquire the capability to receive, process, and archive the images sent to them from the satellite. Typically, the hardware and software cost was between $10 million and $15 million per installation. Because the data from each satellite was different, much of the software could not be used for multiple programs. In exchange, the franchisee was granted an exclusive reception and selling territory. The amount of each contract was dependent on the anticipated size of the market, the number of possible competitors in the market, and the readiness of the local military and civilian agencies to use the imagery. Thus, a contract in Africa would sell for as little as $1 million per year, whereas in several European countries $5–$10 million was not unreasonable. The problem was complicated by the fact that in each market there were usually only one or two companies with the financial strength and market penetration to become a successful franchisee. Therefore, each of the U.S. companies had targeted these companies as their prime prospects.

The Current Problem

Japan was expected to be the third largest market for satellite imagery after the United States and Europe. Imagery sales in Japan were estimated to be from $20 million to $30 million per year. Although the principal user would be the Japanese government, for political reasons the government had made it clear that they would be purchasing data through a local Japanese company. One Japanese company, Higashi Trading Company (HTC), had provided most of the imagery for civilian and military use to the Japanese government.

ISI had been negotiating with HTC for the past six months. It was no secret that HTC had also been meeting with representatives from Lockart and Global Sciences. HTC had sent several engineers to ISI to evaluate the satellite and its construction progress. Jim Willis believed that ISI was currently the front-runner in the quest to sign HTC to a $10 million annual contract. Over five years, that one contract would represent one sixth of the contracts necessary to ensure sufficient venture capital to complete the satellite.

Jim was concerned that if a new launch date was announced, HTC would delay signing a contract. Jim was equally concerned that if HTC learned that Jim and his team knew of the camera design problems and knowingly withheld announcement of a new launch date until after completing negotiations, not only his personal reputation but that of ISI would be damaged. Furthermore, as with any franchise arrangement, mutual trust was critical to the success of each party. Jim was worried that even if only a 12-month delay in launch occurred, trust would be broken between ISI and the Japanese.

Jim's boss, Fred Ballard, had specifically told Jim that launch date information was company proprietary and that Jim was to use the existing published date when talking with clients. Fred feared that if HTC became aware of the delay, they would begin negotiating with one of ISI's competitors, who in Fred's opinion were not likely to meet their launch dates either. This change in negotiation focus by the Japanese would then have ramifications with the venture capitalists whom Fred had assured that a contract with the Japanese would soon be signed.

Jim knew that with the presentation date rapidly approaching, it was time to make a decision.

CASE 4

The Audit

Gamewell D. Gantt, George A. Johnson, and John A. Kilpatrick

SUE WAS PUZZLED AS TO WHAT COURSE OF ACTION TO TAKE. SHE HAD RECENTLY STARTED her job with a national CPA firm, and she was already confronted with a problem that could affect her future with the firm. On an audit, she encountered a client who had been treating payments to a large number, but by no means a majority, of its workers as payments to independent contractors. This practice saves the client the payroll taxes that would otherwise be due on the payments if the workers were classified as employees. In Sue's judgment, this was improper as well as illegal and should have been noted in the audit. She raised the issue with John, the senior accountant to whom she reported. He thought it was a possible problem but did not seem willing to do anything about it. He encouraged her to talk to the partner in charge if she didn't feel satisfied.

She thought about the problem for a considerable time before approaching the partner in charge. The ongoing professional education classes she had received from her employer emphasized the ethical responsibilities that she had as a CPA and the fact that her firm endorsed adherence to high ethical standards. This finally swayed her to pursue the issue with the partner in charge of the audit. The visit was most unsatisfactory. Paul, the partner, virtually confirmed her initial reaction that the practice was wrong, but he said that many other companies in the industry follow such a practice. He went on to say that if an issue was made of it, Sue would lose the account, and he was not about to take such action. She came away from the meeting with the distinct feeling that had she chosen to pursue the issue, she would have created an enemy.

Sue still felt disturbed and decided to discuss the problem with some of her co-workers. She approached Bill and Mike, both of whom had been working for the firm for a couple of years. They were familiar with the problem because they had encountered the same issue when doing the audit the previous year. They expressed considerable concern that if she went over the head of the partner in charge of the audit, they could be in big trouble since they had failed to question the practice during the previous audit. They said that they realized it was probably wrong, but they went ahead because it had been ignored in previous years, and they knew their supervisor wanted them to ignore it again this year. They didn't want to cause problems. They encouraged Sue to be a "team player" and drop the issue.

....

This case was prepared by Professors John A. Kilpatrick, Gamewell D. Gantt, and George A. Johnson of the College of Business, Idaho State University. The names of the organization, individual, location, and/or financial information have been disguised to preserve the organization's desire for anonymity. This case was edited for the *SMBP*–9th, 10th, 11th, 12th, 13th and 14th Editions. Presented to and accepted by the Society for Case Research. All rights reserved to the authors and the SCR. Copyright © 1995 by John A. Kilpatrick, Gamewell D. Gantt, and George A. Johnson. This case may not be reproduced without written permission of the copyright holders. Reprinted by permission.

CASE **5**

Early Warning or False Sense of Security? Concussion Risk and the Case of the Impact-Sensing Football Chinstrap

Clifton D. Petty, Michael R. Shirley
Drury University

> "Anybody who sits down with you and says I have a device that if your child wears it, will either diagnose a concussion or prevent a concussion is lying. Please quote me on that."
> —DAVE HALSTEAD,
> *Technical Director of the Southern Impact Research Center*

It wasn't exactly the sort of quote that would help Battle Sports Science, LLC promote its new impact-sensing football chinstrap. National Public Radio (NPR) interviewed Dave Halstead as part of a story titled *"Can that Mouth Guard Really Prevent a Concussion?"* Armed with a promotional e-mail from Battle Sports Science's founder, Chris Circo, the NPR reporter had asked Halstead's opinion on the new device. And, characteristically, Halstead had offered his blunt assessment. Although Halstead hadn't tested the device himself, he elaborated when asked about the potential for the chinstrap to give an early warning to a coach or player: *"The fear here is that you have an individual who has received not much of an impact . . . but has a significant rotational event (whiplash). They in fact have a significant mild traumatic brain injury. But they have a green light on the chin cup."(NPR 2011).*

Battle Sports Science, LLC

Chris Circo and his partners founded Battle Sports Science in 2009. Headquartered in Omaha, Nebraska, the company was built with a focus on "enhancing safety for athletes" (company website). Specifically, the company wanted to protect young athletes who might have suffered a concussion. An elusive and potentially fatal condition, concussions come with the territory of contact sports. In American football, traditional locker room humor lampooned the antics of the disoriented player, who, following a big hit, wandered toward the wrong huddle. But Circo, who suffered five concussions as a young athlete and today takes anti-seizure medication, considered even the so-called "mild" concussion no laughing matter. Many cases of concussion were tragic, like the case of Nathan Stiles. Stiles, a 17-year-old football player from Spring Hill, Kansas, suffered a concussive blow in a game on October 1, 2010. He collapsed during a game on October 28, and later died. An autopsy revealed a re-bleed of an undetected brain injury (subdural hematoma) (NCCSIR 2012).

Battle Sports Science attempted to gain market attention for its $149.99 Impact Indicator (chin strap) through endorsements, and had enlisted a number of NFL players including Ndamukong Suh, Dexter McCluster, Pierre Thomas, and Eddie Royal. (McKewon 2011). The company hoped to sell the device to sports programs (schools) as well as to individual players. In addition to its Impact Sensing chinstrap, Battle Sports Science made a helmet (Battle Helmet) and mouth-guard (Battle Shield) to protect baseball players at bat (company website).

Chris Circo wondered if he should aggressively challenge Dave Halstead's assessment. Battle Sports Science's design team *had* considered whiplash injuries, and believed that the chinstrap would reliably register "rotational events." He might also challenge Halstead directly. Dave Halstead was a research whiz, but possessed neither M.D. nor college engineering degree credentials. Dave Halstead might not be a completely objective reviewer, given that he was a helmet designer and technical advisor to the NFL.

But within a week of the NPR story, a Congressional panel had expressed skepticism over "anti-concussion" equipment, and Senator Tom Udall (D-N.M.) had asked the Federal Trade Commission (FTC) to investigate the claims of companies in this market—including Battle Sports Science. Now the stakes were growing, and CEO Circo realized that he had reached an important milestone for his young company. Pressing ahead meant defying Dave Halstead and other technical skeptics, and facing scrutiny from Congress and the FTC. From this point on, a product failure was likely to doom his young company.

Football and the Concussion Problem

Football is a contact sport, and has long been associated with serious collision-related injuries. President Theodore Roosevelt called on early football enthusiasts to develop rules that reduced these injuries or face government restrictions. But in recent years, many sports medicine experts have commented on the growing number and severity of concussion injuries. Some also noted that the speed and strength of football players had increased significantly in recent decades. And finally, some aspects of the game—including punt returns and spread offenses—increased the likelihood of high-speed contact, as well as the so-called "defenseless player," or blind spot collision. While both professional (NFL) and college (NCAA) rule-making bodies had recently focused attention on reducing the growing number and severity of traumatic brain injuries, by far the most extensive risk existed at the high school level.

According to the National Federation of State High School Associations, some 1.14 million students annually participated in high school football. Approximately 9%, or at least 140,000 of these young athletes, suffered a concussion each year (Koester 2010). Training programs for high-school football coaches were increasingly focused on concussion recognition. But identification of a player at risk was not an easy matter. According to the Centers for Disease Control (CDC), the symptoms of a concussion were sometimes subtle and athletes often experienced or reported symptoms hours or even days after the concussive event (HHS). Coaches felt pressure to keep talented players on the field, and players often hid their symptoms in order to keep playing. Some high school players took their cues in this regard from professional players:

Both the NFL and NCAA have been sued by players over concussion injuries. A suit was filed against the NCAA on behalf of former Eastern Illinois defensive back Adrian Arrington, 25, who had several concussions between 2006 and 2009. Arrington's suit alleged that the NCAA didn't "set up sufficient guidelines for players with concussions" (Hailey). In addition, 75 former NFL players filed suit in 2010 and alleged that the NFL hid the dangers of concussions from players intentionally (Fendrich 2010).

Product Responsibility and the Impact Indicator

Some recent trends, including the litigation against football leagues and universities, suggest a role for Battle Sports Science's Impact Indicator in both reducing concussive injuries and litigation risk for football organizations and schools. The National Federation of High School (NFHS) has alerted its members that concussion-related litigation is gathering momentum, and is increasingly targeting coaches and school officials at the high school level (Koester). The Impact Indicator identified potential injuries, and helped coaches and players avoid a subsequent collision to an already injured brain. A light on the chin strap shines green until a player is struck in such a way that a head injury is either possible (yellow light) or likely (red light). A coach who spotted the yellow or red light might then sideline the injured player. From this perspective, it might be argued that aggressive promotion of the Impact Indicator should improve safety among players.

Then again, what if Halstead's skepticism was well placed? How will the product have performed in the thousands of complex and high-speed encounters that occur on football fields across the United States? More testing and slower rollout might lower some risk, but it would also provide rivals time to copy the chin strap and beat Battle Science to the market. One thing was certain—the company couldn't stand still now. All the recent publicity—even from critics like Halstead—had pushed the company onto the field with respect to the concussion controversy in football. If Circo had any doubts about his product, it was time to face them before it was too late. Otherwise, it was time to set his strategy for moving forward while managing intense risks and likely controversy.

REFERENCES AND SUGGESTED READINGS

Battle Sports Science, LLC, company website.
Fendrich, Howard (October 20, 2010). NFL concussion saga moves to new phase: Litigation. *Associated Press*.
Hailey, Jim (September 16, 2010). NCAA named in class-action concussion lawsuit. *USA Today*.
Koester, Michael, M.D., (July 2010). NFHS Concussion Rule—What State Associations need to know. *Workshop presentation to the NFHS Sports Medicine Advisory Committee*.
McKewon, Sam (October 14, 2011). Ex-Husker Suh backing safety device. *Omaha World-Herald*.
NPR Interview Transcript (October 5, 2011). Can that mouth guard really prevent a concussion?
(NCCSIR) National Center for Catastrophic Sport Injury Research website.
(HHS) U.S. Department of Health and Human Services, Centers for Disease Control and Prevention (June, 2010). Heads up: Concussion in high school sports.

CASE **6**

A123 Systems: A New Lithium-Ion Battery System for Electric and Hybrid Cars

Alan N. Hoffman
Bentley University

Company Background

A123 systems was founded in 2001 by Dr. Yet-Ming Chiang, Dr. Bart Riley, and Ric Fulop using proprietary nanophosphate technology built on new nanoscale materials initially developed at the Massachusetts Institute of Technology.[1] In 2005, A123 transformed its business by developing a new, high-powered, faster-charging lithium-ion battery system using the nanophosphate technology. Lithium-ion batteries are an advanced technology that have one of the best energy-to-weight ratios on the market and have a slow loss of charge when not in use. In 2005, A123's main business was the commercial market for its batteries. Black and Decker Corporation used these lithium-ion batteries in its Dewalt and VPX brand of power tools. Lithium-ion batteries provided users with increased levels of power and runtime, at a similar or less weight than the traditional corded power tools.[2]

In 2006, A123 Systems was granted a $15 million development contract from the United States Advanced Battery Consortium (USABC) in collaboration with the U.S. Department of Energy (DOE). This contract was for the development of its nanophosphate technology for hybrid electric vehicles. A123 Systems then partnered with General Electric and Ballard Power Services to develop high-voltage battery modules for use in emission-free, energy-efficient transit buses. These new batteries are smaller than existing battery packs currently

The author would like to thank Greg Keller, Ben Davis, Jason Brooks, Felix Lim, and Will Hoffman for their research and contributions to this case. Reprinted by permission of Dr. Alan N. Hoffman, Dept. of Management, Bentley University, 175 Forest Street, Waltham, MA 02452, USA.

available for heavy-duty commercial use.[3] One of the companies that used this new battery was Daimler Buses North America in its Orion VII diesel-electric hybrid bus. The Orion VII was deemed a great success and passed the 3000 units sold mark in 2009, which was considered a great success for A123 and hybrid electric vehicles in general.[4]

A combination of external forces such as increasing oil prices and a desire for consumers to be greener has increased the demand for hybrid vehicles in the consumer market. In 2007, A123 took significant steps toward developing its hybrid electric vehicle business. A123 entered into a partnership with Cobasys to introduce lithium-ion batteries into the automotive market.[5] A123 also entered into an agreement with GM to use their batteries in the Saturn Vue Plug-in Hybrid development program[6] and to co-develop a lithium-ion battery for the Chevrolet Volt.[7] In 2008, A123 Systems entered a partnership with General Electric and Norwegian car manufacture Think Global to develop and supply lithium-ion batteries for Think's new electric crossover SUV.[8] A123's automotive portfolio includes relationships with major global automotive companies such as BMW, Chrysler, Renault/Better Place, and Delphi/Shanghai Automotive Industry Corporation for passenger vehicle models; and Daimler, Magna Steyr, and BAE Systems for heavy-duty transportation vehicles.[9] These joint ventures, partnerships, and strategic alliances have strengthened A123's position in the transportation market.

A123 Systems is also in the electric grid market. A123 developed a lithium-ion battery system named the Smart Grid Stabilization System (SGSS), which helps power plants manage fluctuations in demand that are less expensive and more responsive than traditional methods. The SGSS can respond to changing power needs in milliseconds to ensure power plants are running efficiently and emitting less pollution while optimizing their power output.

A123 Systems currently designs, develops, manufactures, and sells rechargeable lithium-ion batteries and battery systems for the transportation, electric grid, and commercial markets. While they're still involved in all three businesses, A123 Systems has evolved over the past four years. Comparing the total product revenue from 2007, 2008, and 2009, the consumer market has dropped from 93%, to 76%, to 26%, while the transportation market has risen from 7%, to 19%, to 59%, and the electric grid market has grown from 0%, to 5%, to 15%. A123 is shifting away from the consumer market because it has now matured and is focusing on the transportation and electric grid market that has a much larger growth potential. This trend continued through 2010.

On September 24, 2009, A123 Systems announced its IPO on the NASDAQ global market at a price of $13.50 per share. Its shares reached a high of $23.46, but it is now just under $5.00. A123 also received a $249 million grant from the DOE and a $100 million tax credit from the state of Michigan to help build a manufacturing plant in Livonia. This plant was to open on September 13, 2010 and would allow A123 to meet the growing demands of its battery and battery systems.[10]

Strategic Direction

The company's focus on innovation and attracting highly educated employees has allowed it to remain on the forefront of this developing industry. A123's joint ventures, partnerships, and strategic alliances have strengthened their position in the transportation and electric grid market.

The vision of A123 Systems is to combine its portfolio of products that use nanophosphate technology with strategic partner relationships in order to address the next-generation energy storage solutions in the transportation, electric grid services, and consumer markets.[11] Their goal is to use nanotechnology to create the next generation of batteries.[12] The world is focusing on ways to eliminate its dependency on fossil fuels and A123 believes they will help this goal become a reality.

The A123 Systems objective is to utilize their materials science expertise, battery and battery systems engineering expertise, and manufacturing process technologies to provide advanced battery solutions.

A123's Competitors

A123 Systems has a different set of competitors in each of its three product groups. In the transportation industry, its competitors are Panasonic, LiMotive (Bosch and Samsung), Automotive Energy Supply Corporation, Johnson Controls-Saft Advanced Power Solutions, Toshiba, Kokam (Dow Chemical), Hitachi, Ltd., LG, GS Yuasa, Sony, Lithium Energy Japan, EnerDel Inc., Valence and MES-DEA S.A. In the electric grid industry, its competitors are Saft, Altairnano, NGK Insulators Ltd, Prudent Energy, Beacon Power Corp. In the consumer market, its competitors are Panasonic, Sony, Samsung, LG, Valence, and E-One Moli Energy Corp.[13] A123 Systems faces stiff competition for all of its product lines. If some of the larger competitors were to merge through an acquisition or takeover, this could change the competitive landscape and make it very difficult for A123 to compete.

Barriers to entry in the lithium-ion battery business are high. The largest barrier is the proprietary knowledge needed to develop and manufacture this type of technology. Every company in this industry has protected their intellectual property and manufacturing processes with patents, trademarks, and keeping their knowledge as trade secrets.[14] Other barriers to entry are brand recognition and visibility, economies of scale in manufacturing, and the access to strategic partners and distribution networks.[15] While barriers to entry are high right now, it is possible for new technology to come along and turn the entire industry on its head.

A123 Systems is very dependent on transportation manufacturers and electric grid providers. There are multiple lithium-ion battery solutions for their products and if A123 does not meet their demands, they could switch to another provider. There are also a limited number of customers who make up a significant portion of A123's revenue, and the loss of one of those customers could be crippling to their business.[16]

Government Programs

Although lithium-ion batteries have been around in the consumer goods markets since the early 1990s, the industry as it relates to the transportation market, of which A123 is resting much of its future hopes upon, is in many ways still in its embryonic stage, and the products are still heavy and cumbersome. For example, the lithium-ion battery pack used in the Chevy Volt is six-feet, nine-inches long and weighs nearly 400 pounds according to Larry Burns, a former vice-president of research and development at GM.[17]

Perhaps the most influential of the external factors that currently and will continue to affect A123 Systems and its industry peers will be the support that these companies receive from government programs in the form of grants, loans, and incentives. In A123's case, because they have yet to be a profitable company, whose cost of goods sold have historically exceeded the selling price of their products since 2007, the company is, without exaggeration, nearly fully reliant on government funding to operate their business. A123 hope to participate in US Government Programs that stimulate investment in the domestic battery field. This intention is one of their core strategies necessary for success. Clearly, the company is not shy when it comes to signaling their heavy dependence on political opportunities. There are quite a few federal and state government programs of which A123 has elected to be a part of:

American Recovery and Reinvestment Act (ARRA): *When President Obama took office in early 2009, one of the first pieces of legislation that was pushed through with the help of a Democratic*

Congress was the ARRA, meant as a stimulus to a U.S. economy deep in the throes of a painful recession and possibly on the brink of an even more agonizing depression. One of the programs in the nearly $800 billion stimulus package was $2 billion in grants from the Department of Energy to help promote the development of advanced batteries and electric drive components. A123 Systems was able to negotiate an agreement with the DOE in the amount of a $249.1 million grant to fund the construction of new battery plants to be based in Michigan. The terms of the agreement state that the company must spend one dollar for every four dollars it receives, and as of the end of the 2009 fiscal year, A123 had received $6.1 million from the DOE Battery Initiative.

Advanced Technology Vehicles Manufacturing Loan Program (ATVM): *Similar to the ARRA stimulus package, the DOE also has the ATVM Program, which has allowed A123 to borrow four dollars for every one dollar spent. However, unlike the Battery Initiative, funds from this program are in the form of loans that must be paid back as opposed to grants. Under the ATVM Program, A123 will be able to borrow up to $233 million to also help fund their manufacturing expansion.*

State of Michigan Grants and Incentives: *In March 2009, the company received a $10 million grant from the state of Michigan, of which $2.2 million had already been spent as of December 2009 to help with the construction of a new manufacturing facility in Livonia, Michigan. In exchange for the remainder of the grant funds, the company is expected to meet pre-negotiated milestones set forth by the state. Unrelated to the $10 million grant, the state also provided A123 with a $2 million grant in December 2009 as part of a smart grid stabilization program meant to help leverage renewable sources of power in order to power the new plant in Livonia. The city of Livonia has also chipped in by exempting the company from any personal property taxes incurred within the city's limits through December 2023. In exchange, the company must invest at least $24 million in personal property and create 350 new jobs within the district. Lastly, A123 is looking for even more potential tax benefits from the state by having their facility located in one of the designated "Renaissance Zones."*

Michigan Economic Growth Authority (MEGA): There are a number of tax credits and loans being offered under this program in which A123 is taking part. Under the High-Tech Credit, A123 is eligible for a 15-year tax credit worth up to $25.3 million that is dependent upon the number of jobs the company can create in the state of Michigan. Under the Cell Manufacturing Credit, the company is eligible for a 50% credit on their capital expenditures up to $100 million. Finally, the state of Michigan has offered the company $4 million in loans, which is completely forgivable if they create 350 full time jobs by August 2012.

In addition to the grants, loans, and other incentives being offered by the federal, state, and local governments, there are other factors in the political and legal landscape that offer other opportunities to A123 and the industry. First and foremost, as environmental awareness increases and governments in the western world continue to urge their countries' populations to reduce dependence on foreign oil, it is only natural that regulations should follow suit. In 2010, President Obama recently announced new federal standards for all U.S. passenger cars and light trucks to average 35.5 miles per gallon by 2016. Many industry experts predict that by 2020, nearly 50% of all US vehicles will use some form of battery technology to meet the new Corporate Average Fuel Economy (CAFE) regulatory standards. Additionally, rebate programs between $2500 and $7500 were offered directly to consumers under the February 2009 stimulus package that were meant to entice them to purchase plug-in electric vehicles. Obviously, such increases in regulatory standards and direct-to-consumer rebate programs represent a distinct opportunity for A123 Systems and its industry peers.

In addition to the many opportunities that exist, with such a significant stake of the company's future tied to programs initiated by the government, it could be concluded that, the legal and political climate also offers threats to the company and the industry. While there seems to be no shortage of incentives being offered in today's political climate, it remains to be seen how the new Congress, coming to power in January 2011 and with a critical eye on the country's surging deficit, will either continue to support funding for these programs or let them dry up. This could indeed significantly affect the long-term viability of A123 Systems. In fact, after a pointed question was asked about the company's capital expenditure outlook on the latest earnings call in November 2010, David Vieau, the CEO, and Michael Rubino, the outgoing CFO, provided generally vague answers regarding how they intend to fund the company's operations beyond 2012 if all of their current funds become exhausted. Furthermore, they were also unable to provide any revenue visibility into 2011 and beyond, simply stating that "a lot will depend on the scale up of [their] customers" to ramp up production of electric vehicles. If the company is unable to augment the funds received from the government with actual profits from battery sales, then the uncertainty of the political climate could pose a major threat to the company.[18]

In such a highly technical industry that requires a high level of expertise in research and development, the last significant major threat to the livelihood of A123 lies in the protection of its intellectual property, specifically in the proprietary nanophosphate technology that it uses to produce and package its lithium-ion batteries. A large part of the company's success will depend on its ability to protect its patents and trademarks while at the same time not infringing upon other companies'. The company currently owns or licenses 19 patents in the United States and at the time of this writing was in the process of applying for 77 more. In foreign markets, they own or license 29 patents and have applied for 151 that are currently pending.[19] The outcome of the patents currently in the application process could either help to provide A123 with a sustainable competitive advantage in the future if granted, or quickly eliminate any such potential advantage if declined. Furthermore, any lawsuits filed either on behalf of or against the company with regard to patent technology could affect their ability to do business. They are currently involved in two lawsuits with Hydro-Quebec regarding licensed patents it has received from University of Texas. Both Hydro-Quebec and UT allege that some of the electrode technology that A123 uses in its batteries infringe on their patents. In response, A123 has countersued and the lawsuit is ongoing. As of the November 2010 earnings call, the senior managers at A123 have stated that settlement discussions related to the case continued throughout the third quarter, but that no resolution is in sight and that more court activity should pick up in December 2010.

Social and Demographic Trends

Contrary to what some skeptics continue to steadfastly believe, there is significant evidence that worldwide climate change resulting from the effects of greenhouse gases is a real issue that needs real solutions. One of those solutions calls for the reduction in the use of fossil fuels such as coal and oil, and A123 Systems, with its lithium-ion advanced battery systems, was created to help solve that problem. The opportunity is there for A123 to capitalize upon the increasing awareness of environmental issues, as consumers begin to shift away from automobiles with conventional gasoline engines. The company believes that as the technological expertise to create advanced batteries matures, it will continue to drive down manufacturing costs, which can then be passed on to the customer in the form of an economically viable alternative to gasoline-powered vehicles. Once consumers begin to realize the economic benefits of lithium-ion batteries to go along with the environmental benefits, it will create a vast opportunity for A123 and its industry as the adoption of hybrids and plug-in electric vehicles increases dramatically. To take it one step further, the company further believes that the increased adoption of hybrids and plug-in electric vehicles will only help create a positive feedback loop in the form of network effects that benefits the creation of next-generation battery technologies. As mentioned earlier in the political/legal section, the government is also doing its part with stricter regulatory standards, such as CAFE, and by encouraging consumers to purchase hybrid and electric cars through the use of tax credits.

Another opportunity for A123 Systems that results from the environmental movement to reduce dependence on fossil fuels lies in the electric grid services market, which generated

$6 million in revenue for the company in its latest fiscal quarter. As the demand for renewable sources of energy such as wind and solar power increases, the company believes that its advanced battery systems can fill a need in order to smooth out the performance and reliability of these power sources using smart grid technology. Due to the intermittency of solar and wind power sources, battery technology can help store backup power to help supplement the grid during times when the plants are generating excess energy or customer demand is low. Likewise, the batteries can then tap into those reserve sources of power when the plants are not generating any energy or during times of peak electricity usage. As of their latest earnings call in November 2010, the company's senior leaders have set a target for electric grid services to comprise roughly 30% of their entire business in the future, although they did not target a specific date.

A lesser known opportunity for A123 Systems is for it to capitalize on the trend toward increased environmental awareness. Currently, many of the substitute products for lithium-ion batteries include traditional battery technologies that involve toxic metals such as nickel and lead. As a result, many nickel- and lead-based batteries cannot be disposed of through regular means and almost certainly cannot be recycled due to their hazardous nature to other humans and the environment. On the other hand, A123 touts its lithium-ion batteries using nanophosphate technologies as a much cleaner alternative to traditional batteries because they do not use toxic metals such as nickel, lead, or manganese. Additionally, their batteries can either be retrofitted for other uses or their parts can be scrapped and recycled into other materials at the end of their useful lives.

Although many of the social/demographic trends occurring in the macroenvironment represent opportunities for A123, the company highlights one potential threat that could adversely affect its business were it to occur. Even though the trend in gas prices has been heading upward since earlier this decade, there is a minor risk that gasoline prices could decline for an extended period of time. If gasoline prices were to decrease and remain low, it could have an impact on the demand for hybrids and plug-in electric cars, therefore decreasing the demand for the company's batteries. While it deserves mentioning, the likelihood of this risk actually occurring seems low, especially when the growing demand for oil and gas in developing nations such as China and India are taken into consideration.

A123's Technology

A123 currently has three versions of a lithium-ion battery using nanophosphate technology in high-volume production for use in the consumer, transportation, and electric grid services markets; however, it is already working on prototypes of the next-generation of its popular AHR32113 battery, as well as an entirely new line of prismatic, or flat-shaped, batteries meant for use in multiple configurations of different electric vehicles on multiple assembly lines. By devoting resources to the development of low-volume manufacturing of its next-generation products while simultaneously mass-manufacturing its existing products, the company can be sure to stay on the forefront of the innovation curve and ensure that it will be able to capitalize quickly on any future innovations in next-generation nanophosphate technologies. In fact, the company's devotion to innovation is central to its core strategic philosophy.

A123's greatest threat is the potential that better technologies come along that are cheaper and more efficient than lithium-ion batteries based on nanophosphate technologies. Understandably, the company is so new, in an industry that has only just recently begun emerging, that it is most likely unable to devote any more time and energy beyond its own products. However, the company realizes that at any point, better technologies could come along that render batteries, and hence A123's entire product line, obsolete. While these technologies are also in their embryonic stages of development, the company should still keep a watchful eye over any breakthroughs in those areas. These technologies include energy sources such as ultra capacitors, which also store energy and deliver high power albeit at an insufficient energy density, and fuel cells, which generate energy through the consumption of a fuel, such as hydrogen.

Global Opportunities and Threats

The most obvious and glaring example of global opportunities to which A123 is exposed is the explosive growth in the use of automobiles in emerging markets such as China and India. The company has positioned itself well globally by allying closely with international auto manufacturers such as BMW, Renault, and its most recent joint venture, SAIC Motor Company, based in China. Going forward, the joint venture agreement with SAIC will be one of the most important, if not *the* most important, sources of demand and penetration into Chinese markets for A123. As part of the 20-year agreement, the company has agreed to invest $4.7 million in return for a 49% stake in the capital in the joint venture, in which management control will be shared equally. A123 will be responsible for supplying the partnership with enough batteries to meet any production plans while granting technology licenses, under applicable terms and conditions, in exchange for fees and royalties. Finally, SAIC and A123 confirmed their commitment to one another by agreeing not to form any other joint ventures or any other new businesses in China that would compete with their joint venture. The formation of this partnership is just one of the examples of the numerous global opportunities that A123 Systems can leverage for their benefit, which is a concept that the senior leaders at the company clearly recognize. In their most recent quarter earnings call in November 2010, David Vieau, the company's CEO, made it clear that their partnership and their overall presence in China will be key going forward and that they are already in the process of delivering the first prototypes to a second Chinese original equipment manufacturer, with the hope that it will result in a future agreement. Another company senior official, Jason Forcier, anticipates that Chinese annual production of electric vehicles could reach one million by 2020. Because nearly all of their manufacturing facilities are located in China with the exception of the yet-to-be completed Michigan plants, the company has an advantage in that they are located closely to their potential Chinese customers. Therefore, not only are their manufacturing costs kept low, but the transportation costs for their Asian subsidiary, A123 Systems Hong Kong Limited, could also be kept low. Lastly, the government of China is also opening up opportunities for companies such as A123, because they have begun to offer incentives directly to consumers who purchase electric vehicles, much like the United States government has already done.

Although penetration into emerging markets such as China could be especially lucrative for A123 in the future, the decision to become a multinational corporation does not come without potential pitfalls. The company has even clearly demonstrated this point, as they have an entire section in their 10-K report for the fiscal year ended 2009 that is dedicated to the risks associated with doing business in China and Korea. Because A123 is in a highly technical industry that is still arguably in its embryonic stage, one of the most important elements critical to the success or failure of the company is the protection of its intellectual property. If the company cannot protect its intellectual property in foreign markets due to a lack of protectionist laws or otherwise, then it can open the door for competitors to enter their market segment with virtually similar advanced battery systems. In China especially, the legal system is known to be comparatively weak against those in other countries, and by sharing its proprietary licenses with SAIC and potentially other Chinese companies, A123 opens itself up to that kind of threat were the partnership to deteriorate and their intellectual property exposed. In fact, counterfeiting and piracy come at a steep price, costing American businesses (as of 2007) upward of $200 billion each year.[20] The company would thus be in a poor position to defend and enforce its intellectual property rights in the country. In addition, the poor legal system, in general, goes beyond the scope of just intellectual property. Were the company ever to enter into any litigation in China, it realizes that it may be difficult to obtain a quick resolution, judgment, or award issued by a court of law in the country.

Nearly all of its manufacturing capabilities are based in China and anything that adversely affects China could also significantly affect A123's business negatively in a number of ways. The first threat lies with the macroeconomic and political climate of China. Although the consensus is that the economy of China is expected to continue to grow at its rapid pace, and the government has become increasingly capitalistic over the past 20 years, there is no guarantee that these trends will continue in the short- and long-term future. For example, if the economy were to go into a sudden slump, it may affect the consumer demand for electric vehicles and thus affect the demand for the company's lithium-ion batteries. A123's exposure is not only to general market risk but also to firm-specific risk as well. Because much of the company's strategic philosophy is to leverage the benefits of joint ventures in foreign countries, they also expose themselves to their partners' risks. Therefore, some of the company's future livelihood is tied to the fortunes of other companies with whom they are aligned. For example, if the Chinese auto manufacturer, SAIC, were to make poor business decisions in its primary business that hurt the company, it would also hurt its joint venture with A123, and as a result, afflicting some residual damage on A123's primary business.

The government of China also plays a major role in all businesses that operate within its borders, and A123 is no exception. As mentioned earlier, the government has become increasingly capitalistic in recent years, yet they still exert a tremendous amount of influence over the Chinese economy through regulations and state ownership. There is no guarantee that the government of China will continue to support the expansion of foreign companies within its borders, and if they were to view A123 or other foreign businesses in the industry as a threat to their domestic companies, they may simply impose new regulations or increase trade barriers through export tariffs in order to make A123 less competitive in China. Actions such as these by the government would obviously create a negative competitive advantage that the company would need to overcome. Additionally, as a U.S. company, the economic and political relationship between the United States and China are major factors that must be monitored by A123. Currently, China does not float its currency against those of other countries, instead electing to manipulate its currency to keep it artificially low relative to countries such as the United States. Because A123 enjoys normal trade relations status with regard to their significant amount of Chinese operations, they can enjoy the benefits of exporting their Chinese-manufactured products without needing to pay import duties into the United States. This is in addition to the increased purchasing power they enjoy from raw materials and goods purchased in China. However, pressure has been put on China recently by the G20 countries to float its currency, because many view it as a source of China's growing trade surpluses that provide it with an unfair competitive advantage. One day, that pressure could reach the point where the United States introduces retaliatory legislation, such as the introduction of import tariffs, which could affect A123's business negatively.

A123's Finances

A123 has seen increasing absolute revenues from $41.3 million in 2007 to $91 million through December 2010. However, if we look at quarterly sales data since December 2007, we see sales have been relatively flat, with some quarters showing slight gains and others showing slight losses. This discrepancy between annual and quarterly data is due to income reported for only the December 2007 quarter of that year and no reported income in the March 2008 quarter of that year. Looking at Appendix A and B, the annual and quarterly trends of revenues become apparent.

A123 has yet to record a profitable quarter, which is in large part due to the cost of goods sold, sales and marketing, R&D, and capital expenditures. These areas of the company have seen very high levels over the past few years due to management's investment in company infrastructure. Once management is able to complete its desired level of production facilities and personnel, revenues should then be able to start covering their fixed and variable costs, thus moving the company toward positive earnings.

Operating Income has been similar to net income in not producing a positive number thus far. High SG&A expenses are the key reason why this number has continued to increase at a negative rate. Personnel and research and development have been a significant cost to the firm's objectives toward growth. Looking at Appendix A we can see that Operating Income over the past few years has been similar to net income negative growth and has dropped sharply so far through 2010. Flat quarter-to-quarter revenues have not provided the company with enough capital to fund its current operations. This leads us directly into the next financial section on cash and long-term debt, where A123 must look for capital to continue its current operating level.

Since its inception, A123's cash position has been strong relative to its total asset position. Looking at Appendix C, we see their cash position has increased from about $100 million in June 2009 to just about $500 million through September 2009. Much of this large increase can be attributed to the $400 million it raised through its IPO in September 2009. The company was also awarded a $249 million grant from the American Recovery Reinvestment Act and has invoiced about $53 million of this money so far.[21] After September 2009, Appendix C shows us an alarming trend for the company's cash reserves.

It's apparent that A123 has been very reliant on receiving large amounts of capital from investors whether they are venture capitalists, IPOs, or parts of the government. Just as with many technology firms, A123's upfront capital requirements are significant. Management intends on owning the entire production process; a process that includes building or leasing millions of square feet of manufacturing space and large amounts of capital. A123's reported cash position for the quarter ended on September 30, 2010, and was $301 million. Even with government grants and tax incentives, cash reserves have been a significant funding source for the company. Given the company is still young, it's difficult to tell what cash level might be sufficient for them, but management does need to monitor their investments and operating expense needs because the cash reserves may eventually dry up as a source of capital. Management does appear to be concerned with the company's cash level come 2012. The upside of utilizing their cash position for investing and asset growth needs is that the company has been able to keep their debt levels down. They currently have just over $6 million in long-term debt, which is in line with their short-term borrowing history. The highest long-term debt they have carried was $10.5 million in June 2009. If management continues to increase production facilities beyond 2012, issuing debt or taking out loans may become a source of funding for A123.

Inventories and accounts receivable have been increasing since its inception, but Appendix D shows it at a comparable rate to sales. However, the most recent quarter, ending September 2010, shows a spike in both accounts from the quarter ending March 2010, which is concerning. Management should continue to monitor inventories and accounts receivable in order to keep them in line or lower than sales growth.

Areas of Concern for A123

The trend over the last two quarters could prove to be a near-term problem if revenues do not begin to pick up. A123 is currently susceptible to rising inventories due to their business model, that looks to develop agreements, relationships, and partnerships that require large product quantities and long product life cycles. Should a customer's production schedule or input requirements change, an increase in A123's inventories and accounts receivables could materialize.[22]

Management is working to build production capacity that will hopefully allow them to meet customers' orders in a flexible and timely manner. If A123's production infrastructure is built to the level they are seeking, this could certainly prove to be a competitive advantage over other lithium-ion battery producers who do not have similar manufacturing capabilities.

Marketing

A123 employs an experienced sales team with most individuals having engineering sales experience and sector-specific experience. The company sells its products primarily through direct sales from their tiny sales staff of 24. Their staff is comprised of individuals with a strong working knowledge of their products. Most have an engineering background within the energy storage field so they can speak to their potential clients and their needs on their level. The staff is divided between transportation and cell design and development, and the two groups work closely together. The company often uses its strong relations with distributers to close deals.

Over the past decade plus, the United States has felt a strong sentiment in reducing not only its need for foreign oil, but for fossil fuels in general. In the same time frame, the United States has seen a big push toward the development and large-scale adoption of clean energy. The goals of A123's management and potential "green" benefits of their battery products have allowed them to develop a strong government relationship. On the groundbreaking day for the Livonia, Michigan, manufacturing plant, President Obama phoned in to congratulate both the Governor of Michigan as well as A123. As we know, the company was awarded a $249-million-dollar grant toward this plant and further development of its product base.

This strong relationship has also led to the forming of The Government Solutions Group within A123, which is dedicated to developing specific lithium-ion–based products and solutions for various areas of the Government, such as the Department of Defense. This strong relationship gives A123 a significant source of funding and could prove to be vital to their long-term success.

As part of managements overall strategy, the company looks to sell its products to markets and customers that create a competitive advantage.[23] A123's products are essential to the success of these markets and customers and therefore premium prices can be generated. If A123 can prove to be an industry leader within these markets and continue to provide customers with quality products, revenues should grow accordingly.

Another major way A123 markets their products is through partnerships with established energy storage companies abroad. An example is a partnership between A123 and IHI, a Japanese company within the energy sector that can shop A123's products around a new market. This way, A123 can benefit from the position IHI already has within Japan to market more effectively. They believe that this type of international partnership will lead to cost economies of scale. In conjunction with growing the sales force, management keeps the company very active through numerous trade shows and industry conferences. Not only do these shows and conferences help advance lithium-ion battery technology, but they also help solidify A123 as a leader within this industry. These trade shows and conferences typically include attendees such as business partners, strategic investors, industry analysts, and most importantly, customers.

Products include five batteries and battery systems that are applicable to the current markets they target. These markets include transportation, portable power, grid stabilization, and government. They have had successful relationships with DeWalt and Black & Decker in the portable power industry, but have become less reliant on this industry because they believe it is mature and will not produce a high level of revenue. Materials agreements and licenses have allowed the company to develop portable power units tied to specific products such as with DeWalt's 18V Nano line of power tools.[24] A great deal of their marketing is being transitioned toward the adoption of electric vehicles as they expect growth to pick up.

Sales cycles, which include development, qualification, and commercial production phases, can be long for some products, such as batteries for the automotive industry. At the end of 2009, management estimated that technology review took 3 to 9 months, development 12 to 18 months, and total time from initial customer introduction to commercial production could be three to five years for batteries specific to the auto industry.[25] Even though A123 may have a technologically superior product, these lengthy sale-cycles could be very costly to A123 if competitors are able to provide sufficient products at a much quicker pace. We see a similar story with Intel and the chips it produces. While the quality of their chips compared to its competitors is up for debate, they are able to provide significant quantities to customers in a rapid fashion. This has proven to be a big competitive advantage for Intel and will hopefully be the same for A123.

Another challenge they face is that the market for battery solutions in transportation is a new and developing market. This makes it difficult to predict the timing of market demand. They might strike a deal, but if their customer delays their order due to delays in their production, they are left with excess inventory (which is the case they are facing in 2010).[26]

A123 currently employs a small sales team consisting of 20 sales individuals and 4 marketing individuals. Although this current sales team may be sufficient, it will become difficult to manage an increasing customer base with the growth expected by the company and could be a potential issue in the near future.

Research and Development

The nanophosphate technology specifically licensed to them by MIT, is by far the company's biggest strength in R&D. This technology allows A123's management and engineering team to bring an advanced portable battery source to market in a variety of products. It also helps attract top engineering talent to the company's R&D team by giving them the opportunity to work with such an advanced technology. The license also allows A123 to increase the number of applications available for its products and so the company is looking to increase customer specification for these applications.

Dr. Yet-Ming Chiang, a co-founder of A123 Systems and member of the management team, is a full professor at MIT where he helped design the nanophosphate technology used in the company's batteries. Having a close relationship with MIT has given A123 the opportunity to receive a license to use this technology.

As we know from our analysis of the company's financials, R&D costs have been rising over the past few years. Even though R&D and nanophosphate technology are fundamental to A123's business, management needs to keep costs associated with growing this part of the business in line with long-term profitability. If these costs do not begin to decrease as a percent of revenues, then management will need to reevaluate the capital expenditures associated with R&D.

Intellectual property, proprietary technology, and licenses are likely to become obsolete. Although A123 is the only company licensed to use the nanophosphate technology developed at MIT, industry competitors may develop better technologies, offer lower prices, or be faster to market with batteries or power sources that meet current market needs. Although nanophosphate technology appears to be superior to other lithium-ion technologies, it's useless if A123 cannot provide its customers with products that meet specific needs in a timely manner.

Operations

Vertical integration and scalable prismatic battery system architecture allow A123 to adapt to both partner and customer needs throughout the entire battery production process. Vertical integration and scalable battery systems give A123 the ability to respond to markets and customers needs in a faster and more flexible manner.

Through vertical integration management is able to have control of a large percentage of the battery production process, which is a major strategic objective. This internal production control allows A123 to monitor and improve the quality of products as well as protect both materials science and intellectual property. Besides raw materials, A123 does not have to rely on outside suppliers or partners for inputs that can cause both reduced quality and delays, neither of which A123 wants in their business model. This business strategy does require a significant amount of fixed assets, which drives up capital needs as we have seen.

Logistically, having a large company-owned manufacturing facility in Michigan could prove to be very beneficial for not only them, but for the U.S. automotive industry. Assuming A123 systems battery technology is capable of powering electric vehicles (EV) and hybrid electric vehicles (HEV), logistics could become a competitive advantage for A123. If contractual agreements between A123 and U.S automakers pan out, the company could see increased utilization of their Livonia plant.

A123 Systems has a strategy of controlling as much of the production process as feasible. In doing so, they must have adequate operations in areas such as research, design, development, manufacturing, and sales in order to successfully get their products from raw materials to finished batteries.

The largest portion of their operations is the manufacturing associated with producing batteries. As of December 31, 2009, A123 had about 700,000 square feet of manufacturing capabilities, 600,000 of which was located outside the United States. Much of this 600,000 square feet was located in China and Korea, which allows the company to benefit from lower production costs, but can also increase their transportation costs. While they may benefit from cost reductions from international manufacturing plants, they also take on a great deal of risk should any issues arise out of their control associated with these facilities. This in essence is a large weakness for them because it makes manufacturing capabilities dependent on only two major plants. Management has however taken steps to correct this weakness. As we see from economic and political opportunities, more research and manufacturing square feet are being built or leased domestically in such places as Livonia, Michigan.

Building manufacturing facilities in the United States will provide the company with logistical strengths for the domestic battery market, but this currently appears to be a weakness as well because of the dependency on federal, state, and local governments to provide monetary incentives in order to do so. Without this financial help, A123 systems may not have the funds necessary to build such facilities and would need to look to cash reserves or other sources of funding that may decrease company value.

A123 does not currently have a manufacturing presence in Europe, where part of their direct sales force is based. In the long-term, this could prove to be a disadvantage for the company should the market and customer base increase in Europe. Even though production costs are lower in their China and Korea manufacturing facilities, building or leasing a manufacturing facility or facilities in Europe could prove to better serve them as well as their customers. European countries may also offer significant tax incentives or grants for A123, such as the grant and incentives they are currently receiving for their Livonia, Michigan, facility.

With a significant portion of A123's active manufacturing capabilities located in China and Korea, the company faces a number of additional operational threats related to these specific countries. These risks include, but are not limited to, unfavorable political, regulatory, labor, and tax conditions.[27] These additional risks can lead to higher raw material prices, changing employee conditions, difficulties in protecting intellectual property, trouble enforcing agreements or partnerships, and delays in overall operations. Dependency on facilities in China and Korea as a primary source of operations could be harmful to the company as a whole should any of these additional risks materialize. A123 has taken steps to reduce their operational dependency on facilities in China and Korea, but as a long-term strategy they should continue to diversify the locations of their manufacturing facilities.

Challenges Facing A123 Systems

A123 Systems' future success in not a guarantee. The company is facing three serious challenges, given that the future demand of electric cars is uncertain. It is imperative that A123 not run out of cash before demand for electric cars accelerates.

The three challenges facing A123 are:

1. **Depleting cash reserves:** Until revenues begin to pick up significantly and meet the growth the company expects, capital needs will continue to put a strain on the company, as we have seen from their short history of increasing costs and negative cash flows.

2. **Product-centric approach:** A123 focuses its entire strategic philosophy on, and rests its livelihood upon, the fortunes of its product, as opposed to taking a wider view of how it can meet its customers' energy requirements through more than just batteries. Having such a narrowly defined scope is a dangerous path, especially since it could potentially only take one advance in battery or fuel-cell technology to render its products obsolete.

3. **Order timing and overseas competition:** Due to the fact that the long-anticipated electric car market has yet to fully arrive means that it is difficult for A123 to accurately time future demands. This makes it very difficult for A123 to manage their inventories and production, which has left them with large, expensive inventories on hand and with little current demand. When you also consider the fact that countries like Korea and China are producing comparable battery solutions at a lower cost, the traction they have within the industry is in jeopardy.

Appendix A: Revenues, Net Income, and Operating Income Quarterly

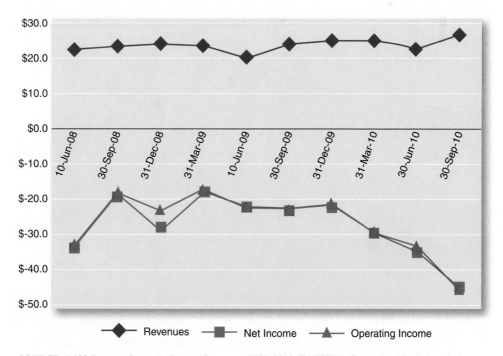

SOURCE: A123 Systems Quarterly Income Statement 2007–2010: FACTSET (CompuStat North America).

Appendix B: Revenues, Net Income, and Operating Income Annual

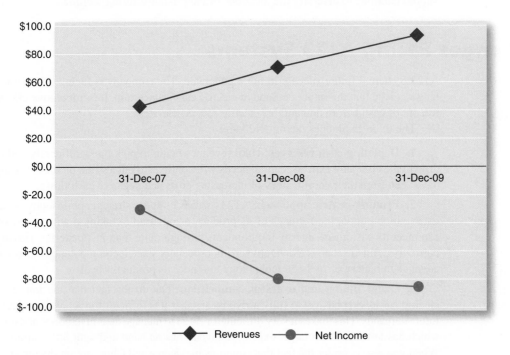

SOURCE: A123 Systems Annual Income Statement 2007, 2009: FACTSET (CompuStat North America).

Appendix C: Cash and Long-Term Debt

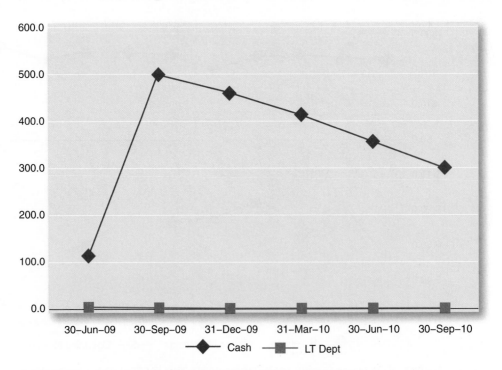

SOURCE: A123 Systems Quarterly Balance Sheet 2007–2010: FACTSET (CompuStat North America).

Appendix D: Inventories and Accounts Receivable

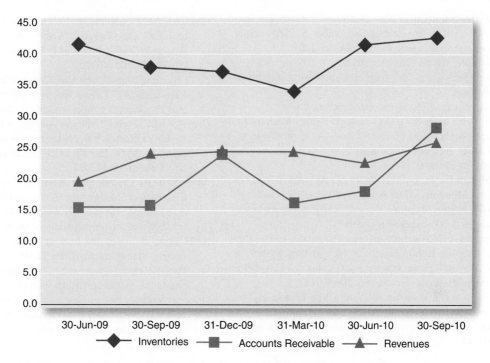

SOURCE: A123 Systems Quarterly Balance Sheet 2007–2010: FACTSET (CompuStat North America).

BIBLIOGRAPHY

A123 Systems Introduces New Generation Lithium-Ion Battery – A123 press release. November 5, 2005. http://www.evworld.com/news.cfm?newsid=10016

A123 website. www.a123systems.com

A123 website. www.a123systems.com/about-us-management-team.htm

A123 website. ir.a123systems.com/directors.cfm

A123 Systems to Develop High-Voltage Battery Modules for Lightweight Fuel-Cell Hybrid Bus – A123 press release. October 26, 2006. http://ir.a123systems.com/releasedetail.cfm?ReleaseID=403113

3,000 Hybrid Buses: Daimler Buses North America Reaches Sales Milestone – Daimler Press Release. September 7, 2009. http://green.autoblog.com/2009/09/08/daimler-buses-na-tops-3-000-hybrid-bus-orders/

Cobasys and A123Systems Announce Partnership to Develop Lithium-Ion Hybrid Electric Vehicle Battery Systems – A123 Press Release. January 3, 2007. http://ir.a123systems.com/releasedetail.cfm?ReleaseID=403112

GM to Use A123 Batteries for Saturn Vue Plug-In Hybrid Development Program – A123 Press Release. January 4, 2007. http://ir.a123systems.com/releasedetail.cfm?ReleaseID=403111

GM and A123 Systems to Co-Develop Lithium-Ion Battery Cell for Chevrolet Volt – A123 Press Release. August 9, 2007. http://ir.a123systems.com/releasedetail.cfm?ReleaseID=403105

A123 Systems Signs Production Contract for Think Electric Vehicles – A123 Press Release. March 5, 2008. http://ir.a123systems.com/releasedetail.cfm?ReleaseID=403100

Chrysler LLC Forms Strategic Alliance with A123Systems for ENVI Electric Vehicle Lineup – A123 Press Release. April 6, 2009. http://ir.a123systems.com/releasedetail.cfm?ReleaseID=403093

A123 Systems Creates New Business Groups Focused on Customized Solutions for Customer Focused Markets – A123 Press Release. November 13, 2009. http://ir.a123systems.com/releasedetail.cfm?ReleaseID=424122

A123 Systems Opens the Largest Lithium-Ion Automotive Battery Manufacturing Plant in North America – A123 Press Release. September 13, 2010. http://ir.a123systems.com/releasedetail.cfm?ReleaseID=506787

"Electric Vehicles Not as Easy as 123," *Fortune* (2010): Accessed 12-5-2010, http://tech.fortune.cnn.com/2010/11/15/electric-vehicles-not-as-easy-as-a123/

NOTES

1. http://www.a123systems.com/a123/company.
2. A123 Press Release - A123Systems Introduces New Generation Lithium-Ion Battery.
3. A123 Press Release - A123 Systems to Develop High-Voltage Battery Modules for Lightweight Fuel-Cell.
4. Daimler Press Release - 3,000 Hybrid Buses: Daimler Buses North America Reaches Sales Milestone.
5. A123 Press Release - Cobasys and A123 Systems Announce Partnership to Develop Lithium-Ion Hybrid Electric Vehicle Battery Systems.
6. A123 Press Release - GM to Use A123 Batteries for Saturn Vue Plug-In Hybrid Development Program.
7. A123 Press Release - GM and A123 Systems to Co-Develop Lithium-Ion Battery Cell for Chevrolet Volt.
8. A123 Press Release - A123 Systems Signs Production Contract for Think Electric Vehicles.
9. A123 Press Release - A123 Systems Creates New Business Groups Focused on Customized Solutions for Customer-Focused Markets.
10. A123 Press Release - A123 Systems Opens the Largest Lithium-Ion Automotive Battery Manufacturing Plant in North America.
11. A123 Systems 10K Report - Page 1.
12. Company website.
13. A123 Systems 10K Report - Page 23.
14. A123 Systems 10K Report - Page 10–11.
15. A123 Systems 10K Report - Pages 4, 15–17, 23.
16. A123 Systems 10K Report - Page 30.
17. Wright, Lawrence. "Can Bolivia become the Saudi Arabia of the electric-car era?" *The New Yorker*. March 22, 2010.
18. http://ir.a123systems.com/events.cfm - 3rd Quarter Earnings Call, November 2010.
19. A123 Systems 10K Report - Page 24.
20. Plafker, Ted. *Doing Business in China: How to Profit in the World's Fastest Growing Market*. 2007. Page 72.
21. http://www.recovery.gov/Transparency/RecipientReportedData/pages/RecipientProjectSummary508.aspx?AwardIdSur=75286&AwardType=Grants.
22. http://tech.fortune.cnn.com/2010/11/15/electric-vehicles-not-as-easy-as-a123/.
23. A123 Systems 10K Report - Page 11.
24. A123 Systems 10K Report - Page 13.
25. A123 Systems 10K Report - Page 20.
26. "Electric Vehicles Not as Easy as 123," *Fortune* (2010): Accessed December 5, 2010: http://tech.fortune.cnn.com/2010/11/15/electric-vehicles-not-as-easy-as-a123/.
27. A123 Systems 10K Report - Page 46.

CASE 7

Guajilote Cooperativo Forestal, Honduras

Nathan Nebbe and J. David Hunger

GUAJILOTE (PRONOUNCED WA-HEE-LOW-TAY) COOPERATIVO FORESTAL WAS A FORESTRY cooperative that operated out of Chaparral, a small village located in the buffer zone of La Muralla National Park in Honduras' Olancho province. Olancho was one of 18 Honduran provinces and was located inland, bordering Nicaragua. The cooperative was one result of a relatively new movement among international donor agencies promoting sustainable economic development of developing countries' natural resources.[1] A cooperative in Honduras was similar to a cooperative in the United States: It was an enterprise jointly owned and operated by members who used its facilities and services.

Guajilote was founded in 1991 as a component of a USAID (United States Agency for International Development) project. The project attempted to develop La Muralla National Park as an administrative and socioeconomic model that COHDEFOR (the Honduran forestry development service) could transfer to Honduras' other national parks. The Guajilote Cooperativo Forestal was given the right to exploit naturally fallen (not chopped down) mahogany trees in La Muralla's buffer zone. Thus far, it was the only venture in Honduras with this right. A buffer zone was the designated area within a park's boundaries but outside its core protected zone. People were allowed to live and engage in economically sustainable activities within this buffer zone.

In 1998, Guajilote was facing some important issues and concerns that could affect not only its future growth but its very survival. For one thing, the amount of mahogany wood was limited and was increasingly being threatened by forest fires, illegal logging, and slash-and-burn agriculture. If the total number of mahogany trees continued to decline, trade in its wood could be restricted internationally. For another, the cooperative had no way to transport its wood to market and was thus forced to accept low prices for its wood from the only distributor in the area. What could be done to guarantee the survival of the cooperative?

This case was prepared by Nathan Nebbe and Professor J. David Hunger of Iowa State University. Copyright © 1999 and 2005 by Nathan Nebbe and J. David Hunger. This case was edited for the *SMBP*–9th, 10th, 11th, 12th, 13th and 14th editions. Presented to the Society for Case Research and published in *Annual Advances in Business Case 1999*. The copyright holders are solely responsible for its content. Further use or reproduction of this material is strictly subject to the express permission of copyright holders. Reprinted by permission of the copyright holders, Nathan Nebbe and J. David Hunger, for the 14th Edition of *SMBP*.

Operations

Guajilote's work activities included three operations using very simple technologies. First, members searched the area to locate appropriate fallen trees. This, in itself, could be very difficult since mahogany trees were naturally rare. These trees were found at elevations up to 1800 meters (5400 feet) and normally were found singly or in small clusters of no more than four to eight trees per hectare (2.2 acres).[2]

Finding fallen mahogany in La Muralla's buffer zone was hampered due to the area's steep and sometimes treacherous terrain. (*La Muralla* means "steep wall of rock" in Spanish.) The work was affected by the weather. For example, more downed trees were available during the wet season due to storms and higher soil moisture—leading to the uprooting of trees.

Second, the cooperative set up a temporary hand-sawmill as close as possible to a fallen tree. Due to the steep terrain, it was often difficult to find a suitable location nearby to operate the hand-sawmill. Once a suitable work location was found, men used a large cross-cut saw to disassemble the tree into various components. The disassembling process was a long and arduous process that could take weeks for an especially large tree. The length of time it took to process a tree depended on the tree's size—mature mahogany trees could be gigantic. Tree size thus affected how many trees Guajilote was able to process in a year.

Third, after a tree was disassembled, the wood was either carried out of the forest using a combination of mule and human power or floated down a stream or river. Even if a stream happened to be near a fallen tree, it was typically usable only during the wet season. The wood was then sold to a distributor who, in turn, transported it via trucks to the cities to sell to furniture makers for a profit.

Guajilote's permit to use fallen mahogany was originally granted in 1991 for a 10-year period by COHDEFOR. The permit was simply written, and stated that if Guajilote restricted itself to downed mahogany, its permit renewal should be granted automatically. The administrator of the area's COHDEFOR office indicated that if things remained as they were, Guajilote should not have any problem obtaining renewal in 2001. Given the nature of Honduran politics, however, nothing could be completely assured.

In 1998, Guajilote's mahogany was still sold as a commodity. The cooperative did very little to add value to its product. Nevertheless, the continuing depletion of mahogany trees around the world meant that the remaining wood should increase in value over time.

Management and Human Resources

Santos Munguia, 29 years old, had been Guajilote's leader since 1995. Although Munguia had only a primary school education, he was energetic and intelligent and had proven to be a very skillful politician. In addition to directing Guajilote, Munguia farmed a small parcel of land and raised a few head of cattle. He was also involved in local politics.

Munguia had joined the cooperative in 1994. Although he had not been one of Guajilote's original members, he quickly became its de facto leader in 1995 when he renegotiated a better price for the sale of the cooperative's wood.

Before Munguia joined the cooperative, Guajilote had been receiving between 3 and 4 lempiras ($0.37, or 11 lempiras to the dollar) per foot of cut mahogany from its sole distributor, Juan Suazo. No other distributors were available in this remote location. The distributor transported the wood to Tegucigalpa or San Pedro Sula and sold it for 16 to 18 lempiras per foot. Believing that Suazo was taking advantage of the cooperative, Munguia negotiated a price increase to 7 to 8 lempiras per foot ($0.60 to $0.62 per foot at the July 15, 1998, exchange rate) by putting political pressure on Suazo. The distributor agreed to the price increase only after a police investigation had been launched to investigate his business dealings. (Rumors circulated that Suazo was transporting and selling illegally logged mahogany by mixing it with that purchased from Guajilote.)

Munguia: El Caudillo

After renegotiating successfully with the cooperative's distributor, Munguia quickly became the group's caudillo (strong man). The caudillo was a Latin American political and social institution. A caudillo was a (typically male) purveyor of patronage. All decisions went through him and were usually made by him. A caudillo was often revered, feared, and hated at the same time because of the power he wielded. Munguia was viewed by many in the area as an ascending caudillo because of his leadership of Guajilote.

Guajilote did not operate in a democratic fashion. Munguia made all the decisions— sometimes with input from his second in command and nephew, Miguel Flores Munguia— and handled all of Guajilote's financial matters. Guajilote's members did not seem to have a problem with this management style. The prevailing opinion seemed to be that Guajilote was a lot better off with Munguia running the show by himself than with more involvement by the members. One man put the members' view very succinctly: "Santos, he saved us (from Suazo, from COHDEFOR, from ourselves)."

Guajilote's organizational structure emphasized Munguia's importance. He was alone at the top in his role as decision maker. If, in the future, Munguia became more involved in politics and other ventures that could take him out of Chaparral (possibly for long periods of time), he would very likely be forced to spend less time with Guajilote's operations. Munguia's leadership has been of key importance to Guajilote's maturing as both a work group and as a business. In 1998, there did not seem to be another person in the cooperative that could take Munguia's place.

Guajilote's Members

When founded, the cooperative had been composed of 15 members. Members were initially selected for the cooperative by employees of USAID and COHDEFOR. The number of employees has held steady over time. Since the cooperative's founding, three original members have quit; four others were allowed to join. Although no specific reasons were given for members leaving, it appeared to be because of personality differences, family problems, or differences of opinion. No money had been paid to them when they left the cooperative. In 1998, there were 16 members in the cooperative.

None of Guajilote's members had any education beyond primary school. Many of the members had no schooling at all and were illiterate. As a whole, the group knew little of markets or business practices.

Guajilote's existence has had an important impact on its members. One member stated that before he had joined Guajilote, he was lucky to have made 2000 lempiras in a year, whereas he now made around 1000 to 1500 in one month as a member of the cooperative. He stated that all five of his children were in school, something that he could not have afforded previously. Before joining the cooperative, he had been involved in subsistence farming and other activities that brought in a small amount of money and food. He said that his children had been required previously to work as soon as they were able. As a simple farmer, he often had to leave his family to find work, mostly migrant farm work, to help his family survive. Because of Guajilote, his family now had enough to eat, and he was able to be home with his family.

This was a common story among Guajilote's members. The general improvement in its members' quality of life also appeared to have strengthened the cooperative members' personal bonds with each other.

Financial Situation

No formal public financial records were available. As head of the cooperative, Munguia kept informal records. Guajilote's 1997 revenues were approximately 288,000 lempiras (US$22,153). (Revenues for 1996 were not available.) Guajilote processed around 36,000 feet of wood during 1997. Very little of the money was held back for capital improvement purchases due to the operation's simple material needs. Capital expenditures for 1997 included a mule plus materials needed to maintain Guajilote's large cross-cut saws.

Each of Guajilote's 16 members was paid an average of about 1,500 lempiras (US$113) per month in 1997 and 1,300 lempiras (US$100) per month in 1996. 1998 payments per month had been similar to 1997's payments, according to Guajilote's members. Money was paid to members based on their participation in Guajilote's operations.

There was conjecture, among some workers, that Munguia and his second in charge were paying themselves more than the other members were receiving. When Munguia was asked if he received a higher wage than the others because of his administrative position in the group, he responded that everything was distributed evenly. An employee of COHDEFOR indicated, however, that Munguia had purchased a house in La Union—the largest town in the area. That person conjectured, based on this evidence, that Munguia was likely receiving more from the cooperative than were the other members.

Issues Facing the Cooperative

Guajilote's size and growth potential were limited by the amount of mahogany it could produce in a year. Mahogany was fairly rare in the forest, and Guajilote was legally restricted to downed trees. Moreover, with the difficulties of finding, processing by hand, and then moving the wood out of the forest, Guajilote was further restricted in the quantity of wood it could handle.

Lack of transportation was a major problem for Guajilote. The cooperative had been unable to secure the capital needed to buy its own truck; lending through legitimate sources was very tight in Honduras and enterprises like Guajilote did not typically have access to lines of credit. Although the prices the cooperative was receiving for its wood had improved, the men still thought that the distributor, Juan Suazo, was not paying them what the wood was worth. It was argued that when demand was high for mahogany, the cooperative gave up as much as 10 lempiras per foot in sales to Suazo. Guajilote could conceivably double its revenues if it could somehow haul its wood to Honduras' major market centers and sell it without use of a distributor. The closest market center was Tegucigalpa—three to four hours from Chaparral on dangerous, often rain-soaked, mountain roads.

A Possibility

Some of the members of Guajilote wondered if the cooperative could do better financially by skipping the distributor completely. It was possible that some specialty shops (chains and independents) and catalogs throughout the world might be interested in selling high-quality mahogany furniture (i.e., chests or chairs) that were produced in an environmentally friendly manner. Guajilote, unfortunately, had no highly skilled carpenters or furniture makers in its membership. There were, however, a couple towns in Honduras with highly skilled furniture makers who worked on a contract basis.

A U.S. citizen with a furniture export business in Honduras worked with a number of independent furniture makers on contract to make miniature ornamental chairs. This exporter reviewed Guajilote's situation and concluded that the cooperative might be able to make and market furniture very profitably—even if it had to go through an exporter to find suitable markets. Upon studying Guajilote's operations, he estimated that Guajilote might be able to more than treble its revenues. In order to do this, however, the exporter felt that Guajilote would have to overcome problems with transportation and upgrade its administrative competence. Guajilote would need to utilize the talents of its members more if it were to widen its operational scope. It would have to purchase trucks and hire drivers to transport the wood over treacherous mountain roads. The role of administrator would become much more demanding, thus forcing Munguia to delegate some authority to others in the cooperative.

Concerns

In spite of Guajilote's improved outlook, there were many concerns that could affect the cooperative's future. A serious concern was the threat of deforestation through fires, illegal logging (i.e., poaching of mahogany as well as clear cutting), and slash-and-burn agriculture.

Small fires were typically set to prepare soils for planting and to help clear new areas for cultivation. Often these fires were either not well supervised or burned out of the control of the people starting them. Due to the 1998 drought, the number of out-of-control forest fires had been far greater than normal. There seemed to be a consensus among Hondurans that 1998 would be one of the worst years for forest fires. Mahogany and tropical deciduous forests are not fire-resistant. Fires not only kill adult and young mahogany trees, but they also destroy their seeds.[3] Mahogany could therefore be quickly eliminated from a site. Each year, Guajilote lost more area from which it could take mahogany.

To make matters worse, many Hondurans considered the area around La Muralla National Park to be a frontier open to settlement by landless campesinos (peasant farmers). In fleeing poverty and desertification, people were migrating to the Olancho province in large numbers.[4] Not only did they clear the forests for cultivation, but they also cut wood for fuel and for use in building their homes. Most of the new settlements were being established in the area's best mahogany growing habitats.

Another concern was that of potential restrictions by CITIES (the international convention on trade in endangered species). Although trade in mahogany was still permitted, it was supposed to be monitored very closely. If the populations of the 12 mahogany species continued to decrease, it was possible that mahogany would be given even greater protection under the CITIES framework. This could include even tighter restrictions on the trade in mahogany or could even result in an outright ban similar to the worldwide ban on ivory trading.

NOTES

1. K. Norsworthy, *Inside Honduras* (Albuquerque, NM: Inter-Hemispheric Education Resource, 1993), pp. 133–138.
2. H. Lamprecht, *Silviculture in the Tropics* (Hamburg, Germany: Verlag, 1989), pp. 245–246.
3. Ibid.
4. K. Norsworthy, *Inside Honduras*, pp. 133–138.

CASE **8**

Google Inc. (2010)

THE FUTURE OF THE INTERNET SEARCH ENGINE

Patricia A. Ryan
Colorado State University

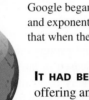

Google began with a mission: to create the ultimate search engine to help users tame the unruly and exponentially growing repository of information that is the Internet. And most would agree that when the word "Google" became a verb, that mission was largely accomplished.[1]

IT HAD BEEN NEARLY SIX YEARS SINCE GOOGLE'S ATTENTION-GRABBING initial public offering and, despite overall stock market weakness, Google remained strong. Although the stock moved with the market in general, the company returned significantly higher returns to its shareholders than did the S&P 500 (**Exhibit 1**). Founders Sergey Brin and Larry Page had created a huge empire in which they now faced challenges of continued growth and innovation. These challenges would carry them through the second decade of the new millennium.

Background[2]

Google was founded in a garage in 1998 by Larry Page and Sergey Brin, two Stanford computer science graduate students, based on ideas generated in 1995. The name *Google* was chosen as a play on *googol*, a mathematical term for the number one followed by one hundred zeros. It is thought the term was appealing to the founders because it related to their mission to organize an exponentially growing Web. Founded on $100,000 from Sun Microsystems, Brin and Page were on their way to creating an Internet engine giant. Google immediately gained the attention of the Internet sector for being a better search engine than its competitors, including Yahoo!

This case was prepared by Professor Patricia A. Ryan of Colorado State University with the research assistance of Ryan A. Neff. Copyright © 2010 by Patricia A. Ryan. The copyright holder is solely responsible for the case content. This case was edited for *Strategic Management and Business Policy*, 14th Edition. Reprinted by permission only for the 14th edition of *Strategic Management and Business Policy* (including international and electronic versions of the book). Any other publication of this case (translation, any form of electronic or media) or sale (any form of partnership) to another publisher will be in violation of copyright law unless Patricia A. Ryan has granted additional written reprint permission.

EXHIBIT 1
Cumulative Returns on
Google (red line) vs.
S&P 500 (blue line)
(2004–2010)

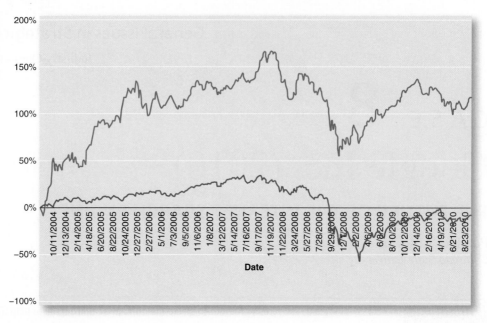

By 2000, Google was operating in 15 languages and gaining international acclaim for its Web search services. The Google toolbar was first released in late 2000. Current Chairman of the Board Eric Schmidt joined Google in that capacity in March 2001. In 2002, Google released Adwords, which was a new cost-per-click pricing system for advertising.

In August 2004, Google went public with 19,605,042 shares at an opening price of $83 per share. **Exhibit 1** traces the growth of Google stock to over $600 per share at the end of 2009. Gmail, an instant messaging and free e-mail service, was released in 2006, just a few months before the announced acquisition of YouTube.

DoubleClick was acquired in 2008. In 2009, Google Docs was introduced. It allowed a user to upload all file types, including ZIP files, in order to work with those files online. The company moved into public education, starting in Oregon with Google Apps for Education. Regarding the transformation of technology in education, Jeff Keltner, a senior manager at Google who worked with educational institutions to increase the use of Google's technology in higher education, commented, "We don't know what the future classrooms will look like. We want to work with schools in a continual evolution to discover what it could look like."[3] The use of Google Docs and Google Spreadsheets in team projects provided the opportunity for increased technological application in the classroom in a manner that business professors had not had the opportunity to apply in the past. Keltner stated that he did not see the biggest challenges as technology-based, but rather culture-based, in that business school professors must be willing and able to accept failure as a part of the process. He believed that the most successful adopters of Google technology will be those that have embraced the willingness to fail in order to drive to a higher level of success.

In 2010, Google was seen as a global leader in technology that was focused on the ways people obtained information. Simply by its growth and product and application development, the company had one of the strongest brand recognitions in the world. There were three primary groups served by Google: (1) Users, (2) Advertisers, and (3) Google Network Members and Other Content Providers. Users gained the ability to find information quickly and easily on the Internet. Advertisers provided 97% of the revenue for Google and gained cost-effective online and offline ads to reach their target market as determined partially by Internet click history. Finally, Google Network Members gained access to AdSense, which allowed for multiple consumer contacts and revenue-sharing among the companies. A full list of products and applications is presented in **Exhibit 2**.

EXHIBIT 2
Products and Services
2010: Google Inc.

GOOGLE.COM—SEARCH ENGINE AND PERSONALIZATIONS
Google Images
Google Books
Google Scholar
Google News
Google Finance
Google Videos
Google Blog Search
iGoogle and Personalized Search
Google Product Search
Google Merchant Search
Google Custom Search
Google Trends
Google Music Search
Google Webmaster Tools

APPLICATIONS
Google Docs
Google Calendar
Gmail
Google Groups
Google Reader
Orkut
Blogger
Google Sites
YouTube

CLIENTS
Google Toolbar
Google Chrome
Google Chrome OS
Google Pack
Picasa
Google Desktop

GOOGLE GEO—MAPS, EARTH, AND LOCAL
Google Local Search
Google Maps
Panoramio
Google Earth
Google SketchUp

ANDROID AND GOOGLE MOBILE
Google Mobile
Mobile Search
Mobile Applications
Mobile Ads

GOOGLE CHECKOUT

GOOGLE LABS

Management and Board of Directors

In 2002, Google hired former Sun Microsystems executive Eric Schmidt to assume the role as Chairman and, later in the same year, CEO. Cofounders Sergey Brin and Larry Page were active members of the Board of Directors. Members of the Executive Team and the Board of Directors are listed in **Exhibit 3**.

Mission

Google's mission was to organize the world's information and make it universally accessible and useful. Management believed that the most effective, and ultimately the most profitable, way to accomplish the company's mission was to put the needs of the users first. They found that offering a high-quality user experience led to increased traffic and strong word-of-mouth promotion. "The perfect search engine would understand exactly what you mean and give back exactly what you want," explained cofounder Larry Page.[4] The complete mission statement is provided in **Exhibit 4**.

EXHIBIT 3
Executive Team and Board of Directors: Google Inc.

A. EXECUTIVE TEAM

Eric Schmidt, 54, Chairman of the Board and CEO, joined Google in 2001 and helped grow the company from a Silicon Valley startup to a global enterprise. Prior to joining Google, Schmidt was the Chief Technology Officer at Sun Microsystems and the President of Sun Technology Enterprises.

Sergey Brin, 36, cofounder, served as a member of the board of directors since Google's inception in September 1998 and as the President of Technology since July 2001. From September 1998 to July 2001, Sergey served as President. Sergey holds a Masters degree in computer science from Stanford University and a Bachelor of Science degree with high honors in mathematics and computer science from the University of Maryland at College Park.

Larry Page, 37, cofounder, has served as a member of the board of directors since Google's inception in September 1998 and as the President of Products since July 2001. Larry served as Chief Executive Officer from September 1998 to July 2001 and as Chief Financial Officer from September 1998 to July 2002. Larry holds a Masters degree in computer science from Stanford University and a Bachelor of Science degree in engineering, with a concentration in computer engineering, from the University of Michigan.

Nikesh Arora, 41, has served as President, Global Sales Operations and Business Development, since April 2009. Prior to that, Nikesh worked for Deutsche Telekom, Putnam Investments, and Fidelity Investments.

David C. Drummond, 46, served as Senior Vice President of Corporate Development since January 2006 and as Chief Legal Officer since December 2006. Prior to joining Google, David served as Chief Financial Officer of SmartForce, an educational software applications company.

Patrick Pichette, 47, served as Chief Financial Officer and Senior Vice President since August 2008. Prior to joining Google, Patrick served as President–Operations for Bell Canada, a telecommunications company.

Jonathan J. Rosenberg, 48, served as Senior Vice President of Product Management since January 2006. Prior to joining Google, Jonathan served as Vice President of Software for palmOne, a provider of handheld computer and communications solutions, and held various executive positions at Excite@Home, an Internet media company.

Shona L. Brown, 43, served as Senior Vice President of Business Operations since January 2006. Prior to joining Google, Shona was at McKinsey & Company, a management consulting firm, where she had been a partner in the Los Angeles office since December 2000.

Alan Eustace, 53, served as Senior Vice President of Engineering and Research since January 2006. Previously, he served as a Vice President of Engineering since July 2002. Prior to joining Google, Alan was at Hewlett-Packard, a provider of technology products, software, and services.

B. BOARD OF DIRECTORS

Eric Schmidt, 54, served as Chairman of the Board from 2001 to 2004 and from 2007 to the present, as well as Chief Executive Officer and board member since 2001.

Sergey Brin, 36, was cofounder and President of Technology. He served on the board since its inception in 1998.

Larry Page, 37, was cofounder and President of Products. He served on the board since its inception in 1998.

L. John Doerr, 58, served as board member since 1999. He has been General Partner of the venture capital firm Kleiner Perkins Caufield since August 1980.

John L. Hennessy, 57, served as Lead Independent Director since 2007. He served on the board since 2004. He has been President of Stanford University since 2000 and previously served as Dean of the Stanford School of Engineering and Chair of the Stanford Department of Computer Science.

Ann Mather, 49, served as board member since 2005. She also served as Executive Vice President and Chief Financial Officer of Pixar from 1999 to 2004 and held various executive positions at Village Roadshow Pictures and Walt Disney Company.

Paul S. Otellini, 59, served as board member since 2004. He has been CEO and President of Intel Corporation since 2005 and served previously in various Intel executive positions.

K. Ram Shriram, 52, served as board member since 1998. He has been Managing Partner of Sherpalo Ventures, an angel venture investment company, since 2000. He previously served as VP of Business Development at Amazon.com.

Shirley M. Tilghman, 63, served as board member since 2005. She has been President of Princeton University since 2001. Previously she served as Professor of Biochemistry and Founding Director of Princeton's multidisciplinary Lewis-Sigler Institute for Integrative Genomics.

....
SOURCE: *Google Forms 10-K and 14-A (2009).*

EXHIBIT 4
Mission Statement:
Google Inc.

Google's mission was to organize the world's information and make it universally accessible and useful. Management believed that the most effective, and ultimately the most profitable, way to accomplish their mission was to put the needs of the users first. They found that offering a high-quality user experience led to increased traffic and strong word-of-mouth promotion. Dedication to putting users first was reflected in three key commitments:

- Google will do its best to provide the most relevant and useful search results possible, independent of financial incentives. Its search results would be objective, and the company did not accept payment for search result ranking or inclusion.

- Google will do its best to provide the most relevant and useful advertising. Advertisements should not be an annoying interruption. If any element on a search result page is influenced by payment to the management, it will make it clear to our users.

- Google will never stop working to improve the user experience, its search technology, and other important areas of information organization.

Management believed that their user focus was the foundation of their success to date. They also believed that this focus was critical for the creation of long-term value. Management stated they did not intend to compromise their user focus for short-term economic gain.

SOURCE: *Google Form 2009 10-K, modified by case author.*

Issues and Risk Factors Facing Google in 2010[5]

Competition

According to top management, Google's industry was characterized by rapid change and converging, as well as new and disruptive, technologies. Google faced formidable competition in every aspect of its business, particularly from companies that sought to connect people with information on the Web and provide them with relevant advertising. Google faced significant direct and indirect competition from:

- **Traditional search engines, such as Yahoo! Inc. and Microsoft Corporation's Bing.** Although Yahoo! was the first search engine to gain widespread acceptance, it lost its dominant position to Google when Google introduced its superior search engine technology. Microsoft's failed attempt to buy Yahoo! in 2008 led to the introduction of Bing, its own search engine, in 2010. Microsoft's marketing power could make Bing a serious competitor to Google.

- **Vertical search engines and e-commerce sites, such as WebMD (for health queries), Kayak (travel queries), Monster.com (job queries), and Amazon.com and eBay (commerce).** Google competed with these sites because they, like Google, were trying to attract users to their websites to search for product or service information, and some users may navigate directly to those sites rather than go through Google.

- **Social networks, such as Facebook, Yelp, or Twitter.** Some users were beginning to rely more on social networks for product or service referrals, rather than seeking information through traditional search engines.

- **Other forms of advertising.** Google competed against traditional forms of advertising, such as television, radio, newspapers, magazines, billboards, and yellow pages, for ad dollars.

- **Mobile applications.** As the mobile application ecosystem developed further, users were increasingly accessing e-commerce and other sites through those companies' stand-alone mobile applications, instead of through search engines.

- **Providers of online products and services.** Google provided a number of online products and services, including Gmail, YouTube, and Google Docs, that competed directly with new and established companies that offered communication, information, and entertainment services integrated into their products or media properties.

Google competed to attract and retain users of its search and communication products and services. Most of the products and services offered to users were free, so Google did not compete on price. Instead, the company competed in this area on the basis of the relevance and usefulness of search results and the features, availability, and ease of use of Google's products and services.

Neither Google's users nor its advertisers were locked into Google. For users, other search engines were literally one click away, and there were no costs to switching search engines. Google's advertisers typically advertised in multiple places, both online and offline. The company competed to attract and retain content providers (Google Network members, as well as other content providers for whom the company distributed or licensed content) primarily based on the size and quality of Google's advertiser base. Google's ability to help these partners generated revenues from advertising and the terms of the agreements. Since 97% of Google's revenues were generated from advertising, this placed the company in a tight position if any advertising contracts were to dissolve or diminish in growth. However, Google was reliant on strong brand recognition and its brand identity.[6]

Legal and Regulatory Issues

Google was subject to increased regulatory scrutiny that may have negatively impacted the business. This was an increased risk with continued growth and corporate expansion. There may be regulatory issues related to potential monopolistic power as the industry faced both growth with expansion and consolidation.

Legal issues were a developing concern for Google. Many laws currently in place had been enacted prior to the Internet age and thus could not have taken into consideration the business practices and implications of the Internet and computer technology. Liability issues, such as laws related to the liability of online services, remained uncertain and were thus a legal risk for Google.

The Digital Millennium Copyright Act contained provisions that limited, but did not eliminate, Google's liability for listing or linking to third-party websites that included materials that infringed on copyrights or other rights, so long as the company complied with the statutory requirements of the act. Various U.S. and international laws restricted the distribution of materials considered harmful to children and imposed additional restrictions on the ability of online services to collect information from minors. Furthermore, in the area of data protection, many states had passed laws requiring notification to users when there was a security breach of personal data. One example was California's Information Practices Act.[7]

International Risk

Google's international revenues were increasing annually, and amounted to 51% of corporate revenues in 2008. Over half of user traffic in 2009 was international. There were increased challenges with international operations which included, but were not limited to, geographic, language, and cultural differences among countries. Countries had different accounting practices, and the credit risk was generally greater for international transactions. Furthermore, exchange rate risk, potential negative tax consequences, foreign exchange controls, and cultural barriers related to customers, employees, and other stakeholders were more prevalent with international dealings. Privacy laws and government censorship often varied among countries.

Government pressure led Google to censor its Web content in numerous locations. For example, it was illegal to publish material in Germany, France, and Poland that denied the Holocaust. Google thus used filters to screen for such material. In Turkey, videos that mocked "Turkishness" were filtered by Google for its *Google.com.tr* website. Since China restricted Internet content and political speech, Google had to agree to censor some of its Internet search results to establish its *Google.com.cn* website in 2006. Google's management made the controversial decision in early 2010 to move its China website from China.cn where it had been under heavy censorship pressure to its site in Hong Kong (Google.hk) that wasn't filtered. According to management, there was clearly a benefit from international transactions that in general outweighed the costs.[8]

Internet Security Issues

Internet security was an issue that plagued the industry, as a security breach would be potentially harmful to Google. Sophisticated software could already track users' Internet activity while they shopped for goods and services on the Web. Skilled hackers from around the world were now able to enter supposedly "secure" websites to obtain user records and credit card information. Identity theft was becoming a major problem for the general population. Security/privacy issues were likely to become even more important as the amount of data and applications available on the Internet increased.

Revenue Growth and Sustainability

Google had experienced remarkable revenue growth in the past six years as evidenced by its financial statements. See **Exhibits 5** and **6** for balance sheets, and income statements for 2004–2009. Google's management recognized that the firm's revenue growth rate may soon decrease due to stronger direct and indirect competition, the developing maturity of the online advertising market, and the growing size of the firm. This could put pressure on operating margins and profits in the future, thus lowering the free cash flow available to investors. Google's management recognized that future profit margins may be tightened further by lower profit margins on revenues received from Google Network members. Furthermore, since 97% of revenue came from advertising, any blockage of online advertising would have a negative effect on operating profits.

Intellectual Property

Google, YouTube, DoubleClick, DART, AdSense, AdWords, Gmail, I'm Feeling Lucky, PageRank, Blogger, orkut, Picassa, SketchUp, and Postini were registered trademarks in the United States. Google also had unregistered trademarks, such as Blog*Spot, Jaiku, Android, Open Handset Alliance, OpenSocial, Panoramio, and Knol. The first version of the PageRank technology was created while Google's cofounders attended Stanford University—thus, Stanford owned a patent to PageRank which was due to expire in 2017. Although Google owned a perpetual license to this patent, the license was due to become non-exclusive at the end of 2011.

Google must fend off threats to their trademarks and secrets. Mainly, the company runs the risk of the name *Google* becoming commonly used by the public to describe "searching" the Internet. Google could actually lose its trademark on the name, as it would become part of the public domain. Trade secrets are also something Google defended, as an internal leak would diminish the value of these secrets.

EXHIBIT 5

Balance Sheet: Google Inc. (Dollar amount in millions)

Year Ending December 31	2004	2005	2006	2007	2008	2009
Assets						
Current assets						
Cash and cash equivalents	$426,873	$3,877,174	$3,544,671	$6,081,593	$8,656,672	$10,197,588
Marketable securities	1,705,424	4,157,073	7,699,243	8,137,020	7,189,099	14,287,187
Accounts receivable	311,836	687,976	1,322,340	2,162,521	2,642,192	3,178,471
Deferred income taxes, net	19,463	49,341	29,713	68,538	286,105	644,406
Income taxes receivable	70,509	0	0	145,253	0	23,244
Prepaid revenue share, expenses, and other assets	159,360	229,507	443,880	694,213	1,404,114	836,062
Total current assets	2,693,465	9,001,071	13,039,847	17,289,138	20,178,182	29,166,958
Prepaid revenue share, expenses, and other assets, noncurrent	35,493	31,310	114,455	168,530	433,846	416,119
Deferred income taxes, net, noncurrent	11,590	0	0	33,219	0	262,611
Nonmarketable equity securities	0	0	1,031,850	1,059,694	85,160	128,977
Property and equipment, net	378,916	961,749	2,395,239	4,039,261	5,233,843	4,844,610
Intangible assets, net	71,069	82,783	346,841	446,596	996,690	774,938
Goodwill	122,818	194,900	1,545,119	2,299,368	4,839,854	4,902,565
Total assets	$3,313,351	$10,271,813	$18,473,351	$25,335,806	$31,767,575	$40,496,778
Liabilities and stockholders' equity						
Current liabilities						
Accounts payable	$32,672	$115,575	$211,169	$282,106	$178,004	$215,867
Accrued compensation and benefits	82,631	198,788	351,671	588,390	811,643	982,482
Accrued expenses and other current liabilities	64,111	114,377	266,247	465,032	480,263	570,080
Accrued revenue share	122,544	215,771	370,364	522,001	532,547	693,958
Deferred revenue	36,508	73,099	105,136	178,073	218,084	285,080
Income taxes payable, net	0	27,774	0	0	81,549	0
Current portion of equipment leases	1,902	0	0	0	0	0
Total current liabilities	340,368	745,384	1,304,587	2,035,602	2,302,090	2,747,467
Deferred revenue, long-term	7,443	10,468	20,006	30,249	29,818	41,618
Liability for stock options exercised early, long-term	5,982	2,083	40,421	0	890,115	1,392,468
Deferred income taxes, net	1	35,419	0	478,372	12,515	0
Other long term liabilities	30,502	59,502	68,497	101,904	294,175	311,001
Commitments and contingencies						
Stockholder's equity						

EXHIBIT 5
(Continued)

Convertible preferred stock, $0.001 par value, 100,000 shares authorized; no shares issued and outstanding	0	0	0	0	0	0
Class A and Class B common stock, $0.001 par value: 9,00,000 shares	267	293	309	313	315	318
Additional paid-in capital	2,582,352	7,477,792	11,882,906	13,241,221	14,450,338	15,816,738
Deferred stock-based compensation	(249,470)	(119,015)	0	0	0	0
Accumulated other comprehensive income	5,436	4,019	23,311	113,373	226,579	105,090
Retained earnings	**590,471**	**2,055,868**	**5,133,314**	**9,334,772**	**13,561,630**	**20,082,078**
Total stockholders' equity	**2,929,056**	**9,418,957**	**17,039,840**	**22,689,679**	**28,238,862**	**36,004,224**
Total liabilities and stockholders' equity	**$3,313,351**	**$10,271,813**	**$18,473,351**	**$25,335,806**	**$31,767,575**	**$40,496,778**

SOURCE: *Google Form 10-K (2009).*

EXHIBIT 6
Income Statement: Google Inc. (Dollar amount in millions)

Year Ending December 31	2004	2005	2006	2007	2008	2009
Revenues	$3,189,223	$6,138,560	$10,604,917	$16,593,986	$21,795,550	$23,650,563
Costs and expenses						
Cost of revenues	1,468,967	2,577,088	4,225,027	6,649,085	8,621,506	8,844,115
Research and development	395,164	599,510	1,228,589	2,119,985	2,793,192	2,843,027
Sales and marketing	295,749	468,152	849,518	1,461,266	1,946,244	1,983,941
General and administrative	188,151	386,532	751,787	1,279,250	1,802,639	1,667,294
Contribution to Google Foundation	0	90,000	0	0	0	0
Nonrecurring portion of settlement of disputes with Yahoo	201,000	0	0	0	0	0
Total costs and expenses	2,549,031	4,121,282	7,054,921	11,509,586	15,163,581	15,338,377
Income from operations	640,192	2,017,278	3,549,996	5,084,400	6,631,969	8,312,186
Interest income and other, net	10,042	124,399	461,044	589,580	316,384	69,003
Impairment of equity investments	0	0	0	0	(1,094,757)	0
Income before income taxes	650,234	2,141,677	4,011,040	5,673,980	5,853,596	8,381,189
Provision for income taxes	251,115	676,280	933,594	1,470,260	1,626,738	1,860,741
Net income	$399,119	$1,465,397	$3,077,446	$4,203,720	$4,226,858	$6,520,448
Net income per share of Class A and Class B common stock						
Basic	$2.07	$5.31	$10.21	$13.53	$13.46	$20.62
Diluted	1.46	5.02	9.94	13.29	13.31	20.41
Shares outstanding (mil)	267	293	309	313	315	318
Year-end stock price	$192.79	$414.86	$460.48	$691.48	$307.65	$619.98

SOURCE: *Google Form 10-K (2009).*

Furthermore, intellectual property rights claims were costly to defend in the legal system. Litigations challenging the IP rights of companies within the technology industry were frequent, and as Google expanded its business, it had experienced more claims against it. Companies had filed trademark infringements against Google, usually over advertisements. Companies have also filed claims against Google for copyright infringement on the features of its website and its products. Examples include the class action settlement with the Authors Guild and the Association of the American Publishers, which will end up costing the company. In addition, some of Google's products have been attacked for patent infringements, for which Google could be required to pay damages or licensing fees. Patent infringement settlements would lead to higher costs and prevent the ability of Google to produce certain services or products, leading to lost profits.

Alternative Technology

Each day, more individuals were using devices other than personal computers to access the Internet. If users of these devices did not widely adopt versions of Google's Web search technology, products, or operating systems developed for these devices, the business could be adversely affected. These alternative devices may make it problematic to use the services provided by Google, and make it challenging for the company to produce products that capture customers' imaginations and loyalties.

Information Technology Issues

Google was susceptible to threats from false or invalid visits to the ads it displayed, and has had to refund fees charged for advertising due to fraudulent clicks. If Google failed to detect click fraud or other invalid clicks, it could lose the confidence of its advertisers, which would harm the company's image and viability.

Additionally, interruption or failure of the information technology and communications systems the company used could hurt its ability to effectively provide products and services, damaging the reputation Google worked to maintain, as well as harming its operating income. Its IT system was exposed to impairment from numerous sources, such as natural disasters, infrastructure failures, and computer hackers. Although management had contingency plans for many of these situations, such plans could not cover every possibility.

Index spammers could harm the integrity of Google's Web service by falsifying users' search attempts. This could damage the company's reputation and lead to users becoming unhappy with Google's products and services, leading to a decline in website visits. This could result in lower advertising revenues from its Google Network partners. Google relied greatly on these members for a significant portion of its revenues, and both parties benefited from their association with each other. The loss of these associates could adversely affect the business.

The future of the business depended upon continued and unimpeded access to the Internet for both the company and its users. Internet access providers may be able to block, degrade, or charge for access to certain Google products and services, which could lead to additional expenses and the loss of users and advertisers.

As Google spread its operations across the globe, more and more of its receivables were being denominated in foreign currencies. If currency exchange rates become unfavorable, the company could lose some revenues in U.S. dollar terms. Although many multinational corporations used hedging strategies to lower or negate the risk of doing business overseas, Google had limited experience with many of these financial strategies. Hedging strategies also had high costs, reducing the company's overall profitability.

Culture and Employees

Like many successful technology firms, Google provided its employees with an open and collaborative culture in which ideas were exchanged and new products and application ideas were developed. Google's management strived to be transparent in their workings, making sure that employees knew about company announcements and new product or application development before the public. The company used both technology and standard processes to convey information. For example, "Tech Talks" blogs and weekly "TGIF" meetings were used to convey information and to communicate with employees.

On December 31, 2009, Google had 19,835 employees, consisting of 7,443 in research and development, 7,338 in sales and marketing, 2,941 in general and administrative, and 2,113 in operations. Given that Google relied on highly skilled workers, its continued success was strongly related to its ability to maintain and grow its strong talent pool. Once the current recession ends, it may become more difficult to attract and maintain skilled, talented employees.[9]

Google experienced rapid and strong growth with strong employee satisfaction. The company worked to gain a globally diverse workforce with different perspectives in which employees were rewarded for performance. Google had historically worked hard to maintain a corporate culture of innovation and performance that aligned the interests of the corporation with those of employees. The company's $1,000 cash bonus and 10% raise paid to all of its employees in 2010 were examples of the lengths to which the company acted to retain top talent. This was important since Google's stock price had dropped 4.7% in 2010. According to Paul Kedrosky, a venture capitalist, "It used to be people were fine taking Google's money and stock, because they believed it would appreciate rapidly. Now it's not as attractive."[10]

The company considered cofounders Brin and Page to be a key corporate resource, even though their spending $15 million for a former Qantas Boeing 767 jet airplane in 2006 to use as a company plane was listed by *Bloomberg Businessweek* as an example of "executive excess."[11]

As the company continues to grow, management will be challenged to find new and innovative ways to maintain a strong corporate culture.

Seasonality

While there were some seasonal effects on Google's business, it was generally not as significant as in retail stores, which earned much of their revenue in the last quarter of the calendar year. In Google's case, there had generally been an increase in business in the last quarter of the calendar year, as represented by commercial queries. Likewise, the summer months tended to be the slowest time of the year. While seasonality might be an issue for Google's business and revenue, it was generally not perceived by management to be a major issue.

Google's Future

Google had thus far thrived in the Internet search engine industry, garnishing a name that, for many, was synonymous with "Internet search." Up to now, growth had been strong, suggesting a bright future. Google appeared to be poised to take advantage of what the future had to offer in new technology by creating new products. In order to continue doing this, it will need to retain the best and brightest minds. For example, one of Google's new concepts was artificial intelligence software for use in automobiles that could drive themselves.[12] The company's stock price had climbed tremendously in the past, but some analysts now felt that Google was maturing as a corporation and that its stock value was leveling off.[13]

As Google continued to grow, it continued purchasing other companies, such as its acquisitions of YouTube, DoubleClick, and Postini.[14] Nevertheless, growth by acquisition may not necessarily lead to increasing growth in revenues or profits. For example, YouTube was a $1.6 billion 2006 acquisition that, as of 2010, had not generated significant additional revenue for Google, despite its growth potential.

There were some indications that acquisitions might become an increasingly difficult strategy in the future. In 2010, Google failed in an attempt to purchase Groupon, a website specializing in local shopping promotions. Google's offer of $6 billion for Groupon was almost double what it had paid for DoubleClick in 2008. Groupon's rejection of the offer reflected a fear common to Web entrepreneurs that their small ventures might get lost inside Google's vastness. For example, several other startups, such as Yelp, that had also been pursued by Google had opted to stay privately owned.[15]

Google's top management needed to consider these and other factors in order to plan strategically. Legal issues will likely continue, such as allegations that Google used Wi-Fi networks to take personal information. Google's management had moved on this quickly with corrective action and similar future responses to legal challenges will be important.[16] The future of mobile computing was an open, uncharted area.[17]

All of these considerations and more were relevant as CEO Schmidt and his executive team pondered the second decade of the new millennium and discussed Google's future strategies.

REFERENCES

Byron Acohido, Kathy Chu, and Calum MacLeod, "Google Clash Highlights How China Does Business: Foreign Companies Have Jumped Through China's Hoops for Years," *USA Today* (January 25, 2010), pp. 1b–2b.

Associated Press. "China Says Dispute Is with Google, Not U.S.," *St. Petersburg Times* (2010, January 22), pp. 4b–5b.

Tricia Bisoux, "First Adopters," *BizEd* (November/December, 2010), pp. 20–26.

Peter Burrows, "Apple vs. Google: How the Battle Between Silicon Valley's Superstars will Shape the Future of Mobile Computing," *Bloomberg Businessweek* (January 25, 2010), pp. 28–34.

Simon Dumenco, "Can We Trust Google to Avoid Chronic AOL-ism?" *Advertising Age,* http://adage.com/print?-article_id=48584 (February 26, 2006).

Bruce Einhorn, "Google and China: A Win for Liberty—and Strategy," *Bloomberg Businessweek* (January 25, 2010), p. 35.

"Exclusive: How Google's Algorithm Rules the Web," http://www.wired.com/magazine/2010/02/ff_google_algorithm/ (November 8, 2010).

"Frequently Asked Questions—Investor Relations—Google," http://investor.google.com/corporate/faq.html (November 18, 2010).

Steven Goldberg, "Tech Titans Are Cheap," *Kiplinger Personal Finance* (September 28, 2010).

Google 10-K form for the year ended December 31, 2009, filed with the SEC.

Google 10-Q form for the third quarter ended on September 30, 2010, filed with the SEC.

"Google: Time to Take Profits? S&P Downgrades on Valuation," http://blogs.barrons.com/techtraderdaily/2010/11/08 (November 8, 2010).

"Google Grabs Personal Info Off of Wi-Fi Networks," http://finance.yahoo.com/news/Google-grabs-personal-info-apf-2162289993.html (November 8, 2010).

"Google to Acquire YouTube for $1.65 Billion in Stock," http://www.google.com/intl/en/press/pressrel/google_youtube.html (November 8, 2010).

"Management Team—Google Corporate Information," http://www.google.com/corporate/execs.html (November 18, 2010).

"Cars Drive Themselves: Google Is Testing Artificial-Intelligence Software in Cars in California," *St. Petersburg Times* (October 10, 2010), p. 1a.

"Our Philosophy—Google Corporate Information," http://www.google.com/corporate/tenthings.html (November 18, 2010).

NOTES

1. Trish Bisoux, "First Adopters," *BizEd* (November/December 2010), p. 20.
2. Much of this section was developed from http://www.google.com/about/company/history/ (September 2, 2013).
3. Trish Bisoux, "First Adopters," p. 22.
4. http://www.google.com/corporate.tenthings.html (October 15, 2010).
5. Much of this information is from Google 10-K, 2009, filed with the SEC.
6. Google Form 10-K, 2009, filed with the SEC.
7. This paragraph was paraphrased from Google's Form 19-K, 2009, filed with the SEC.
8. Peter Burrows, "Apple vs. Google: How the Battle Between Silicon Valley's Superstars will Shape the Future of Mobile Computing," *Bloomberg Businessweek*, http://www.businessweek.com/magazine/content/10_04/b41640284834.htm?chan=magazine+channel_top+stories; (September 2, 2013), pp. 28–34; and Lawrence Carrel, "Apple, Google, and Microsoft: Buy or Avoid?" *Kiplinger Personal Finance*, http://www.kiplinger.com/article/investing/T052-C008-S001-apple-google-and-microsoft-buy-or-avoid.html (September 2, 2013).
9. Google Form 10-K, 2009, filed with the SEC.
10. Brad Stone and Douglas MacMillan, "Groupon's $6 Billion Snub," *Bloomberg Businessweek*, www.businessweek.com/magazine/content/10_51/b4208006060501.htm (December 13–19, 2010).
11. "A Century of Executive Excess," *Bloomberg Businessweek* (December 13–19, 2010), p. 99.
12. "Cars Drive Themselves: Google Is Testing Artificial-Intelligence Software in Cars in California," *St. Petersburg Times* (October 10, 2010), p. 1a.
13. "Google: Time to Take Profits? S&P Downgrades on Valuation," http://blogs.barrons.com/techtraderdaily/2010/11/08 (November 8, 2010); and Lawrence Carrel, "Apple, Google, and Microsoft: Buy or Avoid?"
14. "Google to Acquire YouTube for $1.65 Billion in Stock," http://www.google.com/intl/en/press/pressrel/google_youtube.html (November 8, 2010).
15. Brad Stone and Douglas MacMillan, "Groupon's $6 Billion Snub," pp. 6–7.
16. "Google Grabs Personal Info Off of Wi-Fi Networks," http://www.npr.org/templates/story/story.php?storyId=126837748 (September 2, 2013).
17. Peter Burrows, "Apple vs. Google: How the Battle Between Silicon Valley's Superstars will Shape the Future of Mobile Computing."

CASE 9

Amazon.com, Inc.

RETAILING GIANT TO HIGH-TECH PLAYER?

Alan N. Hoffman
Bentley University

Overview

Founded by Jeff Bezos, online giant Amazon.com, Inc. (Amazon), was incorporated in the state of Washington in July, 1994, and sold its first book in July, 1995. In May 1997, Amazon (AMZN) completed its initial public offering and its common stock was listed on the NASDAQ Global Select Market. Amazon quickly grew from an online bookstore to the world's largest online retailer, greatly expanding its product and service offerings through a series of acquisitions, alliances, partnerships, and exclusivity agreements. Amazon's financial objective was to achieve long-term sustainable growth and profitability. To attain this objective, Amazon maintained a lean culture focused on increasing its operating income through continually increasing revenue and efficiently managing its working capital and capital expenditures, while tightly managing operating costs.

The name "Amazon" was evocative for founder Jeff Bezos of his vision of Amazon as a huge natural phenomenon, like the longest river in the world. He envisioned the company to be the largest online marketplace on earth someday.

By 2008, Amazon had become a global brand, with websites in Canada, the United Kingdom, Germany, France, China, and Japan, with order fulfillment in more than 200 countries.[1] Its operations were organized into two principal segments: North America and International Operations, which grew to include Italy in 2010 and Spain in 2011. By 2012, Amazon employed more than 56,200 people around the world working in the corporate office in Seattle, and in software development, order fulfillment, and customer service centers in North America, Latin America, Europe, and Asia.

The authors would like to thank Barbara Gottfried, Jodi Germann, Lauren-Ashley Higson, Faith Naymie, Faina Shakarova, Jamal Ait Hammou, Muntasir Alam, Shaheel Dholakia, Xinxin Zhu, and Will Hoffman for their research and contributions to this case.
Please address all correspondence to: Dr. Alan N. Hoffman, Dept. of Management, Bentley University, 175 Forest Street, Waltham, MA 02452-4705, voice (781) 891-2287, ahoffman@bentley.edu. Printed by permission of Alan N. Hoffman.

Amazon Corporate Governance

Jeff Bezos is the Chairman of the Board and CEO of Amazon and owns 19.4% of the company.

Amazon has three board committees of which two are standard: the audit committee and the governance committee. The third committee, the Leadership Development and Compensation Committee, is uncommon. Most publicly traded companies have a compensation committee; however, it is unusual for the compensation committee to have leadership development as part of its mandate. The Leadership Development and Compensation Committee "monitors and periodically assesses the continuity of capable management, including succession plans for executive officers."

Amazon's board is not populated by CEOs or retired CEOs. It includes several venture capitalists, a number of senior-level executives from varied industries, an eminent scientist, and a representative from the non-profit sector.

Amazon's board has served together for a long time. This implies a deeper understanding of the company and increasing familiarity and even friendship amongst the group. This tends to discourage independent thinking and objectivity.

All of it is further proof that Jeff Bezos is a strong CEO and runs the company.

Retail Operations/Amazon's Superior Website

As people became more comfortable shopping on line, Amazon developed its website to take advantage of increased Internet traffic and to serve its customers most effectively.[2] The hallmarks of Amazon's appeal were ease of use; speedy, accurate search results; selection, price, and convenience; a trustworthy transaction environment; timely customer service; and fast, reliable fulfillment[3]—all of it enabled by the sophisticated technology the company encouraged its employees to develop to better serve its customers. The site, which offered a huge array of products sold both by itself and by third parties, was particularly designed to create a personalized shopping experience that helped customers discover new products and make efficient, informed buying decisions.

Key to Amazon's success was continual website improvement. A huge part of the technological work done for Amazon was dedicated to identifying problems, developing solutions, and enhancing customers' online experience. Jacob Lepley, in his "Amazon Marketing Strategy: Report One," notes that, "when you visit Amazon . . . you can use [it] to find just about any item on the market at an extremely low price. Amazon has made it very simple for customers to purchase items with a simple click of the mouse. . . . When you have everything you need, you make just one payment and your orders are processed."[4] This simple system is the same whether a customer purchases directly from Amazon or from one of its associates.

Pursuing perfection, Amazon was aggressive in analyzing its website's traffic and modifying the website accordingly. Amazon particularly excelled at customer tracking, collecting data from every visit to its website. Utilizing the information, Amazon then directed users to products that it surmised they might be interested in because the item was either related to a product that they had previously searched for or purchased by another Amazon customer looking for a similar product.

Recommendations were also customized based on the information customers provided about themselves and their interests, and their ratings prior purchased. Amazon also collected data on those who had never visited any of its websites, but who had received gifts from those who had used the site.

One of Amazon's most distinctive features was the community created based on the ratings/reviews provided by private individuals to help others make more informed purchasing decisions. Anyone could provide a narrative review and rate a product on a scale of 1–5 stars, and/or comment on others' reviews. Individuals could also create their own "So You'd Like . . ." guides and "Listmania" lists based on Amazon's products offerings and post them or send them to friends and family. To streamline customer research, Amazon also consolidated different versions of a product (e.g., DVD, VHS, Blu-ray disk) into a single product available for commentary that simplified commentary and user accessibility.[5]

To further target potential customers, Amazon engaged in permission marketing, eliciting permission to e-mail customers regarding specific production promotions based on prior purchases on the assumption that a targeted e-mail was more likely to be read than a blanket e-mail. This strategy was hugely appreciated by Amazon customers, further contributing to Amazon's success.

In addition, Amazon purchased pay-per-click advertisements on search engines such as Google to direct browsing customers to its websites. The ads appeared on the left-hand side of the search list results, and Amazon paid a fee for each visitor who clicked on its sponsored link.

At the same time, as "TV and billboard ads were roughly ten times less effective when compared to direct or online marketing when concerning customer acquisition costs"[6], Amazon reduced its offline marketing. The strategy was simple: as customers shopped online, online marketing was key. However, in 2010, Amazon initiated a small television advertising campaign to increase brand awareness.

Finally, to round out its customer care, Amazon expedited shipping by strategically locating its fulfillment centers near airports[7] where rents were also cheaper, giving Amazon the two-pronged advantage of speed and low cost over its competitors. Furthermore, in the United States, the United Kingdom, Germany, and Japan, Amazon offered subscribers to Amazon Prime the added convenience of free express shipping. Amazon Prime's free next-day delivery endeared it to Amazon customers, again contributing to the customer loyalty that was key to Amazon's success. Amazon Prime cost $79 annually to join and included free access to Amazon Instant Video. The overarching objective of the company was to offer low prices, convenience, and a wide selection of merchandise, a pared down, yet wide-reaching strategy that made Amazon such a huge success.

Diversified Product Offerings

Amazon diversified its product portfolio well beyond simply offering books, which in turn allowed it to diversify its customer mix. In 2007, Amazon successfully launched the Kindle, its $79 e-book reader, which offered users more than one million reasonably priced books and newspapers easily accessed on its handheld device. Competitor Apple, Inc., then introduced the iPad, the first tablet computer, in January 2010, sparking further development of mobile e-readers. E-book sales took off immediately, increasing by more than 100%, according to the Association of American Publishers. Eager to compete in a market for which it was uniquely positioned, Amazon quickly developed its own low-cost tablet, the Kindle Fire, an Android-based tablet with a color touchscreen priced at $199, more than $300 lower than the iPad, sacrificing profit margins in search of sales volume and market-share gains. Other tech giants such as RIMM and HP were unable to compete with the iPad. Only the Sony Nook, the Amazon Kindle and Kindle Fire, and the Samsung Galaxy and Series 7 tablets challenged Apple's consistent 60% of market share. Ultimately, however, Amazon's huge growth derived not simply from the sale of Kindle hardware and the growth of e-book sales, but from its diversification and the continual expansion of the easy website access created by mobile devices.

By 2010, 43% of Amazon net sales were from media, including books, music, DVDs/video products, magazine subscriptions, digital downloads, and video games. More than half of all Amazon sales came from computers, mobile devices including the Kindle, Kindle Fire, and Kindle Touch, and other electronics, as well as general merchandise from home and garden supplies to groceries, apparel, jewelry, health and beauty products, sports and outdoor equipment, tools, and auto and industrial supplies.

Amazon also offered its own credit card, a form of co-branding that benefited all parties: Amazon, the credit card company (Chase Bank), and the consumer. Amazon benefited because it received money from the credit card company both directly from Amazon purchases and indirectly from fees generated from non-Amazon purchases. In addition, Amazon benefited from the company loyalty generated by having its own credit card the consumer sees and uses every day. The credit card company gained from Amazon's high visibility, increasing its potential customer base and transactions. And the consumer earned credit toward gift certificates with each use of the card.

Partnerships

Amazon leveraged its expertise in online order taking and order fulfillment and developed partnerships with many retailers whose websites it hosted and managed, including (currently or in the past) Target, Sears Canada, Bebe Stores, Timex Corporation, and Marks & Spencer. Amazon offered services comparable to those it offered customers on its own websites, thus freeing those retailers to focus on the non-website, non-technological aspects of their operations.[8]

In addition, Amazon Marketplace allowed independent retailers and third-party sellers to sell their products on Amazon by placing links on their websites to Amazon.com or to specific Amazon products. Amazon was "not the seller of record in these transactions, but instead earn[ed] fixed fees, revenue share fees, per-unit activity fees, or some combination thereof."[9] Linking to Amazon created visibility for these retailers and individual sellers, adding value to their websites, increasing their sales, and enabling them to take advantage of Amazon's convenience and fast delivery. Sellers shipped their products to an Amazon warehouse or fulfillment center, where the company stored it for a fee, and when an order was placed, shipped out the product on the seller's behalf. This form of affiliate marketing came at nearly no cost to Amazon. Affiliates used straight text links leading directly to a product page and they also offered a range of dynamic banners that featured different content.

Web Services

As a major tech player, Amazon developed a number of web services, including ecommerce, database, payment and billing, web traffic, and computing. These web services provided access to technology infrastructure that developers were able to utilize to enable various types of virtual businesses. The web services (many of which were free) created a reliable, scalable, and inexpensive computing platform that revolutionized the online presence of small businesses. For instance, Amazon's e-commerce Fulfillment By Amazon (FBA) program allowed merchants to direct inventory to Amazon's fulfillment centers; after products were purchased, Amazon packed and shipped. This freed merchants from a complex ordering process while allowing them control over their inventory. Amazon's Fulfillment Web Service (FWS) added to FBA's program. FWS let retailers embed FBA capabilities straight into their own sites, vastly enhancing their business capabilities.

In 2012, Amazon announced a cloud storage solution (Amazon Glacier) from Amazon Web Services (AWS), a low-cost solution for data archiving, backups, and other long-term storage projects where data not accessed frequently could be retained for future reference. Companies often incurred significant costs for data archiving in anticipation of growing backup demand, which led to under-utilized capacity and wasted money. With Amazon Glacier, companies were able to keep costs in line with actual usage, so managers could know the exact cost of their storage systems at all times. With Amazon Glacier, Amazon continued to dominate the space of cold storage, which had first come into prominence in 2009, amidst competitors such as Rackspace (RAX) and Microsoft (MSFT) offering their own solutions.

By 2012, Amazon Web Services were a crucial facet of Amazon's profit base, and Amazon was one of the lead players in the fast-growing retail ecommerce market. Seeing huge growth potential, Amazon made the decision to expand Amazon Web Services (AWS) internationally and invested heavily in technology infrastructure to support the rapid growth in AWS. Though its investments in ecommerce threatened to suppress its near-term margin growth, Amazon expected to benefit in the long term, given the significant growth potential in domestic and, even more so, in international ecommerce.

Amazon's Acquisition of Zappos, Quidsi, Living Social, and Lovefilm

On July 22, 2009, Amazon acquired Zappos, the online shoe and clothing retailer, for $1.2 billion. At that time, Zappos was reporting over $1 billion in annual sales without any marketing or advertising. According to founder Tony Hsieh, the secret to Zappos' success was superior customer service, from its 365-day return guarantee to the company tours with which it regaled visitors, picking them up at the airport, then returning them to the airport afterward. Zappos' employees were also very well treated, earning it a place at the top of the list of the "best companies to work for." Tony Hsieh felt that Amazon was the perfect partner to fuel Zappo's sales growth going forward.

On November 8, 2010, Amazon announced the acquisition of Quidsi, the parent company of Diapers.com, an online baby care specialty site, and Soap.com, an online site for everyday essentials. Amazon paid $500 million in cash, and assumed $45 million in debt and other obligations. As Jeff Bezos explained, "This acquisition brings together two companies who are committed to providing great prices and fast delivery to parents, making one of the chores of being a parent a little easier and less expensive."[12]

On December 2, 2010, Amazon announced that it had invested $175 million in Groupon competitor LivingSocial, a site whose up-to-the-minute research offered users immediate access to the hottest restaurants, shops, activities, and services in a given area, while saving them 50% to 70% through special site deals.

On January 20, 2011, Amazon acquired Lovefilm for £200 million, a 1.6-million-subscriber-strong European Web-based DVD rental service based in London. Lovefilm had followed Netflix's business model, offering unlimited DVD rentals by mail for a monthly subscription fee of £9.99, but planned to challenge Netflix and expand its digital media business by entering the live-streaming subscription business.

Competitors

Competition was fierce for Amazon on all fronts, from catalogue and mail order houses to retail stores from book, music, and video stores to retailers of electronics, home furnishings, auto parts, and sporting goods. Amazon's Kindle contended with Apple's iPad, among many lesser competitors. And Amazon's competitors in the service sector included other e-commerce and Web service providers. The company faced direct competition from companies such as eBay, Apple, Barnes & Noble, Overstock.com, MediaBay, Priceline.com, PCMall.com, and RedEnvelope.com. Amazon had to compete with companies that provided their own products or services, sites that sold or distributed digital content such as iTunes and Netflix, and media companies such as *The New York Times*. Many of the company's competitors had greater resources (eBay), longer histories (Barnes & Noble), more customers (Apple), or greater brand recognition (iTunes).

The companies offering the most direct threat to Amazon were eBay and Metro AG. Pierre Omidyar founded eBay in 1995, a website that connected individual buyers and sellers, including small businesses to buy and sell virtually anything. In 2010, the total value of goods sold on eBay was $62 billion, making eBay the world's largest online marketplace, serving 39 markets with more than 97 million active users worldwide.[10] eBay and Amazon subscribed to similar growth strategies: each acquired a broad spectrum of companies. Over the 15 years from 1995–2010 eBay acquired PayPal, Shopping.com, StubHub, and Bill Me Later, which have brought new e-commerce efficiencies to eBay.

Metro AG, headquartered in Dusseldorf, Germany, one of the world's leading international retail and wholesale companies, was formed through the merger of retail companies Asko Deutsche Kaufhaus AG, Kaufhof Holding AG and Deutsche SB-Kauf AG. In 2010, the total value of goods sold by Metro AG was €67 billion.[11] Serving 33 countries, Metro AG offered a comprehensive range of products and services designed to meet the specific shopping needs of private and professional customers. Metro AG, like Amazon, focused on customer orientation, efficiency, sustainability, and innovation.

Amazon had to be vigilant, negotiating more favorable terms from suppliers, adopting more aggressive pricing and devoting more resources to technology, infrastructure, fulfillment, and marketing. To maintain competitiveness, Amazon also strengthened its edge by entering into alliances with other businesses (i.e., Amazon Marketplace). Nevertheless, growing competition from global and domestic players continually threatened to erode Amazon's desired share of the market. Across the industries in which it competed, however, Amazon fought to maintain its edge based on its core principles of "selection, price, availability, convenience, information, discovery, brand recognition, personalized services, accessibility, customer service, reliability, speed of fulfillment, ease of use, and ability to adapt to changing conditions, as well as . . . customers' overall experience and trust."[12]

Frustration-Free Packaging

To stay current, Amazon took the initiative to reduce its carbon footprint by implementing a "Frustration Free Packaging" program. Recyclable Frustration Free Packaging came without excess packaging materials such as hard plastic enclosures or wire twists and was designed to be opened by hand without a scissors or a knife. Amazon then went one further and worked with the original manufacturers to package products in Frustration Free Packaging right off the assembly line, further reducing the use of plastic and paper. Units shipped that utilized Frustration Free Packaging has increased very rapidly, from 1.3 million in 2009 to 4.0 million in 2010[13]. Amazon also utilized software to determine the right size box for any product the company shipped, achieving a dramatic reduction in the number of packages shipped in oversized boxes and significantly reducing waste.

EXHIBIT 1A
Income Statement

Income Statement Currency in (Millions of U.S. Dollars) as of:	Dec 31 2008	Dec 31 2009	Dec 31 2010	Dec 31 2011
Revenues	19,166.0	24,509.0	34,204.0	48,077.0
Total Revenues	**19,166.0**	**24,509.0**	**34,204.0**	**48,077.0**
Cost of Goods Sold	14,896.0	18,978.0	26,561.0	37,288.0
Gross Profit	**4,270.0**	**5,531.0**	**7,643.0**	**10,789.0**
Selling, General, & Admin Expenses, Total	2,419.0	3,060.0	4,397.0	6,864.0
R&D Expenses	1,033.0	1,240.0	1,734.0	2,909.0
Other Operating Expenses	29.0	51.0	106.0	154.0
Other Operating Expenses, Total	**3,481.0**	**4,351.0**	**6,237.0**	**9,927.0**
Operating Income	**789.0**	**1,180.0**	**1,406.0**	**862.0**
Interest Expense	–71.0	–34.0	–39.0	–65.0
Interest and Investment Income	83.0	37.0	51.0	61.0
Net Interest Expense	**12.0**	**3.0**	**12.0**	**–4.0**
Income (Loss) on Equity Investments	–9.0	–6.0	7.0	–12.0
Currency Exchange Gains (Loss)	23.0	26.0	75.0	64.0
Other Non-Operating Income (Expenses)	22.0	–1.0	3.0	8.0
Ebt, Excluding Unusual Items	**837.0**	**1,202.0**	**1,503.0**	**918.0**
Gain (Loss) on Sale of Investments	2.0	4.0	1.0	4.0
Gain (Loss) on Sale of Assets	53.0	—	—	—
Other Unusual Items, Total	—	-51.0	—	—
Legal Settlements	—	-51.0	—	—
Ebt, Including Unusual Items	**892.0**	**1,155.0**	**1,504.0**	**922.0**
Income Tax Expense	247.0	253.0	352.0	291.0
Earnings from Continuing Operations	645.0	902.0	1,152.0	631.0
Net Income	**645.0**	**902.0**	**1,152.0**	**631.0**
Net Income to Common Including Extra Items	**645.0**	**902.0**	**1,152.0**	**631.0**
Net Income to Common Excluding Extra Items	**645.0**	**902.0**	**1,152.0**	**631.0**
Report Data Issue				

Financial Operations

Amazon sales doubled from 2009 to 2011, growing from $24,509 million (2009) to $48,077 million (2011) (see **Exhibits 1a** and **1b**), growth attributable especially to increased sales in electronics and other general merchandise, and the adoption of a new accounting standard update, reduced prices (including free shipping offers), increased in-stock inventory availability, and the impact of the acquisition of Zappos in 2009.[14]

Amazon's annual net income for 2009, 2010, and 2011 were $902 million, $1,152 million, and $645 million, respectively. The significant increase from 2009 to 2010 was due in large part to aggressive net sales growth and a large portion of its expenses and investments being fixed. Management explained that net income decreased from 2010 to 2011 as a result of: (1) selling Kindle hardware at a market price slightly below the cost of manufacture; (2) increased spending on technology infrastructure; and (3) increases in payroll expenses.

EXHIBIT 1B
Balance Sheet

Balance Sheet Currency in Millions of U.S. Dollars as of:	Dec 31 2008	Dec 31 2009	Dec 31 2010	Dec 31 2011
Assets				
Cash and Equivalents	2,769.0	3,444.0	3,777.0	5,269.0
Short-Term Investments	958.0	2,922.0	4,985.0	4,307.0
Total Cash and Short-Term Investments	**3,727.0**	**6,366.0**	**8,762.0**	**9,576.0**
Accounts Receivable	827.0	988.0	1,587.0	2,571.0
Total Receivables	**827.0**	**988.0**	**1,587.0**	**2,571.0**
Inventory	1,399.0	2,171.0	3,202.0	4,992.0
Deferred Tax Assets, Current	204.0	272.0	196.0	351.0
Total Current Assets	**6,157.0**	**9,797.0**	**13,747.0**	**17,490.0**
Gross Property Plant and Equipment	1,078.0	1,517.0	2,769.0	5,143.0
Accumulated Depreciation	−396.0	−418.0	−587.0	−1,075.0
Net Property Plant And Equipment	**682.0**	**1,099.0**	**2,182.0**	**4,068.0**
Goodwill	438.0	1,234.0	1,349.0	1,955.0
Deferred Tax Assets, Long Term	145.0	18.0	22.0	28.0
Other Intangibles	332.0	758.0	795.0	996.0
Other Long-Term Assets	560.0	907.0	702.0	741.0
Total Assets	**8,314.0**	**13,813.0**	**18,797.0**	**25,278.0**
Liabilities and Equity				
Accounts Payable	3,594.0	5,605.0	8,051.0	11,145.0
Accrued Expenses	632.0	901.0	1,357.0	2,106.0
Current Portion of Long-Term Debt/Capital Lease	59.0	—	—	395.0
Current Portion of Capital Lease Obligations	—	—	—	395.0
Unearned Revenue, Current	461.0	858.0	964.0	1,250.0
Total Current Liabilities	**4,746.0**	**7,364.0**	**10,372.0**	**14,896.0**
Long-Term Debt	409.0	109.0	184.0	255.0
Capital Leases	124.0	143.0	457.0	1,160.0
Other Non-Current Liabilities	363.0	940.0	920.0	1,210.0
Total Liabilities	**5,642.0**	**8,556.0**	**11,933.0**	**17,521.0**
Common Stock	4.0	5.0	5.0	5.0
Additional Paid in Capital	4,121.0	5,736.0	6,325.0	6,990.0
Retained Earnings	−730.0	172.0	1,324.0	1,955.0
Treasury Stock	−600.0	−600.0	−600.0	−877.0
Comprehensive Income and Other	−123.0	−56.0	−190.0	−316.0
Total Common Equity	**2,672.0**	**5,257.0**	**6,864.0**	**7,757.0**
Total Equity	**2,672.0**	**5,257.0**	**6,864.0**	**7,757.0**
Total Liabilities and Equity	**8,314.0**	**13,813.0**	**18,797.0**	**25,278.0**
Report Data Issue				

Challenges for Amazon

Amazon developed very quickly into a major player in the online retail market, yet challenges remained:

1. From its inception, Amazon was not required to collect state or local sales or use taxes, an exemption upheld by the U.S. Supreme Court. However, in 2012, states began to consider superseding the Supreme Court decision.[15] "If the states were to prevail, Amazon would be forced to collect sales and use tax, creating administrative burdens for it, and putting it at a competitive disadvantage if similar obligations are not imposed on all of its online competitors, potentially decreasing its future sales."[16] Massachusetts and other states were motivated both by the desire (to tap into new sources of revenues for their state budgets and to protect local retailers.

   In 2012, reports had it that Amazon was making deals to collect sales tax in all 50 states, so that they could open warehouses near population centers and provide same-day delivery, a major shift in its business model that would ratchet up competition with big box stores like Best Buy and Target as well as local retailers. However, there were no guarantees of the profitability of same-day delivery, given the added warehouse and delivery costs.

2. With the new social trend of "buying local," Amazon faced the threat of some regular consumers preferring to buy from their local stores rather than from an online retailer.[17]

3. Amazon always had to grapple with the threat of customer preference for instant gratification, the customer's desire to get a product immediately in the store, rather than waiting several days for the product to be shipped to them.

4. Breaches of security from outside parties trying to gain access to its information or data were a continual threat for Amazon.[18] As of 2012, Amazon had systems and processes in place that were designed to counter such attempts; however, failure to maintain these systems or processes could be detrimental to the operations of the company.

5. As more media products were sold in digital formats, Amazon's relatively low-cost physical warehouses and distribution capabilities no longer provided the same competitive advantages. In addition, Amazon had felt that its worldwide free shipping offers and Amazon Prime were effective worldwide marketing tools, and intended to offer them indefinitely, yet it began to suffer from soaring shipping expenses cutting into profits. In quarter three of 2011, Amazon's shipping fees generated $360 million in revenue, which was dwarfed by $918 million in shipping expenses.

6. Amazon had to contend with absorbing losses from its unsuccessful ventures such as its A9 search engine, Amazon Auctions, and Unbox, Amazon's original video-on-demand service.

7. Recent hires from Microsoft, Robert Williams, former senior program manager, and Brandon Watson, head of Windows Phone development prompted speculation that Amazon was developing a smartphone, possibly a Kindle-branded device. Bloomberg reported that Amazon had gone so far as to strike a manufacturing deal with Foxconn, the controversial Taiwanese company responsible for assembling Apple's iPhone and Google Android devices. Amazon has not commented on the reports. A smartphone would have given Amazon another mobile device to sell, but some analysts felt it wouldn't have made sense for Amazon to enter into the already crowded smartphone arena. "Since tablets skew more heavily toward media consumption than smartphones, they are a natural fit for Amazon's commerce and media platform," said Baird & Co. analyst Colin Sebastian, in a research note. "In contrast, smartphones require specialized

native apps (e.g., maps, voice, search, e-mail) that would be costly for Amazon to replicate." Sebastian also noted that hardware is a low-margin business. Amazon's Kindle Fire sold for $199, a price that some analysts believed was below cost, suggesting Amazon hoped the Kindle Fire would more than pay for itself by boosting sales of e-books and other digital content. Thus, by 2012 Amazon had proved itself as a retail giant, yet as with any vibrant company, faced continual challenges, particularly regarding the overarching questions of whether to spend its money developing media products such as the Kindle Smartphone, or to stick with its strengths as an online retailer, perhaps acquiring more holdings such as Zappos, and pushing for same-day delivery despite the added cost to compete with other online retailers, and with the big box stores as well.

In 2012, Amazon was at a crossroads. It needed to decide if it should invest in the infrastructure for same-day delivery, and take on local retailers, or invest in high-technology and compete at a deeper level with Sony, Apple, and Samsung.

REFERENCES

Alexa.com. Amazon.com. 2011. *http://www.alexa.com/siteinfo/ amazon.com*

Amazon.com. 2005 Annual Report. April 2006.

Amazon.com. 2007 Annual Report. April 2008.

Amazon.com. 2008 Annual Report. April 2009.

Amazon.com. 2009 Annual Report. April 2010.

Amazon.com. 2010 Annual Report. April 2011.

Amazon.com. 2011 Corporate Governance: A Message to Shareowners. 2011. *http://phx.corporate-ir.net/phoenix .zhtml?c=97664&p=irol-govHighlights*

Amazon.com. Amazon Leadership Principles. 2011. *http:// www.amazon.com/Values-Careers-Homepage/b?ie=UT F8&node=239365011*

Amazon.com. Locations. 2011. *http://www.amazon.com/ Locations-Careers/b?ie=UTF8&node=239366011*

Amazon.com. Amazon Certified Frusturation-Free Packaging FAQ. (2011). *http://www.amazon.com/gp/help/customer/ display.html?nodeId=200285450*

Amazon.com. Amazon Annual Meeting of Shareholders Presentation (10Q). June 2011. *http://phx.corporate-ir.net/ phoenix.zhtml?c=97664&p=irol-presentations*

Amazon.com. Q3 2011 Amazon.com Inc Earnings Conference Call. Seattle, WA, USA. 2011.

Amazon.com. Company Facts. 2011. Dec. 2011. *http://phx .corporate-ir.net/phoenix.zhtml?c=176060&p= irol-factSheet*

Amazon.com FAQs. 2011. Dec. 2011. *http://phx.corporate-ir.net/phoenix.zhtml?c=97664&p=irol-faq*

Amazon.com. Best Black Friday Ever for Kindle Family: Kindle Sales Increase 4X Over Last Year. Nov. 2011.

Amazon.com. Quarterly Results. *http://phx.corporate-ir.net/ phoenix.zhtml?c=97664&p=irol-reportsother*

Amazon.com. Shipping & Delivery. 2011. *http://www .amazon.com/gp/help/customer/display.html/ ref=hp_468520_tracking?nodeId=468530*

Ante, S. At Amazon, Marketing Is for Dummies. Sept. 2009. *http://www.businessweek.com/magazine/content/09_39/ b4148053513145.htm*

Bange, V. Online Security: Legal Issues. Page 10. New Media Age. Jan. 2007.

Bezos, J. Earth's Most Customer-Centric Company: Differentiating with Technology. MIT, Interviewer. Nov. 2002. *http://mitworld.mit.edu/video/1*

Bofah, Kofi. What Is the Meaning of Foreign Exchange Risk? eHow Money. *http://www.ehow.com/about_6612492_ meaning-foreign-exchange-risk_.html*

Chaffey, D. Amazon.com Case Study. *http://www.davechaffey .com/E-commerce-Internet-marketing-case-studies/ Amazon-case-study/*

CrunchBase.com. Amazon. Nov. 2010. *http://www.crunchbase .com/company/amazon*

Davidson, Paul. Consumers Lifted U.S. Economy Last Quarter. USATODAY.com. Gannett Co. Inc., 27 Oct. 2011. *http:// www.usatoday.com/money/economy/story/2011-10-27/ gdp-q3/50951374/1*

eBay Who We Are. 2011. 10 Dec. 2011. *http://www.ebayinc .com/who*

Elgin, B. Google's Crafty Star Search. UpFront. Sept. 2005.

Federal Trade Commission. About Us. 17 June 2010. *http:// www.ftc.gov/ftc/about.shtm*

Green, Steve. Employee Files lawsuit against Amazon.com. Dec. 2009. *http://www.lasvegassun.com/news/2009/dec/01/ employee-files-lawsuit-against-amazoncom-seeks-cla/*

HR Spectrum. CAHRS Partner Profile: Amazon.com. Nov–Dec 2009. *http://www.ilr.cornell.edu/cahrs/hrSpectrum/HR-Profile-Amazon.html*

Jeffries Group, Inc. Amazon.com: Undergoing ST Pain for LT Gains. 2011.

Kucera, D. Amazon Profit Plunges After New Products Increase Expenses; Shares Tumble. October 2011. *http://www .bloomberg.com/news/2011-10-25/amazon-profit-plunges-after-new-products-increase-expenses-shares-tumble.html*

Layton, J. How Amazon Works. Retrieved from How Stuff Works. *http://money.howstuffworks.com/amazon3.htm*

Legislation.gov.uk. Data Protection Act 1998. *http://www .legislation.gov.uk/ukpga/1998/29/contents*

MarketingPlan.MarketingStrategiesofAmazon.com.*http://www
.marketingplan.net/amazon-com-marketing-strategies/*

Martinez, J. Amazon.com Net Sales, Marketing Expenses
Up. July 2011. *http://www.dmnews.com/amazoncom-
net-sales-marketing-expenses-up/article/208437/*

Metro Group. Corporate Strategy. 2011. *http://www.metrogroup
.de/internet/site/metrogroup/node/10781/Len/index.html*

Mind Tools. PEST Analysis—Problem-Solving Training from
MindTools.com. Management Training, Leadership Training and Career Training. Mind Tools Ltd. 12 Dec. 2011.
http://www.mindtools.com/pages/article/newTMC_09.htm

Morningstar Equity Research. Amazon Is Uniquely Positioned
to Remain a Disruptive Force to the traditional retail channel for years to come. Morningstar Equity Research. 2011.

Morningstar Equity Research. Amazon.com Inc Stock Report.
2011.

Morningstar Equity Research. Amazon's Kindle Fire Poised
to Be Disruptive Force in Digital. 2011.

The Office of Fair Trading. The Office of Fair Trading. Web.
12 Dec. 2011. *http://www.oft.gov.uk/*

Rao, Leena. Amazon has Opened 15 Fulfillment Centers in
2011. July 2011. *http://techcrunch.com/2011/07/26/
amazon-has-opened-15-fulfillment-centers-in-2011-will-
build-a-few-more-by-end-of-the-year/*

Simmonds, Paul. Amazon Strategic Plan. *Scribd.* Web.
12 Dec. 2011. *http://www.scribd.com/doc/24854038/
Amazon-Strategic-Plan#*

Standard & Poor's Capital IQ. Amazon.com Inc. Products.

Steinberg, B. For Amazon, a Focus on the New Helps Push
Sales of the Old. Advertising Age. Nov. 2011. *http://
adage.com/article/special-report-marketer-alist/
marketing-a-list-amazon/230825/*

Supply Chain Digest. Logistics News: Amazon.com in Hot
Corner after Reports of Sweltering DC's.2011, "Urgently"
Buys $2.4 Million in Air Conditioners. Sept. 2011. *http://
www.scdigest.com/ontarget/11-09-26-1.php?cid=4995*

Tozzi, John. To Beat Recession, Indies Launch Buy-Local
Push. Businessweek. Bloomberg L.P., February 2009.
*http://www.businessweek.com/smallbiz/content/feb2009/
sb20090226_752622.htm*

Wikipedia, the Free Encyclopedia. Great Firewall of
China. 12 Dec. 2011. *http://en.wikipedia.org/wiki/
Golden_Shield_Project*

Yahoo.com. Amazon.com Historical Prices. 2011. *http://
finance.yahoo.com/q/hp?s=AMZN+Historical+Prices*

Yarow, J. Here's How Much a Unique Visitor Is Worth.
Jan. 2011. *http://articles.businessinsider.com/2011-01-05
/tech/30039682_1_facebook-visitor-social-networking*

NOTES

1. Chaffey, D. Amazon.com Case Study. http://www.davechaffey
.com/E-commerce-Internet-marketing-case-studies/
Amazon-case-study/

2. Mind Tools. PEST Analysis – Problem-Solving Training from
MindTools.com. Management Training, Leadership Training
and Career Training. Mind Tools Ltd. 12 Dec. 2011. http://www
.mindtools.com/pages/article/newTMC_09.htm

3. Chaffey, D. Amazon.com Case Study. http://www.davechaffey
.com/E-commerce-Internet-marketing-case-studies/
Amazon-case-study/

4. Marketing Plan. Marketing Strategies of Amazon.com. http://
www.marketingplan.net/amazon-com-marketing-strategies/

5. Layton, J. How Amazon Works. Retrieved from How Stuff
Works. http://money.howstuffworks.com/amazon3

6. Marketing Plan. Marketing Strategies of Amazon.com. http://
www.marketingplan.net/amazon-com-marketing-strategies/

7. Amazon.com. 2010 Annual Report. April 2011.

8. Marketing Plan. Marketing Strategies of Amazon.com. http://
www.marketingplan.net/amazon-com-marketing-strategies/

9. Amazon.com. 2010 Annual Report. April 2011.

10. eBay Who We Are. 2011. 10 December 2011 http://www.ebayinc
.com/who

11. Metro Group. Corporate Srategy. 2011. http://www.metrogroup
.de/internet/site/metrogroup/node/10781/Len/index.html

12. AMAZON.COM, INC., FORM 10-K, For the Fiscal Year
Ended December 31, 2006, page 6. http://www.sec.gov/
Archives/edgar/data/1018724/000119312507034081/d10k.htm

13. Amazon.com. Amazon Annual Meeting of Shareholders Presentation (10Q). June 2011. http://phx.corporate-ir.net/phoenix
.zhtml?c=97664&p=irol-presentations

14. Amazon.com. 2010 Annual Report. April 2011.

15. Amazon.com. 2010 Annual Report. Page 13–14. April 2011.

16. Amazon.com. 2010 Annual Report. Page 14. April 2011.

17. Tozzi, John. To Beat Recession, Indies Launch Buy-Local
Push. *Bloomberg's Businessweek.* Bloomberg L.P., February
2009.http://www.businessweek.com/smallbiz/content/feb2009/
sb20090226_752622.htm

18. Amazon.com. 2010 Annual Report. Page 15. April 2011.

CASE 10

Blue Nile, Inc.

"STUCK IN THE MIDDLE" OF THE DIAMOND ENGAGEMENT RING MARKET

Alan N. Hoffman
Bentley University

Built on the premise of making engagement ring selection simpler, Blue Nile, Inc. (formerly known as Internet Diamonds, Inc.) has developed into the largest online retailer of diamond engagement rings. Unlike traditional jewelry retailers, Blue Nile operates completely store-front-free, without in-person consultation services. The business conducts all sales online or by phone and sales include both engagement (70%) and non-engagement (30%) categories.[1] Blue Nile focuses on perfecting its online shopping experience by providing useful guidance and education, extraordinary jewelry, at competitive prices.

Blue Nile's vision is to educate its customer base so that customers can make an informed, confident decision no matter what event they are celebrating.[2] It wants to make the entire diamond-buying process easy and hassle-free.[3] In addition, an important part of Blue Nile's vision, as CEO Diane Irvine said in a recent webinar with Kaihan Krippendorf, is for the company to be seen as the "smart" way to buy diamonds, while saving 20%–40% more than one would in the typical jewelry store. Blue Nile is working to become "the Tiffany for the next generation."[4]

Company Background

Blue Nile started in Seattle, Washington, in 1999, when Mark Vadon, the founder of the company, decided to act upon his and his friends' dissatisfaction with their experience in searching for an engagement ring. As a result, to battle their concerns, he created a company that offered customers education, guidance, quality, and value, allowing customers to shop with confidence.[5]

Blue Nile operates its business through its three websites: www.bluenile.com, www.bluenile.co.uk, and www.bluenile.ca. Customers from the UK and all the member states of the European Union are served by Blue Nile's subsidiary, Blue Nile Worldwide, through the

The author would like to thank Abdullah Al-Hadlaq, Rashid Alhamer, Chris Harbert, Sarah Martin, Adnan Rawji, and Will Hoffman for their research. Please address all correspondence to Dr. Alan N. Hoffman, Dept. of Management, Bentley University, 175 Forest Street, Waltham, MA 02452; ahoffman@bentley.edu. Printed by permission of Dr. Alan N. Hoffman.

UK website. Canadian customers are served through the Canadian website, and U.S. customers, along with 14 additional countries worldwide, are directed to the primary website. In addition, Blue Nile owns another subsidiary in Dublin, Ireland, named Blue Nile Jewelry, Ltd, which acts as a customer service and fulfillment center.

Furthermore, in order to enhance and facilitate the purchasing process to serve both local and foreign demand, Blue Nile has given customers the choice to purchase their products in 22 foreign currencies, as well as in the U.S. dollar.[6] As of the beginning of 2010, the company has offered sales to customers in over 40 countries worldwide.[7]

Not being built as a traditional brick-and-mortar jewelry company, Blue Nile uses its websites to exhibit its fine jewelry offerings, which include diamond, gold, gemstone, platinum, and sterling silver, as well as rings, earrings, pendants, wedding bands, bracelets, necklaces, and watches. Blue Nile's revolutionary and innovative ways of restructuring industry standards did not just stop with its lack of a physical presence. The company offers a "Diamond Search" tool that lets customers examine their entire directory of diamonds to choose the right one in seconds. It also offers the popular "Build Your Own" tool that helps customers customize their own diamond jewelry and then view it on the computer before executing the order. Moreover, Blue Nile offers customers financing options, insurance for the jewelry, a 30-day return policy and free shipping.[8]

Diamond sales represent the majority of Blue Nile's business and revenues. Diamonds, which are certified for high quality by an "independent diamond grading lab,"[9] are differentiated based on "shape, cut, color, clarity and carat weight."[10] Blue Nile uses a just-in-time ordering system from its suppliers, which is initiated once a diamond purchase is made on the website, eliminating the burden and the costs of keeping high-ticket items in inventory. However, the company does keep in inventory rings, earrings, and pendants that it uses as a base to attach the diamond to, in order to be able to customize diamond jewelry to customer requirements. In order to succeed in this industry, Blue Nile maintains a strong relationship with over 40 suppliers.

After its IPO in 2004, Blue Nile shares traded on the NASDAQ (ticker NILE). The company has been awarded the Circle of Excellence Platinum Award, which customers use to rank the best online company in customer service, by Bizrate.com since 2002. Being the only jeweler to be recognized for this excellence is a true testament to Blue Nile's solid business.[11]

Strategic Direction

Blue Nile is in the business of offering "high-quality diamonds and fine jewelry at outstanding prices."[12] It is a publicly traded company, making its ultimate business objective to achieve the highest return possible for its shareholders. In order to do this, Blue Nile focuses on the following:

1. Cause disruption in the diamond industry by creating a "two-horned dilemma." According to Kaihan Krippendorff, Blue Nile has been able to effectively put its competitors in a position where if they try to compete with Blue Nile directly, they compromise an area of their own business (one edge of the horn), and if they do not choose to compete with Blue Nile, they slowly lose market share and competitive positioning (the other edge of the horn). Blue Nile's decision to offer the highest-quality diamonds in spite of it operating in an online environment where it could easily position itself purely as a "discounter" has been key to creating this dilemma. Competitors with brick-and-mortar locations are then left to decide whether they should sell their product online at a lower cost than a customer would find in a store in order to compete (knowing that this could negatively impact the

brick-and-mortar location) or not go head to head with Blue Nile online.[13] This dilemma helps Blue Nile keep its strong position as the largest online jewelry retailer.

2. Keep the consumer in mind and establish relationships with customers during a very important time in their lives. The idea for Blue Nile was born during an unpleasant shopping experience. The company remains focused on perfecting its user experience by investing in online education tools and resources within its website to help customers make educated decisions.[14] Because Blue Nile's customers cannot view the diamonds in person before a purchase, it provides them with grading reports on their diamonds from two independent diamond graders (GIA or AGSL) and a 30-day return policy.

3. Capture market share and emerge after the recession in a strong competitive position. Some competitors have pulled back during the recession by closing locations, while others have closed their doors all together.[15] Blue Nile has been investing in its website and is working to aggressively grow its market share.[16]

The Jewelry Industry

It is estimated that 2010 U.S. jewelry sales finished at US$49.3 billion for the year, a 2.6% growth over 2009.[17] According to First Research.com, the U.S. retail jewelry industry is considered to be fragmented, as "the top 50 jewelry chains generate less than half of (total) revenue" and there are 28,800 specialty stores that generate around US$30 billion in revenue. Diamond jewelry and loose diamonds account for approximately 45% of total jewelry store sales.[18]

A closer look at this industry reveals that 17.2% of total U.S. jewelry sales took place in non-store retailers. Still though, retail locations continue to be the primary source of jewelry sales, accounting for 50% of total U.S. jewelry sales in 2009 in spite of sales decreasing by 7.8% between 2007 and 2009.[19]

According to Compete.com, Blue Nile controls 4.3%[20] of Internet jewelry sales, and as of 2009 Blue Nile had about 4% of the engagement ring business in the United States,[21] which is 50% of the American online engagement jewelry market.[22]

Blue Nile's Competitors

Blue Nile's many competitors include various different retail outlets like department stores, major jewelry store chains, independently owned jewelry stores, online retailers, catalogue retailers, television shopping retailers, discount superstores, and, lastly, wholesale clubs. Many local jewelers have great relations with their clientele in smaller communities, which poses a challenge for Blue Nile to achieve greater market share. Online retailers include Amazon, Overstock.com, and Bidz.com, which are well-known for their discounting, thus creating tremendous competition for Blue Nile. Most major firms who specialize in jewelry have their own online presence as well, such as Zales, Signet, Tiffany, and Helzberg.

DeBeers

DeBeers, which owns 40% of the world's diamond supply,[23] is establishing its presence online as a trusted advisor, just as Blue Nile has done. Upon visiting DeBeers website, it is clear that Blue Nile's consultative approach online has made an impression on DeBeers, as the website has an "Advice" section under Bridal rings and an "Art of Diamond Jewelry" section that both educates and serves as a source of confidence of quality.

Tiffany & Co.

Tiffany & Co., one of the best-known luxury brand names, had revenues in 2010 of US$2.9 billion, compared to Blue Nile's US$302 million.[24] Tiffany & Co. continues to stand out in the jewelry sector by opening stores in urban America and has shown to be a success because many consumers are willing to pay extra for a well-known brand name. Tiffany also offers great service at its stores through product information. Lastly, owning a piece of jewelry from Tiffany's—and receiving the iconic blue box—has an air of prestige all its own that Blue Nile cannot replicate.[25] In spite of the value associated with the Tiffany name, due to its lean business model, Blue Nile's return on capital is three to four times better than Tiffany's.[26]

Blue Nile's many powerful competitors require the business to compete through differentiation, and so Blue Nile gains an advantage over its competition through its unique operating structure. Its strategy, distribution channel, and supply chain help to keep Blue Nile in the market because it also creates barriers to entry. Some competitive advantages include its partnership with Bill Me Later and its direct contracts with major diamond suppliers. Blue Nile partners with Bill Me Later[27] in order to offer financing for fine jewelry and diamond purchases. Blue Nile also has direct contracts with major diamond suppliers, which in turn allow the company to sell stones online at lower prices than brick-and-mortar locations because it has lower overhead costs and fewer distribution interceptions.

Guild Jewelers

It is difficult to find a competitor that can be compared directly to Blue Nile because of the unique way in which the business operates. While Guild Jewelers are not necessarily a united force that Blue Nile must respond to, Blue Nile CEO Diane Irvine considers Guild Jewelers to be the company's major competitor because Guild has local relationships with potential customers that are difficult for Blue Nile to establish online.[28]

Barriers to Entry/Imitation

Barriers to entry in the jewelry industry are high because the following are needed: capital, strong supplier relationships, and reputation. With regard to capital, traditional jewelry stores must fund their brick-and-mortar locations, onsite inventory, and store labor. Supplier relationships with diamond cutters and distributors are also key, and as seen with Blue Nile, they can greatly impact the profitability of a given retailer. Finally, due to the expense associated with jewelry purchases, Blue Nile's "average ticket" is US$2,000.[29] This helps Blue Nile because customers are looking for a trusted source with a strong reputation.

In regard to imitation, Blue Nile leverages a few unique systems and services that are hard for the competition to imitate. First, Blue Nile's "build your own" functionality online differentiates it from competitors by allowing the customer to personally create their ideal diamond ring, earring, pendant, multiple stone rings, and/or multiple stone pendants. The consumer also has access to an interactive search function, which references an inventory of 50,000 diamonds, including signature diamonds that are hand-selected and cut with extreme precision.[30]

Second, Blue Nile has its own customer service team of diamond and jewelry consultants that offer suggestions and assist customers with their purchases. This online interactive customer service approach creates a barrier to entry as the information technology platform for these functions is complex.

Lastly, Blue Nile also offers exclusive colored diamonds, which include rare diamonds that are red and pink.[31] It has a more diversified product range than its competitors because it does not have to hold inventory in stock.

The threat of new entrants is always a concern, but Blue Nile has been successful thus far at staying ahead of new entrants and has established a reputation as a quality, reputable online service.

One of the most significant resources for jewelers is diamonds, and with DeBeers owning 40% of the world's jewelry supply, diamonds are considered scarce and unique. Large diamond suppliers like DeBeers are not as powerful as they were once were—DeBeers at one time sold 80% of the world's diamonds[32]—but their presence is still felt. In addition, diamonds are generally obtained in politically unstable regions of the world, like Africa, and companies must be aware of the risk of obtaining conflict diamonds. The diamond trade is complex with regard to politics and legal issues, as the majority of diamond mines exist in underdeveloped countries, where corruption is prevalent and the rule of law is not easily enforced. Many of the diamond mines are located in African countries such as Botswana, which currently produces 27% of the global diamond supply.[33] However, recent global initiatives, including the Clean Diamond Trade Act of 2003, and the Kimberly Process Certification Scheme of 2002, have made significant impacts on violence and illegal trade in the last decade.[34]

The lack of legal and political stability in many of the diamond source countries represents a threat to Blue Nile and the industry as a whole. With unstable changes in leadership and power, threats to the global supply chain of a valuable commodity are possible, and perhaps even likely to occur. The takeover of diamond mines by militia groups, government claims of eminent domain, diamond smuggling, and obsolescing contract negotiations with foreign governments all have a potential deleterious impact on the jewelry industry. Finally, given the increased valuation of gold in recent years, this jewelry material has become harder to obtain.

Social and Demographic Trends

There are a number of social and demographic trends that offer opportunities for Blue Nile. First, the average age of first-time newlyweds is increasing in the United States, currently 28[35] for men and 26[36] for women.

A *USA TODAY* analysis of the Census figures shows that just 23.5% of men and 31.5% of women ages 20–29 were married in 2006. (The analysis excludes those who are married but separated.) Both the number and percentage of those in their 20s fell from 2000, when 31.5% of men and 39.5% of women were married.[37]

Higher marrying ages tend to translate into greater spending power for marriage-related items, such as engagement rings.

Next, people nowadays are more receptive to handheld technologies and apps. These on-the-go technologies are an opportunity for Blue Nile to reach busy customers who do not have time to drop by a jewelry store to research their product choices and make a purchase. Mobile sites and apps allow a customer with a Smartphone to make purchases on their own schedule, without adhering to a brick-and-mortar schedule. As this generation ages and people become comfortable with technology, Blue Nile will have more segments to cater to and a broader reach. With online purchases becoming more of a cultural norm, with less associated negative stigma, and as higher percentages of the global population gains reliable access to the Internet, Blue Nile is poised to capitalize on its Web-only strategy.

Finally, with historical events like the marriage of Prince William and Kate Middleton dominating the media, Blue Nile and other jewelry retailers reap the benefits of Kate's sapphire ring being displayed and/or mentioned in countless media venues throughout the world.

The jewelers could not have planned such a great publicity stunt, and now have the opportunity to ride the wave for a while.

One social threat Blue Nile faces is tied to issues of Internet fraud and online security in today's environment. The relatively high purchase price for quality jewelry increases the perceived risk for consumers making online purchases.

Another threat is that with each new generation, traditions (such as the purchase and giving of engagement rings) risk becoming outdated or out of fashion. While giving jewelry is highly entrenched in many cultures around the world, it is possible that potential customers in Generation Y and later may perceive lower value in this gifting tradition.

Global Opportunities

Blue Nile wants to expand internationally because it sees great potential in the global marketplace. Currently, non-U.S. sales represent 13% of the total sales at Blue Nile.[38] Blue Nile's international sales have continuously been growing. Recent numbers show that in 2010, sales figures grew by 30.4% compared to the previous year.[39] It is a high priority to grow internationally at Blue Nile. It is important for them to monitor online purchasing rates globally, and expand to those countries accordingly.

One major global threat for Blue Nile is the lack of adoption of online purchasing. Many countries have not yet advanced to American consumer habits. Developed countries are continuing to adopt this as they realize the efficiency, effectiveness, and overall convenience involved. Lack of consumer confidence for high-value online purchases may continue to follow Blue Nile as it expands internationally until it has built a reputation in each foreign country of operations, which may delay return on investment for international expansion programs.

Many consumers in developing nations do not have reliable access to the Internet. Blue Nile currently has no way to tap into the buying power of these would-be customers. Sending huge sums of money and receiving valuable goods when they clear customs is a risk many people are not willing to take, knowing its ramifications. Many countries around the world have a higher incidence of corruption, and thus one cannot be sure that the product will reach the customer safely.

Blue Nile's Finances

Net Sales have been strong each year for Blue Nile since 2006, except in 2008 when the financial crisis impacted the company's performance, as seen in **Exhibit 1**. Sales have grown by US$81.3 million since 2006, a 32% increase. Growth was most substantial in 2007 (26.9%) due to the huge increase in demand for diamond and fine jewelry products ordered through the website. International sales contributed significantly to the surge in demand in 2007, with an increase of 104.8%, due mainly to the new product offerings and the ability of UK and Canadian customers to purchase in their local currency.[40] Sales decreased by 7.5% in 2008, primarily due to the sluggish economy, which negatively impacted the popularity of luxury goods, and the increase in diamond prices worldwide.[41] In 2009, sales rebounded slightly with an increase of 2.3%, due mostly to an increase of 20% in Q4 year over year. The increase in Q4 is attributed to the boost in international sales, which represented 1.9% of the 2.3% total growth, as a result of the new website enhancements and the ability to purchase in 22 other foreign currencies.[42]

In 2010, sales returned to double-digit growth with an increase of 10.2%. Both U.S. sales and international sales grew considerably with 7.7% and 30.4%, respectively, due mainly to the improving economy, which led to increased consumer spending. Increased marketing

EXHIBIT 1
Blue Nile Net Sales
2006–2010
(In Thousands)

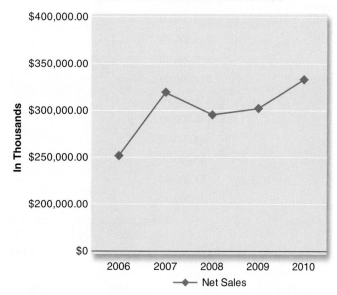

Blue Nile Annual Net Sales

Year	2006	2007	2008	2009	2010
Net Sales	$ 251,587.00	$ 319,264.00	$ 295,329.00	$ 302,134.00	$ 332,889.00
Growth		26.90%	−7.50%	2.30%	10.18%

NOTE: All data in Exhibits 1–6 come from the 2010 Blue Nile Annual Report.

focus, better brand recognition, and the favorable exchange rate of foreign currencies against the U.S. dollar contributed to the strong sales in Q4, which reached an all-time record of US$114.8 million.[43] However, although Q1, Q2, and Q4 numbers are growing annually due to events such as Valentine's Day, Mother's Day, Christmas, and New Year's, Q3 continues to present a challenge due to the lack of a special holiday or event.

Net income levels from 2006 to 2010 tracked the performance of net sales, but were more severe as seen in **Exhibits 2** and **3**. Net income increased by 33.64% in 2007, 10.06% in 2009, and 10.48% in 2010, but decreased by −33.39% in 2008. Not including the decrease in earnings during the financial meltdown, the net income numbers are considered healthy for a company that was started 12 years ago.

Gross profit has grown similarly to net sales from 2006–2010, as can be seen in **Exhibit 4**. However, the most telling difference was in year 2009, when it outpaced net sales growth with an increase of 8.91%. The growth was a result of cost savings achieved with regard to sourcing and selling products, which increased the gross profit margin from 20.2% to 21.6%, as can be seen in **Exhibit 4**. Blue Nile's increasing gross profit margin is a good sign for the company since it shows strict financial management and an emphasis on the bottom line.

Blue Nile has no long-term debt. The company only has lease obligations that it needs to pay every year. The lease obligations decreased from US$880,000 in 2007 to US$748,000 in 2010.[44] The long-term debt-to-equity ratio is effectively zero as a result, and even if we include lease obligations, it is minimal, with a value of 0.01, meaning that equity can cover the remaining debt obligations.

Cash at the company is generated mostly through ongoing operations. The increase in cash from 2009 is a result of an increase in accounts payable and the tax benefits received from the execution of stock options. Investing activities also increased the cash amount with the expiration of short-term investment maturity dates. In addition, a slight increase can be attributed to the financing activities coming from the profits of the stock option execution.[45]

EXHIBIT 2
Blue Nile Net
Income 2006–2010
(In Thousands)

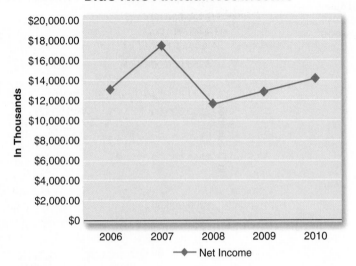

Blue Nile Annual Net Income

Year	2006	2007	2008	2009	2010
Net Income	$ 13,064.00	$ 17,459.00	$ 11,630.00	$ 12,800.00	$ 14,142.00
Growth		33.64%	−33.39%	10.06%	10.48%

EXHIBIT 3
Blue Nile Net Sales
vs. Net Income
(Percentage Change)

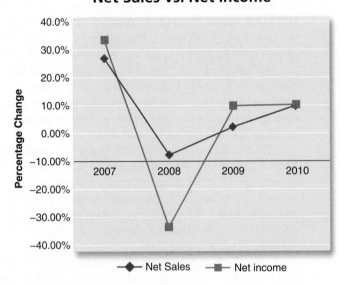

Net Sales vs. Net Income

Growth	2007	2008	2009	2010
Net Sales	26.90%	−7.50%	2.30%	10.18%
Net Income	33.64%	−33.39%	10.06%	10.48%

EXHIBIT 4
Gross Profit Margin
and Operating
Margin

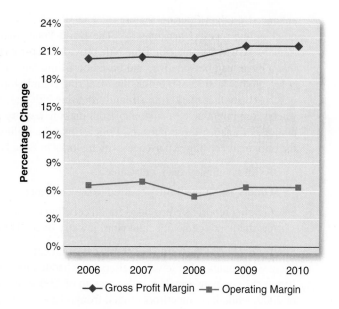

Year	2006	2007	2008	2009	2010
Gross Profit Margin	20.2%	20.4%	20.3%	21.6%	21.6%
Operating Margin	6.600%	7.00%	5.400%	6.400%	6.400%

In 2011, Blue Nile has only US$79 million in cash. In 2008, the company purchased back 1.6 million shares of stock (US$66.5 million) in order to increase consumer confidence in the stock and because Blue Nile's management team believed the stock was being undervalued.

Blue Nile acquires the majority of its inventory on a just-in-time basis. Moreover, the company is successful in growing cash because its uses for it are minimal, such as improving its website and maintaining facilities and warehouses.[46]

Marketing

Blue Nile's marketing strengths include its use of technology to enhance the customer experience, its dedication to making the diamond-buying process as easy and hassle-free as possible, and its ability to capture market share in spite of the recession.

First, in regard to its use of technology, Blue Nile has been investing in introducing and perfecting online technology that enhances its customer experience. For example, the Blue Nile App, which was launched in September of 2010, gives customers instant access to its inventory of 70,000 diamonds and allows a customer to customize a particular diamond or gem with an ideal setting "while standing at a rival's counter."[47]

In 2010, Blue Nile developed and launched its own mobile site that caters to customers wishing to shop using their iPhone, iPod touch, and Android mobile devices. Blue Nile reports that more than 20% of its shoppers are using the mobile site.

Finally, Blue Nile has done an excellent job of making its website educational, easy to navigate, and a trusted advisor for potential diamond buyers. The company completely revamped its website in 2009 in order to include larger images, better zoom functionality, and enhanced product filtering features.[48] The site also utilizes interactive search tools that few other online retailers can match.[49] The Build Your Own Ring component of the site is extremely easy to use, and fun. Blue Nile provides step-by-step guidance on a ring's components that a buyer can personalize, and based on filling out various specifications regarding shape, color, quality, and size, it builds the ideal ring right before the customer's eyes.

Next, another marketing strength for Blue Nile has been its ability to hone in on the obstacles that might deter a customer from making jewelry purchase online, and then providing assurances against those barriers. Policies like the following all work to build confidence in the online purchasing experience, which works in Blue Nile's favor:

- A 30-day money-back guarantee.[50]
- Orders are shipped fully insured to the customer.
- Grading reports are provided for all certified diamonds, as well as professional appraisals for diamond, gemstone, and pearl jewelry over $1,000.[51]

Finally, in spite of the trying economic environment, Blue Nile has been able to capture market share while many other jewelry sellers have had to close their doors. According to CEO Diane Irvine, the company saw U.S. sales growth of 23% year over year in November and December of 2009, while its competitors ranged from a 12% increase to a 12% decline in the same timeframe.[52] In trying economic times, customers have valued the 20%–40% reduced price found at Blue Nile in comparison to brick-and-mortar retailers.

Although Blue Nile has done a good job of anticipating and catering to the barriers that exist in purchasing an expensive piece of jewelry online, the fact still remains that Blue Nile operates with no storefront locations. This means that customers cannot physically touch and inspect their piece of jewelry before making a purchase. Some traditionally minded members of the jewelry market are not comfortable with this limitation and will not consider Blue Nile a viable alternative. It is also more difficult to develop a lasting, long-term relationship with a customer when the transaction lacks the face-to-face experience found at brick-and-mortar stores. Blue Nile's business is completely dependent in online or phone transactions, making it subject to the adjustment period consumers must go through in order to be comfortable with this purchasing experience.

Building on this weakness is the fact that Blue Nile's online traffic and site visits have been in decline. According to 2010 data from Compete.com, Blue Nile saw its number of unique site visitors decrease year over year in a majority of months, while one of its main competitors, Tiffany's, saw its online traffic increase. Similarly, Compete.com reports that when viewing Blue Nile's unique visitor trend between 2007 and 2009, the company has seen a 36% decrease in unique visitors.[53]

Operations and Logistics

Blue Nile aims to offer a wide range of finished and partially customizable jewelry products to online shoppers, made from ethically sourced materials, via a convenient, hassle-free experience. The company looks to leverage its sourcing power to offer exclusive jewels to exclude competition and retain high selling prices, while maximizing profitability through implementation of just-in-time manufacturing tactics to minimize inventory costs.

Blue Nile employs a flexible manufacturing strategy in its operations. The company heavily advertises the ability for people to customize their desired product—"Build Your Own Ring" is an example of how Blue Nile allows a customer to pick a diamond and an engagement ring setting, and get a unique product.[54] Blue Nile also offers a similar type of customization for earrings, pendants, and other jewelry items.

On the one hand, it seems as though the company would be utilizing an "intermittent job shop" approach. However, while the company does offer full customization through a special order service, the "customization" service is basically allowing online shoppers to pick from a predetermined list of jewels and settings. The jewels are listed in a Blue Nile database (maintained in partnership with its source providers), and the materials are prefabricated in mass production–style to minimize cost.[55]

Using the same methods, Blue Nile makes both finished goods (non-customizable products for direct sale over the Web) and customer-directed finished goods. By using the same supply chain and methods, Blue Nile is able to achieve rapid turnaround of "customized" products, adding value to the service offering.[56]

Blue Nile partners with FedEx for both shipping and returns of all of its products. By maintaining one carrier partnership, the company is able to reach economies of scale in shipping expenditures, and also take advantage of FedEx's international shipping capabilities (other carriers, such as UPS, or USPS, are more limited in their international shipping offers). Also, by partnering with FedEx, Blue Nile is able to take advantage of FedEx's best-in-class shipment tracking functions, which alleviates potential customer concerns about expensive online purchases being "lost in the mail."[57]

Although the majority of revenues for Blue Nile come from the sale of diamonds, it typically does not receive diamonds into inventory until an order is placed, following a just-in-time manufacturing strategy. Instead, Blue Nile partners with its diamond sources, many of them in an exclusive agreement, to provide up-to-date records of available diamond inventory. When a customer places an order for a particular diamond, Blue Nile in turn orders the specified diamond from its supplier, receives the stone, finishes the good, enters the product into inventory, and ships it to the customer.[58]

Financially, this puts the company in a strong position, since it does not have to maintain high inventory carrying costs for the diamonds, which can be valued at several hundred to several thousand dollars each. The company actually produces a positive cash flow of approximately 30–45 days, depending on its contract with a particular supplier.[59]

While partnering with a single distribution partner does provide economic and logistical benefits to the company, it also puts Blue Nile at some degree of risk. Although FedEx has yet to experience a strike by its employees, its rival UPS faced this situation some years ago.[60] If the same situation should occur with FedEx, Blue Nile may be hard-pressed to quickly develop new distribution channels, both domestically and abroad.

In addition, there are also risks associated with Blue Nile's just-in-time inventory approach. First, this approach requires that Blue Nile establish and maintain a direct and accurate path of visibility to its suppliers' diamond inventory. Since many of its diamond suppliers are in less developed regions of the world, this is not an insignificant feat.[61]

Second, since the diamonds are not actually in the possession of Blue Nile at the time the customer places order, it is possible that any type of geo-political disruption (natural disaster, governmental turmoil, etc.) could interrupt the flow of the customer's product, and require subsequent customer service follow up and potential product replacement.

Despite these risks, Blue Nile's success in establishing exclusive sourcing agreements with diamond suppliers and cutters has yielded significant benefits, and is one source of competitive advantage for the organization. By negotiating directly with diamond suppliers and cutters, rather than operating through wholesalers, Blue Nile is able to reduce its diamond procurement costs by more than 20%, compared to other diamond retailers.[62] It is therefore able to offer lower prices than its competition, while simultaneously achieving higher profit margins on its products. Blue Nile's exclusive contracts do offer the company opportunities to be a "sole source" for particular diamond cuts or rare colors, although many diamond retailers have also followed this trend, and each major retailer appears to have its own "exclusive" diamonds.[63]

Human Resources and Ethics

Blue Nile employs 193 full-time workers, with 26 of these full-time positions listed at the executive level (see **Exhibits 5** and **6**).[64] The company maintains employee testimonials on its website as part of its career section, with several comments from employees who have been with the organization for 10 years or more.[65] However, when looking for examples of Blue Nile employee satisfaction outside of the company's own website, the picture is not as rosy. The most common complaints pertain to employee development and retention. Unverified reports of hyper-control by senior management, instead of empowerment and distribution of responsibility to managerial staff, if true, may have a significant impact on Blue Nile's ability to attract and retain high-performance employees, and as a result, grow its business.[66] While the company has made a significant leap forward compared to other jewelry retailers, both brick-and-mortar and Internet-based, if the company focuses exclusively on technology, and not on human talent development, it has little chance to continue its recent growth trends.

While Blue Nile has a significant section of its website devoted to its policies around the ethical sourcing of its diamonds and other materials, the company does not detail any of its policies regarding the handling of its own employees. There are no statements regarding employee diversity, the cultural environment, or employee training/advancement programs. Despite listing nine senior managers listed in the company's investor relations section of its website, not one of the nine is involved in Human Resource Management.[67] This absence, taken with the company's wordage from its corporate reports, paints a picture that suggests attention to human assets is limited at Blue Nile, Inc.

Stuck in the Middle

Operating in a niche segment, Blue Nile is "stuck in the middle" of the diamond engagement ring market. It is not at the top end of the jewelry retail market with the likes of Tiffany & Co. or DeBeers. It is neither at the low end of the market, with the likes of Amazon or Over-stock.com. Blue Nile has found a strong growth market by providing high-quality jewelry at discounted prices. Unfortunately, as the company increasingly grows its market share, competitors at the high end and the low end will look to squeeze into the middle niche that Blue Nile currently dominates. Tiffany & Co. and DeBeers have already begun to infuse their online presence with aspects of Blue Nile's approach. Amazon and Overstock.com are likely to look to add higher-priced jewels to their offerings, as broad market acceptance of purchasing jewelry online increases. Michael Porter states that the middle is the worst place to be. The challenge for Blue Nile is how to move up the ladder and become a "high end" diamond retailer—not an easy task for an "online only" retailer.

EXHIBIT 5
Top Management

Harvey Kanter, *Chief Executive Officer, President and Director*

Harvey Kanter, has served as our chief executive officer, president and director since March 30, 2012. He served as the chief executive officer and president of Moosejaw Mountaineering and Backcountry Travel, Inc., a leading multi-channel retailer of premium outdoor apparel and gear, January 2009 to March 2012. From April 2003 to June 2008, Kanter served in various executive positions at Michaels Stores, Inc. ("Michaels"), a specialty retailer of arts and crafts, most recently serving as the Executive Vice President and Managing Director from March 2006 to June 2008. While at Michaels, Kanter also served as the President of Aaron Brothers, Inc., a division of Michaels, from April 2003 to March 2006. From October 1995 to March 2003, Kanter served in various management positions at Eddie Bauer, Inc. ("Eddie Bauer"), a premium outdoor retailer, including serving as the Vice President and Managing Director of Eddie Bauer Home, a division of Eddie Bauer. Prior to Eddie Bauer, Kanter held positions at several other retailers, including Sears Roebuck Company, a multi-line retailer, and Broadway Stores, Inc. (known as, Carter Hawley Hale Department Stores), a department store. Kanter holds an M.B.A from Babson College and a B.S. from Arizona State University.

Vijay Talwar, *General Manager and President of International*

Vijay Talwar has served as our General Manager and President of International since March 30, 2012. He served as our interim chief executive officer from November 2011 to March 2012. He served as our senior vice president and general manager of International from August 2010 to November 2011. From November 2010 to August 2011, he has also served as our interim chief financial officer. From November 2008 to August 2010, Mr. Talwar served as the chief executive officer of the William J. Clinton Foundation India, a global 501©(3) nongovernmental organization established to provide healthcare and sustainability programs across India and South Asia. From February 2008 to September 2008, Mr. Talwar served as the chief operating officer of EL Rothschild LLC, a venture designed to bring international luxury brands to India. From April 2007 to January 2008, Mr. Talwar served as the chief operating officer for the Central Europe, Middle East and Africa region at Nike, Inc., a designer, marketer and distributor of authentic athletic footwear, apparel, equipment and accessories worldwide. From June 2004 to April 2007, Mr. Talwar served as the senior director of strategy and finance at Nike's Global Apparel division. From December 2003 to June 2004, Mr. Talwar served as the director of strategy at Nike's Global Apparel division, and from April 2002 to December 2003, he served as a manager of the global strategic planning group at Nike. Prior to Nike, Mr. Talwar was a consultant at Bain & Company, a management consulting firm; a special projects manager and senior internal auditor at the Kellogg Company, a producer of cereal and convenience foods; and a senior tax consultant and audit assistant at Deloitte & Touche, an accounting firm. Mr. Talwar holds an M.B.A. from University of Chicago, a Master of Accountancy from Miami University and a B.A. in Accountancy from the University of Findlay.

David Binder, *Chief Financial Officer*

David Binder has served as our Chief Financial Officer since August 2011. Mr. Binder joins Blue Nile from Infospace, Inc., an online search and e-commerce company, where he has served as its Chief Financial Officer and Treasurer since January 2008. From October 2004 to December 2007, Mr. Binder was the Vice President of Finance at Infospace. From November 2001 to October 2004, Mr. Binder was the Senior Director of Business Development at Drugstore.com, Inc., an online drugstore. Prior to Drugstore, Mr. Binder served as the Director of Financial Planning and Analysis at Edge2net Inc., a VOIP telecommunications provider; the Director of Finance at HomeGrocer.com, Inc., an e-commerce retailer; and the Director of Planning, Strategy and Competitive Analysis, at AT&T Wireless, a wireless telecommunications business. Mr. Binder holds a master's degree in Economics and Finance and a B.A. degree in Economics from Brandeis University.

Dwight Gaston, *Senior Vice President*

Dwight Gaston has served as Blue Nile's Senior Vice President since September 2005. From July 2003 to March 2005, Mr. Gaston served as Vice President of Operations, and from May 1999 to July 2003, Mr. Gaston served as Blue Nile's Director of Fulfillment Operations. From June 1992 to June 1995 and from August 1997 to May 1999, Mr. Gaston was a consultant with Bain & Company, a management consulting firm. Mr. Gaston holds a B.A. in Economics from Rice University and an M.B.A. from Harvard University.

Terri Maupin, *Chief Accounting Officer*

Terri Maupin has served as Blue Nile's Chief Accounting Officer since August 2011. From July 2004 through August 2011, Ms. Maupin served as Vice President of Finance and Controller, and from October 2004 through January 2010 has served as Corporate Secretary. From September 2003 to July 2004, Ms. Maupin served as Blue Nile's Controller. From February 2001 to September 2003, Ms. Maupin served as the Staff Vice President of Finance and Controller at Alaska Air Group, Inc. From September 1994 to August 1997, Ms. Maupin served as the Manager of Financial Reporting and from September 1997 to January 2001 as the Director of Financial Reporting for Nordstrom, Inc., a fashion specialty retail company. From October 1993 to September 1994, Ms. Maupin served as Controller at Coastal Transportation Inc., a marine transportation company. From January 1987 to October 1993, Ms. Maupin served in various capacities, most recently as audit manager, with Coopers and Lybrand LLP, an accounting firm. Ms. Maupin holds a B.A. in Accounting from Western Washington University and a CPA-Inactive Certificate from the State of Washington.

(continued)

EXHIBIT 5
(Continued)

Lauren Neiswender, *General Counsel and Corporate Secretary*
Lauren Neiswender has served as the Company's General Counsel since October 2004 and has served as the Company's Corporate Secretary since February 2010. Prior to Blue Nile, Ms. Neiswender was an attorney at Wilson Sonsini Goodrich & Rosati, PC. Ms. Neiswender holds a B.A. in Political Science from Emory University and a J.D. from the University of Virginia.

Jon Sainsbury, *Vice President of Marketing*
Jon Sainsbury has served as Blue Nile's Vice President of Marketing since June 2008. From January 2007 to June 2008, Mr. Sainsbury served as Blue Nile's Director of Marketing and from September 2006 to January 2007, he served as Blue Nile's Senior Marketing Manager. From March 2006 to September 2006, Mr. Sainsbury served as Blue Nile's Search Marketing Manager and from October 2004 to March 2006, he served as Blue Nile's International Program Manager. From September 2002 to October 2004, Mr. Sainsbury served as Blue Nile's Senior Marketing Analyst. Prior to Blue Nile, Mr. Sainsbury was an associate consultant with Bain & Company, a management consulting firm. Mr. Sainsbury holds a B.A. in Physics from Pomona College.

EXHIBIT 6
Board of Directors

Mark Vadon, *Chairman of the Board*
Mark Vadon co-founded Blue Nile and has served as Chairman of the Board since its inception. From February 2008 to August 2011, Mr. Vadon served as Executive Chairman. Prior to February 2008, he served as Chief Executive Officer from its inception and served as President from inception to February 2007. From December 1992 to March 1999, Mr. Vadon was a consultant for Bain & Company, a management consulting firm. Mr. Vadon holds a B.A. in Social Studies from Harvard University and an M.B.A. from Stanford University.

Harvey Kanter, *Director*
Harvey Kanter, has served as our chief executive officer, president and director since March 30, 2012. He served as the chief executive officer and president of Moosejaw Mountaineering and Backcountry Travel, Inc., a leading multi-channel retailer of premium outdoor apparel and gear, January 2009 to March 2012. From April 2003 to June 2008, Kanter served in various executive positions at Michaels Stores, Inc. ("Michaels"), a specialty retailer of arts and crafts, most recently serving as the Executive Vice President and Managing Director from March 2006 to June 2008. While at Michaels, Kanter also served as the President of Aaron Brothers, Inc., a division of Michaels, from April 2003 to March 2006. From October 1995 to March 2003, Kanter served in various management positions at Eddie Bauer, Inc. ("Eddie Bauer"), a premium outdoor retailer, including serving as the Vice President and Managing Director of Eddie Bauer Home, a division of Eddie Bauer. Prior to Eddie Bauer, Kanter held positions at several other retailers, including Sears Roebuck Company, a multi-line retailer, and Broadway Stores, Inc. (known as, Carter Hawley Hale Department Stores), a department store. Kanter holds an M.B.A from Babson College and a B.S. from Arizona State University.

Mary Alice Taylor, *Director*
Mary Alice Taylor has served as a director since March 2000. Ms. Taylor is an independent business executive. She held a temporary assignment as Chairman and Chief Executive Officer of Webvan Group, Inc., an e-commerce company, from July 2001 to December 2001. Prior to that, she served as Chairman and Chief Executive Officer of HomeGrocer.com, an e-commerce company, from September 1999 until she completed a sale of the company to Webvan Group, Inc. in October 2000. From January 1997 to September 1999, Ms. Taylor served as Corporate Executive Vice President of Worldwide Operations and Technology for Citigroup, Inc., a financial services organization. Ms. Taylor also served as a Senior Vice President of Federal Express Corporation, a delivery services company, from September 1991 until December 1996. Ms. Taylor holds a B.S. in Finance from Mississippi State University. Ms. Taylor also serves on the Board of Directors of Allstate Corporation, an insurance company.

EXHIBIT 6
(Continued)

Eric Carlborg, *Director*

Eric Carlborg has served as a director since February 2005. Since June 2010, Mr. Carlborg has served as an investment professional at August Capital, an investment company. From April 2006 to May 2010, Mr. Carlborg was a partner at Continental Investors LLC, an investment company. From September 2005 to March 2006, Mr. Carlborg served as Chief Financial Officer of Provide Commerce, Inc., an e-commerce company. From July 2001 to October 2004, Mr. Carlborg was a Managing Director of Investment Banking with Merrill Lynch & Co., focused on the technology and financial sectors. Prior to his tenure at Merrill Lynch, Mr. Carlborg served in various executive financial positions, including Chief Financial Officer at Authorize.net, Inc. and Chief Strategy Officer at Go2Net, Inc., providers of Internet products and services. Mr. Carlborg also previously served as Chief Financial Officer for Einstein/Noah Bagel Corp. In addition, Mr. Carlborg previously served as a member of the Board of Directors of Big Lots, Inc., a Fortune 500 retailer. Mr. Carlborg holds an M.B.A. from the University of Chicago and a B.A. from the University of Illinois.

Leslie Lane, *Lead Independent Director*

Leslie Lane, age 44, has served as a director since December 2008. Mr. Lane has served as Operating Partner at Altamont Capital Partners, a venture capital company, since May 2011. He served as the Vice President and Managing Director of the Nike Foundation at Nike, Inc., a leading designer, marketer, and distributor of authentic athletic footwear, apparel, equipment, and accessories, from June 2010 to April 2011. From October 2006 to June 2010, he served as Vice President and General Manager of Global Running for Nike, Inc. From March 2004 to October 2006, he served as the Director of Nike Global Footwear Finance and Strategic Planning and, from March 2003 to March 2004, he served as the Director of Nike Subsidiaries. From 1998 to 2002, Lane held various positions at Roll International Corporation, a private holding company, including serving as the Chief Operating Officer of PomWonderful LLC, the Chief Financial Officer of Paramount Citrus, and the Vice President of Strategy of Roll International Corporation. From 1990 to 1998, Lane was a consultant with Bain & Company. He holds an M.A. in Chemistry from Oxford University and an M.B.A. from Harvard University.

Michael Potter, *Director*

Michael Potter has served as a director since October 2007. Mr. Potter served as Chairman and Chief Executive Officer of Big Lots, Inc., a Fortune 500 retailer, from June 2000 to June 2005. Prior to serving as Chief Executive Officer, Mr. Potter served in various capacities at Big Lots, including the role of Chief Financial Officer. Prior to Big Lots, Mr. Potter held various positions at The Limited, Inc., May Department Stores, and Meier & Frank, all retail companies. Mr. Potter currently serves on the Board of Directors of Coldwater Creek, Inc., a triple channel retailer of women's apparel, gifts, and accessories, as well as Newegg, Inc., an online-only retailer specializing in high-tech products. Mr. Potter holds an M.B.A. from Capital University in Ohio and a B.S. in Finance and Management from the University of Oregon.

Steve Scheid, *Director*

Steve Scheid has served as director since October 2007. Mr. Scheid currently serves as the Chairman of the Board of Janus Capital Group, Inc. ("Janus"). From April 2004 until December 2005, Mr. Scheid served as Chief Executive Officer and Chairman of the Board of Janus. Scheid joined the Janus Board in December 2002 and was appointed Chairman in January 2004. Scheid served as Vice Chairman of The Charles Schwab Corporation and President of Schwab's retail group from 2000 to 2002. Prior thereto, Mr. Scheid headed Schwab's financial products and services group and was the firm's Chief Financial Officer from 1996 through 1999. From 2001 to 2002, Mr. Scheid served on the Federal Advisory Council, which provides oversight to the Federal Reserve Board in Washington, D.C. Mr. Scheid holds a B.S. from Michigan State University.

Chris Bruzzo, *Director*

Chris Bruzzo has served as director since July 2011. Mr. Bruzzo has served as the Senior Vice President and Chief Marketing Officer for Seattle's Best Coffee, a subsidiary of Starbucks Corporation, a specialty coffee retailer, since July 2011. From June 2008 to July 2011, he served as Vice President of Global Advertising & Digital Marketing at Starbucks Corporation. From January 2007 to January 2008, Mr. Bruzzo served as the Vice President of Digital Strategy at Starbucks Corporation and from January 2008 to May 2008 he served as the Chief Technology Officer and interim Chief Information Officer at Starbucks Corporation. From July 2006 to October 2006, Mr. Bruzzo served as the Vice President of Marketing and Public Relations at Amazon.com, Inc., an online retailer. From July 2003 to February 2006, Mr. Bruzzo served in various roles at Amazon.com, Inc., including Vice President of Strategic Communications, Content and Initiatives. Prior to Amazon.com, Inc., Mr. Bruzzo was an Assistant Vice President at Regence Blue Shield. Mr. Bruzzo holds a B.A. in Political Studies from Whitworth College.

NOTES

1. Blue Nile, Inc. Datamonitor. www.datamonitor.com. September 10, 2010.
2. http://www.bluenile.com/blue-nile-advantage
3. http://www.bluenile.com/about-blue-nile
4. http://www.kaihan.net/vpw_login.php?img=blue-nile
5. http://www.bluenile.com/blue-nile-history
6. http://www.reuters.com/finance/stocks/companyProfile?symbol=NILE.O
7. Ibid.
8. http://www.bluenile.com/blue-nile-history
9. http://www.bluenile.com/about-blue-nile
10. http://www.reuters.com/finance/stocks/companyProfile?symbol=NILE.O
11. http://www.bluenile.com/about-blue-nile
12. http://www.bluenile.com/blue-nile-advantage
13. Krippendorff, Kaihan. "Creating a Two-Horned Dilemma." *Fast Company.com.* September 8, 2010.
14. http://www.kaihan.net/vpw_login.php?img=blue-nile
15. Blue Nile, Inc. Datamonitor. www.datamonitor.com. September 10, 2010.
16. MacMillan, Douglas. "How Four Rookie CEOs Handled the Great Recession." *Bloomberg Businessweek.* February 18, 2010.
17. Mintel. Accessed May 8, 2011. http://academic.mintel.com/sinatra/oxygen_academic/search_results/show&/display/id=482738/display/id=540585#hit1.
18. Jewelry Retail Industry Profile. *First Research.com.* February 14, 2011.
19. Mintel. Accessed May 8, 2011. http://academic.mintel.com/sinatra/oxygen_academic/search_results/show&/display/id=482738/display/id=540590#hit1
20. DeFotis, Dimitra. "No Diamond in the Rough." *Barron's.* February 15, 2010.
21. Plourd, Kate. "I Like Innovative, Disruptive Businesses." *CFO Magazine.* February 1, 2009.
22. Blue Nile, Inc. Datamonitor. *www.datamonitor.com.* September 10, 2010.
23. Jewelry Retail Industry Profile. *First Research.com.* February 14, 2011.
24. DeFotis, Dimitra. "No Diamond in the Rough." *Barron's.* February 15, 2010.
25. https://collab.itc.virginia.edu/access/content/group/dff17973-f012-465d-9e73-a05fa4456644/Research/Memos/MII%20Memos/Archive/Short/S%20-NILE_2.pdf
26. http://www.kaihan.net/vpw_login.php?img=blue-nile
27. http://www.bluenile.com/services_channel.jsp
28. http://www.kaihan.net/vpw_login.php?img=blue-nile
29. "Blue Nile CEO interview." CEO Wire. November 29, 2010. http://ezp.bentley.edu/login?url=http://search.proquest.com/?url=http://search.proquest.com/docview/814841480?accountid=8576
30. http://www.bluenile.com/why-choose-blue-nile
31. http://www.bluenile.com/diamonds/fancy-color-diamonds?keyword_search_value=colored+diamonds
32. Levine, Joshua. "A Beautiful Mine." *The New York Times.* April 17, 2011.
33. (2008), DIAMONDS: Kimberley Process Effective. *Africa Research Bulletin: Economic, Financial and Technical Series,* 44: 17640A–17641A.
34. http://www.kimberleyprocess.com/background/index_en.html
35. http://factfinder.census.gov/servlet/GRTTable?_bm=y&-geo_id=01000US&-_box_head_nbr=R1204&-ds_name=ACS_2009_1YR_G00_&-redoLog=false&-mt_name=ACS_2005_EST_G00_R1204_US30&-format=US-30
36. http://factfinder.census.gov/servlet/GRTTable?_bm=y&-geo_id=D&_box_head_nbr=R1205&ds_name=ACS_2009_1YR_G00_&-_lang=en&-redoLog=false&-format=D&mt_name=ACS_2009_1YR_G00_R1204_US30
37. DeBarros, Anthony and Jayson, Sharon. "Young Adults Delaying Marriage; Data Show 'Dramatic' Surge in Single Twenty-somethings." *USA Today.* September 12, 2007.
38. 2010 Blue Nile Annual Report. Pg 27.
39. 2010 Blue Nile Annual Report. Pg 27.
40. Annual report 2008. Pg 31.
41. Ibid. Pg 30.
42. Annual report 2010. Pg 31.
43. Ibid. Pg 30.
44. Annual report 2010. Pg 33.
45. Ibid. Pg 32.
46. Ibid. Pg 33.
47. Birchall, Jonathan. " Smartphone Apps: Competition Set to Intensify for Online Retailers." *FT.com.* Nov 13, 2010.
48. Byron Acohido and Edward C. Baig. "Blue Nile Gets a New Look." *USA Today.* September 2, 2009.
49. Blue Nile, Inc. Datamonitor. www.datamonitor.com. September 10, 2010.
50. Ibid.
51. "Blue Nile Unwraps Cyber Monday Promotions." *Information Technology Newsweekly.* December 8, 2009.
52. DeFotis, Dimitra. "No Diamond in the Rough." *Barron's.* February 15, 2010.
53. DeFotis, Dimitra. "No Diamond in the Rough." *Barron's.* February 15, 2010.
54. http://www.bluenile.com/build-your-own-diamond-ring?track=head
55. http://www.glassdoor.com/Reviews/Blue-Nile-Reviews-E11944.htm
56. http://www.glassdoor.com/Reviews/Blue-Nile-Reviews-E11944.htm
57. http://www.fedex.com/us/track/index.html
58. http://www.reuters.com/finance/stocks/companyProfile?symbol=NILE.O
59. http://seekingalpha.com/article/11593-the-bull-and-bear-cases-for-blue-nile-nile
60. http://www.businessweek.com/smallbiz/news/date/9811/e981119.htm
61. http://seekingalpha.com/article/11593-the-bull-and-bear-cases-for-blue-nile-nile
62. http://seekingalpha.com/article/11593-the-bull-and-bear-cases-for-blue-nile-nile
63. http://www.diamondsnews.com/hearts_on_fire.htm
64. http://www.hoovers.com/company/Blue_Nile_Inc/rffxhxi-1.html
65. http://www.bluenile.com/employee_testimonials.jsp
66. http://www.glassdoor.com/Reviews/Blue-Nile-Reviews-E11944.htm
67. http://investor.bluenile.com/management.cfm

C A S E **11**

Groupon, Inc.

DAILY DEAL OR LASTING SUCCESS?

Nick Falcone, Eric Halbruner, Ellie A. Fogarty, and Joyce Vincelette

Andrew Mason sat in his office in Chicago, Illinois, thinking about the city. His adult life began there—he graduated from Northwestern in 2003. His business originated there not long after—Groupon began as a local Chicago discount service and became a global phenomenon seemingly overnight. Mason knew that Groupon was a great idea. The company was the first of its kind and changed the way consumers spend, shop, and think about discounts. But how could Groupon, based in such innovation and having experienced such exceptional growth, be in such a precarious position? A wave of competition had swelled, including the likes of technology giants and both general and niche daily deals services, all replicating Groupon's business model. How could Groupon compete against large companies and their expansive resources? Would consumers and merchant partners flock to other services that better suited their needs? Mason worried about the increasingly downward trajectory of Groupon's stock price since the company's initial public offering. The year 2012 had brought additional scrutiny of Groupon from the SEC, as well as the unfortunate title of Worst CEO of 2012 for Mason.[1] He thought about the barrage of competition facing his firm and the related questions regarding the sustainability of its business model. Groupon was a star as it grew from its Illinois roots, but it now had problems on a global scale. Mason looked out his window over the city where it all started, nostalgic for a time when business was easier and wondered what to do.

History

In 2006, three years after graduating from Northwestern University with a degree in Music, Andrew Mason became frustrated when trying to cancel a cell phone contract. He thought about the likely large group of people in similar circumstances and figured "if [he and they] were united in some way, [they] could leverage [their] collective power."[2] He began developing a Web platform based on the "tipping point" principle (the number at which an idea or cause reaches critical mass, popularized by Malcolm Gladwell) that would utilize social media to organize collective action.[3] The company he created was aptly named ThePoint and was designed to be a tool for raising money for various causes. The "tipping point" for a particular cause, which would be set by the fundraiser, was a certain amount of money or signatures needed for the plan to become active.[4] Users could donate with minimal risk because credit cards were not charged unless and until the threshold was met and the cause "tipped."

But ThePoint lacked the focus necessary to survive on its own. "The big problem. . ." Mason said, "is that it's this huge, abstract idea. You can use this platform to do anything from boycotting a multinational company to getting 20% off a subscription to *The Economist* . . . we needed to pick one application of the larger abstract idea and execute it really, really well."[5] The service was too broad to achieve success, but the tipping point element had noticeable potential.

Mason found his "one application" in the most effective campaigns on The Point—those that gave a group of consumers buying power.[6] He began recruiting merchants to offer discounts in online deals that centered on the tipping point principle. In deals that tipped (when enough coupons were purchased), consumers saved money and merchants benefitted from both large-scale sales and market exposure. The concept grew into an entirely new venture: a daily deals service that relied on the power of groups. Groupon—the name is a combination of the words "group" and "coupon"—launched its first deal in October 2008: Buy two pizzas for the price of one from the Motel Bar, located on the first floor of Groupon's Chicago headquarters.[7]

From there, the company grew at an unprecedented rate. In six months, Groupon parlayed its 5000-person Chicago e-mail list into daily deals operations in Boston, New York, and Washington, DC. Groupon's estimated worth was over US$1 billion after just 16 months in business, becoming the second-fastest website to reach that milestone (YouTube reached the mark in 12 months).[8] By 2010, Groupon was serving more than 150 markets in North America, 100 markets in Europe, Asia, and South America, and was boasting 35 million registered users.[9] *Forbes* magazine declared Groupon to be the "fastest growing company ever"[10] in August 2010 and Groupon rejected a US$6 billion acquisition offer from technology giant Google in December of the same year.[11]

In November 2011, the company raised US$700 million in its initial public offering, the largest IPO by a United States Internet company since Google's US$1.7 billion in 2004.[12] But the growth seen in the company's infancy had been largely elusive since its IPO. In the 10 subsequent months, Groupon's stock fell 84% from US$26.11 to close at US$4.15 on August 31, 2012.

Business Model

Groupon described itself as "a local commerce marketplace that connects merchants to consumers by offering goods and services at a discount."[13] The company saw opportunity in bringing the brick-and-mortar world of local commerce onto the Internet, which it said was creating a new way for local merchant partners to attract customers.[14] The "Groupon Promise" was core to the company's customer-service philosophy:

> We're confident in the businesses we feature on Groupon and back them with the Groupon Promise. If the experience using your Groupon ever lets you down, we'll make it right or return your purchase. Simple as that.[15]

Groupon followed specific processes in dealings with consumers and merchants to keep its promise. The company used its technology and scale to target relevant deals based on individual customer preferences.[16] Deals were disseminated primarily via e-mail; consumers subscribed to Groupon's mailing list, chose their locations, and were sent information on deals in their areas. Groupon's mobile application and website were set up to distribute deals to current and potential customers based on proximity to the sponsoring merchant partner.[17] Customers purchased coupons online, which became active only when a deal reached its predetermined critical number of purchases. The coupons had expiration dates.

Merchants wishing to partner with Groupon and feature their products or services in deals were vetted by the company. Only one in eight applicants was accepted. Winning merchants had to be receiving praise on review sites like Yelp, CitySearch, and TripAdvisor, and their Groupon deals had to offer a substantial discount from normal prices and not be similar to other promotions regularly offered by the vendor.[18] A merchant partner signed a contract that specified the percentage of revenue Groupon would collect from a deal (typically 50%) and the number of coupons that would have to be purchased for a deal to "tip" and for the discount to become active. Groupon collected revenue from the deals immediately and made payments to merchants over a 60-day period.[19]

Merchants were not completely at ease with the general model, now utilized by other deal providers, citing the heavy discounts required and low repeat rates from customers as their two biggest concerns.[20] Twenty-three percent of respondents to a merchant survey on daily deals companies said that the discounts were their biggest concern, but 45% said they acquired more customers as a result of offering the promotions.[21] Eighty percent were satisfied with daily-deal companies. Merchant satisfaction and retention were critical to Groupon's strategy for success.

Mission and Strategy

CEO Andrew Mason explained his vision for Groupon in a 2011 Letter to Stockholders. Upon the shoulders of its business model, he wrote, Groupon was setting out to reinvent the multitrillion-dollar local commerce ecosystem. "Today, Groupon is a marketing tool that connects consumers and merchants. Tomorrow, we aim to move upstream and serve as the entry point for local transactions." Groupon's mission, according to Mason, was "to become the operating system for local commerce."[22]

Groupon's objective was to become an essential part of everyday local commerce for consumers and merchants. Key elements of its strategy included the following:[23]

- **Grow subscriber and customer base.** Groupon made significant investments to acquire subscribers through online marketing initiatives, such as search engine marketing, display advertisements, referral programs, and affiliate marketing. In addition, Groupon's subscriber base increased by word of mouth. The company intended to continue to invest in acquiring subscribers; however, it continued to shift its efforts toward converting subscribers into customers who purchase Groupons. Groupon's investment in the growth of its subscriber base and achieving optimal subscriber levels was directly linked to the breadth and location of its merchant partners. As such, while the number of total subscribers was a key metric to measure Groupon's progression over the long term, it was not a key operational metric in the same manner as was the active customer base.

- **Grow the number of merchant partners.** Groupon expanded the number of ways in which consumers could discover deals through its marketplace. The company made significant investments in its sales force, which built merchant partner relationships and local expertise. Merchant partner retention efforts were focused on providing merchant partners with a positive experience by offering targeted placement of their deals to the subscriber base, high-quality customer service, and tools to manage deals more effectively. Groupon routinely solicited feedback from merchant partners to ensure their objectives were met and they were satisfied with its services. Based on this feedback, Groupon believed that merchant partners considered the profitability of the immediate deal, potential revenue generated by repeat customers, and increased brand awareness for the merchant partner and the resulting revenue stream that brand awareness might generate over time. Some merchant partners viewed deals as a marketing expense and might be willing to offer deals with little or no immediate profitability in an effort to gain future customers and increased brand awareness.

- **Position Groupon to benefit from technological changes that may affect consumer behavior.** Groupon believed that as technological advances continued, particularly with the proliferation of affordable Smartphones and tablet computers, the ways in which customers and local merchant partners interacted would change significantly. For example, in December 2011, one quarter of all purchases in its North America segment were made through mobile devices. Groupon believed that it was well positioned to benefit from, and to drive, these changes. The company continued to invest heavily in technology, including through acquisitions.

- **Increase the number and variety of products through innovation.** Groupon launched a variety of new products in 2011 and planned to continue to launch new products to increase the number of customers and merchant partners transacting business through its marketplace. As its local commerce marketplace grew, Groupon believed that consumers would use Groupon not only as a discovery tool for local merchant partners, but also as an ongoing connection point to their favorite merchants.

- **Expand with acquisitions and business development partnerships.** Historically, the core assets Groupon gained from acquisitions were local management teams and small subscriber and merchant partner bases, to which the company then applies its expertise, resources, and brand to scale the business. More recently, Groupon's focus shifted to acquiring businesses with technology and technology talent that could help expand its business. In addition to acquisitions, Groupon entered into agreements with local partners to expand its international presence. Groupon entered into affiliate programs with companies such as eBay, Microsoft, Yahoo, and Zynga, that allowed these partners to display, promote, and distribute Groupon's deals to their users in exchange for a share of the revenue the deals generate.

Corporate Governance

Groupon's Global Code of Conduct and Corporate Governance Guidelines were adopted in the fall of 2011. These documents, and the charters for the Audit, Compensation, and Nominating & Governance Committees, can be found on the company's website at http://investor.groupon.com/governance.cfm.

Board of Directors.[24]   The biographies of the eight members of the Board of Directors are as follows:

Eric Lefkofsky, 42, is a co-founder and the Executive Chairman of Groupon. He is also a founder and director of several firms, including InnerWorkings, Inc., a global provider of managed print and promotional solutions; Echo Global Logistics, Inc., a technology-enabled transportation and logistics outsourcing firm; MediaBank, LLC, a leading provider of integrated media procurement technology; and LightBank, a venture fund focused on helping disruptive technology businesses. Eric serves on the board of directors of Children's Memorial Hospital and the board of trustees of the Steppenwolf Theatre, the Art Institute of Chicago, and the Museum of Contemporary Art. Eric is also an adjunct professor at the University of Chicago Booth School of Business. He holds a bachelor's degree from the University of Michigan and a Juris Doctor from the University of Michigan Law School.

Peter Barris, 59, joined New Enterprise Associates (NEA) in 1992 and has served as Managing General Partner since 1999. Since joining NEA, Peter has led investments in over 20 information technology companies that have completed public offerings or successful mergers. These include such industry pioneering companies as Amisys, CareerBuilder, InnerWorkings, Neutral Tandem, UUNET, and Vonage. Prior to joining NEA, Peter was President and

Chief Operating Officer of Legent Corporation (LGNT) and Senior Vice President of the Systems Software Division of UCCEL Corporation (UCE). Both companies were ultimately acquired at valuations that were record breaking for their time. Earlier, Peter spent almost a decade at General Electric Company in a variety of management positions, including Vice President and General Manager at GE Information Services. Outside interests include serving on the Northwestern University Board of Trustees and the Dartmouth Tuck School Board of Overseers. Peter previously served on the Executive Committee of the Board of the National Venture Capital Association and was also a founding member of Venture Philanthropy Partners, a philanthropic organization in the Washington, DC, area. He has a BS degree in Electrical Engineering from Northwestern and an MBA from Dartmouth. Mr. Barris is the chair of the Compensation Committee and a member of the Nominating and Governance Committee.

Mellody Hobson, 42, is president of Ariel Investments, a Chicago-based money management firm serving institutional clients and individual investors; she also serves as chairman of the board of trustees for Ariel's no-load mutual funds. Beyond her work at Ariel, Mellody has become a nationally recognized voice on financial literacy and investor education. Specifically, she is a regular financial contributor on *Good Morning America*, the featured consumer finance expert on Tom Joyner's *Money Mondays* radio program, and a regular columnist for *Black Enterprise*. Mellody is a director of three public companies: DreamWorks Animation SKG, Inc., The Estée Lauder Companies Inc., and Starbucks Corporation. In addition, she serves on the boards of various civic organizations including The Field Museum, The Chicago Public Education Fund, and the Sundance Institute. Mellody is a graduate of Princeton University where she received her AB degree from the Woodrow Wilson School of Public and International Affairs. She is a member of both the Compensation Committee and the Nominating and Governance Committee.

Brad Keywell, 42, is a founder of MediaBank LLC, Echo Global Logistics, Inc., Groupon Inc., Starbelly, and several other companies. He has served on the Board since Groupon's inception. He is on the Board of the Zell-Lurie Entrepreneurship Institute at the University of Michigan, Big Communications, Warrior Productions, and University of Michigan Hillel Foundation. He was formerly on the Board of Columbia College, as well as the Advisory Committee of the University of Chicago Graduate School of Business Directors' College. Mr. Keywell is a member of the Compensation Committee and the chair of the Nominating and Governance Committee.

Ted Leonsis, 55, is Vice Chairman Emeritus of AOL LLC with more than a decade of experience in global Internet services and media at AOL, where he also served as Vice Chairman and President of several business units. In addition to his work at AOL, Leonsis is the majority owner of the National Hockey League's Washington Capitals and the Women's National Basketball Association's Washington Mystics. He is also the producer of "Nanking," a documentary film that made its premiere at the 2007 Sundance Film Festival. Mr. Leonsis is the chair of the Audit Committee and a member of the Compensation Committee.

Andrew Mason, 31, is a founder of Groupon and has served as its Chief Executive Officer since its inception in November 2008. Prior to co-founding Groupon and ThePoint, Andrew worked as a software developer with Innerworkings, Inc. Andrew received his Bachelor of Arts in Music from Northwestern University.

Daniel Henry, 62, has been the Chief Financial Officer of American Express Company since October 2007. Henry is responsible for leading American Express Company's finance organization and representing American Express to investors, lenders, and rating agencies. He also served as Executive Vice President and Chief Financial Officer of U.S. Consumer, Small Business and Merchant Services and joined American Express as Comptroller in 1990. Prior to joining American Express, Henry was a partner with Ernst & Young. Mr. Henry is a member of the Audit Committee.

Robert Bass, 62, served as a Vice Chairman of Deloitte LLP from 2006 through June 2012, and was a partner in Deloitte from 1982 through June 2012. Mr. Bass specializes in e-commerce, mergers and acquisitions, and SEC filings. At Deloitte, Mr. Bass was responsible for all services provided to Forstmann Little and its portfolio companies and is the advisory partner for Blackstone, DIRECTV, McKesson, IMG, and CSC. He has also previously been the advisory partner for priceline.com, RR Donnelley, Automatic Data Processing, Community Health Systems, and Avis Budget. He is a member of the American Institute of Certified Public Accountants and the New York and Connecticut State Societies of Certified Public Accountants. Mr. Bass is a member of the Audit Committee.

Daniel Henry and Robert Bass joined the Board on April 26 and June 19, 2012, respectively, in a move to bring more accounting and financial expertise to the Board. Mr. Henry replaced Howard Schultz, CEO of Starbucks. Mr. Bass replaced Kevin Efrusy, a partner at the venture-capital firm Accel Partners.[25]

Top Management.[26]   The biographical sketches for Groupon's top management team are as follows:

Andrew D. Mason, 31, is a co-founder of Groupon and has served as its Chief Executive Officer and a director since its inception. In 2007, Mr. Mason co-founded ThePoint, a Web platform that enables users to promote collective action to support social, educational, and civic causes, from which Groupon evolved. Prior to co-founding ThePoint, Mr. Mason worked as a computer programmer with InnerWorkings, Inc. Mr. Mason received his Bachelor of Arts from Northwestern University. Mr. Mason brings to the Board the perspective and experience as one of Groupon's founders and as Chief Executive Officer. Mr. Mason was elected to the Board pursuant to voting rights granted to the former holders of Groupon's common stock and preferred stock under Groupon's voting agreement, which terminated as a result of the company's initial public offering.

Jason E. Child, 43, has served as Chief Financial Officer since December 2010. From March 1999 through December 2010, Mr. Child held several positions with Amazon.com, Inc., including Vice President of Finance, International from April 2007 to December 2010, Vice President of Finance, Asia from July 2006 to July 2007, Director of Finance, Amazon Germany from April 2004 to July 2006, Director of Investor Relations from April 2003 to April 2004, Director of Finance, Worldwide Application Software from November 2001 to April 2003, Director of Finance, Marketing and Business Development from November 2000 to November 2001, and Global Controller from October 1999 to November 2000. Prior to joining Amazon.com, Mr. Child spent more than seven years as a C.P.A. and a consulting manager at Arthur Andersen. Mr. Child received his Bachelor of Arts from the Foster School of Business at the University of Washington.

Joseph M. Del Preto II, 36, has served as Chief Accounting Officer since April 2011. From January 2011 to April 2011, Mr. Del Preto served as Groupon's Global Controller. Prior to joining Groupon, Mr. Del Preto served as Controller and Vice President, Finance of Echo Global Logistics, Inc. from April 2009 to December 2010. From January 2006 to March 2009, Mr. Del Preto served as Controller of InnerWorkings, Inc. Mr. Del Preto began his career at PricewaterhouseCoopers LLP. Mr. Del Preto received his Bachelor of Science degree from Indiana University.

Jason D. Harinstein, 36, has served as Senior Vice President-Corporate Development since March 2011. From June 2005 to February 2011, Mr. Harinstein served in several capacities at Google, Inc., including most recently as Director of Corporate Development. From July 2003 to June 2005, Mr. Harinstein worked as an Equity Research Associate at Deutsche Bank Securities, Inc. where he covered Internet advertising, online search, eCommerce and video game companies. Previously, Mr. Harinstein served as a strategy consultant at iXL, Inc. (now part of Razorfish) from June 1999 to June 2001, and at Andersen Consulting Strategic Services (now Accenture) from September 1997 to June 1999. Mr. Harinstein received his Bachelor of Arts in Economics from Northwestern University and his Master's in Business Administration from the University of Chicago.

Jeffrey Holden, 43, has served as Senior Vice President-Product Management since April 2011. In 2006, Mr. Holden co-founded Pelago, Inc. and served as its Chief Executive Officer until Groupon acquired Pelago in April 2011. Prior to co-founding Pelago, Mr. Holden held several positions at Amazon.com, Inc., including Senior Vice President, Worldwide Discovery, from March 2005 to January 2006, Senior Vice President, Consumer Applications, from April 2004 to March 2005, Vice President, Consumer Applications, from April 2002 to April 2004, and Director, Automated Merchandising and Discovery from February 2000 to April 2002. Mr. Holden joined Amazon.com in May 1997 as Director, Supply Chain Optimization Systems. Mr. Holden received his Bachelor of Science and Master of Science degrees in Computer Science from the University of Illinois at Urbana-Champaign.

David R. Schellhase, 48, has served as General Counsel since June 2011. From March 2010 to May 2011, Mr. Schellhase served as Executive Vice President, Legal of salesforce.com, inc. From December 2004 to March 2010, Mr. Schellhase served as the Senior Vice President and General Counsel of salesforce.com, and he served as Vice President and General Counsel of salesforce.com from July 2002 to December 2004. From December 2000 to June 2002, Mr. Schellhase was an independent legal consultant and authored a treatise entitled Corporate Law Department Handbook. Previously, he served as General Counsel at Linuxcare, Inc., The Vantive Corporation and Premenos Technology Corp. Mr. Schellhase received a Bachelor of Arts from Columbia University and a Juris Doctor from Cornell University.

Brian J. Schipper, 51, has served as Senior Vice President–Human Resources since June 2011. From October 2006 to May 2011, Mr. Schipper served as Senior Vice President and Chief Human Resources Officer of Cisco Systems, Inc. From November 2003 to October 2006, Mr. Schipper served as the Corporate Vice President, Human Resources of Microsoft Corporation. From February 2002 to March 2003, Mr. Schipper was Partner and Head of Human Resources and Administration for Andor Capital Management LLC. From March 2000 to February 2002, Mr. Schipper served as Senior Vice President of Human Resources and Administration at DoubleClick, Inc. Prior to joining DoubleClick, Mr. Schipper served as Vice President, Human Resources at PepsiCo, Inc. from May 1995 to March 2000. Prior to joining PepsiCo, Mr. Schipper worked at Compaq Computer Corporation, where he was global head of compensation and benefits and head of Human Resources for North America. Mr. Schipper received his Bachelor's from Hope College and his Master's in Business Administration from Michigan State University.

Brian K. Totty, 45, Ph.D., has served as Senior Vice President—Engineering and Operations since November 2010. Dr. Totty was the Chief Executive Officer of Ludic Labs, Inc., a startup venture developing a new class of software applications from January 2006 through November 2007. We acquired Ludic Labs in November 2010. Dr. Totty also was a co-founder and Senior Vice President of Research and Development of Inktomi Corporation from February 1996 to August 2002. Dr. Totty received his Ph.D. in computer science from the University of Illinois at Urbana-Champaign, his Master of Public Administration from Harvard's Kennedy School and his Bachelor of Science from the Massachusetts Institute of Technology.

Operations

Groupon's operations were divided into North America (United States and Canada) and International segments.

EXHIBIT 1

	2009	% of total	2010	% of total	2011	% of total
			Year Ended December 31			
			(dollars in thousands)			
North America	$ 14,540	100.0%	$ 200,412	64.0%	$ 634,980	39.4%
International	—	—	112,529	36.0%	975,450	60.6%
Revenue	$ 14,540	100.0%	$ 312,941	100.0%	$ 1,610,430	100.0%

SOURCE: Groupon, Inc. *10-K* (March 30, 2012), p. 45.

One trend that contributed to Groupon's growth was its investment in international markets. In 2009, the company's operations focused entirely on North America. In 2010, however, Groupon began looking abroad for growth, targeting key markets in both Europe and Asia. As a result, the International segment accounted for 36% of total revenues in 2010. As Groupon continued to see growth in 2011, the segment accounted for 60.6%, as shown in **Exhibit 1**. While this rapid expansion of the International segment contributed substantially to the company's growth, it also contributed to its annual net losses. In fact, management blamed the net loss in 2011 primarily on the "rapid expansion of [its] International segment during the year, which involved investing heavily in upfront marketing, sales and infrastructure related to the build out of [its] operations" in early stage countries.[27] Groupon's international segment often felt the impact of unfavorable foreign exchange rates.

To accompany this expansion, Groupon made changes to its distribution of resources, including corporate facilities and employees. The company's principal executive properties are described in **Exhibit 2**. Other facilities were located throughout the world.

The size and geographic distribution of Groupon's sales force over time is shown in **Exhibit 3**. Considering Groupon's two-pronged dependence on subscribers and on merchants, many of whom were very small businesses, the company maintained high-touch relationships with its merchants. In addition to its sales team, Groupon employed customer service representatives, editorial staff, marketing planners, merchant research and services teams, and "city planners" who created the schedules for each Groupon city every week.[28]

The growth in Groupon's sales force reflected international operations that began in May 2010 with the acquisition of CityDeal Europe GmbH. CityDeal was founded by Oliver Samwer and Marc Samwer, who have served since the acquisition as consultants and been extensively involved in the development and operations of Groupon's international segment.[29]

EXHIBIT 2

Description of Use	Square Footage	Operating Segment	Location	Lease Expiration
Corporate office facilities	550,000	North America	Chicago, IL	From 2012 through 2018
Corporate office facilities	30,000	International	Berlin, Germany; Schaffhausen, Switzerland	From 2012 through 2022

SOURCE: Groupon, Inc. *10-K* (March 30, 2012), p. 33.

EXHIBIT 3

Size of sales force	Mar. 31, 2010	June 30, 2010	Sept. 30, 2010	Dec. 31, 2010	Mar. 31, 2011	June 30, 2011	Sept. 30, 2011	Dec. 31, 2011
North America	128	201	348	493	661	990	1,004	1,062
International	—	1,080	1,224	2,080	2,895	3,860	3,849	4,134
Total	128	1,291	1,572	2,573	3,556	4,850	4,853	5,196

SOURCE: Groupon, Inc. *10-K* (March 30, 2012), p. 8.

Agreements under which Oliver and Marc Samwer provided consulting services were set to expire in October 2012 and October 2013, respectively.[30]

In January 2011, Groupon B.V., a subsidiary, entered into a joint venture along with Rocket Asia GmbH & Co. KG, an entity controlled by the Samwers.[31] Groupon B.V. became part owner of GaoPeng.com, which operates a group buying site offering discounts for products and services to individual consumers and businesses via Internet websites and social and interactive media.[32] GaoPeng.com began offering daily deals in Beijing and Shanghai in March 2011 and subsequently began offering daily deals in other major cities in China.[33]

Such acquisitions and joint ventures were an important part of Groupon's growth strategy. Groupon acquired eight firms in 2010, another nine in 2011, and an additional eight firms as of May 2012.[34]

Finance

Exhibits **4** and **5** show Groupon's consolidated statement of operations and consolidated balance sheet for the fiscal years ended 2008 through 2011.

For the years ended 2009, 2010, and 2011, Groupon reported revenue of US$14.5 million, US$312.9 million, and US$1.6 billion, respectively.[35] This represented an annual compound growth rate of 380%. From 2010 to 2011 specifically, revenue increased by US$1.3 billion. The company attributed this growth mainly to expanding the scale of its business both domestically and internationally through acquisitions, as well as by entering new markets. Initiatives that contributed to this expansion included an increase in marketing expenditures, as well as an increase in the company's sales force.[36]

Despite such significant revenue growth, operating income remained negative in 2011 (see **Exhibit 4**). Total operating expenses reached over US$1.8 billion in fiscal year 2011, an increase of 151.4% from that of 2010. Groupon attributed this rise to an increase of US$216 million in the cost of revenue due to increases in credit card processing fees, refunds, and editorial salary costs. Higher volumes of merchant partner transactions and a larger subscriber base contributed to these costs.[37]

The company's greatest increases in operating expenses, however, were in marketing, selling, general, and administrative expenses. For the years ended December 31, 2009, 2010, and 2011, the company reported marketing expenses of US$5.1 million, US$290.6 million, and US$768.5 million, respectively.[38] In its annual report, Groupon made it clear that such increases in marketing expenses have been necessary, stating that "Since our inception, we have prioritized growth, and investments in our marketing initiatives have contributed to our losses."[39] Management viewed investments in marketing as a necessary cost to acquire subscribers. When compared to the profits generated from these subscribers over time, the cost to maintain a subscriber was relatively inexpensive, as interaction was largely limited to e-mails and mobile applications. As its business continued to grow and became established in more markets, Groupon expected that its marketing expense would decrease as a percentage of revenue.

EXHIBIT 4

Groupon, Inc. Consolidated Statement of Operations (In thousands, except share and per-share amounts)

	Year Ended December 31			
	2008	2009	2010	2011
	(dollars in thousands, except share data)			
Consolidated Statements of Operations Data:				
Revenue (gross billings of $94, $34,082, $745,348 and $3,985,501, respectively)	$ 5	$ 14,540	$ 312,941	$ 1,610,430
Costs and expenses:				
Cost of revenue	88	4,716	42,896	258,879
Marketing	163	5,053	290,569	768,472
Selling, general, and administrative	1,386	5,848	196,637	821,002
Acquisition-related	—	—	203,183	(4,537)
Total operating expenses	1,637	15,617	733,285	1,843,816
Loss from operations	(1,632)	(1,077)	(420,344)	(233,386)
Interest and other income (expense), net	90	(16)	284	5,973
Equity-method investment activity, net of tax	—	—	—	(26,652)
Loss before provision for income taxes	(1,542)	(1,093)	(420,060)	(254,065)
Provision (benefit) for income taxes	—	248	(6,674)	43,697
Net loss	(1,542)	(1,341)	(413,386)	(297,762)
Less: Net loss attributable to non-controlling interests	—	—	23,746	18,335
Net loss attributable to Groupon, Inc.	(1,542)	(1,341)	(389,640)	(279,427)
Dividends on preferred shares	(277)	(5,575)	(1,362)	—
Redemption of preferred stock in excess of carrying value	—	—	(52,893)	(34,327)
Adjustment of redeemable non-controlling interests to redemption value	—	—	(12,425)	(59,740)
Preferred stock distributions	(339)	—	—	—
Net loss attributable to common stockholders	$ (2,158)	$ (6,916)	$ (456,320)	$ (373,494)
Net loss per share of common stock				
Basic	$ (0.01)	$ (0.04)	$ (2.66)	$ (1.03)
Diluted	$ (0.01)	$ (0.04)	$ (2.66)	$ (1.03)
Weighted average number of shares outstanding				
Basic	333,476,258	337,208,284	342,698,772	362,261,324
Diluted	333,476,258	337,208,284	342,698,772	362,261,324

SOURCE: Groupon, Inc. *10-K* (March 30, 2012), p. 38.

EXHIBIT 5
Groupon, Inc. Consolidated Balance Sheets (In thousands, except share and per-share amounts)

	December 31	
	2010	2011
Assets		
Current assets:		
Cash and cash equivalents	$ 118,833	$ 1,122,935
Accounts receivable, net	42,407	108,747
Prepaid expenses and other current assets	12,615	91,645
Total current assets	173,855	1,323,327
Property and equipment, net	16,490	51,800
Goodwill	132,038	166,903
Intangible assets, net	40,775	45,667
Investments in equity interests	—	50,604
Deferred income taxes, non-current	14,544	46,104
Other non-current assets	3,868	90,071
Total assets	$ 381,570	$ 1,774,476
Liabilities and stockholders' equity		
Current liabilities:		
Accounts payable	$ 57,543	$ 40,918
Accrued merchant payable	162,409	520,723
Accrued expenses	98,323	212,007
Due to related parties	13,321	246
Deferred income taxes, current	17,210	76,841
Other current liabilities	21,613	144,427
Total current liabilities	370,419	995,162
Deferred income taxes, non-current	604	7,428
Other non-current liabilities	1,017	70,766
Total liabilities	372,040	1,073,356
Commitments and contingencies (see Note 8)		
Redeemable noncontrolling interests	2,983	1,653
Groupon, Inc. Stockholders' Equity		
Series D, convertible preferred stock, $.0001 par value, 6,560,174 shares authorized and issued, 6,258,297 shares outstanding at December 31, 2010, and no shares outstanding at December 31, 2011	1	—
Series F, convertible preferred stock, $.0001 par value, 4,202,658 shares authorized, issued, and outstanding at December 31, 2010, and no shares outstanding December 31, 2011	1	—
Series G, convertible preferred stock, $.0001 par value, 30,075,690 shares authorized, 14,245,018 shares issued and outstanding at December 31, 2010 and no shares outstanding at December 31, 2011, liquidation preference of $450,000 at December 31, 2010	1	—

(continued)

EXHIBIT 5
(Continued)

	December 31	
	2010	**2011**
Voting common stock, $.0001 par value, 1,000,000,000 shares authorized, 422,991,996 shares issued and 331,232,520 shares outstanding at December 31, 2010 and no shares outstanding at December 31, 2011	4	—
Class A common stock, par value $0.0001 per share, no shares authorized, issued, and outstanding at December 31, 2010; 2,000,000,000 shares authorized, 641,745,225 shares issued and outstanding at December 31, 2011	—	64
Treasury stock, at cost, 93,328,656 shares at December 31, 2010 and no shares outstanding at December 31, 2011	(503,173)	—
Additional paid-in capital	921,122	1,388,253
Stockholder receivable	(286)	—
Accumulated deficit	(419,468)	(698,704)
Accumulated other comprehensive income	9,875	12,928
Total Groupon, Inc. Stockholders' Equity	**8,077**	**702,541**
Noncontrolling interests	(1,530)	(3,074)
Total equity	**6,547**	**699,467**
Total liabilities and equity	**$ 381,570**	**$ 1,774,476**

SOURCE: Groupon, Inc. 10-K (March 30, 2012), p. 65.

Selling expenses reported in **Exhibit 4** consisted of "payroll and sales commissions for sales representatives, as well as costs associated with supporting the sales function such as technology, telecommunications, and travel."[40] For the years 2009, 2010, and 2011, total selling, general, and administrative expenses were reported at US$5.8 million, US$196.6 million, and US$821.0 million, respectively.[41] Groupon attributed these increases largely to the expansion of its global sales force as well as investments in technology and corporate infrastructure.[42] Like its marketing expense, Groupon expected that selling, general, and administrative expenses would decrease as a percentage of revenue as its operations matured over time.

The underlying concern regarding Groupon's financials was that the company realized a total net loss in income every year since its inception. For the years 2008 through 2011, these losses amounted to US$1.5 million, US$1.3 million, US$413.3 million, and US$297.7 million, respectively.[43] As shown in the statement of retained earnings in **Exhibit 6**, these losses led to an accumulated deficit of US$698.7 million in 2011. In this light, management decided not to pay dividends, intending instead "to retain all of our earnings for the foreseeable future to finance the operation and expansion of our business."[44]

EXHIBIT 6
Consolidated Statement of Retained Earnings (thousands)

Report Date	12/31/2011	12/31/2010	12/31/2009	12/31/2008
Previous retained earnings (accumulated deficit)	(419,468)	(29,828)	(2,574)	(1,032)
Common stock dividends	—	—	20,338	—
Preferred stock dividends	—	—	5,575	—
Forfeiture of dividends	(191)	—	—	—
Retained earnings (accumulated deficit)	(698,704)	(419,468)	(29,828)	(2,574)

SOURCE: Mergent Online.

In 2012, Groupon continued to see exceptional growth in revenues. **Exhibit 7** compares the results of operations from the quarter ended March 31, 2012 to the quarter ended March 31, 2011. For the first quarter of 2012, the company reported revenues of US$559.3 million, compared to US$295.5 million for the first quarter of 2011.[45] Total operating expenses continue to rise in 2012, increasing by US$106.9 million from the first quarter of 2011, reflecting significant increases in cost of revenue and selling expenses. Groupon made strides toward cutting marketing spending in 2012, reporting US$116.6 million in marketing expenses compared to US$230.1 million in the first quarter of 2011. The company attributed this expense cut to a strengthening brand name that allowed it to become more established in markets around the globe. As of March 31, 2012, Groupon reported 36.8 million active customers, more than double the 15.3 million reported on March 31, 2011.[46] The amount of revenue that Groupon received per customer had not increased, however; revenue per average active customer was

EXHIBIT 7
Groupon, Inc.
Condensed Consolidated Statements
of Operations (In
thousands, except
share and per-
share amounts)
(unaudited)

	Three Months Ended March 31	
	2011	2012
(Restated)		
Revenue (gross billings of $668, 174 and $1,354,800, respectively)	$ 295,523	$ 559,283
Costs and expenses:		
Cost of revenue	39,765	119,498
Marketing	230,085	116,615
Selling, general, and administrative	142,821	283,583
Acquisition-related	—	(52)
Total operating expenses	412,671	519,644
(Loss) income from operations	(117,148)	39,639
Interest and other income (expense), net	1,060	(3,539)
Equity-method investment activity, net of tax	(882)	(5,128)
(Loss) income before provision for income taxes	(116,970)	30,972
Provision (benefit) for income taxes	(3,079)	34,565
Net loss:	(113,891)	(3,593)
Less: Net loss (income) attributable to noncontrolling interests	11,223	(880)
Net loss attributable to Groupon, Inc.	(102,668)	(4,473)
Redemption of preferred stock in excess of carrying value	(34,327)	—
Adjustment of redeemable noncontrolling interests to redemption value	(9,485)	(7,222)
Net loss attributable to common stockholders	$ (146,480)	$ (11,695)
Net loss per share:		
Basic	$ (0.48)	$ (0.02)
Diluted	$ (0.48)	$ (0.02)
Weighted average number of shares outstanding:		
Basic	307,849,412	644,097,375
Diluted	307,849,412	644,097,375

SOURCE: Groupon, Inc. *10-Q* (May, 15, 2012), p. 5.

reported at US$72.41 on March 31, 2011, compared to US$71.77 on March 31, 2012.[47] Rather than adding revenue solely by acquiring more customers, Groupon was searching for ways to increase the amount of revenue it received per subscriber from its existing base.

"We Don't Measure Ourselves in Conventional Ways"

Investors and the Securities and Exchange Commission began to question management's reporting of Groupon's financials. Although Groupon disclosed all financial data required by the SEC, management stressed the importance of other, more unconventional metrics. The company, which said that it did not "measure [itself] in conventional ways," placed more importance on metrics such as adjusted consolidated segment operating income, free cash flow, and gross billings, rather than net income.[48] Groupon reported net losses in each of the past three years and believed that unique metrics better reflected its financial progress.

Groupon defined adjusted consolidated segment operating income (CSOI) as "the consolidated segment operating income before new subscriber acquisition costs and certain non-cash charges."[49] It believed that adjusted CSOI was an important measure of the performance of its business since adjusted CSOI excluded expenses that management believed were not indicative of future operating expenses. Free cash flow was defined as cash flow from operations reduced by "purchases of property and equipment"[50] and although the measure could be revealing, Groupon acknowledged that it was a non-GAAP financial measure. Gross billings, another proprietary metric, was the gross amount collected from customers for Groupons sold. Management viewed gross billings as a measurement of growth, but its use in revenue recognition was a source of controversy. Wall Street observers argued that Groupon's use of these non-GAAP measures was simply a strategy to portray its financials favorably in light of its lack of profitability.[51]

In 2011, Groupon had to restate its earnings for the three months ended March 31, 2011 "to correct for an error in its presentation of revenue."[52] Groupon historically reported its revenue as the gross amounts billed to its subscribers. The revision required revenue to be restated as the net of the amounts related to merchant fees. This error prompted the company to report a "material weakness" in its internal control over financial reporting.[53] The Condensed Statement of Operations shown in **Exhibit 8** for the three months ended March 31, 2011, was restated to show the net amount the company retained after paying merchant fees. Several other income statement expenses were changed as well to align with the reporting of revenue on a net basis.

Then, on March 30, 2012, the company announced that it would also have to restate earnings for the fourth quarter of 2011 after a higher-than-expected number of customers demanded refunds.[54] Going forward, management planned to improve its internal controls for financial reporting. With significant errors and multiple financial restatements present in

EXHIBIT 8
Groupon, Inc. Notes to Condensed Consolidated Financial Statements for the Three Months Ended March 31, 2011, In Thousands (Unaudited)

	As previously reported (unaudited)	Restatement adjustment	As restated
Revenue	$ 644,728	(349,205)	$ 295,523
Cost of revenue	$ 374,728	(334,963)	$ 39,765
Marketing	$ 208,209	21,876	$ 230,085
Selling, general, and administrative	$ 178,939	(36,118)	$ 142,821

SOURCE: Groupon, Inc. *10-Q* (May 15, 2012), p. 11.

Groupon's first year as a publicly traded company, investors continued to question the company's disclosure methods and the reliability of its internal reports. Five federal class action securities complaints, and six federal and two state stockholder derivative lawsuits had been brought against Groupon and its current and former directors and officers since the restatement.[55] The addition of new members of the Board of Directors with accounting and financial expertise was considered necessary to regain investor confidence.[56]

Information Technology

Groupon did not equivocate regarding technology's importance to its operations and business strategy:

> We employ technology to improve the experience we offer subscribers and merchant partners, increase the rate at which our customers purchase Groupons, and enhance the efficiency of our business operations. A component of our strategy is to continue developing and refining our technology.[57]

Almost all of the company's communication with both customers and merchant partners was electronic. It was important for Groupon to adopt an information system that would facilitate efficient communication with both merchants and customers. Groupon used a common information technology platform that enhanced communication while also providing management and merchant partners the ability to track deal performance and analytics for demographic data and capacity. The platform included business operations tools to track internal workflow; applications and infrastructure to serve content at scale; dashboards and reporting tools to display operating and financial metrics for historical and ongoing deals; and a publishing and purchasing system for consumers.[58] Groupon used the platform only in North American operations in 2012, but management planned to merge the system with the company's more segmented international information technology platforms. While there was no timetable in place for this move, Groupon reported that it planned to "enable greater efficiencies and consistency across [its] global organization."[59]

Information system platforms, as well as websites, applications, and back-end business intelligence systems were hosted at data centers in Florida, Texas, California, and overseas in Asia and Europe. For security purposes, Groupon used commercial antivirus, firewall, and patch-management technologies to protect and maintain systems located at the data centers. To ensure the security of its website as well as customer transactions, Groupon also invested in intrusion and pattern detection tools, as well as Secure Socket Layer (SSL) to provide encryption for transferring data. These security measures were easily scalable to accommodate increasing numbers of subscribers.[60]

Marketing

Since the company's founding, marketing had been at the core of Groupon's business strategy. Management's aggressive marketing efforts fueled revenue approaching US$2 billion in three years of existence. A first mover in the daily deal industry, Groupon owned number-one market share in 37 of 48 countries served as of the first quarter of 2012.[61] Specifically in North America, Groupon held 53% market share, as of the second quarter of 2012.[62]

Critical to Groupon's strategy was growing its subscriber and customer base. As stated earlier, the vast majority of its investments to fuel this growth were through online marketing initiatives: search engine marketing, display advertisements, referral programs, and affiliate marketing.[63] Groupon also marketed to merchant partners to grow the number and variety of deals it could offer customers. To further increase merchant partner growth, Groupon utilized a sales force of over 5000 inside and outside representatives. The sales force was responsible for building partner relationships as well as providing local expertise.

The company focused the majority of its marketing efforts on demographics most likely to use a Groupon: relatively young consumers more prone to search for discounts when shopping and most likely to use the Internet or mobile applications to do so. According to Morpace Inc., the majority of Groupon's customers (40.2%) were between the ages of 18 and 34,[64] and although women were historically more likely to purchase online coupons, men and women had been found almost equally likely to use Groupon deals. As with all coupon users, Groupon users had higher income.[65]

Groupon's attempt to participate in national television ads during the 2011 Super Bowl was widely criticized. A series of ads meant to "spoof" typical celebrity-endorsed public service announcements fell flat and many found the ads offensive.[66] Groupon dropped the ads and ultimately stopped working with the advertising agency that created the spots.[67]

Groupon's investments in marketing were substantial. Marketing expenses were largely variable, increasing significantly as revenues grew. For the years ended 2008 through 2011, marketing expenses were reported at US$163 thousand, US$5.05 million, US$290.57 million, and US$768.47 million, respectively (see **Exhibit 4**).

Distribution. The distribution of Groupon's deals relied heavily on technology. Deals were distributed to customers directly through daily e-mails, websites, and mobile applications, as well as through social networks. In an effort to reach more potential customers, Groupon also utilized various online affiliates to display and promote deals on their websites. The company's "online affiliates" included eBay, Microsoft, Yahoo, and Zynga.[68] Partnerships allowed for the distribution of daily deals to not only Groupon's customer base, but also to the affiliate's user base. Groupon also partnered with thousands of smaller online affiliates that could embed a Groupon widget on their websites and earn a commission whenever their site's visitors purchased Groupons through the link.[69] Management believed that leveraging affiliate relationships online in this manner would extend the distribution of Groupon deals to a larger customer base.

In an effort to attract more customers and to ease communication with existing customers, Groupon launched a mobile application in March 2010. Deals were offered at no additional cost on the iPhone, Android, BlackBerry, and Windows mobile operating systems. The applications allowed consumers to "browse, purchase, manage and redeem deals on their mobile devices as well as access Groupon Now! Deals that were offered based on the location of the mobile user."[70] In this way, the mobile applications promoted immediate deals based on the customer's desire and location. As of December 31, 2011, the Groupon App had been downloaded over 26 million times.[71]

Groupon began targeting online social networks as another possible distribution channel. Daily deals were published through various social networks, while website and mobile application interfaces also allowed consumers to push notifications of deals to their personal social network. Groupon acknowledged that social networks were not yet a "material portion of customer acquisition."[72]

Products. Founded strictly as a daily deals service, Groupon historically did not offer much variety in terms of deal categories. As its operations grew, however, Groupon made an effort to transition "from offering deals only through email to having a local commerce marketplace where customers can purchase Groupons for a variety of services and products from local, national and online merchants."[73] In 2012, Groupon offered the following types of deals:[74]

- *Featured Daily Deals* were distributed by targeting technology to current and potential customers based on location and personal preferences. Daily deals were sent to subscribers through mass e-mails and posted on the website and mobile application. This product was launched in October 2008 and was offered in all North American and International markets.

- Groupon's primary focus was on local deals, but the company also offered *National Deals* from national merchants to build brand awareness and acquire new customers in the North American market. It featured deals from over 100 national merchant partners, including Domino's Pizza, Sony Electronics, and The Body Shop.

- *Groupon Now!* deals were initiated by a merchant on demand and offered instantly to customers through mobile devices and the Groupon website. These deals targeted current and potential customers within close proximity of the merchant, and the purchased Groupons typically expired within a few hours of the deal launch. This product was launched in the second quarter of 2011.

- *Groupon Goods* enabled customers to purchase vouchers for products directly from the website or mobile application. Deals were offered for a variety of product categories, including electronics, home and garden, and toys. This product was launched in September 2011 in select North American and International markets.

- *Groupon Getaways* are travel deals that feature domestic and international hotels, airfare, and package deals. Groupon Getaways was launched in July 2011.

- *GrouponLive* is a partnership with LiveNation whereby Groupon serves as a local resource for LiveNation events and clients of its global ticketing business, Ticketmaster. GrouponLive is offered as part of the featured daily deals and was launched in May 2011.

- *Groupon Rewards*, a free service to merchant partners that allowed customers to earn reward points through repeat visits that could be used to unlock special deals, were launched in October 2011.

Competition

Groupon rose to prominence in uncertain economic conditions—during the Great Recession and its slow recovery. Consumers began spending less as a result of the financial crisis, and so the demand for coupons increased. At the same time, merchants began looking for new and effective ways of attracting business. This combination could explain why Groupon might owe some of its unprecedented growth to the economic environment into which it was born, but it also explained the more recent blitz of competition Groupon has faced.

Andrew Mason's idea to apply the tipping point principle to online commerce and facilitate the leveraging of consumers' collective power was innovative and established Groupon as a first mover in the daily deals segment. The ease with which the business model could be replicated, however—in concert with the strong demand for discounts—ensured that Groupon would not be the only company competing for market share.

Groupon's competition was fairly broad; the company competed with traditional offline coupon and discount services, as well as newspapers, magazines, and other traditional media companies that provided coupons and discounts on products and services.[75] The most intense competition was with companies utilizing the online daily deals business model—to whatever extent and with whatever focus. Some such competitors offered deals as an add-on to their core business, while others adopted a business model similar to Groupon's.[76] These included GiltCity, DailyDeals.com, Bloomspot, and Eversave. Competition also existed in more narrowly positioned companies that offered services more focused on particular merchant categories or markets. They included Daily Pride, for the Lesbian, Gay, Bisexual, and Transgendered community; Jewpon, for the Jewish community; My Pet Savings, for pet owners; and GroupPrice, for online businesses, among others.

Groupon's most directly matched competitor was LivingSocial, a Washington DC, daily-deals website that operated a similar e-mail-based business model. As of December 2011, LivingSocial had about 46 million subscribers spread across 25 countries.[77] The company's deal categories, somewhat more expansive than Groupon's, included nationwide deals and deals for families, escapes, and adventures.[78] LivingSocial, a private company valued in 2010 at US$200 million, was valued in 2011 at US$3 billion after rounds of investing that included funding from the likes of Amazon.com.[79]

Amazon operated its own daily-deals service in addition to its ties to LivingSocial. AmazonLocal launched in mid-2011 and offered customers savings from select businesses in their neighborhoods and nationwide.[80] Around the same time, Google—after its offer to acquire Groupon was rejected in late 2010—began testing its own service, Google Offers.[81] Both Google Offers and AmazonLocal had extensive, available resources from their established and wealthy parent companies, and both Amazon and Google typified the competitors that Groupon expressed concern about in its annual report:

> Many of our current and potential competitors have longer operating histories, significantly greater financial, technical, marketing, and other resources, and larger customer bases than we do. These factors may allow our competitors to benefit from their existing customer base with lower acquisition costs or to respond more quickly than we can to new or emerging technologies and changes in customer requirements. These competitors may engage in more extensive research and development efforts, undertake more far-reaching marketing campaigns and adopt more aggressive pricing policies, which may allow them to build a larger subscriber base or to monetize that subscriber base more effectively than we do. Our competitors may develop products or services that are similar to our products and services or that achieve greater market acceptance than our products and services.[82]

Legal Issues[83]

Regulation.   Groupon was subject to a variety of regulations across the jurisdictions where it conducted its business, including, for example, consumer protection, marketing practices, tax and privacy rules, and regulations. Additional areas of concern included the evolving regulation of Internet business, the Credit Card Responsibility and Disclosure (CARD) Act of 2009, gift certificates/cards, disclosure of security breaches of personal data, and liability under the Digital Millennium Copyright Act (DMCA) for linking to third-party websites that include materials that infringe copyrights or other rights.[84] Some of Groupon's merchants raised concerns within their own industries about the appearance of fee-splitting, kickbacks for referrals, and the ethics of using Groupons and other daily deals for health services and the purchase of alcohol.[85, 86]

Litigation.   As described earlier, Groupon and its current and former directors and officers faced numerous class action lawsuits following its restatement of earnings in 2012. Groupon was also involved in, and at risk of, litigation concerning intellectual property infringement suits and suits by customers (individually or as class actions) alleging, among other things, violation of the Credit Card Accountability, Responsibility and Disclosure Act and state laws governing gift cards, stored value cards, and coupons. The company believed that additional lawsuits alleging that Groupon had violated patent, copyright, or trademark laws would be filed against it.

Looking to the Future

As Groupon continued to grow over the past year, it reported a net loss of only US$3.6 million in the first quarter of 2012, compared to US$113.9 million for that of 2011.[87] Marketing expenses were coming under control. The number of subscribers and merchants continued to grow, and promising new products were being pilot tested in specific markets. The company's prospects looked brighter in 2012 than in years past, but it had yet to record a profit. The question remained whether or not Andrew Mason's Groupon could do so in the future.

NOTES

1. Herb Greenberg, "The Worst CEO for 2012?" *Market Insider, CNBC.* April 12, 2012. http://www.cnbc.com/id/47030593 (last visited August 20, 2012).
2. The Amazing Rise (and Inevitable Fall?) of Groupon. *Online MBA.* http://www.onlinemba.com/the-amazing-rise-of-groupon/ (last visited July 16, 2012).
3. Ibid.
4. Leah Goldman and Alyson Shontell, "Groupon: From The Ashes Of a Dead Startup to a Billion-Dollar Company In 2 Years." *Business Insider.* June 4, 2011.
5. Ibid.
6. Ibid.
7. Bari Weiss, "Groupon's $6 Billion Gambler." *The Wall Street Journal.* December 20, 2010.
8. The Amazing Rise (and Inevitable Fall?) of Groupon.
9. Ibid.
10. Christopher Steiner, "Meet the Fastest Growing Company Ever." *Forbes.* August 30, 2010.
11. Evelyn M. Rusli and Jenna Wortham. "Groupon Said to Reject Google's Offer." *The New York Times, DealBook.* December 3, 2010.
12. Alistair Barr and Clare Baldwin. "Groupon's IPO Biggest by U.S. Web Company since Google." *Reuters.* November 4, 2011.
13. Groupon, Inc. *10-K* (March 30, 2012), p. 3.
14. Ibid.
15. Ibid., p. 6.
16. Ibid.
17. Ibid.
18. Christopher Steiner, "Meet the Fastest Growing Company Ever."
19. Sarah E. Needleman and Shayndi Raice. "Groupon Holds Cash Tight." *The Wall Street Journal.* November 10, 2011.
20. Ari Levy. "Groupon Declines on Concern that Merchants Are Retreating from Daily Deals." *Bloomberg Businessweek.* January 3, 2012.
21. Ibid.
22. Andrew Mason. Groupon, Inc. 2011 Letter to Stockholders. p. 1.
23. Groupon, Inc. *10-K* (March 30, 2012), p. 7–8. This section was quoted directly with minor editing.
24. Groupon, Inc. Investor Relations, http://investor.groupon.com/directors.cfm, (last visited July 15, 2012). This section was quoted directly with minor editing.
25. Brian Womack, "Groupon Bolsters Board with AmEx's Henry, Deloitte's Bass." *Bloomberg Businessweek.* May 1, 2012. http://www.bloomberg.com/news/2012-04-30/groupon-adds-amex-s-henry-deloitte-s-bass-to-bolster-board-1-.html.
26. Groupon, Inc. *10-K* (March 30, 2012), p. 14. This section was quoted directly with minor editing.
27. Groupon, Inc. *10-Q* (May 15, 2012), p. 40.
28. Groupon, Inc. "Meet the Team, Merchant Resources." http://www.grouponworks.com/merchant-resources/meet-the-team (last visited August 25, 2012).
29. Groupon, Inc. *10-K* (March 30, 2012), p. 21.
30. Ibid.
31. Ibid., p. 101.
32. Groupon, Inc. 2012 Proxy Statement (June 19, 2012), p. 13.
33. Ibid.
34. Privco. Groupon Inc. Report on Groupon complied by Privco. March 2012. http://www.privco.com/private-company/groupon-inc.
35. Groupon, Inc. *10-K* (March 30, 2012), p. 38.
36. Ibid., p. 45.
37. Ibid., p. 46.
38. Ibid., p. 44.
39. Ibid., p. 8.
40. Ibid., p. 74.
41. Ibid., p. 44.
42. Ibid., p. 48
43. Mergent Inc., *Mergent Online.* http://www.mergentonline.com.
44. Groupon, Inc. *10-K* (March 30, 2012), p. 31.
45. Groupon, Inc. *10-Q* (May 15, 2012), p. 5.
46. Ibid., p. 25.
47. Ibid.
48. Groupon, Inc. *S-1* (June 2, 2011), p. 1.
49. Ibid., p. 9.
50. Groupon, Inc. *10-K* (March 30, 2012), p. 41.
51. Marielle Segarra. "Groupon CFO Defends Use of Non-GAAP Measures." CFO.com, February 10, 2012. http://www3.cfo.com/article/2012/2/accounting-tax_groupon-cfo-jason-child-defends-non-gaap-metrics.
52. Groupon, Inc. *10-Q* (May, 15, 2012), p. 10.
53. Ibid., p. 15.
54. Shayndi Raice and John Letzing, "Groupon Forced to Revise Results." *The Wall Street Journal.* April 2, 2012.
55. Groupon, Inc. *10-Q* (August 14, 2012), p. 16.
56. Douglas MacMillan, "Groupon Is Said to Seek New Directors After Restatement." Bloomberg Businessweek, April 24, 2012. http://www.bloomberg.com/news/2012-04-24/groupon-is-said-to-seek-new-directors-after-revenue-restatement.html.
57. Groupon, Inc. *10-K* (March 30, 2012), p. 11.
58. Ibid.
59. Ibid.
60. Ibid.
61. Groupon, Inc. Investor Presentation. June 2012.
62. Douglas MacMillan, "Groupon Loses Market Share as Online Daily Deals Decline." *Bloomberg Businessweek,* August 15, 2012. http://www.businessweek.com/news/2012-08-15/groupon-loses-market-share-as-online-daily-deals-decline.
63. Groupon, Inc. *10-K* (March 30, 2012), p. 8.
64. eMarketer, "Groupon and the Online Deal Revolution." *eMarketer,* June 7, 2011.
65. Ibid.
66. Philip Caulfield. "Groupon Super Bowl Ad Falls Flat; Slammed for Making Fun of China-Tibet Conflict." New York Daily News. February 7, 2011. http://articles.nydailynews.com/2011-02-07/entertainment/28536983_1_groupon-ceo-andrew-mason-tibetans-ads-and-one.

67. Rupal Parekh. "Groupon CEO: We Placed Too Much Trust in Agency for Super Bowl Ads." *Advertising Age*. March 21, 2011. http://adage.com/article/news/groupon-ceo-relied-agency-bowl-ads/149498/.

68. Groupon, Inc. *10-K* (March 30, 2012), p. 8.

69. Ibid., p. 10.

70. Ibid.

71. Ibid.

72. Ibid.

73. Ibid., p. 9.

74. Ibid. This section was quoted directly with minor editing.

75. Ibid., p. 11

76. Ibid.

77. Evelyn M. Rusli. "LivingSocial Looks to Raise $400 Million." *The New York Times, DealBook*. December 7, 2011.

78. LivingSocial, home page. www.LivingSocial.com.

79. Thomas Heath and Steven Overly. "LivingSocial, Based in D.C., Raises $400 Million as It Vies with Groupon." *The Washington Post*. April 5, 2011.

80. "Growing Up Fast: AmazonLocal Celebrates First Birthday with Sweepstakes." *The New York Times*. June 1, 2012.

81. Miguel Helft. "Google vs. Groupon." *The New York Times, Bits Blog*. June 1, 2011.

82. Groupon, Inc. 10-K (March 30, 2012), p. 12.

83. Ibid., p. 82.

84. Ibid., p. 12.

85. Kelly Soderlund. "Dental Groupons, Incentives." *ADA News*, November 21, 2011. http://www.ada.org/news/6576.aspx

86. Donna Goodison. "State: Groupon, Online Discounters Can't Offer Alcohol Deals." *Boston Herald.com,* March 14, 2011. http://bostonherald.com/jobfind/news/technology/view/2011_0314massachusetts_groupon_online_discounters_cant_offer_happy_hour_alcohol_deals_state_groupon_online_discounters_cant_offer_alcohol_deals

87. Groupon, Inc. *10-Q* (May, 15, 2012), p. 5.

CASE 12

Netflix, Inc.

THE 2011 REBRANDING/PRICE INCREASE DEBACLE

Alan N. Hoffman
Bentley University

In 2011, Netflix was the world's largest online movie rental service. Its subscribers paid to have DVDs delivered to their homes through the U.S. mail, or to access and watch unlimited TV shows and movies streamed over the Internet to their TVs, mobile devices, or computers. The company was founded by Marc Randolph and Reed Hastings in August, 1997 in Scotts Valley, California, after they had left Pure Software. Hastings was inspired to start Netflix after being charged US$40 for an overdue video.[1] Initially, Netflix provided movies at US$6 per rental, but moved to a monthly subscription rate in 1999, dropping the single-rental model soon after. From then on, the company built its reputation on the business model of flat fee unlimited rentals per month without any late fees, or shipping and handling fees.

In May 2002, Netflix went public with a successful IPO, selling 5.5 million shares of common stock at the IPO price of US$15 per share to raise US$82.5 million. After incurring substantial losses during its first few years of operations, Netflix turned a profit of US$6.5 million during the fiscal year 2003.[2] The company's subscriber base grew strongly and steadily from one million in the fourth quarter of 2002 to over 27 million in July 2012.[3]

By 2012, Netflix had over 100,000 titles distributed via more than 50 shipment centers, insuring customers received their DVDs in one to two business days, which made Netflix one of the most successful dotcom ventures in the past two decades.[4] The company employed almost 4100 people, 2200 of whom were part-time employees.[5] In September 2010, Netflix began international operations by offering an unlimited streaming plan without DVDs in Canada. In September 2011, Netflix expanded its international operations to customers in the Caribbean, Mexico, and Central and South America.

Key to Netflix's success was its no late fee policy. Netflix's profits were directly proportional to the number of days the customer kept a DVD. Most customers wanted to view a new DVD release as soon as possible. If Netflix imposed a late fee, it would have to have multiple copies of the new releases and find a way to remain profitable. However, because of the no-late-fee rule,

....

The authors would like to thank Barbara Gottfried, Ashna Dhawan, Emira Ajeti, Neel Bhalaria, Tarun Chugh, and Will Hoffman for their research and contributions to this case. Please address all correspondence to: Dr. Alan N. Hoffman, Dept. of Management, Bentley University, 175 Forest Street, Waltham, MA 02452-4705, voice (781) 891-2287, ahoffman@bentley.edu. Printed by permission of Alan N. Hoffman.

the demand for the newer movies was spread over a period of time, ensuring an efficient circulation of movies.[6]

On September 18, 2011, Netflix CEO and co-founder Reed Hastings announced on the Netflix blog that the company was splitting its DVD delivery service from its online streaming service, rebranding its DVD delivery service Qwikster as a way to differentiate it from its online streaming service, and creating a new website for it. Three weeks later, in response to customer outrage and confusion, Hastings rescinded rebranding the DVD delivery service Qwikster and reintegrating it into Netflix. Nevertheless, by October 24, 2011, only five weeks after the initial split, Netflix acknowledged that it had lost 800,000 U.S. subscribers and expected to lose yet more, thanks both to the Qwikster debacle and the price hike the company had decided was necessary to cover increasing content costs.[7]

Despite this setback, Netflix continued to believe that by providing the cheapest and best subscription-paid, commercial-free streaming of movies and TV shows it could still rapidly and profitably fulfill its envisioned goal to become the world's best entertainment distribution platform.

Online Streaming

By the end of 2011, Netflix had 24.4 million subscribers, making it the largest provider of online streaming content in the world.[8] Subscription numbers had grown exponentially, increasing 250% from 9.3 million in 2008. At the same time, Netflix proactively recognized that the demand for DVDs by mail had peaked, and the future growth would be in online streaming. With 245 million Internet users in the U.S., and 2.2 billion[9] worldwide, Netflix saw the opportunity to expand its online streaming base both domestically and internationally to become a dominant world player. In 2011, Netflix expanded into Canada and Central America, and in 2012 into Ireland and the United Kingdom.[10]

The scarce resource for the online video industry was bandwidth, the amount of data that can be carried from one point to another in a given time period.[11] With the introduction of Blu-ray discs, the demand for higher- and better-quality picture and sound streaming increased, which in turn increased the demand for higher bandwidths. At the same time, cheaper Internet connections and faster download speeds made it easier and more affordable for customers to take advantage of the services Netflix and its competitors offered. If the cost of Internet access was to increase, it would directly affect sales in the industry's streaming segment.

Netflix was a leader in developing streaming technologies, increasing its spending on technology and development from US$114 million (2009) to US$258 million in 2011[12] (8% of its revenue),[13] and initiating a US$1 million five-year prize in to improve the existing algorithm of Netflix's recommendation service by at least 10%. Because Netflix had already developed proprietary streaming software and an extensive content library, it had a head start in the online streaming market, and with continued investments in technological enhancements, hoped to maintain its lead.[14] However, increased competition in streaming, ISP fair-use charges, and piracy were some of the major challenges it faced.

In March 2011, Netflix made its services readily available to consumers through Smartphones, tablets and video game consoles when only 35% of the total U.S. market were using Internet-enabled Smartphones.[15] Thus, the expansion potential for Netflix in this market was substantial. The Great Recession of 2008–2010 was a boon for Netflix as people cut down on high-value discretionary spending, choosing "value for money" Internet offerings instead.[16] However, in its annual letter to shareholders, Netflix acknowledged that many of its customers were among the highest users of data on an ISPs network and in the near future it expected that such users might be forced to pay extra for their data usage, which could be a major deterrent for the growth of Netflix because most of its customers are highly price sensitive.

Demographics

The number of Internet users in the United States had increased from about 205 million in 2005 to 245 million in 2012.[17] According to a research report by Mintel investment research database, the percentage of people using the Internet to stream video has jumped from 5% (2005) to 17% (2011), significantly growing the market for online streaming services such as Netflix. At the same time, the recession of 2008–2010, with its high unemployment and slow economic growth had a significant impact on the spending habits of U.S. consumers. More and more people chose to forego an evening at the movie theatre in favor of home movie rentals to save on costs.[18] By 2011, the crucial 18- to 34-year-old demographic saw the Internet as its prime source of access to entertainment. However, this demographic, was particularly sensitive to price fluctuations. When Netflix changed its pricing structure in the third quarter of 2011, subscriptions immediately dropped off 3%. Mintel Research reported that only 15% of the under 18–25 age bracket of its customers were ready to pay US$16/month for premium content via Netflix. In addition, the proliferation of free content over the Internet—Mega video, for example, with around 81 million unique visitors and a maximum exposure in the 18–33 demographic became a strong competitor for Netflix, further limiting the pricing power Netflix could exercise.[19]

The Mintel report also found that American households with two or more children and a household income of US$50,000 or more had a very favorable attitude toward Netflix;[20] Netflix fostered this trend by cutting a deal with Disney[21] that gave it access to content exclusively targeting young children.

At the same time that Netflix was increasing its customer base among the 18- to 34-year-olds and households with young children, both of whom preferred streaming, it lost ground with affluent Baby Boomers who still preferred to rent the DVDs over the Internet. Thus, Netflix needed to fine-tune its strategy to include this older demographic since people over 60 had US$1 trillion in discretionary income per year, and fewer familial responsibilities, making them a prime target demographic for expanding Netflix's customer base.[22]

The availability of high-speed Internet at home and the shift to online TVs created opportunities for Netflix. The company recognized that to fully leverage the current world of technological convergence, it needed to compete on as many platforms as possible, and created applications for the Xbox, Wii, PS3, iPad, Apple TV, Windows phone, and Android. The company also collaborated with TV manufacturers to integrate Netflix directly into the latest televisions.[23]

Netflix's Competitors

Netflix's great operational advantage in the DVD rental market was its nationwide distribution network, which prevented the entry of many of its potential competitors. While only Netflix provided both mail delivery and online rentals, with the growth of online streaming, Netflix's advantage shrank and it faced increasing competition from Blockbuster, Wal-Mart, Amazon, Hulu, and Redbox.

Netflix's one-time strongest competitor, **Blockbuster** LLC, founded in 1985, and headquartered in McKinney, Texas, provided in-home movie and game entertainment, originally through over 5000 video rental stores throughout the Americas, Europe, Asia, and Australia, and later by adding DVD-by-mail, streaming video on demand, and kiosks. Its business model emphasized providing convenient access to media entertainment across multiple channels, recognizing that the same customer might choose different ways to access media entertainment on different nights. Competition from Netflix and other video rental companies forced

Blockbuster to file for bankruptcy on September 23, 2010, and on April 6, 2011, satellite television provider Dish Network bought it at auction for US$233 million.[24]

Redbox Automated Retail, LLC, a wholly owned subsidiary of Coinstar Inc., specialized in DVD, Blu-ray, and rentals via automated retail kiosks. By June 2011, Redbox had over 33,000 kiosks in over 27,800 locations worldwide,[25] and was considering launching an online streaming service, perhaps for as cheaply as US$3.95 per month.

Vudu, Inc., formerly known as Marquee, Inc., founded in 2004, a content delivery media technology company acquired by **Wal-Mart** in March 2010, worked by allowing users to stream movies and TV shows to Sony PlayStation3, Blu-ray players, HDTVs, computers, or home theaters. VUDU Box and VUDU XL provided access to movies and television shows; users also needed a VUDU Wireless Kit to connect VUDU Box/VUDU XL to the Internet. Based in Santa Clara, California, the company was the third most popular online movie service, with a market share of 5.3%.[26] Vudu had no monthly subscription fee, instead users deposited funds to an online account which was reduced depending on how many movies the user rented. In other words, you paid for only what you watched.

In February 2011, Amazon.com, a multinational electronic commerce company, announced the launch for Amazon Prime members of unlimited, commercial-free instant streaming of all movies and TV shows to members' computers or HDTVs. In addition, Amazon Prime members were given access to the Kindle Owners' Lending Library, allowing them to borrow selected popular titles for free with no due date. For non-Amazon Prime members, 48-hour on-demand rentals were available for US$3.99, or the title could be bought outright.[27]

Hulu Plus was the first ad-supported subscription service for TV shows and films that could be accessed by computers, television sets, mobile phone, or other digital devices. Like Netflix, the streaming service cost US$8 per month, but unlike Netflix, Hulu offered more recent TV episodes and seasons. However, subscribers had to put up with ads, and Hulu's movie selection was much more limited than Netflix's selection.

Marc Schuh, an early financial backer of Netflix, observed that copying software was relatively simple.[28] Anyone could buy the best servers, processors, operating systems, and databases—but timing was crucial.[29] Barnes & Noble waited 17 months to enter the fray against Amazon, so that by 2012, Amazon had eight times the profit and 30 times the market capitalization of Barnes & Noble. Similarly, in the same year that Netflix's profits increased sevenfold, Blockbuster lost over one billion dollars.[30] Technology with correct timings can help a company gain competitive advantage over rivals. Other barriers to entry include investments in infrastructure aiding supply chain and delays from major production houses for gaining permission to stream their titles.

Rising Content Costs

In the DVD rental business, the rental company had the first sale doctrine, in which the company was permitted to rent a single disc many times to recover the cost of the content. But this doctrine did not apply to digital content, and the technological shift away from the DVD rental business was in part responsible for the excessive increase in content cost for Netflix.[31]

In addition, Netflix's dependence on outside content suppliers such as the six major movie studios and the top television networks contributed significantly to rising costs for the company. As an example, Liberty Media Corporation's Starz LLC had been an early Netflix supplier. In 2011, Starz demanded US$300 million to renew its deal with Netflix, testament to the power of suppliers in relation to market demand from an increasing number of competitors. On September 1, 2011, Netflix customers learned they would lose access to newer films from the Walt Disney Company and the Sony Corporation after talks to obtain those movies from Starz broke down. The loss created the impression of a major setback, even though the films were making up a smaller share of viewing than previously.

However, Netflix did sign new deals with the CW Network, DreamWorks Animation, and Discovery Communications in 2011.

Global Expansion

Beginning in 2007, Netflix shifted its focus to its streaming business in response to their customers' move to streaming in preference to DVD rentals and the rising cost of mailing DVDs. Conveniently, expanding its streaming business did not require expanding its physical infrastructure. This strategy has proven to be a major differentiator as it expands internationally in the Americas and Europe.

By the end of 2011, the company had started operations in Canada and 43 countries in Latin America, and planned to start European operations in early 2012. At the end of the third quarter of 2011, Netflix had 1.48 million international subscribers with predictions of 2 million by the end of the year.[32] The UK was considered a huge potential market. Twenty million UK households had broadband Internet, and 60% of those households subscribed to a paid movie service. In Latin America, four times that number had Internet access,[33] making international expansion there especially attractive to subscriber-hungry Netflix.

However, international expansion was potentially risky, as Netflix faced rising content costs from higher studio charges. In addition, international expansion required both broadening its content offerings and tailoring those offerings to meet the specific needs of each of its international markets, which Netflix feared would further increase content costs. It was clear that the correct content mix was crucial, yet a huge challenge for Netflix.

In addition, as Canada and the UK were already developed markets, Netflix faced local competition from a proliferation of DVD rental/streaming services. In the UK, for instance, Virgin and Sky already had strong brand recognition and balance sheets, and the Sky network had already contracted exclusive first-pay window rights to movies from all six major American studios, tough competition that could easily delay profitability from international operations.

Lower per capita income and slower Internet speeds, especially in Latin America, were further potential problems for Netflix's international expansion. In Canada, low data usage limits per subscriber were a concern for a data hungry service such as Netflix.

Financial Results

In 2011, Netflix surpassed US$3.2 billion in sales, an annual revenue growth of 50% over 2010 (US$2.1 billion, see **Exhibits 1–3**). Subscriber growth was the most important metric for Netflix because its revenue growth was directly correlated to its subscriber growth. Netflix grew from 12 million subscribers in 2009 to 20 million in 2010, and then to 27 million in 2012. International operations were set to expand to become a major source of sales growth for the company in the coming years.

However, by 2012, Netflix faced challenges from its pricing changes in the United States and its expansion into international markets, even stating that it expected revenue per subscriber to drop from its 2011 level of US$11.56[34] as subscribers choose the streaming only option of US$7.99 over the more expensive streaming and DVD delivery option. For future revenue growth, Netflix needed to increase its subscribers numbers both domestically and internationally.

EXHIBIT 1
Netflix, Inc.
Consolidated
Statements of
Operations[55] (in
thousands, except
per-share data)

	Year ended December 31		
	2011	**2010**	**2009**
Revenues	$3,204,577	$2,162,625	$1,670,269
Cost of revenues:			
Subscription	1,789,596	1,154,109	909,461
Fulfillment expenses	250,305	203,246	169,810
Total cost of revenues	2,039,901	1,357,355	1,079,271
Gross profit	1,164,676	805,270	590,998
Operating expenses:			
Marketing	402,638	293,839	237,744
Technology and development	259,033	163,329	114,542
General and administrative	117,937	64,461	46,773
Legal settlement	9,000	—	—
Total operating expenses	788,608	521,629	399,059
Operating income	376,068	283,641	191,939
Other income (expense):			
Interest expense	(20,025)	(19,629)	(6,475)
Interest and other income	3,479	3,684	6,728
Income before income taxes	359,522	267,696	192,192
Provision for income taxes	133,396	106,843	76,332
Net income	$226,126	$160,853	$115,860
Net income per share:			
Basic	$4.28	$3.06	$2.05
Diluted	$4.16	$2.96	$1.98
Weighted-average common shares outstanding:			
Basic	52,847	52,529	56,560
Diluted	54,369	54,304	58,416

EXHIBIT 2
Netflix, Inc.
Consolidated
Balance Sheets[55]
(in thousands,
except share and
per-share data)

	As of December 31	
	2011	**2010**
Assets		
Current assets:		
Cash and cash equivalents	$508,053	$194,499
Short-term investments	289,758	155,888
Current content library, net	919,709	181,006
Prepaid content	56,007	62,217
Other current assets	57,330	43,621
Total current assets	1,830,857	637,231
Non-current content library, net	1,046,934	180,973
Property and equipment, net	136,353	128,570
Other non-current assets	55,052	35,293
Total assets	$3,069,196	$982,067

EXHIBIT 2
(Continued)

As of December 31		
	2011	**2010**
Liabilities and stockholders' equity		
Current liabilities:		
Content accounts payable	$924,706	$168,695
Other accounts payable	87,860	54,129
Accrued expenses	63,693	38,572
Deferred revenue	148,796	127,183
Total current liabilities	1,225,055	388,579
Long-term debt	200,000	200,000
Long-term debt due to related party	200,000	—
Non-current content liabilities	739,628	48,179
Other non-current liabilities	61,703	55,145
Total liabilities	2,426,386	691,903
Commitments and contingencies (Note 5)		
Stockholders' equity:		
Preferred stock, $0.001 par value; 10,000,000 shares authorized at December 31, 2011 and 2010; no shares issued and outstanding at December 31, 2011 and 2010	—	—
Common stock, $0.001 par value; 160,000,000 shares authorized at December 31, 2011 and 2010; 55,398,615 and 52,781,949 issued and outstanding at December 31, 2011 and 2010, respectively	55	53
Additional paid-in capital	219,119	51,622
Accumulated other comprehensive income	706	750
Retained earnings	422,930	237,739
Total stockholders' equity	642,810	290,164
Total liabilities and stockholders' equity	$3,069,196	$982,067

EXHIBIT 3
Netflix, Inc. Consolidated Statements of Cash Flows[55] (in thousands)

Year Ended December 31			
	2011	**2010**	**2009**
Cash flows from operating activities:			
Net income	$226,126	$160,853	$115,860
Adjustments to reconcile net income to net cash provided by operating activities:			
Additions to streaming content library	(2,320,732)	(406,210)	(64,217)
Change in streaming content liabilities	1,460,400	167,836	(4,014)
Amortization of streaming content library	699,128	158,100	48,192
Amortization of DVD content library	96,744	142,496	171,298
Depreciation and amortization of property, equipment, and intangibles	43,747	38,099	38,044
Stock-based compensation expense	61,582	27,996	12,618

....

SOURCE: http://files.shareholder.com/downloads/NFLX/2097321301x0x561754/3715da18-1753-4c34-8ba7-18dd28e50673/NFLX_10K.pdf

(continued)

EXHIBIT 3
(Continued)

Year Ended December 31	2011	2010	2009
Excess tax benefits from stock-based compensation	(45,784)	(62,214)	(12,683)
Other non-cash items	(4,050)	(9,128)	(7,161)
Deferred taxes	(18,597)	(962)	6,328
Gain on sale of business	—	—	(1,783)
Changes in operating assets and liabilities:			
Prepaid content	6,211	(35,476)	(5,643)
Other current assets	(4,775)	(18,027)	(5,358)
Other accounts payable	24,314	18,098	1,537
Accrued expenses	68,902	67,209	13,169
Deferred revenue	21,613	27,086	16,970
Other non-current assets and liabilities	2,883	645	1,906
Net cash provided by operating activities	317,712	276,401	325,063
Cash flows from investing activities:			
Acquisition of DVD content library	(85,154)	(123,901)	(193,044)
Purchases of short-term investments	(223,750)	(107,362)	(228,000)
Proceeds from sale of short-term investments	50,993	120,857	166,706
Proceeds from maturities of short-term investments	38,105	15,818	35,673
Purchases of property and equipment	(49,682)	(33,837)	(45,932)
Proceeds from sale of business	—	—	7,483
Other assets	3,674	12,344	11,035
Net cash used in investing activities	(265,814)	(116,081)	(246,079)
Cash flows from financing activities:			
Principal payments of lease financing obligations	(2,083)	(1,776)	(1,158)
Proceeds from issuance of common stock upon exercise of options	19,614	49,776	35,274
Proceeds from public offering of common stock, net of issuance costs	199,947	—	—
Excess tax benefits from stock-based compensation	45,784	62,214	12,683
Borrowings on line of credit, net of issuance costs	—	—	18,978
Payments on line of credit	—	—	(20,000)
Proceeds from issuance of debt, net of issuance costs	198,060	—	193,917
Repurchases of common stock	(199,666)	(210,259)	(324,335)
Net cash provided by (used in) financing activities	261,656	(100,045)	(84,641)
Net increase (decrease) in cash and cash equivalents	313,554	60,275	(5,657)
Cash and cash equivalents, beginning of year	194,499	134,224	139,881
Cash and cash equivalents, end of year	$508,053	$194,499	$134,224
Supplemental disclosure:			
Income taxes paid	$79,069	$56,218	$58,770
Interest paid	19,395	20,101	3,878

In terms of net income, Netflix had steadily improved its bottom line in conjunction with strong top line growth. The company had a net income of US$226 million in 2011 for a growth rate of 40% over the previous year's US$160 million net income. Over the five years from 2006–2011, the company saw an average net income growth of 31% per year that, coupled with high revenue growth, was instrumental to Netflix's high stock valuation. However, recently, its operating margin slid from 15% in 2010 to 2.9% in 2012, a drop directly attributable to the higher cost of content acquisition.

Until the end of 2007, Netflix had no long-term debt on its books, but it began to acquire long-term debt in 2008 as a result of its decision to invest in building a strong content library and expand overseas. At the end of 2011, Netflix had US$508 million in cash and US$200 million in long-term debt.

Netflix's Success

Netflix went from being a company that exclusively mailed DVDs to the largest media delivery company in the world by making some smart strategic decisions. For instance, Netflix jumped on the streaming bandwagon even though it was not really ready. At the time, the online content available for streaming was extremely limited—less than 10% of the content that was available from Netflix's DVDs holdings.

At that time, Netflix's mail-order DVD business was very popular, and customers did not seem to mind waiting a day or two for their DVDs. Netflix then went ahead and offered streaming content, a bold decision that anticipated an as yet unexpressed need for the immediate gratification of streaming, and made Netflix the first entrant into the market for streamed video. It was clear to Netflix that the use of DVDs would gradually decline, and Netflix's aggressive adoption of streaming videos was a sharp marketing move, that gave it an edge in the global economy.

After its initial launch of online streaming, Netflix kept up to date with new trends and customer preferences, especially the quickly changing preferences of Generation Y, which were influenced by branding, social media, and media saturation. Netflix utilized all the platforms that Generation Y would find appealing, from computers and TVs, to Smartphones and tablets.

Continually bearing in mind that the two most important things for Netflix's customers were price per content, and quality of content, Netflix kept its priorities straight and never stopped improving the quality of its content, or the platforms for delivering that content.

Netflix also focused on increasing customer engagement. It allowed customers to rate movies they viewed, thereby enhancing the customer experience and creating a community of viewers. And, by tracking the movies a customer viewed, Netflix was able to track customer preferences, and offer targeted recommendations for viewing. Netflix also exploited customer loyalty to attract new customers, for instance, through its "refer-a-friend" offer of one free month of service for both the new customer and the referrer to attract new users who wanted to try the service risk-free.

The 2011 Price Increase/Rebranding Debacle

Netflix continued to grow robustly by offering a combined DVD mail and unlimited streaming service at a flat rate of US$9.99 a month, a rate that was key to Netflix's ability to offer a great value for money service. But with increased competition and expensive new content deals, the company found it increasingly difficult to maintain its operating margin levels. In the third quarter of 2011, Netflix implemented a 60% price increase, from US$10 to US$16 a month for unlimited streaming and DVDs by mail, which immediately resulted in the loss of 800,000 subscribers, pointing to the company's very limited latitude with regard to pricing.[35]

In response, Netflix took action that very shortly proved disastrous. In addition to raising its prices and shifting its business model to focus on online streaming. Netflix also attempted to restructure its operations by spinning off its DVD delivery service and rebranding it Qwikster. Rebranding a well-known product or service such as Netflix usually only works if a company was trying to simplify its brand, almost never the other way around, which was, unfortunately what Netflix tried to do. Netflix attempted to introduce a new entity, Qwikster, by splitting the old entity into two: with two separate websites, two separate queues, two separate sets of recommendations, two separate customer bases, two separate billing avenues, and two new sets of rules customer had to learn about. While Netflix had banked on the competitive advantage of offering "affordability, instant access and usability," the introduction of a separate website undercut instant access and usability. Customers, critics, and Wall Street responded harshly.

Apart from losing over 800,000 subscribers after its price increase, and losing half of its market capitalization, Netflix's rebranding strategy did not seem justifiable to its customers.

Netflix botched the rebranding because it neglected due diligence prior to launching it and its price increases. Market research would surely have indicated customer resistance to both. Heavily focused on increasing profits, Netflix did not effectively strategize the rebranding/ repricing plan, nor did it anticipate resistance or prepare strategy implementation scenarios. A new strategy should not only increase revenues and profits, it should consider relationship and brand image gains and losses. In springing the rebranding on customers, Netflix undercut the quality of the experience it had previously offered, and the negative reaction was not mitigated by the company's public apology or its rescinding of its decision to split its services. The botched rebranding led to a dilution of Netflix's brand, and loss of customer trust. Reestablishing its brand image became a priority for Netflix, though it was not very easy to do. The company needed to offer something genuinely useful to its customers at just the right cost, while increasing the quality of the content offered and enhancing customer experience.

Finally, in order for Netflix to expand internationally, it needed to invest in the technological infrastructure in the international markets that it lacked but which it desperately needs due to heavy competitions and other legal concerns that appear there

Strategic Challenges Ahead for Netflix

Netflix's top management needed to address many issues to maintain the company's leading position in the home video market. A strategic plan was needed to:

1. Repair the PR damage from the rebranding and price increases of 2011.
2. Focus on growing its subscriber base both at home and abroad.
3. Maintain a healthy cash position to meet the growing content cost obligations.
4. Invest in innovative user interface and streaming technologies to create a solid platform for the shift from DVD delivery to streaming.

REFERENCES

Blockbuster Wins 3-Month Restructuring Extension. *Reuters*. 20 Jan 2011. URL: http://t.co/iZPsUi5

Video On Demand, Wikipedia, Accessed: 31-Jan-2011, URL: http://en.wikipedia.org/wiki/Video_on_demand

Netflix Annual SEC Report (2010) URL: http://files. shareholder.com/downloads/NFLX/1159919179x 0xS1193125-10-36181/1065280/filing.pdf

http://www.funginguniverse.com/company-histories/Netflix-Inc-company-History.html

2 10-K Netflix Annual Report – 2010

Hoovers company profile—Netflix Inc.

Datamonitor. Netflix Inc. Company Profile. 23 Jun. 2010

http://money.cnn.com/2011/10/24/technology/netflix_earnings/index.htm

Datamonitor. Blockbuster Inc. Company Profile. 30 Dec. 2010

http://www.redbox.com/release_20110811

http://www.theatlanticwire.com/business/2011/08/walmarts-facebook-powered-future/41843/

http://www.csmonitor.com/Innovation/2011/0713/Five-alternatives-to-Netflix/Amazon-Prime-instant-video

http://facstaff.uww.edu/mohanp/netflix.html

Information System: A Manager's Guide to Harnessing – John Gallaugher

FY 2008, and June 2009 market cap figures for both firms

http://www.barnesandnobleinc.com/newsroom/financial_only.html

http://phx.corporate-ir.net/phoenix.zhtml?c= 97664&p=irol-reportsOther

Movies to Go. *The Economist*. July 9, 2005

http://insight.kellogg.northwestern.edu/index.php/Kellogg/article/a_surprising_secret_to_netflixs_runaway_success

http://searchenterprisewan.techtarget.com/definition/bandwidth

http://slatest.slate.com/posts/2011/06/02/nnessee_netflix_law_new_measure_makes_it_illegal_to_share_login_.html

http://www.wired.com/threatlevel/2011/09/netflix-video-privacy/

http://www.reelseo.com/time-warner-netflix-sued-providing-captions-video-streams/

http://news.cnet.com/8301-13578_3-20072619-38/netflix-sued-by-deaf-group-over-lack-of-subtitles/

http://arxiv.org/PS_cache/cs/pdf/0610/0610105v2.pdf

http://www.nytimes.com/2010/03/13/technology/13netflix.html

http://news.cnet.com/8301-10784_3-9926311-7.html

S&P Net Advantage

IDC Technology Research Firm Source: S&P Industry Survey

10-Q Netflix Quarterly Fillings-Q3-2011

10-K Netflix Annual Report – 2010

http://www.cnn.com/2011/08/31/tech/mobile/smartphone-market-share-gahran/index.html

S&P Industry Survey

10-Q Netflix Quarterly Fillings-Q3-2011

Morningstar Analyst Report

Euromonitor Bentley Library Database

http://www.emarketer.com/blog/index.php/time-spent-watching-tv-tops-internet/

Media Usage & Online Behavior—Mintel Report Oct 2011

http://www.reuters.com/article/2011/10/31/us-netflixdisney-idUSTRE79U0O420111031

http://www.businessweek.com/magazine/content/05_43/b3956201.htm

Mintel Investment Research

Annual Shareholder letter Netflix 2011

Consolidated Financial Statement 10k

Netflix 10k 2011

Netflix Factsheet

https://www.google.com/adplanner/planning/site_profile#site Details?identifier=megaupload.com

Quarterly Letter to the shareholders 3Q 2011

http://www.ibtimes.com/articles/256810/20111128/netflix-estimates-revised-jefferies-guidance-capital-raise.htm

Company Fillings 8k 3Q

Blockbuster Creditors Should Call It Quits, Poll Says, TheStreet, 30 Jan 2011. URL: http://t.co/TcSPlun

Blockbuster Wins 3-month Restructuring Extension, *Reuters*, 20 Jan 2011. URL: http://t.co/iZPsUi5

Grossman, Robert J. Tough Love at Netflix. *HR Magazine* (Apr 2010): 36–41

Fuoco-Karasinski. Netflix Bucks Traditional Total Rewards, WorldatWork workspan (8/07)

Goldfarb, Jeffrey, & Holding, Reynolds. Incentives Play Role in Success of Netflix. *The New York Times* (May 8, 2011)

http://files.shareholder.com/downloads/NFLX/2097321301 x0x561754/3715da18-1753-4c34-8ba7-18dd28e50673/NFLX_10K.pdf

http://ir.netflix.com/management.cfm

NOTES

1. http://www.fundinguniverse.com/company-histories/Netflix-Inc-company-History.html.
2. 10-K Netflix Annual Report – 2010.
3. Hoovers company profile – Netflix Inc.
4. Datamonitor, Netflix Inc. Company Profile. 23 Jun. 2010.
5. Datamonitor, Netflix Inc. Company Profile. 23 Jun. 2010.
6. http://insight.kellogg.northwestern.edu/index.php/Kellogg/article/a_surprising_secret_to_netflixs_runaway_success
7. http://money.cnn.com/2011/10/24/technology/netflix_earnings/index.htm
8. S&P Advantage
9. IDC Technology Research Firm Source: S&P Industry Survey
10. 10-Q Netflix Quarterly Filings – Q3-2011
11. http://searchenterprisewan.techtarget.com/definition/bandwidth
12. Consolidated Financial Statement 10-K
13. 10-K Netflix Annual Report – 2010
14. 10-K Netflix Annual Report – 2010
15. http://www.cnn.com/2011/08/31/tech/mobile/smartphone-market-share-gahran/index.html
16. S&P Industry Survey
17. Euromonitor, Bentley University Library Database
18. S&P Industry Survey
19. https://www.google.com/adplanner/planning/site_profile#siteDetails?identifier=megaupload.com
20. Media Usage & Online Behavior – Mintel Report Oct. 2011
21. http://www.reuters.com/article/2011/10/31/us-netflixdisney-idUSTRE79U0O420111031
22. http://www.businessweek.com/magazine/content/05_43/b3956201.htm
23. Annual Shareholder Letter – Netflix 2011
24. Datamonitor, Blockbuster Inc. Company Profile. 30 Dec. 2010
25. http://www.redbox.com/release_20110811
26. http://www.theatlanticwire.com/business/2011/08/walmarts-facebook-powered-future/41843/
27. http://www.csmonitor.com/Innovation/2011/0713/Five-alternatives-to-Netflix/Amazon-Prime-instant-video
28. http://facstaff.uww.edu/mohanp/netflix.html
29. Information System: A manager's guide to harnessing – John Gallaugher
30. Movies to Go. *The Economist*. July 9, 2005
31. Morningstar Investment Report
32. Quarterly letter to the shareholders 3Q 2011
33. Quarterly letter to the shareholders 3Q 2011
34. Company Filings – 8K 3Q
35. 10-Q Netflix Quarterly Filings – Q3-2011

CASE **13**

Carnival Corporation & plc (2010)

**Michael J. Keeffe, John K. Ross III, Sherry K. Ross,
Bill J. Middlebrook, and Thomas L. Wheelen**

IT WAS EARLY MORNING ON NOVEMBER 2010 AS MICKEY ARISON, Chairman and CEO, drove up the palm-lined entryway to the headquarters of Carnival Corporation. In front of the building, the large Carnival red, white, and blue logo (shaped like a ship's funnel) reminded him that his ships were not only still afloat, but doing well in this down economy.

As he reflected back on the year, he was delighted that the company had weathered the global recession. Despite reduced leisure travel demand, the U.S. government's advisory against travel to Mexico as a result of the flu virus, terrorist fears, fuel price uncertainty, and a host of other factors, Carnival managed to carry a record 8.5 million guests. Although 2009 sales were below the 2008 record, the company still posted a US$1.8 billion net income. Quick responses by management offset the revenue declines through cost containment efforts, most notably a 5% reduction in fuel consumption, and through expansion in its European market. This expansion represented 39% of the company's operations.

Third-quarter results (through August 31, 2010) showed improvement over the same period in 2009, nearing the record levels of 2008. In the Western Hemisphere, the gulf oil spill had not materially affected cruise operations and the hurricane season had not been as bad as predicted. European expansion proceeded smoothly and expansion initiatives in Australia and Asia produced positive results. Given a global economic recovery, the company should see a return to the historical growth patterns it experienced in previous years.

The strategic outlook through 2012 and beyond was projected to be highly favorable. Carnival Corporation's management believed that only 20% of the U.S. population, 9%–10% of the UK population, and 4%–5% of the continental European population had ever taken a cruise. This left a large number of potential cruise guests. European growth potential was consistent with the North American market 12 years ago. Anticipating this growth, Carnival Corporation intended to continue average annual capacity growth in North America at a 3% rate and European capacity growth at 9% through 2012.

....
This case was prepared by Michael J. Keefe, John K. Ross III, Sherry K. Ross, Bill J. Middlebrook, and Thomas L. Wheelen. Copyright © 2010 by Kathryn E. Wheelen, Michael J. Keeffe, John K. Ross III, Sherry K. Ross, Bill J. Middlebrook, and Thomas L. Wheelen. Reprinted by permission only for the 13th edition of *Strategic Management and Business Policy* (including international and electronic versions of the book). Any other publication of this case (translation, any form of electronic or media) or sale (any form of partnership) to another publisher will be in violation of copyright law unless Kathryn E. Wheelen, Michael J. Keeffe, John K. Ross III, Sherry K. Ross, Bill Middlebrook, and Thomas L. Wheelen have granted additional written reprint permission.

Overview

In 1972, Ted Arison founded Carnival Cruise Lines with one ship, the *Mardi Gras*. Ted Arison's son, Mickey Arison, now served as Chairman and CEO. **Exhibit 1** shows the brands, passenger capacity, number of ships, and primary market from the 2010 Annual Report. By late 2010, the number of operating ships had increased to 98 ships serving seven continents.

Ships added during 2010 included the *Costa Deliziosa*, *Nieuw Amsterdam*, *Azura*, *AIDAblu*, *Queen Elizabeth*, and the *Seabourn Sojourn*. Carnival's 98 ships had a capacity of over 190,000 passenger berths. Given that fleet-wide occupancy rates usually hover at or above 100% (ship berths are at double occupancy and additional berths can be made available), and with over 70,000 shipboard employees, more than 260,000 people were sailing aboard the Carnival fleet at any given time (**Exhibit 2**). Additionally, Carnival Corporation

EXHIBIT 1
Cruise Brands, Passenger Capacity, Number of Cruise Ships, and Primary Markets

Cruise Brands	Passenger Capacity (a)	Number of Cruise Ships	Primary Markets
North America			
Carnival Cruise Lines	54,480	22	North America
Princess	37,608	17	North America
Holland America Line	23,492	15	North America
Seabourn	1,524	5	North America
North America Cruise Brands	117,104	59	
Europe, Australia, & Asia ("EAA")			
Costa	29,202	14	Italy, France, and Germany
P&O Cruises (UK) (b)	15,098	7	United Kingdom ("UK")
AIDA	12,054	7	Germany
Cunard	6,676	3	UK and North America
P&O Cruises (Australia)	6,322	4	Australia
Ibero	5,008	4	Spain and South America
EAA Cruise Brands	74,360	39	
	191,464	98	

Notes:

(a) In accordance with cruise industry practice, passenger capacity is calculated based on two passengers per cabin even though some cabins can accommodate three or more passengers.

(b) Includes the 1,200-passenger capacity *Artemis*, which was sold in October 2009 to an unrelated entity and is being operated by P&O Cruises (UK) under a bareboat charter agreement until April 2011.

SOURCE: *Carnival Corporation & plc 2010 Annual Report.*

EXHIBIT 2
Passengers, Capacity, and Occupancy

Fiscal Year	Cruise Passengers	Year-End Passenger Capacity	Occupancy
2005	6,848,000	136,960	105.6%
2006	7,008,000	143,676	106.0%
2007	7,672,000	158,352	105.6%
2008	8,183,000	169,040	105.7%
2009	8,519,000	180,746	105.5%
2010	9,147,000	191,464	105.6%

SOURCE: *Carnival Corporation & plc 2010 Annual Report.*

expected delivery of nine ships by the end of 2014 (Carnival–2; Costa–2; AIDA–2; Seabourn–1; Princess–2).

Carnival not only owned ships but also owned a chain of 16 hotels and lodges in Alaska and the Canadian Yukon with 3000 guest rooms to complement Alaska cruises. For "Alaskan cruise tours," Carnival operated two luxury day trips to the glaciers in Alaska and the Yukon River, and owned 30 domed rail cars operated by the Alaska Railroad as sight-seeing trains.

The Evolution of Cruising

When aircraft replaced ocean liners as the primary means of transoceanic travel during the 1960s, the opportunity for developing the modern cruise industry was created. Ships that were no longer required to ferry passengers from destination to destination became available to investors who envisioned new alternative vacations that complemented the increasing affluence of Americans. Ted and Mickey Arison envisioned travelers experiencing classical cruise elegance, along with the latest modern conveniences, at a price comparable to land-based vacation packages sold by travel agents. Carnival's all-inclusive packages, when compared to packages at resorts or theme parks such as Walt Disney World, often were priced below those destinations, especially when the array of activities, entertainment, and meals were considered. Once the purview of the rich and leisure class, cruising was now targeted at the middle class, with service and amenities similar to the grand days of first-class ocean travel.

According to *Cruise Travel* magazine, the increasing popularity of taking a cruise as a vacation can be traced to two serendipitously timed events. First, television's *Love Boat* series dispelled many myths associated with cruising and depicted people of all ages and backgrounds enjoying the cruise experience. During the 1970s, the show was among the top 10 television programs and provided extensive publicity for cruise operators. Second, the increasing affluence of Americans and the increased participation of women in the workforce gave couples and families more disposable income for discretionary purposes, especially vacations. As the myths were dispelled and disposable income grew, younger couples and families realized the benefits of cruising as a vacation alternative, creating a large new target market for the cruise product and accelerating growth in the number of Americans taking cruises as a vacation.

Over the last 20 years, the cruise industry and cruise vacation have matured with the development of ships designed specifically for cruise vacations and varied itineraries worldwide. Current cruise liners bear little resemblance to early industry cruise liners and are truly a floating vacation resort. Modern cruise ships are much larger than previous ships, have little motion due to computer-controlled stabilization systems, are environmentally friendly with full recycling capabilities, and have a multitude of activities, entertainment, clubs, and deck spaces for guests to explore. The common misconception of being perpetually seasick or bored on a ship would be hard to fathom given the evolution and development of modern cruise ships and the many and varied ports of call.

Carnival History

In 1972, Ted Arison, backed by the American Travel Services Inc. (AITS), purchased an aging ocean liner from Canadian Pacific Empress Lines for US$6.5 million. The new AITS subsidiary, Carnival Cruise Lines, refurbished the vessel from bow to stern and renamed it the *Mardi Gras* to capture the party spirit. (Also included in the deal was another ship later renamed the *Carnivale*.) The company's beginning was less than promising when the *Mardi Gras* ran aground in Miami Harbor with more than 300 invited travel agents aboard. The ship was slow and guzzled expensive fuel, which limited the number of ports of call and lengthened the minimum stay of passengers on the ship needed to break even. Arison then bought another older vessel from the Union Castle Lines to complement the *Mardi Gras* and the *Carnivale* and named it the *Festivale*. To attract customers, Arison began adding onboard diversions such as planned activities, a casino, discos, and other forms of entertainment designed to enhance the shipboard experience.

Carnival lost money for the next three years, and in late 1974 Ted Arison bought out the Carnival Cruise subsidiary from AITS Inc. for US$1 cash and the assumption of US$5 million in debt. One month later, the *Mardi Gras* began showing a profit and, through the remainder of 1975, operated at more than 100% capacity. (Normal ship capacity was determined by the number of fixed berths [referred to as lower berths available]. Ships, like hotels, operate beyond this fixed capacity by using rollaway beds, pullmans, and upper bunks.)

Ted Arison, Chairman, along with his son Mickey Arison, President, and Bob Dickinson, Vice President of Sales and Marketing, began to alter the current approach to cruise vacations. Carnival targeted first-time cruisers and young people with a moderately priced vacation package that included airfare to the port of embarkation and airfare home after the cruise. Per-diem rates were very competitive with other vacation packages. Carnival offered passage to multiple exotic Caribbean ports, several meals served daily with premier restaurant service, and all forms of entertainment and activities included in the base fare. The only items not included in the fare were items of a personal nature, liquor purchases, gambling, and tips for the cabin steward, table waiter, and busboy. Carnival continued to add to the shipboard experience with a greater variety of activities, nightclubs, and other forms of entertainment. It also used multimedia-advertising promotions and established the theme of "Fun Ship" cruises, primarily promoting the ship as the destination and ports of call as secondary. Carnival told the public it was throwing a shipboard party and everyone was invited. Today, the "Fun Ship" theme still permeates all Carnival Cruise brand ships.

Throughout the 1980s, Carnival was able to maintain a growth rate of approximately 30%, about three times that of the industry as a whole. Between 1982 and 1988, its ships sailed with an average capacity of 104%. Targeting younger, first-time passengers by promoting the ship as a destination proved to be extremely successful. Carnival's customer profile showed that approximately 30% of passengers at that time were between the ages of 25 and 39, with household incomes of US$25,000 to US$50,000.

In 1987, Ted Arison sold 20% of his shares of Carnival Cruise Lines and immediately generated over US$400 million for further expansion. In 1988, Carnival acquired the Holland America Line, which had four cruise ships with 4500 berths. Holland America was positioned to appeal to higher-income travelers with cruise prices averaging 25%–35% more than similar Carnival cruises. The deal included two Holland America subsidiaries, Windstar Sail Cruises and Holland America Westours. This purchase allowed Carnival to begin an aggressive "superliner" building campaign for its core subsidiary. By 1989, the cruise segments of Carnival Corporation carried more than 75,000 passengers in one year, a "first" in the cruise industry.

Ted Arison relinquished the role of Chairman to his son Mickey in 1990, a time when the explosive growth of the industry began to subside. Higher fuel prices and increased airline costs began to affect the industry as a whole. The first Persian Gulf War caused many cruise operators to divert ships to the Caribbean, increasing the number of ships competing directly with Carnival. Carnival's stock price fell from US$25 in June of 1990 to US$13 later in the year. The company also incurred a US$25.5 million loss during fiscal 1990 for the operation of the Crystal Palace Resort and Casino in the Bahamas. In 1991, Carnival reached a settlement with the Bahamian government (effective March 1, 1992) to surrender the 672-room Riviera Towers to the Hotel Corporation of the Bahamas in exchange for debt cancellation incurred in constructing and developing the resort. The corporation took a US$135 million write-down on the Crystal Palace that year.

In the early 1990s, Carnival attempted to acquire Premier Cruise Lines, which was then the official cruise line for Walt Disney World in Orlando, Florida, for approximately US$372 million. The deal was never consummated because the involved parties could not agree on price. In 1992, Carnival acquired 50% of Seabourn, gaining the cruise operations of K/S Seabourn Cruise Lines, and formed a partnership with Atle Brynestad. Seabourn served the ultra-luxury market with destinations in South America, the Mediterranean, Southeast Asia, and the Baltic.

The 1993 to 1995 period saw the addition of the superliner *Imagination* to Carnival Cruise Lines and *Ryndam* for Holland America Lines. In 1994, the company discontinued the operations of Fiestamarina Lines, which had attempted to serve Spanish-speaking clientele. Fiestamarina had been beset with marketing and operational problems and had never reached continuous operation. Many industry analysts and observers were surprised at the failure of Carnival to successfully develop this market. In 1995, Carnival sold 49% interest in the Epirotiki Line, a Greek cruise operation, for US$25 million and purchased US$101 million (face amount) of senior secured notes of Kloster Cruise Limited, the parent of competitor Norwegian Cruise Lines, for US$81 million. Carnival Corporation continued to expand through internally generated growth by adding new ships. Additionally, Carnival seemed to be willing to continue with its external expansion through acquisitions, if the right opportunity arose.

In June 1997, Royal Caribbean made a bid to buy Celebrity Cruise Lines for US$500 million and the assumption of its US$800 million debt. Within a week, Carnival had responded by submitting a counteroffer to Celebrity for US$510 million and the assumption of debt. Two days later, Carnival raised the bid to US$525 million. Nevertheless, Royal Caribbean announced on June 30, 1997, the final merger arrangements with Celebrity. The resulting company had 17 ships, with more than 30,000 berths.

Not to be thwarted in its expansion, Carnival announced in June 1997 the purchase of Costa, an Italian cruise company and the largest European cruise line, for US$141 million. The purchase was finalized in September 2000. External expansion continued when Carnival announced the acquisition of the Cunard Line for US$500 million from Kvaerner ASA on May 28, 1998. Cunard was then operationally merged with Seabourn Cruise Line. Carnival announced on December 2, 1999, a hostile bid for NCL Holding ASA, the parent company of Norwegian Cruise Lines. Carnival was unsuccessful in this acquisition attempt.

The terrorist attacks on New York's twin towers on September 11, 2001, caused tourists to cancel cruise plans and affected the leisure travel industry worldwide. It forced several smaller cruise line companies into bankruptcy, while others reduced the size and scope of operations. Other competitors discounted cruise prices to maintain historic occupancy levels. Carnival was well positioned in the market and soon recovered once public fears subsided. It also made a focused effort to expand into the German and Spanish markets in Europe.

Consolidation in the industry continued in 2003 when Carnival and P&O Princess Cruises finalized an agreement to combine and created the first truly global cruise line. Carnival remained the parent company and added P&O Cruises, Ocean Village, AIDA, P&O Cruises Australia, and tour operator Princess Tours. The new Carnival now offered an ever expanding selection of price points, alternative destinations, and varied accommodations that allowed for even greater market penetration.

In 2007, Carnival sold Windstar Cruise Line to Ambassadors International Cruise Group, and Swan Hellenic to Lord Sterling.

Carnival's Corporate Governance

Board of Directors

Exhibit 3A shows the 14 members of Carnival's Board of Directors, three of whom served as internal officers and four others who were retired company employees or had previous ties to Carnival Corporation or one of its subsidiaries. Mickey Arison owned approximately one-third of the company's stock. (He also owned the Miami Heat, a basketball team which won the 2006 NBA Championship.) The Arison family and its trusts controlled roughly 36% of the stock. All other directors and executive officers, as a group, owned or controlled approximately 30% of the total shares outstanding.

According to the Board's by-laws, each outside director must own at least 5000 shares of stock. Additionally, external board members are yearly granted 10,000 stock options, and are paid an annual retainer fee of US$40,000 for serving on the Board. Fees are also paid for attending board and committee meetings.

Exhibit 3B lists Carnival's executive officers. **Exhibit 4** shows compensation for the key executives.

EXHIBIT 3A
Board of Directors

Mickey Arison
Chairman of the Board
and Chief Executive Officer
Carnival Corporation & plc

Sir Jonathon Band
Former First Sea Lord and Chief of Naval
Staff British Navy

Robert H. Dickinson
Former President
and Chief Executive Officer
Carnival Cruise Lines

Arnold W. Donald
Former President
and Chief Executive Officer
Juvenile Diabetes Research Foundation
International

Pier Luigi Foschi
Chairman and Chief Executive Officer
Costa Crociere S.p.A.

Howard S. Frank
Vice Chairman of the Board
and Chief Operating Officer
Carnival Corporation & plc

Richard J. Glasier
Former President
and Chief Executive Officer
Argosy Gaming Company

Modesto A. Maidique
President Emeritus and Professor of
Management and Executive Director, FIU
Center for Leadership
Florida International University

Sir John Parker
Chairman, National Grid plc, Chairman,
Anglo American plc, and Vice Chairman,
DP World (Dubai)

Peter G. Ratcliffe
Former Chief Executive Officer
P&O Princess Cruises International

Stuart Subotnick
General Partner
and Executive Vice President
Metromedia Company

Laura Weil
Chief Executive Officer
Urban Brands, Inc.

Randall J. Weisenburger
Executive Vice President
and Chief Financial Officer
Omnicom Group Inc.

Uzi Zucker
Private Investor

EXHIBIT 3B
Principal Officers

Mickey Arison
Chairman of the Board
and Chief Executive Officer

Howard S. Frank
Vice Chairman of the Board
and Chief Operating Officer

David Bernstein
Senior Vice President
and Chief Financial Officer

Richard D. Ames
Senior Vice President—Shared Services

Arnaldo Perez
Senior Vice President, General Counsel
and Secretary

Larry Freedman
Chief Accounting Officer
and Vice President–Controller

OPERATIONS SEGMENTS

AIDA CRUISES
Michael Thamm
President

CARNIVAL CRUISE LINES
Gerald R. Cahill
President and Chief Executive Officer

CARNIVAL AUSTRALIA
Ann Sherry AO
Chief Executive Officer
Carnival Australia

CARNIVAL UK
David K. Dingle
Chief Executive Officer

COSTA CROCIERE S.p.A.
Pier Luigi Foschi
Chairman and Chief Executive Officer
Gianni Onorato
President

HOLLAND AMERICA LINE
Stein Kruse
President and Chief Executive Officer

PRINCESS CRUISES
Alan B. Buckelew
President and Chief Executive Officer

SEABOURN CRUISE LINE
Pamela C. Conover
President and Chief Executive Officer

Corporate Organization

Headquartered in Miami, Florida, and London, England, Carnival Corporation is incorporated in Panama, while Carnival plc is incorporated in England and Wales. Fleet operations are worldwide, with the majority of operations in the North American market and secondarily in Europe. The company's total worldwide share of the cruise line vacation market was at or above 50%, and distinctly higher in some geographically defined or segmented markets.

According to Carnival's investor relations site, Carnival Corporation & plc operated under a dual listed company structure whereby Carnival Corporation and Carnival plc functioned as a single economic entity through contractual agreements between separate legal entities. Shareholders of both Carnival Corporation and Carnival plc had the same economic and voting interest, but their shares were listed on different stock exchanges and not fungible. Carnival Corporation common stock was traded on the New York Stock Exchange under the symbol CCL. Carnival plc was traded on the London Stock Exchange under the symbol CCL and as ADS on the New York Stock Exchange under the symbol CUK. Carnival was the only company in the world to be included in both the S&P 500 index in the United States and the FTSE 100 index in the United Kingdom.

EXHIBIT 4
Annual Compensation: Carnival Corporation & plc

Name and Principal Position	Fiscal Year	Salary ($)	Bonus ($)	Stock Awards ($)	Option Awards ($)	Non-Equity Incentive Plan Compensation ($)	Change in Pension Value and Nonqualified Deferred Compensation Earnings ($)	All Other Compensation ($)	Total ($)
Micky Arison	2009	880,000	—	4,772,807	930,546	2,206,116	255,581	496,513	9,541,563
Chairman of the	2008	880,000	—	5,561,856	1,538,673	—	112,718	404,329	8,497,576
Board & CEO	2007	850,000	—	3,689,123	1,879,529	2,925,000	69,875	336,688	9,750,215
David Bernstein	2009	450,000	83,915	274,181	91,013	383,585	—	107,269	1,389,963
Senior Vice	2008	350,000	155,860	107,122	128,795	428,260	—	105,088	1,275,125
President & CFO	2007	269,596	—	—	158,043	350,000	—	77,193	854,832
Gerald R. Cahill	2009	750,000	194,310	1,094,676	423,413	655,441	884,716	58,869	4,061,425
President and CEO	2008	750,000	—	708,717	569,727	1,162,288	675,536	48,775	3,915,043
of Carnival Cruise Lines	2007	625,000	—	168,248	654,499	1,000,000	343,435	42,841	2,834,023
Pier Luigi Foschi	2009	1,320,500	—	791,735	315,915	1,794,143	—	340,033	4,562,326
Chairman and CEO	2008	1,415,500	996,810	486,451	583,118	800,441	—	402,830	4,685,150
of Costa Crociere S.p.A.	2007	1,244,400	909,840	194,428	1,663,810	668,430	—	312,149	4,993,057
Howard S. Frank	2009	780,000	—	3,015,393	513,577	2,137,175	—	267,303	6,713,448
Vice Chairman of the	2008	780,000	—	2,893,800	827,976	2,709,400	3,899,136	355,255	11,465,567
Board & COO	2007	750,000	—	2,610,000	1,113,260	2,825,000	—	243,383	7,541,643

Mission

According to management, "Our mission is to deliver exceptional vacation experiences through the world's best-known cruise brands that cater to a variety of different lifestyle and budgets, all at an outstanding value unrivaled on land or at sea."

The 11 cruise lines competed in all of the three operational sectors of the cruise market (contemporary, premium, and luxury).

Operating Segments and Corporate Brands

Carnival Cruise Lines (www.carnival.com)

Carnival Cruise Lines was the most popular and most profitable cruise line in the world. Operating in the contemporary cruise sector, as of late 2010, Carnival operated 22 ships with a total passenger capacity of 54,480. Occupancy rates typically exceeded 100% on average, and the brand was the market leader in the contemporary segment of the industry. Carnival still utilized the theme of the "Fun Ships," and had embarked on a US$250 million enhancement program of its eight fantasy-class ships. Carnival ships cruised to destinations in the Bahamas, Canada, the Caribbean, the Mexican Riviera, New England, the Panama Canal, Alaska, and Hawaii, as well as limited operations in Europe, with most cruises ranging from three to seven days.

Princess Cruises (www.princesscruises.com)

Princess Cruises offered a "complete escape" from the daily routine. This segment operated 17 ships with a total passenger capacity of 37,588. Princess treated its passengers to world-class cuisine, exceptional service, and myriad resort-like amenities onboard, including the Lotus Spa, Movies Under the Stars, lavish casinos, nightclubs, and lounges. Princess was a pioneer in offering a choice of dining experiences so guests could dine when and where it was convenient. The Princess fleet cruised to all seven continents and boasted more than 280 destinations. Princess was classified in the industry as contemporary to premium. The company offered cruises ranging in length principally from 7 to 14 days.

Holland America Line (www.hollandamerica.com)

The Holland America Line was a leader in the premium cruise sector. Holland America operated a five-star fleet of 15 ships, with a 23,484 passenger capacity. Holland America consistently set a standard in the premium segment with feature programs and amenities such as culinary arts demonstrations, greenhouse spas, and cabins with flat-panel TVs and Sealy plush-top Mariner's Dream beds. The company offered cruises from 7 to 21 days. Its ships sailed to more than 300 ports of call on all seven continents with more than 500 cruises per year.

Seabourn Cruises (www.seabourn.com)

Seabourn Cruise Line epitomized luxury cruising aboard each of its five intimate all-suite ships. The Yachts of Seabourn were lavishly appointed with virtually one staff member for every guest, to ensure the highest quality service. Typical cruises were from 7 to 14 days.

Costa Cruises (www.costacruises.com)

Costa Cruises was the leading cruise company in Europe and South America. Headquartered in Genoa, Italy, Costa offered guests on its 14 ships a multiethnic, multicultural, and multilingual ambiance. A Costa cruise was distinguished by its "Cruising Italian Style" shipboard ambiance. Costa's fleet cruised the Caribbean, the Mediterranean, Northern Europe, South America, Dubai, the Far East, and transoceanic crossings.

P&O Cruises (www.pocruises.com)

P&O Cruises was the largest cruise operator and the best-known contemporary cruise brand in the United Kingdom, and has cruised Australia for 78 years. The seven-ship main fleet and the three-ship Australian fleet offered cruises to the Mediterranean, the Baltic, the Norwegian Fjords, the Caribbean, and the Atlantic Islands, as well as Australia and the Far East. Total passenger capacity was approaching 20,000 for both operational fleets, and its principal market was the United Kingdom.

AIDA (www.aida.com)

AIDA was the best-known cruise brand in the fast-growing German cruise market. With its seven club ships and a capacity of over 12,000, AIDA offered cruises to the Mediterranean, the Baltic, the Norwegian Fjords, the Canary Islands, and the Caribbean. AIDA emphasized elements of the upmarket clubs and resorts in the premium and four-star range, and its facilities and activities attracted younger, more active vacationers.

Cunard Line (www.cunard.com)

The Cunard Line offered the only regular transatlantic crossing service aboard the world-famous ocean liner *Queen Mary 2* and the brand new *Queen Elizabeth*. Her equally famous retired sister, *Queen Elizabeth 2*, sailed on unique itineraries worldwide serving both U.S. and UK guests and still evoked memories of the grand days of ocean travel. The passenger capacity of the three Cunard ships was 6700 (double occupancy), and Cunard's primary market was the United Kingdom and North America. The line proudly carried the legacy of the era of sophisticated floating palaces into the 21st century. These ships were classified in the luxury sector of the cruise market.

Ocean Village (http://www.oceanvillageholidays.co.uk)

Ocean Village was founded in 2004 in the United Kingdom. Its one ship sailed throughout the Mediterranean and the Caribbean, and targeted individuals in the 30 to 50 age range who liked to explore and wanted a change from traditional cruising. Although performance had been good, there have been indications that the ship may be transferred to the P&O brand at some future date.

IberoCruceros (www.iberocruceros.com/)

IberoCruceros was one of the top operators in the fast-growing Spanish and Portuguese language cruise markets. The company operated four ships with a berth capacity of 5010. Ibero vessels operated in Mediterranean, Brazilian, Northern Europe, and Caribbean waters.

Industry Projections

The leisure cruise vacation industry has fared very well over the last 25 years, originating from transatlantic crossings and leisure cruises for the wealthy to being a staple vacation alternative for the middle class. Cruise Market Watch, a cruise vacation research company, estimated that all cruise lines will carry an annualized total passenger count worldwide of 18.4 million in 2010 and projected an increase to 21.3 million in 2013, a 15.7% increase from 2010. Giving perspective to the 2010 numbers, cruise travel accounted for less than half (50%) of all visitors to Las Vegas, when including all cruise ships, from all lines, filled to capacity all year long. Cruise companies can move ships to match demand patterns over the globe, while Las Vegas was a fixed destination.

According to Cruise Lines International Association's 2010 *Cruise Market Overview*, growth in the number of North American passengers (95% U.S. and 5% Canadian) was currently flat. Mickey Arison estimated the number of people in the United States that have taken a cruise at 20%. He based his estimate on the total U.S. population. Arison's estimate did not reflect the *core market*, the number of people who fit the cruiser potential profile: over 25, sufficient income, leisure time, and other factors. Cruise Market Watch estimated the core market at 130 million, and approximately 60 million individuals in the core market had taken a cruise. The North American market was a more mature market than other geographic markets internationally. Still, as of 2009, the North American market was the largest and was valued at US$15.95 billion with Carnival holding a commanding 55% market share.

Despite the 2008–2009 economic slump, industry growth worldwide had been between 5% and 8% per year due to the growth in the number of international passengers. This annual growth was expected to exceed that of the U.S. and Canadian market for the next several years. Europe's market was valued at US$7.2 billion and the Asia/Australian markets combined was valued at US$2.9 billion. Faster market growth combined with a weakening U.S. dollar would strengthen overseas earnings and create a greater focus to capture the fast-growing markets. In these two market areas, as of 2009, Carnival held a 52% market share.

Industry capacity continued to increase (up 6.9% over 2009 capacity) and should continue through 2013. Industry occupancy (per ship) hovered between 102% and 104% in 2008–2009, depending on the market. Ticket prices and onboard spending was predicted to improve slightly in 2010 compared to 2009, but still remain below 2008 levels. *Cruise Market Watch* estimated that the average cruise revenue, per passenger, per diem for all cruise lines worldwide was projected to be approximately US$208, of which US$157 would be attributed to ticket price and US$51 would constitute onboard spending.

Advertising

According to the Nielsen Company, hospitality and total travel advertising expenditures showed a slight increase for the industry in 2009 over 2008 levels. Total industry advertising in 2008 of US$3.89 billion was roughly a 4% increase over 2007. While hospitality firms such as Intercontinental Hotels, the Blackstone Group, and Southwest Airlines all increased advertising expenditures, Carnival Corporation decreased U.S. advertising expenditures as of January 2009 to US$89.3 million, a 21% decrease from the previous calendar year. The brand with the greatest reduction in ad spending in the Carnival portfolio was Princess Cruises. *Hoover's* reported that, beginning in 2009, Carnival increased online and social media advertising utilizing Facebook, YouTube, Twitter, Flickr, and podcasts, to allow for two-way conversations with consumers and also create brand fans.

Human Resources Management

Carnival Corporation's shore operations had approximately 10,000 full-time and 5000 part-time/seasonal employees. Carnival also employed approximately 70,000 officers, crew, and staff onboard the 98 ships at any one time. Because of the highly seasonal nature of the Alaskan and Canadian operations, Holland America Tours and Princess Tours increased their workforce during the late spring and summer months in connection with the Alaskan cruise season, employing additional seasonal personnel. Carnival had entered into agreements with unions covering certain employee categories, and union relations were considered to be generally good. Nonetheless, the American Maritime union had cited Carnival (and other cruise operators) several times for exploitation of its crews.

Onboard service was labor-intensive, employing help from almost 100 nations, many from third-world countries, with reasonable returns to employees. For example, waiters on a Carnival Cruise Lines ship could earn approximately US$18,000 to US$27,000 per year (base salary and tips), significantly greater than could be earned in their home countries for similar employment. Waiters typically worked 10 hours per day, six to seven days per week, and had a tenure of approximately eight years with the company. Even with these work parameters, applicants exceeded demand for all cruise positions.

Suppliers

The company's largest purchases were for travel agency services, fuel, advertising, food and beverages, hotel and restaurant supplies and products, airfare, repairs and maintenance, dry-docking, port facility utilization, and communication services. Most capital outlays were for the construction of new ships as well as upgrades and refurbishment of current ships. Although Carnival utilized a select number of suppliers for most of its food and beverages and hotel and restaurant supplies, most of these items were available from numerous sources at competitive prices. The use of a select number of suppliers enabled management to, among other things, obtain volume discounts. The company purchased fuel and port facility services at some of its ports of call from a limited number of suppliers. To better manage price fluctuations, the company hedged the price of fuel oil. In addition, the company performed major dry-dock and ship improvement work at dry-dock facilities in the Bahamas, British Columbia, Canada, the Caribbean, Europe, and the United States. Management believed there were sufficient dry-dock and shipbuilding facilities to meet the company's anticipated requirements.

Government Regulations

All of Carnival's ships were registered in a country outside the United States and each ship flew the flag of its country of registration. Carnival's ships were regulated by various international, national, state, and local port authorities' laws, regulations, and treaties in force in the jurisdictions in which the ships operated. Internationally, all ships and operations conformed to the SOLAS (Safety of Life at Sea) regulations adopted by most seafaring nations. In U.S. waters and ports, the ships had to comply with U.S. Coast Guard and U.S. Public Health regulations, the Maritime Transportation Security Act, International Ship and Port Facility Security Code, U.S. Oil Pollution Act of 1990, U.S. Maritime Commission, local port authorities, local and federal law enforcement agencies, and all laws pertaining to the hiring of foreign workers. All cruise ships were inspected for health issues and received a rating that was published on the Center for Disease Control (CDC) website for potential cruisers to review. Terrorist threats had tightened U.S. security of ports regarding docking facilities, cargo containers, and storage areas, and crews had to comply with various Homeland Security agencies.

Sustainability

Carnival Corporation had adopted the requirements of International Standard ISO 14001:2004 for the environmental management systems of all subsidiary lines. It had internal policies concerning the reduction of its carbon and environmental footprint, energy reduction, shipboard waste management, the environmental training of crew members, health, safety, and security, and corporate social responsibility.

Legal Issues

Carnival Corporation, like all cruise companies and hospitality providers, usually had several lawsuits pending at any point in time. Although consuming the time of corporate officers and sometimes requiring substantial financial remuneration, the principal danger of lawsuits results from the negative media publicity that may influence current and potential guests.

Some of the more publicized personal lawsuits came from passengers injured while onboard a Carnival vessel, sexual assaults by crewmembers or other passengers, negligence of the onboard medical staff, food contamination lawsuits, pay and working conditions lawsuits brought by crewmembers, and a host of other related court filings.

Legal issues for the company also tarnished its corporate image and reputation. Carnival had been sued by various entities for pollution, ship dumping of bilge and other waste contaminants in international and jurisdictional waters, and filing false statements with the U.S. Coast Guard. Fuel surcharges for passengers that were not part of the stated cruise fare and various other class actions have also led to legal proceedings. The company had also been sued over copyright infringement in its production of entertainment shows and materials onboard ship.

Carnival attempted to aggressively protect its corporate reputation and brand image by attempting to minimize damage while ensuring that violations and actions were promptly corrected. Management wanted the company to be perceived as a responsible corporate citizen for guests, workers, and the world community.

Competitors

According to Cruise Lines International Association, there were several large cruise line companies worldwide and a host of smaller companies totaling more than 100 ships competing with the Carnival fleet. Carnival's primary competitors were Royal Caribbean, Disney, and Norwegian Cruise Line, although several other companies competed with Carnival brands in selected geographical markets and specific targeted cruise segments.

Royal Caribbean Cruises Ltd. operated five brands—Royal Caribbean International, Celebrity Cruises, Pullmantur, Azamara Cruises, and CDF Croisieres de France—and had a 50% joint venture with TUI cruises. Royal Caribbean operated 38 cruise ships with a passenger capacity of over 84,000. The company planned to add four new ships by 2012, bringing the capacity to 100,000 berths. The fleet visited approximately 400 destinations worldwide. The Royal Caribbean brand competed with the Carnival Cruise Lines brand and was perceived as being slightly more upscale than Carnival ships. It competed secondarily with Costa and other Carnival brands. Celebrity cruises competed in the premium segment against Carnival's Princess and Holland America brands. The Royal Caribbean company had a 27% market share in North America and a 22% share in the remaining world markets.

Disney Cruise Line, had two cruise ships, each having 877 staterooms (3508 berths). Disney had its own private island, Castaway Bay, exclusive for Disney Cruise Line passengers, and catered primarily to family vacations. One analyst said, "Carnival should thank Disney for taking children off their ships." Specific areas of the ships were designated for activities preferred by adults, families, teens, and children. Disney Cruise Line used its ships primarily as a complement to its theme park vacations, and had a 2% market share in North America.

Norwegian Cruise Line had 11 ships with a berth capacity of over 23,000, and marketed "Freestyle Cruising," which allowed guests freedom of choice with regard to a multiplicity of dining venues and times. The atmosphere in the ships was "resort casual"; the fleet competed with Royal Caribbean and Carnival ships, and, to a lesser extent, brands targeted to the premium segment. The company was Hawaii's cruise leader. NCL had a market share of 10% of the North American Market and its affiliated companies had a small market share primarily in European markets.

Other Competitive Concerns

Carnival's management described the firm's competitors in the following manner:

First: Carnival competed with land-based vacation alternatives throughout the world including resorts, hotels, theme parks, and vacation ownership properties located in Las Vegas, Nevada, Orlando, Florida, various parts of the Caribbean and Mexico, Bahamian and Hawaiian Island destination resorts, and numerous other vacation destinations throughout Europe and the rest of the world.

Second: Carnival's primary cruise competitors in the contemporary and/or premium cruise segments for North American passengers were Royal Caribbean Cruise Ltd., Norwegian Cruise Line, and Disney Cruise Line. The three primary cruise competitors for European passengers were: (1) My Travel's Sun Cruises, Fred Olsen, Saga and Thomson in the United Kingdom; (2), Festival Cruises, Hapag-Lloyd, Peter Deilmann, Phoenix Reisen, and Tranocean Cruises in Germany; and (3) Mediterranean Shipping Cruises, Louis Cruise Line, Festival Cruises, and Spanish Cruise Line in Southern Europe. Carnival also competed for passengers throughout Europe with Norwegian Cruise Line, Orient Lines, Royal Caribbean International, and Celebrity Cruises.

Third: The company's primary competitors in the luxury cruise segment for the Cunard and Seabourn brands included Crystal Cruises, Radisson Seven Seas Cruise Line, and Silversea Cruises.

Fourth: Carnival brands also competed with similar or overlapping product offerings across all segments.

Financials

Stock

Like most corporations in the last five years, Carnival (CCL) stock had been a rollercoaster ride ranging from approximately US$55 per share common to US$17 and back to US$42 as of the third quarter, 2010. With a beta of 1.51 the stock has moved parallel to both the DOW and S&P 500 but had underperformed both indexes. However, with a market cap of US$33.51 billion and a forward P/E of 14.59, market analysts were generally recommending Carnival as a "hold" in October, 2010.

In 2006, the Board of Directors authorized the repurchase of US$1 billion (maximum) of Carnival Corporation common stock and Carnival plc. A repurchase authorization of approximately US$787 million was still in effect.

Because Carnival Corporation & plc operated under a dual-listed company structure, an unusual "Stock Swap" arrangement had been created. Each year the Boards of Directors authorized the repurchase of a set dollar amount of Carnival plc ordinary shares and a set dollar amount of Carnival Corporation common stock shares under the "Stock Swap" program. The boards then used the "Stock Swap" program in situations where an economic benefit can be obtained because either Carnival Corporation common stock or Carnival plc ordinary shares were trading at a price that was at a premium or discount to the price of Carnival plc ordinary shares or Carnival Corporation common stock, as the case may be. In effect, the company would sell overpriced stock in one company to buy undervalued stock in the other company.

Income and Balance Sheet

Cash dropped from US$1.1 billion to US$0.5 billion over the last five years and remained steady with a slight rise quarter over quarter during the third quarter of 2010. (See **Exhibits 5** to **7**.)

EXHIBIT 5
Consolidated
Statements of
Operations: Carnival
Corporation & plc
(Dollar amounts
in millions, except
per-share data)

Year Ending November 30	2009	2008	2007
Revenues			
Cruise			
Passenger tickets	$ 9,985	$ 11,210	$ 9,792
Onboard and other	2,885	3,044	2,846
Other	287	392	395
	13,157	14,646	13,033
Costs and expenses			
Operating			
Cruise			
Commissions, transportation, and other	1,917	2,232	1,941
Onboard and other	461	501	495
Payroll and related	1,498	1,470	1,336
Fuel	1,156	1,774	1,096
Food	839	856	747
Other ship operating	1,997	1,913	1,717
Other	236	293	296
Total	8,104	9,039	7,628
Selling and administrative	1,590	1,629	1,579
Depreciation and amortization	1,309	1,249	1,101
	11,003	11,917	10,308
Operating income	2,154	2,729	2,725
Nonoperating (expense) income			
Interest income	14	35	67
Interest expense, net of capitalized interest	(380)	(414)	(367)
Other income (expense), net	18	27	(1)
	(348)	(352)	(301)
Income before income taxes	1,806	2,377	2,424
Income tax expense, net	(16)	(47)	(16)
Net income	$ 1,790	$ 2,330	$ 2,408
Earnings per share			
Basic	$ 2.27	$ 2.96	$ 3.04
Diluted	$ 2.24	$ 2.90	$ 2.95
Dividends declared per share		$ 1.60	$ 1.375

Reflecting the increase in the number of ships ordered and going online, property and equipment steadily increased over the last five years from US$21 billion to over US$30 billion (3Q 2010). For this same reason, by 2009 long-term debt also increased from US$5.7 billion to over US$9 billion, but dropped to US$7.6 billion by 3Q 2010.

Revenues had also seen a steady increase until the recession, but 3Q 2010 results indicated the company was on the road to recovery and could reach the net profits of 2008.

Although both revenues and profits had begun to recover, trends in ROA, ROI, gross profit margin, and net margin had steadily decreased over the last five years. Additionally, cost of goods sold as a percentage of revenues had shown a slow, but steady increase over the last five years. This increase had been partially offset by careful management of selling, general, and administrative expenses.

EXHIBIT 6
Consolidated
Balance Sheets:
Carnival
Corporation &
plc (Dollar amounts
in millions, except
par values)

Year Ending November 30		
Assets		
Current assets		
Cash and cash equivalents	$ 538	$ 650
Trade and other receivables, net	362	418
Inventories	320	315
Prepaid expenses and other	298	267
Total current assets	1,518	1,650
Property and equipment, net	29,870	26,457
Goodwill	3,451	3,266
Trademarks	1,346	1,294
Other assets	650	733
Total assets	$36,835	$33,400
Liabilities and shareholders' equity		
Current liabilities		
Short-term borrowings	$135	$256
Current portion of long-term debt	815	1,081
Convertible debt subject to current put option		271
Accounts payable	568	512
Accrued liabilities and other	874	1,142
Customer deposits	2,575	2,519
Total current liabilities	4,967	5,781
Long-term debt	9,097	7,735
Other long-term liabilities and deferred income	736	786
Commitments and contingencies		
Shareholders' equity		
Common stock of Carnival Corporation; $0.01 par value; 1,960 shares authorized; 644 shares at 2009 and 643 shares at 2008 issued	6	6
Ordinary shares of Carnival plc; $1.66 par value; 226 shares authorized; 213 shares at 2009 and 2008 issued	354	354
Additional paid-in capital	7,707	7,677
Retained earnings	15,770	13,980
Accumulated other comprehensive income (loss)	462	(623)
Treasury stock; 24 shares at 2009 and 19 shares at 2008 of Carnival Corporation and 46 shares at 2009 and 52 shares at 2008 of Carnival plc, at cost	(2,264)	(2,296)
Total shareholders' equity	22,035	19,098
Total liabilities and shareholders' equity	$36,835	$33,400

Geographic, Segment, and Cost

Exhibit 8 shows the revenues by geographic region. Although revenues across the board dropped in 2009, the percent of revenues from North America declined (−7.7%) with a corresponding increase in Europe (up 5.5%) and Others (up 2.3%).

Carnival offered both cruises and tours. **Exhibit 9** shows the breakdown of revenues and costs for each segment. Cruises brought in the greatest revenue and had the least cost structure. Tours, although profitable, were offered primarily to enhance the cruise experience and differentiate one destination from another.

EXHIBIT 7
Selected Ratios and
Common-Sized
Data: Carnival
Corporation & plc

Selected Ratios	11/30/09	11/30/08	11/30/07	11/30/06	11/30/05
Return on assets	5.80	7.69	8.18	8.43	8.82
Return on invested capital	6.73	9.08	9.65	9.87	10.29
Cost of goods sold to sales	61.59	61.72	58.53	57.36	56.07
Net margin	13.60	15.91	18.48	19.25	20.36
From common-sized income statement					
Cost of goods sold	61.59%	61.72%	58.53%	57.36%	56.07%
Selling, general, & admin expenses	12.08%	10.94%	12.12%	12.22%	11.99%

SOURCE: *Tompson One Banker, October 28, 2010.*

EXHIBIT 8
Revenues by
Geographic Area
(Dollar amount in
millions)

	Years Ended November 30		
	2009	**2008**	**2007**
North America	$ 6,855	$ 8,090	$ 7,803
Europe	5,119	5,443	4,355
Others	1,183	1,113	875
	$ 13,157	$ 14,646	$ 13,033

SOURCE: *Carnival Corporation & plc 2010 Annual Report, p. F24.*

EXHIBIT 9 Revenue by Segment: Carnival Corporation & plc (Dollar amount in millions)

	Nine Months Ended August 31				
	Revenues	**Operating Expenses**	**Selling and Administrative**	**Depreciation and Amortization**	**Operating Income**
2010					
Cruise	$ 10,475	$ 6,306	$ 1,158	$ 1,019	$ 1,992
Tour and other	346	279	23	30	14
Intersegment elimination	(105)	(105)	—	—	—
	$ 10,716	$ 6,480	$ 1,181	$ 1,049	$ 2,006
2009					
Cruise	$ 9,698	$ 5,765	$ 1,142	$ 937	$ 1,854
Tour and other	373	316	24	27	6
Intersegment elimination	(120)	(120)	—	—	—
Total revenue	$ 9,951	$ 5,961	$ 1,166	$ 964	$ 1,860

SOURCE: *Carnival 2010 10-Q, p. 7.*

Exhibits 10 and **11** provide a further breakdown of costs associated with cruising and the dramatic impact fuel costs have on the net profitability.

EXHIBIT 10
Selected
Cruise and Other
Information: Carnival
Corporation & plc

	Year Ending Three Months Ended August 31		Year Ending Nine Months Ended August 31	
	2010	**2009**	**2010**	**2009**
Passengers carried (in thousands)	2,617	2,485	6,888	6,383
Occupancy percentage (a)	111.1%	111.4%	106.2%	106.4%
Fuel consumption (metric tons in thousands)	838	807	2,473	2,359
Fuel cost per metric ton (b)	$ 473	$ 405	$ 489	$ 330
Currencies				
U.S. dollar to €1	$ 1.27	$ 1.41	$ 1.32	$ 1.37
U.S. dollar to £1	$ 1.52	$ 1.64	$ 1.54	$ 1.53

Notes:
(a) In accordance with cruise industry practice, occupancy is calculated using a denominator of two passengers per cabin even though some cabins can accommodate three or more passengers. Percentages in excess of 100% indicate that on average more than two passengers occupied some cabins.
(b) Fuel cost per metric ton is calculated by dividing the cost of fuel by the number of metric tons consumed.

SOURCE: *Carnival 2010 10-Q, p. 16.*

EXHIBIT 11
Selected Overall and
ALBD* Expenses

(Dollar amounts in millions except ALBDS* and cost per ALBD)	Three Months Ended August 31		
	2010	**2010 Constant Dollar**	**2009**
	(in millions, except ALBDs and costs per ALBD)		
Cruise operating expenses	$ 2,160	$ 2,224	$ 2,081
Cruise selling and administrative expenses	373	384	372
Gross cruise costs	2,533	2,608	2,453
Less cruise costs included in net cruise revenues			
Commissions, transportation, and other	(517)	(542)	(515)
Onboard and other	(131)	(134)	(131)
Net cruise costs	1,885	1,932	1,807
Less fuel	(396)	(396)	(327)
Net cruise costs excluding fuel	$ 1,489	$ 1,536	$ 1,480
ALBDs	17,255,120	17,255,120	16,241,798
Gross cruise costs per ALBD	$ 146.84	$ 151.15	$ 151.07
Net cruise costs per ALBD	$ 109.24	$ 111.96	$ 111.29
Net cruise costs excluding fuel per ALBD	$ 86.28	$ 89.00	$ 91.16

Notes:
ALBD stands for Available Lower Berth Day

SOURCE: *Carnival 2010 10-Q, p. 18.*

Carnival in the Future

Carnival currently held approximately 50% of the cruising market. The company's strategy of "do one thing and do it better than anyone else" had been very successful. This concentration strategy had been so successful, in fact, that continued expansion in the cruise market was likely to become increasingly competitive and additional market share difficult to capture.

However, improving economic conditions may release pent-up demand for vacations with corresponding increase in the entire cruising market. An improving economy may be offset by increased terrorist activity in Europe and North America, a double dip recession, or rising fuel prices.

Carnival seemed to be positioned to take advantage of changes in the cruising industry by focusing more on Europe and differentiating with destinations, shipboard activities, and ship size. As Mickey Arison pondered the future of Carnival, he knew his vision had to extend many years into the future (ships must be ordered five or more years in advance) and attempt to forecast the world of 2016 and beyond to be successful.

C A S E **14**

Zynga, Inc. (2011): Whose Turn Is It?

Zachary Burkhalter, Daniel Zuller, Concetta Bagnato, Joyce Vincelette, and Ellie A. Fogarty

Introduction

As Mark Pincus waited for his friend to play a word, he could not help but think how the Facebook IPO and the growth in mobile gaming would affect his company over the long term. Mr. Pincus, founder and Chief Executive Officer (CEO) of Zynga, had built a company around social gaming. This new type of gaming had transformed the gaming industry on multiple levels and across various platforms. Zynga had originally built its games using the Facebook platform and had capitalized on the company's unique method of social networking that had captured audiences around the world. However, this strong reliance on Facebook and changes in consumer gaming practices caused some concern for outside investors and the future of Zynga. As a result of these concerns, by 2012, Zynga had expanded beyond its almost total reliance on the Facebook platform. The company had developed browser-based games that worked both stand-alone on mobile platforms such as Apple iOS and Google Android and as an application on social networking websites such as Facebook, Zynga.com, Google+, and Tencent.[1]

Zynga was built entirely around the concept of social gaming. It could then be inferred that social gaming took playing video games to a new level. When playing games on platforms such as computers, cell phones, tablets, or other devices, gamers were no longer required to play alone or with a friend physically present. Social gamers were able to play with others, over the Internet, at each other's pace. This was exactly how Zynga's games were played. For example, *Words with Friends* was a game similar to Scrabble. One person initiated a game with a friend or random opponent, played a word on a board game, and then waited for the friend to see that it was their move, which could take minutes or days. The friend then played a word and the move was sent back to the other player. This went back and forth until the game was done and, of course, the player with the most points won. All social games followed a somewhat similar format. In some games, like *FarmVille*, a player could plant, plow, and harvest crops without waiting for another player. However, players could help each other farm by sending necessary supplies and fertilizing their friends' crops. Players could even send each other gifts, which could either be bought with coins gathered from harvesting crops or by purchasing coins via real money.

Social games had been known to generate considerable competition between players. In one instance, a *Words with Friends* game became so heated that a celebrity player was kicked-off an airplane for refusing to turn off his cell phone during his turn. However, in the heat of the social gaming battle, Mark Pincus could not help but wonder about a few things concerning Zynga's future. How could Zynga continue to generate new social games to attract the masses? Did Zynga's business model need modifications? Would it be a wise decision to move away from Facebook and toward Zynga's own platform? What was the future of mobile gaming? Where else could Zynga spend its marketing dollars to gain more users and effectively grow its fan base? Were there alternative methods for generating revenues more consistently in the future? How should Zynga spend the approximate US$1 billion generated from its IPO? In addition, Pincus knew that Zynga had to remain aware of the trends in the company's external environment, including its competition, customers, changing technology (cloud computing, apps, increasing and changing platforms, etc.), and the global legal landscape and yet continually create or acquire games that attracted large audiences.

History

After three failed companies, Mark Pincus decided to try yet again and founded Zynga in April 2007 under the name Presidio Media, as a California limited liability company. Presidio converted to a Delaware corporation in October 2007 and its name was changed to Zynga in November 2010.[2] Zynga was named for Mark Pincus's late American Bulldog, Zinga, and the company used an image of a bulldog as their logo.[3] Zynga's first game, *Texas Hold'EM Poker*, now known as *Zynga Poker*, was released on Facebook in July 2007.

The company received two rounds of venture capital financing in 2008 totaling US$39 million. By June of 2008, Zynga had launched *Mafia Wars* on multiple platforms, including Facebook and MySpace and acquired the *YoVille* game in order to expand its game portfolio.[4] Zynga Poker was free to players, and Zynga's revenues were generated through advertisements. Because of its popularity, Zynga decided to sell chips to users in 2008 to generate additional revenues.[5]

In April 2009, Zynga became the #1 Facebook app developer with 40 million monthly active users (MAUs).[6] Soon afterward, Zynga opened a game studio, Zynga East, in Baltimore. In June 2009, Zynga launched *FarmVille*, which quickly became the most popular game on Facebook with 20 million daily active users (DAUs). In the second half of 2009, Zynga launched several other new games, including *Café World*.

In 2010, Zynga saw continued growth from existing games and new game launches, including *FrontierVille* and *CityVille*. In February 2010, Zynga opened a studio in Los Angeles and also the company's first office outside of the United States, Zynga India, in Bangalore.[7] During the second quarter of 2010, Zynga acquired both XPD Media and Challenge Games, which would later become known as Zynga China and Zynga Austin, respectively. In August 2010, Zynga acquired Conduit Labs and renamed it Zynga Boston. At this time, Zynga began its expansion into Europe and acquired Dextrose AG, renamed Zynga Germany. Also during this year, Zynga acquired Bonfire Studios, renamed Zynga Dallas, and Texas-based mobile game developer, Newtoy, Inc., renamed Zynga with Friends. With Newtoy, Zynga acquired the games *Words with Friends* and *Chess with Friends*. Additional smaller studios were also opened in 2010 in Japan and Seattle. In 2010, Facebook began requiring the use of Facebook Credits for monetization in Zynga games and on May 18, 2010, Zynga and Facebook entered into a five-year relationship to expand the use of Facebook Credits in Zynga games.[8] In December 2010, *CityVille* surpassed *FarmVille* as the company's most popular game with over 61 million MAUs and a base of over 16 million DAUs.[9]

In early 2011, Zynga announced numerous acquisitions, including the New York–based game developer Area/Code, renamed Zynga New York; Boston-based game developer Floodgate Entertainment; and MarketZero, renamed Zynga ATX, an online poker tracker company;

Five Mobile, renamed Zynga Toronto, specializing in mobile platforms; as well as a number of smaller acquisitions. Zynga also launched a number of games in 2011, including *Empires and Allies*, the company's first strategy combat game; *Hanging with Friends*, a mobile game that was developed in the company's Zynga with Friends studio; *Indiana Jones Adventure World*; *Words with Friends on Facebook*; and *CastleVille*. In October 2011, Zynga announced plans to create the company's own platform on which users could play games.[10] Although the platform, Project Z, would have ties to Facebook, it would be the first step away from reliance on Facebook. This new platform would be operated as Zynga.com.

Zynga completed its initial public offering in December 2011 and the company's Class A common stock was listed on NASDAQ Global Select Market under the symbol "ZNGA."[11] During its IPO, Zynga issued and sold 100 million shares of Class A common stock at a public offering price of US$10 per share. The company raised a total of US$961.4 million of net proceeds.[12]

In early 2012, Zynga added a puzzle game, *Hidden Chronicles*, to its game portfolio, and also launched *Zynga Slingo*, a casino type game, and *Bubble Safari*, the first game created by Zynga San Diego and the first to be launched simultaneously on two platforms: Zynga .com and Facebook.[13] In March 2012, Zynga announced the purchase of the game company OMGOP, creator of *Draw Something*, a popular mobile game. The largest and most controversial of Zynga's acquisitions, OMGOP cost the company US$180 million.[14] In June 2012, CBS was the winner of a bidding war for the pilot of a TV game show based on *Draw Something*.[15]

In order to develop new titles, in early 2012 Zynga acquired four small mobile game companies, including German company, GameDoctors, maker of the *ZombieSmash* game; U.S.-based company Page44 Studios, creator of the *World of Goo* game for the Apple iOS platform; San Francisco–based HipLogic; and New York–based Astro Ape Studios.[16] In June 2012, Zynga announced the purchase of video game maker Buzz Monkey, renamed Zynga Eugene. Buzz Monkey was known for working on successful video games such as *Tomb Raider* and *Tony Hawk*, as well as *Zynga's FrontiersVille*.[17]

In March 2012, Zynga launched the new Zynga Platform, Zynga.com, designed to bring players a new way to play social games. On Zynga.com, players were able to play not only Zynga-created games, but also games created by third-party game developers, called Platform Partners. Zynga planned to open up the new Platform and make it more widely available to all third-party game developers through an API by the end of 2012.[18] When launched, Zynga.com was available in 16 languages, including English, French, Italian, German, Spanish, Portuguese, Turkish, Indonesian, Norwegian, Danish, Dutch, Swedish, Chinese, Korean, Japanese, and Thai, and was totally integrated with Facebook.[19] An additional goal was to connect players of various Zynga game titles across multiple platforms. Players could create profiles to show their activity, message friends, discover which games friends were playing, and meet new people based on shared gaming interests.[20]

On June 26, 2012, Zynga launched the cross-platform *Zynga with Friends* network. Zynga described the network as a social lobby where all players could meet and play across all social networks and platforms. This meant that a player on Facebook would be able to play a game with a player on an iOS device.[21] Key features included activity feeds, a new chat interface, multiplayer leaderboards, and a variety of other additions designed to unify the company's titles. The *Zynga with Friends* network put Zynga in direct competition with Facebook as a social networking site.

Mission, Strategy, and Business Model

Mark Pincus, always thought that he would love to work with games and had been quoted as saying, "I've always said that social games are like a great cocktail party. . . . What I thought was the ultimate thing you can do—once you bring all of your friends and their friends together—is play games."[22] The concept behind all of Zynga's games was for them to be available for friends to play with or against each other over the Internet across platforms such as Facebook, mobile phones, Internet connected devices, social networking sites, and any platform that could help enhance a user's experience.[23]

This was consistent with Zynga's mission to: Connect the world through games.[24] To support this mission, Zynga encouraged entrepreneurship and innovation to produce break-through innovations, called bold beats.[25]

With the mission in mind, Zynga had achieved significant growth in a short period of time using a unique business model that had been questioned by analysts for its long-term sustainability. Essentially, Zynga's social games were free to play and the company generated revenue through the in-game sale of virtual goods and advertising. Initially, the primary method Zynga used to deliver its games to consumers had been the Facebook platform. Consumers would log on to Facebook to access Zynga games. By 2011, the number of people who played games on Facebook was shrinking. This decline had come as people shifted to playing games on their mobile devices instead of on personal computers. According to Zynga, the number of people who played its games on mobile devices was growing three times faster than the number of those who played on the Internet.

Recognizing these trends, by the fourth quarter of 2011 Zynga had begun investing in its own network infrastructure, with the goal of reducing its reliance on third-party, web-hosting services. By 2012, the company was hosting a significant portion of its game traffic on its own network infrastructure. Zynga also began investing in new distribution channels such as mobile and other platforms, including other social networks and in international markets, to expand its reach and grow its business. The company continued to hire additional employees and acquired companies with experience in developing mobile applications. Zynga also invested resources in integrating and operating some of the company's games on additional platforms, including Google+, mixi, and Tencent.[26]

As a result of the changes in consumer playing habits, Zynga's core business with its Facebook games had suffered. For Zynga, these trends made moving into mobile games and figuring out how to make money from them more important than ever. Zynga's CEO said his vision for mobile games was to connect a large network of game players across a variety of platforms. "I think that there's an opportunity on mobile devices for there to be a connector of these experiences," he said.[27]

Corporate Governance

Zynga's Code of Business Conduct was adopted on October 12, 2011, and Zynga's Corporate Governance Guidelines were adopted in March of 2012. These documents can be found on the company's website at http//:://investor.zynga.com/governance.cfm.

In September 2011, Zynga adopted a three-class common stock structure which had the effect of concentrating voting control with those stockholders who held the stock prior to the company's initial public offering, including Mark Pincus, founder and CEO, and other executive officers, employees, directors, and their affiliates. Zynga's Class C common stock had 70 votes per share. Mark Pincus was the only holder of Class C common stock. Class B common stock had seven votes per share. Class A common stock has one vote per share. As of December 31, 2011, there were approximately 1461 stockholders of Class B common stock and approximately 109 holders of Class A common stock. The holders of Class C and B common stock collectively held approximately 97.8% of the voting power of the company's outstanding capital stock, with Mark Pincus owning approximately 36.0% of the voting power. Future sales or transfers of Class B or Class C common stock would result in those shares converting to Class A common stock.[28]

Board of Directors. Zynga's board of directors was comprised of two internal and six external members including: Mark Pincus founder, Chairman, and CEO; John Schappert,

Chief Operating Officer (COO); William "Bing" Gordon, Reid Hoffman, Jeffrey Katzenberg, Stanley J. Meresman, Sunil Paul, and Owen Van Natta. Cash compensation had not been granted to non-employee directors for their services. Instead, non-employee directors had been granted options or restricted stock units (ZSUs) to purchase shares of Zynga's common stock under the company's equity incentive plans.[29]

The Zynga Way

Zynga attributed its success to its ability to identify, hire, integrate, develop, motivate, and retain talented employees, particularly game designers, product managers, and engineers under the leadership of Chief People Officer, Colleen McCreary. Zynga had historically hired a number of key personnel through acquisitions. As of March 31, 2012, Zynga was comprised of 2267 full-time employees domestically and internationally.[30] As of December 31, 2011, approximately 54% of Zynga employees had been with the company for less than one year, and approximately 84% for less than two years.[31]

Zynga's corporate headquarters, located in San Francisco, California, was nicknamed The Dog House.[32] Zynga employees enjoyed unique benefits including a gym and personal training, free gourmet meals, access to a nutritionist, pet insurance, massages, haircuts, acupuncture, a coffee shop, gaming arcade, basketball court, lounges with big-screen TVs, poker nights, and a beer bar in the basement with happy hours. Zynga also offered generous benefits packages to its employees. The company paid 100% of the premiums for medical, dental, and vision coverage, life and accident insurance, and short- and long-term disability protection for all U.S. full-time employees, as well as 75% of the premiums for dependents. The company had a unique vacation policy in that there was no formal policy. Instead, Zynga employees were encouraged to take days off when they felt the need.[33]

Zynga was known for its entrepreneurial, execution-focused, fiercely competitive, and stressful culture that worked well for the company pre-IPO but appeared to be more difficult to maintain as a public company obtaining most of its employees through acquisitions. Zynga's culture could be described as one where employees were encouraged to work hard and play hard. Many Zynga employees chose to work and thrived in the hard-driving, performance-driven, results-oriented culture that was often described as meritocratic, but others may not have been willing participants, particularly those who came on board through acquisitions. This had led to varying reports from employees about what it was like to work at Zynga, some very positive and some extremely negative.

Since its beginnings, Zynga utilized an organization structure where the company's studios operated independently from each other in game creation. When Zynga acquired small gaming companies, often their name was changed but the management and creative teams remained intact. The reason for this organizational structure was to encourage and reward creativity. Studio heads set goals and were given the freedom to achieve them any way that was possible.[34] Those who succeeded were rewarded with cash, stock bonuses, and extra resources, such as the ability to hire extra staff. Mark Pincus called this structure "true meritocracy." The approach was designed to motivate everyone to succeed in an environment where all winners were rewarded.[35]

Turning Games to Revenue

In 2012, Zynga generated revenue in primarily two ways: (1) through the in-game sale of virtual goods, and (2) through advertisements.[36]

Sale of Virtual Goods.   All Zynga games were offered as live services that allowed players to play for free. Within these games, Zynga provided the opportunity for players to purchase virtual currency to obtain virtual goods that could enhance their game-playing experience. Examples of virtual goods were items used to decorate farms in Farmville, VIP access and chips in Zynga Poker, and gifts that players could buy for their online friends. Gamers could also advance through a game based on their time invested and level of skill, or purchase goods that would allow them to advance more quickly through a game and "skip the line," giving people the option of paying with time, or money.[37] Some forms of virtual currency could be earned through game play, while other forms could only be acquired for cash or, in some cases, by accepting promotional offers from the company's advertising partners.[38]

Virtual goods were the primary source of Zynga's revenues and the company generated US$969 million from the sales of these goods in 2011. Surprisingly, only a small percentage of gamers actually spent money on virtual goods in Zynga games. It was estimated that less than 1% of gamers were responsible for up to half of Zynga's sales, the majority of Zynga gamers did not spend any money.[39]

Zynga believed its players chose to pay for virtual goods for the same reasons they were willing to pay for other forms of entertainment. They enjoyed the additional playing time or added convenience, the ability to personalize their game boards, the satisfaction of leveling up, and the opportunity for sharing creative expressions. Zynga believed players were more likely to purchase virtual goods when they were connected to and playing with friends, whether those friends played for free or also purchased virtual goods.

According to Zynga's May 2010 agreement with Facebook, virtual goods purchased by gamers playing Zynga games on the Facebook Platform must purchase their virtual goods using Facebook Credits as the primary method of payment. Players could purchase Facebook Credits from Facebook, directly through Zynga games, or through game cards purchased from retailers and distributors. When playing Zynga games on platforms other than Facebook, players were able to purchase virtual goods through various payment methods offered in the games, including credit cards, PayPal, Apple iTunes accounts, and direct wires. Players could also purchase game cards from retailers and distributors for use on these platforms.[40]

Advertisements.   The second way Zynga generated revenue was through the company's online advertisements. Although advertising had not been the company's primary emphasis, Zynga was beginning to focus more on online ads as a source of revenue. The types of advertisements that Zynga used included: branded virtual goods and sponsorships that integrated advertising within game play; engagement ads and offers where players could answer certain questions or sign up for third-party services to receive virtual currency; mobile ads through ad-supported free versions of Zynga mobile games; and display ads in Zynga's online Web games that included banner advertisements.[41] Zynga generated US$55 million in revenues in 2011 from advertisements, which accounted for only 5% of the company's total revenues.

Zynga realized the importance of sustaining growth in the sale of virtual goods and increasing advertising revenues. Zynga's revenue growth depended on its ability to attract and retain players and more effectively monetize its player base through the sale of virtual goods and advertising.[42]

Partnerships

Facebook.   Facebook was the primary distribution, marketing, promotion, and payment platform for all Zynga games. In 2012, Zynga generated most of its bookings, revenue, and players through the Facebook platform.[43] In addition, the largest amount of marketing dollars Zynga spent was spent on Facebook ads.[44] In 2011, an estimated 93.25% of Zynga's yearly bookings and revenues were generated through the Facebook platform.[45]

Although Zynga had stated it would like to lessen its reliance on Facebook, it was also aware that if its relationship with Facebook were to deteriorate or if Facebook itself became less popular with consumers, the company's business would suffer and alternatives would have to be created. This would be costly and more than likely not as efficient in generating such large amounts of attention from gamers.[46] Zynga's relationship with Facebook was mutually beneficial. Not only did Zynga generate revenue and a large portion of its players from Facebook, Zynga contributed 12% of Facebook's US$3.711 billion in revenue or US$445 million during 2011.[47]

In May 2010, Zynga entered into a five-year deal with Facebook in order to promote the launch of their new games. This deal required that Zynga be subject to Facebook's standard terms and conditions for application developers that governed the promotion, distribution, and operation of Zynga games through the Facebook platform. These included: that Zynga must notify Facebook a week before a new game launch, that Facebook had control over the release date, and that Zynga game players must be actively logged into Facebook in order to play.[48] In addition to the standard terms, Zynga had an addendum with Facebook that modified the terms and required the use of Facebook Credits as the primary payment method for Zynga games on the Facebook platform. The addendum also required Facebook to remit to Zynga an amount equal to 70% of the face value of Facebook Credits purchased by Zynga game players for use in Zynga games. This addendum with Facebook expires in May 2015.[49]

Hasbro.   In mid-2012, Zynga announced a comprehensive partnership that granted Hasbro Inc. the rights to develop a wide range of toy and gaming experiences based on Zynga's popular social games and brands, such as *Farmville*, *Mafia Wars*, *Words With Friends*, and others. This deal also created opportunities for co-branded merchandise featuring a combination of both Hasbro and Zynga brands. The two companies expected that the first products would be available beginning fall 2012.[50]

New Platform Partners.   In early 2012, Zynga announced new Zynga Platform Partners including: Mob Science, Row Sham Bow, Sava Transmedia, Konami Digital Entertainment, Playdemic, Rebellion, 50 Cubes, Majesco Entertainment, and Portalarium. These partners were able to publish and promote their games on Zynga's new platform, Zynga.com, and not only have access to Zynga players but also the ability to tap into other Zynga features and metrics.[51] Zynga also announced partners for the company's new Zynga Partners for Mobile Program including Atari, Crash Lab, Fat Pebble, Phosphor Games Studio, and Sava Transmedia to help increase Zynga's presence on mobile devices.[52]

American Express.   In May 2012, Zynga and American Express announced a partnership that would link everyday spending to online rewards for Zynga game players through a co-branded prepaid card called Zynga Serve Rewards. Players would be able to add money to their Serve account through any funding source, including a bank account, debit card, credit card, or cash. The Serve Rewards card would be accepted everywhere in the United States that American Express cards were accepted for purchases and would receive online, in-game rewards.[53]

Acquisitions

Acquisitions had become an integral source of new games, international expansion, and employees for Zynga, and the foundation of Zynga's growth strategy. Zynga spent US$147.2 million for 22 companies during 2010 and 2011.[54] In order to develop new game titles for a variety of platforms, this strategy was continued into 2012 with the purchase

EXHIBIT 1
Zynga Headquarters,
Acquisitions, Studios
and Facilities in
June 2012

- Zynga Corporate Headquarters, San Francisco, CA
- Zynga East-Baltimore, Maryland, 2009
- Zynga India-Bangalore, 2010
- Zynga Los Angeles, 2010
- Zynga China, Beijing (formerly XPD media), 2010
- Zynga Austin (formerly Challenge Games), 2010
- Zynga Boston (formerly Conduit Labs), 2010
- Zynga Japan, Tokyo (formerly UNOH games), 2010
- Zynga Germany, Frankfurt (formerly Dextrose AG), 2010
- Zynga Dallas (formerly Bonfire Studios), 2010
- Zynga with Friends, McKinney, Texas (formerly Newtoy, Inc.), 2010
- Zynga ATX (formerly MarketZero, Inc.), 2011
- Zynga New York (formerly Area/Code), 2011
- Zynga Seattle, opened 2010
- Floodgate Entertainment, 2011
- Zynga Toronto (formerly Five Mobile), 2011
- OMGOP, 2012
- Wild Needle (casual gaming company specializing in games appealing to females), 2012
- Zynga Eugene (formerly Buzz Monkey Software), 2012
- GameDoctors, Germany, 2012
- Page44 Studios, 2012
- HipLogic, 2012
- Astro Ape Studios, 2012
- Zynga San Diego, 2012
- Additional smaller studios and facilities

of six domestic and international companies by mid-year, including OMGOP, creator of *Draw Something*, a popular mobile game.[55] *Draw Something* was the #1 word game in 80 countries when acquired by Zynga, and then experienced a noticeable drop in popularity following the acquisition, as DAUs dropped from 15 million to 10 million in the first month after the acquisition.[56] Mark Pincus was quoted as saying, "We love finding great, accomplished teams that share our mission and vision."[57]

To be successful with the company's acquisition strategy, Zynga must be able to successfully integrate acquired companies into its business and manage the growth associated with these multiple acquisitions. Zynga must also be able to integrate highly talented and creative employees from these acquired companies into Zynga's highly competitive culture. Zynga's headquarters, acquisitions, and studios are listed in **Exhibit 1**.

Operations

In 2007, Zynga was able to meet the demand for its games like Zynga Poker with a simple IT infrastructure using servers stacked in a rented retail data center. Then Zynga released *FarmVille* in 2009 and the company's IT needs changed overnight. Within five months of the game's release, 25 million users were hitting *FarmVille* servers. Zynga was not able to scale its internal infrastructure quickly enough to keep up with demand, so the company shifted most of its IT needs to Amazon Web Services (AWS). AWS allowed Zynga to buy virtual server and storage space, scaling capacity up and down as needed. Zynga relied on Amazon for most of its IT needs throughout 2009 and 2010, and then realized that they could develop a proprietary system that would be more aligned with the company's business needs and yet be entirely within their own control. For example, with its own system, Zynga could customize its hardware and software to meet the specific needs of *FarmVille*, *Words with Friends*, and all of its other games.[58]

In 2010, Zynga started building data centers on both the east and west coasts. By the end of 2011, about 80% of Zynga game users at any given time were logged onto servers in the company's own data centers, while the other 20% were playing in the Amazon cloud. By 2012, Zynga's internal infrastructure, called zCloud, was able to not only serve the company's social gaming needs but also provide a platform to help third-party developers build social games.[59] Zynga planned to continue to use Amazon to meet some of its server needs and provide increased capacity when needed.

In March 2011, Zynga announced the launch of a new platform, Zynga.com, where players were able to play not only Zynga-created games, but also games created by third-party game developers, called Platform Partners. Zynga planned to open up the new Platform and make it more widely available to all third-party game developers through an API by the end of 2012.[60] The Zynga API would allow third-party game developers to take advantage of Zynga's technology and servers and build their own games on top of Zynga's technology, enhancing online gaming opportunities for smaller startups.

In 2012, Zynga had one operating segment with one business activity, developing, and monetizing social games.[61] In the past, the company's studios specialized in certain types of social games for specific devices. By 2012, all studios created games for mobile devices, indicating the increased importance placed on the development of mobile games for the future success of Zynga.

Marketing

In 2012, Zynga developed, marketed, and operated online social games as live services played over the Internet, on social gaming sites, and on mobile platforms.[62] In 2011, Zynga was the world's leading provider of social games with 240 million MAUs in over 175 countries. Zynga launched the most successful social games in the industry in 2009, 2010, and 2011 and generated over US$1.85 billion in cumulative revenue and over US$2.35 billion in cumulative bookings since the company's inception in 2007.[63]

Products.   Zynga had historically depended on a small number of games for the majority of its revenue. Company growth depended on the ability to launch and enhance games that attracted and retained a significant number of players. The games that constituted Zynga's top three games varied over time, but historically, the top three revenue-generating games in any period contributed the majority of Zynga's revenue. Zynga's top three games accounted for 57%, 78%, and 83% of Zynga's online game revenue in 2011, 2010, and 2009, respectively.[64]

From 2007 to 2012, Zynga had regularly created and launched new social games and had improved upon well establish games. All Zynga's games were accessible to players worldwide on mobile platforms such as Apple iOS and Google Android and as an application on social networking websites such as Facebook, Zynga.com, Google+, and Tencent.[65] In 2012, Zynga was actively attempting to increase the number of games offered on multiple platforms, especially mobile platforms, through both internal game development and acquisitions. A list of Zynga Games in mid-2012 can be found in **Exhibit 2**.

EXHIBIT 2
Zynga Games
July 2012

Blackjack	Matching with Friends
Bubble Safari	Pathwords
CastleVille	PetVille
CaféWorld	The Pioneer Trail (formerly FrontierVille)
ChefVille	Ruby Blast
Chess with Friends	Scramble with Friends
CityVille	Sudoku
CityVille Holidaytown	The Ville
CityVille Hometown	Treasure Isle
Draw Something	Vampires: Bloodlust
Dream Heights	Vampire Wars
Dream Pethouse	Word Twist
Dream Zoo	Words with Friends
Drop7	Yakuza Lords
Empires & Allies	YoVille
FarmVille	Zynga Bingo
FarmVille Mobile	Zynga Elite Slots
FishVille	Zynga Poker+
ForestVille	Zynga Slingo
Hanging with Friends	Zynga Slots
Hidden Chronicles (F	Zombie Swipeout
Indiana Jones Adventure World	ZombieSmash
Live Poker	

Upcoming Games
FarmVille2

In 2012, Zynga created and launched new games in what Zynga called popular "genres." In the *Ville* genre, Zynga was about to launch *FarmVille 2*, and had created *The Ville*, *ChefVille*, and other popular games. In the *Casino* genre, Zynga built on the legacy of *Zynga Poker* and *Zynga Bingo* and created *Zynga Slots* and *Zynga Elite Slots*. Casino games using real money rather than virtual currency were also in the works. In the *Arcade* genre, a new game called *Ruby Blast* became the first game from both Zynga China and Zynga Seattle and the first international cross-collaboration for a game launch. In the *Words with Friends* genre, Zynga was building on the popularity *of Words with Friends* with the creation of *Scramble with Friends*, a find a word game, and *Matching with Friends*, a puzzle game involving matching colors. Additional "genres" were planned.

Zynga's "products" were classified as social games for a variety of platforms, but it needed to be understood that Zynga gave these products to game players for free. Customers were not charged for these products. Zynga generated real revenue and posted real profits from the sale of virtual goods and to a lesser extent advertising.[66] Social game developers found it more difficult to make money from mobile games than from computer console–based games because the smaller screen size resulted in less room for advertisements. In addition, players on mobile devices tended to be more casual players who spent less money for ways to advance quickly in a game, than did the more dedicated players on PCs. These concerns had led to debates about whether mobile games should be free or if players should pay to play up front.[67]

Customers.   To sustain revenue levels, it was necessary to attract, retain, and increase the number of players or more effectively monetize the company's existing players.[68] Mark

Pincus said, "The most important predictor of next month's usage is how many people you play with this month."[69]

It was important for Zynga to understand the characteristics of its players for the effective expense of marketing dollars. With over 247 million MAUs in 2011, Zynga had found it difficult to pinpoint the exact characteristics of the company's average gamer.[70] However, studies suggested, somewhat surprisingly, that the average person that engaged in social games was a 43-year-old woman.[71] This demographic made more sense when the characteristics of social games were considered. Social games were simple to play, could be played in a short period of time, and were for the most part offered for free. Women outpaced men with 38% and 29%, respectively, playing social games several times a day. The study also cited that women were more likely to play with real-world friends than men, and men were more likely than women to play with strangers met online. Roughly 95% of social gamers played multiple times per week and almost two-thirds played at least daily.[72] Another survey discovered that gamer age correlated to whether or not the player purchased in-game virtual goods. It was found that the older the gamer, the more inclined they were to spend money on goods. Forty-two percent of all virtual goods purchases were made by gamers 35 and older, while 18% of virtual good purchases were made by players 18 to 25 years of age.[73]

The number of individuals who accessed the Internet through devices other than a personal computer, such as Smartphones, tablets, televisions, and set-top box devices had increased dramatically and the trend was likely to continue. These devices typically had lower processing speed, power, functionality, and memory and made playing Zynga games through these devices more difficult and the versions developed less compelling to players.

It was estimated that in mid-2012 nearly half of U.S. cell phone subscribers had a Smartphone, up from 36% in 2011. This almost 14% increase was not surprising considering two out of three people who purchased a new device chose a Smartphone.[74] The tablet industry had also been on the rise and in 2012 boasted just under 60 million users.[75] The consumer transition from playing social games on desktop computers to playing these games on mobile platforms happened in a very short period of time requiring social game developers to scramble to make the transition in order to remain profitable.

Advertising.   Zynga generated advertising revenue through paid advertisements and also spent considerable advertising dollars to attract new players to Zynga games and to advertise new games and game upgrades. During 2011, Zynga spent about US$234 million dollars on marketing. This equated to the company spending roughly 36 cents to earn one dollar in sales, up from 14 cents in the third quarter of 2011.[76] Most of the traditional advertising dollars were spent on Facebook advertisements. Zynga, however, acquired most players through unpaid channels and had gained users by the viral and sharing features available on social networking sites.[77] In addition, Zynga tried to stay connected with players through fan pages, generally on Facebook, Twitter, and occasionally hosted live and online player events.[78]

Zynga operated in a highly competitive and fast-paced environment. Zynga competed for the leisure time, attention, and discretionary spending of its players with other social game developers, on a number of factors, including quality-of-player experience, brand awareness and reputation, and access to distribution channels. For Zynga to be successful, the company must fully understand the competition and the changing nature of the company's external environment.

The Legal Landscape

Government Regulations.   Zynga is subject to a number of foreign and domestic laws and regulations that affect companies conducting business on the Internet, many of which are still evolving and subject to interpretation. Because some of Zynga's games, such as *Zynga Poker*, are based on traditional casino games, the company had structured and operated these games with the gambling laws in mind. Zynga also sometimes offered its players various types of sweepstakes, giveaways, and promotional opportunities.[79] Because the U.S. Justice Department has signaled that states could begin developing regulations for online gambling, Zynga had begun investing in state and federal lobbying efforts around gambling with real money. Zynga reported spending some US$75,000 during the second quarter of 2012 on these lobbying efforts. Zynga planned on releasing its first real money gambling program in early 2013.

Privacy issues.   Zynga was subject to federal, state, and foreign laws regarding privacy and protection of player data. This regulatory framework for privacy issues worldwide was currently in flux. During the course of its business, Zynga received, stored, processed, and used personal information and other player data, and enabled its players to share their personal information with each other and third parties, on both the Internet and mobile platforms. These practices had come under increased public scrutiny, and civil claims alleging the liability for the breach of data privacy had been asserted against Zynga.[80]

Cheating Programs and Scams.   Unauthorized third parties operated cheating programs that enabled players to exploit Zynga games, play them in an automated way or obtain unfair advantages over players who played fairly. In addition, unauthorized parties had attempted to scam players with fake offers for virtual goods, disrupting the virtual economy of Zynga games.[81]

Intellectual Property.   Intellectual property in the gaming industry was a very valuable asset; however, it was sometimes hard to protect because the laws were so loosely defined. The laws protected expressions, or codes used to create games, but not ideas. For example, the idea of a farm game could not be protected because of its generality, but the code used to create the games could be protected.[82] Based on the law, if Zynga or any other developer could create a game with the company's own code but used the same concept as another, it was legal. This interpretation of the law had provided a challenge for all game companies in the industry. Copying of successful game ideas had been rampant in the industry with numerous lawsuits filed.

Zynga and its competitors had extensively used this "copying" strategy. If another game developer created a game that saw positive results, Zynga launched a similar version of its own. When Psycho Monkey launched the popular game *Mob Wars*, Zynga came out with *Mafia Wars*.[83] Zynga responded to Playfish's *Restaurant City* with their *Café World*.[84] After Slashkey's *Farm Town* appeared successful, Zynga's quickly created *Farmville*.[85] Many examples could also be found of competitors engaged in similar practices. Mark Pincus believed that the copying of competitor's products was a sound business level strategy.

Industry players had engaged in this strategy because it had worked. It had proven to be a cost-effective formula. Competitors had been able to quickly launch games while making slight improvements based on player experiences. The downside of the strategy was the cost of lawsuits and potential damage to a company's image. Just one lawsuit with Psycho Monkey over the copying of *Mob Wars* cost Zynga US$7 to US$9 million in an out-of-court settlement.[86]

In June 2012, Zynga appeared to have stepped on bigger toes with potentially deeper pockets. Electronic Arts (EA) hit Zynga with a copyright infringement suit stating similarities that were more than coincidental and superficial between *The Sims Social* (launched in August 2011) and Zynga's *The Ville* (released in June 2012) and deemed it a "clear violation" of copyright laws. The lawsuit alleged that Zynga copied everything from design choices and animations to visual style and character motions. Reginald Davis, Zynga's General Counsel, had responded that Zynga planned to defend itself against the EA lawsuit and has stated that *The Ville* was much more innovative than *The Sims Social*.[87]

Lawsuits.   Typing in the keywords "Zynga" and "lawsuit" together in Google's search bar resulted in a whopping 1,210,000 hits as of this writing, which gives the reader an idea of the scope of Zynga's legal concerns. Most of these lawsuits dealt with alleged intellectual property law violations. In July 2012, Zynga was hit with an insider-trading lawsuit alleging that some top executives and investors, including CEO Mark Pincus and Google, engaged in insider trading. Following Zynga's IPO in December 2011, employees and investors were "locked up," unable to sell their shares until May 28th. A group of top executives and shareholders hired underwriters to manage the sale of some of their shares, creating a loophole that allowed them to sell some of their stock at US$12 on April 3. Zynga actually beat Q1 2012 earnings estimates and the "insiders" were not aware of Q2 results prior to selling their stock, but the stock price declined to approximately US$3 per share shortly after the sale, raising investor concerns.[88]

Corporate Philanthropy

Through Zynga's philanthropic arm, Zynga.org, the company raised over US$13 million for its nonprofit partners, including UCSF Benioff Children's Hospital, Save the Children, the World Food Programme, Habitat for Humanity, St. Jude's Children's Research Hospital, Wildlife Conservation Society, Half the Sky Foundation, Direct Relief International, Every Mother Counts, and many others, by selling virtual goods in Zynga games and donating some of the proceeds to charity.[89] In addition, the Knight Foundation and Zynga collaborated to look into the creation of digital games that were not just for entertainment, but also had a philanthropic or social edge. Zynga.org was also focused on working with nonprofits to help them develop suitable online games to raise money for their organizations.

Finance

In addition to traditional financial measures of the company's performance, Zynga used a number of proprietary metrics to evaluate the company's financial and operating results. A description of these metrics can be found in **Exhibit 3**. Zynga's balance sheets, statement of operations, and cash flow statements can be found in **Exhibits 4** through **6**.

From 2008 to 2011, Zynga reported revenue of US$19.4 million, US$121.5 million, US$597.5 million, and US$1.14 billion, respectively, and bookings of US$35.9 million, US$328.1 million, US$838.9 million, and, US$1.16 billion, respectively.[90] The resulting net income from 2008 to 2011 was a loss of US$22.1 million, US$52.8 million, and US$404.3 million in 2008, 2009, and 2011, respectively, and a gain of US$90.6 million in 2010. International revenue as a percentage of the total accounted for 36%, 33%, and 27% in 2011, 2010, and 2009, respectively.[91]

Exhibit 6 shows Zynga's statement of operations for the six months ended June 30, 2012 compared to the six months ended June 30, 2011. As can be seen, Zynga's total revenue was up 25% to US$653.5 million from US$522 million in the prior year. During this same period, the company's cost of revenue had also increased significantly to US$184 million from US$145 million in June 2011. More importantly, Zynga's total costs and expenses as of June 2012 increased nearly 65% to US$777 million from US$472 million during the same

EXHIBIT 3
Zynga Proprietary
Key Financial and
Operating Metrics

Bookings were equal to the revenue recognized in the period in addition to the change in deferred revenue during the period. Bookings were used to evaluate the results of operations, generate future operating plans, and assess company performance. Bookings were the fundamental metric used by Zynga to manage its business. Zynga believed it was a better indicator of the sales activity in a given period.

Adjusted EBITDA was calculated as net income (loss), adjusted for benefit from income taxes; other income (expense), net; interest income; gain (loss) from legal settlements; depreciation; amortization; stock-based compensation; and change in deferred revenue.

DAUs (daily active users of Zynga games) were the number of individuals who played a game during a particular day. Under this metric, an individual who played two different games on the same day was counted as two DAUs. Similarly, an individual who played the same game on two different platforms or on two different social networks on the same day was counted as two DAUs. Average DAUs was the average of the DAUs for each day during the period recorded. Zynga used DAU as a measure of audience engagement.

MAUs (mean monthly active users of Zynga games) were the number of individuals who played a particular game during a 30-day period. Under this metric, an individual who played two different games in the same period was counted as two MAUs. Similarly, an individual who played the same game on two different platforms or on two different social networks during the period was counted as two MAUs. Average MAUs were the average of the MAUs at each month-end during the period. Zynga used MAUs as a measure of total game audience size.

MUUs (mean monthly unique users of Zynga games) were the number of unique individuals who played any Zynga game on a particular platform in a 30-day period. Any individual who played more than one Zynga game during the period was counted as a single MUU. Because many Zynga players played more than one game during a given 30-day period, MUUs were always lower than MAUs in any given period. Average MUUs for a particular period were the average of the MUUs at each month-end. Zynga used MUU as a measure of total audience reach across the company's network of games.

MUPs (monthly unique payers) were the number of unique players who made a payment at least once during the applicable month. If a player made a payment in Zynga games on two different platforms in a period, the player was counted as two unique players in that period. MUPs were presented as a quarterly average of the three months in the applicable quarter.

ABPU (average bookings per user) were defined as Zynga total bookings in a given period, divided by the number of days in that period, divided by the average DAUs during the period. Zynga used ABPU as a measure of overall monetization across all of the company's players through the sale of virtual goods and advertising.

....
SOURCE: Zynga, Inc., *2011 Form 10-K*, pp. 35–36.

period in 2011. As a result, Zynga's stock price dropped to US$5.44 as of the close on June 29, 2012. After Zynga announced second-quarter results on July 25, 2012, and slashed the company's 2012 earnings outlook, Zynga's stock plunged to US$3.05, down nearly 70% from the company's IPO price of US$10 in December 2011.

Correspondingly, Zynga's ending cash balance had reduced to US$435 million as of June 2012, compared with US$535 million as of June 2011. This decrease in cash, on top of a falling stock price and costs and expenses increasing more than revenue, suggested concerns about Zynga's future. The Zynga management team listed several reasons for the results, including changes to Facebook's gaming platform making Zynga's most profitable games harder to find, the shift to mobile platforms, a delayed game release, and several games that were poorly rated by users. Zynga had also struggled to get users of its mostly free games to pay real money for virtual items in games.[92]

EXHIBIT 4
Consolidated Balance Sheets: Zynga Inc. (Dollar amounts in thousand, except share and per share information)

	For the Fiscal Year Ended		
	December 31, 2011	December 31, 2010	December 31, 2009
Assets			
Current assets:			
Cash and cash equivalents	$ 1,582,343	$ 187,831	$ 127,336
Marketable securities	225,165	550,259	72,622
Accounts receivable, net of allowance of $163 and $325 at December 31, 2011 and 2010, respectively	135,633	79,974	7,157
Income tax receivable	18,583	36,577	11,298
Deferred tax assets	23,515	24,399	—
Restricted cash	3,846	2,821	653
Other current assets	34,824	24,353	3,082
Total current assets	2,023,909	906,214	222,140
Long-term marketable securities	110,098	—	—
Goodwill	91,765	60,217	—
Other intangible assets, net	32,112	44,001	1,045
Property and equipment, net	246,740	74,959	34,827
Restricted cash	4,082	14,301	—
Other long-term assets	7,940	12,880	836
Total assets	$ 2,516,646	$ 1,112,572	$ 258,848
Liabilities and stockholders' equity (deficit)			
Current liabilities:			
Accounts payable	44,020	33,431	21,503
Other current liabilities	167,271	78,749	35,024
Deferred revenue	457,394	408,470	178,109
Total current liabilities	668,685	520,650	234,636
Deferred revenue	23,251	56,766	45,690
Deferred tax liabilities	13,950	14,123	—
Other non-current liabilities	61,221	38,818	—
Total liabilities	767,107	630,357	28,326
Stockholders' equity			
Convertible preferred stock, $.00000625 par value:			
Authorized, 0 and 351,199 at December 31,2011 and 2010, respectively. Issued and outstanding, 0 and 276,702 shares at December 21, 2011 and 2010, respectively (aggregate liquidation preference of $849,380 at December 31, 2010.	—	394,026	47,672
Common stock, $.00000625 par value:			
Authorized, 2,020,517 (Class A 1,100,000, Class B 900,000, Class C 20,517) and 965,632 (Class A 0, Class B 945,115, Class C 20,517) shares at December 31, 2011 and 2010, respectively. Issued and Outstanding, 721,592 (Class A 121,381, Class B 579, 694, Class C 20,517) and 291,524 (Class A 0, Class B 271,007, Class C 20,517) shares at December 31, 2011 and 2010, respectively;	4	2	2

(continued)

EXHIBIT 4
(Continued)

	For the Fiscal Year Ended		
	December 31, 2011	December 31, 2010	December 31, 2009
Additional paid-in capital	2,426,164	79,335	6,610
Treasury stock	(282,897)	(1,484)	—
Other comprehensive income	362	114	21
Retained earnings (accumulated deficit)	(394,094)	10,222	(75,783)
Total stockholders' equity	1,749,539	482,215	(21,478)
Total equity and liabilities	$ 2,516,646	$ 1,112,572	$ 258,848

....
SOURCE: Zynga, Inc., 2011, 10-K, p.57.

EXHIBIT 5
Consolidated Statement of Operations Data: Zynga Inc. (In thousands, except per share, users, and ABPU data)

	For the Fiscal Year Ended (1)				Period from Inception (April 19, 2007) to December 31,
	Year Ended December 31,				
	2011	2010	2009	2008	2007
Consolidated statements of operations data:					
Revenue	$ 1,140,100	$ 597,459	$ 121,467	$ 19,410	$ 693
Costs and expenses:					
Cost of revenue	330,043	176,052	56,707	10,017	189
Research and development	727,018	149,519	51,029	12,160	869
Sales and marketing	234,199	114,165	42,266	10,982	231
General and administrative	254,456	32,251	24,243	8,834	277
Total costs and expenses	1,545,716	471,987	174,245	41,993	1,566
Income (loss) from operations	(405,616)	125,472	(52,778)	(22,583)	(873)
Interest income	1,680	1,222	177	319	22
Other income (expense), net	(2,206)	365	(209)	187	8
Income (loss) before income taxes	(406,142)	127,059	(52,810)	(22,077)	(843)
(Provision for)/ benefit from income taxes	1,826	(36,464)	(12)	(38)	(3)
Net income (loss)	$ (404,316)	$ 90,595	$ (52,822)	$ (22,115)	$ (846)
Deemed dividend to a Series B-2 convertible preferred stockholder	—	4,590	—	—	—
Net income attributable to participating securities	—	58,110	—	—	—
Net income (loss) attributable to common stockholders	$(404,316)	$27,895	$52,822	$22,115	$(846)
Net income (loss) per share attributable to common stockholders					
Basic	$(1.40)	$0.12	$(0.31)	$(0.18)	$(0.06)
Diluted	$(1.40)	$0.11	$(0.31)	$(0.18)	$(0.06)

	For the Fiscal Year Ended (1)				Period from Inception (April 19, 2007) to December 31,
	Year Ended December 31,				
	2011	2010	2009	2008	2007
Weighted average common shares used to compute net income (loss) per share attributable to common stockholders:					
Basic	288,599	223,881	171,751	119,990	14,255
Diluted	288,599	329,256	171,751	119,990	14,255
Other financial and operational data:					
Bookings	1,155,509	$838,896	$328,070	$35,948	$1,351
Adjusted EBITDA	303,274	$392,738	$168,187	$4,549	−$185
Average DAUs (in millions)	57	56	41	NA	NA
Average MAUs (in millions)	233	217	153	NA	NA
Average MUUs (in millions)	151	116	86	NA	NA
ABPU	$ 0.055	$0.041	$0.035	NA	NA

NOTE: Definitions and calculations for "Other Financial and Operational Data" can be found in Exhibit 3.
SOURCE: Zynga, Inc. *2011 Form 10-K*, pp. 29–30.

EXHIBIT 6 Consolidated Statements of Operations for Six Months Ended June 30, 2011 and 2010: Zynga Inc. (In thousands, except per share data) (Unaudited)

	Six Months Ended June 30,	
	2012	2011
Revenue		
Online game	$584,328	$493,872
Advertising	69,137	28,162
Total revenue	653,465	522,034
Cost and expenses:		
Cost of revenue	184,963	145,738
Research and development	358,192	167,507
Sales and marketing	112,892	78,254
General and administrative	121,445	81,328
Total costs and expenses	777,492	472,827
Income (loss) from operations	(124,027)	49,207
Interest income	2,375	961
Other income (expense), net	20,108	(536)
Income (loss) before income taxes	(101,544)	49,632
Provision for income taxes	(6,618)	(31,483)
Net income (loss)	$(108,162)	$18,149

SOURCE: Zynga, Inc. Form 10-Q filed on July 30, 2012.

Future Outlook

In the company's short history, Zynga had been able to capitalize on the growth of social gaming and the popularity of the Facebook platform. By mid-2012, Facebook had been showing signs of weakness, and Zynga's growth in bookings had been slowing down. In addition, there was a rapid shift in demand from console-based social games to mobile gaming. Zynga had been preparing for the shift by acquiring companies with mobile gaming experience and developing games for mobile platforms. In addition, Zynga had lessened its reliance on Facebook and had invested considerable resources in infrastructure, including new platforms and networks. The social gaming industry had changed rapidly in just two years and more changes appeared to be on the horizon. Zynga will need to rethink the sustainability of the company's current business model as it plans for future success.

NOTES

1. "About Zynga" (http://company.zynga.com/about).
2. Zynga, Inc., *2011 Form 10-K*, p. 2.
3. http://www.crunchbase.com/company/zynga
4. Zynga, Inc., *2011 Form 10-K*, p. 33.
5. http://venturebeat.com/2011/12/12/zynga-history/view-all/
6. Mack, Christopher, "Zynga Making $100 Million/Year," April 30, 2009, (http://www.insidesocialgames.com/2009/04/30/zynga-making-100-millionyear/)
7. "Zynga Opens First International Office in India," http://www.businesswire.com/news/home/20100217005531/en/Zynga-Opens-International-Office-India
8. "Facebook and Zynga Enter into a Long-Term Relationship" (http://www.facebook.com/press/releases.php?p=162172)
9. "CityVille Dethrones FarmVille as Biggest Game on Facebook: What's Next for Zynga?" (http://www.Socialtimes.com/2010/12/cityville-dethrones-farmville-as-biggest-game-on-facebook-whats-next-for-zynga/)
10. Anderson, Ash, "Zynga Unveils New Games and a New Platform, Project Z," http://www.hollywoodreporter.com/news/zynga-unveils-new-games-own-246702
11. Zynga, Inc., *2011 Form 10-K*, p. 2.
12. Ibid., p. 63.
13. Zynga company website, http://company.zynga.com/games/featured-games
14. http://www.bloomberg.com/news/2012-04-17/zynga-flashes-1-8-billion-searching-for-the-new-farmville-tech.html
15. Wallenstein, Andrew, "CBS to Adapt Zynga game 'Draw Something' for TV," June 15, 2012, (http://www.variety.com/article/VR1118055570)
16. "Zynga Acquires Four Mobile Gaming Companies," January 19, 2012, (http://www.telecompaper.com/news/zynga-acquires-four-mobile-gaming-companies)
17. Cutler, Kim-Mai, "Zynga Adds 50 People Through Talent Acquisition of Video Game Maker Buzz Monkey," June 4, 2012, (http://techcrunch.com/2012/06/04/zynga-acquires-buzz-monkey/)
18. www.Zynga.com, Press Release, "Zynga Unveils New Platform for Play," March 2012.
19. Ibid.
20. Chang, Alexandra, "Zynga Unleashes New Games and Its Own 'With Friends' Social Network," *Wired*, June 26, 2012, (http://www.wired.com/gadgetlab/2012/06/zynga-unleashed-its-own-social-network-new-games)
21. Eldon, Eric, "Zynga Launches Cross-Platform *Zynga with Friends*, Multiplayer, New Chat Features, and More Games," June 26, 2012, (http://www.techcrunch.com/2012/06/26/zynga-network-adds-social-lobby-for-users-across-all-devices)
22. http://venturebeat.com/2011/12/12/zynga-history/view-all/
23. Zynga, Inc., *2011 Form 10-K*, p. 2.
24. Ibid., p. 2.
25. Ibid., p. 2.
26. Ibid., p. 38.
27. Rice, Shayndi, *The Wall Street Journal*, August 6, 2012, pp. B1—2. http://online.wsj.com/article/SB10000872396390443545504577567762954064098.html?mod=djem_jiewr_MG_domainid
28. Zynga. Inc., Proxy Statement, June 8, 2012, p. 21.
29. Ibid., pp. 9–12.
30. http://investor.zynga.com/faq.cfm
31. Zynga, Inc., *2011 Form 10-K*, p. 4.
32. "Zynga Slashes Outlook, Denting Iits Stock and Facebook's," http://mobile.reuters.com/article/idUSL2E8IPJFS20120725?irpc=932
33. Hintz-Zambrano, Katie, "Zynga's Stylish Power Players Give Us a Tour of Their Extra-Fun Office!" April 12, 2012, (http://www.refinary29.com/zynga-offoce-tour).
34. http://www.cenedella.com/job-search/zynga-org-structure-follows-business-needs/
35. http://blogs.atlassian.com/2010/03/zynga_on_game_development_tools/
36. http://files.shareholder.com/downloads/AMDA-KX1KB/1956019531x0x562957/69c06a79-9713-43a3-8f3a-cead638f00d0/2011_Annual_Report.pdf. Also Zynga, Inc., *2011 Form 10-K*, p. 49.
37. http://mashable.com/2012/03/23/zynga-economics/
38. Zynga, Inc., *2011 Form 10-K*, p. 3.
39. http://images.businessweek.com/cms/2011-07-13/tech_zynga29_01_popup.jpg
40. Zynga, Inc., *2011 Form 10-K*, pp. 49 and 34.
41. Ibid, pp. 4 and 34.
42. http://files.shareholder.com/downloads/AMDA-KX1KB/1956019531x0x562957/69c06a79-9713-43a3-8f3a-cead638f00d0/2011_Annual_Report.pdf

43. Zynga, Inc., *2011 Form 10-K*, p. 7.

44. Ibid., p. 4.

45. Ibid., p. 38.

46. Ibid., pp. 7–8.

47. http://seekingalpha.com/article/365781-estimates-on-zynga-s-4q-revenues-from-facebook-s-latest-filing

48. http://articles.businessinsider.com/2011-07-19/tech/29993613_1_zynga-games-facebook-integration-playfish

49. Zynga, Inc., *2011 Form 10-K*, pp. 4, 7, 50 and 65.

50. http://online.wsj.com/article/SB10001424052970204642604577213590333947130.html

51. www.Zynga.com, Zynga Press Releases, "Zynga Welcomes New Platform Partners: Konami, Playdemic, and Rebellion," and "Zynga Unveils New Platform for Play," March 12, 2012.

52. Marlowe, Chris, "Zynga Powers Up Social Gaming Network, Mobile and More," June 26, 2012, (http://www.dmwmedia.com/news.com/news/2012/06/26/zynga-powers-up-social-gaming-network-mobile-and-more)

53. www.Zynga.com. Zynga Press Release, "Zynga and American Express Launch Zynga Serve Rewards Program," May 22, 2012.

54. Zynga, *2011 Form 10-K*, pp. 71–72.

55. http://www.bloomberg.com/news/2012-04-17/zynga-flashes-1-8-billion-searching-for-the-new-farmville-tech.html

56. http://www.forbes.com/sites/insertcoin/2012/05/04/draw-something-loses-5m-users-a-month-after-zynga-purchase/

57. http://www.bloomberg.com/news/2012-04-17/zynga-flashes-1-8-billion-searching-for-the-new-farmville-tech.html

58. Brodkin, John, "How Amazon Saved Zynga's Butt—and Why Zynga Built a Cloud of Its Own," May 8, 2012, (http://arstechnica.com/business/2012/05/how-amazon-saved-zyngas-buttand-why-zynga-built-a-cloud-of-its-own)

59. http://seekingalpha.com/article/430761-zynga-moves-highlight-amazon-web-services-and-adverse-selection

60. www.Zynga.com. Press Release, "Zynga Unveils New Platform for Play," March 2012.

61. Ibid., p. 63

62. Zynga, Inc., *2011 Form 10-K*, p. 63.

63. Ibid., p. 33.

64. Ibid., p. 34.

65. "About Zynga" (http://company.zynga.com/about)

66. http://online.wsj.com/article/SB10001424053111904823804576502442835413446.html

67. Letzing, John, "Zynga Puts Real Money in Gambling Lobby," pp. B1–B2.

68. Zynga, Inc., *2011 Form 10-K*, p. 9.

69. http://news.cnet.com/8301-1023_3-57461989-93/zyngas-quest-for-player-liquidity/

70. appdata.com/leaderboard/developers?metric_select=mau

71. http://gigaom.com/2010/02/17/average-social-gamer-is-a-43-year-old-woman/

72. Ibid.

73. http://www.forbes.com/sites/johngaudiosi/2011/12/20/new-report-details-demographics-of-mobile-gamers-buying-virtual-goods/

74. http://www.nielsen.com/us/en/newswire/2012/smartphones-account-for-half-of-all-mobile-phones-dominate-new-phone-purchases-in-the-us.html

75. http://mashable.com/2012/06/07/mobile-commerce-infographic/

76. http://www.businessinsider.com/zynga-sees-limits-to-growth-sales-flatten-as-marketing-costs-double-2012-2?op=1

77. Zynga, Inc., *Form 10-K*, p. 4. http://www.astproxyportal.com/ast/17382/index.html?where=eengine.goToPage(1,1)

78. Ibid., p. 4.

79. Ibid., pp. 7 and 18.

80. Zynga, Inc., *2011 Form 10-K*, p. 17.

81. Ibid, p. 15.

82. http://lawofthegame.blogspot.com/2012/03/zynga-vs-every-body-battle-over-online_07.html

83. http://techcrunch.com/2009/02/14/mob-wars-creator-sues-zynga-for-copyright-infringement/

84. http://arstechnica.com/gaming/news/2009/12/cloning-or-theft-ars-explores-game-design-with-jenova-chen.ars

85. http://www.sfweekly.com/2010-09-08/news/farmvillains/

86. http://techcrunch.com/2009/02/14/mob-wars-creator-sues-zynga-for-copyright-infringement/

87. Silwinski, Alexander, "Highlights from EA's lawsuit against Zynga," August 3, 2012, (http://www.joystiQ.com/2012/08/03/highlights-from-eas-lawsuit-against-zzynga/) and Eric Kain, "CloneWars: Zynga vs. EA and The Baffling Laziness of Copycat Games," August 10, 2012, (http://www.forbes.com/sites/erikkain/2012/08/10/clone-wars-zynga-vs-ea-and-the-baffling-laziness-of-copycat-games)

88. Primack, Dan, "Fraudville? Zynga Sued for Insider Trading," July 31, 2012, http://finance.fortune.cnn.com/2012/07/31/fraudville-zynga-sued-for-insider-trading/

89. http://www.sfgate.com/technology/article/Zynga-teams-up-with-nonprofits-for-games-3782858.php

90. Zynga, Inc., *2011 Form 10-K*, pp. 2, 31, and 32.

91. Ibid., pp. 40 and 42.

92. Steitfield, David and Wortham, Jenna, "The New Isn't Good in FarmVille," July 25, 2012, (http://www.nytimes.com/2012/07/26/technology/for-zynga-a-reversal-of-fortune.html)

CASE 15

The Boston Beer Company

BREWERS OF SAMUEL ADAMS BOSTON LAGER (MINI CASE)

Alan N. Hoffman

Company History

THE BOSTON BEER COMPANY WAS FOUNDED BY JIM KOCH IN 1984 after the discovery of his great-great-grandfather's family microbrew recipe in the attic of his home in Cincinnati, Ohio. In his kitchen, Jim Koch brewed the first batch of what is today known as Samuel Adams Boston Lager. Through use of the family recipe, Jim handcrafted a higher-quality, more flavorful beer than what was currently available in the United States.

Samuel Adams beers were known for their distinct taste and freshness. Although different brewers had access to the rare, expensive Noble hops that Samuel Adams used, its special ingredients remained a secret and were what gave its brews their distinct flavor. Jim Koch refused to compromise on the components that made up the full, rich, flavorful taste of Samuel Adams beer.

As his business began to grow, Jim moved his brewing operations into an old, abandoned brewery in Pennsylvania. This was subsequently followed by the opening of the extremely popular Boston Brewery in 1988. In the mid-1990s, Jim further expanded his business operations by purchasing the Hudepohl-Schoenling Brewery in his hometown of Cincinnati, Ohio. In 1995, The Boston Beer Company Inc. went public.

Jim Koch was viewed as the pioneer of the American craft beer revolution. He founded the largest craft brewery, brewing over 1 million barrels of 25 different styles of Boston Beer

This case was prepared by Professor Alan N. Hoffman, Bentley University and Erasmus University. Copyright © 2010 by Alan N. Hoffman. The copyright holder is solely responsible for case content. Reprint permission is solely granted to the publisher, Prentice Hall, for *Strategic Management and Business Policy*, 13th Edition (and the international and electronic versions of this book) by the copyright holder, Alan N. Hoffman. Any other publication of the case (translation, any form of electronics or other media) or sale (any form of partnership) to another publisher will be in violation of copyright law, unless Alan N. Hoffman has granted an additional written permission. Reprinted by permission. The author would like to thank MBA students Peter Egan, Marie Fortuna, Jason McAuliffe, Lauren McCarthy, and Michael Pasquarello at Bentley University for their research.

No part of this publication may be copied, stored, transmitted, reproduced, or distributed in any form or medium whatsoever without the permission of the copyright owner, Alan N. Hoffman.

products and employing 520 people. Nevertheless, Boston Beer was only the sixth-largest brewer in the United States, producing less than 1% of the total U.S. beer market in 2010.

Since its inception, Jim Koch has had numerous offers from the large brewing companies to buy him out, but he has consistently declined them. He wanted to remain independent and never compromise on the full, rich, flavorful, and fresh taste of Samuel Adams beer. Jim never altered his great-great-grandfather's original recipe created over a century ago.

Corporate Mission and Vision

The mission of the Boston Beer Company was "to seek long-term profitable growth by offering the highest quality products to the U.S. beer drinker."[1] As the largest craft brewer, the Boston Beer Company had been successful for several reasons: (1) premium products produced from the highest-quality ingredients; (2) an unwavering commitment to the freshness of its beer; (3) constant creativity and innovation that resulted in the introduction of a new flavor of beer every year; and (4) the passion and dedication of its employees.

The Boston Beer Company's vision was "to become the leading brewer in the Better Beer category by creating and offering high quality full-flavored beers."[2] The Better Beer category was comprised of craft brewers, specialty beers, and a large majority of the imports. As of 2010, Samuel Adams was the largest craft brewer and "the third largest brand in the Better Beer category of the United States brewing industry, trailing only the imports Corona and Heineken."[3]

In 2007, the Boston Beer Company had revenues of $341 million with COGS of $152 million and $22.5 million of net income. From 2007 to 2009, revenues grew by 22% to $415 million with COGS of $201 million and $31.1 million in net income. Management expected sales to be $430 million in 2010. The Boston Beer Company had no long-term debt and only 14 million shares outstanding. In August 2010, the stock price was $67.

The Beer Industry

The domestic beer market in 2010 was facing many challenges. In 2010, domestic beer overall sales declined 1.2%. Industry analysts predicted inflation-adjusted growth to be only 0.8% through 2012.[4] Decreases in domestic beer sales as a whole were mainly due to decreased alcohol consumption per person. U.S. consumers were drinking less beer because of health concerns, increased awareness of the legal consequences of alcohol abuse, and an increase in options for more flavorful wines and spirits.

To gain more market share in a highly competitive market, the industry was shifting to the mass production of beers, leading to industry consolidation. There were two major players in the brewing industry in the United States: AB InBev (Anheuser-Busch) and SABMiller PLC (SABMiller). SABMiller PLC was a 2007 joint venture of SABMiller and Molson Coors. Anheuser-Busch had been purchased in 2008 by Belgium producer InBev, the second-largest beer producer in the world.

The domestic beer industry also contained some opportunities. Although sales of domestic beer were flat, the past decade showed increases in the domestic consumption of light beer and the craft beer categories. The Better Beer category (comprised of craft, specialty, and import beers) was growing at an annual rate of 2.5% and comprised roughly 19% of all U.S. sales. Beers were classified as "better beers" mainly because of higher quality, taste, price, and image, compared to mass-produced domestic beers. The craft beer segment grew an estimated 9% in 2010. In an industry dominated by male customers, females were viewed as an opportunity. Research showed that women were most concerned about the calories in beer. However, 28% of these same women answered that they were presently drinking more wine.[5]

The growth in craft beer sales was good news for the Boston Beer Company, which positioned itself in this category and was the largest and most successful craft brewer in the United States. It ranked third overall in the U.S. Better Beer category, trailing only two imports: Corona from Mexico and Heineken from The Netherlands.

Domestic Beers

Two major players in the U.S. domestic beer market—AB InBev and MillerCoors—accounted for roughly 95% of all U.S. beer production and sales, minus imports.

MillerCoors LLC controlled roughly 30% of the U.S. beer market. MillerCoors recently entered the Better Beer category by acquiring, in whole or in part, existing craft brewers and by importing and distributing foreign brewers' brands. In 2010, the company experienced double-digit growth with its Blue Moon, Leinenkugel's, and Peroni Nastro Azzurro brands.

AB Inbev was the number-one brewer in the U.S. market in terms of both volume and revenues. Its dominant position allowed it to exert significant influence over distributors, making it difficult for smaller brewers to maintain their market presence or access new markets. Inbev was created in the 2004 merger of the Belgian company Interbrew and the Brazilian brewer AmBev, and subsequently purchased Anheuser-Busch in 2008.

Craft Beer Segment

Sierra Nevada Brewing Company was the second-largest craft beer maker in the United States. Founded in Chico, California, in 1980, the company's mission was to produce the finest-quality beers and ales, and believed that its mission could be accomplished "without compromising its role as a good corporate citizen and environmental steward." Its most successful brands included the hop-flavored Pale Ale, as well as Porter, Stout, and wheat varieties. Sierra Nevada, like Samuel Adams, produced seasonal brews including Summer Fest, Celebration, and Big Foot. Although Sierra Nevada beer had been distributed nationally for some time, sales were still strongest on the West Coast.

New Belgium Brewing Company was founded in 1991 in Fort Collins, Colorado. Its Fat Tire brand made up two-thirds of the company's total sales.[6] New Belgium currently had nine total craft beer brands, in addition to seasonal and limited brands. Its products were offered in 25 western and midwestern states. New Belgium, like Sierra Nevada, focused on being eco-friendly and stressed employee ownership in its mission.

Imports

Grupo Modelo was founded in 1925 and was the market leader in Mexico. Its most successful product, Corona Extra, was the United States' number-one beer import out of 450 imported beers. AB Inbev held a 50% noncontrolling interest in Grupo Modelo.

Heineken, the third-largest brewer by revenue, positioned itself as the world's most valuable international premium beer. Heineken had over 170 international, regional, and local specialty beers and 115 breweries in 65 countries. It had the widest presence of all international brewers due to the sales of Heineken and Amstel products.

Flavored Malt Beverage Category

Samuel Adams also competed in the "flavored malt beverage" (FMB) category with Twisted Tea. The FMB category accounted for roughly 2% of U.S. alcohol consumption. Twisted Tea competed mainly with beverages such as Smirnoff Ice, Bacardi Silver, and Mike's Hard Lemonade. FMB products all targeted relatively the same consumers. Since pricing was similar, these products relied heavily upon advertising and promotions.

Current Challenges

The Boston Beer Company had been growing revenues by 22% over the past two years, and the craft beer industry as a whole continued to experience double-digit growth as well. However, there were some challenges ahead if the company was to successfully achieve its mission and continue this level of growth.

1. Probably the most critical challenge was the increased level of competition in the craft beer industry. "Volume sales within the craft beer industry increased 20% during 2002–2010 to 220 million cases,"[7] and this astonishing growth attracted many players into this market, especially imported beers such as Corona and Heineken, and the top two brewers AB Inbev and MillerCoors.

2. Through mergers and acquisitions, the major competitors achieved cost savings and greater leverage with suppliers and distributors and preferential shelf space and placement with retailers.

3. A continuous increase in production costs of all basic beer ingredients, such as barley malt and hops, as well as packaging materials like glass, cardboard, and aluminum continued into 2010 with further increases in fuel and transportation costs. The global inventory of the company's "Noble" hops declined, and the harvest in recent years of its two key hops suppliers in Germany did not meet the high standards of the Boston Beer Company. As a result, Boston Beer received a lower quantity at a higher price than expected.

4. The company purchased a brewery in Breinigsville, Pennsylvania, in 2008 for $55 million. Although this brewery was expected to increase capacity by 1.6 million barrels of beer annually, it required significant renovations before it could produce quality beer.

United Airlines Dilemma

United Airlines recently approached the Boston Beer Company with an interesting opportunity. United wanted to offer Samuel Adams Boston Lager to fliers on all of its flights. This would provide the Boston Beer Company increased national exposure and could result in a significant increase in beer sales. However, United Airlines would only sell Samuel Adams Boston Lager in cans, not bottles.

The Boston Beer Company had never sold any of its beers in cans because management believed that metal detracts from the flavor of the beer. Management felt that the "full-flavor" of Samuel Adams could only be realized using glass bottles. Should Boston Beer's management rethink its decision not to distribute its beer in cans to take advantage of this opportunity? Many years ago, Jim Koch said that there would never be a "Sam Adams Light Beer," but he eventually reversed that decision and Sam Light became a huge success.

NOTES

1. 2007 Annual Report, http://thomson.mobular.net/thomson/7/2705/3248/.
2. Ibid.
3. Ibid.
4. Mintel—US–Domestic Beer December 2007.
5. Ibid.
6. http://www.rockymountainnews.com/news/2007/nov/24/reuteman-colorado-rides-on-fat-tire-to-beer/.
7. Mintel Report, "Domestic Beer–US–December 2007–Executive Summary," http://academic.mintel.com.ezp.bentley.edu/sinatra/mintel/print/id=311747 (July 15, 2008).

CASE 16

Panera Bread Company (2010): Still Rising Fortunes?

Joyce P. Vincelette and Ellie A. Fogarty

BREAD—ESSENTIAL AND BASIC, but nonetheless special—has transcended millennia. A master baker combined simple ingredients to create what has been an integral part of society and culture for over 6000 years. Sourdough bread, a uniquely American creation, was made from a "culture" or "starter." Sourdough starter contained natural yeasts, flour, and water and was the medium that made bread rise. In order to survive, a starter had to be cultured, fed, and tended to by attentive hands in the right environment. Without proper care and maintenance, the yeast, or the growth factor, would slow down and die. Without a strong starter, bread would no longer rise.

Ronald Shaich, CEO and Chairman of Panera Bread Company, created the company's "starter." Shaich, the master baker, combined the ingredients and cultivated the leavening agent that catalyzed the company's phenomenal growth. Under Shaich's guidance, Panera's total systemwide (both company and franchisee) revenues rose from US$350.8 million in 2000 to US$1,353.5 million in 2009, consisting of US$1,153.3 million from company-owned bakery-café sales, US$78.4 million from franchise royalties and fees, and US$121.9 million from fresh dough sales to franchisees. Franchise-operated bakery-café sales, as reported by franchisees, were US$1,640.3 million in fiscal 2009.[1] Panera shares have outperformed every major restaurant stock over the last 10 years.[2] Panera's share price has risen over 1600% from US$3.88 a share on December 31, 1999, to US$67.95 a share on December 28, 2009.[3] Along the way, Panera largely led the evolution of what became known as the "fast casual" restaurant category.

Ronald Shaich had clearly nurtured the company's "starter" and had been the vision and driving force behind Panera's success from the company's beginnings until his resignation as CEO and Chairman effective May 13, 2010. For Panera to continue to rise, the company's new CEO, William Moreton, would need to continue to feed and maintain Panera's "starter." In addition to new unit growth, new strategies and initiatives must be folded into the mix.

History

Panera Bread grew out of the company that could be considered the grandfather of the fast casual concept: Au Bon Pain. In 1976, French oven manufacturer Pavailler opened the first Au Bon Pain (a French colloquialism for "where good bread is") in Boston's Faneuil Hall as a demonstration bakery. Struck by its growth potential, Louis Kane, a veteran venture capitalist, purchased the business in 1978.[4] Between 1978 and 1981, Au Bon Pain opened 13, and subsequently closed 10, stores in the Boston area and piled up US$3 million in debt.[5] Kane was ready to declare bankruptcy when he gained a new business partner in Ronald Shaich.[6]

Shortly after opening the Cookie Jar bakery in Cambridge, Massachusetts, in 1980, Shaich, a recent Harvard Business graduate, befriended Louis Kane. Shaich was interested in adding bread and croissants to his menu to stimulate morning sales. He recalled that "50,000 people a day were going past my store, and I had nothing to sell them in the morning."[7] In February 1981, the two merged the Au Bon Pain bakeries and the cookie store to form one business, Au Bon Pain Co. Inc. The two served as co-CEOs until Kane's retirement in 1994. They had a synergistic relationship that made Au Bon Pain successful: Shaich was the hard-driving, analytical strategist focused on operations, and Kane was the seasoned businessperson with a wealth of real estate and finance connections.[8] Between 1981 and 1984, the team expanded the business, worked to decrease the company's debt, and centralized facilities for dough production.[9]

In 1985, the partners added sandwiches to bolster daytime sales as they noticed a pattern in customer behavior—that is, customers were buying sliced baguettes and making their own sandwiches. It was a "eureka" moment, and the birth of the fast casual restaurant category.[10] According to Shaich, Au Bon Pain was the "first place that gave white collar folks a choice between fast food and fine dining."[11] Au Bon Pain became a lunchtime alternative for urban dwellers who were tired of burgers and fast food. Differentiated from other fast-food competitors by its commitment to fresh, quality sandwiches, bread, and coffee, Au Bon Pain attracted customers who were happy to pay more money (US$5 per sandwich) than they would have paid for fast food.[12]

In 1991, Kane and Shaich took the company public. By that time, the company had US$68 million in sales and was a leader in the quick service bakery segment. By 1994, the company had 200 stores and US$183 million in sales, but that growth masked a problem. The company was built on a limited growth concept, what Shaich called, "high density urban feeding."[13] The main customers of the company were office workers in locations like New York, Boston, and Washington, DC. The real estate in such areas was expensive and hard to come by. This strategic factor limited expansion possibilities.[14]

Au Bon Pain acquired the Saint Louis Bread Company in 1993 for US$24 million. Shaich saw this as the company's "gateway into the suburban marketplace."[15] The acquired company, founded in 1987 by Ken Rosenthal, consisted of a 19-store bakery-café chain located in the Saint Louis, Missouri, area. The concept of the café was based on San Francisco sourdough bread bakeries. The acquired company would eventually become the platform for what is now Panera.

Au Bon Pain management spent two years studying Saint Louis Bread Co., looking for the ideal concept that would unite Au Bon Pain's operational abilities and quality food with the broader suburban growth appeal of Saint Louis Bread. The management team understood that a growing number of consumers wanted a unique expression of tastes and styles, and were tired of the commoditization of fast-food service. Shaich and his team wrote a manifesto that spelled out what Saint Louis Bread would be, from the type of food it would serve, to the kind of people behind the counters, and to the look and feel of the physical space.[16]

Au Bon Pain began pouring capital into the chain when Shaich had another "eureka" moment in 1995. He entered a Saint Louis Bread store and noticed a group of business people meeting in a corner. The customers explained that they had no other place to talk.[17] This experience helped Shaich realize that the potential of the neighborhood bakery-café concept was greater than that of Au Bon Pain's urban store concept. The bakery-café concept capitalized on a confluence of current trends: the welcoming atmosphere of coffee shops, the food of sandwich shops, and the quick service of fast food.[18]

While Au Bon Pain was focusing on making Saint Louis Bread a viable national brand, the company's namesake unit was faltering. Rapid expansion of its urban outlets had resulted in operational problems, bad real estate deals,[19] debt over US$65 million,[20] and declining operating margins.[21] Stiff competition from bagel shops and coffee chains such as Starbucks compounded operational difficulties. Au Bon Pain's fast-food ambiance was not appealing to customers who wanted to sit and enjoy a meal or a cup of coffee. At the same time, the café style atmosphere of Saint Louis Bread, known as Panera (Latin for "time for bread") outside the Saint Louis area, was proving to be successful. In 1996, comparable sales at Au Bon Pain locations declined 3% while same-store sales of the Panera unit were up 10%.[22]

Lacking the capital to overhaul the ambiance of the Au Bon Pain segment, the company decided to sell the unit. This allowed the company to strategically focus its time and resources on the more successful Panera chain. Unlike Au Bon Pain, Panera was not confined to a small urban niche and had greater growth potential. On May 16, 1999, Shaich sold the Au Bon Pain unit to investment firm Bruckman, Sherrill, and Co. for US$73 million. At the time of the divestiture, the company changed its corporate name to Panera Bread Company. The sale left Panera Bread Company debt-free, and the cash allowed for the immediate expansion of its bakery-café stores.[23]

Throughout the 2000s, Panera grew through franchise agreements, acquisitions (including the purchase of Paradise Bakery & Café, Inc.), and new company-owned bakery-cafés. By 2009, Panera had become a national bakery-café concept with 1380 company-owned and franchise-operated bakery-café locations in 40 states and in Ontario, Canada. Panera had grown from serving approximately 60 customers a day at its first bakery-café to serving nearly six million customers a week systemwide, becoming one of the largest food-service companies in the United States. The company believed its success was rooted in its ability to create long-term dining concept differentiation.[24] The company operated under the Panera, Panera Bread, Saint Louis Bread Co., Via Panera, You Pick Two, Mother Bread, and Paradise Bakery & Café design trademark names registered in the United States. Others were pending. Panera also had some of its marks registered in foreign countries.[25]

May 13, 2010, marked a significant change in the history of Panera Bread Company. After 28 years, Ronald Shaich stepped down as CEO and Chairman effective immediately following the Annual Stockholders Meeting, and William Moreton, previously the Executive Vice President and co-Chief Operating Officer, assumed the role of CEO. Shaich planned to remain as the company's Executive Chairman. He announced that he expected to focus his time and energy within Panera on a range of strategic and innovation projects and mentoring the senior team. In typical Panera fashion, the transition had been planned for one-and-a-half years to ensure its success.

Concept and Strategy[26]

Concept

At the time when Panera was created, the fast-food industry was described as featuring low-grade burgers, greasy fries, and sugared colas. Shaich decided to create a casual but comfortable place where customers could eat fresh-baked artisan breads and fresh sandwiches, soups, and salads without worrying about whether it was nutritious.[27]

Panera's restaurant concept focused on the specialty bread/bakery-café category. Bread was Panera's platform and entry point to the Panera experience at its bakery-cafés. It was the symbol of Panera quality and a reminder of "Panera Warmth," the totality of the experience the customer received and could take home to share with friends and family. The company endeavored to offer a memorable experience with superior customer service. The company's associates were passionate about sharing their expertise and commitment with Panera customers. The company strove to achieve what Shaich termed "Concept Essence," Panera's blueprint for attracting targeted customers that the company believed differentiated it from competitors. Concept Essence included a focus on artisan bread, quality products, and a warm, friendly, and comfortable environment. It called for each of the company's bakery-cafés to be a place customers could trust to serve high-quality food. Bread was Panera's passion, soul, expertise, and the platform that made all of the company's other food items special.

The company's bakery-cafés were principally located in suburban, strip mall, and regional mall locations and featured relaxing décor and free Internet access. Panera's bakery-cafés were designed to visually reinforce the distinctive difference between its bakery-cafés and those of its competititors.

Panera extended its strong values and concept of fresh food in an unpretentious, welcoming atmosphere to the nonprofit community. The company's bakery-cafés routinely donated bread and baked goods to community organizations in need. Panera's boldest step was the May 2010 opening of the Panera Cares bakery-café in Missouri, which had no set prices; instead, customers were asked to pay what they wanted.[28]

Panera's success in achieving its concept was often acknowledged through customer surveys and awards from the press. From *Advertising Age*[29] to *Zagat*,[30] Panera was touted as one of America's hottest brands and most popular chains. Customers rated Panera fifth overall in the restaurant industry in 2008 and highest among fast casual eateries in an annual customer satisfaction and quality survey conducted by Dandelman & Associates, a restaurant market research firm.[31] In 2009, Panera also was named number one on the "Healthiest for Eating on the Go" list by *Health* magazine for its variety of health menu options, whole grain breads, and half-sized items. Numerous other national and local awards had been received each year for the company's sandwiches, breads, lunches, soups, vegetarian offerings, cleanliness, Wi-Fi, community responsibility, workplace quality, and kids' menu.[32] Panera's own consumer panel testing of 1000 customers showed consistently high value perceptions of the company's products.[33]

Strategy

Panera operated in three business segments: company-owned bakery-café operations, franchise operations, and fresh dough operations. As of December 29, 2009, the company-owned bakery-café segment consisted of 585 bakery-cafés, all located in the United States, and the franchised operations segment consisted of 795 franchise-operated bakery-cafés, located throughout the United States and in Ontario, Canada. The company anticipated 80 to 90 systemwide bakery-cafés opening in 2010 with average weekly sales for company-owned new units of US$36,000 to US$38,000.[34] **Exhibit 1** shows the total number of systemwide

EXHIBIT 1 Company-Owned and Franchise-Operated Bakery-Cafés: Panera Bread Company

	For the Fiscal Year Ended				
	December 29, 2009	December 30, 2008	December 25, 2007	December 26, 2006	December 27, 2005
Number of bakery-cafés					
company-owned					
Beginning of period	562	532	391	311	226
Bakery-cafés opened	30	35	89	70	66
Bakery-cafés closed	(7)	(5)	(5)	(3)	(2)
Bakery-cafés acquired from franchisees (1)	—	—	36	13	21
Bakery-cafés acquired (2)	—	—	22	—	—
Bakery-cafés sold to a franchisees (3)	—	—	(1)	—	—
End of period	585	562	532	391	311
Franchise-operated					
Beginning of period	763	698	636	566	515
Bakery-cafés opened	39	67	80	85	73
Bakery-cafés closed	(7)	(2)	(5)	(2)	(1)
Bakery-cafés sold to company (1)	—	—	(36)	(13)	(21)
Bakery-cafés acquired (2)	—	—	22	—	—
Bakery-cafés purchased from company (3)	—	—	1	—	—
End of period	795	763	698	636	566
Systemwide					
Beginning of period	1,325	1,230	1,027	877	741
Bakery-cafés opened	69	102	169	155	139
Bakery-cafés closed	(14)	(7)	(10)	(5)	(3)
Bakery-cafés acquired (2)	—	—	44	—	—
End of period	1,380	1,325	1,230	1,027	877

Notes:

(1) In June 2007, Panera acquired 32 bakery-cafés and the area development rights from franchisees in certain markets in Illinois and Minnesota. In February 2007, the company acquired four bakery-cafés, as well as two bakery-cafés still under construction, and the area development rights from a franchisee in certain markets in California.
In October 2006, Panera acquired 13 bakery-cafés (one of which was under construction) and the area development rights from a franchisee in certain markets in Iowa, Nebraska, and South Dakota. In September 2006, the company acquired one bakery-café in Pennsylvania from a franchisee. In November 2005, Panera acquired 23 bakery-cafés (two of which were under construction) and the area development rights from a franchisee in certain markets in Indiana.

(2) In February 2007, Panera acquired 51% of the outstanding capital stock of Paradise Bakery & Café Inc., which then owned and operated 22 bakery-cafés and franchised 22 bakery-cafés, principally in certain markets in Arizona and Colorado.

(3) In June 2007, Panera sold one bakery-café and the area development rights for certain markets in Southern California to a new area developer.

....

SOURCES: Panera Bread Company Inc., *2009 Form 10-K*, p. 25 and *2006 Form 10-K*, p. 20.

bakery-cafés for the last five years. As of December 29, 2009, the company's fresh dough operations segment, which supplied fresh dough items daily to most company-owned and franchise-operated bakery-cafés, consisted of 23 fresh dough facilities. Company-owned bakery-café operations accounted for 85.2% of revenues in 2009, up from 78% in 2005. Royalties and fees from franchise operations made up 5.8% of revenues in 2009, down from 8.5% in 2005, and fresh dough operations accounted for 9% of total revenues in 2009, down from 13.5% in 2005.[35]

In addition to the dine-in and take-out business, the company offered Via Panera, a nationwide catering service that provided breakfast assortments, sandwiches, salads, and soups using the same high-quality ingredients offered in the company's bakery-cafés. Via Panera was supported by a national sales infrastructure. The company believed that Via Panera would be a key component of long-term growth.

The key initiatives of Panera's growth strategy focused on growing store profit, increasing transactions and gross profit per transaction, using its capital smartly, and putting in place drivers for concept differentiation and competitive advantage.[36] The company paid careful attention to the development of new markets and further penetration of existing markets by both company-owned and franchised bakery-cafés, including the selection of sites that would achieve targeted returns on invested capital.[37] Panera's strategy in 2009 was different from many of its competitors. When many restaurant companies were focused on surviving the economic meltdown by downsizing employees, discounting prices, and lowering quality, Panera chose to stay the course and continued to execute its long-term strategy of investing in the business to benefit the customer. The result, according to Shaich: "Panera zigged while others zagged."[38]

During the economic downturn, Panera stuck to a simple recipe: Get more cash out of each customer, rather than just more customers. While other recession-wracked restaurant chains discounted and offered meals for as little as US$5 to attract customers, Panera bucked conventional industry wisdom by eschewing discounts and instead targeted customers who could afford to shell out an average of about US$8.50 for lunch. While many of its competitors offered less expensive meals, Panera added a lobster sandwich for US$16.99 at some of its locations. Panera was able to persuade customers to pay premiums because it had been improving the quality of its food.[39] "Most of the world seems to be focused on the Americans who are unemployed," said CEO Ronald Shaich. "We're focused on the 90 percent that are still employed."[40]

Panera's positive financial results contrasted with those of many other casual dining chains, which had posted negative same-store sales due partly to declining traffic and lower-priced food. Some chains found that discounting not only hurt margins but also failed to lure as many customers as hoped. Shaich seemed to thrive on doing the opposite of his competition. During 2009, instead of slashing prices, he raised them twice, one on bagels and once on soup. "We're contrarians to the core," said Shaich. "We don't offer a lower-end strategy. In a world where everyone is cutting back, we want to give more not less."[41] "This is the time to increase the food experience," insisted Shaich, "that is, when consumers least expect it."[42]

Also crucial to Panera's success in 2009 was the company's approach to operations during the recession. Over the years, many restaurant companies told investors they were able to improve labor productivity while running negative comparable store sales. Panera believed that reducing labor in a restaurant taxed the customer by creating longer waits, slower service, and more frazzled team members. Panera took the approach of keeping labor consistent with sales and continuing to invest in its employees as a way to better serve its customers.[43]

The results for 2009 showed that Panera's strategy of zigging while others were zagging paid off. Panera met or exceeded its earnings targets in each quarter of 2009. Panera delivered 25% earnings per share (EPS) growth in 2009 on top of 24% EPS growth in 2008. Panera's stock price increased 115% from December 31, 2007, to March 30, 2010.

Panera's objectives for 2010 included a target of 17%–20% EPS growth through the execution of its key initiatives. To further build transactions, Panera planned to focus on differentiation through innovative salads utilizing new procedures to further improve quality. Panera also planned to test a new way to make paninis using newly designed grills. The company expected to roll out improved versions of several Panera classics while continuing to focus on improving operations, speed of service, and accuracy.[44]

In early 2010, to increase gross profit per transaction and further improve margins while still providing overall value to customers, Panera introduced an initiative called the Meal Upgrade Program. With this program, a customer who ordered an entrée and a beverage was offered the opportunity to purchase a baked good to complete their meal at a "special" price point. Panera intended to test other impulse add-on initiatives, bulk baked goods, and bread as a gift.[45]

"I worry about keeping the concept special," said Shaich. "Is it worth walking across the street to? It doesn't matter how cheap it is. If it isn't special, there's no reason the business needs to exist."[46]

The Fast Casual Segment

Panera's predecessor, Au Bon Pain, was a pioneer of the fast casual restaurant category. Dining trends caused fast casual to emerge as a legitimate trend in the restaurant industry as it bridged the gap between the burgers-and-fries fast-food industry and full service, sitdown, casual dining restaurants.

Technomic Information Services, a food-service industry consultant, coined the term to describe restaurants that offered the speed, efficiency, and inexpensiveness of fast food with the hospitality, quality, and ambiance of a full-service restaurant. Technomic defined a fast casual restaurant by whether or not the restaurant met the following four criteria: (1) The restaurant had to offer a limited service or self-service format. (2) The average check had to be between US$6 and US$9, whereas fast-food checks averaged less than US$5. This pricing scheme placed fast casual between fast food and casual dining. (3) The food had to be made-to-order, as consumers perceived newly prepared, made-to-order foods as fresh. Fast casual menus usually also had more robust and complex flavor profiles than the standard fare at fast-food restaurants. (4) The décor had to be upscale or highly developed. Décor inspired a more enjoyable experience for the customer as the environment of fast casual restaurants was more akin to a neighborhood bistro or casual restaurant. The décor also created a generally higher perception of quality.[47]

The fast casual market was divided into three categories: bread-based chains, traditional chains, and ethnic chains. According to a Mintel 2008 report, bread-based chains, such as Panera, and ethnic chains, such as Chipotle Mexican Grill, had sales momentum and were predicted to grow at the expense of traditional chains such as Steak 'n Shake, Boston Market, Fuddruckers, and Fazoli's, which were weighted down by older concepts. The report also suggested that bread-based and ethnic chains had an edge with respect to consumer perceptions about food healthfulness.[48] Most fast casual brands did not compete in all dayparts (breakfast, lunch, dinner, late-night), but instead focused on one or two. While almost all competitors in this segment had a presence at lunch, many grappled with the question of whether and how to participate in other dayparts.[49] In addition, unlike fast-food restaurants that constructed stand-alone stores, fast casual chains were typically located in strip malls, small-town main streets, and preexisting properties.

According to Technomic, by offering high-quality food with fast service, fast casual chains had experienced increased traffic in 2009 as diners "traded-down" from casual dining chains and "traded-up" from fast-food restaurants to lower-priced but still higher-quality fresh food.[50] In other words, the desire to eat out did not diminish; only the destination changed. Sales in 2009 for the top 100 fast casual chains reached US$17.5 billion, a 4.5% increase over 2008; and units grew by 4.3% to 14,777 locations,[51] compared to a 3.2% sales decline in the overall restaurant industry.[52] The growth in the fast casual segment was also due to the maturation of two large segments of the U.S. population: baby boomers and their children. Both age groups had little time for cooking and were tired of fast food.

Bakery-café/bagel remained the largest of the fast casual restaurant clusters and the largest menu category, generating US$4.8 billion in U.S. sales in 2009 and jumping from 17% to 21% of the top 100 fast casual restaurants. In 2009, Mexican, with total sales of US$3.8 billion, was the second-largest fast casual cluster of restaurants.[53] Technomic's 2009 Top 100 Fast-Casual Restaurant Report noted that besides burgers (up 16.7%), the fastest growing menu categories reflected the growing interest of consumers in international flavors: Asian/noodle (up 6.4%) and Mexican (up 6.3%).[54]

Exhibit 2 provides a list of the 20 largest fast casual franchises in 2010. Even though Chipotle Mexican Grill was one of Panera's key competitors, it was not included on this list because it did not franchise.

EXHIBIT 2
2010's Twenty Largest Fast Casual Franchises

	2009 United States Sales
1. Panera Bread	$2,796,500
2. Zaxby's	718,250
3. El Polio Loco	582,000
4. Boston Market	545,000
5. Jason's Deli	475,870
6. Five Guys Burgers and Fries	453,500
7. Qdoba Mexican Grill	436,500
8. Einstein Bros. Bagels	378,444
9. Moe's Southwestern Grill	358,000
10. McAlister's Deli	351,960
11. Fuddruckers	320,500
12. Wingstop	306,606
13. Baja Fresh Mexican Grill	300,000
14. Schlotzky's	248,000
15. Corner Bakery Café	235,029
16. Fazoli's	235,000
17. Noodles & Company	230,000
18. Bruegger's Bagel Bakery	196,000
19. Donatos Pizza	185,000
20. Cosi	168,500

Note:
(a) Not all key fast casual competitors are franchised restaurants.

SOURCES: Technomic's 2010 Top 100 Fast-Casual Chain Restaurant Report, www.bluemaumau.cor/9057/2010's-top-twenty-largest-fastcausual-franchises.

Competition

Panera experienced competition from numerous sources in its trade areas. The company's bakery-cafés competed with specialty food, casual dining and quick service cafés, bakeries, and restaurant retailers, including national, regional, and locally owned cafés, bakeries, and restaurants. The bakery-cafés competed in several segments of the restaurant business based on customers' needs for breakfast, AM "chill," lunch, PM "chill," dinner, and take-home through both on-premise sales and Via Panera catering. The competitive factors included location, environment, customer service, price, and quality of products. The company competed for leased space in desirable locations and also for hourly employees. Certain competitors or potential competitors had capital resources that exceeded those available to Panera.[55]

Panera's 2009 sales of nearly US$2.8 billion ranked as the largest of the fast casual chains. The company saw an increase in sales of 7.1% and an increase in units of 4.3% to 1380 stores over 2008. Chipotle Mexican Grill held on to the number two spot, growing U.S. sales 13.9% to US$1.5 billion, and units by 14.2% to 955 locations in 2009.[56]

Panera and Chipotle Mexican Grill, which together made up more than 25% of the fast casual segment, posted double-digit percentage increases in first-quarter 2010 sales over the same period in 2009, driven by opening new outlets and robust increases in same-store sales. By contrast, United States revenues at McDonald's suffered in 2009, and for the first five months of 2010, same-store sales were up 3% over the same period in 2009. Burger King struggled during the same period with revenues in the United States and Canada down 4% for the first three months of 2010.[57] Established restaurant chains were beginning to take notice of the opportunities in the fast casual segment and were considering options. For example, Subway started testing an upscale design in the Washington, DC, market in 2008. New competitors, such as Otarian, were also entering the fast casual segment and testing new concepts, many having a health and wellness or sustainability component to them.

Although Panera continued to learn from its competitors, none of its competitors had yet figured out the formula to Panera's success. While McDonald's had rival Burger King, and Applebee's had T.G.I. Friday's, there was no direct national competitor that replicated Panera's business model. Like Panera, Chipotle sold high-quality food made with fine ingredients—but it was Mexican. Cosi sold quality sandwiches and salads, but lacked pastries and gourmet coffees. Starbucks had fine coffee and pastries but not Panera's extensive food menu. According to Shaich, the reason is that "this is hard to do, . . . what seems simple can be tough. It is not so easy to knock us off."[58]

Corporate Governance

Panera was a Delaware corporation and its corporate headquarters were located in Saint Louis, Missouri.

Board of Directors

Panera's Board was divided into three classes of membership. The terms of service of the three classes of directors were staggered so that only one class expired at each annual meeting. At the time of the May 2010 annual meeting, the Board consisted of six members. Class I consisted of Ronald M. Shaich and Fred K. Foulkes, with terms expiring in 2011; Class II consisted of Domenic Colasacco and Thomas E. Lynch, with terms expiring in 2012; and Class III consisted of Larry J. Franklin and Charles J. Chapmann III, with terms ending in 2010. Mr. Franklin and Mr. Chapman were both nominated for reelection with terms ending in 2013, if elected.[59]

The biographical sketches for the board members are shown next.[60]

Ronald M. Shaich (age 56) was a Director since 1981, co-founder, Chairman of the Board since May 1999, Co-Chairman of the Board from January 1988 to May 1999, Chief Executive Officer since May 1994, and Co-Chief Executive Officer from January 1988 to May 1994. Shaich served as a Director of Lown Cardiovascular Research Foundation, as a trustee of the nonprofit Rashi School, as Chairman of the Board of Trustees of Clark University, and as Treasurer of the Massachusetts Democratic Party. He had a Bachelor of Arts degree from Clark University and an MBA from Harvard Business School. Immediately following the 2010 Annual Meeting, Mr. Shaich planned to resign as Chief Executive Officer and the Board intended to elect him as Executive Chairman of the Board.

Larry J. Franklin (age 61) was a Director since June 2001. Franklin had been the President and Chief Executive Officer of Franklin Sports Inc., a leading branded sporting goods manufacturer and marketer, since 1986. Franklin joined Franklin Sports Inc. in 1970 and served as its Executive Vice President from 1981 to 1986. Franklin served on the Board of Directors of Bradford Soap International Inc. and the Sporting Goods Manufacturers Association (Chairman of the Board and member of the Executive Committee).

Fred K. Foulkes (age 68) was a Director since June 2003. Dr. Foulkes had been a Professor of Organizational Behavior and had been the Director (and founder) of the Human Resources Policy Institute at Boston University School of Management since 1981. He had taught courses in human resource management and strategic management at Boston University since 1980. From 1968 to 1980, Foulkes had been a member of the Harvard Business School faculty. Foulkes wrote numerous books, articles, and case studies. He served on the Board of Directors of Bright Horizons Family Solutions and the Society for Human Resource Management Foundation.

Domenic Colasacco (age 61) was a Director since March 2000, and Lead Independent Director since 2008. Colasacco had been President and Chief Executive Officer of Boston Trust & Investment Management, a banking and trust company, since 1992. He also served as Chairman of its Board of Directors. He joined Boston Trust in 1974 after beginning his career in the research division of Merrill Lynch & Co. in New York City.

Charles J. Chapman III (age 47) was a Director since 2008. Chapman had been the Chief Operating Officer and a Director of the American Dairy Queen Corporation since October 2005. From 2001 to October 2005, Chapman held a number of senior positions at American Dairy Queen. Prior to joining American Dairy Queen, Chapman served as Chief Operating Officer at Bruegger's Bagel's Inc., where he was also President and co-owner of a franchise. He also held marketing and operations positions with Darden Restaurants and served as a consultant with Bain & Company.

Thomas E. Lynch (age 50) was a Director since March 2010 and previous Director from 2003–2006. Lynch served as Senior Managing Director of Mill Road Capital, a private equity firm, since 2005. From 2000 to 2004, Lynch served as Senior Managing Director of Mill Road Associates, a financial advisory firm that he founded in 2000. From 1997 through 2000, Lynch was the founder and Managing Director of Lazard Capital Partners. From 1990 to 1997, Lynch was a Managing Director of the Blackstone Group, where he was a senior investment professional for Blackstone Capital Partners. Prior to Blackstone, Lynch was a senior consultant at the Monitor Company. He also had previously served on the Board of Directors of Galaxy Nutritional Foods Inc.

The Board had established three standing committees, each of which operated under a charter approved by the Board. The *Compensation and Management Development Committee* included Foulkes (Chair), Franklin, and Colasacco. The *Committee on Nominations and*

Corporate Governance included Franklin (Chair), Chapman, and Foulkes. The *Audit Committee* included Colasacco (Chair), Foulkes, and Franklin.[61]

The compensation package of non-employee directors consisted of cash payments and stock and option awards. Total non-employee director compensation ranged from US$29,724 to US$124,851 in fiscal 2009 depending on services rendered.[62]

Top Management

The biographical sketches for some of the key executive officers follow.[63]

Ronald Shaich (age 56) planned to resign as Chief Executive Officer immediately following the May 2010 Annual Meeting. The Board of Directors announced its intentions to elect him as Executive Chairman of the Board at that time. The Board intended to appoint William W. Moreton to succeed Mr. Shaich as Chief Executive Officer and President and to elect him to the Board of Directors.[64]

William M. Moreton (age 50) re-joined Panera in November 2008 as Executive Vice President and Co-Chief Operating Officer. He previously served as Executive Vice President and Chief Financial Officer from 1998 to 2003. From 2005 to 2007, Moreton served as President and Chief Financial Officer of Potbelly Sandwich Works, and from 2004–2005 as Executive Vice President-Subsidiary Brands, and Chief Executive Officer of Baja Fresh, a subsidiary of Wendy's International Inc. Immediately following the conclusion of the 2010 Annual Meeting, upon the resignation of Mr. Shaich, the Board planned for Mr. Moreton to succeed Mr. Shaich as Chief Executive Officer, and the Board intended to appoint him as President and elect him to the Board.

John M. Maguire (age 44) had been Chief Operating Officer and subsequently Co-Chief Operating Officer since March 2008 and Executive Vice President since April 2006. He previously served as Senior Vice President, Chief Company, and Joint Venture Operations Officer from August 2001 to April 2006. From April 2000 to July 2001, Maguire served as Vice President, Bakery Operations, and from November 1998 to March 2000, as Vice President, Commissary Operations. Maguire joined the company in April 1993; from 1993 to October 1998, he was a Manager and Director of Au Bon Pain/Panera Bread/St. Louis Bread.

Cedric J. Vanzura (age 46) had been Executive Vice President and Co-Chief Operating Officer since November 2008 and Executive Vice President and Chief Administrative Officer from March to November 2008. Prior to joining the company, Vanzura held a variety of roles at Borders International from 2003 to 2007.

Mark A. Borland (age 57) had been Senior Vice President and Chief Supply Chain Officer since August 2002. Borland joined the company in 1986 and held management positions within Au Bon Pain and Panera Bread divisions until 2000, including Executive Vice President, Vice President of Retail Operations, Chief Operating Officer, and President of Manufacturing Services. From 2000 to 2001, Borland served as Senior Vice President of Operations at RetailDNA, and then rejoined Panera as a consultant in the summer of 2001.

Jeffrey W. Kip (age 42) had been Senior Vice President and Chief Financial Officer since May 2006. He previously served as Vice President, Finance and Planning, and Vice President, Corporate Development, from 2003 to 2006. Prior to joining Panera, Mr. Kip was an Associate Director and then Director at UBS from 2002 to 2003 and an Associate at Goldman Sachs from 1999 to 2002.

Michael J. Nolan (age 50) had been Senior Vice President and Chief Development Officer since he joined the company in August 2001. From December 1997 to March 2001,

Nolan served as Executive Vice President and Director for John Harvard's Brew House, L.L.C., and Senior Vice President, Development, for American Hospitality Concepts Inc. From March 1996 to December 1997, Nolan was Vice President of Real Estate and Development for Apple South Incorporated, a chain restaurant operator, and from July 1989 to March 1996, Nolan was Vice President of Real Estate and Development for Morrison Restaurants Inc. Prior to 1989, Nolan served in various real estate and development capacities for Cardinal Industries Inc. and Nolan Development and Investment.

Other key Senior Vice Presidents included Scott Davis, Chief Concept Officer; Scott Blair, Chief Legal Officer; Rebecca Fine, Chief People Officer; Thomas Kish, Chief Information Officer; Michael Kupstas, Chief Franchise Officer; Michael Simon, Chief Marketing Officer; and William Simpson, Chief Company and Joint Venture Operations Officer. In 2009, the total compensation for the top five highest-paid executive officers ranged from US$939,919 to US$3,354,708.[65]

At year-end 2009, there were two classes of stock: (1) Class A common stock with 30,491,278 shares outstanding and one vote per share, and (2) Class B common stock with 1,392,107 shares outstanding and three votes per share.[66] Class A common stock was traded on NASDAQ under the symbol PNRA. As of March 15, 2010, all directors, director nominees, and executive officers as a group (20 persons) held 1,994,642 shares or 6.22% of Class A common stock and 1,311,690 shares or 94.22% of Class B common stock with a combined voting percentage of 13.23%. Ronald Shaich owned 5.5% of Class A common stock and 94.22% of Class B common stock for a combined voting percentage of 12.42%.[67] In November 2009, Panera's Board of Directors approved a three-year share repurchase program of up to US$600 million of Class A common stock.[68]

Menu[69]

Panera's value-oriented menu was designed to provide the company's target customers with affordably priced products built on the strength of the company's bakery expertise. The Panera menu featured proprietary items prepared with high-quality fresh ingredients as well as unique recipes and toppings. The key menu groups were fresh-baked goods, including a variety of freshly baked bagels, breads, muffins, scones, rolls, and sweet goods; made-to-order sandwiches; hearty and unique soups; hand-tossed salads; and café beverages including custom-roasted coffees, hot or cold espresso, cappuccino drinks, and smoothies.

The company regularly reviewed and updated its menu offerings to satisfy changing customer preferences, to improve its products, and to maintain customer interest. To give its customers a reason to return, Panera had been rolling out new products with fresher ingredients such as antibiotic-free chicken (Panera is the nation's largest buyer[70]). The roots of most new Panera dishes could be traced to its R&D team's twice-yearly retreats to the Adirondacks, where staffers took turns trying to out-do each other in the kitchen. "We start with: What do we think tastes good," said Scott Davis. "We're food people, and if we're not working on something that gets us really excited, it's kind of not worth working on."[71] Panera did not have test kitchens and instead tested all new menu items directly in its cafés.

Panera integrated new product rollouts into the company's periodic or seasonal menu rotations, referred to as "Celebrations." Examples of products introduced in fiscal 2009 included the Chopped Cobb Salad and Barbeque Chicken Chopped Salad, introduced during the 2009 summer salad celebration. Other menu changes in 2009 included a reformulated French baguette, a new line of smoothies, new coffee, a new Napa Almond Chicken Salad sandwich, a new Strawberry Granola Parfait, the Breakfast Power Sandwich, and a new line of brownies and blondies. Three new salmon options, five years in the making, were introduced in early 2010 along with a new Low-Fat Garden Vegetable Soup and a new Asiago Bagel

Breakfast Sandwich. New chili offerings were in the planning stages. During this time Shaich had also been busy tweaking things he wanted Panera to do better, such as improving the freshness of Panera's lettuce by cutting the time from field to plate in half. He also improved the freshness of the company's breads by opting to bake all day long, not just in the early morning hours. Panera's changes and improvements were all designed to build competitive advantage by strengthening value. Value, according to the company, meant offering guests an even better "total experience."

In 2008, Panera introduced the antithesis to the microwaved, processed breakfast sandwich, by introducing a made-to-order grilled breakfast sandwich. The new line of breakfast sandwiches were made fresh daily with quality ingredients—a combination of all-natural eggs, Vermont white cheddar cheese, Applewood-smoked bacon or all natural sausage, grilled between two slices of fresh baked ciabatta. Many of the company's competitors had also moved to more protein-based breakfast sandwich offerings because of the growth opportunities in this segment of the market. In order to be competitive, Panera needed to be different.

Not all of Panera's menu innovations had been successful with customers or had added much to the bottom line. Panera redesigned its menu boards in 2009 to draw the customers' eyes toward meals with higher margins, like the soup and salad combo, rather than pricier items, like a strawberry poppy-seed salad, that did not bring as much to the bottom line. The Crispani pizza was discontinued in 2008 after it failed to drive business during evening hours.

To improve margins, Panera was able to anticipate and react to changes in food and supply costs including, among other things, fuel, proteins, dairy, wheat, tuna, and cream cheese costs through increased menu prices and to use its strength at purchasing to limit cost inflation in efforts to drive gross profit per transaction.

Panera believe in being transparent with regard to the ingredients it used. They were one of the first restaurants to serve antibiotic-free chicken even though it was more expensive. Panera chose to be ahead of the curve again when it announced in early 2010 that it would post calorie information on all systemwide bakery-café menu boards by the end of 2010. Panera had for a number of years provided a nutritional calculator on its website so customers could find nutritional information for individual products or build a meal according to their dietetic specifications. Recognizing the health risks associated with transfats, Panera had completely removed all transfat from its menu by 2006.[72] Panera also offered a wide range of organic food products including cookies, milk, and yogurt, which were incorporated into the company's children's menu, Panera Kids, in 2006. Because of its healthy choices, Panera was named "One of the 10 Best Fast-Casual Family Restaurants" by *Parents* magazine in its July 2009 issue.[73]

Site Selection and Company-Owned Bakery-Cafés[74]

As of December 29, 2009, the company-owned bakery-café segment consisted of 585 company-owned bakery-cafés, all located in the United States. During 2009, Panera focused on using its cash to build new high-ROI bakery-cafés and executed a disciplined development process that took advantage of the recession to drive down costs while selecting locations that delivered strong sales volume. In 2009, Panera believed the best use of its capital was to invest in its core business, either through the development of new bakery-cafés or through the acquisition of existing bakery-cafés from franchisees or other similar restaurant or bakery-café concepts, such as the acquisition of Paradise Bakery & Café Inc.

All company-owned bakery-cafés were in leased premises. Lease terms were typically 10 years with one, two, or three 5-year renewal option periods thereafter. Leases typically had charges for a proportionate share of building and common area operating expenses and real estate taxes, and a contingent percentage rent based on sales above a stipulated sales level. Because Panera was considered desirable as a tenant due to its profitable balance sheet and national reputation, the company enjoyed a favorable leasing environment in lease terms and the availability of desirable locations.

The average size of a company-owned bakery-café was approximately 4600 square feet as of December 29, 2009. The average construction, equipment, furniture and fixtures, and signage costs for the 30 company-owned bakery-cafés opened in fiscal 2009 was approximately US$750,000 per bakery-café after landlord allowances and excluding capitalized development overhead. The company expected that future bakery-cafés would require, on average, an investment per bakery-café of approximately US$850,000.

In evaluating potential new locations for both company-owned and franchised bakery-cafés, Panera studied the surrounding trade area, demographic information within the most recent year, and publicly available information on competitors. Based on this analysis and utilizing predictive modeling techniques, Panera estimated projected sales and a targeted return on investment. Panera also employed a disciplined capital expenditure process focused on occupancy and development costs in relation to the market, designed to ensure the right-sized bakery-café and costs in the right market. Panera's methods had proven successful in choosing a number of different types of locations, such as in-line or end-cap locations in strip or power centers, regional malls, drive-through, and freestanding units.

Franchises[75]

Franchising was a key component of Panera's growth strategy. Expansion through franchise partners enabled the company to grow more rapidly as the franchisees contributed the resources and capabilities necessary to implement the concepts and strategies developed by Panera.

The company began a broad-based franchising program in 1996, when the company actively began seeking to extend its franchise relationships. As of December 29, 2009, there were 795 franchise-operated bakery-cafés open throughout the United States and in Ontario, Canada, and commitments to open 240 additional franchise-operated bakery-cafés. At this time, 57.6% of the company's bakery-cafés were owned by franchises comprised of 48 franchise groups. The company was selective in granting franchises, and applicants had to meet specific criteria in order to gain consideration for a franchise. Generally, the franchisees had to be well capitalized to open bakery-cafés, with a minimum net worth of US$7.5 million and meet liquidity requirements (liquid assets of US$3 million),[76] have the infrastructure and resources to meet a negotiated development schedule, have a proven track record as multi-unit restaurant operators, and have a commitment to the development of the Panera brand. A number of markets were still available for franchise development.

Panera did not sell single-unit franchises. Instead, they chose to develop by selling market areas using Area Development Agreements, referred to as ADAs, which required the franchise developer to open a number of units, typically 15 bakery-cafés, in a period of four to six years. If franchisees failed to develop bakery-cafés on schedule or defaulted in complying with the company's operating or brand standards, the company had the right to terminate the ADA and to develop company-owned locations or develop locations through new area developers in that market.

The franchise agreement typically required the payment of an up-front franchise fee of US$35,000 (broken down into US$5000 at the signing of the area development agreement and US$30,000 at or before the bakery-café opens) and continued royalties of 4%–5% on sales from each bakery-café. The company's franchise-operated bakery-cafés followed the same protocol for in-store operating standards, product quality, menu, site selection, and bakery-café construction as did company-owned bakery-cafés. Generally, the franchisees were required to purchase all of their dough products from sources approved by the company.

The company did not generally finance franchise construction or area development agreement purchases. In addition, the company did not hold an equity interest in any of the franchise-operated bakery-cafés. However, in fiscal 2008, to facilitate expansion into Ontario, Canada, the company entered into a credit facility with the Canadian franchisee. By March 2010, Panera had repurchased the three franchises in Toronto in order to be more directly involved in the Canadian market. While the company thought the geographic market represented a good growth opportunity, Panera decided to study and learn from other U.S. firms that had expanded successfully in Canada.[77]

Bakery Supply Chain[78]

According to Ronald Shaich, "Panera has a commitment to doing the best bread in America."[79] Freshly baked bread made with fresh dough was integral to honoring this commitment. System-wide bakery-cafés used fresh dough for sourdough and artisan breads and bagels.

Panera believed its fresh dough facility system and supply chain function provided competitive advantage and helped to ensure consistent quality at its bakery-cafés. The company had a unique supply-chain operation in which dough was supplied daily from one of the company's regional fresh dough facilities to substantially all company-owned and franchise-operated bakery-cafés. Panera bakers then worked through the night shaping, scoring, and glazing the dough by hand to bring customers fresh-baked loaves every morning and throughout the day. In 2009, the company began baking loaves later in the morning to ensure freshness throughout the day and altered the fermentation cycle of its baguettes to make them sweeter.

As of December 29, 2009, Panera had 23 fresh dough facilities, 21 of which were company-owned, including a limited production facility that was co-located with one of the company's franchised bakery-cafés in Ontario, Canada, to support the franchise-operated bakery-cafés located in that market (2 of the fresh dough facilities were franchise operated). All fresh dough facilities were leased. In fiscal 2009, there was an average of 62.5 bakery-cafés per fresh dough facility compared to an average of 62.0 in fiscal 2008.[80]

Distribution of the fresh dough to bakery-cafés took place daily through a leased fleet of 184 temperature-controlled trucks driven by Panera employees. The optimal maximum distribution range for each truck was approximately 300 miles; however, when necessary, the distribution ranges might be up to 500 miles. An average distribution route delivered dough to seven bakery-cafés.

The company focused its expansion in areas served by the fresh dough facilities in order to continue to gain efficiencies through leveraging the fixed cost of its fresh dough facility structure. Panera expected to enter selectively new markets that required the construction of additional facilities until a sufficient number of bakery-cafés could be opened that permitted efficient distribution of the fresh dough.

In addition to its need for fresh dough, the company contracted externally for the manufacture of the remaining baked goods in the bakery-cafés, referred to as sweet goods. Sweet goods products were completed at each bakery-café by professionally trained bakers. Completion included finishing with fresh toppings and other ingredients and baking to established artisan standards utilizing unique recipes.

With the exception of products supplied directly by the fresh dough facilities, virtually all other food products and supplies for the bakery-cafés, including paper goods, coffee, and smallwares, were contracted externally by the company and delivered by vendors to an independent distributor for delivery to the bakery-cafés. In order to assure high-quality food and supplies from reliable sources, Panera and its franchisees were required to select from a list of approved suppliers and distributors. The company leveraged its size and scale to improve the quality of its ingredients, effect better purchasing efficiency, and negotiate purchase agreements with most approved suppliers to achieve cost reduction for both the company and its customers. One company delivered the majority of Panera's ingredients and other products to the bakery-cafés two or three times weekly. In addition, company-owned bakery-cafés and franchisees relied on a network of local and national suppliers for the delivery of fresh produce (three to six times per week).

Marketing[81]

Panera focused on customer research to plan its marketing and brand-building initiatives. According to Panera executives, "everything we do at Panera goes through the customer filter first."[82] Panera's target customers were between 25 and 50 years old, earned US$40,000 to US$100,000 a year, and were seeking fresh ingredients and high-quality choices.[83] The company's customers spent an average of US$8.50 per visit.[84]

Panera was committed to improving the customer experience in ways the company believed rare in the industry. The company leveraged its nationwide presence as part of a broader marketing strategy of building name recognition and awareness. As much as possible, the company used its store locations to market its brand image. When choosing a location to open a new store, Panera carefully selected the geographic area. Better locations needed less marketing, and the bakery-café concept relied on a substantial volume of repeat business.

In 2009, Panera executed a more aggressive marketing strategy than most of its competitors. While many competitors discounted to lure customers back through 2009, Panera focused on offering guests an even better "total experience." Improvements to the "total experience" included new coffee and breakfast items, new salads, new china, smoothies, and mac and cheese. The company focused on improving store profit by increasing transactions as well as increasing gross profit per transaction through the innovation and sales of higher gross profit items. Panera also had a successful initiative to drive add-on sales through the Meal Upgrade program.[85]

In 2010, Panera began modest increases in advertising and additional investments in its marketing infrastructure because the company recognized the importance of marketing as a driver of earnings and sales increases.[86] In spite of these increases, Panera remained very cautious about its marketing investments and focused on the appropriate mix for each market. Panera primarily used radio and billboard advertising, with some television, social networking, and in-store sampling days. Panera found that it benefited when other companies advertised products that Panera also carried, such as McDonald's early 2010 promotion of smoothies. Panera was testing additional television advertising in 20 markets but considered any significant growth in this medium to be a few years away.[87]

Panera's franchise agreements required franchisees to pay the company advertising fees based on a percentage of sales. In fiscal 2009, franchise-operated bakery-cafés contributed 0.7% of their sales to a company-run national advertising fund, paid a marketing administration fee of 0.4% of sales, and were required to spend 2.0% of their sales on advertising in their respective local markets. The company contributed the same sales percentages from company-owned bakery-cafés toward the national advertising fund and marketing administration fee. For fiscal 2010, the company increased the contribution rate to the national advertising fund to 1.1% of sales.[88]

Panera invested in cause-related marketing efforts and community activities through its Operation Dough-Nation program. These programs included sponsoring runs and walks, helping nonprofits raise funds, and the Day-End Dough-Nation program through which unsold bakery products were packaged at the end of each day and donated to local food banks and charities.[89]

Management Information Systems[90]

Each company-operated bakery-café had programmed point-of-sale registers to collect transaction data used to generate pertinent information, including transaction counts, product mix, and average check. All company-owned bakery-café product prices were programmed into the system from the company's corporate headquarters. The company allowed franchisees to have access to certain proprietary bakery-café systems and systems support. The fresh dough facilities had information systems that accepted electronic orders from the bakery-cafés and monitored delivery of the ordered product. The company also used proprietary online tools such as eLearning to provide online training for retail associates and online baking instructions for its bakers.

Panera's intranet site, The Harvest, allowed the company to monitor important analytics and provide support to its bakery-cafés. For example, Panera used a weather application on its intranet that tied a bakery-café's historic local weather to the store's historic sales, allowing managers to forecast sales based on weather for any given day. "That helps in staffing and how you're going to allocate labor and what you need in terms of materials," said Greg Rhoades, Panera's senior manager in information services. He called The Harvest "our single source of information." Panera shared news with its employees about food safety and customer satisfaction websites and provided information on daily sales, hourly sales, staffing, product sales, labor costs, and ingredient costs.[91]

The company began offering Wi-Fi in its bakery-cafés in 2003. By 2010, most bakery-cafés provided customers with free Internet access through a managed Wi-Fi network. As a result, Panera hosted one of the largest free public Wi-Fi networks in the country.[92]

In 2010, Panera began to pilot test a loyalty program, "My Panera," in 23 stores. Rather than just a food-discounting program, "My Panera" was intended to provide a deeper relationship with the customer by including participants in events such as the food tasting of new products. The company expected to complete the pilot by year-end 2010 and hoped to begin leveraging the data to better understand its high-frequency customers and to "surprise and delight" them in a way that was tailored to the customers' buying habits.[93]

Human Resources[94]

From the beginning, Panera realized that the key ingredients to the successful development of the Panera brand ranged from the type of food it served to the kind of people behind the counters. The company placed a priority on staffing its bakery-cafés, fresh dough facilities, and support center operations with skilled associates and invested in training programs to ensure the quality of its operations. As of December 29, 2009, the company employed approximately 12,000 full-time associates (defined as associates who average 25 hours or more per week), of whom approximately 600 were employed in general or administrative functions, principally in the company's support centers; approximately 1200 were employed in the company's fresh dough facility operations; and approximately 10,300 were employed in the company's bakery-café operations as bakers, managers, and associates. The company also had approximately 13,200 part-time hourly associates at the bakery-cafés. There were no collective bargaining agreements. The company considered its employee relations to be good.

Panera believed that providing bakery-café operators the opportunity to participate in the success of the bakery-cafés enabled the company to attract and retain experienced and highly motivated personnel, which resulted in a better customer experience. Through a Joint Venture Program, the company provided selected general managers and multi-unit managers with a multi-year bonus program based upon a percentage of the cash flows of the bakery-café they operated. The intent of the program's five-year period was to create team stability, generally resulting in a higher level of stability for that bakery-café and thus lead to stronger associate engagement and customer loyalty. In December 2009, approximately 50% of company-owned bakery-café operators participated in the Joint Venture program.[95]

Finance

Panera reported a 48% increase in net income of US$25,845 million, or US$0.82 per diluted share, during the first quarter of 2010, compared to US$17,432 million, or US$0.57 per diluted share, during the first quarter of 2009. For this same period, Panera reported revenues of US$364,210 million, a 14% gain over revenues of US$320,709 for the same period in 2009.[96] Company-owned comparable bakery-café sales in the first quarter of fiscal 2010 increased 10.0%, due to transaction growth of 3.5% and average check growth of 6.5% over the comparable period in 2009. Franchise-operated comparable bakery-café sales increased 9.2% in the first quarter of 2010 compared to the same period in 2009. As a result, total comparable bakery-café sales increased 9.5% in the first quarter of fiscal 2010 compared to the comparable period in 2009.[97] In addition, average weekly sales (AWS) for newly opened company-owned bakery-cafés during the first quarter of 2010 were US$56,111 compared to US$41,922 in the first quarter of 2009. During the first quarter of 2010, Panera and its franchises opened eight new bakery-cafés systemwide. No bakery-cafés were closed during this period.[98]

Exhibits **3** to **5** provide Panera's consolidated statement of operations, common size income statements, and consolidated balance sheets, respectively, for the company for the fiscal years ended 2005 through 2009.

In fiscal 2009, during an uncertain economic environment, Panera bucked industrywide trends and increased performance on the following key metrics: (1) systemwide comparable bakery-café sales growth of 0.5% (0.7% for company-owned bakery-cafés and 0.5% for franchise-operated bakery-cafés); (2) systemwide average weekly sales increased 1.8% to US$39,926 (US$39,050 for company-owned bakery-cafés and US$40,566 for franchise-operated bakery-cafés); and (3) 69 new bakery-cafés opened systemwide (7 company-owned bakery-cafés and 39 franchise-operated bakery-cafés). In fiscal 2009, Panera earned US$2.78 per diluted share.[99] In addition, average weekly sales (AWS) for newly opened company-owned bakery-cafés in 2009 reached a six-year high for new units.[100] **Exhibit 6** provides 2005–2009 selected financial information about Panera.

Total company revenue in fiscal 2009 increased 4.2% to US$1,353.5 million from US$1,298.9 million in fiscal 2008. This growth was primarily due to the opening of 69 new bakery-cafés systemwide in fiscal 2009 (and the closure of 14 bakery-cafés) and, to a lesser extent, the 0.5% increase in systemwide comparable bakery sales.

Company-owned bakery-café sales increased 4.2% in fiscal 2009 to US$1,153.3 million compared to US$1,106.3 million in fiscal 2008. This increase was due to the opening of 30 new company-owned bakery-cafés and to the 0.7% increase in comparable company-owned bakery-café sales in 2009. Company-owned bakery-café sales as a percentage of revenue remained consistent at 85.2% in both fiscal 2009 and fiscal 2008. In addition, the increase in average weekly sales for company-owned bakery-cafés in fiscal 2009 compared to the prior fiscal year was primarily due to the average check growth that resulted from the company's initiative to drive add-on sales. Franchise royalties and fees in fiscal 2009 were up 4.8% to US$78.4 million, or 5.8% of total revenues, up from US$74.8 million in 2008. Fresh dough sales to franchises increased 3.5% in fiscal 2009 to US$121.9 million compared to US$117.8 million in fiscal 2008.[101]

Panera believed that its primary capital resource was cash generated by operations. The company's principal requirements for cash have resulted from the company's capital expenditures for the development of new company-owned bakery-cafés; for maintaining

EXHIBIT 3 Consolidated Statement of Operations: Panera Bread Company

	(Dollar amounts in thousands, except per share information) For the Fiscal Year Ended (1)				
	December 29, 2009	December 30, 2008	December 25, 2007	December 26, 2006	December 27, 2005
Revenues					
Bakery-café sales	$ 1,153,255	$ 1,106,295	$ 894,902	$ 666,141	$ 499,422
Franchise royalties and fees	78,367	74,800	67,188	61,531	54,309
Fresh dough sales to franchisee	121,872	117,758	104,601	101,299	86,544
Total revenue	1,353,494	1,298,853	1,066,691	828,971	640,275
Costs and expenses					
Bakery-café expenses					
Cost of food and paper products	$ 337,599	$ 332,697	$271,442	$ 196,849	$ 143,057
Labor	370,595	352,462	286,238	204,956	151,524
Occupancy	95,996	90,390	70,398	48,602	35,558
Other operating expenses	155,396	147,033	121,325	92,176	70,003
Total bakery-café expenses	959,586	922,582	749,403	542,583	400,142
Fresh dough cost of sales to franchisees	100,229	108,573	92,852	85,951	74,654
Depreciation and amortization	67,162	67,225	57,903	44,166	33,011
General and administrative expenses	83,169	84,393	68,966	59,306	46,301
Pre-opening expenses	2,451	3,374	8,289	6,173	5,072
Total costs and expenses	1,212,597	1,186,147	977,413	738,179	559,180
Operating profit	140,897	112,706	89,278	90,792	81,095
Interest expense	700	1,606	483	92	50
Other (income) expense, net	273	883	333	(1,976)	(1,133)
Income before income taxes	139,924	110,217	88,462	92,676	82,178
Income taxes	53,073	41,272	31,434	33,827	29,995
Net income	86,851	68,945	57,028	58,849	52,183
Less: income (loss) attributable to noncontrolling interest	801	1,509	(428)		
Net income attributable to Panera Bread	$ 86,050	$ 67,436	$ 57,456	$ 58,849	$ 52,183
Per share data					
Earnings per common share attributable to Panera Bread Company					
Basic	$ 2.81	$ 2.24	$ 1.81	$ 1.88	$ 1.69
Diluted	$ 2.78	$ 2.22	$ 1.79	$ 1.84	$ 1.65
Weighted average shares of common and common equivalent shares outstanding					
Basic	30,667	30,059	31,708	31,313	30,871
Diluted	30,979	30,422	32,178	32,044	31,651

Notes:

(1) Fiscal 2008 was a 53-week year consisting of 371 days. All other fiscal years presented contained 52 weeks consisting of 364 days with the exception of fiscal 2005. In fiscal 2005, the company's fiscal week was changed to end on Tuesday rather than Saturday. As a result, the 2005 fiscal year ended on December 27, 2005, instead of December 31, 2005, and, therefore, consisted of 52 and a half weeks rather than the 53 week year that would have resulted without the calender change.

....

SOURCES: Panera Bread Company Inc., *2009 Form 10-K*, pp. 20–21.

EXHIBIT 4   Common Size Statement: Panera Bread Company

	(Percentages are in relation to total revenues except where otherwise indicated) **For the Fiscal Year Ended**				
	December 29, 2009	**December 30, 2008**	**December 25, 2007**	**December 26, 2006**	**December 27, 2005**
Revenues					
Bakery-café sales	85.2%	85.2%	83.9%	80.4%	78.0%
Franchise royalties and fees	5.8	5.8	6.3	7.4	8.5
Fresh dough sales to franchisee	9.0	9.1	9.8	12.2	13.5
Total revenue	100.0%	100.0%	100.0%	100.0%	100.0%
Costs and expenses					
Bakery-café expense (1)					
Cost of food and paper products	29.3%	30.1%	30.3%	29.6%	28.6%
Labor	32.1	31.9	32.0	30.8	30.3
Occupancy	8.3	8.2	7.9	7.3	7.1
Other operating expenses	13.5	13.3	13.6	13.8	14.0
Total bakery-café expenses	83.2	83.4	83.7	81.5	80.0
Fresh dough cost of sales to franchisees (2)	82.2	92.2	88.8	84.5	86.7
Depreciation and amortization	5.0	5.2	5.4	5.3	5.2
General and administrative expenses	6.1	6.5	6.5	7.2	7.2
Pre-opening expenses	0.2	0.3	0.8	0.7	0.8
Total costs and expenses	**89.6**	**91.3**	**91.6**	**89.0**	**87.3**
Operating profit	10.4	8.7	8.4	11.0	12.7
Interest expense	0.1	0.1	0.1	—	—
Other (income) expense, net	—	0.1	—	-0.2	-0.2
Income before income taxes	10.3	8.5	8.3	11.2	12.8
Income taxes	3.9	3.2	2.9	4.1	4.7
Net income	**6.4**	**5.3**	**5.4**	**7.1**	**8.2**
Less: net income attributable to noncontrolling interest	0.1	0.1	—	—	—
Net income attributable to Panera Bread Company	**6.4%**	**5.2%**	**5.4%**	**7.1%**	**8.2%**

Notes:
(1) As a percentage of bakery-café sales.
(2) As a percentage of fresh dough facility sales to franchisees.

SOURCES: Panera Bread Company, Inc. *2009 Form 10-K*, p. 24 and *2006 Form 10-K*, p. 19.

EXHIBIT 5 Consolidated Balance Sheets: Panera Bread Company

	(Dollar amounts in thousands, except share and per share information) For the Fiscal Year Ended				
	December 29, 2009	December 30, 2008	December 25, 2007	December 26, 2006	December 27, 2005
Assets					
Current assets					
Cash and cash equivalents	$ 246,400	$ 74,710	$ 68,242	$ 52,097	$ 24,451
Short-term investments	—	2,400	23,198	20,025	36,200
Trade accounts receivable, net	17,317	15,198	25,122	19,041	18,229
Other accounts receivable	11,176	9,944	11,640	11,878	6,929
Inventories	12,295	11,959	11,394	8,714	7,358
Prepaid expenses	16,211	14,265	5,299	12,036	5,736
Deferred income taxes	18,685	9,937	7,199	3,827	3,871
Total current assets	322,084	138,413	152,124	127,618	102,774
Property and equipment, net	403,784	417,006	429,992	345,977	268,809
Other assets					
Goodwill	87,481	87,334	87,092	57,192	48,540
Other intangible assets, net	19,195	20,475	21,827	6,604	3,219
Long-term investments	—	1,726	—	—	10,108
Deposits and other	4,621	8,963	7,717	5,218	4,217
Total other assets	111,297	118,498	116,636	69,014	66,084
Total assets	$ 837,165	$ 673,917	$ 698.752	$ 542,609	$ 437,667
Liabilities and stockholders' equity					
Current liabilities					
Accounts payable	6,417	4,036	6,326	5,800	4,422
Accrued expenses	135,842	109,978	121,440	102,718	81,559
Deferred revenue	—	—	—	1,092	884
Total current liabilities	142,259	114,014	127,766	109,610	86,865
Long-term debt	—	—	75,000	—	—
Deferred rent	43,371	39,780	33,569	27,684	23,935
Deferred income taxes	28,813	—	—	—	5,022
Other long-term liabilities	25,686	21,437	14,238	7,649	4,867
Total liabilities	240,129	175,231	250,573	144,943	120,689
Stockholders' equity					
Common stock, $.0001 par value: Class A, 75,000,000 shares authorized: 30,364,915 issued and 30,196,808 outstanding in 2009; 29,557,849 issued and 29,421,877 outstanding in 2008; 30,213,869 issued and 30,098,275 outstanding in 2007.	3	3	3	3	3
Class B, 10,000,000 shares authorized; 1,392,107 issued and outstanding in 2009; 1,398,242 in 2008; 1,398,588 in 2007; 1,400,031 in 2006 and 1,400,621 in 2005.	—	—	—	—	—

(continued)

EXHIBIT 5 (Continued)

Treasury stock, carried at cost;	(3,928)	(2,204)	(1,188)	(900)	(900)
Additional paid-in capital	168,288	151,358	168,386	176,241	154,402
Accumulated other comprehensive income (loss)	224	(394)	—	—	—
Retained earnings	432,449	346,399	278,963	222,322	163,473
Total stockholders' equity	597,036	495,162	446,164	397,666	316,978
Noncontrolling interest	—	3,524	2,015	—	—
Total equity	$ 597,036	$ 498,686	$ 446,164	$ 397,666	$ 316,978
Total equity and liabilities	$ 837,165	$ 673,917	$ 698,752	$ 542,609	$ 437,667

SOURCES: Panera Bread Company, Inc., *2009 Form 10-K*, p. 45; *2008 Form 10-K*, p. 43; and *2006 Form 10-K*, p. 36.

EXHIBIT 6 Selected Financial Information: Panera Bread Company

(Dollar amounts in thousands)

A. Year to Year Comparable Sales Growth (not adjusted for differing number of weeks)

	For the Fiscal Year Ended				
	December 29, 2009 (52 weeks)	December 30, 2008 (53 weeks)	December 25, 2007 (52 weeks)	December 26, 2006 (52 weeks)	December 27, 2005 (52-1/2 weeks)
Company-owned	0.7%	5.8%	1.9%	3.9%	7.4%
Franchise-operated	0.5%	5.3%	1.5%	4.1%	8.0%
Systemwide	0.5%	5.5%	1.6%	4.1%	7.8%

B. System Wide Average Weekly Sales

	For the Fiscal Year Ended				
	December 29, 2009	December 30, 2008	December 25, 2007	December 26, 2006	December 27, 2005
Systemwide average weekly sales	$ 39,926	$ 39,239	$ 38,668	$ 39,150	$ 38,318

C. Company-owned Bakery-Café Average Weekly Sales

	For the Fiscal Year Ended				
	December 29, 2009	December 30, 2008	December 25, 2007	December 26, 2006	December 27, 2005
Company-owned average weekly sales	39,050	38,066	37,548	37,833	37,348
Company-owned number of operating weeks	29,533	29,062	23,834	176,077	13,280

D. Franchise-owned Bakery-Café Average Weekly Sales

	For the Fiscal Year Ended				
	December 29, 2009	December 30, 2008	December 25, 2007	December 26, 2006	December 27, 2005
Franchise average weekly sales	40,566	40,126	39,433	39,894	38,777
Franchise number of operating weeks	40,436	38,449	34,905	31,220	28,090

SOURCES: Panera Bread Company, Inc., *2009 Form 10-K*, pp. 26–30; *2008 Form 10-K*, pp. 25–27; and *2006 Form 10-K*, pp. 20–23.

or remodeling existing company-owned bakery-cafés; for purchasing existing franchise-operated bakery-cafés or ownership interests in other restaurant or bakery-café concepts; for developing, maintaining, or remodeling fresh dough facilities; and for other capital needs such as enhancements to information systems and infrastructure. The company had access to a US$250 million credit facility which, as of December 29, 2009, had no borrowings outstanding. Panera believed its cash flow from operations and available borrowings under its existing credit facility to be sufficient to fund its capital requirements for the foreseeable future.[102]

According to Nicole Miller Regan, an analyst at Piper Jaffray, "the key to Panera's success during the recessionary period lies in what the company hasn't done. . . . It hasn't tried to change."[103] "For us, the recession has been the best of times," said CEO Shaich.[104]

NOTES

1. Panera Bread Company Inc., *2009 Form 10-K*, pp. 1–2.
2. John Jannarone, "Panera Bread's Strong Run," *The Wall Street Journal* (January 23, 2010).
3. Christopher Tritto, "Panera's Rosenthal Cashes In," *St. Louis Business Journal* (January 5, 2010), http://stlouis.bizjournals.com/stlouis/stories/2010/01/04/story2.html.
4. "Overview: Panera Bread Company," *Hoover's Inc.*
5. Linda Tischler, "Vote of Confidence," *Fast Company* 65 (December 2002), pp. 102–112.
6. Peter O. Keegan, "Louis I. Kane & Ronald I. Shaich: Au Bon Pain's Own Dynamic Duo," *Nation's Restaurant News* 28 (September 19, 1994), p. 172.
7. Tischler, pp. 102–112.
8. Keegan, p. 172.
9. Robin Lee Allen, "Au Bon Pain's Kane Dead at 69; Founded Bakery Chain," *Nation's Restaurant News* 34 (June 26, 2000), pp. 6–7.
10. Tischler, pp. 102–112.
11. Ibid.
12. Powers Kemp, "Second Rising," *Forbes* 166 (November 13, 2000), p. 290.
13. Tischler, pp. 102–112.
14. Ibid.
15. "Overview: Panera Bread Company," *Hoover's Inc.*
16. Robin Lee Allen, "Au Bon Pain Co. Pins Hopes on New President, Image," *Nation's Restaurant News* 30 (December 2, 1996), pp. 3–4.
17. Tischler, pp. 102–112.
18. Chern Yeh Kwok, "Bakery-Café Idea Smacked of Success from the Very Beginning; Concept Gives Rise to Rapid Growth in Stores, Stock Price," *St. Louis Dispatch* (May 20, 2001), p. E1.
19. Allen (December 2, 1996), pp. 3–4.
20. Kemp, p. 290.
21. Richard L. Papiernik, "Au Bon Pain Mulls Remedies, Pares Back Expansion Plans," *Nation's Restaurant News* 29 (August 28, 1995), pp. 3–4.
22. "Au Bon Pain Stock Drops 11% on News that Loss Is Expected," *The Wall Street Journal* (October 7, 1996), p. B2.
23. Andrew Caffrey, "Heard in New England: Au Bon Pain's Plan to Reinvent Itself Sits Well with Many Pros," *The Wall Street Journal* (March 10, 1999), p. NE.2.
24. Panera Bread Company Inc., *2009 Form 10-K*, p. 1.
25. Ibid., pp. 6–7.
26. Panera Bread Company Inc., *2009 Form 10-K*, pp. 1–2.
27. Bruce Horovitz, "Panera Bakes a Recipe for Success," *USA Today* (July 23, 2009), p. 1.
28. Christopher Leonard, "New Panera Location Says Pay What You Want," Associated Press (May 18, 2010).
29. Emily Bryson York. "Panera: An America's Hottest Brands Case Study," *Advertising Age* (November 16, 2009), http://adage.com/article?article_id=140482.
30. Zagat Survey, http://www.zagat.com/FASTFOOD.
31. Tritto.
32. Panera Company Overview, www.panerabread.com/about/company/awards.php.
33. Panera Bread Company Inc., Second Quarter Earnings Conference Call, July 28, 2010.
34. Panera Press Release (314-633-4282), *Panera Bread Reports Q1 EPS of $.82, up 44% Over Q1 2009, on a 10% Company-owned Comparable Bakery-Café Sales Increase*, pp. 1–10.
35. Ibid., p. 20.
36. Panera Bread Company Inc., Second Quarter Earnings Conference Call, July 28, 2010.
37. Ibid., p. 10.
38. Panera, April 12, 2010 Letter to Stockholders, p. 1.
39. Julie Jargon, "Slicing the Bread but Not the Prices," *The Wall Street Journal* (August 18, 2009), B1.
40. Ibid.
41. Horovitz, p. 1.
42. Ibid.
43. Panera, April 12, 2010 Letter to Stockholders.
44. Ibid.
45. Ibid.
46. Sean Gregory, "How Panera Bread Defies the Recession," *Time* (December 23, 2009), p. 2, www.time.com/time/printout/0,8816,1949371,00.html.
47. G. LaVecchia, "Fast Casual Enters the Fast Lane," *Restaurant Hospitality* 87 (February 2003), pp. 43–47.
48. *MINTEL 2008.*
49. Ibid.
50. Paul Ziobro, "Panera Looks to Bake Up Profit," *The Wall Street Journal* (August 13, 2008), p. B3C.
51. "Fast-Casual Chains Thriving During Tough Economy" (June 24, 2010), www.foodproductdesign.com/news/2010/06/fast-casual-chains-thriving-during-tough-economy.aspx.

52. Lauren Shephard, "Convenience Key to Driving Fast-Casual Sales," *Nations Restaurant News* (June 16, 2010).

53. "Fast-Casual Chains Thriving. . . ."

54. Bob Vosburgh, "The Future of Fast Casual Restaurants" (June 24, 2010), http://supermarketnews.com/blog/future-fast-casual-restaurants

55. Panera Bread Company Inc., *2009 Form 10-K*, p. 8.

56. "Fast-Casual Chains Thriving. . . ."

57. Greg Farrell, "Appetite Grows for US 'Fast Casual Food,'" *Financial Times* (June 18, 2010), http://www.ft.com/cms/s/0/0f452038-7b06-11df-8935-00144feabdc0.html

58. Horovitz, p. 1.

59. Panera Bread Company Inc. Notice of Annual Stockholders Meeting, April 12, 2010, pp. 4–5.

60. Ibid., pp. 5–8.

61. Ibid., pp. 10–12.

62. Ibid., p. 37.

63. Ibid., pp. 14–16.

64. Ibid., p. 5.

65. Ibid., p. 29.

66. Ibid., p. 3.

67. Ibid., p. 40.

68. Ibid., p. 1.

69. Panera Bread Company Inc., *2009 Form 10-K*, p. 4.

70. Kate Rockwood, "Rising Dough: Why Panera Bread Is on a Roll," *Fastcompany.com* (October 1, 2009), www.fastcompany.com//magazine/139/rising-dough.html.

71. Ibid.

72. www.Datamonitor.com (December 15, 2008), p. 8.

73. www.panerabread.com/menu/cafe/kids.php.

74. Panera Bread Company Inc., *2009 Form 10-K*, pp. 5–6.

75. Panera Bread Company Inc., *2009 Form 10-K*, p. 7.

76. Panera Bread Franchise Information, www.panerabread.com/about/franchise/, pp. 1–8.

77. Panera Bread Company Inc., Second Quarter Earnings Conference Call, July 28, 2010.

78. Panera Bread Company Inc., *2009 Form 10-K*, p. 7.

79. Tischler, pp. 102–112.

80. Panera Bread Company Inc., *2009 Form 10-K*, p. 28.

81. Panera Bread Company Inc., *2009 Form 10-K*, pp. 3–4.

82. Panera Bread Company Inc., Second Quarter Earnings Conference Call, July 28, 2010.

83. Jargon, p. B1.

84. Ibid.

85. Panera, April 12, 2010 Letter to Stockholders.

86. Panera Bread Company Inc., Second Quarter Earnings Conference Call, July 28, 2010.

87. Ibid.

88. Panera Bread Company Inc., *2009 Form 10-K*, p. 3.

89. Panera Bread Company Inc. http://www.panerabread.com/about/community/.

90. Panera Bread Company Inc., *2009 Form 10-K*, p. 6.

91. Gregg Cebrzynski, "Panera Bread Managers 'Harvest' Key Sales Data via Intranet to Support Internal Marketing Goals," *Nation's Restaurant News* (November 3, 2008), www.nrn.com/article/panera-bread-managers-%E2%80%98harvest%E2%80%99-key-sales-data-intranet-support-internal-marketing-goals.

92. Panera, *2009 Form 10-K*, p. 6.

93. Panera Bread Company Inc., Second Quarter Earnings Conference Call, July 28, 2010.

94. Panera Bread Company Inc., *2009 Form 10-K*, p. 8.

95. Ibid. p. 5.

96. Panera Press Release (314-633-4282), *Panera Bread Reports Q1 EPS of $.82, up 44% Over Q1 2009, on a 10.0% Company-owned Comparable Bakery-Café Sales Increase*, pp. 1–10.

97. Ibid., pp. 1–2.

98. Ibid., p. 2.

99. Panera Bread Company Inc., *2009 Form 10-K*, p. 23.

100. Panera Bread Company Inc., *2009 Form 10-K*, *Annual Letter to Stockholders*, p. 2.

101. Panera Bread Company Inc., *2009 Form 10-K*, pp. 26–28.

102. Panera Bread Company Inc., *2009 Form 10-K*, pp. 4 and 32–33.

103. Sean Gregory, "How Panera Bread Defies the Recession," *Time* (December 23, 2009), pp. 1–2, www.time.com/time/printout/0,8816,1949371,00.html.

104. Ibid., p. 1.

C A S E **17**

Whole Foods Market 2010: How to Grow in an Increasingly Competitive Market? (Mini Case)

Patricia Harasta and Alan N. Hoffman

REFLECTING BACK OVER HIS THREE DECADES OF EXPERIENCE IN THE GROCERY BUSINESS, John Mackey smiled to himself over his previous successes. His entrepreneurial history began with a single store that he has now grown into the nation's leading natural food chain. Whole Foods is not just a food retailer but instead represents a healthy, socially responsible lifestyle that customers can identify with. The company has differentiated itself from competitors by focusing on quality, excellence, and innovation that allow it to charge a premium price for premium products. While proud of the past, John had concerns about the future direction in which Whole Foods should head.

Company Background

Whole Foods carries both natural and organic food, offering customers a wide variety of products. "Natural" refers to food that is free of growth hormones or antibiotics, whereas "certified organic" food conforms to the standards, as defined by the U.S. Department of Agriculture (USDA) in October 2002. Whole Foods Market is the world's leading retailer of natural and organic foods, with 193 stores in 31 states, Canada, and the United Kingdom.

This case was prepared by Patricia Harasta and Professor Alan N. Hoffman, Bentley University and Erasmus University. Copyright © 2010 by Alan N. Hoffman. The copyright holder is solely responsible for case content. Reprint permission is solely granted to the publisher, Prentice Hall, for *Strategic Management and Business Policy*, 13th Edition (and the international and electronic versions of this book) by the copyright holder, Alan N. Hoffman. Any other publication of the case (translation, any form of electronics or other media) or sale (any form of partnership) to another publisher will be in violation of copyright law, unless Alan N. Hoffman has granted an additional written permission. Reprinted by permission. The authors would like to thank Will Hoffman, Christopher Ferrari, Robert Marshall, Julie Giles, Jennifer Powers, and Gretchen Alper for their research and contributions to this case. No part of this publication may be copied, stored, transmitted, reproduced, or distributed in any form or medium whatsoever without the permission of the copyright owner, Alan N. Hoffman.

According to the company, Whole Foods Market is highly selective about what it sells, dedicated to stringent quality standards, and committed to sustainable agriculture. It believes in a virtuous circle entwining the food chain, human beings, and Mother Earth: Each is reliant upon the others through a beautiful and delicate symbiosis. The message of preservation and sustainability are followed while providing high-quality goods to customers and high profits to investors.

Whole Foods has grown over the years through mergers, acquisitions, and new store openings. The US$565 million acquisition of its lead competitor, Wild Oats, in 2007 firmly set Whole Foods as the leader in the natural and organic food market and led to 70 new stores. The U.S. Federal Trade Commission (FTC) focused its attention on the merger on antitrust grounds. The dispute was settled in 2009, with Whole Foods closing 32 Wild Oats stores and agreeing to sell the Wild Oats Markets brand.

Although the majority of Whole Foods' locations are in the United States, European expansion provides enormous potential growth due to the large population there and because it has access to a more sophisticated organic-foods market than the United States in terms of suppliers and acceptance by the public. Whole Foods targets its locations specifically by an area's demographics. The company targets locations where 40% or more of the residents have a college degree because its citizens are more likely to be aware of nutritional issues.

Whole Foods Market's Philosophy

Whole Foods Market's company philosophy is to be a sustainable company. While Whole Foods recognizes it is only a supermarket, management is working toward fulfilling their vision within the context of the industry. In addition to leading by example, they strive to conduct business in a manner consistent with their mission and vision. By offering minimally processed, high-quality food, engaging in ethical business practices, and providing a motivational, respectful work environment, the company believes it is on the path to a sustainable future.

Whole Foods incorporates the best practices of each location back into the chain. This can be seen in the company's store product expansion from dry goods to perishable produce, including meats, fish, and prepared foods. The lessons learned at one location are absorbed by all, enabling the chain to maximize effectiveness and efficiency while offering a product line customers love. Whole Foods carries only natural and organic products. The best tasting and most nutritious food available is found in its purest state—unadulterated by artificial additives, sweeteners, colorings, and preservatives.

Employee and Customer Relations

Whole Foods encourages a team-based environment allowing each store to make independent decisions regarding its operations. Teams consist of up to 11 employees and a team leader. The team leaders typically head up one department or another. Each store employs anywhere from 72 to 391 team members. The manager is referred to as the "store team leader." The "store team leader" is compensated by an Economic Value Added (EVA) bonus and is also eligible to receive stock options.

Whole Foods tries to instill a sense of purpose among its employees and has been named for 13 consecutive years as one of the "100 Best Companies to Work For" in America by *Fortune* magazine. In employee surveys, 90% of its team members stated that they always or frequently enjoy their job.

The company strives to take care of its customers, realizing they are the "lifeblood of our business," and the two are "interdependent on each other." Whole Foods' primary objective goes beyond 100% customer satisfaction with the goal to "delight" customers in every interaction.

Competitive Environment

At the time of Whole Foods' inception, there was almost no competition with less than six other natural food stores in the United States. Today, the organic foods industry is growing and Whole Foods finds itself competing hard to maintain its elite presence.

Whole Foods competes with all supermarkets. With more U.S. consumers focused on healthful eating, environmental sustainability, and the green movement, the demand for organic and natural foods has increased. More traditional supermarkets are now introducing "lifestyle" stores and departments to compete directly with Whole Foods. This can be seen in the Wild Harvest section of Shaw's, or the "Lifestyle" stores opened by conventional grocery chain Safeway.

Whole Foods' competitors now include big box and discount retailers who have made a foray into the grocery business. Currently, the United States' largest grocer is Wal-Mart. Not only does Wal-Mart compete in the standard supermarket industry, but it has even begun offering natural and organic products in its supercenter stores. Other discount retailers now competing in the supermarket industry include Target, Sam's Club, and Costco. All of these retailers offer grocery products, generally at a lower price than what one would find at Whole Foods.

Another of Whole Foods' key competitors is Los Angeles–based Trader Joe's, a premium natural and organic food market. By expanding its presence and product offerings while maintaining high quality at low prices, Trader Joe's has found its competitive niche. It has 215 stores, primarily on the west and east coasts of the United States, offering upscale grocery fare such as health foods, prepared meals, organic produce, and nutritional supplements. A low-cost structure allows Trader Joe's to offer competitive prices while still maintaining its margins. Trader Joe's stores have no service department and average just 10,000 square feet in store size.

A Different Shopping Experience

The setup of the organic grocery store is a key component to Whole Foods' success. The store's setup and its products are carefully researched to ensure that they are meeting the demands of the local community. Locations are primarily in cities and are chosen for their large space and heavy foot traffic. According to Whole Foods' 10-K, "approximately 88% of our existing stores are located in the top 50 statistical metropolitan areas." The company uses a specific formula to choose store sites that is based upon several metrics, which include but are not limited to income levels, education, and population density.

Upon entering a Whole Foods supermarket, it becomes clear that the company attempts to sell the consumer on the entire experience. Team members (employees) are well trained and the stores themselves are immaculate. There are in-store chefs to help with recipes, wine tasting, and food sampling. There are "Take Action food centers" where customers can access information on the issues that affect their food such as legislation and environmental factors. Some stores offer extra services such as home delivery, cooking classes, massages, and valet parking. Whole Foods goes out of its way to appeal to the above-average income earner.

Whole Foods uses price as a marketing tool in a few select areas, as demonstrated by the 365 Whole Foods brand name products priced less than similar organic products that are carried within the store. However, the company does not use price to differentiate itself from competitors. Rather, Whole Foods focuses on quality and service as a means of standing out from the competition.

Whole Foods spends much less than other supermarkets on advertising, approximately 0.4% of total sales in fiscal year 2009. It relies heavily on word-of-mouth advertising from its customers to help market itself in the local community. The company advertises in several health-conscious magazines, and each store budgets for in-store advertising each fiscal year.

Whole Foods also gains recognition via its charitable contributions and the awareness that they bring to the treatment of animals. The company donates 5% of its after-tax profits to not-for-profit charities. It is also very active in establishing systems to make sure that the animals used in their products are treated humanely.

The Green Movement

Whole Foods exists in a time where customers equate going green and being environmentally friendly with enthusiasm and respect. In recent years, people began to learn about food and the processes completed by many to produce it. Most of what they have discovered is disturbing. Whole Foods launched a nationwide effort to trigger awareness and action to remedy the problems facing the U.S. food system. It has decided to host 150 screenings of a 12-film series called "Let's Retake Our Plates," hoping to inspire change by encouraging and educating consumers to take charge of their food choices. Jumping on the bandwagon of the "go green" movement, Whole Foods is trying to show its customers that it is dedicated to not only all natural foods, but to a green world and healthy people. As more and more people become educated, the company hopes to capitalize on them as new customers.[1]

Beyond the green movement, Whole Foods has been able to tap into a demographic that appreciates the "trendy" theme of organic foods and all natural products. Since the store is associated with a type of affluence, many customers shop there to show they fit into this category of upscale, educated, new-age people.

The Economic Recession of 2008

The uncertainty of today's market is a threat to Whole Foods. The expenditure income is low and "all natural foods" are automatically deemed as expensive. Because of people being laid off, having their salaries cut, or simply not being able to find a job, they now have to be more selective when purchasing things. While Whole Foods has been able to maintain profitability, it's questionable how long this will last if the recession continues or worsens. The reputation that organic products have of being costly may be enough to motivate people to never enter Whole Foods. In California, the chain is frequently dubbed "Whole Paycheck."[2]

However, management understood that it must change a few things if the company was to survive the decrease in sales felt because customers were not willing to spend their money so easily. They have been working to correct this "pricey" image by expanding offerings of private-label products through their "365 Everyday Value" and "365 Organic" product lines. Private-label sales accounted for 11% of Whole Foods' total sales in 2009, up from 10% in 2008. They have also instituted a policy that their 365 product lines must match prices of similar products at Trader Joe's.[3]

Organic Foods as a Commodity

When Whole Foods first started in the natural foods industry in 1980, the industry was a relatively new concept. During its first decade, Whole Foods enjoyed the benefits of offering a unique value proposition to consumers wanting to purchase high-quality natural foods from a trusted retailer. Over the last few years, however, the natural and organic foods industry has attracted the attention of general food retailers that have started to offer foods labeled as natural or organic at reasonable prices.

By 2007, the global demand for organic and natural foods far exceeded the supply. This is becoming a huge issue for Whole Foods, as more traditional supermarkets with higher purchasing power enter the premium natural and organic foods market. The supply of organic food has been significantly impacted by the entrance of Wal-Mart into the competitive arena. Due to the limited resources within the United States, Wal-Mart began importing natural and organic foods from China and Brazil, which led to it coming under scrutiny for passing off non-natural or organic products as the "real thing." Additionally, the quality of natural and organic foods throughout the entire market has been decreased due to constant pressure from Wal-Mart.

The distinction between what is truly organic and natural is difficult for the consumer to decipher because general supermarkets have taken to using terms such as "all natural," "free-range," and "hormone-free," thus confusing customers. Truly organic food sold in the United States bears the "USDA Organic" label and needs to have at least 95% of the ingredients organic before it can get this distinction.[4]

In May 2003, Whole Foods became America's first Certified Organic grocer by a federally recognized independent third-party certification organization. In July 2009, California Certified Organic Growers (CCOF), one of the oldest and largest USDA-accredited third-party organic certifiers, individually certified each store in the United States, complying with stricter guidance on federal regulations. This voluntary certification tells customers that Whole Foods has gone the extra mile by not only following the USDA's Organic Rule, but opening its stores up to third-party inspectors and following a strict set of operating procedures designed to ensure that the products sold and labeled as organic are indeed organic—procedures that are not specifically required by the Organic Rule. This certification verifies the handling of organic goods according to stringent national guidelines, from receipt through repacking to final sale to customers. To receive certification, retailers must agree to adhere to a strict set of standards set forth by the USDA, submit documentation, and open their facilities to onsite inspections—all designed to assure customers that the chain of organic integrity is preserved.

Struggling to Grow in an Increasingly Competitive Market

Whole Foods has historically grown by opening new stores or acquiring stores in affluent neighborhoods targeting the wealthier and more educated consumers. This strategy has worked in the past; however, the continued focus on growth has been impacting existing store sales. Average weekly sales per store have decreased over the last number of years despite the fact that overall sales have been increasing. It is likely that this trend will continue unless Whole Foods starts to focus on growing sales within the stores it has and not just looking to increase overall sales by opening new stores. It is also increasingly difficult to find appropriate locations for new stores that are first and foremost in an area where there is limited competition and also to have the store in a location that is easily accessible by both consumers and the distribution network. Originally, Whole Foods had forecast to open 29 new stores in 2010 but this has since been revised downward to 17.

Opening up new stores or acquiring existing stores is also costly. The average cost to open a new store ranges from US$2 to US$3 million, and it takes on average 8 to 12 months. A lot of this can be explained by the fact that Whole Foods custom builds the stores, which reduces the efficiencies that can be gained from the experience of having opened up many new stores previously. Opening new stores requires the company to adapt its distribution network, information management, supply, and inventory management, and adequately supply the new stores in a timely manner without impacting the supply to the existing stores. As the company expands, this task increases in complexity and magnitude.

The organic and natural foods industry overall has become a more concentrated market with few larger competitors having emerged from a more fragmented market composed of a large number of smaller companies. Future acquisitions will be more difficult for Whole Foods because the FTC will be monitoring the company closely to ensure it does not violate any federal antitrust laws through the elimination of any substantial competition within this market.

Over the last number of years, there has been an increasing demand by consumers for natural and organic foods. Sales of organic foods increased by 5.1% in 2009 despite the fact that U.S. food sales overall only grew by 1.6%.[5] This increase in demand and high-margin availability on premium organic products led to an increasing number of competitors moving into the organic foods industry. Conventional grocery chains such as Safeway have remodeled stores at a rapid pace and have attempted to narrow the gap with premium grocers like Whole Foods in terms of shopping experience, product quality, and selection of takeout foods. This increase in competition can lead to the introduction of price wars where profits are eroded for both existing competitors and new entrants alike.

Unlike low-price leaders such as Wal-Mart, Whole Foods dominates because of its brand image, which is trickier to manage and less impervious to competitive threats. As competitors start to focus on emphasizing organic and natural foods within their own stores, the power of the Whole Foods brand will gradually decline over time as it becomes more difficult for consumers to differentiate Whole Foods' value proposition from that of its competitors.

NOTES

1. "Whole Foods Market; Whole Foods Market Challenge: Let's Retake Our Plates!" *Food BusinessWeek* (April 15, 2010).
2. "Eating Too Fast at Whole Foods," *BusinessWeek* (2005).
3. Katy McLaughlin, "As Sales Slip, Whole Foods Tries Health Push," *The Wall Street Journal* (August 15, 2009).
4. "Whole Foods Markets Organic China California Blend," http://www.youtube.com/watch?v=JQ31Ljd9T_Y (April 10, 2010).
5. Organic Trade Association, http://www.organicnewsroom.com/2010/04/us_organic_product_sales_reach_1.html.

CASE **18**

Burger King (Mini Case)

J. David Hunger

ORIGINALLY CALLED INSTA-BURGER KING, the company was founded in Florida in 1953 by Keith Kramer and Matthew Burns. Their Insta-Broiler oven was so successful at cooking hamburgers that they required all of their franchised restaurants to use the oven. After the chain ran into financial difficulties, it was purchased by its Miami-based franchisees, James McLamore and David Edgerton, in 1955. The new owners renamed the company Burger King, and the restaurant chain introduced the first *Whopper* sandwich in 1957. Expanding to over 250 locations in the United States, the company was sold in 1967 to Pillsbury Corporation.

The company successfully differentiated itself from McDonald's, its primary rival, when it launched the *Have It Your Way* advertising campaign in 1974. Unlike McDonald's, which had made it difficult and time-consuming for customers to special-order standard items (such as a plain hamburger), Burger King restaurants allowed people to change the way a food item was prepared without a long wait.

Pillsbury (including Burger King) was purchased in 1989 by Grand Metropolitan, which in turn merged with Guinness to form Diageo, a British spirits company. Diageo's management neglected the Burger King business, leading to poor operating performance. Burger King was damaged to the point that major franchises went out of business and the total value of the firm declined. Diageo's management decided to divest the money-losing chain by selling it to a partnership private equity firm led by TPG Capital in 2002.

The investment group hired a new advertising agency to create (1) a series of new ad campaigns, (2) a changed menu to focus on male consumers, (3) a series of programs designed to revamp individual stores, and (4) a new concept called the BK Whopper Bar. These changes led to profitable quarters and reenergized the chain. In May 2006, the investment group took Burger King public by issuing an Initial Public Offering (IPO). The investment group continued to own 31% of the outstanding common stock.

Business Model

Burger King was the second-largest fast-food hamburger restaurant chain in the world as measured by the total number of restaurants and systemwide sales. As of June 30, 2010, the company owned or franchised 12,174 restaurants in 76 countries and U.S. territories, of which 1,387 were company-owned and 10,787 were owned by franchisees. Of Burger King's restaurant total, 7,258 or 60% were located in the United States. The restaurants featured flame-broiled hamburgers, chicken and other specialty sandwiches, French fries, soft drinks, and other low-priced food items.

According to management, the company generated revenues from three sources: (1) retail sales at company-owned restaurants; (2) royalty payments on sales and franchise fees paid by franchisees; and (3) property income from restaurants leased to franchisees. Approximately 90% of Burger King restaurants were franchised, a higher percentage than other competitors in the fast-food hamburger category. Although such a high percentage of franchisees meant lower capital requirements compared to competitors, it also meant that management had limited control over franchisees. Franchisees in the United States and Canada paid an average of 3.9% of sales to the company in 2010. In addition, these franchisees contributed 4% of gross sales per month to the advertising fund. Franchisees were required to purchase food, packaging, and equipment from company-approved suppliers.

Restaurant Services Inc. (RSI) was a purchasing cooperative formed in 1992 to act as purchasing agent for the Burger King system in the United States. As of June 30, 2010, RSI was the distribution manager for 94% of the company's U.S. restaurants, with four distributors servicing approximately 85% of the U.S. system. Burger King had long-term exclusive contracts with Coca-Cola and with Dr Pepper/7UP to purchase soft drinks for its restaurants.

Management touted its business strategy as growing the brand, running great restaurants, investing wisely, and focusing on its people. Specifically, management planned to accelerate growth between 2010 and 2015 so that international restaurants would comprise 50% of the total number. The focus in international expansion was to be in (1) countries with growth potential where Burger King was already established, such as Spain, Brazil, and Turkey; (2) countries with potential where the firm had a small presence, such as Argentina, Colombia, China, Japan, Indonesia, and Italy; and (3) attractive new markets in the Middle East, Eastern Europe, and Asia.

Management was also working to update the restaurants by implementing its new 20/20 design and complementary Whopper Bar design introduced in 2008. By 2010, more than 200 Burger King restaurants had adopted the new 20/20 design that evoked the industrial look of corrugated metal, brick, wood, and concrete. The new design was to be introduced in 95 company-owned restaurants during fiscal 2011.

Management was using a "barbell" menu strategy to introduce new products at both the premium and low-priced ends of the product continuum. As part of this strategy, the company introduced in 2010 the premium Steakhouse XT burger line and BK Fire-Grilled Ribs, the first bone-in pork ribs sold at a national fast-food hamburger restaurant chain. At the other end of the menu, the company introduced in 2010 the quarter-pound Double Cheeseburger, the Buck Double, and the US$1 BK Breakfast Muffin Sandwich.

Management continued to look for ways to reduce costs and boost efficiency. By June 30, 2010, point-of-sale cash register systems had been installed in all company-owned restaurants, and in 57% of its franchise-owned restaurants. It had also installed a flexible batch broiler to maximize cooking flexibility and facilitate a broader menu selection while reducing energy costs. By June 30, 2010, the flexible broiler was in 89% of company-owned restaurants and 68% of franchise restaurants.

Industry

The fast-food hamburger category operated within the quick service restaurant (QSR) segment of the restaurant industry. QSR sales had grown at an annual rate of 3% over the past 10 years and were projected to continue increasing at 3% from 2010 to 2015. The fast-food hamburger restaurant (FFHR) category represented 27% of total QSR sales. FFHR sales were projected to grow 5% annually during this same time period. Burger King accounted for around 14% of total FFHR sales in the United States.

The company competed against market-leading McDonald's, Wendy's, and Hardee's restaurants in this category and against regional competitors, such as Carl's Jr., Jack in the Box, and Sonic. It also competed indirectly against a multitude of competitors in the QSR restaurant segment, including Taco Bell, Arby's, and KFC, among others. As the North American market became saturated, mergers occurred. For example, Taco Bell, KFC, and Pizza Hut became part of Yum! Brands. Wendy's and Arby's merged in 2008. Although the restaurant industry as a whole had few barriers to entry, marketing and operating economies of scale made it difficult for a new entrant to challenge established U.S. chains in the FFHR category.

The quick-service restaurant market segment appeared to be less vulnerable to a recession than other businesses. For example, during the quarter ended May 2010, both QSR and FFHR sales decreased 0.5%, compared to a 3% decline at both casual dining chains and family dining chains. The U.S. restaurant category as a whole declined 1% during the same time period.

America's increasing concern with health and fitness was putting pressure on restaurants to offer healthier menu items. Given its emphasis on fried food and saturated fat, the quick service restaurant market segment was an obvious target for likely legislation. For example, Burger King's recently introduced Pizza Burger was a 2,530-calorie item that included four hamburger patties, pepperoni, mozzarella, and Tuscan sauce on a sesame seed bun. Although the Pizza Burger may be the largest hamburger produced by a fast-food chain, the foot-long cheeseburgers of Hardee's and Carl's Jr. were similar entries. A health reform bill passed by the U.S. Congress in 2010 required restaurant chains with 20 or more outlets to list the calorie content of menu items. A study by the National Bureau of Economic Research found that a similar posting law in New York City caused the average calorie count per transaction to fall 6%, and revenue increased 3% at Starbucks stores where a Dunkin Donuts outlet was nearby. One county in California attempted to ban McDonald's from including toys in its high-calorie "Happy Meal" because legislators believed that toys attracted children to unhealthy food.

Issues

Even though Burger King was the second-largest hamburger chain in the world, it lagged far behind McDonald's, which had a total of 32,466 restaurants worldwide. McDonald's averaged about twice the sales volume per U.S. restaurant and was more profitable than Burger King. McDonald's was respected as a well-managed company. During fiscal year 2009 (ending December 31), McDonald's earned US$4.6 billion on revenues of US$22.7 billion. Although its total revenues had dropped from US$23.5 billion in 2008, net income had actually increased from US$4.3 billion in 2008. In contrast to most corporations, McDonald's common stock price had risen during the 2008–2010 recession, reaching an all-time high in August 2010.

In contrast, Burger King was perceived by industry analysts as having significant problems. As a result, Burger King's share price had fallen by half from 2008 to 2010. During fiscal year 2010 (ending June 30), Burger King earned US$186.8 million on revenues of US$2.50 billion. Although its total revenues had dropped only slightly from US$2.54 billion in fiscal 2009 and increased from US$2.45 billion in 2008, net income fell from

US$200.1 million in 2009 and US$189.6 million in 2008. Even though same-store sales stayed positive for McDonald's during the recession, they dropped 2.3% for Burger King from fiscal 2009 to 2010. In addition, some analysts were concerned that expenses were high at Burger King's company-owned restaurants. Expenses as a percentage of total company-owned restaurant revenues were 87.8% in fiscal 2010 for Burger King compared to only 81.8% for McDonald's in fiscal 2009.

McDonald's had always emphasized marketing to families. The company significantly outperformed Burger King in both "warmth" and "competence" in consumers' minds. When McDonald's recently put more emphasis on women and older people by offering relatively healthy salads and upgraded its already good coffee, Burger King continued to market to young men by (according to one analyst) offering high-calorie burgers and ads featuring dancing chickens and a "creepy-looking" king. These young men were the very group who had been hit especially hard by the recession. According to Steve Lewis, who operated 36 Burger King franchises in the Philadelphia area, "overall menu development has been horrible. . . . We disregarded kids, we disregarded families, we disregarded moms." For example, sales of new, premium-priced menu items like the Steakhouse XT burger declined once they were no longer being advertised. One analyst stated that the company had "put a lot of energy into gimmicky advertising" at the expense of products and service. In addition, analysts commented that franchisees had also disregarded their aging restaurants.

Some analysts felt that Burger King may have cannibalized its existing sales by putting too much emphasis on value meals. For example, Burger King franchisees sued the company in 2009 over the firm's double-cheeseburger promotion, claiming it was unfair for them to be required to sell these cheeseburgers for only US$1 when they cost US$1.10. Even though the price was subsequently raised to US$1.29, the items on Burger King's "value menu" accounted for 20% of all sales in 2010, up from 12% in 2009.

New Owners: Time for a Strategic Change?

On September 2, 2010, 3G Capital, an investment group dominated by three Brazilian millionaires, offered US$4 billion to purchase Burger King Holdings Inc. At US$24 a share, the offer represented a 46% premium over Burger King's August 31 closing price. According to John Chidsey, Burger King's Charman and CEO, "It was a call out of the blue." Both the board of directors and the investment firms owning 31% of the shares supported acceptance of the offer. New ownership should bring a new board of directors and a change in top management. What should new management propose to ensure the survival and long-term success of Burger King?

CASE 19

Church & Dwight:
Time to Rethink the Portfolio?

Roy A. Cook

"A DECADE AGO, CHURCH & DWIGHT WAS A LARGELY HOUSEHOLD DOMESTIC PRODUCTS COMPANY with one iconic brand, delivering less than US$1 billion in annual sales. Today, the company has been transformed into a diversified packaged goods company with a well-balanced portfolio of leading household and personal care brands delivering over US$2.5 billion in annual sales worldwide."[1] Now, after a decade of rapid growth fueled by a string of acquisitions, the top management team is faced with a new challenge. It must now rationalize the firm's expanded consumer products portfolio of 80 brands into the existing corporate structure while continuing to scout for new avenues of growth. This is no easy task as it competes for market share with such formidable consumer products powerhouses as Colgate-Palmolive, Clorox, and Procter & Gamble, commanding combined sales of over US$100 billion. Future decisions will determine if the company can compete successfully with these other well-known giants in the consumer products arena or remain in their shadows.

Background

For over 160 years, Church & Dwight Co. Inc. has been working to build market share on a brand name that is rarely associated with the company. When consumers are asked, "Are you familiar with Church & Dwight products?" the answer is typically "No." Yet, Church & Dwight products can be found among a variety of consumer products in 95% of all U.S. households. As the world's largest producer and marketer of sodium bicarbonate–based products, Church & Dwight has achieved fairly consistent growth in both sales and earnings as new and expanded uses were found for its core sodium bicarbonate products. Although Church & Dwight may not be a household name, many of its core products bearing the ARM & HAMMER name are easily recognized.

Shortly after its introduction in 1878, ARM & HAMMER Baking Soda became a fundamental item on the pantry shelf as homemakers found many uses for it other than baking, such as cleaning and deodorizing. The ingredients that can be found in that ubiquitous yellow box of baking soda can also be used as a dentrifice, a chemical agent to absorb or neutralize odors and acidity, a kidney dialysis element, a blast media, an environmentally friendly cleaning agent, a swimming pool pH stabilizer, and a pollution-control agent.

Finding expanded uses for sodium bicarbonate and achieving orderly growth have been consistent targets for the company. Over the past 30 years, average company sales have increased 10%–15% annually. While top-line sales growth has historically been a focal point for the company, a shift may have occurred in management's thinking, as more emphasis seems to have been placed on bottom-line profitability growth. Since President and Chief Executive Officer James R. Cragie took over the helm of Church & Dwight from Robert A. Davies III in July of 2004, he has remained focused on "building a portfolio of strong brands with sustainable competitive advantages."[2] At that time, he proposed a strategy of reshaping the company through acquisitions and organic growth and he continues to state that "Our long-term objective is to maintain the company's track record of delivering outstanding TSR (Total Shareholder Return) relative to that of the S&P 500. Our long-term business model for delivering this sustained earnings growth is based on annual organic growth of 3%–4%, gross margin expansion, tight management of overhead costs and operating margin improvement of 60–70 basis points resulting in sustained earnings growth of 10%–12% excluding acquisitions."[3] In addition, Cragie noted that ". . . [W]e have added $1 billion in sales in the past five years, a 72% increase, while reducing our total headcount by 5%, resulting in higher revenue per employee than all of our major competitors."[4] The results of these efforts can be seen in the financial statements shown in **Exhibits 1**, **2**, and **3**.

Management

The historically slow but steady course Church & Dwight has traveled over the decades reflected stability in the chief executive office and a steady focus on long-term goals. The ability to remain focused may be attributable to the fact that about 25% of the outstanding shares of common stock were owned by descendants of the company's co-founders. Dwight C. Minton, a direct descendant of Austin Church, actively directed the company as CEO from 1969 through 1995 and remained on the board as Chairman Emeritus. He passed on the duties of CEO to the first non-family member in the company's history, Robert A. Davies III, in 1995 and leadership at the top has remained a stable hallmark of the company.

Many companies with strong brand names in the consumer products field have been susceptible to leveraged buy-outs and hostile takeovers. However, a series of calculated actions has spared Church & Dwight's board and management from having to make last-minute decisions to ward off unwelcome suitors. Besides maintaining majority control of the outstanding common stock, the board amended the company's charter, giving current shareholders four votes per share. However, they required future shareholders to buy and hold shares for four years before receiving the same privilege. The board of directors was also structured into three classes with four directors in each class serving staggered three-year terms. According to Minton, the objective of these moves was to "[give] the board control so as to provide the best results for shareholders."[5]

EXHIBIT 1
Consolidated State-
ments of Income:
Church & Dwight
Co. Inc. (Dollars in
thousands, except
per share data)

Year Ending December 31	2009	2008	2007
Net sales	$ 2,520,922	$ 2,422,398	$ 2,220,940
Cost of sales	1,419,932	1,450,680	1,353,042
Gross profit	1,100,990	971,718	867,898
Marketing expenses	353,588	294,130	256,743
Selling, general, and administrative expenses	354,510	337,256	306,121
Patent litigation settlement, net	(20,000)	—	—
Income from operations	412,892	340,332	305,034
Equity in earnings of affiliates	12,050	11,334	8,236
Investment earnings	1,325	6,747	8,084
Other income (expense), net	1,537	(3,208)	2,469
Interest expense	(35,568)	(46,945)	(58,892)
Income before income taxes	392,236	308,260	264,931
Income taxes	148,715	113,078	95,900
Net income	243,521	195,182	169,031
Non-controlling interest	(12)	8	6
Net income	$ 243,533	$ 195,174	$ 169,025
Weighted average shares outstanding—Basic	70,379	67,870	65,840
Weighted average shares outstanding—Diluted	71,477	71,116	70,312
Net income per share—Basic	$ 3.46	$ 2.88	$ 2.57
Net income per share—Diluted	$ 3.41	$ 2.78	$ 2.46
Cash dividends per share	$ 0.46	$ 0.34	$ 0.30

SOURCES: Church & Dwight Co. Inc., 2009 Annual Report, p. 43.

As a further deterrent to would-be suitors or unwelcome advances, the company entered into an employee severance agreement with key officials. This agreement provided sever-ance pay of up to two times (three times for Mr. Cragie) the individual's highest annual sal-ary and bonus plus benefits for two years (three years for Mr. Cragie) if the individual was terminated within one year after a change in control of the company. Change of control was defined as the acquisition by a person or group of 50% or more of company common stock; a change in the majority of the board of directors not approved by the pre-change board of directors; or the approval by the stockholders of the company of a merger, consolidation, liquidation, dissolution, or sale of all the assets of the company.[6]

As Church & Dwight pushed aggressively into consumer products outside of sodium bicarbonate–related products and into the international arena in the early 2000s, numerous changes were made in key personnel. Many of the new members of the top management team brought extensive marketing and international experience from organizations such as Spald-ing Sports Worldwide, Johnson & Johnson, FMC, and Carter-Wallace.

In addition to the many changes that have taken place in key management positions, changes have also been made in the composition of the board of directors. Four members of the ten-member board have served for 10 years or more, whereas the other six members have served for five years or less. Two women serve on the board, and the ages of members range from 50 to 74, with six members being younger than 60. All but one of the newer additions to the board brought significant consumer products and service industry insights from their ties

EXHIBIT 2 Consolidated Balance Sheets: Church & Dwight Co. Inc. (Dollars in thousands, except share and per share data)

Year Ending December 31	2009	2008	2007
Assets			
Current assets			
Cash and cash equivalents	$ 447,143	$ 197,999	$ 249,809
Accounts receivable, less allowances of $5,782 and $5,427	222,158	211,194	247,898
Inventories	216,870	198,893	213,651
Deferred income taxes	20,432	15,107	13,508
Prepaid expenses	11,444	10,234	9,224
Other current assets	10,218	31,694	1,263
Total current assets	**928,265**	**665,121**	**735,353**
Property, plant, and equipment, net	455,636	384,519	350,853
Notes receivable	—	—	3,670
Equity investment in affiliates	12,815	10,061	10,324
Long-term supply contracts	—	—	2,519
Tradenames and other intangibles	794,891	810,173	665,168
Goodwill	838,078	845,230	688,842
Other assets	88,761	86,334	75,761
Total assets	**$ 3,118,446**	**$ 2,801,438**	**$ 2,532,490**
Liabilities and stockholders' equity			
Current liabilities			
Short-term borrowings	$ 34,895	$ 3,248	$ 115,000
Accounts payable and accrued expenses	332,450	310,622	303,071
Current portion of long-term debt	184,054	71,491	33,706
Income taxes payable	15,633	1,760	6,012
Total current liabilities	**567,032**	**387,121**	**457,789**
Long-term debt	597,347	781,402	707,311
Deferred income taxes	201,256	171,981	162,746
Deferred and other long-term liabilities	112,440	93,430	87,769
Pension, postretirement, and postemployment benefits	38,599	35,799	36, 416
Minority interest	—	—	194
Total liabilities	**1,516,674**	**1,469,733**	**1,452,225**
Commitments and contingencies stockholders' equity			
Preferred stock–$1.00 par value			
Authorized 2,500,000 shares, none issued	—	—	—
Common stock–$1.00 par value			
Authorized 300,000,000 shares, issued 73,213,775 shares	73,214	73,214	69,991
Additional paid-in capital	276,099	252,129	121,902
Retained earnings	1,275,117	1,063,928	891,868
Accumulated other comprehensive income (loss)	10,078	(20,454)	39,128
Common stock in treasury, at cost:			
2,664,312 shares in 2009 and 3,140,931 shares in 2008	(32,925)	(37,304)	(42,624)
Total church & dwight Co. Inc. stockholders' equity	**1,601,583**	**1,331,513**	**—**
Noncontrolling interest	189	192	—
Total stockholders' equity	**1,601,772**	**1,331,705**	**1,080,265**
Total liabilities and stockholders' equity	**$ 3,118,446**	**$ 2,801,438**	**$ 2,532,490**

SOURCES: Church & Dwight Co. Inc., 2009 Annual Report, p. 44.

EXHIBIT 3
Business Segment
Results: Church &
Dwight Co. Inc.

	Consumer Domestic	Consumer International	Specialty Products	Corporate	Total
Net sales					
2009	$1,881,748	$393,696	$245,478	$ —	$2,520,922
2008	1,716,801	420,192	285,405	—	2,422,398
2007	1,563,895	398,521	258,524	—	2,220,940
Income before					
Income taxes					
2009	$325,633	$38,562	$15,991	$12,050	$392,236
2008	236,956	34,635	25,335	11,334	308,260
2007	205,688	34,656	16,351	8,236	264,931

....
SOURCES: Church & Dwight Co. Inc., 2009 Annual Report, p. 30.

with companies such as Revlon, ARAMARK, VF Corporation, Welch Foods, and H.J. Heinz. Although in a less active role as Chairman Emeritus, Dwight Church Minton, who became a board member in 1965, continued to provide leadership and a long legacy of "corporate memory."

Changing Directions

Entering the 21st century, ". . . [m]anagement recognized a major challenge to overcome . . . was the company's small size compared to its competitors in basic product lines of household and personal care. They also recognized the value of a major asset, the company's pristine balance sheet, and made the decision to grow."[7] According to Cragie, "Church & Dwight has undergone a substantial transformation in the past decade largely as a result of three major acquisitions which doubled the size of the total company, created a well-balanced portfolio of household and personal care businesses, and established a much larger international business."[8] The Mentadent, Pepsodent, Aim, and Close-Up brands of toothpaste products were purchased from Unilever in October of 2003; the purchase of the remaining 50% of Armkel, the acquisition vehicle that had been used to purchase Carter-Wallace's consumer brands such as Trojan, was completed in May of 2004; and Spinbrush was purchased from Procter & Gamble in October of 2005.

Five years later, another major acquisition was finalized when the stable of Orange Glow International products, including the well-known OxiClean brand, were added to the portfolio. The acquisitions didn't stop as Del Pharmaceutical's Orajel brands were added in 2008. What impact has this string of acquisitions made? The numbers speak for themselves, as revenues have been pumped up from less than US$500 million in 1995 to over US$1 billion in 2001, then to US$1.7 billion in 2005, and finally topping US$2.5 billion in 2009.

Explosive growth through acquisitions transformed this once small company focused on a few consumer and specialty products into a much larger competitor, not only across a broader range of products, but also across a greater geographic territory. Consumer products now encompassed a broad array of personal care, deodorizing and cleaning, and laundry products while specialty products offerings were expanded to specialty chemicals, animal nutrition, and specialty cleaners. International consumer product sales, which were an insignificant portion of total revenue at the turn of the century, now accounted for 16% of sales. In the face of consumer products behemoths such as Clorox, Colgate-Palmolive, and Procter & Gamble, Church & Dwight had been able to carve out a respectable position with several leading brands. Regardless, the firm was not a major market force and needed to evaluate its portfolio of 80 different consumer brands.

Consumer Products

Prior to its acquisition spree, the company's growth strategy had been based on finding new uses for sodium bicarbonate. Using an overall family branding strategy to penetrate the consumer products market in the United States and Canada, Church & Dwight introduced additional products displaying the ARM & HAMMER logo. This logoed footprint remained significant as the ARM & HAMMER brand controlled a commanding 85% of the baking soda market. By capitalizing on its easily recognizable brand name, logo, and established marketing channels, Church & Dwight moved into such related products as laundry detergent, carpet cleaners and deodorizers, air deodorizers, toothpaste, and deodorant/antiperspirants. This strategy worked well, allowing the company to promote multiple products using only one brand name, but it limited growth opportunities ". . . in highly competitive consumer product markets, in which cost efficiency, new product offering and innovation are critical to success."[9]

From the company's founding until 1970, it produced and sold only two consumer products: ARM & HAMMER Baking Soda and a laundry product marketed under the name Super Washing Soda. In 1970, under Minton, Church & Dwight began testing the consumer products market by introducing a phosphate-free, powdered laundry detergent. Several other products, including a liquid laundry detergent, fabric softener sheets, an all-fabric bleach, tooth powder and toothpaste, baking soda chewing gum, deodorant/antiperspirants, deodorizers (carpet, room, and pet), and clumping cat litter have been added to the expanding list of ARM & HAMMER brands. However, simply relying on baking soda extensions and focusing on niche markets to avoid a head-on attack from competitors with more financial resources and marketing clout limited growth opportunities.

So, in the late 1990s, the company departed from its previous strategy of developing new product offerings in-house and bought several established consumer brands such as Brillo, Parsons Ammonia, Cameo Aluminum & Stainless Steel Cleaner, RainDrops water softener, Sno Bol Toilet Bowl Cleaner, and Toss 'N Done dryer sheets from one of its competitors, the Dial Corporation. An even broader consumer product assortment including Trojan, Nair, and First Response was added to the company's mix of offerings with the acquisition of the consumer products business of Carter-Wallace in partnership with the private equity group, Armkel. The list of well-known brands was further enhanced with the acquisition of Crest's Spinbrush, Coty's line of Orajel products, and OxiClean, as well as other brands from Orange Glow International. In fact, acquisitions have been so important that seven of the company's eight brands are the result of these moves. The company has achieved significant success in the consumer products arena.

Church & Dwight faced the same dilemma as other competitors in mature domestic and international markets for consumer products. New consumer products had to muscle their way into markets by taking market share from larger competitors' current offerings. With the majority of company sales concentrated in the United States and Canada where sales were funneled through mass merchandisers, such as Wal-Mart (accounting for 22% of sales), supermarkets, wholesale clubs, and drugstores, it was well-equipped to gain market share with its low-cost strategy. In the international arena where growth was more product-driven and less marketing sensitive, the company was less experienced. To compensate for this weakness, Church & Dwight relied on acquisitions and management changes to improve its international footprint and reach.

With its new stable of products and expanded laundry detergent offerings, Church & Dwight found itself competing head-on with both domestic and international consumer product giants such as Clorox, Colgate-Palmolive, Procter & Gamble, and Unilever. The breadth of its expanded consumer product offerings, composed of 60% premium and 40% value brand names.

According to Minton, as the company grew, "We have made every effort to keep costs under control and manage frugally."[10] A good example of this approach to doing business can be seen in the Armkel partnership. "Armkel borrowed money on a non-recourse basis so a failure would have no impact on Church & Dwight, taking any risk away from shareholders."[11] As mentioned previously, the remaining interest in Armkel was purchased in 2005. This important move cleared the way to increase marketing efforts behind Trojan, a brand which controlled 71% of the market.[12]

As more and more products were added to the consumer line-up, Church & Dwight brought many of its marketing tasks in-house as well as stepping out with groundbreaking and often controversial marketing campaigns. The first major in-house marketing project was in dental care. Although it entered a crowded field of specialty dental products, Church & Dwight rode the crest of increasing interest by both dentists and hygienists in baking soda for maintaining dental health—enabling it to sneak up on the industry giants. The company moved rapidly from the position of a niche player in the toothpaste market to that of a major competitor.

In a groundbreaking marketing campaign that some considered controversial, the company aired commercials for condoms on prime-time television. The campaign was controversial and targeted people who don't think they need to use condoms. Other campaigns, such as when the Trojan brand advertised its own stimulus package at the same time as the federal stimulus package was enacted, stated, "because we believe we should ride out these hard times together."[13] A Valentine's Day ad featuring condoms in place of candy in a heart-shaped box of chocolates continued to highlight the shock theme.[14]

The company's increasing marketing strength caught the attention of potential partners, as is evidenced by its partnership with Quidel Corporation, a provider of point-of-care diagnostic tests, to meet women's health and wellness needs. "The partnership combined Church & Dwight's strength in the marketing, distribution, and sales of consumer products with Quidel's strength in the development and manufacture of rapid diagnostic tests."[15] Other product tie-ins, especially with ARM & HAMMER Baking Soda, have been created with air filter, paint, and vacuum cleaner bag brands.

For the most part, Church & Dwight's acquired products and entries into the consumer products market have met with success. However, potential marketing problems may be looming on the horizon for its ARM & HAMMER line of consumer products. The company could be falling into the precarious line-extension snare. Placing a well-known brand name on a wide variety of products could cloud the brand's image, leading to consumer confusion and loss of marketing pull. In addition, competition in the company's core laundry detergent market continues to heat up as the market matures and sales fall with major retailers such as Wal-Mart and Target wringing price concessions from all producers.[16] Will the addition of such well-known brand names as Orajel, OxiClean, and Spinbrush continue the momentum gained from the Xtra, Nair, Trojan, and First Response additions? Where would new avenues for their consumer products' growth come from?

Specialty Products

In addition to a large and growing stable of consumer products, Church & Dwight also has a very solid core of specialty products. The Specialty Products Division basically consists of the manufacture and sale of sodium bicarbonate for three distinct market segments: specialty chemicals, animal nutrition products, and specialty cleaners. Manufacturers utilize sodium bicarbonate performance products as a leavening agent for commercial baked goods; an antacid in pharmaceuticals; a chemical in kidney dialysis; a carbon dioxide release agent in fire extinguishers; and an alkaline in swimming pool chemicals, detergents, and various textile and tanning applications. Animal feed producers use sodium bicarbonate nutritional products predominantly as a buffer, or antacid, for dairy cattle feeds and make a nutritional supplement that enhances milk production of dairy cattle. Sodium bicarbonate has also been used as an additive to poultry feeds to enhance feed efficiency.

"Church & Dwight has long maintained its leadership position in the industry through a strategy of sodium bicarbonate product differentiation, which hinges on the development of special grades for specific end users."[17] Management's apparent increased focus on consumer products has only recently impacted the significance of specialty products in the overall corporate mix of revenues, as is shown in **Exhibit 4**.

Church & Dwight was in an enviable position to profit from its dominant niche in the sodium bicarbonate products market since it controlled the primary raw material used in its production. The primary ingredient in sodium bicarbonate is produced from the mineral trona, which is extracted from the company's mines in southwestern Wyoming. The other ingredient, carbon dioxide, is a readily available chemical that can be obtained from a variety of sources. Production of the final product, sodium bicarbonate, for both consumer and specialty products is completed at one of the two company plants located in Green River, Wyoming, and Old Fort, Ohio.

The company maintained a dominant position in the production of the required raw materials for both its consumer and industrial products. It manufactures almost two-thirds of the sodium bicarbonate sold in the United States and, until recently, was the only U.S. producer of ammonium bicarbonate and potassium carbonate. The company has the largest share (approximately 75%) of the sodium bicarbonate capacity in the United States and is the largest consumer of baking soda as it fills its own needs for company-produced consumer and industrial products.[18]

The Specialty Products Division focused on developing new uses for the company's core product, sodium bicarbonate. Additional opportunities continue to be explored for ARMEX Blast Media. This is a sodium bicarbonate–based product used as a paint-stripping compound. It gained widespread recognition when it was utilized successfully for the delicate task of stripping the accumulation of years of paint and tar from the interior of the Statue of Liberty without damaging the fragile copper skin. It is now being considered for other specialized applications

EXHIBIT 4
Revenues by Product Category as a Percent of Net Sales: Church & Dwight Co. Inc.

	2009	2008	2007	2006	2005	2004
Consumer domestic						
Household	47	45	45	43	41	47
Personal car	27	26	26	29	29	27
Consumer international	16	17	17	17	17	12
Specialty products	10	12	12	11	13	14
Total	100	100	100	100	100	100

SOURCES: Company records.

in the transportation and electronics industries and in industrial cleaning because of its apparent environmental safety. ARMEX also has been introduced into international markets.

Specialty cleaning products are found in blasting (similar to sand blasting applications) as well as many emerging aqueous-based cleaning technologies such as automotive parts cleaning and circuit board cleaning. Safety-Kleen and Church & Dwight teamed up through a 50–50 joint venture, ARMAKLEEN, to meet the parts cleaning needs of automotive repair shops. Safety-Kleen's 2800 strong sales and service team markets Church & Dwight's aqueous-based cleaners as an environmentally friendly alternative to traditional solvent-based cleaners.[19]

The company's ARMAKLEEN product is also used for cleaning printed circuit boards. This nonsolvent-based product may have an enormous potential market because it may be able to replace chlorofluorocarbon-based cleaning systems. Sodium bicarbonate also has been used to remove lead from drinking water and, when added to water supplies, coats the inside of pipes and prevents lead from leaching into the water. This market could grow in significance with additions to the Clean Water Bill. The search for new uses of sodium bicarbonate from pharmaceutical to environmental protection continues in both the consumer and industrial products divisions.

International Operations

Church & Dwight has traditionally enjoyed a great deal of success in North American markets and is attempting to gain footholds in international markets through acquisitions. The company's first major attempt to expand its presence in the international consumer products market was with the acquisition of DeWitt International Corporation, which manufactured and marketed personal care products including toothpaste. The DeWitt acquisition not only provided the company with increased international exposure but also with much-needed toothpaste production facilities and technology. However, until the 2001 acquisition of the Carter-Wallace line of products, only about 10% of sales were outside the United States. By 2009, 19% of revenue was derived from sales outside the United States. Most of the growth in international markets was being fueled by consumer products.

As the company cautiously moved into the international arena of consumer products, it also continued to pursue expansion of its specialty products into international markets. Attempts to enter international markets have met with limited success, probably for two reasons: (1) lack of name recognition and (2) transportation costs. Although ARM & HAMMER was one of the most recognized brand names in the United States (in the top 10), it did not enjoy the same name recognition elsewhere. In addition, on a historic basis, international transportation costs were at least four times as much as domestic transportation costs. However, export opportunities continued to present themselves, as 10% of all U.S. production of sodium bicarbonate was exported. While Church & Dwight dominated the United States sodium bicarbonate market, Solvay Chemicals was the largest producer in Europe and Ashi Glass was the largest producer in Asia. Although demand was particularly strong in Asia, Church & Dwight did not export sodium bicarbonate to Asia because of the high transportation costs involved.

Streamlining

Two significant projects were completed in 2009. One was the completion and startup of a major new manufacturing facility, and the other was the disposition of some non-core assets.

With the completion of a 1.1 million square foot manufacturing plant for laundry detergent, the company consolidated into one facility the functions that had previously been completed in five separate facilities with room to grow. This move took place in an industry facing slowing growth. Global laundry detergent sales had grown by 8% between 2003 and 2008, but were only forecast to grow by 3% between 2008 and 2013.[20]

Although the company had made some minor asset sales in the past, the disposition in 2009 of five domestic and international consumer product brands acquired during the 2008 Del Laboratories transaction marked the first major jettisoning of non-core assets for the company. This was followed by the disposition of the Lambert Kay pet supplies line, and then the Brillo brand in March of 2010. These changes were just the beginning. To remain competitive in a volatile retail market with major competitors jockeying for shelf space and retailers seeking to rationalize their breadth of product offerings, more changes may be considered.

The core business and foundation on which the company was built remained the same after more than 160 years. However, as management looks to the future, can it successfully achieve a balancing act based on finding growth through expanded uses of sodium bicarbonate while assimilating a divergent group of consumer products into an expanding international footprint? Will the current portfolio of products continue to deliver the same results in the face of competitors who, unlike consumers, know the company and must react to its strategic and tactical moves?

NOTES

1. *Church & Dwight Co. Inc. Annual Report*, 2009, p. 2.
2. *Church & Dwight Co. Inc. Annual Report*, 2005, p. 3.
3. *Church & Dwight Co. Inc. Annual Report*, 2009, p. 5.
4. Ibid.
5. Minton, Dwight Church, personal interview, October 2, 2002.
6. *8-K*, 2006.
7. *Church & Dwight Co. Inc. Proxy Statement*, 2004.
8. *Church & Dwight Co. Inc. Annual Report*, 2006, p. 3.
9. *10-k*, 2006, p. 20.
10. Minton, Dwight Church, personal interview, October 2, 2002.
11. Ibid.
12. Jack Neff, "Trojan," *Advertising Age* 76 (November 7, 2005).
13. "BEST of BRANDFREAK 2010," *Brandweek* 50 (December 14, 2009), p. 58.
14. Stuart Elliot, "This Campaign Is Wet (and Wild)," *The New York Times on the Web* (February 9, 2010), Business/Financial Desk; CAMPAIGN SPOTLIGHT.
15. Press release, 2006, p. 1.
16. Doris de Guzman, "Household Products Struggle," *Chemical Market Reporter* 269 (2006).
17. *Church & Dwight Co. Inc. Annual Report*, 2000, p. 17.
18. Lisa Jarvis, "Church & Dwight Builds Sales Through Strength in Bicarbonate," *Chemical Market Report* 257 (April 10, 2002).
19. Helena Harvilicz, "C&D's Industrial Cleaning Business Continues to Grow," *Chemical Market Reporter* 257 (May 15, 2000).
20. Kerri Walsh, "Stocking Up on Innovation," *Chemical Week* (January 18–25, 2010), p. 19.

CASE **20**

Under Armour

Ram Subramanian
Montclair State University

Pradeep Gopalakrishna
Lubin School of Business Pace University

Kevin A. Plank, the founder and Chief Executive Officer of Under Armour (UA), reviewed the press briefing that was to accompany the company's release of the financial performance for the second quarter of fiscal 2010. Plank noted that the second quarter saw the second consecutive decline in footwear sales. UA's footwear sales had declined by 4.5% over second quarter 2009 and was showing a 16.6% decline for the first six months of 2010 over 2009. This was in contrast to apparel, the company's core category, which saw a 32.2% uptick over 2009, and accessories that had gone up by 28% (**Table 1** shows summary performance for the first two quarters of fiscal 2010).[1]

TABLE 20–1	Under Armour's Summary Financials for First Two Quarters of 2010 (in US$ millions)			
	First Quarter 2010	**First Quarter 2009**	**Second Quarter 2010**	**Second Quarter 2009**
Apparel	172,636	132,239	150,205	112,040
Footwear	42,958	56,931	35,820	37,496
Accessories	7,518	5,776	8,857	7,012
Licensing	6,295	5,054	9,904	8,100
Total	229,407	200,000	204,786	164,648

SOURCE: Under Armour 10Q, 2010.

Industry Background

The Sporting Goods Manufacturers Association (SGMA) projected the industry's revenues in the United States to hit US$75.03 billion (wholesale) in 2010, an increase of 4.5% over 2009.[2] Sports apparel and athletic footwear were two important industry categories. Sports apparel accounted for approximately US$30 billion in revenues and was projected to grow at 2.4%, while footwear was US$12.9 billion with a projected growth rate of 5.1%. The women's segment of the sports apparel category was the fastest growing industry segment with an anticipated 42% growth rate. The sporting goods industry was cyclical in nature and was impacted by the macroeconomic business cycle. There was a high correlation between disposable income and industry sales. The 4.3% drop in 2009 industry revenues over 2008 was due to the 2008–2009 recession, and as the economy recovers so will consumer spending on fitness and athletic apparel.

Ten brands accounted for 30% of the sports apparel market share. The rest were spread out among numerous small companies that focused on specific segments. Apparel made from synthetic products was the fastest growing segment of the sports apparel market. This category was referred to as "performance apparel" (the category created by UA), and products in this category were purchased for use in active sports or exercise. Performance apparel consisted of apparel that provided compression, moisture management, and temperature control.

The sports apparel market was fragmented, with Nike (16.4% market share in 2008) and Adidas (13.8%) accounting for less than one-third of the market. Champion, a brand owned by Hanesbrands Inc., was regarded as an up-and-coming player in this segment. The performance apparel segment was concentrated with UA holding a 78% market share in 2009.[3]

The athletic footwear market was dominated by Nike and Adidas (that also owned the Reebok brand). In 2009, Nike had an estimated 35% market share, Adidas 22%, followed by New Balance and Puma.[4]

Sporting goods companies typically designed the product and outsourced manufacturing to contract manufacturers in various Asian countries. In the footwear segment, Vietnam, China, and Indonesia were the leading countries for contract manufacture, while China, Thailand, and Indonesia were the most used by sports apparel companies. Many leading sporting goods companies (Nike, Adidas, and UA, among them) sourced inputs (such as synthetic rubber and fiber, leather, and canvas) to take advantage of purchasing power and pass on the inputs to the contract manufacturers. Nike, for example, also used a Japanese company for global procurement of key inputs. The contract manufacturers were responsible for shipping the finished products either to the client (for sale through company stores or online) or to the warehouses of retail chains. All the leading sporting goods companies had local offices to monitor their contract manufacturers.

Sporting goods were sold in the United States through department stores (such as Sears), mass merchandisers (such as Target and Wal-Mart), sports specialty chains (such as Dick's Sporting Goods, Modell's, and The Sports Authority), and thousands of independent stores, both freestanding and mall-based.[5] According to Standard & Poor's, in 2009,[6] sports specialty stores accounted for 30% of sporting goods sales, followed by 22% for mass merchandisers, and 14% for department stores. Internet retailers, factory stores, and independent outlets accounted for the rest of the retail sales. Leading companies in the industry sold their products through a wide variety of channels, including company owned "flagship" and factory-outlet stores, as well as via the Internet. Consumers faced a number of choices in each category of sporting goods, with some categories like athletic footwear offering 30 plus well-known brands. Sporting goods companies competed on a variety of price points, with most product categories offering some variation of the "good," "better," "best" possibilities.

Competitors

UA regarded its key competitors as Nike and adidas. In addition, Champion competed with UA in the apparel category.

Nike[7]

Founded in 1964 by Bill Bowerman and Phil Knight, Nike was the world's leading supplier of athletic footwear and apparel. It reported revenues of US$19.014 billion, gross margins of 46.3%, and net income of US$1.907 billion in 2010. It sold US$10.332 billion worth of footwear, US$5.037 of apparel, and US$1.035 million of equipment (the rest of the revenues came from licensing and its other brands such as Cole Haan). Fifty-eight percent of its revenues came from international markets. It sold its products in over 170 countries., and it employed around 30,000 people. The company identified its target market as any individual playing a sport anywhere in the world. It's slogan in this regard was, "If you have a body, you are an athlete." Nike was positioned as a premium brand and the company sought to maximize its brand equity. It sold through 23,000 U.S. and 24,000 international outlets. Its 2010 marketing budget was US$2.356 billion. The company's athletic endorsers included Tiger Woods, Kobe Bryant, LeBron James, and Cristiano Ronaldo. In its 2010 annual report, Nike's CEO, Mark Parker, spoke about China being the next great opportunity for the company. In addition, he identified "action sports" as a key growth category and emphasized the need to leverage the company's Nike, Converse, and Hurley brands in this category. He spoke about the strength of the Nike brand:

> *"The NIKE brand will always be our greatest competitive advantage. It's the source of our most advanced R&D. It delivers insight and scale and leverage to every NIKE, Inc. brand and business. It's the source of our culture and personality that connects so strongly with consumers around the world. The NIKE brand is a source of instant credibility and opportunity that we never take for granted."*[8]

adidas[9]

The Adidas Group was a Germany-based global industry leader. It was the largest athletic products company in Europe and second in the world, after Nike. It reported 2009 revenues of 10.381 billion euros, a gross profit of 4.712 billion euros, and net income of 245 million euros. It employed 39,596 people and sold products under the adidas, Reebok, Rockport, and Taylor Made brand names. It used leading athletes such as Lionel Messi and David Beckham to endorse its products. Each of the company's subsidiaries created brands that catered to specific target markets, such as Taylor Made for golf, Rockport for the metropolitan professional, and Reebok Classic for the lifestyle consumer.

Champion[10]

Champion, a leading sports apparel company, was part of Hanesbrands, Inc. Hanesbrands, Inc. was spun off from Sara Lee Corporation and owned brands such as Hanes, Champion, Playtex, and L'eggs. Champion competed in the sports apparel and performance sports apparel segments with T-shirts, shorts, fleece, sports bras, and thermals. The company obtained 89% of its revenues from the United States. It reported revenues of US$3.691 billion in fiscal 2010, gross profits of US$1.265 billion, and net income of US$51.83 million. It employed 47,400 employees.

Under Armour's History[11]

In 1995, Kevin Plank was a walk-on special teams player for the University of Maryland football team. He played on the field goal, punting, and kicking teams. At 5'11" and 228 pounds, Plank tended to sweat a lot during the long, arduous practice sessions. Frustrated by being weighed down by the accumulated sweat in his cotton T-shirt, Plank began to search for alternatives. He began looking for synthetic material that would wick the sweat from his body and make him lighter and faster. He took various promising fabrics to a local fabric store to be sewn as a T-shirt. After spending US$450 on seven prototypes, Plank found a fabric usually used in women's lingerie to work very well as a tight-fitting compression T-shirt. The T-shirt (inner wear) wicked away sweat, thus keeping the outerwear light. Plank used his savings of US$17,000 from a campus flower business to order 500 shirts. Plank gave these shirts to his high school and college teammates and also mailed them to college and professional football player friends from around the country. Plank talked about the importance of player recommendation to the success of the startup company.

These early influencers included Jim Druckenmiller, then a backup quarterback for the San Francisco 49ers, and his teammate, Frank Wycheck (a teammate of Plank's at the University of Maryland). The first big exposure for Plank came serendipitously. A front-page photograph in *USA Today* of then–Oakland Raiders quarterback, Jeff George, showed George wearing the UA mock turtleneck T-shirt visibly under his uniform. This surprised Plank because he hadn't sent a sample to George. While the George photograph gave the fledgling company publicity, it did not turn into sales. Plank sent samples to every equipment manager in the Atlantic Coast Conference. His first big break came when the equipment manager for Georgia Tech University placed an order for 350 T-shirts. North Carolina State University followed with an order and the network of equipment managers soon resulted in sales to other colleges and National Football League teams.

Further exposure came with the release of Oliver Stone's football movie *Any Given Sunday*. Plank had heard about the movie from a former high school classmate and sent samples of his product to the costume designer. It resulted in the movie's star, Jamie Foxx wearing a UA jockstrap prominently in a locker room scene. Anticipating publicity from the movie, Plank paid US$25,000 for an advertisement in *ESPN The Magazine*. The advertisement generated orders worth US$750,000 and the three-year old company was on its way. In effect, Plank had created, using US$17,000 of his own cash and a US$40,000 credit card debt, a new category of sports apparel, one that focused on the athlete's performance, and hence dubbed "performance apparel."

Plank talked about how the company was able to create an entirely new category:

> *"Analysts often ask me: "How was the door left so wide open for UA's entry into the industry?" I tell them that my many detractors did not think consumers would pay $25 to $35 for a T-shirt. But, when you give consumers some tangible benefit, you're able to reinvent entire product categories."*[12]

Plank took the company public in a 2005 IPO. Under Armour was granted the rights to outfit the fictitious Dillon Panthers high school football team when the television show *Friday Night Lights* premiered in 2006 on NBC. The company, headquartered in Baltimore, Maryland, had a market cap of US$2.28 billion in September 2010. Plank owned 25% of UA shares and also controlled 77% of the company's voting shares.[13]

Under Armour's Activities

Products[14]

UA sold products in three categories: apparel, footwear, and accessories (**Table 2** contains a sample list of UA's products). UA sold a wide variety of innerwear and outerwear in the apparel segment, a broad line of footwear, and a line of accessories for both men and women.

UA's price points were comparable to those of competitors like Nike, adidas, and Champion (**Table 3** provides a price comparison of selected products for UA and its competitors).

Under Armour created the performance apparel segment, a sub-segment of the sports apparel category, and had a 78% market in 2009. UA's core apparel product was the tight-fitting compression T-shirt. It was a three-layered synthetic fabric that used moisture wicking technology to speed up the evaporation of sweat.

In tests, UA demonstrated that its T-shirt was 52% lighter than a cotton T-shirt after 60 minutes of exercise. In addition, tests indicated that a UA T-shirt released 80% of its moisture after 30 minutes, in comparison to a cotton T-shirt that released 39% of its moisture after the same period. UA's T-shirt was also able to keep the body 3.5 degrees cooler than cotton.[15]

The initial product was marketed as HeatGear. The same microfiber technology was used to develop a line of cold weather T-shirts called ColdGear. In 2010, UA had additional

TABLE 20–2   Sample List of Under Armour Products

Apparel

Men
- ColdGear Longsleeve Mock
- Men's Armour Fleece
- UA Tech Short Sleeve
- ColdGear Action Legging
- UA Barrage Jacket (Rainwear)
- HeatGear Zone Socks

Footwear
- Men's UA Fleet (Running)
- Women's UA Proto Interval (Training)
- Men's UA Blur (Football)
- Men's UA Twin Bill II Mid (Baseball)

Women
- UA Victory Burnout T
- UA HeartGear Fitted Shortsleeve
- UA Form Cardio Tank
- UA Duplicity (A/B Cup)
- UA Surge Jacket (Rainwear)
- QuickStep Lo Cut Liner socks

Accessories
- Men's Cage III Batting Glove (Baseball)
- Thief (Eyewear)
- UA Surge Backpack
- Performance Bottle (Water Bottle)

SOURCE: www.underarmour.com

TABLE 20–3   Sample Price Comparison Apparel

Apparel Type	Nike	Under Armour	Champion
Men's Graphic Tee	$25.00	$24.99	$11.99
Men's Jersey	$30.00	$34.99	$40.00
Men's Shorts	$22.00	$24.99	$22.00
Women's Short Sleeve Tee	$20.00	$19.99	$22.00
Women's Track Pant	$60.00	$54.99	$40.00

| | Footwear | | |
Shoe Type	Nike	Under Armour	adidas
Men's Football Cleats	$129.99	$119.99	$99.99
Men's Baseball Cleats	$104.99	$ 99.99	$89.99
Men's Performance Training Shoes	$ 89.99	$ 89.99	$99.99
Women's Running Shoes	$ 89.99	$ 84.99	$84.99
Women's Performance Training Shoes	$ 84.99	$ 89.99	$75.00

SOURCE: Company websites and www.dickssportinggoods.com

products embodying the same technology and was sold under the LooseGear and AllSeasons-Gear trade names. In addition to the microfiber technology for temperature control, UA also developed "Lockertag" technology to prevent skin irritation from tags and labels. UA's technology heat-sealed the label onto the shirt, thereby preventing the irritation caused by the tag rubbing against the skin. The company's other product technologies included UA Metal and UA Tech for men, and Duplicity Sports Bras for women.

UA sold a line of sports accessories that featured items such as sweatbands, headbands, running goggles, backpacks, and water bottles.

The footwear line was launched in 2006 in the form of football cleats, followed by baseball cleats. The company soon established itself as the number-two player (in terms of market share) behind Nike in the niche segment of athletic cleats. A four-product running shoe line (running shoes were a US$5 billion market and the largest segment in athletic footwear) was launched on January 31, 2009. The running shoes featured a proprietary technology, Cartilage, that has, according to a company press release, an "independent suspension system [that] serves as the connective tissue between a runner and his environment to enhance performance and provide an exceptionally stable and smooth ride." Plank believes that Under Armour will surpass Nike as the preferred brand of today's teenagers.

In spite of the high-profile launch, Under Armour couldn't meet their sales expectations for running shoes. UA replaced its head of footwear operations and decided to revamp the line. The company had to mark down its prices to clear inventory, and Wall Street responded by pummeling its stock price. UA announced that it was forgoing any new footwear launch until late 2010 or early 2011. Plank cautioned analysts to be patient while the company navigated its way through the 18-month cycle necessary to bring new models to market.

Operations[16]

UA outsourced almost all of its manufacturing to contract manufacturers in Asia and Latin America. In 2009, 22 manufacturers operating in 17 countries manufactured the company's products. A team from UA evaluated potential contract manufacturers on quality, social compliance, and financial strength prior to certifying them. UA's Hong Kong and Guangzhou, China offices supported and monitored the company's outsourced manufacturing activities for apparel and footwear. Manufacturers procured raw materials (specialty fabrics, canvas, etc.) and provided finished products to the company's distribution facilities. Manufacturing contracts were typically for the short-term and UA ensured that it had multiple manufacturers for a single product.

UA operated a small manufacturing facility in Glen Burnie, Maryland, called Special Make-Up Shop. This 17,000-square-foot shop manufactured apparel products for the company's high-profile athletes, leagues, and teams. The purpose of this operation was to provide superior (and quick) service to special customers. The company treated the cost of operating this facility as a marketing expense.

Distribution[17]

UA operated two leased distribution facilities in Glen Burnie, Maryland, a short distance away from the company's headquarters in Baltimore, Maryland. The first was a 359,000-square-foot facility, while the second occupied 308,000 square feet. Products were shipped to retailers and company stores via a third-party logistics provider, both in the United States and in Europe. Inventory management was critical because of two factors. Industry practice was for retailers to return defective or improperly shipped merchandise. In addition, because of overseas sourcing, the lead times for design and production was long, which meant that production orders were to be made much before customer orders for new products.

Marketing

UA's 2009 annual report summed up the company's vision as: "The athletic brand of this generation. And next." To guide its marketing, UA also developed a brand mission: "To make all athletes better through passion, science and the relentless pursuit of innovation." UA spent between 12% and 13% of revenues on marketing.[18]

The market for sporting apparel and gear spanned the entire population, although primary users were the sports-oriented and/or active and health conscious segments. Young males constituted a large segment of this market, although recent trends indicated an upsurge in the female and older age group segments. UA targeted individuals in the 15–25 age group.

From the inception of UA, Plank relied on what he called "influencers" to market his products. After high school, determined to get a scholarship to play Division I football, Plank enrolled in Fork Union Military Academy to bulk up, play with top high school athletes, and attract the attention of major programs. Fork Union Military Academy was well-known as a "football mill," that sent a lot of athletes to the top college football programs. The contacts that Plank made at Fork helped him select his first influencers.

An early series of influencers included former and current NFL players such as Jim Druckenmiller, Frank Wycheck, and Eddie George. Later influencers included Brandon Jacobs (of the NFL New York Giants), Heather Mitts (U.S. women's soccer player), Brandon Jennings (of the NBA Milwaukee Bucks), and Lindsay Vonn (a gold medal–winning U.S. skier from the Vancouver Olympics). Plank's former teammate, Eric Ogbogu (who played seven years in the NFL and was dubbed "The Big E") was the company's brand spokesman.

UA's marketing budget was spent on athlete influencers, print, digital and television advertising, and payments to college teams to wear the company's products. Steve Battista, UA's senior vice president of brand, wanted UA's ads featuring professional athletes wearing Under Armour apparel to come across as similar to comic book superheroes.

UA's signature commercial "Protect This House" was featured in numerous college football and NFL stadiums in both print and video forms. Other commercials included "Click-Clack, I Think You Hear Us Coming" (for the footwear line launch), "Athlete's Run" (for running shoes), and "Protect This House, I Will" (for the women's line of products). UA was the official outfitter for around 50 universities (including Auburn University, University of Maryland, and Texas Tech University), while Nike had over a 100 universities under contract. UA paid its universities for the privilege of being named the "Official Outfitter."[19]

UA priced its products competitively on a par with Nike and adidas. The company supported its product positioning with a policy of full retail pricing, rarely allowing its brand to be discounted. The idea was to add to the company's up-market appeal and position its brand as distinct from competing brands. UA, however, was forced to discount its prices in the running shoe line because of overstock.

In 2009, UA generated approximately 78% of its revenues from its U.S. wholesale distribution channel. UA was highly dependent on its two primary retailers—Dick's Sporting Goods and The Sports Authority—which accounted for 30% of its wholesale distribution. In addition to the two retailers, UA also sold through stores such as Modell's Sporting Goods, Academy Sports and Outdoors in the United States, and Sportcheck International and Sportsman International in Canada. UA's distribution channels also included independent and specialty retailers, institutional athletic departments, leagues and teams, and company-owned stores, as well as its website. When UA got into footwear, it extended its distribution to include footwear chains such as Finish Line and Foot Locker. Worldwide, UA sold its product in over 20,000 stores.

Personnel[20]

In September 2010, UA employed approximately 3,000 people. About half of the employees worked at the company's manufacturing facility, the Special Make-Up Shop, and various company-owned stores. The rest worked at UA's distribution facilities and the corporate headquarters. The company's employees were non-unionized. The company reported that in 2008 it received about 26,000 resumes, of which it hired 215 employees.

Eight executives made up UA's top management team. Kevin A. Plank was the President, Chief Executive Officer, and Chairman of the Board, Wayne A. Marino was the Chief Operating Officer, and Brad Dickerson was the Chief Financial Officer. The operations of the company were divided into apparel (led by Senior Vice President, Henry B. Stafford) and footwear (headed by Senior Vice President, Gene McCarthy). Distribution was the responsibility of Dan J. Sawall (Vice President of Retail), and John S. Rogers (Vice President/General manager of e-Commerce). Finally, Kevin Plank's older brother, J. Scott Plank headed the company's domestic and global business development efforts as an Executive Vice President.

Culture

Football, the sport that gave UA its start, not only dominated the company's product categories, but also permeated its culture. For example, employees were referred to as "teammates." Further, posted on the walls of company offices were "Under Armour Huddles," short, pithy statements that provided guidance to all. Examples were "manage the clock," "execute the play," and "run the huddle."

Plank himself set the aggressive tone for the company by never considering UA to be too small to take on giants such as Nike.

Plank and Marino, the COO, had developed a tradition of meeting at Plank's house every Saturday morning at 6:00 A.M. Accompanied by personal trainers, the two would engage in a strenuous physical workout while talking about UnderArmour.

Tori Hanna, UA's director of women's sports marketing, talked about how Plank's belief in playing offense even in a tough economy percolated throughout the company.

Finances

Table 4 contains UA's financials for the last three years. The company broke down its revenues into apparel, footwear, accessories, and licensing.[21] It did not, however, provide category-wise operating margins. The company explained that the 2009 decline in gross profit margins was due to a less favorable footwear and apparel product mix and the liquidation of unsold footwear inventory. The company's finances were affected by seasonality with the last two quarters showing better numbers because of the Fall football season. The company did not break down revenues geographically, although one report indicated that in 2009, UA obtained nearly 94% of its revenues from the United States and Canada.

TABLE 4	Under Armour's Financial Statements Consolidated Balance Sheets (In thousands, except share data)		
	December 31, 2009	**December 31, 2008**	**December 31, 2007**
Assets			
Current assets			
Cash and cash equivalents	$ 187,297	102,042	40,588
Accounts receivable, net	79,356	81,302	93,515
Inventories	148,888	182,232	166,082
Prepaid expenses and other current assets	19,989	18,023	11,642
Deferred income taxes	12,870	12,824	10,418
Total current assets	448,000	396,423	322,245
Property and equipment, net	72,926	73,548	52,332
Intangible assets, net	5,681	5,470	6,470
Deferred income taxes	13,908	8,687	8,173
Other long term assets	5,073	3,427	1,393
Total assets	$ 545,588	487,555	390,613
Liabilities and Stockholders' Equity			
Current liabilities			
Revolving credit facility	$ —	25,000	—
Accounts payable	68,710	72,435	55,012
Accrued expenses	40,885	25,905	36,111
Current maturities of long-term debt	9,178	7,072	4,111
Current maturities of capital lease obligations	97	361	465
Other current liabilities	1,292	2,337	—
Total current liabilities	120,162	133,110	95,699
Long-term debt, net of current maturities	10,948	13,061	9,298
Capital lease obligations, net of current maturities	—	97	458
Other long-term liabilities	14,481	10,190	4,673
Total liabilities	$ 145,591	156,458	110,128
Stockholders' equity			
Class A Common Stock, $.0003 1/3 par value; 100,000,000 shares authorized as of December 31, 2009 and 2008; 37,747,647 shares issued and outstanding as of December 31, 2009 and 36,808,750 shares issued and outstanding as of December 31, 2008	13	12	12
Class B Convertible Common Stock, $.0003 1/3 par value; 12,500,000 shares authorized, issued and outstanding as of December 31, 2009 and 2008	4	4	4
Additional paid-in capital	197,342	174,725	162,362
Retained earnings	202,188	156,011	117,782
Unearned compensation	(14)	(60)	(182)
Accumulated other comprehensive income	464	405	507
Total stockholders' equity	399,997	331,097	280,485
Total liabilities and stockholders' equity	$ 545,588	487,555	390,613

SOURCE: Under Armour Annual Report, 2009.

Consolidated Statements of Income (In thousands, except per-share amounts)

	December 31, 2009	December 31, 2008	December 31, 2007
Net revenues	$856,411	725,244	606,561
Cost of goods sold	443,386	370,296	301,517
Gross profit	413,025	354,948	305,044
Operating expenses			
Selling, general, and administrative expenses	327,752	278,023	218,779
Income from operations	85,273	76,925	86,265
Interest income (expense), net	(2,344)	(850)	749
Other income (expense), net	(511)	(6,175)	2,029
Income before income taxes	82,418	69,900	89,043
Provision for income taxes	35,633	31,671	36,485
Net income	$ 46,785	38,229	52,558
Net income available per common share			
Basic	$0.94	0.78	1.09
Diluted	$0.92	0.76	1.05
Weighted average common shares outstanding			
Basic	49,848	49,086	48,345
Diluted	50,650	50,342	50,141

SOURCE: Under Armour Annual Report, 2009.

Consolidated Statements of Cash Flows (In thousands)

	December 31, 2009	December 31, 2008	December 31, 2007
Cash flows from operating activities			
Net income	$46,785	38,229	52,558
Adjustments to reconcile net income to net cash provided by (used in) operating activities: Depreciation and amortization	28,249	21,347	14,622
Unrealized foreign currency exchange rate (gains) losses	(5,222)	5,459	(2,567)
Loss on disposal of property and equipment	37	15	—
Stock-based compensation	12,910	8,466	4,182
Deferred income taxes	(5,212)	(2,818)	(4,909)
Changes in reserves for doubtful accounts, returns, discounts and inventories	1,623	8,711	4,551
Changes in operating assets and liabilities:			
Accounts receivable	3,792	2,634	(24,222)
Inventories	32,998	(19,497)	(83,966)
Prepaid expenses and other assets	1,870	(7,187)	(2,067)
Accounts payable	(4,386)	16,957	11,873
Accrued expenses and other liabilities	11,656	(5,316)	11,825
Income taxes payable and receivable	(6,059)	2,516	3,492
Net cash provided by (used in) operating activities	119,041	69,516	(14,628)

(Continued)

	December 31, 2009	December 31, 2008	December 31, 2007
Cash flows from investing activities			
Purchase of property and equipment	(19,845)	(38,594)	(33,959)
Purchase of intangible assets	—	(600)	(125)
Purchase of trust owned life insurance policies	(35)	(2,893)	—
Proceeds from sales of property and equipment	—	21	—
Purchases of short-term investments	—	—	(62,860)
Proceeds from sales of short-term investments	—	—	62,860
Net cash used in investing activities	(19,880)	(42,066)	(34,084)
Cash flows from financing activities			
Proceeds from revolving credit facility	—	40,000	14,000
Payments on revolving credit facility	(25,000)	(15,000)	(14,000)
Proceeds from long-term debt	7,649	13,214	11,841
Payments on long-term debt	(7,656)	(6,490)	(2,973)
Payments on capital lease obligations	(361)	(464)	(794)
Excess tax benefits from stock-based compensation arrangements	5,127	2,131	6,892
Proceeds from exercise of stock options and other stock issuances	5,128	1,990	3,182
Payments of debt financing costs	(1,354)	—	—
Net cash provided by (used in) financing activities	(16,467)	35,381	18,148
Effect of exchange rate changes on cash and cash equivalents	2,561	(1,377)	497
Net increase (decrease) in cash and cash equivalents	85,255	61,454	(30,067)
Cash and cash equivalents			
Beginning of year	102,042	40,588	70,655
End of year	$187,297	102,042	40,588
Non-cash financing and investing activities			
Fair market value of shares withheld in consideration of employee tax obligations relative to stock-based compensation	$ 608	—	—
Purchase of property and equipment through certain obligations	4,784	2,486	1,110
Purchase of intangible asset through certain obligations	2,105	—	—
Other supplemental information			
Cash paid for income taxes	40,834	29,561	30,502
Cash paid for interest	1,273	1,444	525

SOURCE: Under Armour Annual Report, 2009.

The Pursuit of Three Percent

Several experts criticized the company's foray into footwear. Laura Ries, a marketing expert, was quite critical of UA's entry into footwear:

> *"The key to remember is that Under Armour isn't just a great brand; Under Armour pioneered and dominates a great category. Its power comes from the category it owns in the mind, not the brand name it puts on the package. "Under Armour" are the words that represent that category in mind. So putting the Under Armour brand name on another category is not going to guarantee success, especially if that category has little to do with performance clothing. Under Armour is an apparel brand. Nike is a footwear brand. Each might sell other stuff too, but the brands are rooted in these categories and can't grow too far from them. Here is a company (UA) with no credibility in athletic shoes attacking one of the world's most iconic and dominant brands for athletic footwear. Furthermore, Under Armour was doing so with no clear-cut product advantage and with a name that defined a totally different strategy."*[22]

John Horan, publisher of *Sporting Goods Intelligence*, an industry newsletter, talked about the U.S. sports apparel/footwear market becoming a duopoly with Nike and Under Armour. He believes that Under Armour is one of a very small number of companies that has successfully challenged Nike in the marketplace.

But Plank and his team were attracted by the US$31 billion international branded footwear market. Their contention was that even a 3% share of the market would nearly double UA's total revenues. They based their support of the footwear foray on the strength of UA's brand.

In addition, UA's team believed that the strong relationships they had with the distribution channel was a viable foundation to succeed in the new category.

In a number of interviews, Plank and his top management team members had reiterated the importance of the international markets for its apparel products. In fact, Plank's favorite line was "We haven't sold a single T-shirt in China." UA was a company that was largely dependent on the U.S. market for its revenues.

As Plank reflected on UA's second quarter 2010 financial results, he thought about what he wanted UA to be. Should the company attempt to be a leading athletic brand with products beyond apparel, or should UA cement its reputation as the leading U.S. performance apparel maker and extend its dominance globally?

ENDNOTES

1. Under Armour Press Release, July 27, 2010, http://investor.underarmour.com/releases.cfm.
2. http://sgma.com, extracted September 20, 2010.
3. Michels, W, How Stealth Stocks Make it Big, *The Motley Fool*, http://www.fool.com/investing/high-growth/2008/07/09/how-stealth-stocks-make-it-big.aspx, 2008, retrieved on September 20, 2010.
4. Heath, Thomas, Taking on the Giants: How Under Armour Founder Kevin Plank Is Going Head-to-Head with the Industry's Biggest Players, *The Washington Post*, January 24, 2010, www.washingtonpost.com.
5. Websites of Nike and Under Armour.
6. Standard & Poor's Industry Surveys, Apparel and Footwear: Retailers and Brands, September 3, 2009.
7. www.nike.com.
8. Ibid., 2010 Annual Report.
9. www.adidas.com.
10. www.hanesbrands.com.
11. This section is drawn from the following sources: Palmisano, Trey, From Rags to Microfiber: Inside the Rapid Rise of Under Armour, http://si.com, April 9, 2009; Dessauer, Carin, For Under Armour CEO and Kensington Native Kevin Plank, It's Always Been About the Huddle, *Bethesda Magazine*, www.bethesdamagazine.com, March 2009; De Lollis, Barbara, No Sweat: Idea for Athletic Gear Takes Him to Top, *USA Today*, December 12, 2004, http://usatoday.com; and, Heath, Thomas, op. cit.
12. Under Armour, 2006 Annual Report.
13. Yahoo Finance and Heath, Thomas, op. cit.
14. Under Armour, 2009 10K.
15. Under Armour, various 10Ks.
16. Under Armour, 2009 10K.
17. Ibid.
18. Under Armour, 2009 Annual Report.
19. Under Armour, 2009 10K.
20. Under Armour, Investor Relations Website.
21. Under Armour, 2009 10K.
22. http://ries.typepad.com/ries_blog/2009/11/under-armour-too-big-for-its-shirt.html, extracted September 28, 2010.

CASE **21**

TOMS Shoes (Mini Case)

J. David Hunger

FOUNDED IN 2006 BY BLAKE MYCOSKIE, TOMS Shoes was an American footwear company based in Santa Monica, California. Although TOMS Shoes was a for-profit business, its mission was more like that of a not-for-profit organization. The firm's reason for existence was to donate to children in need one new pair of shoes for every pair of shoes sold. Blake Mycoskie referred to it as the company's "One for One" business model.

While vacationing in Argentina during 2006, Mycoskie befriended children who had no shoes to protect them during long walks to obtain food and water, as well as attend school. Going barefoot was a common practice in rural farming regions of developing countries, where many subsistence farmers could not afford even a single pair of shoes. Mycoskie learned that going barefoot could lead to some serious health problems. Podoconiosis was one such disease in which feet and legs swelled, formed ulcers, emitted a foul smell, and caused intense pain. It affected millions of people across 10 countries in tropical Africa, Central America, and northern India. For millions, not wearing shoes could deepen the cycle of poverty and ruin lives. Upset that such a simple need was being unmet, Mycoskie founded TOMS Shoes in order to provide them the shoes they needed. "I was so overwhelmed by the spirit of the South American people, especially those who had so little,"[1] Mycoskie said. "I was instantly struck with the desire—the responsibility—to do more."[1] The name of his new venture was TOMS Shoes.

History

Blake Mycoskie started his entrepreneurial career by creating a college laundry service in 1997 when he was a student at Southern Methodist University. In his words, "After we expanded EZ Laundry to four colleges, I sold my share. I moved to Nashville to start an outdoor media company that Clear Channel scooped up three years later."[1] In 2002, Blake and his sister Paige formed a team to compete on the CBS reality show *The Amazing Race*, coming in second. One of the places that they visited during the filming was Argentina. Fascinated by South America, Blake returned to Argentina in 2006 for a vacation. "On my visit I saw lots of kids with no shoes who were suffering from injuries to their feet. I decided a business would be the most sustainable way to help, so I founded TOMS, which is short for a 'better tomorrow,'"[1] explained Mycoskie.

While in Argentina, Mycoskie had taken to wearing *alpargatas*—resilient, light-weight, slip-on shoes with a breathable canvas top and soft leather insole traditionally worn by Argentine workers, but worn casually by most people in that country. Mycoskie spent two months meeting with shoe and fabric makers in Argentina. Although he modeled his shoe after the espadrille-like alpargata, he used brighter colors and different materials. "No one looked twice at alpargatas, but I thought they had a really cool style,"[1] said Mycoskie. "I'm a fan of Vans, but they can be clunky and sweaty. These aren't. They fit your foot like a glove but are sturdy enough for a hike, the beach, or the city."[1]

Founding his new company that year in Santa Monica, California, the 30-year-old Blake Mycoskie began his third entrepreneurial venture. With a staff of seven full-time employees (including former Trovata clothing line designer John Whitledge), six sales representatives, and eight interns, TOMS Shoes introduced 15 styles of men's and women's shoes plus limited-edition artist versions in June 2006. The shoes were quickly selected for distribution by stores like American Bag and Fred Segal in Los Angeles and Scoop in New York City. By Fall 2006, the company had sold 10,000 pairs of shoes, averaging US$38 each, online and through 40 retail stores.

As promised, Mycoskie returned to Argentina in October 2006 with two dozen volunteers to give away 10,000 pairs of shoes along 2,200 miles of countryside. Mycoskie wryly explained what he learned from this experience. "I always thought that I'd spend the first half of my life making money and the second half giving it away. I never thought I could do both at the same time."[1] The next year, TOMS Shoes gave away 50,000 pairs of shoes in "shoe drops" to children in Argentina plus shoe drops to South Africa. More countries were added to the list over the next three years.

Business Model

Realizing that a not-for-profit organization would be heavily dependent upon sponsors and constant fundraising, Mycoskie chose to create an innovative for-profit business model to achieve a charitable purpose. For every pair of shoes the company sold, it would donate one pair to a child in need. Mycoskie felt that this model would be more economically sustainable than a charity because sales would be used to achieve the company's mission. He saw this to be a form of social entrepreneurship in which a new business venture acted to improve society through product donations at the same time it lived off society through its sales.

Mycoskie believed that the firm's One-for-One model would be self-sustaining because the company could make and sell shoes at a price similar to other shoe companies, but with lower costs. "Selling online (www.toms.com) has allowed us to grow pretty rapidly, but we're not going to make as much as another shoe company, and the margins are definitely lower,"[1] he admits. "But what we do helps us to get publicity. Lots of companies give a percentage of their revenue to charity, but we can't find anyone who matches one for one."[1]

Marketing and Distribution

TOMS Shoes kept expenses low by spending only minimally on marketing and promotion. The company's marketing was primarily composed of presentations by Blake Mycoskie, fan word-of-mouth, and promotional events sponsored by the firm. The company won the

2007 People's Design Award at Cooper-Hewitt's National Design Awards. Two years later, Mycoskie and TOMS received the annual ACE award given by U.S. Secretary of State Hillary Clinton. This award recognized companies' commitment to corporate social responsibility, innovation, exemplary practices, and democratic values worldwide. Mycoskie spoke along with President Bill Clinton at the Opening Plenary session of the Second Annual Clinton Global Initiative Conference in 2007. With other business leaders, he also met with President Obama's senior administration in March 2009 to present solutions and ideas to support small businesses. In addition, he was featured in a CNBC segment titled "The Entrepreneurs," in which he and TOMS Shoes was profiled.

Mycoskie explained why he spent so much time speaking to others about TOMS Shoes. "My goal is to inspire the next generation of entrepreneurs and company leaders to think differently about how they incorporate giving into their business models. Plus, many of the people who hear me speak eventually purchase a pair of Toms, share the story with others, or support our campaigns like *One Day Without Shoes*, which has people go barefoot for one day a year to raise awareness about the children we serve."

Celebrities like Olivia Wilde, Karl Lagerfeld, and Scarlett Johansson loved the brand and what it stood for. Actress Demi Moore promoted the 2010 *One Day Without Shoes* campaign on *The Tonight Show with Jay Leno*. It didn't hurt that Mycoskie's fame was supported by his Bill Clinton–like charisma, Hollywood good looks, and his living on a boat in Marina del Rey with "TOMS" sails. Famed designer Ralph Lauren asked Mycoskie to work with him on a few styles for his Rugby collection, the first time Lauren had collaborated with another brand.

TOMS Shoes and Blake Mycoskie were profiled in the *Los Angeles Times*, as well as *Inc.*, *People*, *Forbes*, *Fortune*, *Fast Company*, and *Time* magazines. Mycoskie pointed out that the 2009 *Los Angeles Times* article, "TOMS Shoes the Model: Sell 1, Give 1," resulted in 2,200 orders for shoes in just 12 hours after the article appeared. In February 2010, *FastCompany* listed TOMS Shoes as #6 on its list of "Top Ten Most Innovative Retail Companies."[1]

By early 2007, TOMS Shoes had orders from 300 retail stores, including Nordstrom's, Urban Outfitters, and Bloomingdale's, for 41,000 pairs of shoes from its spring and summer collections. The company introduced a line of children's shoes called Tiny TOMS in May 2007 and unveiled a pair of leather shoes in Fall of that year. By September 2010, the company added Whole Foods to its distribution network and had given over 1,000,000 pairs of new shoes to children in need living in more than 20 countries in the Americas (Argentina, El Salvador, Guatemala, Haiti, Honduras, Nicaragua, and Peru), Africa (Burundi, Ethiopia, Lesotho, Malawi, Mali, Niger, Rwanda, South Africa, Swaziland, Uganda, and Zambia), Asia (Cambodia and Mongolia), and Eurasia (Armenia). The shoes were now selling for US$45 to US$85 a pair.

Operations and Management

TOMS shoes were manufactured in Argentina, China, and Ethiopia. The company required the factories to operate under sound labor conditions, pay fair wages, and follow local labor standards. A code of conduct was signed by all factories. In addition to its production staff routinely visiting the factories to ensure that they were maintaining good working standards, third parties annually audited the factories. The company's original line of alpargata shoes was expanded to include children's shoes, leather shoes, cordones youth shoes, botas, and wedges. In January 2009, the company collaborated with Element Skateboards to create a line of shoes, skateboard decks, and longboards. For each pair of TOMS Element shoes and/or skateboard bought, one of the same was given to children at the Indigo Skate Camp in the village of Isithumba in Durban, South Africa.

Blake Mycoskie was the company's Chief Executive Officer and joked that he was also its "Chief Shoe Giver." He spent much of his time traveling the country to speak at universities and companies about the TOMS Shoes' business model. According to CEO Mycoskie in a June 2010 article in *Inc.*, "The reason I can travel so much is that I've put together a strong team of about ten people who pretty much lead the company while I am gone. Candice Wolfswinkel is my chief of staff and the keeper of the culture. . . . I have an amazing CFO, Jeff Tyler, and I'll check in with him twice a week. I talk to my sales managers on a weekly basis. I also call my younger brother, Tyler, a lot—he's head of corporate sales."[1] The company had 85 employees plus interns and volunteers. In 2009, more than 1000 people applied for 15 summer internship positions.

The company depended upon many volunteers to promote the company and to distribute its shoes to needy children. For example, Friends of TOMS was a registered nonprofit affiliate of TOMS Shoes that had been formed to coordinate volunteer activities and all shoe drops. The company sponsored an annual "Vagabond Tour" to reach college campuses. Volunteers were divided into five regional teams to reach campuses throughout the United States to spread information about the One-for-One movement. To capture volunteer enthusiasm, the company formed a network of college representatives at 200 schools to host events, screen a documentary about the brand, or throw shoe decorating parties.

Mycoskie believed that a key to success for his company was his generation's desire to become involved in the world. "This generation is one that thrives off of action. We don't dream about change, we make it happen. We don't imagine a way to incorporate giving into our daily lives—we do it. TOMS has so many young supporters who are passionate about the One-for-One movement, and who share the story and inspire others every day they wear their TOMS. Seeing them support this business model is proof that this generation is ready and able to create a better tomorrow."

Mission Accomplished: Next Steps?

When Blake Mycoskie originally proposed his One-for-One business model in 2006, few had much confidence in his ability to succeed. He never generated a business plan or asked for outside support. Mycoskie used the money he had earned from his earlier entrepreneurial ventures to fund the new business. Looking back on those days, Mycoskie stated, "A lot of people thought we were crazy. They never thought we could make a profit."[1] Much to everyone's surprise, TOMS Shoes had its first profitable year in 2008, only two years after being founded. The company's sales kept increasing throughout the "great recession" of 2008–2009 and continued being marginally profitable. Mycoskie admitted that the company would have to sell about a million pairs of shoes annually to be really profitable. Nevertheless, TOMS Shoes did not take on any outside investors and did not plan to do so.

In September 2010, Blake Mycoskie celebrated TOMS Shoes' total sales of one million pairs of shoes by returning to Argentina to give away the millionth pair. Looking forward to returning to where it all began, Mycoskie mused: "To reach a milestone like this is really amazing. We have been so busy giving shoes that we don't even think about the scope of what we've created and what we've done."[1]

What should be next for TOMS Shoes? Blake Mycoskie invested a huge amount of his own time, energy, and enthusiasm in the growth and success of TOMS Shoes. Was the company too dependent upon its founder? How should it plan its future growth?

NOTE

1. Source: http://www.toms.com/corporate-info

CASE 22

Best Buy Co. Inc. (2009): Sustainable Customer-Centricity Model?

Alan N. Hoffman
Bentley University

BEST BUY CO. INC., HEADQUARTERED IN RICHFIELD, MINNESOTA, was a specialty retailer of consumer electronics. It operated over 1100 stores in the United States, accounting for 19% of the market. With approximately 155,000 employees, it also ran more than 2800 stores in Canada, Mexico, China, and Turkey. The company's subsidiaries included Geek Squad, Magnolia Audio Video, and Pacific Sales. In Canada, Best Buy operated under both the Best Buy and Future Shop labels.

Best Buy's mission was to make technology deliver on its promises to customers. To accomplish this, Best Buy helped customers realize the benefits of technology and technological changes so they could enrich their lives in a variety of ways through connectivity: "To make life fun and easy,"[1] as Best Buy put it. This was what drove the company to continually increase the tools to support customers in the hope of providing end-to-end technology solutions.

As a public company, Best Buy's top objectives were sustained growth and earnings. This was accomplished in part by constantly reviewing its business model to ensure it was satisfying customer needs and desires as effectively and completely as possible. The company strived to have not only extensive product offerings but also highly trained employees with extensive product

This case was prepared by Professor Alan N. Hoffman, Bentley University and Erasmus University. Copyright © 2015 by Alan N. Hoffman. The copyright holder is solely responsible for case content. Reprint permission is solely granted to the publisher, Prentice Hall, for *Strategic Management and Business Policy*, 14th Edition (and the international and electronic versions of this book) by the copyright holder, Alan N. Hoffman. Any other publication of the case (translation, any form of electronics or other media) or sale (any form of partnership) to another publisher will be in violation of copyright law, unless Alan N. Hoffman has granted an additional written permission. Reprinted by permission. The author would like to thank MBA students Kevin Clark, Leonard D'Andrea, Amanda Genesky, Geoff Merritt, Chris Mudarri, and Dan Fowler for their research. No part of this publication may be copied, stored, transmitted, reproduced, or distributed in any form or medium whatsoever without the permission of the copyright owner, Alan N. Hoffman.

knowledge. The company encouraged its employees to go out of their way to help customers understand what these products could do and how customers could get the most out of the products they purchased. Employees recognized that each customer was unique and thus determined the best method to help that customer achieve maximum enjoyment from the product(s) purchased.

From a strategic standpoint, Best Buy moved from being a discount retailer (a low-price strategy) to a service-oriented firm that relied on a differentiation strategy. In 1989, Best Buy changed the compensation structure for sales associates from commission-based to non-commissioned-based, which resulted in consumers having more control over the purchasing process and in cost savings for the company (the number of sales associates was reduced). In 2005, Best Buy took customer service a step further by moving from peddling gadgets to a customer-centric operating model. It was now gearing up for another change to focus on store design and providing products and services in line with customers' desire for constant connectivity.

Company History[2]

From Sound of Music to Best Buy

Best Buy was originally known as Sound of Music. Incorporated in 1966, the company started as a retailer of audio components and expanded to retailing video products in the early 1980s with the introduction of the videocassette recorder to its product line. In 1983, the company changed its name to Best Buy Co. Inc. (Best Buy). Shortly thereafter, Best Buy began operating its existing stores under a "superstore" concept by expanding product offerings and using mass marketing techniques to promote those products.

Best Buy dramatically altered the function of its sales staff in 1989. Previously, the sales staff worked on a commission basis and was more proactive in assisting customers coming into the stores as a result. Since 1989, however, the commission structure has been terminated and sales associates have developed into educators that assist customers in learning about the products offered in the stores. The customer, to a large extent, took charge of the purchasing process. The sales staff's mission was to answer customer questions so that the customers could decide which product(s) fit their needs. This differed greatly from their former mission of simply generating sales.

In 2000, the company launched its online retail store: BestBuy.com. This allowed customers a choice between visiting a physical store and purchasing products online, thus expanding Best Buy's reach among consumers.

Expansion Through Acquisitions

In 2000, Best Buy began a series of acquisitions to expand its offerings and enter international markets:

2000: Best Buy acquired Magnolia Hi-Fi Inc., a high-end retailer of audio and video products and services, which became Magnolia Audio Video in 2004. This acquisition allowed Best Buy access to a set of upscale customers.

2001: Best Buy entered the international market with the acquisition of Future Shop Ltd, a leading consumer electronics retailer in Canada. This helped Best Buy increase revenues, gain market share, and leverage operational expertise. The same year, Best Buy also opened its first Canadian store. In the same year, the company purchased Musicland, a mall-centered music retailer throughout the United States (divested in 2003).

2002: Best Buy acquired Geek Squad, a computer repair service provider, to help develop a technological support system for customers. The retailer began by incorporating in-store Geek Squad centers in its 28 Minnesota stores, then expanding nationally, and eventually internationally in subsequent years.

2005: Best Buy opened the first Magnolia Home Theater "store-within-a-store" (located within the Best Buy complex).

2006: Best Buy acquired Pacific Sales Kitchen and Bath Centers Inc. to develop a new customer base: builders and remodelers. The same year, Best Buy also acquired a 75% stake in Jiangsu Five Star Appliance Co., Ltd, a China-based appliance and consumer electronics retailer. This enabled the company to access the Chinese retail market and led to the opening of the first Best Buy China store on January 26, 2007.

2007: Best Buy acquired Speakeasy Inc., a provider of broadband, voice, data, and information technology services, to further its offering of technological solutions for customers.

2008: Through a strategic alliance with the Carphone Warehouse Group, a UK-based provider of mobile phones, accessories, and related services, Best Buy Mobile was developed. After acquiring a 50% share in Best Buy Europe (with 2414 stores) from the Carphone Warehouse, Best Buy intended to open small-store formats across Europe in 2011.[3] Best Buy also acquired Napster, a digital download provider, through a merger to counter the falling sales of compact discs. The first Best Buy Mexico store was opened.

2009: Best Buy acquired the remaining 25% of Jiangsu Five Star. Best Buy Mobile moved into Canada.

Industry Environment

Industry Overview

Despite the negative impact the financial crisis had on economies worldwide, in 2008 the consumer electronics industry managed to grow to a record high of US$694 billion in sales—a nearly 14% increase over 2007. In years immediately prior, the growth rate was similar: 14% in 2007 and 17% in 2006. This momentum, however, did not last. Sales dropped 2% in 2009, the first decline in 20 years for the electronics giant.

A few product segments, including televisions, gaming, mobile phones, and Blu-ray players, drove sales for the company. Television sales, specifically LCD units, which accounted for 77% of total television sales, were the main driver for Best Buy, as this segment alone accounted for 15% of total industry revenues. The gaming segment continued to be a bright spot for the industry as well, as sales were expected to have tremendous room for growth. Smartphones were another electronics industry segment predicted to have a high growth impact on the entire industry.

The consumer electronics industry had significant potential for expansion into the global marketplace. There were many untapped markets, especially newly developing countries. These markets were experiencing the fastest economic growth while having the lowest ownership rate for gadgets.[4] Despite the recent economic downturn, the future for this industry was optimistic. A consumer electronics analyst for the European Market Research Institute predicted that the largest growth will be seen in China (22%), the Middle East (20%), Russia (20%), and South America (17%).[5]

Barriers to Entry

As globalization spread and use of the Internet grew, barriers to entering the consumer electronics industry were diminished. When the industry was dominated by brick-and-mortar companies, obtaining the large capital resources needed for entry into the market was a barrier for those looking to gain any significant market share. Expanding a business meant purchasing or leasing large stores that incurred high initial and overhead costs. However, the Internet significantly reduced the capital requirements needed to enter the industry. Companies like Amazon.com and Dell utilized the Internet to their advantage and gained valuable market share.

The shift toward Internet purchasing also negated another once strong barrier to entry: customer loyalty. The trend was that consumers would research products online to determine which one they intended to purchase and then shop around on the Internet for the lowest possible price.

Even though overall barriers were diminished, there were still a few left, which a company like Best Buy used to its advantage. The first, and most significant, was economies of scale. With over 1000 locations, Best Buy used its scale to obtain cost advantages from suppliers due to high quantity orders. Another advantage was in advertising. Large firms had the ability to increase advertising budgets to deter new entrants into the market. Smaller companies generally did not have the marketing budgets for massive television campaigns, which were still one of the most effective marketing strategies available to retailers. Although Internet sales were growing, the industry was still dominated by brick-and-mortar stores. Most consumers looking for electronics—especially major electronics—felt a need to actually see their prospective purchases in person. Having the ability to spend heavily on advertising helped increase foot traffic to these stores.

Internal Environment

Finance

While Best Buy's increase in revenue was encouraging (see **Exhibit 1**), recent growth had been fueled largely by acquisition, especially Best Buy's fiscal year 2009 revenue growth. At the same time, net income and operating margins had been declining (see **Exhibits 2** and **3**). Although this could be a function of increased costs, it was more likely due to pricing pressure. Given the current adverse economic conditions, prices of many consumer electronic products had been forced down by economic and competitive pressures. These lower prices caused margins to decline, negatively affecting net income and operating margins.

Best Buy's long-term debt increased substantially from fiscal 2008 to 2009 (see **Exhibit 4**), which was primarily due to the acquisition of Napster and Best Buy Europe. The trend in available cash has been a mirror image of long-term debt. Available cash increased from fiscal 2005 to 2008 and then was substantially lower in 2009 for the same reason.

EXHIBIT 1
Quarterly Sales, Best
Buy Co., Inc.

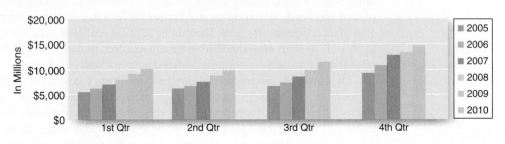

SOURCE: Best Buy Co., Inc.

EXHIBIT 2
Quarterly Net
Income, Best
Buy Co., Inc.

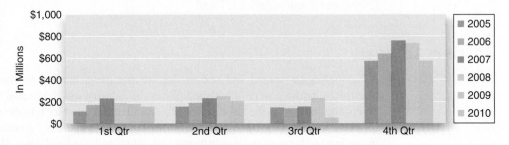

SOURCE: Best Buy Co., Inc.

EXHIBIT 3
Operating Margin,
Best Buy Co., Inc.

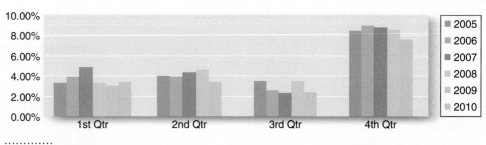

SOURCE: Best Buy Co., Inc.

EXHIBIT 4
Long-Term Debt
and Cash, Best
Buy Co., Inc.

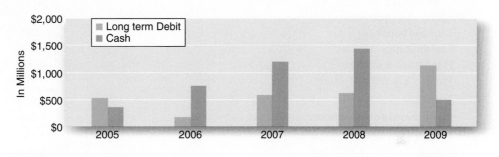

SOURCE: Best Buy Co., Inc.

While the change in available cash and long-term debt were not desirable, the bright side was that this situation was due to the acquisition of assets, which led to a significant increase in revenue for the company. Ultimately, the decreased availability of cash would seem to be temporary due to the circumstances. The more troubling concern was the decline in net income and operating margins, which Best Buy needed to find a way to turn around. If the problems with net income and operating margins were fixed, the trends in cash and long-term debt would also begin to turn around.

At first blush, the increase in accounts receivable and inventory was not necessarily alarming since revenues were increasing during this same time period (see **Exhibit 5**). However, closer inspection revealed a 1% increase in inventory from fiscal 2008 to 2009 and a 12.5% increase in revenue accompanied by a 240% increase in accounts receivable. This created a potential risk for losses due to bad debts. (For complete financial statements, see **Exhibits 6** and **7**.)

EXHIBIT 5
Accounts Receivable
and Inventory, Best
Buy Co., Inc.

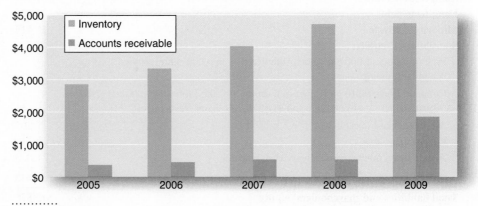

SOURCE: Best Buy Co., Inc.

EXHIBIT 6 Consolidated Balance Sheets, Best Buy Co., Inc. ($ in millions, except per share and share amounts)

	February 28, 2009	March 1, 2008
Assets		
Current assets:		
Cash and cash equivalents	$498	$1,438
Short-term investments	11	64
Receivables	1,868	549
Merchandise inventories	4,753	4,708
Other current assets	1,062	583
Total current assets	8,192	7,342
Property and equipment:		
Land and buildings	755	732
Leasehold improvements	2,013	1,752
Fixtures and equipment	4,060	3,057
Property under capital lease	112	67
	6,940	5,608
Less accumulated depreciation	2,766	2,302
Net property and equipment	4,174	3,306
Goodwill	2,203	1,088
Tradenames	173	97
Customer relationships	322	5
Equity and other investments	395	605
Other assets	367	315
Total assets	$15,826	$12,758
Liabilities and shareholders' equity		
Current liabilities:		
Accounts payable	$4,997	$4,297
Unredeemed gift card liabilities	479	531
Accrued compensation and related expenses	459	373
Accrued liabilities	1,382	975
Accrued income taxes	281	404
Short-term debt	783	156
Current portion of long-term debt	54	33
Total current liabilities	8,435	6,769
Long-term liabilities	1,109	838
Long-term debt	1,126	627
Minority interests	513	40
Shareholders' equity:		
Preferred stock, $1.00 par value: Authorized — 400,000 shares; Issued and outstanding — none	—	—
Common stock, $0.10 par value: Authorized — 1.0 billion shares; Issued and outstanding — 413,684,000 and 410,578,000 shares, respectively	41	41
Additional paid-in capital	205	8
Retained earnings	4,714	3,933
Accumulated other comprehensive (loss) income	(317)	502
Total shareholders' equity	4,643	4,484
Total liabilities and shareholders' equity	$15,826	$12,758

SOURCE: *Best Buy Co., Inc. 2009 Form 10-K*, p. 56.

EXHIBIT 7
Consolidated
Statements of
Earnings, Best
Buy Co., Inc. ($ in
millions, except per
share amounts)

Fiscal Years Ended	February 28, 2009	March 1, 2008	March 3, 2007
Revenue	$45,015	$40,023	$35,934
Cost of goods sold	34,017	30,477	27,165
Gross profit	10,998	9,546	8,769
Selling, general and administrative expenses	8,984	7,385	6,770
Restructuring charges	78	—	—
Goodwill and tradename impairment	66	—	—
Operating income	1,870	2,161	1,999
Other income (expense)			
Investment income and other	35	129	162
Investment impairment	(111)	—	—
Interest expense	(94)	(62)	(31)
Earnings before income tax expense, minority interests and equity in income (loss) of affiliates	1,700	2,228	2,130
Income tax expense	674	815	752
Minority interests in earnings	(30)	(3)	(1)
Equity in income (loss) of affiliates	7	(3)	—
Net earnings	$1,003	$1,407	$1,377
Earnings per share			
Basic	$2.43	$3.20	$2.86
Diluted	$2.39	$3.12	$2.79
Weighted-average common shares outstanding (in millions)			
Basic	412.5	439.9	482.1
Diluted	422.9	452.9	496.2

SOURCE: *Best Buy Co., Inc. 2009 Form 10-K,* p. 57.

Marketing

Best Buy's marketing goals were four-fold: (1) to market various products based on the customer-centricity operating model, (2) to address the needs of customer lifestyle groups, (3) to be at the forefront of technological advances, and (4) to meet customer needs with end-to-end solutions.

Best Buy prided itself on customer centricity that catered to specific customer needs and behaviors. Over the years, the retailer created a portfolio of products and services that complemented one another and added to the success of the business. These products included seven distinct brands domestically, as well as other brands and stores internationally:

Best Buy: This brand offered a wide variety of consumer electronics, home office products, entertainment software, appliances, and related services.

Best Buy Mobile: These stand-alone stores offered a wide selection of mobile phones, accessories, and related e-services in small-format stores.

Geek Squad: This brand provided residential and commercial product repair, support, and installation services both in-store and onsite.

Magnolia Audio Video: This brand offered high-end audio and video products and related services.

Napster: This brand was an online provider of digital music.

Pacific Sales: This brand offered high-end home improvement products, primarily including appliances, consumer electronics, and related services.

Speakeasy: This brand provided broadband, voice, data, and information technology services to small businesses.

Starting in 2005, Best Buy initiated a strategic transition to a customer-centric operating model, which was completed in 2007. Prior to 2005, the company focused on customer groups such as affluent professional males, young entertainment enthusiasts, upscale suburban mothers, and technologically advanced families.[6] After the transition, Best Buy focused more on customer lifestyle groups such as affluent suburban families, trendsetting urban dwellers, and the closely knit families of Middle America.[7] To target these various segments, Best Buy acquired firms with aligned strategies, which were used as a competitive advantage against its strongest competition, such as Circuit City and Wal-Mart. The acquisitions of Pacific Sales, Speakeasy, and Napster, along with the development of Best Buy Mobile, created more product offerings, which led to more profits.

Marketing these different types of products and services was a difficult task. That was why Best Buy's employees had more training than competitors. This knowledge service was a value-added competitive advantage. Since the sales employees no longer operated on a commission-based pay structure, consumers could obtain knowledge from salespeople without being subjected to high-pressure sales techniques. This was generally seen to enhance customer shopping satisfaction.

Operations

Best Buy's operating goals included increasing revenues by growing its customer base, gaining more market share internationally, successfully implementing marketing and sales strategies in Europe, and having multiple brands for different customer lifestyles through M&A (Merger and Acquisition).

Domestic Best Buy store operations were organized into eight territories, with each territory divided into districts. A retail field officer oversaw store performance through district managers, who met with store employees on a regular basis to discuss operations strategies such as loyalty programs, sales promotion, and new product introductions.[8] Along with domestic operations, Best Buy had an international operation segment, originally established in connection with the acquisition of Canada-based Future Shop.[9]

In fiscal 2009, Best Buy opened up 285 new stores in addition to the European acquisition of 2414 Best Buy Europe stores. It relocated 34 stores and closed 67 stores.

Human Resources

The objectives of Best Buy's human resources department were to provide consumers with the right knowledge of products and services, to portray the company's vision and strategy on an everyday basis, and to educate employees on the ins and outs of new products and services. Best Buy employees were required to be ethical and knowledgeable. This principle started within the top management structure and filtered down from the retail field officer through district managers, and through store managers to the employees on the floor. Every employee had to have the company's vision embedded in their service and attitude.

Despite Best Buy's efforts to train an ethical and knowledgeable employee force, there were some allegations and controversy over Best Buy employees, which gave the company a black eye in the public mind. One lawsuit claimed that Best Buy employees had misrepresented the manufacturer's warranty in order to sell its own product service and replacement plan. The lawsuit accused Best Buy of "entering into a corporate-wide scheme to institute high-pressure sales techniques involving the extended warranties" and "using artificial barriers to discourage consumers who purchased the 'complete extended warranties' from making legitimate claims."[10]

In a more recent case (March 2009), the U.S. District Court granted Class Action certification to allow plaintiffs to sue Best Buy for violating its "Price Match" policy. According to the ruling, the plaintiffs alleged that Best Buy employees would aggressively deny consumers the ability to apply the company's "price match guarantee."[11] The suit also alleged that Best Buy had an undisclosed "Anti-Price Matching Policy," where the company told its employees not to allow price matches and gave financial bonuses to employees who complied.

Competition

Brick-and-Mortar Competitors

Wal-Mart Stores Inc., the world's largest retailer, with revenues over US$405 billion, operated worldwide and offered a diverse product mix with a focus on being a low-cost provider. In recent years, Wal-Mart increased its focus on grabbing market share in the consumer electronics industry. In the wake of Circuit City's liquidation,[12] Wal-Mart was stepping up efforts by striking deals with Nintendo and Apple that would allow each company to have their own in-store displays. Wal-Mart also considered using Smartphones and laptop computers to drive growth.[13] It was refreshing 3500 of its electronics departments and was beginning to offer a wider and higher range of electronic products. These efforts should help Wal-Mart appeal to the customer segment looking for high quality at the lowest possible price.[14]

GameStop Corp. was the leading video game retailer with sales of almost US$9 billion as of January 2009, in a forecasted US$22 billion industry. GameStop operated over 6000 stores throughout the United States, Canada, Australia, and Europe, as a retailer of both new and used video game products including hardware, software, and gaming accessories.[15]

The advantage GameStop had over Best Buy was the number of locations: 6207 GameStop locations compared to 1023 Best Buy locations. However, Best Buy seemed to have what it took to overcome this advantage—deep pockets. With significantly higher net income, Best Buy could afford to take a hit to its margins and undercut GameStop prices.[16]

RadioShack Corp. was a retailer of consumer electronics goods and services, including flat panel televisions, telephones, computers, and consumer electronics accessories. Although the company grossed revenues of over US$4 billion from 4453 locations, RadioShack consistently lost market share to Best Buy. Consumers had a preference for RadioShack for audio and video components, yet preferred Best Buy for their big box purchases.[17]

Second tier competitors were rapidly increasing. Wholesale shopping units were becoming more popular, and companies such as Costco and BJ's had increased their piece of the consumer electronics pie over the past few years. After Circuit City's bankruptcy, mid-level electronics retailers like HH Gregg and Ultimate Electronics were scrambling to grab Circuit City's lost market share. Ultimate Electronics, owned by Mark Wattles, who was a major investor in Circuit City, had a leg up on his competitors. Wattles was on Circuit City's board of executives and had firsthand access to profitable Circuit City stores. Ultimate Electronics planned to expand its operations by at least 20 stores in the near future.

Online Competitors

Amazon.com Inc., since 1994, had grown into the United States' largest online retailer with revenues of over US$19 billion in 2008 by providing just about any product imaginable through its popular website. Created as an online bookstore, Amazon soon ventured into various consumer electronics product categories including computers, televisions, software, video games, and much more.[18]

Amazon.com gained an advantage over its supercenter competitors because it was able to maintain a lower cost structure compared to brick-and-mortar companies like Best Buy. Amazon was able to push those savings through to its product pricing and selection/diversification. With an increasing trend in the consumer electronics industry to shop online, Amazon.com was positioned perfectly to maintain strong market growth and potentially steal some market share away from Best Buy.

Netflix Inc. was an online video rental service, offering selections of DVDs and Blu-ray discs. Since its establishment in 1997, Netflix had grown into a US$1.4 billion company. With over 100,000 titles in its collection, the company shipped for free to approximately 10 million subscribers. Netflix began offering streaming downloads through its website, which eliminated the need to wait for a DVD to arrive.

Netflix was quickly changing the DVD market, which had dramatically impacted brick-and-mortar stores such as Blockbuster and Hollywood Video and retailers who offered DVDs for sale. In a responsive move, Best Buy partnered with CinemaNow to enter the digital movie distribution market and counter Netflix and other video rental providers.[19]

Core Competencies

Customer-Centricity Model

Most players in the consumer electronics industry focused on delivering products at the lowest cost (Wal-Mart—brick-and-mortar; Amazon—web-based). Best Buy, however, took a different approach by providing customers with highly trained sales associates who were available to educate customers regarding product features. This allowed customers to make informed buying decisions on big-ticket items. In addition, with the Geek Squad, Best Buy was able to offer and provide installation services, product repair, and ongoing support. In short, Best Buy provided an end-to-end solution for its customers.

Best Buy used its customer-centricity model, which was built around a significant database of customer information, to construct a diversified portfolio of product offerings. This let the company offer different products in different stores in a manner that matched customer needs. This in turn helped keep costs lower by shipping the correct inventory to the correct locations. Since Best Buy's costs were increased by the high level of training needed for sales associates and service professionals, it had been important that the company remain vigilant in keeping costs down wherever it could without sacrificing customer experience.

The tremendous breadth of products and services Best Buy was able to provide allowed customers to purchase all components for a particular need within the Best Buy family. For example, if a customer wanted to set up a first-rate audio-visual room at home, he or she could go to the Magnolia Home Theater store-within-a-store at any Best Buy location and use the knowledge of the Magnolia or Best Buy associate in the television and audio areas to determine which television and surround sound theater system best fit their needs. The customer could then employ a Geek Squad employee to install and set up the television and home theater system. None of Best Buy's competitors offered this extensive level of service.

Successful Acquisitions

Through its series of acquisitions, Best Buy had gained valuable experience in the process of integrating companies under the Best Buy family. The ability to effectively determine where to expand was important to the company's ability to differentiate itself in the marketplace. Additionally, Best Buy was also successfully integrating employees from acquired companies. Best Buy had a significant global presence, which was important because of the maturing domestic market. This global presence provided the company with insights into worldwide trends in the consumer electronics industry and afforded access to newly developing markets. Best Buy used this insight to test products in different markets in its constant effort to meet and anticipate customer needs.

Retaining Talent

Analyzing Circuit City's demise, many experts concluded one of the major reasons for the company's downfall was that Circuit City let go of their most senior and well-trained sales staff in order to cut costs. Best Buy, on the other hand, had a reputation for retaining talent and was widely recognized for its superior service. Highly trained sales professionals had become a unique resource in the consumer electronics industry, where technology was changing at an unprecedented rate, and was a significant source of competitive advantage.

Challenges Ahead

Economic Downturn

Electronics retailers like Best Buy sold products that could be described as "discretionary items, rather than necessities."[20] During economic recessions, however, consumers had less disposable income to spend. While there was optimism about a possible economic turnaround in 2010 or 2011, if the economy continued to stumble, this could present a real threat to sellers of discretionary products.

In order to increase sales revenues, many retailers, including Best Buy, offered customers low-interest financing through their private-label credit cards. These promotions were tremendously successful for Best Buy. From 2007 to 2009, these private-label credit card purchases accounted for 16%–18% of Best Buy's domestic revenue. Due to the credit crisis, however, the Federal Reserve issued new regulations that could restrict companies from offering deferred interest financing to customers. If Best Buy and other retailers were unable to extend these credit lines, it could have a tremendous negative impact on future revenues.[21]

Pricing and Debt Management

The current depressed economic conditions, technological advances, and increased competition put a tremendous amount of pricing pressure on many consumer electronics products. This was a concern for all companies in this industry. The fact that Best Buy did not compete strictly on price structure alone made this an even bigger concern. Given the higher costs that Best Buy incurred training employees, any pricing pressure that decreased margins put stress on Best Buy's financial strength. In addition, the recent acquisition of Napster and the 50% stake in Best Buy Europe significantly increased Best Buy's debt and reduced available cash. Even in prosperous times, debt management was a key factor in any company's success, and it became even more important during the economic downturn. (See **Exhibits 6** and **7** for Best Buy's financial statements.)

Products and Service

As technology improved, product life cycles, as well as prices, decreased. As a result, margins decreased. Under Best Buy's service model, shorter product life cycles increased training costs. Employees were forced to learn new products with higher frequency. This was not only costly but also increased the likelihood that employees would make mistakes, thereby tarnishing Best Buy's service record and potentially damaging one of its most important, if not its most important, differentiators. In addition, more resources would be directed at research of new products to make sure Best Buy continued to offer the products consumers desire.

One social threat to the retail industry was the growing popularity of the online marketplace. Internet shoppers could browse sites searching for the best deals on specific products. This technology allowed consumers to become more educated about their purchases, while creating increased downward price pressure. Ambitious consumers could play the role of a Best Buy associate themselves by doing product comparisons and information gathering without a trip to the store. This emerging trend created a direct threat to companies like Best Buy, which had 1023 stores in its domestic market alone. One way Best Buy tried to continue the demand for brick-and-mortar locations and counter the threat of Internet-based competition was by providing value-added services in stores. Customer service, repairs, and interactive product displays were just a few examples of these services.[22]

Leadership

The two former CEOs of Best Buy, Richard Shultze and Brad Anderson, were extremely successful at making the correct strategic moves at the appropriate times. With Brad Anderson stepping aside in June 2009, Brian Dunn replaced him as the new CEO. Although Dunn worked for the company for 24 years and held the key positions of COO and President during his tenure, the position of CEO brought him to a whole new level and presented new challenges, especially during the economic downturn. He was charged with leading Best Buy into the world of increased connectivity. This required a revamping of products and store setups to serve customers in realizing their connectivity needs. This was a daunting task for an experienced CEO, let alone a new CEO who had never held the position.

Wal-Mart

Best Buy saw its largest rival, Circuit City, go bankrupt. However, a new archrival, Wal-Mart, was expanding into consumer electronics and stepping up competition in a price war Wal-Mart hoped to win. Best Buy needed to face the competition not by lowering prices, but by coming up with something really different. Best Buy had to determine the correct path to improve its ability to differentiate itself from competitors, which was increasingly difficult given an adverse economic climate and the company's financial stress. How Best Buy could maintain innovative products, top-notch employees, and superior customer service while facing increased competition and operational costs was an open question.

NOTES

1. Best Buy Co. Inc., *Form 10-K*. Securities and Exchange Commission, February 28, 2009.
2. Ibid.
3. Ibid.
4. Greg Keller, "Threat Grows by iPod and Laptop," *The Columbus Dispatch*, May 18, 2009, http://www.dispatch.com/live/content/business/stories/2009/05/18/greener_gadgets.ART_ART_05-18-09_A9_TMDSJR8.html (July 10, 2009).
5. Larry Magid, "Consumer Electronics: Future Looks Bright," *CBSNews.com*, May 2, 2008, http://www.cbsnews.com/stories/2008/05/02/scitech/pcanswer/main4067008.shtml (July 10, 2009).
6. Best Buy Co. Inc., *Form 10-K*, 2009.

7. Ibid.
8. Ibid.
9. Ibid.
10. Manhattan Institute for Policy Research, "They're Making a Federal Case Out of It . . . in State Court," *Civil Justice Report* 3, 2001, http://www.manhattan-institute.org/html/cjr_3_part2.htm.
11. "Best Buy Bombshell!" *HD Guru*, March 21, 2009, http://hdguru.com/best-buy-bombshell/.
12. Circuit City Stores Inc. was an American retailer in brand-name consumer electronics, personal computers, entertainment software, and (until 2000) large appliances. The company opened its first store in 1949 and liquidated its final American retail stores in 2009 following a bankruptcy filing and subsequent failure to find a buyer. At the time of liquidation, Circuit City was the second-largest U.S. electronics retailer, after Best Buy.
13. Z. Bissonnette, "Wal-Mart Looks to Expand Electronics Business," *Bloggingstocks.com*, May 18, 2009, http://www.bloggingstocks.com/2009/05/18/wal-mart-looks-to-expand-electronics-business/.
14. N. Maestrie, "Wal-Mart Steps Up Consumer Electronics Push," *Reuters*, May 19, 2009, http://www.reuters.com/article/technologyNews/idUSTRE54I4TR20090519.
15. Capital IQ, "GameStop Corp. Corporate Tearsheet," *Capital IQ*, 2009.
16. E. Sherman, "GameStop Faces Pain from Best Buy, Downloading," *BNET Technology*, June 24, 2009, http://industry.bnet.com/technology/10002329/gamestop-faces-pain-from-best-buy-downloading/.
17. T. Van Riper, "RadioShack Gets Slammed," *Forbes.com*, February 17, 2006, http://www.forbes.com/2006/02/17/radioshack-edmondson-retail_cx_tr_0217radioshack.html.
18. Capital IQ, "Amazon.com Corporate Tearsheet," *Capital IQ*, 2009.
19. T. Kee, "Netflix Beware: Best Buy Adds Digital Downloads with CinemaNow Deal," *paidContent.org*, June 5, 2009, http://paidcontent.org/article/419-best-buy-adds-digital-movie-downloads-with-cinemanow-deal/.
20. Best Buy Co., Inc., *Form 10-K*, 2009.
21. Ibid.
22. Ibid.

CASE **23**

Rosetta Stone Inc.

CHANGING THE WAY PEOPLE LEARN LANGUAGES

Christine B. Buenafe and Joyce P. Vincelette

Introduction

ROSETTA STONE'S MISSION WAS TO CHANGE the way people learn languages. The company blended language learning with technology at a time when globalization connected more and more individuals and institutions to each other.

The potential for profit in the language-learning industry encouraged management to become more proactive and aggressive about Rosetta Stone's growth. In 2007, an industry analysis commissioned from The Nielsen Company, a market research firm, found that the language-learning industry produced over US$83 billion in consumer spending.[1] Of this amount, US$32 billion, or 39% of the total, was spent on self-study options. In the United States, the industry generated US$5 billion in consumer spending in 2007, of which US$2 billion was for self-study.[2] Over 90% of the US$83 billion was spent outside the United States.

The company's debut on the New York Stock Exchange brought capital and resources that placed Rosetta Stone in an exciting and promising position. In 2007, online education was a growing market, and with these new added financial resources, coupled with future profits from operations, Rosetta Stone could potentially consider other acquisition candidates in the future.

How should the company move forward in order to sustain its momentum? Would it be appropriate for Rosetta Stone to offer products like audio books or services such as language classrooms in order to increase market share? Which international markets would provide the company with a strategic and guaranteed return? Could changes in the company's advertising and financial strategies improve Rosetta Stone's position? Should the company maintain anti-piracy initiatives as a priority or could its efforts be better allocated elsewhere? Companies that depend on technology face environmental risks that include economic conditions; federal, state, and local regulations; and taxes and supplier or vendor concerns.[3] To effectively compete, Rosetta Stone will have to push product and service development, as well as attract and retain talented personnel.

Rosetta Stone Inc. sold computer-based, self-study language-learning programs. It developed, marketed, and sold their products to individuals, educational institutions, the armed forces, government agencies, and corporations. It referred to its teaching method as *Dynamic Immersion*.

History[4]

The idea for Rosetta Stone originated in the 1980s, when Allen Stoltzfus set out to learn Russian. Stoltzfus was having a difficult time with the language and he attributed his slow progress to his study methods. Years earlier, he lived and studied in Germany. His control of German was facilitated by the language immersion he experienced while abroad. To learn Russian, Stoltzfus realized that he needed to create an environment conducive to learning a language naturally, rather than sitting in a classroom reviewing grammar rules and translating texts.

Stoltzfus turned to computer technology, along with contextualized inputs like pictures and conversations, to simulate the way people acquired their first language. He discussed his idea with his brother-in-law, John Fairfield, who had a PhD in Computer Science. They believed that technology was not yet ready for their ambitions.

By 1992, technology had improved. Allen Stoltzfus founded Fairfield Language Technologies in Harrisonburg, Virginia, and became the company's Chairman and President. He recruited his brother, Eugene Stoltzfus, to be Fairfield's Executive Vice President. Eugene had a background in architecture and he contributed his expertise in designing the program's appearance and organization. Allen and Eugene Stoltzfus, along with John Fairfield, named their product Rosetta Stone, after the artifact that served as the key to understanding Egyptian hieroglyphics. Like that artifact, their product was meant to unlock language-learning success.

Allen Stoltzfus passed away in 2002 and Eugene filled the role of President and Chairman until the end of 2005. In 2003, Tom Adams was named CEO and began guiding the company's expansionary strategies. In 2005, the company opened an office in the United Kingdom.[5] In 2006, investment firms ABS Capital Partners and Northwest Equity Partners bought Fairfield Language Technologies, renaming the company Rosetta Stone.

At the end of that year, the company paid an upfront fee for a perpetual, irrevocable, and worldwide license allowing Rosetta Stone Inc. to use speech recognition technology developed at the University of Colorado.[6] The University of Colorado, Boulder, was ranked 24th and 25th on *U.S. News & World Report*'s lists of Top Speech–Language Pathology Programs and Top Audiology Programs, respectively.[7] The company also hired some of the technology's original developers to build on its speech recognition expertise. Rosetta Stone opened an office in Japan in 2007 and in Korea in 2009.[8]

The company sold its products in more than 30 different languages and in more than 150 countries when it had its initial public offering. Rosetta Stone Inc. (RST) began public trading on the New York Stock Exchange in April 2009. Its shares were priced at US$18, above the estimated US$15–$17 range. The price for RST jumped 42% from US$18 to US$25.55 in late-morning trading.[9] Rosetta Stone sold 6.25 million shares for a total of US$112.5 million. Analysts tied the company's success to a lack of publicly held competitors.[10]

In November 2009, Rosetta Stone acquired assets from SGLC International Co. Ltd., a software reseller in Seoul, South Korea. The purchase price consisted of an initial cash payment of US$100,000, followed by three annual cash installment payments, based on revenue performance in South Korea.[11] Rosetta Stone's total revenue for the year ended December 31, 2009, was US$252.3 million.

Products and Services

As of December 31, 2009, Rosetta Stone offered the language-learning market 31 languages from which to choose. Six languages were available in up to five levels of proficiency. Nineteen languages were available in up to three levels. Six languages were available in only one level of proficiency. The company's language offerings are listed in **Exhibit 1**, which also shows the available levels and software versions. Each level provided approximately 40 hours of the target language broken down into units, lessons, and activities.[12] Rosetta Stone offered four different editions of its language offerings: personal, enterprise, classroom, and home school. **Exhibit 2** lists the intended market for each edition and provides descriptions of any special features.

The company had Version 2 and Version 3 of its programs available at the end of fiscal year 2009. Version 2 of its software was available in 31 languages and Version 3 was available in 25 languages. The newer version of the program featured improvements in the images and audio samples used, as well as in the organization and presentation of content. Other benefits of Version 3 included speaking activities, grammar and spelling components, simulated conversations, advanced speech recognition technology, and Adaptive Recall.[13] Adaptive Recall referred to algorithms developed by the company that had students review problem areas at longer and longer intervals, thereby improving language learners' long-term retention.[14] In July 2009, the company introduced Rosetta Stone TOTALe. These online offerings of integrated courses with coach-led practice sessions included language games, encouraged interaction with native speakers, and provided live support from customer service.[15]

The company also developed Rosetta Stone products for the exclusive use of Native American communities to help preserve their languages. Examples included Mohawk, Chitmacha, Innutitut, and Iñupiaq.[16] In addition, the company offered a customized version of its learning solutions that focused on military-specific content for the United States Army.[17]

Customers could choose to enjoy Rosetta Stone's services on a CD-ROM or online. For the year ended December 31, 2009, the company made 87% of its revenue from CD-ROM sales and 13% from online subscriptions.[18] Customers could choose to purchase each language level separately or pay a discounted price by purchasing all available levels of a language together. Prices ranged from US$219 for Level 1 of Indonesian to US$1199 for TOTALe Korean.

The company also supported an online peer-to-peer practice environment called SharedTalk at www.SharedTalk.com.[19] Anyone was able to register on the website for free in order to find language partners across the world and acquire pen pals for e-mail exchange. SharedTalk had more than 125,000 active users in 2009.

EXHIBIT 1   Intangible Assets: Rosetta Stone Inc. (Dollar amount in millions)

	December 31, 2009			December 31, 2008		
	Gross Carrying Amount	Accumulated Amortization	Net Carrying Amount	Gross Carrying Amount	Accumulated Amortization	Net Carrying Amount
Trade name/trademark	$10,607	$ —	$10,607	$10,607	$ —	$10,607
Core technology	2,453	(2,453)	—	2,453	(2,453)	—
Customer relationships	10,842	(10,747)	95	10,739	(10,706)	33
Website	12	(10)	2	12	(7)	5
Total	$23,914	$(13,210)	$10,704	$23,811	$(13,166)	$10,645

SOURCE: Rosetta Stone Inc., *2009 Form 10-K*, p. F-20.

EXHIBIT 2 Consolidated Statement of Operations: Rosetta Stone Inc. (Dollar amounts in thousands except per share amount)

Exchange Rate Used Is That of the Year End Reported Date

Year Ending December 31	2009	% Change	2008	% Change	2007	% Change	2006	% Change	Jan. 4 2006
Revenue									
Product	218,549	18.7	184,182	53.6	119,897	48.7	80,604	45,183.1	178
Subscription & service	33,722	33.8	25,198	44.6	17,424	62.9	10,694	11,276.6	94
Total revenue	252,271	20.5	209,380	52.5	137,321	50.4	91,298	33,465.4	272
Cost of product revenue	30,264	14.0	26,539	39.3	19,055	65.0	11,549	5,703.5	199
Cost of subscription & service revenue	3,163	48.0	2,137	30.9	1,632	64.5	992	24,700.0	4
Total cost of revenue	33,427	16.6	28,676	38.6	20,687	65.0	12,541	6,077.8	203
Gross profit	218,844	21.1	180,704	54.9	116,634	48.1	78,757	114,040.6	69
Operating expenses									
Sales & marketing expenses	114,899	23.0	93,384	42.7	65,437	42.7	45,854	6,497.7	695
Research & development*	26,239	42.7	18,387	42.6	12,893	58.8	20,714	19,697.6	41
General & administrative expenses	57,174	44.5	39,577	32.9	29,786	79.5	16,590	11,583.1	142
Lease abandonment	—		1,831		—		—		—
Total operating expenses	198,312	29.5	153,179	41.7	108,116	30.0	83,158	—	—
Other income and expense									
Interest income	159	(65.0)	454	(32.5)	673	9.8	613	—	—
Interest expense	356	(60.0)	891	(33.1)	1,331	(14.7)	1,560	—	—
Other income	112	(53.1)	239	55.2	154	156.7	60	1,900.0	3
Total other income (expense)	(85)	(57.1)	(198)	(60.7)	(504)	(43.2)	(887)	(29,666.7)	3
Income (loss) before income taxes	20,447	(25.2)	27,327	241.0	8,014	(251.6)	(5,288)	(52.5)	(11,121)
Income tax provision (benefit)	7,084	(47.3)	13,435	147.2	5,435	(538.3)	(1,240)	—	—
Net income (loss)	13,363	(3.8)	13,892	438.7	2,579	(163.7)	(4,048)	(63.6)	(11,121)
Preferred stock accretion					80	(49.7)	159	—	—
Net income (loss) attributable to common stockholders	13,363	(3.8)	13,892	455.9	2,499	(159.4)	(4,207)	(62.2)	(11,121)
Year end shares outstanding	20,440	955.8	1,936	5.4	1,837	14.0	1,612	—	—
Net earnings (loss) per share—basic	1	(87.8)	7	395.9	1	(155.9)	(3)	(979.6)	0
Net earnings (loss) per share—diluted	1	(18.3)	1	446.7	0	(105.7)	(3)	(979.6)	0
Weighted average shares outstanding—basic	14,990	686.9	1,905	11.9	1,702	6.5	1,598	(104.3)	(37,194)
Weighted average shares outstanding—diluted	19,930	17.8	16,924	2.4	16,533	934.6	1,598	(104.3)	(37,194)

*In 2006, Research and Development expenses included $12,597 of acquired in-process R&D.

SOURCE: Rosetta Stone Inc., *2009 Form 10-K*, p. F-4.

The company's growth strategies centered on expanding its offerings and target market. Rosetta Stone planned to develop advanced course levels and add new languages. The company also recognized that adding skill development and remediation courses to its product line could attract advanced language learners to the brand. In addition, the company could develop customized versions of its programs for industries like health care, business, real estate, and retail. Rosetta Stone Version 4 TOTALe was planned for release in September 2010.[20] It would integrate the Version 3 language-learning software solution with the online features of Rosetta Stone TOTALe.

Content and Curriculum[21]

Rosetta Stone's curriculum encouraged students to progress from seeing and recognizing pictures and vocabulary and hearing native speakers to actually speaking the target language. Language learners reviewed the alphabet, vocabulary, and intuitive grammar, as well as the skills of reading, listening, pronunciation, and conversation without the use of translation exercises or detailed explanations. Lessons combined the introduction of new concepts, a review of recent material, and the production of key phrases. The curriculum was designed to be flexible so learners could focus on meeting particular goals or developing certain abilities.

The company's products relied on a library of more than 25,000 photographic images and 400,000 professionally recorded sound files. The images, along with their combinations, aimed to convey a universal meaning. This enabled the company to apply the same curriculum across multiple languages and conveniently sped up the rate at which the company could add new languages to its product line. Rosetta Stone implemented a specific sequencing method devised to teach the user the most important and relevant language skills. It also incorporated languages' specific nuances, such as dual forms for parts of speech in Arabic. Any localization tailored by the company was minimal because Rosetta Stone did not rely on translations from the target language to the learner's native language.

Technology[22]

Rosetta Stone developed most of its own technology. It created content development tools that allowed curriculum specialists to write, edit, manage, and publish course materials. These tools allowed authors, translators, voicers, photographers, and editors to work efficiently and cooperatively across multiple locations. The company developed the software's intuitive user interface which assisted in the learner's transition from listening comprehension to speaking. Rosetta Stone established a student management system designed to allow teachers and administrators to configure lesson plans and to review student progress reports. The company, with the help of software firm Parature Inc., offered customer service via Facebook.[23]

The technology supporting Rosetta Stone's programs was specially designed to handle the complexities of languages. For example, the company's software was able to support languages written from right-to-left such as Arabic and Hebrew, along with languages with characters such as Chinese and Japanese. Rosetta Stone's speech recognition technology was included in Version 3. This technology targeted the different challenges language learners encountered when speaking. For example, this technology recognized non-native speech understanding and highlighted pronunciation feedback, reinforcing correct pronunciation. The speech recognition models used by the program also included languages and dialects that had not been supported by speech recognition software in the past, such as Irish.

For the year ended December 31, 2009, the company's research and development expenses were US$26.2 million, or 10.4% of total revenue. Rosetta Stone intended to advance its software platform and its speech recognition technology. The company also sought to build on its success with www.SharedTalk.com. The company was evaluating opportunities to extend its offerings to mobile technology. For example, it was developing a mobile application called Rosetta Stone Mini for release during the second half of 2010.

Manufacturing and Fulfillment[24]

Rosetta Stone focused on minimizing costs and achieving efficiency as it met its production goals. It obtained most of its products and packaging components from third-party contract manufacturers. It also had alternative sources to turn to in the event that its main manufacturers and suppliers were unavailable.

The company's fulfillment facility in Harrisonburg, Virginia, was its primary facility for packaging and distributing products. Rosetta Stone also contracted with third-party vendors in Munich for fulfillment services such as order processing, inventory control, and e-commerce; the Netherlands for consumer orders in Europe; and Tokyo, Japan, for orders in Japan.

Language-Learning Success[25]

In 2009, Rosetta Stone Inc. commissioned Roumen Vesselinov, PhD, a visiting professor at Queens College, City University of New York, as well as Rockman et al., an independent evaluation research and consulting firm, to study the effectiveness of Rosetta Stone's offerings. Their results, along with the numerous awards and recognition the company received, supported the company's initiatives and accomplishments.

Vesselinov discovered that after 55 hours of study using the company's Spanish program, a student would be able to achieve a WebCAPE score at a level sufficient to fulfill the requirements for one semester of Spanish in a college that offered six semesters of the language, with 95% confidence. WebCAPE, or the Web-based Computer Adaptive Placement Exam, was a standardized test used by over 500 colleges and universities for language-level placement. Sixty-four percent of the students from this study improved their oral proficiency by at least one level on a seven-level scale based on the American Council on the Teaching of Foreign Languages (ACTFL) OPIc test. This test was used worldwide by academic institutions, government agencies, and private corporations for evaluating oral language proficiency.

Rockman's study showed that after 64 hours of study with Rosetta Stone Spanish (Latin American) and six hours of Rosetta Stone Studio sessions, 78% of the students participating in its study increased their oral proficiency by at least one level on the seven-level scale developed by ACTFL. Rosetta Stone Studio provided an interactive online environment in real-time where learners communicated with students and native-speaking coaches.

In 2009, the company placed #14 on the Inc. 5000 list for the education industry. It also received the National Parenting Publications Awards (NAPPA) Honors Award for Rosetta Stone Version 3 Personal Edition, four classroom-specific awards for Classroom Version 3, as well as two enterprise-specific awards for its products. In 2008, it received the CODiE awards for best corporate learning solution and best instructional solution in other curriculum areas from the Software & Information Industry Association. In 2007, the company won the EDDIE multilevel foreign language award for Chinese levels 1 and 2 and a multilevel English-as-a-second-language, or ESL, award for English levels 1, 2, and 3 from *ComputED Gazette*.

Marketing, Sales, and Distribution[26]

The company's growth and profitability were dependent upon the effectiveness and efficiency of Rosetta Stone's direct marketing expenditures. In 2009, 82% of Rosetta Stone's revenue was generated through the company's direct sales channels, which included its call centers, websites, institutional sales force, and kiosks.

Rosetta Stone's advertising campaigns encompassed radio, television, and print. The company had advertisements in national publications such as *Time*, *The Economist*, *The New Yorker*, and *National Geographic*. The company's strategy was to purchase "remnant" advertising segments.[27] These segments were random time slots and publication dates that had remained unsold and were offered at discounts. There was a limited supply of this type of advertising, and it was not guaranteed that the company would be able to stay within its marketing budget if these discounted slots were unavailable. Past Rosetta Stone advertisements featured U.S. Olympic gold medal swimmer Michael Phelps. Another marketing campaign depicted a farmer hoping to impress a supermodel with his Italian-speaking abilities.[28]

The company's online media advertising strategy included banner and paid search advertising, as well as affiliate relationships. Rosetta Stone worked with online agencies to buy impression-based and performance-based traffic. The company tracked the effectiveness of its advertising by asking customers to indicate the marketing campaigns that caught their attention. The company's website provided a space for users to leave testimonials and reviews. Positive stories and comments served as free word-of-mouth advertising favoring Rosetta Stone's products and services.

Marketing research supported the success of the company's advertising programs. According to an August 2008 survey commissioned from Global Market Insite Inc., a market research services firm, Rosetta Stone was the most recognized language-learning brand in the United States. Of those surveyed who had an opinion of the brand, over 80% had associated it with high quality and effective products and services for teaching foreign languages. In addition, internal studies from January and February 2009 showed that aided brand awareness for Rosetta Stone in the United States was approximately 74%–79%, based on general population surveys. Aided brand awareness refers to customers' recollection of a particular brand name after seeing or hearing about the product.

Sales and marketing expenses were 46% of total revenue for the year ended December 31, 2009.[29] That year, Rosetta Stone expanded its direct marketing activities, and sales and marketing expenses increased by US$21.5 million, or by 23%, to US$114.9 million. During 2009, the company increased direct advertising expenses by 25% to US$42.4 million. Advertising expenses related to television and radio media and Internet marketing grew by US$8.6 million. Rosetta Stone Inc. also increased its number of kiosks from 150 to 242 in 2009, which resulted in US$6.2 million of additional kiosk operating expenses, which included rent and sales compensation-related expenses. Personnel costs related to growth in the institutional sales channel and marketing and sales support activities increased by US$6.4 million since 2008.

The Consumer Channel[30]

For the year ended December 31, 2009, consumer sales accounted for 79% of total revenue. The consumer distribution model encompassed call centers, websites, kiosks, and select retail resellers. Language products were also offered in a limited number of ZoomShop unmanned automated kiosks. The company's growth strategy for its consumer channel involved the purchase of additional advertising services and exploration of new media channels. Rosetta Stone also intended to add retail relationships and kiosks.

The direct-to-consumer channel produced 57% of consumer revenue for the year ended December 31, 2009. This channel included sales from websites and call centers. Sales to retailers such as Amazon.com, Apple, Barnes & Noble, Books-A-Million, Borders, London Drugs retail outlets, and Office Depot accounted for 23% of consumer revenue. Sales from kiosks made up 20%.

Rosetta Stone operated 242 retail kiosks, including three full service retail outlets, in airports, malls, and other strategic high-traffic locations in 39 states and the District of Columbia. Sales associates at these kiosks promoted interest with personal demonstrations. These kiosks were considered an efficient use of retail space. Most kiosk site licenses ranged between three to six months with renewal options; the company closed underperforming kiosks.

Rosetta Stone also offered products in unmanned ZoomShop automated kiosks. ZoomShop kiosks were owned by ZoomSystems and worked like vending machines. These kiosks provided interactive demonstrations on their touchscreens with audio that helped illustrate teaching techniques. These devices required low capital commitment and allowed Rosetta Stone to quickly establish a presence in retail locations. Other retailers that relied on ZoomSystems to sell their products from kiosks included Apple, Best Buy, Proactive Solution, Sephora, and the Body Shop.

The Institutional Channel[31]

For the year ended December 31, 2009, institutional sales accounted for 21% of total revenue. Rosetta Stone's institutional distribution model served four markets: primary and secondary schools, colleges, and universities; the U.S. armed forces and federal government agencies; corporations; and not-for-profit organizations.

Sales to educational institutions represented 44% of institutional sales for the year ended December 31, 2009. Sales to governmental agencies, the armed forces, and not-for-profit organizations accounted for 25% of institutional sales. Examples of not-for-profit groups purchasing Rosetta Stone products included those that trained volunteers to teach ESL students, sent members overseas for work, and established literacy programs. Home school sales represented 19% and corporations 12% of institutional revenue.

Regional sales managers were assigned to sales territories and supervised account managers who maintained the customer base. The company expanded its sales force to keep up with its institutional marketing activities. Rosetta Stone promoted interest within this channel with onsite visits, speaking engagements, trade show and conference demonstrations, seminar attendance, direct mailings, advertising in institutional publications, and responses to request for proposals and to calls based on recommendations from existing customers. Request for proposals were statements seeking certain services through a bidding process that were made to vendors.

International

International sales accounted for 8% of revenue for the year ended December 31, 2009. In addition to its international subsidiaries in the United Kingdom, Germany, South Korea, and Japan, the company operated 9 kiosks in the United Kingdom, 12 in Japan, and 20 in South Korea.[32] To facilitate growth, the company planned to develop its international business through its subsidiaries and to explore opportunities in additional markets in Europe, Asia, and Latin America.

Protecting Rosetta Stone

The company relied on patents, trade secrets, trademarks, copyrights, and nondisclosure and other contractual arrangements to protect its intellectual property.[33] **Exhibit 1** lists the company's intangible assets. Rosetta Stone also protected its trade dress, or the visual appearance of its products and its packaging. The company believed that its yellow box and blue logos were important in building Rosetta Stone's brand image and distinguishing its solutions from those of its competitors.[34] In addition, individuals who worked for Rosetta Stone were required to sign agreements that prohibited the unauthorized disclosure of the company's proprietary rights, information, and technology.[35]

Each CD-ROM came with a product key that verified that the disc was not illegally copied. The key activated the program after installation and prevented multiple accesses to the product. Rosetta Stone customers had to agree to terms listed in a license agreement in order to use the programs. Software could be installed on more than one personal computer, but not more than one person was allowed to use the program at the same time.[36] Those who purchased the CD-ROM were not allowed to make backup copies. Online users were forbidden to transfer their user name, password, or activation ID to any other person.

Rosetta Stone Inc. was sensitive to software piracy and how unauthorized access to its language programs affected the company's reputation and profitability. Peer-to-peer file sharing network sites like eDonkey, BitTorrent, and Direct Connect provided individuals with a means of distributing and downloading illegal copies of Rosetta Stone.[37] Unauthorized users took advantage of paid subscribers' information, using corporate or educational logins in order to access the company's online offerings. Those who disregarded Rosetta Stone's protection measures were subject to civil and criminal laws. Violators could be fined up to US$250,000, face up to five years in prison, or both.[38] The company provided links on its website where individuals could report instances of piracy.

The company also attempted to educate users about the various risks they were exposed to as a result of Internet fraud.[39] On its website, Rosetta Stone explained that buying from unauthorized dealers leaves users subject to identity theft and exposed to defective or corrupted software and software viruses. In addition, using unauthorized products excluded users from access to warranties, proper manuals, support services, and software upgrades.

The Language-Learning Industry

Rosetta Stone's target customers had a number of reasons for learning a second, third, or fourth language. The language-learning industry served a replenishing global customer base. For some people, learning a language provided a means of personal enjoyment and enrichment.[40] It allowed learners to participate in new cultures and travel abroad. Many individuals also took advantage of language instruction to improve their earning power and career flexibility. In addition, people learned languages to communicate with friends and family and allow for opportunities to extend relationships past language borders. Institutions like businesses and schools especially took note of this interest in language learning in developing products, services, or advertisements in order to reach more people.

Among the most studied languages were Chinese (Mandarin), Spanish, English, and Arabic.[41] According to Simple-Chinese.com, there were 40 million people learning Chinese as a second language in 2009. This number had increased by 60% since 2004, reflecting a 10% increase in Chinese learners every year.[42] The growth in the Spanish-speaking population in the United States influenced the popularity of the language. In 2009, the Pew Hispanic Research Center estimated that there were 44 million Hispanics living in the United States. It projected that this number would grow exponentially to over 100 million people by 2050, when Hispanics would make up 25% of the total population.[43]

There were 328 million native English speakers in 2009.[44] English was the predominant language for careers in business, science, and technology. According to Asiaone.com, 33% of the world's population would be learning English by 2016.[45] British Prime Minister Gordon Brown estimated that 300 million people from China and 350 million people from India spoke English. The demand for Arabic speakers in the United States increased after the September 11, 2001, attacks and the movement of American troops into Afghanistan and Iraq.[46] Companies like Sakhr Software took advantage of this demand and their technology to market services to the U.S. government. Sakhr Software was an Egyptian company that developed a mobile application that could transmit audio translations of spoken phrases.[47]

The demand for language-learning products and services created a fragmented industry influenced by trends and consumer preferences. The industry provided language students with many alternative educational materials and environments in which to practice. Students could seek language lessons from textbook publishers, audio CD and MP3 download providers, schools and universities, language centers like Berlitz and Inlingua, and online tutoring services.[48] Students also relied on online dictionaries, translation services, and online social environments for language aid. Some services required students to pay, and others provided their offerings for free. Students could pay anywhere from US$1.99 for a mobile application to US$54,410 for one year of undergraduate education at Sarah Lawrence College in Bronxville, New York.[49]

Students differentiated language references and instruction by their teaching methods, effectiveness, convenience, fun and likelihood of continued practice, advertising, reputation, and price.[50] The industry took advantage of trends such as increased online accessibility and dependence, interactive games, social networking, and the use of mobile applications. According to a 2008 report by Euromonitor International Inc., a market research firm, there were more than one billion personal computers in use and 1.7 billion people using the Internet by 2009.[51] According to a 2007 report by Global Industry Analysts Inc., a market research firm, the global demand for the delivery of instructional content through the use of electronic technology, or eLearning, would grow an average of 21% annually between 2007 and 2010, reaching a total estimated value of US$53 billion by 2010.[52]

Competitors

Rosetta Stone's primary competitors, most of which were privately held and divisions of larger corporations, included Berlitz International Inc., Simon & Schuster, Inc. (Pimsleur), Random House Ventures LLC (Living Language), Disney Publishing Worldwide, McGraw-Hill Education, and Pearson. These companies differentiated their products and services by means of the following features: teaching methods, effectiveness, convenience, fun and likelihood of continued practice, advertising, reputation, and price.[53]

Berlitz International Inc. presented the Berlitz Method as a teaching style that contextualized vocabulary and grammar in real-life situations and simulated natural conversations.[54] The Berlitz School of Language was founded in 1878 and marketed to individuals, businesses, and institutions. The company had over 500 locations in 70 countries and provided access to more than 50 languages. Examples of Berlitz's offerings included online courses, study abroad programs, and cultural consulting. Language students could participate in Berlitz's virtual semi-private instruction, which started at US$1445.

Simon & Schuster, Inc. (Pimsleur) was founded in 1924.[55] It was the publishing arm of CBS Corporation, a media company. The Audio Division's Pimsleur Language Program was a series of audio books available in more than 50 languages. It was even accessible on the iPhone as an application. The Pimsleur Method relied on graduated interval recall, anticipation of correct responses, and utilization of core vocabulary. The program encouraged students to understand and speak from the start. Prices for Pimsleur products ranged from US$11.95 to US$345.

Random House Ventures LLC (Living Language) was originally developed by U.S. government experts in 1946 for overseas-bound service personnel and diplomats.[56] It offered books, CDs, digital downloads, and online courses in 28 different languages. Among its offerings were applications for the iPod or iPhone and niche references on language learning for babies and bilingual children. Prices for Living Language products ranged from US$9.95 to US$99.95.

Disney Publishing Worldwide was the publishing arm of Walt Disney's Consumer Products Division.[57] The company licensed its characters to English-training ventures in China until it decided to develop its own schools there for children ages 1 to 11. Disney planned to increase the number of its schools from 11 to 148 and earn over US$100 million from 2010 to 2015. The company sought to reach 150,000 children whose parents were willing to pay US$2200 a year for tuition that would cover two hours of instruction per week. In China, Disney also considered initiatives such as establishing an English distance-learning program, which could involve lessons via web conferencing, e-mail, or recorded video, and developing English learning products to sell in retail outlets.

McGraw-Hill Education was a division of The McGraw-Hill Companies, founded in 1888.[58] It provided educational materials and references for the following markets: Pre-K to 12, Assessment, Higher Education, and Professional. The company had offices in 33 countries and works published in more than 65 languages. Within the language-learning industry, the company offered materials for students of all ages. Abroad, McGraw-Hill Education partnered with the Tata Group to offer English training courses tailored for the Banking/Financial Services sector.[59] In 2009, the company partnered with the Chinese vocational-training firm Ambow to launch an English-language program specifically for IT engineers.[60] The McGraw-Hill Companies had sales of US$5.95 billion in 2009.

Pearson had businesses in education, business information, and consumer publishing.[61] It employed 37,000 individuals in 60 countries and provided products and services ranging from textbooks and software to assessment and teacher development materials. Pearson's English language division, Pearson Longman, provided English programs for more than 20 million students. The company also owned the Learning Education Center chain of language schools in China and developed digitally deliverable products, such as English language materials on mobile phones, for institutional and individual customers. The company made US$9.1 billion in revenue fiscal year 2009.

Rosetta Stone's online competitors provided students with myriad language aids and opportunities to practice their skills. Some websites offered all of their services for free, while some programs charged users as their skills progressed. GermanPod101.com and ChinesePod.com offered audio and video language lessons in addition to tutoring. RhinoSpike.com, launched in March 2010, supported a library of almost 2500 recordings spoken by native speakers.[62] Language learners frequented the site to improve their pronunciation. WordReference.com hosted forums where individuals could post and answer questions about correct phrasing and grammar.

A number of competitors took advantage of the Internet and social networking trends to help individuals feel more engaged during the learning process. Livemocha.com, a company with US$14 million in venture capital financing, offered language lessons on a social network environment for more than 38 languages.[63] Users corrected each other's writing assignments and their profiles displayed points and medals won from language games. In August 2009, LiveMocha partnered with Pearson to co-develop and launch an English conversational program available on LiveMocha's online platform.[64]

MyLanguageExchange.com, founded in 2000, listed profiles of people who want to share their language expertise with others trying to learn the language.[65] MyLanguageExchange users could pay US$24 per year to e-mail other users for one-on-one practice. In 2009, this website boasted 1.5 million members studying 115 languages. UsingEnglish.com, Englishcage.com, and Englishbaby.com allowed users to share photos and interests.[66] Skype, a software application that allowed users to make voice calls over the Internet, set up forums where people from around the world could practice with native speakers.

Financial Analysis

From 2004 to 2009, Rosetta Stone's revenue increased from US$25.4 million to US$252.3 million, representing a 58% compound annual growth rate.[67] The company's consolidated statement of operations from 2006 to 2009 is available in **Exhibit 2**. Select data from the consolidated statement of operations featuring figures from 2006 to 2009 is shown as a percent of revenue in **Exhibit 3**. Revenue from 2009 reflected an increase of US$42.9 million or 21% from the amount produced in 2008. **Exhibit 4** compares revenue from 2009 to revenue from 2008. Rosetta Stone's 2008 revenue included a US$2.6 million initial stocking order from Barnes & Noble to support the bookstore's expansion of Rosetta Stone products to over 650 of its national stores.[68] In 2009, Rosetta Stone did not have any comparable stocking orders. Rosetta Stone's consolidated balance sheet is available in **Exhibit 5**.

EXHIBIT 3 Consolidated Statement of Operations: Rosetta Stone Inc. (Dollar amount in thousands except per share amounts)

As a Percent of Total Revenue Exchange Rate Used Is That of the Year End Reported Date

| | | | | | | | | | January 4, | |
| | | | | Year Ended December 31, | | | | | | |
Year Ending December 31	2009	% of Revenue	2008	% of Revenue	2007	% of Revenue	2006	% of Revenue	2006	% of Revenue
Revenue										
Product	218,549	86.6	184,182	88.0	119,897	87.3	80,604	88.3	178	65.4
Subscription & service	33,722	13.4	25,198	12.0	17,424	12.7	10,694	11.7	94	34.6
Total revenue	252,271		209,380		137,321		91,298		272	
Cost of product revenue	30,264		26,539		19,055		11,549		199	
Cost of subscription & service revenue	3,163		2,137		1,632		992		4	
Total cost of revenue	33,427		28,676		20,687		12,541		203	
Gross profit	218,844		180,704		116,634		78,757		69	
Operating expenses										
Sales & marketing expenses	114,899	45.5	93,384	44.6	65,437	47.7	45,854	50.2	695	255.5
Research & development*	26,239	10.4	18,387	8.8	12,893	9.4	20,714	8.9	41	15.1
General & administrative expenses	57,174	22.7	39,577	18.9	29,786	21.7	16,590	18.2	142	52.2
Lease abandonment	—	—	1,831.0	0.9	—	—	—	—	—	—
Total operating expenses	198,312	78.6	153,179	73.2	108,116	78.7	83,158	91.1	878	322.8

*In 2006, Research and Development expenses included $12,597 of acquired in-process R&D.

SOURCE: Rosetta Stone Inc., *2009 Form 10-K*, p. F-4.

EXHIBIT 4 Revenue Comparison for 2009 and 2008: Rosetta Stone Inc.

| | Year Ended December 31 | | | | Change | % Change |
| | 2009 | | 2008 | | | |
			(dollars in thousands)			
Product revenue	$218,549	86.6%	$184,182	88.0%	$34,367	18.7%
Subscription and service revenue	33,722	13.4%	25,198	12.0%	$8,524	33.8%
Total revenue	$252,271	100.0%	$209,380	100.0%	$42,891	20.5%
Revenue by sales channel						
Direct-to-consumer	$114,002	45.2%	$96,702	46.2%	$17,300	17.9%
Kiosk	40,418	16.0%	36,314	17.3%	$4,104	11.3%
Retail	44,850	17.8%	34,638	16.5%	$10,212	29.5%
Total consumer	199,270	79.0%	167,654	80.1%	31,616	18.9%
Institutional	53,001	21.0%	41,726	19.9%	$11,275	27.0%
Total revenue	$252,271	100.0%	$209,380	100.0%	$42,891	20.5%

SOURCE: Rosetta Stone Inc., *2009 Form 10-K*, p. 53.

EXHIBIT 5 Consolidated Balance Sheet: Rosetta Stone Inc. (in thousands, except per share amounts)

Exchange Rate Used Is That of the Year End Reported Date

Year Ending December 31	2009	% Change	2008	% Change	2007
Assets					
Current assets					
Cash & cash equivalents	95,188	210.8	30,626	41.2	21,691
Restricted cash	50	47.1	34	(91.3)	393
Accounts receivable, net	37,400	41.1	26,497	123.6	11,852
Inventory, net	8,984	82.9	4,912	27.2	3,861
Prepaid expenses & other current assets	7,447	12.9	6,598	70.4	3,872
Deferred income taxes	6,020	163.8	2,282	169.1	848
Total current assets	**155,089**	118.6	**70,949**	66.9	**42,517**
Property & equipment, net	18,374	16.8	15,727	17.0	13,445
Goodwill	34,838	1.9	34,199	0.0	34,199
Intangible assets, net	10,704	0.6	10,645	(22.1)	13,661
Deferred income taxes	5,565	(18.5)	6,828	12.2	6,085
Other assets	872	85.5	470	0.2	469
Total assets	**225,442**	62.4	**138,818**	25.8	**110,376**
Liabilities					
Current liabilities					
Accounts payable	1,605	(50.0)	3,207	(30.8)	4,636
Accrued compensation	10,463	22.1	8,570	73.5	4,940
Other current liabilities	25,638	20.1	21,353	87.0	11,421
Deferred revenues	24,291	68.9	14,382	19.4	12,045
Income taxes payable	4,184	—	—	—	—
Current maturities of long-term debt—related party	—	—	4,250	25.0	3,400
Total current liabilities	**66,181**	27.9	**51,762**	42.0	**36,442**
Long-term debt, related party	—	—	5,660	(42.9)	9,909
Deferred revenue	1,815	33.3	1,362	52.3	894
Other long-term liabilities	1,011	5.0	963	15,950.0	6
Total liabilities	**69,007**	15.5	**59,747**	26.4	**47,251**
Stockholders' equity					
Class B redeemable convertible preferred stock	—	—	—	—	5,000
Class A, series A-1 convertible preferred stock	—	—	26,876	0.0	26,876
Class A, series A-2 convertible preferred stock	—	—	17,820	0.0	17,820
Class B convertible preferred stock	—		11,341	78.9	6,341
Common stock, net	2	100.0	1	0.0	1
Additional paid-in capital	130,872	1,110.2	10,814	25.6	8,613
Accumulated income (loss)	25,785	107.6	12,422	(945.0)	(1,470)
Accumulated other comprehensive income (loss)	(224)	10.3	(203)	262.5	(56)
Total stockholders' equity (deficit)	**156,435**	97.8	**79,071**	36.0	**63,125**
Total liabilities and stockholders' equity	**225,442**	62.4	**138,818**	31.7	**110,376**

....
SOURCE: Rosetta Stone Inc., *2009 Form 10-K*, p. F-3.

For fiscal year 2009, consumer revenue was US$199.3 million, up 19% from the previous year. The company attributed this growth to a 14% increase in unit sales and a 4% increase in the average selling price of each unit.[69] The increase in sales resulted in a US$23.8 million increase in revenue, and the price increase accounted for a US$7.8 million increase in revenue. The increase in units sold was traced to Rosetta Stone's planned expansion of its direct marketing strategies as well as growth in its retail distribution network.[70] Product revenue represented 96% of total consumer revenue, and subscription and service revenue represented the remaining 4%.

Institutional revenue amounted to US$53.0 million in 2009, increasing by US$11.3 million, or 27%, since 2008. The increase in institutional revenue was primarily due to the expansion of Rosetta Stone's direct sales force.[71] This expansion increased education revenue by US$4.8 million, government revenue by US$3.9 million, and corporate revenue by US$2.0 million. Product revenue represented 52% of total institutional revenue for the year ended December 31, 2009, and subscription and service revenue represented 48% of total institutional revenue.

According to Tom Adams, "Strong demand from both consumers and institutions for (its) industry-leading language-learning solution drove record revenues and earnings in Rosetta Stone's fourth quarter (of 2009). Rosetta Stone's consumer business delivered solid results on the back of record demand . . ."[72] The company's international revenue accounted for 11% of fourth quarter 2009 revenue, up from 5% for the same period in 2008. It grew to US$8.5 million, or 76% over the third quarter of 2009, and more than 160% over the fourth quarter of 2008.

NOTES

1. Rosetta Stone, Inc., *2009 Form 10-K*, p. 3.
2. Ibid.
3. "Top 20 Risks Facing U.S. Tech Companies," *EWeek*, http://www.eweek.com/c/a/IT-Management/Top-20-Risks-Facing-US-Tech-Companies-879264/ (September 7, 2010).
4. *History | Rosetta Stone*, http://www.rosettastone.com/ (August 21, 2010).
5. Rosetta Stone, Inc., *2009 Form 10-K*, p. 15.
6. Ibid.
7. "Best Graduate Schools 2008," *US News*, http://grad-schools.usnews.rankingsandreviews.com/best-graduate-schools/ (September 6, 2010).
8. Rosetta Stone, Inc., *2009 Form 10-K*, p. 15.
9. Phil Wahba, "Rosetta Stone IPO Prices Above Estimate Range | Reuters," *Reuters.co.uk* (April 16, 2009), http://uk.reuters.com/article/idUKTRE53E7GP20090416 (September 7, 2010).
10. Ibid.
11. Rosetta Stone, Inc., *2009 Form 10-K*, p. 18.
12. Rosetta Stone, Inc., *2009 Form 10-K*, p. 6.
13. *Language Learning | Rosetta Stone*, http://www.rosettastone.com/ (August 21, 2010).
14. Rosetta Stone, Inc., *2009 Form 10-K*, p. 5.
15. *Language Learning | Rosetta Stone*, http://www.rosettastone.com/ (August 21, 2010).
16. Rosetta Stone, Inc., *2009 Form 10-K*, p. 11.
17. Ibid., p. 12.
18. Ibid., p. 10.
19. IBID., P. 11.
20. Ibid., p. 8.
21. Ibid., p. 12.
22. Ibid., p. 11. This section was directly quoted, except for minor editing.
23. Susan J. Campbell, "Rosetta Stone Now Offering Dedicated Customer Support on Facebook via 'Parature for Facebook,'" *TMCnet.com* (August 13, 2010), http://www.tmcnet.com/channels/customer-support-software/articles/95152-rosetta-stone-now-offering-dedicated-customer-support-facebook.htm (August 21, 2010).
24. Rosetta Stone, Inc., *2009 Form 10-K*, p. 16.
25. Ibid., pp. 7–8. This section was directly quoted, except for minor editing.
26. Ibid., pp. 3, 13–15. This section was directly quoted, except for minor editing.
27. Ibid., p. 21.
28. Phil Wahba, "Rosetta Stone IPO Prices Above Estimate Range | Reuters," *Reuters.co.uk* (April 16, 2009), http://uk.reuters.com/article/idUKTRE53E7GP20090416 (September 7, 2010).
29. Rosetta Stone, Inc., *2009 Form 10-K*, p. 45. This section was directly quoted, except for minor editing.
30. Rosetta Stone, Inc., *2009 Form 10-K.*, pp. 3, 13–14. This section was directly quoted, except for minor editing.
31. Ibid., pp. 14–15.
32. Ibid., p. 14.
33. Rosetta Stone, Inc., *2009 Form 10-K.*, p. 17.
34. Ibid.
35. Ibid.
36. "Global End User Agreement," *Rosetta Stone*. (September 6, 2010). http://www.rosettastone.com/us_assets/eulas/eula-global-eng.pdf.

37. "Rosetta Stone Continues Strong Stand on Piracy and Distribution of Counterfeit Products | Rosetta Stone | Rosetta Stone," *Rosetta Stone* (February 13, 2009), http://www.rosettastone .co.uk/global/press/releases/20090213-rosetta-stone-continues-strong-stand-on-piracy-and-distribution-of-counterfeit-products (September 7, 2010).

38. "Anti Piracy," *Rosetta Stone*, http://www.rosettastone.com/global/anti-piracy (September 7, 2010).

39. Ibid.

40. Rosetta Stone, Inc., *2009 Form 10-K*, p. 3.

41. "Most Popular Languages in the World by Number of Speakers—Infoplease.com," *Infoplease: Encyclopedia, Almanac, Atlas, Biographies, Dictionary, Thesaurus. Free Online Reference, Research & Homework Help—Infoplease.com*, http://www.infoplease.com/ipa/A0775272.html (September 7, 2010).

42. "Chinese Language Becomes More Popular Worldwide," *Simple-Chinese.com*, http://www.simple-chinese.com/china-blog/chinese-language-becomes-more-popular-worldwide/ (September 7, 2010).

43. "Why Is It Important to Learn Spanish?" *Learn Spanish Abroad: IMAC Spanish Language Schools | Spanish Language Courses*, http://www.spanish-school.com.mx/learnspanish.php (September 7, 2010).

44. "State of Global Translation Industry (2009)," *MyGengo.com,* http://www.slideshare.net/dmc500hats/mygengocom-state-of-global-translation-industry-2009 (September 7, 2010).

45. "India Falling behind China in English," *Asiaone,* http://www.asi-aone.com/News/Education/Story/A1Story20091120-181251.html (September 6, 2010).

46. "US Scrambles to Find Linguists for Afghan Surge," *The Journal of Turkish Weekly,* http://www.turkishweekly.net/news/78751/-us-scrambles-to-find-linguists-for-afghan-surge.html (September 5, 2010).

47. "Now, Smartphones That Translate Languages—The Economic Times," *The Economic Times: Business News, Personal Finance, Financial News, India Stock Market Investing, Economy News, SENSEX, NIFTY, NSE, BSE Live, IPO News*, http://economic-times.indiatimes.com/Now-smartphones-that-translate-languages/articleshow/4724646.cms (September 7, 2010).

48. Jane L. Levere, "As Many Software Choices as Languages to Learn," *The New York Times* (November 26, 2006). http://www.nytimes.com/2006/11/26/business/yourmoney/26language.html?_r=1&scp=3&sq=rosettastone,languages&st=nyt (August 21, 2010).

49. Lindsay Dittman, "The Most EXPENSIVE Colleges and Universities (PHOTOS)," *The Huffington Post* (March 29, 2010), http://www.huffingtonpost.com/2010/03/29/the-most-expensive-colleg_n_517861.html (September 7, 2007).

50. Rosetta Stone, Inc., *2009 Form 10-K*, pp. 16–17.

51. Ibid., p. 5. This section was directly quoted, except for minor editing.

52. Ibid. This section was directly quoted, except for minor editing.

53. Rosetta Stone, Inc., *2009 Form 10-K*, p. 16.

54. *Berlitz Home*, http://www.berlitz.com/ (September 7, 2010).

55. *Foreign Language Learning Programs from Pimsleur*, http://www.pimsleur.com/ (September 7, 2010).

56. *Living Language*, http://www.randomhouse.com/livinglanguage/ (September 6, 2010).

57. Matthew Garrahan and Annie Saperstein, "Disney to Expand Language Schools in China," *Financial Times* [Los Angeles] (July 6, 2010).

58. "About Us," *The McGraw-Hill Companies,* http://www.mcgraw-hill.com/site/about-us (September 7, 2010).

59. "McGraw-Hill Education and Tata Expand Partnership in Education and Professional Training," *Investor Relations—The McGraw-Hill Companies* (March 17, 2010), http://investor.mcgraw-hill.com/phoenix.zhtml?c=96562&p=irol-newsArticle&ID=1403377&highlight= (August 21, 2010).

60. "McGraw-Hill Deepens Commitment to China's $4 Billion Professional Development Education Market through New Relationship with Ambow Education," *Investor Relations—The McGraw-Hill Companies* (November 11, 2009), http://investor.mcgraw-hill.com/phoenix.zhtml?c=96562&p=irol-newsArticle&ID=1354199&highlight= (September 7, 2010).

61. *Pearson,* http://www.pearson.com/ (September 7, 2010).

62. Peter Wayner, "Learning a Language From an Expert, on the Web," *The New York Times* (July 28, 2010).

63. Ibid.

64. Ibid.

65. Ibid.

66. Ibid.

67. Rosetta Stone, Inc., *2009 Form 10-K*, p. 3.

68. Ibid., p. 53.

69. Ibid.

70. Ibid.

71. Ibid.

72. "Rosetta Stone Inc. Reports Fourth Quarter 2009 Results," *Rosetta Stone* (February 25, 2010), http://pr.rosettastone.com/phoenix.zhtml?c=228009&p=irol-newsarticle&ID=1395780&highlight= (September 7, 2010).

CASE 24

Dollar General Corporation:

2011 GROWTH EXPANSION PLANS (MINI CASE)

Kathryn E. Wheelen

Expansion Plan

On January 6, 2011, the management of Dollar General announced its 2011 expansion plan for the company. Dollar General had plans to open 625 stores, add 6000 employees, and open stores in three additional states—Connecticut, Nevada, and New Hampshire. Recently, the company announced plans to open stores in Colorado. In addition, the company intended to remodel or relocate 550 of its 9200 stores in 35 states.

Each store averaged 6 to 10 employees, a combination of full-time and part-time employees. Employees had the option of flex-time, and wages were competitive to the local market wages. The company had 79,800 employees altogether.[1]

Industry

The dollar discount store industry's primary competitors were Dollar General, the largest company, with revenues of US$12.73 billion; Family Dollar Stores, with revenues of US$8.04 billion; and Dollar Tree in third place with revenues of US$5.71 billion. The industry's total revenue was US$36.98 billion.[2] See **Exhibit 1** for information on each of the three major players in this industry segment.

The discount variety store industry's main competitor was Wal-Mart, with revenues of US$419.24 billion, 2,100,000 employees, and an income of US$15.11 billion. Wal-Mart operated more than 3500 stores and supercenters and 596 Sam's Clubs in the United States.

EXHIBIT 1
Direct Competitors
of Dollar General
(Data is trailing
12 months)

A. Dollar Discount Stores' Competitive Information

	Dollar General	Family Dollar	Dollar Tree
Net sales (millions)	$12,735	$8,041	$5,716
YoY Chg	8.00%	7.6%	13.0%
3-Year CAGR	10.3%	5.1%	10.3%
Comparable sales Chg	5.8%	5.9%	7.1%
Gross margin	32.0%	35.7%	35.3%
Operating margin	9.0%	7.3%	10.3%
Profit margin	3.9%	4.5%	6.5%
Operating income (millions)	$1,145	$588	$590
YoY Chg (in bps)	27.6%	23.8%	7.1%
Net income (millions)	$493	$365	$370
YoY Chg	47.4%	21.8%	27.2%
3-YR GAGR	N/A	14.9%	21.9%
Diluted EPS	$1.43	$2.72	$2.84
YoY Chg	36.2%	27.1%	33.1%
3-YR CAGR	N/A	18.6%	27.6%
Store count	9,273	6,852	4,009
Retail selling Sq. Ft	66,270,000	48,721,000	34,400,000
Employees	79,800	50,000	54,480

B. Average Sales

	Dollar General	Family Dollar	Dollar Tree
Avg. sales/selling sq. ft	$198	$167	$172
Avg. sales/stores (1,000s)	$1,408	$1,189	$1,464
Avg. sales/employee	$155,758	$162,116	$172,671

SOURCE: http://seekingalpha.com/article/245097-discount-retail-throwdown-a-closer-look-at-dollar-stores?source=yahoo. Used by permission of the author, Josh Ramer of RetailSails.com.

Wal-Mart also had stores overseas in several countries, with its largest non-U.S. markets consisting of 371 stores in the UK and 279 stores in China.

Target was in second place with revenues of US$66.91 billion, 351,000 employees, and net income of US$2.82 billion. It operated 1746 stores in 49 states. Other large discount store companies were Costco Wholesale Corporation and Kmart Corporation.[3]

Corporate Ownership

KKR (Koldberg Kravis Roberts & Co. L.P.) owned 79.17% (7,898,796,886 shares) of the company stock on September 30, 2010. On March 12, 2007, KKR acquired Dollar General for US$732 billion. KKR, a private equity company, paid a 31% premium for the stock at US$16.78. Goldman Sachs Group Inc. owned 17.17% (1,712,829,454 shares) of the company's stock. Combined, these two companies owned 96.37% of Dollar General's stock. Goldman Sachs was KKR's advisor on this deal, while Lazard and Lehman Brothers were Dollar General's advisor.[4]

Dollar General's sales growth objective in the present depressed economy was contingent on the hiring of employees with wages to support a family, and not jobs at minimum wages and no health care. If the former occurs, this plays into the customers who will shop at Dollar General.

According to the Federal Reserve Chairman, Ben S. Bernanke, wages in 2010 increased only 1.7%. The country needed to add 230,000 jobs just to keep up with the growth in the yearly population (college and high school graduates, etc.). If inflation returned to the economy, wages must exceed the annual wage increase so consumers would have more money to spend.

The U.S unemployment rate in January, 2011 was around 9.4%–9.6%. The actual total unemployment rate was 16.6%.[5]

The Dollar General Store and Merchandise

The average Dollar General store had approximately 7100 square feet of selling space and was typically operated by a manager, an assistant manager, and three or more sales clerks. Approximately 55% of the stores were in freestanding buildings, 43% in strip malls, and 2% in downtown buildings. Most of its customers lived within three miles, or a 10-minute drive, of the stores. The Dollar General store strategy featured low initial capital expenditures, limited maintenance capital, low occupancy and operating costs, and a focused merchandise offering within a broad range of categories, allowing the company to deliver low retail prices while generating strong cash flows and investment returns. A typical new store in 2009 required approximately US$230,000 of equipment, fixtures, and initial inventory, net of payables.

Dollar General generally had not encountered difficulty locating suitable store sites in the past. Given the size of the communities it was targeting, Dollar General believed there was ample opportunity for new store growth in existing and new markets. In addition, the current real estate market was providing an opportunity for Dollar General to access higher-quality sites at lower rates than in recent years. Also, Dollar General believed it had significant opportunities available for its relocation and remodel programs. Remodeled stores required approximately US$65,000 for equipment and fixtures, while the cost of relocations was approximately US$110,000 for equipment, fixtures, and additional inventory, net of payables. Dollar General has increased the combined number of remodeled and relocated stores to 450 in 2009, as compared to 404 in 2008 and 300 in 2007.[6]

The following chart shows Dollar General's four major categories of merchandise:[7]

	2009	2008	2007
Consumables	70.8%	69.3%	66.5%
Seasonal	14.5%	14.6%	15.9%
Home products	7.4%	8.2%	9.2%
Apparel	7.3%	7.9%	8.4%

Finance

Exhibit 2 shows the consolidated balance sheets, and **Exhibit 3** displays the consolidated statements of income for Dollar General. The key financial metrics shown here were developed by management for 2010.[8]

Management recognized that the company had *substantial debt*, which included a US$1.964 billion senior secured term loan facility, which matures on July 6, 2014; US$979.3 million aggregate principal amount of 10.623% senior notes due 2015; and US$450.7 million aggregate principal amount of 11.875%/12.625% senior subordinated toggle notes due 2017. This debt could have important negative consequences to the business, including:

- Same-store sales growth
- Sales per square floor
- Gross profit, as a percentage of sales;

EXHIBIT 2
Dollar General
Corporation and
Subsidiaries
Consolidated
Balance Sheets
(In thousands,
except per share
amounts)

	January 28, 2011	January 29, 2010
Assets		
Current assets:		
Cash and cash equivalents	$ 497,446	$ 222,076
Merchandise inventories	1,765,433	1,519,578
Income taxes receivable	—	7,543
Prepaid expenses and other current assets	104,946	96,252
Total current assets	2,367,825	1,845,449
Net property and equipment	1,524,575	1,328,386
Goodwill	4,338,589	4,338,589
Intangible assets, net	1,256,922	1,284,283
Other assets, net	58,311	66,812
Total assets	$ 9,546,222	$ 8,863,519
Liabilities and shareholders' equity		
Current liabilities:		
Current portion of long-term obligations	$ 1,157	$ 3,671
Accounts payable	953,641	830,953
Accrued expenses and other	347,741	342,290
Income taxes payable	25,980	4,525
Deferred income taxes payable	36,854	25,061
Total current liabilities	1,365,373	1,206,500
Long-term obligations	3,287,070	3,399,715
Deferred income taxes payable	598,565	546,172
Other liabilities	231,582	302,348
Commitments and contingencies		
Redeemable common stock	9,153	18,486
Shareholders' equity:		
Preferred stock, 1,000 shares authorized	—	—
Common stock; $0.875 par value, 1,000,000 shares authorized, 341,507 and 340,586 shares issued and outstanding at January 28, 2011 and January 29, 2010, respectively	298,819	298,013
Additional paid-in capital	2,945,024	2,293,377
Retained earnings	830,932	203,075
Accumulated other comprehensive loss	(20,296)	(34,167)
Total shareholders' equity	4,054,479	3,390,298
Total liabilities and shareholders' equity	$ 9,546,222	$ 8,863,519

SOURCE: Dollar General Corporation, 2010 Form 10-K, p. 64.

EXHIBIT 3
Dollar General Corporation and Subsidiaries Consolidated Statements of Income (In thousands, except per share amounts)

	For the Year Ended		
	January 28, 2011	January 29, 2010	January 30, 2009
Net sales	$ 13,035,000	$ 11,796,380	$ 10,457,668
Cost of goods sold	8,858,444	8,106,509	7,396,571
Gross profit	4,176,556	3,689,871	3,061,097
Selling, general and administrative expenses	2,902,491	2,736,613	2,448,611
Litigation settlement and related costs, net	—	—	32,000
Operating profit	1,274,065	953,258	580,486
Interest income	(220)	(144)	(3,061)
Interest expense	274,212	345,744	391,932
Other (income) expense	15,101	55,542	(2,788)
Income before income taxes	984,972	552,116	194,403
Income tax expense	357,115	212,674	86,221
Net income	$ 627,857	$ 339,442	$ 108,182
Earnings per share:			
Basic	$ 1.84	$ 1.05	$ 0.34
Diluted	$ 1.82	$ 1.04	$ 0.34
Weighted average shares:			
Basic	341,047	322,778	317,024
Diluted	344,800	324,836	317,503

. . . .
SOURCE: Dollar General Corporation, 2010 Form 10-K, p. 65.

- Operating profit
- Inventory turnover
- Cash flow
- Net income
- Earnings per share
- Earnings before interest, income taxes, depreciation, and amortization
- Return on invested capital

Management's position on the impact of debt on the company was stated in the following:

- Increasing the difficulty of our ability to make payments on our outstanding debt
- Increasing our vulnerability to general economic and industry conditions because our debt payment obligations may limit our ability to use our cash to respond to our cash flow to fund our operations, capital expenditures, and future business opportunities or pay dividends;
- Limiting our ability to obtain additional financing for working capital expenditures, debt service requirements, acquisitions, and general corporate or other purposes
- Placing us at a disadvantage compared to our competitors who are less highly leveraged and may be better able to use their cash flow to fund competitive response to changing industry, market, or economic conditions[9]

NOTES

1. Greg Stushinisu, "Dollar General Forges Ahead," January 20, 2011, and company announcement on January 6, 2011, and company documents.

2. Yahoo–Finance–competitors of Dollar General.

3. Yahoo–Finance–for both Wal-Mart and Target.

4. Parla B. Kavilana, "Dollar General to Be Acquired by KKR," *CNNMoney.com*, March 12, 2007.

5. CNN Finance and MSNBC—both had Chairman Bernanke on the news.

6. Dollar General Corporation, "SEC 10-K," January 29, 2010, p. 7. These two paragraphs are directly quoted.

7. Ibid.

8. Ibid., p. 11.

9. Ibid., P. 31.

CASE 25

iRobot:

FINDING THE RIGHT MARKET MIX?

Alan N. Hoffman
Bentley University

IROBOT CORPORATION, FOUNDED IN 1990 IN DELAWARE, has designed and built a vast array of behavior-based robots for home, military, and industrial uses, and is among the first companies to introduce robotic technology into the consumer market. Home care robots are iRobot's most successful products, with over 5 million units sold worldwide, accounting for over half of its total annual revenue. iRobot also had a long-standing contractual relationship with the U.S. government to produce robots for military defense.

The company is fully gauged toward first-mover radical innovation with an extensive R&D budget. Made up of over 500 of the most distinguished robotics professionals in the world, it aims at leading the robotics industry. By forming alliances with companies like Boeing and Advanced Scientific Concepts, it is able to develop and improve upon products that it otherwise is incapable of obtaining solely through its own technology. The company also has a healthy financial position with an excellent cash and long-term debt rate.

Despite these competencies, iRobot still has serious concerns. Although the robotics industry is not highly competitive, iRobot needs more competition to help build up the total scale and visibility of the fledgling industry it has pioneered. Home care robots, its biggest revenue source, is a luxury supplemental good. Times of economic recession, however, could prove to be a problem for the sales of iRobot's consumer goods, given that discretionary budgets are likely decreased. In addition, iRobot had over 70 patents, many of which will begin to expire in 2019. In a rapidly advancing industry, technology can also become obsolete quickly

....

This case was prepared by Professor Alan N. Hoffman, Bentley University and Erasmus University. Copyright © 2010 by Alan N. Hoffman. The copyright holder is solely responsible for case content. Reprint permission is solely granted to the publisher, Prentice Hall, for *Strategic Management and Business Policy*, 13th Edition (and the international and electronic versions of this book) by the copyright holder, Alan N. Hoffman. Any other publication of the case (translation, any form of electronics or other media) or sale (any form of partnership) to another publisher will be in violation of copyright law, unless Alan N. Hoffman has granted an additional written permission. Reprinted by permission. The author would like to thank MBA students Jeremy Elias, Ryan Herrick, Steven Iem, Jaspreet Khambay, and Marina Smirnova at Bentley University for their research. RSM Case Development Centre prepared this case to provide material for class discussion rather than to illustrate either effective or ineffective handling of a management situation. Copyright © 2010, RSM Case Development Centre, Erasmus University. No part of this publication may be copied, stored, transmitted, reproduced or distributed in any form or medium whatsoever without the permission of the copyright owner, Alan N. Hoffman.

and render patents useless. Additionally, iRobot is highly dependent on several third-party suppliers to manufacture its consumer products. It also depends on the U.S. government for the sales of its military products. Any volatility in its supply chain or in government fiscal policy will have grave consequences upon the company's future.

Company History

In the late 1980s, the coolest robots in the world were being developed at the MIT Artificial Intelligence Lab. These robots, modeled on insects, captured the imagination of researchers, explorers, military, and dreamers alike. iRobot cofounders, MIT professor Rodney Brooks and graduates Colin Angle and Helen Greiner, saw this technology as the basis for a whole new class of robots that could make people's lives easier and more fun. In 1990, iRobot was incorporated in the state of Delaware.[1]

After leaving the MIT extraterrestrial labs, the three entrepreneurs focused their business on extraterrestrial exploration, introducing the Genghis for robotic researchers in 1990. In 1998, the founders shifted their focus onto military tactile robots and consumer robots after landing a pivotal contract with the U.S. Defense Advanced Research Project Agency (DARPA). This contract provided funding for the necessary R&D to develop new technologies. As a direct result, iRobot delivered the PacBot to the government in 2001 to assist in the search at the NYC World Trade Center. In 2010, thousands of PacBots were serving the country on the war front.

In 2002, iRobot began selling its first practical and affordable home robot, the Roomba vacuuming robot. With millions of Roomba vacuums sold, iRobot has continued to develop and unveil new consumer robots such as a robotic gutter cleaner and a pool vacuum. In 2005, iRobot raised US$120 million in its IPO and began trading on the NASDAQ stock exchange.

iRobot's Products and Distribution

iRobot designs and builds robots for consumer, government, and industrial use, as shown in **Exhibit 1**. On the consumer robots front, the company offers floor cleaning robots, pool cleaning robots, gutter cleaning robots, and programmable robots. iRobot sells its home robots through a network of over 30 national retailers. Internationally, iRobot relies on a network of in-country distributors to sell these products to retail stores in their respective countries. iRobot also sells its products through its own online store and other online stores like Amazon and Wal-Mart.

Home robots have been the company's most successful products, with over 5 million units sold worldwide. Sales of home robots accounted for 55.5% and 56.4% of iRobot's total revenue in 2009 and 2008, respectively.[2] Currently, iRobot is exploring new technological opportunities, including those that can automatically clean windows, showers, and toilets. The potential to fully clean one's house using automated robots is appealing to customers.

On the government and industrial robotics front, iRobot offered both ground and maritime unmanned vehicles, selling the vehicles directly to end-users or through prime contractors and distributors.[3] Its government customers included the U.S. Army, U.S. Marine Corp, U.S. Army and Marine Corps Robotic Systems Joint Program office, U.S. Navy EOD Technical Division, U.S. Air Force, and Domestic Police and First Responders. For 2009 and 2008, 36.9% and 40.3% (respectively) of iRobot total revenue came from the U.S. government.

Consumer Products:

- **Roomba** floor vacuuming robot: vacuum floors and rugs at the press of a button (US$129–US$549).

- **Scooba** floor washing robot: preps, washes, scrubs, and dries hard floor surfaces (US$299–US$499).

- **Verro** pool cleaning robot: cleans a standard size pool in about an hour while removing debris as small as two microns from the pool floor, walls, and stairs (US$399–US$999).

- **Looj** gutter cleaning robot: simplifies the difficult and dangerous job of gutter cleaning (US$69–US$129).

- **Create** programmable robot: a fully assembled programmable robot based on the Roomba technology that is compatible with Roomba's rechargeable batteries, remote control, and other accessories (US$129–US$299).

Government and Industrial Products:

- iRobot 510 PackBot (advanced EOD configuration)
- iRobot 510 PackBot (FasTac configuration)
- iRobot 510 PackBot (First responder configuration)
- iRobot 510 PackBot (Engineer configuration)
- iRobot 210 Negotiator
- 310 SUGV
- iRobot 1Ka Seaglider
- iRobot 710 Warrior
- Daredevil Project
- LANdroids Project

Competition

The robot-based products market is an emerging market with high entry barriers because it requires new entrants to have access to advanced technology, as well as large amounts of capital to invest in R&D. As a result, the market has relatively few companies competing with each other.

iRobot competes with large and small companies, government contractors, and government-sponsored laboratories and universities. It also competes with companies producing traditional push vacuum cleaners, such as Dyson and Oreck.

Many of iRobot's competitors have significantly more financial resources. These include Sweden-based AB Electrolux, German-based Kärcher, South Korea–based Samsung, UK-based QinetiQ, and U.S.-based Lockheed, all of whom compete against iRobot mainly in the robot vacuum cleaning market and the unmanned ground vehicle market. The iRobot product (for example, its Roomba vacuum robot) is not the most expensive product, but is rated the highest across the majority of comparison points.

AB Electrolux

Founded in 1910, Electrolux is headquartered in Stockholm, Sweden. It does business in 150 countries with sales of 109 billion SEK (US$15 billion), and is engaged in the manufacture and sales of household and professional appliances. Its Electrolux Trilobite vacuum cleaner competed with the iRobot's Roomba vacuum cleaner in international markets. Although Electrolux Trilobite is currently unavailable in the United States, it will likely soon be sold on the company's website. An Electrolux Trilobite is priced at about US$1800, much more than a Roomba, which retails for between US$200 and US$500.

Alfred Kärcher GmbH & Co.

Founded in 1935, Kärcher is a German manufacturer of cleaning systems and equipment, and is known for its high-pressure cleaners. Kärcher does business worldwide, with sales of €1.3 billion (US$1.7 billion). In 2003, it launched Kärcher RC 3000, the world's first autonomous cleaning system, which competes with the iRobot Roomba vacuum cleaner in international markets. Kärcher RC 3000 is not currently sold in the United States but can be purchased and shipped directly from Germany for approximately US$1500.

Samsung Electronics Co., Ltd

Founded in 1969, Samsung is headquartered in South Korea. It is the world's largest electronics company, with a revenue of US$117.4 billion in 2009. It is a prominent player in the world market for more than 60 products, including home appliances such as washing machines, refrigerators, ovens, and vacuum cleaners. In November 2009, Samsung launched Tango, its autonomous vacuum cleaner robot, which is available in South Korea. In March 2010, the company premiered the Samsung NaviBot, an autonomous vacuum cleaner, in Europe. It was priced at €400 to €600 (US$516 to US$774).

QinetiQ

Founded in 2001, QinetiQ is a defense technology company headquartered in the UK with revenues of £1.6 billion (US$2.4 billion). It produces aircraft, unmanned aerial vehicles, and energy products. iRobot's stiffest competitor in the unmanned aerial vehicles market is QinetiQ, which has 2500 Talon robots deployed in Iraq and Afghanistan. iRobot had delivered more than 3000 PackBot robots worldwide.

Lockheed Martin Corporation

Based in Maryland, the U.S.-based Lockheed is the world's second-largest defense contractor by revenue and employs 140,000 people worldwide. It was formed by the merger of Lockheed and Martin Marietta in 1995, and competed with iRobot in the unmanned ground vehicle market.

Research and Development at iRobot

Research and development (R&D) is a critical part of iRobot's success. The company spends nearly 6% of its revenue on R&D. In 2009, its total R&D costs were US$45.5 million, of which US$14.7 million was internally funded, while the remaining amount was funded by government-sponsored research and development contracts. iRobot believes that by utilizing R&D capital it will be able to respond and stay ahead of customer needs by bringing new, innovative products to the market. As of 2009, iRobot had 538 full-time employees, 254 of which were in R&D.[4]

The company's core technology areas are collaborative systems, semi-autonomous operations, advanced platforms, and human-robot interaction. Each area provides a unique benefit to the development and advancement of robot technology. Research in these fields is done using three different methods: team organization, spiral development, and the leveraged model.

Team organization revolves around small teams that focus on certain specific projects or robots. They work together with all the different lines of the business to ensure that a product is well integrated. Primary locations for these teams are Bedford, Massachusetts; Durham, North Carolina; and San Luis Obispo, California.

Spiral development is used for military products. Newly created products are sent into the field and tested by soldiers with an in-field engineer nearby to receive feedback from the soldiers on the product's performance. Updates and improvements are made in a timely manner, and the product is sent back to the field for retesting. This method of in-field testing has allowed iRobot to quickly improve its technology and design so it can truly fulfill the needs of its end-users.

The leveraged model uses other organizations for funding, research, and product development. iRobot's next generation of military products are supported by various U.S. government organizations. Although the government has certain rights to these products, iRobot does "retain ownership of patents and know-how and are generally free to develop other commercial products, including consumer and industrial products, utilizing the technologies developed during these projects."[5] The same methodology holds true when designing consumer products. If expertise is developed that will assist in governmental projects, it is transferred to the appropriate team.

iRobot's continued success depends on its proprietary technology, the intellectual skills of its employees, and its ability to innovate. The company holds at least 71 U.S. patents, 150 pending U.S. patents, 34 international patents, and more than 108 pending foreign applications. The patents held, however, will start to expire in 2019.

Financial Results

Sales, Net Income, and Gross Margins

From 2005 through 2009, iRobot's total revenue more than doubled, from US$142 million to US$299 million. Revenues received from products accounted for nearly 88% of total revenue, far greater than the remaining 12% received from contract revenue, though contract revenue showed a record high of US$36 million by the end of 2009. (See **Exhibit 2**).

Revenues from 2009 showed a decline of US$9 million from 2008 that was mainly attributable to a 6.3% decrease in home robots shipped. This decrease resulted from softening demand in the domestic market. On a more positive note, the total US$30.9 million decrease in domestic sales was partially offset by an increase in international sales (US$23.2 million). Even though revenues declined in 2009, iRobot was able to control its costs and operating expenses, resulting in an increase in net income of over four-fold, from US$756,000 in 2008 to US$3.3 million in 2009.

Cash and Long-Term Debt

iRobot is in a strong financial position regarding cash and long-term debt. In 2009, iRobot increased its cash position by over US$31 million while decreasing the amount of long-term debt by about US$400,000. Its cash position by the end of 2009 was US$72 million versus US$41 million in 2010, an increase of over 77%. This put iRobot in a good position to continue investing in research and development even if sales began to slow. At the end of 2009, iRobot's long-term debt was just over US$4 million (see **Exhibit 3**). iRobot's financial status gives it a competitive edge, as it should be able to withstand both current and future unforeseen swings in sales, supplier issues, and the cancellation of government contracts.

Marketing

iRobot's promotion strategies vary by product group, but neither its defense product group nor its home care product group utilize television or radio advertising. Since defense products are produced solely for the U.S. government, promotion is unnecessary. Home care products, on

EXHIBIT 2

Consolidated Statement of Operations: iRobot Corporation (Dollar amounts in thousands)

Year Ending	January 2, 2010	December 27, 2008	December 29, 2007	December 30, 2006	December 31, 2005
Revenue					
Product revenue	$262,199	$281,187	$227,457	$167,687	$124,616
Contract revenue	36,418	26,434	21,624	21,268	17,352
Total revenue	298,617	307,621	249,081	188,955	141,968
Cost of revenue					
Cost of product revenue	176,631	190,250	147,689	103,651	81,855
Cost of contract revenue	30,790	23,900	18,805	15,569	12,534
Total cost of revenue	207,421	214,150	166,494	119,220	94,389
Gross margin	91,196	93,471	82,587	69,735	47,579
Operating expenses					
Research and development	14,747	17,566	17,082	17,025	11,601
Selling and marketing	40,902	46,866	44,894	33,969	21,796
General and administrative	30,110	28,840	20,919	18,703	12,072
Litigation and related expenses	—	—	2,341	—	—
Total operating expenses	85,759	93,272	85,236	69,697	45,469
Operating (loss) income	5,437	199	(2,649)	38	2,110
Net income	$3,330	$756	$9,060	$3,565	$2,610
Net income attributable to common stockholders	$3,330	$756	$9,060	$3,565	$1,553
Net income per common share					
Basic	$0.13	$0.03	$0.37	$0.15	$0.13
Diluted	$0.13	$0.03	$0.36	$0.14	$0.11
Shares used in per common share calculations					
Basic	24,998	24,654	24,229	23,516	12,007
Diluted	25,640	25,533	25,501	25,601	14,331

the other hand, need to be marketed to generate public demand. iRobot aggressively utilizes social media tools such as Facebook and Twitter primarily for promoting support services and brand recognition. For example, Facebook had at least 10 fan pages for either iRobot Corporation or selected iRobot home cleaning products like Roomba.

Another branding strategy used by iRobot education concerns how the company recognized that fewer and fewer American children go into STEM (science, technology, engineering, math) areas. Because of this, it launched the SPARK (Starter Programs for the Advancement of Robotics Knowledge) program to stimulate an interest in science and technology. The program caters to students ranging from elementary school to the university level. iRobot also initiated an annual National Robotics Week program to educate the public on how robotics technology impacts society. The first national robotics week was held in April 2010 in the Museum of Science in Boston.

iRobot developed an education and research robot, the Create(R) programmable mobile robot, to provide educators, students, and developers with an affordable, preassembled platform for hands-on programming and development. Students can learn the fundamentals of robotics, computer science, and engineering; program behaviors, sounds, and movements; and attach accessories like sensors, cameras, and grippers. It also runs a unique and multifaceted Educational Outreach Program that includes classroom visits and tours of its company headquarters. This is all designed to inspire students to choose careers in the robotics industry and become future roboticists.

EXHIBIT 3

Consolidated Balance Sheet: iRobot Corporation (Dollar amount in thousands)

Year Ending	January 2, 2010	December 27, 2008
Assets		
Current assets		
Cash and cash equivalents	$71,856	$40,852
Short-term investments	4,959	—
Accounts receivable, net of allowance of $90 and $65 at January 2, 2010, and December 27, 2008, respectively	35,171	35,930
Unbilled revenue	1,831	2,014
Inventory	32,406	34,560
Deferred tax assets	8,669	7,299
Other current assets	4,119	3,340
Total current assets	159,011	123,995
Property and equipment, net	20,230	22,929
Deferred tax assets	6,089	4,508
Other assets	14,254	12,246
Total assets	**$199,584**	**$163,678**
Liabilities, redeemable convertible preferred stock, and stockholders'equity		
Current liabilities		
Accounts payable	$30,559	$19,544
Accrued expenses	14,384	10,989
Accrued compensation	13,525	6,393
Deferred revenue and customer advances	3,908	2,632
Total current liabilities	62,376	39,558
Long-term liabilities	4,014	4,444
Commitments and contingencies:		
Redeemable convertible preferred stock, 5,000,000 shares authorized zero outstanding	—	—
Common stock, $0.01 par value, 100,000,000 and 100,000,000 shares authorized and 25,091,619 and 24,810,736 shares issued and outstanding at January 2, 2010, and December 27, 2008, respectively	251	248
Additional paid-in capital	140,613	130,637
Deferred compensation	(64)	(314)
Accumulated deficit	(7,565)	(10,895)
Accumulated other comprehensive loss	(41)	—
Total stockholders' equity	133,194	119,676
Total liabilities, redeemable convertible preferred stock, and stockholders' equity	**$199,584**	**$163,678**

Despite multiple methods of reaching out to current and potential consumers, some industry analysts claim iRobot lacks aggressiveness toward customer acquisition. Many observers believe that iRobot will benefit from more competition to help build industry visibility among consumers.

Operations

iRobot is not a manufacturing company, nor has it ever claimed to be. Its core competency is to design, develop, and market robots, not manufacture them. All non-core activities are outsourced to third parties skilled in manufacturing. While third-party manufacturers provide the raw materials and labor, iRobot concentrates on developing and optimizing prototypes.

Up until April 2010, iRobot used only two third-party manufacturers for its consumer products: Jetta Co. Ltd. and Kin Yat Industrial Co. Ltd., both located in China. iRobot did not have a long-term contract with either company, and the manufacturing was done on a purchase-order basis. This changed in April 2010, when iRobot entered a multi-year manufacturing agreement with electronic parts maker Jabil Circuit Inc., which henceforth would make, test, and supply iRobot's consumer products, including the Roomba.[6]

The Robotic Industry

Robots serve a wide variety of industries, such as the consumer, automotive, military, construction, agricultural, space, renewable energy, medical, law enforcement, utilities, manufacturing, entertainment, mining, transportation, space, and warehouse industries.

In 2008, before the economic downturn, the global market for industry robot systems was estimated to be about 110,000 units.[7] Industrial robot sales worldwide in 2009 slumped by about 50% compared to 2008. The sales started to improve from the third quarter of 2009 onward, with the slow recovery coming from emerging markets in Asia and especially from China. In North America and Europe, sales were also seen slowly improving from late 2009.[8]

The sales of professional services robots, including military and defense robots, were about US$11 billion at the end of 2008 and were expected to grow by US$10 billion for the period of 2009 to 2012.[9]

Twelve million units of household and entertainment robots were expected to be sold from 2009 to 2012 in the mass market, with an estimated value of US$3 billion.[10]

New Markets

The 2009 economic recession had negative impacts on consumer spending. iRobot domestic sales of robot vacuum cleaners, predominantly the Roomba, were down comparable to other US$400 discretionary purchases, and its international sales also experienced a slowdown.[11] In addition to lower consumer demand, the national and international credit crunches led to a scarcity of credit, tighter lending standards, and higher interest rates on consumer and business loans. Continued disruptions in credit markets may limit consumer credit availability and impact home robot sales.

If the robot market does not experience significant growth, the entire industry may not survive. "Fallout has forced the robotics industry to look outside of its comfort zone and move into emerging energy technologies like batteries, wind, and solar power," said Roger Christian, Vice President of Marketing and International Groups at Motoman Inc. He also predicted growing demand for robotics in health care and the food and beverage industry.[12] Under the Obama administration, there were economic incentives devoted to R&D in alternative energy industries. For example, "the Stimulus Act passed by Congress in early 2009, a US$787 billion package of tax cuts, state aid, and government contracts, has made some impact on the alternative energy market in favor of robotics."[13]

In addition to its home care and military markets, iRobot hoped to expand into the civil law enforcement market and the maritime market. It also explored possibilities in the health care market.[14] It partnered with the toy company Hasbro to enter the toy market with My Real Baby—an evolutionary doll that has animatronics and emotional response software.

iRobot continued to grow its international presence by entering new markets. The percentage of its international sales rose from 38% in 2008 to 53.8% in 2009.[15] Its growing focus on international sales resulted in an increase of US$23.2 million in international home robots revenue for 2009 compared to 2008. iRobot also sold its military products overseas in compliance with the International Traffic in Arms Regulations.

Challenges Ahead

Consumer Marketplace

iRobot was competing in a new and emerging market. Although the industry had relatively low competition, analysts believed iRobot needed "more competition, not less, to help build up the total scale and visibility of the fledgling industry it had been pioneering."[16] If the demand for the home robots became stagnant or declined, this would greatly impact the vitality of iRobot and put it under pressure to remain innovative and adaptive to consumer needs in the event that it did gain widespread popularity.

iRobot's consumer products were primarily a luxury supplemental good gauged toward the middle and upper class. iRobot's home cleaning robots were reasonably priced from US$129 to US$1000, depending on the model and accessories. Such a price range was comparable with luxury brands of vacuum machines. However, times of economic recession could prove to be a problem for iRobot's consumer goods sales given that discretionary budgets have contracted. To save money, iRobot's base customers may revert to manual labor.

Supply Chain

For many years, iRobot had only two China-based manufacturers to produce its home cleaning robots and no long-term contract with either of those companies. Its best-selling Roomba 400 series and Scooba series, for example, were both produced by Jetta at a single plant in China. This put iRobot in a high-risk situation if Jetta was unable to deliver products for any unforeseen reason, or if quality started to dip below standards.

Fortunately, iRobot was aware of the problem and signed a new manufacturing agreement with U.S.-based Jabil Circuit. This relationship provided iRobot with numerous benefits, including diversifying key elements of its supply chain, providing geographic flexibility to address new markets, and expanding overall capacity to meet growing demands, explained Jeffrey Beck, president of iRobot's Home Robots Division. Whether this attempt to diversify its supply chain with a new partnership will work out is of crucial importance for iRobot.

Intellectual Property

Continued development of products that are difficult to duplicate through reverse engineering will be the key to success in the area of intellectual property. By maintaining strong relationships and giving superior service to customers such as government agencies, iRobot can create an advantage even if they are unable to ultimately protect their technology from being duplicated. At the same time, iRobot also needs to ensure that its employees will continue to be innovative and create new technologies to keep iRobot competitive for years to come.

Government Contracts

Nearly 40% of iRobot's revenues are from government-contracted military robots. As a contractor or a subcontractor to the U.S. government, iRobot is subject to federal regulations. Fiscal policy and expenditure can be volatile, not only through a single presidency, but certainly during the transition from one presidency to the next. The volatility and unknown demand of the U.S. government presents a problem. The economic fallout from the recession also impacted U.S. federal budgetary considerations. Emphasis and focus was placed on larger, more troubled industries, with large bailout packages made available to financial and automotive companies. It remains to be seen how these large outlays will affect the federal government's ability to continue to fund contracts for robotics.

Strategic Alliances

iRobot relied on strategic alliances to provide technology, complementary product offerings, and better and quicker access to markets. It entered an agreement with The Boeing Company to develop and market a commercial version of the SUGV that was being developed under the Army's BCTM (formerly FCS) program. It also formed an alliance with Advanced Scientific Concepts Inc. for exclusive rights to use the latter's LADAR technology of unmanned ground vehicles. In exchange, iRobot commited itself to purchase units from Advanced Scientific Concepts.

iRobot's Challenge

iRobot's focus on home cleaning products differentiates it from all the other manufacturers in the robotics industry, which are mainly focused on manufacturing robots for the automotive sector. iRobot's focus on two entirely different markets—consumer and military—allows it (1) the ability to leverage its core capabilities and diversification, and (2) provides it with a hedge against slower demand in one sector. By introducing robotics to the consumer market, iRobot has created a "blue ocean of new opportunities." However, iRobot had numerous competitors with more experience in the consumer marketplace.

An analyst wondered if the long-term success in the consumer market would require iRobot to develop more "blue oceans." Also, did it make sense for iRobot to continue to develop new consumer products or would it be better off focusing on the military and aerospace marketplace?

NOTES

1. http://investor.irobot.com/phoenix.zhtml?c=193096&p=irol-faq_pf

2. iRobot *2009 Annual Report, Form 10K*, filed February 19, 2010.

3. Ibid.

4. iRobot *2009 Annual Report*, 2010.

5. Ibid.

6. "iRobot Enters Manufacturing Deal with Jabil," *The Lowell Sun*, (April 28, 2010). http://www.lowellsun.com/latestnews/ci_14830219.

7. http://www.ifr.org/industrial-robots/statistics/

8. Gudrun Litzenberger, IFR Statistical Department, "The Robotics Industry Is Looking Ahead with Confidence to 2010," http://www.emeraldinsight.com/journals.htm?issn=0143-991X&volume=37&issue=5&articleid=1876691&show=html

9. Ibid.

10. Ibid.

11. M. Raskino, (a), 2010, "Insights on a Future Growth Industry." An interview with Colin Angle, CEO, iRobot. http://my.gartner.com/portal/server.pt?open=512&objID=260&mode=2&PageID=3460702&resId=1275816&ref=QuickSearch&sthkw=irobot.

12. B. Brumson, 2010, "Robotics Market Cautiously Optimistic for 2010." Robotic Industries Association. http://www.robotics.org/content-detail.cfm/Industrial-Robotics-Feature-Article/Robotics-Market-Cautiously-Optimistic-for-2010/content_id/1936.

13. Ibid.

14. *Robotreviews*, 2010, "iRobot Celebrates Two Decades of Innovation in Robotics," http://www.robotreviews.com/news/its-national-robotics-week.

15. iRobot *2009 Annual Report*, 2010.

16. M. Raskino, (b), 2010, Cool Vendors in Emerging Technologies," 2010. http://my.gartner.com/portal/server.pt?open=512&objID=260&mode=2&PageID=3460702&resId=133843&ref=QuickSearch&sthkw-irobot.

CASE **26**

Tesla Motors, Inc.:

THE FIRST U.S. CAR COMPANY IPO SINCE 1956

Alan N. Hoffman
Bentley University

Tesla Motors, Inc. is in the business of developing, manufacturing, and selling technology for high-performance electric automotives and power train components. Hoping to develop a greater worldwide acceptance of electric vehicles as an alternative to the traditional internal combustion, petroleum-based vehicles that dominate the market, Tesla is the first company that commercially produced a federally compliant electric vehicle with the design styling and performance characteristics of a high-end performance automobile. Tesla currently offers one vehicle, the Roadster, for sale, as well as supplying electric power train components to Daimler for use in its Smart EV automobile. Additionally, Tesla has a partnership with Toyota Motors to develop and supply an electric power train for Toyota's Rav4 SUV.

Company Background

Tesla Motors was founded in Silicon Valley in 2003 by Martin Eberhard and Marc Tarpenning to create efficient electric cars for driving aficionados. The founders acquired their first round of financing from PayPal and SpaceX founder Elon Musk who subsequently took over as CEO in 2008. The company unveiled its first car, a two-seat sports car named the Roadster, in 2006 after raising $150 million and going through four years of technological and internal struggles.[1] Powered by a three-phase, four-pole AC induction motor, the Roadster has a top speed of 130 mph and accelerates from 0 to 60 mph in under four seconds, all completely silent.[2] Production of the Roadster began in March of 2008 with a first-year production run of 600 vehicles.[3] In June 2008, Tesla announced that it would be building a four-door,

This teaching case was compiled from published sources. The author would like to thank Lindsay Pacheco, Patrick Toomey, Ned Coffee, William Gormly, and Will Hoffman for their research. Please address all correspondence to Dr. Alan N. Hoffman, Dept. of Management, Bentley University, 175 Forest Street, Waltham, MA 02452; ahoffman@bentley.edu. Printed by permission of Dr. Alan N. Hoffman.

five-passenger sedan called the Model S to be built in California and be available for sale in 2012.[4] The Model S is slated to retail for approximately $57,400 and be offered with battery options for 160-, 230-, or 300-mile ranges per charge. The company went public in June 2010 with an initial public offering at $17 a share, raising about $226.1 million in the first stock debut of a car maker since the Ford Motor Company held its initial public offering in 1956.[5]

Tesla has also used its innovative technology to partner with traditional automobile manufacturers on their electric vehicle offerings. In 2009, Tesla signed a deal to provide Daimler with the battery technology to power 1000 electric Smart city cars.[6] Tesla will supply battery packs and electric power trains to Daimler and in return it will receive auto manufacturing and design expertise in areas including safety requirements and mass production of vehicles.[7] Later in that same year, Daimler announced that it had acquired a "nearly 10 percent" stake in Tesla.[8] On October 6, 2010, Tesla entered into a Phase 1 Contract Services Agreement with Toyota Motor Corporation for the development of a validated power train system, including a battery, power electronics module, motor, gearbox, and associated software, which will be integrated into an electric vehicle version of the RAV4 for which Tesla received US$60 million.[9]

In May 2010, Tesla purchased the former NUMMI factory in Fremont, California, one of the largest, most advanced and cleanest automotive production plants in the world, where it will build the Model S sedan and future Tesla vehicles.[10] Additionally, Toyota invested US$50 million in Tesla and together the two companies will cooperate on the development of electric vehicles, parts, and production system and engineering support.[11]

Strategic Direction

Tesla desires to develop alternative energy electric vehicles for people who love to drive. While most car companies are developing small, compact electric cars, Tesla has focused on a high-priced, high-performance electric vehicle that competes against traditional performance cars such as those offered by BMW and Porsche. The company has also devoted many resources to research and development in an effort to produce an electric power train that has both long mileage between recharges and the high performance that car enthusiast's desire.

Tesla's main objectives are to achieve both growth in sales and profits, provide technological leadership in the field of electric vehicles, and foster sustainability and social responsibility. The company desires for growth are served with its development and sale of the Model S vehicle that is expected to retail for almost half of the Roadster price and thus create higher demand and revenue. The company further strives for growth through its strategic partnerships with Toyota and Daimler to supply electric power trains to those companies for use in their electric vehicle designs.

The company's objectives of sustainability and social responsibility are shown through its desire to develop automobiles that are not powered by petroleum products and produce very little carbon emissions. The company won the Globe Sustainability Innovation Award 2009.

Tesla's Competition

Tesla's products participate in the automotive market based on its power train technology. It currently competes with a number of vehicles in the non-petroleum powered (alternative fuel) automobile segment from companies such as Mitsubishi, Nissan, General Motors (Chevy), Toyota, BMW, and Honda to name a few. Within this market segment, there are four primary means of power train propulsion which differentiate the various competitors in this market:

- *Electric Vehicles (EV)* are vehicles powered completely by a single on-board energy storage system (battery pack or fuel cell) which is refueled directly from an electricity source. Both the Tesla Roadster and the Model S are examples of electric vehicles.

- *Plug-in Hybrid Vehicles (PHEV)* are vehicles powered by both a battery pack with an electric motor and an internal combustion engine that can be refueled both with traditional petroleum fuels for the engine and electricity for the battery pack. The internal combustion engine can either work in parallel with the electric motor to power the wheels, such as in a parallel plug-in hybrid vehicle, or be used only to recharge the battery, such as in a series plug-in hybrid vehicle like the Chevrolet Volt.

- *Hybrid Electric Vehicles (HEV)* are vehicles powered by both a battery pack with an electric motor and an internal combustion engine but which can only be refueled with traditional petroleum fuels as the battery pack is charged via regenerative braking, such as used in a hybrid electric vehicle like the Toyota Prius.[12]

- *Hydrogen Vehicles* are vehicles powered by liquefied hydrogen fuel cells. The power plants of such vehicles convert the chemical energy of hydrogen to mechanical energy either by burning hydrogen in an internal combustion engine, or by reacting hydrogen with oxygen in a fuel cell to run electric motors.[13] These vehicles are required to refuel their hydrogen fuel cells at special refueling stations. Examples of these types of vehicles are the BMW Hydrogen 7 and the Honda Clarity.

Mitsubishi i-MiEV

Established in Japan in 1970, Mitsubishi Motors Corporation is a member of the Mitsubishi conglomerate of 25 distinct companies. Mitsubishi Motors is headquartered in Tokyo, Japan, and employs roughly 31,000 employees. The company sells automobiles in 160 countries worldwide and in 2010 sold 960,000 units.[14] Within the United States, the company had a meager 0.5% of the market share in 2010 with 55,683 units sold.[15] Along with traditional gasoline engine automobiles, the company has long been involved in the R&D of electric vehicles. Mitsubishi has been involved in electric vehicle research and development since the 1960s with a partnership with the Tokyo Electric Power Company (TEPCO).[16] Since 1966 to the present, the company has dabbled in electric vehicle and battery research and development with numerous prototype vehicles produced.

In 2009. Mitsubishi released its newest EV car called the i-MiEV (Mitsubishi Innovative Electric Car). The i-MiEV is a small, four-passenger, all-electric car with a top speed of approximately 80 MPH and a quoted range of 75 miles on a single charge based on U.S. driving habits and terrain.[17] The car is based on lithium-ion battery technology. In October 2010, the company announced that it had reached the 5000 production unit mark for the car.[18] Currently the i-MiEV is being sold in Japan, other Asian countries, Costa Rica, and 14 countries in Europe. The Japanese price of the i-MiEV was originally US$50,500 but was reduced to US$42,690 in mid-2010 due to competition from other car companies. Mitsubishi plans on introducing the i-MiEV to the U.S. market in the fall of 2011.

Nissan LEAF

The Nissan Motor Company, formed in 1933, is headquartered in Yokohama, Japan and employs over 158,000 workers. Currently, it builds automobiles in 20 countries and offers products and services in 160 countries around the world.[19] In 2010, it sold globally over 3 million vehicles in its first three fiscal quarters (April 2010–December 2010) with over 700,000 of those being sold in the United States.[20] The company operates two brands, Nissan and Infinity, which design and sell both passenger vehicles and luxury passenger vehicles.

On December 3, 2010, Nissan introduced the LEAF, which it billed as the world's first 100% electric, zero-emission car designed for the mass market.[21] The LEAF is a five-passenger electric car with a top speed of 90 mph and a quoted range of 100 miles on a single charge using lithium-Ion battery technology. The current 2011 price in the United States for the LEAF is approximately US$33,000, which is also eligible for the US$7500 electric vehicle tax credit. It is reported that Nissan had sold 3657 LEAFs by the end of February 2011 with 173 of the sales within the United States and the rest in Japan.[22]

Chevy Volt

Chevrolet Motor Company was formed in 1911 and joined the General Motors Corporation in 1918.[23] GM has its global headquarters in Detroit, Michigan, and employs 209,000 people in every major region of the world and does business in more than 120 countries.[24] In 2010, Chevrolet sold 4.26 million vehicles worldwide and 1.57 million in the United States.[25]

In mid-December 2010, Chevy began delivery of a four-passenger, plug-in hybrid electric vehicle called the Volt. The Volt operates by using an electric engine until the batteries are discharged and then a gasoline engine kicks in for what Chevy calls "extended-range" driving. The car is quoted as having a range of 35 miles in electric mode and an additional 340 miles of extended driving using the gasoline engine.[26] It is reported that Chevy had sold 928 Volts by the end of February 2011; all within the United States.[27] The current 2011 price in the United States for the Volt is approximately US$42,000, which is also eligible for the US$7500 electric vehicle tax credit.

Toyota Prius

The Toyota Motor Company was established in 1937 and is headquartered in Toyota City, Japan. It employs over 320,000 employees worldwide with 51 overseas manufacturing companies in 26 countries and regions.[28] Toyota's vehicles are sold in more than 170 countries and regions. For fiscal year 2010, Toyota sold over 7.2 million vehicles worldwide, of which 1.76 million were sold in the United States.[29]

In 1997, Toyota introduced a five-passenger, gasoline-electric hybrid automobile called the Prius. The Prius has both a gasoline engine and an electric motor, which is used under lighter load conditions to maximize the car's fuel economy. The electric batteries are recharged via the gasoline engine only. On April 5, 2011, Toyota announced that it had sold its 1 millionth Prius in the United States and had surpassed 2 million global sales 6 months earlier in October 2010.[30] Currently, Toyota offers four versions of the Prius in the United States with prices ranging from US$23,000 to US$28,000. The company has announced a plug-in version of the Prius, which is slated for sale in 2012.

BMW Hydrogen 7

Bayerische Motoren Werke (BMW) was established in 1916 in Bavaria, Germany. Originally, the company started manufacturing airplane engines, but after World War I, Germany was not allowed to manufacture any airplane components as part of the terms of the armistice.[31] The company turned its focus to motorcycle engine development and subsequently, in 1928, developed its first automobile. Presently, the company is headquartered in Munich, Germany, and employs approximately 95,000 workers. In 2010, BMW sold approximately 1.2 million vehicles.[32]

In 2006, BMW introduced the four-passenger Hydrogen 7 automobile that was the world's first hydrogen-drive luxury performance automobile.[33] The car is a dual-fuel vehicle capable of running on either liquid hydrogen or gasoline with just the press of a button on the steering wheel.[34] The combined range for the car is approximately 425 miles with the hydrogen tank contributing 125 miles and the gasoline providing the rest. To date, BMW has only produced 100 units of the vehicle, which have been leased/loaned to public figures. The car has not been made available for purchase to the general public and no sale price has been quoted.

Honda Clarity

The Honda Motor Company was established in the 1940s in Japan originally as a manufacturer of engines for motorcycles.[35] Honda produced its first production automobile in 1963 and has been a global supplier since then. In 2010, Honda sold 3.4 million automobiles worldwide with 1.4 million being sold in the United States.[36] In 2008, Honda began production of its four-passenger FCX Clarity, the world's first hydrogen-powered fuel-cell vehicle intended for mass production.[37] The FCX Clarity FCEV is basically an electric car because the fuel cell combines hydrogen with oxygen to make electricity which powers an electric motor, which in turn propels the vehicle.[38] The car can drive 240 miles on a tank, almost as far as a gasoline car, and also gets higher fuel efficiency than a gasoline car or hybrid, the equivalent of 74 miles per gallon of gas.[39] The company planned to ship 200 of the Clarity to customers in Southern California who can lease it for three years at US$600 a month.

Barriers to Entry and Imitation

The barriers to entry into the non-petroleum-powered automobile market segment are high. The hybrid technology for vehicles such as the Prius is well understood by the major automobile companies and many of them have developed and marketed their own version of electric/gasoline hybrid vehicles. The all-electric and hydrogen fuel-cell automobiles are unique technologies that require resources to develop. In this segment, the energy storage and motor technologies are barriers to new competitors. Rechargeable battery systems and fuel cells are newer technologies that require large investments in research and development. A competitor would need to develop its own technologies or partner with another company to acquire these resources.

Proprietary Technology

As electric vehicles are a newer technology, Tesla's innovation has led it to have some unique resources in technology and intellectual property over its competitors. Tesla's proprietary technology includes cooling systems, safety systems, charge balancing systems, battery engineering for vibration and environmental durability, customized motor design and the software and electronics management systems necessary to manage battery and vehicle performance under demanding real-life driving conditions. These technology innovations have resulted in an extensive intellectual property portfolio—as of February 3, 2011, the company had 35 issued patents and approximately 280 pending patent applications with the United States Patent and Trademark Office and internationally in a broad range of areas.[40] These patents and innovations are not easily duplicated by competitors.

A second unique resource that a company developing electric vehicles would require would be its battery cell design. Tesla's current battery strategy incorporates proprietary packaging using cells from multiple battery suppliers.[41] This allows the company to limit the power of its battery supply chain. The company also has announced a partnership with Panasonic to jointly collaborate on next-generation battery development.

Inherent to the requirements for an electric automobile company is the knowledge and skills of the workforce. Tesla believes that its roots in Silicon Valley have enabled it to recruit engineers with strong skills in electrical engineering, power electronics, and software engineering to aid it in development of its electric vehicles and components.[42] Being one of the first to market with a high-performance EV also gives the company a first-mover advantage in experience and branding.

Tesla has an agreement with the automobile manufacture Lotus for the supply of its Roadster vehicle bodies. The company entered into a supply agreement in 2005 with Lotus that requires Tesla to purchase a certain number of vehicle chassis and any additional chassis will require a new contract of redesign to a new supplier.[43] This places a large dependence on Lotus to both fulfil the existing contract and also gives them significant power in the event that Tesla requires additional Roadster units.

Tesla is dependent on its single battery cell supplier. The company designed the Roadster to be able to use cells produced by various vendors, but to date there has only been one supplier for the cells fully qualified. The same is also true for the battery cells used for battery packs that Tesla supplies to other OEMs.[44] Any disruption in the supply of battery cells from its vendors could disrupt production of the Roadster or future vehicles and the battery packs produced for other automobile manufacturers.[45]

External Opportunities and Threats

Electric vehicle companies may be able to take advantage of many of the opportunities with the continuous shift toward green energy. President Barack Obama has publicly committed to funding "green" or alternative energy initiatives through various vehicles.[46] In his 2011 State of the Union Address, the President set a goal of getting one million electric cars on the road by 2015.[47] Within the United States, various federal and state governmental agencies are currently supporting loan programs through the likes of the Department of Energy and the California Zero-Emission Vehicle (ZEV) program. The tragic Louisiana BP oil spill that took place from April to May 2010 intensified the focus on decreasing U.S. dependence on petroleum products. It also highlighted the fact that while alternative energy is currently more expensive to produce than conventional energy, there are hidden environmental and human costs that must be taken into consideration when making this comparison. This increased focus on alternative energy has been beneficial for the EV industry, benefiting both Tesla and its competitors. Due in part to this increase in funding, Tesla is competing in an industry that is expanding, making its absolute market share less relevant than how fast it is growing its market share.

Despite the new dawn of interest and pledges for funding alternative energy, many plans for funding will never come to fruition. Currently in the United States, there is a massive budget deficit, and members of the Republican Party have focused their demands for budget cuts in the "discretionary spending" arena, which is where alternative energy funding falls. Notably, some of the cuts proposed would seriously affect programs funding energy efficiency, renewable energy, and the DOE Loan Guarantee Authority.[48] The EV industry has very few lobbyists compared to the traditional car and petroleum industry, and so is more vulnerable to being targeted in budget cuts. These cuts represent a serious threat to the continued development of the alternative energy and electric car industry. For EVs to come into widespread use, the United States must develop an EV-charging infrastructure, and this will need the support of both state and federal government in the form of both funding and regulation.

Not only is the federal government facing budget cuts, but the state of California is also dealing with massive shortfalls and reductions in services and funding. This is especially important to Tesla since it operates its manufacturing in California, and one of its largest target markets is California, due to the strict emissions regulation and traditional green focus of Californians.

There are also many regulations to which companies developing electric vehicles are subjected. A topic of current interest is the upcoming change in how the range of electric vehicles is calculated—a regulation determined by the EPA. It is thought that the new calculation will result in a lower advertised range for all the electric vehicles, which may make their superiority over traditional petroleum-based vehicles less prevalent. There are also numerous safety requirements that EVs must adhere to, governed by the National Highway Traffic Safety Administration. Companies that produce less than 5000 cars for sale and have three product lines or less can qualify for a gradual phase-in regulation for advanced airbag systems and other safety requirements. Similarly, in Europe, smaller companies are currently exempt from many of the safety testing regulations, and are currently allowed to operate under the "Small Series Whole Vehicle Type Approval."

Additionally, battery safety and testing is regulated by the Pipeline and Hazardous Materials Safety Administration, which is based on UN guidelines regarding the safe transport of hazardous materials. These guidelines ensure that the batteries will perform or travel safely when undergoing changes in altitude, temperature, vibrations, shocks, external short circuiting, and overcharging.

Other regulatory issues include automobile manufacturer and dealer regulations, which are set on a state-by-state basis. In some United States states, such as Texas, it is not legal for the dealer and manufacturer to be owned by the same company. Therefore, these regulations would impact the market penetration levels that a company wishing to utilize a distribution model based on being able to both manufacture and sell its cars through its own wholly owned dealerships would be able to reach in certain states.

An interesting, though potentially costly, new regulation is the minimum noise requirements, mandated by the Pedestrian Safety Enhancement Act of 2010 signed in January 2011. There have been concerns that since electric cars are so much quieter than their combustion-engine counterparts that their design must be somehow altered to increase the amount of noise they generate in order to make them easier to hear by people with impaired vision. These regulations are likely to take effect by 2013 and could alter electric vehicle designs.

The macroeconomic conditions of 2011 and the outlook for the near future is slow but continued growth,[49] in contrast to the past several years of economic retraction. In recent years, American buyers, and indeed buyers in most parts of the world, have cut back on discretionary purchases in light of high unemployment and general economic uncertainty. The economic recovery has created more demand for higher-priced luxury vehicles.

The largest component of what makes an electric vehicle attractive from a financial standpoint is the savings in traditional fuel costs. There is a huge difference between the cost of electricity to recharge an electric vehicle versus the cost of gas to fuel a conventional vehicle. Hence, as oil prices increase, the financial incentive to purchase an electric vehicle increases as well. Additionally, the variability of oil prices means that owners of conventionally powered vehicles cannot predict what their fuel costs for the year will be with any confidence. Thus, the much more stable costs of electricity make an electric vehicle more desirable. It is not likely that the cost of oil will ever see a sustained and significant drop in price, nor is it likely that the cost of oil will ever be as stable as the cost of electricity, creating a sustained advantage over traditionally powered vehicles.

Electric vehicle manufacturers are currently riding the wave of environmental consciousness that began in the 1960s, and has been slowly gaining momentum since. The "Green movement" encourages people to make choices that lessen their negative impact on the environment, and to use resources that are renewable. Alternative fuel products fit this description, by both reducing consumer demand for oil and eliminating harmful emissions during use. For the time being, electric vehicles still leave a noticeable "footprint," though one not nearly as large as a conventional car.

Challenges to Adoption of Electric Cars: Consumer Perceptions

Consumer perceptions of electric vehicles are a huge challenge to adoption. Many people think of electric vehicles as being underpowered, clunky looking, hard to charge, quirky, and undependable. Public experience with traditional vehicles and their concerns about the newness of alterative fuel vehicles must be overcome.

Additionally, the absence of a public infrastructure for recharging electric vehicle batteries introduces a "Which came first – the chicken or the egg?" paradox: There is no infrastructure because there are not enough electric vehicles, and part of the reason why there are not many electric vehicles is because there is no infrastructure to support them. For the time being, consumers must charge their vehicles either at home, or possibly at their place of work. This limits the electric vehicle driving range, which has a negative impact on the image of electric vehicles with consumers.

Another concern that consumers have when considering an alternative energy vehicle is the cost. Electric vehicles, as well as most alternative fuel vehicles, cost significantly more than traditional vehicles of similar style and performance. This is due both to the cost of the research and development and the high cost of materials, particularly for the battery cells.[50] Additionally, the production of low environmental impact products is in most cases more expensive than their conventionally produced counterparts. So long as there are areas of the world willing to sacrifice the environment (natural resources, air, water, waste production) to create low-cost products, this dynamic will continue.

The EV industry is hampered by the public view of the limited range of vehicles in comparison to traditional gasoline cars. In recent years, there has been much advancement in the ways of sustainable energy. High gas prices along with increased awareness on environmental impacts have become the catalysts for new research into sustainability. There has been an increase in new battery technology that is an opportunity for the electric vehicle industry. Currently, the most viable battery for an electric vehicle, that also provides performance, is the lithium-ion battery (is the same type found in your laptop). Companies like Planar Energy are now coming out with "solid state, ceramic-like" batteries that could potentially provide more energy for a lower cost.[51] With these new advances, there is a distinct opportunity for electric car companies to create a better performing and less expensive vehicle. Electric vehicle companies that can develop battery architectures that cross this limited mileage chasm will have positive implications in the public view. Tesla is credited to have one of the industry's best batteries, and it is on the cutting edge of innovative technology. This type of innovative technology is what distinguishes Tesla from other competitors in its industry, and will continue to set it apart across contexts in the market.

Electric vehicles are also reliant on a network of available power sources. Though infrastructure is currently limited, companies like GE are already planning a rollout of EV charging stations to be sold to households, companies, and local governments.[52] The U.S. government has set out to aid in the building of electric vehicle charging stations, with government grants supporting the installation of the electric-car charging stations in areas such as San Francisco and Oregon, which will soon host 15,000 stations around the state, some of them public.[53] An increase in charging station technology and infrastructure should broaden the demand for electric vehicles that is still encumbered by beliefs of limited service and "refueling" capabilities.

Along with the advantages of technological innovations in electric vehicle designs, there are also respective weaknesses to consider, including the amount of time necessary to charge a battery and the limited driving range per charge. Currently, Tesla has reduced the recharge time of its battery cell to 45 minutes, but this is a long time compared to the few minutes that it takes cars to refuel at the gas pump. Coupled with the recharge time of the battery cells is the limited range of electric vehicles. For owners of conventional cars who are used to having a range of 300 miles or more, with a refilling time of 3 to 4 minutes, the limited range and recharging options of EVs can seem very restrictive. However, the average American driver travels only 35 miles per day, and the average trip length is only 10 miles.[54] More importantly, long distance trips (more than 100 miles, accounting for less than 1% of all trips) made by American drivers have a median distance of 194 miles.[55] This indicates that most drivers will very infrequently be driving non-stop for more than 245 miles, making range a virtual non-issue. However, while the facts may be different from perception, it is the perception of consumers that will drive their purchasing behavior, thus still making the range issue a serious concern for EV manufacturers.

The second issue with batteries is their end-of-life concerns. Rechargeable batteries, over time, will become less efficient, and will no longer hold their charge as well as when the battery was new. The same issue exists with electric vehicle batteries. Tesla estimates that after 100,000 miles or seven years, the Roadster's battery will only operate at 60%–65% efficiency.[56] This decrease in battery performance will decrease the range of the car, and will start taking place well before the 100,000 mile/7-year marker. Proper battery disposal is another issue. At this time, there are not many battery disposal facilities due to the limited electric vehicle market to date.

Finally, maintenance of electric vehicles is a concern, given the paucity of many adequately trained repair facilities and the low market penetration of the cars. There simply are not many EVs on the road, and conventional car repair shops do not have proper training in the repair of electric vehicles. This can have a detrimental effect on adoption of EVs.

In recent years, international emerging markets have increased their infrastructures and stratification of wealth and the current consumer demographic is better equipped to afford more expensive vehicles as a result. Additionally, there is a growing global awareness and commitment to developing sustainable and "green" energy and innovations. These factors may increase opportunities for sales of EVs in these markets.

Oil Price

The rising cost of oil is also a major opportunity for electric vehicle manufacturers to cultivate a great presence in the market, due to the demand of consumers to seek alternative types of vehicles, including electric. The global future of the EV market is promising based on the current trends in oil cost, consumption, and awareness about conservation.

Global economic policies, such as the Kyoto protocol, advance the cause of environmentally sustainable products, such as electric vehicles. However, every country has the choice to either ratify these protocols, or not. This lack of accountability means that the financial and political support of environmentally sustainable products are highly variable, and can affect the favorability and feasibility of selling electric vehicles in every country in which they are sold or manufactured.

Finances

Revenues at Tesla Motors are derived from sales that are recognized from two sources, sales of the Roadster and sales of Tesla's patented electric power train components (see **Exhibit 1**). Coinciding with the sales of the Roadster, Tesla recognizes income from the sale of vehicle options and accessories, vehicle service and maintenance, and the sale of Zero-Emission Vehicle (ZEV) credits.

EXHIBIT 1
Tesla Projected
Sales, in US$ millions

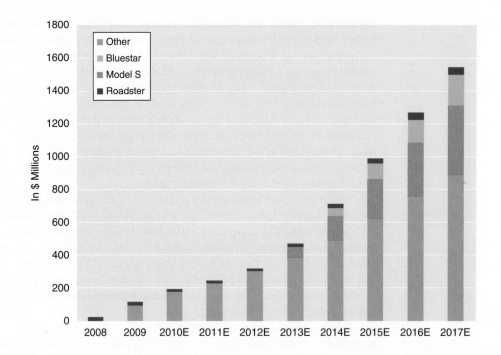

Zero-Emission Vehicle credits are required by the State of California to ensure auto manufacturers design vehicles to meet strict eco-friendly guidelines. Credits are acquired by producing and selling vehicles that meet a minimum emission level in an attempt to offset the pollutants produced by mainstream vehicles. If a manufacturer chooses not to design ZEV vehicles, it is able to purchase credits from companies such as Tesla, who only produces electric vehicles and does not have to accrue credits. Tesla has realized sales of US$14.5 (see **Exhibit 2**), million in ZEV credits since 2008.

Total quarterly revenues at Tesla have been increasing steadily throughout 2010, but no definitive year-over-year positive trends can be established from Tesla's sales data. Two trends that do appear to be gaining in the most recent fiscal year are foreign sales and sales of power train components and related sales.

Tesla's cash position (see **Exhibit 5**) is currently in a less than optimal position. Through its IPO, Tesla was able to raise US$226 million in June of 2010 and has also been able to take advantage of state and federal programs to raise capital at low prices due to its investment in alternative energy programs. These sources of cash offer the company the ability to meet its current obligations, but revenues (see **Exhibits 3** and **4**) have not been able to match expenses, resulting in the company's largest net loss yet of US$51 million in December of 2010. The United States Department of Energy (DOE) loaned Tesla US$465 million at the beginning of the year, so no matter what, Tesla has to manage a "mountain of debt."[57] This specific

EXHIBIT 2
Automotive Sales

Automotive sales consisted of the following for the periods presented (in thousands):			
	2010	**2009**	**2008**
Vehicle, options and related sales	US$75,459	$111,555	$14,742
Power train component and related sales	21,619	388	—
	$97,078	$111,943	$14,742

EXHIBIT 3
Income Statement
(2010)

The following table includes selected quarterly results of operations data for the years ended December 31, 2010 and 2009 (in thousands, except per share data):

| | Three Months Ended | | | |
	Mar 31	Jun 30	Sept 30	Dec 31
2010				
Total Revenue	US$20,812	$28,405	$31,241	$36,286
Gross profit	3,852	6,261	9,296	11,321
Net loss	(29,519)	(38,517)	(34,935)	(51,158)
Net loss per share, basic and diluted	(4.04)	(5.04)	(0.38)	(0.54)
2009				
Total Revenue	$20,886	$26,945	$45,527	$18,585
Gross profit	(2,046)	2,101	7,699	1,781
Net loss	(16,016)	(10,867)	(4,615)	(24,242)
Net loss per share, basic and diluted	(2.31)	(1.56)	(0.66)	(3.43)

EXHIBIT 4
Revenue by Region

The following table sets forth revenue by geographic area (in thousands):

Revenues	2010	2009	Cf 2008
North America	$ 41,866	$ 90,833	$14,742
Europe	70,542	21,110	—
Asia	4,336	—	—
	$116,744	$111,943	$14,742

EXHIBIT 5
Tesla 2010 Financial
Highlights

All info as of 12/31/2010 (in thousands)

Sales: US$97,078
Net Profit: (US$154,328)
Operating Margin: (125.78%)
Receivables: US$6710
Cash Assets: US$99,558
Inventory: US$45,182
Total Debt: US$71,828

loan has various restrictions that are structured around the progress of the Model S and several financial ratios. Tesla stands to lose revenue if the Model S delays, since the DOE loan pays in installments as the Model S reaches various development and production benchmarks. Although debt as a percent of total capital increased at Tesla Motors, Inc. over the last fiscal year to 25.96%, it is still in line with the automobile industry's norm. Additionally, there are enough liquid assets to satisfy current obligations.[58]

Marketing

Tesla's internal marketing situation has to operate with many limitations stemming from the company's infancy and its lack of resources. Looking at the product offerings, the only vehicle Tesla currently has on the market is the Roadster, a sporty two-seater priced at US$108,000 and up. The high price tag puts it firmly in competition with other luxury vehicles as opposed to other electric vehicles. The key demographic market for luxury cars are white males, 45 and older, who are married, have no kids, and make over US$75,000 a year. Primary considerations for this group when purchasing a luxury vehicle are performance, design, and safety, while factors such as financing, the environment, and gas mileage are not important.[59] The Roadster does deliver on aesthetics and performance, but it is questionable whether or not its electric motor will be an effective differentiator. Bearing this in mind, Tesla needs to focus on early adopters and environmentalists, who also have the resources to afford their car. One could argue that this is a narrow market segment.

In 2012, Tesla will roll out the Model S, a premium four-door sedan that will be variably priced at US$57,000 for the lowest range, US$67,000 for the mid range, and US$77,000 at the top of the range. This lower-priced vehicle will target larger families and a greater-sized market. Unless it can lower the price point, this will still be a difficult sell, as households with children have less disposable income and accumulated wealth. Demand for electric cars is also estimated to remain below 10% until at least 2016, because of perceptions of high cost for marginal utility.[60] Two advantages Tesla does have on price, however, are the US$7500 government tax credit for buying fuel-efficient vehicles, and the low cost of maintenance and fuel.

Aside from a minimal product offering, Tesla is also limited by its distribution and fulfilment infrastructure. At the moment, Tesla has a mix of brick-and-mortar dealerships in premium locations, along with regional sales representatives, and online ordering. North America has 10 stores and four reps, Europe has seven stores and four reps, and Asia has one store and two reps. Over the next few years, Tesla plans to open 50 stores in preparation of the Model S rollout. To ease its current lack of fulfilment capabilities, Tesla sales representatives will arrange a test drive in your location and organize vehicle delivery. This is an inexpensive way to increase its distribution capabilities without investing in physical stores. This might also hinder sales though, given that the key demographic for luxury vehicles rely on car dealerships as the second most influential outlet on what car to buy.[61]

Tesla could ramp up distribution by allowing existing dealerships to sell its cars but chooses not to, preferring a customized sales approach where it has complete control over its message. To compliment direct sales, the company has avoided traditional advertising in lieu of product placement, Internet ads, and event marketing. It is adept at turning current customers into vocal brand ambassadors. The company website is littered with quotes from owners and industry reviewers singing its praises. This promotion strategy is a clear strength for Tesla, especially considering that recommendations from friends and relatives, as well as general word of mouth, are the most influential factors for a luxury/sports car's key demographic.

The Tesla brand is also inherently tied to the environmental/green movement. Because of this, it has been able to generate a lot of free media publicity.

Operations

Tesla is headquartered in Palo Alto, California, where it also manufactures its power trains, battery packs, motors, and gearbox. The body and chassis for the Roadster are manufactured by Lotus in Hethel, England, and then are fully assembled in Menlo Park, California, for U.S. buyers, or Wymondham, England, for European and Asian customers. For the upcoming launch of the Model S, Tesla is building a new factory in Fremont, California, that will have a capacity of 20,000 cars per year.

Tesla's main operating strength lies in its intellectual property and its patents. Currently, Tesla has 35 issued patents with another 280 pending. Proprietary components include power train technology, safety systems, charge balancing, battery engineering for vibration and environmental durability, motor design, and the electricity management system. The company also owns the proprietary software systems that are used to manage efficiency, safety, and controls. Tesla's software is designed to be updatable, and many aspects of the vehicle architecture have been designed so it can be used on multiple future models.

To boost operational know-how and supplement the revenue Tesla gets from sales of the Roadster, it also sells Zero-Emission Vehicle credits, and supplies power train and battery pack components to original equipment manufacturers. Currently, Tesla has strategic partnerships with Daimler and Toyota, and is providing their electric vehicle expertise in the development of Daimler's Smart Car and Toyota's new RAV4. These partnerships are an opportunity for Tesla to diversify its revenue streams and network and access greater supply chains.

As previously mentioned, Tesla has decided to distribute through its own network of stores and regional sales staff as opposed to selling through established dealer networks. Despite fulfilment implications, Tesla considers owning its own distribution channel as a competitive advantage. Channel ownership not only allows for greater operating efficiency through inventory control, but also gives Tesla control over its sales message, warranty, price, brand image, and user feedback. The drawbacks to this strategy include the high capital costs of buying real estate and constructing showrooms and the cost of additional sales staff.

Currently, over 2000 parts are sourced from 150 suppliers. One major issue with the current supply structure is that many vendors are the single source. This leaves Tesla vulnerable to delays and increased costs. Due to limited economies of scale, (as of December 31, 2010 only 1500 Roadsters were sold) production costs also run high. The first Roadster was sold in early 2008, but revenues didn't exceed the costs of production until the second quarter of 2009. Tesla is still struggling to bring the costs of the Model S down so it can be profitably sold at US$57,000.

Servicing vehicles presents another challenge for Tesla. Given the complex and proprietary components of their cars, the average mechanic won't be able to diagnose and fix issues. Lacking the appropriate physical infrastructure, Tesla sends maintenance technicians (which it refers to as Rangers) to wherever the car owner lives. The cars themselves also have advanced diagnostic systems that link up to a server at Tesla's headquarters. Issues can be determined prior to sending Rangers out to fix the car, which saves time and resources. Overall though, this system isn't as convenient as having a worldwide infrastructure of third-party repair shops.

This Ranger service system may work for the time being, with only 1500 cars on the road, but with the anticipated sales of the Model S and subsequent vehicles, the services infrastructure will have to be greatly expanded. Two ideas that Tesla hopes will come to fruition are an increase in fast charge stations, and the creation of a battery replacement network. The latter harkens back to the days where cowboys would exchange tired horses for fresh steeds. In anticipation of this, the Model S will incorporate removable battery packs.

Human Resources

Tesla Motors operates more like a software company than a car company, and innovation is top priority. CEO Elon Musk is a serial entrepreneur who has stocked his executive team with half-techie, half-business hybrid employees who are former industry leaders. Taking a cue from Google, the environment is fast paced and culturally unstructured. Employees are encouraged to challenge norms, think outside the box, and commit time to innovation. In order to boost teamwork and eliminate departmental silos, most staff work in an open room with no walls. Tesla prides itself on solutions created through an integration of all departments working side by side. An explanation for this corporate culture can be found in the hiring of Human

Resources director, Arnnon Geshuri, who was the former director of staffing and operations at Google. Because of the emphasis on technology and innovation, the majority of manufacturing is done in California, as opposed to areas with lower labor costs, due to the abundance of top-quality engineers.

Due to the extreme importance of Tesla's intellectual capital, it is imperative to have happy employees. Aside from being able to get in on the ground floor of an innovative new company, employees are also given competitive salaries, benefits, an aesthetically pleasing office space, and "meaningful equity."

Currently, Tesla has about 900 employees, including 212 in the power train and R&D department, 170 in vehicle design and engineering, 121 in sales and marketing, 79 in the service department, and 213 in the manufacturing department. Tesla is currently looking to hire more graduating engineering students and sales staff, especially those who have had some hands-on experience. Recruiting and retaining the best talent is a paramount goal, because of difficulties arising from Tesla's capacity to design, test, manufacture, and sell at the same time.

Tesla's Future: Success or Bust?

In a nutshell, Tesla has limited sales in a limited market, and is making low margins due to high product costs and the lack of economies of scale. However, if oil prices continue to climb toward US$200 a barrel and new electric cars, such as the Chevy Volt and Nissan Leaf, catch on with consumers, the upside for Tesla could be enormous. Can Tesla reach the tipping point? Or will it become just a footnote in automotive history? Time will tell.

NOTES

1. NYTimes.com. (2010) Tesla Motors. http://topics.nytimes.com/top/news/business/companies/tesla_motors/index.html

2. Blanco, Sebastian. (2006) Roadster Unveiled in Santa Monica. http://green.autoblog.com/2006/07/20/tesla-roadster-unveiled-in-santa-monica/

3. U.S. Dept. of Energy. (2008) Tesla Motors Starts Production of Its Electric-Only Roadster http://apps1.eere.energy.gov/news/news_detail.cfm/news_id=11645

4. Tesla Motors. (2008) Tesla Motors to Manufacture Sedan in California. http://www.teslamotors.com/about/press/releases/tesla-motors-manufacture-sedan-california

5. http://topics.nytimes.com/top/news/business/companies/tesla_motors/index.html

6. Chuck Squatriglia. "Tesla Motors Joins Daimler on a Smart EV," Wired.com, January 13, 2009. http://www.wired.com/autopia/2009/01/tesla-motors-jo/

7. Eric Loveday. AllCarsElectric.com. "Daimler Announces New Strategic Partner Tesla Motors." http://www.allcarselectric.com/blog/1020804_daimler-announces-new-strategic-partner-tesla-motors

8. Jim Motavalli. "Daimler Takes a Stake in Tesla Motors," The New York Times, May 9, 2011. http://wheels.blogs.nytimes.com/2009/05/19/daimler-takes-a-stake-in-tesla-motors/

9. Tesla Motors. (2010) Tesla Notifies SEC of Agreement with Toyota to Develop Electric Version of RAV4. http://www.tesla-motors.com/about/press/releases/tesla-notifies-sec-agreement-toyota-develop-electric-version-rav4

10. Tesla Motors. (2010) Tesla Motors Announces Factory in Northern California. http://www.teslamotors.com/about/press/releases/tesla-motors-announces-factory-northern-california

11. Edmunds InsideOnline.com. (2010, May 21). Toyota and Tesla to Make Electric Vehicles at Mothballed NUMMI Plant. http://www.insideline.com/tesla/toyota-and-tesla-to-make-electric-vehicles-at-mothballed-nummi-plant.html

12. Tesla Motors, Inc. (March 3, 2011) 2010 10-K Annual Report. Pg. 28.

13. Wikipedia. Hydrogen vehicle. http://en.wikipedia.org/wiki/Hydrogen_vehicle

14. Mitsubishi Motors. (2011). Overview of Mitsubishi Motors. Retrieved from http://www.mitsubishi-motors.com/en/corporate/aboutus/profile/index.html

15. Wall Street Journal.com. (2011, May 3). Sales and Share of Total Market by Manufacturer. http://online.wsj.com/mdc/public/page/2_3022-autosales.html#autosalesE

16. Mitsubishi Motors. (2011). History of Mitsubishi Motors' EV Development. Retrieved from http://global.ev-life.com/

17. Brad Berman. (2010, March 9). Mitsubishi i. Retrieved from http://www.plugincars.com/mitsubishi-i-miev/review

18. PureGreenCars.com. (2010, November 24) http://puregreencars.com/Green-Cars-News/markets-finance/mitsubishi-i-miev-production-hits-5000-units.html

19. Nissan Motors. (2011). Corporate Information. Retrieved from http://www.nissan-global.com/EN/COMPANY/PROFILE/

20. Nissan Motors. (2011, February 9).FY2010 3rd Quarter Financial Results [Press Release]. http://www.nissan-global.com/EN/IR/FINANCIAL/

21. Nissan Motors. 100% Electric Zero-Emission Nissan LEAF Debuts in Japan Start of Sales on December 20th [Press Release]. http://www.nissan-global.com/EN/NEWS/2010/_STORY/101203-01-e.html

22. Eric Loveday. (2011, March 11). AutoBlog.com. "Nissan Leaf sales hit 3,657; that's like four times more than the Chevy Volt." http://green.autoblog.com/2011/03/11/nissan-leaf-sales-3657-four-times-more-chevy-volt/

23. Chevrolet. (2011) History & Heritage. Retrieved from http://www.chevrolet.com/experience/history/

24. GM. (2011). About GM. http://www.gm.com/content/gmcom/home/company/aboutGM.html

25. GM. (2011). http://www.gm.com/investors/sales-production/pressrelease.jsp?id=/content/Pages/news/cn/en/2011/Jan/0118.html

26. Chevrolet. (2011). 2011 Volt. Retrieved from http://www.chevrolet.com/volt/

27. Eric Loveday. "Nissan Leaf sales hit 3,657; that's like four times more than the Chevy Volt."

28. Toyota Motor Corporation. (2011). Worldwide Operations. Retrieved from http://www.toyota-global.com/company/profile/facilities/worldwide_operations.html

29. Toyota Motor Corporation. (2011). Overview. Retrieved from http://www.toyota-global.com/company/profile/overview/

30. Toyota Motor Corporation. (2011, April 6). *Toyota Sells One-Millionth Prius in the U.S.* [Press Release]. http://pressroom.toyota.com/article_display.cfm?article_id=2959

31. BMW. (2011). BMW History. Retrieved from http://www.bmwdrives.com/bmw_history/bmw-1910.php

32. BMW Group. (2011). BMW Group in Figures. Retrieved from http://annual-report.bmwgroup.com/2010/gb/en/facts-and-figures-2010/bmw-group-in-figures.html

33. DistroCars.com. (2006, Sept. 12). 2007 BMW Hydrogen 7 Series Reducing Fuel Consumption. http://www.distrocars.com/2007-bmw-hydrogen-7-series

34. Hydrogen Fuel Cars Now. (2011). BMW Hydrogen 7. http://www.hydrogencarsnow.com/bmw-hydrogen7.htm

35. Honda. (2011) History. http://world.honda.com/history/limitlessdreams/encounter/text01/index.html

36. Honda Motor Company, LTD. Annual Report 2010. Retrieved May 2, 2011 from http://world.honda.com/investors/library/annual_report/2010/honda2010ar-all-e.pdf

37. Martin Fackler. "Latest Honda Runs on Hydrogen, Not Petroleum," The New York Times, June 17, 2008. http://www.nytimes.com/2008/06/17/business/worldbusiness/17fuelcell.html

38. Honda Motor Company. (2011) How FCX Clarity FCEV Works. Retrieved from http://automobiles.honda.com/fcx-clarity/how-fcx-works.aspx

39. Martin Fackler. "Latest Honda Runs on Hydrogen, Not Petroleum"

40. Tesla Motors, Inc. (March 3, 2011) 2010 10-K Annual Report. Pg 29

41. Tesla Motors, Inc. (2010, Jan. 11). *Tesla and Panasonic Collaborate to Develop Next-Generation Battery Cell Technology* [Press Release]. http://www.teslamotors.com/about/press/releases/tesla-and-panasonic-collaborate-develop-nextgeneration-battery-cell-technology

42. Tesla Motors, Inc. (March 3, 2011) 2010 10-K Annual Report. Pg 4

43. Ibid. Pg 48

44. Ibid. Pg 50

45. Ibid. Pg 50

46. http://apps1.eere.energy.gov/news/progress_alerts.cfm/pa_id=152

47. http://www.washingtonpost.com/wp-dyn/content/article/2011/02/07/AR2011020705616.html

48. http://www.nationaljournal.com/house-gop-proposes-cuts-to-scores-of-sacred-cows-20110209

49. http://dailyreckoning.com/us-data-indicate-slow-economic-growth/

50. http://green.autoblog.com/2010/06/10/ask-abg-why-are-electric-vehicles-so-expensive/

51. Planar Energy, "Department of Energy Awards $4 million to Planar Energy Under Its Advanced Research Project Agency–Energy Initiative," http://www.planarenergy.com/Press%20Releases/DOE%20Awards%20Planar%20Energy%20$4M%20Grant.pdf, April 29, 2010.

52. "Electric Vehicle Equipment from GE." *GE Industrial Systems.* Web. May 11, 2011. http://www.geindustrial.com/products/static/ecomagination-electric-vehicles/?kmed=ppc.

53. http://techland.time.com/2011/05/10/san-francisco-to-offer-free-electric-car-charging-stations/

54. http://www.bts.gov/publications/highlights_of_the_2001_national_household_travel_survey/html/executive_summary.html

55. http://www.bts.gov/publications/highlights_of_the_2001_national_household_travel_survey/html/table_a22.html

56. Tesla Motors, Inc. (March 3, 2011) 2010 10-K Annual Report. Pg 37

57. Tyler Matuella, J. and Ajayi, Mannie (March 28, 2011). Why Electric Carmaker Tesla Motors Will Likely Be Acquired. *Business Insider.* Retrieved on April 21, 2011, from, http://www.businessinsider.com/why-electric-carmaker-tesla-motors-is-unlikely-to-succeed-on-its-own-2011-3.

58. Bloomberg Businessweek (May 3, 2011) from, http://investing.businessweek.com/businessweek/research/stocks/financials/financials.asp?ticker=TSLA:US&dataset=balanceSheet&period=A&currency=native

59. Mintel – Auto Market – Sports and Luxury Cars – U.S. 2003

60. Bloomburg.com, "Hybrid, Battery Car Demand Limited by Cost, Utility, J.D. Power Says," Alan Ohnsman, April 2011

61. Mintel – Auto Market – Sports and Luxury Cars – U.S. 2003

CASE 27
Delta Air Lines (2012)

NAVIGATING AN UNCERTAIN ENVIRONMENT

Alan N. Hoffman
Bentley University

J. David Hunger
St. John's University and Iowa State University

Delta Air Lines Inc. (Delta), headquartered in Atlanta, Georgia, was the world's second-largest airline providing air transportation for passengers, cargo, and mail. Delta operated an extensive domestic and international network across all continents in the world except Antarctica. It was also a founding partner of the SkyTeam airline alliance.

Delta had used mergers and acquisitions (M&A) successfully to solidify its strong position as a leader in the airline industry. It had gone through five M&As since 1953, including the most recent acquisition of Northwest Airlines (Northwest), which turned Delta into an airline with major operations in every region of the world. On the other hand, the Northwest merger took a toll on Delta's financial position by contributing to its high long-term debt.

In 2012, top management was cautiously exploring opportunities for entering new markets, routes, and partnerships in order to boost market share. The airline industry was known for being extremely competitive with significant market share volatility, strong price competition, and low brand loyalty. Management was also searching for ways to reduce costs and expenses in an industry that was rapidly consolidating into fewer major national and international players.

....

The authors thank MBA students Beth Davis, Honore Djambou, Priscila Mattozo, Kelly Nugent, and Steve Paris at Bentley University for their research assistance for a previous version of this case.

The authors prepared this case to provide material for class discussion rather than to illustrate either effective or ineffective handling of a management situation.

Delta Becomes the World's Second-Largest Airline

Company History

Delta's history begins in 1924 with the formation of Huff Daland Dusters in Mason, Georgia. Huff Daland Dusters was the first commercial agricultural flying company in the US and commenced carrying passengers and mail as its business expanded. Recognizing the success and value of the company, C.E. Woolman, acquired the firm and renamed it Delta Air Services.

Throughout the 1930s and 1940s, Woolman focused on defining Delta's mission to ensure that it would be a viable company in the long term. During this period, Delta broadened its services and expanded its horizons: It secured a contract with the U.S. Postal Service to carry mail, participated in the war effort by modifying over one thousand aircraft, developed a regularly scheduled cargo service, and introduced night service. The company changed its name to Delta Air Lines. All these events laid a solid foundation for Woolman and his young company.

Over the next few decades, a series of mergers and key alliances enabled Delta to expand its operations and gain market share in the airline industry. The first merger took place in 1953 with Chicago and Southern Airlines, allowing Delta to become the first service provider in the United States with flights to the Caribbean and South America. The acquisition of Northeast Airlines in 1972 gave Delta a major presence in the northeastern United States In 1984, Delta formed a strategic partnership with Comair Airline, which soon became a Delta wholly-owned subsidiary and connection carrier. Between 1986 and 1991, Delta acquired both Western Airlines and Pan American World Airways. With these acquisitions, Delta gained routes and became a major carrier on the U.S. West Coast and across the Atlantic to Europe. Finally, Delta was able to emerge from bankruptcy by acquiring Northwest Airlines in 2008, which made it the airline with the most worldwide traffic.

In 2012, Delta serviced 572 destinations in 65 countries on six continents, including North America, South America, Europe, Asia, Africa, and Australia. It operated 714 aircraft in 5,766 daily flights and employed more than 80,000 employees worldwide. With over 160 million customers every year, Delta was the world's second-largest airline. Delta was named domestic "Airline of the Year" by the readers of *Travel Friendly* magazine and was named the "Top Tech-Friendly U.S. Airline" by *PC World* magazine for its innovation in technology.

Delta attempted to operate low-cost carrier subsidiaries through launching Delta Shuttle in 1991, Delta Express in 1996, and Song in 2003. None of these subsidiaries were successful, however, and were discontinued not long after being established. In 2010, Delta sold Compass and Mesaba, two regional subsidiaries of Northwest Airlines. Delta continued to operate Comair as a wholly-owned subsidiary (based in Cincinnati) as part of its Delta Connection. Delta had originally bought 20% of Comair in 1984, followed by full ownership in 1999 for US$2 billion, but by 2012 many of Comair's 50-seat turbo-prop aircraft were getting old and had high unit costs per flight hour.

Merger with Northwest

In early 2008, Delta and Northwest announced a merger while both companies were emerging from Chapter 11 bankruptcy. This merger would permit Delta to gain all the routes, landing slots, gates, and other operational assets of Northwest, while allowing Delta to lay off excess personnel and reduce excess flights.[1] It would also enable Delta to compete more effectively against its two biggest rivals: United Airlines and American Airlines.

While many were hesitant about the merger, analysts predicted the annual savings would be US$200 million in 2009, US$500 to US$700 million in 2010, US$800 million to US$1 billion in 2011, and US$1 to US$1.2 billion in 2012.[2] One of the major contributors to these savings for Delta came from the streamlining of operations. The two airlines were able to combine technology and scheduling platforms, which reduced overhead costs for the larger Delta. The additional planes and resources gained from Northwest, combined with Delta's existing fleet and staff, allowed Delta to better match its services to travel demand. The company was able to designate its new, smaller planes to less popular destinations to eliminate empty seats, while utilizing the larger planes for more popular legs out of New York and Atlanta.

Another major financial benefit of the merger was the buying power it offered when purchasing contracts for jet fuel. Fuel was the largest operating expense of any airline company. All airlines used a hedging strategy in an attempt to secure and stabilize exposure to fluctuations in fuel costs. While Delta has historically hedged a larger percentage of its fuel consumption than Northwest, the combined fuel use of these two companies gave Delta a volume discount, resulting in significant savings.

Even though the merger was officially closed in October 2008 after receiving regulatory and shareholder approval, it took until January 2010 for Delta and Northwest to fly as a single carrier. On that date, all Northwest bookings were canceled and transferred to Delta—requiring computer engineers to perform 8856 separate steps over several days. More than 140,000 electronic devices had to be replaced. The new Delta had to reduce 1199 computer systems to about 600. Even though the pilot unions of both airlines had agreed to a common contract by the end of 2009, flight attendants continued to work during 2012 under separate agreements, each with their own work rules. Thus, attendants from Delta and Northwest could not work together on the same flights. It would take until May 2012 for the last Northwest airplane to be repainted as a Delta plane.

The cultures of the two airlines were different. Delta had always thought of itself as the gracious host—hence, flight attendants personally poured requested drinks. Since Northwest saw itself as the practical carrier, flight attendants just gave customers the drink cans. When implementing the merger, no difference between the two airlines was too small to cause problems. For example, Delta had traditionally cut its limes into 10 slices, while Northwest had cut them into 16. Richard Anderson, CEO of the combined airline, was informed at a meeting that Northwest had saved about US$500,000 a year by cutting the limes into smaller slices. In the end, it was decided to stay with Delta's 10 slices, but to carry fewer limes on each flight. Compromises had to be made. Even though Northwest carried Pepsi and Delta carried Coke products (also based in Atlanta with Delta), it was agreed that the combined airline would serve Coke's drinks and Pepsi's snacks.

Although the merger had been deemed a financial success by both Delta's management and industry analysts, with the new Delta earning its highest profit in years in 2011, Delta's operations continued to struggle. Customer complaints per passenger were double the industry average in 2009. By 2011, Delta had the worst record among large carriers for on-time arrivals and accounted for a third of all customer complaints, the worst of any airline, for categories like service and lost bags.[3]

Competitors

Over the past decade, there have been a number of mergers and acquisitions among the major airlines in North America and Europe. For example, Air France and KLM merged in 2004, US Airways and America West in 2005, Delta and Northwest in 2008, plus Southwest and AirTran, and British Airways and Iberia in 2010. According to industry analysts, US Airways and Delta were expressing some interest in each other in early 2012, while independently considering American Airlines.[4]

Delta's major competitors in the United States were United Airlines and American Airlines at the high end, US Airways in the middle, and carriers such as Southwest and JetBlue at the low end. American Airlines, United Airlines, US Airways, and Delta had similar business models with hub-and-spoke service, extensive hubs and network infrastructure, global operations, broad service portfolios and relatively high ticket prices. They constituted what was called "legacy," major, or traditional network carriers.

Southwest and JetBlue had point-to-point connections between cities that permitted direct, nonstop routing, minimizing connections, delays, and total trip time. These carriers did not offer many of the amenities that major carriers offered, but were known as budget airlines because of their low fares.

United Continental Holdings was the holding company for United Airlines, the largest air carrier in the world, as well as United Express. United Continental was headquartered in Chicago, Illinois and employed about 88,253 people. United and Houston-based Continental Airlines had merged in July 2011, but was still in the process of combining the two companies using 33 merger teams. Prior to the merger, it had been agreed that Continental's CEO Jeff Smisek would become CEO of the combined airline. It was also agreed that the airline would retain its United name and be based in Chicago. All other implementation decisions, such as information systems and labor negotiations, had been postponed until after the merger was approved. Continental had built a culture around making its employees happy while catering to customers. In contrast, United's relations between management and workers had been openly hostile. United's new management saw the merger as an opportunity to examine how things were done and to correct any problems.

The new United Airlines operated 5574 flights each day to 377 domestic and international airports through its mainline and United Express services. It had 10 hubs throughout the United States including four of its largest cities. It was rated the world's most admired airline on *Fortune* magazine's 2012 airline industry list of the "World's Most Admired Companies." It was a member of the global Star Alliance network, which contained 27 member airlines from around the world. United's management proudly stated that United had the world's "most comprehensive global network."

United Continental Holdings generated US$37,110 million in revenues, US$1822 million in operating income, and US$36 million in net income during 2011.[5]

AMR Corporation was the holding company for American Airlines and American Eagle. The company provided domestic and long-haul flight services throughout the United States, Mexico, Puerto Rico, the Caribbean, and Canada, and the Latin American, European, and Pacific region. It was headquartered in Fort Worth, Texas, and employed 80,100 people.

American Airlines was also an important scheduled air freight carrier and provided a range of freight and mail services to shippers. It operated five hubs in Dallas/Fort Worth, Chicago O'Hare, Miami, St. Louis, and San Juan (Puerto Rico). American was the largest airline in the United States in 2007, but by 2012 had fallen to become the third-largest airline.

AMR Eagle owned and operated two regional airlines, American Eagle Airlines and Executive Airlines. American Eagle carriers provided connections at American Airlines' hubs and other major airports such as the Boston/Logan and New York/John F. Kennedy airports. It also conducted business with three independently owned regional airlines, which collectively operated as the AmericanConnection. American Airlines was a founding member of the One World Alliance network.

American Airlines, AMR Eagle, and the AmericanConnection airlines served 250 cities in 50 countries with more than 3400 daily flights. The combined network fleet numbered approximately 900 aircraft. AMR Corporation generated revenues of US$23,979 million, US$1054 in an operating loss, and US$1979 in a net loss during 2011. 2011 was AMR's fourth straight year of net losses. Not surprisingly, AMR filed for Chapter 11 bankruptcy in November 2011.[6] Immediately, rumors surfaced that US Airways was seriously interested in acquiring AMR. Although US Airways CEO Doug Parker had not yet made a formal bid for AMR in early 2012, he was working to reach labor agreements with American's three largest labor unions.[7]

US Airways was the smallest of the major U.S. airlines. Based in Tempe, Arizona, it was a member of the Star Alliance Network. The airline utilized a fleet of 338 mainline jet aircraft and 285 regional jet and turbo-prop aircraft, connecting 204 destinations in North America, South America, Europe, and the Middle East. The carrier operated the US Airways Shuttle, a US Airways brand providing hourly service between Boston, New York, and Washington, D.C. Regional airline service was branded as US Airways Express, operated by contract and subsidiary airline companies.

US Airways and America West Airlines merged in 2005. As of 2012, US Airways employed 32,306 people worldwide and operated 3197 daily flights (1268 US Airways Mainline and 1929 US Airways Express). Among the 10 largest domestic airlines, consumers scored US Airways last for overall customer satisfaction in a May 2011 *Consumer Reports* survey. Conversely, US Airways earned the top spot in the 2011 Airline Quality Rating (AQR) report among the hub-and-spoke major carriers.

US Airways Group generated US$13,055 million in revenues, US$426 million in operating income, and US$71 million in net income during 2011. In January 2012, CEO Doug Parker expressed interest in taking over bankrupt American Airlines. In terms of capacity, both American and US Airways were significantly smaller than both Delta and United. A US Airways/American combination would be slightly larger and very competitive with both United and Delta. Whereas US Airways had lower unit labor costs than either United or Delta, American had the highest labor costs in the industry. Aircraft on order for both American and US Airways would move American from having one of the oldest, inefficient fleets to one of the youngest and most fuel-efficient fleets. It was estimated that fuel expense would be reduced by 10%–20% as newer aircraft replace the current old fleet.[8]

Southwest Airlines was the largest and most successful of the low-cost U.S.-based airlines. Headquartered in Dallas, Texas, Southwest employed more than 46,000 people and primarily provided point-to-point, high-frequency, low-fare services to 103 destinations in 41 states, the District of Columbia, Puerto Rico, and six near-international countries. In addition to serving major airports, Southwest served many secondary or downtown airports such as Dallas Love Field, Houston Hobby, Chicago Midway, and Baltimore-Washington International. Southwest took pride in differentiating itself from other low-fare carriers by providing excellent customer service in terms of on-time arrivals and no baggage fees.

In May 2011, Southwest purchased Air Tran Airways. At the time, Southwest operated about 3400 flights per day, with Air Trans operating nearly 700 flights. This gave Southwest its first service to Atlanta, Delta's headquarters. Management expected to spend the next several years integrating the two airlines. This acquisition made Southwest a "national" discount airline and better positioned it to attract more business travelers. Southwest Airlines generated US$15.7 billion in revenues, US$693 million in operating income, and US$178 million in net income during 2011.[9]

Corporate Governance

The Board of Directors of Delta Airlines, Inc. was composed of 11 people, three of whom were employed by the corporation. Richard Anderson served as Chief Executive Officer. Edward Bastian served as Delta's President. Kenneth Rogers was a Delta Pilot who had been nominated by the Delta MEC (Master Executive Council of ALPA, the pilot's union). Although the Board did not have a formal policy on whether the same person should serve as the Chairman of the Board and the Chief Executive Officer, these roles had been separated since 2003. Daniel Carp served as Chairman of the Board. The Board established the following committees: audit, corporate governance (proposed nominations to the board), finance, personnel & compensation, and safety & security.

The directors and executive officers as a group beneficially owned 1.3% of the 849,639,086 shares of common stock in 2012. None of the Board members or executive officers owned more than 1% of the shares. Five institutional investors were each beneficial owners of more than 5% of the common stock: BlackRock, Inc. (5.51%), Janus Capital Management, LLC (7.50%), Janus Overseas Fund (6.37%), and Wellington Management Company, LLP (6.67%) for a total of 26% of Delta's common stock. For their service on the Board of Directors, non-employee (inside) directors received during 2011 an annual retainer of US$85,000, approximately US$115,000 in restricted stock, plus US$10,000 retainer for each committee membership. Committee chairs received US$20,000 as retainers, while the board chairman received an annual retainer of US$175,000. The board required each non-employee director to own at least 35,000 shares of Delta common stock no later than three years after his or her election to the Board.

The board had established pay for performance as a key component of executive compensation. The CEO compensation mix for 2011 was composed of salary (7%), annual incentive (11%), and long-term incentive (82%). The vast majority of compensation for Delta's executive officers was determined by the company's financial, operational, customer service, stock price performance, and the officer's continued employment with Delta. This at-risk compensation constituted 93% of the CEO's compensation and 85% of other executive officers' compensation.

Two of Delta's executive officers had previously been employees of Northwest Airlines. CEO Richard Anderson had served as Northwest's CEO from 2001 to 2004 before he became Executive Vice President of UnitedHealth Group. Mickey Foret had served as executive vice-president and Chief Financial Officer of Northwest from 1998 to 2002 before he joined a consulting firm as its President.

Financial Results

Net income earned by Delta in 2011 was US$854 million, US$261 million higher than in 2010 despite higher fuel costs. Total operating revenue increased US$3.4 billion on an 11% increase in passenger mile yield, primarily due to higher passenger revenues. Total operating income decreased to US$1975 in 2011 from US$2217 million in 2010. Total operating expense increased US$3.6 billion, driven primarily by a US$2.9 billion increase in fuel expenses. (See **Exhibits 1, 2,** and **3** for Delta's financial statements.)

EXHIBIT 1
Delta Airlines, Inc.
Consolidated
Balance Sheets
(In millions,
except share data)

	December 31,	
	2011	**2010**
Assets		
Current assets:		
Cash and cash equivalents	$ 2,657	$ 2,892
Short-term investments	958	718
Restricted cash, cash equivalents, and short-term investments	305	409
Accounts receivable, net of an allowance for uncollectible accounts of $33 and $40 at December 31, 2011 and 2010, respectively	1,563	1,456
Expendable parts and supplies inventories, net of an allowance for obsolescence of $101 and $104 at December 31, 2011 and 2010, respectively	367	318
Deferred income taxes, net	461	355
Prepaid expenses and other	1,418	1,159
Total current assets	7,729	7,307

EXHIBIT 1
(Continued)

	December 31,	
	2011	**2010**
Property and equipment, net:		
Property and equipment, net of accumulated depreciation and amortization of $5,472 and $4,164 at December 31, 2011 and 2010, respectively	20,223	20,307
Other assets:		
Goodwill	9,794	9,794
Identifiable intangibles, net of accumulated amortization of $600 and $530 at December 31, 2011 and 2010, respectively	4,751	4,749
Other noncurrent assets	1,002	1,031
Total other assets	15,547	15,574
Total assets	$ 43,499	$ 43,188
Liabilities and stockholders' (deficit) equity		
Current liabilities:		
Current maturities of long-term debt and capital leases	$ 1,944	$ 2,073
Air traffic liability	3,480	3,306
Accounts payable	1,600	1,713
Frequent flyer deferred revenue	1,849	1,690
Accrued salaries and related benefits	1,367	1,370
Taxes payable	594	579
Other accrued liabilities	1,867	654
Total current liabilities	12,701	11,385
Noncurrent liabilities:		
Long-term debt and capital leases	11,847	13,179
Pension, postretirement, and related benefits	14,200	11,493
Frequent flyer deferred revenue	2,700	2,777
Deferred income taxes, net	2,028	1,924
Other noncurrent liabilities	1,419	1,533
Total noncurrent liabilities	32,194	30,906
Commitments and contingencies stockholders' (deficit) equity:		
Common stock at $0.0001 par value; 1,500,000,000 shares authorized, 861,499,734 and 847,716,723 shares issued at December 31, 2011 and 2010, respectively	—	—
Additional paid-in capital	13,999	13,926
Accumulated deficit	(8,398)	(9,252)
Accumulated other comprehensive loss	(6,766)	(3,578)
Treasury stock, at cost, 16,253,791 and 12,993,100 shares at December 31, 2011 and 2010, respectively	(231)	(199)
Total stockholders' (deficit) equity	(1,396)	897
Total liabilities and stockholders' (deficit) equity	$ 43,499	$ 43,188

SOURCE: *Delta Airlines, Inc. 2011 Form 10-K*, pp. 46–47.

EXHIBIT 2
Delta Airlines,
Inc. Consolidated
Statements of
Operations
(In millions, except
per share data)

Operating Revenue:	Year Ended December 31,		
	2011	**2010**	**2009**
Passenger:			
Mainline	$ 23,864	$ 21,408	$ 18,522
Regional carriers	6,393	5,850	5,285
Total passenger revenue	30,257	27,258	23,807
Cargo	1,027	850	788
Other	3,831	3,647	3,468
Total operating revenue	35,115	31,755	28,063
Operating expense:			
Aircraft fuel and related taxes	9,730	7,594	7,384
Salaries and related costs	6,894	6,751	6,838
Contract carrier arrangements	5,470	4,305	3,823
Aircraft maintenance materials and outside repairs	1,765	1,569	1,434
Passenger commissions and other selling expenses	1,682	1,509	1,405
Contracted services	1,642	1,549	1,595
Depreciation and amortization	1,523	1,511	1,536
Landing fees and other rents	1,281	1,281	1,289
Passenger service	721	673	638
Aircraft rent	298	387	480
Profit sharing	264	313	—
Restructuring and other items	242	450	407
Other	1,628	1,646	1,558
Total operating expense	33,140	29,538	28,387
Operating income (loss)	1,975	2,217	(324)
Other (expense) income:			
Interest expense, net	(901)	(969)	(881)
Amortization of debt discount, net	(193)	(216)	(370)
Loss on extinguishment of debt	(68)	(391)	(83)
Miscellaneous, net	(44)	(33)	77
Total other expense, net	(1,206)	(1,609)	(1,257)
Income (loss) before income taxes	769	608	(1,581)
Income tax benefit (provision)	85	(15)	344
Net income (loss)	$ 854	$ 593	$ (1,237)
Basic earnings (loss) per share	$ 1.02	$ 0.71	$ (1.50)
Diluted earnings (loss) per share	$ 1.01	$ 0.70	$ (1.50)

....
SOURCE: *Delta Airlines, Inc. 2011 Form 10-K*, p. 48.

EXHIBIT 3
Delta Airlines, Inc.
Consolidated State-
ments of Cash Flow

Cash Flows From Operating Activities:	Year Ended December 31, (in millions)		
	2011	2010	2009
Net income (loss)	$ 854	$ 593	$ (1,237)
Adjustments to reconcile net income (loss) to net cash provided by operating activities:			
Depreciation and amortization	1,523	1,511	1,536
Amortization of debt discount, net	193	216	370
Loss on extinguishment of debt	68	391	83
Fuel hedge derivative contracts	135	(136)	(148)
Deferred income taxes	(2)	9	(329)
Pension, postretirement and postemployment expense (less than) in excess of payments	(308)	(301)	307
Equity-based compensation expense	72	89	108
Restructuring and other items	142	182	—
Changes in certain assets and liabilities:			
Receivables	(76)	(141)	147
Hedge margin receivables	(24)	—	1,132
Restricted cash and cash equivalents	153	16	79
Prepaid expenses and other current assets	(16)	(7)	(61)
Air traffic liability	174	232	(286)
Frequent flyer deferred revenue	82	(345)	(298)
Accounts payable and accrued liabilities	303	516	143
Other assets and liabilities	(373)	(98)	(138)
Other, net	(66)	105	(29)
Net cash provided by operating activities	$ 2,834	$ 2,832	$ 1,379
Cash Flows From Investing Activities:			
Property and equipment additions:			
Flight equipment, including advance payments	(907)	(1,055)	(951)
Ground property and equipment, including technology	(347)	(287)	(251)
Purchase of investments	(1,078)	(815)	—
Redemption of investments	844	149	256
Other, net	(10)	(18)	(62)
Net cash used in investing activities	(1,498)	(2,026)	(1,008)
Cash Flows From Financing Activities:			
Payments on long-term debt and capital lease obligations	(4,172)	(3,722)	(2,891)
Proceeds from long-term obligations	2,395	1,130	2,966
Fuel card obligation	318	—	—
Debt issuance costs	(63)	(19)	—
Restricted cash and cash equivalents	(51)	—	—
Other, net	2	90	(94)
Net cash used in financing activities	(1,571)	(2,521)	(19)
Net (Decrease) Increase in Cash and Cash Equivalents	(235)	(1,715)	352

(continued)

EXHIBIT 3
(Continued)

	Year Ended December 31, (in millions)		
Cash Flows From Operating Activities:	**2011**	**2010**	**2009**
Cash and cash equivalents at beginning of period	2,892	4,607	4,255
Cash and cash equivalents at end of period	$ 2,657	$ 2,892	$ 4,607
Supplemental disclosure of cash paid for interest	$ 925	$ 1,036	$ 867
Non-cash transactions:			
Flight equipment under capital leases	$ 117	$ 329	$ 57
JFK redevelopment project funded by third parties	126	—	—
Debt relief through vendor negotiations	—	160	—
Debt discount on American Express agreements	—	110	—
Aircraft delivered under seller financing	—	20	139

....
SOURCE: *Delta Airlines, Inc. 2011 Form 10-K, p. 49.*

Fuel price volatility continued to plague Delta's management. Fuel cost per gallon increased 31% from 2010 to 2011 and amounted to 36% of Delta's total operating expense, compared to 30% in 2010. During 2011, gains from Delta's hedging program reduced fuel expense by US$420 million. Including fuel hedging activity, the company's average cost per fuel gallon in 2011 was US$3.06 compared to US$2.33 in 2010. (See **Exhibit 4**.)

In finalizing its merger with Northwest, Delta took on US$904 million in debt.[10] In order to make this debt more manageable, Delta made an offering to sell US$500 million of five-year secured bonds to help the company recover from its massive debt accumulation. Most of the proceeds from this offering went toward refinancing the Northwest bank loans as a result of the merger.[11] Management was working diligently to reduce this debt. For example, the company sold two of its wholly owned regional subsidiaries, Mesaba and Compass Airlines, for a total of US$82.5 million in July 2010. By the end of 2011, total debt and capital leases, including current maturities, was US$13.8 billion, a US$1.5 billion reduction from 2010 and a US$3.4 billion reduction from 2009.

Delta's management admitted in the corporation's 2011 annual report that "our substantial indebtedness may limit our financial and operating activities and may adversely affect our ability to incur additional debt to fund future needs." They also admitted that a significant

EXHIBIT 4
Delta Airlines, Inc.
Fuel Cost and
Consumption

	2006	2007	2008	2009	2010	2011
Gallons Consumed	2111	2534	2740	3853	3,823	3856
Cost (US$ Millions)	$4,319	$5,676	$8,686	$8,291	$8,901	$11,783
Average Cost Per Gal	$ 2.04	$ 2.24	$ 3.16	$ 2.15	$ 2.33	$ 3.06
% of Operating Expenses	25%	31%	38%	29%	30%	36%

....
SOURCE: *Delta Airlines, Inc. Annual Reports for 2008 and 2011.*

portion of the corporation's assets were currently subject to liens, which could further limit management's ability to obtain additional financing on acceptable terms for working capital, capital expenditures, and other purposes.

Marketing

Delta's target market was the business class passenger segment. Delta's SkyMiles was a free program that allowed members to earn miles or points accrued for free travel, upgrades, or other products and services. Members could earn miles by flying with Delta or any of Delta's over 20 affiliate airlines, including Air France, Korean Air, Aeromexico, Alitalia, and Alaska Air. Delta had also teamed with other businesses such as Budget Rent-A-Car and several leading hotels to provide SkyMiles members with new mileage-earning opportunities that encompass their global travel experience.

The SkyMiles program encouraged return purchases and increased brand loyalty. A customer could choose Delta or an affiliate over another airline for the added benefit of earning miles, even if the flight was slightly more expensive. Also, by creating and maintaining this membership program, Delta was able to distribute information and updates to its customers directly via e-mail or to a physical address, both of which were items required for registration with the program.

Delta also provided special services and amenities to its business travelers through the Business Elite Services program. This program was similar to flying first class with other airlines. When a member booked a flight, the passenger can choose to fly coach or business/first class. By branding what other airlines would typically call first class as "Business Elite," Delta created a higher perceived value for this service for its customers. Business Elite passengers received premium service during their travel experience from start to finish. There were Business Elite check-in desks; larger, more comfortable seats; free food and beverages on most flights; access to the Delta Sky Clubs in participating airports; flat bed seats for transatlantic flights; priority baggage claim; and 150% earned miles over the typical SkyMiles member flying in coach.

Another marketing strength employed by Delta was its use of affiliate marketing. Affiliate marketing allowed Delta to join forces with other businesses to advertise and promote its services. Even for small businesses, Delta paid a commission for every ticket sale that resulted in a referral from another business' website displaying a link to Delta. Delta also paired with large organizations such as the PGA tour, Walt Disney World, and the Minnesota Twins, where it was advertised as the airline of choice. By creating these relationships, both Delta and its affiliates reaped the advertising benefits of reaching more people and the hope of potential sales.

Following the online revolution, Delta jumped on board by creating a blog to post the airline's news and events. The blog allowed its followers to directly comment on any of the posts and participate in any discussion. With an entity as large as Delta, this gave customers a feeling of worth and inclusion by being heard and being allowed to participate. The subject of the blog posts included day-to-day living to service upgrades, green initiatives and new plane paint jobs to snack selection and destination reviews, as well as many other topics.

One of Delta's marketing weaknesses, however, was a lack of differentiation with respect to its services. While air travel was a commodity, some of Delta's competitors had differentiated their services from the competition, while Delta failed to set itself apart from other airlines. Because of this, Delta was forced to compete on price and quality to earn its customers and their loyalty. In addition, the use of television advertising was almost nonexistent for Delta; whereas, other airlines used television as their primary source of advertising.

Operations

Delta was a founding member of SkyTeam, a global airline alliance that included Aeroflot, Aeromexico, Air France, Alitalia, China Southern Airlines, CSA Czech Airlines, Delta Air Lines, KLM Royal Dutch Airlines, Korean Air, Air Europa, and Kenya Airways. Combined, this alliance offered over 13,000 flights daily to almost 900 destinations worldwide. This expansive network gave Delta flexibility to fly literally anywhere in the world with the support of the other SkyTeam carriers. It also allowed shorter connections and consolidated hubs that share gates and baggage transfer systems to increase efficiency and reduce costs for the airlines. Furthermore, Delta was able to offer cargo customers a consistent international product line through its SkyTeam Cargo membership.

Delta had a significant number of U.S. domestic hub airports, plus three foreign hubs in Amsterdam, Paris, and Tokyo. Hub operation required more gates, and therefore, acted to shut out competition from many lower-fare competitors.[12] Delta's hub operations in Atlanta, Cincinnati, Detroit, Memphis, Minneapolis-St. Paul, New York-JFK, and Salt Lake City took place at some of the busiest and largest airports in the United States, thus preventing many other carriers from competing in those markets.

In early 2009, Delta and newly merged Air France-KLM created a joint venture (JV) agreement to expand transatlantic travel for both companies. This agreement gave the two companies a total of 25% of the global transatlantic air travel market. It allowed them to share revenues and costs for transatlantic flights and should boost both partners' revenues by US$150 million, according to both Delta and Air France-KLM CEOs.[13] It also allowed the companies to share pricing and marketing data to better improve their international travel.

As part of the operations strategy, Delta's management worked to strengthen the company's position in New York. In December 2011, Delta traded 42 slots at Reagan National plus the rights to operate additional daily service to Sao Paulo, Brazil, and US$66.5 million in cash to US Airways for 132 slot pairs at LaGuardia Airport in order to operate a new domestic hub at LaGuardia. This enabled management to announce the expansion of Delta's domestic service at LaGuardia to include more than 100 new flights and 29 new destinations. In addition, Delta was creating a "state-of-the-art" facility at New York's John F. Kennedy International Airport for international travelers. The project would cost approximately US$1.2 billion and would be completed over a five-year period beginning in 2010.

Delta also operated a maintenance and service division, Delta TechOps. This service division provided airframe maintenance, component and part maintenance, engine maintenance, line maintenance, logistics, fleet engineering support, and technical operations training to not only Delta, but other commercial airlines as well. Having these services in-house was a tremendous strength for Delta, which could maintain the quality of its fleet in-house and then market these services to other airlines to make a profit.

Delta struggled to effectively match capacity and demand. In order to provide good service to its customers, the company offered flights to as many destinations as possible. In order to be profitable, however, management must fill planes with enough travelers to cover, and hopefully exceed, the fixed operational expenses of that specific flight. While the recession made this match difficult with lower demand and higher fuel prices, Delta tried to combat this by using smaller planes and retiring older ones.[14] It also tried to reduce costs by eliminating some of its operations staff. Thanks to various codesharing agreements and its merger with Northwest, Delta increased its passenger load factor from 68.1% in 2001 to 83% in 2010 and 82.1% in 2011. A combination of raising the load factor and cutting costs helped reduce the airlines' operating cost per available seat mile from 18.72 cents in 2008 to 14.12 cents in 2011 (compared to 12.41 cents for Southwest Airlines).[15]

Delta had learned over the decades that it was incapable of operating as a low-cost carrier to compete with airlines like JetBlue and Southwest. Its attempt in the early 2000s to operate Song Airline was a major failure that forced Delta to return to relying on its original operating structure. In its attempts to establish a budget airline, Delta had pulled resources away from its main business. While trying to be more competitive, it had essentially created a competitor to its own mainline business.[16]

Human Resources and Social Responsibility

Delta has struggled with people problems. Most of its workforce, except for flight operations personnel and pilots, was non-unionized. With unionized employees, compensation and benefits had always been a hot topic of discussion. Over the years, Delta had attempted to impose pay cuts to lower operating costs. While in bankruptcy court, Delta pilots, represented by the Air Line Pilots Association, fought hard for fair compensation, even threatening total liquidation of Delta if an agreement could not be reached.[17] During the merger with Northwest, both airlines met with the union to garner their support for the agreement. Although Delta has not experienced the same degree of domestic labor disruptions that other airlines have experienced, its workers in European countries are much more active in labor unions and political protests.

Delta's corporate governance policies promoted diversity inside and outside of the organization. It participated in an initiative to promote small businesses, minority-and female-owned businesses. Top management understood that the global economy depended on the well being of all businesses and tried to distribute its sales to promote and grow these smaller companies.

Delta's focus on social responsibility was exemplified through Delta's Force for Global Good program. In this program, Delta supported global diversity, global wellness and health, improving the environment, and promoting arts and culture. It participated in and sponsored thousands of events every year and partnered with well-known organizations like the Red Cross, Habitat for Humanity, UNICEF, the Nature Conservatory, the Tribeca Film Festival, the National Black Arts Festival, and many other charitable organizations.

Technology

Delta had a lengthy history of embracing technology, from early adoption of jet aircraft to the use of mainframe computers, and most recently, integrating the Delta and Northwest websites, operations and reservation systems. Delta was at the forefront of developing technologies to increase the total customer experience. Passengers were able to view, select, or change seat assignments at its online website. They could also receive boarding passes via self-service kiosks. Delta, along with the Transportation Security Administration (TSA), initiated the paperless mobile check-in for domestic travel from some airports in the United States. It was now offering upgraded video, music, game, and power options on many of its newer aircraft.[18]

The Airline Industry

Deregulation

The U.S. domestic airline industry was largely deregulated in 1978,[19] and entry barriers for new entrants were lower from a legislative standpoint. Airlines were free to negotiate their own operating arrangements with different airports, enter and exit routes easily, and set fares and flight volumes according to market conditions.

Deregulation resulted in spectacular industry growth. The number of air passengers increased from 207.5 million in 1974 to 721.1 million in 2010. Unfortunately, this growth resulted in a flight-choked Northeastern U.S. corridor, overcrowded airports, delays, and terrorist risks. More competition led to fare cutting. For example, the cheapest round-trip New York–Los Angeles flight in 1974 was US$1442 (inflation-adjusted dollars). By 2010, that same flight cost US$268. Consequently, this resulted in an average decrease in revenue per passenger mile from an inflation-adjusted 33.3 cents in 1974 to 13 cents in 2010.[20]

Deregulation did not free airlines from oversight by a number of domestic and international agencies. A short list included the U.S. Department of Transportation, the U.S. Department of Homeland Security, and air transport and safety organizations of the various countries the airlines served. For example, Delta was a member of the International Air Transport Association (IATA) and was subject to applicable conventions such as the "Warsaw Conditions of Contract and Other Important Notices." It was also subject to scheduling and landing slot rules by the foreign countries it serves and various airport management authorities.

Entry Barriers

There was a large amount of bureaucracy involved in setting up a new airline. For example, a new company in the United States must apply to the Federal Aviation Authority (FAA) for an air carrier certificate. In order to operate aircraft, new airlines must obtain an operating license, which was usually a lengthy process. These procedures dissuaded many from entering the industry because generation of revenues can take a long time.

The large capital outlay that was required to start an airline business can also be a serious deterrent for new entrants. An entrant must have sufficient resources to pay the staff required and to either lease or buy a fleet of aircraft.

Even if a new entrant had the capital to launch a business, it would encounter obstacles in accessing airports. Established airlines had an edge over potential entrants, for they held a monopoly over time slots at certain airports, making it harder for new airlines to gain entry to those airports. This created immense difficulties for new airlines to negotiate prime slots at busy airports and may result in a new airline being restricted to offering flights only at off-peak times, or having to fly to airports further away from popular destinations.

Established airlines formed strategic alliances such as SkyTeam, Oneworld, and Start, in order to be more competitive both locally and globally. Airlines partnered with one another not only to achieve network size economies through initiatives such as code sharing, but also to achieve scale economies in the purchase of fuel and even of aircraft. A new entrant faced a potentially high cost of operation because it took a long time to gain access to these types of arrangements and take advantage of the cost reductions that resulted from alliance building.

Fuel Economy

The cost of fuel had become a significant and growing cost of doing business for the entire airline industry. If oil once again significantly rose in price, the effects could be profound and long lasting. Analysts openly contemplate the end of mass international air travel, an event that could reconfigure world economics and make flying an option for only the wealthy. A flight across the Atlantic can easily consume 60,000 liters of fuel—more than a motorist would use in 50 years of driving—and generate 140 tons of carbon dioxide. The world fleet of jetliners burned about 130 million tons of fuel each year.[21]

Until recently, the airline industry predicted a doubling of flights by 2050.[22] But another war in the Middle East, the world's largest source of oil-derived products, could devastate supplies and easily lead to a severe curtailment in flights worldwide. Even without armed conflict, there were leaders who could use oil—and the threat of shutting down production—for political purposes. Finally, rising economies, such as those in Brazil, India, and China, were using more of these limited resources.

Brand Loyalty

The airline industry was highly competitive. The key buyers in the airline industry were leisure and business travelers. While the leisure pool was somewhat fragmented and lacked real bargaining power, business travelers from major corporations had some leverage. Since customers were sensitive to price and could easily switch from one airline to another, brand loyalty in the industry was low. As a counter move, airlines had used loyalty schemes to entice and retain customers.

Even with loyalty programs, airlines were still struggling to keep customers on board. The recession of 2008 dampened demand for air travel.[23] In a bad economy, individuals were able to substitute air travel with other choices—car, bus or train, or by using lower-cost regional airlines, such as Southwest. Customers were far less loyal today than in former years. Travel sites such as Orbitz and Travelocity could be instructed to search by lower fares, fewer connecting flights, and so forth. Air and credit card rewards programs were less generous than in years past, so there was less incentive for passengers to remain loyal to any one airline.[24]

Supplier Power

Fuel suppliers, aircraft manufacturers, and skilled employees were the key suppliers in the airline industry. The industry was characterized by strong supplier power, given the duopoly of the large, jet engine–powered aircraft manufacturers of Boeing and Airbus. Airlines entered into contracts when buying or leasing aircraft from suppliers, and breaking these contracts often invoked heavy financial penalties.

Fuel suppliers were also in a strong position, since no viable substitute for jet fuel had yet been discovered. Staffing costs for an airline were substantial, with large numbers of highly trained flight and ground personnel, including mechanics, reservation, and transportation ticketing agents being required in order to provide an efficient service. Labor costs were difficult to cut, given that most large airlines were unionized.

Consumer Attitudes

Customers in recent years had become increasingly hostile toward the airline industry as a result of travel delays, intrusive screening, and "nickel and dime" issues such as checked baggage fees and even a recent proposal by Spirit Airline to charge for overhead baggage.[25] Both Delta and United led the industry by charging US$100 for a second checked bag on international flights. U.S. airlines collected US$3.4 billion in baggage fees in 2011, helping to offset fuel costs and reducing the need for baggage handlers.[26] Customers were increasingly vocal in their discontent with "cattle car" treatment and multiple fees. Consumer groups, such as the International Airline Passengers Association, the Air Travelers Association, FlyerRights.org, and the Coalition for an Airline Passengers' Bill of Rights, had been fighting for increased oversight of airlines. In 2009, a video on YouTube titled, "United Breaks Guitars," received widespread notice.

One professor argued that compared to the early 1980s, air fares were lower in 2012, but everything else (except for in-flight entertainment) was worse. There was less leg room, less food, less service, more-crowded airplanes, and more time wasted going through the airport.[27]

Calls for an airplane passenger's "Bill of Rights" had become more frequent, culminating in 2011 with U.S. legislation stating that if a boarded international commercial airplane sat on a runway for more than four hours, the airline would be charged up to US$27,500 per passenger. The law also stated that airlines must prominently post bag, meal, and cancellation fees on their website and compensate "bumped" passengers at least double the price of their ticket.

According to the American Customer Satisfaction Index, the airline industry as a whole received a score in 2011 of 65% out of 100% possible. This compared to 82% for the full-service restaurant industry. In order of highest customer satisfaction for 2011 were Southwest (81%), Continental (64%), American (63%), US Airways and United (61%), and Delta (56%).

Natural and Social Calamities

Some events, such as blizzards, earthquakes, and even a volcanic eruption in Iceland, were beyond the control of any airline. There were no technological "fixes" for these natural disasters. The enormous ash cloud from the Icelandic volcano that shut down European air space in 2010 cost U.S.-based airlines tens of millions of dollars per day. Since Delta had the biggest presence in Europe, it lost the most money—up to US$6.5 million per day.[28]

Airlines also faced threats from wars, political instability, and social unrest. Protesters in Thailand, for instance, forced the closure of its main airport terminal in 2008, causing airport operations to cease for a time.[29] Similarly, the 2001 terrorist attacks in the United States caused all air traffic to be halted for a period of several days and led to a sharp decline in the economy and air travel.[30]

Industry Outlook

According to IBIS*World*'s "2012 Domestic Airlines in the U.S. Industry Market Research Report" the U.S. airline industry had been unstable over the past decade with revenue growing marginally at an annualized rate of 0.3% over the five years leading up to 2012. Revenue was up 9.0% during 2010 and 3.6% in 2011. The overall trend over the past five years had been an increase in market share for low-cost carriers such as US Airways, JetBlue, and Southwest Airlines, to the detriment of American and United Airlines.

The IBIS*World* report predicted that the U.S. airline industry should experience a modest recovery and positive growth over the next five years. Nevertheless, high fuel costs should continue cutting into profitability. Major carriers were expected to continue merging in order to boost profitability and gain a competitive advantage.

Outside the United States, many nations had traditionally subsidized their national air carriers. There had been an economic benefit in having a nationally branded airline flying the flag overseas, bringing tourists into the country, and generating income for local businesses. National pride also played a role. An increasingly competitive global airline industry meant that small national airlines had become less cost effective. Airlines had been forced to ask for more money from their governments or else go out of business. This was why New Zealand stepped in to prop up Air New Zealand in 2001. For their part, many governments no longer had the money to support airlines as they did in the past. In January 2012, Spain's Spanair and Hungary's Malev foundered when their governments reduced airline subsidies. State investors in Sweden's SAS, Ireland's Aer Lingus, Portugal's TAP, and the flag carriers of Poland and the Czech Republic indicated in 2012 that because of the European debt crisis they would be reducing financial support and seeking new investors. Turkish Airlines was working to buy a stake in LOT Polish Airlines from the Polish government, which had been trying to sell its 25% share of the carrier since 2009. These state-supported European airlines found themselves falling behind Europe's three big airline groups: Air France-KLM

Group, Deutsche Lufthansa (including carriers in Austria, Belgium, and Switzerland), and International Consolidated Group (merger of British Airways and Iberia). It was logical to expect that mergers among state-supported airlines would soon occur as governments chose to privatize their national airlines by selling their ownership shares.[31]

The International Air Transport Association (IATA) forecasted that the global airline industry would post a second consecutive year of net profit declines in 2012 as the deepening European debt crisis would offset lower fuel prices, stronger-than-expected growth in passenger traffic, and an improved freight market. Although the IATA expected modest profit growth for carriers in North America, carriers in the Asia Pacific region should see the most increase in net profits in 2012. In contrast, European airlines should report a US$1.1 billion loss. According to John Leahy, Chief Operating Office for Airbus, "There's no doubt about it that 2012 is a softer year than 2011 in terms of orders and in terms of the health of some of the airlines."[32]

Challenges Facing Delta

Delta had emerged from bankruptcy and proven that it could be a profitable company. The SkyTeam Alliance, a substantial flight network, and the recent merger with Northwest had contributed to its success in this industry. Like many successful companies, however, Delta continued to struggle with how to remain a viable company in the long term. While mergers and acquisitions had enabled the company to become the world's largest airline carrier, Delta still needed to focus on maintaining its profitability. Significant challenges for Delta remained.

Possible Strategic Options

Delta was competing in an uncertain environment with many players, limited growth prospects, and little room to differentiate itself from others. The company's cost structure, service portfolio, brand loyalty, and ability to manage debt and crises will affect its future development. Further exploration of new business initiatives was also essential for Delta to move out of this crowded, stagnant market to create a new space for itself. With the successful merger of Northwest, the JV with Air France-KLM, and its ongoing success with SkyTeam, should Delta's management continue to pursue other M&A and JV opportunities, such as pursuing a merger with bankrupt American Airlines? While Delta's history has shown that it cannot successfully maintain a low-cost subsidiary on its own, a main question became, would it be beneficial to acquire or merge with a low-cost carrier, such as JetBlue, while keeping the carrier's current business model and brand?

In early 2012, Delta's top management became aware of an intriguing business opportunity. ConocoPhillips was planning to sell or close its 185,000 barrels-per-day Trainer, Pennsylvania, refinery, the latest struggling East Coast refinery to fall victim to low profit margins. East Coast refineries were typically reliant on expensive Brent crude oil imports from the North Sea and West Africa and could no longer compete with Midwest refineries that used cheaper West Texas Intermediate crude oil. No pipelines existed to bring highly discounted crude oil from the Bakken shale field of North Dakota. The Trainer refinery near Philadelphia was the third-largest of 12 East Coast refineries. Two of the twelve were idled in 2010 and two more, including Trainer, were idled in 2011.

Conoco's management announced that they would close the Trainer refinery if they didn't soon find a buyer. They planned to make Conoco's downstream operations (including pipelines, refineries, and retail stations) a separate company in 2013 and had repeatedly said that they were prepared to sell less sophisticated refining assets and other oil and gas properties they considered obsolete. Conoco's management said that they would entertain offers to buy the Trainer refinery through May, 2012. It was common knowledge in the industry that except for a brief period from 2005 to 2008, refining was an unprofitable business. This would explain why no new refinery had been built in the United States in decades.

Preliminary meetings between Delta and Conoco revealed that Delta could purchase the Trainer refinery for US$180 million. Delta's management realized that even if they bought the refinery, they would have to spend another US$100 million to modify the refinery to maximize its production of jet fuel. On a positive note, any environmental cleanup risks previous to a sale would stay with the refinery's previous operator. The State of Pennsylvania announced that it would be willing to contribute US$30 million in job creation assistance to anyone who would buy and operate the refinery with at least 402 full-time workers for at least five years. A purchase of the refinery would also include the pipelines and transportation assets necessary to supply fuel to Delta's operations throughout the northern United States.[33]

Delta's management was aware that operating a refinery profitably would be a tougher business than profitably operating an airline. The refinery was not making money and probably wouldn't in the future without a series of investments to make it competitive. Nevertheless, it would be one alternative to reduce the high cost of jet fuel, a major issue in airline profitability in 2012 and probably for many years to come. But, was this the best use of Delta's limited funds, especially when it was already committed to spending large sums of money to upgrade its New York facilities?

NOTES

1. Yamanouchi, Kelly. "Delta loses $161 million: Some charges date to Northwest merger. Domestic flight capacity, more jobs to be trimmed next year." *The Atlanta Journal–Constitution.* October 23, 2009. (accessed via ProQuest.com, April 23, 2010)
2. Bailey, Jeff. "Delta and Northwest promote benefits of merger." The New York Times. April 15, 2008.
3. Mouawas, Jad. "Delta-Northwest merger's long and complex path." *The New York Times.* May 18, 2011. A print version of this article appeared in *The New York Times* on May 19, 2011, p. B1.) Esterl, Mike. "Delta's full integration of northwest gets final clearance." The Wall Street Journal Online. January 2, 2010.
4. Credeur, Mary Jane. "Marriage at 30,000 feet." Bloomberg Businessweek. February 6–February 12, 2012, pp. 58–63.
5. United Continental 10-K Form. 2011.
6. AMR Corporation Form 10-K. 2011.
7. Ahles, Andrea. "American Airlines bankruptcy." *Star-Telegram.* June 16, 2012.
8. Herbst, Bob. American Airlines and US Airways – Will they fly together?" Airline Financials.com LLC. April 20, 2012.
9. Southwest Airlines Form 10-K. 2011.
10. Webber, Harry. "Delta Air Lines plans $500M private debt offering." *USA Today.* September 16, 2009.
11. Haywood, Kate. "Delta Air plans $500 million debt offering." NASDAQ.com. September 16, 2009.
12. McCartney, Scott. "The middle seat: Why travelers benefit when an airline hub closes; As gates free up, discounters move in and fares drop; Lessons from Pittsburgh." The Wall Street Journal. November 1, 2005. Eastern edition: ABI/INFORM Global. (accessed via ProQuest.com, April 23, 2010).
13. Michaels, Daniel. "Air France-KLM, Delta form trans-Atlantic joint venture." *The Wall Street Journal.* May 25, 2009.
14. Delta Airlines Inc. *Annual Report for the fiscal year ended December 31, 2009.* http://www.delta.com/about_delta/investor_relations/annual_report_proxy_statement/.
15. Delta Air Lines Form 10-K. 2011.
16. Williams, Paula and John. "Why good companies go bad." July 17, 2009. http://www.ravenwerks.com/?page_id=426.
17. Associated Press. "Delta warns of possible pilot strike." MSNBC. November 14, 2005. http://www.msnbc.msn.com/id/10028262/.
18. Aviation Explorer. http://www.aviationexplorer.com/delta_airlines.htm
19. Ignatius, David. "Failing airlines, failing government." *The Washington Post.* June 22, 2008. (accessed via ProQuest.com, April 23, 2010)
20. Breyer, Stephen. "Airline deregulation revisited." Bloomberg Businessweek. Winter 2011. P. 68.
21. "Limits turn some rewards programs into no-fly zones." *Palm Beach Post.* March 29, 2010. (accessed via ProQuest.com, April 23, 2010)
22. Ibid.
23. Jones, Charisse and Reed, Dan. "2009 was worst year for airlines: 2010 looks better, but losses of $5.6 billion expected globally." *USA Today.* January 28, 2010. (accessed via ProQuest.com, April 23, 2010)
24. "Limits turn some rewards programs into no-fly zones." *Palm Beach Post.* March 29, 2010. (accessed via ProQuest.com, April 23, 2010)
25. Croghan, Lore. "That's the spirit!! Airlines won't charge for carry-ons" *New York Daily News.* April 19, 2010. (accessed via ProQuest.com, April 23, 2010)
26. Ford, Andrea. "Sky high." *Time.* July 2, 2012. P. 18.
27. Borenstein, Severin. "Why U.S. airlines need to adapt to a slow-growth future." Bloomberg.com. June 3, 2012.

28. Smith, Aaron. "Iceland volcano ash costing U.S. airlines $20 million a day." *CNN Money*, April 19, 2010. http://money.cnn.com/2010/04/19/news/companies/airlines_volcano/index.htm

29. Onsanit, Rattaphol and Kate, Daniel Ten, "Thai protesters force airport closure, bomb injures 4 (Update2)" Bloomberg.com. November 26, 2008. http://www.bloomberg.com/apps/news?pid=20601100&sid=aLYa1IkGDOTw&refer=germany.

30. Bhadra, Dipasis and Texter, Pamela (2004). "Airline networks: An econometric framework to analyze domestic U.S. air travel." United States Department of Transportation. April 22, 2010.

http://www.bts.gov/publications/journal_of_transportation_and_statistics/volume_07_number_01/html/paper_06/

31. Baigorri, Manuel, Rothwell, Steve, and Webb, Alex. "Turbulence for Europe's state-owned airlines." *Bloomberg Businessweek*. February 6–12, 2012. Pp. 28–29.

32. Chiu, Joanne and Ng, Jeffrey. "Aviation industry leaders cautious on near-term industry growth prospects." Dow Jones Newswires. June 11, 2012.

33. Kahn, Chris, Mayerowitz, and Levy, Marc. "Delta Air Lines is getting into fuel business." Associated Press. May 1, 2012.

CASE 28

TomTom

NEW COMPETITION EVERYWHERE!

Alan N. Hoffman
Bentley University

TOMTOM WAS ONE OF THE LARGEST PRODUCERS OF SATELLITE NAVIGATION SYSTEMSIN THE WORLD. Its products were comprised of both stand-alone devices and applications. TomTom led the navigation systems market in Europe and was second in the United States. TomTom attributed its position as a market leader to the following factors: the size of its customer and technology base, its distribution power, and its prominent brand image and recognition.[1]

With the acquisition of Tele Atlas, TomTom became vertically integrated and also controlled the map creation process. This helped TomTom establish itself as an integrated content, service, and technology business. The company was Dutch by origin and had its headquarters based in Amsterdam, The Netherlands. In terms of geography, the company's operations spanned from Europe to Asia Pacific, covering North America, the Middle East, and Africa.[2]

TomTom was supported by a workforce of 3300 employees from 40 countries. The company's revenues had grown from €8 million in 2002 to €1.674 billion in 2008. (See **Exhibits 1** and **2**.)

....

This case was prepared by Professor Alan N. Hoffman, Bentley University and Erasmus University. Copyright © 2015 by Alan N. Hoffman. The copyright holder is solely responsible for the case content. Reprint permission is solely granted to the publisher, Prentice Hall, for *Strategic Management and Business Policy*, 14th Edition (and the international and electronic versions of this book) by the copyright holder, Alan N. Hoffman. Any other publication of the case (translation, any form of electronics or other media) or sale (any form of partnership) to another publisher will be in violation of copyright law, unless Alan N. Hoffman has granted an additional written permission. The author would like to thank Will Hoffman, Mansi Asthana, Aakashi Ganveer, Hing Lin, and Che Yii for their research. Please address all correspondence to: Professor Alan N. Hoffman, Bentley University, 175 Forest Street, Waltham, MA 02452 or ahoffman@bentley.edu. Printed by permission of Dr. Alan N. Hoffman.

RSM Case Development Centre prepared this case to provide material for class discussion rather than to illustrate either effective or ineffective handling of a management situation. Copyright © 2010, RSM Case Development Centre, Erasmus University. No part of this publication may be copied, stored, transmitted, reproduced, or distributed in any form or medium whatsoever without the permission of the copyright owner, Alan N. Hoffman.

EXHIBIT 1
Sales Revenue and
Net Income (€):
TomTom (Amount in
millions of €)

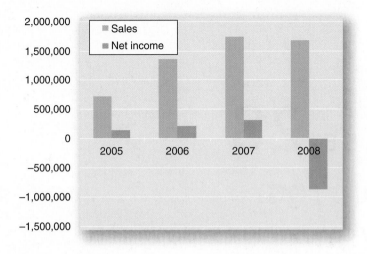

EXHIBIT 2
Quarterly Sales:
TomTom (Amount in
millions of €)

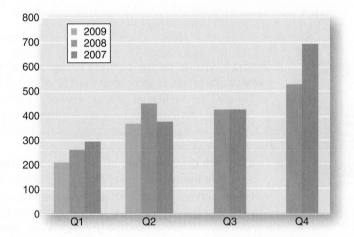

However, because of the Tele Atlas acquisition and the current economic downturn, the company has recently become a cause of concern for investors. On July 22, 2009, TomTom reported a decline in its net income at the end of the second quarter of 2009.

TomTom was in the business of navigation-based information services and devices. The company had been investing structurally and strategically in research and development to bring new and better products and services to its customers. The company's belief in radical innovation helped it remain at the cutting edge of innovation within the navigation industry.

The vision of TomTom's management was to improve people's lives by transforming navigation from a "don't-get-lost solution" into a true travel companion that gets people from one place to another safer, faster, cheaper, and better informed. This vision helped the company become a market leader in every marketplace in the satellite navigation information services market.[3]

The company's goals focused around radical advances in three key areas:

- **Better maps:** This goal was achieved by maintaining TomTom's high-quality map database, which was continuously kept up to date by a large community of active users who provided corrections, verifications, and updates to TomTom. This was supplemented by inputs from TomTom's extensive fleet of surveying vehicles.[4]

- **Better routing:** TomTom had the world's largest historical speed profile database IQ Routes, facilitated by TomTom HOME, the company's user portal.[5]

- **Better traffic information:** TomTom possessed a unique, real-time traffic information service called TomTom HD traffic, which provided users with high-quality, real-time traffic updates.[6] These three goals formed the base of satellite navigation, working in conjunction to help TomTom achieve its mission.

TomTom's Products

TomTom offered a wide variety of products ranging from portable navigation devices to software navigation applications and digital maps. The unique features in each of these products made them truly "the smart choice in personal navigation."[7] Some of these products are described next.

TomTom Go and TomTom One

These devices came with an LCD screen that made it easy to use with fingertips while driving. They provided Points of Interest (POI) that helped in locating petrol stations, restaurants, and places of importance and traffic information.

TomTom Rider

These were portable models especially designed for bikers. The equipment consisted of an integrated GPS receiver that could be mounted on any bike, and a wireless headset inside the helmet. Similar to the car Portable Navigation Devices (PNDs), the TomTom Rider models had a number of POI applications. The interfaces used in TomTom Rider were user-friendly and came in a variety of languages.[8]

TomTom Navigator and TomTom Mobile

These applications provided navigation software along with digital maps. Both of these applications were compatible with most mobiles and PDAs provided by companies like Sony, Nokia, Acer, Dell, and HP. These applications came with TomTom HOME, which could be used to upgrade to the most recent digital maps and application versions.[9]

TomTom for iPhone

On August 17, 2009, TomTom released TomTom for the iPhone.

The TomTom app for iPhone 3G and 3GS users included a map of the United States and Canada from Tele Atlas, and was available for US$99.99.

The TomTom app for iPhone included the exclusive IQ Routes technology. Instead of using travel time assumptions, IQ Routes based its routes on the actual experience of millions of TomTom drivers to calculate the fastest route and generate the most accurate arrival times in the industry. TomTom IQ Routes empowered drivers to reach their destination faster up to 35% of the time.

Company History

TomTom was founded as "Palmtop" in 1991 by Peter-Frans Pauwels and Pieter Geelen, two graduates from Amsterdam University, The Netherlands. Palmtop started out as a software development company and was involved in producing software for handheld computers, one of the most popular devices of the 1990s. In the following few years, the company diversified into producing commercial applications including software for personal finance, games, a dictionary, and maps. In the year 1996, Corinne Vigreux joined Palmtop as the third partner. In the same year, the company announced the launch of Enroute and RouteFinder, the first navigation software titles. As more and more people using PCs adopted Microsoft's operating system, the company developed applications which were compatible with it. This helped the company increase its market share. In 2001, Harold Goddijn, the former Chief Executive of Psion, joined the company as the fourth partner. This proved to be a turning point in the history of TomTom. Not only did Palmtop get renamed to TomTom, but it also entered the satellite navigation market. TomTom launched TomTom Navigator, the first mobile car satnav system.

In 2002, the company generated revenue of €8 million by selling the first GPS-linked car navigator, the TomTom Navigator, for PDAs. The upgraded version, Navigator 2, was released in early 2003. Meanwhile, the company made efforts to gain technical and marketing personnel. TomTom took strategic steps to grow its sales. The former CTO of Psion, Mark Gretton, led the hardware team, while Alexander Ribbink, a former top marketing official, looked after sales of new products introduced by the company.

TomTom Go, an all-in-one car navigation system, was the company's next major launch. With its useful and easy-to-use features, TomTom Go was included in the list of successful products of 2004. In the same year, the company launched TomTom Mobile, a navigation system that sat on top of Smartphones.[10]

TomTom completed its IPO on the Amsterdam Stock Exchange in May 2005, raising €469 million (US$587 million). The net worth of the company was nearly €2 billion after the IPO. A majority of the shares were held by the four partners.[11] From the years 2006 to 2008, TomTom strengthened itself by making three key strategic acquisitions. Datafactory AG was acquired to power TomTom WORK through WEBfleet technology, while Applied Generics gave its technology for Mobility Solutions Services. However, the most prominent of these three was the acquisition of Tele Atlas.[12]

In July of 2007, TomTom bid for Tele Atlas, a company specializing in digital maps. The original bid price of €2 billion was countered by a €2.3 billion offer from Garmin, TomTom's biggest rival. When TomTom raised its bid price to €2.9 billion, the two companies initiated a bidding war for Tele Atlas. Although there was speculation that Garmin would further increase its bid price, in the end management decided not to pursue Tele Atlas any further. Rather, Garmin struck a content agreement with Navteq. TomTom's shareholders approved the takeover in December 2007.[13]

TomTom's Customers

TomTom was a company that had a wide array of customers, each with their own individual needs and desires. TomTom had a variety of products to meet the requirements of a large and varied customer base. As an example, its navigational products ranged from US$100–$500 in the United States, spanning lower-end products with fewer capabilities to high-end products with advanced features.

The *first* group was the individual consumers who bought stand-alone portable navigation devices and services. The *second* group was automobile manufacturers. TomTom teamed with companies like Renault to develop built-in navigational units to install as an option in cars. A *third* group of customers was the aviation industry and pilots with personal planes. TomTom produced navigational devices for air travel at affordable prices. A *fourth* group of customers was business enterprises. Business enterprises referred to companies such as Wal-Mart, Target, or The Home Depot, huge companies with large mobile workforces. To focus on these customers, TomTom formed a strategic partnership with a technology company called Advanced Integrated Solutions to "optimize business fleet organization and itinerary planning on the TomTom pro series of navigation devices." This new advanced feature on PNDs offered ways for fleet managers and route dispatchers to organize, plan, and optimize routes and to provide detailed mapping information about the final destination. TomTom's *fifth* group of customers, the Coast Guard, was able to use TomTom's marine navigational devices for its everyday responsibilities.

Mergers and Acquisitions

TomTom made various mergers and acquisitions as well as partnerships, which positioned the company well. In 2008, TomTom acquired a digital mapping company called Tele Atlas. The acquisition significantly improved TomTom customers' user experience and created other benefits for the customers and partners of both companies, including more accurate navigation information, improved coverage, and new enhanced features such as map updates and IQ Routes.

In 2005, TomTom partnered with Avis, adding its user-friendly navigation system to all Avis rental cars. This partnership began in Europe, and soon the devices had made their way into Avis rental cars in North America as well as many other countries where Avis operated.

TomTom acquired several patents for its many different technologies. By having these patents for each of its ideas, the company protected itself against its competition and other companies trying to enter into the market.

TomTom prided itself on being the industry innovator and always being a step ahead of the competition in terms of its technology.

TomTom had a strong brand name/image. It positioned itself well throughout the world as a leader in portable navigation devices. The company marketed its products through its very user-friendly online website and also through large companies such as Best Buy and Wal-Mart. TomTom also teamed up with Locutio Voice Technologies and Twentieth Century Fox Licensing & Merchandising to bring the original voice of Homer Simpson to all TomTom devices via download. "Let Homer Simpson be your TomTom co-pilot" was one of the many interesting ways TomTom marketed its products and name to consumers.[14]

TomTom's Resources and Capabilities

The company believed that there were three fundamental requirements to a navigation system—digital mapping, routing technology, and dynamic information. Based on these requirements, three key resources could be identified that really distinguished TomTom from its competition.

The first of these resources was the in-house **routing algorithms**. These algorithms enabled TomTom to introduce technologies like IQ Routes that provided a "community based information database." IQ Routes calculated customer routes based on the real average speeds measured on roads at that particular time.

The second unique resource was Tele Atlas and the **digital mapping technology** that the TomTom group specialized in. Having the technology and knowledge in mapping that the company brought to TomTom allowed it to introduce many unique features to its customers. First, TomTom came out with a map update feature. The company recognized that roads around the world were constantly changing and, because of this, it used the technology to come out with four new maps each year, one per business quarter. This allowed its customers to always have the latest routes to incorporate into their everyday travel. A second feature it introduced is its Map Share program. The idea behind this is that customers of TomTom who notice mistakes in a certain map are able to go in and request a change to be made. The change was then verified and checked directly by TomTom and was shared with the rest of the global user community.

The third unique resource was **automotive partnerships** with two companies in particular: Renault and Avis. At the end of 2008, TomTom reached a deal with Renault to install its navigation devices in its cars as an option. The clincher was the new price of the built-in navigation units. The cost of a navigation device installed in Renault's cars before TomTom was €1500. Now, with the TomTom system, it cost only €500. As mentioned earlier, TomTom also partnered with Avis in 2005 to offer its navigation devices, specifically the model GO 700, in all Avis rental cars, first starting in Europe and then expanding into other countries where Avis operated.

Traditional Competition

TomTom faced competition from two main companies. The first of these was Garmin, which held 45% of the market share, by far the largest and double TomTom's market share (24%). Garmin was founded in 1989 by Gary Burrell and Min H. Kao. The company was known for its on-the-go directions since its introduction into GPS navigation in 1989. At the end of 2008, Garmin reported annual sales of US$3.49 billion. Garmin had competed head to head in 2009 with TomTom in trying to acquire Tele Atlas for its mapmaking. Garmin withdrew its bid when it became evident that it was becoming too expensive to own Tele Atlas. Garmin executives made a decision that it was cheaper to work out a long-term deal with its current supplier, Navteq, than to try to buy out a competitor.

The second direct competitor was Magellan, which held 15% of the market share. Magellan was part of a privately held company under the name of MiTac Digital Corporation. Similar to Garmin, Magellan products used Navteq-based maps. Magellan was the creator of Magellan NAV 100, the world's first commercial handheld GPS receiver, which was created in 1989. The company was also well-known for its award-winning RoadMate and Maestro series portable car navigation systems.

Together these three dominant players accounted for about 85% of the total market. Other competitors in the personal navigation device market were Navigon, Nextar, and Nokia. Navigon and Nextar competed in the personal navigation devices with TomTom, Magellan, and Garmin, who were the top three in the industry. But Navigon competed in the high-end segment, which retailed for more than any of the competitors but offered a few extra features in its PNDs. Nextar competed in the low-end market and its strategy was low cost. Finally, Nokia was mentioned as a competitor in this industry because the company acquired Navteq, a major supplier of map services in this industry. Along with that, Nokia had a big market share in the cell phone industry and planned on incorporating GPS technology in every phone, making it a potential key player to look for in the GPS navigation industry.

New Competition Everywhere!

Cell Phones

Cell phones were widely used by people all around the world. With the 2005 FCC mandate that required the location of any cell phone used to call 911 to be tracked, phone manufacturers included a GPS receiver in almost every cell phone. Due to this mandate, cell phone manufacturers and cellular services were able to offer GPS navigation services through the cell phone for a fee.

AT&T Navigator

GPS Navigation with AT&T Navigator and AT&T Navigator Global Edition feature real-time GPS-enabled turn-by-turn navigation on AT&T mobile Smartphones (iPhones and BlackBerrys) or static navigation and Local Search on a non-GPS AT&T mobile Smartphone.

AT&T Navigator featured Global GPS turn-by-turn navigation—Mapping and Point of AT&T Interest content for three continents, including North America (United States, Canada, and Mexico), Western Europe, and China, where wireless coverage was available from AT&T or its roaming providers. The AT&T Navigator was sold as a subscription service and cost US$9.99 per month.

Online Navigation Applications

Online navigation websites that were still popular among many users for driving directions and maps were MapQuest, Google Maps, and Yahoo Maps. Users were able to use these free sites to get detailed directions on how to get to their next destination. In the current economic downturn, many people were looking for cheap (or if possible, free) solutions to solve their problems. These online websites offered the use of free mapping and navigation information that would allow them to get what they needed at no additional cost. However, there were downsides to these programs: They were not portable and could have poor visualization designs (such as vague images or text-based output).[15]

Built-in Car Navigation Devices

In-car navigation devices first came about in luxury, high-end vehicles. Currently, it has become more mainstream and is now being offered in mid- to lower-tier vehicles. These built-in car navigation devices offered similar features to the personal navigation device but didn't have the portability, so users wouldn't have to carry multiple devices. However, they came with a hefty price. Some examples of these are Kenwood, Pioneer, and Eclipse units, which are all installed in cars. These units tended to be expensive and overpriced because they were brand-name products and required physical installation. For example, the top-of-the-line Pioneer unit was US$1,000 for the monitor and another US$500 for the navigation device plus the physical labor. When buying such products, a customer spent a huge amount of money on a product that was almost identical to a product TomTom offered at a significantly lower price.

Physical Maps

Physical maps were the primary option for navigating for decades until technology improved them. Physical maps provided detailed road information to help a person get from point A to point B. Although more cumbersome to use than some of the modern technology alternatives, it was an alternative for people who were not technically savvy or for whom a navigation device was an unnecessary luxury.

Potential Adverse Legislation and Restrictions

In the legal and political realm, TomTom faced two issues that were not critical now, but that might have significant ramifications to not only TomTom in the future, but also the entire portable navigation device industry. The reaction of TomTom's management to each of these issues will determine whether or not there was an opportunity for gain or a threat of a significant loss to the company.

The most important issue TomTom dealt with was the possible legislative banning of all navigational devices from automobiles. In Australia, the government was considering banning PNDs completely from automobiles. There was a similar sentiment in Ontario, Canada, where a law that was currently under review would ban all PNDs that were not mounted either to the dashboard or to the windshield itself.[16]

With the increase in legislation adding to the restrictions placed on PND devices, the threat that the PND market in the future will be severely limited could not be ignored. All of the companies within the PND industry, not just TomTom, must create a coordinated and united effort to stem this wave of restrictions as well as provide reassurance to the public that they were also concerned with the safe use of their products. This effort can be seen in the heavily regulated toy industry. Many companies within the toy industry had combined to form the International Council of Toy Industries[17] to be proactive in regard to safety regulations, as well as lobby governments against laws that may unfairly threaten the toy industry.[18]

The other issue within the legal and political spectrum that TomTom must focus on was the growing use of GPS devices as tracking devices. Currently, law enforcement agents were allowed to use their own GPS devices to track the movements and locations of individuals they deemed suspicious. However, if budget cuts reduced the access to these GPS devices, then the simple solution will be to use the PND devices already installed in many automobiles.

This issue also required the industry as a whole to proactively work with the consumers and the government to come to an amicable resolution. The threat of having every consumer's GPS information at the fingertips of either the government or surveillance company will most certainly stunt or even completely halt any growth within the PND industry.

Another alarming trend was the rise in PND thefts around the country.[19] With the prices for PNDs at a relatively high level, thieves were targeting vehicles that had visible docking stations for PNDs either on the dashboard or the windshield. The onus will be on TomTom to create new designs that will not only hide PNDs from would-be thieves but also deter them from trying to steal one. Consumers who were scared to purchase PNDs because of this rise in crime will become an issue if this problem is not resolved.

There was also a current trend, labeled the GREEN movement,[20] that aimed to reduce any activities that would endanger the environment. This movement was a great opportunity for TomTom to tout its technology as the smarter and more environmentally safe tool if driving is an absolute necessity. Not only can individuals tout this improved efficiency, but more importantly on a larger scale, businesses that require large amounts of materials to be transported across long stretches can show activists that they too are working toward becoming a green company.

It is ironic that the core technology used in TomTom's navigation system, the GPS system, has proliferated into other electronic devices at such a rapid pace that it has caused serious competition to the PND industry. GPS functionality was a basic requirement for all new Smartphones that entered the market and soon will become a basic functionality in regular cellular phones. TomTom will be hard pressed to compete with these multifunctional devices unless it can improve upon its designs and transform itself into a single focused device.

Another concern for not only TomTom, but also every company that relies heavily on GPS technology, was the aging satellites that supported the GPS system. Analysts predicted that these satellites will be either replaced or fixed before there are any issues, but this issue was unsettling due to the fact that TomTom had no control over it.[21] TomTom will have to devise contingency plans in case of catastrophic failure of the GPS system, much like what happened to Research in Motion when malfunctioning satellites caused disruption in its service.

TomTom was one of the leading companies in the PND markets in both Europe and the United States. Although they were the leader in Europe, that market was showing signs of becoming saturated. Even though the U.S. market was currently growing, TomTom could not wait for the inevitable signs of that market's slowdown as well.

The two main opportunities for TomTom to expand—creating digital maps for developing countries and creating navigational services—can either be piggybacked or can be taken in independent paths. The first-mover advantage for these opportunities will erect a high barrier of entry for any companies that do not have large amounts of resources to invest in the developing country. TomTom was already playing catch-up to Garmin and its already established service in India.

Globalization of any company's products did not come without a certain set of issues. For TomTom, the main threat brought on by foreign countries was twofold. The first threat, which may be an isolated instance, but could also be repeated in many other countries, was the restriction of certain capabilities for all of TomTom's products. Due to security and terrorism concerns, GPS devices have not been allowed in Egypt since 2003.[22] In times of global terrorism, TomTom must be vigilant of the growing trend for countries to become overly protective of foreign companies and their technologies.

Internal Environment

Finance

TomTom's financial goals were to diversify and become a broader revenue-based company. The company not only sought to increase the revenue base in terms of geographical expansion but also wanted to diversify its product and service portfolio. Additionally, another important goal the company strived to achieve was reducing its operating expenses.

Sales Revenue and Net Income

Exhibit 2 shows that from 2005 to 2007 there was a consistent growth in sales revenue, as well as a corresponding increase in net income. However, year 2008 was an exception to this trend. In this year, sales revenue decreased by 3.7% and the net income decreased by 136%. In fact, in the first quarter the net income was actually negative, totaling –€37 million. The decrease in sales can be accounted for by the downturn in the economy. According to its 2008 annual report, the sales are in line with market expectations. However, the net income plummeted much more than the decrease in sales. This was actually triggered by its acquisition of the digital mapping company—Tele Atlas—which was funded by both cash assets and debt.

Quarterly sales.   In the second quarter of 2009, TomTom received sales revenue of €368 million, compared to €213 million in the first quarter and €453 million in the same quarter in 2008 (**Exhibit 3**). By evaluating quarterly sales for a three-year period from 2007 until the present, it was apparent that the sales followed a seasonal trend in TomTom, with highest sales in the last quarter and lowest in the first quarter. However, focusing on just the first and second quarter for three years, one can infer that the sales revenue as a whole was also going down year after year. To investigate further on the causes of this scenario, the company will have to delve deeper into its revenue base. TomTom's sources of revenue can be broadly grouped into two categories—market segment and geographic location.

EXHIBIT 3
Revenue per Segment: TomTom (Amount in millions of €)

(in € millions)	Q 1'09	Q 1'08	y.o.y	Q 4'08	q.o.q.
Revenue	172	264	–35%	473	–64%
PNDs	141	234	–40%	444	–68%
Others	31	29	5%	29	5%
# of PNDs sold (in thousands)	1,419	1,997	–29%	4,443	–68%
Average Selling Price (€)	99	117	–15%	100	–1%

Revenue per Segment

TomTom's per segment revenue stream can be divided into PNDs and others, where others consisted of services and content. Evaluating the first quarter of 2008 against that of 2009 and the last quarter of 2008, TomTom experienced steep declines of 40% and 68% (see **Exhibit 4**). This could be a consequence of the compounded effect of the following: (1) The number of devices (PNDs) decreased by a similar amount during both time periods. (2) The average selling price of PNDs had also been decreasing consistently. In a technology company, a decrease in average selling price is a part of doing business in a highly competitive and dynamic marketplace. Nevertheless, the revenue stream from business units other than PNDs had seen a steady increase in both the scenarios.

Revenue per Region

TomTom's per region revenue stream can be further divided into Europe, North America, and the rest of the world. Comparing the first quarter of 2009 against 2008, it can be seen that revenue from both Europe and North America was on the decline, with a decrease of 22% and 52%, respectively (see **Exhibit 5**). At the same time, revenue from the rest of the world had seen a huge increase of 90%. Both of these analyses supported TomTom's current goal to increase its revenue base and is aligned with its long-term strategy of being a leader in the navigation industry.

Long-term debt. In 2005, TomTom was a cash-rich company. However, the recent acquisition of Tele Atlas, which amounted to €2.9 billion, was funded by cash, the release of new shares, and long-term debt (see **Exhibit 6**), in this case a €1.2 billion loan. These combined to use up TomTom's cash reserves. Currently, TomTom's debt was €1,006 million.

EXHIBIT 4
Revenue per Region: TomTom (Amount in millions of €)

	Quarter 1 of 2009	Quarter 1 of 2009	Difference
Europe	178,114	146,549	–22%
North America	84,641	55,558	–52%
Rest of world	1,087	10,976	90%
Total	263,842	213,083	–24%

EXHIBIT 5
Cash versus Long-Term Debt (Amount in thousands of €)

	2005	2006	2007	2008	2009
Long Term Debt	301	338	377	4,749	4,811
Cash Assets	178,377	437,801	463,339	321,039	422,530
Borrowings	0	0	0	1,241,900	1,195,715

EXHIBIT 6
Operating Margin:
TomTom

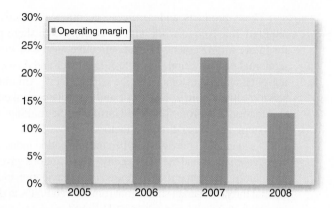

Operating margin. TomTom saw a consistent increase in operating margin until 2006. However, since 2007, operating margin has been decreasing for the firm. In fact, by the end of 2008 it came down to 13%, compared to 26% in 2006.

Marketing

Traditionally, high quality and ease of use of solutions have been of utmost importance to TomTom. In a 2006 interview, TomTom's Marketing Head, Anne Louise Hanstad, emphasized the importance of simplicity and ease of use with its devices. This underlined TomTom's belief that people prefer fit-for-purpose devices that are developed and designed to do one specific thing very well. At that time, both of these were core to TomTom's strategy as its targeted customers were *early adopters*. Now, however, as the navigation industry moved from embryonic to a growth industry, TomTom's current customers were *early majority*. Hence, simplicity and ease alone could no longer provide it with a competitive advantage.

Recently, to be in line with its immediate goal of diversifying into different market segments, TomTom was more focused on strengthening its brand name. In December 2008, TomTom's CEO stated " . . . we are constantly striving to increase awareness of our brand and strengthen our reputation for providing smart, easy-to-use, high-quality portable navigation products and services."[23]

Along with Tele Atlas, the TomTom group has gained depth and breadth of expertise over the last 30 years, which made it a trusted brand. Three out of four people were aware of the TomTom brand across the markets. The TomTom group has always been committed to the three fundamentals of navigation: mapping, routing algorithm, and dynamic information. Tele Atlas' core competency was the digital mapping database, while TomTom's was routing algorithms and guidance services using dynamic information. Together, the group created synergies that enabled it to introduce products almost every year that advanced on one or a combination of these three elements. Acquiring its long-time supplier of digital maps, Tele Atlas, in 2008 gave TomTom an edge with in-house digital mapping technology.

TomTom provided a range of PND devices like TomTom One, TomTom XL, and the TomTom Go Series. Periodically, it tried to enhance those devices with new features and services that were built based on customer feedback. Examples of services were IQ Routes and LIVE services. While IQ Routes provided drivers with the most efficient route planning, accounting for situations as precise as speed bumps and traffic lights, LIVE services formed a range of information services delivered directly to the LIVE devices. The LIVE services bundle included Map Share and HD Traffic, bringing the content collected from vast driving communities directly to the end-user.

These products and services accentuated effective designs and unique features, and required TomTom to work with its customers to share precise updates and also get feedback for future improvements. Hence, effective customer interaction became essential to its long-term goal of innovation. In 2008, J. D. Power and Associates recognized TomTom for providing outstanding customer service experience.[24] Although it awarded TomTom for customer service satisfaction, J. D. Power and Associates ranked Garmin highest in overall customer satisfaction. TomTom followed Garmin in the ranking, performing well in the routing, speed of system, and voice direction factors.[25]

As mentioned previously, when the navigation industry was still in its embryonic stages, features, ease of use, and the high quality of its solutions gave TomTom products a competitive edge. Eventually, the competition increased in the navigation industry and even substitutes posed a substantial threat to market share. TomTom offered PNDs in different price ranges, broadly classified into high-range and mid-range PNDs, with an average selling price of €99. There were entry-level options that allowed a savvy shopper to put navigation in his/her car for just over US$100. Higher-end models added advanced features and services that were previously described.

TomTom sold its PNDs to consumers through retailers and distributors. After acquiring Tele Atlas, it was strategically placed to gain the first mover advantage created by its rapid expansion of geographical coverage.[26] This was of key importance when it came to increasing its global market share.

TomTom directed its marketing expenditure toward B2B advertising that was directed to retailers and distributors. TomTom also invested in an official blog website, as well as search optimization, which placed it in premium results in online searches. This enabled TomTom to do effective word-of-mouth promotion while keeping flexible marketing spending, in accordance with changes in the macroeconomic environment or seasonal trends.[27] Although this approach gave TomTom spending flexibility, it lacked a direct B2C approach. In 2009, only 21% of U.S. adults owned PNDs, whereas 65% of U.S. adults neither owned nor used navigation.[28] By not spending on B2C marketing, TomTom discounted on the opportunity both to attract first-tier noncustomers and glean an insight of needs of second-tier noncustomers.[29]

Operations

The focus of operations had always been on innovation. More recently, TomTom's operational objective had been to channel all its resources and core capabilities to create economies of scale so as to be aligned with its long-term strategy. TomTom aimed to focus and centralize R&D resources to create scale economies to continue to lead the industry in terms of innovation.[30]

Implementation of this strategy was well underway and the changes were visible. By the second quarter of 2009, mid-range PNDs were introduced with the capabilities of high-range devices. In addition, 50% of PNDs were sold with IQ Routes technology. The first in-dash product was also launched in alliance with Renault, and the TomTom iPhone application was also announced.[31]

After acquiring Tele Atlas to better support the broader navigation solutions and content and services, the group underwent restructuring. The new organizational structure consisted of four business units that had a clear focus on a specific customer group and were supported by two shared development centers.

The four business units were CONSUMER (B2C), composed of retail sales of PND, on-board, and mobile; AUTOMOTIVE (B2B), composed of auto industry sales of integrated solutions and content & services; LICENSING (B2B), composed of PND, automotive, mobile, Internet, and GIS content and services; and WORK (B2B), composed of commercial fleet sales of Webfleet & Connected Solutions.

TomTom's supply chain and distribution model was outsourced. This increased TomTom's ability to scale up or down the supply chain, while limiting capital expenditure risks. At the same time, however, it depended on a limited number of third parties—and in certain instances sole suppliers—for component supply and manufacturing, which increased its dependency on these suppliers.

TomTom's dynamic content sharing model used high-quality digital maps along with the connected services, like HD Traffic, Local Search with Google, and weather information. This provided customers with relevant real-time information at the moment they needed it, which helped them deliver the benefits of innovative technology directly to the end-user at affordable prices. Although the network externalities previously mentioned were among the advantages of TomTom's LIVE, it had also increased TomTom's dependency on the network of the connected driving community. The bigger the network, the more effective the information gathered from the guidance services.

Furthermore, in order to reduce operating expenses and strengthen the balance sheet, heavy emphasis had been placed on the cost-cutting program. In 2009, the cost reductions were made up of reduction of staff, restructuring and integration of Tele Atlas, reduced discretionary spending, and reduction in the number of contractors and marketing expenditures. However, if not executed wisely, it could hamper TomTom's long-term objective of being a market leader. For example, one of the core capabilities of any technology company was its staff; reducing it could hinder future innovative projects. This may also occur when reducing the marketing expenditures in a market that still held rich prospects of high growth. Among U.S. adults, 65% did not own any kind of navigation system.[32]

Human Resources

Like in any other technology company, the success of individual employees was very important to TomTom. Additionally, TomTom had a vision that company success should also mean success for the individual employee. Therefore, at TomTom, employee competency was taken very seriously and talent development programs were built around it. There was a personal navigation plan that provided employees with a selection of courses based on competencies in their profile. In 2008, TomTom completed its Young Talent Development Program, which was aimed at broadening the participants' knowledge while improving their technical and personal skills.

TomTom's motto was to do business efficiently and profitably, as well as responsibly. This underlined its corporate social responsibility. TomTom's headquarters was one of the most energy-efficient buildings in Amsterdam. As previously mentioned, earlier navigation was oriented toward making the drivers arrive at their destination without getting lost. TomTom was the pioneer in introducing different technology that actually helped drivers make their journeys safer and more economical. This showed TomTom's commitment to its customer base as well as to the community as a whole.

Issues of Concern for TomTom

First, TomTom was facing increasing competition from other platforms using GPS technology, such as cell phones and Smartphones. In the cell phone industry, Nokia was leading the charge in combining cell phone technology with GPS technology. Around the same time TomTom acquired Tele Atlas, Nokia purchased Navteq, a competitor to Tele Atlas. With the acquisition of Navteq, Nokia hoped to shape the cell phone industry by merging cell phone, Internet, and GPS technology.

The Smartphone industry was emerging with the iPhone and the Palm Pre. There was also a shift in how people were able to utilize these technologies as a navigation tool. A big trend in Smartphones was applications. Because of the ease of developing software on platforms for Smartphones, more and more competitors were coming to the forefront and developing GPS navigation applications. On October 28, 2009, Google announced the addition of Tom Tom and Garmin Ltd. as competitors. Google was adding driving directions to its Smartphones.

For TomTom, both of these sectors might signal that major change was on the horizon and that there was no longer a need for hardware for GPS navigation devices. The world seemed to be heading toward a culture where consumers wanted an all-in-one device such as a cell phone or Smartphone that would do everything needed, including offering GPS navigation services. A recent study done by Charles Golvin for Forrester suggested that by 2013 phone-based navigation will dominate the industry. The reason was due to Gen Y and Gen X customers who were increasingly reliant on their mobile phone and who would demand that social networking and other connected services be integrated into their navigation experience.[33]

Secondly, TomTom faced a maturing U.S. and European personal navigation device market. After three years of steady growth in the PND market, TomTom had seen decreasing growth rates for PND sales. Initially entering the European market 12 months before entering the U.S. market, TomTom witnessed a 21% dip in sales for the European market. Although TomTom experienced some growth in the U.S. market for 2008, the growth rate was not as good as in prior years.

NOTES

1. TomTom AR-08, "TomTom Annual Report 2008," *TomTom Annual Report 2008*, December 2008.
2. Ibid.
3. TomTom, "TomTom, Portable GPS Car Navigation Systems," http://investors.tomtom.com/overview.cfm.
4. Ibid.
5. Ibid.
6. Ibid.
7. TomTom AR-08, "TomTom Annual Report 2008," *TomTom Annual Report 2008*, December 2008.
8. Ibid.
9. Ibid.
10. Ibid.
11. "TomTom NV," http://www.answers.com/topic/tomtom-n-v.
12. Ibid.
13. Thomson Reuters, "TomTom Launches 2.9 bln Euro Bid for Tele Atlas," http://www.reuters.com/article/technology-media-telco-SP/idUSL1839698320071119 (November 19, 2007).
14. *Boston Business* Article, http://www.boston.com/business/ticker/2009/06/let_homer_simps.html.
15. Magellan website, http://www.magellangps.com/Company/About-Us.
16. Tanya Talaga and Rob Ferguson, *TheStar.com*, October 28, 2008, http://www.thestar.com/News/Ontario/article/525697 (July 29, 2009).
17. ICTI, 2009, http://www.toy-icti.org/ (July 29, 2009).
18. Ibid.
19. *GPS Magazine*, September 23, 2007, http://gpsmagazine.com/2007/09/gps_thefts_rise.php (July 29, 2009).
20. "Webist Media," *Web Ecoist*, August 17, 2008, http://webecoist.com/2008/08/17/a-brief-history-of-the-modern-green-movement/ (July 29, 2009).
21. Nick Jones, *Garnter*, January 5, 2009, http://www.gartner.com/id=1007612
22. *US News*, October 14, 2008, http://usnews.rankingsandreviews.com/cars-trucks/daily-news/081014-GPS-Devices-Banned-in-Egypt/ (July 29, 2009).
23. TomTom AR-08, "TomTom Annual Report 2008," *TomTom Annual Report 2008*, December 2008.
24. Reuters, "TomTom Inc. Recognized for Call Center Customer Satisfaction Excellence by J.D. Power," January 7, 2008, http://www.reuters.com/article/pressRelease/idUS141391+07-Jan-2008+PRN20080107.
25. J. D. Power and Associates, "Garmin Ranks Highest in Customer Satisfaction with Portable Navigation Devices," October 23, 2008, http://www.jdpower.com/corporate/news/releases/pressrelease.aspx?ID=2008221.
26. TomTom AR-08, "TomTom Annual Report 2008," *TomTom Annual Report 2008*, December 2008.
27. Ibid.
28. Forrestor Research, "Phone-Based Navigation Will Dominate by 2013," March 27, 2009.
29. W. Chan Kim and Mauborgne, *Blue Ocean Strategy* (Boston: Harvard Business School Press, 2005).
30. TomTom AR-08, "TomTom Annual Report 2008," *TomTom Annual Report 2008*, December 2008.
31. Ibid.
32. Forrestor Research, "Phone-Based Navigation Will Dominate by 2013," March 27, 2009.
33. Ibid.

CASE **29**

General Electric, GE Capital, and the Financial Crisis of 2008:

THE BEST OF THE WORST IN THE FINANCIAL SECTOR?

Alan N. Hoffman
Bentley University

Company Background

For more than a century, General Electric (GE), has been a global leader and iconic brand known for innovation and leadership in a wide range of endeavors. Its diversified portfolio of products is organized into four strategic business units: energy, technology infrastructure, GE Capital, and home and business solutions.

GE began in 1878 when Thomas Edison formed the Edison General Electric Company (EGEC). Though Edison was best known for inventing the first incandescent light bulb, he also pioneered systems design for generating and distributing electricity, eventually holding over 1000 patents. Within a few years, the rival Thomas Houston Company, which held key patents in the same area, challenged EGEC's position in the marketplace. In 1892, the two companies merged, forming General Electric. GE then parlayed the demand for electricity into the invention of home heating, stoves and other appliances, and refrigeration, transforming American households, and went on to become an innovator in myriad fields, from medicine, aviation, and transportation to plastics and financial services. GE created the GE Credit Corporation (later GE Capital) in the wake of the Great Depression to facilitate the sale of household appliances and provide the option of extended payments for consumers. Innovation defined the organization, and the commitment to research and development remained key.[1]

....

The authors would like to thank Barbara Gottfried, Patrick DeCourcy, Keith Dugas, Kaitlin Mackie, Desiree Ouellette, Jason Tate, and Will Hoffman for their research and contributions to this case.

Please address all correspondence to: Dr. Alan N. Hoffman, Dept. of Management, Bentley University, 175 Forest Street, Waltham, MA 02452-4705, voice (781) 891-2287, ahoffman@bentley.edu. Printed by permission of Alan N. Hoffman.

GE was one of the original 12 companies that formed the Dow Jones Industrial Average, and the only one of those companies that was still part of the DJIA in 2012. GE was also recognized for cultivating leaders such as Charles Wilson, Ralph Cordiner, Fred Borch, Reginald Jones, and John Welch.[2] In the early 1970s under Fred Borch, GE was one of the first companies with a diversified infrastructure to formalize strategic planning at both corporate and business unit levels with its creation of strategic business units.[3]

GE always saw itself as striving to create a world that worked better, "making what few in the world can, but everyone needs."[4] The company's strategic philosophy centered on innovation, superior technology, and demonstrating leadership in growth markets. GE sought to maintain a strong competitive advantage through innovation, smart capital allocation, and solidifying customer relationships. The strategy also included transitioning from an industrial conglomerate to an infrastructure leader to maximize the core strengths of its existing businesses. Diversification and expansion of its business portfolio was a central focus, designed to minimize volatility and create stability through varying growth cycles. Another facet of GE's strategy was to invest for the long-term in high-growth market opportunities that were closely related to its core businesses. For instance, in 2010 the company launched the GE Advantage Program that focused on process excellence and innovation to improve margins in industrial projects.[5]

One of GE's biggest operational strengths lay in its ability to cut costs and maximize return for shareholders. In the 1990s, GE CEO Jack Welch implemented the Six Sigma approach to business management. This approach helped decrease variability and errors to help cut down waste and build a consistent product, one of the many ways GE trained employees to succeed and build their expertise. GE was also able to cut costs because its reputation as a market leader with a large network of businesses and strong alliances with other major corporations enabled it to leverage long-standing relationships to employ the best human, equipment, and capital resources to ensure quality and consistency at a low cost. It acquired many businesses that provided useful resources, and sold off business units that did not contribute to its success.

In 2011, GE's strategic accomplishments included 22% growth (defined as a 22% increase in operating EPS excluding impact of the preferred stock redemption) and a 20% rise in operating earnings. Over the two-year period through 2011, GE's dividends increased a total of 70%. GE was positioned for continued success in 2012 with a record industrial backlog of US$200 billion, US$85 billion cash, and equivalents offering significant financial flexibility. Internationally, GE saw 18% growth in industrial revenue, and U.S. exports were up US$1 billion from 2010. At the same time, GE's management demonstrated their continued commitment to innovation by investing 6% of the firm's industrial revenue in R&D.[6] General Electric was divided into six Operating Segments (five Industrial): Aviation, Energy Infrastructure, Healthcare, Home & Business Solutions, Transportation, and GE Capital.

By 2012, under the leadership of Jeffrey Immelt, General Electric was a powerful conglomerate employing approximately 300,000 people globally and operating in more than 100 countries,[7] ranked the sixth-largest American corporation and the 14th most profitable by *Forbes*. Immelt had replaced the highly regarded Jack Welch as CEO and Chairman of the Board in 2001 and had been named as one of the "World's Best CEOs" three times by *Barron's*. GE's board of directors was composed of 17 members, of whom two-thirds were considered to be "independent." The board was in continuous dialogue with GE's top management. Together they emphasized strategy and risk management while monitoring strategic initiatives personally through site visits.

Fast Company ranked GE the 19th most innovative company; *Fortune* listed GE as the 15th most admired company; and Interbrand cited GE as the number 5 best global brand.[8] General Electric's objectives were, and continued to be, earnings growth, increasing margins, and returning cash to investors, as well as organic growth, increased financial flexibility, and larger U.S. exports. While pursuing these ambitious objectives, GE, at the same time, committed itself to social and environmental responsibility

GE's Diversified Industrial Products Competitors

Diversified international industrial conglomerates, such as GE, have by definition many strong, direct competitors spanning many industries, as the total market capitalization for this industry is over US$137 billion.[9] Aside from GE, the three industrial conglomerates with the best relative performance (based on fundamental and technical strength) were Siemens, Phillips Electronics, and 3M.[10]

Siemens AG, the largest European electronic engineering and manufacturing conglomerate, based in Munich, Germany, and operating worldwide,[11] is split into four sectors: Energy, Healthcare, Industry, and Infrastructure and Cities, yielding 19 divisions with over 360,000 employees and €73.5 billion (US$96.2 billion) in sales in 2011. Its focus is on sustainable value creation, innovation-driven growth markets, customer relations, and capitalizing on core competencies.

Royal Phillips Electronics, based in the Netherlands, is split into three overlapping sectors: Healthcare, Lighting, and Consumer Lifestyle, with many subdivisions in 60 countries,[12] over 125,000 employees, and €20.1 billion (US$26.3 billion) in sales in 2011. Phillips' focus is on improving people's lives through meaningful innovation, delivering a quality product, and building value for customers and shareholders.

3M, based in Minnesota, operates in the markets of consumer goods, office supplies, display and graphics, health care, industrial goods, transportation goods, and safety, security, and protection services. With over 80,000 employees and a presence in more than 65 countries, 3M amassed more than US$27 billion of sales revenue in 2011. As a diversified technology company, 3M focuses on ingenious, innovative products and building global market share.[13]

GE Capital

GE Capital, the largest of GE's four strategic business units in 2012, was created in 1932 as GE Contracts, an internal business unit to help finance consumer purchases of GE appliances (see **Exhibits 1** and **2**).[14] Particularly in the midst of the Great Depression, consumers were hesitant to invest in what at the time were considered superfluous products. To encourage consumers, GE Contracts offered comparatively low monthly payments to make its parent company's products more affordable.

EXHIBIT 1

GE Capital (in millions)	2011	2010	2009	2008	2007
Revenues	45,730	46,422	48,906	65,900	65,625
Net Income	6,549	3,158	1,325	7,841	12,179

EXHIBIT 2

GE (Parent Company) (in millions)	2011	2010	2009
Revenues	147,300	149,593	154,438
Net Income	13,120	11,344	10,725

Renamed GE Capital in 1987, the former appliance financing unit grew to incorporate interests beyond those of its GE corporate parent, such as investment banking, retail stores, television channels, and auto/truck leasing. It also acquired a significant market share in private-label credit cards, including those of JCPenney, Montgomery Ward, and Wal-Mart. Early on in its history, GE Capital benefited particularly from its association with its GE parent's strong asset base and creditworthiness, garnering both lower borrowing rates and easy access to cheap capital to generate investment beyond its profits. Through the early 2000s, GE Capital continued to expand its product lines, delving into property and casualty insurance, life insurance, mortgages, and real estate.[15]

As the unit grew, GE Capital became an increasingly significant contributor to its GE parent's success. While in the past most people had thought of GE as an industrial company, GE Capital, a finance company, grew to represent nearly half of its GE parent's annual profits.[16] As of 2012, there were five major components of GE Capital:[17]

1. **Commercial Lending and Leasing:** This division provides loans to outside businesses for a range of uses, including company acquisition, internal restructuring, and even leasing office space. Additionally, the Commercial Lending unit maintains fleets of cars and heavy industrial equipment available for leasing.

2. **Consumer Financing:** Within the U.S., GE Capital's retail financing arm represents their private-label credit card interests, and retail purchase financing that includes automobiles, furniture, and other costly items consumers often don't pay for with cash.

3. **Energy Financial Services:** GE Energy owned stakes in energy interests worldwide, providing financing for companies to invest and expand, often in conjunction with its GE parent's efforts to educate and supply companies with necessary equipment.

4. **Aviation Services:** GE Capital Aviation is involved in passenger aircraft purchasing and leasing, and aircraft part financing, including various engines that its GE parent produced, and airport expansion financing.

5. **Real Estate:** GE Capital Real Estate specializes in various real estate transactions, including property acquisition, debt refinancing, and joint venture investments. Many of its properties are office buildings, but it also owns stakes in multi-family developments and hotels.

GE Capital's Strategic Direction

GE Capital's main expertise is in mid-market banking, providing financing for a range of industries from aviation and energy to health care, and for the purchase, lease, distribution, and maintenance of large fleets and equipment.[18] It also provides capital for corporate acquisitions and restructuring. It is GE Capital's vision to be more than just a banker—to align itself with GE's corporate objective of supporting growth not simply by providing capital, but by helping customers invent more and build more[19] through leveraging its global experience and industry expertise.[20]

However, the financial services industry was, by definition, volatile, and GE Capital was particularly hard hit by the economic recession of 2008. With the credit markets illiquid and financial markets falling, GE Capital found that it was overexposed to commercial real estate and foreign residential mortgages. At this point, GE's parent corporation stepped in, began reorganizing GE Capital, and significantly downsized the unit. GE Capital sold most of its insurance lines, completely left the U.S. mortgage market, and substantially tightened its consumer underwriting guidelines. However, the company still was on the lookout for underpriced assets, and purchased several lending lines from even more troubled Citigroup, as well as a large commercial real estate portfolio from Merrill Lynch financing.

By 2012, GE Capital was smaller, leaner, and more focused on specialty financing especially mid-market lending and leasing.[21] However, like its parent company, GE Capital hoped to see continued sustainable earnings growth with growing margins and lower portfolio risk, and to return money to investors and resume paying dividends to its parent company.[22]

GE Capital's Competitors

GE Capital's main competition came primarily from specialty corporate financial lenders, such as CIT Group, and larger companies that offered diverse and comprehensive financial services, such as Bank of America and Citigroup, according to Hoovers.[23]

In 2012, *Bank of America*[24] was one of the largest and most identifiable banks in the United States with over US$2.1 trillion in assets. Its goal was to be accessible to every sort of customer at any stage of their financial lives by offering both a variety of products and easy accessibility with over 5700 locations and 17,000 ATMs. Beyond the arena of specialty lending, Bank of America served consumers and companies ranging from small sole proprietorships to multinational global corporations with banking, investments, and asset management. While the company was successful in building market share, it faced a multitude of difficulties from major lawsuits deriving from its acquisitions of Countrywide and Merrill Lynch, and from its "robo-signing" foreclosure practices.

Bank of America attempted to return to profitability after declaring a US$2.2 billion loss in 2010 and only a US$1.5 billion profit in 2011, focusing on strengthening its capital reserves and integrating lean initiatives to cut costs and improve efficiency. However, legislation that reduced its two major sources of revenue, interest earnings and fee revenue, in conjunction with depressed consumer and investor confidence levels, heralded a difficult road ahead for the company.

Like Bank of America, *Citigroup* is a behemoth in the financial services industry, made up of a number of units including brokerage, investment bank, and wealth management and consumer lending divisions, with over US$1.9 trillion in total assets and maintaining more than 200 million customer accounts in over 160 countries. The 2008 financial crisis and its aftermath hit Citigroup very hard, resulting in US$90 billion in losses, which led to selling off or divesting from underperforming industries. Citigroup then sold several commercial lending lines to GE Capital, fully exited the student loan market, and planned to sell its CitiMortgage and CitiFinancial divisions. Going forward, Citigroup refocused on traditional banking and continued unloading toxic assets and non-core business units.

Perhaps most similar to GE Capital, *CIT Group Inc*[25] specialized in commercial lending and financing for small and mid-sized businesses, managing US$45 billion in total assets. In addition to its general corporate finance arm, CIT group offered transportation equipment financing, vendor finance, and a smaller branch of consumer lending. Hit severely by the financial crisis, CIT Group briefly declared chapter 11 in 2009, stemming from extreme losses in its subprime mortgage and student loan portfolios. It subsequently improved its balance sheet and reduced debt obligations, refocusing on its commercial lending division by building up its loan and lease accounts and hoping to increase deposit accounts by acquiring already established banks.

Financials

With operations in over 100 countries and 53% of its revenues coming from outside the United States, GE's growth depended on its ability to successfully navigate the political risks associated with international business dealings that could affect its growth and profitability.[26]

Change and instability in the financial markets had a significant effect on GE, especially GE Capital. Historically, GE had relied on commercial paper and long-term debt as major sources of its funding, but the increasing difficulty and cost of obtaining those sources of funding potentially threatened GE's ability to grow and maintain its level of profitability.[27] After the financial crisis of 2008, the deterioration of the real estate market, for example, adversely affected GE Capital. GE Capital subsequently tried to secure other sources of funding, including bank deposits, securitization, and other asset-based funding to mitigate its risks. These economic setbacks affected not only GE and GE Capital, but trickled down to the corporations, large and small, they did business with, along with GE's governmental customers around the world.

Nevertheless, GE's credit rating with the major analysts helped stem the tide of negativity and control the costs of funds, margins, and access to capital markets. As of 2012, GE boasted a AA+ Rating (2nd out of 21 ratings) from Standard and Poor's and an Aa2 rating (3rd out of 21 ratings) from Moody's, solidifying its rating with the major analysts. Any reduction in these ratings would negatively impact GE's profitability.[28]

In the three years after the financial crisis, from 2009 to 2011, both GE and GE Capital's sales revenue declined sharply (see also **Exhibits 3** thru **8**).

EXHIBIT 3
Quarterly Sales
Growth[50]

Quarterly Sales Growth			
Year		**GE**	**GE Capital**
2008	Q1	7.7%	3.2%
	Q2	13.3%	10.4%
	Q3	10.8%	1.7%
	Q4	−3.2%	−18.4%
2009	Q1	−8.7%	−19.9%
	Q2	−15.5%	−29.3%
	Q3	−20.0%	−30.8%
	Q4	−10.8%	−14.5%
2010	Q1	−6.0%	−11.5%
	Q2	−6.2%	−5.0%
	Q3	−5.8%	−5.1%
	Q4	−1.1%	−5.1%
2011	Q1	−4.8%	−4.6%
	Q2	−4.5%	−9.1%
	Q3	−1.1%	−7.9%
	Q4	−7.8%	−16.1%
2012	Q1	3.4%	−6.6%

EXHIBIT 4
Quarterly Net Income Growth[51]

		Quarterly Net Income Growth	
Year		GE	GE Capital
2008	Q1	−11.7%	−27.9%
	Q2	−3.5%	14.8%
	Q3	−12.4%	−37.6%
	Q4	−43.4%	−84.2%
2009	Q1	−34.5%	−60.1%
	Q2	−46.6%	−86.8%
	Q3	−45.2%	−94.4%
	Q4	−21.6%	−79.2%
2010	Q1	−19.4%	−48.7%
	Q2	11.3%	100.0%
	Q3	26.6%	590.3%
	Q4	28.7%	807.2%
2011	Q1	47.0%	252.2%
	Q2	10.5%	117.0%
	Q3	3.7%	86.3%
	Q4	0.6%	60.7%
2012	Q1	−11.2%	1.4%

EXHIBIT 5
Quarterly Net Profit Margins[52]

		Quarterly Net Profit Margins	
Year		GE	GE Capital
2007	Q1	12.7%	19.5%
	Q2	13.7%	14.0%
	Q3	12.1%	17.8%
	Q4	14.3%	17.4%
2008	Q1	10.4%	13.6%
	Q2	11.7%	14.6%
	Q3	9.6%	10.9%
	Q4	8.3%	3.4%
2009	Q1	7.5%	6.8%
	Q2	7.4%	2.7%
	Q3	6.6%	0.9%
	Q4	7.3%	0.8%
2010	Q1	6.4%	3.9%
	Q2	8.8%	5.7%
	Q3	8.8%	6.4%
	Q4	9.5%	7.9%
2011	Q1	9.9%	14.5%
	Q2	10.1%	13.7%
	Q3	9.3%	13.0%
	Q4	10.4%	15.1%

EXHIBIT 6
GE Income
Statement[53] (All
numbers in
thousands)

Period Ending	31-Dec-11	31-Dec-10	31-Dec-09
Total Revenue	147,300,000	149,593,000	154,438,000
Cost of Revenue	71,190,000	74,725,000	78,938,000
Gross Profit	76,110,000	74,868,000	75,500,000
Operating Expenses			
Research and Development	—	—	—
Selling, General, and Administrative	37,384,000	38,054,000	37,354,000
Non-recurring	4,083,000	7,176,000	10,585,000
Others	—	—	—
Total Operating Expenses	—	—	—
Operating Income or Loss	34,643,000	29,638,000	27,561,000
Income from Continuing Operations			
Total Other Income/Expenses Net	—	—	—
Earnings Before Interest and Taxes	34,643,000	29,638,000	27,561,000
Interest Expense	14,545,000	15,553,000	17,697,000
Income Before Tax	20,098,000	14,085,000	9,864,000
Income Tax Expense	5,732,000	1,033,000	−1,142,000
Minority Interest	−292,000	−535,000	−200,000
Net Income From Continuing Ops	14,366,000	13,052,000	11,006,000
Non-recurring Events			
Discontinued Operations	77,000	−873,000	219,000
Extraordinary Items	—	—	—
Effect of Accounting Changes	—	—	—
Other Items	—	—	—
Net Income	14,151,000	11,644,000	11,025,000
Preferred Stock and Other Adjustments	−1,031,000	−300,000	−300,000
Net Income Applicable to Common Shares	13,120,000	11,344,000	10,725,000

. . . .
NOTE: Currency in USD.

EXHIBIT 7
GE Balance Sheet[54]
(All numbers in thousands)

Period Ending	30-Dec-11	30-Dec-10	30-Dec-09
Assets			
Current Assets			
Cash and Cash Equivalents	84,501,000	78,943,000	70,488,000
Short-Term Investments	47,374,000	43,938,000	51,343,000
Net Receivables	307,470,000	329,204,000	30,514,000
Inventory	13,792,000	11,526,000	11,987,000
Other Current Assets	—	—	—
Total Current Assets	453,137,000	463,611,000	164,332,000
Long-Term Investments	—	—	319,247,000
Property, Plant, and Equipment	66,450,000	103,099,000	103,081,000
Goodwill	72,625,000	64,388,000	65,076,000
Intangible Assets	12,068,000	9,971,000	11,751,000
Accumulated Amortization	—	—	—
Other Assets	112,962,000	106,724,000	118,414,000
Deferred Long-Term Asset Charges	—	—	—
Total assets	**717,242,000**	**747,793,000**	**781,901,000**
Liabilities			
Current Liabilities			
Accounts Payable	58,373,000	56,943,000	32,860,000
Short/Current Long-Term Debt	166,869,000	147,977,000	129,869,000
Other Current Liabilities	59,891,000	67,328,000	50,788,000
Total Current Liabilities	285,133,000	272,248,000	213,517,000
Long-Term Debt	243,459,000	293,323,000	336,172,000
Other Liabilities	70,647,000	55,271,000	104,995,000
Deferred Long-Term Liability Charges	−131,000	2,753,000	2,081,000
Minority Interest	1,696,000	5,262,000	7,845,000
Negative Goodwill	—	—	—
Total liabilities	**600,804,000**	**628,857,000**	**664,610,000**
Stockholders' equity			
Misc Stocks Options Warrants	—	—	—
Redeemable Preferred Stock	—	—	—
Preferred Stock	—	—	—
Common Stock	702,000	702,000	702,000
Retained Earnings	137,786,000	131,137,000	126,363,000
Treasury Stock	−31,769,000	−31,938,000	−32,238,000
Capital Surplus	—	—	—
Other Stockholder Equity	9,719,000	19,035,000	22,464,000
Total stockholder equity	**116,438,000**	**118,936,000**	**117,291,000**
Net tangible assets	**31,745,000**	**44,577,000**	**40,464,000**

....
NOTE: Currency in USD.

EXHIBIT 8 Summary of Operating Segments[55] (In millions)

	General Electric Company and consolidated affiliates				
	2011	2010	2009	2008	2007
Revenues					
Energy infrastructure	$ 43,694	$ 37,514	$ 40,648	$ 43,046	$ 34,880
Aviation	18,859	17,619	18,728	19,239	16,819
Healthcare	18,083	16,897	16,015	17,392	16,997
Transportation	4,885	3,370	3,827	5,016	4,523
Home & business solutions	8,465	8,648	8,443	10,117	11,026
Total industrial revenues	93,986	84,048	87,661	94,810	84,245
GE Capital	45,730	46,422	48,906	65,900	65,625
Total segment revenues	139,716	130,470	136,567	160,710	149,870
Corporate items and eliminations[a]	7,584	19,123	17,871	19,127	20,094
Consolidated revenues	$147,300	$149,593	$154,438	$179,837	$169,964
Segment profit					
Energy infrastructure	$ 6,650	$ 7,271	$ 7,105	$ 6,497	$ 5,238
Aviation	3,512	3,304	3,923	3,684	3,222
Healthcare	2,803	2,741	2,420	2,851	3,056
Transportation	757	315	473	962	936
Home & business solutions	300	457	370	365	983
Total industrial segment profit	14,022	14,088	14,291	14,359	13,435
GE Capital	6,549	3,158	1,325	7,841	12,179
Total segment profit	20,571	17,246	15,616	22,200	25,614
Corporate items and eliminations[a]	(359)	(1,105)	(593)	1,184	1,441
GE interest and other financial charges	(1,299)	(1,600)	(1,478)	(2,153)	(1,993)
GE provision for income taxes	(4,839)	(2,024)	(2,739)	(3,427)	(2,794)
Earnings from continuing operations	14,074	12,517	10,806	17,804	22,268
Earnings (loss) from discontinued operations, net of taxes	77	(873)	219	(394)	(60)
Consolidated net earnings attributable to the company	$ 14,151	$ 11,644	$ 11,025	$ 17,410	$ 22,208

NOTE:
See accompanying notes to consolidated financial statements in Part II, Item 8. "Financial Statements and Supplementary Data" of this Form 10-K Report.

[a]Includes the result of NBCU, our formerly consolidated subsidiary, and our current equity method investment in NBCUniversal LLC.

Consistent quarterly revenue losses slightly rebounded beginning in Q1 2010 (from double-digit to single-digit losses in both GE and GE Capital), yet sales revenue at GE Capital declined again from US$12.814 billion to US$10.745 billion from Q4 2010 to Q4 2011, marking a return to double-digit quarterly revenue losses. GE Capital's Q1 2012 revenue loss shrank again to single digits at 6.6%, while revenue grew at GE as a whole in Q1 2012 by 3.4% from the industrial division's strong performance (14% quarterly revenue growth).[29] Annually from 2010 to 2011, GE and GE Capital respectively reported 1.9% and 1.5% sales revenue losses. Much of the poor performance was attributable to macroeconomic risk factors, causing unstable demand for the products of the industrial business units, as well as restrictions in the global credit markets, which severely hampered GE Capital's ability to perform as it did prior to the recession (US$65.435 billion revenue in FY 2007, US$45.730 billion in FY 2011). From FY2009 on, GE Capital began strategically transforming its portfolio to be less focused on risky lending and more focused on middle market lending and specialty finance to industrial division customers.[30] This strategy required reducing leverage, improving liquidity, and shedding assets—all of which cut into previous top-line sales revenue performance.[31]

Despite the overall top-line losses, GE was organized as a global corporation that generated revenue in a number of regions worldwide. Although U.S. revenues were down 7.9% in 2011 (from US$75.8 billion in FY2010 to US$69.8 billion in FY2011) and Western European revenues decreased 12%, global revenues (excluding the U.S.) increased 4% overall, from US$74.5 billion in 2010 to US$77.5 billion in 2011.[32] The strong international performance was tied to revenue growth in emerging markets such as Latin America (29%), China (28%), and Australia (46%).

GE recorded massive net income losses from FY2007 to FY2009, peaking between FY2008 and FY2009 (with net income losses of 38% for GE and 78.3% for GE Capital), driven by the global financial crisis and recession. The performance of GE as a whole was largely tied to that of GE Capital, its largest and formerly most profitable business unit. GE Capital had become deeply ensnared in both the collapse of the credit markets through the excessive use of leverage leading up to FY2009 and the subprime mortgage crisis because it had bought a subprime mortgage company and heavily invested in commercial real estate.[33]

GE Capital had made some ill-advised marketing decisions prior to the financial collapse in 2008. Rather than retaining its focus on middle market and specialty finance for GE industrial product customers, GE Capital began to market itself as a credit card financing entity as well as a mortgage financier.[34] Financing subprime mortgages and commercial real estate soon followed, and eventually GE Capital was engaging in the financing of very risky assets, including derivatives and credit default swaps. This market strategy led to the highly leveraged structure that almost caused the entire corporation to collapse in 2008 during the financial crisis.

GE's long-term debt began growing in FY2007 and hit a high of US$377 billion in 2009, but was reduced slightly in FY2010 and FY2011, resulting in flat growth for the five years from 2007–12. Most of the debt on GE's balance sheet was from GE Capital. During the financial crisis of 2008–09, GE Capital's highly leveraged structure—combined with its risky ventures in interest rate swaps, subprime mortgages, commercial real estate, and massive commercial paper—almost led to the financial collapse of the entire GE Corporation.[35] A record influx of equity capital and the sale of preferred stock stabilized a 10% daily hemorrhage in the stock price that began on October 1, 2008. After that, GE capital aggressively cut its long-term debt from US$304 billion in FY2007 to US$234 billion in FY2011 through strategic de-leveraging and restructuring of the scope of its financing activities.

Both GE and GE capital also took steps to significantly increase their cash balances to better manage risk. From FY2007 to FY2011, GE increased its cash balance from US$18 billion to US$87 billion, and GE Capital's increased from US$11 billion to US$43 billion. However, as of 2012, neither GE nor GE Capital was on completely solid footing, with a LT debt-to-equity ratio of 2.67 and 2.93, respectively.

GE Capital had been forced to scale back in the wake of the recession, and due to pressures to meet stricter regulatory standards. These strictures streamlined GE Capital's operations, helping it better understand its best practices for lending and its other financial endeavors. GE Capital also moved to expand its operational base in the aftermath of the recession by creating new partnerships with companies like Ducati and Sophos. These new partnerships were important to GE Capital's operations to offset "shrinking its asset base and tightening underwriting standards."[36] Nevertheless, the decrease in year-over-year earnings was evidence that

GE Capital had to operate with fewer resources and adjust its internal infrastructure to utilize more limited resource availability.

GE Capital returned some of its profits to its GE parent company through the issuance of a dividend. GE Capital resumed paying a dividend to GE in May 2012.

New Directions for Growth: Green Energy and Health Care

In the new millennium, General Electric was uniquely positioned to take advantage of financial incentives, subsidies, and lucrative partnerships available for innovators in the green energy sector.[37] It was spurred both by an interest in the environment, and the desire for financial security due to volatility in fossil fuel prices and concerns over climate change. Having spent more money than any other single corporation on governmental lobbying, General Electric used its political capital for growth opportunities.[38] For example, GE, especially its electrical energy divisions, was able to leverage its political strength to benefit from tax incentives associated with the green energy movement.

In addition, the GE Energy Group took a leadership role in the manufacture and distribution of wind turbines—a critical component of the renewable energy sector, particularly in Oregon, where the largest wind turbine farm in the United States was powered entirely by GE-built wind turbines.[39] GE also branched out into the management and financing of solar energy projects, including a solar farm in Australia developed by a consortium of companies, including GE.[40] GE was one of the leading manufacturers of LED lighting and had signed a distribution deal with Marriot hotels that saved it 66% in power use for lighting, without compromising on the look or quality of the light.[41] GE perceived the opportunity to become the best-in-class manufacturer and distributor of certain elements of clean energy infrastructure, as well as other innovative forms of clean energy, and is poised to continue to innovate as the sector grows.

Over the past decade GE Healthcare Group established itself as a leading innovator in emerging health care technology. Diagnostic medicine became a key area of health care sector investment—the market is projected to grow 11% annually from US$232 billion,[42] and GE developed some creative tools for diagnostic imaging, including a handheld ultrasound device, with which primary care doctors could be more accurate in their initial diagnoses, prior to ordering expensive follow up diagnostics.[43] GE also launched a US$100 million open innovation competition related to cancer diagnostics[44] and invested in life science offerings, with a US$4 billion portfolio that projects to double over the next few years.[45] As the Baby Boomer generation entered retirement age, the health care demand began to rise, expanding the need for new health care technologies. GE Healthcare was poised to capitalize on this new demand.

Core Competencies

General Electric's key strengths—its operational efficiencies, sheer size, history, and reputation—all worked to create competitive advantages for GE. One of GE's biggest operational strengths lay in its ability to cut costs and maximize return for shareholders, as with GE CEO Jack Welch's implementation of the Six Sigma approach in the 1990s to business management, as mentioned earlier. GE was also able to cut costs because its reputation as a market leader, its large network of businesses, and its strong alliances with other major corporations, enabled it to leverage long-standing relationships to employ the best human, equipment, and capital resources to ensure quality and consistency at a low cost. It acquired many businesses that provided useful resources, and sold off business units that did not contribute to its success. In addition, GE's history of innovation, from Edison inventing the light bulb to its pioneering of green energy medical diagnostic technology contributed to GE's long-term success.

In addition to the operational excellence that came from GE's experience and unparalleled commitment to growth, the sheer size of GE also created a tremendous competitive advantage, from distribution channels in over a hundred companies to dozens of lines of business. Few other companies were big enough to compete with the variety and breadth of resources GE brought to the table.

Globally recognized and ubiquitous in American homes, GE's history and reputation was also a key competitive advantage. Its reputation and political influence garnered favorable treatment from the U.S. and other governments. Smaller firms tried to compete with GE in individual industries, but GE's reputation and brand awareness made it difficult for them to succeed.

Finally, GE's strong company culture empowered and motivated employees, creating a workforce that stayed with the company long-term and moved internally, building a strong, knowledgeable employee base, and its focus on sustainability and the greater community helped inspire employees and improve GE's image overall.

Challenges Facing GE

By the end of 2012, GE faced many challenges. First, the parent company's comfort in mature industries such as industrial appliances and jet engines rendered it reluctant to explore different markets, or identify and move into innovative industries at the beginning of their life cycles when potential growth and earnings are greatest. While this defensive strategy was more pronounced with former CEO Jack Welch, under whose direction GE maintained a near-zero marketing budget and focus on efficiency, many within the company perceived that there was still room for growth in innovative markets, particularly the green energy market, where GE could utilize its strength of scalability to establish a competitive advantage.

Second, for many years, GE relied on its staunch traditional methods to train workers, especially general managers. Throughout the 1990s, CEO Jack Welch focused on the bottom line through lean practices and overall cost cutting, creating an extremely efficient, process-conscious organization that prioritized meeting budgets, but lagged in innovation. While these strategies did increase net earnings, it became clear that they would not yield sustainable growth, as cutting additional costs began to outweigh the savings. GE began to see that the long-term solution was to train employees and management to focus on creating new technology and products that both earn profitable returns and open new growth opportunities.

GE also needed to acknowledge potential weaknesses stemming from being such a large and diverse organization. For instance, it occasionally underperformed in Asian and European markets. Greater understanding of the operational differences and difference in business practices between the U.S. and these countries could explain in part why GE's growth there did not meet projections.

Another challenge for GE was potential changes to the tax code. In 2012, GE filed a 57,000-page tax return, the single largest tax return in the United States.[46] While GE benefited from a number of tax incentives, tax code reform constantly loomed on the horizon, and GE would be one of the companies most affected by changes to the tax code.

Although GE had a strong global brand associated with product excellence and market leadership in several industrial categories, it came under attack for being synonymous with corporate greed. GE was accused of not paying its fair share of taxes, and protestors forcefully interrupted Jeff Immelt's speeches alleging that[47] using legitimate accounting techniques to pay lower effective tax rates, GE only paid an effective tax rate of 2.3% for more than 10 years, and that GE realized US$14 billion in profits yet paid no taxes in 2011.[48] Also, GE was the recipient of a US$140 billion bailout in 2008, to cover massive losses at GE Capital.[49] These allegations did not help their name, tarnishing the reputation of an otherwise well-managed brand. Furthermore, GE was the fourth-largest producer air and water pollution globally. Although top management's focus on sustainability was considered a strength, GE needed to develop ways to become more "green" without hurting its bottom line.

What to Do with GE Capital?

Despite General Electric's market-leading portfolio and strong brand-name recognition, in the recent financial crisis, the dangers of a company's reliance on financial services became apparent. What had begun as a financing arm to catalyze GE appliance sales had grown into a dominating financial services company that surpassed the earnings of the rest of the company to account for over 50% of GE's total net income.

This concentration of resources in GE Capital paid excellent dividends during strong economic times, yet the financial sector's volatility rendered GE Capital vulnerable to large, rapid losses. Unless GE hedged against financial slowdowns by reducing its exposure to GE Capital, it might occasionally suffer losses that could put the company as a whole at risk. Further, like many financial firms, GE Capital was tempted by the large potential returns of what were later seen as risky investments, such as mortgage-backed securities and real estate. Unless GE Capital decreased its portfolio of risky assets, it could be prone to future losses that might have a negative impact on its GE parent.

In the years leading up to the financial crisis, GE, according to some industry analysts, had become complacent, and corporate growth and earnings consequently stagnated. GE focused too heavily on cutting costs and relied too heavily on the fortunes of GE Capital, which suffered from massive losses during the 2008–2009 financial crisis. When the recession forced GE to reduce the scope of GE Capital's activities, GE was not able to invest and innovate elsewhere to bolster its financials and satisfy stockholders. GE also did not have enough significant new ideas to mitigate GE Capital's financial setback, such that GE Capital's losses had a major negative impact on the growth and earnings of the corporation as a whole.

The key question facing GE's top management and board of directors at the end of 2012 was to what degree should they reduce GE Capital as a percentage of the entire company. Or, more to the point, should GE Capital be spun off altogether to allow the GE parent corporation to focus on the industrial products segment it had historically excelled in and where there is less competition and government regulation?

NOTES

1. "Explore GE Innovations by Title." General Electric Company. Web. 21 Apr. 2012. http://www.ge.com/innovation/timeline/index.html.

2. "GE Past Leaders." General Electric Company. Web. 21 Apr. 2012. http://www.ge.com/company/history/past_leaders.html.

3. Joseph, John and Ocasio, William. *Rise and Fall-or Transformation? The evolution of Strategic Planning at the General Electric Company.* http://www.elsevier.com/locate/lrp.

4. *GE 2011 Annual Report.* http://www.ge.com/ar2011/pdf/GE_AR11_EntireReport.pdf.

5. Ibid.

6. *GE 2011 Annual Report.* http://www.ge.com/ar2011/pdf/GE_AR11_EntireReport.pdf.

7. *GE 2011 Annual Report.* http://www.ge.com/ar2011/pdf/GE_AR11_EntireReport.pdf.

8. "General Electric." *Wikipedia.* Wikimedia Foundation, 05 Apr. 2012. Web. 21 Apr. 2012. http://en.wikipedia.org/wiki/General_Electric.

9. "Industrial Conglomerates Industry Snapshot - NYTimes.com." *NYTimes.com.* New York Times, 02 May 2012. Web. 02 May 2012. http://markets.on.nytimes.com/research/markets/usmarkets/industry.asp?industry=52311.

10. Stone, Mallory. "Top 5 Companies in the Industrial Conglomerates Industry with the Best Relative Performance (SI, GE, PHG, MMM, TYC)." *Comtex News Network.* Comcast, 16 Mar. 2012. Web. 02 May 2012. http://finance.comcast.net/stocks/news_body.html?ID_OSI=85473.

11. *Siemens USA.* Web. 05 May 2012. http://www.usa.siemens.com/entry/en/.

12. *Phillips Global.* Web. 05 May 2012. http://www.philips.com/global/index.page.

13. 3M Global. Web. 05 May 2012. http://www.3m.com/.

14. Ramirez, Diane. "General Electric Capital Corporation Profile." *Hoovers* D&B Company. http://www.hoovers.com/company/General_Electric_Capital_Corporation/.

15. Ramirez, Diane. "General Electric Capital Corporation Profile." *Hoovers* D&B Company. http://www.hoovers.com/company/General_Electric_Capital_Corporation/

16. Colvin, Geoffrey. "GE under Siege (pg. 2)." *CNNMoney.* Cable News Network, 10 Oct. 2008. Web. 23 Apr. 2012. http://money.cnn.com/2008/10/09/news/companies/colvin_ge.fortune/index2.htm

17. *GE Capital: Our Businesses.* 2012. General Electric. http://www.gecapital.com/en/our-company/our-businesses.html?gemid2=gtnav0502

18. "Start Building." *GE Capital Business Model & Fact Sheet*. Web. 21 Apr. 2012. http://www.gecapital.com/en/our-company/company-overview.html?gemid2=gtnav0501.

19. "GE Capital: The Capital Difference." *Fact Sheet*. General Electric Company. Web. 21 Apr. 2012. http://www.gecapital.com/en/pdf/GE_Capital_Fact_Sheet.pdf.

20. Ibid.

21. *GE 2011 Annual Report*. http://www.ge.com/ar2011/pdf/GE_AR11_EntireReport.pdf.

22. Ibid.

23. Ramirez, Diane. "General Electric Capital Corporation Profile." *Hoovers* D&B Company. http://www.hoovers.com/company/General_Electric_Capital_Corporation/.

24. Ramirez, Diane. "Bank of America Corporation Profile." *Hoovers* D&B Company. http://www.hoovers.com/company/Bank_of_America_Corporation/.

25. Ramirez, Diane. "CIT Group IncProfile." *Hoovers* D&B Company. http://www.hoovers.com/company/CIT_Group_Inc.

26. *GE 2011 Annual Report*. http://www.ge.com/ar2011/pdf/GE_AR11_EntireReport.pdf.

27. Ibid.

28. *GE 2011 Annual Report*. http://www.ge.com/ar2011/pdf/GE_AR11_EntireReport.pdf.

29. General Electric. *GE Q1'12 Earnings*. Www.ge.com. General Electric Company, 20 Apr. 2012. Web. 25 Apr. 2012. http://www.ge.com/pdf/investors/events/04202012/ge_webcast_pressrelease_04202012.pdf.

30. Protess, Ben. "Revenue Drops at GE Capital." *The New York Times*. The New York Times Company, 20 Apr. 2012. Web. 23 Apr. 2012. http://dealbook.nytimes.com/2012/04/20/revenues-drop-at-ge-capital/.

31. GE *2011 Annual Report*. Page 5 http://www.ge.com/ar2011/pdf/GE_AR11_EntireReport.pdf.

32. Ibid., page 47.

33. Protess, Ben. "Revenue Drops at GE Capital." *The New York Times*. The New York Times Company, 20 Apr. 2012. Web. 23 Apr. 2012. http://dealbook.nytimes.com/2012/04/20/revenues-drop-at-ge-capital/.

34. Colvin, Geoffrey. "GE under Siege (pg. 2)." *CNNMoney*. Cable News Network, 10 Oct. 2008. Web. 23 Apr. 2012. http://money.cnn.com/2008/10/09/news/companies/colvin_ge.fortune/index2.htm.

35. Ibid.

36. Andrejczak, Matt. "Industrial Operations Key to GE Earnings Report." *Market Watch*. The Wall Street Journal, 19 Apr. 2012. Web. 29 Apr. 2012. http://articles.marketwatch.com/2012-04-19/industries/31366115_1_ge-capital-ge-shares-chief-executive-jeff-immelt.

37. "DSIRE: DSIRE Home." *DSIRE USA*. Web. 28 Apr. 2012. http://www.dsireusa.org/.

38. Mosk, Matthew. "General Electric Wages Never-Say-Die Campaign for Jet Engine Contract." ABD News 7 March 2012.

39. *GE 2011 Annual Report*. Page 18 http://www.ge.com/ar2011/pdf/GE_AR11_EntireReport.pdf.

40. "GE Set to Soar on Clean Energy Projects—Seeking Alpha." *Stock Market News & Financial Analysis*. 17 Apr. 2012. Web. 28 Apr. 2012. http://seekingalpha.com/article/503701-ge-set-to-soar-on-clean-energy-projects.

41. Ibid.

42. "$232 Billion Personalized Medicine Market to Grow 11 Percent Annually, Says PricewaterhouseCoopers." *NEW YORK, Dec. 8 / PRNewswire/*. Web. 28 Apr. 2012. http://www.prnewswire.com/news-releases/232-billion-personalized-medicine-market-to-grow-11-percent-annually-says-pricewaterhousecoopers-78751072.html.

43. "DOTmed.com - GE Launches Handheld Ultrasound Tool." *Dotmed.com*. 2010. Web. 28 Apr. 2012. http://www.dotmed.com/news/story/11669.

44. *GE 2011 Annual Report*. Page 27 http://www.ge.com/ar2011/pdf/GE_AR11_EntireReport.pdf.

45. Ibid., page 5.

46. McCormack, John. "GE Filed 57,000-Page Tax Return, Paid No Taxes on $14 Billion in Profits." Weekly Standard. 17 November 2011.

47. Shepardson, David. "GE CEO Defends Tax Rate after Protestors Disrupt Speech." *The Detroit News*. 24 Apr. 2012. Web. 24 Apr. 2012. http://www.detroitnews.com/article/20120424/BIZ/204240397/GE-CEO-defends-tax-rate-after-protesters-disrupt-speech?odyssey=tab|topnews|text|FRONTPAGE.

48. "GE Filed 57,000-Page Tax Return, Paid No Taxes on $14 Billion in Profits." *The Weekly Standard*. 17 Nov. 2011. Web. 24 Apr. 2012. http://www.weeklystandard.com/blogs/ge-filed-57000-page-tax-return-paid-no-taxes-14-billion-profits_609137.html.

49. Hill, Vernon. "General Electric Gets a $140B Bailout - What's the Point of AAA? - Seeking Alpha." *Stock Market News & Financial Analysis*. 14 Nov. 2008. Web. 24 Apr. 2012. http://seekingalpha.com/article/105984-general-electric-gets-a-140b-bailout-what-s-the-point-of-aaa.

50. Source: http://www.ge.com/ar2011/.

51. Ibid.

52. Ibid.

53. Ibid.

54. Ibid.

55. Ibid.

CASE **30**

AB Electrolux

CHALLENGING TIMES IN THE APPLIANCE INDUSTRY

Alan N. Hoffman
Rotterdam School of Management, Erasmus University and Bentley University

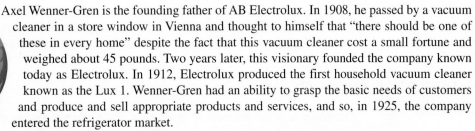

Axel Wenner-Gren is the founding father of AB Electrolux. In 1908, he passed by a vacuum cleaner in a store window in Vienna and thought to himself that "there should be one of these in every home" despite the fact that this vacuum cleaner cost a small fortune and weighed about 45 pounds. Two years later, this visionary founded the company known today as Electrolux. In 1912, Electrolux produced the first household vacuum cleaner known as the Lux 1. Wenner-Gren had an ability to grasp the basic needs of customers and produce and sell appropriate products and services, and so, in 1925, the company entered the refrigerator market.

As World War II paralyzed many of Electrolux's manufacturing plants, the company reorganized some of its production facilities and made air filters and steel fittings for the Swedish defence forces. Following the end of the war, the company continued on its path to dominating the household appliance industry by introducing the first household washing machine in 1951 and the first household dishwasher in 1959. Acquisitions of other companies played an important role in the growth of Electrolux throughout the past 90 years, and it helped the company become a global player in the industry. It has acquired over 300 companies from various countries throughout the world, providing Electrolux with better production capabilities and access to large mature markets and established brand names, such as Eureka, Frigidaire, and Kelvinator. In 1997, following years of acquisitions, Eletrolux began a two-year restructuring

....

This teaching case was compiled from published sources and written with the assistance of Tao Yue from the RSM Case Development Centre.

RSM Case Development Centre prepared this teaching case to provide material for class discussion rather than to illustrate either effective or ineffective handling of a management situation. The author has disguised identifying information to protect confidentiality.

program in an effort to improve its bottom line. It divested several of its sectors including industrial products, sewing machines, and vending machines and laid off 11,000 employees and closed 23 plants and 50 warehouses. Following its success in the European markets, Electrolux-branded appliances were introduced in North America in 2004. Hans Stråberg was appointed Electrolux's President & CEO in 2002 and remains in that position today. The company is currently the world's second-largest appliance maker, behind Whirlpool, and has over 50,000 employees in more than 50 countries around the world. Its headquarters are in Stockholm, Sweden.

Product Offerings and Brands

Electrolux sells over 40 million products to customers in more than 150 different global markets every year in two product categories: consumer durables and professional products. Its consumer product offerings are broken down into three segments: kitchen products (for example, fridges and freezers); laundry products (such as washers and dryers); and floor-care products like vacuums. Electrolux also sells spare parts and services associated with its products. In its professional products division, it offers food-service equipment for restaurants and industrial-kitchens, as well as laundry equipment for the health care industry and apartment buildings. Consumer durables are a core piece of Electrolux's business, representing 93% of overall sales in 2009. Kitchen products represent a majority of the Electrolux consumer product category with 57% of overall company sales. Electrolux's roots are in the floor-care business, and today those products only contribute 8% of the company's annual sales. The professional products business makes up a smaller portion of its sales at only 7% (in 2009). Through its acquisition strategy in the 1980s and 1990s, Electrolux acquired many different brands in several global markets, with various brands offered in different regions of the world. Approximately half of the 40 million products Electrolux sold in 2009 were sold under the global Electrolux brand.

Strategic Direction

Electrolux is in the business of developing and marketing premium household and professional appliances. The guiding principle that the company follows is to offer products and services that consumers prefer, that benefit both people and the environment, and for which consumers are willing to pay a higher price. The company is truly in the premium market category of household appliances. Electrolux is also a very consumer-driven company. The "Thinking of You" slogan indicates the high importance the company places on understanding customer needs. Whether it's in product development, design, production, marketing or service, the customer is always at the forefront of Electrolux's mind.

The vision of Electrolux coincides with the vision of its founding father 90 years ago when he believed that there should be a vacuum cleaner in every home. The company's vision is to surpass Whirlpool and become the world's largest manufacturer of household appliances. Their aim is "To be the world leader in making life easier and more enjoyable with the help of powered appliances."[1] This vision is illustrated throughout their marketing campaign in North America featuring Kelly Ripa with the tag line "be even more amazing." The focus is on the customer and helping to make their day-to-day life simpler with its products.

Industry Environment

Recently, the appliance industry has seen sluggish sales moving through the current recession. There have been several government programs similar to the Cash for Clunkers program but instead implemented for the appliance industry. These programs are intended to rid homes of non energy-efficient appliances but also have a second motive, to spur demand. In an attempt to satisfy consumer demand, appliance companies have been developing more and more Energy Star approved efficient products. Further, appliance companies have been producing their products in a more environmentally friendly manner.[2,3]

According to a paper published in 2008, the income elasticity of appliances is less than one, and in the case of washers and dryers, income elasticity was found to be merely 0.26—a figure proving that appliance sales are quite inelastic. This means that if a person's income was to increase or decrease, their expenditures on appliances would, on average, not increase or decrease at a similar rate. This makes sense, as many consumer appliances are considered a necessity to which a family cannot live without. It can also be inferred that with such a low-income elasticity, the appliance industry could be insulated from a recession.[4] Finally, the appliance industry is mainly dominated by Electrolux and Whirlpool. The industry market capitalization is about US$12 billion with an industry profit margin of approximately 8.42%.[5,6]

Competition

Whirlpool Corporation, a company devoted strictly to the appliance market, has a market capitalization of over US$6 billion and is currently the largest appliance manufacturer in the world. Prior to 2006, Electrolux held that title; however, following Whirlpool's acquisition of Maytag, it surpassed Electrolux as the world's largest appliance maker. Whirlpool currently produces products under the brand names Kitchen-aid, Jenn-Air, and Amana and has approximately US$20 billion in sales, an operating margin of 5.8%, and a growth rate of 8.8%. This is quite below the industry average growth rate of over 29%. Whirlpool's current product mix is one of medium cost and quality. Many of the company's products excel beyond their generic counterparts but fall behind in features that many luxury appliance brands offer. Whirlpool Corporation employs approximately 67,000 people.[7,8]

GE Appliances, a subsidiary division owned by General Electric, currently has a product mix that is most similar to that of Electrolux. It produces high-quality ranges, ovens, and refrigerators that have many of the same features as Electrolux products, including an induction cook top. This type of cook top has become quite desirable as it uses electromagnetism to create precise heat in half the time while using much less energy than a classic gas or electric stove. While financial information specific to GE Appliances is not widely available, General Electric, the parent company, currently has a market capitalization of over US$167 billion. One benefit to a diversified large company, such as General Electric, is that it can use resources from another division and reallocate the resources to the appliance subsidiary if needed.[9,10]

LG Electronics, a privately owned subsidiary of LG, Lucky Goldstar, offers a lower-cost product mix with a few high-end appliances, but does not have certain features other brands offer, including induction cook tops. The financial information specific to the appliance division of LG Electronics is not readily available, but it is estimated that it employs 28,895 people. LG Electronics also has the benefit of being part of a very large diversified parent company that can transfer resources to the appliances division if needed.[11,12]

Sustainability

For the past six years, Electrolux has been implementing a production restructuring program that involves relocating approximately 60% of its manufacturing to low-cost countries such as Mexico and China. Electrolux also has a goal of reducing its overall energy consumption by 15% of the 2008 levels by 2012 in an effort to achieve more efficient energy consumption in its manufacturing process. The company also has goals specific to its sustainability focused on four issues: climate change, sound business practices, responsible sourcing, and restructuring. Every business sector of Electrolux has launched a "green" range of products in its efforts to increase awareness of the company's energy-efficient and climate-smart products.

Increasingly, sustainability initiatives are creeping into the collective consciousness of governments and the general consumer. There is an awareness level around sustainability that is pervasive and now influences consumers' purchasing behavior. In addition, this movement has become so strong that it is now a major part of nearly every legislative agenda around the world. The American Recovery and Reinvestment Act, passed into law in 2009, has earmarked a whopping US$27.2 billion to energy efficiency and renewable energy research and investment.[13] Going "green" is no longer a fad—it's a behavior incentivized by governments. For example, in the near future there will be criteria for lower energy consumption when appliances are in standby mode as well as smart electricity meters that distribute power consumption more evenly throughout day and night. Currently, these types of incentives generally take the form of rebates offered to the consumer for buying brands that have met a standard level of energy conservation requirements. In the future, it is likely that governments will not only provide rebates on the purchase of energy-efficient appliances, but mandate it as well. Industries like home and commercial lighting are already feeling the impact of this type of directive with the law that incandescent bulbs will no longer be available on shelves after 2014. These mandates are a significant opportunity for Electrolux. The company is in a prime position to capitalize on this trend by rapidly rolling out energy-efficient products that capitalize on today's consumer awareness and positions it well for tomorrow's mandates.

The 2008–09 Global Recession

The appliance market is impacted greatly by the fluctuations of the credit market. Clearly, the current state of the global economy has taken its toll on major appliance makers such as Electrolux. Retailers had limited credit to stock appliances, and consumers were operating with shoestring budgets. Instead of purchasing new appliances, many were forgoing the purchase altogether and opting to repair an outdated appliance. Of course, the economy is cyclical and by most accounts has already hit bottom. As the recovery moves forward, the credit markets will open and provide a new opportunity for Electrolux. This expanding credit market will inevitably lead to an increased rate of new appliance purchases. The purchase of new appliances is also inextricably linked to home buying. People tend to buy major appliances in the midst of a new home purchase or remodel. As credit becomes available, home buying will surge upward and serve as the tailwind needed to jumpstart appliances.

Like the automotive industry before it, the appliance market is facing stiff competition from Asian companies such as LG, Haier, and Samsung. These companies will pose a significant challenge to the success of an established brand like Electrolux. In addition, as Electrolux looks to outsource production to developing nations—it needs to be mindful of the increasing cost of labor in these countries. China, once the epicenter of global outsourcing, is already being viewed as a risk when it comes to outsourcing due to the inevitable increase in wages. In July of 2010, 18 provinces in China increased the minimum wage by an average of 20%.[14] This increase in wages could offset the cost advantages Electrolux hopes to achieve by moving production. Finally, Electrolux has recently churned out a few encouraging quarters in a row and have trumpeted the fact that its operating margin is slowly creeping upward. Part of this is because commodity prices are cyclically low. This is a natural reaction to a down economy. When the economy suffers, commodity prices tend to fall. Electrolux has benefited from this reduction in commodity prices because it has helped to reduce the company's costs throughout the supply chain. A manufacturer like Electrolux relies heavily on commodities like steel for the production of its appliances. As the recovery continues, commodity prices will increase and impact the operating margin and bottom-line earnings of the company. Some of this increase should be offset by the ability to charge higher prices, but the threat is still present.

The Growing Middle Class in Asia

As the social and demographic trends continue to evolve, so do the opportunities afforded to Electrolux. The most significant demographic shift globally is the growing middle class in Asia, which includes families with incomes between US$6000 and US$30,000. It is estimated that by 2020 there will be one billion more people in the global middle class than there were in 2010.[15] Correlated with rising incomes worldwide, homeownership has also increased at a substantial rate giving rise to increased demand for consumer durables such as refrigerators, washing machines, and dishwashers.[16]

Consumers worldwide are also working longer hours with increased workplace demands, and consequently their "free" time to maintain their domiciles is shrinking.[17] Consumers are expecting more out of their appliances to fit their unique needs, including faster cycle times for washers and dryers and the automation of processes. For example, consumers are looking for ovens that automatically determine at what temperature food needs to be cooked, how long it needs to be cooked for, and an automatic shut-off when the food is done cooking. For refrigerators, consumers are more focused on the freshness of stored food and are using this as a guiding principle in appliance comparisons.[18]

Consumers are no longer simply concerned about the usability of their appliances, but who makes the appliance, how the appliance was made, and what happens to the appliance after its use. Corporate social responsibility is a growing factor in differentiating companies for consumers and it has become more and more important for companies to invest in the communities of their target customer. Consumers are also more concerned about the environment, now more than ever, and companies have to be creative in incorporating environmentally friendly practices. Energy consumption, pollution, and recyclability of appliances are all variables that consumers keep in mind when selecting their home appliances.

Aside from practical and environmentally conscious concerns, there are also the continually evolving tastes of consumers. The kitchen has become the favored entertainment space for people, which has led to a more fashionably conscious consumer in picking out kitchen appliances. It is important to recognize new consumer tastes of aesthetics rather than just focusing on the practicability of appliances.

The greatest social and demographic threats to Electrolux are the erroneous perceptions of consumers about appliances in regards to energy consumption and ease of use. Currently, less than half of the households in Europe own dishwashers.[19] A substantial segment of consumers in Europe still believe that dishwashers consume an exorbitant amount of water for each cycle. With the development of energy-efficient dishwashers, the average dishwashing cycle consumes only 10–15 liters of water.[20] A comparable load of dishes washed by hand would use nearly 80–90 liters of water.[21]

Technical Advancements

The evolution of technology has allowed companies like Electrolux to meet the ever-changing consumer demands and tastes for appliances. One of the most important factors for consumers in selecting home appliances is the level of energy consumption. Consumers are not only now using this as a variable in selecting fuel-efficient cars and electricity-saving light bulbs, but also in choosing dishwashers, stoves, and refrigerators. The AEG-Electrolux Super-Eco washing machine is a great example of energy efficiency, in that it features a cycle that only uses cold water.[22]

The ability to create appliances like AEG-Electrolux Super-Eco has come from several technical advancements. Refrigerators now have the ability to store food with sustained freshness and frost-free freezers.[23] In line with becoming more environmentally friendly, the Electrolux Lagoon is a system for washing, drying, and finishing using only water and biologically degradable detergents. This system can even wash and dry linens that normally would only allow for dry cleaning.[24] These technological advancements are most significant for cookers, ovens, and hobs where technical differentiation is extremely important to customers.[25] As previously mentioned, the Inspiro oven is just one example of Electrolux's aim at incorporating new technologies in its products.

Driven by consumer preferences, there has been a growing demand for lower noise–emitting vacuums. With this in mind, Electrolux has focused on developing vacuums that are much less noisy than past models. One of Electrolux's vacuum models focuses on air flow, enhances the performance of the vacuum, and reduces the noise level, resulting in an effectively silent vacuum cleaner.[26]

While the demand to incorporate new technologies into appliances to increase the standard of living persists, the ability to use different recyclable raw materials in developing appliances is also another technological opportunity. Environmentally conscious consumers look for appliances that use at least some recycled material and are taking into consideration the recyclability of their appliances after their use. This presents a unique opportunity for Electrolux to use new technologies to meet these environmentally conscious consumers.

One of the more significant threats for Electrolux is the Internet. The Internet allows consumers faster and more extensive access to information about products and services, which in turn leads to greater price awareness.[27] Products like refrigerators and dishwashers, which have low profit margins in geographic areas like Europe and are more difficult to differentiate except by price, suffer the most from the use of tools like the Internet. Consumers can easily shop online to discover the lowest-priced appliance without ever interfacing with a sales person or traveling to an appliance store.

In general, kitchen appliances like refrigerators, stoves, and dishwashers are heavy and bulky, which makes shipping these goods much more expensive.[28] Products like these need to be manufactured and produced near their end-market to reduce the cost of shipping. As mentioned before, many of these appliances already have a low-profit margin, so any reduction in cost to produce and ship allows Electrolux the ability to be more competitive based on price. In a push by the appliance industry to produce in low-cost countries, heavy and bulky appliances create a complex problem that companies must overcome in order to remain price competitive.

Global Opportunities and Threats

One of the most important opportunities for any manufacturing company is the ability to manufacture at low costs. There are several regions and countries of the world that allow companies to establish manufacturing plants that reduce the cost of goods sold, especially in the production of appliances. For Electrolux, all vacuum cleaners are produced in low-cost countries.[29] As previously mentioned, part of Electrolux's campaign to relocate production facilities to low-cost countries has resulted in Electrolux plants in Poland, Hungary, Mexico, China, and Thailand to reach the company's global market.[30] As indicated before, certain bulky appliances must be produced near the end-market. For example, the Mexico manufacturing facilities for Electrolux serve its North American market.[31] Manufacturing facilities in Thailand, on the other hand, serve the Australian market.[32]

With rising incomes and increasing worldwide homeownership, there are several attractive markets for appliances including Southeast Asia, Latin America, Mexico, Argentina, and Brazil.[33] For dishwashers in particular, the European market has experienced tremendous growth with increased demand for dishwashers of 20% since 2004.[34]

It's important for companies to also identify countries where governments have introduced economic recovery plans that favor appliance corporations. For example, Brazil's government has rolled out a stimulus package that led directly to an increase in demand for consumer durables supported by lower taxes on domestically produced appliances, as well as lower interest rates and greater access to credit.[35]

While predicting the next boom of consumer durable demand globally is difficult, there is one variable that helps companies determine when to ramp up production and prepare for increased demand. As previously stated, there is a direct positive correlation between raw material prices and strong economic periods.[36] As the price of raw materials increases, Electrolux can use this relationship phenomenon to identify future economic booms.

With the opportunities available for companies that take advantage of the global market, there are certainly threats that make it difficult to maintain a competitive advantage. For Electrolux, operating and manufacturing in dozens of countries across the globe opens the company up to currency risk exposure in fluctuating markets. With such economic uncertainty, as witnessed from this most recent economic recession, it is now more important than ever to hedge currency risks and identify, and respond to, markets that are a detriment to the business.

Raw material prices also fluctuate with great volatility and are difficult to forecast. A complicating factor, supporting price volatility for companies, is the scarcity of natural resources used to manufacture appliances like steel.[37] Companies must balance short fluctuating prices of raw materials and adjust menu prices as needed while keeping in mind what consumers must be willing to accept and pay for the price variations.

Financials

Consumer products make up 93% of Electrolux's sales. North America and Europe are its largest markets in both sales and income. However, sales in Latin America have continued to increase over the past few years as the company gains greater market share in Brazil. As discussed in the global opportunities section, the Asian market is growing at a rapid pace, and as such, the company has seen an increase in sales and market share in this region as well. The company's income in all regions increased in 2009 primarily due to the lower cost of raw materials and cost-cutting measures taken by the company.

The company has had a tough time increasing its sales since 2002 and its year-over-year sales growth has been less than 10% in that time period. In 2005, the company's net income loss was mainly due to the higher cost of raw materials, namely steel. Raw material costs make up approximately 20% of the price of an Electrolux appliance, so the fluctuation in cost has a significant impact on the company's profitability. During 2005, the company also faced a weakening market in North America and significant competitive challenges in the Chinese market. These factors all contributed to their 2005 loss. Despite the global economic crisis in 2008, the company's sales remained flat year over year. Due to the decreasing demand for Electrolux premium appliances in 2008, the company decreased their prices in an effort to keep their sales flat; however, this had a negative impact on their bottom-line profitability. The company also took cost-cutting measures in order to prepare for the uncertain economic climate in 2009 by reducing headcount and transferring production to low-cost countries such as Thailand, China, and Mexico. In 2009, Electrolux was able to slightly increase its sales by 4% and significantly improve its income from SEK 366M to SEK 2.6B. The increase in income was a result of the company's cost savings initiatives and a lower cost for raw materials. Some of the cost-cutting methods the company took in 2009 include closing 16 plants, reducing headcount by over 3000 employees and reducing the number of component variants in its products. Electrolux has moved 60% of its production to low-cost countries and expects that this manufacturing restructure will generate annual savings of approximately

SEK 3 billion. The company also cut its plant capacity to respond to the decrease in demand so that Electrolux's capacity utilization is only 60% versus a normal of over 85%. Electrolux's laser focus on maintaining cost efficiency helped it to survive and emerge stronger from the recession. Electrolux needs to maintain a lean cost structure and focus investments on marketing to strengthen its brand.

Operations

The operational structure of Electrolux provides a glimpse into its overall strategy. Electrolux has four global regions for the sale of major appliances: Europe, North America, Latin America, and Asia Pacific. For the remaining product divisions, the company established a single global entity that manages the entire line—floor care and small appliances, along with professional products. This operational structure aligns with the strategy of focusing on high-end, premium appliances. More attention has been devoted to the appliance business because it represents the largest growth sector and the highest-margin products for the company.

The primary objective of Electrolux from an operational standpoint is to achieve an operating margin of 6%. For the last few years, the company has been focused on improving its operating margin. This focus developed as the company realized its cost base was significantly higher than the majority of the industry. In addition, Electrolux strives to be an innovation-driven company focused on the consumer. It does this by maintaining a focus on the consumer during product development, design, production, marketing, logistics, and service.

Because of this continued focus on improving the operating margin, one of the strengths of the company's operations is the diminishing cost of its supplier and production network. By the end of 2010, Electrolux will have moved 60% of its production to low-cost countries, saving the company SEK 3 billion annually.[38] Another strength is that the company is not blindly relocating production facilities on the basis of price alone. Electrolux is making a strategic decision with each new production facility based on current and future costs of labor, transportation parameters, access to local suppliers, and proximity to growing markets. Because of this, the company has made strategic decisions to keep some production in high- or medium-cost countries. For example, the company has determined that plants for built-in ovens and cookers for Europe must remain local due to advanced technology and high transportation costs. Likewise, refrigerators and washing machines must be produced close to the end market because the items are expensive to ship and labor costs make up a small fraction of the total cost of the product. The two production plants in Juarez, Mexico, are a prime example of this strategy. While Mexico is not a country with high labor costs, it is not considered low either. Two plants have been established in the country to serve the North American markets—one for kitchen appliances and one for washing machines and dryers. This helps to reduce the cost of labor but also maintain a facility in close proximity to the end market. Conversely, vacuums are inexpensive to ship and labor makes up the bulk of the final price of the product. As such, 100% of Electrolux vacuum cleaners are made in low-cost countries—primarily Thailand. This represents a significant strength for Electrolux because it makes strategic decisions around its production facilities rather than constantly chasing the lowest-cost labor.

Though Electrolux has been improving its operating position, the company still has a number of weaknesses. As mentioned earlier, the company has undergone a strategic initiative to significantly reduce its cost structure to achieve an operating margin of 6%. The company is nearing its goal with an operating margin of 4.82 %. But even at 6%, Electrolux is well below the industry standard of 8.42%. This slim margin is a glaring weakness. Another weakness of Electrolux is that its margins are impacted greatly by an over-reliance on low-cost items like vacuum cleaners where margins are much tighter. As the company pushes toward the stated goal of a 6% operating margin, it will need to continue to emphasize high-end appliances over vacuums.

Marketing

A key strength for Electrolux is that after many years of continuously declining prices, the company managed to increase prices in Europe at the beginning of 2009 and at the same time maintained its price position in the American market. This is indicative of a strong brand that consumers are willing to pay a premium for—especially in the face of declining demand.[39] A second strength of the Electrolux marketing function is that the company has multiple customer touch points and entry points into the home, similar to GE. Also, the company has roots in door-to-door sales. This type of relationship selling is becoming even more crucial in today's market. While it's not door-to-door sales, consumers expect a one-to-one relationship with companies and are increasingly reluctant to engage with a brand that focuses on pushing messages to the masses. Electrolux is uniquely positioned in this regard. The company is also strongly positioned when it comes to sustainability initiatives. Many companies have jumped on the sustainability bandwagon, but few have done it with a clear plan on how they will cut energy consumption and how that will save the company resources in the long run. By year-end 2012, Electrolux factories, offices, and warehouses will use 15% less energy than in 2008. These reductions will result in CO_2 savings of over 73,000 tons—the equivalent of the yearly emissions from more than 32,000 cars. This reflects Electrolux's continued commitment to reducing energy use that has been ongoing and allow the company to save approximately US$100 million per year.[40] Finally, the company's marketing function is strong in the fact that the department is engaged in the product development process from the start. This helps to produce key innovations such as an induction cook top that can boil water in 90 seconds and a washer dryer that can complete a load of laundry in 36 minutes.

Because Electrolux is such a large company with several brands, a primary weakness of the marketing function is that the sub-brands are often more well-known than the premium brands. For example, many people in the North American market are familiar with the Frigidaire brand but have only a minimal awareness of the Electrolux brand outside of vacuum cleaners. This could pose a challenge for the company as it aims to move upstream and focus on high-end appliances. In addition, another key weakness of the Electrolux marketing team is its roots in door-to-door sales. While it is also a strength due to the heritage in relationship selling, it runs counter to the idea of a premium brand. When people think of high-end appliances, they don't immediately consider brands that sell vacuums door to door. If Electrolux hopes to move more squarely into the high-end appliance segment, it will have to distance itself from this history.

Innovation

Electrolux's core competency is its unique focus on comprehensive innovation and its ability to successfully create differentiated value in its products. Electrolux has been able to take cutting-edge technologies and integrate them into household appliances, catering to new consumer preferences and tastes. This ability to combine practicability and aesthetics has supported Electrolux as a prospector in the appliance industry.

The Ultra Silencer Green vacuum cleaner is a perfect example of combing the unique consumer tastes with new technologies. As previously described, the Ultra Silencer Green vacuum is comprised of 55% recycled plastic material and is the most energy-efficient vacuum cleaner on the market. Its high-efficiency motor reduces the Ultra Silencer's energy consumption by 33% compared to the standard 2000-watt vacuum cleaner.[41] With a sleek black finish, highlighted with green buttons, this vacuum cleaner sets the pace for an aesthetically pleasing model with the environment in mind.

Another example of Electrolux's focus on innovation is the new 200G Compass Control Electrolux industrial washer machine with the ability to send text message updates to users of the machine when cycles are completed.[42] With this, Electrolux has been able to capture more of an already mature market by introducing washers and dryers that clean clothes that would have normally only allowed for dry cleaning. The Electrolux Calima is a premium washing machine that is fitted with a fold-out heat map for sensitive garments such as woolen pullovers.[43] This ability to capture some of the substitute competitors market is a testament to Electrolux's ability to identify new opportunities in what was believed to be a mature market.

The supporting factor in Electrolux's core competency is its ability to listen to its customer, and recognize evolving consumer demands and tastes. The Ultra Silencer vacuum cleaner originated from a comprehensive study that Electrolux completed in which consumers were surveyed and focus groups were assembled, to assess the most important variables in selecting vacuum cleaners. A growing factor in vacuum selection was noise level.[44] By focusing on the air-flow system of vacuum cleaners, Electrolux was able to take this growing trend and develop the Ultra Silencer, which effectively eliminates all noise pollution from the vacuum cleaner. This technological advancement allows customers to play music and have a conversation with someone while vacuuming.

Challenges

Although Electrolux has differentiated itself as a prospector and prided its business on innovation and incorporating cutting-edge technology, there are a few key weaknesses that negatively affect its potential. Electrolux has been unable to maintain sales of high-profit margin appliances in Germany, Spain, the UK, and China.[45] Due to low-priced competition, and an inability to differentiate products such as refrigerators and dishwashers, Electrolux has squeezed only low profits from these mature markets. In relation to other markets and products offered, refrigerators and dishwashers sold in the aforementioned markets require significant company resources but return little in the form of profits.

In 2009, capacity utilization was only 60% for Electrolux.[46] With significant resources tied up in capital of production facilities, Electrolux suffers financially from high overhead costs and costs of goods sold. The return on the company's current manufacturing facility assets has declined significantly as a result of the past recession. Although Electrolux has closed 16 plants and cut back production in 5 others, low capacity utilization is still a major issue that Electrolux must resolve in order to compete on price against other low-priced competitors.[47]

Electrolux has always positioned itself as an appliance company focused on value over volume. Although the company chose to lower its production utilization and lessen its inventory levels due to the abrupt decline of consumer demand during the last recession, Electrolux has been stuck with inventory in its factories.[48] Electrolux's competitors have experienced the same over-production, which leads to an industrywide problem of increased supply with decreased consumer demand. This basic economic dilemma leads to downward pressure on prices and lower profit margins for Electrolux.

Electrolux has not maintained the same level of innovation, value, and competitive advantage in all of its strategic business units. With multiple brands and hundreds of products, it has not been able to sustain high-profit margin products that are highly differentiated from its competitors. Although Electrolux excels in sales and profits in the Professional Products segment of the business, it falls behind its competitors in specific product categories like refrigerators.[49] Electrolux can be regarded as a prospector when it develops products like the Inspiro oven, but it can be seen as a defender in Europe with its line of standard, price-differentiated refrigerators. How can Electrolux identify and strengthen its weaker strategic business units in order to maintain its competitive advantage?

NOTES

1. Electrolux 2009 Annual Report. http://ir.electrolux.com/files/Elux_ENG_Ars09_Del1.pdf
2. Market Research, http://www.marketresearch.com/product/display.asp?productid=2614446
3. USA Today, http://www.usatoday.com/tech/news/2010-02-23-energyrebates23_ST_N.htm
4. Relative Price Elasticity of Demand for Appliances, Larry Dale
5. Appliances Industry Overview, http://biz.yahoo.com/ic/310.html
6. Whirlpool Competitors, http://finance.yahoo.com/q/co?s=WHR+Competitors
7. Appliances Industry Overview
8. Whirlpool Competitors
9. GE Appliances, http://www.geappliances.com/?cid=3113&omni_key=ge_appliances
10. Google Finance, http://www.google.com/finance?q=ge&rls=com.microsoft:en-us&oe=UTF-
11. Whirlpool Competitors
12. LG, www.lg.com
13. "United States Government American Recovery and Reinvestment Act." www.recovery.gov
14. China Daily. "No Cheap Labor? "China Increase Minimum Wages." July 2, 2010. http://www.chinadaily.com.cn/china/2010-07/02/content_10053553.htm
15. Goldman Sachs, http://www2.goldmansachs.com/ideas/global-economic-outlook/expanding-middle.pdf
16. Ibid.
17. Ibid.
18. Ibid.
19. Ibid.
20. Ibid.
21. Ibid.
22. Ibid.
23. Ibid.
24. Ibid.
25. Ibid.
26. Ibid.
27. Ibid.
28. Ibid.
29. Ibid.
30. Ibid.
31. Ibid.
32. Ibid.
33. Ibid.
34. Ibid.
35. Ibid.
36. Ibid.
37. Ibid.
38. Ibid.
39. Ibid.
40. Ibid.
41. Ibid.
42. Electrolux Professional Laundry Systems, http://www.laundry-systems.electrolux.com/node237.aspx?lngNewsId=1122
43. Electrolux 2009 Annual Report
44. Ibid.
45. Ibid.
46. Ibid.
47. Ibid.
48. Ibid.
49. Ibid.

CASE 31

Apple Inc.: Performance in a Zero-Sum World Economy

Moustafa H. Abdelsamad, Hitesh (John) Adhia, David B. Croll, Bernard A. Morin, Lawrence C. Pettit Jr., Kathryn E. Wheelen, Richard D. Wheelen, Thomas L. Wheelen II, and Thomas L. Wheelen

ON NOVEMBER 1, 2010, JOHN TARPEY, SENIOR FINANCIAL ANALYST at a securities firm, was sitting at his conference table to begin the task of fully analyzing the 2010 financial performance and strategic strategies of Apple Inc. On his table were hundreds of articles, reports, SEC documents, and company documents. The basic question he sought answers to with this in-depth analysis was how Apple's performance continued to be outstanding, while the world and U.S. economy was flat to negative.

A second, and more important question, was whether Apple could sustain this high level of performance and major innovation. **Exhibit 1** shows unit sales by key products, net sales by the same products, net sales by the company's operating segments, and Mac unit sales by operating segments. John noted that there were nine positive increases versus three negative ones. He saw that the positive increases outnumbered the negative changes three to one. In 2010, there were only three negative changes compared with nine changes for 2009. Net sales of desktop computers were up 43% in 2010, compared with a 23% drop in sales in 2009.

John considered Apple's Consolidated Statement of Operations (see **Exhibit 2**) and Balance Sheet (see **Exhibit 3**).

EXHIBIT 1 Selected Sales Information: Apple Inc. (Sales in millions, except unit sales in thousands)

	2010	Change	2009	Change	2008
Net sales by operating segment					
Americas net sales	$24,498	29%	$18,981	15%	$16,552
Europe net sales	18,692	58%	11,810	28%	9,233
Japan net sales	3,981	75%	2,279	32%	1,728
Asia-Pacific net sales	8,256	160%	3,179	18%	2,686
Retail net sales	9,798	47%	6,656	-9%	7,292
Total net sales	$65,225	52%	$42,905	14%	$37,491
Mac unit sales by operating segment					
Americas Mac unit sales	4,976	21%	4,120	4%	3,980
Europe Mac unit sales	3,859	36%	2,840	13%	2,519
Japan Mac unit sales	481	22%	395	2%	389
Asia-Pacific Mac unit sales	1,500	62%	926	17%	793
Retail Mac unit sales	2,846	35%	2,115	4%	2,034
Total Mac unit sales	13,662	31%	10,396	7%	9,715
Net sales by product					
Desktops	$6,201	43%	$4,324	–23%	$5,622
Portables	11,278	18%	9,535	9%	8,732
Total Mac net sales	17,479	26%	13,859	9%	14,354
iPod	8,274	2%	8,091	–12%	9,153
Other music-related products/ services	4,948	23%	4,036	21%	3,340
iPhone and related products/ services	25,179	93%	13,033	93%	6,742
iPad and related products/ services	4,958	—	0	—	0
Peripherals and other hardware	1,814	23%	1,475	–13%	1,694
Software, service, and other sales	2,573	7%	2,411	9%	2,208
Total net sales	$65,225	52%	$42,905	14%	$37,491
Unit sales by product					
Desktops	4,627	45%	3,182	–14%	3,712
Portables	9,035	23%	7,214	20%	6,003
Total Mac unit sales	13,662	31%	10,396	7%	9,715
Net sales per Mac unit sold	$1,279	–4%	$1,333	–10%	$1,478
iPod unit sales	50,312	–7%	54,132	–1%	54,828
Net sales per iPod unit sold	$164	10%	$149	–11%	$167
iPhone units sold	39,989	93%	20,731	78%	11,627
iPad units sold	7,458	—	0	—	0

SOURCE: *Apple Inc., SEC 10-K Report, (September 25, 2010), p. 33.*
NOTE: The notes were deleted.

EXHIBIT 2
Consolidated
Statements of
Operations: Apple
Inc. (Amounts in
millions, except
share amounts
which are reflected
in thousands and
per share amounts)

Year Ending September 25	2010	2009	2008
Net sales	$65,225	$42,905	$37,491
Cost of sales	39,541	25,683	24,294
Gross margin	25,684	17,222	13,197
Operating expenses:			
Research and development	1,782	1,333	1,109
Selling, general and administrative	5,517	4,149	3,761
Total operating expenses	7,299	5,482	4,870
Operating income	18,385	11,740	8,327
Other income and expenses	155	326	620
Income before provision for income taxes	18,540	12,066	8,947
Provision for income taxes	4,527	3,831	2,828
Net income	$14,013	$8,235	$6,119
Earnings per common share:			
Basic	$15.41	$9.22	$6.94
Diluted	$15.15	$9.08	$6.78
Shares used in computing earnings per share:			
Basic	909,461	893,016	881,592
Diluted	924,712	907,005	902,139

SOURCE: *Apple Inc., SEC 10-K Form* (September 25, 2010), p. 46.

Management's View of the Company[1]

John searched and found in the 10-K report management's views on the company's performance in 2010 as stated next.

First, the company designed, manufactured, and marketed a range of personal computers, mobile communication and media devices, and portable digital music players, and sold a variety of related software, services, peripherals, networking solutions, and third-party digital content and applications. The company's products and services included Mac computers, iPhone, iPad, iPod, Apple TV, Xserve, a portfolio of consumer and professional software applications, the Mac OS X and iOS operating systems, third-party digital content and applications through the iTunes Store, and a variety of accessory, service, and support offerings. The company sold its products worldwide through its retail stores, online stores, and direct sales force, as well as third-party cellular network carriers, wholesalers, retailers, and value-added resellers. In addition, the company sold a variety of third-party Mac, iPhone, iPad, and iPod compatible products, including application software, printers, storage devices, speakers, headphones, and various other accessories and peripherals through its online and retail stores. The company sold to SMB, education, enterprise, government, and creative markets.

Second, the company was committed to bringing the best user experience to its customers through its innovative hardware, software, peripherals, services, and Internet offerings. The company's business strategy leverages its unique ability to design and develop its own operating systems, hardware, application software, and services to provide its customers new products and solutions with superior ease-of-use, seamless integration, and innovative industrial design. The company believed continual investment in research and development was critical to the development and enhancement of innovative products and technologies. In conjunction with its strategy, the company continued to build and host a robust platform for the discovery

EXHIBIT 3
Consolidated
Balance Sheets:
Apple Inc. (Dollar
amounts in
millions, except
share amounts)

Years Ending September 30	2010	2009
Assets		
Current assets		
Cash and cash equivalents	$ 11,261	$ 5, 263
Short-term marketable securities	14,359	18,201
Accounts receivable, less allowances of $55 and $52, respectively	5,510	3,361
Inventories	1,051	455
Deferred tax assets	1,636	1,135
Vendor non-trade receivables	4,414	1,696
Other current assets	3,447	1,444
Total current assets	41,678	31,555
Long-term marketable securities	$ 25,391	$ 10,528
Property, plant, and equipment, net	4,768	2,954
Goodwill	741	206
Acquired intangible assets, net	342	247
Other assets	2,263	2,011
Total assets	$ 75,183	$ 47,501
Liabilities and shareholders' equity		
Current liabilities		
Accounts payable	$ 12,015	$ 5,601
Accrued expenses	5,723	3,852
Deferred revenue	2,984	2,053
Total current liabilities	20,722	11,506
Deferred revenue—non-current	1,139	853
Other non-current liabilities	5,531	3,502
Total liabilities	27,392	15,861
Commitments and contingencies		
Shareholders' equity		
Common stock, no par value; 1,800,000,000 shares authorized; 915,970,050, and 899,805,500 shares issued and outstanding, respectively	10,668	8,210
Retained earnings	37,169	23,353
Accumulated other comprehensive (loss)/income	–46	77
Total shareholders' equity	47,791	31,640
Total liabilities and stockholders' equity	$ 75,183	$ 47,501

SOURCE: *Apple Inc., SEC 10-K Form (September 25, 2010).*

and delivery of third-party digital content and applications through the iTunes Store. Within the iTunes Store, the company expanded its offerings through the App Store and iBookstore, which allowed customers to browse, search for, and purchase third-party applications and books through either a Mac or Windows-based computer or by wirelessly downloading directly to an iPhone, iPad, or iPod touch. The company also worked to support a community for the development of third-party software and hardware products and digital content that complement the company's offerings. Additionally, the company's strategy included expanding its distribution network to effectively reach more customers and provide them with a high-quality sales and post-sales support experience. The company was therefore uniquely positioned to offer superior and well-integrated digital lifestyle and productivity solutions.

Third, the company participated in several highly competitive markets, including personal computers with its Mac computers; mobile communications and media devices with its iPhone, iPad, and iPod product families; and distribution of third-party digital content and applications with its online iTunes Store. While the company was widely recognized as a leading innovator in the markets where it competes, these markets were highly competitive and subject to aggressive pricing. To remain competitive, the company believed that increased investment in research and development, marketing, and advertising was necessary to maintain or expand its position in these markets. The company's research and development spending was focused on further developing its existing Mac line of personal computers; the Mac OS X and iOS operating systems; application software for the Mac; iPhone, iPad, and iPod and related software; development of new digital lifestyle consumer and professional software applications; and investments in new product areas and technologies. The company also believed increased investment in marketing and advertising programs was critical to increasing product and brand awareness.

The company utilized a variety of direct and indirect distribution channels, including its retail stores, online stores, and direct sales force, as well as third-party cellular network carriers, wholesalers, retailers, and value-added resellers. The company believed that sales of its innovative and differentiated products were enhanced by knowledgeable salespersons who could convey the value of the hardware, software, and peripheral integration; demonstrate the unique digital lifestyle solutions that were available on its products; and demonstrate the compatibility of the Mac with the Windows platform and networks. The company further believed providing direct contact with its targeted customers was an effective way to demonstrate the advantages of its products over those of its competitors, and that providing a high-quality sales and after-sales support experience is critical to attracting new—and retaining existing—customers. To ensure a high-quality buying experience for its products in which service and education were emphasized, the company continued to expand and improve its distribution capabilities by expanding the number of its own retail stores worldwide. Additionally, the company invested in programs to enhance reseller sales by placing high-quality Apple fixtures, merchandising materials, and other resources within selected third-party reseller locations. Through the Apple Premium Reseller Program, certain third-party resellers focused on the Apple platform by providing a high level of integration and support services, as well as product expertise.

History of Apple Inc.[2]

The history of Apple can be broken into five separate time periods, each with its own strategic issues and concerns.

1976–84: The Founders Build a Company

Founded in a California garage on April 1, 1976, Apple created the personal computer revolution with powerful yet easy-to-use machines for the desktop. Steve Jobs sold his Volkswagen bus and Steve Wozniak hocked his HP programmable calculator to raise US$1300 in seed money to start their new company. Not long afterward, a mutual friend helped recruit A. C. "Mike" Markkula to help market the company and give it a million-dollar image. Even though all three founders had left the company's management team during the 1980s, Markkula continued serving on Apple's Board of Directors until August 1997.

The early success of Apple was attributed largely to marketing and technological innovation. In the high-growth industry of personal computers in the early 1980s, Apple grew quickly, staying ahead of competitors by contributing key products that stimulated the development of software for the computer. Landmark programs such as Visicalc (forerunner to Lotus 1-2-3 and other spreadsheet programs) were developed first for the Apple II. Apple also secured early dominance in the education and consumer markets by awarding hundreds of thousands of dollars in grants to schools and individuals for the development of education software.

Even with enormous competition, Apple revenues continued to grow at an unprecedented rate, reaching US$583.3 million by fiscal 1982. The introduction of the Macintosh graphical user interface in 1984, which included icons, pull-down menus, and windows, became the catalyst for desktop publishing and instigated the second technological revolution attributable to Apple. Apple kept the architecture of the Macintosh proprietary; that is, it could not be cloned like the "open system" IBM PC. This allowed the company to charge a premium for its distinctive "user-friendly" features.

A shakeout in the personal computer industry began in 1983 when IBM entered the PC market, initially affecting companies selling low-priced machines to consumers. Companies that made strategic blunders or that lacked sufficient distribution or brand awareness of their products disappeared.

1985–97: Professional Managers Fail to Extend the Company

In 1985, amid a slumping market, Apple saw the departure of its founders, Jobs and Wozniak. As Chairman of the Board, Jobs had recruited John Sculley, an experienced executive from PepsiCo, to replace him as Apple's CEO in 1983. Jobs had challenged Sculley when recruiting him by saying, "Do you want to spend the rest of your life selling sugared water, or do you want to change the world?" Jobs willingly gave up his title as CEO so that he could have Sculley as his mentor. In 1985, a power struggle took place between Sculley and Jobs. With his entrepreneurial orientation, Jobs wanted to continue taking the company in risky new directions. Sculley, in contrast, felt that Apple had grown to the point where it needed not only to be more careful in its strategic moves, but also better organized and rationally managed. The board of directors supported Sculley's request to strip Jobs of his duties, since it felt that the company needed an experienced executive to lead Apple into its next stage of development.

Jobs then resigned from the company he had founded and sold all but one share of his Apple stock. Under the leadership of John Sculley, CEO and Chairman, the company engineered a remarkable turnaround. He instituted a massive reorganization to streamline operations and expenses. During this time, Wozniak left the company. Macintosh sales gained momentum throughout 1986 and 1987. Sales increased 40% from US$1.9 billion to US$2.7 billion in fiscal 1987, and earnings jumped 41% to US$217 million.

In the early 1990s, Apple sold more personal computers than any other computer company. Net sales grew to over US$7 billion, net income to over US$540 million, and earnings per share to US$4.33. The period from 1993 to 1995 was, however, a time of considerable change in the management of Apple. The industry was rapidly changing. Personal computers using Microsoft's Windows operating system and Office software plus Intel microprocessors began to dominate the personal computer marketplace. (The alliance between Microsoft and Intel was known in the trade as Wintel.) Dell, Hewlett-Packard, Compaq, and Gateway replaced both IBM and Apple as the primary makers of PCs. The new Windows system had successfully imitated the user-friendly "look and feel" of Apple's Macintosh operating system. As a result, Apple lost its competitive edge. In June 1993, Sculley was forced to resign and Michael H. Spindler was appointed CEO of the company. At this time, Apple was receiving a number of offers to acquire the company. Many of the company's executives advocated Apple's merging with another company. However, when no merger took place, many executives chose to resign.

Unable to reverse the company's falling sales, Spindler was soon forced out and Gilbert Amelio was hired from outside Apple to serve as CEO. Amelio's regime presided over an accelerated loss of market share, deteriorating earnings, and stock that had lost half of its value. Apple's refusal to license the Mac operating system to other manufacturers had given Microsoft the opening it needed to take the market with its Windows operating system. Wintel PCs now dominated the market—pushing Apple into a steadily declining market niche composed primarily of artisans and teachers. By 1996, Apple's management seemed to be in utter disarray.

Looking for a new product with which Apple could retake the initiative in personal computers, the company bought NeXT for US$402 million on December 20, 1996. Steve Jobs, who formed the NeXT computer company when he left Apple, had envisioned his new company as the developer of the "next generation" in personal computers. Part of the purchase agreement was that Jobs would return to Apple as a consultant. In July of 1997, Amelio resigned and was replaced by Steve Jobs as Apple's interim CEO (iCEO). This ended Steve Jobs' 12-year exile from the company that he and Wozniak had founded. In addition to being iCEO of Apple, Jobs also served as CEO of Pixar, a company he had personally purchased from Lucasfilm for US$5 million. Receiving only US$1.00 a year as CEO of both Pixar and Apple, Jobs held the Guinness World Record as the "Lowest Paid Chief Executive Officer."

1998–2001: Jobs Leads Apple "Back to the Future"

Once in position as Apple's CEO, Steve Jobs terminated many of the company's existing projects. Dropped were the iBook and the AirPort products series, which had helped popularize the use of wireless LAN technology to connect a computer to a network.

In May 2001, the company announced the reopening of Apple Retail Stores. Like IBM and Xerox, Apple had opened its own retail stores to market its computers during the 1980s. All such stores had been closed, however, when Wintel-type computers began being sold by mass merchandisers, such as Sears and Circuit City, as well as through corporate websites.

Apple introduced the iPod portable digital audio player, and the company opened its own iTunes music store to provide downloaded music to iPod users. Given the thorny copyright issues inherent in the music business, analysts doubted if the new product would be successful.

2002–06: A Corporate Renaissance?

In 2002, Apple introduced a redesigned iMac using a 64-bit processor. The iMac had a hemispherical base and a flat-panel, all-digital display. Although it received a lot of press, the iMac failed to live up to the company's sales expectations.

In 2004 and 2005, Apple opened its first retail stores in Europe and Canada. By November 2006, the company had 149 stores in the United States, 4 stores in Canada, 7 stores in the United Kingdom, and 7 stores in Japan.

In 2006, Jobs announced that Apple would sell an Intel-based Macintosh. Previously, Microsoft had purchased all of its microprocessors from Motorola. By this time, Microsoft's operating system with Intel microprocessors was running on 97.5% of the personal computers sold, with Apple having only a 2.5% share of the market. The company also introduced its first Intel-based machines, the iMac and MacBook Pro.

By this time, Apple's iPod had emerged as the market leader of a completely new industry category, which it had created. In 2006, Apple controlled 75.6% of the market, followed by SunDisk with 9.7%, and Creative Technology in third place with 4.3%. Although one analyst predicted that more than 30 million iPods would be sold in fiscal 2006, Apple actually sold 41,385,000. Taking advantage of its lead in music downloading, the company's next strategic move was to extend its iTunes music stores by offering movies for US$9.99 each. An analyst reviewing this strategic move said that Apple was able to create a US$1 billion-a-year market for the legal sale of music. Apple may be able to provide the movie industry with a similar formula.

2007–Present: Mobile Consumer Electronics Era

While delivering his keynote speech at the Macworld Expo on January 9, 2007, Jobs announced that Apple Computer Inc. would from that point on be known as Apple Inc., due to the fact that computers were no longer the singular focus for the company. This change reflected the company's shift of emphasis to mobile electronic devices from personal computers. The event also saw the announcement of the iPhone and the Apple TV. The following day, Apple shares hit US$97.80, an all-time high at that point. In May, Apple's share price passed the US$100 mark. In an article posted on Apple's website on February 6, 2007, Steve Jobs wrote that Apple would be willing to sell music on the iTunes Store with DRM (which would allow tracks to be played on third-party players) if record labels would agree to drop the technology. On April 2, 2007, Apple and EMI jointly announced the removal of DMR technology from EMI's catalog in the iTunes Store, effective in May. Other record labels followed later that year.

In July of the following year, Apple launched the App Store to sell third-party applications for the iPhone and iPod Touch. Within a month, the store sold 60 million applications and brought in US$1 million daily on average, with Jobs speculating that the App Store could become a billion-dollar business for Apple. Three months later, it was announced that Apple had become the third-largest mobile handset supplier in the world due to the popularity of the iPhone.

On December 16, 2008, Apple announced that, after over 20 years, 2009 would be the last year Steve Jobs would be attending the Macworld Expo, and that Phil Schiller would deliver the 2009 keynote speech in lieu of the expected Jobs. Almost exactly one month later, on January 14, 2009, an internal Apple memo from Jobs announced that Jobs would be taking a six-month leave of absence, until the end of June 2009, to allow him to better focus on his health and to allow the company to better focus on its products without having the rampant media speculating about his health. Despite Jobs' absence, Apple recorded its best non-holiday quarter (Q1 FY 2009) during the recession with revenue of US$8.16 billion and a profit of US$1.21 billion.

After years of speculation and multiple rumored "leaks," Apple announced a large screen, tablet-like media device known as the iPad on January 27, 2010. The iPad ran the same touch-based operating system that the iPhone used and many of the same iPhone apps were compatible with the iPad. This gave the iPad a large app catalog on launch even with very little development time before the release. Later that year on April 3, 2010, the iPad was launched in the United States and sold more than 300,000 units on that day, reaching 500,000 by the end of the first week. In May 2010, Apple's market cap exceeded that of competitor Microsoft for the first time since 1989.

In June 2010, Apple released the fourth-generation iPhone, which introduced video calling, multitasking, and a new insulated stainless steel design that served as the phone's antenna. Because of this antenna implementation, some iPhone 4 users reported a reduction in signal strength when the phone was held in specific ways. Apple offered buyers a free rubber "bumper" case until September 30, 2010, as cases had been developed to solve/improve the signal strength issue.

In September 2010, Apple refreshed its iPod line of MP3 players, introducing a multitouch iPod Nano, iPod Touch with FaceTime, and iPod Shuffle with buttons. In October 2010, Apple shares hit an all-time high, eclipsing US$300. Additionally, on October 20, Apple updated its MacBook Air laptop, iLife suite of applications, and unveiled Mac OS X Lion, the latest installment in its Mac OS X operating system. On November 16, 2010, Apple Inc., after years of negotiations, finalized a deal to allow iTunes to sell The Beatles' music at US$1.29 per song. The five major Web-TV boxes were (1) Apple TV, (2) Boxee, (3) Google TV, (4) WD TV Hub, and (5) Roku.

Steven P. Jobs: Entrepreneur and Corporate Executive[3]

In 2010, Steve Jobs was chosen as "Executive of the Decade" by *Fortune* magazine. He has also been referred to as the "Henry Ford" of the current world business market. Steven P. Jobs was born on February 24, 1955, in San Francisco. He was adopted by Paul and Clara Jobs in February 1955. In 1972, Jobs graduated from Homestead High School in Los Altos, California. His high school electronics teacher said, "He was somewhat of a loner and always had a different way of looking at things." After graduation, Jobs was hired by Hewlett-Packard as a summer employee. This is where he met Steve Wozniak, a recent dropout from The University of California at Berkeley. Wozniak had a genius IQ and was an engineering whiz with a passion for inventing electronic gadgets. At this time, Wozniak was perfecting his "blue box," an illegal pocket-sized telephone attachment that allowed the user to make free long-distance calls. Jobs helped Wozniak sell this device to customers.[4]

In 1972, Jobs enrolled at Reed College in Portland, Oregon, but dropped out after one semester. He remained around Reed for a year and became involved in the counterculture. During that year, he enrolled in various classes in philosophy and other topics. In a later speech at Stanford University, Jobs explained, "If I had never dropped in on that single course (calligraphy), that Mac would have never had multiple typefaces or proportionally spaced fonts."[5]

In early 1974, Jobs took a job as a video-game designer for Atari, a pioneer in electronic arcade games. After earning enough money, Jobs went to India in search of personal spiritual enlightenment. Later that year, Jobs returned to California and began attending meetings of Steve Wozniak's "Homebrew Computer Club." Wozniak converted his TV monitor into what would become a computer. Wozniak was a very good engineer and extremely interested in creating new electronic devices. Although Jobs was not interested in developing new devices, he realized the marketability of Wozniak's converted TV. Together they designed the Apple I computer in Jobs' bedroom and built the first prototype in Jobs' garage. Jobs showed the Apple I to a local electronics retailer, the Byte Shop, and received a US$25,000 order for 50 computers. Jobs took this purchase order to Cramer Electronics to order the components needed to assemble the 50 computers.

Jobs and Wozniak decided to start a computer company to manufacture and sell personal computers. They contributed US$1300 of their own money to start the business. Jobs selected the name Apple for the company based on his memories of a summer job as an orchard worker. On April 1, 1976, Apple Computer company was formed as a partnership.

During Jobs' early tenure at Apple, he was a persuasive and charismatic evangelist for the company. Some of his employees have described him at that time as an erratic and tempestuous manager. An analyst said that many persons who look at Jobs' management style forget that he was 30 years old in 1985 and he received his management and leadership education on the job. Jobs guided the company's revenues to US$1,515,616,000 and profits of US$64,055,000 in 1984. Jobs was cited in several articles as having a demanding and aggressive personality. One analyst said that these two attributes described most of the successful entrepreneurs. Jobs strategically managed the company through a period of new product introduction, rapidly changing technology, and intense competition—a time during which many companies have failed.

In 1985, after leaving Apple, Jobs formed a new computer company, NeXT Computer Inc. Jobs served as Chairman and CEO.[6] NeXT was a computer company that built machines with futuristic designs and ran the UNIX-derived NeXT step operating system. It was marketed to academic and scientific organizations. NeXT was not a commercial success, however, in part because of its high price.

In 1986, Jobs purchased Pixar Animation from Lucasfilm for US$5 million. He provided another US$5 million in capital, owned 50.6% of the stock, and served as Chairman and CEO.

Pixar created three of the six highest-grossing domestic (gross revenues) animated films of all time—*Toy Story* (1995), *A Bug's Life* (1998), and *Toy Story 2* (1999). Each of these films, released under a partnership with the Walt Disney Company, was the highest grossing animated film for the year in which it was released. During this period, Jobs delegated more to his executives. Many analysts felt that the excellent executive staff and animators were prime reasons that Disney management subsequently wanted to acquire Pixar. Jobs served as CEO of NeXT and Pixar from 1985 to 1997. Jobs ultimately sold NeXT in 1996 to Apple for US$402 million and became iCEO of Apple in July 1997.[7]

At Pixar, Jobs focused on business duties, which was different than his earlier management style at Apple. The creative staff was given a great deal of autonomy. Sources say he spent less than one day a week at the Pixar campus in Emeryville, just across the San Francisco Bay from Apple's headquarters.

Michael D. Eisner, CEO of the Walt Disney Company, did not have a smooth relationship with Jobs during the years of the Pixar/Disney partnership. Critics explained that Eisner was unable to work with Jobs because both men were supremely confident (some said arrogant) that their own judgment was correct—regardless of what others said. In 2005, in response to Eisner's unwillingness to modify Disney's movie distribution agreement with Pixar, Jobs refused to renew the contract. At the time, Disney's own animation unit was faltering and unable to match Pixar's new computer technology and creativity. Concerned with Eisner's leadership style and his inability to support the company's distinctive competence in animation, Roy Disney led a shareholders' revolt. On October 1, 2005, Eisner was replaced by Robert A. Iger as CEO of Disney.[8]

On January 24, 2006, CEO Iger announced that Disney had agreed to pay US$7.4 billion in stock to acquire Pixar Animation Studios. Since this deal made Jobs the largest stockholder (6.67%) in Disney, he was appointed to Disney's board of directors.[9]

Peter Burrows and Ronald Grover stated in an article: "The alliance between Jobs and Disney is full of promise. If he can bring to Disney the same kind of industry-sharing, boundary-busting energy that has lifted Apple and Pixar sky-high, he could help the staid company become the leading laboratory for media convergences. It's not hard to imagine a day when you could fire up your Apple TV and watch net-only spin-offs of popular TV shows from Disney's ABC Inc. (DIS). Or use your Apple iPhone to watch Los Angeles Lakers superstar Kobe Bryant's video blog delivered via Disney's ESPN Inc. 'We've been talking about a lot of things,' said Jobs. 'It's going to be a pretty exciting world looking ahead over the next five years.'"[10]

An expert on Jobs asked, "*So what is Jobs' secret?*" His answer: "There are many, but it starts with focus and a non-religious faith in his strategy." In his return to Apple, he took a proprietary approach as he cut dozens of projects and products. Many on Wall Street were not initially happy with Jobs' new directions for the company, but soon were impressed by Apple's successful turnaround.[11]

Jim Cramer, host of *Mad Money*, has said several times on his television program that Steve Jobs is the "Henry Ford" of this period of America's industry. Others claim Steve is the present Thomas Edison. Steve Jobs over the years has received many honors, such as the National Medal of Technology (with Steve Wozniak) from President Reagan in 1985. Jobs was among the first people to ever receive the honor, and a Jefferson Award for Public Service in the category "Greatest Public Service by an Individual 35 Years or Under" (a.k.a., the *Samuel S. Beard Award*) in 1987. On November 27, 2007, California Governor Arnold Schwarzenegger and First Lady Maria Shriver inducted Jobs into the California Hall of Fame, located at The California Museum for History, Women and the Arts. In August 2009, Jobs was selected the most admired entrepreneur among teenagers on a survey by Junior Achievement. On November 5, 2009, Jobs was named the CEO of the decade by *Fortune* magazine. On November 22, 2010, *Forbes* magazine named Steve Jobs the "17th Most Powerful Person on Earth." The list had only 68 individuals out of the world population of 6.8 billion people.[12]

Health Concerns

In 2004, Jobs informed Apple employees that he had been diagnosed with a cancerous tumor in his pancreas. Jobs underwent a pancreaticoduodenectomy (or "Whipple procedure") to remove the tumor. During Jobs' absence, Timothy D. Cook, head of worldwide sales and operations, was acting CEO.

In 2008, there were concerns about Jobs health after his WWDC keynote address. Jobs said that he was suffering from a "common bug" and that he was taking antibiotics. During a July conference call discussing Apple earnings, participants were told that Steve Jobs' health was a "private matter."

On August 28, 2008, Bloomberg mistakenly published a 2500-word obituary of Jobs in its corporate news service, containing blank spaces for his age and cause of death.

Jobs responded by quoting Mark Twain: "Reports of my death are greatly exaggerated."

On January 14, 2009, Jobs health had taken a turn for the worse and announced a six-month leave of absence until the end of June 2009. Tim Cook, who previously served as acting CEO in Jobs' 2004 absence, again became acting CEO of Apple. Jobs was consulted on important strategic initiatives at Apple.

In April 2009, Jobs underwent a liver transplant at Methodist University Hospital Transplant Institute in Memphis, Tennessee. The surgery was successful and his prognosis was excellent."[13]

On June 29, 2010, Steve Jobs returned to his position as CEO. And began discussions with Apple employees about the possibility of him not returning to active management at Apple.[14]

Surprised Leave of Absence Announced—2011

On January 17, 2011, Steve Jobs sent an e-mail to all Apple employees informing them that the Apple Board of Directors had granted him a leave of absence for health reasons and that Tim Cook would now be in charge of Apple, Inc.

This was Job's second leave of absence. The first one was from January 2009 until June 2009.

Tim Cook, chief operating officer, again took over the day-to day activities of the CEO position, but Jobs kept the title as he did on his first leave of absence. After Jobs' first medical leave of absence was granted in January 2009, a 10% drop occurred in the stock. On January 19, 2011, the stock's close price was US$348.48; as of the last trade January 20, it was US$340.65 (a change down US$7.83 or 2.25%).[15] This was not in line with the trading in the past month.

Business Strategy[16]

Apple was committed to bringing the best user experience to its customers through its innovative hardware, software, peripherals, services, and Internet offerings. The company's business strategy leveraged its unique ability to design and develop its own operating systems, hardware, application software, and services to provide its customers with new products and solutions that offered superior ease-of-use, seamless integration, and innovative industrial design. The company believed continual investment in research and development was critical to the development and enhancement of innovative products and technologies. In conjunction with its strategy, the company continued to build and host a robust platform for the discovery and delivery of third-party digital content and applications through the iTunes Store. The iTunes Store included the App Store and iBookstore, which allowed customers to discover and download third-party applications and books through either a Mac or Windows-based computer or wirelessly through an iPhone, iPad, or iPod touch. The company also worked to support a community for the development of third-party software and hardware products and digital content that complemented the company's offerings. Additionally, the company's strategy included expanding its distribution to effectively reach more customers and provided them with a high-quality sales and post-sales support experience. The company was therefore uniquely positioned to offer superior and well-integrated digital lifestyle and productivity solutions.

Consumer and Small and Mid-Sized Business

The company believed a high-quality buying experience with knowledgeable salespersons who could convey the value of the company's products and services greatly enhanced its ability to attract and retain customers. Apple sold many of its products and resells certain third-party products in most of its major markets directly to consumers and businesses through its retail and online stores. The company has also invested in programs to enhance reseller sales by placing high-quality Apple fixtures, merchandising materials, and other resources within selected third-party reseller locations. Through the Apple Premium Reseller Program, certain third-party resellers focused on the Apple platform by providing a high level of integration and support services, as well as product expertise.

As of September 25, 2010, the company had opened a total of 317 retail stores—233 stores in the United States and 84 stores internationally. The company typically located its stores at high-traffic locations in quality shopping malls and urban shopping districts. By operating its own stores and locating them in desirable high-traffic locations, the company was better positioned to control the customer buying experience and attract new customers. The stores were designed to simplify and enhance the presentation and marketing of the company's products and related solutions. To that end, retail store configurations had evolved into various sizes to accommodate market-specific demands. The company believed providing direct contact with its targeted customers was an effective way to demonstrate the advantages of its products over those of its competitors. The stores employed experienced and knowledgeable personnel who provided product advice, service, and training. The stores offered a wide selection of third-party hardware, software, and various other accessories and peripherals that complemented the company's products.

Education

Throughout its history, the company focused on the use of technology in education and was committed to delivering tools to help educators teach and students learn. The company believed effective integration of technology into classroom instruction can result in higher levels of student achievement, especially when used to support collaboration, information access, and the expression and representation of student thoughts and ideas. The company designed a range of products, services, and programs to address the needs of education customers, including individual laptop programs and education roadshows. In addition, the company supported mobile learning and real-time distribution and accessibility of education-related materials through iTunes U, which allowed students and teachers to share and distribute educational media directly through their computers and mobile communication and media devices. The company sold its products to the education market through its direct sales force, select third-party resellers, and its online and retail stores.

Enterprise, Government, and Creative

The company also sold its hardware and software products to customers in enterprise, government, and creative markets in each of its geographic segments. These markets were also important to many third-party developers who provided Mac-compatible hardware and software solutions. Customers in these markets utilized the company's products because of their high-powered computing performance and expansion capabilities, networking functionality, and seamless integration with complementary products. The company designed its high-end hardware solutions to incorporate the power, expandability, compatibility, and other features desired by these markets.

Other

In addition to consumer, SMB, education, enterprise, government, and creative markets, the company provided hardware and software products and solutions for customers in the information technology and scientific markets.

Business Organization[17]

The company managed its business primarily on a geographic basis. The company's reportable operating segments consisted of the Americas, Europe, Japan, Asia-Pacific, and Retail. The Americas, Europe, Japan, and Asia-Pacific reportable segments did not include activities related to the Retail segment. The Americas segment included both North and South America. The Europe segment included European countries, as well as the Middle East and Africa. The Asia-Pacific segment included Australia and Asia, but did not include Japan. The Retail segment operated Apple-owned retail stores in the United States and in international markets. Each reportable operating segment provided similar hardware and software products and similar services.

Each of the five operating centers is discussed next.

1. Americas

During 2010, net sales in the Americas segment increased US$5.5 billion or 29% compared to 2009. This increase in net sales was driven by increased iPhone revenue, strong demand for the iPad, continued demand for Mac desktop and portable systems, and higher sales of third-party digital content and applications from the iTunes Store. Americas Mac net sales and unit sales increased 18% and 21%, respectively, during 2010 compared to 2009, largely due to strong demand for MacBook Pro. The Americas segment represented 37% and 44% of the company's total net sales in 2010 and 2009, respectively.

During 2009, net sales in the Americas segment increased US$2.4 billion or 15% compared to 2008. The increase in net sales during 2009 was attributable to the significant year-over-year increase in iPhone revenue, higher sales of third-party digital content and applications from the iTunes Store, and increased sales of Mac portable systems, partially offset by a decrease in sales of Mac desktop systems and iPods. Americas Mac net sales decreased 6% due primarily to lower average selling prices, while Mac unit sales increased by 4% on a year-over-year basis. The increase in Mac unit sales was due primarily to strong demand for the MacBook Pro. The Americas segment represented approximately 44% of the company's total net sales in both 2009 and 2008.

2. Europe

During 2010, net sales in Europe increased US$6.9 billion or 58% compared to 2009. The growth in net sales was due mainly to a significant increase in iPhone revenue attributable to continued growth from existing carriers and country and carrier expansion, increased sales of Mac desktop and portable systems, and strong demand for the iPad, partially offset by a stronger U.S. dollar. Europe Mac net sales and unit sales increased 32% and 36%, respectively, during the year due to strong demand for MacBook Pro and iMac. The Europe segment represented 29% and 28% of the company's total net sales in 2010 and 2009, respectively.

During 2009, net sales in Europe increased US$2.6 billion or 28% compared to 2008. The increase in net sales was due mainly to increased iPhone revenue and strong sales of Mac portable systems, offset partially by lower net sales of Mac desktop systems, iPods, and a stronger U.S. dollar. Mac unit sales increased 13% in 2009 compared to 2008, which was driven primarily by increased sales of Mac portable systems, particularly MacBook Pro, while total Mac net sales declined as a result of lower average selling prices across all Mac products. iPod net sales decreased year-over-year as a result of lower average selling prices, partially offset by increased unit sales of the higher-priced iPod touch. The Europe segment represented 28% and 25% of total net sales in 2009 and 2008, respectively.

3. Japan

During 2010, Japan's net sales increased US$1.7 billion or 75% compared to 2009. The primary contributors to this growth were significant year-over-year increases in iPhone revenue, strong demand for the iPad, and to a lesser extent strength in the Japanese yen. Mac net sales increased by 8%, driven by a 22% increase in unit sales due primarily to strong demand for MacBook Pro and iMac, partially offset by lower average selling prices in Japan on a year-over-year basis. The Japan segment represented 6% and 5% of the company's total net sales for 2010 and 2009, respectively.

Japan's net sales increased US$551 million or 32% in 2009 compared to 2008. The primary contributors to this growth were increased iPhone revenue, stronger demand for certain Mac portable systems and iPods, and strength in the Japanese yen, partially offset by decreased sales of Mac desktop systems. Net sales and unit sales of Mac portable systems increased during 2009 compared to 2008, driven primarily by stronger demand for the MacBook Pro. Net sales and unit sales of iPods increased during 2009 compared to 2008, driven by strong demand for the iPod touch and iPod nano. The Japan segment represented approximately 5% of the company's total net sales in both 2009 and 2008.

4. Asia-Pacific

Net sales in the Asia-Pacific segment increased US$5.1 billion or 160% during 2010 compared to 2009. The significant growth in Asia-Pacific net sales was due mainly to increased iPhone revenue, which was primarily attributable to country and carrier expansion and continued growth from existing carriers. Asia-Pacific net sales were also favorably affected by strong demand for Mac portable and desktop systems and for the iPad. Particularly strong year-over-year growth was experienced in China, Korea, and Australia. The Asia-Pacific segment represented 13% and 7% of the company's total net sales for 2010 and 2009, respectively. Net sales in Asia-Pacific increased US$493 million or 18% during 2009 compared to 2008, reflecting strong growth in sales of iPhone and Mac portable systems, offset partially by a decline in sales of iPods and Mac desktop systems, as well as a strengthening of the U.S. dollar against the Australian dollar and other Asian currencies. Mac net sales and unit sales grew in the Asia-Pacific region by 4% and 17%, respectively, due to increased sales of the MacBook Pro. The Asia-Pacific segment represented approximately 7% of the company's total net sales in both 2009 and 2008.

5. Retail

Retail net sales increased US$3.1 billion or 47% during 2010 compared to 2009. The increase in net sales was driven primarily by strong demand for iPad, increased sales of Mac desktop and portable systems, and a significant year-over-year increase in iPhone revenue. Mac net sales and unit sales grew in the retail segment by 25% and 35%, respectively, during 2010. The company opened 44 new retail stores during the year, 28 of which were international stores, ending the year with 317 stores open compared to 273 stores at the end of 2009. With an average of 288 stores and 254 stores opened during 2010 and 2009, respectively, average revenue per store increased to US$34.1 million in 2010, compared to US$26.2 million in 2009. The Retail segment represented 15% and 16% of the company's total net sales in 2010 and 2009, respectively.

Retail net sales decreased US$636 million or 9% during 2009 compared to 2008. The decline in net sales was driven largely by a decrease in net sales of iPhones, iPods, and Mac desktop systems, offset partially by strong demand for Mac portable systems. The year-over-year decline in Retail net sales was attributable to continued third-party channel expansion, particularly in the United States where most of the company's stores were located, and also reflects the challenging consumer-spending environment in 2009. The company opened 26 new retail stores during 2009, including 14 international stores, ending the year with 273 stores open. This compared to 247 stores open as of September 27, 2008. With an average of 254 stores and 211 stores opened during 2009 and 2008, respectively, average revenue per store decreased to US$26.2 million for 2009 from US$34.6 million in 2008.

The Retail segment reported operating income of US$2.4 billion during 2010 and US$1.7 billion during both 2009 and 2008. The increase in Retail operating income during 2010 compared to 2009 was attributable to higher overall net sales. Despite the decline in Retail net sales during 2009 compared to 2008, the Retail segment's operating income was flat at US$1.7 billion in 2009 compared to 2008, due primarily to a higher gross margin percentage in 2009 consistent with that experienced by the overall company.

Expansion of the Retail segment has required, and will continue to require, a substantial investment in fixed assets and related infrastructure, operating lease commitments, personnel, and other operating expenses. Capital asset purchases associated with the Retail segment since its inception totaled US$2.2 billion through the end of 2010. As of September 25, 2010, the Retail segment had approximately 26,500 full-time equivalent employees and had outstanding lease commitments associated with retail space and related facilities of US$1.7 billion. The company would incur substantial costs if it were to close multiple retail stores, and such costs could adversely affect the company's financial condition and operating results.

Product Support and Services[18]

AppleCare offered a range of support options for the company's customers. These options included assistance that was built into software products, printed and electronic product manuals, online support including comprehensive product information as well as technical assistance, and the AppleCare Protection Plan ("APP"). APP was a fee-based service that typically included two to three years of phone support and hardware repairs, dedicated Web-based support resources, and user diagnostic tools.

Markets and Distribution[19]

The company's customers were primarily in the consumer, SMB, education, enterprise, government, and creative markets. The company utilized a variety of direct and indirect distribution channels, such as its retail stores, online stores, and direct sales force, as well as third-party cellular network carriers, wholesalers, retailers, and value-added resellers. The company believed that sales of its innovative and differentiated products were enhanced by knowledgeable salespersons who could convey the value of the hardware, software, and peripheral integration; demonstrate the unique digital lifestyle solutions that were available on its products; and demonstrate the compatibility of the Mac with the Windows platform and networks. The company further believed providing direct contact with its targeted customers was an effective way to demonstrate the advantages of its products over those of its competitors and providing a high-quality sales and after-sales support experience was critical to attracting new—and retaining existing—customers. To ensure a high-quality buying experience for its products in which service and education were emphasized, the company continued to expand and improve its distribution capabilities by expanding the number of its own retail stores worldwide. Additionally, the company invested in programs to enhance reseller sales by placing high-quality Apple fixtures, merchandising materials, and other resources within selected third-party reseller locations. Through the Apple Premium Reseller Program, certain third-party resellers focused on the Apple platform by providing a high level of integration and support services, as well as product expertise. One of the company's customers accounted for 11% of net sales in 2009; there was no single customer that accounted for more than 10% of net sales in 2010 or 2008.

Competition[20]

The company was confronted by aggressive competition in all areas of its business. The markets for the company's products and services were highly competitive. These markets were characterized by frequent product introductions and rapid technological advances that had substantially increased the capabilities and use of personal computers, mobile communication and media devices, and other digital electronic devices. The company's competitors who sold personal computers based on other operating systems had aggressively cut prices and lowered their product margins to gain or maintain market share. The company's financial condition and operating results could be adversely affected by these and other industrywide downward pressures on gross margins. The principal competitive factors included price, product features, relative price/performance, product quality and reliability, design innovation, availability of software and peripherals, marketing and distribution capability, service and support, and corporate reputation.

The company was focused on expanding its market opportunities related to mobile communication and media devices, including iPhone and iPad. The mobile communications and media device industries were highly competitive and included several large, well-funded, and experienced participants. The company expected competition in these industries to intensify significantly as competitors attempted to imitate some of the iPhone and iPad features and applications within their own products or, alternatively, collaborate with each other to offer solutions that were more competitive than those they currently offered. These industries were characterized by aggressive pricing practices, frequent product introductions, evolving design approaches and technologies, rapid adoption of technological and product advancements by competitors, and price sensitivity on the part of consumers and businesses.

The company's iPod and digital content services faced significant competition from other companies promoting their own digital music and content products and services, including those offering free peer-to-peer music and video services. The company believed it offered superior innovation and integration of the entire solution including the hardware (personal computer, iPhone, iPad, and iPod), software (iTunes), and distribution of digital content and applications (iTunes Store, App Store, and iBookstore). Some of the company's current and potential competitors had substantial resources and may have been able to provide such products and services at little or no profit or even at a loss to compete with the company's offerings. Alternatively, these competitors may have collaborated with each other to offer solutions that were more integrated than those they currently offered.

The company's future financial condition and operating results were substantially dependent on the company's ability to continue to develop and offer new innovative products and services in each of the markets it competed in. In 2010, only AT&T was the carrier for the iPhone. Verizon began selling a version of the iPhone in early 2011. AT&T activated 11 million iPhone accounts in the first nine months of 2010. Before Verizon, the iPhone had been exclusive to AT&T since its launch in 2007.

Supply of Components[21]

Although most components essential to the company's business were generally available from multiple sources, certain key components including but not limited to microprocessors, enclosures, certain liquid crystal displays (LCDs), certain optical drives, and application-specific integrated circuits (ASICs) were currently obtained by the company from single or limited sources, which subjected the company to significant supply and pricing risks. Many of these and other key components that were available from multiple sources, including but not limited to NAND flash memory, dynamic random access memory (DRAM), and certain LCDs, were subject at times to industrywide shortages and significant commodity pricing fluctuations. In addition, the company entered into certain agreements for the supply of key components including but not limited to microprocessors, NAND flash memory, DRAM, and LCDs at favorable pricing. However, there was no guarantee the company would be able to extend or renew these agreements on similar favorable terms, or at all, upon expiration, or otherwise obtain favorable pricing in the future. Therefore, the company remained subject to significant risks of supply shortages and/or price increases that could materially adversely affect its financial condition and operating results.

The company and other participants in the personal computer and mobile communication and media device industries also competed for various components with other industries that experienced increased demand for their products. In addition, the company used some custom components that were not common to the rest of these industries, and introduced new products that often utilized custom components available from only one source. When a component or product used new technologies, initial capacity constraints existed until the suppliers' yields had matured or manufacturing capacity had increased. If the company's supply of a key single-sourced component for a new or existing product was delayed or constrained, if such components were available only at significantly higher prices, or if a key manufacturing vendor delayed shipments of completed products to the company, the company's financial condition and operating results could be materially adversely affected. The company's business and financial performance could also be adversely affected depending on the time required to obtain sufficient quantities from the original source, or to identify and obtain sufficient quantities from an alternative source. Continued availability of these components at acceptable prices, or at all, may be affected if those suppliers decided to concentrate on the production of common components instead of components customized to meet the company's requirements.

Substantially all of the company's Macs, iPhones, iPads, iPods, logic boards, and other assembled products were manufactured by outsourcing partners, primarily in various parts of Asia. A significant concentration of this outsourced manufacturing was performed by only a few outsourcing partners of the company, including Hon Hai Precision Industry Co. Ltd. and Quanta Computer Inc. The company's outsourced manufacturing was often performed in single locations. Among these outsourcing partners were the sole-sourced supplier of components and manufacturing outsourcing for many of the company's key products, including but not limited to final assembly of substantially all of the company's Macs, iPhones, iPads, and iPods. Although the company worked closely with its outsourcing partners on manufacturing schedules, the company's operating results would be adversely affected if its outsourcing partners were unable to meet their production commitments. The company's purchase commitments typically covered the company's requirements for periods ranging from 30 to 150 days.

The company sources components from a number of suppliers and manufacturing vendors. The loss of supply from any of these suppliers or vendors, whether temporary or permanent, would materially adversely affect the company's business and financial condition.

Research and Development[22]

Because the industries in which the company competed were characterized by rapid technological advances, the company's ability to compete successfully was heavily dependent upon its ability to ensure a continual and timely flow of competitive products, services, and technologies to the marketplace. The company continued to develop new products and technologies and to enhance existing products that expanded the range of its product offerings and intellectual property through licensing and acquisition of third-party business and technology. Total research and development expenses were US$1.8 billion, US$1.3 billion, and US$1.1 billion in 2010, 2009, and 2008, respectively.

Patents, Trademarks, Copyrights, and Licenses[23]

The company currently held rights to patents and copyrights relating to certain aspects of its Macs; iPhone, iPad, and iPod devices; peripherals; software; and services. In addition, the company registered and/or applied to register trademarks and service marks in the United States and a number of foreign countries for "Apple," the Apple logo, "Macintosh," "Mac," "iPhone," "iPad," "iPod," "iTunes," "iTunes Store," "Apple TV," "MobileMe," and numerous other trademarks and service marks. Although the company believed the ownership of such patents, copyrights, trademarks, and service marks was an important factor in its business and that its success depended in part on the ownership thereof, the company relied primarily on the innovative skills, technical competence, and marketing abilities of its personnel.

The company regularly filed patent applications to protect inventions arising from its research and development, and was currently pursuing thousands of patent applications around the world. Over time, the company had accumulated a portfolio of several thousand issued patents in the United States and worldwide. In addition, the company held copyrights relating to certain aspects of its products and services. No single patent or copyright was solely responsible for protecting the company's products. The company believed the duration of the applicable patents it had been granted was adequate relative to the expected lives of its products. Due to the fast pace of innovation and product development, the company's products were often obsolete before the patents related to them expired—and sometimes were obsolete before the patents related to them were even granted.

Many of the company's products were designed to include intellectual property obtained from third parties. While it may be necessary in the future to seek or renew licenses relating to various aspects of its products and business methods, the company believed, based upon past experience and industry practice, that such licenses generally could be obtained on commercially reasonable terms; however, there was no guarantee such licenses could be obtained at all. Because of technological changes in the industries in which the company competed, current extensive patent coverage, and the rapid rate of issuance of new patents, it was possible certain components of the company's products and business methods may unknowingly infringe upon existing patents or the intellectual property rights of others. From time to time, the company had been notified that it may be infringing upon certain patents or other intellectual property rights of third parties.

Foreign and Domestic Operations and Geographic Data[24]

The United States represented the company's largest geographic marketplace. Approximately 44% of the company's net sales in 2010 came from sales to customers inside the United States. Final assembly of the company's products was performed in the company's manufacturing facility in Ireland, and by external vendors in California, Texas, the People's Republic of China, the Czech Republic, and the Republic of Korea. The supply and manufacture of many critical components was performed by sole-sourced third-party vendors in the United States, China, Germany, Ireland, Israel, Japan, Korea, Malaysia, the Netherlands, the Philippines, Taiwan, Thailand, and Singapore. Sole-sourced third-party vendors in China performed final assembly of substantially all of the company's Macs, iPhones, iPads, and iPods. Margins on sales of the company's products in foreign countries, and on sales of products that include components obtained from foreign suppliers, can be adversely affected by foreign currency exchange rate fluctuations and by international trade regulations, including tariffs and anti-dumping penalties.

Seasonal Business[25]

The company historically experienced increased net sales in its first and fourth fiscal quarters compared to other quarters in its fiscal year due to the seasonal demand of consumer markets related to the holiday season and the beginning of the school year; however, this pattern was less pronounced following the introductions of the iPhone and iPad. This historical pattern should not be considered a reliable indicator of the company's future net sales or financial performance.

Warranty[26]

The company offered a basic limited parts and labor warranty on most of its hardware products, including Macs, iPhones, iPads, and iPods. The basic warranty period was typically one year from the date of purchase by the original end-user. The company also offered a 90-day basic warranty for its service parts used to repair the company's hardware products. In addition, consumers may purchase the APP, which extended service coverage on many of the company's hardware products in most of its major markets.

Backlog[27]

In the company's experience, the actual amount of product backlog at any particular time was not a meaningful indication of its future business prospects. In particular, backlog often increased in anticipation of or immediately following new product introductions as dealers anticipated shortages. Backlog was often reduced once dealers and customers believed they were able to obtain sufficient supply. Because of the foregoing, backlog should not be considered a reliable indicator of the company's ability to achieve any particular level of revenue or financial performance.

Environmental Laws

Compliance with federal, state, local, and foreign laws enacted for the protection of the environment has to date had no significant effect on the company's capital expenditures, earnings, or competitive position. In the future, however, compliance with environmental laws could materially adversely affect the company.

Production and marketing of products in certain states and countries may subject the company to environmental and other regulations including, in some instances, the requirement to provide customers with the ability to return a product at the end of its useful life, as well as place responsibility for environmentally safe disposal or recycling with the company. Such laws and regulations had been passed in several jurisdictions in which the company operates, including various countries within Europe and Asia and certain states and provinces within North America. Although the company does not anticipate any material adverse effects in the future based on the nature of its operations and the thrust of such laws, there is no assurance that such existing laws or future laws will not materially adversely affect the company's financial condition or operating results.

Employees

As of September 25, 2010, the company had approximately 46,600 full-time equivalent employees and an additional 2800 full-time equivalent temporary employees and contractors.

Legal Proceedings

As of September 25, 2010, the company was subject to the various legal proceedings and claims as well as certain other legal proceedings and claims that had not been fully resolved and that had arisen in the ordinary course of business. In the opinion of management, the company did not have a potential liability related to any current legal proceeding or claim that would individually or in the aggregate materially adversely affect its financial condition or operating results. However, the results of legal proceedings could not be predicted with certainty. Should the company fail to prevail in any of these legal matters or should several of these legal matters be resolved against the company in the same reporting period, the operating results of a particular reporting period could be materially adversely affected. The company settled certain matters during the fourth quarter of 2010 that did not individually or in the aggregate have a material impact on the company's financial condition and results of operations.

Software Development Costs

Research and development costs were expensed as incurred. Development costs of computer software to be sold, leased, or otherwise marketed were subject to capitalization, beginning when a product's technological feasibility has been established and ending when a product is made available for general release to customers. In most instances, the company's products are released soon after technological feasibility has been established. Therefore, costs incurred subsequent to achievement of technological feasibility are usually not significant, and generally most software development costs have been expensed as incurred.

The company did not capitalize any software development costs during 2010. In 2009 and 2008, the company capitalized US$71 million and US$11 million, respectively, of costs associated with the development of Mac OS X.

Properties

The company's headquarters are located in Cupertino, California. As of September 25, 2010, the company owned or leased approximately 10.6 million square feet of building space, primarily in the United States and, to a lesser extent, in Europe, Japan, Canada, and the Asia-Pacific regions. Of that amount, approximately 5.6 million square feet was leased, of which approximately 2.5 million square feet was retail building space. Additionally, the company owned a total of 480 acres of land in various locations.

As of September 25, 2010, the company owned a manufacturing facility in Cork, Ireland, that also housed a customer support call center and facilities in Elk Grove, California, that included warehousing and distribution operations and a customer support call center. In addition, the company owned facilities for research and development and corporate functions in Cupertino, California, including land for the future development of the company's second corporate campus. The company also owned a data center in Newark, California, and land in North Carolina for a new data center facility currently under construction. Outside the United States, the company owned additional facilities for various purposes.

John Tarpey's Decision

After analyzing Apple's most recent balance sheets and income statements and integrating that information with his knowledge of the company, John Tarpey was unsure of his next move. As a senior financial analyst of a securities firm, he was obligated to make a recommendation. Should he tell his clients to buy, hold, or sell Apple's common stock?

He had a number of concerns about the company's future. For example, how dependent was Apple on Steve Jobs? The shareholder proposal at the most recent shareholder meeting asking the board to develop an executive succession plan indicated that current shareholders were certainly worried about Jobs' health and ability to lead the company. In addition, how long would it take for Apple's competitors to catch up with the company's lead in product development and perhaps even surpass Apple? There was no doubt in John's mind that Apple's stock price had done very well over the past few years. Even *Mad Money's* Jim Cramer was still touting Apple as the industry's leader and "best of breed." Was this a good time to be buying more Apple stock or was the smarter move to sell the stock and take some profit while it was still a solid performer?

Given Apple's history of boom-and-bust performance over its lifetime, what should the company be doing to cement its market leadership in this constantly evolving industry?

NOTES

1. This section was directly quoted from *Apple Inc.*, "SEC 10-K," p. 22, September 25, 2010, p. 32.
2. This section, History of Apple, is a combination of information from previous revisions of the Apple Case in this book, *Strategic Management and Business Policy*, over the past 20 years, and Wikipedia, the free encyclopedia, "History of Apple, Inc.," pp. 1–20.
3. "Steve Jobs," Wikipedia, the free encyclopedia, pp. 1–8.
4. Ibid., pp. 1–2.
5. Ibid.
6. Previous Apple Case.
7. Pixar, "Corporate Overview," p. 1.
8. "Steve Jobs Magic Kingdom," *Business Week*, pp. 1–5, and Vandana Sinna, "Disney, Pixar Give Marriage Second Chance," pp. 1–3.
9. "Steve Jobs Magic Kingdom," p. 1.
10. Ibid.
11. Ibid.
12. "The Most Powerful People on Earth," *Forbes*, November 22, 2010, p. 88, and Peter Newcomb, "Business-Person of the Year," pp. 136–137.
13. This section was directly quoted from "Steve Jobs—Health Concerns," Wikipedia, the free encyclopedia, p. 11.

14. This section was directly quoted from *Apple Inc.*, "SEC 10-K," September 23, 2010.
15. These five sections below were directly quoted from *Apple Inc.*, "SEC 10-K," September 25, 2010, p. 1.
16. Ibid., p. 8.
17. Ibid., pp. 8–9.
18. Ibid., p. 9.
19. Ibid.
20. Ibid.
21. Ibid.
22. Ibid., p. 10.
23. Ibid., p. 10.
24. Ibid., p. 22.
25. Ibid., p. 8.
26. Ibid., p. 21.
   Note: Footnotes 16-26 were directly quoted from Apple, Inc., "SEC 10-K," September 25, 2010.
27. Peter Oppenheimer (Chief Financial Officer of Apple Inc.), "Live Update: Apple 4Q Financial Report." Presented at Macworld live conference. www.macworld.com.

CASE 32

Dell Inc.:

CHANGING THE BUSINESS MODEL (MINI CASE)

J. David Hunger

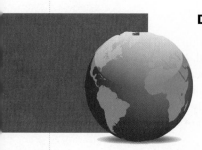

DELL INC. was founded in 1984 by Michael Dell at age 19 while he was a student living in a dormitory at the University of Texas. As a college freshman, he bought personal computers (PCs) from the excess inventory of local retailers, added features such as more memory and disk drives, and sold them out of the trunk of his car. He withdrew US$1000 in personal savings, used his car as collateral for a bank loan, hired a few friends, and placed ads in the local newspaper offering computers at 10%–15% below retail price. Soon he was selling US$50,000 worth of PCs a month to local businesses. Sales during the first year reached US$600,000 and doubled almost every year thereafter. After his freshman year, Dell left school to run the business full time.

Michael Dell began assembling his own computers in 1985 and marketed them through ads in computer trade publications. Two years later, his company witnessed tremendous change: It launched its first catalog, initiated a field sales force to reach large corporate accounts, went public, changed its name from PCs Limited to Dell Computer Corporation, and established its first international subsidiary in Britain. Michael Dell was selected "Entrepreneur of the Year" by *Inc.* in 1989, "Man of the Year" by *PC Magazine* in 1992, and "CEO of the Year" by *Financial World* in 1993. In 1992, the company was included for the first time among the *Fortune 500* roster of the world's largest companies.

By 1995, with sales of nearly US$3.5 billion, the company was the world's leading direct marketer of personal computers and one of the top five PC vendors in the world. In 1996, Dell supplemented its direct mail and telephone sales by offering its PCs via the Internet at dell.com. By 2001, Dell ranked first in global market share and number one in the United States for shipments of standard Intel architecture servers. The company changed its name to Dell Inc. in 2003 as a way of reflecting the evolution of the company into a diverse supplier of technology products and services. In 2005, Dell topped *Fortune*'s list of "Most Admired Companies." Fiscal year 2005 (Dell's fiscal year ended in early February or late January of the same calendar year) was an outstanding year in which the company earned US$3.6 billion in net income on US$55.8 billion in net revenue.

Soon, however, increasing competition and cost pressures began to erode Dell's margins. Even though the company's net revenue continued to increase to US$57.4 billion in fiscal year 2007 and US$61.1 billion during fiscal year 2008, its net income dropped to US$2.6 billion in 2007, with a slight increase to US$2.9 billion in 2008. The "great recession" of 2008–2009 took its toll on both Dell and the computer industry. Dell's fiscal 2010 (ending January 29, 2010) net income fell further to US$1.4 billion on US$52.9 billion in net revenue. Sales improved during calendar year 2010 as the global economy showed signs of recovery. Net revenue for February through July 2010 increased to US$30.4 billion compared to only US$25.1 billion during the first half of 2009, while first half net income rose to US$886 million in 2010 compared to US$762 million during the same period in 2009. Nevertheless, Dell's net income was only 2.91% of net revenue during the first half of 2010, compared to a much rosier 6.45% during 2006. (Note: Dell's financial reports are available via the company's website at www.dell.com.)

Problems of Early Growth

The company's early rapid growth resulted in disorganization. Sales jumped from US$546 million in fiscal 1991 to US$3.4 billion in 1995. Growth had been pursued to the exclusion of all else, but no one seemed to know how the numbers really added up. When Michael Dell saw that the wheels were beginning to fly off his nine-year-old entrepreneurial venture, he sought older, outside management help. He temporarily slowed the corporation's growth strategy while he worked to assemble and integrate a team of experienced executives from companies like Motorola, Hewlett-Packard, and Apple.

The new executive team worked to get Dell's house in order so that the company could continue its phenomenal sales growth. Management decided in 1995 to abandon distribution of Dell's products through U.S. retail stores and return solely to direct distribution. This enabled the company to refocus Dell's efforts in areas that matched its philosophy of high emphasis on customer support and service. In July 2004, Kevin Rollins replaced Michael Dell as Chief Executive Officer, allowing the founder to focus on being Chairman of the Board. This situation did not last long, however. Rising sales coupled with rapidly falling net income caused Michael Dell to rethink his retirement and resume his role as CEO in January 2007. Although Michael Dell in 2010 owned only 11.7% of the corporation's stock, at age 45 he owned the largest block of stock and continued to be the "heart and soul" of the firm. The rest of the directors and executive officers owned less than 1% of the stock.

Business Model

Dell's original business model was very simple: Dell machines were made to order and delivered directly to the customer. The company had no distributors or retail stores. Dell PCs had consistently been listed among the best PCs on the market by *PCWorld* and *PC Magazine*. Cash flow was never a problem because Dell was paid by customers long before Dell paid its suppliers. The company held virtually no parts inventory. As a result, Dell made computers more quickly and cheaply than any other company.

Dell became the master of process engineering and supply chain management. It spent less on R&D than did Apple or Hewlett-Packard, but focused its spending on improving its manufacturing process. (Dell spent 1% of sales on R&D versus the 5% typically invested by other large computer firms.) Instead of spending its money on new computer technology, Dell waited until a new technology became a standard. Michael Dell explained that soon after a technology product arrived on the market, it was a high-priced, high-margin item made differently by each company. Over time, the technology standardized—the way PCs standardized around Intel microprocessors and Microsoft operating systems. At a certain point between the development of the standard and its becoming a commodity, that technology became ripe for Dell. When the leaders were earning 40% or 50% profit margins, they were vulnerable to Dell making a profit on far smaller margins. Dell drove down costs further by perfecting its manufacturing processes and using its buying power to obtain cheaper parts. Its reduction of overhead expenses to only 9.6% of revenue meant that Dell earned nearly US$1 million in revenue per employee—three times the revenue per employee at IBM and almost twice HP's rate.

Although the company outsourced some operations, such as component production and express shipping, it had its own assembly lines in the United States, Malaysia, China, Brazil, India, and Poland. A North Carolina plant had been opened in 2005 as Dell's third American desktop plant. Cost pressures had, however, caused management to rethink its manufacturing strategy. They closed the company's desktop plants in Texas and Tennessee in 2008 and 2009, respectively, and were planning to close the firm's last desktop assembly plant in North Carolina in January 2011. From then on, desktop assembly for the North American market would take place in Dell's factories in other countries and by contract manufacturers in Asia and Mexico. In Europe, the company closed its Ireland plant and sold its plant in Poland to Foxconn Technology, a unit of Hon Hai, the world's largest contract manufacturer. They then contracted with Foxconn for manufacturing services. In contrast to its global desktop manufacturing strategy, 95% of Dell's notebook computers were assembled in Dell's plants in Malaysia and China.

After its failed experiment with distribution through U.S. retail stores in the 1990s, management again changed its mind regarding its reliance on direct marketing. Over time, Dell's competitors had imitated Dell's direct marketing model, but were also successfully selling through retail outlets. A presence in retail was becoming especially important in countries outside North America. Sales in these countries were often based on the advice of sales staff, putting Dell's "direct only" business model at a disadvantage. In response, Dell began shipping its products in 2007 to major U.S. and Canadian retailers, such as Wal-Mart, Sam's Club, Staples, and Best Buy. This was soon followed by sales elsewhere in the world through DSGI, GOME, and Carrefour, among others, to number over 56,000 outlets worldwide.

Product Line and Structure

Over the years, Dell Inc. has broadened its product line to include not only desktop and laptop (listed under mobility) computers, but also servers, storage systems, printers, software, peripherals, and services, such as infrastructure services. By 2010, net revenue by product line was composed of desktop PCs (25%), mobility (31%), software and peripherals (18%), servers and networking (11%), services (11%), and storage (4%). Desktop PCs' net revenue dropped from 38% in 2006, with each of the other product lines (especially mobility) increasing as a percentage of total revenue. Although the 2010 gross margin for all Dell products was only 14.1% of sales, due to a lower average selling price, the gross margin for services, including software, was a much fatter 33.7%.

Dell's corporate headquarters was located in Round Rock, Texas, near Austin. In 2009, the company was reorganized from a geographic structure into four global business units based on customers: *Large Enterprise*, *Public*, *Small & Medium Business*, and *Consumer*. Its 2010 revenue by segment was 27% from Large Enterprise, 27% from Public, 23% from Small & Medium Business, and 23% from the Consumer unit. Interestingly, operating income as a percentage of total revenue totaled 9% for both Public and Small & Medium Business units,

6% from Large Enterprise, and only 1% from the Consumer unit. Commercial customers accounted for 77% of total revenue. Dell was dependent upon the U.S. market for 53% of its total 2010 revenues.

The Industry Matures

By 2006, the once torrid growth in PC sales had slowed to about 5% a year. Sales fell significantly during the "great recession" of 2008–09 as companies and consumers deferred computer purchases. With the economy improving, the output of U.S. computer manufacturers was forecast to grow at an annual compounded rate of 7% between 2010 and 2015. Nevertheless, margins were getting progressively smaller for the desktop PC, Dell's flagship product. Competitors were becoming increasingly competitive in both desktop and mobile computers.

Gateway, for example, found ways to reduce its costs and fight its way back to profitability. The same was true for Hewlett-Packard (HP) once it had digested its acquisition of Compaq. Asian manufacturers, such as Acer, Toshiba, and Lenovo, with strengths in laptops were becoming major global competitors. Ironically, by driving down supplier costs, Dell also reduced its rivals' costs. In addition, the sales growth in the computer industry was in the consumer market and in emerging countries rather than in the corporate market and developed countries in which Dell sold most of its products. Between 2006 and 2010, HP replaced Dell as the company with the largest global market share in personal computers. Using price reductions, Dell was now battling with Acer for second place in global PC market share.

As the personal computer became more like a commodity, consumers were no longer interested in paying top dollar for a computer unless it was "unique." Wal-Mart and Best Buy were selling basic laptop computers for less than US$300 in 2010 and intended to maintain this pricing so long as manufacturers continued to supply low-cost products. PC notebook sales had been falling during 2010, primarily due to the introduction of Apple's highly featured iPad and the consequent rise in "tablet" PC sales. According to Morgan Stanley, Apple's iPad cannibalized about 25% of PC notebook sales since its introduction in April through August, 2010. Dell countered the iPad with a tablet computer called Streak in May 2010, but failed to generate much enthusiasm or sales for this product.

As corporate buyers increasingly purchased their computer equipment as part of a package of services to address specific problems, service-oriented rivals like IBM, HP, and Oracle had an advantage over Dell. All of these competitors had made large commitments to servers, software, and consulting—all having higher margins than personal computers. IBM had sold its laptop, hard drive, and printer businesses to focus on building its services business. Hewlett-Packard acquired Electronic Data Systems in 2008 to boost its expertise in services. By offering customers a package of servers, software, and storage, HP dominated the server business with 32% market share, with IBM closely following with a 28% share of the market. Oracle's acquisition of Sun Microsystems gave it 8% of the server market. IBM and Oracle offered proprietary server platforms in enterprise accounts. In contrast, Dell (along with HP) offered x86 open-system servers. In order to better compete in the large enterprise market segment, Dell purchased Perot Systems, an IT services company, in 2009. Even after this acquisition, however, services accounted for only 13% of Dell's sales. In 2010, Dell attempted to acquire 2PAR, a data storage firm, but was outbid by HP.

Issues and Strategy

Since 2007, when Michael Dell resumed being the company's CEO, Dell has made more than 10 acquisitions, cut about 10,000 jobs, and hired executives from Motorola and Nike to add more excitement to its product line. Its US$3.6 billion purchase of Perot Systems allowed it to expand into higher-margin computing services. Nevertheless, Dell's stock fell 42% following January 2007, during a period when Hewlett-Packard's stock gained 11% and IBM gained 31%.

The industry's focus shifted from desktop PCs to mobile computing, software, and technology services—areas of relative weakness at Dell. Due to a changing industry, the company's original business model based on direct sales and value chain efficiencies had been abandoned. It was now using the same distribution channels, component providers, and assembly contractors as its competitors. Unfortunately, Dell's emphasis on cost reduction and competitive pricing meant that it was no longer perceived as providing high-quality personal computers or the quality service to go with them. Previously a strength of the company, its customer service rating in 2005 fell to a score of 74 (average for the industry) in a survey by the University of Michigan. Complaints about Dell's service more than doubled in 2005 to 1,533. Although the company successfully worked to improve customer satisfaction by adding more service people, more people meant increased costs and smaller margins.

In order to improve the company's competitive position, Dell's management initiated a three-pronged strategy:

- *Improve the core business* by profitably growing the desktop and mobile computer business and enhancing the online experience for customers. This involved cost-savings initiatives and simplifying product offerings.

- *Shift the portfolio to higher-margin and recurring revenue offerings* by expanding the customer solutions business in servers, storage, services, and software. This involved growing organically as well as through acquisitions.

- *Balance liquidity, profitability, and growth* by maintaining a strong balance sheet with sufficient liquidity to respond to the changing industry. This provided the capability to develop and acquire more capabilities in enterprise products and solutions.

Future Prospects

A number of industry analysts felt that Dell was not well positioned either for a future of low-priced, commodity-like personal computers or one of highly featured innovative digital products like the iPad and iPod. To continue as a major player in the industry, they argued that Dell needed an acquisition similar to HP's US$13.2 billion purchase of EDS in order to compete in business information services. Overall, analysts were ambivalent about the firm's prospects in a changing industry. Should Dell continue with its current strategy of following the consumer market down in price and adjusting its costs accordingly or, like IBM, should it change its focus to more profitable business services, or, like HP, should it try to do both?

CASE 33

Logitech (Mini Case)

Alan N. Hoffman
Bentley University

Company Background

LOGITECH, HEADQUARTERED IN ROMANEL-SUR-MORGES, SWITZERLAND, was the world's leading provider of computer peripherals in 2010. Personal computer peripherals were input and interface devices that were used for navigation, Internet communications, digital music, home-entertainment control, gaming, and wireless devices. Derived from the French word *logiciel*, meaning software, Logitech was originally established as a software development and hardware architecture company by two Stanford graduate students in Apples, Switzerland. Shortly after establishing itself as a quality software development company, Logitech saw a new hardware product opportunity that was emerging in the mid 1980s, the computer mouse. The mouse was standard equipment on the original Macintosh computer launched in January 1984. Logitech viewed the mouse as a growth opportunity and it became a turning point in the company's future. Logitech introduced its first hardware device, the P4 mouse, for users of graphics software. An OEM sales contract with HP followed, and in 1985 it entered the retail market, selling 800 units in the first month.

In July of 1988, Logitech's executives decided to take the company public to help finance its rapid growth. Then, in the early 1990s, while facing increasingly strong competition in the mouse business, Logitech identified a larger market opportunity for computer peripherals and began growing its business beyond the mouse. In the next few years, Logitech introduced products such as (1) computer keyboards, (2) a digital still camera, (3) a headphone/microphone, (4) a joystick gaming peripheral, and (5) a Web camera on a flexible arm. While these new products were being introduced under the Logitech name, the company also continued innovation in its core mouse business. New and revolutionary technologies that were being developed by Logitech allowed it to continue to be an industry leader in the mouse and keyboard business.

In the mid-1990s, the PC market exploded due to the popularity of the Internet and new home/office software applications. This growth of the PC industry created demand for the peripheral products that Logitech produced. The Internet allowed computer users to access new areas such as music, video, communications, and gaming. From this point forward, Logitech continued to grow both organically and through acquisition as new opportunities arose to expand its portfolio of products.

Between 1998 and 2006, Logitech made a number of significant acquisitions to expand its product portfolio. It acquired companies such as Connectix for its line of webcams, Labtec for its audio business presence, Intrigue Technologies for its "Harmony" remote controls, and Slim Devices for its music systems. All of these acquisitions were done strategically to help Logitech position itself in all aspects of the personal computer peripherals world.

In addition to growing significantly through strategic acquisitions, Logitech also continued to innovate and grow its core business. It made significant innovations in the area of cordless mice and keyboards and also introduced the industry's first retail pointing device with Bluetooth wireless technology. It then expanded its Bluetooth technology to many other products in the digital world, such as cordless gaming controllers and a personal digital pen.

Logitech provided consumers with cutting-edge innovation while maintaining its product quality. It maintained its product leadership by combining continued innovation, award-winning industrial design, and excellent price performance with core technologies such as wireless, media-rich communications, and digital entertainment.

Competitors

Within the specialized personal peripherals industry, Logitech had three major competitors: Creative Technology Ltd., Microsoft Corporation, and Royal Philips Electronics N.V.

Creative Technology Ltd. was one of the worldwide leaders in digital entertainment products for the personal computer (PC) and the Internet. Creative Technology was founded in Singapore in 1981, with the vision that multimedia would revolutionize the way people interact with their PCs. The product line offered by Creative Technology included MP3 players, portable media centers, multimedia speakers and headphones, digital and Web cameras, graphics solutions, revolutionary music keyboards, and PC peripherals. Creative had a net profit margin of (−29.58%) in FY 2009 and (−32.82%) in the first quarter of 2010.

Microsoft Corporation provided software and hardware products and solutions worldwide. Founded in 1975 by Bill Gates and Paul Allen, Microsoft's core business was to create operating systems and computer software applications. Microsoft expanded into markets such as mice, keyboards, video game consoles, customer relationship management applications, server and storage software, and digital music players. In FY 2009, Microsoft Corporation had annual sales of US$58.4 billion and a net income of US$14.5 billion.

Royal Philips Electronics was a Netherlands-based company that focused on improving people's lives through innovation. Philips was a well-diversified company with products in many different businesses: consumer electronics, televisions, VCRs, DVD players, and fax machines, as well as light bulbs, electric shavers and other personal care appliances, medical systems, and silicon systems solutions. With this diversified portfolio of products, Royal Philips had FY 2009 revenues of US$30.76 billion and a gross profit of US$11.59 billion.

Logitech was the only company exclusively focused on personal computer peripheral products, whereas all of its competitors had products and resources invested in a variety of other industries as well.

Trends

Logitech implemented a strategy of innovation, mixed with strategic acquisitions, to enhance its products with the technologies and software of other companies in order to create the safest, most advanced, innovative, and collaborative experience for its customers. As Logitech had always been on the forefront of mouse and keyboard technology, it had also been a leader in videoconferencing technology since the early stages of the Logitech mountable computer camera.

From 1998–2004, Logitech made many important strategic acquisitions in order to enhance future portfolios and expand the depth of the peripheral product lines. Its first acquisition was the video camera division, QuickCam PC, of Connectix Corporation. This led to an influx of peripherals such as cameras and wireless cameras, and served as a very early introduction to the current videoconferencing division of Logitech. The second successful acquisition for Logitech was Labtec Inc., an audio peripheral maker, in 2001. Following this acquisition, with a hunger to expand product focus, Logitech acquired Intrigue Technologies Inc. in 2004. This acquisition positioned Logitech as a leader in advanced remote control–making, allowing peripherals to accommodate more than just computer and video game uses. This positioned it for its next acquisition—Slim Devices, a manufacturer of music systems—in 2006. Logitech used these acquisitions to expand its multibusiness unit corporation into a diverse and specialized company appealing to a large group of technology users. Finally, with its acquisition of Paradial AS, Logitech was able to combine its peripheral products with the software, video effects, and security features of Paradial. This allowed Logitech to deliver a complete and intuitive HD videoconferencing experience for companies of any size.

Future industry trends revolved around content strategy and consumer expectations of the mobile Web and smartphone applications. Content strategy involved decisions about what information/features to incorporate into a product, including those that provided the most benefit or fulfilled the most needs—anything else was just noise and diluted the product. In terms of the mobile Web and smartphone application trends, Logitech had three options: (1) develop closed partnerships with specific platforms (iPhone or BlackBerry); (2) produce apps (applications) for each platform; or (3) produce "platform-neutral" apps by using the mobile Web.

Global Presence

As the global economy has expanded and become more reliant on technology, Logitech has seen an increase in the desire for ease of use when it comes to portable computers, games, and videoconferencing technology. Logitech has consistently expanded its product offerings to satisfy this growing demand for computer peripherals. In FY 2009, 85% of its revenue came from retail sales of peripheral products such as mice, keyboards, speakers, webcams, headsets, headphones, and notebook stands. Logitech has also seen global demand sharpen for devices designed for specific purposes such as gaming, digital music, multimedia, audio and visual communication over the Internet, and PC-based video security. The company's products combined essential core technologies, continued innovation, award-winning industrial design, and excellent value that were necessary to come out on top of a rapidly changing and evolving technological industry. Since its inception in 1981 in Apples, Switzerland, Logitech has been a growing player in the technological product market and distributed products to over 100 different countries.

For Logitech, opportunities arose as the desire for global communication did. The trend of wireless and portable communication, such as Skype and Apple's Facetime, has opened up a window of opportunity for new and more advanced products to enable video communication and conferencing.

As computers age, Logitech has been able to sell add-on peripherals to users who want to add newer applications to their older computers. It has sold products at the end of the product life cycle such as mice and keyboards and generated profits to fund new product development like the new Logitech Revue with Google TV. As its consumers became more globally conscious and connected, Logitech was able to tailor its products toward the many uses of video communication and high-speed Internet capabilities.

Logitech created a global presence and reputation for its brand and products. In 2009, Logitech's sales were distributed globally with 45.3% in the Eastern Europe, Middle East, and North Africa regions; 35.6% in the Americas; and 19.1% in the Asia Pacific region. By expanding its presence globally, Logitech became the leading provider of personal peripherals in the world. In addition to being an innovator in its industry, Logitech has also maintained reasonably priced products as well. In 2009, 67% of its sales stemmed from products that were priced less than US$60. This innovative mindset, in addition to reasonable prices, has also contributed to large sales and, in the end, Logitech's good financial health as a company.

Finance

The recession in 2008–09 hit Logitech's business hard. For fiscal year 2010, sales were US$2.0 billion, down from US$2.2 billion in fiscal 2009. Operating income was US$78 million, down from US$110 million the previous year. Net income was US$65 million (US$0.36 per share), compared to US$107 million (US$0.59 per share) in the prior year. Gross margin for fiscal 2010 was 31.9% compared to 31.3% in fiscal 2009. As a result of the economic downturn, Logitech found it necessary to restructure its workforce. In early 2009, Logitech reduced its salaried workforce globally by 15%.

Logitech's stock price spiked to US$40 in late 2007, as a result of record sales and profits from its successful launch of iPod-capable peripherals. Its iPod peripherals—speakers, docks, and headphones—made the increasingly popular iPod easier to use.

In 2009, Logitech's operating margin was 5.15%, far below its 2007 high of 12% due to increasing price competition.

It did not issue dividends to shareholders so it could reinvest its net income back into research and development and product advertising, as well as have moneys available for strategic acquisitions, thus causing a continuous cycle.

Logitech outlined specific financial objectives it sought to reach. It wanted to achieve sales growth between 13% and 19% and a gross margin between 32% and 34%. Logitech also intended to invest 5% of its sales revenue in R&D and 12%–14% in marketing. By continuously investing resources in research and development, Logitech took a strategic approach to maintaining long-term growth and profitability.

Operations

One of the initial weaknesses that Logitech faced regarding operations was that it had numerous manufacturing locations dispersed throughout the world. The problem with having so many locations was that these facilities were not cost effective. Many of its plants were located in countries where it was expensive to operate and the labor costs for qualified employees was high. Logitech saw that, in the early 1990s, the personal computer industry was becoming increasingly competitive. Having recognized this, Logitech made two primary operations decisions that allowed it to increase its competitiveness. First, it consolidated manufacturing, which was once widely dispersed in China. This allowed the company to maintain lower prices on its products and increase its competitiveness. In addition to its China manufacturing facilities, Logitech established a second center for R&D, located in Cork, Ireland, a prime location for innovation in the technology and IT sectors. This resolved the issue of Logitech having several expensive locations by instead moving into fewer, more cost-effective facilities. In addition to moving manufacturing, Logitech also knew its category was changing and that it would no longer be able to compete by only manufacturing computer mice. Therefore, Logitech expanded its product line beyond the mouse and introduced a variety of products including a handheld scanner, Fotoman (a digital camera), Audioman (a speaker/microphone), and Wingman (the first gaming peripheral).

These operational decisions not only helped Logitech remain innovative and competitive within the industry, but also positioned it for success during the personal computing industry boom in the mid- to late 1990s, when the Internet and online industries took off. Logitech, known as a leading personal peripheral provider, was both innovative, with more than 130 personal computer peripheral products, and reasonably priced. When the PC industry jumped into high gear, Logitech was already established as an industry leader and its sales soared.

It was also a leader in the wireless peripherals sector. By following consumer trends, Logitech saw the personal peripherals sector was moving into a new digital era, where wireless peripherals was on the rise. In light of this, Logitech created an entirely new product category with the Logitech Cordless Desktop, a wireless mouse and keyboard bundle. By staying on top of consumer trends, Logitech sold over 100 million cordless mice and keyboards.

The Changing Landscape Ahead

Logitech became a leader in computer peripherals by developing innovative products and focusing on the consumer's experience. Between 2007 and 2010 alone, Logitech received 11 different awards for 19 products in 14 categories. In a market that was saturated with deep-pocketed competitors such as Microsoft and Philips, Logitech used innovation as its means of survival.

In 2010, Logitech faced a significant challenge in that the way that people interacted with its devices was changing. The iPhone and iPad used touchscreen technology with built-in accelerometers, eliminating the need for mice and trackpads. Secondly, cameras and higher-quality speakers became standard equipment built into the iPhone, iPad, and Windows laptop computers. In fact, Apple introduced the "magic pad" to replace the mouse altogether. And so the need for consumers to buy add-on peripherals was slowly evaporating as more of these peripherals became standard equipment designed into new mobile technologies.

Logitech could see its peripherals market beginning to disintegrate before its own eyes. Because of this, the company needed to decide if it should invest more in videoconferencing and television all-in-one remote controls and/or focus on developing partnerships with computer and telecom manufacturers and mobile carriers such as AT&T, Verizon, T-Mobile, and Sprint. Once again, the computer industry was changing and Logitech needed to formulate diversification strategies to ensure its long-term survival.

CASE 34

Daktronics (A): The U.S. Digital Signage Industry in 2010

Joseph Kavanaugh
Sam Houston State University

Joshua Warne and Carol J. Cumber
South Dakota State University

The U.S. signage industry is almost as old as organized urban commerce in the colonies. The earliest signs were associated with taverns and coffeehouses. Tradesmen identified their shops with pictorial signage representing their trade or the product offered. Names painted above entryways were augmented by protruding signs (most often of wood—barber poles, wooden Indians) that identified the establishment, although such signage was largely confined to on-premises signs. Printed handbills announcing auctions, stagecoach timetables, and traveling theatrical groups appeared as early as the middle of the eighteenth century, but it was another century before the outdoor advertising industry gained major impetus from the colorful posters of Phineas Taylor Barnum who first used them in the mid-1800's to advertise his circus.[1] Later, with the growth of the American highway system, the industry evolved from such early shop signage and posters into the development of roadside signage for promoting approaching services and general products. From Burma Shave and Mail Pouch Tobacco[2] to an array of services (e.g., food, lodging, gasoline, and attractions), America's roadsides were embellished (apologies to Lady Bird Johnson)[3] with signage targeting the needs of the traveler.

Eventually these signs were lighted, creating the first major segmentation of the market—electrified versus other forms of print signage. Luminous tube, fluorescent lamp, and incandescent bulb signs evolved as the market developed and retailers, manufacturers, and others sought more and better ways to identify their facilities, products, and services, and communicate their marketing message.

Copyright © 2012 by the *Case Research Journal* and the authors. The authors developed this industry note for class discussion rather than to illustrate either effective or ineffective handling of the situation. The industry note was presented at the North American Case Research Association Annual Meeting on October 29, 2010, in Gatlinburg, Tennessee. This project was made possible with financial support via a NACRA case research grant and South Dakota State University.

Driven by new technologies in microprocessors, graphics software, digital controllers, wireless communications, and low-energy Liquid Crystal Display (LCD) and Light Emitting Diode (LED) light sources,[4] by the turn of the twenty-first century the latest evolution in the industry was the emergence of digital signage.

The digital signage industry came into being to meet the emerging commercial and communications need for more dynamic messaging. It was a nexus between two industries—those who manufactured the equipment and those who created the messaging content. Together, they created an industry that provided instantaneous messaging at the speed of light.

In 2010, the market was a technically complex, multi-product, multi-segment, multi-channel, highly fragmented market with few dominant firms, rapidly evolving technologies, and relatively low entry barriers for many parts of the industry. Those firms that emerged as dominant competitors tended to have higher levels of vertical integration, greater financial strength, and broader product lines; served multiple segments; and had the design and engineering capabilities to provide high-level product customization. These capabilities enabled them to meet the demands of top-tier customers with challenging product requirements for one-of-a-kind installations like sports stadiums, large-venue advertising such as Times Square (New York), and major communications/display installations such as the Beijing Olympic Games. Increased capabilities in design, product engineering, fabrication, and technology integration led to broader and more diversified product lines and the ability to meet demanding customer requirements in multiple market segments.

The U.S. Digital Signage Industry

The emerging digital signage industry represented the nexus (intersection) between two established industries, the Billboard and Sign Manufacturing industry (NAICS code 33995) and the Billboard and Outdoor Display Advertising industry (NAICS code 54185). The first focused primarily on manufacturing hardware (e.g., paper and digital display outdoor billboards often viewed along highways, in-store digital displays, and electronic price signs at your local gas station) while the second established industry focused on the development of content—the actual words, images, and graphics that convey the advertiser's message. Companies that competed in the digital signage industry integrated hardware and content to deliver digital messaging to consumer markets that sought rapidly changing information. The advertising industry often referred to these markets as the digital-out-of-home (DOOH) market, while manufacturers referred to their products as digital signage or messaging systems. The industry was not uniform in its language and many terms were used interchangeably: out-of-home advertising; billboard, sign manufacturing, and advertising display; digital signage; DOOH; outdoor and display advertising; outdoor advertising; and billboard and sign manufacturing were often used contextually to represent the same essential elements of the industry: 1) content that delivered the message; 2) the hardware through which it was displayed; and 3) the integration of the two.

Overview of Industry Structure

The structure of the industry in 2010 is presented in **Exhibit 1**. Each manufacturer faced choices about how to "go to market" and which application segments of the market they wished to target. Generally, large projects were sold direct to the final customer or through partners or national accounts (franchises or companies with multiple locations). Smaller applications were sold through resellers or integrators who delivered turnkey installations to their clients. Resellers included advertising and marketing firms; integrators included consultants, architects, engineers and project managers. End user market segments (also called "verticals") ranged from retailing, transportation, and advertising/messaging, to entertainment/sports venues.

EXHIBIT 1 Structure of the U.S. Digital Signage Industry in 2010

Producer		Company		
Distributor	Resellers: Advertising and Marketing Companies	Integrators: Consultants, Architects, Engineers, and Project Managers	Company Direct, Partners or National Accounts	
End User	Entertainment Venues	Commercial Indoor/Outdoor Advertising	Transportation	Mobile and Modular	Other

Exhibit produced by authors.

Product and Market Segments

Table 1 outlines some of the applications for which digital signs could be used in the different market segments. For each application end users could choose from a variety of different products available from a multitude of vendors. The table illustrates the market's complexity with many products and segments in 2010.

In addition to the market, products were also complex. A digital sign had several essential elements all of which came from a different set of vendors: the plasma, LED, or LCD screen; a player, either a small computer or digital controller; software that configured the image and drove display of the content; content of the message; and peripherals related to the

TABLE 1 Examples of Applications with Digital Signage Market Segments
Market Segments

Entertainment Venues	Commercial Indoor/Outdoor Advertising	Transportation	Mobile and Modular	Other
Large sports stadiums	Convenience and retail stores	Airports and aviation	Concerts and staging	Campus communications
Small sports venues	Financial, medical, and pharmacies	Mass transit (railways and buses)	Auto shows	Control rooms and simulators
Amusement and theme parks	Restaurants, gaming, and hospitality	Freeways, tollways and roadways	Festivals and sporting events	Manufacturing
Cinemas and theatres	Billboards	Fixed gighway signs	Award shows	Landmarks and spectaculars
Fairs and expos	Shopping, civic, and convention centers	Parking	Trade shows	
Performing arts	Auto dealers			
Casinos	Worship			

SOURCE: Table produced by authors.

installation of the sign. All of these components were acquired by the system integrator which assembled the sign package, installed it, and might provide after-sale service and support. For the sign to work it had to be able to communicate with a network source via cable or wireless connectivity to receive the digital signal provided by content specialists who designed the messaging—text, graphics, photos, streaming video—that were the actual set of images displayed on the sign.[5]

Because of these complexities, employing an experienced vendor, preferably with industry-specific knowledge, added significant value.[6] For this reason, many of the industry-leading firms sought higher levels of vertical integration where they could better control quality and the total end-user interface.

International Market

Because of the bulky size and weight of large digital signs, relatively few were either exported or imported. Fabrication generally occurred within the region where the product would be installed. In 2010 imports represented only 1.8% of domestic demand, while exports accounted for only 0.8% of industry revenue. However, U.S. sign manufacturers sometimes outsourced production to firms in foreign countries by sending design requirements and orders electronically, which reduced turnaround time and limited production problems.[7]

The two largest markets were the U.S. and China, half a world away from one another, suggesting that any significant market penetration would necessitate in-country fabrication and installation. Design, engineering, and content could still be handled in the home country of the manufacturer.

From 2005 to 2008 digital display was the fastest growing segment of the Chinese advertising market with a compound growth rate of 80%, from 1.1 billion Yuan in 2005 to 6.53 billion Yuan in 2008. VisionChina, the leading operator of outdoor digital TV advertising networks in China, grew 2008 revenues by over 250% and profits grew almost 400%.[8] China overtook the United States in 2008 as the top digital signage consumer as it prepared for the 2008 Olympics.[9] China had the most site deployments, while the United States still led in advertising dollars committed to digital signage.[10] Besides China, other major international markets for digital-out-of-home (DOOH) advertising included the UK, Japan, France, Germany, and Russia.[11] In early July 2009 Samsung Electronics Co. announced that it was entering Japan's market for digital signs with 46-inch ultra-high definition (UD) LCD panels.[12]

A major industry analyst observed in September 2009 that "digital signage networks tend to be country or region-specific. . . . Each major region also tends to have its own set of solution leaders . . . (T)echnology winners will emerge and be defined by major geographic marketplaces: North America, Europe, Asia, Australia, South America and Africa."[13] To emerge as a global leader would require consolidation of a home market first. According to the same analyst, "True globalization will likely be fueled by entry of truly global entities."[14]

Emergence of the Industry

Sony introduced the "Jumbotron," based on cathode ray technology (CRT), at the 1985 International Science and Technology Expo. By 1989, Sony moved to LED technology when it installed the then-largest screen in Toronto's SkyDome. Daktronics, the industry's current market leader, was founded in 1968 and installed its first digital billboard in 2001. Over the next decade, the industry grew rapidly driven by developments in technology, visibility of high-profile installations, and the changing needs of the various industry "verticals" (end user market segments). Industry technical standards evolved, as did the ability to measure the impact of investment in digital signage.

2001–2007

In the early years, growth in the billboard and sign manufacturing industry was driven by commercial construction (especially retail); outdoor advertising expenditures; improvements in technology, especially the advent of plasma, LED, and LCD digital technologies; and the rate at which retailers and others adopted digital signage for information and promotional purposes. For the period 2001–2007, annual outdoor advertising expenditures in the U.S. grew from $5.56 billion to $7.77 billion.[15] Of this, the digital portion (DOOH advertising) was estimated to be $2.43 billion.[16]

The industry also faced major issues during this early stage, including the plethora of competing technology options available and the difficulty of proving return on investment (ROI) in network development and deployment. The array of competing technology options available was a substantial challenge to system integrators, and made system integration a key to any sustainable business model.[17] Aggregators helped unify technology platforms as dominant technologies emerged. In turn, the establishment of industry standards for communications protocols further enhanced the confidence of those timid to invest in emerging technologies.

A proprietary market research survey assessed the market status of digital displays in 2007 and their future potential. The sites surveyed were used primarily for "third-party advertising in an ambience of consumption, locations where people are required to wait, and locations where people are in transit."[18] According to this survey, the number of screens deployed at each site averaged three to four, ranging from ten to twenty-five per location for retail establishments to one to eight for hotels, pubs and bars; and one to five for healthcare sites. The number of sites at the end of 2007 was 300,000+, projected to grow to 850,000, while advertising revenue from digital signage was estimated at $1.1 billion, projected to grow to $2.7 billion by the end of 2013. The greatest concentration of digital displays was in the United States, followed by Asia, Australia, Canada, Europe, the former Soviet Union, and parts of Latin America. Retail accounted for 29% of the sites and 71% of the revenue. Hospitality, healthcare, and transportation were also important verticals.

2008

By 2008 digital signage had become a major segment of the billboard and sign manufacturing industry[19] As **Table 2** shows, digital signage was estimated to be $2.86 billion (23.8% of industry revenue of $12.1 billion dollars).[20] This revenue was not highly concentrated. The four largest firms accounted for approximately 11.2% of sign manufacturing revenue whereas the eight largest firms summed only to 15% of revenue.[21]

According to a 2008 study conducted by Multimedia Intelligence, retail, transportation, and restaurants/bars were the three largest digital signage verticals, while education and corporate communications were making impressive gains.[22] Other segments of significance were corporate, healthcare, transportation, entertainment, and hospitality.[23]

Advancements in technology resulting in declining costs was a major factor in development of the DOOH segment and helped account for the segment's resistance to the 2008 down

TABLE 2	Billboard and Sign Manufacturing in the U.S. in 2008

Industry Segments and Percentages of Revenues						
Non-electric printed signs 33.2%	Digital signs 23.8%	Non-electric screen printed signs 14.0%	Luminous tube signs 13.3%	Fluorescent lamp signs 10.8%	Incandescent lamp signs 4.9%	Total revenues (billions) $12.1

SOURCE: IBIS *World* Billboard & Sign Manufacturing in the U.S. 33995, July, 2008.

turn in overall advertising expenditures. Other factors that were driving the global digital signage market included urbanization and the growth of retail spaces, flourishing tourism, people spending more time out of their homes, and huge investments in the transportation infrastructure for outdoor advertising in emerging markets.[24]

Expertise in measuring advertising impact was advancing; for example, one study established that a relatively high percentage of all adults (62%) were aware of advertising on digital signs, but the results were even more effective when targeted to specific life patterns. More college students noticed this media (75%), while 59% of Hispanics versus 48% of the general adult population found the advertising entertaining. Such studies established the basis for highly targeted marketing and were critical for preparing ROI estimates based on advertising efectiveness.[25]

2009

In early 2009, the largest digital sign installed in the U.S. was at Walgreen's Times Square location. It was 17,000 square feet in surface, comprised thirteen interconnected plasma screens, and rose to 340 feet. Additionally, thirteen digital signs at street level offered a wide range of advertising options for Walgreen's suppliers. Each hour of programmed content contained 30 minutes of paid advertising and 30 minutes of Walgreen's promotions and Times Square nostalgia.[26]

National sports also provided great visibility for the industry as broadcasters highlighted the "wow" factors of the Dallas Cowboys' new stadium in Arlington, Texas, that opened fall 2009. In addition to the largest HD screen to date, the Stadium Vision installation by Cisco included nearly 3000 digital signage screens throughout the complex that delivered "entertainment, pre-event, in-event, and post-event, using video and content, such as out-of-town games and scores, trivia, weather, track and news, in addition to the action on the field,"[27] all controlled by internal IT infrastructure. Stadiums in New York, Miami, Kansas City, and many in Europe received similar Stadium Vision installations in 2009. The trend was projected to continue as fan expectations escalated for a total entertainment experience.[28] It was no longer just about the game on the field; the total multi-media environment within the stadium elevated the fan experience to a higher level. Industry observers saw that the future would belong to equipment manufacturers and content providers who could continuously enhance the product and meet or exceed ever-increasing fan expectations.

Another notable development was greater continuity between the digital screen and the other four screens (cinema, TV, PC, and mobile) with interactivity possible.[29] As an example, the nation's first free, over-the-air broadcast of mobile digital television to the public was launched in April 2009, a collaboration between Harris Corporation and WRAL, Raleigh, N.C. Raleigh bus riders with a lot of "dwell time"[30] could watch monitors with hyper-local content that changed depending on their location in the city; and they could interact via their mobile phones.[31] More such interactions of digital signage and mobile were on the way.[32]

Industry standards were further solidified in 2009 when the industry's first comprehensive training and certification program exclusively for the installation and support of digital signage was launched.[33]

The overall outdoor and display advertising industry was affected significantly by the recession in 2008 and 2009. Estimates were that 2009 revenues declined 11.6% to $6.29 billion.[34] However, the DOOH sector outperformed the signage industry as a whole, growing 25% in 2009, as it approached its one millionth networked screen. The 4Q2009 North American digital signage industry index, a major industry performance measure, rose by 10.8%, reflecting increased firm revenue, screens deployed, the number of DOOH networks, and increased capital expenditures and employment.[35]

The emergence of digital signage, both indoor and outdoor, was changing the economics of the advertising industry. DOOH required much higher front-end investment but yielded lower long-term operating costs than traditional signage media. And this medium had only begun to penetrate the advertising market. For instance, of Lamar Advertising's 159,000 billboards, only an estimated 1100 were digital in 2009. Although there would be reduced direct labor costs in changing displays at these sites, other maintenance costs associated with the displays would likely increase. Some of these costs were recouped through higher demand and, therefore, higher prices commanded by these sites. Additional savings would be realized from reduced printing and installation costs.[36]

2010

Among the 2010 trends foreseen by industry observers were the continuing emergence of content, progress in the development of industry content standards, and the continuing shift of investors and advertising dollars as new ad-based networks proliferated. Software for managing content continued in its development as advertisers sought to better target micro-markets.[37]

In February 2010, the tenth convention of the industry's largest trade show, the Digital Signage Expo, had over 3400 participants. Reflective of an emerging industry, 56 of the estimated 200 trade booths that showcased their products and services were first-time exhibitors.[38] Only a few were recognizable multinational firms (Mitsubishi, Hyundai, Intel, Philips, Samsung, Sharp, and Sony) but these had already established a position in this young industry.

Manufacturers of digital signs and the peripherals required to run them were only a portion of the industry. The driver of the industry was the content providers who designed the messages that filled these signs for various locations—point-of-purchase, point-of-dwell, in-store promotional screens, digital networks, and outdoor advertising. The key to this marketing medium was the development of networks of signs linked by cable or wirelessly to servers that delivered content across the network—within a store or across an entire franchise system. Examples operational by 2010 were Walgreen's exterior signage, Wal-Mart TV, and numerous fast-food franchisers that offered content through their own in-store network of digital screens.[39]

While some content providers sought to compete as cutting edge video and graphic designers (e.g., Scala, MiniComm), others like RedPost, a Goshen, Indiana company, saw a whole new opportunity at the low end of the market. Using digital signs as bulletin boards, its products enabled local independent retailers and business owners who could not afford sophisticated installations to manage content through web-based software. For menu boards, employee announcements, in-store promotions, and other simple content, the systems included basic text and graphic packages and were easily managed.[40]

Another industry trend was the emergence of companies that could provide complete end-to-end solutions rather than customers having to rely on aggregators to assemble the technology platform; content providers for video, graphics, and text; installers to put the system in place; and others for after-installation service and support. Wireless Ronin Technologies, which specialized in menu signage for food installations at places such as stadiums, was one example of a firm that provided a complete turnkey digital signage system that could be managed from one central location. Its services included consulting, creative development, project management, installation, and training.[41]

Many industry insiders suggested that 2010 would be the tipping point for the industry. High growth, increased advertising revenues, standardization of communications protocols, the continued growth in the number of industry participants and associations, and merger and acquisition activity constrained by the recession suggested that the industry was approaching its next stage of development.[42] Market evidence suggested so as well, as major players who had been sitting on the edge of the industry appeared to be ready to enter the market in much bigger ways. Dell, IBM, Cisco, Oracle, and others were preparing new digital platforms or software, not to mention Google (which had patents pending) and Microsoft who had been absent from the market thus far.[43] Some analysts believed the "table was set" in the industry for an infusion of serious investment capital and the entry of major technology leaders with global reach.[44]

Environment of the U.S. Digital Signage Industry in 2010

Significant factors determining the industry environment in 2010 included its suppliers, technologies, political and regulatory context, and the economic outlook.

Suppliers

In 2010, with the exception of the LED light source, the resources needed to create digital signs were available abundantly either locally or regionally. These included aluminum or steel sheet metal, plastics, semiconductors, circuits, wiring, and hardware. Screen types including liquid crystal, plasma, and other fluorescent light were also abundant. Content providers were also plentiful.

It was a time of transition for the industry as manufacturers began to produce digital signs with plastic cases rather than steel. Design advantages of plastic included its abundance, durability, lower cost, and lower weight than metal, making plastic cases easier and less expensive to transport. It was also easy for manufacturers to work with suppliers on standard and custom design specifications like abstract shapes.

By 2010 LED was becoming the preferred light source for digital signs and other peripherals. It was also being used to backlight LCD screens as well as for indoor and outdoor lighting solutions. LEDs offered manufacturers and end users dynamic lighting that was durable, long-lasting, bright, and energy efficient.

While LED demand was projected to be 20% to 30% greater than supply in 2010, LED supply was expected to grow rapidly[45] Taiwan and China were the largest producers and expected to expand along with manufacturers in Japan, India, and Russia. **Table 3** shows the number of fabricators in 2010. The production output of many of these fabricators was not scheduled to come on line until 2012. Some industry analysts expected even more global firms to enter the LED supply chain and help alleviate the bottleneck, improve productivity, and bring down costs.

Technologies

Digital signage powered with LED or LCD lights stood in contrast to the broad billboard and signage industry, where the level of technology development was low and the preference of the industry's customers was for traditional billboard advertising at much lower cost.[46] Digital displays cost more and depreciated faster than traditional billboards. IBIS*World* reported that

TABLE 3	Global Dedicated LED Fabricators in 2010
Global Region	**# of Fabricators**
North America	4
Europe	4
China	22
Korea	7
Japan	11
Taiwan	36
Southeast Asia	2

SOURCE: SEMI® Opto/LED Fab Watch Database, March 2010.

"digital billboards need to be replaced about every five years at an estimated cost of $250,000 per unit."[47]

Digital billboards offered numerous advantages over traditional billboards despite their higher cost. Their messages could be changed constantly; they could be made interactive with the cell phones of passersby; and they were backlit for greater nighttime visibility—all features that were projected to command rate premiums from advertisers.[48]

A negative factor was that digital signage required a power source and would demand more power as the industry expanded. The positive side was that the messaging could be changed instantaneously without the need to print new billboards, flyers, newspapers, and other forms of messaging that consumed paper stock as a medium and power for machines to produce them.

Some new technologies under development that would continue to enhance the value proposition of digital signage included:

- GPS modems that instantly updated billboards on buses and cars.

- LED billboards that used Bluetooth and infrared technology to display multiple messages during the course of a day.

- Interactive billboards that sent messages directly to cell phones with product offers.

- Billboards utilizing scanning technology that could identify consumers' gender to further tailor advertising.[49]

- Technology innovation based on wireless penetration, 3D, holographic displays, and touch screen.[50]

Political and Regulatory Environment

Outdoor advertising was subject to governmental regulation at the federal, state, and local levels. Visual pollution from signs along highways had long been a concern. Regulations generally restricted the size, spacing, lighting, and other aspects of advertising structures and posed significant impediments to expansion in many markets. Federal law, principally the Highway Beautification Act of 1965 (the "HBA"), regulated outdoor advertising on Federal Aid Primary, Interstate, and National Highway Systems roads. The HBA required states to "effectively control" outdoor advertising along these roads, and mandated a state compliance program and state standards regarding size, spacing, and lighting. All states had passed billboard control statutes and regulations at least as restrictive as the federal requirements.

Municipal and county governments generally also had sign controls as part of their zoning laws and building codes. Using federal funding for transportation enhancement programs, state governments in the past had purchased and removed billboards for beautification, and might do so again in the future. Since digital billboards had only been developed and introduced into the market on a large scale within the past five years, existing regulations that did not apply to them in 2010 could be revised in the future to impose greater restrictions, potentially because of concerns over aesthetics or driver safety.[51]

As external digital signage became more prevalent, regulation at the local level[52] had heated up as people reacted to the intrusive brightness of nighttime digital signage, and the potential negative impact on urban aesthetics and traffic safety[53] A July 2010 article in *Planning* magazine addressed the issue of community response to digital signage and its potential as a traffic hazard, noting that "Los Angeles, El Paso, and St. Louis had adopted moratoria, and outright bans had been enacted against such signs in Maine; Vermont; Montana; Pima County, Arizona; Amarillo, Texas; Durham, North Carolina; Knoxville, Tennessee, and Denver, Colorado. Surely, since then, other municipalities have followed."[54] However, other studies, conducted in Cleveland, OH and Rochester, NY, by the Outdoor Advertising Association of

America, found that "not only was there no correlation between signs and accidents, traffic accidents decreased by 4% within a half-mile radius of the signs."[55]

More positively, the industry made major contributions to enhancing the infrastructure of the nation's transportation system. Local, state, and federal agencies were the primary operators of the country's transportation network. Highways, airports, and local transit systems (bus, train, subway) all required signage and increasingly were using digital messaging systems to alert passengers and drivers to changing conditions (e.g., changes in schedule, lane closings, traffic conditions, and Amber alerts).[56]

Economic Outlook

The U.S. economy was predicted to show signs of recovery in 2010 as reflected in **Table 4**. Economists anticipated that as disposable income rose, consumers would spend more money on the goods and services which the industry's clients advertised. As corporate profits rose, companies would allot more money to advertising and the industry would return to growth. Although modest recovery was expected in 2010, strong signs of improvement would not be seen until 2011, when the economic and operating environment was forecasted to be more robust.

Overall, the billboard and sign manufacturing industry was projected to grow to $13.3 billion by 2015, an average annualized rate of 2.9%. During the outlook period (2010–2014), out-of-home advertising was forecasted to increase as a proportion of total media expenditure while traditional media (e.g., newspapers and television) continued to decline. The Internet and social media networks made it harder to reach a mass audience, leaving outdoor advertising as one of the few ways to do so. An increase in digital display advertising accounted for much of the revenue growth projected for the outlook period. Advancements in digital technology would make digital displays more affordable and efficient, increasing their profitability.[57] Following the recession, expenditures from 2010–2015 for outdoor advertising were expected to grow from $6.3 billion to $8.1 billion based on increased corporate profits, increased total media expenditures, and overall performance as the economy recovered and consumer sentiment improved. It was the fastest growing segment of the advertising industry.[58]

Trends that would drive domestic demand included the continuing replacement of luminous and fluorescent signage with digital signage; the upgrading of stadium signage and scoreboards to better LED, LCD, or plasma technologies; and the increased use of digital signage for messaging by business and many other types of organizations. Profitability would continue to improve due to restraint of prices in supply markets, increased margins associated with more technologically advanced products, and an increased level of customization achievable with digital technologies that could deliver higher-valued solutions to customers' signage needs.[59]

	TABLE 4	Economic Factors Outlook for the U.S.: 2010 to 2014		
Year	Dollars Per Capita Disposable Income	Percent Growth	Index of Consumer Sentiment	Percent Growth
2010	29,296	1.4	71.9	13.6
2011	30,087	2.7	80.5	12.0
2012	30,840	2.5	86.4	7.3
2013	31,611	2.5	86.9	0.6
2014	32,369	2.4	89.0	2.4

SOURCE: IBIS *World,* 2009.

However, industry growth would continue to be hampered by government controls on the number, location and content of outdoor displays. Increased demands from environmental groups to reduce billboards on highways would continue to inhibit growth. Furthermore, an increased proportion of clients' marketing budgets targeted toward such "below-the-line" advertising as promotions, trade shows, and sponsorships, would continue to drag on industry revenue growth.[60,61]

There were challenges ahead. A survey of industry advertisers identified proof of effectiveness as a primary concern, followed by the heavy capital investment to deploy a network, and the industry's need for standardization to ensure hardware, software, and network compatibility. Managing content across multiple networks, the need for industry consolidation, and the integration of mobile devices and the Internet with digital signs were also mentioned.[62]

Return on Investment

Over the next few years, the industry was expected to experience increased demand by clients for more targeted and direct forms of advertising, and proof of impact. Demands for improved measurability would be met by continuing technological advancements that generated above-average returns to advertisers. Digital displays offered the distinct advantage of being able to change constantly throughout the day, allowing different demographics to be targeted for specific times. Improvements in audience measurement would assist companies in market research and allow companies to place advertisements at the right place and at the right time. Better market research would help operators improve return on clients' investments by allowing advertisers to target more specific audiences. While earlier efforts had developed models for measuring ROI for both sign owners and their advertisers,[63] the new era of digital signs would need to deliver "customization of content at any level, near-real-time diagnostics, and accurate proof-of-play reporting"[64] in order to prove ROI for investors and advertisers.

Competitive Environment

By 2010, there were hundreds of firms that competed in the U.S. market but most were minor, segment-specific competitors with sales less than $20 million. For 2010, **Table 5** lists major manufacturers across the industry indicating their locations and size (revenue and profits) where available.

Appendices A and B provide a more detailed profile of each competitor's market position based on the types of technology, market segments targeted, distribution channels employed, and their customization capabilities.

TABLE 5	Major Competitors of the Digital Signage Industry in 2010[65]				
Company	HQ Location	Website	2009 Net Income	2009? Company Revenues (USD)	
Adaptive Micro Systems (AMS)	USA	www.adaptivedisplays.com	P	52,000,000	*
ANC Sports	USA	www.ancsports.com	P	57,000,000	*
BARCO	Belgium	www.barco.com	(86,000,000)	919,200,000	***
Capturion	USA	www.capturion.com	P	n/a	*
Daktronics, Inc.	USA	www.daktronics.com	26,428,000	581,900,000	*
Hibino Corp	Japan	www.hibino.co.jp/english www.hitechled.com	(3,253,853)	173,574,544	***
Hi-Tech LED Displays	USA		P	30,000,000	**

(continued)

TABLE 5   Major Competitors of the Digital Signage Industry in 2010[65] (Continued)

Company	HQ Location	Website	2009 Net Income	2009? Company Revenues (USD)	
Imago, (ADDCO, Odeco)	Spain	www.imagoscreens.com	P	46,630,000	*
Ledstar, Inc.	Canada	www.ledstar.com	P	4,600,000	*
LG Corporation[1]	Korea	www.LGsolutions.com	979,914,738	26,068,124,151	***
Lighthouse Technologies	Hong Kong	www.lighthouse-tech.com www.lsi-idustries.com	P	59,260,000	*
LSI Industries, Inc.	USA		(13,414,000)	233,800,000	***
Mitsubishi Electric[1]	Japan	www.mitusbishielectric.com	1,593,538,170	36,970,616,123	***
Nevco, Inc.	USA	www.nevco.com	P	10,800,000	*
Optec Displays, Inc.	USA	www.optec.com	P	12,400,000	*
Optotech Corporation	Taiwan	www.opto.com.tw	6,732,540	172,970,994	***
Panasonic Corporation[1]	Japan	www.panasonic.com	(3,822,637,589)	78,331,857,247	***
SignCoEDS (EDS)	USA	www.signcoeds.com	P	7,000,000	*
Skyline Products, Inc.	USA	www.skylineproducts.com	(15,434,000)	26,400,000	*
Sony Corporation[1]	Japan	www.sony.com	(998,002,744)	77,973,622,095	***
Telegra	Croatia	www.telegra-europe.com	P	60,220,000	*
Toshiba[1]	Japan	www.toshiba.com/led	(3,488,793,000)	67,125,141,220	***
Trans-Lux Corporation	USA	www.trans-lux.com	(8,795,999)	36,700,000	***
Watchfre Signs	USA	www.watchfresigns.com	P	10,800,000	*
Young Electric Sign Co. (YESCO)	USA	www.yesco.com	13,148,000	1,032,000,000	***

*Estimates were found at http://www.hoovers.com on 06/07/2010

**Estimate from http://www.usitoday.com/article_view.asp?ArticleID=2034

***Financials from investors section of company websites.

[1]Mitsubishi, LG, Panasonic, Sony, and Toshiba had revenues that were much larger than other firms in the industry, much of which was earned producing products other than digital signs.

P = Privately held. Hoover's does not report net income for privately held companies.

SOURCE: Table produced by authors from sources cited in the footnotes to the table.

Summary Analysis of Industry Competitiveness in 2010

In 2010, the competitive environment primarily depended on the type of products a company sold, and the market segments it was targeting. For a product that had a "standard" design without much variation from one company to the next, like the LED text or graphic sign, companies primarily competed for business based on price. Purchase decisions that were focused heavily on product design features however, would change the competitive scope of things. While price was still important, considering the investment a digital sign required, other variables like the reputation of the company manufacturing the sign and its history of after-sale support and service tended to become bigger factors in the purchase decision process.

Products

There were hundreds of products available in the DOOH market place, some of which had many applications and others only a few. In some instances, a product design varied little from company to company, and in others one company may have had a product that was completely unique. One example of a design that varied very little from company to company was a LED sign capable of displaying basic text or graphics, which might have been seen outside of a McDonalds or Burger King. The sign itself probably varied no more than the cheeseburger you would buy from either store; it's the same product with slightly different design variations. On the other hand, the giant Mitsubishi video display at Dallas Cowboy Stadium and the Daktronics' Coca-Cola spectacular in Times Square, New York were completely unique, one-of-a-kind designs.

In fact, nearly every sign application received some design modification, and customers were able to demand this given the large number of products and companies that were competing in the industry. End-users were looking to maximize ROI as they sought increased revenues and sales, or tried to enhance the physical environment of their venue. Increasingly, sign features like viewing angle, display brightness and contrast, software and controllers, networking capabilities, number of LED diodes used, or high definition capabilities, among others, were becoming more important as technology advanced and became more affordable. Also, outdoor products had to be designed to withstand harsh conditions including rain, snow, hail, ice, blowing winds, sand, salt, sea air and debris, as well as extreme temperatures.

In addition to sign design and features, the quality and durability of the sign were important. The quality of materials used should be in line with the prices, and the warranty should reflect some indication of the product's durability. Customers in the DOOH market wanted a product that was durable, functional, and attractive, and may have been willing to pay a higher price for one that lasted longer than a less expensive one that would need to be replaced in a short time.

Finally, economies of scope were important for companies in the industry. A diverse product line enabled companies to serve several different market segments, and sell multiple products to existing customers and attract new customers.

Sales and Marketing

A company's sales and marketing capabilities were not only determined by its financial resources, but also by the structure and networks it was able to build to get its products to the market. A company that had the ability to establish sales and service locations across multiple regions/countries may have had some advantages over a company that was attempting to operate out of a centralized location, and hence greater growth potential.

However, company owned and operated sales and service offices were not the only way to accomplish a vast sales and marketing network. Many of the companies in the digital sign industry used dealer networks (resellers) to sell, service, and provide after-sale support. Some companies used both. In most cases, a dealer network was used to sell and service "standard" commercial or retail signs, where there was not a lot, if any, customized product design—i.e., signs that could be produced in large numbers through a standardized manufacturing process. Tis made it easier for manufacturers to train the dealers on how to operate, sell, and service the signs.

National accounts were another important sales channel for companies in the DOOH industry. National accounts included franchises and large companies with multiple locations like Walgreens, McDonalds, Sonic, and WalMart. When a potential customer chose to make a DOOH advertising network part of its business model, it created an opportunity for an industry competitor to pick up a contract that included supplying all of the DOOH signs for the organization. This type of large volume sale could be very stabilizing to a company for years to come.

Distribution channels were vitally important in this industry. The ability to be in direct contact with the end-user or decision maker allowed one company to set itself apart from the next. In some instances, like with large venue video score board displays, the sales cycle could be extremely long and oftentimes a customer was dealing with an integrator (e.g., architect or consultant). The ability to convince the integrator that your company's product was the best could lead to not only a sale today, but future sales through them as well.

Reviewing the distribution channels puts into perspective why it was important for a company to develop a sales and service network, whether it involved company owned and operated branches or a dealer network. The capacity of a company to use all distribution channels and disperse representatives across the prospective sales area would ultimately increase the amount of face-to-face time with decision makers. This was vital to these companies because only a handful of the companies competing in the industry were recognizable multinational firms. Even industry leader Daktronics was not a household name.

Reliable after-sale support and service was another benefit of a strong company network of sales and service locations. Tis allowed a company to quickly respond to maintenance and service inquiries. Given the fact that many of the customers would not be able to service their own products due to the technology and engineering involved, customers wanted some reassurance that their investment would be maintained and in good operation for the expected life of the product. For companies with global offices, this would also give them an advantage as they were able to have their own technicians provide after-sale service in the foreign country, eliminating the concern of who would maintain the customer's investment.

Providing reliable after-sale support was one way to build a strong reputation in the industry. With increasing levels of competition, companies had to find a way to set themselves apart. Building a reputation for one or more aspects of the business was vital. The number of products and companies available made it easy for customers to find alternatives or create bidding wars. It was often the intangibles that set companies apart. Companies in the DOOH marketplace often got their reputation from one or more of the following: 1. word of mouth; 2. completing highly recognizable projects (e.g., Dallas Cowboys Stadium); 3. developing new products and innovation; and 4. capacity to deliver based on engineering capabilities, breadth of product lines, after-sale support, or other factors that enhanced capabilities to meet customer requirements.

Firms were often constrained by how much they could do in any given year. While Daktronics, Mitsubishi, or Toshiba may have been able to complete two, three, or more large-venue projects in a year, some of the smaller competitors did not have the manufacturing space, capacity, or financial strength to take on several large projects at once.

Research and Development

As product and market development were important aspects of the growth of the DOOH industry, companies generally invested in some form of research and development. Industry leader Daktronics invested 4% of net sales into product design and development. In comparison, some of its competitors including Barco, Toshiba, and Mitsubishi invested 10.6%, 5.7%, and 4% of net sales respectively in 2009 on research and development. While the industry average was unknown, and there was no rule of thumb as to how much a company should invest in R&D, nearly all firms in the industry were engaged in some level of R&D, whether it was simply adapting their digital signs to new improved technologies, like better LEDs, or a more involved process of creating new products, designs, and technologies. Such investments were considered necessary if firms expected to merely maintain their competitive position or sought to stay on the leading edge of the industry.

Manufacturing

The strength of a company began with its engineering and manufacturing capabilities. Companies in the DOOH industry had to not only be able to develop and engineer quality products, but also manufacture them extremely efficiently. The downward price pressures in the industry left very little room for firms to operate without careful management of the supply chain, manufacturing process, quality controls, and waste reduction.

Many of the firms in the DOOH industry tried to be vertically integrated, relying on as few input suppliers as possible. This helped control costs and eliminate the need for large materials inventories. It ensured that when the company needed inputs, they were able to get them, and were not waiting on suppliers or competing with other companies looking for the same materials. Many firms were moving to lean manufacturing as a way to increase production efficiencies, decrease waste, and cut costs. Ultimately this would make the entire industry more competitive, and put even more downward pressure on prices.

Quality controls were another important aspect of the manufacturing process. Large investments were needed to meet demanding customer requirements. Companies wanted to make sure they took every step necessary to produce a reliable, durable, and quality product, which was what the customer expected to receive.

Looking to the Future

For the digital signage industry, 2010 was a year of recovery from the worst economic decline since the Great Depression of the 1930s. As unemployment slowly declined and consumer confidence returned, household consumption was expected to expand and the U.S. and global economies would be on the road to recovery.

The DOOH advertising market was important as a driver of future demand for both signage and content. Expansion in the retailing sector, hospitality, and other verticals could be expected to generate additional demand to replenish the balance sheets of firms positioned to seize the opportunities presented by global recovery. China and the Indian sub-continent had not been as severely impacted by the global recession and could be expected to continue their migration to the digital advertising age.

After 10 years of dramatic growth, the digital signage industry had established its viability and whetted consumer appetites for ever-more-dynamic messaging, not only in retailing, but in transportation, travel, and especially large sports and entertainment venues. The number of spectators, the distances from the field or stage, and the up-close-and-personal real-time images of the action elevated the entertainment experience to new heights.

The industry also faced challenges. In 2010, the industry was highly fragmented, disaggregated, and multi-domestic. International trade was highly constrained by the logistics demands of transporting heavy, bulky signage around the globe. New business models would be needed before the industry would see true multi-national competitors and consolidation of the industry beyond country or regional boundaries.

Technological development in light sources created the industry and would continue to drive its development. Other emerging technologies in materials science (nanotechnology) and solar power could be anticipated to have future impact. The interactivity of mobile devices with digital advertising content had just entered the market and presented unexplored opportunity to advertisers and marketers who could define bankable value propositions.

For those industry participants with vision, technical capabilities, market power, financial strength, and business acumen, industry observers foresaw a very bright future indeed.

Appendix A: Market Focus of Major Competitors in 2010

Company	Private	Public	Standardized	Low	Median	High	LED Text	LED Video	LCD	Rear Projection	Front Projection	Other	Entertainment	Commercial	In/Outdoor Adv.	Transportation	Mobile/Modular	Other	Direct	Resellers	Integrators
			Custom Displays				Display Technology						Application						Distribution		
Adaptive Micro Systems (AMS)	X		X				X	X				X	X	X	X	X				X	
ANC Sports[2]	X				X	X	X	X	X			X	X	X	X	X			X		X
BARCO		X	X	X	X	X	X	X	X	X	X		X	X	X		X	X	X	X	X
Capturion	X		X	X	X	X	X	X	X	X	X		X	X	X		X	X	X		X
Daktronics, Inc.		X	X	X	X	X	X	X	X			X	X	X	X	X	X	X	X	X	X
Hibino Corp[2]		X	X	X	X		X	X				X	X				X	X	X		
Hi-Tech LED Displays	X		X	X			X	X					X	X	X				X	X	
Imago	X		X	X			X	X					X	X	X			X		X	X
Ledstar, Inc.	X		X	X			X							X	X	X			X		
Lighthouse Technologies	X		X	X	X		X	X					X	X	X		X	X	X		X
LG Electronics[1]		X	X	X	X		X	X	X				X	X	X	X	X	X	X	X	X
LSI Industries, Inc.		X	X	X	X		X	X	X			X	X	X	X		X	X	X	X	X
Mitsubishi Electric[1]		X	X	X	X	X	X	X	X	X	X		X	X	X	X	X	X	X		X
Nevco, Inc.	X		X	X			X	X				X	X						X		X
Optec Displays, Inc.	X		X		X		X	X					X	X	X				X	X	
Optotech Corporation		X	X	X	X		X	X		X	X	X	X	X	X	X		X	X	X	X
Panasonic Corporation[1]		X	X	X			X	X	X				X	X	X				X		X
SignCoEDS	X		X	X			X	X	X			X	X	X	X						X
Skyline Products, Inc.	X		X				X	X						X	X	X			X	X	
Sony Corporation[1]		X	X	X	X		X	X	X				X	X	X				X	X	
Telegra[2]	X		X	X	X		X	X				X		X	X	X		X	X		X
Toshiba[1]		X	X	X	X	X	X	X	X	X	X	X	X	X	X	X	X		X	X	X
Trans-Lux Corporation		X	X	X			X	X	X	X	X		X	X	X	X	X		X	X	X
Watchfire Signs	X		X			X	X	X					X	X	X			X	X	X	X
Young Electric Sign Co	X		X	X	X		X	X				X	X	X	X	X		X	X	X	X

[1] Mitsubishi, Sony, Panasonic, LG and Toshiba had revenues that were much larger than other firms in the industry, much of which was earned producing products other than digital signs.

[2] Company specialized in one or a few applications.

SOURCE: Table produced by authors from company websites and company reports.

Key to Appendix A

Display Customization

Standardized (none): Products are manufactured to the same specifications in every production run.

Low Customization: Products are primarily manufactured to the same specifications across production runs with slight variations in product color, user content, or some other small variation that does not change the basic function or operation of the display, nor the manufacturing process.

Moderate Customization: Company can manufacture products to customer specifications as far as size, shape, color, and installation requirements are concerned. A company in this category may be limited to the number of custom displays they can manufacture in any given year, limited in a manufacturing aspect like the display size or shape, or limited in the size of job they can complete.

High Customization: Company can manufacture or custom fabricate products to customer specifications of any kind, and are not limited in the number or size of custom jobs they can complete in a year. The companies also do not have any type of manufacturing limitation when it comes to designing, manufacturing, and assembling displays.

Display Technology

LED: Short for light-emitting diode, an LED is an electronic semiconductor that emits light when electricity passes through it. LED lights are more efficient than other types of light sources and can be used to make a variety of text, graphic, animations, and video displays, as well as other types of light sources. LEDs can also be used to make ropes, floors, and wound to make any type of shapes.

LCD: Short for liquid crystal display, an LCD is a low power, flat screen device used to display text, graphics, animations, and images.

Rear and Front Projection: A type of display that uses lenses and/or mirrors to project images on a screen.

Other: DLP (Digital Light Processing) Technology, CRT technology, and Neon Lighting.

Application

Entertainment Venues: Large sports venues, small sports venues, amusement and theme parks, cinemas and theatres, fairs and expos, performing arts theatres, and casinos.

Commercial Indoor/Outdoor Advertising: Billboards, convenience and retail stores, financial, medical, pharmacy, restaurants, gaming, hospitality, shopping, civic centers, convention centers, auto dealers and worship.

Transportation: Airports and aviation, mass transit (bus and railways), roadways, fixed highway signs, parking, and intelligent transportation systems.

Mobile and Modular: Concerts and staging, festivals and sporting events, auto shows, trade shows, and award shows.

Other: Campus communications, control rooms, simulators, manufacturing, landmarks and spectaculars.

Distribution Channels

Direct: Company direct, partners, and national accounts.

Resellers: Dealer networks, installation companies, and advertising and marketing companies.

Integrators: Consultants, architects, engineers, and project managers.

Appendix B

Profile of Major Digital Signage Industry Competitors

The following brief profiles represent the breadth of firms that competed in the digital signage industry in 2010.

Adaptive Micro Systems, LLC, was founded in 1978 and manufactured standard LED text and video displays primarily applicable to indoor/outdoor commercial advertising and transportation markets. The company had manufacturing and sales sites in the U.S., Malaysia, and Europe and used an authorized dealer network to sell its products.

ANC Sports specialized in manufacturing and selling LED video displays directly to large sports venues. It had worked with many collegiate and professional sports teams on custom LED video display designs. It had also worked with other LED display manufacturing companies, like Mitsubishi Electric, to complete projects using ANC's software and controllers that were used to power large, high-definition LED video displays.

Barco was a leading global technology company that designed and sold visualization solutions for a variety of markets including the digital-out-of-home (DOOH) industry. Its manufacturing sites in Europe, North America, and Asia-Pacific built standard and custom LED video displays as well as LCD and rear- or front-projection displays. Barco had sales offices around the globe and also sold to customers through resellers and system integrators.

Capturion was a privately owned multi-format LED video display company based in Laurel, Mississippi with manufacturing facilities owned and operated in Asia. It was striving to advance its indoor and outdoor products towards a better, "greener" LED system.

Daktronics was considered by many to be the industry leader in manufacturing LED displays. In business since 1968, the company had products installed in nearly 100 countries. Daktronics manufactured a wide variety of custom and standard LED text and video displays as well as LCD screens. Daktronics used a vast dealer network as well as selling its custom products directly and through system integrators.

Hibino Corp., in business since 1964, manufactured LED video displays primarily for use in mobile and modular applications. The company reported it could custom design and construct completely mobile audio visual systems for nearly any event. Hibino sold directly to its customers.

Hi-Tech LED Displays had been manufacturing electronic displays since 1984. It mostly manufactured standard LED text and video displays for a variety of applications, but also manufactured some custom displays. Hi-Tech sold primarily to U.S. sign installation companies, but also sold directly to customers, and had completed projects world-wide.

Imago (Odeco Electronica in Europe and ADDCO in the United States) had offices and partners around the world. Its assembly plants in Europe, North America, South America, and India manufactured a variety of standard LED text and video displays. Imago was best known for its intelligent transportation systems, but also did some low-end custom LED displays. The company sold through integrators and resellers to customers.

Ledstar, Inc., specialized in manufacturing LED text variable message signs (VMS) for transportation applications since 1988. The VMS used on highways across North America provided information to motorists. Ledstar's products could be purchased directly from the company.

LG Electronics, located in Korea, was established in 1958. Globally, it had 9.4% of the LCD TV market and 13.5% of the fat panel TV market in 2010. It had leveraged its TV capabilities—including high definition (HD) TV—into commercial products for the public venue market as well as many other market segments, including healthcare, transportation, education, financial, retail, hospitality, quick service restaurants (QSR), food services, government, and small business.

Lighthouse Technologies offered a line of LED text and video displays for almost any application. The company had sales offices around the world and was recognized for its custom mobile and modular units, as well as some of its displays in large sports venues. Lighthouse was known as one of the industry's leading companies for new products and technologies. The company sold direct and through systems integrators to customers.

LSI Industries entered the DOOH industry with its 2006 purchase of SACO Technologies, Inc., of Montreal, which gave it the ability to produce large-format LED displays. The company manufactured LED text and video displays and LCD displays for nearly every application. LSI also had the ability to design and manufacture custom displays and sold them direct and through integrators and resellers.

Mitsubishi Electric rated in 2009 as the world's 215th largest company by Fortune Global 500, manufactured standard and custom LED text and video displays, and a variety of other products. It had sales locations around the globe and was capable of manufacturing some of the largest custom LED video displays through its subsidiary Mitsubishi Diamond Vision. The company sold its products through several distribution channels including direct and through partners, resellers, and system integrators.

Nevco, Inc., manufactured its first scoreboard in 1934, and had been considered the largest private scoreboard manufacturer for some time until Daktronics displaced it. Most recognized for its LED scoreboards. The first also manufactured LED text and video displays. Nevco was capable of small custom scoreboard designs and sold directly to end users and integrators mainly in North America, but also around the world.

Optec Display, Inc., in business since the late 1980s, primarily manufactured standard outdoor LED text and video commercial advertising displays. It used manufacturing sites in the United States, China, and Taiwan and had a 300^+ dealer network that sold its displays primarily in the United States, with some global sales.

Optotech Corporation, established in 1983, manufactured both standard and custom LED text and video displays for a variety of applications, its best known being digital billboards. It also made LCD screens and other products. It had locations in Taiwan and China, as well as sales locations throughout the world. To sell its products Optotech used resellers and integrators, but also sold directly to the customer.

Panasonic Corporation, headquartered in Japan, was one of the largest electronic product manufacturers in the world, comprised of over 634 companies. The company offered a wide range of digital signage solutions, from all-inclusive bundled solutions, to custom-designed enterprise networks. Panasonic provided hardware, software installation and support for its customers.

SigtiCoEDS manufactured signage for sports and commercial applications. It manufactured LED text and video signs as well as LCD video walls and DLP (digital light processing) displays. SignCoEDS primarily used a dealer network to sell to customers, but also sold through integrators when doing custom projects.

Skyline Products, Inc., manufactured LED text displays primarily for the transportation industry. Skyline's VMS provided information to travelers on highways and as a part of intelligent transportation systems. Skyline also manufactured renewable energy sources and did aluminum fabrication. Skyline products could be purchased directly from the company.

Sony was a Japanese multinational conglomerate corporation headquartered in Tokyo, Japan. Convergent Media systems, a Sony company, developed Prodokol, a fully managed, end-to-end, digital signage platform. Prodokol supported applications such as interactive touchscreen, digital menu boards, and single display or multi-display signage. Its leading managed solutions were banking, retail and quick service restaurants (QSR).

Telegra was a leading manufacturer of advanced traffic management systems for roadways, tunnels, and other transportation applications. It had manufacturing sites in Croatia and the United State, as well as sales sites around the world. The company reported the ability to custom design transportation systems for nearly any application and sold directly through integrators and resellers to customers.

Toshiba, rated in 2009 as the world's 97th largest company by Fortune Global, manufactured a variety of standard and custom LED text and video displays, LCD and plasma screens, rear- and front-projection screens, as well as a number of other communications and electronics products. Toshiba sales locations around the globe sold products for use in a variety of applications. Toshiba sold direct, and through system integrators and resellers around the world.

Trans-Lux Corporation manufactured standard and custom LED text and video displays as well as LCD and plasma screens for a variety of applications. Trans-Lux had locations across North America and the globe to sell its products. Trans-Lux worked with resellers, partners, and integrators to sell its products to customers.

Watchfre manufactured standard LED text and video displays for the commercial indoor/outdoor advertising market. The company's products were manufactured completely in the United States and were sold through a dealer network to customers across North America.

Young Electric Sign Company (YESCO) started building custom signs and displays in 1920. The company manufactured LED text and video displays as well as other different styles of signs, and was often featured on the Las Vegas strip. YESCO had several manufacturing and sales locations in the United States capable of custom building many styles of signs. It sold directly, and through resellers and integrators.

NOTES

1. Hendon, Donald W. and William F. Muhs, "Origin and early development of outdoor advertising in the United States." *Journal of Advertising History,* 9(1), 1986, 7–17.
2. Burma Shave signs "dotted the landscape along the nation's two-lane highways from 1926 to '63," while the Bloch Brothers Tobacco Company of Wheeling, W. Va., manufacturers of Mail Pouch Tobacco, began painting barns with their roadside messages in 1890.
3. Lady Bird Johnson, wife of President Lyndon Baines Johnson, is largely recognized as the force behind passage of the 1966 Highway Beautification Act that strongly regulated signage on Federal highways.
4. By 2000, Liquid crystal displays (LCD) replaced cathode ray tubes (CRT) in television and other display screens and in small consumer electronics—video players, clocks, watches, instrument panels, and small signs—as they were more energy efficient. However, as they had no power source, they had to be arrayed in front of a light source (backlit). Light-emitting diodes (LED) supplanted LCDs as they were an even more energy efficient light source, smaller, provided extraordinary color range, radiated little heat, and had extremely long life, among many positive characteristics that made them highly flexible for use in a very broad range of lighting applications, including outdoor and indoor signage.
5. www.nsr.com, "Global market and digital signage." May, 2008.
6. *Credit Union Times,* "Before you buy, know how to kick the tires of a digital signage system." November 4, 2009, v20, 144, p. 201(1).
7. IBIS*World, Industry Report, Billboard & Sign Manufacturing in the U.S.: 33995,* July 07 2008, p. 23.
8. *Xinhua Economic News,* "China's outdoor digital display market to boost: Analysis International." March 6, 2009, p. NA.
9. *Wireless News,* November 1, 2008, "MultiMedia Intelligence: Digital signage market growth continues as IP drives next generation advertising," p. NA.
10. *Investment Weekly News.* "The research, 'Tink Narrow, Win Large: Advertising, Analytics, and Applications in Digital Signage' discusses new trends in digital signage as witnessed in 1Q2009." August 22, 2009, p. 454.
11. www.seesawnetworks.com, "Global digital out-of-home media forecast 2008– 2012," published by Northern Sky Research, Cambridge, MA 02138.
12. *AsiaPulse News,* "Samsung enters Japan's digital signage market," July 3, 2009, p. NA.
13. www.digitalsignagetoday.com. "Digital signage industry prognostications for fall 2009." Ken Goldberg, September 29, 2009.
14. Ibid.
15. IBIS*World, Industry Report, Billboard & Outdoor Display Advertising in the U.S.: 54185,* November, 2010.
16. www.seesawnetworks.com.
17. www.nsr.com, *Global Digital Out of Home Media Forecast 2008–2012,* published by Northern Sky Research, Cambridge, MA 02138.
18. www.nsr.com, Ibid.
19. NAICS Code 33995 (Billboard & Sign Manufacturing in the U.S.), SIC Code 3993 (Signs & Advertising Displays), and NAICS Code 54185 (Billboard & Outdoor Display Advertising in the U.S.)

20. IBIS*World, Industry Report*, 2008, p. 8.

21. Ibid., p. 10.

22. *Wireless News,* 2008, p. NA.

23. Ibid., p. NA.

24. *Wireless News,* November 2, 2009, "Research and Markets Adds Report: Global Digital Signage Market: 2008 Edition," p. NA.

25. *Internet Wire*, June 12, 2008. The study was commissioned from OTX by See Saw Networks, a company that offers extensive DOOH media.

26. *Digital Signage Magazine,* "Landmark digital signage: Walgreens goes big to stand out in the digital signage capitol of the world—Times Square." February 2009 v5, i1, p. 14.

27. www.digitalsignagetoday.com, "Digital signage: The top 10 trends for 2010, Part 1 & 2", Keith Kelson, December 29–30, 2009.

28. www.digitalsignagetoday.com, "5 great digital signage moments in 2009." Bill Yackey, December 23, 2009.

29. www.digitalsignagetoday.com, Kelson.

30. "Dwell time" is a term for audiences that are captive and thus available for exposure to advertising messaging for a longer duration. Examples are bus and train riders, and passengers waiting in terminals and boarding lounges who experience significant sit time.

31. www.digitalsignagetoday.com, Yackey.

32. www.digitalsignagetoday.com, Kelson.

33. *Digital signage magazine,* "Flat is the new up? Tink again . . .", February 2009, v5, i1, p. 5.

34. IBIS*World, Industry Report, Billboard & Outdoor Display Advertising in the U.S.: 54185,* December 29, 2009, p. 30.

35. www.digitalsignageexpo.net, "Platt Retail Institute announces quarterly digital signage industry index," November 17, 2009.

36. IBIS*World, Industry Report, 54185,* 2009, 20.

37. www.digitalsignagetoday.com, Kelson.

38. www.digitalsignageexpo.net/DigitalSignageExpo/ExhibitorsList.aspx. Lists 2010 Exhibitors as of January 5, 2010.

39. www.digitalsignagetoday.com, Kelson.

40. *Sound and Video Contractor (Online Exclusive),* April 22, 2008, p. NA.

41. *GlobeNewswire,* "Wireless Ronin completes digital signage installation at home of NHL's Minnesota Wild," November 4, 2009.

42. www.digitalsignagetoday.com, Kelson.

43. www.digitalsignagetoday.com, Goldberg.

44. Ibid.

45. www.semi.org/en/IndustrySegments/LED/ctr035763.

46. IBIS*World, Industry Report, 33995,* 2008.

47. IBIS*World, Industry Report, 54185,* 2010, p. 20.

48. Ibid.

49. Ibid.

50. *Investment Weekly News* 2009, p 454.

51. IBIS*World, Industry Report, 33995,* 2008, p.19–20.

52. Nichols, Christopher L., "Billboard Sign Regulation: Recent Cases and Trends." Paper presented to the Texas City Attorneys Association, June, 2011, South Padre Island, Tx.

53. For updated information, visit the website of Scenic America. www.scenic.org/billboards/digital.

54. *Planning,* "Sign World: What other nations can teach us about sign control," Jef Soule, FAICP. July, 2010.

55. www.americancityandcounty.com, "Dim your sign, please: Cities adjust ordinances to regulate digital billboards," Peter Barnes, August, 2009, p. 19.

56. http://www.amberalert.gov/about.htm. The AMBER Alert System began in 1996 when Dallas-Fort Worth broadcasters teamed with local police to develop an early warning system to help find abducted children. AMBER stands for America's Missing: Broadcast Emergency Response.

57. IBIS*World, 54185,* 2009, p. 35.

58. Ibid.

59. IBIS*World, Industry Report, Billboard & Sign Manufacturing in the U.S.: 33995,* August 2010, p. 5.

60. IBIS*World, 54185,* 2009, p. 36–37.

61. Below-the-line advertising referred to advertising by means other than the five major media (newspapers, magazines, television, radio, and outdoor).

62. North American Digital Signage Index (2009), Vol. 1, Issue 1, pps. 18–20. Platt Retail Institute.

63. www.nsr.com.

64. *Sound & Video Contractor* (Online Exclusive). "Expert viewpoint: Digital signage trends," June 2, 2009, p. NA.

65. Based on presentation by Chairman of the Board, Daktronics Corporation, Annual Shareholder's Meeting, August, 2009, Brookings, South Dakota.

GLOSSARY

360-degree performance appraisal An evaluation technique in which input is gathered from multiple sources.

80/20 rule A rule of thumb stating that one should monitor those 20% of the factors that determine 80% of the results.

Absorptive capacity A firm's ability to value, assimilate, and utilize new external knowledge.

Acquisition The purchase of a company that is completely absorbed by the acquiring corporation.

Action plan A plan that states what actions are going to be taken, by whom, during what time frame, and with what expected results.

Activity-based costing (ABC) An accounting method for allocating indirect and fixed costs to individual products or product lines based on the value-added activities going into that product.

Activity ratios Financial ratios that indicate how well a corporation is managing its operations.

Adaptive mode A decision-making mode characterized by reactive solutions to existing problems, rather than a proactive search for new opportunities.

Advisory board A group of external business people who voluntarily meet periodically with the owners/managers of the firm to discuss strategic and other issues.

Affiliated directors Directors who, though not really employed by the corporation, handle the legal or insurance work for the company or are important suppliers.

Agency theory A theory stating that problems arise in corporations because the agents (top management) are not willing to bear responsibility for their decisions unless they own a substantial amount of stock in the corporation.

Altman's Z-Value Bankruptcy Formula A formula used to estimate how close a company is to declaring bankruptcy.

Analytical portfolio manager A type of general manager needed to execute a diversification strategy.

Andean Community A South American free-trade alliance composed of Columbia, Ecuador, Peru, Bolivia, and Chile.

Annual report A document published each year by a company to show its financial condition and products.

Assessment center An approach to evaluating the suitability of a person for a position by simulating key parts of the job.

Assimilation A strategy that involves the domination of one corporate culture over another.

Association of Southeast Asian Nations (ASEAN) A regional trade association composed of the Asian countries of Brunei Darussalam, Cambodia, Indonesia, Laos, Malaysia, Myanmar, Philippines, Singapore, Thailand, and Vietnam. ASEA+3 includes China, Japan, and South Korea.

Autonomous (self-managing) work teams A group of people who work together without a supervisor to plan, coordinate, and evaluate their own work.

Backward integration Assuming a function previously provided by a supplier.

Balanced scorecard Combines financial measures with operational measures on customer satisfaction, internal processes, and the corporation's innovation and improvement activities.

Bankruptcy A retrenchment strategy that forfeits management of the firm to the courts in return for some settlement of the corporation's obligations.

Basic R&D Research and development that is conducted by scientists in well-equipped laboratories where the focus is on theoretical problem areas.

BCG (Boston Consulting Group) Growth-Share Matrix A simple way to portray a corporation's portfolio of products or divisions in terms of growth and cash flow.

Behavior control A control that specifies how something is to be done through policies, rules, standard operating procedures, and orders from a superior.

Behavior substitution A phenomenon that occurs when people substitute activities that do not lead to goal accomplishment for activities that do lead to goal accomplishment because the wrong activities are being rewarded.

Benchmarking The process of measuring products, services, and practices against those of competitors or companies recognized as industry leaders.

Best practice A procedure that is followed by successful companies.

Blind spot analysis An approach to analyzing a competitor by identifying its perceptual biases.

Board of director responsibilities Commonly agreed obligations of directors, which include: setting corporate strategy, overall direction, mission or vision; hiring and firing the CEO and top management; controlling, monitoring, or supervising top management; reviewing and approving the use of resources; and caring for shareholder interest.

Board of directors' continuum A range of the possible degree of involvement by the board of directors (from low to high) in the strategic management process.

BOT (build-operate-transfer) concept A type of international entry option for a company. After building a facility, the company operates the facility for a fixed period of time during which it earns back its investment, plus a profit.

Brainstorming The process of proposing ideas in a group without first mentally screening them.

Brand A name that identifies a particular company's product in the mind of the consumer.

Budget A statement of a corporation's programs in terms of money required.

Business model The mix of activities a company performs to earn a profit.

Business plan A written strategic plan for a new entrepreneurial venture.

Business policy A previous name for strategic management. It has a general management orientation and tends to look inward with primary concern for integrating the corporation's many functional activities.

Business strategy Competitive and cooperative strategies that emphasize improvement of the competitive position of a corporation's products or services in a specific industry or market segment.

Cannibalize To replace popular products before they reach the end of their life cycle.

Capability A corporation's ability to exploit its resources.

Cap-and-trade A government-imposed ceiling (cap) on the amount of allowed greenhouse gas emissions combined with a system allowing a firm to sell (trade) its emission reductions to another firm whose emissions exceed the allowed cap.

Capital budgeting The process of analyzing and ranking possible investments in terms of the additional outlays and additional receipts that will result from each investment.

Captive company strategy Dedicating a firm's productive capacity as primary supplier to another company in exchange for a long-term contract.

Carbon footprint The amount of greenhouse gases being created by an entity and released into the air.

Cash cow A product that brings in far more money than is needed to maintain its market share.

Categorical imperatives Kant's two principles to guide actions: A person's action is ethical only if that person is willing for that same action to be taken by everyone who is in a similar situation, and a person should never treat another human being simply as a means but always as an end.

Cautious profit planner The type of leader needed for a corporation choosing to follow a stability strategy.

Cellular/modular organization A structure composed of cells (self-managing teams, autonomous business units, etc.) that can operate alone but can interact with other cells to produce a more potent and competent business mechanism.

Center of excellence A designated area in which a company has a core or distinctive competence.

Center of gravity The part of the industry value chain that is most important to the company and the point where the company's greatest expertise and capabilities lay.

Central American Free Trade Agreement (CAFTA) A regional trade association composed of El Salvador, Guatemala, Nicaragua, Honduras, Costa Rica, the United States, and the Dominican Republic.

Clusters Geographic concentrations of interconnected companies and industries.

Code of ethics A code that specifies how an organization expects its employees to behave while on the job.

Codetermination The inclusion of a corporation's workers on its board of directors.

Collusion The active cooperation of firms within an industry to reduce output and raise prices in order to get around the normal economic law of supply and demand. This practice is usually illegal.

Commodity A product whose characteristics are the same regardless of who sells it.

Common-size statements Income statements and balance sheets in which the dollar figures have been converted into percentages.

Common thread A unifying theme for the whole organization to rally around and provide focus for organizational efforts.

Competency A cross-functional integration and coordination of capabilities.

Competitive intelligence A formal program of gathering information about a company's competitors.

Competitive scope The breadth of a company's or a business unit's target market.

Competitive strategy A strategy that states how a company or a business unit will compete in an industry.

Competitors The companies that offer the same products or services as the subject company.

Complementor A company or an industry whose product(s) works well with another industry's or firm's product and without which that product would lose much of its value.

Concentration A corporate growth strategy that concentrates a corporation's resources on competing in one industry.

Concentric diversification A diversification growth strategy in which a firm uses its current strengths to diversify into related products in another industry.

Concurrent engineering A process in which specialists from various functional areas work side by side rather than sequentially in an effort to design new products.

Conglomerate diversification A diversification growth strategy that involves a move into another industry to provide products unrelated to its current products.

Conglomerate structure An assemblage of legally independent firms (subsidiaries) operating under one corporate umbrella but controlled through the subsidiaries' boards of directors.

Connected line batch flow A part of a corporation's manufacturing strategy in which components are standardized and each machine functions like a job shop but is positioned in the same order as the parts are processed.

Consensus A situation in which all parties agree to one alternative.

Consolidated industry An industry in which a few large companies dominate.

Consolidation The second phase of a turnaround strategy that implements a program to stabilize the corporation.

Constant dollars Dollars adjusted for inflation.

Continuous improvement A system developed by Japanese firms in which teams strive constantly to improve manufacturing processes.

Continuous systems Production organized in lines on which products can be continuously assembled or processed.

Contraction The first phase of a turnaround strategy that includes a general across-the-board cutback in size and costs.

Cooperative strategies Strategies that involve working with other firms to gain competitive advantage within an industry.

Co-opetition A term used to describe simultaneous competition and cooperation among firms.

Core competency A collection of corporate capabilities that cross divisional borders and are widespread within a corporation, and that a corporation can do exceedingly well.

Core rigidity/deficiency A core competency of a firm that over time matures and becomes a weakness.

Corporate brand A type of brand in which the company's name serves as the brand name.

Corporate capabilities See *capability.*

Corporate culture A collection of beliefs, expectations, and values learned and shared by a corporation's members and transmitted from one generation of employees to another.

Corporate culture pressure A force from existing corporate culture against the implementation of a new strategy.

Corporate entrepreneurship Also called intrapreneurship; the creation of a new business within an existing organization.

Corporate governance The relationship among the board of directors, top management, and shareholders in determining the direction and performance of a corporation.

Corporate parenting A corporate strategy that evaluates the corporation's business units in terms of resources and capabilities that can be used to build business unit value as well as generate synergies across business units.

Corporate reputation A widely held perception of a company by the general public.

Corporate scenario Pro forma balance sheets and income statements that forecast the effect that each alternative strategy will likely have on return on investment.

Corporate stakeholders Groups that affect or are affected by the achievement of a firm's objectives.

Corporate strategy A strategy that states a company's overall direction in terms of its general attitude toward growth and the management of its various business and product lines.

Corporation A mechanism legally established to allow different parties to contribute capital, expertise, and labor for their mutual benefit.

Cost focus A low-cost competitive strategy that concentrates on a particular buyer group or geographic market and attempts to serve only that niche.

Cost leadership A low-cost competitive strategy that aims at the broad mass market.

Cost proximity A process that involves keeping the higher price a company charges for higher quality close enough to that of the competition so that customers will see the extra quality as being worth the extra cost.

Crisis of autonomy A time when people managing diversified product lines need more decision-making freedom than top management is willing to delegate to them.

Crisis of control A time when business units act to optimize their own sales and profits without regard to the overall corporation. See also *suboptimization*.

Crisis of leadership A time when an entrepreneur is personally unable to manage a growing company.

Cross-functional work teams A work team composed of people from multiple functions.

Cultural integration The extent to which units throughout an organization share a common culture.

Cultural intensity The degree to which members of an organizational unit accept the norms, values, or other culture content associated with the unit.

Deculturation The disintegration of one company's culture resulting from unwanted and extreme pressure from another to impose its culture and practices.

Dedicated transfer line A highly automated assembly line making one mass-produced product and using little human labor.

Defensive centralization A process in which top management of a not-for-profit retains all decision-making authority so that lower-level managers cannot take any actions to which the sponsors may object.

Defensive tactic A tactic in which a company defends its current market.

Delphi technique A forecasting technique in which experts independently assess the probabilities of specified events. These assessments are combined and sent back to each expert for fine-tuning until an agreement is reached.

Devil's advocate An individual or a group assigned to identify the potential pitfalls and problems of a proposal.

Dialectical inquiry A decision-making technique that requires that two proposals using different assumptions be generated for consideration.

Differentiation A competitive strategy that is aimed at the broad mass market and that involves the creation of a product or service that is perceived throughout its industry as unique.

Differentiation focus A differentiation competitive strategy that concentrates on a particular buyer group, product line segment, or geographic market.

Differentiation strategy See *differentiation*.

Dimensions of national culture A set of five dimensions by which each nation's unique culture can be identified.

Directional strategy A plan that is composed of three general orientations: growth, stability, and retrenchment.

Distinctive competencies A firm's competencies that are superior to those of their competitors.

Diversification A corporate growth strategy that expands product lines by moving into another industry.

Divestment A retrenchment strategy in which a division of a corporation with low growth potential is sold.

Divisional structure An organizational structure in which employees tend to be functional specialists organized according to product/market distinctions.

Dogs A business that does not seem to provide any remaining opportunities for growth.

Downsizing Planned elimination of positions or jobs.

Due care The obligation of board members to closely monitor and evaluate top management.

Durability The rate at which a firm's underlying resources and capabilities depreciate or become obsolete.

Dynamic industry expert A leader with a great deal of experience in a particular industry appropriate for executing a concentration strategy.

Dynamic capabilities Capabilities that are continually being changed and reconfigured to make them more adaptive to an uncertain environment.

Dynamic pricing A marketing practice in which different customers pay different prices for the same product or service.

Earnings per share (EPS) A calculation that is determined by dividing net earnings by the number of shares of common stock issued.

Economic value added (EVA) A shareholder value method of measuring corporate and divisional performance. Measures after-tax operating income minus the total annual cost of capital.

Economies of scale A process in which unit costs are reduced by making large numbers of the same product.

Economies of scope A process in which unit costs are reduced when the value chains of two separate products or services share activities, such as the same marketing channels or manufacturing facilities.

EFAS (External Factor Analysis Summary) table A table that organizes external factors into opportunities and threats and how well management is responding to these specific factors.

Electronic commerce The use of the Internet to conduct business transactions.

Engineering (or process) R&D R&D concentrating on quality control and the development of design specifications and improved production equipment.

Enterprise resource planning (ERP) software Software that unites all of a company's major business activities, from order processing to production, within a single family of software modules.

Enterprise risk management (ERM) A corporatewide, integrated process to manage the uncertainties that could negatively or positively influence the achievement of the corporation's objectives.

Enterprise strategy A strategy that explicitly articulates a firm's ethical relationship with its stakeholders.

Entrepreneur A person who initiates and manages a business undertaking and who assumes risk for the sake of a profit.

Entrepreneurial characteristics Traits of an entrepreneur that lead to a new venture's success.

Entrepreneurial mode A strategy made by one powerful individual in which the focus is on opportunities, and problems are secondary.

Entrepreneurial venture Any new business whose primary goals are profitability and growth and that can be characterized by innovative strategic practices.

Entry barrier An obstruction that makes it difficult for a company to enter an industry.

Environmental scanning The monitoring, evaluation, and dissemination of information from the external and internal environments to key people within the corporation.

Environmental sustainability The use of business practices to reduce a company's impact upon the natural, physical environment.

Environmental uncertainty The degree of complexity plus the degree of change existing in an organization's external environment.

Ethics The consensually accepted standards of behavior for an occupation, trade, or profession.

European Union (EU) A regional trade association composed of 27 European countries.

Executive leadership The directing of activities toward the accomplishment of corporate objectives.

Executive succession The process of grooming and replacing a key top manager.

Executive type An individual with a particular mix of skills and experiences.

Exit barrier An obstruction that keeps a company from leaving an industry.

Expense center A business unit that uses money but contributes to revenues only indirectly.

Experience curve A conceptual framework that states that unit production costs decline by some fixed percentage each time the total accumulated volume of production in units doubles.

Expert opinion A nonquantitative forecasting technique in which authorities in a particular area attempt to forecast likely developments.

Explicit knowledge Knowledge that can be easily articulated and communicated.

Exporting Shipping goods produced in a company's home country to other countries for marketing.

External environment Forces outside an organization that are not typically within the short-run control of top management.

Externality Costs of doing business that are not included in a firm's accounting system, but that are felt by others.

External strategic factor Environmental trend with both a high probability of occurrence and a high probability of impact on the corporation.

Extranet An information network within an organization that is available to key suppliers and customers.

Extrapolation A form of forecasting that extends present trends into the future.

Family business A company that is either owned or dominated by relatives.

Family directors Board members who are descendants of the founder and own significant blocks of stock.

Financial leverage The ratio of total debt to total assets.

Financial strategy A functional strategy to make the best use of corporate monetary assets.

First mover The first company to manufacture and sell a new product or service.

Flexible manufacturing A type of manufacturing that permits the low-volume output of custom-tailored products at relatively low unit costs through economies of scope.

Follow-the-sun-management A management technique in which modern communication enables project team members living in one country to pass their work to team members in another time zone so that the project is continually being advanced.

Forward integration Assuming a function previously provided by a distributor.

Four-corner exercise An approach to analyzing a competitor in terms of its future goals, current strategy, assumptions, and capabilities, in order to develop a competitor's response profile.

Fragmented industry An industry in which no firm has large market share and each firm serves only a small piece of the total market.

Franchising An international entry strategy in which a firm grants rights to another company/individual to open a retail store using the franchiser's name and operating system.

Free cash flow The amount of money a new owner can take out of a firm without harming the business.

Full integration Complete control of the entire value chain of the business.

Full vertical integration A growth strategy under which a firm makes 100% of its key supplies internally and completely controls its distributors.

Functional strategy An approach taken by a functional area to achieve corporate and business unit objectives and strategies by maximizing resource productivity.

Functional structure An organizational structure in which employees tend to be specialists in the business functions important to that industry, such as manufacturing, sales, or finance.

Geographic-area structure A structure that allows a multinational corporation to tailor products to regional differences and to achieve regional coordination.

Global industry An industry in which a company manufactures and sells the same products, with only minor adjustments for individual countries around the world.

Globalization The internationalization of markets and corporations.

Global warming A gradual increase in the Earth's temperature leading to changes in the planet's climate.

Goal An open-ended statement of what one wants to accomplish, with no quantification of what is to be achieved and no time criteria for completion.

Goal displacement Confusion of means with ends, which occurs when activities originally intended to help managers attain corporate objectives become ends in themselves or are adapted to meet ends other than those for which they were intended.

Good will An accounting term describing the premium paid by one company in its purchase of another company that is listed on the acquiring company's balance sheet.

Grand strategy Another name for directional strategy.

Green-field development An international entry option to build a company's manufacturing plant and distribution system in another country.

Greenwash A derogatory term referring to a company's promoting its environmental sustainability efforts with very little action toward improving its measurable environmental performance.

Gross domestic product (GDP) A measure of the total output of goods and services within a country's borders.

Growth strategies A directional strategy that expands a company's current activities.

Hierarchy of strategy A nesting of strategies by level from corporate to business to functional, so that they complement and support one another.

Horizontal growth A corporate growth concentration strategy that involves expanding the firm's products into other geographic locations and/or increasing the range of products and services offered to current markets.

Horizontal integration The degree to which a firm operates in multiple geographic locations at the same point in an industry's value chain.

Horizontal strategy A corporate parenting strategy that cuts across business unit boundaries to build synergy across business units and to improve the competitive position of one or more business units.

House of quality A method of managing new product development to help project teams make important design decisions by getting them to think about what users want and how to get it to them most effectively.

HRM strategy A functional strategy that makes the best use of corporate human assets.

Human diversity A mix of people from different races, cultures, and backgrounds in the workplace.

Hypercompetition An industry situation in which the frequency, boldness, and aggressiveness of dynamic movement by the players accelerates to create a condition of constant disequilibrium and change.

Idea A concept that could be the foundation of an entrepreneurial venture if the concept is feasible.

IFAS (Internal Factor Analysis Summary) table A table that organizes internal factors into strengths and weaknesses and how well management is responding to these specific factors.

Imitability The rate at which a firm's underlying resources and capabilities can be duplicated by others.

Index of R&D effectiveness An index that is calculated by dividing the percentage of total revenue spent on research and development into new product profitability.

Index of sustainable growth A calculation that shows how much of the growth rate of sales can be sustained by internally generated funds.

Individual rights approach An ethics behavior guideline that proposes that human beings have certain fundamental rights that should be respected in all decisions.

Individualism-collectivism (IC) The extent to which a society values individual freedom and independence of action compared with a tight social framework and loyalty to the group.

Industry A group of firms producing a similar product or service.

Industry analysis An in-depth examination of key factors within a corporation's task environment.

Industry matrix A chart that summarizes the key success factors within a particular industry.

Industry scenario A forecasted description of an industry's likely future.

Information technology strategy A functional strategy that uses information systems technology to provide competitive advantage.

Input control A control that specifies resources, such as knowledge, skills, abilities, values, and motives of employees.

Inside director An officer or executive employed by a corporation who serves on that company's board of directors; also called management director.

Institutional advantage A competitive benefit for a not-for-profit organization when it performs its tasks more effectively than other comparable organizations.

Institution theory A concept of organizational adaptation that proposes that organizations can and do adapt to changing conditions by imitating other successful organizations.

Integration A process that involves a relatively balanced give-and-take of cultural and managerial practices between merger partners, with no strong imposition of cultural change on either company.

Integration manager A person in charge of taking an acquired company through the process of integrating its people and processes with those of the acquiring company.

Intellectual property Special knowledge used in a new product or process developed by a company for its own use, and which is usually protected by a patent, copyright, or trademark, and is sometimes treated as a trade secret.

Interlocking directorate A condition that occurs when two firms share a director or when an executive of one firm sits on the board of a second firm.

Intermittent system A method of manufacturing in which an item is normally processed sequentially, but the work and the sequence of the processes vary.

Internal environment Variables within the organization not usually within the short-run control of top management.

Internal strategic factors Strengths (core competencies) and weaknesses that are likely to determine whether a firm will be able to take advantage of opportunities while avoiding threats.

International transfer pricing A method of minimizing taxes by declaring high profits in a subsidiary located in a country with a low tax rate, and small profits in a subsidiary located in a country with a high tax rate.

Intranet An information network within an organization that also has access to the Internet.

Investment center A unit in which performance is measured in terms of the difference between the unit's resources and its services or products.

ISO 9000 Standards Series An internationally accepted way of objectively documenting a company's high level of quality operations.

ISO 14000 Standards Series An internationally accepted way to document a company's impact on the environment.

Job characteristics model An approach to job design that is based on the belief that tasks can be described in terms of certain objective characteristics, and that those characteristics affect employee motivation.

Job design The design of individual tasks in an attempt to make them more relevant to the company and more motivating to the employee.

Job enlargement Combining tasks to give a worker more of the same type of duties to perform.

Job enrichment Altering jobs by giving the worker more autonomy and control over activities.

Job rotation Moving workers through several jobs to increase variety.

Job shop One-of-a-kind production using skilled labor.

Joint venture An independent business entity created by two or more companies in a strategic alliance.

Justice approach An ethical approach that proposes that decision makers be equitable, fair, and impartial in the distribution of costs and benefits.

Just-in-time A purchasing concept in which parts arrive at the plant just when they are needed rather than being kept in inventories.

Key performance measures Essential measures for achieving a desired strategic option—used in the balanced scorecard.

Key success factors Variables that significantly affect the overall competitive position of a company within a particular industry.

Late movers Companies that enter a new market only after other companies have done so.

Law A formal code that permits or forbids certain behaviors.

Lead director An outside director who calls meetings of the outside board members and coordinates the annual evaluation of the CEO.

Lead user A customer who is ahead of market trends and has needs that go beyond those of the average user.

Leading Providing direction to employees to use their abilities and skills most effectively and efficiently to achieve organizational objectives.

Lean Six Sigma A program incorporating the statistical approach of Six Sigma with the lean manufacturing program developed by Toyota.

Learning organization An organization that is skilled at creating, acquiring, and transferring knowledge and at modifying its behavior to reflect new knowledge and insights.

Levels of moral development Kohlberg proposed three levels of moral development: preconventional, conventional, and principled.

Leveraged buyout An acquisition in which a company is acquired in a transaction financed largely by debt—usually obtained from a third party, such as an insurance company or an investment banker.

Leverage ratio An evaluation of how effectively a company utilizes its resources to generate revenues.

Licensing An agreement in which the licensing firm grants rights to another firm in another country or market to produce and/or sell a branded product.

Lifestyle company A small business in which the firm is purely an extension of the owner's lifestyle.

Line extension Using a successful brand name on additional products, such as Arm & Hammer brand first on baking soda, and then on laundry detergents, toothpaste, and deodorants.

Linkage The connection between the way one value activity (for example, marketing) is performed and the cost of performance of another activity (for example, quality control).

Liquidation The termination of a firm in which all its assets are sold.

Liquidity ratio The percentage showing to what degree a company can cover its current liabilities with its current assets.

Logical incrementalism A decision-making mode that is a synthesis of the planning, adaptive, and entrepreneurial modes.

Logistics strategy A functional strategy that deals with the flow of products into and out of the manufacturing process.

Long-term contract Agreements between two separate firms to provide agreed-upon goods and services to each other for a specified period of time.

Long-term evaluation method A method in which managers are compensated for achieving objectives set over a multiyear period.

Long-term orientation (LT) The extent to which society is oriented toward the long term versus the short term.

Lower-cost strategy A strategy in which a company or business unit designs, produces, and markets a comparable product more efficiently than its competitors.

Management audit A technique used to evaluate corporate activities.

Management By Objectives (MBO) An organization-wide approach ensuring purposeful action toward mutually agreed-upon objectives.

Management contract Agreements through which a corporation uses some of its personnel to assist a firm in another country for a specified fee and period of time.

Market development A marketing functional strategy in which a company or business unit captures a larger share of an existing market for current products through market penetration or develops new markets for current products.

Marketing mix The particular combination of key variables (product, place, promotion, and price) that can be used to affect demand and to gain competitive advantage.

Marketing strategy A functional strategy that deals with pricing, selling, and distributing a product.

Market location tactics Tactics that determine where a company or business unit will compete.

Market position Refers to the selection of specific areas for marketing concentration and can be expressed in terms of market, product, and geographical locations.

Market research A means of obtaining new product ideas by surveying current or potential users regarding what they would like in a new product.

Market segmentation The division of a market into segments to identify available niches.

Market value added (MVA) The difference between the market value of a corporation and the capital contributed by shareholders and lenders.

Masculinity-femininity (MF) The extent to which society is oriented toward money and things.

Mass customization The low-cost production of individually customized goods and services.

Mass production A system in which employees work on narrowly defined, repetitive tasks under close supervision in a bureaucratic and hierarchical structure to produce a large amount of low-cost, standard goods and services.

Matrix of change A chart that compares target practices (new programs) with existing practices (current activities).

Matrix structure A structure in which functional and product forms are combined simultaneously at the same level of the organization.

Mercosur/Mercosul South American free-trade area including Argentina, Brazil, Uruguay, and Paraguay.

Merger A transaction in which two or more corporations exchange stock, but from which only one corporation survives.

Mission The purpose or reason for an organization's existence.

Mission statement The definition of the fundamental, unique purpose that sets an organization apart from other firms of its type and identifies the scope or domain of the organization's operations in terms of products (including services) offered and markets served.

Modular manufacturing A system in which preassembled subassemblies are delivered as they are needed to a company's assembly-line workers who quickly piece the modules together into finished products.

Moore's law An observation of Gordon Moore, co-founder of Intel, that microprocessors double in complexity every 18 months.

Morality Precepts of personal behavior that are based on religious or philosophical grounds.

Moral relativism A theory that proposes that morality is relative to some personal, social, or cultural standard, and that there is no method for deciding whether one decision is better than another.

Most-favored nation A policy of the World Trade Organization stating that a member country cannot grant one trading partner lower customs duties without granting them to all WTO member nations.

Multidomestic industry An industry in which companies tailor their products to the specific needs of consumers in a particular country.

Multinational corporation (MNC) A company that has significant assets and activities in multiple countries.

Multiple sourcing A purchasing strategy in which a company orders a particular part from several vendors.

Multipoint competition A rivalry in which a large multibusiness corporation competes against other large multibusiness firms in a number of markets.

Mutual service consortium A partnership of similar companies in similar industries that pool their resources to gain a benefit that is too expensive to develop alone.

Natural environment That part of the external environment that includes physical resources, wildlife, and climate that are an inherent part of existence on Earth.

Net present value (NPV) A calculation of the value of a project that is made by predicting the project's payouts, adjusting them for risk, and subtracting the amount invested.

Network structure An organization (virtual organization) that outsources most of its business functions.

New entrants Businesses entering an industry that typically bring new capacity to an industry, a desire to gain market share, and substantial resources.

New product experimentation A method of test marketing the potential of innovative ideas by developing products, probing potential markets with early versions of the products, learning from the probes, and probing again.

No-change strategy A decision to do nothing new; to continue current operations and policies for the foreseeable future.

North American Free Trade Agreement (NAFTA) Regional free trade agreement between Canada, the United States, and Mexico.

Not-for-profit organization Private nonprofit corporations and public governmental units or agencies.

Objectives The end result of planned activity stating what is to be accomplished by when, and quantified if possible.

Offensive tactic A tactic that calls for competing in an established competitor's current market location.

Offshoring The outsourcing of an activity or function to a provider in another country.

Open innovation A new approach to R&D in which a firm uses alliances and connections with corporate, government, and academic labs to learn about new developments.

Operating budget A budget for a business unit that is approved by top management during strategy formulation and implementation.

Operating cash flow The amount of money generated by a company before the costs of financing and taxes are figured.

Operating leverage The impact of a specific change in sales volume on net operating income.

Operations strategy A functional strategy that determines how and where a product or service is to be manufactured, the level of vertical integration in the production process, and the deployment of physical resources.

Opportunity A strategic factor considered when using the SWOT analysis.

Orchestrator A top manager who articulates the need for innovation, provides funding for innovating activities, creates incentives for middle managers to sponsor new ideas, and protects idea/product champions from suspicious or jealous executives.

Organizational analysis Internal scanning concerned with identifying an organization's strengths and weaknesses.

Organizational learning theory A theory proposing that an organization adjusts to changes in the environment through the learning of its employees.

Organizational life cycle How organizations grow, develop, and eventually decline.

Organizational structure The formal setup of a business corporation's value chain components in terms of work flow, communication channels, and hierarchy.

Organization slack Unused resources within an organization.

Output control A control that specifies what is to be accomplished by focusing on the end result of the behaviors through the use of objectives and performance targets.

Outside directors Members of a board of directors who are not employees of the board's corporation; also called non–management directors.

Outsourcing A process in which resources are purchased from others through long-term contracts instead of being made within the company.

Parallel sourcing A process in which two suppliers are the sole suppliers of two different parts, but they are also backup suppliers for each other's parts.

Parenting strategy The manner in which management coordinates activities and transfers resources and cultivates capabilities among product lines and business units

Pattern of influence A concept stating that influence in strategic management derives from a not-for-profit organization's sources of revenue.

Pause/proceed-with-caution strategy A corporate strategy in which nothing new is attempted; an opportunity to rest before continuing a growth or retrenchment strategy.

Penetration pricing A marketing pricing strategy to obtain dominant market share by using low price.

Performance The end result of activities, actual outcomes of a strategic management process.

Performance appraisal system A system to systematically evaluate employee performance and promotion potential.

Performance gap A performance gap exists when performance does not meet expectations.

Periodic statistical report Reports summarizing data on key factors such as the number of new customer contracts, volume of received orders, and productivity figures.

Phases of strategic management A set of four levels of development through which a firm generally evolves into strategic management.

Piracy The making and selling of counterfeit copies of well-known name-brand products, especially software.

Planning mode A decision-making mode that involves the systematic gathering of appropriate information for situation analysis, the generation of feasible alternative strategies, and the rational selection of the most appropriate strategy.

Policy A broad guideline for decision making that links the formulation of strategy with its implementation.

Political strategy A strategy to influence a corporation's stakeholders.

Population ecology A theory that proposes that once an organization is successfully established in a particular environmental niche, it is unable to adapt to changing conditions.

Portfolio analysis An approach to corporate strategy in which top management views its product lines and business units as a series of investments from which it expects a profitable return.

Power distance (PD) The extent to which a society accepts an unequal distribution of influence in organizations.

Prediction markets A forecasting technique in which people make bets on the likelihood of a particular event taking place.

Pressure-cooker crisis A situation that exists when employees in collaborative organizations eventually grow emotionally and physically exhausted from the intensity of teamwork and the heavy pressure for innovative solutions.

Primary activity A manufacturing firm's corporate value chain, including inbound logistics, operations process, outbound logistics, marketing and sales, and service.

Primary stakeholders A high priority group that affects or is affected by the achievement of a firm's objectives.

Prime interest rate The rate of interest banks charge on their lowest-risk loans.

Private nonprofit corporation A nongovernmental not-for-profit organization.

Privatization The selling of state-owned enterprises to private individuals. Also the hiring of a private business to provide services previously offered by a state agency.

Procedures A list of sequential steps that describe in detail how a particular task or job is to be done.

Process innovation Improvement to the making and selling of current products.

Product champion A person who generates a new idea and supports it through many organizational obstacles.

Product development A marketing strategy in which a company or unit develops new products for existing markets or develops new products for new markets.

Product innovation The development of a new product or the improvement of an existing product's performance.

Product life cycle A graph showing time plotted against sales of a product as it moves from introduction through growth and maturity to decline.

Product/market evolution matrix A chart depicting products in terms of their competitive positions and their stages of product/market evolution.

Product-group structure A structure of a multinational corporation that enables the company to introduce and manage a similar line of products around the world.

Production sharing The process of combining the higher labor skills and technology available in developed countries with the lower-cost labor available in developing countries.

Product R&D Research and development concerned with product or product-packaging improvements.

Professional liquidator An individual called on by a bankruptcy court to close a firm and sell its assets.

Profitability ratios Ratios evaluating a company's ability to make money over a period of time.

Profit center A unit's performance, measured in terms of the difference between revenues and expenditures.

Profit-making firm A firm depending on revenues obtained from the sale of its goods and services to customers, who typically pay for the costs and expenses of providing the product or service plus a profit.

Profit strategy A strategy that artificially supports profits by reducing investment and short-term discretionary expenditures.

Program A statement of the activities or steps needed to accomplish a single-use plan in strategy implementation.

Propitious niche A portion of a market that is so well suited to a firm's internal and external environment that other corporations are not likely to challenge or dislodge it.

Public governmental unit or agency A kind of not-for-profit organization that is established by government or governmental agencies (such as welfare departments, prisons, and state universities).

Public or collective good Goods that are freely available to all in a society.

Pull strategy A marketing strategy in which advertising pulls the products through the distribution channels.

Punctuated equilibrium A point at which a corporation makes a major change in its strategy after evolving slowly through a long period of stability.

Purchasing power parity (PPP) A measure of the cost, in dollars, of the U.S.-produced equivalent volume of goods that another nation's economy produces.

Purchasing strategy A functional strategy that deals with obtaining the raw materials, parts, and supplies needed to perform the operations functions.

Push strategy A marketing strategy in which a large amount of money is spent on trade promotion in order to gain or hold shelf space in retail outlets.

Quality of work life A concept that emphasizes improving the human dimension of work to improve employee satisfaction and union relations.

Quasi-integration A type of vertical growth/integration in which a company does not make any of its key supplies but purchases most of its requirements from outside suppliers that are under its partial control.

Question marks New products that have the potential for success and need a lot of cash for development.

R&D intensity A company's spending on research and development as a percentage of sales revenue.

R&D mix The balance of basic, product, and process research and development.

R&D strategy A functional strategy that deals with product and process innovation.

Ratio analysis The calculation of ratios from data in financial statements to identify possible strengths or weaknesses.

Real options An approach to new project investment when the future is highly uncertain.

Red flag An indication of a serious underlying problem.

Red tape crisis A crisis that occurs when a corporation has grown too large and complex to be managed through formal programs.

Reengineering The radical redesign of business processes to achieve major gains in cost, service, or time.

Regional industry An industry in which multinational corporations primarily coordinate their activities within specific geographic areas of the world.

Relationship-based governance A government system perceived to be less transparent and have a higher degree of corruption.

Repatriation of profits The transfer of profits from a foreign subsidiary to a corporation's headquarters.

Replicability The ability of competitors to duplicate resources and imitate another firm's success.

Resources A company's physical, human, and organizational assets that serve as the building blocks of a corporation.

Responsibility center A unit that is isolated so that it can be evaluated separately from the rest of the corporation.

Retired executive directors Past leaders of a company kept on the board of directors after leaving the company.

Retrenchment strategy Corporate strategies to reduce a company's level of activities and to return it to profitability.

Return on equity (ROE) A measure of performance that is calculated by dividing net income by total equity.

Return on investment (ROI) A measure of performance that is calculated by dividing net income before taxes by total assets.

Revenue center A responsibility center in which production, usually in terms of unit or dollar sales, is measured without consideration of resource costs.

Reverse engineering Taking apart a competitor's product in order to find out how it works.

Reverse stock split A stock split in which an investor's shares are reduced for the same total amount of money.

RFID A technology in which radio frequency identification tags containing product information are used to track goods through inventory and distribution channels.

Risk A measure of the probability that one strategy will be effective, the amount of assets the corporation must allocate to that strategy, and the length of time the assets will be unavailable.

Rule-based governance A governance system based on clearly stated rules and procedures.

Rules of thumb Approximations based not on research, but on years of practical experience.

Sarbanes–Oxley Act Legislation passed by the U.S. Congress in 2002 to promote and formalize greater board independence and oversight.

Scenario box A tool for developing corporate scenarios in which historical data are used to make projections for generating pro forma financial statements.

Scenario writing A forecasting technique in which focused descriptions of different likely futures are presented in a narrative fashion.

SEC 10-K form An SEC form containing income statements, balance sheets, cash flow statements, and information not usually available in an annual report.

SEC 10-Q form An SEC form containing quarterly financial reports.

SEC 14-A form An SEC form containing proxy statements and information on a company's board of directors.

Secondary stakeholders Lower-priority groups that affect or are affected by the achievement of a firm's objectives.

Sell-out strategy A retrenchment option used when a company has a weak competitive position resulting in poor performance.

Separation A method of managing the culture of an acquired firm in which the two companies are structurally divided, without cultural exchange.

SFAS (Strategic Factors Analysis Summary) matrix A chart that summarizes an organization's strategic factors by combining the external factors from an EFAS table with the internal factors from an IFAS table.

Shareholder value The present value of the anticipated future stream of cash flows from a business plus the value of the company if it were liquidated.

Short-term orientation The tendency of managers to consider only current tactical or operational issues and ignore strategic ones.

Simple structure A structure for new entrepreneurial firms in which the employees tend to be generalists and jacks-of-all-trades.

Six Sigma A statistically based program developed to identify and improve a poorly performing process.

Skim pricing A marketing strategy in which a company charges a high price while a product is novel and competitors are few.

Small-business firm An independently owned and operated business that is not dominant in its field and that does not engage in innovative practices.

Social capital The goodwill of key stakeholders, which can be used for competitive advantage.

Social entrepreneurship A business in which a not-for-profit organization starts a new venture to achieve social goals.

Social responsibility The ethical and discretionary responsibilities a corporation owes its stakeholders.

Societal environment Economic, technological, political-legal, and sociocultural environmental forces that do not directly touch on the short-run activities of an organization but influence its long-run decisions.

Sole sourcing Relying on only one supplier for a particular part.

SO, ST, WO, WT strategies A series of possible business approaches based on combinations of opportunities, threats, strengths, and weaknesses.

Sources of innovation Drucker's proposed seven sources of new ideas that should be monitored by those interested in starting entrepreneurial ventures.

Sponsor A department manager who recognizes the value of a new idea, helps obtain funding to develop the innovation, and facilitates the implementation of the innovation.

Stability strategy Corporate strategies to make no change to the company's current direction or activities.

Staffing Human resource management priorities and use of personnel.

Stages of corporate development A pattern of structural development that corporations follow as they grow and expand.

Stages of international development The stages through which international corporations evolve in their relationships with widely dispersed geographic markets and the manner in which they structure their operations and programs.

Stages of new product development The stages of getting a new innovation into the marketplace.

Stage-gate process A method of managing new product development to increase the likelihood of launching new products quickly and successfully. The process is a series of steps to move products through the six stages of new product development.

Staggered board A board on which directors serve terms of more than one year so that only a portion of the board of directors stands for election each year.

Stakeholder An individual or entity with an interest in the activities of the organization

Stakeholder analysis The identification and evaluation of corporate stakeholders.

Stakeholder measure A method of keeping track of stakeholder concerns.

Stakeholder priority matrix A chart that categorizes stakeholders in terms of their interest in a corporation's activities and their relative power to influence the corporation's activities.

Stall point A point at which a company's growth in sales and profits suddenly stops and becomes negative.

Standard cost center A responsibility center that is primarily used to evaluate the performance of manufacturing facilities.

Standard operating procedures Plans that detail the various activities that must be carried out to complete a corporation's programs.

Star Market leader that is able to generate enough cash to maintain its high market share.

Statistical modeling A quantitative technique that attempts to discover causal or explanatory factors that link two or more time series together.

STEEP analysis An approach to scanning the societal environment that examines socio-cultural, technological, economic, ecological, and political-legal forces. Also called PESTEL analysis.

Steering control Measures of variables that influence future profitability.

Stewardship theory A theory proposing that executives tend to be more motivated to act in the best interests of the corporation than in their own self-interests.

Strategic alliance A partnership of two or more corporations or business units to achieve strategically significant objectives that are mutually beneficial.

Strategic audit A checklist of questions by area or issue that enables a systematic analysis of various corporate functions and activities. It's a type a management audit.

Strategic audit worksheet A tool used to analyze a case.

Strategic business unit (SBU) A division or group of divisions composed of independent product-market segments that are given primary authority for the management of their own functions.

Strategic choice The evaluation of strategies and selection of the best alternative.

Strategic choice perspective A theory that proposes that organizations adapt to a changing environment and have the opportunity and power to reshape their environment.

Strategic decision-making process An eight-step process that improves strategic decision making.

Strategic decisions Decisions that deal with the long-run future of an entire organization and are rare, consequential, and directive.

Strategic factors External and internal factors that determine the future of a corporation.

Strategic flexibility The ability to shift from one dominant strategy to another.

Strategic-funds method An approach that separates developmental expenses from expenses required for current operations.

Strategic group A set of business units or firms that pursue similar strategies and have similar resources.

Strategic inflection point The period in an organization's life in which a major change takes place in its environment and creates a new basis for competitive advantage.

Strategic management A set of managerial decisions and actions that determine the long-run performance of a corporation.

Strategic management model A rational, prescriptive planning model of the strategic management process including environmental scanning, strategy formulation, strategy implementation, and evaluation and control.

Strategic myopia The willingness to reject unfamiliar as well as negative information.

Strategic piggybacking The development of a new activity for a not-for-profit organization that would generate the funds needed to make up the difference between revenues and expenses.

Strategic planning staff A group of people charged with supporting both top management and business units in the strategic planning process.

Strategic R&D alliance A coalition through which a firm coordinates its research and development with another firm(s) to offset the huge costs of developing new technology.

Strategic rollup A means of consolidating a fragmented industry in which an entrepreneur acquires hundreds of owner-operated small businesses resulting in a large firm with economies of scale.

Strategic sweet spot A market niche in which a company is able to satisfy customers' needs in a way that competitors cannot.

Strategic type A category of firms based on a common strategic orientation and a combination of structure, culture, and processes that are consistent with that strategy.

Strategic vision A description of what the company is capable of becoming.

Strategic window A unique market opportunity that is available only for a particular time.

Strategic-funds method An evaluation method that encourages executives to look at development expenses as being different from expenses required for current operations.

Strategies to avoid Strategies sometimes followed by managers who have made a poor analysis or lack creativity.

Strategy A comprehensive plan that states how a corporation will achieve its mission and objectives.

Strategy-culture compatibility The match between existing corporate culture and a new strategy to be implemented.

Strategy formulation Development of long-range plans for the effective management of environmental opportunities and threats in light of corporate strengths and weaknesses.

Strategy implementation A process by which strategies and policies are put into action through the development of programs, budgets, and procedures.

Structure follows strategy The process through which changes in corporate strategy normally lead to changes in organizational structure.

Stuck in the middle A situation in which a company or business unit has not achieved a generic competitive strategy and has no competitive advantage.

Suboptimization A phenomenon in which a unit optimizes its goal accomplishment to the detriment of the organization as a whole.

Substages of small business development A set of five levels through which new ventures often develop.

Substitute products Products that appear to be different but can satisfy the same need as other products.

Supply chain management The formation of networks for sourcing raw materials, manufacturing products or creating services, storing and distributing goods, and delivering goods or services to customers and consumers.

Support activity An activity that ensures that primary value-chain activities operate effectively and efficiently.

SWOT analysis Identification of strengths, weaknesses, opportunities, and threats that may be strategic factors for a specific company.

Synergy A concept that states that the whole is greater than the sum of its parts; that two units will achieve more together than they could separately.

Tacit knowledge Knowledge that is not easily communicated because it is deeply rooted in employee experience or in a corporation's culture.

Tactic A short-term operating plan detailing how a strategy is to be implemented.

Takeover A hostile acquisition in which one firm purchases a majority interest in another firm's stock.

Taper integration A type of vertical integration in which a firm internally produces less than half of its own requirements and buys the rest from outside suppliers.

Task environment The part of the business environment that includes the elements or groups that directly affect the corporation and, in turn, are affected by it.

Technological competence A corporation's proficiency in managing research personnel and integrating their innovations into its day-to-day operations.

Technological discontinuity The displacement of one technology by another.

Technological follower A company that imitates the products of competitors.

Technological leader A company that pioneers an innovation.

Technology sourcing A make-or-buy decision that can be important in a firm's R&D strategy.

Technology transfer The process of taking a new technology from the laboratory to the marketplace.

Time to market The time from inception to profitability of a new product.

Timing tactics Tactics that determine when a business will enter a market with a new product.

Tipping point The point at which a slowly changing situation goes through a massive, rapid change.

Top management responsibilities Leadership tasks that involve getting things accomplished through, and with, others in order to meet the corporate objectives.

Total Quality Management (TQM) An operational philosophy that is committed to customer satisfaction and continuous improvement.

TOWS matrix A matrix that illustrates how external opportunities and threats facing a particular company can be matched with that company's internal strengths and weaknesses to result in four sets of strategic alternatives.

Transaction cost economics A theory that proposes that vertical integration is more efficient than contracting for goods and services in the marketplace when the transaction costs of buying goods on the open market become too great.

Transferability The ability of competitors to gather the resources and capabilities necessary to support a competitive challenge.

Transfer pricing A practice in which one unit can charge a transfer price for each product it sells to a different unit within a company.

Transformational leader A leader who causes change and movement in an organization by providing a strategic vision.

Transparent The speed with which other firms can understand the relationship of resources and capabilities supporting a successful firm's strategy.

Trends in governance Current developments in corporate governance.

Triggering event Something that acts as a stimulus for a change in strategy.

Trigger point The point at which a country has developed economically so that demand for a particular product or service is increasing rapidly.

Turnaround specialist A manager who is brought into a weak company to salvage that company in a relatively attractive industry.

Turnaround strategy A plan that emphasizes the improvement of operational efficiency when a corporation's problems are pervasive but not yet critical.

Turnkey operation Contracts for the construction of operating facilities in exchange for a fee.

Turnover A term used by European firms to refer to sales revenue. It also refers to the amount of time needed to sell inventory.

Uncertainty avoidance (UA) The extent to which a society feels threatened by uncertain and ambiguous situations.

Union of South American Nations An organization formed in 2008 to unite Mercosur and the Andean Community.

Utilitarian approach A theory that proposes that actions and plans should be judged by their consequences.

Value chain A linked set of value-creating activities that begins with basic raw materials coming from suppliers and ends with distributors getting the final goods into the hands of the ultimate consumer.

Value-chain partnership A strategic alliance in which one company or unit forms a long-term arrangement with a key supplier or distributor for mutual advantage.

Value disciplines An approach to evaluating a competitor in terms of product leadership, operational excellence, and customer intimacy.

Vertical growth A corporate growth strategy in which a firm takes over a function previously provided by a supplier or distributor.

Vertical integration The degree to which a firm operates in multiple locations on an industry's value chain from extracting raw materials to retailing.

Virtual organization An organizational structure that is composed of a series of project groups or collaborations linked by changing nonhierarchical, cobweb-like networks.

Virtual team A group of geographically and/or organizationally dispersed co-workers who are assembled using a combination of telecommunications and information technologies to accomplish an organizational task.

Vision A view of what management thinks an organization should become.

VRIO framework Barney's proposed analysis to evaluate a firm's key resources in terms of value, rareness, imitability, and organization.

Web 2.0 A term used to describe the evolution of the Internet into wikis, blogs, RSSs, social networks, podcasts, and mash-ups.

Weighted-factor method A method that is appropriate for measuring and rewarding the performance of top SBU managers and group-level executives when performance factors and their importance vary from one SBU to another.

Whistle-blower An individual who reports to authorities incidents of questionable organizational practices.

World Trade Organization A forum for governments to negotiate trade agreements and settle trade disputes.

Z-value A formula that combines five ratios by weighting them according to their importance to a corporation's financial strength to predict the likelihood of bankruptcy.

NAME INDEX

SUBJECT INDEX